Criminology

and the Criminal Justice System

Reviewers

Criminology
and the Criminal Justice System

FOURTH EDITION

Freda Adler
Distinguished Professor of Criminal Justice
School of Criminal Justice, Rutgers University

Gerhard O. W. Mueller
Distinguished Professor of Criminal Justice
School of Criminal Justice, Rutgers University

William S. Laufer
Associate Professor of Legal Studies
Wharton School, University of Pennsylvania

Boston   Burr Ridge, IL   Dubuque, IA   Madison, WI   New York   San Francisco   St. Louis
Bangkok   Bogotá   Caracas   Lisbon   London   Madrid
Mexico City   Milan   New Delhi   Seoul   Singapore   Sydney   Taipei   Toronto

McGraw-Hill Higher Education ⌖

A Division of The McGraw-Hill Companies

CRIMINOLOGY AND THE CRIMINAL JUSTICE SYSTEM
Published by McGraw-Hill, an imprint of The McGraw-Hill Companies, Inc. 1221 Avenue of the Americas, New York, NY, 10020. Copyright © 2001, 1998, 1995, 1991 by The McGraw-Hill Companies, Inc. All rights reserved. No part of this publication may be reproduced or distributed in any form or by any means, or stored in a database or retrieval system, without the prior written consent of The McGraw-Hill Companies, Inc., including, but not limited to, in any network or other electronic storage or transmission, or broadcast for distance learning.
Some ancillaries, including electronic and print components, may not be available to customers outside the United States.

This book is printed on acid-free paper.

1 2 3 4 5 6 7 8 9 0 VNH/VNH 0 9 8 7 6 5 4 3 2 1 0

ISBN 0-07-232149-0

Editorial director: *Phillip A. Butcher*
Senior sponsoring editor: *Carolyn Henderson*
Developmental editor: *Roz Sackoff*
Editorial coordinator: *Suzanne Driscoll*
Marketing manager II: *Leslie A. Kraham*
Project manager: *Susanne Riedell*
Production supervisor: *Rose Hepburn*
New media: *James Fehr*
Director of design: *Keith J. McPherson*
Interior design: *Z Graphics*
Cover design: *Z Graphics/Keith J. McPherson*
Cover image: *Bruce Quist Photography*
Photo research coordinator: *Sharon Miller*
Supplement coordinator: *Matthew Perry*
Compositor: *Carlisle Communications, Ltd.*
Typeface: *10.5/12 Palatino*
Printer: *Von Hoffman Press, Inc.*

Library of Congress Cataloging-in-Publication Data
Adler, Freda.
    Criminology and the criminal justice system / Freda Adler, Gerhard O. W. Mueller, William S. Laufer.—4th ed.
        p. cm.
    Updated ed. of: Criminology. 3rd ed. 1998.
    Includes indexes.
    ISBN 0-07-232149-0 (softcover : alk. paper)
    1. Criminology.   I. Mueller, Gerhard O. W.   II. Laufer, William S. III. Title.
    HV6025 .A35 2001
    364—dc21   00-036134

www.mhhe.com

FREDA ADLER is Distinguished Professor of Criminal Justice at Rutgers University, School of Criminal Justice. She received her BA in sociology, her MA in criminology, and her PhD in sociology from the University of Pennsylvania. Dr. Adler began her career in criminal justice as an evaluator of drug and alcohol treatment programs for federal and state governments. Since 1968, she has taught such subjects as criminal justice, criminology, comparative criminal justice systems, statistics, and research methods. She has served as criminal justice advisor to the United Nations, as well as to federal, state, and foreign governments. Dr. Adler's published works include 13 books as author or coauthor, 9 books as editor or coeditor, and over 90 journal articles. She has served on the editorial boards of the *Journal of Criminal Justice, Criminology,* and the *Journal of Research on Crime and Delinquency.* Dr. Adler serves as editorial consultant to the *Journal of Criminal Law and Criminology* and coeditor of *Advances in Criminological Theory.* She also has served as president of the American Society of Criminology (1994–1995).

GERHARD O. W. MUELLER is Distinguished Professor of Criminal Justice at Rutgers University, School of Criminal Justice. After earning his JD degree from the University of Chicago, he went on to receive a master of laws degree from Columbia University. He was awarded the degree of Dr-Jur (hc) by the University of Uppsala, Sweden. His career in criminal justice began in 1945, when he served as a chief petty officer in the British Military Government Water Police, where he commanded a Coast Guard cutter. His teaching in criminal justice, begun in 1953, was partially interrupted between 1974 and 1982, when, as Chief of the United Nations Crime Prevention and Criminal Justice Branch, he was responsible for all United Nations programs dealing with problems of crime and justice worldwide. He continues his service to the United Nations as Chairman ad interim of the Board of the International Scientific and Professional Advisory Council of the United Nations Crime Prevention and Criminal Justice Programme. Professor Mueller has been a member of the faculties of law at the University of Washington, West Virginia University, New York University, and the National Judicial College. He is the author or editor of some 50 books and 270 scholarly articles.

WILLIAM S. LAUFER is Associate Professor of Legal Studies at the Wharton School of the University of Pennsylvania. Dr. Laufer received his BA in social and behavioral sciences at the Johns Hopkins University, his JD at Northeastern University School of Law, and his PhD at Rutgers University, School of Criminal Justice. Since 1987, he has taught such subjects as corporate and white-collar crime, business ethics, criminal law and criminal procedure, and criminology. Dr. Laufer's research has appeared in law reviews and a wide range of criminal justice, legal, and psychology journals, such as the *Journal of Research in Crime and Delinquency, American Journal of Criminal Law, American Criminal Law Review, Law and Human Behavior, Journal of Personality and Social Psychology,* and *Business Ethics Quarterly.* He is coeditor of the *Handbook of Psychology and Law; Personality, Moral Development and Criminal Behavior;* and *Crime, Values and Religion.* Dr. Laufer is coeditor with Freda Adler of *Advances in Criminological Theory.*

To

David S., Daniel A., Julia A., Noah A., Zoë A., Hannah M., Nicolai A.,
John J., Lauren E., Stephen W., and Anna L.

Contents in Brief

Contents

PART III
Types of Crimes 263

List of Boxes

 Window to the World

 Where Do We Go from Here?

 Of Immediate Concern

Preface

Criminology is a young discipline—in fact, the term "criminology" is only a little over a century old. But in this brief time, criminology has emerged as an important social and behavioral science devoted to the study of crime as a social phenomenon. Criminology fosters theoretical debates, contributes ideas, and suggests solutions to deal with a crime problem that many consider intolerable. Problems as vital and urgent as those addressed in this book are challenging, exciting and, at the same time, disturbing and tragic. Moreover, these problems are immediately relevant to students' lives. Our goal with this book has always been, and remains, to discuss these problems, their origins, and their possible solutions in a clear, practical, straightforward fashion that brings the material to life for students. We invite teachers and students alike to join us in traveling along criminology's path, exploring its domain and mapping out its future.

THE FOURTH EDITION

In the three preceding editions of this text, we have prepared students of criminology to understand the contemporary problems with which criminology is concerned and to anticipate those problems that society would have to face in the twenty-first century. We have now entered that century. It is time to face the new century's problems as we simultaneously continue to work on solutions to old problems. Because of the forward-looking orientation of previous editions of *Criminology* and the wide respect and acceptance that those editions have enjoyed, we have chosen not to depart from the book's established structure and approach. We have, however, vigorously researched, refined, and updated every chapter of the text—not only to maintain the book's scholarly integrity, but also to ensure its relevance for today's students. In addition to updating every chapter's research base and statistical information, we have significantly expanded coverage of some of the most critical issues for criminologists in the twenty-first century:

- The chapter on labeling, conflict, and radical theory features many new opportunities for students to think critically about current controversies in crime and justice (why genocide is rarely examined by criminologists, for instance, and how racial profiling is an extension of labeling theory).

- We have added, to the chapter on violent crime, a new section that covers recent terrorist attacks, illegal "militia" activities, hate crimes, and school shootings, as well as their criminological significance.

- In the chapter on property crime, we have substantially broadened our coverage of high-tech crime, including new types of insurance frauds (especially medical), telemarketing scams, characteristics of high-tech criminals, and the large contemporary range of computer and computer-facilitated crimes, such as child pornography, illegal gambling, theft of information, siege attacks (viruses), cybervandalism, break-ins, industrial espionage, software piracy, and credit card fraud.

- In the chapter on organizational crime, we have expanded our discussion of the latest theories and statistics on crimes committed by corporations or employees of corporations.

- The chapter on comparative criminology provides extended coverage of crime trends worldwide as well as the means of gauging those trends. This chapter also includes expanded coverage of the work of the international criminal courts in dealing with crime in the global community.

Inasmuch as media reports often have an impact on developments in criminology, the student will find discussion of recent events of national significance:

- The Columbine High School killing spree.
- The Matthew Shepard torture killing.
- The terrorist bombing of American embassies abroad.
- The killings in a Texas church.
- The deviant behavior of super athletes.
- The arrest of gangsta rapper Sean "Puffy" Combs.
- The alleged insurance swindle by financier Marvin Frankel.

As in previous editions, we have endeavored not only to reflect developments and change, but to anticipate them on the basis of trend data. After all, those who study criminology with our text today must be ready to resolve new criminological problems tomorrow when they are decision makers, researchers, teachers, and planners. The aim, however, remains constant: to reach a future as free from crime as possible.

ORGANIZATION

As with previous editions, there are two versions of this text. *Criminology* consists of three parts; *Criminology and the Criminal Justice System* has four parts. For schools that retain the traditional criminology course, which includes criminological coverage of criminal justice, *Criminology and the Criminal Justice System* would be the ideal text. For schools that offer both an Introduction to Criminology course and an Introduction to Criminal Justice course, *Criminology* is the more appropriate text, since it omits Part IV, "A Criminological Approach to the Criminal Justice System."

Part I, "Understanding Criminology," presents an overview of criminology and describes the vast horizon of this science. It explains techniques for measuring the number and characteristics of crimes and criminals. It also traces the history of criminological thought through the era that witnessed the formation of the major schools of criminology, classicism and positivism (eighteenth and nineteenth centuries).

Part II, "Explanations of Crime and Criminal Behavior," includes explanations of crime and criminal behavior based on the various theories developed in the twentieth century. Among the subjects covered are theories that offer biological, psychological, sociological, sociopolitical, and integrated explanations. Coverage of research by radical, socialist, and feminist criminologists has been updated. Theories that discuss why offenders choose to commit one offense rather than another at a given time and place are also covered in this part.

Part III, "Types of Crime," covers the various types of crimes from a legal and sociological perspective. The familiar street crimes, such as homicide and robbery, are assessed, as are other criminal activities, such as high-tech crimes that have been highlighted by researchers only in recent years. The chapter on comparative criminology—an area with vastly increased practical and policy implications—has been expanded and updated in view of the growing research in the field.

Part IV, "A Criminological Approach to the Criminal Justice System" (only in *Criminology and the Criminal Justice System*), includes an explanation of the component parts and the functioning of the system. It explains contemporary criminological research on how the people who run the system operate it, the decision-making processes of all participants, and the interaction of all the system components.

PEDAGOGICAL AIDS

Working together, the authors and the editors have developed a format for the text that supports the goal of a readable, practical, and attractive text. In addition to all the changes already mentioned, the number of photographs has been doubled in this edition in order to make the book even more approachable. Redesigned tables and figures highlight and amplify the text coverage. Chapter outlines, lists of key terms, chapter review sections, and a comprehensive glossary all help students master the material. Always striving to help students see the relevance of criminology in their lives, we have added a number of innovative features to this edition:

- "Crime Surfing"   Particularly interesting Web addresses are accompanied by mini-exercises that allow students to explore chapter topics further.

- "Did You Know?" Surprising factual realities provide eye-opening information about chapter topics.
- "Theory Informs Policy" Brief sections in theory chapters demonstrate how problems identified by criminologists have led to practical solutions.

We are particularly proud of our new box program. In these boxes, we highlight criminologically significant issues that deserve special discussion. Each chapter has three boxes—"Where Do We Go from Here?" "Of Immediate Concern," and "Window to the World."

- "Where Do We Go from Here?" boxes present issues and existing solutions—and ask provocative questions about the future. For example, how do we deal with rapidly changing drug markets? What are the policy implications of widening sports doping scandals? How can we handle the proliferation of computer viruses caused by the virtual explosion of computer use around the world? How can the already taxed law enforcement agencies, as yet ill-equipped to deal with global issues, deal with the globalization of crime, especially the emergence of transnational crime? In other words, "Where do we go from here?"
- "Of Immediate Concern" boxes highlight problems that are "of the moment" as a result of their technological nature or human implications; they challenge us to come up with specific, effective responses right now. Thus, in the wake of school killings, should we create maximum-security schools? In view of our experience with hate-motivated crimes, are harsher laws called for? Cyberporn is viewed as a major global problem; what can we do about it?
- "Window to the World" boxes examine developments abroad that affect America's crime situation. Since international terrorist threats plague nations around the globe, in countries as diverse as the United States and Russia, what can be done to deter them? Now that ethnic gangs have emerged around the world, conducting activities such as forcibly transporting women and young girls to be sex slaves, how can nations deal with the problem?

SUPPLEMENTS PACKAGE

As a full-service publisher of quality educational products, McGraw-Hill does much more than just sell textbooks. The company creates and publishes an extensive array of print, video, and digital supplements for students and instructors. This edition of *Criminology* and of *Criminology and the Criminal Justice System* is accompanied by an extensive, comprehensive supplements package:

For the Student

- *Making the Grade* CD-ROM. Interactive CD-ROM packaged free of charge with every text includes chapter quizzes, an Internet guide, a study skills primer, and much more.
- Student's Online Learning Center. Web-based, interactive study guide with quizzes and a wealth of other study and review tools.
- Interactive E-Source. Fully functional, nonlinear electronic book, ideal for visual learners.

For the Instructor

- Instructor's Manual/Testbank. Chapter outlines, key terms, overviews, lecture notes, discussion questions, a complete testbank, and more.
- Computerized Testbank. Easy-to-use computerized testing program for both Windows and Macintosh computers.
- PowerPoint Slides. Chapter-by-chapter slide shows featuring text, photos, tables, and illustrations.
- Instructor's Online Learning Center. Password-protected access to important instructor support materials and additional resources.

- PageOut. Easy-to-use tool that allows the instructor to create his or her own course Web page and to access all material on the *Criminology* Online Learning Center.
- Videotapes. A wide variety of videotapes from the *Films for the Humanities and Social Sciences* series is available to adopters of the text.

All the above supplements are provided free of charge to students and instructors. Orders of new (versus used) textbooks help defray the substantial cost of developing such supplements. Please contact your local McGraw-Hill representative for more information on any of the above supplements.

IN APPRECIATION

We gratefully acknowledge the assistance and support of a number of dedicated professionals. At Rutgers University, the librarian of the N.C.C.D./Criminal Justice Collection, Phyllis Schultze, has been most helpful in patiently tracking and tracing sources. We thank Professor Sesha Kethineni, Illinois State University, for her tireless assistance on the first edition; and Deborah Leiter-Walker for her help on the second; and Laura Shepard and Nhung Tran from the University of Pennsylvania for their assistance on the third. Gratitude is also owed to the many former and current Rutgers University students who have valiantly contributed their labors to all editions. These include Susanna Cornett, Dory Dickman, Lisa Maher, Susan Plant, Mangai Natarajan, Dana Nurge, Sharon Chamard, Marina Myhre, Diane Cicchetti, Emmanuel Barthe, Illya Lichtenberg, Peter Heidt, Vanja Stenius, Christine Tartaro, Megan McNally, Danielle Gunther, and Jim Roberts. Joan Schroeder has done a superb job of word processing for all editions; we could not have produced the book without her.

Many academic reviewers (listed facing title page) offered invaluable help in planning and drafting chapters. We thank them for their time and thoughtfulness and for the experience they brought from their teaching and research.

We thank our colleagues overseas who have prepared translations of *Criminology* with a view to familiarizing students of foreign cultures with criminological problems that are now global, with our theories, and with our efforts to deal with the persistent problem of crime in the years to come:

The Arabic translation: Dr. Mohammed Zeid, Cairo, Egypt, and Rome, Italy
The Japanese translation: Dr. Toyoji Saito, Kobe, Japan, and his colleagues
The Hungarian translation: Dr. Miklos Levai, Miskolc, Hungary, and his colleagues

Finally, we owe a special debt to the team at McGraw-Hill: to Editorial Director Phil Butcher and Senior Editor Carolyn Henderson for their encouragement and support; to Development Editor Roz Sackoff, whose ideas and suggestions helped refine this edition; to Sue Driscoll, Editorial Coordinator, for her attention to the day-to-day details; and to the Production staff in Burr Ridge as well as to Barbara Salz for their design, photo research, and copyediting.

A combined total of 100 years of teaching criminology and related subjects provide the basis for the writing of *Criminology and the Criminal Justice System, Fourth Edition.* We hope the result is a text that is intellectually provocative, factually rigorous, and scientifically sound, and that offers a stimulating learning experience for the student.

Freda Adler
Gerhard O. W. Mueller
William S. Laufer

Watch for these useful learning tools and study aids as you work your way through *Criminology and the Criminal Justice System*, Fourth Edition.

PART I Understanding Criminology   5

Heartbreak
THE DENVER POST
High School Massacre

USA TODAY
Students massacred in Colo.

Newspaper headlines, local and national, focus on the rash of school killings.

April 20, 1999, Littleton, Colorado (2 perpetrators): 13 dead, 23 injured.
April 15, 1999, Salt Lake City, Utah: 2 dead, 4 wounded.

Five other mass killings took place in 1997 and 1998. Criminologists are very much interested in studying this sequence of events. Is there a connection between the events? Who are the perpetrators? What was their motivation? What weapons did they use? Do any of the existing theories of crime causation explain these mass killings? What can (and should) be done to prevent these crimes from occurring? How can policy makers be reached with criminologists' recommendations?

• In 1989, news photographs depicted the supertanker *Exxon Valdez* aground in Prince William Sound, Alaska, exuding oil through a rupture in its hull. This accident caused North America's largest ecological disaster. (The captain was eventually convicted on a misdemeanor charge.) Tankers have run aground before and since the *Exxon Valdez* disaster (Table 1.1). On February 15, 1996, the tanker *Sea Em-*

press ran aground off Wales, spilling 20 million gallons of oil, far exceeding the *Exxon Valdez* spillage. In all probability the cause once again was human error. But criminologists have many questions: How can we prevent such disasters from happening in the future? Should corporations like Exxon be held criminally liable for the acts of their employees? What sanctions are appropriate?

Criminologists study the sanctions used against i... tions. How can h... be controlled... Are new la... tion aga... will n... efic... ve...

Up-to-Date Coverage of Criminological Theories, Topics, and Issues

Extensive updating of research and statistical information along with detailed discussion of important current events like Columbine, the doping of athletes, and so on—when combined with the text's expanded coverage of political criminology (terrorism, etc.) and in-depth treatment of high-tech crimes—make this the most current book available for the course.

Unique *Making the Grade* Student CD-ROM

This terrific study tool—packaged free with every copy of the text—features online quizzing with feedback explaining why responses are right or wrong as well as plentiful other materials students will find helpful in their college careers.

making the A+ grade

...ven...le...to...er...o...flo...
dropped by two-thirds.

Parking Facilities[64] Parking garages are said to be dangerous places: Individuals are alone in a large space, there are many hiding places, the amount of valuable property (cars and their contents) is high, they are open to the public, an offender's car can go unnoticed, and lighting is usually poor. Yet statistics indicate that because of the small amount of time and the relatively limited number of trips that each person takes to and from parking facilities, an individual's chances of being raped, robbed, or assaulted in a parking facility are very low. Nevertheless, the fear of victimization in these facilities is high. Efforts to improve conditions include better lighting, stairways and elevators that are open to the air or glass-enclosed, ticket-booth personnel

...creased dramatically. The risks of stealing a motorcycle became too high because a would-be offender could not drive it away without wearing a helmet. At this point researchers expected to see a rise in the numbers of cars or bikes stolen. They did not. In other words, there was very little displacement. Of course, some offenders will look for other crime opportunities, but many others will quit for some time, perhaps forever.

THEORY INFORMS POLICY

The study of targets and victims is crucial to preventing crime. Understanding how offenders make decisions helps policy makers allocate resources efficiently. For example, if it is possible to significantly reduce convenience-store robbery by relatively simple measures, isn't it better to spend time and money doing those

Classic *Theory Informs Policy* Sections

Acclaimed coverage of the interrelated nature of theory, policy, and practice highlights the practical aspects of what criminologists do.

Plentiful Photographs, Charts, and Tables

Completely re-drawn charts and tables and a dramatically enhanced photo program make chapter material clearer, more understandable, and more inviting than ever before.

Chapter-Opening Previews

Succinct chapter-opening outlines, key terms lists, and overviews help students focus on the chapter's critical theories, concepts, and terminology.

tles of drugs involved. Respondents generally agreed that violent crime is more serious than property crime. They also considered white-collar crimes, such as engaging in consumer fraud, cheating on income taxes, polluting, and accepting bribes, to be as serious as many violent and property crimes.

MEASURING CHARACTERISTICS OF CRIMINALS

Information on the characteristics of crimes is not the only sort of data analyzed by criminologists. They also want to know the characteristics of the people who commit those crimes.

Behind each crime is a criminal or several criminals. Criminals can be differentiated by age, ethnicity, gender, socioeconomic level, and other criteria. These characteristics enable us to group criminals into categories, and it is these categories that researchers find useful. They study the various offender groups to determine why some people are more likely than others to

these arrests were distributed among the offenses. During the 10 years between 1988 and 1997, the number of arrests rose 16 percent. Let us take a close look at the characteristics of the persons arrested.[33]

Age and Crime

Six armed men who have been called the "over-the-hill gang" were arrested trying to rob an elegant bridge and backgammon club in midtown New York City. The robbery began at 10:25 P.M. when the men, wearing rubber gloves and ski masks and armed with two revolvers, a shotgun, and a rifle, forced the customers and employees to lie down

Crime Surfing

www.uncjin.org

The United Nations Crime and Justice Information Network (UNCJIN) is a resource for investigating crime and criminal justice systems in various countries around the world. The URL above will take you to reported crime data for many countries. Use these data to determine whether other countries have crime patterns similar to those of the United States.

Unique *Crime Surfing* Inserts

Brief internet exercises integrated into every chapter enable students to explore the Web in a directed fashion.

---

ence validation directly causes delinquency is lacking.[18]

So far we have considered psychological theories that attribute the causes of delinquency or criminality to unconscious problems and failures in moral development. Not all psychologists agree with these explanations of criminal behavior. Some argue that human behavior develops through learning. They say that we learn by observing others and by watching the responses to other people's behavior (on television or in the movies, for instance) and to our own. Social learning theorists reject the notion that internal

functioning alone makes us prone to act aggressively or violently.

Learning Aggression and Violence

Social learning theory maintains that delinquent behavior is learned through the same psychological processes as any other behavior. Behavior is learned when it is reinforced or rewarded; it is not learned when it is not reinforced. We learn behavior in various ways: observation, direct experience, and differential reinforcement.

Observational Learning Albert Bandura, a leading proponent of social learning theory, argues that individuals learn violence and aggression through **behavioral modeling:** Children learn how to behave by fashioning their behavior after that of others. Behavior is socially transmitted through examples, which come pri-

Did You Know

. . . that, while evidence is lacking that deprivation directly causes delinquency, research on the impact of family-based crime-prevention programs is promising? Programs that target family risk factors in multiple settings (ecological contexts) have achieved success. (See Table 4.2.)

Fascinating *Did You Know?* Asides

Intriguing, little-known facts related to specific chapter topics engage students' natural curiosity about criminology.

Where Do We Go from Here?
Changing Drug Markets

A decade ago the Bushwick neighborhood of Brooklyn was one of the most notorious drug bazaars in the country. Today dealers no longer sell on street corners, but use beepers and sell behind closed doors. Businesses are returning to the neighborhood, land once used by drug dealers for pit bull fights is now a garden, children and adults fill the parks by day, and the nightly gunfire in the park has been replaced by the voices of boys arguing over who the greatest baseball player is.

How did this change come about? The generation that started using crack in the 1980s has not stopped using it, but their children are not following in their footsteps. A Harlem resident whose mother was a crack addict noted that children of crack addicts "wanted to get as far away from that drug as [they] could." (1) Using crack is no longer a socially desirable option. In fact, "[p]eople look down on them so much that even crackheads don't want

The neighborhood fights back.

to be crackheads anymore."(1) These comments are reflected in a drug use survey of male arrestees in New York

which found that 35.7 percent of males over the age of 36 had recently used crack compared with 4 percent of

Intriguing *Where Do We Go From Here?* Boxes

Unique coverage of current issues in criminology and their corresponding existing solutions pose provocative questions about where we go from here (discussion questions included).

Of Immediate Concern

Obituary for Tupac Amaru Shakur (1971–1996)

Don't shed a tear for me nigga, I ain't happy here
I hope they bury me and send me to my rest
headlines reading 'murdered to death'
my last breath.(1)
From Tupac's "If I Die 2nite"

At 4:03 P.M. on September 13, 1996, Tupac Amaru Shakur, rapper and actor, died at the University of Nevada Medical Center, in Las Vegas. The cause of death: gunshot wounds received 6 days earlier in a drive-by shooting. Tupac Shakur, known as 2Pac, was 25 years old.(2)

If you had been assigned to write Tupac Shakur's obituary, how would you have captured the contradiction of his artistic achievement and self-destructive life? The gangsta rapper Tupac was a sensitive poet and film actor with an innocent, endearing smile. His records were making millions of dollars. He was also a violent, abusive alcoholic. Tupac was a sweet and kind mother's boy. He was also a frightening street thug, a former drug dealer, and a convicted rapist. He was a product of the Marin Public Housing project—an impoverished group of buildings called "the jungle" by many residents.(3)

How would you have explained the unnerving convergence of violent rap and street crime that marked his death? Tupac made light of urban gangsta violence in rap, and died in the middle of the night from a flurry of gangland gunfire that had the look and feel of a well-choreographed music video. He challenged his own death in lyrics and song: "I heard a rumor I died/murdered in cold blood, dramatized/pictures of me in my final state, you know how I cried."(4) In an ultimate pairing of life and art, two of the gunshots fired on that fateful Saturday night hit Tupac's *thug life* tattoo, causing the internal bleeding that took his life.

In just five years, from 1991 to 1996, Tupac released four solo albums: *2Pacalypse Now* (1991), *Strictly 4 My Ni'gaz* (1993), *Me Against the World* (1995), and *All Eyez on Me* (1996); he also appeared in five films: *Juice* (1991), *Poetic Justice* (1993), *Above the Rim* (1994), *Gang Related* (1996), and *Gridlock* (1996). During the same five years, he was also

Tupac and beyond: Gangsta rap musicians seem to be linked to violence. Depicted are Sean (Puffy) Combs and his girlfriend Jennifer Lopez. Around them on December 27, 1999, at Club New York, gunshots injured three. Combs and Lopez left in a Lincoln owned by Combs' Bad Boy Entertainment Company. Arrested after a high speed chase, Puff Daddy was indicted on felony weapons charges; Lopez was cleared.

- Charged with beating a video director in Los Angeles (5 days in jail).
- Charged with threatening another rapper with a baseball bat (charges dropped).
- Arrested in Atlanta for allegedly shooting two off-duty cops (charges dropped).
- Charged in the sexual abuse of a fan in a New York City hotel room (convicted by a jury and sentenced to jail).
- Arrested on charges of gun and marijuana possession in LA.
- Shot five times in a midtown New York City recording studio (crime unsolved).
- Jailed for 8 months (served sentence for sexual abuse conviction).
- Sentenced to 120 days for probation violation in New York and Los Angeles (freed pending appeal).

Now, put aside the contradictions of achievement and self-destruction that mark Tupac Shakur's life and death. Forget the unnerving convergence of life

and art. Instead, consider how you would have captured the real meaning of Tupac Shakur's success. How would you have explained our attraction to and fascination with Dr. Dre, Eazy-E, Snoop Doggy Dog, Tha Dogg Pound, Run-DMC, and Outkast? What does the rise of gangsta rap say about the way we define artistic and commercial success; the image that is fashioned of ghetto life and young black males; and our fear of and fascination with criminal violence?

Following Tupac's death, one music critic and friend noted, "It would be easy to cull the meaning of Tupac's short and turbulent life from his lyrics. If you listened hard enough, the sketchy outline of his soul revealed itself. His lyrics were a series of bloody, open sores, summing up the trials of Black boys reared in crack-crazed neighborhoods everywhere. With his mix of tough guy charisma and true ghetto flavor, Tupac captivated a nation with songs that possessed a defiant spirit almost unrivaled in mod[ern] . . .

Rap music h[as] . . . nation and capti[vated] . . . parts of the world . . . concern in many . . . countries, rap ha[s] . . . criminogenic, as[sociated with] . . . and violence. Ye[t] . . . out that rap star[s] . . . example for you[th] . . . to make it in life . . .

Sources
1. Frank Willia[ms,] . . . *The Source,* . . .
2. Kevin Powe[ll,] . . . Violent Deat[h] . . . Bury Me Lik[e] . . . Oct. 31, 199[ ] . . .
3. Michael Mar[ ] . . . Angry Voice[s] . . . Streets," *Ne[wsweek]* . . . 16, 1996, p. [ ] . . .
4. Tupac Shak[ur] . . .
5. Williams, p. [ ] . . .

Questions for [Discussion]
1. How real is . . . produces cr[ime?] . . . find out? . . .
2. What would . . . want to ban[ ] . . .

Timely *Of Immediate Concern* Boxes

Detailed discussion of the kinds of issues students are hearing about in the media relates the theories presented in each chapter back to the real world (discussion questions included).

Window to the World

A Social System Breaks Down

The American anthropologist Kenneth Good committed—for anthropologists— the unpardonable sin of marrying a young woman of the tribe he studied, the Yanomamö. The young bride returned with her husband to suburban New Jersey in 1988, and there they raised their children.(1) But in 1993 the Yanomamö wife slipped back into the Amazon jungle to live among her own people.

Who are the Yanomamö?

When another anthropologist Robert Carneiro went to the Amazon jungle in 1975 to study the Yanomamö, he found them to be a remote, stone-age, people dedicated to frequent intervillage warfare.(2)

Indeed, the Yanomamö are the last major remaining Stone Age people on earth, living their lives in harmony with nature, but also engaging in tribal warfare, according to their customs.

But all went awry in the 1980s, when gold was discovered in the Yanomamö territory.(3) As many as 40,000 prospectors had invaded by 1987, clearing the jungle for airstrips, bringing diseases—venereal and others—against which the Yanomamö had no immunity, importing modern weapons to replace Stone Age clubs, and raising the homicide rate.(4) What once was a nation of 100,000 was reduced to 22,000 (9400 in Brazil; 12,600 in Venezuela). A severe drought in the late 1990s added to the suffering of the Yanomamös, who use ancient incantations to bring rain as well as to quench forest fires and to drive out invaders.(2)

Help is under way and more is promised. The United Nations sent an emergency team of firefighters to deal with the forest fires. The Brazilian government clamped down on encroachments by rogue miners. The U.S. Congress

A Yanomamö man with the trappings of modern civilization.

made some assistance available to protect the rain forests, but did not designate preservation of the Yanomamö territory and lifestyle a priority.

Too little, too late? The Yanomamö's traditional way of life has broken down. The chances that they can withstand the attack of the Western culture invasion are slim. The large deposits of gold, diamonds, tin, and other minerals in the soil of their land will continue to attract invaders, with their attack on the traditional culture. Yanomamös are dying faster than ever before, hunting and fishing are increasingly difficult, alcohol and prostitution are taking their toll, firearms are escalating the death rate, and infant mortality is 24 times that of the United States.(5)

What are we to do about the Yanomamö? It does not seem possible to transplant Yanomamö into suburban

New Jersey. Forcing modern capitalism on them is even more destructive.

Should we just build a fence around the Yanomamö territory and allow them to live their accustomed lifestyle? The spectre of an entrepreneur flying in tourists in jumbo jets and charging admission to view "unspoiled," stone-aged Yanomamö is just too daunting.

Are we witnessing a genocide in the making?

Are you wondering about the Yanomamö wife? Well, you can see her adorned with tribal decoration in a photo at the American Museum of Natural History, Amazon exhibit.

Sources
1. Kenneth Good with David Chernoff, *Into the Heart* (New York: Simon and Schuster, 1991).
2. Robert L. Carneiro, "War and Peace: Alternating Realities in Human History," in *Studying War—Anthropological Perspectives,* ed. S. P. Reyns and R. E. Downs (City: Gordon and Bresch, 1994), pp. 3–27.
3. Lynne Wallis, "Quiet Genocide: Miners Seeking Precious Metals Are Causing Deaths of the Yanomami," *Ottawa Citizen,* June 28, 1993, p. A6.
4. "Aid for an Ancient Tribe," *Newsweek,* Apr. 9, 1990, p. 34.
5. "Genocide in the Amazon," *Newsweek,* Aug. 30, 1993, p. 61.

Questions for Discussion
1. As the Yanomamö culture is being destroyed, how would you expect the tribe's traditional ways of dealing with crime to be affected? Explain.
2. What measures might be effective in protecting indigenous peoples in all parts of the world from suffering a fate similar to that of the Yanomamö?

Merton's Theory of Anomie

Merton argued that in a class-oriented society, opportunities to get to the top are not equally distributed. Very few members of the lower class ever get there. His anomie theory emphasizes the importance of two elements in any society: (1) cultural aspirations, or goals that people believe are worth striving for, and (2) institutionalized means or accepted ways to attain the desired ends. If a society is to be stable, these

Classic *Window to the World* Boxes

Acclaimed thematic box highlights the international dimensions of criminology and lets students begin to understand the global ramifications of what they are studying (discussion questions included).

A Walk Through of the Fourth Edition

Easy-to-Use End-of-Chapter Reviews

Clear, concise chapter summaries and key terms lists—tabbed along the side of the page for easy reference when studying for an exam—provide students with essential review materials.

REVIEW

When psychologists have attempted to explain criminality, they have taken four general approaches. First, they have focused on failures in psychological development—an overbearing or weak conscience, inner conflict, insufficient moral development, and maternal deprivation, with its concomitant failure of attachment. Second, they have investigated the ways in which aggression and violence are learned through modeling and direct experience. Third, they have investigated the personality characteristics of criminals and found that criminals tend to be more impulsive, intolerant, and irresponsible than noncriminals. Fourth, psychologists have investigated the relation of criminality to such mental disorders as psychosis and psychopathy.

Biocriminologists investigate the biological correlates of criminality, including a genetic predisposition to commit crime. The XYY syndrome, though now generally discounted as a cause of criminality, suggests that aggressive and violent behavior may be at least partly determined by genetic factors. Studies of the behavior of identical and fraternal twins and of the rates of criminality among adopted children with both criminal and noncriminal biological and adoptive parents tend to support this hypothesis. Investigators have also found a strong correlation between low IQ and delinquency. Criminologists are still debating what public policy issues are raised by the possible role of genetics in crime.

Biocriminologists' most recent and perhaps most important discovery is the relation of criminal behavior to biochemical factors (food allergies, dietary deficiencies, hormonal imbalances) and neurophysiological factors (EEG abnormalities and minimal brain dysfunction). Most scientists agree that if some people are biologically predisposed to certain behaviors, both psychological and environmental factors shape the forms of those behaviors.

YOU BE THE CRIMINOLOGIST

For many years psychologists searched for the criminal personality, a common set of personality characteristics associated with criminals. If you were asked to assist in this effort, what methods would you use to capture the criminal personality? Would you use objective personality inventories? If you were successful, what would you do with your findings? How could this common personality profile be used in the criminal justice system?

KEY TERMS

The numbers next to the terms refer to the pages on which the terms are defined.

attachment (89)
behavioral modeling (92)
biocriminology (104)
chromosomes (105)
conditioning (99)
cortical arousal (99)
differential association-reinforcement (97)
dizygotic (DZ) twins (106)
ego (87)
extroversion (99)
fundamental psycholegal error (103)
hypoglycemia (111)
id (87)
minimal brain dysfunction (MBD) (112)
monozygotic (MZ) twins (106)
neuroticism (99)
psychoanalytic theory (87)
psychopathy (100)
psychosis (100)
psychoticism (99)
social learning theory (92)
superego (87)

NOTES

1. See Ronald Blackburn, *The Psychology of Criminal Conduct: Theory, Research, and Practice* (Chichester, England: Wiley, 1993); and Hans Toch, *Violent Men: An Inquiry into the Psychology of Violence*, rev. ed. (Washington, D.C.: American Psychological Association, 1992).
2. See, e.g., Cathy Spatz Widom, "Cycle of Violence," *Science*, **244** (1989): 160–165; and Nathaniel J. Pallone and J. J. Hennessey, *Criminal Behavior: A Process Psychology Analysis* (New Brunswick, N.J.: Transaction, 1992).
3. See, e.g., Sigmund Freud, *A General Introduction to Psychoanalysis* (New York: Liveright, 1920); and Sigmund Freud, *The Ego and the Id* (London: Hogarth, 1927).
4. August Aichhorn, *Wayward Youth* (New York: Viking, 1935).
5. Kate Friedlander, *The Psycho-Analytic Approach to Juvenile Delinquency* (New York: International Universities Press, 1947).
6. See Hans Eysenck, *The Rise and Fall of the Freudian Empire* (New York: Plenum, 1987).
7. Lawrence Kohlberg, "The Development of Modes of Moral Thinking and Choice in the Years Ten to Sixteen," Ph.D. dissertation, University of Chicago, 1958.
8. Lawrence Kohlberg, "Stage and Sequence: The Cognitive-Developmental Approach to Socialization," in *Handbook of Socialization Theory and Research*, ed. David A. Goslin (Chicago: Rand McNally, 1969).
9. Carol Gilligan has studied moral development in women—extending Kohlberg's role-taking theory of moral development. She found that moral reasoning differed in women. Women, according to Gilligan, see morality as the responsibility to take the view of others and to ensure their well-being. See Carol Gilligan, *In a Different Voice: Psychological Theory and Women's Development* (Cambridge, Mass.: Harvard University Press, 1982).
10. William S. Jennings, Robert Kilkenny, and Lawrence Kohlberg, "Moral Development Theory and Practice for Youthful Offenders," in *Personality Theory, Moral Development, and Criminal Behavior*, ed. William S. Laufer and James M. Day (Lexington, Mass.: Lexington Books, 1983). See also Daniel D. Macphail, "The Moral Education Approach in Treating Adult Inmates," *Criminal Justice and Behavior*, **15** (1989): 81–97; Jack Arbuthnot and Donald A. Gordon, "Crime and Cognition: Community Applications of Sociomoral Reasoning Development," *Criminal Justice and Behavior*, **15** (1988): 379–393; and J. E. LeCapitaine, "The Relationships between Emotional Development and Moral Development and the Differential Impact of Three Psychological Interventions on Children," *Psychology in the Schools*, **15** (1987): 379–393.
11. John Bowlby, *Attachment and Loss*, 2 vols. (New York: Basic Books, 1969, 1973). See also Bowlby's "Forty-Four Juvenile Thieves: Their Characteristics and Home Life," *International Journal of Psychoanalysis*, **25** (1944): 19–52.
12. John Bowlby, *The Making and Breaking of Affectional Bonds* (London: Tavistock, 1979). See also Michael Rutter, *Maternal Deprivation Reassessed* (Harmondsworth, England: Penguin, 1971).
13. Michael Lewis, Candice Feiring, Carolyn McGuffog, and John Jaskir, "Predicting Psychopathology in Six-Year-Olds from Early Social Relations," *Child Development*, **55** (1984): 123–136.
14. L. Sroufe, "Infant Caregiver Attachment and Patterns of Adaptation in Preschool: The Roots of Maladaption and Competence," in *Minnesota Symposium on Child Psychology*, vol. 16, ed. Marion Perlmutter (Hillsdale, N.J.: Erlbaum, 1982).
15. Alicia F. Lieberman, "Preschoolers' Competence with a Peer: Influence of Attachment and Social Experience," *Child Development*, **48** (1977): 1277–1287.
16. Joan McCord, "Some Child-Rearing Antecedents of Criminal Behavior," *Journal of Personality and Social Psychology*, **37** (1979): 1477–1486; Joan McCord, "A Longitudinal View of the Relationship between Paternal Absence and Crime," in *Abnormal Offenders, Delinquency, and the Criminal Justice System*, ed. John Gunn and David P. Farrington (London: Wiley, 1982). See also Scott W. Henggeler, Cindy L. Hanson, Charles M. Borduin, Sylvia M. Watson, and Molly A. Brunk, "Mother-Son Relationships of Juvenile Felons," *Journal of Consulting and Clinical Psychology*, **53** (1985): 942–943; and Francis I. Nye, *Family Relationships and Delinquent Behavior* (New York: Wiley, 1958).
17. Sheldon Glueck and Eleanor T. Glueck, *Unraveling Juvenile Delinquency* (New York: Commonwealth Fund, 1950); Lee N. Robins, "Aetiological Implications in Studies of Childhood Histories Relating to Antisocial Personality," in *Psychopathic Behaviour*, ed. Robert D. Hare and Daisy Schalling (Chichester, England: Wiley, 1970); Lee N.

CHAPTER 4

Review • You Be the Criminologist • Key Terms • Notes

Unique *You Be the Criminologist* Exercises

Chapter-ending exercises challenge students to use their critical thinking skills to apply what they have read about in the chapter.

Understanding Criminology

Criminology is the scientific study of the making of laws, the breaking of laws, and society's reaction to the breaking of laws. Sometimes these laws are arrived at by consensus; sometimes they are imposed by those in power. Today, most people share certain common interests. As a result, criminological research and crime-prevention strategies are becoming globalized, even though the reach of laws may not yet be global. Nationally and internationally, criminological research has become influential in policy making (Chapter 1).

Criminologists have adopted methods of study from all the social and behavioral sciences. Like all other scientists, criminologists measure. They assess crime over time and place, and they measure the characteristics of criminals and crimes (Chapter 2).

Throughout history, thinkers and rulers have written about crime and criminals and the control of crime. Yet the term "criminology" is little more than a century old, and the subject has been of scientific interest for only two centuries. Two schools of thought contributed to modern criminology: the classical school, associated predominantly with Cesare Beccaria (eighteenth century), which focused on crime, and the positivist school, associated with Cesare Lombroso, Enrico Ferri, and Raffaele Garofalo (nineteenth and early twentieth centuries), which focused on criminals (Chapter 3). Contemporary American criminology owes much to these European roots.

CHAPTER 1
An Overview of Criminology

KEY TERMS
conflict model
consensus model
crime
criminology
deviance

Criminologists study crime from a broad scientific perspective, in an effort to understand its causes and, ultimately, its prevention. They are not, as most of the world learned during O.J. Simpson's televised trial, the scientists who engage in crime scene investigations. (The people who do that are called criminalists or forensic scientists.) Another popular misunderstanding is that criminologists are only, or at least primarily, interested in street crime as it affects our lives and our fears, largely as a result of media portrayal. It is true that criminologists are very much concerned with murders, robberies, burglaries, and thefts. But consider for a moment that while all of America's thieves (excluding automobile thieves) cause us a loss of $4 billion annually, a single rogue trader may cause losses of billions. So criminologists must extend their focus beyond street crime and include other criminal activities that may be less visible, but may cause far greater harm to human beings all over the globe.

• Let us begin with a few select wealthy investment bankers and traders in trouble with the law. Ivan F. Boesky was convicted of insider trading scams committed in the 1980s, went to prison, and paid a $100 million fine. Marc Rich was indicted (60 counts) for trading with the enemy and tax fraud in 1983 and fled to Switzerland. Nicholas W. Leeson, rogue trader and financier, is alleged to have caused $1.3 billion in bank losses. He sits in a Singapore prison. Michael R. Milken paid $1 billion in fines and restitution and spent 2 years in prison for financial fraud. Martin A. Siegel pled guilty to conspiracy and tax evasion and paid $9 million in fines. Toshihide Iguchi of the New York branch of Daiwa Bank, after being convicted of bank fraud in the amount of $1.1 billion, is in prison. Money manager Martin Frankel, accused of swindling American insurance companies out of $350 million, was finally arrested in Hamburg, Germany, in September 1999. Criminologists are interested in the crimes these traders and bankers have committed. They are also interested in their deviance and in the trust they have breached.

While criminologists are interested in the punishments imposed on these criminals (and whether such sanctions have the expected effect), they are also interested in the reactions of their families and their colleagues (punishments beyond the law). Nearly all the traders mentioned have lost their respected status on Wall Street and have been barred from trading. Most have lost their spouses through divorce. Criminologists are interested in the controls and sanctions, legal or social, that guard the safety of our money and financial institutions.

The crimes we have just described—financial and tax fraud—belong to an area known as white-collar crime. Much research has been conducted to understand why middle- and upper-class people commit these crimes that affect broad sectors of the population. Criminologists are called upon by industry and government to measure, describe, and explain white-collar and corporate crime and to assist in devising strategies to prevent and control future offending.

• On February 11, 1998, U.S. District Court Judge Reena Raggi imposed a 20-year prison sentence on Lee Peng Fei, mastermind of the *Golden Venture* smuggling operation. On June 6, 1993, the Taiwan-registered rust-bucket freighter *Golden Venture* had grounded on the beach at Rockaway in New York City. The ship's captain and 12-man crew, along with 281 "passengers," jumped overboard in 6-foot swells, as the ship creaked and rolled in the surf. Six died in the effort to swim ashore. Most of the others were rounded up by officers of the U.S. Coast Guard, the Immigration and Naturalization Service, and the New York City police.

By now the Coast Guard has identified or intercepted over 50 of the many rust buckets that ferry an estimated 100,000 illegal Chinese immigrants to U.S. shores every year, for fees of between $20,000 and $60,000. The "lucky ones" must pay off these fees to gang enforcers through years of slavery in sweatshops or massage parlors.

Scholars of many disciplines are concerned with the causes and control of illegal migrations. Criminologists are expert at studying the criminal exploitation of human desires and ambitions, the organizational structure of the large and pervasive syndicates that resort to many kinds of crime in order to enrich themselves at the expense of individual victims and the public at large. Criminologists also study the links between alien, drug, arms, and contraband smuggling, and their impact on social structures and, indeed, on world peace.

• On August 10, 1999, a white supremacist shot up a summer-school camp for Jewish children, injuring five people; he then shot and killed a postal worker. And on September 15, 1999, a troubled loner opened fire on people assembled for a prayer meeting at the Wedgwood Baptist Church in Texas, killing seven people and wounding seven more. These were but the latest in a seemingly endless stream of mass killings, including six others in 1999, mostly in schools and libraries, mostly by single perpetrators:

August 5, 1999, Pelham, Alabama: 3 dead.
July 29, 1999, Atlanta, Georgia: 12 dead, 13 wounded.
July 2–4, 1999, Illinois and Indiana: 2 dead, 9 injured.
May 20, 1999, Conyers, Georgia: 6 injured.

Newspaper headlines, local and national, focus on the rash of school killings.

April 20, 1999, Littleton, Colorado (2 perpetrators): 13 dead, 23 injured.
April 15, 1999, Salt Lake City, Utah: 2 dead, 4
wounded.

Five other mass killings took place in 1997 and
1998. Criminologists are very much interested
in studying this sequence of events. Is there a
connection between the events? Who are the
perpetrators? What was their motivation? What
weapons did they use? Do any of the existing
theories of crime causation explain these mass
killings? What can (and should) be done to prevent these crimes from occurring? How can policy makers be reached with criminologists' recommendations?

• In 1989, news photographs depicted the supertanker *Exxon Valdez* aground in Prince
William Sound, Alaska, exuding oil through a
rupture in its hull. This accident caused North
America's largest ecological disaster. (The captain was eventually convicted on a misdemeanor charge.) Tankers have run aground before and since the *Exxon Valdez* disaster (Table
1.1). On February 15, 1996, the tanker *Sea Em-*
press ran aground off Wales, spilling 20 million
gallons of oil, far exceeding the *Exxon Valdez*
spillage. In all probability the cause once again
was human error. But criminologists have many
questions: How can we prevent such disasters
from happening in the future? Should corporations like Exxon be held criminally liable for the
acts of their employees? What sanctions are appropriate?

Criminologists study the criminal sanctions used against individuals and corporations. How can human and corporate behavior
be controlled to safeguard the environment?
Are new laws likely to provide greater protection against negligence and error? How much
will new measures cost, and are they cost-beneficial? To do such studies, criminologists develop research questions, select the most appropriate methods, and then assemble and
analyze the results.

• After a long civil war in the former Yugoslavia, the guns are now largely silent. U.N.
peacekeeping troops are patrolling the former
battlegrounds, and a U.N. international war
crimes tribunal has issued indictments and be-

The disastrous pollution of the oceans by tanker sinkings continues: The stern section of the Maltese oil tanker "Erika" points skyward as it flounders in heavy seas off the coast of France, December 13, 1999. The broken tanker, holding up to 20,000 tons of fuel oil, sank while it was being towed further out to sea.

TABLE 1.1 Some Major Marine Oil Spills

Tanker	Gallons	Date	Location
Amoco Cadiz	68 million	Mar. 16, 1978	Off Brittany, France
Torrey Canyon	36 million	Mar. 18, 1967	Isles of Scilly, United Kingdom
Braer	25 million	Jan. 5, 1993	Off Garths Ness, near Scotland
Nova	21 million	Dec. 6, 1985	Arabian Gulf
Sea Empress	20 million	Feb. 15, 1996	Milford Haven, Wales
Exxon Valdez	11 million	Mar. 24, 1989	Prince William Sound, Alaska
Estrella Pampeana	9 million	Jan. 19, 1999	Rio de la Plata, Argentina
North Cape	1 million	Jan. 19, 1999	South Kingston, Rhode Island

gun trials on charges of genocide, war crimes, and massive criminal violations of human rights, including ethnic cleansing through at least 21,000 murders (by at least 5000 perpetrators) and tens of thousands of rapes. These international crimes were rooted in deep-seated ethnic hatred and bigotry, whipped up by political opportunists.

Let us ask a challenging question: Are we in America free from ethnic hatred and bigotry? Far from it. Hate groups are on the increase, advocating white supremacy or black power and vowing death to those who oppose them, including government itself. Between January 1995 and September 1996, there were 102 suspicious fires at black churches, 122 at white churches, 6 at syna-

In a spate of hate crimes, houses of worship of many religions have been torched. Depicted here are the smoldering remnants of Mt. Zion Church burned by arsonists in Boligee, Alabama.

gogues, and 2 at mosques. While insurance fraud and vandalism account for some of the incidents, racial hatred appears to account for the majority.

Here, too, criminologists are searching for answers, not just those to be found in criminal sanctions, but also those of peaceful conflict resolution and education.

Did You Know

. . . that terrorism is not a new crime? From the seventeenth to nineteenth centuries, pirates flying the skull and crossbones, and dressed in grotesque and fear-inspiring garb, made wild and ear-shattering noises, thus using terror as a weapon.

• Most people remember the terrorist bomb that destroyed Pan Am flight 103 over Lockerbie, Scotland in December 1988, with a loss of 270 lives. Most of the victims were Americans returning home for the holidays. Finally, more than a decade later, two Libyans are on trial for conspiracy before a court composed of Scottish judges in The Hague, the Netherlands. The suspects were finally surrendered by the government of Libya, after the U.N. Security Council placed economic sanctions on that country.

People in Italy, France, Germany, and Ireland, as well as in Asia, Latin America, and the Middle East, have long been familiar with terrorism; many have dealt with it successfully. For Americans, terrorism at home is something new and shocking. The number of terrorist acts, whether domestic or foreign, has been increasing to the point where we have had between 1000 and 2000 terrorist bombings annually since 1989 (Figure 1.1).

Terrorism poses a particular challenge to criminologists. Who are the terrorists? What prompts them to commit what types of terrorist crimes against whom, and when? What measures can be adopted to prevent terrorism, a crime that can cripple an economy and destroy a government? What international strategies can be adopted to deal with this form of crime?

Having surveyed the broad spectrum of criminologists' interests, we now define criminology, delineate its place among the sciences, and describe its major areas of concern: the making of laws, the breaking of laws, and society's reaction to the breaking of laws. We turn first to history.

FIGURE 1.1　Bombing incidents reported to or investigated by the Bureau of Alcohol, Tobacco and Firearms, by type of incident, United States, 1976–97.

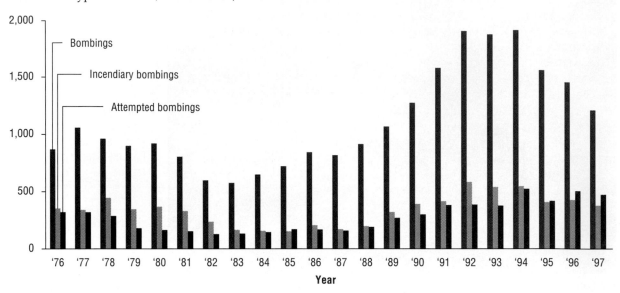

Note: "Bombings" are incidents in which high explosives, low explosives, or blasting agents explode. "Incendiary bombings" are bombings in which incendiary/chemical devices induce burning. "Attempted bombings" are incidents in which a device fails to function.

Source: U.S. Department of the Treasury, Bureau of Alcohol, Tobacco and Firearms, *Explosives Incidents Report 1985,* p. 9; *1990,* p.11; *1993,* p. 13 (Washington, DC: U.S. Department of the Treasury); and U.S. Department of the Treasury, Bureau of Alcohol, Tobacco and Firearms, *1995 Arson and Explosives Incidents Report,* p. 13; *1997,* p. 13 (Washington, DC: U.S. Department of the Treasury).

WHAT IS CRIMINOLOGY?

In the Middle Ages human learning was commonly divided into four areas: law, medicine, theology, and philosophy. Universities typically had four faculties, one for each of these fields. Imagine a young person in the year 1392—100 years before Columbus came ashore in America—knocking at the portal of a great university with the request: "I would like to study criminology. Where do I sign up?" A stare of disbelief would have greeted the student, because the word had not yet been coined. Cautiously the student would explain: "Well, I'm interested in what crime is, and how the law deals with criminals." The university official might smile and say: "The right place for you to go is the law faculty. They will teach you everything there is to know about the law."

The student might feel discouraged. "That's a lot more than I want to know about the law. I really don't care about inheritance laws and the law of contracts. I just want to study all about crime and criminality. For example, why are certain actions considered wrong or evil in the first place,

and . . ." The official would interrupt: "Then you must go to the faculty of theology. They know all there is to know about good and evil, heaven and hell." The student might persist. "But could they teach me what it is about the human body and mind that could cause some people and not others to commit crime?" "Oh, I see," the official would say. "You really should study medicine." "But, sir, medicine probably is only part of what I need to know, and really only part of medicine seems relevant. I want to know all there is to know about . . ." And then would come the official's last attempt to steer the student in the right direction: "Go and study philosophy. They'll teach you all there is to know!"

For centuries, all the knowledge the universities recognized continued to be taught in these four faculties. It was not until the eighteenth and nineteenth centuries that the natural and social sciences became full-fledged disciplines. In fact, the science of criminology has been known as such for only a little more than a century.

In 1885 the Italian law professor Raffaele Garofalo coined the term "criminology" (in Italian, *criminologia*).[1] The French anthropologist Paul Topinard used it for the first time in French (*criminologie*) in 1887.[2] "Criminology" aptly described and encompassed the scientific concern with the phenomenon of crime. The term immediately gained acceptance all over the world, and criminology became a subject taught at universities. Unlike their predecessors in 1392—or even in 1892—today's entering students will find that teaching and learning are distributed among 20 or 30 disciplines and departments. And criminology or criminal justice is likely to be one of them.

Criminology is a science, an empirical science. More particularly, it is one of the social, or behavioral, sciences. It has been defined in various ways by its scholars. The definition provided in 1934 by Edwin H. Sutherland, one of the founding scholars of American criminology, is widely accepted:

> **Criminology** is the body of knowledge regarding crime as a social phenomenon. It includes within its scope the process of making laws, of breaking laws, and of reacting toward the breaking of laws. . . . The objective of criminology is the development of a body of general and verified principles and of other types of knowledge regarding this process of law, crime, and treatment or prevention.[3]

This definition suggests that the field of criminology is narrowly focused on crime, yet broad in scope. By stating as the objective of criminology the "development of a body of general and verified principles," Sutherland mandates that criminologists, like all other scientists, collect information for study and analysis in accordance with the research methods of modern science. As we shall see in Chapter 3, it was in the eighteenth century that serious investigations into criminal behavior were first conducted. The investigators, however, were not engaged in empirical research, although they based their conclusions on factual information. It was only in the nineteenth century that criminologists began to systematically gather facts about crime and criminals and evaluate their data in a scientific manner.

Among the first researchers to analyze empirical data (facts, statistics, and other observable information) in a search for the causes of crime was Cesare Lombroso (1835–1909) of Italy (Chapter 3). His biologically oriented theories influenced American criminology at the turn of the twentieth century. At that time the causes of crime were thought to rest within the individual: Criminal behavior was attributed to feeblemindedness and "moral insanity."

Crime Surfing

http://www.ussc.gov/moneylaw/monisum.htm

One of the components of Sutherland's definition of criminology focuses on the making of laws. For example, Congress creates the offense of money laundering in 1986. How did Congress define this crime?

From then on, psychologists and psychiatrists played an important role in the study of crime and criminals.

By the 1920s other scholars attributed the cause of crime to the influx of immigrants and their alien behaviors. The search then moved on to cultural and social interpretations. Crime was explained not only in terms of the offender but also in terms of social, political, and economic problems.

In increasing numbers, sociologists, political scientists, legal scholars, and economists have entered the arena of criminology. Architects too have joined the ranks of criminologists in an effort to design housing units that will be relatively free from crime. Engineers are working to design cars that are virtually theftproof. Pharmacologists play a role in alleviating the problem of drug addiction. Satellites put into space by astrophysicists can help control the drug trade. Specialists in public administration work to improve the functioning of the criminal justice system. Educators have been enlisted to prepare children for a life as free from delinquency as possible. Economists and social workers are needed to help break the cycle of poverty and crime. Biologists and endocrinologists have expanded our understanding of the relationship between biology and deviant behavior. Clearly, criminology is a discipline composed of the accumulated knowledge of many other disciplines. Criminologists acknowledge their indebtedness to all contributing disciplines, but they consider theirs a separate science.

In explaining what is meant by Sutherland's definition—"making laws," "breaking laws,"

FIGURE 1.2   The funnel of deviance.

Most inclusive

 I. Feeling that something is
    vaguely wrong, strange, peculiar
 II. Feelings of dislike, repugnance
 III. Feeling that something violates values or rules
 IV. Feeling that something violates moral values
    or moral rules
 V. Judgment that something violates values or rules
 VI. Judgment that something violates moral
    values or moral rules
 VII. Judgment that something violates morally
    legitimate misdemeanor laws
 VIII. Judgment that something violates morally
    legitimate felony laws
 IX. Judgment that something violates moral human nature
 X. Judgment that something is absolutely evil

Least inclusive

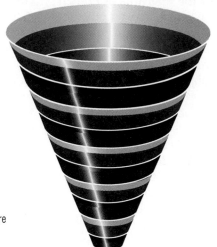

Source: Adapted from Jack D. Douglas and Frances C. Waksler, *The Sociology of Deviance* (Boston: Little, Brown, 1982), p. 11.

and "reacting toward the breaking of laws"—we will use a contemporary as well as a historical perspective on these processes, and a global as well as a local focus.

THE MAKING OF LAWS

Conjure up a picture of a crowded supermarket just after working hours when most people are eager to get home after a busy day. The checkout counters have long lines of carts overflowing with groceries. One counter—an express line—takes 10 items only. You have 15, but you get in line anyway. People behind you in the line stare. Your behavior is not acceptable. You are a nonconformist, a deviant.

Deviance

Criminologists use the term **deviance** to describe behavior that violates social norms, including laws. The customary ways of doing everyday things (like not exceeding the posted limit of items at supermarket express lines) are governed by norms other than laws. More serious deviant behavior, like taking someone else's property, is governed by laws. Criminologists are interested in all social norms and in how society reacts to success or failure of com-

pliance.[4] They are interested in what society does when customary ways of doing things no longer prove effective in controlling conduct perceived as undesirable. New Yorkers concerned over the problem of dog droppings provide an example.

Disciplined city dwellers had always observed the custom of curbing their dogs. Street signs warned them to do this. But as more and more dog owners failed to comply, New Yorkers decided that the cleanliness of the sidewalks was an important issue. Laws were enacted making it an offense not to clean up after one's dog. In Beijing, China, and Reykjavik, Iceland, dogs have been severely restricted or banned from the city altogether.

The difference between crime and other forms of deviance is subject to constant change, and may vary from one state or country to another and from one time to another. What yesterday was only distasteful or morally repugnant may today be illegal. Criminologists are therefore interested in all norms that regulate conduct. Making something that is distasteful into a crime may be counterproductive and detrimental to the social order. If everything deviant (inconsistent with the majority's norms) were to be made criminal, society would become very rigid. The more rigid a society, the more behavior defined as violating social norms is prohibited by law.

Jack D. Douglas and Frances C. Waksler have presented the continuum of deviance as a funnel (Figure 1.2). This funnel consists of definitions ranging from the broadest (a "feeling that something is vaguely wrong, strange, peculiar") to the narrowest (a "judgment that something is absolutely evil"). Somewhere between these two extremes, deviant behavior becomes criminal behavior. The criminologist's interest in understanding the process begins at the earliest point—when a behavior is first labeled deviant.[5]

Although criminologists are interested in all deviant behavior—even that of no interest to the law—their primary interest is in criminal behavior, that which violates the law.

The Concept of Crime

A **crime** is any human conduct that violates a criminal law and is subject to punishment. What leads a society to designate some deviant behavior as a crime and leave other wrongs to be settled by private or civil remedies? For centuries, natural-law philosophers, believing in the universal rightness and wrongness of certain human behavior, held the view that some forms of behavior are innately criminal and that all societies condemn them equally. Homicide and theft were thought to be among these.

This notion is no longer supported. Raffaele Garofalo, who gave our discipline its name, defended the concept of natural crime, by which he meant behavior that offends basic moral sentiments, such as respect for the property of others and revulsion against infliction of suffering. Nevertheless, he admitted that although we might think such crimes as murder and robbery would be recognized by all existing legal systems, "a slight investigation seems to dispel this idea."[6]

Garofalo was right. The earliest codes, including the Babylonian Code of Hammurabi (about 1750 B.C.) and the Roman Law of the Twelve Tables (451–450 B.C.), do not list homicide or ordinary theft as crimes. Problems like these were settled without resorting to pun-

The Code of Hammurabi, king of ancient Babylonia, is the oldest complete legal code in existence (approximately 1750 B.C.). The 8.2-foot carving, found in Iran in 1902, is now on display in the Louvre in Paris. The only exact replica is at the United Nations building in New York.

ishment. But all early societies imposed punishment for acts detrimental to their own existence: treason. Other crimes depended on socioeconomic needs (destroying a bridge was a crime among the Incas; stealing a beehive was a crime among the ancient Germanic tribes; stealing a horse or a blanket was a crime among American Plains Indians).

The question arises: Who in a society decides—and when and under what circumstances—which acts that are already considered deviant in that society should be elevated to the level of gross deviance or crime, subject to punishment?

Did You Know

. . . that in the early days of the common law, judges made the laws? Legislatures (parliament) took over lawmaking only about three centuries ago.

The Consensus and Conflict Views of Law and Crime

In the traditional interpretation of the historical development of legal systems, and of criminal justice in particular, lawmaking is an accommodation of interests in a society, whether that society is composed of equals (as in a democracy) or of rulers and ruled (as in absolute monarchies), so as to produce a system of law and enforcement to which everybody basically subscribes. This is the **consensus model.** According to this view, certain acts are deemed so threatening to the society's survival that they are designated crimes. If the vast majority of a group shares this view, we can say the group has acted by consensus.

The model assumes that members of a society by and large agree on what is right and wrong, and that codification of social values becomes law, with a mechanism of control which settles disputes that arise when some individuals stray too far from what is considered acceptable behavior. In the words of the famous French sociologist Émile Durkheim, "We can . . . say that an act is criminal when it offends strong and defined states of the collective conscience."[7] Consensus theorists view society as a stable entity in which laws are created for the general good. Laws function to reconcile and to harmonize most of the interests that most of us accept, with the least amount of sacrifice.

Some criminologists view the making of laws in a society from a different theoretical perspective. In their interpretation, known as the **conflict model,** the criminal law expresses the values of the ruling class in a society, and the criminal justice system is a means of controlling the classes that have no power. Conflict theorists claim that a struggle for power is a far more basic feature of human existence than is consensus. It is through power struggles that various interest groups manage to control lawmaking and law enforcement. Accordingly, the appropriate object of criminological investigation is not the violation of laws but the conflicts within society.

Traditional historians of crime and criminal justice do not deny that throughout history there have been conflicts that needed resolution. Traditionalists claim that differences have been resolved by consensus, while conflict theorists claim that the dominant group has ended the conflicts by imposing its will. This difference in perspective marks one of the major criminological debates today, as we shall see in Chapter 8. It also permeates criminological discussion of who breaks the criminal laws and why.

THE BREAKING OF LAWS

Sutherland's definition of criminology includes within its scope investigating and explaining the process of breaking laws. This may seem simple if viewed from a purely legal perspective. A prosecutor is not interested in the fact that hundreds of people are walking on Main Street. But if one of those hundreds grabs a woman's purse and runs away with it, the prosecutor is interested, provided the police have brought the incident to the prosecutor's attention. What alerts the prosecutor is the fact that a law has been broken, that one of those hundreds of people on Main Street has turned from a law-abiding citizen into a lawbreaker. This event, if detected, sets in motion a legal process that ultimately will determine whether someone is indeed a lawbreaker.

Sutherland, in saying that criminologists have to study the process of lawbreaking, had much more in mind than determining whether or not someone has violated the criminal law. He was referring to the process of breaking laws. That process encompasses a series of events, perhaps starting at birth or even earlier, which results in the commission of crime by some individuals and not by others.

Let us analyze the following rather typical scenario: In the maximum-security unit of a Midwestern penitentiary is an inmate we will call Jeff. He is one of three robbers who held up a check-cashing establishment. During the robbery, another of the robbers killed the clerk. Jeff has been sentenced to life imprisonment.

Born in an inner-city ghetto, Jeff was the third child of an unwed mother. He had a succession of temporary "fathers." By age 12 he had run away from home for the first time, only to be brought back to his mother, who really did not care much whether he returned or not. He

Let us start this box with the question, Where have we come from?

Have you ever wondered about the wolf who accosts Little Red Riding Hood as she makes her way through the forest to her grandmother's house? Later he devours both Grandma and Little Red Riding Hood. Who is that wolf who speaks like a man?

THE WOLF-OUTLAW

Scholarly research suggests that he is a wolf of the two-legged variety—a convicted criminal banished to the woods. Fairy tales embody ancient folk wisdom and law. Before there were written legal codes, law was transmitted orally from generation to generation. The Red Riding Hood fairy tale reflects a time when the punishment for the most serious crimes was to be a wolf. Like the four-legged variety, the offender was banished from human society and condemned to the forest, there to live or die among the four-legged wolves, shunned or hunted like one of them.

The ancient European tribes, ever on the move, could not rely on prisons as punishment for offenders. Outlawry seemed to be the perfect solution, and the wolf provided a model.

Imprisonment as a punishment for crime does not appear in any of the Grimms' fairy tales, another accurate reflection of historical fact: German principalities began to use imprisonment only in the fourteenth century, and the tales collected by the Grimm brothers generally predated that period.

CATALOGS OF CRIME AND PUNISHMENT

Fairy tales are rich in criminological lore. Every category of crime and the punishments that were in vogue in the early Middle Ages appear in the Grimms' tales. Death by fire was the punishment of choice for witchcraft, as in "Hansel and Gretel," where the witch is incinerated in her own stove. Murderers were drowned, burned, or banished to the forest, and grand larceny was punished by hanging, as in the fairy tale "The Master-Thief" (although the ruler commuted the sentence). Petty larceny was punished corporally, and impersonation and involuntary servitude, as in "Cinderella," were punished by blinding, a penalty German tribes regarded as very severe. Tarring also appeared as a punishment for serious crimes, both in the fairy tales and in law documents from the period.

In the fairy tale "The Twelve Brothers," perverting justice and attempting to cause an innocent person to be executed was punished by being boiled in oil into which vipers were thrown, the most unusual penalty that appears in the Grimms' collection. But it, too, reflects historical fact; a similar punishment is recorded in early Roman law.

PSYCHOLOGICAL TREATISES

These tales can tell us about more than just types of crimes and punishments. The author of a research report entitled "The Criminal Element in German Folk Tales," published in 1910, used a criminological psychology approach to analyze the Grimms' tales and those collected by others. This report uncovered "every conceivable criminal motivation, from base greed to the grossest form of psychopathology." Perhaps fairy tales would be useful required reading for students of criminology.

Source

Gerhard O. W. Mueller, "The Criminological Significance of the Grimms' Fairy Tales," in *Fairy Tales and Society: Illusion, Allusion, and Paradigm,* ed. Ruth B. Bottigheimer (Philadelphia: University of Pennsylvania Press, 1986), pp. 217–227.

Questions for Discussion

We can now conclude this box with the question, Where do we go from here?
1. Since fairy tales—the product of folk wisdom—are so full of sound information about crime, law, and criminals, are modern criminologists and lawyers simply trying to catch up with the community at large?
2. What might be the modern equivalent of fairy tales in terms of an unofficial recording of the types of crimes and punishments in use today?
3. The Grimms' fairy tales provide information about European crime and punishment. Is there any similar source of information about early forms of crime and punishment in North America?

rarely went to school because, he said, "all the guys were bigger." At age 16, after failing two grades, Jeff dropped out of school completely and hung around the streets of his deteriorated, crime-ridden neighborhood. He had no job. He had no reason to go home, since usually no one was there.

One night he was beaten up by members of a local gang. He joined a rival gang for protection and soon began to feel proud of his membership in one of the toughest gangs in the neighborhood. Caught on one occasion tampering with parking meters and on another trying to steal a car CD player, he was sentenced to 2 months in a county correctional institution for boys. By the age of 18 he had moved from petty theft to armed robbery.

Many people reading the story of Jeff would conclude that he deserves what is coming to him and that his fate should serve as a warning to others. Other people would say that with his background, Jeff did not have a chance. Some may even marvel at Jeff's ability to survive at all in a very tough world.

To the criminologist, popular interpretations of Jeff's story do not explain the process of breaking laws in Sutherland's terms. Nor do these interpretations explain why people in general break a certain law. Sutherland demanded scientific rigor in researching and explaining the process of breaking laws. As we will see later in the book (Parts II and III), scientists have thoroughly explored Jeff's story and the stories of other lawbreakers. They ask: Why are some people prone to commit crime and others are not? There is no agreement on the answer as yet. Researchers have approached the question from different perspectives. Some have examined delinquents (juvenile offenders) and criminals from a biological perspective in order to determine whether some human beings are constitutionally more prone to yield to opportunities to commit criminal acts. Are genes to blame? Hormones? Diet? Others have explored the role played by moral development and personality. Is there a criminal personality? (These questions are discussed in Chapter 4.)

Most contemporary criminologists look to such factors as economic and social conditions, which can produce strain among social groups and lead to lawbreaking (Chapter 5). Others point to subcultures committed to violent or illegal activities (Chapter 6). Yet another argument is that the motivation to commit crime is simply part of human nature. So some criminologists examine the ability of social groups and institutions to make their rules effective (Chapter 7).

The findings of other scholars tend to show that lawbreaking depends less on what the offender does than on what society, including the criminal justice system, does to the offender (Chapter 8). This is the perspective of the labeling, conflict, and radical theorists, who have had great influence on criminological thinking since the 1970s.

Scholars have also researched the question of why people who are inclined to break laws engage in particular acts at particular times. They have demonstrated that opportunity plays a great role in the decision to commit a crime. Opportunities are suitable targets inadequately protected. In these circumstances, all that is required for a crime to be committed is a person motivated to offend. These claims are made by criminologists who explain crime in terms of two perspectives, called routine activities and rational choice (Chapter 9).

SOCIETY'S REACTION TO THE BREAKING OF LAWS

Criminologists' interest in understanding the process of breaking a law (or any other social norm) is tied to understanding society's reaction to deviance. The study of reactions to lawbreaking demonstrates that society has always tried to control or prevent norm breaking.

In the Middle Ages, the wayfarer entering a city had to pass the gallows, on which the bodies of criminals swung in the wind. Wayfarers had to enter through gates in thick walls, and the drawbridges were lowered only during the daylight hours; at nightfall the gates were closed. In front of the town hall, stocks and pillory warned dishonest vendors and pickpockets. Times have changed, but perhaps less than we think. Today penitentiaries and jails dot the countryside. Teams of work-release convicts work along highways under guard. Signs proclaim "Drug-Free School Zone," and decals on doors announce "Neighborhood

Don't shed a tear for me nigga, I ain't
happy here
I hope they bury me and send me to
my rest
headlines reading 'murdered to death'
my last breath.(1)
From Tupac's "If I Die 2nite"

At 4:03 P.M. on September 13, 1996, Tupac Amaru Shakur, rapper and actor, died at the University of Nevada Medical Center, in Las Vegas. The cause of death: gunshot wounds received 6 days earlier in a drive-by shooting. Tupac Shakur, known as 2Pac, was 25 years old.(2)

If you had been assigned to write Tupac Shakur's obituary, how would you have captured the contradiction of his artistic achievement and self-destructive life? The gangsta rapper Tupac was a sensitive poet and film actor with an innocent, endearing smile. His records were making millions of dollars. He was also a violent, abusive alcoholic. Tupac was a sweet and kind mother's boy. He was also a frightening street thug, a former drug dealer, and a convicted rapist. He was a product of the Marin Public Housing project—an impoverished group of buildings called "the jungle" by many residents.(3)

How would you have explained the unnerving convergence of violent rap and street crime that marked his death? Tupac made light of urban gangsta violence in rap, and died in the middle of the night from a flurry of gangland gunfire that had the look and feel of a well-choreographed music video. He challenged his own death in lyrics and song: "I heard a rumor I died/murdered in cold blood, dramatized/pictures of me in my final state, you know how I cried."(4) In an ultimate pairing of life and art, two of the gunshots fired on that fateful Saturday night hit Tupac's *thug life* tattoo, causing the internal bleeding that took his life.

In just five years, from 1991 to 1996, Tupac released four solo albums: *2Pacalypse Now* (1991), *Strictly 4 My Ni*Gaz* (1993), *Me Against the World* (1995), and *All Eyez on Me* (1996); he also appeared in five films: *Juice* (1991), *Poetic Justice* (1993), *Above the Rim* (1994), *Gang Related* (1996), and *Gridlock* (1996). During the same five years, he was also

Tupac and beyond: Gangsta rap musicians seem to be linked to violence. Depicted are Sean (Puffy) Combs and his girlfriend Jennifer Lopez. Around them on December 27, 1999, at Club New York, gunshots injured three. Combs and Lopez left in a Lincoln owned by Combs' Bad Boy Entertainment Company. Arrested after a high speed chase, Puff Daddy was indicted on felony weapons charges; Lopez was cleared.

- *Charged with beating a video director in Los Angeles (5 days in jail).*
- *Charged with threatening another rapper with a baseball bat (charges dropped).*
- *Arrested in Atlanta for allegedly shooting two off-duty cops (charges dropped).*
- *Charged in the sexual abuse of a fan in a New York City hotel room (convicted by a jury and sentenced to jail).*
- *Arrested on charges of gun and marijuana possession in LA.*
- *Shot five times in a midtown New York City recording studio (crime unsolved).*
- *Jailed for 8 months (served sentence for sexual abuse conviction).*
- *Sentenced to 120 days for probation violations in New York and Los Angeles (freed pending appeal).*

Now, put aside the contradictions of achievement and self-destruction that mark Tupac Shakur's life and death. Forget the unnerving convergence of life

and art. Instead, consider how you would have captured the real meaning of Tupac Shakur's success. How would you have explained our attraction to and fascination with Dr. Dre, Eazy-E, Snoop Doggy Dog, Tha Dogg Pound, Run-DMC, and Outkast? What does the rise of gangsta rap say about the way we define artistic and commercial success; the image that is fashioned of ghetto life and young black males; and our fear of and fascination with criminal violence?

Following Tupac's death, one music critic and friend noted, "It would be easy to cull the meaning of Tupac's short and turbulent life from his lyrics. If you listened hard enough, the sketchy outline of his soul revealed itself. His lyrics were a series of bloody, open sores, summing up the trials of Black boys reared in crack-crazed neighborhoods everywhere. With his mix of tough guy charisma and true ghetto flavor, Tupac captivated a nation with songs that possessed a defiant spirit almost unrivaled in modern pop music."(5)

Rap music has reached beyond our nation and captivated youth in nearly all parts of the world, causing great concern in many societies. In some countries, rap has been banned as criminogenic, as glorifying drug use and violence. Yet some observers point out that rap stardom sets a good example for youngsters who are trying to make it in life.

Sources

1. Frank Williams, "The Living End," *The Source*, November 1996, p. 103.
2. Kevin Powell, "The Short Life and Violent Death of Tupac Shakur: Bury Me Like a G," *Rolling Stone*, Oct. 31, 1996, p. 40.
3. Michael Marriott, "Shots Silence Angry Voice Sharpened by the Streets," *New York Times*, Sept. 16, 1996, p. A1.
4. Tupac Shakur, "Ain't Hard to Find."
5. Williams, p. 106.

Questions for Discussion

1. How real is the fear that rap music produces crime? How would you find out?
2. What would you say to those who want to ban or abolish rap music?

Crime Watch." Police patrol cars are as visible as they are audible.

These overt signs of concern about crime provide us with only a surface view of the apparatus society has created to deal with lawbreaking; they tell us little of the research and policy making that have gone into the creation of the apparatus. Criminologists have done much of the research on society's reaction to the breaking of laws, and the results have influenced policy making and legislation aimed at crime control. The research has also revealed that society's reaction to lawbreaking has often been irrational, arbitrary, emotional, politically motivated, and counterproductive.

Research on society's reaction to the breaking of laws is more recent than research on the causes of crime. It is also more controversial. For some criminologists, the function of their research is to assist government in the prevention or repression of crime. Others insist that such a use of science only supports existing power structures that may be corrupt. The position of most criminologists is somewhere in between. Researchers often discover inhumane and arbitrary practices and provide the database and the ideas for a humane, effective, and efficient criminal justice system.

Criminology and the Criminal Justice System

The term "criminal justice system" is relatively new. It became popular only in 1967, with the publication of the report of the President's Commission on Law Enforcement and Administration of Justice, *The Challenge of Crime in a Free Society.* The discovery that various ways of dealing with lawbreaking form a system was itself the result of criminological research. Research into

Crime Surfing

http://www.albany.edu/sourcebook

If you want to know more about the criminal justice system, its characteristics, its function, its cost, and its impact, go to the "Sourcebook of Criminal Justice Statistics."

the functioning of the system and its component parts, as well as into the work of functionaries within the system, has provided many insights over the last few decades.

Scientists who study the criminal justice system are frequently referred to as "criminal justice specialists." This term suggests a separation between criminology and criminal justice. In fact, the two fields are closely interwoven. Scholars of both disciplines use the same scientific research methods. They have received the same rigorous education, and they pursue the same goals. Both fields rely on the cooperation of many other disciplines, including sociology, psychology, political science, law, economics, management, and education. Their origins, however, do differ. Criminology has its roots in European scholarship, though it has undergone refinements, largely under the influence of American sociology. Criminal justice is a recent American innovation.

The two fields are also distinguished by a difference in focus. Criminology generally focuses on scientific studies of crime and criminality, whereas criminal justice focuses on scientific studies of decision-making processes, operations, and such justice-related concerns as the efficiency of police, courts, and corrections systems; the just treatment of offenders; the needs of victims; and the effects of changes in sentencing philosophy.

The United States has well over 50 criminal justice systems—those of the 50 states and of the federal government, the District of Columbia, Puerto Rico, Guam, the U.S. Virgin Islands, American Samoa, the Commonwealth of the Northern Mariana Islands, Palau, and the military. They are very similar: All are based on constitutional principles and on the heritage of the common law. All were designed to cope with the problem of crime within their territories, on the assumption that crime is basically a local event calling for local response. Crimes that have an interstate or international aspect are under the jurisdiction of federal authorities, and such offenses are prosecuted under the federal criminal code.

The Global Approach to the Breaking of Laws

Until fairly recently there was rarely any need to cooperate with foreign governments, as crime

Despite many differences, Americans and Russians had one thing in common: freedom from terrorism at home. This commonality was shattered for Americans on February 26, 1993, when a bomb tore a huge hole in the World Trade Center (WTC) in New York City, killing 6 people. Russians were awakened to the reality of terrorism on August 31, 1999, when a bomb exploded at Moscow's upscale Manezh shopping center near the Kremlin, killing 1 person and injuring 40. So, once again, Americans and Russians have something in common: domestic terrorism and the fear that goes with it. In America, the WTC terrorist attack was followed by the Oklahoma City bombing, on April 19, 1995, which killed 168 people, and the Olympic Park bomb explosion in Atlanta, Georgia, on July 30, 1996, which killed 1 person and injured many. Of course, Americans have been victimized by terrorist attacks outside the country, including, among many others:

- The destruction of Pan Am flight 103 over Lockerbie, Scotland , in 1988 (270 dead).
- The destruction of a U.S. military residence in Dhahran, Saudi Arabia, in 1996 (19 dead, many injured).
- The destruction of the U.S. embassies in Nairobi, Kenya, and Dar-es-Salaam, Tanzania, in 1998 (224 dead, 4300 injured).

Russians suffered five brutal terrorist attacks within the span of 3 weeks:

1. August 31, 1999. Manezh Shopping Center, near the Kremlin, Moscow (1 killed, 40 injured).
2. September 4, 1999. Dagestan, Russia (64 killed).
3. September 9, 1999. Moscow apartment building (94 killed).
4. September 13, 1999. Moscow apartment building (118 killed).
5. September 16, 1999. Volgodansk, Russia, apartment building (18 killed).

There was a time when terrorism could be categorized in terms of political versus profit motive, foreign versus domestic, and so on. These lines have become blurred, and the profit motive seems to have disappeared. While there may still be a domestic form of terrorism, such as the terrorism

Terrorism against Americans at home: A truck bomb explodes outside the federal building in Oklahoma City, on April 19, 1995, killing 168 Americans and seriously injuring many others.

perpetrated by fanatics and by cultlike private militias who see the government as an enemy, most terrorism appears to have an international base and is directed against people and their governments. In particular, Islamic fanatic fundamentalist terrorists are increasingly identified with attacks against U.S. and Russian targets.

There also was a time when terrorists enjoyed the support, both financial and material, of some foreign governments. That support no longer exists. Very few countries can be counted among the supporters of current terrorist groups.

In 1993—before most of the terrorist events discussed here took place—a meeting of over 200 counterterrorism experts and Pentagon officials concluded "that the proliferation of ethnic and regional conflicts will spawn new radical movements, leading inevitably to new terrorism." "We're going to see a global increase in anarchy," said one Defense

Terrorism against Russians at home: Explosion destroys buildings in Moscow, September 9, 1999.

Department analyst. Some at the meeting worried about what they term "mass terrorism," like that spawned by ethnic conflicts. Others were more concerned about what they are calling "single-issue" terrorism, attacks by radicals who share no ideology, only the hatred for a particular enemy.(1)

Americans have been very active in bringing terrorists to justice. The WTC and Oklahoma City terrorists have been convicted. The Pan Am 103 terrorists are on trial in the Netherlands, and air-strike retaliation has taken place against the embassy terrorist groups in Africa. Russian law enforcement authorities have tentatively identified some Chechen terrorists, although no arrests have been made yet. But Russia has conducted retaliatory air strikes against Chechen targets.

Source

1. Douglas Waller, "Counterterrorism: Victim of Success?" *Newsweek*, July 5, 1993, pp. 22–23.

Questions for Discussion

1. International terrorism is a criminal activity that can involve an almost limitless number of specific crimes, individuals, and countries. How would you devise a strategy to combat it at the national and international levels?
2. How would you go about studying trends in terrorism and the impact of terrorist attacks on society and the economy?

---

had few international connections. This situation has changed drastically: Crime, like life itself, has become globalized, and responses to lawbreaking have inevitably extended beyond local and national borders. In the first 3½ decades after World War II, from 1945 until the late 1970s, the countries of the world gradually became more interdependent. Commercial relations among countries increased. The jet age brought a huge increase in international travel and transport. Satellite communications facilitated intense and continuous public and private relationships. The Internet added the final touch to globalization.

Beginning in the 1980s, the internationalization of national economies accelerated sharply, and with the collapse of Marxism in Eastern Europe in the 1990s, a global economy is being created. These developments, which turned the world into what has been called a global village, have also had considerable negative consequences. As everything else in life became globalized, so did crime. Transnational crimes, those that violate the laws of more than one country, suddenly boomed. Among these are drug trafficking, commercial fraud, environmental offenses, and the smuggling of aliens. Then there are the truly international crimes—those that are proscribed by international law—such as crimes against the peace and security of mankind, genocide, and war crimes. But even many apparently purely local crimes, whether local drug crime or handgun violence, now have international dimensions. In view of the rapid globalization of crime, we devote an entire chapter (Chapter 15) to the international dimensions of criminology. In addition, a "Window to the World" box in each chapter explores the international implications of various topics.

RESEARCH INFORMS POLICY

Skeptics often ask: With so many criminologists at work in the United States, and so many studies conducted over the last half century, why do we have so much crime, why is some of it increasing, and why do new forms of crime emerge constantly? There are several answers. Crime rates go up and down. Through the 1990s and recently, crime has actually been decreasing. The popular perception that the crime problem is increasing rests on a fear of crime that is fueled by media portrayals. Obviously, the various elements of the mass media are very competitive, and such competitiveness determines the focus on crime. Sensational reports often sell newspapers and TV programs.[8] Politicians, in turn, seek security in office by catering to public perceptions of crime, rather than its reality.[9] They therefore propose and enact measures that respond to popular demands and that often are more symbolic than result-oriented.[10] At the moment, this means ever harsher and more punitive measures for dealing with the crime problem.

Few criminologists believe that at present enough research exists to justify such an approach. In fact, some criminological research demonstrates the futility of escalating punishments and often points to measures of quite a different nature as more promising, more humane, and more cost-beneficial. So why do

criminologists not make themselves heard?[11] The answer is that criminologists are social scientists, not politicians. Criminologists are not voted into Congress or to the presidency or a governorship. Yet criminologists have served on virtually every federal and state commission dealing with problems of crime or criminal justice. But just as the Pentagon cannot declare war, criminologists cannot dictate national or state crime-control policies. They can, however, provide pertinent research findings that inform national policy making.[12] Recently, for example, the attorney general of the United States asked criminologists to formulate policy recommendations based on their research findings in areas such as delinquency prevention, drug control, global crime, youth violence, and violence against women.[13] In subsequent chapters that deal with the causes of crime, we continue this discussion under the heading "Theory Informs Policy."

REVIEW

Very little happens on earth that does not concern criminology. Yet criminology as a science is only a century old. Edwin H. Sutherland provided the most widely accepted definition: "The body of knowledge regarding crime as a social phenomenon. It includes within its scope the process of making laws, of breaking laws, and of reacting toward the breaking of laws."

Criminologists study behavior that violates all social norms, including laws. They distinguish between two conflicting views of the history of criminal law: the consensus view, which regards lawmaking as the result of communal agreement about what is to be prohibited, and the conflict view, according to which laws are imposed by those with power over those without power.

The breaking of laws (the subject to which much of this book is devoted) is not merely a formal act that may lead to arrest and prosecution, but an intricate process by which some people violate some laws under some circumstances. Many disciplines contribute to understanding the process of breaking laws or other norms, but as yet there is no consensus on why people become criminals. Society has always reacted to lawbreaking, although the scientific study of lawbreaking is of very recent origin. Today criminologists analyze the methods and procedures society uses in reacting to crime; they evaluate the success or failure of such methods; and on the basis of their research, they propose more effective and humane ways of controlling crime.

Criminologists have discovered that the various agencies society has created to deal with lawbreaking constitute a system that, like any other system, can be made more efficient. Research on the system depends on the availability of a variety of data, especially statistics. The gathering and analysis of statistics on crime and criminal justice are among the primary tasks of criminologists. The effectiveness of their work depends on reliable data.

The province of criminology today is the entire world: Every aspect of life, including crime, has become increasingly globalized in recent years as a result of both rapid advances in technology and economic integration.

Criminology is a politically sensitive discipline. Its findings inform public policy. While criminologists cannot dictate what the branches of government—the legislative, the judicial, and the executive—should do about crime, their research findings are being used increasingly in making governmental decisions.

YOU BE THE CRIMINOLOGIST

How would you teach the ideal course on criminology? (Don't answer until you have completed the course!)

KEY TERMS

The numbers next to the terms refer to the pages on which the terms are defined.

conflict model (12)
consensus model (12)
crime (11)
criminology (9)
deviance (10)

NOTES

1. Raffaele Garofalo, *Criminologia* (Naples, 1885), published in English as *Criminology,*

trans. Robert W. Millar (Boston: Little, Brown, 1914; rpt., Montclair, N.J.: Patterson Smith, 1968).

2. Paul Topinard, "L'Anthropologie criminelle," *Revue d'anthropologie,* **2** (1887).

3. Edwin H. Sutherland, *Principles of Criminology,* 2d ed. (Philadelphia: Lippincott, 1934), originally published as *Criminology,* 1924.

4. Some legal scholars argue that criminologists should study only lawbreaking. See Paul W. Tappan, *Crime, Justice and Correction* (New York: McGraw-Hill, 1960).

5. Jack D. Douglas and Frances C. Waksler, *The Sociology of Deviance* (Boston: Little, Brown, 1982).

6. Garofalo, *Criminologia,* p. 5.

7. Émile Durkheim, *Rules of Sociological Method,* trans. S. A. Solaway and J. H. Mueller (Glencoe, Ill.: Free Press, 1958), p. 64.

8. See Rick Marin and Peter Katel, "Miami's Crime Time Live," *Newsweek,* June 20, 1994, pp. 71–72.

9. See David C. Anderson, "Expressive Justice Is All the Rage—Fired by Occasional 'Willie Horton' Crimes, the Public Insists: Let the Punishment Fit the Rage," *New York Times*

Magazine, Jan. 15, 1995, pp. 36–7; Wendy Kaminer, *It's All the Rage: Crime and Culture* (Reading, Mass.: Addison-Wesley, 1995).

10. Nancy E. Marion, *A History of Federal Crime Control Initiatives, 1960–1993* (Westport, Conn.: Praeger, 1994); Nancy E. Marion, "Symbolism and Federal Crime Control Legislation: 1960–1990," *Journal of Crime and Justice,* **17** (1994): 69–91.

11. Samuel H. Pillsbury, "Why Are We Ignored? The Peculiar Place of Experts in the Current Debate about Crime and Justice," *Criminal Law Bulletin,* **31**(4) (1995): 305–336.

12. Jerome H. Skolnick, "What to Do about Crime—The American Society of Criminology 1994 Presidential Address," *Criminology,* **33** (1995): 1–15; Freda Adler, "Our American Society of Criminology, the World, and the State of the Art—The American Society of Criminology 1995 Presidential Address," *Criminology,* **34** (1995): 1–9.

13. *Critical Criminal Justice Issues: Task Force Reports to Attorney General Janet Reno* (Washington, D.C.: National Institute of Justice / American Society of Criminology, 1995).

CHAPTER 2
Measuring Crime and Criminal Behavior Patterns

In one of many versions of Aesop's fable about the three blind men and the elephant, a circus comes to town, and the residents of a home for the blind are invited to "experience" an elephant. When one blind man is led to the elephant, he touches one of its legs. He feels its size and shape. Another man happens to touch the tail, and still another feels the trunk. Back at their residence they argue about the nature of the beast. Says the first man, "An elephant is obviously like the trunk of a tree." "No," says the second, "it's like a rope." "You're both wrong," says the third. "An elephant is like a big snake." All three are partly right, for each has described the part of the animal he has touched.

Assessment of the nature and extent of crime often suffers from the same shortcomings as the three blind men's assessments of the elephant. Researcher A may make assessments on the basis of arrest records. Researcher B may rely on conviction rates to describe crime. Researcher C may use the number of convicts serving prison sentences. None of the researchers, however, may be in a position to assess the full nature and extent of crime; each is limited by the kinds of data he or she uses.

Questions about how crime is measured and what those measurements reveal about the nature and extent of crime are among the most important issues in contemporary criminology. Researchers, theorists, and practitioners need information in order to explain and prevent crime and to operate agencies that deal with the crime problem. After we look at the objectives and methods of collecting information, we will consider the limitations of the information sources criminologists most frequently use to estimate the nature and extent of crime in the United States. We then explore measurement of the characteristics of crimes and criminals.

MEASURING CRIME

There are three major reasons for measuring characteristics of crimes and criminals. First of all, researchers need to collect and analyze information in order to test theories about why people commit crime. One criminologist might record the kinds of offenses committed by people of different ages; another might count the number of crimes committed at different times of the year. But without ordering these observations in some purposeful way, without a **theory**, a systematic set of principles that explain how two or more phenomena are related, scientists would be limited in their ability to make predictions from the data they collect.

The types of data that are collected and the way they are collected are crucial to the research process. Criminologists analyze these data and use their findings to support or refute theories. In Part II we examine several theories (including the one outlined briefly here) that explain why people commit crime, and we will see how these theories have been tested.

One theory of crime causation, for example, is that high crime rates result from the wide disparity between people's goals and the means available to them for reaching those goals. Those who lack legitimate opportunities to achieve their goals (primarily, people in the lower class) try to reach them through criminal means. To test this theory, researchers might begin with the **hypothesis** (a testable proposition that describes how two or more factors are related) that lower-class individuals engage in more serious crimes and do so more frequently than middle-class individuals. (See "Social Class and Crime," later in this chapter.) Next they would collect facts, observations, and other pertinent information—called **data**—on the criminal behavior of both lower-class and middle-class individuals. A finding that lower-class persons commit more crimes would support the theory that people commit crimes because they do not have legitimate means to reach their goals.

The second objective of measurement is to enhance our knowledge of the characteristics of various types of offenses. Why are some more likely to be committed than others? What situational factors, such as time of day or type of place, influence the commission of crime? Experts have argued that this information is needed if we are to prevent crime and develop strategies to control it (Chapter 9 deals with this subject).

Measurement has a third major objective: Criminal justice agencies depend on certain kinds of information to facilitate daily operations and to anticipate future needs. How many persons flow through county jails? How many will receive prison sentences? Besides the questions that deal with the day-to-day functioning of the system (number of beds, distribution and hiring of personnel), other questions affect legislative and policy decisions. For instance, what effect does a change in law have on the amount of crime committed? Consider legislation on the death penalty. Some people claim that homicides decrease when a death penalty is instituted. Others claim that capital punishment laws make no difference. Does fear of crime go down if we put more police officers in a neighborhood? Does drug smuggling move to another entry point if old access routes are cut off? These and other potential changes need to be evaluated—and evaluations require measurement.

Methods of Collecting Data

Given the importance of data for research, policy making, and the daily operation and planning of the criminal justice system, criminologists have been working to perfect data collection techniques. Through the years these methods have become increasingly more sophisticated.

Depending on what questions they are asking, criminologists can and do collect their data in a variety of ways: through survey research, experiments, observation, and case studies. One of the most widely used methods is survey research, which is a cost-effective method of measuring characteristics of groups. Experimental studies are difficult and costly to conduct, and for that reason they are used infrequently. But they have been, and still are, an important means of collecting data on crime. Participant observation involves the direct participation of the researcher in the activities of the people who are the subjects of the research. A variation of this technique is nonparticipant observation, in which the researcher collects data without joining in the activity. Another way to collect information about crime, and especially about criminal careers, is to examine biographical and autobiographical accounts of individual offenders (the case-study method).

Data can be found in a wide variety of sources, but the most frequently used sources are statistics compiled by government agencies, private foundations, and business. Familiarity with the sources of data and the methods used to gather data will help in understanding the studies we discuss throughout this book. The facts and observations researchers gather for the purpose of a particular study are called **primary data.** Those they find in government sources, or data that were previously collected for a different investigation, are called **secondary data.**

Surveys Most of us are familiar with surveys—in public opinion polls, marketing research, and election-prediction studies. Criminologists use surveys to obtain quantitative data. A **survey** is the systematic collection of respondents' answers to questions asked in questionnaires or interviews; interviews may be conducted face-to-face or by telephone. Generally, surveys are used to gather information about the attitudes, characteristics, or behavior of a large group of persons, who are called the **population** of the survey. Surveys conducted by criminologists measure, for example, the amount of crime, attitudes toward police or toward the sentencing of dangerous offenders, assessment of drug abuse, and fear of crime.

Instead of interviewing the total population under study, most researchers interview a representative subset of that population—a **sample.** If a sample is carefully drawn, researchers can generalize the results from the sample to the population. A sample determined by random selection, whereby each person in the population to be studied has an equal chance of being selected, is called a **random sample.**

Surveys are a cost-effective method, but they have limitations. If a study of drug use by high school students were done one time only,

The year 2000 census started when Harold Johnson visited the Eskimo village of Unalkleet, Alaska, on January 19, 2000. The U.S. Census will provide information on all Americans, their lifestyles and problems, including, through random survey done in cooperation with the Bureau of Justice Statistics, data on crime victimization.

the finding of a relationship between drug use and poor grades would not tell us whether drug use caused bad grades, whether students with bad grades turned to drugs, or whether bad grades and drug taking resulted from some other factor, such as lack of a stable family.

Experiments The **experiment** is a technique used in the physical and biological sciences, and in the social sciences as well. An investigator introduces a change into a process and makes measurements or observations in order to evaluate the effects of the change. Through experimentation, scientists test hypotheses about how two or more **variables** (factors that may change) are related. The basic model for an experiment involves changing one variable, keeping all other factors the same (controlling them, or holding them constant),

Despite experimental evidence that the Scared Straight experience may be counter-productive, the program continues at East Jersey State Prison (formerly Rahway State Prison). Here, a member of the Lifer's group appears in a Scared Straight 1999 video. The film is an update of the original Scared Straight video that shows how inmates give young people in trouble a taste of prison life.

and observing the effect of that change on another variable. If you change one variable while keeping all other factors constant and then find that another variable changes as well, you may safely assume that the change in the second variable was caused by the change in the first.

Most experiments are done in laboratories, but it is possible to do them in real-world, or field, settings (hence the name **field experiment**). A field experiment was done at New Jersey's Rahway State Prison to test the hypothesis that if youngsters were shown the horrors of prison, they would not commit crimes. The object was to scare young people out of crime; consequently, the project became known as "Scared Straight!" Several agencies were asked to propose male juveniles for the experiment. All were given a series of tests to determine their attitudes toward crime, punishment, prison, the police, and so forth. Afterward some of the juveniles were randomly assigned to the experimental group, which would actually go to the prison. The rest were assigned to a control group, which would not go.

After the experimental group had participated in the program, both groups were again given the same attitude tests to find out if the prison experience had changed the attitudes of the experimental group. Six months later the juvenile records of the two groups were checked to find out how many of the youths in both groups had committed crimes during the 6-month period. Had fewer of the youngsters who had supposedly been scared straight been arrested than those who had not made the prison visit? No, according to James Finckenauer's analysis. In fact, many more of the boys in the experimental group had been arrested than had boys in the control group, and the boys in the experimental group also tended to commit more serious offenses than those in the control group.[1]

Experiments in the real world are costly and difficult to carry out, but they have the advantage of increasing scientists' ability to establish cause and effect.

Participant and Nonparticipant Observation Researchers who engage in participant and nonparticipant observation use methods that provide detailed descriptions of life as it actually is lived—in prisons, gangs, and other settings.

Observation is the most direct means of studying behavior. Investigators may play a variety of roles in observing social situations. When they engage in **nonparticipant observation,** they do not join in the activities of the groups they are studying; they simply observe the activities in everyday settings and record what they see. Investigators who engage in **participant observation** take part in many of the activities of the groups in order to gain acceptance, but they generally make clear the purpose of their participation. Anne Campbell, a criminologist who spent 2 years as a participant observer of the lifestyles of girl gang members, explains:

> My efforts to meet female gang members began with an introduction through the New York City Police Department's Gang Crimes Unit. Through one of their plain-clothes gang liaison officers, John Galea, I was introduced first to the male gang members of a number of Brooklyn gangs. On being reassured that I "only" wanted to talk to the female members, the male leaders gave their OK and I made arrangements to meet with the girls' leaders or "godmothers." At first they were guarded in their disclosures to me. They asked a lot about my life, my background and my reasons for wanting to hang out with them. Like most of us, however, they enjoyed talking about themselves and over the period of six months that I spent with each of three female gangs they opened up a good deal—sitting in their kitchens, standing on the stoops in the evenings or socializing at parties with allied gangs.[2]

Observations of groups in their natural setting afford the researcher insights into behavior and attitudes that cannot be obtained through such techniques as surveys and experiments.

Case Studies   A **case study** is an analysis of all pertinent aspects of one unit of study, such as an individual, an institution, a group, or a community. The sources of information are documents such as life histories, biographies, diaries, journals, letters, and other records. A classic demonstration of criminologists' use of the case-study method is found in Edwin Suther-

land's *The Professional Thief,* which is based on interviews with a professional thief.

Sutherland learned about the relationship between amateur and professional thieves, how thieves communicate, how they determine whether to trust each other, and how they network. From discussions with the thief and an analysis of his writings on topics selected by the researcher, Sutherland was able to draw several conclusions that other techniques would not have yielded. For instance, a person is not a professional thief unless he is recognized as such by other professional thieves. Training by professional thieves is necessary for the development of the skills, attitudes, and connections required in the "profession."[3] One of the drawbacks of the case-study method is that the information given by the subject may be biased or wrong and by its nature is limited. For these reasons it is difficult to generalize from one person's story—in this instance, to all professional thieves.

Using Available Data in Research   Besides collecting their own data, researchers often depend on secondary data collected by private and public organizations. The police, the courts, and corrections officials, for example, need to know the number of persons passing through the criminal justice system at various points in order to carry out day-to-day administrative tasks and to engage in long-range planning. It is not always feasible to collect new data for a research project, nor is it necessary to do so when such vast amounts of relevant information are already available.

To study the relationship between crime and variables such as average income or single-parent households, one might make use of the Uniform Crime Reports (see "Police Statistics" later in this chapter), together with information found in the reports of the Bureau of the Census. Various other agencies, among them the Federal Bureau of Prisons, the Drug Enforcement Agency, the Treasury Department, and the Labor Department, are also excellent sources of statistics useful to criminologists. At the international level, U.N. world crime surveys contain information on crime, criminals, and criminal justice systems in countries on all continents.

www.jrsainfo.org/ibrrc/index.html

Crime Surfing

The Justice Research and Statistics Association (JRSA) is a national nonprofit group of state-level statistical analysis centers. The group gathers data from across the country, conducts studies on criminal justice issues, and helps people find information on topics relating to criminal justice programs and research. The JRSA website discusses the National Incident-Based Reporting System (NIBRS).

Researchers who use available data can save a great deal of time and expense. However, they have to exercise caution in fitting data not collected for the purpose of a particular study into their research. Many official records are incomplete or the data have been collected in such a way as to make them inadequate for the research. It is also frequently difficult to gain permission to use agency data that are not available to the public because of a concern about confidentiality.

Ethics and the Researcher

In the course of their research, criminologists encounter many ethical issues. Chief among such issues is confidentiality. Consider the dilemma faced by a group of researchers in the late 1960s. In interviewing a sample of 9945 boys born in 1945, the team collected extensive self-reported criminal histories of offenses the boys had committed before and after they turned 18. Among the findings were four unreported homicides and 75 rapes. The researchers were naturally excited about capturing such interesting data. More important, the researchers had feelings of grave concern. How should they handle their findings?

Should the results of these interviews be published?

Could the failure of the research staff to disclose names be considered the crime of obstructing justice?

Does an obligation to society as a whole to release the names of the offenders transcend a researcher's obligation to safeguard a subject's confidentiality?

What is the best response to a demand by the police, a district attorney, or a court for the researcher's files containing the subjects' names?

Should criminologists be immune to prosecution for their failure to disclose the names of their subjects?

Is it possible to develop a technique that can ensure against the identification of a subject in a research file?[4]

Such questions have few clear-cut answers. When researchers encounter these problems, however, they can rely on standards for ethical human experimentation. Human-experimentation review committees at most universities and government agencies check all proposals for research projects to ensure the protection of human subjects. In addition, researchers are required to inform their subjects about the nature of the study and to obtain written and informed agreement to participate.

Because of heightened awareness of the ethical issues involved in human experimentation—particularly in correctional institutions, where coercion is difficult to avoid—the field of criminology and criminal justice is in the process of adopting formal codes of ethics. The guidelines include full reporting of experimental findings, honoring commitments made to respondents, not misleading respondents, and protecting respondents' confidentiality. Special provisions for what are called vulnerable populations (e.g., the illiterate, the mentally ill, children, those of low social status, and those under judicial or penal supervision) include taking appropriate steps to secure informed consent and to avoid invasions of privacy.[5] In the end, however, as Seth Bloomberg and Leslie Wilkins have noted, "the responsibility for safeguarding human subjects ultimately rests with the researcher. . . . A code of ethics may provide useful guidelines, but it will not relieve the scientist of moral choice."[6]

THE NATURE AND EXTENT OF CRIME

As we have seen, criminologists gather their information in many ways. The methods they choose depend on the questions they want to

FIGURE 2.1 The process of bringing crime to the attention of police.

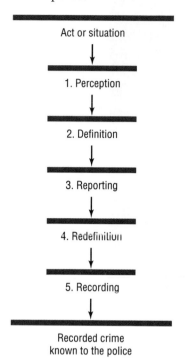

Act or situation

1. Perception

2. Definition

3. Reporting

4. Redefinition

5. Recording

Recorded crime
known to the police

Source: R. F. Sparks, H. G. Genn, and D. J. Dodd, *Surveying Victims: A Study of the Measurement of Criminal Victimization, Perceptions of Crime, and Attitudes to Criminal Justice* (Chichester, England: Wiley, 1977), p. 6.

answer. To estimate the nature and extent of crime in the United States, they rely primarily on the Uniform Crime Reports, data compiled by the police; on the National Crime Victimization Survey, which measures crime through reports by victims; and on various self-report surveys, which ask individuals about criminal acts they have committed, whether or not these acts have come to the attention of the authorities.

Official statistics gathered from law enforcement agencies provide information available on the crimes actually investigated and reported by these agencies. But not all crimes appear in police statistics. In order for a criminal act to be "known to the police," the act first must be *perceived* by an individual (the car is not in the garage where it was left). It must then be *defined,* or classified, as something that places it within the purview of the criminal justice system (a theft has taken place), and it must be *reported* to the police. Once the police are notified,

they classify the act and often *redefine* what may have taken place before *recording* the act as a crime known to the police (Figure 2.1). Information about criminal acts may be lost at any point along this processing route, and many crimes are never discovered to begin with.

Police Statistics

In 1924 the director of the Bureau of Investigation, J. Edgar Hoover, initiated a campaign to make the bureau responsible for gathering national statistics. With support from the American Bar Association (ABA) and the International Association of Chiefs of Police (IACP), the House of Representatives in 1930 passed a bill authorizing the bureau (later renamed the Federal Bureau of Investigation, or FBI) to collect data on crimes known to the police. These data are compiled into reports called the Uniform Crime Reports (UCR). At present approximately 17,000 city, county, and state law enforcement agencies, which cover 95 percent of the total population, voluntarily contribute information on crimes brought to their attention. These agencies represent over 254 million United States inhabitants, with higher representation in large urban areas (97 percent) than in smaller cities (90 percent) or rural areas (87 percent). If the police verify that a crime has been committed, that crime goes into the report, whether or not an arrest has been made. Each month, reporting agencies provide data on offenses in 29 categories.

Part I and Part II Offenses The UCR divides offenses into two major categories: Part I and Part II. Part I offenses include eight crimes, which are aggregated as **crimes against the person** (criminal homicide, forcible rape, robbery, and aggravated assault) and **crimes against property** (burglary, larceny-theft, motor vehicle

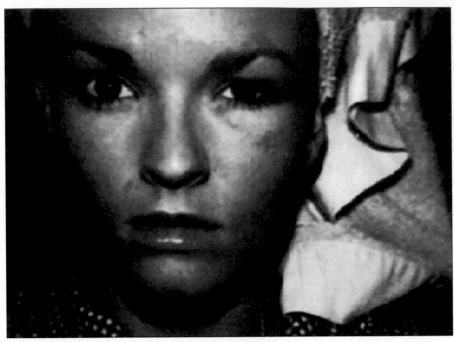

This photograph of Nicole Brown Simpson, bruised and battered, was shown to the jurors in the O. J. Simpson trial. Lawyers documented the abusive relationship by playing the voice recording of Nicole's 911 reports to the police. (Excerpt from 911 report: Ms. Simpson: "Could you just send somebody over here?" Unidentified 911 operator: "O.K. What is he doing there?" Ms. Simpson: "He's going nuts again. Could you please send somebody over?")

theft, and arson). Collectively, Part I offenses are called **Index crimes.** Because they are serious, these crimes tend to be reported to the police more reliably than others and therefore can be used in combination as an index, or indicator, of changes over time. All other offenses, except traffic violations, are Part II crimes. These 21 crimes include fraud, embezzlement, weapons offenses, vandalism, and simple assaults.

Crime Rates   To analyze crime data, experts frequently present them as crime rates. Crime rates are computed by the following formula:

$$\text{Crime rate} = \frac{\begin{array}{c}\text{number of}\\\text{reported crimes}\end{array}}{\text{total population}} \times 100,000$$

Crime rates may be computed for groups of offenses (such as the Index crimes or crimes against the person) or for specific offenses (such as homicide). If we say, for example, that the homicide rate is 10.2, we mean that there were 10.2 homicides for every 100,000 persons in the population under consideration (total U.S. population, say, or all males in the United States). Expressing the amount of crime in terms of rates over time shows whether an increase or a decrease in crime results from a change in the population or a change in the amount of crime committed.

In addition to data on reported crimes, the UCR includes the number of offenses cleared by arrest. Crimes may be cleared in one of two ways: by the arrest, charging, and turning over to the courts of at least one person for prosecution, or by disposition of a case when an arrest is not possible, as when the suspect has died or fled the jurisdiction. Besides reported crimes and crimes cleared by arrest, the reports contain data on characteristics of crimes (such as geographical location, time, and place), characteristics of criminals (such as gender, age, and race), and distri-

Crime Surfing

http://www.crime.org/

Examine this annotated list of links to websites that have data on crime, an explanation of what crime data are, where they come from, and how accurate they are likely to be.

bution of law enforcement personnel. We shall look at what these statistics reveal about the characteristics of crime and criminals in more detail later, but first we must recognize their limitations.

Limitations of the Uniform Crime Reports Despite the fact that the UCR is among the main sources of crime statistics, its research value has been questioned. The criticisms deal with methodological problems and reporting practices. Some scholars argue, for example, that figures on reported crime are of little use in categories such as larceny, in which a majority of crime is not reported. The statistics present the amount of crime known to law enforcement agencies, but they do not reveal how many crimes have actually been committed. Another serious limitation is the fact that when

several crimes are committed in one event, only the most serious offense is included in the UCR; the others go unreported. At the same time, when certain other crimes are committed, each individual act is counted as a separate offense. If a person robs a group of six people, for example, the UCR lists one robbery. But if a person assaults six people, the UCR lists six assaults. UCR data are further obscured by the fact that they do not differentiate between completed acts and attempted acts.

Police reports to the FBI are voluntary and vary in accuracy. In a study conducted on behalf of the Police Foundation, Lawrence Sherman and Barry Glick found that while the UCR requires that arrests be recorded even if a suspect is released without a formal charge, all 196 departments surveyed recorded an arrest only after a formal booking procedure.[7] In addition, police departments may want to improve their image by showing that their crime rate has either declined (meaning the streets are safer) or risen (justifying a crackdown on, say, prostitution).[8] New record-keeping procedures can also create significant changes (the New York robbery

One offense.

Six offenses.

rate appeared to increase 400 percent in 1 year).[9] Many fluctuations in crime rates may therefore be attributable to events other than changes in the actual numbers of crimes committed.

Finally, the UCR data suffer from several omissions. Many arsons go unreported because not all fire departments report to the UCR.[10] Federal cases go unlisted. Most white-collar offenses are omitted because they are reported not to the police but to regulatory authorities, such as the Securities and Exchange Commission and the Federal Trade Commission.[11]

To deal with the limitations of the UCR, in 1986 the International Association of Chiefs of Police, the National Sheriffs' Association, and the state-level UCR programs joined forces with the FBI.[12] A new reporting system was developed, called the National Incident-Based Reporting System (NIBRS). Reporting to the NIBRS is voluntary and coexists with the UCR.[13] The NIBRS is a major attempt to improve the collection of crime data.[14] But it deals only with crimes that come to the attention of the police. What about crimes that remain unreported? For what is called the "dark figure of crime," we have to rely on victimization data and self-report studies.

Victimization Surveys

Victimization surveys measure the extent of crime by interviewing individuals about their experiences as victims. The Bureau of the Census, in cooperation with the Bureau of Justice Statistics, collects information annually about persons and households that have been victimized. The report is called the National Crime Victimization Survey (NCVS). Researchers for the NCVS estimate the total number of crimes committed by asking respondents from a national sample of approximately 43,000 households, representing 80,000 persons over the age of 12 (parental permission is needed for those under 14 years old), about their experiences as victims during a specific time period. Interviewers visit (or sometimes telephone) the homes selected for the sample. Each housing unit remains in the sample for 3 years. Every 6 months 10,000 households are rotated out of the sample and replaced by a new group.

The NCVS measures the extent of victimization by rape, robbery, assault, larceny, burglary, personal theft, and motor vehicle theft. Note that two of the UCR Part I offenses—criminal homicide and arson—are not included (see Table 2.1).[15] Homicide is omitted because the NCVS covers only crimes whose victims can be interviewed. The designers of the survey also decided to omit arson, a relative newcomer to the UCR, because measuring it with some validity by means of a victimization survey was deemed to be too difficult. Part II offenses have been excluded altogether because many of them are considered victimless (prostitution, vagrancy, drug abuse, drunkenness) or because victims are willing participants (gambling, con games) or do not know they have been victimized (forgery, fraud).

The survey covers characteristics of crimes such as time and place of occurrence, number of offenders, use of weapons, economic loss, and time lost from work; characteristics of victims, such as gender, age, race, ethnicity, marital status, household composition, and educational attainment; perceived characteristics of offenders, such as age, gender, and race; circumstances surrounding the offenses and their effects, such as financial loss and injury; and patterns of police reporting, such as rates of reporting and reasons for reporting and for not reporting. Some questions also encourage interviewees to discuss family violence.

Limitations of Victimization Surveys While victimization surveys give us information about crimes that are not reported to the police, these data, too, have significant limitations. The NCVS covers crimes in a more limited way than the UCR; the NCVS includes only 7 offenses, whereas there are 8 offenses in Part I of the UCR and an additional 21 in Part II. Although the NCVS is conducted by trained interviewers, some individual variations in interviewing and recording style are inevitable, and as a result, the information recorded may vary as well.

Since the NCVS is based on personal reporting, it also suffers from the fact that memories may fade over time, so some facts are forgotten while others are exaggerated. Moreover,

For 70 years, information about crimes reported to the police has been compiled in a format known as the Uniform Crime Reports (UCR). This system has some quirks that make the UCR of limited use to criminologists who wish to study more closely how criminal events happen. For example, assume someone robs a convenience store and, while in the act, pushes one customer to the floor, shoots another in the foot, and then rapes and strangles the clerk. Under the "hierarchy rule," only the felony murder (the strangling of the clerk), because it is the most serious crime, will be counted in the UCR. The robbery, simple assault, aggravated assault, and rape will not be reported to the UCR. Another odd example is the "hotel rule." If you and five neighbors in your apartment house are burglarized, six burglaries would be reported to the UCR. But if you and your five neighbors happen to be on vacation in the same hotel and each has his or her separate hotel room burglarized, only one burglary would be reported to the UCR.

The UCR is also what is known in criminological jargon as "aggregated data." This means the information is available only as total counts of offenses, victims, and offenders. Thus, for those who wish to learn more about criminal events, the greatest criticism of the UCR is the lack of detail. Suppose you are interested in studying aggravated assault. You could go to the UCR to find out how many crimes of aggravated assault occurred last year in specific police jurisdictions. However, you could not get information on the nature of each aggravated assault. Imagine three very different scenarios: Casual acquaintances get into a bar brawl and crack each other over the head with bar stools; a married heterosexual couple has a fight, and the husband is stabbed with a kitchen knife; a toddler is injured by a stray bullet

fired by a drive-by shooter. Each of these incidents would count as one case of aggravated assault, even though they are very different in terms of circumstances, participants, weapons, and location. But since the UCR does not break down and categorize specifics, you could not get any detailed information. So what is a hapless researcher to do in this situation? The National Incident-Based Reporting System (NIBRS) has the answer.

The NIBRS collects data on incidents and allows for rich detail. Each incident can have up to 10 different offense types (as opposed to the UCR, which allows only 1), 999 victims, and 99 offenders. Information collected on victims includes race, gender, age, and ethnicity, as well as where they lived at the time of the incident, what type of injury they sustained, and what their relationship was to the offender(s). As for offenders, data are collected on race, gender, age, ethnicity, residence, and weapon used, as well as what happened to them after they were arrested. With all this information, you could find out, for example, if victims are assaulted in the towns or cities where they live and the relationship, if any, they have with their attacker(s).

Criminologists want more crime-specific data in order to understand how particular types of crime happen and to learn about characteristics of those incidents. With the NIBRS, a researcher can look very closely at, for example, muggings that occur in schools. Knowledge of the type of weapons used, the injuries that result, the time incidents occur, and the interaction between victims and offenders can provide valuable insights to be used in developing crime-prevention strategies. A researcher looking at burglary can use the NIBRS to focus on incidents that are of special interest, perhaps burglaries that occur during

the day as opposed to those that occur at night. The NIBRS makes it possible to find out which techniques burglars use to break into homes and whether a pattern exists with regard to items that are stolen during the day versus items that are stolen at night. As we shall see in Chapter 9, there is tremendous potential in the idea of preventing crime using crime-specific strategies. The NIBRS is one of the best tools criminologists have to assist them in this difficult task.

Some experts claim that the NIBRS will enhance the capacity for crime analysis at all jurisdictional levels, thus allowing law enforcement agencies to more effectively and efficiently define their needs, justify expenditures, and allocate resources. The NIBRS is a computerized system; therefore, local agencies can download their crime data directly to state- and federal-level agencies, reducing the need for standardized reporting forms. In this respect, the NIBRS is more efficient than the cumbersome UCR.

Source

Michael G. Maxfield, "The National Incident-Based Reporting System: Research and Policy Applications," *Journal of Quantitative Criminology*, **15** (1999): 119–149.

Questions for Discussion

1. Suppose you are designing a crime-prevention program for an inner-city college campus. What kinds of information would you look for in the data collected by the NIBRS?

2. If crime statistics were calculated nationally using the NIBRS, would you expect crime rates for most offenses to go up or down? How does the hierarchy rule used in the UCR influence the number of crimes that are counted when determining official crime rates?

TABLE 2.1   How Do the Uniform Crime Reports and the National Crime Victimization Survey Differ?

	Uniform Crime Reports	National Crime Victimization Survey
Offenses measured	Homicide Rape Robbery (personal and commercial) Assault (aggravated) Burglary (commercial and household) Larceny (commercial and household) Motor vehicle theft Arson	Rape Robbery (personal) Assault (aggravated and simple) Household burglary Larceny Personal theft Motor vehicle theft
Scope	Crimes reported to the police in most jurisdictions; considerable flexibility in developing small-area data	Crimes both reported and not reported to police; all data are for the nation as a whole; some data are available for a few large geographical areas
Collection method	Police department reports to FBI	Survey interviews; periodically measures the total number of crimes committed by asking a national sample of 43,000* households representing 80,000* persons over the age of 12 about their experiences as victims of crime during a specified period
Kinds of information	In addition to offense counts, provides information on crime clearances, persons arrested, persons charged, law enforcement officers killed and assaulted, and characteristics of homicide victims	Provides details about victims (such as age, race, sex, education, and income, and whether the victim and offender were related to each other) and about crimes (such as time and place of occurrence, whether or not reported to police, use of weapons, occurrence of injury, and economic consequences)
Sponsor	Department of Justice, Federal Bureau of Investigation	Department of Justice, Bureau of Justice Statistics

*Figures have been updated.

Source: Adapted from U.S. Department of Justice, Bureau of Justice Statistics, *Report to the Nation on Crime and Justice,* 2d ed. (Washington, D.C.: U.S. Government Printing Office, 1988), p. 11; U.S. Department of Justice, Bureau of Justice Statistics, *Criminal Victimization 1997* (Washington, D.C.: U.S. Government Printing Office, December 1998), pp. 1-2.

some interviewees may try to please the interviewer by fabricating crime incidents.[16] Respondents also have a tendency to telescope events—that is, to move events that took place in an earlier time period into the time period under study. Like the UCR, the NCVS records only the most serious offense committed during an event in which several crimes are perpetrated.

Self-Report Surveys

Another way to determine the amount and types of crime actually committed is to ask people to report their own criminal acts in a confidential interview or, more commonly, on an anonymous questionnaire. These investigations are called **self-report surveys.**

Findings of Self-Report Surveys   Self-reports of delinquent and criminal behavior have produced several important findings since

their development in the 1940s. First, they quickly refuted the conventional wisdom that only a small percentage of the general population commits crimes. The use of these measures over the last several decades has demonstrated very high rates of law-violating behavior by seemingly law-abiding people. Almost everyone, at some point in time, has broken a law.

In 1947, James S. Wallerstein and Clement J. Wyle questioned a group of 1698 individuals on whether or not they had committed any of 49 offenses that were serious enough to require a maximum sentence of not less than 1 year. They found that over 80 percent of the men reported committing malicious mischief, disorderly conduct, and larceny. More than 50 percent admitted a history of crimes including reckless driving and driving while intoxicated, indecency, gambling, fraud, and tax evasion. The authors acknowledged the lack of scientific rigor of their study. No attempt was made to ensure a balanced or representative cross section of the individuals surveyed.[17] However, these findings do suggest that the distinction between criminals and noncriminals may be more apparent than real.

Studies conducted since the 1940s have provided a great deal more information. They suggest a wide discrepancy between official and self-report data as regards the age, race, and gender of offenders.[18] Unrecorded offenders commit a wide variety of offenses, rather than specializing in one type of offense.[19] It also appears that only one-quarter of all serious, chronic juvenile offenders are apprehended by the police. Moreover, an estimated 90 percent of all youths commit delinquent or criminal acts, primarily truancy, use of false identification, alcohol abuse, larceny, fighting, and marijuana use.[20]

From 1991 to 1993, the first International Self-Report Delinquency (ISRD) study was conducted in Finland, Great Britain, the Netherlands, Belgium, Germany, Switzerland, Portugal, Spain, Italy, Greece, the United States, and New Zealand. Each country used the same questionnaire, which had been translated into the respective languages. The studies used various sampling techniques, so the results from each country are not strictly comparable. Nonetheless, the findings support much of what is found in the self-report literature. Boys commit about twice as many offenses as girls. The peak age of offending in the participating countries is 16 to 17 years. Violence is strongly related to lower educational levels. No relationship was found between socioeconomic status and delinquency. Drug use seems related to leaving school early and unemployment. School failure is related to violent offenses.[21]

Limitations of Self-Report Surveys Self-report surveys have taught us a great deal about criminality. But they, like the other methods of data collection, have drawbacks. The questionnaires are often limited to petty acts, such as truancy, and therefore do not represent the range of criminal acts that people may commit. Michael Hindelang, Travis Hirschi, and Joseph Weis argue that researchers who find discrepancies with respect to gender, race, and class between the results produced by official statistics and those collected by self-report methods are in fact measuring different kinds of behavior rather than different amounts of the same behavior. They suggest that if you take into account the fact that persons who are arrested tend to have committed more serious offenses and to have prior records (criteria that affect decisions to arrest), then the two types of statistics are quite comparable.[22]

Another drawback of self-reports is that most of them are administered to high school or college students, so the information they yield applies only to young people attending school. And who can say that respondents always tell the truth? The information obtained by repeated administration of the same questionnaire to the same individuals might yield different results. Many self-report measures lack validity; the data obtained do not correspond with some other criterion (such as school records) that measures the same behavior. Finally, samples may be biased. People who choose not to participate in the studies may have good reason for not wanting to discuss their criminal activities.

Each of the three commonly used sources of data—police reports, victim surveys, and self-report surveys—adds a different dimension to our knowledge of crime. All of them are useful in our search for the characteristics of crimes, criminals, and victims.

MEASURING CHARACTERISTICS OF CRIME

Streets in Charlotte, North Carolina, with tranquil names—Peaceful Glen, Soft Wind, Gentle Breeze—were killing lanes.[23] The city that had hoped to displace Atlanta as the "Queen City of the South" had 115 homicides in 1992, more than double the number it had 6 years earlier. It seemed that the city was out of control. Experts pointed to drugs and to a growing number of swap shops and flea markets that served as unregulated outlets for buying guns as the reasons for the high number of homicides. Most of the killings took place in a 26-square-mile area inhabited primarily by low-income African-American families. Fortunately, within 5 years the situation reversed itself. In 1997 the number of homicides in Charlotte was reduced to 59.[24]

It has been a few years since the dramatic drop in the rate for violent crime in New York City and many other jurisdictions across the country. Criminologists in policing circles have spent much of that time trying to understand why this drop occurred and debating various explanations. The number of ideas about what accounts for the decline in violent crime in the mid-1990s is growing as more researchers carry out studies to examine this phenomenon closely. Here are some opinions and findings:

- University of Chicago economist Steven Levitt and Stanford University law professor John Donohue III argue that legalizing abortion in 1973 (as a consequence of the *Roe v. Wade* decision) may account for as much as half of the drop in crime. This notion has generated a torrent of criticism from those on both sides of the abortion debate, as well as from some criminologists, who say the research does not examine other factors that may explain the drop in crime.(1)
- On the basis of data from the NCVS, Warren Friedman estimates that Americans devote almost 4 billion hours each year to "organized safety activity." He argues that what ordinary people contribute in these grassroots efforts is overlooked by most researchers, with their focus on punishment, police, and prisons. Crime prevention at the community level may well have had an important impact on the decline of violent crime.(2)
- In a study comparing alcohol consumption with homicide rates, researchers concluded that declining alcohol consumption is related to the drop in murders in the United States. They argue that violent crime may be reduced and prevented through "tighter regulation of alcohol availability, taxation, and restrictions on the age of purchase."(3)
- University of New Mexico criminologist Gary LaFree argues that changes in the "legitimacy of social institutions" explain the rapid changes in street-crime trends over the past 50 years. Declining crime rates in the 1990s, he asserts, may be the result of increased trust in political institutions, increased economic well-being, increased viable alternatives to the traditional two-parent family, as well as increased support for criminal justice, welfare, and educational institutions.(4)
- George Kelling and William Bratton (who was the New York City police commissioner during one of the most dramatic drops in that city's crime rate) claim that the decline in violent crime is largely a result of a change in police tactics and strategies. Rather than focusing on serious crimes, the police began to address disorderly behavior and so-called quality-of-life offenses (such as public drunkenness and vagrancy). When these seemingly petty crimes were brought under control, citizens felt less fearful and hard-core criminals found it more difficult to move into certain communities. In addition, New York

Crackdown on quality of life offenses. Here New York City police officers removed the homeless from Tomkins Square.

City was one of the first places in the country to implement COMPSTAT, a process involving ongoing analysis of crime data and accountability for crime reduction at the precinct level.(5)
- In his decade-long ethnographic study of several Brooklyn communities, Rick Curtis concluded that one explanation for the drop in violent crime was that the people themselves took back their neighborhoods. Young people "shared a conviction that they would not succumb to the same fate that nearly erased the previous generation." They turned away from the things that would put them in danger: the open-

This information not only gives us general insights into the crime problem in Charlotte, but also enables us to examine the changes in the homicide rate over time, the high-risk areas, and the racial and economic composition of those areas, to provide a full picture of the crime history.

Criminologists use these kinds of data about crimes in their research. Some investigators, for example, may want to compare drug use to crime in major cities. Others may want to explain a decrease or an increase in the crime rate in a single city (Charlotte), in a single neighborhood (the impoverished inner city), or perhaps in the nation as a whole.

Crime Trends

One of the most important characteristics of any crime is how often it is committed. From such figures we can determine crime trends, the increases and decreases of crime over time. The

market sale of drugs, rampant violence, and hard-drug use.(6)

- Other criminologists point to the stabilization of the drug markets in inner cities. In business management parlance, drug markets are said to have "matured," which translates into fewer conflicts between rival drug dealers and fewer drug-related murders. Because this type of murder accounts for so many of the homicides occurring in cities, maturation of the drug market could explain a significant part of the drop in murder rates. In addition, the crack epidemic of the 1980s has largely subsided. There seems to have been a switch among users from cocaine, which agitates the user, to heroin, which mellows the user.(7)
- One school of thought holds that demographic changes, specifically a temporary dip in the high-crime population aged 18 to 24, can account for some of the drop in violent crime.(8)
- Another theory is that the most dangerous criminals are now in prison. In New York State alone, the number of felons behind bars is nearly 70,000, almost three times what it was 15 years ago.(9)

It has been said that criminologists are luckier than economists. Economists are judged on their ability to predict the future of the economy, while criminologists just have to explain what happened after the fact.(10) But explaining is harder than it seems, and the stakes can be high. The better that criminologists become at understanding past crime rates, the better they will be at predicting future crime rates. The implications of these predictions can be huge. Criminologists' predictions about crime patterns in the future can mean changes in, for example, policing strategies, the length of prison sentences, the amount of money to be earmarked for rehabilitation and child welfare programs, and politicians' and citizens' attitudes about crime and crime policy.

Sources

1. Erica Goode, "Linking Drop in Crime to Rise in Abortion," *New York Times,* Aug. 20, 1999, p. 14.
2. Warren Friedman, "Volunteerism and the Decline of Violent Crime," *Journal of Criminal Law and Criminology,* **88** (1999): 1453–1474.
3. Robert Nash Parker and Randi S. Cartmill, "Alcohol and Homicide in the United States 1934–1995—or One Reason Why U.S. Rates of Violence May Be Going Down," *Journal of Criminal Law and Criminology,* **88** (1999): 1369–1398.
4. Gary LaFree, "Social Institutions and the Crime 'Bust' of the 1990s," *Journal of Criminal Law and Criminology,* **88** (1999): 1325–1386.
5. George L. Kelling and William J. Bratton, "Declining Crime Rates: Insiders' Views of the New York City Story," *Journal of Criminal Law and Criminology,* **88** (1999): 1217–1232.
6. Richard Curtis, "The Improbable Transformation of Inner-City Neighborhoods: Crime, Violence, Drugs and Youth in the 1990s," *Journal of Criminal Law and Criminology,* **88** (1999): 1233–1276.
7. Clifford Krauss, "The Mystery of New York, the Suddenly Safer City," *New York Times,* July 23, 1995, p. 4A.
8. Gregory Beals and Evan Thomas, "A Crimebuster's Fall," Newsweek, Apr. 8, 1996, p. 42.
9. Camille Graham Camp and George M. Camp, *The Corrections Yearbook 1998* (Middletown, Conn.: Criminal Justice Institute, Inc., 1998), p. 6.
10. Michael D. Maltz, "Which Homicides Decreased? Why?" *Journal of Criminal Law and Criminology,* **88** (1999): 1489–1495.

Questions for Discussion

1. Why is there so much disagreement about what has caused the drop in violent crime? Do you think criminologists have vested interests in one explanation over another?
2. Is it possible for the police to have the great impact on crime that Kelling and Bratton claim? To what extent is crime something that can be controlled by the police?
3. Crime rates continue to drop across the country. Have you noticed any changes in your community in the past few years that may be a result of lower crime rates? For example, are there more businesses in downtown areas, do the streets seem safer, is there less drug-related violence?

UCR shows that about 13.2 million Index crimes (excluding arson) were reported to the police in 1997 (Figure 2.2b). Of the total number of Index crimes, violent crimes make up a small portion—12 percent—with a murder rate of 6.8 per 100,000. Most Index crimes are property offenses (88 percent), and 67 percent of the property offenses are larcenies.[25]

The 1997 NCVS presents a somewhat different picture (Figure 2.2a). Though the data presented in the NCVS and the UCR are not entirely comparable because the categories differ, the number of crimes reported to the police and the number reported in the victimization survey are clearly far apart. According to the NCVS, there were over 34 million victimizations. Indeed, the NCVS reports more thefts than the total number of UCR Index offenses.[26]

According to UCR data, the crime rate increased slowly between 1930 and 1960. After 1960 it began to rise much more quickly. This trend continued until 1980 (Figure 2.3), when

FIGURE 2.2 National Crime Victimization Survey and Uniform Crime Reports: A comparison of number of crimes reported. (a) National Crime Victimization Survey: Total number of victimizations, 1997. (b) Uniform Crime Reports: Total number of Index offenses, 1997.

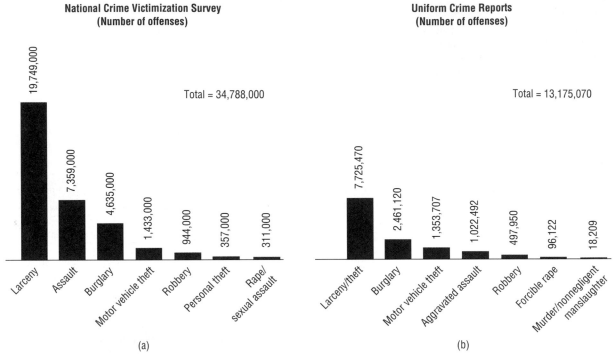

Source: (a) Adapted from U.S. Department of Justice, Bureau of Justice Statistics, *Criminal Victimization 1997* (Washington D.C.: U.S. Government Printing Office, December 1998), p. 3. (b) Adapted from U.S. Department of Justice, Federal Bureau of Investigation, *Crime in the United States, 1997* (Washington D.C.: U.S. Government Printing Office, 1998), p. 67.

the crime rate rose to 5950 per 100,000. From that peak the rate steadily dropped until 1984, when there were 5031.3 crimes per 100,000. After that year the rate rose again until 1991. Since then, it has decreased every year, to 4922.7 in 1997, the lowest rate since 1974.[27] The NCVS also shows that the victimization rate peaked from 1979 to 1981, but that in the 5-year span from 1993 to 1998, the victimization rates for all crimes dropped.[28]

The gradual decline in the crime rate after 1980 is an important phenomenon that requires a bit more analysis. One important factor is the age distribution of the population. Given the fact that young people tend to have the highest crime rate, the age distribution of the population has a major effect on crime trends (Figure 2.4). After World War II, the birthrate increased

FIGURE 2.3 Uniform Crime Reports: Rate of all Index crimes per 100,000 population, 1960–1994.

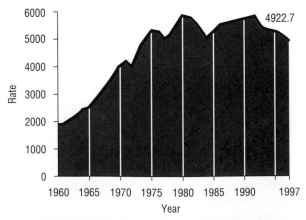

Source: U.S. Department of Justice, Federal Bureau of Investigation, *Crime in the United States, 1975; 1980; 1992; 1994; 1997* (Washington D.C.: U.S. Government Printing Office, 1976, 1981, 1993, 1995, 1998), pp. 41, 49, 58, 67.

FIGURE 2.4   Relationships between murder and age.

A new view of murder

Some relationships can be summarized in two-dimensional graphs; other relationships require a more complex picture. To provide a more comprehensive representation of murders, Michael Maltz proposed using three-dimensional plots to show the relationship between the ages of victims and offenders. One such plot is presented in the surface graph to the right.

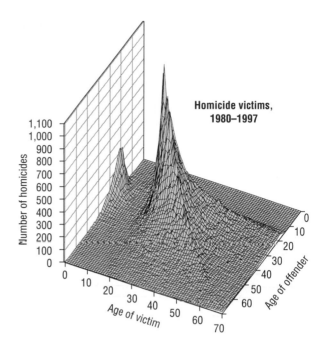

The contours of its surface reveal some attributes of murder in the United States. The large central peak shows that most offenders are between the ages of 18 and 34, as are their victims. The smaller peak off to the left shows that many very young children are killed by persons in their twenties and thirties—mostly incidents of infants being killed by their parents. There is an area between the two peaks in which very few murders occur (victim ages 4 to 12). The diagonal ridge running from the top of the central peak to the lower right-hand corner shows that adult offenders tend to kill victims in their own age group. The ridge running along the line of 20-year-old offenders shows that older juveniles and young adults kill victims in a wide age range.

Source: Analyses of the FBI's *Supplementary Homicide Reports* for the years 1980–1997 [machine-readable data files], *Juvenile Offenders and Victims: 1999 National Report.*

sharply in what is known as the baby boom. The baby-boom generation reached its crime-prone years in the 1960s, and the crime rate duly rose. As the generation grew older, the crime rate became more stable and in the 1980s began to decline. Some researchers claim that the children of the baby boomers may very well expand the ranks of the crime-prone ages once again and that crime will again increase.

During the period when the baby-boom generation outgrew criminal behavior, U.S. society was undergoing other changes. We adopted a get-tough crime-control policy, which may have deterred some people from committing crimes. Mandatory prison terms meant judges had less discretion in sentencing, and fewer convicted felons were paroled. In addition, crime-prevention programs, such as Neighborhood Watch groups, became popular. These and other factors have been suggested to explain why the crime rate dropped, but we have no definitive answers.

Did You Know

. . . that in one-third of all sexual assaults reported to police, the victim was under the age of 12?

Crime Surfing

http://www.albany.edu/sourcebook

The "Sourcebook of Criminal Justice Statistics" is an excellent place to look for official data on all parts of the criminal justice system. Go to this website to find the most recent arrest data for the area in which you live. Which three offenses have the most arrests?

Locations and Times of Criminal Acts

Statistics on the characteristics of crimes are important not only to criminologists who seek to know why crime occurs but also to those who want to know how to prevent it (Chapter 9). Two statistics of use in prevention efforts are those on *where* crimes are committed and *when* they are committed.

Most crimes are committed in large urban areas rather than in small cities, suburbs, or rural areas. This pattern can be attributed to a variety of factors—population density, age distribution of residents, stability of the population, economic conditions, and the quality of law enforcement, to name but a few. The statistics for Charlotte, North Carolina, for example, show that most arrests took place in the poverty-ridden ghetto areas. The fact that the majority of those arrests were made in neighborhoods where drug dealers were visibly present on the streets fits the national picture.

NCVS data tell us the safest place to be is at home, although we are likely to be victimized when we are in familiar territory. In 1995, only one-quarter of violent crimes took place near or at the victim's home. Almost three-quarters of violent crimes occurred within 5 miles of home. Common locations for violent crimes are streets other than those near the victim's home (19 percent), at school (14 percent), or at a commercial establishment (12 percent).[29]

As for the time of day when crimes are committed, NCVS data reveal that over 58 percent of all violent crimes involving strangers are committed at night, between 6 P.M. and 6 A.M. Household crimes follow the same pattern: Of crimes committed within a known period, 70 percent of household larcenies and 75 percent of motor vehicle thefts are committed at night. Most personal thefts, however, are committed during the day. For juveniles, 19 percent of violent crimes occur in the 4 hours (3 P.M. to 7 P.M.) immediately after the close of school (Figure 2.5).[30]

Nationwide crime rates also vary by season. Personal and household crimes are more likely to be committed during the warmer months of the years, perhaps because in summer people spend more time outdoors, where they are more vulnerable to crime.[31] People also often leave doors and windows open when they go out in warm weather.

Severity of Crime

We have seen that crime rates vary by time and place. They also vary in people's perception of

FIGURE 2.5 Serious juvenile crime by time of day. On school days serious juvenile crimes cluster in the hours immediately after the close of school. On school days, serious violent crimes by juveniles peak at 3 P.M.

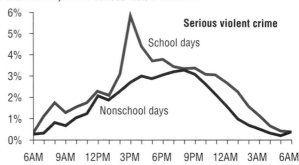

Percent of all juvenile serious violent incidents

On nonschool days the temporal pattern of juvenile violence is similar to the overall pattern for adults; juvenile violence peaks at night on nonschool days.

Note: Serious violent crimes include murder, violent sex assaults, robbery, and aggravated assault.

Source: Analyses of the FBI's *National Incident-Based Reporting System master files* for the years 1991–1996 [machine-readable data files], as cited in *Juvenile Offenders and Victims: 1999 National Report.*

their severity. To some extent, legislation sets a standard of severity by the punishments it attaches to various crimes. But let us take a critical look at such judgments.

Do you believe that skyjacking an airplane is a more serious offense than smuggling heroin? Is forcible rape more serious than kidnapping? Is breaking into a home and stealing $1000 more serious than using force to rob a person of $10? A yes answer to all three questions conforms with the findings of the National Survey of Crime Severity, which in 1977 measured public perceptions of the seriousness of 204 events, from planting a bomb that killed 20 people to playing hooky from school.[32]

The survey, conducted by Marvin E. Wolfgang and his colleagues, found that individuals generally agree about the relative seriousness of specific crimes (Table 2.2). In ranking severity, people seem to base their decisions on such factors as the ability of victims to protect themselves, the amount of injury and loss suffered, the type of business or organization from which property is stolen, the relationship between of-

TABLE 2.2   How Do People Rank the Severity of Crime?

Severity Score	Ten Most Serious Offenses	Severity Score	Ten Least Serious Offenses
72.1	Planting a bomb in a public building. The bomb explodes and 20 people are killed.	1.3	Two persons willingly engage in a homosexual act.
52.8	A man forcibly rapes a woman. As a result of physical injuries, she dies.	1.1	Disturbing the neighborhood with loud, noisy behavior.
43.2	Robbing a victim at gunpoint. The victim struggles and is shot to death.	1.1	Taking bets on the numbers.
39.2	A man stabs his wife. As a result, she dies.	1.1	A group continues to hang around a corner after being told to break up by a police officer.
35.7	Stabbing a victim to death.	0.9	A youngster under 16 years old runs away from home.
35.6	Intentionally injuring a victim. As a result, the victim dies.	0.8	Being drunk in public.
33.8	Running a narcotics ring.	0.7	A youngster under 16 years old breaks a curfew law by being out on the street after the hour permitted by law.
27.9	A woman stabs her husband. As a result, he dies.	0.6	Trespassing in the backyard of a private home.
26.3	An armed person skyjacks an airplane and demands to be flown to another country.	0.3	A person is a vagrant. That is, he has no home and no visible means of support.
25.8	A man forcibly rapes a woman. No other physical injury occurs.	0.2	A youngster under 16 years old plays hooky from school.

Source: Adapted from Marvin E. Wolfgang, Robert Figlio, Paul E. Tracey, and Simon I. Singer, *National Survey of Crime Severity* (Washington, D.C.: U.S. Government Printing Office, 1985).

fender and victim, and (for drug offenses) the types of drugs involved. Respondents generally agreed that violent crime is more serious than property crime. They also considered white-collar crimes, such as engaging in consumer fraud, cheating on income taxes, polluting, and accepting bribes, to be as serious as many violent and property crimes.

MEASURING CHARACTERISTICS OF CRIMINALS

Information on the characteristics of crimes is not the only sort of data analyzed by criminologists. They also want to know the characteristics of the people who commit those crimes.

Behind each crime is a criminal or several criminals. Criminals can be differentiated by age, ethnicity, gender, socioeconomic level, and other criteria. These characteristics enable us to group criminals into categories, and it is these categories that researchers find useful. They study the various offender groups to determine why some people are more likely than others to commit crimes or particular types of crimes. It has been estimated that 15.3 million arrests were made in 1997 for all criminal offenses ex-cept traffic violations. Figure 2.6 shows how these arrests were distributed among the offenses. During the 10 years between 1988 and 1997, the number of arrests rose 16 percent. Let us take a close look at the characteristics of the persons arrested.[33]

Age and Crime

Six armed men who have been called the "over-the-hill gang" were arrested trying to rob an elegant bridge and backgammon club in midtown New York City. The robbery began at 10:25 P.M. when the men, wearing rubber gloves and ski masks and armed with two revolvers, a shotgun, and a rifle, forced the customers and employees to lie down in a back room while they loaded a nylon bag with wallets, players' money, and the club's cash box. A club worker slipped out a side door to

Crime Surfing

www.uncjin.org

The United Nations Crime and Justice Information Network (UNCJIN) is a resource for investigating crime and criminal justice systems in various countries around the world. The URL above will take you to reported crime data for many countries. Use these data to determine whether other countries have crime patterns similar to those of the United States.

In the early 1970s, the General Assembly of the United Nations requested the Secretary-General to conduct a global survey on the prevalence of crime in Member States. Governments may have had various reasons for wanting to know the amount of crime in the world, but they all seemed to agree that crime impedes national development and imposes great burdens on individual victims.

The U.N. Crime Prevention and Criminal Justice Branch (now called the Centre for International Crime Prevention) surveyed all Member States by means of a questionnaire. This exercise has been repeated every 5 years so that by now, statistical information about the extent of crime (and the operations of criminal justice systems) is available for the period from 1970 through 1995. (The sixth survey, covering 1996 and beyond, is in progress.) The number of participating countries has increased over the years, from 72 to over 100. Many difficulties had to be overcome to obtain data and to assess their validity, such as national differences in the definitions of crimes, varying methods of reporting and recording those to be considered, as well as a variety of factors which prompt officials to understate or overstate the amount of some crimes. Victimization surveys and self-report studies, which have been conducted more recently, have helped in the analysis of the prevalence of crime.

While it is impossible to present the global picture here, a few statistical snapshots are indicative of the challenges posed by the UNCJS to statisticians and policy makers. The figure depicts the percentages of various crime types reported globally.

The global picture shows property crime to account for most criminality.

Crime types reported to the UNCJS, 1994.

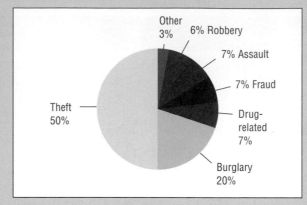

Source: Fifth United Nations Crima and Justice Survey Global Report on Crime and Justice.

Obviously, patterns vary somewhat from country to country, and from region to region.

In sample years from all five world crime surveys, a global comparison of homicide rates grouped by developing countries versus industrialized countries reveals a startling development, namely, a complete reversal of incident rates. In 1974, developing countries had over twice as many homicides as industrialized countries. By 1994, industrialized countries had twice as many homicides as the more rural developing countries.

This trend gives criminologists, statisticians, and policy makers much to think about: What accounts for this enormous shift to homicides in industrialized countries? Would one not have expected a far greater rise in homicides in developing countries, where ethnic strife and civil wars are exacting a great toll in lives? They must also address other startling findings in the never-ending effort to track down crime's root causes, to determine the relation between crime and socioeconomic development, and to evaluate the interplay between official (public) crime-prevention efforts and other forms of social control. Ultimately, they must devise policy guidelines that will be useful to nations and communities in dealing with the problem of crime *now,* before it victimizes more of the world's citizens and their countries.

Source

Graeme Newman, ed., *Global Report on Crime and Justice* (New York: United Nations; Oxford: Oxford University Press, 1999).

Questions for Discussion

1. Since every country has its own notions on what constitutes crime and how a particular crime is defined, how would you go about making statistical information received from 100 or more countries comparable?
2. Why would governments understate or overstate their "official" crime rates?
3. What methods can a statistician use to obtain a true picture of crime rates?

FIGURE 2.6 Distribution of total number of arrests, 1997 (estimated).

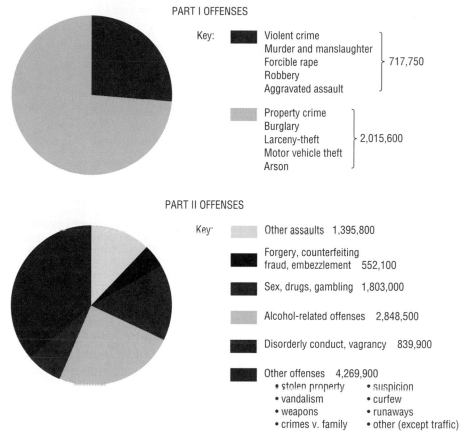

PART I OFFENSES

Key:

■ Violent crime
Murder and manslaughter
Forcible rape   } 717,750
Robbery
Aggravated assault

▩ Property crime
Burglary
Larceny-theft   } 2,015,600
Motor vehicle theft
Arson

PART II OFFENSES

Key:

▨ Other assaults 1,395,800

■ Forgery, counterfeiting
fraud, embezzlement 552,100

■ Sex, drugs, gambling 1,803,000

▩ Alcohol-related offenses 2,848,500

■ Disorderly conduct, vagrancy 839,900

■ Other offenses 4,269,900
• stolen property   • suspicion
• vandalism   • curfew
• weapons   • runaways
• crimes v. family   • other (except traffic)

Source: U.S. Department of Justice, Federal Bureau of Investigation, *Crime in the United States, 1997* (Washington D.C.: U.S. Government Printing Office, 1998), p. 222.

alert police, who arrived within minutes. They surprised and disarmed one member of the gang, a 48-year-old, whom they found clutching a .22-caliber revolver. They took a .38-caliber revolver from another gang member, 41 years old. During the scuffle with the officers, one suspect tried to escape, fell, and broke his nose. The officers then found and arrested a 40-year-old man standing in the hallway with a 12-gauge Winchester shotgun. Meanwhile, the other gang members abandoned their gloves and masks and lay down among the people they had robbed. One of the suspects, aged 72, who wore a back brace, complained of chest and back pain as police locked handcuffs on him. He was immediately hospitalized.[34]

In another case, 94-year-old career criminal Wesley (Pop) Honeywood, from Jacksonville,

Florida, was sentenced to 7 years after he pointed an unloaded gun at another man who warned him not to eat grapes growing in the man's yard. Mr. Honeywood was given the option to go to a nursing home instead of prison, but he resisted, saying, "If I go to jail, I may be out in a couple of years. If I go to a nursing home, I may be there the rest of my life."[35]

These cases are extraordinary for at least two reasons. First, in any given year approximately half of all arrests are of individuals under the age of 25; and second, gang membership is ordinarily confined to the young. Though juveniles (people under the age of 18) constitute about 8 percent of the population, they account for almost one-third of the arrests for Index crimes. Arrest rates begin to decline after age 30 and taper off to about 2 percent or less from age

50 on (Figure 2.7).[36] In fact, although people aged 65 and over constitute 12.6 percent of the population, they make up fewer than 1 percent of arrests.[37] This decline in criminal activities with age is known as the **aging-out phenomenon.** The reasons for it have sparked a lively scientific debate. Michael Gottfredson and Travis Hirschi contend there is a certain inclination to commit crimes which peaks in the middle or late teens and then declines throughout life. This relationship between crime and age does not change, "regardless of sex, race, country, time, or offense."[38]

Crime decreases with age, the researchers add, even among people who commit frequent offenses. Thus differences in crime rates found among young people of various groups, such as males and females or lower class and middle class, will be maintained throughout the life cycle. If lower-class youths are three times more likely to commit crimes than middle-class youths, for instance, then 60-year-old lower-class persons will be three times more likely to commit crimes than 60-year-old middle-class persons, though crimes committed by both lower-class and middle-class groups will constantly decline.[39] According to this argument, all offenders commit fewer crimes as they grow older because they have less strength, less mobility, and so on.

James Q. Wilson and Richard Herrnstein support the view that the aging-out phenomenon is a natural part of the life cycle.[40] Teenagers may become increasingly independent of their parents yet lack the resources to support themselves; they band together with other young people who are equally frustrated in their search for legitimate ways to get money, sex, alcohol, and status. Together they find illegitimate sources. With adulthood, the small gains from criminal behavior no longer seem so attractive. Legitimate means open up. They marry. Their peers no longer endorse lawbreaking. They learn to delay gratification. Petty crime is no longer adventurous.[41] It is at this time that the aging-out process begins for most individuals. Even the ones who continue to commit offenses will eventually slow down with increasing age.[42]

The opposing side in this debate, sometimes called the life-course perspective, argues

FIGURE 2.7   Violent crime Index arrests by age.

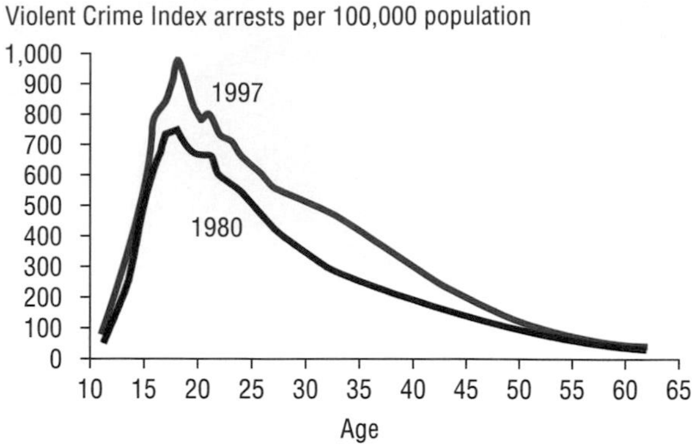

Violent Crime Index arrests per 100,000 population

Source: Analysis of arrest data from an unpublished FBI report for 1980 and the FBI's *Crime in the United States 1997* and population data from the Bureau of the Census for 1980 from *Current Population Reports*, P25–1095 and for 1997 from *Estimates of the Population of States by Age, Sex, Race, and Hispanic Origin: 1997* [machine-readable data file], as cited in *Juvenile Offenders and Victims: 1999 National Report.*

that the decrease in crime rates after adolescence does not imply that the number of crimes committed by all individual offenders declines. In other words, the frequency of offending may go down for most offenders, but some chronic active offenders may continue to commit the same amount of crime over time. Why might this be so? Because the factors that influence any individual's entrance into criminal activity vary, the number and types of offenses committed vary, and the factors that eventually induce the individual to give up criminal activity vary.[43]

According to this argument, the frequency of criminal involvement, then, depends on such social factors as economic situation, peer pressure, and lifestyle; and it is these social factors that explain the aging-out phenomenon. A teenager's unemployment, for example, may have very little to do with the onset of criminal activity because the youngster is not yet in the labor force and still lives at home. Unemployment may increase an adult's rate of offending, however, because an adult requires income to support various responsibilities. Thus the relationship between age and crime is not the same for all offenders. Various conditions during the life cycle affect individuals' behavior in different ways.[44]

To learn how the causes of crime vary at different ages, Alfred Blumstein and his colleagues

Two very old inmates in the geriatric unit at Estelle Prison, Huntsville, Texas: an increasing burden for custodial care.

suggest that we study **criminal careers,** a concept that describes the onset of criminal activity, the types and amount of crime committed, and the termination of such activity.[45] **Longitudinal studies** of a particular group of people over time should enable researchers to uncover the factors that distinguish criminals from noncriminals and those that differentiate criminals in regard to the number and kinds of offenses they commit.

Those who are involved in research on criminal careers assume that offenders who commit 10 crimes may differ from those who commit 1 or 15. They ask: Are the factors that cause the second offense the same ones that cause the fourth or the fifth? Do different factors move one offender from theft to rape or from assault to shoplifting? How many persons in a **birth cohort** (a group of people born in the same year) will become criminals? Of those, how many will become career criminals (chronic offenders)?

In the 1960s, researchers at the Sellin Center of the University of Pennsylvania began a search for answers. Their earliest publication, in 1972, detailed the criminal careers of 9945 boys (a cohort) born in Philadelphia in 1945. Marvin Wolfgang, Robert Figlio, and Thorsten Sellin obtained their data from school records and official police reports. Their major findings were that 35 percent of the boys had had contact with the police before reaching their eighteenth birthday; of those boys, 46 percent were one-time offenders and 54 percent were repeat offenders. Of those with police contact, 18 percent had committed five or more offenses; they represented 6 percent of the total. The "chronic 6 percent," as they are now called, were responsible for more than half of all the offenses committed, including 71 percent of the homicides, 73 percent of the rapes, 82 percent of the robberies, and 69 percent of the assaults.[46]

Research continued on 10 percent of the boys in the original cohort until they reached the age of 30. This sample was divided into three groups: those who had records of offenses only as juveniles, those who had records only as adults, and those who were persistent offenders with both juvenile and

Did You Know

. . . that one in every three delinquents with a history of violent offenses has a juvenile court record before reaching age 14?

adult records. Though they made up only 15 percent of the follow-up group, those who had been chronic juvenile offenders made up 74 percent of all the arrests. Thus chronic juvenile offenders do indeed continue to break laws as adults.[47]

The boys in the original cohort were born in 1945. Researchers questioned whether the same behavior patterns would continue over the years. Criminologist Paul Tracy and his associates found the answer in a second study, which examined a cohort of 13,160 males born in 1958. The two studies show similar results. In the second cohort, 33 percent had had contact with the police before reaching their eighteenth birthday, 42 percent were one-time offenders, and 58 percent were repeat offenders. Chronic delinquents were found in both cohorts. The chronic delinquents in the second cohort, however, accounted for a greater percentage of the cohort—7.5 percent. They also were involved in more serious and injurious acts than the previous group.

The 1945 cohort study did not contain females, so no overall comparisons can be made over time. But comparing females and males in the 1958 cohort, we see significant gender differences. Of the 14,000 females in the cohort, 14 percent had had contact with the police before age 18. Among the female delinquents, 60 percent were one-time offenders, 33 percent were repeat offenders, and 7 percent were chronic offenders. Overall, female delinquency was less frequent and less likely to involve serious charges.[48]

In another longitudinal study, researchers followed about 4000 youngsters in Denver, Pittsburgh, and Rochester, New York, for 5 years, 1988 through 1992. By the age of 16, over half the youngsters admitted to committing violent criminal acts. According to Terence P. Thornberry, the principal investigator in Rochester, chronic offenders also accounted for a high percentage of all violent offenses: 15 percent of the youths in the sample were responsible for 75 percent of the acts.[49]

The policy implications of such findings are clear. If a very small group of offenders is committing a large percentage of all crime, the crime rate should go down if we incarcerate those of-fenders for long periods of time. Many jurisdictions around the country are developing sentencing policies to do just that, but such policies are quite controversial.

Gender and Crime

Except for such crimes as prostitution, shoplifting, and welfare fraud, males traditionally commit more crimes than females at all ages. According to the UCR for 1997, the arrest ratio is typically about 4 male offenders to 1 female offender.[50] The NCVS of 1993 reports a wider gap: For personal crimes of violence involving a single offender, 83 percent of victims perceived the gender of the offender as male.[51]

Since the 1960s, however, there have been some interesting developments in regard to gender and crime data. In 1960 females accounted for 11 percent of the total number of arrests across the country. They now account for about 22 percent. And while the female arrest rate is still much lower than that of males, the rate of increase for women has risen faster than the rate for men (Figure 2.8 shows juvenile rates).[52]

Self-report surveys, which show more similarities in male and female criminal activity than official reports do, find that males commit more offenses than females. However, several of these studies suggest that gender differences in crime may be narrowing. They demonstrate that the patterns and causes of male and female delinquent activity are becoming more alike.[53] John Hagan and his associates agree, but only with respect to girls raised in middle-class egalitarian families in which husband and wife share similar positions of power at home and in the workplace. They argue that girls raised in lower-class, father-dominated households grow up in a cult of domesticity that reduces their freedom and thus the likelihood of their delinquency.[54] Researchers Merry Morash and Meda Chesney-Lind disagree. In a study of 1427 adolescents and their caretakers, they found gender differences in delinquency between girls and boys regardless of the type of family in which the youngsters were raised.[55]

Because women traditionally have had such low crime rates, the scientific community and the mass media had generally ignored the subject of

FIGURE 2.8 Juvenile male and female arrest rates.

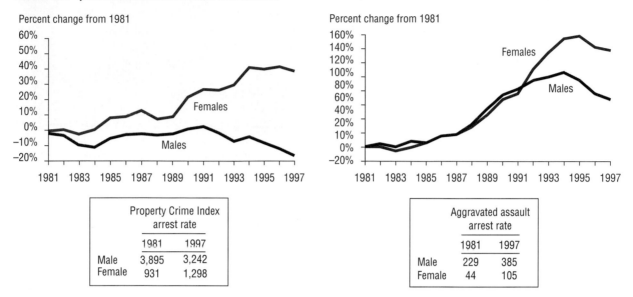

Percent change from 1981

	Property Crime Index arrest rate	
	1981	1997
Male	3,895	3,242
Female	931	1,298

	Aggravated assault arrest rate	
	1981	1997
Male	229	385
Female	44	105

While juvenile male arrest rates for Property Crime Index offenses declined during the 1990s, the female rate increased. Between 1981 and 1997, male juvenile property crime rates declined 17 percent, while female rates increased 39 percent.

While male arrest rates for aggravated assault leveled off between 1992 and 1995, female arrest rates continued to increase. In 1997, male arrest rates for aggravated assault were nearly four times the female rates. Between 1981 and 1997, female arrest rates increased twice as much as male rates increased.

Note: Arrest rates are arrests per 100,000 males or females ages 10 to 17.

Source: Analyses of arrest data from unpublished FBI reports for 1980 through 1994 and the FBI's *Crime in the United States* reports for 1995, 1996, and 1997 and population data from the Bureau of the Census for 1980 through 1989 from *Current Population Reports*, P25–1095 and for 1990 through 1997 from *Estimates of the Population of States by Age, Sex, Race, and Hispanic Origin: 1990–1997* [machine-readable data files], as cited in *Juvenile Offenders and Victims: 1999 National Report*.

female criminality. Both have tended to view female offenders as misguided children who are an embarrassment rather than a threat to society. Only a handful of the world's criminologists have deemed the subject worthy of independent study. Foremost among them was Cesare Lombroso (whom we shall meet again in Chapter 3). His book *The Female Offender* (coauthored by William Ferrero), which appeared in 1895, detailed the physical abnormalities that would predestine some girls to be criminal from birth.[56] Lombroso's findings on male criminals, however, have not stood the test of later scientific research, and his portrayal of the female criminal has been found to be similarly inaccurate.

A little over a generation later, in the 1930s, Sheldon and Eleanor Glueck launched a massive research project on the biological and environmental causes of crime, with a separate inquiry into female offenders. Their conclusions were decidedly sociological. They said, in essence, that in order to change the incidence of female criminality, there would have to be a change in the social circumstances in which females grow up.[57]

Otto Pollack shared the Gluecks' views on sociological determinants. In 1952 he proposed that female crime has a "masked character" that keeps it from being properly recorded or otherwise noted in statistical reports. Protective attitudes toward women make police officers less willing to arrest them, make victims less eager to report their offenses, make district attorneys less enthusiastic about prosecuting them, and make juries less likely to find them guilty. Moreover, Pollack noted that women's social roles as homemakers, child rearers, and shoppers furnish them with opportunities for concealed criminal activity and with victims who are the least likely to complain and/or cooperate with the police. He also argued that female crime was limited by the various psychological and physiological characteristics inherent in the female anatomy.[58]

A quarter century after Pollack's work, two researchers, working independently, took a fresh look at female crime in light of women's new roles in society. In 1975 Freda Adler posited that as social and economic roles of women changed in the legitimate world, their participation in crime would also change. According to this argument, the temptations, challenges, stresses, and strains to which women have been increasingly subjected in recent years cause them to act or react in the same manner in which men have consistently reacted to the same stimuli. In other words, equalization of social and economic roles leads to similar behavior patterns, both legal and illegal, on the part of both men and women. To steal a car, for example, one needs to know how to drive. To embezzle, one needs to be in a position of trust and in control of funds. To get into a bar fight, one needs to go to a bar. To be an inside trader on Wall Street, one needs to be on the inside.[59]

Rita Simon has taken a similar position. She, too, has argued that female criminality has undergone changes. But these changes, according to Simon, have occurred only in regard to certain property crimes, such as larceny/theft and fraud/embezzlement. Women are becoming more involved in these crimes because they have more opportunities to commit them. Simon hypothesizes that since the propensity of men and women to commit crime is not basically different, as more women enter the labor force and work in a much broader range of jobs, their property crime rate will continue to go up.[60]

Some criminologists have challenged the views of Adler and Simon. Many questions have been asked about the so-called new female criminal. Does she exist? If so, does she commit more crimes than the old female criminal did? What types of crimes? Is she still involved primarily in offenses against property, or has she

Mary Kay Letourneau, 35 years old, the teacher who had sex with a thirteen-year-old student and gave birth to his child, is sentenced to 6 months in jail in a Seattle, Washington, court (Nov. 1997). Ms. Letourneau had pleaded guilty to second degree child rape. Shortly after her release from jail, she resumed her relationship with the boy and was sentenced to seven years in prison for violating the conditions of her release. (She subsequently had a second child with the boy.)

turned to more violent offenses? Researchers differ on the answers. Some contend that the extent of female criminality has not changed through the years but that crimes committed by women are more often making their way into official statistics simply because they are more often reported and prosecuted. In other words, the days of chivalry in the criminal justice system are over.[61]

Others argue that female crime has indeed increased, but they attribute the increase to nonviolent, petty property offenses that continue to reflect traditional female gender roles.[62] Moreover, some investigators claim, the increased involvement in these petty property offenses suggests that women are still economically disadvantaged, still suffering sexism in the legitimate marketplace.[63] Other researchers support the contention of Adler and Simon that female roles have changed and that these changes have indeed led women to commit the same kinds of crimes as men, violent as well as property offenses.[64]

Though scholars disagree on the form and extent of female crime, they do seem to agree that the crimes women commit are closely associated with their socioeconomic position in society. The controversy has to do with whether or not that position has changed. In any case, the association between gender and crime has become a recognized area of concern in the growing body of research dealing with contemporary criminological issues.[65]

Social Class and Crime

Researchers agree on the importance of age and gender as factors related to crime, but they disagree strongly about whether social class is related to crime. First of all, the term "class" can have many meanings. If "lower class" is defined by income, then the category might include graduate students, unemployed stockbrokers, pensioners, welfare mothers, prison inmates, and many others who have little in common except low income. Furthermore, "lower class" is often defined by the low prestige associated with blue-collar occupations. Some delinquency studies determine the class of young people by the class of their fathers, even though the young people may have jobs quite different from those of their fathers.

Another dispute focuses on the source of statistics used by investigators. Many researchers attribute the relatively strong association between class and crime found in arrest statistics to class bias on the part of the police. If the police are more likely to arrest a lower-class suspect than a middle-class suspect, they say, arrest data will show more involvement of lower-class people in criminality whether or not they are actually committing more crimes. When Charles Tittle, Wayne Villemez, and Douglas Smith analyzed 35 studies of the relationship between social class and crime rates in 1978, they found

little support for the claim that crime is primarily a lower-class phenomenon. An update of that work, which evaluates studies done between 1978 and 1990, again found no pervasive relationship.[66]

Many scholars have challenged such conclusions. They claim that when self-report studies are used for analysis, the results show few class differences because the studies ask only about trivial offenses. Delbert Elliott and Suzanne Ageton, for example, looked at serious crimes among a national sample of 1726 young people ages 11 to 17. According to the youths' responses to a self-report questionnaire, lower-class young people were much more likely than middle-class young people to commit such serious crimes as burglary, robbery, assault, and sexual assault.[67] A follow-up study concluded that middle-class and lower-class youths differed significantly in both the nature and the number of serious crimes they committed.[68]

Controversies remain about the social class of people who commit crimes. There is no controversy, however, about the social class of people in prison. The probability that a person such as Dan Rostenkowski, former chairman of the federal House of Representatives Ways and Means Committee, who was convicted for mail fraud, will get a prison sentence is extremely low. Rostenkowski does not fit the typical profile of the hundreds of thousands of inmates of our nation's jails and prisons. He is educated. Only 28 percent of prison inmates have completed high school.[69] His income was that of a high-ranking politician. The average yearly income of jail inmates who work is $5600. He had a white-collar job. Eighty-five percent of prison inmates are blue-collar workers. He committed a white-collar offense. Only 18 percent of those convicted of such offenses go to prison for more than 1 year, whereas 39 percent of the violent offenders and 26 percent of the property offenders do.[70] Finally, Dan Rostenkowski is white in a criminal justice system where blacks are disproportionately represented.

Race and Crime

Statistics on race and crime show that while African-Americans constitute 12 percent of the

Martin Frankel was arrested at this luxury Hamburg, Germany, hotel on charges of money laundering and wire fraud in the amount of $350 million. Traveling with a counterfeit British passport, he alluded capture from May to August 1999.

population, they account for 30.4 percent of all arrests for Index crimes.[71] Other statistics confirm their disproportionate representation in the criminal justice system. Fifty percent of black urban males are arrested for an Index crime at least once during their lives, compared with fourteen percent of white males. The likelihood that any man will serve time in jail or prison is estimated to be 18 percent for blacks and 3 percent for whites. Moreover, the leading cause of death among young black men is murder.[72]

These statistics raise many questions. Do blacks actually commit more crimes? Or are they simply arrested more often? Are black neighborhoods under more police surveillance than white neighborhoods? Do blacks receive differential treatment in the criminal justice system? If blacks commit more crimes than whites, why?

Some data support the argument that there are more African-Americans in the criminal justice system because bias operates from the time of arrest through incarceration. Other data support the argument that racial disparities in official statistics reflect an actual difference in crim-inal behavior. Much of the evidence comes from the statistics of the NCVS, which are very similar to the statistics on race found in arrest data.

When interviewers asked victims about the race of offenders in violent crimes, 28 percent identified the assailants as black.[73] Similarly, while self-report data demonstrate that less serious juvenile offenses are about equally prevalent among black and white youngsters, more serious ones are not: Black youngsters report having committed many more Index crimes than do whites of comparable ages.[74]

If the disparity in criminal behavior suggested by official data, victimization studies, and self-reports actually exists, and if we are to explain it, we have to try to discover why people commit crimes. A history of hundreds of years of abuse, neglect, and discrimination against black Americans has left its mark in the form of high unemployment, residence in socially disorganized areas, one-parent households, and negative self-images.[75]

In 1968, in the aftermath of the worst riots in modern American history, the National Advisory Commission on Civil Disorders alluded to the reasons blacks had not achieved the successes accomplished by other minority groups that at one time or another were discriminated against as well. European immigrants provided unskilled labor needed by industry. By the time blacks migrated from rural areas to cities, the U.S. economy was changing and soon there was no longer much demand for unskilled labor. Immigrant groups had also received economic advantages by working for local political organizations. By the time blacks moved to the cities, the political machines no longer had the power to offer help in return for votes. Though both immigrants and blacks arrived in cities with little money, all but the very youngest members of the cohesive immigrant family contributed to the family's income. As slaves, however, black persons had been forbidden to marry, and the unions they formed were subject to disruption at the owner's convenience and therefore tended to be unstable. We will have more to say about the causal factors associated with high crime rates and race in Chapters 5 and 6.

REVIEW

Researchers have three main objectives in measuring crime and criminal behavior patterns. They need (1) to collect and analyze data to test theories about why people commit crime, (2) to learn the situational characteristics of crimes in order to develop prevention strategies, and (3) to determine the needs of the criminal justice system on a daily basis. Data are collected by surveys, experiments, nonparticipant and participant observation, and case studies. It is often cost-effective for researchers to use repositories of information gathered by public and private organizations for their own purposes. The three main sources of data for measuring crime are the Uniform Crime Reports, the National Crime Victimization Survey, and self-report questionnaires. Though each source is useful for some purposes, all three have limitations.

By measuring the characteristics of crime and criminals, we can identify crime trends, the places and times at which crimes are most likely to be committed, and the public's evaluation of the seriousness of offenses. Current controversies concerning offenders focus on the relationship between crime and age throughout the life cycle, the changing role of women in crime, and the effects of social class and race on the response of the criminal justice system. Crime is an activity disproportionately engaged in by young people, males, and minorities.

YOU BE THE CRIMINOLOGIST

Your agency has been asked by the mayor's office to develop a program to reduce youth violence. Of course, you must first determine the extent of youth violence before going out into the field to talk to people. You plan to use information that is publicly available. What specifically will you measure, and what data will you use?

KEY TERMS

The numbers next to the terms refer to the pages on which the terms are defined.

aging-out phenomenon (44)

birth cohort (45)

case study (27)

Review • You Be the Criminologist • Key Terms • Notes

NOTES

1. James O. Finckenauer and Patricia W. Gavin, *Scared Straight: The Panacea Phenomenon Revisited* (Prospect Heights, Ill.: Waveland, 1999).
2. Personal communication from Anne Campbell. Based on Campbell, *The Girls in the Gang: A Report from New York City* (New York: Basil Blackwell, 1984).
3. Edwin H. Sutherland, *The Professional Thief* (Chicago: University of Chicago Press, 1937).
4. Marvin E. Wolfgang, "Ethics and Research," in *Ethics, Public Policy, and Criminal Justice*, ed. A. F. Ellison and N. Bowie (Cambridge, Mass.: Oelgeschlager, Gunn & Hain, 1982).
5. *Draft of ASC Code of Ethics, Criminologist*, **24** (July–August 1999): 13–21.
6. Seth A. Bloomberg and Leslie Wilkins, "Ethics of Research Involving Human Subjects in Criminal Justice," *Crime and Delinquency*, **23** (1977): 435–444.
7. Lawrence Sherman and Barry Glick, "The Quality of Arrest Statistics," *Police Foundation Reports*, **2** (1984): 1–8.
8. Michael Couzens, "Getting the Crime Rate Down: Political Pressure and Crime Reporting," *Law and Society Review*, **8** (1974): 457–493.
9. President's Commission on Law Enforcement and Administration of Justice, *The Challenge of Crime in a Free Society* (Washington, D.C.: U.S. Government Printing Office, 1967), p. 25.
10. Patrick Jackson, "Assessing the Validity of Official Data on Arson," *Criminology*, **26** (1988): 181–195.
11. For a new method of describing statistics of UCR, see James J. Hennessy and Laurie Kepecs-Schlussel, "Psychometric Scaling Techniques Applied to Rates of Crime and Victimization: I. Major Population Centers," *Journal of Offender Rehabilitation*, **18** (1992): 1–80.
12. Patrick G. Jackson, "Sources of Data," in *Measurement Issues in Criminology*, ed. Kimberly L. Kempf (New York: Springer-Verlag, 1990), p. 42. For a comparison of the NCVS, UCR, and NIBRS, with a particular emphasis on what can be learned from incident-based police data that cannot be learned from other sources, see Michael G. Maxfield, "The National Incident-Based Reporting System: Research and Policy Applications," *Journal of Quantitative Criminology*, **15** (1999): 119–149.
13. *Demonstrating the Operational Utility of Incident-Based Data for Local Crime Analysis* (Washington, D.C.: Bureau of Justice Statistics, 1994), p. 1.
14. Victoria L. Major, "UCR's Blueprint for the Future," *FBI Law Enforcement Bulletin*, **61** (1992): 15–21. See also Brian A. Reaves, *Using NIBRS Data to Analyze Violent Crime* (Washington, D.C.: Bureau of Justice Statistics, 1993).
15. For a comparison of victimization data with official police data, see Alfred Blumstein, Jacqueline Cohen, and Richard Rosenfeld, "Trend and Deviation in Crime Rates: A Comparison of UCR and NCS Data for Burglary and Robbery," *Criminology*, **29** (1991):

237–263; Scott Menard, "Residual Gains, Reliability, and the UCR-NCS Relationship: A Comment on Blumstein, Cohen, and Rosenfeld," *Criminology*, **30** (1992): 105–113; Alfred Blumstein, Jacqueline Cohen, and Richard Rosenfeld, "The UCR-NCR Relationship Revisited: A Reply to Menard," *Criminology*, **30** (1992): 115–124; and David McDowall and Colin Loftin, "Comparing the UCR and NSC over Time," *Criminology*, **30** (1992): 125–132. For a discussion of disparity in rape rates between UCR and NCVS, see Gary F. Jensen and Mary Altani Karpos, "Managing Rape: Exploratory Research on the Behavior of Rape Statistics," *Criminology*, **31** (1993): 363–385.

16. James Levine, "The Potential for Crime Overreporting in Criminal Victimization Surveys," *Criminology*, **14** (1976): 307–330. See also Helen M. Eigenberg, "The National Crime Survey and Rape: The Case of the Missing Question," *Justice Quarterly*, **7** (1990): 655–672.

17. James S. Wallerstein and Clement J. Wyle, "Our Law-Abiding Law-Breakers," *Probation*, **25** (March–April 1947): 107–112.

18. Martin Gold, "Undetected Delinquent Behavior," *Journal of Research in Crime and Delinquency*, **3** (1966): 27–46; David Farrington, "Self-Reports of Deviant Behavior: Predictive and Stable?" *Journal of Criminal Law and Criminology*, **64** (1973): 99–110.

19. D. Wayne Osgood, Lloyd Johnston, Patrick O' Malley, and Jerald Bachman, "The Generality of Deviance in Late Adolescence and Early Adulthood," *American Sociological Review*, **53** (1988): 81–93.

20. Franklin Dunford and Delbert Elliott, "Identifying Career Offenders Using Self-Reported Data," *Journal of Research in Crime and Delinquency*, **21** (1983): 57–86.

21. Josine Junger-Tas, Gert-Jan Terlouw, and Malcolm W. Klein, eds., *Delinquent Behavior among Young People in the Western World* (Amsterdam: Kugler, 1994).

22. Michael Hindelang, Travis Hirschi, and Joseph Weis, *Measuring Delinquency* (Beverly Hills, Calif.: Sage, 1981).

23. Tom Squitieri, "Soaring Murder Rate 'Tears Apart' Charlotte," *USA Today*, Jan. 31, 1992, p. 6A.

24. U.S. Department of Justice, Federal Bureau of Investigation, *Crime in the United States, 1992* (hereafter cited as Uniform Crime Reports) (Washington, D.C.: U.S. Government Printing Office, 1993), p. 140; Uniform Crime Reports, 1986, p. 94; Uniform Crime Reports, 1997, p. 147.

25. Uniform Crime Reports, 1997, p. 67.

26. U.S. Department of Justice, Bureau of Justice Statistics, *Criminal Victimization, 1997* (Washington, D.C.: U.S. Government Printing Office, December 1998), p. 3.

27. Uniform Crime Reports, 1997, p. 7.

28. *Criminal Victimization*, 1997, p. 9. For a discussion of the relationship of unemployment, drugs, and family breakdown to rising crime rates, see George B. Palermo, Maurice B. Smith, John J. Di Motto, and Thomas P. Christopher, "Soaring Crime in a Midwestern American City: A Statistical Analysis," *International Journal of Offender Therapy and Comparative Criminology*, **36** (1992): 291–305.

29. Bureau of Justice Statistics, *Crime and Victim Statistics*, found at http://www.ojp.usdoj.gov/bjs/cvict_c.htm#place, Oct. 9, 1999.

30. U.S. Department of Justice, Bureau of Justice Statistics, *Highlights from 20 Years of Surveying Crime Victims* (Washington, D.C.: U.S. Government Printing Office, October 1993), pp. 6–7.

31. Derral Cheatwood, "The Effects of Weather on Homicide," *Journal of Quantitative Criminology*, **11** (1995): 51–70.

32. U.S. Department of Justice, *The Severity of Crime*, Bureau of Justice Statistics Bulletin (Washington, D.C.: U.S. Government Printing Office, January 1984).

33. Uniform Crime Reports, 1997, p. 221.

34. James C. McKinley, Jr., "Six Armed Men, Aged 40–72, Held in Bungled Robbery of a Club," *New York Times*, Apr. 20, 1989, p. D6.

35. *New York Times*, Nov. 6, 1994, p. 24.

36. Uniform Crime Reports, 1997, pp. 232–233.

37. U.S. Bureau of the Census, *Statistical Abstract of the United States: 1998* (Washington, D.C.: U.S. Government Printing Office, 1998), p. 15.

38. Michael Gottfredson and Travis Hirschi, "The True Value of Lambda Would Appear

to Be Zero: An Essay on Career Criminals, Criminal Careers, Selective Incapacitation, Cohort Studies, and Related Topics," *Criminology*, **24** (1986): 213–234.

39. Michael Gottfredson and Travis Hirschi, "Science, Public Policy, and the Career Paradigm," *Criminology*, **26** (1988): 37–55. For a critique of Hirschi and Gottfredson's contentions, see Darrell J. Steffensmeier, Emilie Anderson Allan, Miles D. Harer, and Cathy Streifel, "Age and the Distribution of Crime," *American Journal of Sociology*, **94** (1989): 803–831. For a test of those contentions, see Sung Joon Jang and Marvin D. Krohn, "Developmental Patterns of Sex Differences in Delinquency among African American Adolescents: A Test of the Sex-Invariance Hypothesis," *Journal of Quantitative Criminology*, **11** (1995): 195–222.

40. James Q. Wilson and Richard Herrnstein, *Crime and Human Nature* (New York: Simon & Schuster, 1985), pp. 126–147.

41. Gordon Trasler, "Some Cautions for a Biological Approach to Crime Causation," in *The Causes of Crime: New Biological Approaches*, ed. Sarnoff Mednick, Terrie Moffitt, and Susan Stack (Cambridge: Cambridge University Press, 1987), pp. 7–24.

42. Charles Tittle, "Two Empirical Regularities (Maybe) in Search of an Explanation: Commentary on the Age/Crime Debate," *Criminology*, **26** (1988): 75–85.

43. Alfred Blumstein, Jacqueline Cohen, and David Farrington, "Criminal Career Research: Its Value for Criminology," *Criminology*, **26** (1988): 1–35.

44. Dawn R. Jeglum Bartusch, Donald R. Lynum, Terrie E. Moffitt, and Phil A. Silva, "Is Age Important? Testing a General versus a Developmental Theory of Antisocial Behavior," *Criminology*, **35** (1997): 13–48.

45. Alfred Blumstein, Jacqueline Cohen, Jeffrey Roth, and Christy Visher, *Criminal Careers and "Career Criminals"* (Washington, D.C.: National Academy Press, 1986). On the relationship between crime and age, see Robert J. Sampson and John H. Laub, *Crime in the Making: Pathways and Turning Points through Life* (Cambridge, Mass.: Harvard University Press, 1993); Neal

Shover and Carol Y. Thompson, "Age, Differential Expectations, and Crime Desistance," *Criminology*, **30** (1992): 89–104; David F. Greenberg, "The Historical Variability of the Age-Crime Relationship," *Journal of Quantitative Criminology*, **10** (1994): 361–373; Daniel S. Nagin, David P. Farrington, and Terrie E. Moffitt, "Life-Course Trajectories of Different Types of Offenders," *Criminology*, **33** (1995): 111–139; and Julie Horney, Wayne Osgood, and Ineke Haen Marshall, "Criminal Careers in the Short-Term: Intra-individual Variability in Crime and Its Relation to Local Life Circumstances," *American Sociological Review*, **60** (1995): 655–673.

46. Marvin Wolfgang, Robert Figlio, and Thorsten Sellin, *Delinquency in a Birth Cohort* (Chicago: University of Chicago Press, 1972). For a discussion of how each delinquent act was weighted for seriousness, see Thorsten Sellin and Marvin Wolfgang, *The Measurement of Delinquency* (New York: Wiley, 1964). See also Douglas A. Smith, Christy A. Visher, and G. Roger Jarjoura, "Dimensions of Delinquency: Exploring the Correlates of Participation, Frequency, and Persistence of Delinquent Behavior," *Journal of Research in Crime and Delinquency*, **28** (1990): 6–32.

47. Marvin E. Wolfgang, Terence Thornberry, and Robert Figlio, *From Boy to Man, from Delinquency to Crime* (Chicago: University of Chicago Press, 1987).

48. Paul E. Tracy, Marvin E. Wolfgang, and Robert M. Figlio, *Delinquency Careers in Two Birth Cohorts* (New York: Plenum, 1990), pp. 275–280; Paul E. Tracy, Marvin E. Wolfgang, and Robert M. Figlio, Executive Summary, *Delinquency in Two Birth Cohorts*, U.S. Department of Justice (Washington, D.C.: U.S. Government Printing Office, September 1985), pp. 5–11.

49. Terence P. Thornberry, "What's Working and What's Not Working in Safeguarding Our Children and Preventing Violence," Safeguarding Our Youth: Violence Prevention for Our Nation's Children, speech presented at Department of Education, Washington, D.C., July 20, 1993.

50. Uniform Crime Reports, 1997, p. 229.

51. *Criminal Victimization in the United States, 1993*, p. 43.

52. Uniform Crime Reports, 1997, p. 229.

53. Delbert Elliott and Suzanne Ageton, "Reconciling Race and Class Differences in Self-Reported and Official Estimates of Delinquency," *American Sociological Review*, **45** (1980): 95–110; and Roy L. Austin, "Recent Trends in Official Male and Female Crime Rates: The Convergence Controversy," *Journal of Criminal Justice*, **21** (1993): 447–466.

54. John Hagan, John Simpson, and A. R. Gillis, "Class in the Household: A Power Control Theory of Gender and Delinquency," *American Journal of Sociology*, **92** (1987): 788–816. See also Gary F. Jensen, John Hagan, and A. R. Gillis, "Power-Control vs. Social Control Theories of Common Delinquency: A Comparative Analysis," in *New Directions in Criminological Theory*, ed. Freda Adler and William S. Laufer (New Brunswick, N.J.: Transaction, 1993), pp. 363–398.

55. Merry Morash and Meda Chesney-Lind, "A Reformulation and Partial Test of the Power Control Theory of Delinquency," *Justice Quarterly*, **8** (1991): 347–377. For an examination of sexual abuse of girls and how it leads to later delinquency, as well as a discussion of how the double standard influences female criminality, see Meda Chesney-Lind, *The Female Offender: Girls, Women, and Crime* (Thousand Oaks, Calif.: Sage, 1997). For a discussion about the role family controls have on female delinquency, see Karen Keimer and Stacy De Coster, "The Gendering of Violent Delinquency," *Criminology*, **37** (1999): 277–318. For an application of strain theory to female crime, see Lisa Broidy and Robert Agnew, "Gender and Crime: A General Strain Theory Perspective," *Journal of Research in Crime and Delinquency*, **34** (1997): 275–306. For a discussion of the implications of the feminization of poverty and welfare on property crime and assault, see Anne Campbell, Steven Muncer, and Daniel Bibel, "Female–Female Criminal Assault: An Evolutionary Perspective," *Journal of Research in Crime and Delinquency*, **35** (1998): 413–428, and Lance Hannon and James DeFronzo, "Welfare and Property Crime," *Justice Quarterly*, **15** (1998): 273–288.

56. Cesare Lombroso and William Ferrero, *The Female Offender* (London: T. Fisher Unwin, 1895).

57. Sheldon Glueck and Eleanor T. Glueck, *Five Hundred Delinquent Women* (New York: Knopf, 1934).

58. Otto Pollack, *The Criminality of Women* (Philadelphia: University of Pennsylvania Press, 1950).

59. Freda Adler, *Sisters in Crime* (New York: McGraw-Hill, 1975), pp. 6–7.

60. Rita Simon, *The Contemporary Woman and Crime* (Rockville, Md.: National Institute of Mental Health, 1975).

61. Meda Chesney-Lind, "Female Offenders: Paternalism Reexamined," in *Women, the Courts, and Equality*, ed. Laura Crites and Winifred Hepperle (Newbury Park, Calif.: Sage, 1987).

62. Darrell J. Steffensmeier, "Crime and the Contemporary Woman: An Analysis of Changing Levels of Female Property Crimes, 1960–1975," *Social Forces*, **57** (1978): 566–584; Lee H. Bowker, *Women, Crime, and the Criminal Justice System* (Lexington, Mass.: Heath, 1978). For a description of the typical female offender, see Nancy T. Wolfe, Francis T. Cullen, and John B. Cullen, "Describing the Female Offender: A Note on the Demographics of Arrests," *Journal of Criminal Justice*, **12** (1984): 483–492.

63. Mary E. Gilfus, "From Victims to Survivors to Offenders: Women's Routes of Entry and Immersion into Street Crime," *Women and Criminal Justice*, **4** (1992): 63–89; and Sally S. Simpson and Lori Ellis, "Doing Gender: Sorting Out the Caste and Crime Conundrum," *Criminology*, **33** (1995): 47–81. For a discussion of the internalization of gender roles by female prisoners, see Edna Erez, "The Myth of the New Female Offender: Some Evidence from Attitudes toward Law and Justice," *Journal of Criminal Justice*, **16** (1988): 499–509.

64. Nanci Koser Wilson, "The Masculinity of Violent Crime—Some Second Thoughts," *Journal of Criminal Justice*, **9** (1981): 111–123; Ronald L. Simons, Martin G. Miller, and

Stephen M. Aigner, "Contemporary Theories of Deviance and Female Delinquency: An Empirical Test," *Journal of Research in Crime and Delinquency,* **17** (1980): 42–57.

65. For a discussion of a unisex theory of crime, see Coramae Richey Mann, *Female Crime and Delinquency* (Tuscaloosa: University of Alabama Press, 1984). For an analysis of the relation of both gender and race to crime, see Vernetta D. Young, "Women, Race, and Crime," *Criminology,* **18** (1980): 26–34; Gary D. Hill and Elizabeth M. Crawford, "Women, Race, and Crime," *Criminology,* **28** (1990): 601–626; and Sally S. Simpson, "Caste, Class, and Violent Crime: Explaining Differences in Female Offending," *Criminology,* **29** (1991): 115–136. For a discussion of female crime in countries around the world, see Freda Adler, ed., *The Incidence of Female Criminality in the Contemporary World* (New York: New York University Press, 1984). See also Freda Adler and Rita James Simon, eds., *The Criminology of Deviant Women* (Boston: Houghton Mifflin, 1979). For other sources on the subject of female crime, see Victoria E. Brewster and M. Dwayne Smith, "Gender Inequality and Rates of Female Homicide Victimization across U.S. Cities," *Journal of Research in Crime and Delinquency,* **32** (1995): 175–190; R. Barri Flowers, *Female Crime, Criminals and Cellmates: An Exploration of Female Criminality and Delinquency* (Jefferson, N.C.: McFarland & Company, 1995); R. Emerson Dobash, Russell P. Dobash, and Lesley Noaks, eds., *Gender and Crime* (Cardiff: University of Wales Press, 1995); and Ruth Triplett and Laura B. Myers, "Evaluating Contextual Patterns of Delinquency: Gender-Based Differences," *Justice Quarterly,* **12** (1995): 59–84. For an examination of women who commit murder, see Coramae Richey Mann, *When Women Kill* (Albany, N.Y.: SUNY Press, 1996).

66. Charles Tittle, Wayne Villemez, and Douglas Smith, "The Myth of Social Class and Criminality: An Empirical Assessment of the Empirical Evidence," *American Sociological Review,* **43** (1978): 643–656; Charles R. Tittle and Robert F. Meier, "Specifying the SES/Delinquency Relationship," *Criminology,* **28** (1990): 271–299. For a discussion of the relationship between crime and aspects of social class that influence juveniles' personality and behavior, see G. Roger Jarjoura and Ruth A. Triplett, "Delinquency and Class: A Test of the Proximity Principle," *Justice Quarterly,* **14** (1997): 763–792. For an elaboration on the relationship between socioeconomic status (SES) and delinquency, see Bradley R. Entner Wright, Avshalom Caspi, Terrie E. Moffitt, Richard A. Miech, and Phil A. Silva, "Reconsidering the Relationship between SES and Delinquency: Causation but Not Correlation," *Criminology,* **37** (1999): 175–194.

67. Elliott and Ageton, "Reconciling Race and Class Differences."

68. Delbert Elliott and David Huizinga, "Social Class and Delinquent Behavior in a National Youth Panel: 1976–1980," *Criminology,* **21** (1983): 149–177.

69. The data on socioeconomic factors come from U.S. Department of Justice, *Report to the Nation on Crime and Justice,* pp. 48–49.

70. U.S. Department of Justice, Bureau of Justice Statistics, *Annual Report, Fiscal 1986* (Washington, D.C.: U.S. Government Printing Office, April 1987), p. 39.

71. Uniform Crime Reports, 1997, p. 240. See also Gary LaFree, Kriss A. Drass, and Patrick O'Day, "Race and Crime in Postwar America: Determinants of African-American and White Rates, 1957–1988," *Criminology,* **30** (1992): 157–188.

72. Joan Petersilia, "Racial Disparities in the Criminal Justice System: A Summary," *Crime and Delinquency,* **31** (1985): 15–34.

73. *Criminal Victimization in the United States, 1993,* p. 44.

74. Delbert Elliott and Harwin Voss, *Delinquency and Dropout* (Lexington, Mass.: Lexington Books, 1974).

75. Robert J. Sampson, "Urban Black Violence: The Effect of Male Joblessness and Family Disruption," *American Journal of Sociology,* **93** (1987): 348–382.

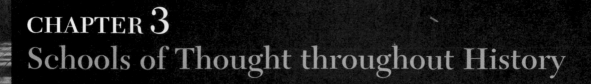

CHAPTER 3
Schools of Thought throughout History

Children now love luxury. They have bad manners, contempt for authority. They show disrespect for elders. They contradict their parents, chatter before company, cross their legs and tyrannize their teachers.

The ideal condition would be, I admit, that men should be right by instinct; but since we are all likely to go astray, the reasonable thing is to learn from those who can teach.

When there is an income tax, the just man will pay more and the unjust less on the same amount of income.[1]

C riminologists traditionally consider that their field has its origins as a science in the eighteenth century, when Cesare Beccaria established what came to be known as the classical school of criminology. But when we look at what some much earlier thinkers had to say about crime, we may have to reconsider this assumption. Look again at the preceeding quotations. The first may appear to be a modern description of delinquent youth, but Socrates made this observation over 2300 years ago. The second quotation, about instinct and learning and their association with criminality, was an observation made by Sophocles, who lived almost 2500 years ago. The final quotation, about income tax fraud, is not taken from a study of American white-collar crime: Plato voiced this insight, in his treatise *The Republic,* in the fourth century B.C.

Scholars, philosophers, and poets have speculated about the causes of crime and possible remedies since ancient times, and modern criminology owes much to the wisdom the ancient philosophers displayed. The philosophical approach culminated in the middle of the eighteenth century in the **classical school of criminology.** It is based on the assumption that individuals choose to commit crimes after weighing the consequences of their actions. According to classical criminologists, individuals have free will. They can choose legal or illegal means to get what they want; fear of punishment can deter them from committing crime; and society can control behavior by making the pain of punishment greater than the pleasure of the criminal gains.

Public punishment: painting depicts beheading of the king's wife Marie Antoinette at the Guillotine, October 16, 1793.

The classical school did not remain unchallenged for long. In the early nineteenth century great advances were made in the natural sciences and in medicine. Physicians in France, Germany, and England undertook systematic studies of crimes and criminals. Crime statistics became available in several European countries. There emerged an opposing school of criminology, the **positivist school.** This school posits that human behavior is determined by forces beyond individual control and that it is possible to measure those forces. Unlike classical criminologists, who claim that people rationally choose to commit crime, positivist criminologists view criminal behavior as stemming from biological, psychological, and social factors.

The earliest positivist theories centered on biological factors, and studies of those factors dominated criminology during the last half of the nineteenth century. In the twentieth century, biological explanations were ignored (and even targeted as racist after World War II). They did not surface again until the 1970s, when scientific advances in psychology shifted the emphasis from defects in criminals' bodies to defects in

their minds. Throughout the twentieth century, psychologists and psychiatrists have played a major role in the study of crime causation. A third area of positivist criminology focuses on the relation of social factors to crime. Sociological theories, developed in the second half of the nineteenth century and advanced throughout the twentieth, continue to dominate the field of criminology today.

An understanding of the foundations of modern criminology helps us understand contemporary developments in the field. Let us begin with the developments that led to the emergence of the classical school.

CLASSICAL CRIMINOLOGY

In the late eighteenth to the mid-nineteenth centuries, during what is now called the neoclassical period, the classical culture of the ancient Mediterranean was rediscovered. This was also a period of scientific discoveries and the founding of new scholarly disciplines. One of these was criminology, which developed as an attempt to apply rationality and the rule of law to brutal and arbitrary criminal justice processes.

On a fine Thursday afternoon in September 1991, vacationers from Germany, on an alpine hiking trip, spotted a head protruding from the glacial ice. They hurried to a nearby guest house and reported their find to the innkeeper, who promptly called both the Italian and the Austrian police. It became immediately apparent that this corpse was no ordinary mountain casualty. Rather, this was an ancient mountain casualty. Experts were brought in from Austrian universities, and the body was freed from its icy embrace. It was dubbed "Oetzi," after the Oetztal Alps of the discovery.

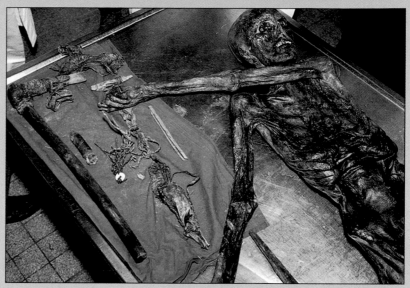

Oetzi, who was preserved in the glacial crevice in which he died five thousand years ago.

Oetzi is 5300 years old, a robust young man, 25 to 30 years old at the time of his death. Completely mummified, he was found in the position in which he had placed himself, in a crevice, probably to escape a snowstorm. He was fully dressed, in an unlined fur robe. Originally fashioned with great skill, the robe was badly repaired with sinew and plant fiber, suggesting that he could not have relied on the services of his wife or the village seamstress for some time. Oetzi had placed his equipment by his side, most of it of the best Stone Age craftsmanship. What is surprising is that he did not carry with him a ready-to-shoot bow.

Investigators determined that Oetzi was an outdoor type, a shepherd who sought refuge in the crevice, froze to death, and was preserved for 5 millennia by permafrost and glacial ice. But what was Oetzi doing at 3210 meters (nearly 10,000 feet) above sea level on a fall day? Obviously, he was not a herder since he was far above the grazing range of a herd. Nor was he a trader trying to cross the Alps in the fall. So what was he doing up there, where nothing grows and where it is hard to breathe? One answer, based on all the evidence available so far, is that Oetzi may have been an outlaw.

Oetzi was a Late Stone Age (Neolithic) man, likely to have come from a herding community of, at most, 200 persons. Robert Carneiro of the American Museum of Natural History has figured out that a community of 200 produces 20,000 one-on-one disagreement possibilities. Oetzi may have had such interpersonal problems.

The tasks of social control even within such a small community stagger the imagination. Fighting could have erupted within the community. Jealousy could be engendered about who deserves more respect as the best hunter, the best storyteller, the best healer, or the wisest person. A dispute could have happened over the distribution of food or the sharing of tools.

The evidence about Neolithic society permits us to conclude that these societies had no institution that we could compare with modern criminal justice, although they had problems that today might be referred to a criminal justice system. How were such problems solved? Minor problems were dealt with by the use of shaming, by dispute resolution, by compensation, and by sacrifices. Major unforgivable offenses led to casting out the wrongdoers: They would be declared outlaws. They had to leave camp instantly, without gathering weapons or tools, and flee to the wilderness. Oetzi fits the description of such an outlaw, literally, a person cast outside the protection of the laws, the customs, and the protection of his group, to take to the wilderness and perhaps to die there. If Oetzi was a criminal banished from his village, the punishment clearly was effective.

Source

Adapted from Gerhard O. W. Mueller and Freda Adler, "The Emergence of Criminal Justice: Tracing the Route to Neolithic Times," in *Festskrift till Jacob W. F Sundberg*, ed. Erik Nerep and Wiweka Warnling Nerep (Stockholm: Jurisförlaget, 1993), pp. 151–170.

Questions for Discussion

1. For purposes of improving modern crime-control techniques, can we learn anything from Stone Age societies?
2. What crimes do you think might result in the banishment of one of the members of such a community?

The work of criminology's founders—scholars like Cesare Beccaria and Jeremy Bentham—became known as classical criminology.

The Historical Context

Classical criminology grew out of a reaction against the barbaric system of law, punishment, and justice that existed before the French Revolution of 1789. Until that time, there was no real system of criminal justice in Europe. There were crimes against the state, against the church, and against the crown. Some of these crimes were specified; some were not. Judges had discretionary power to convict a person for an act not even legally defined as criminal.[2] Monarchs often issued what were called in French *lettres de cachet,* under which an individual could be imprisoned for almost any reason (disobedience to one's father, for example) or for no reason at all.

Many criminal laws were unwritten, and those that had been drafted, by and large, did not specify the kind or amount of punishment associated with various crimes. Arbitrary and often cruel sentences were imposed by judges who had unbounded discretion to decide questions of guilt and innocence and to mete out punishment. Due process in the modern sense did not exist. While there was some official consensus on what constituted crime, there was no real limit to the amount and type of legal sanction a court could command. Punishments included branding, burning, flogging, mutilating, drowning, banishing, and beheading.[3] In England a person might receive the death penalty for any of more than 200 offenses, including what we today call petty theft.

Public punishments were popular events. When Robert-François Damiens was scheduled to be executed on March 2, 1757, for the attempted murder of Louis XV, so many people wanted to attend the spectacle that window seats overlooking the execution site were rented for high prices. Torture to elicit confessions was common. A criminal defendant in France might be subjected to the *peine forte et dure,* which consisted of stretching him on his back and placing over him an iron weight as heavy as he could bear. He was left that way until he died or spoke. A man would suffer these torments and

lose his life in order to avoid trial and therefore conviction so that his lands and goods would not be confiscated and would be preserved for his family. This proceeding was not abolished until 1772.[4]

Even as Europe grew increasingly modern, industrial, and urban in the eighteenth century, it still clung to its medieval penal practices. With prosperity came an increasing gulf between the haves and the have-nots. Just before the French Revolution, for example, a Parisian worker paid 97 percent of his daily earnings for a 4-pound loaf of bread.[5] Hordes of unemployed people begged by day and found shelter under bridges by night. One of the few ways in which the established upper class could protect itself was through ruthless oppression of those beneath it, but ruthless oppression created more problems. Social unrest grew. And as crime rates rose, so did the brutality of punishment. Both church and state became increasingly tyrannical, using violence to conquer violence.

The growing educated classes began to see the inconsistency in these policies. If terrible tortures were designed to deter crime, why were people committing even more crimes? Something must be wrong with the underlying reasoning. By the mid-eighteenth century, social reformers were beginning to suggest a more rational approach to crime and punishment. One of them, Cesare Beccaria, laid the foundation for the first school of criminology—the classical school.

Cesare Beccaria

Cesare Bonesana, Marchese di Beccaria (1738–1794), was rather undistinguished as a student. After graduating with a law degree from the University of Pavia, he returned home to Milan and joined a group of articulate and radical intellectuals. Disenchanted with contemporary European society, they organized themselves into the Academy of Fists, one of many young men's clubs that flourished in Italy at the time. Their purpose was to discover what reforms would be needed to modernize Italian society.

In March 1763 Beccaria was assigned to prepare a report on the prison system. Pietro Verri,

Cesare Beccaria, the young Italian nobleman-dissident who became the father of modern criminology with his monograph, On Crimes and Punishment.

the head of the Academy of Fists, encouraged him to read the works of English and French philosophers—David Hume (1711–1776), John Locke (1632–1704), Claude Adrien Helvétius (1715–1771), Voltaire (1694–1778), Montesquieu (1600–1755), and Jean Jacques Rousseau (1712–1778). Another member of the academy, the protector of prisons, revealed to him the inhumanities that were possible under the guise of social control. Beccaria learned well. He read, observed, and made notes on small scraps of paper. These notes, Harry Elmer Barnes has observed, were destined to "assure to its author immortality and would work a revolution in the moral world" upon their publication in July 1764 under the title *Dei delitti e delle pene (On Crimes and Punishment).*[6] Beccaria presented a coherent, comprehensive design for an enlightened criminal justice system that was to serve the people rather than the monarchy.

The climate was right: With the publication of this small book, Cesare Beccaria became the "father of modern criminology." The controversy between the rule of men and the rule of law was at its most heated. Some people defended the old order, under which judges and administrators made arbitrary or whimsical decisions. Others fought for the rule of law, under which the decision making of judges and administrators would be confined by legal lim-

itations. Beccaria's words provided the spark that ultimately ended medieval barbarism.

According to Beccaria, the crime problem could be traced not to bad people but to bad laws. A modern criminal justice system should guarantee all people equal treatment before the law. Beccaria's book supplied the blueprint. That blueprint was based on the assumption that people freely choose what they do and are responsible for the consequences of their behavior. Beccaria proposed the following principles:

- *Laws should be used to maintain the social contract.* "Laws are the conditions under which men, naturally independent, united themselves in society. Weary of living in a continual state of war, and of enjoying a liberty, which became of little value, from the uncertainty of its duration, they sacrificed one part of it, to enjoy the rest in peace and security."

- *Only legislators should create laws.* "The authority of making penal laws can only reside with the legislator, who represents the whole society united by the social compact."

- *Judges should impose punishment only in accordance with the law.* "[N]o magistrate then, (as he is one of the society), can, with justice inflict on any other member of the same society punishment that is not ordained by the laws."

- *Judges should not interpret the laws.* "Judges, in criminal cases, have no right to interpret the penal laws, because they are not legislators. . . . Every man hath his own particular point of view, and, at different times, sees the same objects in very different lights. The spirit of the laws will then be the result of the good or bad logic of the judge; and this will depend on his good or bad digestion."

- *Punishment should be based on the pleasure/pain principle.* "Pleasure and pain are the only springs of actions in beings endowed with sensibility. . . . If an equal punishment be ordained for two crimes that injure society in different degrees, there is nothing to deter men from committing the greater as often as it is attended with greater advantage."

- *Punishment should be based on the act, not on the actor.* "Crimes are only to be measured by the injuries done to the society. They err, therefore, who imagine that a crime is greater or less according to the intention of the person by whom it is committed."

- *The punishment should be determined by the crime.* "If mathematical calculation could be applied to the obscure and infinite combinations of human actions, there might be a corresponding scale of punishments descending from the greatest to the least."

- *Punishment should be prompt and effective.* "The more immediate after the commission of a crime a punishment is inflicted, the more just and useful it will be. . . . An immediate punishment is more useful; because the smaller the interval of time between the punishment and the crime, the stronger and more lasting will be the association of the two ideas of crime and punishment."

- *All people should be treated equally.* "I assert that the punishment of a nobleman should in no wise differ from that of the lowest member of society."

- *Capital punishment should be abolished.* "The punishment of death is not authorized by any right; for . . . no such right exists. . . . The terrors of death make so slight an impression, that it has not force enough to withstand the forgetfulness natural to mankind."

- *The use of torture to gain confessions should be abolished.* "It is confounding all relations to expect . . . that pain should be the test of truth, as if truth resided in the muscles and fibres of a wretch in torture. By this method the robust will escape, and the feeble be condemned."

- *It is better to prevent crimes than to punish them.* "Would you prevent crimes? Let the laws be clear and simple, let the entire force of the nation be united in their defence, let them be intended rather to favour every individual than any particular classes. . . . Finally, the most certain method of preventing crime is to perfect the system of education."[7]

Perhaps no other book in the history of criminology has had so great an impact. Beccaria's ideas were so advanced that Voltaire, the great French philosopher of the time, who wrote the commentary for the French version, referred to Beccaria as "brother."[8] The English version appeared in 1767; by that time, 3 years after the book's publication, it had already gone through six Italian editions and several French editions.

Crime Surfing

www.utm.edu/research/iep/b/beccaria.htm

If Beccaria were alive today, what arguments would he use in a debate on capital punishment?

After the French Revolution, Beccaria's basic tenets served as a guide for the drafting of the French penal code, which was adopted in 1791. In Russia, Empress Catherine II (the Great) convened a commission to prepare a new code and issued instructions, written in her own hand, to translate Beccaria's ideas into action. The Prussian King Friedrich II (the Great) devoted his reign to revising the Prussian laws according to Beccaria's principles. Emperor Joseph II had a new code drafted for Austria-Hungary in 1787—the first code to abolish capital punishment. The impact of Beccaria's treatise spread across the Atlantic as well: It influenced the first 10 amendments to the U.S. Constitution (the Bill of Rights).

Did You Know?

. . . that it took the 26-year-old Cesare Beccaria just 9 months to write *On Crimes and Punishment*, the brief book that has influenced criminology all over the world? And did you know that he published the book anonymously out of fear that the authorities, with their interest in perpetuating the existing brutal system, would persecute him?

Jeremy Bentham's Utilitarianism

Legal scholars and reformers throughout Europe proclaimed their indebtedness to Beccaria,

Few people can be credited for their contribution to Anglo-American criminal law philosophy as much as Jeremy Bentham (1748–1832), the foremost spokesperson for the utilitarian approach to the management of people in general, and criminals and potential criminals in particular. Above all, he is remembered for his proposition that the purpose of all legislation is to achieve "the greatest happiness of the greatest number." Punishments, he argued, should be no greater (nor less) than necessary to achieve government's purpose to control crime.(1)

According to Princeton University professor Peter Singer, utilitarianism—the greatest good of the greatest number—implies that a child born with incurable birth defects should be killed, as its life would impose a far greater emotional and financial burden on its family and the community, than its death.(2) Thus Singer argues that "some infanticide is not even as important as, say, killing a happy cat."(3) Among his principal examples for justifiable infanticide are babies born with Down's syndrome. Singer's argument fails to take into account the many adults with Down's syndrome who take a bus to work every day, earn a salary, and pay taxes on their earnings.(2)

Putting aside the difficulty of making a prognosis about a baby's chance to have a productive and content life, how would society determine where to put the limit on legalizing infanticide? Mr. Justice Holmes ruled in *Buck v. Bell* that "three generations of imbeciles are enough" in upholding a state statute that mandated the sterilization of "imbeciles" with a family record of imbecility.(4) By those utilitarian standards, killing *all* imbecile babies would be even more cost-beneficial. Should a similar mandate apply to three generations of criminals, as determined by convictions? And would society not be better off (in terms of cost-benefit calculations) if it were to get rid of *all* troublemakers? Would Professor Singer go that far?

Bentham had nothing of that sort in mind when he set forth his utilitarian principles. In fact, he was not even an

Demonstrators picket Princeton University over its appointment of a controversial bioethics professor, Peter Singer, in Princeton, New Jersey, April 1999.

advocate of capital punishment, considering it to be "unfrugal" and "irremissible."(1)

To demonstrate his utilitarianism, Jeremy Bentham decreed that upon his death (June 6, 1832), his body be dissected in the presence of his friends and the skeleton be reconstructed, supplied with a wax head to replace the original (to be mummified), dressed in his own clothes, and placed upright in a glass case so that he, himself, could be useful as a reminder of his principles. Until recently, once a year at meetings of the Bentham Society in London, Bentham's body was wheeled out and celebrated with a feast.

Sources

1. Jeremy Bentham, *An Introduction to the Principles of Morals and Legislation* (1789; New York: Haffner Library of Classics, 1948), esp. pp. 197, 200.

2. Peter Singer, *Rethinking Life and Death: The Collapse of Our Traditional Ethics* (New York: St. Martin's Press, 1996); *How Are We to Live? Ethics in an Age of Self-Interest* (New York: Prometheus Books, 1995).

3. George F. Will, "Life and Death at Princeton," *Newsweek,* Sept. 13, 1999, pp. 80–81.

4. *Buck v. Bell,* 274 U.S. 200, 207 (1927).

Questions for Discussion

1. According to utilitarian principles, is capital punishment preferable to a life sentence?

2. Should abortion be legalized when a baby can be profiled (by family history) as a high risk for a life in crime?

3. Can you think of a way to use utilitarian principles to reduce the use and duration of imprisonment?

but none owed more to him than the English legal philosopher Jeremy Bentham (1748–1832). Bentham had a long and productive career. He inspired many of his contemporaries, as well as criminologists of future generations, with his approach to rational crime control.

Bentham devoted his life to developing a scientific approach to the making and breaking of laws. Like Beccaria, he was concerned with achieving "the greatest happiness of the greatest number."[9] His work was governed by utilitarian principles. **Utilitarianism** assumes that all human actions are calculated in accordance with their likelihood of bringing happiness (pleasure) or unhappiness (pain). People weigh the probabilities of present and future pleasures against those of present and future pain.

Bentham proposed a precise pseudomathematical formula for this process, which he called "felicific calculus." According to his reasoning, individuals are "human calculators" who put all the factors into an equation in order to decide whether or not a particular crime is worth committing. This notion may seem rather whimsical today, but at a time when there were over 200 capital offenses, it provided a rationale for reform of the legal system.[10] Bentham reasoned that if prevention was the purpose of punishment, and if punishment became too costly by creating more harm than good, then penalties needed to be set just a bit in excess of the pleasure one might derive from committing a crime, and no higher. The law exists in order to create happiness for the community. Since punishment creates unhappiness, it can be justified only if it prevents greater evil than it produces. Thus, Bentham suggested, if hanging a man's effigy produced the same preventive effect as hanging the man himself, there would be no reason to hang the man.

Sir Samuel Romilly, a member of Parliament, met Jeremy Bentham at the home of a mutual friend. He became interested in Bentham's idea that the certainty of punishment outweighs its severity as a deterrent against crime. On February 9, 1810, in a speech before Parliament, he advocated Benthamite ideas:

> So evident is the truth of that maxim that if it were possible that punishment, as the consequence of guilt, could be reduced to an absolute certainty, a very slight penalty would be sufficient to prevent almost every species of crime.[11]

Although conservatives prevented any major changes during Romilly's lifetime, the program of legislative pressure he began was continued by his followers and culminated in the complete reform of English criminal law between 1820 and 1861. During that period the number of capital offenses was reduced from 222 to 3: murder, treason, and piracy. Gradually, from the ideals of the philosophers of the Age of Enlightenment and the principles outlined by the scholars of the classical school, a new social order was created, an order that affirmed a commitment to equal treatment of all people before the law.

The Classical School: An Evaluation

Classical criminology had an immediate and profound impact on jurisprudence and legislation. The rule of law spread rapidly through Europe and the United States. Of no less significance was the influence of the classical school on penal and correctional policy. The classical principle that punishment must be appropriate to the crime was universally accepted during the nineteenth and early twentieth centuries. Yet the classical approach had weaknesses. Critics attacked the simplicity of its argument: The responsibility of the criminal justice system was simply to enforce the law with swiftness and certainty and to treat all people in like fashion, whether the accused were paupers or nobles; government was to be run by the rule of law rather than at the discretion of its officials. In other words, the punishment was to fit the crime, not the criminal. The proposition that human beings had the capacity to choose freely between good and evil was accepted without question. There was no need to ask why people behave as they do, to seek a motive, or to ask about the specific circumstances surrounding criminal acts.

During the last half of the nineteenth century, scholars began to challenge these ideas. Influenced by the expanding search for scientific explanations of behavior in place of philosophical ones, criminologists shifted their attention from the act to the actor. They argued that people did not choose of their own free will to commit crime; rather, factors beyond their control were responsible for criminal behavior.

POSITIVIST CRIMINOLOGY

During the late eighteenth century, significant advances in knowledge of both the physical and the social world influenced thinking about crime. Auguste Comte (1798–1857), a French sociologist, applied the modern methods of the physical sciences to the social sciences in his six-volume *Cours de philosophie positive (Course in Positive Philosophy)*, published between 1830 and 1842. He argued that there could be no real knowledge of social phenomena unless it was based on a positivist (scientific) approach. Positivism alone, however, was not sufficient to bring about a fundamental change in criminological thinking. Not until Charles Darwin (1809–1882) challenged the doctrine of creation with his theory of the evolution of species did the next generation of criminologists have the tools with which to challenge classicism.

The turning point was the publication in 1859 of Darwin's *Origin of Species*. Darwin's theory was that God did not make all the various species of animals in 2 days, as proclaimed in Genesis 1:20–26, but rather that the species had evolved through a process of adaptive mutation and natural selection. The process was based on the survival of the fittest in the struggle for existence. This radical theory seriously challenged traditional theological teaching. It was not until 1871, however, that Darwin publicly took the logical next step and traced human origins to an animal of the anthropoid group—the ape.[12] He thus posed an even more serious challenge to a religious tradition that maintained that God created the first human in his own image (Genesis 1:27).

The scientific world would never be the same again. The theory of evolution made it possible to ask new questions and to search in new ways for the answers to old ones. New biological theories replaced older ones. Old ideas that demons and animal spirits could explain human behavior were replaced by knowledge based on new scientific principles. The social sciences were born.

The nineteenth-century forces of positivism and evolution moved the field of criminology from a philosophical to a scientific perspective.

But there were even earlier intellectual underpinnings of the scientific criminology that emerged in the second half of the nineteenth century.

BIOLOGICAL DETERMINISM: THE SEARCH FOR CRIMINAL TRAITS

Throughout history a variety of physical characteristics and disfigurements have been said to characterize individuals of "evil" disposition. In the earliest pursuit of the relationship between biological traits and behavior, a Greek scientist who examined Socrates found his skull and facial features to be those of a person inclined toward alcoholism and brutality.[13] The ancient Greeks and Romans so distrusted red hair that actors portraying evil persons wore red wigs. Through the ages cripples, hunchbacks, people with long hair, and a multitude of others were viewed with suspicion. Indeed, in the Middle Ages laws indicated that if two people were suspected of a crime, the uglier was the more likely to be guilty.[14]

The belief that criminals are born, not made, and that they can be identified by various physical irregularities is reflected not only in scientific writing but in literature as well. Shakespeare's Julius Caesar states:

> Let me have men about me that are fat;
> Sleek-headed men, and such as sleep o' nights.
> Yond Cassius has a lean and hungry look;
> He thinks too much: such men are dangerous.

Although its roots can be traced to ancient times, it was not until the sixteenth century that the Italian physician Giambattista della Porta (1535–1615) founded the school of human **physiognomy,** the study of facial features and their relation to human behavior. According to Porta, a thief had large lips and sharp vision. Two centuries later Porta's efforts were revived by the Swiss theologian Johann Kaspar Lavater (1741–1801).[15] They were elaborated by the German physicians Franz Joseph Gall (1758–1828) and Johann Kaspar Spurzheim (1776–1832), whose science of **phrenology** posited that bumps on the head were indications of psychological propensities.[16] In the United States these views

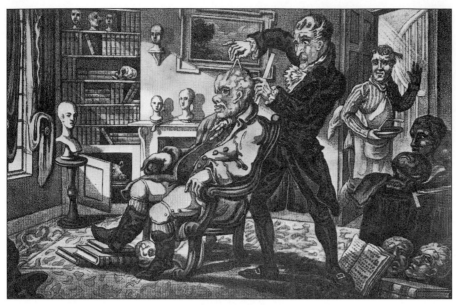

A criminological examination according to an 1890 caricature.

were supported by the physician Charles Caldwell (1772–1853), who searched for evidence that brain tissue and cells regulate human action.[17] By the nineteenth century, the sciences of physiognomy and phrenology had introduced specific biological factors into the study of crime causation.

Lombroso, Ferri, Garofalo: The Italian School

Cesare Lombroso (1835–1909) integrated Comte's positivism, Darwin's evolutionism, and the many pioneering studies of the relation of crime to the body. In 1876, with the publication of *L'uomo delinquente (The Criminal Man)*, criminology was permanently transformed from an abstract philosophy of crime control through legislation to a modern science of investigation into causes. Lombroso's work replaced the concept of free will, which had reigned for over a century as the principle that explained criminal behavior, with that of determinism. Together with his followers, the Italian legal scholars Enrico Ferri and Raffaele Garofalo, Lombroso developed a new orientation, the Italian, or positivist, school of criminology, which seeks explanations for criminal behavior through scientific experimentation and research.

Cesare Lombroso   After completing his medical studies, Cesare Lombroso served as an army physician, became a professor of psychiatry at the University of Turin, and later in life accepted an appointment as professor of criminal anthropology. His theory of the "born criminal" states that criminals are a lower form of life, nearer to their apelike ancestors than noncriminals in traits and dispositions. They are distinguishable from noncriminals by various **atavistic stigmata**—physical features of creatures at an earlier stage of development, before they became fully human.

He argued that criminals frequently have huge jaws and strong canine teeth, characteristics common to carnivores who tear and devour meat raw. The arm span of criminals is often greater than their height, just like that of apes, who use their forearms to propel themselves along the ground. An individual born with any five of the stigmata is a **born criminal.** This category accounts for about a third of all offenders.

The theory became clear to Lombroso "one cold grey November morning" while he pored over the bones of a notorious outlaw who had died in an Italian prison:

This man possessed such extraordinary agility, that he had been known to scale steep mountain heights

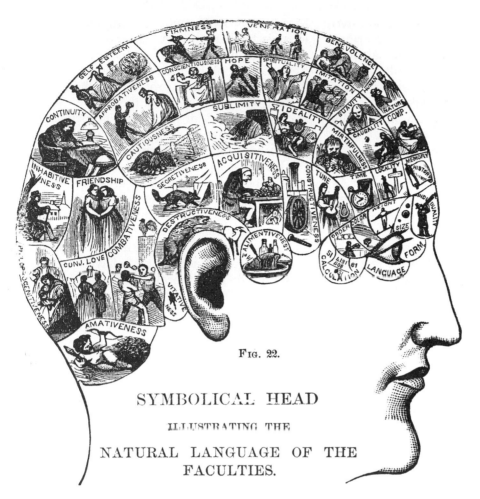

FIG. 22.

SYMBOLICAL HEAD

ILLUSTRATING THE

NATURAL LANGUAGE OF THE
FACULTIES.

This depiction of the human brain appeared in an 1890s scientific book, How to Read Character: A New Illustrated Hand-Book of Physiology, Phrenology and Physiognomy for Students and Examiners.

bearing a sheep on his shoulders. His cynical effrontery was such that he openly boasted of his crimes. On his death . . . I was deputed to make the post-mortem, and on laying open the skull I found . . . a distinct depression . . . as in inferior animals.

Lombroso was delighted by his findings:

> This was not merely an idea, but a revelation. At the sight of that skull, I seemed to see all of a sudden, lighted up as a vast plain under a flaming sky the problem of the nature of the criminal—an atavistic being who reproduces in his person the ferocious instincts of primitive humanity.[18]

Criminal women, according to Lombroso, are different from criminal men. It is the prostitute who represents the born criminal among them:

We also saw that women have many traits in common with children; that their moral sense is different; they are revengeful, jealous, inclined to vengeance of a refined cruelty. . . . When a morbid activity of the psychical centres intensifies the bad qualities of women . . . it is clear that the innocuous semi-criminal present in normal women must be transformed into a born criminal more terrible than any man. . . . The criminal woman is consequently a monster. Her normal sister is kept in the paths of virtue by many causes, such as maternity, piety, weakness, and when these counter influences fail, and a woman commits a crime, we may conclude that her wickedness must have been enormous before it could triumph over so many obstacles.[19]

To the born criminal, Lombroso added two other categories, insane criminals and criminoloids. *Insane criminals* are not criminal from birth; they become criminal as a result of some change in their brains which interferes with their ability to distinguish between right and wrong.[20] *Criminoloids* make up an ambiguous group that includes habitual criminals, criminals by passion, and other diverse types.

Most scientists who followed Lombroso did not share his enthusiasm or his viewpoint. As happens so often in history, his work has been kept alive more by criticism than by agreement. The theory that criminals were lodged on the lower rungs of the evolutionary ladder did not stand up to scientific scrutiny. But the fact that Lombroso measured thousands of live and dead prisoners and compared these measurements with those obtained from control groups (however imperfectly derived) in his search for determinants of crime changed the nature of the questions asked by the generations of scholars who came after him.

His influence continues in contemporary European research; American scientists, as the criminologist Marvin Wolfgang says, use him "as a straw man for attack on biological analyses of criminal behavior."[21] Thorsten Sellin has noted: "Any scholar who succeeds in driving hundreds of fellow-students to search for the truth, and whose ideas after half a century possess vitality, merits an honorable place in the history of thought."[22] At his death, true to his lifetime pursuits, Lombroso willed his body to the laboratory of legal medicine and his brain to the Institute of Anatomy at the University of Turin, where for so many years the father of empirical criminology had espoused biological determinism.[23]

Enrico Ferri   The best known of Lombroso's associates was Enrico Ferri (1856–1929).

Did You Know?

. . . that certain Nazi anthropologists and physicians made use of Lombroso's ideas about born criminals? They proposed "scientific" classification of Arians and non-Arians (and ultimately death or denial of civil rights to non-Arians) on the basis of skull measurements.

Member of Parliament, accomplished public lecturer, brilliant lawyer, editor of a newspaper, and esteemed scholar, Ferri had published his first major book by the time he was 21. By age 25 he was a university professor. Although Ferri agreed with Lombroso on the biological bases of criminal behavior, his interest in socialism led him to recognize the importance of social, economic, and political determinants.

Ferri was a prolific writer on a vast number of criminological topics. His greatest contribution was his attack on the classical doctrine of free will, which argued that criminals should be held morally responsible for their crimes because they must have made a rational decision to commit these acts. Ferri believed criminals could not be held morally responsible because they did not choose to commit crimes but, rather, were driven to commit them by conditions in their lives. He did, however, stress that society needed protection against criminal acts and that it was the purpose of the criminal law and penal policy to provide that protection.

Although he advocated conventional punishments and even the death penalty for individuals he assumed would never be fit to live in society, he was more interested in controlling crime through preventive measures—state control of the manufacture of weapons, inexpensive housing, better street lighting, and so forth.

Ferri claimed that strict adherence to preventive measures based on scientific methods would eventually reduce crime and allow people to live together in society with less dependence on the penal system. Toward the end of his life he proudly admitted that he was an idealist, a statement with which generations of scholars have agreed. Though his prescription for crime reduction was overly optimistic, Ferri's importance to the development of modern criminology is undisputed. "When Enrico Ferri died on April 12, 1929," writes Thorsten Sellin, "one of the most colorful, influential figures in the history of criminology disappeared."[24]

Raffaele Garofalo   Another follower of Lombroso was the Italian nobleman, magistrate, senator, and professor of law Raffaele Garofalo (1852–1934). Like Lombroso and Ferri, Garofalo rejected the doctrine of free will and supported the position that the only way to understand crime was to study it by scientific methods. Influenced by Lombroso's theory of atavistic stigmata, in which he found many shortcomings, Garofalo traced the roots of criminal behavior not to physical features but to their psychological equivalents, which he called "moral anomalies." According to this theory, natural crimes are found in all human societies, regardless of the views of lawmakers, and no civilized society can afford to disregard them.[25]

Natural crimes, according to Garofalo, are those that offend the basic moral sentiments of probity (respect for the property of others) and piety (revulsion against the infliction of suffering on others). An individual who has an organic deficiency in these moral sentiments has no moral constraints against committing such crimes. Garofalo argued that these individuals could not be held responsible for their actions. But, like Ferri, he also emphasized that society needed protection and that penal policy should be designed to prevent criminals from inflicting harm.[26]

Influenced by Darwinian theory, Garofalo suggested that the death penalty could rid society of its maladapted members, just as the natural selection process eliminated maladapted organisms. For less serious offenders, capable of adapting themselves to society in some measure, other types of punishments were preferable: transportation to remote lands, loss of privileges, institutionalization in farm colonies, or perhaps simply reparation. Clearly, Garofalo was much more interested in protecting society than in defending the individual rights of offenders.

Challenges to Lombrosian Theory Although Lombroso, Ferri, and Garofalo did not always agree on the causes of criminal behavior or on the way society should respond to it, their combined efforts marked a turning point in the development of the scientific study of crime. These three were responsible for developing the positivist approach to criminality, which influences criminology to the present day. Nevertheless, they had their critics. By using the scientific method to explore crime causation, they paved the way for criminologists to support or refute the theories they had created. The major challenge to Lombrosian theory came from the work of Charles Buckman Goring.

From 1901 until 1913 Charles Buckman Goring (1870–1919), a medical officer at Parkhurst Prison in England, collected data on 96 traits of more than 3000 convicts and a large control group of Oxford and Cambridge university students, hospital patients, and soldiers. Among his research assistants was a famous statistician, Karl Pearson. When Goring had completed his examinations, he was armed with enough data to refute Lombroso's theory of the anthropological criminal type. Goring's report to the scientific community proclaimed:

> From a knowledge only of an undergraduate's cephalic [head] measurement, a better judgment could be given as to whether he were studying at an English or Scottish university than a prediction could be made as to whether he would eventually become a university professor or a convicted felon.[27]

This evaluation still stands as the most cogent critical analysis of Lombroso's theory of the born criminal. Although Goring rejected the claim that specific stigmata identify the criminal, he was convinced that poor physical condition plus a defective state of mind were determining factors in the criminal personality.

A Return to Biological Determinism

After Goring's challenge, Lombrosian theory lost its academic popularity for about a quarter century. Then in 1939 Ernest Hooten (1887–1954), a physical anthropologist, reawakened an interest in biologically determined criminality with the publication of a massive study comparing American prisoners with a noncriminal control group. He concluded:

> [I]n every population there are hereditary inferiors in mind and in body as well as physical and mental deficients. . . . Our information definitely proves that it is from the physically inferior element of the population that native born criminals from native parentage are mainly derived.[28]

Like his positivist predecessors, Hooten argued for the segregation of those he referred to as the "criminal stock," and he recommended their sterilization as well.[29]

One afternoon in the late 1970s, deep in the labyrinthine interior of a massive Gothic tower in New Haven, an unsuspecting employee of Yale University opened a long-locked room in the Payne Whitney Gymnasium and stumbled upon something shocking and disturbing.

Shocking, because what he found was an enormous cache of nude photographs, thousands and thousands of photographs of young men in front, rear, and side poses. Disturbing, because on closer inspection the photos looked like the record of a bizarre body-piercing ritual: sticking out from the spine of each and every body was a row of sharp metal pins.(1)

Half a generation after the "bizarre body-piercing rituals" (the metal pins had not been inserted into the skin, but had been attached by tape), it was a *New York Times Magazine* journalist who was shocked and disturbed, particularly so because he had been exposed to the ritual while at Yale. And the same ritual might have been imposed upon him had he been a student at Mount Holyoke, Vassar, Smith, Princeton, or Wellesley.

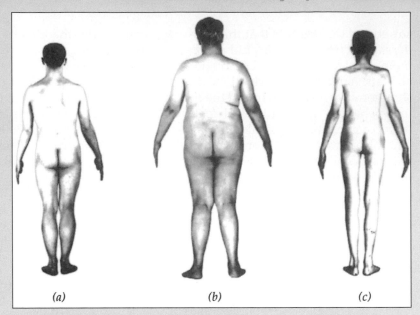

Sheldon's body types: (a) mesomorphic; (b) endomorphic; (c) ectomorphic

The implications were mind-boggling: A routine freshman procedure, supposedly aimed at assessing and improving posture, had yielded a cache of nude photographs, including ones of those of many well-known people. While most of the schools shredded the photographs

10 or more years ago, thousands are still being kept under lock and seal at the Smithsonian in Washington. And what do all the photographs have to do with criminology?

In 1949 the physician William H. Sheldon reported that 200 boys living in

The Somatotype School In the search for the source of criminality, other scientists, too, looked for the elusive link between physical characteristics and crime. The **somatotype school of criminology,** which related body build to behavior, became popular during the first half of the twentieth century. It originated with the work of a German psychiatrist, Ernst Kretschmer (1888–1964), who distinguished three principal types of physiques: (1) the asthenic—lean, slightly built, narrow shoulders; (2) the athletic—medium to tall, strong, muscular, coarse bones; and (3) the pyknic—medium height, rounded figure, massive neck, broad face. He then related these physical types to various psychic disorders: pyknics to manic depression, asthenics and athletics to schizophrenia, and so on.[30]

Kretschmer's work was brought to the United States by William Sheldon (1898–1977), who formulated his own group of somatotypes: the *endomorph,* the *mesomorph,* and the *ectomorph.* Sheldon's father was a dog breeder who used a point system to judge animals in competition, and Sheldon worked out a point system of his own for judging humans. Thus one could actually measure on a scale from 1 to 7 the relative dominance of each body type in any given individual. People with predominantly mesomorph traits (physically powerful, aggressive, athletic physiques), he argued, tend more than others to be involved in illegal behavior.[31] This finding was later supported by Sheldon Glueck (1896–1980) and Eleanor Glueck (1898–1972), who based their studies of delinquents on William Sheldon's somatotypes.[32]

Boston's Hayden Goodwill Inn had body builds significantly different from a control group of 4000 college students. That control group came out of the Ivy League's posture photos in the buff.

SHELDON'S BODY TYPES

Sheldon classified physiques into three categories: mesomorphs, ectomorphs, and endomorphs. A mesomorph tends to be muscular, strong, heavy-boned, and firm; an ectomorph is fragile, thin, and delicate; and an endomorph has a predominance of soft roundness throughout the body. Sheldon used his classifications to show that body types were related to behavior, temperament, and even life expectancy.

Sheldon's 200 young males included alcoholics, mental defectives, and psychopaths, nondelinquents and criminals. He found that the criminal types were more mesomorphic.

A follow-up study of these 200 youths 30 years later identified 14 "primary criminals," individuals who had felony convictions as adults. These persistent criminals were relatively mesomorphic as compared with the others in the follow-up group.

SOMATOTYPING: PRO AND CON

In *Crime and Human Nature* (1985), James Q. Wilson and Richard J. Herrnstein evaluated a number of studies relating physique to delinquency, including Sheldon's. They stated: "[T]he main conclusions have been confirmed wherever they have been tested, despite the initial skepticism of criminologists."(2)

Somatotyping is not without its critics, however. In an extensive review of Wilson and Herrnstein's conclusions, Leon J. Kamin ridicules their presentation of the topic, claiming that they completely ignore a number of studies that have appeared since 1949.(3)

Wilson and Herrnstein themselves present information that raises questions about the value of somatotyping to criminology. They cite studies in which, while the tendency toward the mesomorphic was clear, "mesomorphs could be found among the nondelinquents and ectomorphs among the delinquents." And they emphasize the difference between correlation and causation, stating clearly, "Physique does not cause crime."(1)

A major question remains: Even if a significant relationship between body build and crime could be found, do you believe it is ethical to do this kind of research? Could it lead to arresting the wrong person because he or she "looks" like a criminal? Or could it raise the possibility of picking the wrong person out of a police lineup?

Sources

1. Ron Rosenbaum, "The Great Ivy League Nude Posture Photo Scandal," *New York Times Magazine,* Jan. 15, 1995, pp. 26–31, 40, 46, 55–56; quote from p. 26.
2. James Q. Wilson and Richard J. Herrnstein, *Crime and Human Nature* (New York: Simon & Schuster, 1985), p. 87.
3. Leon J. Kamin, "Crime and Human Nature," *Scientific American,* **254** (February 1986): 22.

Questions for Discussion

1. If criminals were shown conclusively to be "skewed toward the mesomorph," what use might crime-prevention strategists make of such information?
2. Did Sheldon violate standards of ethics in research by utilizing nude photographs taken for other purposes?

By and large, studies based on somatotyping have been sharply criticized for methodological flaws, including nonrepresentative selection of their samples (bias), failure to account for cultural stereotyping (our expectations of how muscular, physically active people should react), and poor statistical analyses. An anthropologist summed up the negative response of the scientific community by suggesting that somatotyping was "a New Phrenology in which the bumps on the buttocks take the place of the bumps on the skulls."[33] After World War II, somatotyping seemed too close to **eugenics** (the science of controlled reproduction to improve hereditary qualities), and the approach fell into disfavor. During the 1960s, however, the discovery of an extra sex chromosome in some criminal samples (see Chapter 4) revived interest in this theory.

Inherited Criminality During the period when some researchers were measuring skulls and bodies of criminals in their search for the physical determinants of crime, others were arguing that criminality was an inherited trait passed on in the genes. To support the theory, they traced family histories. Richard Dugdale (1841–1883), for example, studied the lives of more than a thousand members of the family he called "Jukes." His interest in the family began when he found six related people in a jail in upstate New York. Following one branch of the family, the descendants of Ada Jukes, whom he referred to as the "mother of criminals," Dugdale found among the thousand of descendants 280 paupers, 60 thieves, 7 murderers, 40 other criminals, 40 persons with venereal disease, and 50 prostitutes.

His findings indicated, Dugdale claimed, that since some families produce generations of criminals, they must be transmitting a degenerate trait down the line.[34] A similar conclusion was reached by Henry Goddard (1866–1957). In a study of the family tree of a Revolutionary War soldier, Martin Kallikak, Goddard found many more criminals among the descendants of Kallikak's illegitimate son than among the descendants of his son by a later marriage with "a woman of his own quality."[35]

These early studies have been discredited primarily on the grounds that genetic and environmental influences could not be separated. But in the early twentieth century they were taken quite seriously. On the assumption that crime could be controlled if criminals could be prevented from transmitting their traits to the next generation, some states permitted the sterilization of habitual offenders. Sterilization laws were held constitutional by the U.S. Supreme Court in a 1927 opinion written by Justice Oliver Wendell Holmes, Jr., which included the following well-known pronouncement:

> It is better for all the world, if instead of waiting to execute degenerate offspring for crime, or to let them starve for their imbecility, society can prevent those who are manifestly unfit from continuing their kind. . . . Three generations of imbeciles are enough.[36]

Clearly the early positivists, with their focus on physical characteristics, exerted great influence. They were destined to be overshadowed, though, by investigators who focused on psychological characteristics.

PSYCHOLOGICAL DETERMINISM

On the whole, scholars who investigated criminal behavior in the nineteenth and early twentieth centuries were far more interested in the human body than in the human mind. During that period, however, several contributions were made in the area of psychological explanations of crime. Some of the earliest

contributions came from physicians interested primarily in the legal responsibility of the criminally insane. Later on, psychologists entered the field and applied their new testing techniques to the study of offenders (see Chapter 4).

Pioneers in Criminal Psychology

Isaac Ray (1807–1881), acknowledged to be America's first forensic psychiatrist, was interested throughout his life in the application of psychiatric principles to the law. He is best known as the author of *The Medical Jurisprudence of Insanity*, a treatise on criminal responsibility that was widely quoted and influential.[37] In it he defended the concept of moral insanity, a disorder first described in 1806 by the French humanitarian and psychiatrist Philippe Pinel (1745–1826).[38] "Moral insanity" was a term used to describe persons who were normal in all respects except that something was wrong with the part of the brain that regulates affective responses. Ray questioned whether we could hold people legally responsible for their acts if they had such an impairment, because such people committed their crimes without an intent to do so.

Born in the same year as Lombroso, Henry Maudsley (1835–1918), a brilliant English medical professor, shared Ray's concerns about criminal responsibility. According to Maudsley, some people may be considered either "insane or criminal according to the standpoint from which they are looked at." He believed that for many persons crime is an "outlet in which their unsound tendencies are discharged; they would go mad if they were not criminals."[39] Most of Maudsley's attention focused on the borderline between insanity and crime.

Psychological Studies of Criminals

Around the turn of the twentieth century, psychologists used their new measurement techniques to study offenders. The administering of intelligence tests to inmates of jails, prisons, and other public institutions was especially popular at that time, because it was a period of major controversy over the relation of mental deficiency to criminal behavior. The new technique seemed to provide an objective basis for differentiating criminals from noncriminals.

In 1914 Henry H. Goddard (1866–1957), research director of the Vineland, New Jersey, Training School for the Retarded, examined some intelligence tests that had been given to inmates and concluded that 25 to 50 percent of the people in prison had intellectual defects that made them incapable of managing their own affairs.[40] This idea remained dominant until it was challenged by the results of intelligence tests administered to World War I draftees, whose scores were found to be lower than those of prisoners in the federal penitentiary at Leavenworth. As a result of this study and others like it, intelligence quotient (IQ) measures largely disappeared as a basis for explaining criminal behavior.

SOCIOLOGICAL DETERMINISM

During the nineteenth and early twentieth centuries, some scholars began to search for the social determinants of criminal behavior. The approach had its roots in Europe in the 1830s, the time between Beccaria's *On Crimes and Punishment* and Lombroso's *The Criminal Man.*

Adolphe Quételet and André Michel Guerry

The Belgian mathematician Adolphe Quételet (1796–1874) and the French lawyer André Michel Guerry (1802–1866) were among the first scholars to repudiate the classicists' free-will doctrine. Working independently on the relation of crime statistics to such factors as poverty, age, sex, race, and climate, both scholars concluded that society, not the decisions of individual offenders, was responsible for criminal behavior.

The first modern criminal statistics were published in France in 1827. Guerry used those statistics to demonstrate that crime rates varied with social factors. He found, for example, that the wealthiest region of France had the highest rate of property crime but only half the national rate of violent crime. He concluded that the main factor in property crime was opportunity: There was much more to steal in the richer provinces.

Quételet did an elaborate analysis of crime in France, Belgium, and Holland. After analyzing criminal statistics, which he called "moral statistics," he concluded that if we look at overall patterns of behavior of groups across a whole society, we find a startling regularity of rates of various behaviors. According to Quételet:

> We can enumerate in advance how many individuals will soil their hands in the blood of their fellows, how many will be frauds, how many prisoners; almost as one can enumerate in advance the births and deaths that will take place.[41]

By focusing on groups rather than individuals, he discovered that behavior is indeed predictable, regular, and understandable. Just as the physical world is governed by the laws of nature, human behavior is governed by forces external to the individual. The more we learn about those forces, the easier it becomes to predict behavior. A major goal of criminological research, according to Quételet, should be to identify factors related to crime and to assign to them their "proper degree of influence."[42] Though neither he nor Guerry offered a theory of criminal behavior, the fact that both studied social factors scientifically, using quantitative research methods, made them key figures in the subsequent development of sociological theories of crime causation.

Gabriel Tarde

One of the earliest sociological theories of criminal behavior was formulated by Gabriel Tarde (1843–1904), who served 15 years as a provincial judge and then was placed in charge of France's national statistics. After an extensive analysis of these statistics, he came to the following conclusion:

The majority of murderers and notorious thieves began as children who had been abandoned, and the true seminary of crime must be sought for upon each public square or each crossroad of our towns, whether they be small or large, in those flocks of pillaging street urchins who, like bands of sparrows, associate together, at first for marauding, and then for theft, because of a lack of education and food in their homes.[43]

Tarde rejected the Lombrosian theory of biological abnormality, which was popular in his time, arguing that criminals were normal people who learned crime just as others learned legitimate trades. He formulated his theory in terms of **laws of imitation**—principles that governed the process by which people became criminals. According to Tarde's thesis, individuals emulate behavior patterns in much the same way that they copy styles of dress. Moreover, there is a pattern to the way such emulation takes place: (1) Individuals imitate others in proportion to the intensity and frequency of their contacts; (2) inferiors imitate superiors—that is, trends flow from town to country and from upper to lower classes; and (3) when two behavior patterns clash, one may take the place of the other, as when guns largely replaced knives as murder weapons.[44] Tarde's work served as the basis for Edwin Sutherland's theory of differential association, which we shall examine in Chapter 5.

Émile Durkheim

Modern criminologists take two major approaches to the study of the social factors associated with crime. Tarde's approach asks how individuals become criminal. What is the process? How are behavior patterns learned and transmitted? The second major approach looks at the social structure and its institutions. It asks how crime arises in the first place and how it is related to the functioning of a society. For answers to these questions, scholars begin with the work of Émile Durkheim (1858–1917).

Of all nineteenth-century writers on the relationship between crime and social factors,

Emile Durkheim (1858–1917), one of the founders of sociology.

none has more powerfully influenced contemporary criminology than Durkheim, who is universally acknowledged as one of the founders of sociology. On October 12, 1870, when Durkheim was 12 years old, the German army invaded and occupied his hometown, Epinal, in eastern France. Thus at a very early age he witnessed social chaos and the effects of rapid change, topics with which he remained preoccupied throughout his life. At the age of 24 he became a professor of philosophy, and at 29 he joined the faculty of the University of Bordeaux. There he taught the first course in sociology ever to be offered by a French university.

By 1902 he had moved to the University of Paris, where he completed his doctoral studies.

His *Division of Social Labor* became a landmark work on the organization of societies. According to Durkheim, crime is as normal a part of society as birth and death. Theoretically, crime could disappear altogether only if all members of society had the same values, and such standardization is neither possible nor desirable. Furthermore, some crime is in fact necessary if a society is to progress:

> The opportunity for the genius to carry out his work affords the criminal his originality at a lower level. . . . According to Athenian law, Socrates was a criminal, and his condemnation was no more than just. However, his crime, namely, the independence of his thought, rendered a service not only to humanity but to his country.[45]

Durkheim further pointed out that all societies have not only crime but sanctions. The rationale for the sanctions varies in accordance with the structure of the society. In a strongly cohesive society, punishment of members who deviate is used to reinforce the value system—to remind people of what is right and what is wrong—thereby preserving the pool of common belief and the solidarity of the society. Punishment must be harsh to serve these ends. In a large, urbanized, heterogeneous society, on the other hand, punishment is used not to preserve solidarity but rather to right the wrong done to a victim. Punishment thus is evaluated in accordance with the harm done, with the goal of restitution and reinstatement of order as quickly as possible. The offense is not considered a threat to social cohesion, primarily because in a large, complex society criminal events do not even come to the attention of most people.

The most important of Durkheim's many contributions to contemporary sociology is his concept of **anomie,** a breakdown of social order as a result of a loss of standards and values. In a society plagued by anomie (see Chapter 5), disintegration and chaos replace social cohesion.

Crime Surfing

www.runet.edu/~lridener/DSS/INDEX.HTML

According to Durkheim, what role does religion play in society?

HISTORICAL AND CONTEMPORARY CRIMINOLOGY: A TIME LINE

Classical criminologists thought the problem of crime might be solved through limitations on governmental power, the abolition of brutality, and the creation of a more equitable system of justice. They argued that the punishment should fit the crime. For over a century this perspective dominated criminology. Later on, positivist criminologists influenced judges to give greater consideration to the offender than to the gravity of the crime when imposing sentences. The current era marks a return to the classical demand that the punishment correspond to the seriousness of the crime and the guilt of the offender. Table 3.1 presents a chronology of all the pioneers in criminology we have discussed.

As modern science discovered more and more about cause and effect in the physical and social universes, the theory that individuals commit crimes of their own free will began to lose favor. The positivists searched for determinants of crime in biological, psychological, and social factors. Biologically based theories were popular in the late nineteenth century, fell out of favor in the early part of the twentieth, and emerged again in the 1970s (see Chapter 4) with studies of hormone imbalances, diet, environmental contaminants, and so forth. Since the studies of criminal responsibility in the nineteenth century centering on the insanity defense and of intelligence levels in the twentieth century, psychiatrists and psychologists have continued to play a major role in the search for the causes of crime, especially after Sigmund Freud developed his well-known theory of human personality (Chapter 4). The sociological perspective became popular in the 1920s and has remained the predominant approach of criminological studies. (We will examine contemporary theories in Chapters 5 through 9.)

CHAPTER 3

TABLE 3.1   Pioneers in Criminology: A Chronology

Classical Criminology

Free Will

Cesare Beccaria (1738–1794). Devised the first design for comprehensive, enlightened criminal justice system based on law
Jeremy Bentham (1748–1832). Developed utilitarian principles of punishment

Positivist Criminology

Biological Determinism

Giambattista della Porta (1535–1615). Was the founder of the school of physiognomy, which is the study of facial features and their relation to human behaviors
Johann Kaspar Lavater (1741–1801). Espoused a biological approach to crime causation; developed phrenology
Franz Joseph Gall (1758–1828). Espoused a biological approach to crime causation; further developed phrenology
Charles Caldwell (1772–1853). Was a physician who searched for evidence that brain tissue and cells regulate human behavior.
Johann Kaspar Spurzheim (1776–1832). Espoused a biological approach; continued studies of phrenology
Charles Darwin (1809–1882). Formulated theory of evolution, which changed explanations of human behavior
Cesare Lombroso (1835–1909). Saw determinism as explanatory factor in criminal behavior; posited the "born criminal"; father of modern criminology
Richard Dugdale (1841–1883). Related criminal behavior to inherited traits (Jukes family)
Raffaele Garofalo (1852–1934). Traced roots of criminal behavior to "moral anomalies" rather than physical characteristics
Enrico Ferri (1856–1929). Produced first penal code based on positivist principles; replaced moral responsibility with social accountability
Ernest Hooten (1887–1954). Related criminality to hereditary inferiority
Ernst Kretschmer (1888–1964). Introduced the somatotype school of criminology
William Sheldon (1898–1977). Related body types to illegal behavior

Psychological Determinism

Isaac Ray (1807–1881). Questioned whether those who were "morally insane" could be held legally responsible for their acts
Henry Maudsley (1835–1918). Pioneered criteria for legal responsibility
Henry H. Goddard (1866–1957). Related criminal behavior to intelligence (Kallikak family)

Social Determinism

Adolphe Quételet (1796–1874). Was one of the first to repudiate classical free-will doctrine; studied social determinants of behavior
Auguste Comte (1798–1857). Brought modern scientific methods from physical to social sciences
André Michel Guerry (1802–1866). Was one of the first to repudiate free-will doctrine; related crime statistics to social factors
Gabriel Tarde (1843–1904). Explained crime as learned behavior
Émile Durkheim (1858–1917). Was one of the founders of sociology; developed theory of anomie and idea that crime is normal in all societies
Charles Buckman Goring (1870–1919). Used empirical research to refute Lombroso's theory of criminal types
Sheldon Glueck (1896–1980) and Eleanor Glueck (1898–1972). Espoused primarily social causes of delinquency, but also psychological and biological explanations

REVIEW

In the history of criminology from ancient times to the early twentieth century, its many themes at times have clashed and at times have supported one another. There is no straight-line evolutionary track that we can follow from the inception of the first "criminological" thought to modern theories. Some scholars concentrated on criminal law and procedure; others, on criminal behavior. Some took the biological route; others, the psychological; still others, the sociological. And the work of some investigators has encompassed a combination of factors. Toward the end of the nineteenth century a discipline began to emerge.

Tracing the major developments back in time helps us understand how criminology grew into the discipline we know today. Many of the issues that appear on the intellectual battlefields as we enter the twenty-first century are the same issues our academic ancestors grappled with for hundreds, indeed thousands, of years. With each new clash, some old concepts died, while others were incorporated within competing doctrinal boundaries, there to remain until the next challenge. The controversies of one era become the foundations of knowledge for the next. As societies develop and are subjected to new technologies, the crime problem becomes ever more complex. So do the questions it raises. In Part II we will see how twentieth-century theorists have dealt with those questions.

 ## YOU BE THE CRIMINOLOGIST

An historical society has invited you to represent criminology in a discussion group made up of experts from various disciplines. The topic is: How do the foundations of your discipline help us to understand contemporary developments in the field? What would you discuss?

KEY TERMS

The numbers next to the terms refer to the pages on which the terms are defined.

anomie (77)

atavistic stigmata (68)

born criminal (68)

classical school of criminology (59)

eugenics (73)

laws of imitation (76)

phrenology (67)

physiognomy (67)

positivist school of criminology (60)

somatotype school of criminology (73)

utilitarianism (66)

NOTES

1. First quote: attributed to Socrates by Plato, wording unconfirmed by researchers; see *Respectfully Quoted*, ed. Suzy Platt (Washington, D.C.: Library of Congress, 1989), p. 42. Second quote: Sophocles, *Antigone*, I, 720. Third quote: Plato, *The Republic, I*, 343 d.

2. Leon Radzinowicz, *Ideology and Crime* (New York: Columbia University Press, 1966), p. 2; Marc Ancel, *Introduction to the French Penal Code*, ed. G. O. W. Mueller (South Hackensack, N.J.: Fred B. Rothman, 1960), pp. 1–2.

3. Thorsten Sellin, *Slavery and the Penal System* (New York: Elsevier, 1976); Thorsten Eriksson, *The Reformers: An Historical Survey of Pioneer Experiments in the Treatment of Criminals* (New York: Elsevier, 1976).

4. Marcello T. Maestro, *Cesare Beccaria and the Origins of Penal Reform* (Philadelphia: Temple University Press, 1973), p. 16.

5. George Rude, *The Crowd in the French Revolution* (New York: Oxford University Press, 1959), appendix.

6. Harry Elmer Barnes, *The Story of Punishment: A Record of Man's Inhumanity to Man*, 2d ed. (Montclair, N.J.: Patterson Smith, 1972), p. 99.

7. Cesare Beccaria, *On Crimes and Punishment*, 2d ed., trans. Edward D. Ingraham (Philadelphia: Philip H. Nicklin, 1819), pp. 15, 20, 22–23, 30–32, 60, 74–75, 80, 97–98, 149, 156. For a debate on the contribution of Beccaria to modern criminology, see G. O. W. Mueller, "Whose Prophet Is Cesare Beccaria? An Essay on the Origins of Criminological Theory," *Advances in Criminological Theory*, **2** (1990): 1–14; Graeme Newman and Pietro Marongiu, "Penological Reform and the Myth of Beccaria," *Criminology*, **28** (1990): 325–346; and Piers Beirne, "Inventing Criminology: The 'Science of Man,' in Cesare Beccaria's *Dei delitti e delle pene*," *Criminology*, **29** (1991): 777–820.

8. Marcello T. Maestro, *Voltaire and Beccaria as Reformers of Criminal Law* (New York: Columbia University Press, 1942), p. 73.

9. Jeremy Bentham, *A Fragment on Government and an Introduction to the Principles of Morals and Legislation*, ed. Wilfred Harrison (Oxford: Basil Blackwell, 1967), p. 21.

10. Barnes, *The Story of Punishment*, p. 102.

11. Quoted in Leon Radzinowicz, *A History of English Criminal Law and Its Administration from 1750*, vol. 1 (New York: Macmillan, 1948), p. 330.

12. Charles Darwin, *Origin of Species* (1854; Cambridge, Mass.: Harvard University Press,

1859); Charles Darwin, *The Descent of Man and Selection in Relation to Sex* (1871; New York: A. L. Burt, 1874).

13. Havelock Ellis, *The Criminal*, 2d ed. (New York: Scribner, 1900), p. 27.

14. Christopher Hibbert, *The Roots of Evil* (Boston: Little, Brown, 1963), p. 187.

15. Arthur E. Fink, *The Causes of Crime: Biological Theories in the United States, 1800–1915* (Philadelphia: University of Pennsylvania Press, 1938), p. 1.

16. Hermann Mannheim, *Comparative Criminology* (Boston: Houghton Mifflin, 1965), p. 213.

17. George B. Vold, *Theoretical Criminology* (New York: Oxford University Press, 1958), pp. 44–49.

18. Gina Lombroso Ferrero, *Criminal Man: According to the Classification of Cesare Lombroso*, with an Introduction by Cesare Lombroso (1911; Montclair, N.J.: Patterson Smith, 1972), pp. xxiv–xxv.

19. Cesare Lombroso and William Ferrero, *The Female Offender* (New York: Appleton, 1895), pp. 151–152.

20. Cesare Lombroso, *Crime, Its Causes and Remedies* (Boston: Little, Brown, 1918).

21. Marvin Wolfgang, "Cesare Lombroso," in *Pioneers in Criminology*, ed. Hermann Mannheim (London: Stevens, 1960), p. 168.

22. Thorsten Sellin, "The Lombrosian Myth in Criminology," *American Journal of Sociology*, **42** (1937): 898–899. For Lombroso's impact on American anthropological criminology, see Nicole Hahn Rafter, "Criminal Anthropology in the United States," *Criminology*, **30** (1992): 525–545.

23. Wolfgang, "Cesare Lombroso."

24. Thorsten Sellin, "Enrico Ferri: Pioneer in Criminology, 1856–1929," in *The Positive School of Criminology: Three Lectures by Enrico Ferri*, ed. Stanley E. Grupp (Pittsburgh: University of Pittsburgh Press, 1968), p. 13.

25. Raffaele Garofalo, *Criminology*, trans. Robert Wyness Millar (Montclair, N.J.: Patterson Smith, 1968), pp. 4–5.

26. Marc Ancel, *Social Defense: The Future of Penal Reform* (Littleton, Colo.: Fred B. Rothman, 1987).

27. Charles B. Goring, *The English Convict: A Statistical Study* (London: His Majesty's Stationery Office, 1913), p. 145. For a critique of Goring's work, see Piers Beirne, "Heredity versus Environment," *British Journal of Criminology*, **28** (1988): 315–339.

28. E. A. Hooten, *The American Criminal* (Cambridge, Mass.: Harvard University Press, 1939), p. 308.

29. E. A. Hooten, *Crime and the Man* (Cambridge, Mass.: Harvard University Press, 1939), p. 13.

30. Ernst Kretschmer, *Physique and Character* (New York: Harcourt Brace, 1926).

31. William H. Sheldon, *Varieties of Delinquent Youth: An Introduction to Constitutional Psychiatry* (New York: Harper, 1949). See also Emil M. Hartl, Edward P. Monnelly, and Ronald D. Elderkin, *Physique and Delinquent Behavior: A Thirty-Year Follow-Up of William H. Sheldon's Varieties of Delinquent Youth* (New York: Academic Press, 1982).

32. Eleanor Glueck and Sheldon Glueck, *Unraveling Juvenile Delinquency* (Cambridge, Mass.: Harvard University Press, 1950). See also Sheldon Glueck and Eleanor Glueck, *Of Delinquency and Crime* (Springfield, Ill.: Charles C. Thomas, 1974), p. 2. For a recent reanalysis of the Gluecks' data, see John H. Laub and Robert J. Sampson, "Unravelling Families and Delinquency: A Reanalysis of the Gluecks' Data," *Criminology*, **26** (1988): 355–380. For the life and work of Eleanor Touroff Glueck, see John H. Laub and Jinney S. Smith, "Eleanor Touroff Glueck: An Unsung Pioneer in Criminology," *Women in Criminal Justice*, **6** (1995): 1–22.

33. S. L. Washburn, book review, "Varieties of Delinquent Youth, An Introduction to Constitutional Psychiatry," *American Anthropologist*, **53** (1951): 561–563.

34. Richard L. Dugdale, *The Jukes: A Study in Crime, Pauperism, Disease, and Heredity*, 5th ed. (New York: Putnam, 1895), p. 8.

35. Henry H. Goddard, *The Kallikak Family: A Study in the Heredity of Feeble-Mindedness* (New York: Macmillan, 1912), p. 50.

36. *Buck v. Bell*, 274 U.S. 200, 207 (1927).

37. Isaac Ray, *The Medical Jurisprudence of Insanity* (Boston: Little, Brown, 1838).

38. Philippe Pinel, *A Treatise on Insanity* (1806; New York: Hafner, 1962).

39. Peter Scott, "Henry Maudsley," *Journal of Criminal Law, Criminology, and Police Science,* **46** (March–April 1956): 753–769.

40. Henry H. Goddard, *The Criminal Imbecile* (New York: Macmillan, 1915), pp. 106–107.

41. Adolphe Quételet, *A Treatise on Man,* facs. ed. of 1842 ed., trans. Salomon Diamond (1835; Gainesville, Fla.: Scholars Facsimiles and Reprints, 1969), p. 97.

42. Quételet, *A Treatise on Man,* p. 103. For Quételet's influence on modern scholars, see Derral Cheatwood, "Is There a Season for Homicide?" *Criminology,* **26** (1988): 287–306.

43. Gabriel Tarde, *Penal Philosophy,* trans. R. Howell (Boston: Little, Brown, 1912), p. 252.

44. Gabriel Tarde, *Social Laws: An Outline of Sociology* (New York: Macmillan, 1907).

45. Émile Durkheim, *The Rules of Sociological Method,* ed. George E. G. Catlin (Chicago: University of Chicago Press, 1938), p. 71.

Review • You Be the Criminologist • Key Terms • Notes

PART II

Explanations of Crime and Criminal Behavior

Having explored the history of criminology, the early explanations of criminal behavior, and the scientific methods used by criminologists, we turn now to contemporary theories and research. Current explanations of criminal behavior focus on biological, psychological, social, and economic factors. Biological and psychological theories assume that criminal behavior results from underlying physical or mental conditions that distinguish criminals from noncriminals (Chapter 4). These theories yield insight into individual cases, but they do not explain why crime rates vary from place to place and from one situation to another.

Sociological theories seek to explain criminal behavior in terms of the environment. Chapter 5 examines strain and cultural deviance theories, which focus on the social forces that cause people to engage in criminal behavior. Both theories assume that social class and criminal behavior are related. Strain theorists argue that people commit crimes because they are frustrated by not being able to achieve their goals through legitimate means. Cultural deviance theorists claim that crime is learned in socially disorganized neighborhoods where criminal norms are transmitted from one generation to the next. In Chapter 6 we examine subcultures that have their own norms, beliefs, and values, which differ significantly from those of the dominant culture. Chapter 7 explains how people remain committed to conventional behavior in the face of frustration, poor living conditions, and other criminogenic factors. In Chapter 8 we discuss three theoretical perspectives that focus on society's role in creating criminals and defining them as such. Finally, in Chapter 9 we explain why offenders choose to commit one offense rather than another at a given time and place.

CHAPTER 4
Psychological and Biological Perspectives

KEY TERMS
attachment
behavioral modeling
biocriminology
chromosomes
conditioning
cortical arousal
differential association-
reinforcement
dizygotic (DZ) twins
ego
extroversion
fundamental psycholegal error
hypoglycemia
id
minimal brain dysfunction (MBD)
monozygotic (MZ) twins
neuroticism
psychoanalytic theory
psychopathy
psychosis
psychoticism
social learning theory
superego

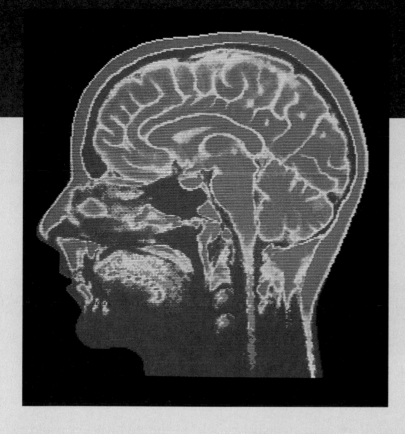

Heriberto Seda was a loner from birth. In a neighborhood overrun with crime, his mother tried to shield her only son from the dangers that lurked around every corner. She never let Heriberto have friends over or let him venture too far from home. Each day, Heriberto would return from school to his apartment where, in the solitude of his room, he watched television, looked at basketball trading cards, and developed a fascination with the concept of God.

In 1984, Heriberto was suspended for discharging a starter's pistol in class. A few months shy of graduation, Heriberto dropped out of Francis K. Lane High School and took to spreading the word of God on a full-time basis. He roamed the streets of his neighborhood to do "the will of God." Dressed in black, with his hair neatly restrained in a ponytail, Heriberto would emerge from his home after dark and berate the drug dealers that conducted business in the hallways and on the streets. He preached by night and returned to the seclusion of his home by day. Here, his previously innocent hobbies had taken a sinister turn—basketball trading cards were replaced by those of serial murderers from the True Crime Series; the magazines now had a militaristic twist: *Soldier of Fortune* and mail-order catalogs for military supplies; models of boats and ships were replaced by filed-down zip guns and homemade pipe bombs, with a generous sprinkling of gas masks, machetes, and hundreds of rounds of ammunition.

On March 8, 1990, Heriberto embarked on the first of many shootings in his crusade to eradicate evil—to dispose of the enemies of God. During the course of the next few years, Heriberto Seda shot eight people, killing three. All his victims were vulnerable: a homeless man asleep on a park bench, a crippled factory worker on his way home, a 78-year-old man who turned his back to get his murderer a glass of water.

Heriberto vowed to shoot and kill a person born under each astrological sign.

After several of the shootings, cryptic messages with astrological underpinnings were found nearby, scrawled on pieces of paper. Similar letters were sent to *60 Minutes* and the *New York Post,* declaring him the Zodiac, all sealed with the same trademark signature: an encircled cross with three 7s. This signature at the end of each message would prove to be his downfall.

Heriberto Seda, confessed Zodiac Killer, terrorized East New York for six years with random shootings. In 1999, he was convicted of eight counts of attempted murder, among other charges. He was sentenced to 152 1/2 years to life in prison.

In 1994, Heriberto Seda was arrested for illegal possession of a firearm, but the charges were dropped a few days later when the weapon was deemed inoperable for safety reasons; in no time, Heriberto was back on the streets of New York. On June 18, 1996, Heriberto shot his 19-year-old sister in the back, after an alleged dispute over her promiscuity. A 3-hour standoff with the police ensued, ending in his capture.

Did You Know

. . . that there are as many as 50 serial killers living (and killing) in the United States today?

Down at the police station, Heriberto Seda gave a signed statement sealed with his trademark: an encircled cross with three 7s. This evidence, in addition to expert fingerprint analysis linking him to four of the shootings in 1990, sealed the fate of the Zodiac Killer. In 1998 Heriberto was convicted of three murders and one attempted murder in a Queens, New York, courthouse. He was sentenced to 83 years to life in prison. In July 1999 a Brooklyn, New York, jury convicted him of attempting to murder eight people, including his 19-year-old sister. The judge added another 152 ½ years to his sentence.

In the United States, explanations of criminal behavior have been dominated by sociological theories. These theories focus on lack of opportunity and the breakdown of the conventional value system in urban ghettos, the formation of subcultures whose norms deviate from those of the middle class, and the increasing inability of social institutions to exercise control over behavior. Criminological texts have treated psychological and biological theories as peripheral, perhaps because criminology's disciplinary allegiance is to sociology. When psychological theories were first advanced to explain criminal behavior, their emphasis was largely psychoanalytic, so they may have seemed not quantitative enough to some criminologists.[1] Others may have considered the early work of Lombroso, Goring, and Hooten too scientifically naive to be taken seriously.

Sociological theories focus on crime rates of groups that experience frustration in their efforts to achieve accepted goals, not on the particular individual who becomes a criminal.

Sociological theories cannot explain how one person can be born in a slum, be exposed to family discord and abuse, never attend school, have friends who are delinquents, and yet resist opportunities for crime, while another person can grow up in an affluent suburban neighborhood in a two-parent home and end up firing a gun at the president. In other words, sociologists do not address individual differences.[2] Psychologists and biologists are interested in finding out what may account for individual differences.

It is clear that psychological, biological, and sociological explanations are not competing to answer the same specific questions. Rather, all three disciplines are searching for answers to different questions, even though they study the same act, status, or characteristic. We can understand crime in a society only if we view criminality from more than one level of analysis: why a certain individual commits a crime (psychological and biological explanations) and why some groups of individuals commit more or different criminal acts than other groups (sociological explanations).

Sociological theory and empirical research often ignore such factors as personality and human biology, almost as if they were irrelevant. And psychological theory often focuses on the individual, with little regard for the fact that while each one of us comes into the world with certain predispositions, from the moment we are born we interact with others in complex situations that influence our behavior.

PSYCHOLOGY AND CRIMINALITY

Psychologists have considered a variety of possibilities to account for individual differences— defective conscience, emotional immaturity, inadequate childhood socialization, maternal deprivation, poor moral development. They study how aggression is learned, which situations promote violent or delinquent reactions, how crime is related to personality factors, and how various mental disorders are associated with criminality.

Psychological Development

The **psychoanalytic theory** of criminality attributes delinquent and criminal behavior to at least three possible causes:

- A conscience so overbearing that it arouses feelings of guilt.

- A conscience so weak that it cannot control the individual's impulses.

- The need for immediate gratification.

Consider the case of Richard. Richard was 6 when he committed his first delinquent act: He stole a comic book from the corner drugstore. Three months before the incident, his father, an alcoholic, had been killed in an automobile accident, and his mother, unable to care for the family, had abandoned the children.

For the next 10 years the county welfare agency moved Richard in and out of foster homes. During this time he actively pursued a life of crime, breaking into houses during daylight hours and stealing cars at night. By age 20, while serving a 10-year prison sentence for armed robbery, he had voluntarily entered psychoanalysis. After 2 years, Richard's analyst suggested three reasons for his criminality:

1. Being caught and punished for stealing made him feel less guilty about hating both his father for dying and thus abandoning him as well as his mother for deliberately abandoning him.

2. Stealing did not violate his moral and ethical principles.

3. Stealing resulted in immediate gratification and pleasure, both of which Richard had great difficulty resisting.

Sigmund Freud (1856–1939), the founder of psychoanalysis, suggested that an individual's psychological well-being is dependent on a healthy interaction among the id, ego, and superego—the three basic components of the human psyche. The **id** consists of powerful urges and drives for gratification and satisfaction. The **ego** is the executive of the personality, acting as a moderator between the superego and id. The **superego** acts as a moral code or conscience. Freud proposed that criminality may result from an overactive superego or conscience. In treating patients, he noticed that those who were suffering from unbearable guilt committed crimes in order to be apprehended and punished.[3] Once they had been punished, their feelings of guilt were relieved. Richard's psychoanalyst suggested that Richard's anger over his father's death and his mother's abandonment created unconscious feelings of guilt, which he sought to relieve by committing a crime and being punished for it.

The psychoanalyst also offered an alternative explanation for Richard's persistent criminal activities: His conscience was perhaps not too strong, but too weak. The conscience, or superego, was so weak or defective that he was unable to control the impulses of the id. Because the superego is essentially an internalized parental image, developed when the child assumes the parents' attitudes and moral values, it follows that the absence of such an image may lead to an unrestrained id and thus to delinquency.[4]

Psychoanalytic theory suggests yet another explanation for Richard's behavior: an insatiable need for immediate reward and gratification. A defect in the character formation of delinquents drives them to satisfy their desires at once, regardless of the consequences.[5] This urge, which psychoanalysts attribute to the id, is so strong that relationships with people are important only so long as they help satisfy it. Most analysts view delinquents as children unable to give up their desires for instant pleasure.

The psychoanalytic approach is still one of the most prominent explanations for both normal and asocial functioning. Despite criticism,[6] three basic principles still appeal to psychologists who study criminality:

1. The actions and behavior of an adult are understood in terms of childhood development.

2. Behavior and unconscious motives are intertwined, and their interaction must be unraveled if we are to understand criminality.

3. Criminality is essentially a representation of psychological conflict.

In spite of their appeal, psychoanalytic treatment techniques devised to address these principles have been controversial since their introduction by Freud and his disciples. The controversy has involved questions about improvement following treatment and, perhaps more important, the validity of the hypothetical conflicts the treatment presupposes.

Moral Development

Consider the following moral dilemma:

> In Europe, a woman is near death from a special kind of cancer. There is one drug that the doctors think might save her. It is a form of radium that a druggist in the same town has recently discovered. The drug is expensive to make, and the druggist is charging ten times that cost. He paid $200 for the radium and is charging $2,000 for a small dose of the drug. The sick woman's husband, Heinz, goes to everyone he knows to borrow the money, but he can get together only $1,000. He tells the druggist that his wife is dying and asks him to sell the drug more cheaply or to let him pay later. The druggist says, "No, I discovered the drug and I'm going to make money from it." Heinz is desperate and considers breaking into the man's store to steal the drug for his wife.[7]

This classic dilemma sets up complex moral issues. While you may know that it is wrong to steal, you may believe that this is a situation in which the law should be circumvented. Or is it always wrong to steal, no matter what the circumstances? Regardless of what you decide, the way you reach the decision about whether or not to steal reveals much about your moral development.

The psychologist Lawrence Kohlberg, who pioneered moral developmental theory, has found that moral reasoning develops in three phases.[8] In the first, the preconventional level, children's moral rules and moral values consist of dos and don'ts to avoid punishment. A desire to avoid punishment and a belief in the superior power of authorities are the two central reasons for doing what is right. According to the theory, until the ages of 9 to 11, children usually reason at this level. They think, in effect, "If I steal, what are my chances of getting caught and being punished?"

Adolescents typically reason at the conventional level. Here individuals believe in and have adopted the values and rules of society. Moreover, they seek to uphold these rules. They think, in effect, "It is illegal to steal and therefore I should not steal, under any circumstances." Finally, at the postconventional level, individuals examine customs and social rules according to their own sense of universal human rights, moral principles, and duties. They think, in effect, "One must live within the law, but certain universal ethical principles, such as respect for human rights and for the dignity of human life, supersede the written law when the two conflict." This level of moral reasoning is generally seen in adults after the age of 20. (See Table 4.1.)

According to Kohlberg and his colleagues, most delinquents and criminals reason at the preconventional level. Low moral development or preconventional reasoning alone, however, does not result in criminality. Other factors, such as the presence or the absence of significant social bonds, may play a part. Kohlberg has argued that basic moral principles and social norms are learned through social interaction and role playing. In essence, children learn how to be moral by reasoning with others who are at a higher level of moral development.[9]

Students of Kohlberg have looked at practical applications of his theory. What would happen, for instance, if delinquents who were poor moral reasoners were exposed to individuals who reasoned at a higher level? Joseph Hickey, William Jennings, and their associates designed programs for Connecticut and Florida prisons and applied them in school systems throughout the United States. The "just-community intervention" approach involves a structured educational curriculum stressing democracy, fairness, and a sense of community. Above all, the focus is on the growth and development of moral reasoning. A series of evaluations of just-community programs has revealed significant improvement in moral development.[10]

Maternal Deprivation and Attachment Theory

In a well-known psychological experiment, infant monkeys were provided with the choice between two wire "monkeys." One, made of uncovered cage wire, dispensed milk. The other, made of cage wire covered with soft fabric, did not give milk. The infant monkeys in the experiment gravitated to the warm cloth monkey, which provided comfort and security even though it did not provide food. What does this have to do with criminality? Research has demonstrated that a phenomenon important to social development takes place shortly after the birth of any mammal: the construction of an emotional bond between the infant and its mother. The strength of this emotional bond, or **attachment,** will determine, or at least materially affect, a child's ability to form attachments in the future. In order to form a successful attachment, a child needs a warm, loving, and interactive caretaker.

Studies of Attachment. The British psychiatrist John Bowlby has studied both the need for warmth and affection from birth onward and the consequences of not having it. He has proposed a theory of attachment with seven important features:

- *Specificity.* Attachments are selective, usually directed to one or more individuals in some order of preference.

- *Duration.* Attachments endure and persist, sometimes throughout the life cycle.

- *Engagement of emotion.* Some of the most intense emotions are associated with attachment relationships.

- *Ontogeny (course of development).* Children form an attachment to one primary figure in the first 9 months of life. That principal attachment figure is the person who supplies the most social interaction of a satisfying kind.

- *Learning.* Though learning plays a role in the development of attachment, Bowlby finds that attachments are the products not of rewards or reinforcements, but of basic social interaction.

- *Organization.* Attachment behavior follows cognitive development and interpersonal maturation from birth onward.

- *Biological function.* Attachment behavior has a biological function—survival. It is

TABLE 4.1 Kohlberg's Sequence of Moral Reasoning

Level	Stage	Sample Moral Reasoning	
		In Favor of Stealing	Against Stealing
Level 1: Preconventional morality. At this level, the concrete interests of the individual are considered in terms of rewards and punishments.	Stage 1: Obedience and punishment orientation. At this stage, people stick to rules in order to avoid punishment, and there is obedience for its own sake.	If you let your wife die, you will get in trouble. You'll be blamed for not spending the money to save her, and there'll be an investigation of you and the druggist for your wife's death.	You shouldn't steal the drug because you'll be caught and sent to jail if you do. If you do get away, your conscience will bother you, thinking how the police will catch up with you at any minute.
	Stage 2: Reward orientation. At this stage, rules are followed only for one's own benefit. Obedience occurs because of rewards that are received.	If you do happen to get caught, you could give the drug back and you wouldn't get much of a sentence. It wouldn't bother you much to serve a little jail term, if you have your wife when you get out.	You may not get much of a jail term if you steal the drug, but your wife will probably die before you get out, so it won't do much good. If your wife dies, you shouldn't blame yourself; it wasn't your fault she had cancer.
Level 2: Conventional morality. At this level, moral problems are approached by an individual as a member of society. People are interested in pleasing others by acting as good members of society.	Stage 3: "Good boy" morality. Individuals at this stage show an interest in maintaining the respect of others and doing what is expected of them.	No one will think you're bad if you steal the drug, but your family will think you're an inhuman husband if you don't. If you let your wife die, you'll never be able to look anybody in the face again.	It isn't just the druggist who will think you're a criminal; everyone else will too. After you steal it, you'll feel bad, thinking how you've brought dishonor on your family and yourself; you won't be able to face anyone again.
	Stage 4: Authority and social-order-maintaining morality. People at this stage conform to society's rules and consider that "right" is what society defines as right.	If you have any sense of honor, you won't let your wife die just because you're afraid to do the only thing that will save her. You'll always feel guilty that you caused her death if you don't do your duty to her.	You're desperate and you may not know you're doing wrong when you steal the drug. But you'll know you did wrong after you're sent to jail. You'll always feel guilty for your dishonesty and lawbreaking.
Level 3: Postconventional morality. People at this level use moral principles which are seen as broader than those of any particular society.	Stage 5: Morality of contract, individual rights, and democratically accepted law. People at this stage do what is right because of a sense of obligation to laws which are agreed upon within society. They perceive that laws can be modified as part of changes in an implicit social contract.	You'll lose other people's respect, not gain it, if you don't steal. If you let your wife die, it will be out of fear, not out of reasoning. So you'll just lose self-respect and probably the respect of others too.	You'll lose your standing and respect in the community and violate the law. You'll lose respect for yourself if you're carried away by emotion and forget the long-range point of view.
	Stage 6: Morality of individual principles and conscience. At this final stage, a person follows laws because they are based on universal ethical principles. Laws that violate the principles are disobeyed.	If you don't steal the drug, if you let your wife die, you'll always condemn yourself for it afterward. You won't be blamed and you'll have lived up to the outside rule of the law, but you won't have lived up to your own standards of conscience.	If you steal the drug, you won't be blamed by other people, but you'll condemn yourself because you won't have lived up to your own conscience and standards of honesty.

Source: Adapted from Robert S. Feldman, *Understanding Psychology* (New York: McGraw-Hill, 1987), p. 378.

found in almost all species of mammals and in birds.[11]

Bowlby contends that a child needs to experience a warm, intimate, and continuous relationship with either a mother or a mother sub-stitute in order to be securely attached. When a child is separated from the mother or is rejected by her, anxious attachment results. Anxious attachment affects the capacity to be affectionate and to develop intimate relationships with oth-

Experiments with young monkeys and surrogate mothers reveal the power of attachment in behavioral development. Here a frightened baby rhesus monkey holds on to a terry-cloth mother.

ers. Habitual criminals, it is claimed, typically have an inability to form bonds of affection:

> More often than not the childhoods of such individuals are found to have been grossly disturbed by death, divorce, or separation of the parents, or by other events resulting in disruption of bonds, with an incidence of such disturbance far higher than is met with in any other comparable group, whether drawn from the general population or from psychiatric casualties of other sorts.[12]

Considerable research supports the relationship between anxious attachment and subsequent behavioral problems:

- In a study of 113 middle-class children observed at 1 year and again at 6 years, researchers noted a significant relationship

between behavior at age 6 and attachment at age 1.[13]

- In a study of 40 children seen when they were 1 year old and again at 18 months, it was noted that anxiously attached children were less empathetic, independent, compliant, and confident than securely attached children.[14]

- Researchers have noted that the quality of one's attachment correlates significantly with asocial preschool behavior—being aggressive, leaving the group, and the like.[15]

Family Atmosphere and Delinquency Criminologists also have examined the effects of the mother's absence, whether because of death, divorce, or abandonment. Does her absence cause delinquency? Empirical research is equivocal. Perhaps the most persuasive evidence comes from longitudinal research conducted by Joan McCord, who has investigated the relationship between family atmosphere (such as parental self-confidence, deviance, and affection) and delinquency.

In one study, she collected data on the childhood homes of 201 men and their subsequent court records in order to identify family-related variables that would predict criminal activity. Such variables as inadequate maternal affection and supervision, parental conflict, the mother's lack of self-confidence, and the father's deviance were significantly related to the commission of crimes against persons and/or property. The father's absence by itself was not correlated with criminal behavior.[16]

Other studies, such as those by Sheldon and Eleanor Glueck and the more recent studies by Lee N. Robins, which were carried out in schools, juvenile courts, and psychiatric hospitals, suggest a moderate to strong relation between crime and childhood deprivation.[17] However, evi-

Crime Surfing

www.ncjrs.org

Material deprivation can be related to delinquent behavior. What happens to deprived (often abused and neglected) children? Is there a cycle of violence?

TABLE 4.2   Family-Based Crime Prevention by Ecological Context

Ecological Context	Program	Prevention Agent
Home	Regular visits for emotional, informational, instrumental, and educational support for parents of preschool (or older) children	Nurses, teachers, paraprofessionals, preschool teachers
	Foster care outplacement for the prevention of physical and sexual abuse or neglect	Family services, social workers
	Family preservation of families at risk of outplacement of child	Private family-preservation teams
	Personal alarm for victims of serious domestic violence	Police
	In-home proactive counseling for domestic violence	Police, social workers
Preschool	Involvement of mothers in parent groups, job training, parent training	Preschool teachers
School	Parent training	Psychologists, teachers
	Simultaneous parent and child training	Psychologists, child care workers, social workers
Clinics	Family therapy	Psychologists, psychiatrists, social workers
	Medication—psychostimulants for treatment of hyperactivity and other childhood conduct disorders	Psychiatrists, psychologists, pediatricians
Hospitals	Domestic violence counseling	Nurses, social workers
	Low-birthweight baby mothers' counseling and support	Nurses, social workers
Courts	Prosecution of batterers	Police, prosecutors
	Warrants for unarrested batterers	Police, prosecutors
	Restraining orders or "stay away" order of protection	Police, prosecutors, judges, victims' advocates
	Hot line notification of victim about release of incarcerated domestic batterer	Probation, victim advocates
Battered women's shelters	Safe refuge during high-risk 2 to 7 days' aftermath of domestic assault; counseling; hot lines	Volunteers, staff

dence that deprivation directly causes delinquency is lacking.[18]

So far we have considered psychological theories that attribute the causes of delinquency or criminality to unconscious problems and failures in moral development. Not all psychologists agree with these explanations of criminal behavior. Some argue that human behavior develops through learning. They say that we learn by observing others and by watching the responses to other people's behavior (on television or in the movies, for instance) and to our own. Social learning theorists reject the notion that internal functioning alone makes us prone to act aggressively or violently.

Learning Aggression and Violence

Social learning theory maintains that delinquent behavior is learned through the same psychological processes as any other behavior. Behavior is learned when it is reinforced or rewarded; it is not learned when it is not reinforced. We learn behavior in various ways: observation, direct experience, and differential reinforcement.

Observational Learning   Albert Bandura, a leading proponent of social learning theory, argues that individuals learn violence and aggression through **behavioral modeling:** Children learn how to behave by fashioning their behavior after that of others. Behavior is socially transmitted through examples, which come pri-

Mark Martone was 16 when he shot his father to death. [He] remembers abuse back to age five, when he told his dad he was scared of the dark. "Oh, Jesus Christ," said the parent in disgust. Then he led the terrified boy down to the cellar, handcuffed his arms over a rafter, turned off the light and shut the door. Mark dangled in silence for hours. When Mark was nine, his father held the boy's hand over a red-hot burner as punishment for moving a book of matches on a bureau. And when he was 15, his dad, angered by a long-distance phone bill, stuck a gun in his son's mouth and "told me he was going to blow my brains out."(1)

Sylvester Hobbs III, a 20-year-old, said to be depressed and withdrawn, stabbed and killed his stepfather and wounded his mother.(2)

Eleven-year-old identical twins were charged with murdering their father and attempting to kill their mother and 16-year-old sister in their house.(3)

James Brian Hill, 28, said he was defending his own life when he killed his father, who had previously assaulted his mother.(2)

Carlton Akee Turner Jr., 19, killed his parents because his father was said to be abusive.(2)

An estimated 5.7 million children in the United States are physically, mentally, and sexually abused by their parents annually, and the problem is not lessening. Of those millions of children, maybe a few hundred each year fight back with the ultimate weapon: They kill the abusive parent. In the past such children were regarded as particularly evil, and the law reserved the most terrible forms of capital punishment for parricides. With the growing understanding of the horrors of child abuse, however, these youths are being treated with increasing sympathy. "They know what they're doing is wrong," comments a psychologist at the University of Virginia. "But they are desperate and helpless, and they don't see alternatives."(1)

The typical case involves a 16- to 18-year-old from a white middle-class family. Sons are more likely than daughters to commit murder, and the victim is more likely to be a father than a mother. While children who kill nonabusive parents usually display some sign of mental disorder, the killers of abusive parents generally are seen as well adjusted.(4)

The increasing sympathy for these teenagers has led to verdicts of not guilty by reason of self-defense or guilty of reduced charges (for example, manslaughter instead of first-degree murder). A battered-child-syndrome defense sometimes is successful, but the killings do not usually fit the typical idea of self-defense: Most happen when the parent is in a vulnerable position instead of in the middle of an attack on the child. But mental health experts think that treatment is more appropriate than punishment for children who kill their abusive parents. "These kids don't need to be locked up for our protection," says one attorney and psychologist. "Some may benefit in the sense that they've been able to atone and overcome some guilt. But beyond that, it's really Draconian."(1)

CHARACTERISTICS ASSOCIATED WITH ADOLESCENT PARRICIDE OFFENDERS

1. Patterns of family violence (parental brutality and cruelty toward child and/or toward one another).
2. Adolescent's attempts to get help from others fail.
3. Adolescent's efforts to escape family situation fail (e.g., running away, thoughts of suicide, suicide attempts).
4. Adolescent is isolated from others/fewer outlets.
5. Family situation becomes increasingly intolerable.
6. Adolescent feels increasingly helpless, trapped.
7. Adolescent's inability to cope leads to loss of control.
8. Prior criminal behavior is minimal or nonexistent.
9. Availability of gun.
10. Homicide victim is alcoholic.
11. Evidence to suggest dissociative state in some cases.
12. Victim's death perceived as relief to offender/family; initial absence of remorse.

Sources

1. Hannah Bloch and Jeanne McDowell, "When Kids Kill Abusive Parents," *Time,* Nov. 23, 1992, p. 60.
2. Nancy Calaway, "Spotlight Intensifies on Children Who Murder Parents; Recent Focus on Crime Doesn't Mean It's Increasing, Analyst Says," *Dallas Morning News,* Aug. 30, 1999, p. 1A.
3. Anne Saker, "Twin Boys Face Trial in Father's Killing," (Raleigh, NC) *News and Observer,* Aug. 1, 1999, p. A1.
4. Kathleen M. Heide, *Why Kids Kill Parents* (Columbus: Ohio State University Press, 1992), pp. 40–41.

Questions for Discussion

1. If you were on a jury, would you be willing to consider that what appears to be cold-blooded murder might have been a form of self-defense for a battered child?
2. An attorney specializing in parricide feels that such cases "open a window on our understanding of child abuse." How would you go about determining which of millions of child abuse cases are likely to lead to parricide for which a standard defense should be recognized?

Source: Excerpted from Kathleen M. Heide, *Why Kids Kill Parents* (Columbus: Ohio State University Press, 1992), table 3.1, pp. 40–41.

GameWorks, a popular video entertainment center franchise, attracts children who enjoy electronic games of action and violence. GameWorks, increasingly concerned about the possibility that simulated violence may provoke real violence, issues two smart cards: a regular card that plays all games and the V-card, which restricts children to non–violent games.

marily from the family, the subculture, and the mass media.[19]

Psychologists have been studying the effects of family violence (Chapter 11) on children. They have found that parents who try to resolve family controversies by violence teach their children to use similar tactics. Thus a cycle of violence may be perpetuated through generations. Observing a healthy and happy family environment tends to result in constructive and positive modeling.

To understand the influence of the social environment outside the home, social learning theorists have studied gangs, which often provide excellent models of observational learning of violence and aggression. They have found, in fact, that violence is very much a norm shared by some people in a community or gang. The highest incidence of aggressive behavior occurs where aggressiveness is a desired characteristic, as it is in some subcultures.

Observational learning takes place in front of the television set and at the movies, as well. Children who have seen others being rewarded for violent acts often believe that violence and aggression are acceptable behaviors.[20] And today children can see a lot of violence. The psy-

chologist Leonard Eron has argued that the "single best predictor of how aggressive a young man would be when he was 19 years old was the violence of the television programs he preferred when he was 8 years old."[21]

Results from the 3-year landmark *National Television Violence Study* initiated in 1994 suggest that the problem is one not only of violence, but also of the portrayal of violence—the absence of consequences for violent acts and the glamorization of violence.[22] (See Figure 4.1.)

FIGURE 4.1 Overall television industry averages: 3-year comparisons.

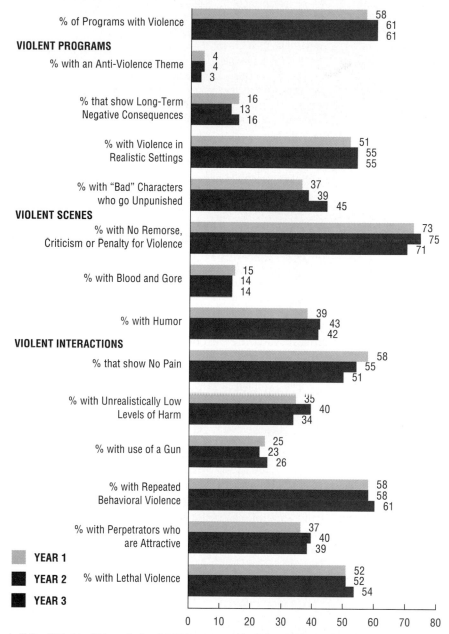

Source: J. Federman, ed., *National Television Violence Study,* vol. 3 (University of California, Santa Barbara, Center for Communications and Social Policy, 1998).

Direct Experience What we learn by observation is determined by the behavior of others. What we learn from direct experience is determined by what we ourselves do and what happens to us. We remember the past and use its lessons to avoid future mistakes. Thus we learn through trial and error. According to social learning theorists, after engaging in a given

On December 19, 1996, the U.S. television industry announced a voluntary TV ratings system. All TV shows are now rated as follows:

- TV-Y, material suitable for children of all ages. Show contains little or no violence, strong language, or sexual content.
- TV-Y7, material suitable for children 7 and older.
- TV-G, material suitable for all audiences.
- TV-PG, parental guidance is suggested. Program may contain infrequent coarse language, limited violence, some suggestive sexual dialogue and situations.
- TV-14, material may be inappropriate for children under 14. Program may contain sophisticated themes, strong language, and sexual content.
- TV-M, for mature audiences only. Program may contain profane language, graphic violence, and explicit sexual content.

What prompted this unprecedented move? Many Americans had for some time been concerned about the ever-increasing amount of violence on television and its effects on children.(1)

SOCIAL CONTROL VERSUS CENSORSHIP

While many people saw the networks' plans for ratings as a disappointingly small contribution to a big problem, others began worrying about freedom of expression. Representative Edward J. Markey pushed for a plan that would require "V-block" computer chips in all new TV sets—the chip would allow parents to block all V-rated (violent) shows. V-chips are now mandatory on all television sets with screens 13 inches and larger.(1) "I am totally opposed to the government getting involved in any way that infringes on the First Amendment," argues Jack Valenti, president of the Motion Picture Association of America.(1) " 'That's getting awfully close to censorship,' frets Peggy Charren, founder of Action for Children's Television."(2)

If such warnings and "zappings" do constitute censorship, the United States is ahead of other countries. In Egypt, both radio and television are owned by the state, and all broadcasts are supervised by the government.(3) In Singapore, television also is state-controlled.(4) India, despite being open to satellite-dish broadcasting, was still using its government-run network in 1992 to censor the violence that occurred during religious riots across the country.(5) Indonesia's government announced in 1993 that censoring all materials citizens could watch on private and foreign networks had become "too onerous a task" for its National Film Censorship Board; it stated that the people themselves should judge what to watch and should avoid "morally unsuitable" programs, such as those containing pornography and violence.(6)

The Chinese Example

Perhaps China provides the most prominent example of the use of television for social control: "In the hands of Chinese media experts, TV is both an instrument to instill terror and obedience and an educational tool," wrote Newsday reporter Thomas Collins after the Tiananmen Square protests. "The . . . important thing was to control and limit what a billion Chinese people would believe had happened."(7) According to Collins, the event was portrayed as follows:

> Rather than a demonstration for democratic reforms involving millions of people throughout the country, the protests were the work of a handful of "counterrevolutionaries" and "hoodlums." Instead of the massacre of hundreds, possibly thousands of students and workers, the Chinese populace is being told that the only casualties were soldiers. No students were killed.

Sources

1. Ann Scott, "The Role of Washington in Curbing Youth Violence," *Christian Science Monitor,* May 6, 1999, p. 2.
2. Harry F. Waters, "Networks under the Gun," *Newsweek,* July 12, 1993, pp. 64–66.
3. "Middle East Watch Report," *Middle East News Network,* Nov. 17, 1991.
4. "Singapore: Opening Up to a Little Sex and Nudity," *Inter Press Service,* Apr. 15, 1991.
5. Molly Moore, "Satellite TV Shows Asia a World beyond Reach of State Censors," *Washington Post,* Apr. 10, 1993, p. A12.
6. "Indonesia to Revamp Film Censorship," *Straits Times,* Apr. 29, 1993, p. 13.
7. Thomas Collins, "In China, the Carnage That Never Was," *Newsday,* June 14, 1989, p. 67.

Questions for Discussion

1. Research suggests an association between children's exposure to TV violence and the likelihood that they will resolve their own conflicts by violent means. Are we then justified in censoring TV violence?
2. Suppose censorship were imposed. How could we then measure the impact of censorship on rates of violent crime?

behavior, most of us examine the responses to our actions and modify our behavior as necessary to obtain favorable responses. If we are praised or rewarded for a behavior, we are likely to repeat it. If we are subjected to verbal or physical punishment, we are likely to refrain from such behavior. Our behavior in the first instance and our restraint in the second are said to be "reinforced" by the rewards and punishments we receive.

The psychologist Gerald Patterson and his colleagues examined how aggression is learned

With 15,577 fans watching, rookie Joe Thornton took on the 6-foot-2, 217-pound Canucks forward Dave Scatchard who just ran him into the boards near the penalty box after some words were exchanged. What was the reaction of the fans? Violent fights are the highlight of hockey games. Fans, young and old, cheered Thornton for standing up to Scatchard.

by direct experience. They observed that some passive children at play were repeatedly victimized by other children but were occasionally successful in curbing the attacks by counteraggression. Over time, these children learned defensive fighting, and eventually they initiated fights. Other passive children, who were rarely observed to be victimized, remained submissive.[23] Thus children, like adults, can learn to be aggressive and even violent by trial and error.

While violence and aggression are learned behaviors, they are not necessarily expressed until they are elicited in one of several ways. Albert Bandura describes the factors that elicit behavioral responses as "instigators." Thus social learning theory describes not only how aggression is acquired but also how it is instigated. Consider the following instigators of aggression:

- *Aversive instigators.* Physical assaults, verbal threats, and insults; adverse reductions in conditions of life (such as impoverishment) and the thwarting of goal-directed behavior.

- *Incentive instigators.* Rewards, such as money and praise.

- *Modeling instigators.* Violent or aggressive behaviors observed in others.

- *Instructional instigators.* Observations of people carrying out instructions to engage in violence or aggression.

- *Delusional instigators.* Unfounded or bizarre beliefs that violence is necessary or justified.[24]

Differential Reinforcement In 1965 the criminologist C. Ray Jeffery suggested that learning theory could be used to explain criminality.[25] Within one year Ernest Burgess and Ronald Akers combined Bandura's psychologically based learning theory with Edwin Sutherland's sociologically based differential association theory (Chapter 5) to produce the theory of **differential association-reinforcement.** This theory suggests that (1) the persistence of criminal behavior depends on whether or not it is rewarded or punished, and (2) the most meaningful rewards and punishments are those given by groups that are important in an individual's life—the peer group, the family, teachers in school, and so forth. In other words, people respond more readily to the reactions of the most significant people in their lives. If criminal behavior elicits more positive reinforcement or rewards than punishment, such behavior will persist.[26]

Social learning theory helps us understand why some individuals who engage in violent and aggressive behavior do so: They learn to behave that way. But perhaps something within the personality of a criminal creates a susceptibility to aggressive or violent models in the first place. For example, perhaps criminals are more extroverted, irresponsible, or unsocialized than noncriminals. Or perhaps criminals are more intolerant and impulsive or have lower self-esteem.

Personality

Four distinct lines of psychological research have examined the relation between personality and criminality.[27] First, investigators have looked at the differences between the personality structures of criminals and noncriminals. Most of this work has been carried out in state and federal prisons, where psychologists have administered personality questionnaires such as the Minnesota Multiphasic Personality Inventory (MMPI) and the California Psychological Inventory (CPI) to inmates. The evidence from these studies shows that inmates are typically more impulsive, hostile, self-centered, and immature than noncriminals.[28]

Second, a vast amount of literature is devoted to the prediction of behavior. Criminologists want to determine how an individual will respond to prison discipline and whether he or she will avoid crime after release. The results are equivocal. At best, personality characteristics seem to be modest predictors of future criminality.[29] Yet when they are combined with such variables as personal history, they tend to increase the power of prediction significantly.[30]

Third, many studies examine the degree to which normal personality dynamics operate in criminals. Findings from these studies suggest that the personality dynamics of criminals are often quite similar to those of noncriminals. Social criminals (those who act in concert with others), for example, are found to be more sociable, affiliative, outgoing, and self-confident than solitary criminals.[31]

Finally, some researchers have attempted to quantify individual differences between types and groups of offenders. Several studies have compared the personality characteristics of first-time offenders with those of repeat or habitual criminals. Other investigators have compared violent offenders with nonviolent offenders, and murderers with drug offenders. In addition, prison inmates have been classified according to personality type.[32]

In general, research on criminals' personality characteristics has revealed some important associations. However, criminologists have been skeptical of the strength of the relationship of personality to criminality. A review of research on that relationship published in 1942 by Milton Metfessel and Constance Lovell dismissed personality as an important causal factor in criminal behavior.[33] In 1950 Karl Schuessler and Donald Cressey reached the same conclusion.[34] Twenty-seven years later, Daniel Tennenbaum's updated review agreed with earlier assessments. He found that "the data do not reveal any significant differences between criminal and noncriminal psychology. . . . Personality testing has not differentiated criminals from noncriminals."[35]

Despite these conclusions, whether or not criminals share personality characteristics continues to be debated. Are criminals in fact more aggressive, dominant, and manipulative than noncriminals? Are they more irresponsible? Clearly, many criminals are aggressive; many have manipulated a variety of situations; many assume no responsibility for their acts. But are such characteristics common to all criminals? Samuel Yochelson and Stanton Samenow addressed these questions. In *The Criminal Personality,* this psychiatrist-psychologist team described their growing disillusion with traditional explanations of criminality.

From their experience in treating criminals in the Forensic Division of St. Elizabeth's Hospital in Washington, D.C., they refuted psychoanalysts' claims that crime is caused by inner conflict. Rather, they said, criminals share abnormal thinking patterns that lead to decisions to commit crimes. Yochelson and Samenow identified as many as 52 patterns of thinking common to the criminals they studied. They argued that criminals are angry people who feel a sense of superiority, expect not to be held accountable for their acts, and have a highly inflated self-image. Any perceived attack on their glorified self-image elicits a strong reaction, often a violent one.[36]

Other researchers have used different methods to study the association between criminality and personality. For example, criminologists have reviewed the findings of a large sample of studies that use the California Psychological Inventory. Their research revealed a common personality profile: The criminals tested showed remarkable similarity in their deficient self-control, intolerance, and lack of responsibility.[37]

Though studies dealing with personality correlates of criminals are important, some psychologists are concerned that by focusing on the personalities of criminals in their search for explanations of criminal behavior, investigators may overlook other important factors, like the complex social environment in which a crime is committed.[38] A homicide that began as a barroom argument between two intoxicated patrons who backed different teams to win the Super Bowl, for example, is very likely to hinge on situational factors that interact with the participants' personalities.

Eysenck's Conditioning Theory For over 20 years Hans J. Eysenck has been developing and refining a theory of the relationship between personality and criminality that considers more than just individual characteristics.[39] His theory has two parts. First, Eysenck claims that all human personality may be seen in three dimensions—psychoticism, extroversion, and neuroticism. Individuals who score high on measures of **psychoticism** are aggressive, egocentric, and impulsive. Those who score high on measures of **extroversion** are sensation-seeking, dominant, and assertive. High scorers on scales assessing **neuroticism** may be described as having low self-esteem, excessive

anxiety, and wide mood swings. Eysenck has found that when criminals respond to items on the Eysenck Personality Questionnaire (EPQ), they uniformly score higher on each of these dimensions than do noncriminals.

The second part of Eysenck's theory suggests that humans develop a conscience through **conditioning.** From birth, we are rewarded for social behavior and punished for asocial behavior. Eysenck likens this conditioning to training a dog. Puppies are not born house-trained. You have to teach a puppy that it is good to urinate and defecate outside your apartment or house by pairing kind words and perhaps some tangible reward (such as a dog treat) with successful outings. A loud, angry voice will convey disapproval and disappointment when mistakes are made inside.

In time most dogs learn and, according to Eysenck, develop a conscience. But as Eysenck also has noted, some dogs learn faster than others. German shepherds acquire good "bathroom habits" faster than basenjis, who are most difficult to train. It is argued that the same is true of humans; there are important individual differences. Criminals become conditioned slowly and appear to care little whether or not their asocial actions bring disapproval.

Eysenck has identified two additional aspects of a criminal's poor conditionability. First, he has found that extroverts are much more difficult to condition than introverts and thus have greater difficulty in developing a conscience. Youthful offenders tend to score highest on measures of extroversion. Second, differences in conditionability are dependent on certain physiological factors, the most important of which is **cortical arousal,** or activation of the cerebral cortex.

The cortex of the brain is responsible for higher intellectual functioning, information processing, and decision making. Eysenck found that individuals who are easily conditionable and develop a conscience have a high level of cortical arousal; they do not need intense external stimulation to become aroused. A low level of cortical arousal is associated with poor conditionability, difficulty in developing a conscience, and need for external stimulation.

MENTAL DISORDERS AND CRIME

It has been difficult for psychiatrists to derive criteria that would help them decide which offenders are mentally ill. According to psychiatrist Seymour L. Halleck, the problem lies in the evolving conceptualization of mental illness. Traditionally, the medical profession viewed mental illness as an absolute condition or status—either you are afflicted with **psychosis** or you are not. Should such a view concern us? Halleck suggests that it should. "Although this kind of thinking is not compatible with current psychiatric knowledge," he writes, "it continues to exert considerable influence upon psychiatric practice. . . . As applied to the criminal, it also leads to rigid dichotomies between the 'sick criminal' and the 'normal criminal.' "[40]

Halleck and other psychiatrists, such as Karl Menninger, conceptualize mental functioning as a process.[41] Mental illness should not be considered apart from mental health—the two exist on the same continuum. At various times in each of our lives we move along the continuum from health toward illness.[42] For this reason, a diagnosis of "criminal" or "mentally ill" may overlook potentially important gradations in mental health and mental illness. This issue is perhaps no more apparent than in the insanity defense, which calls for proof of sanity or insanity and generally does not allow for gradations in mental functioning (see Chapter 10).

Estimates vary, but between 20 and 60 percent of state correctional populations suffer from a type of mental disorder that in the nineteenth century was described by the French physician Philippe Pinel as *manie sans délire* ("madness without confusion"), by the English physician James C. Prichard as "moral insanity," and by Gina Lombroso Ferrero as "irresistible atavistic impulses." Today such mental illness is called **psychopathy,** sociopathy, or antisocial personality—a personality characterized by the inability to learn from experience, lack of warmth, and absence of guilt.

The psychiatrist Hervey Cleckley views psychopathy as a serious illness even though patients may not appear to be ill. According to

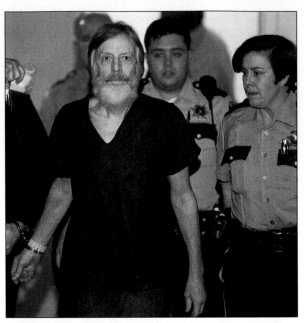

John Dupont, heir to the Dupont fortune, who imagined himself to be the Christ child, the Dali Lama, and the crown prince of Russia, killed the Olympic wrestler he had hired as a coach. Dupont was found guilty but mentally ill at trial and was sentenced to 13 to 30 years in prison.

Cleckley, psychopaths appear to enjoy excellent mental health; but what we see is only a "mask of sanity." Initially, they seem free of any kind of mental disorder and appear to be reliable and honest. After some time, however, it becomes clear that they have no sense of responsibility whatsoever. They show a disregard for truth, are insincere, and feel no sense of shame, guilt, or humiliation. Psychopaths lie and cheat without hesitation and engage in verbal as well as physical abuse without any thought. Cleckley describes the following case:

> A sixteen-year-old boy was sent to jail for stealing a valuable watch. Though apparently . . . untouched by his situation, after a few questions were asked he began to seem more like a child who feels the unpleasantness of his position. He confessed that he had worried much about masturbation, saying he had been threatened and punished severely for it and told that it would cause him to become "insane."
>
> He admitted having broken into his mother's jewelry box and stolen a watch valued at $150.00. He calmly related that he exchanged the watch for 15 cents' worth of ice cream and seemed entirely satisfied with what he had done. He readily

Criminologists who study the most famous connection between mental illness and crime—the insanity defense—have had little to say over the past 20 years. Empirical research on the number of cases where the defense has been raised provides few novel insights and findings.(1) Retentionists and abolitionists occasionally renew their calls.(2) The print and television media exploit efforts to raise the insanity defense in cases of unspeakable and senseless violence.(3) National, state, and local politicians join the fray with calls for legislative reform designed to limit the use of the insanity defense.(4) Americans recoil at the image of factually guilty offenders using a defense to criminal responsibility that allows for acquittal in the face of conclusive inculpatory evidence.(5) And, some say, we are all held prisoner by stereotypes and myths about the insanity defense.

It has been argued that the insanity defense is a prisoner of a host of myths and symbols rooted in medieval folklore and fundamentalist visions of mental illness and crime. These myths and symbols reveal our collective "punitive spirit" and "moralized aggression."(6) They reject the value of psychiatry and psychology, including psychodynamic explanations of human behavior.(7) The use of the insanity defense creates so much controversy because the public recognizes that in a few select cases the defense is necessary. At the same time, most people are convinced that in virtually all cases of criminal violence, some punishment is required and deserved. Reconciling the limited need for the defense with a strong desire for an exacting punishment is often too much of a challenge.

Myths about the insanity defense survive even though they are not grounded in scientific and behavioral evidence (see table). Unpacking these

Empirical Myths

Myth 1	The insanity defense is overused.
Myth 2	Use of the insanity defense is limited to murder cases.
Myth 3	There is no risk to the defendant who pleads insanity.
Myth 4	Not Guilty by Reason of Insanity (NGRI) acquittees are quickly released from custody.
Myth 5	NGRI acquittees spend much less time in custody than do defendants convicted of the same offenses.
Myth 6	Criminal defendants who plead insanity are usually faking.
Myth 7	Most insanity defense trials feature "battles of the experts."
Myth 8	Criminal defense attorneys—perhaps inappropriately—employ the insanity defense solely to "beat the rap."

myths reveals four common misconceptions:

1. That those claiming the insanity defense are feigning mental illness.
2. That mental illness is really different from other illness.
3. That a legally insane defendant must have a different "look" or appearance from one who is sane.
4. That mental illness should generally not permit an otherwise guilty person to escape punishment.(8)

Most of these myths persist because we harbor distorted assumptions about the legally insane.(9) Many are made more believable by the often distorted portrayal of the mentally ill offender on television and in the newspapers.

Sources

1. Perlin, *The Jurisprudence of the Insanity Defense*, 100–132 (1994).
2. See Morris, *Psychiatry and the Dangerous Criminal*, 41 S. Cal. L. Rev. 514 (1968); Morse, *Excusing the Crazy: The Insanity Defense Revisited*, 58 S. Cal. L. Rev. 777 (1985).
3. Id at 14–16.
4. Id at 96–97.
5. Perlin considers the *Hinkley* case as a paradigm for understanding public furor. See Perlin supra note 1 at 14–16.
6. Id at 29
7. Id at 444. According to Perlin: "Insanity defense decision making is often irrational. It rejects empiricism, science, psychology and philosophy, and substitutes myth, stereotype, bias and distortion." Id at 307.
8. Id at 232–233.
9. See Perlin, *Morality and Precon-textuality, Psychiatry and Law: Of "Ordinary Common Sense," Heuristic Reasoning, and Cognitive Dissonance*, 19 Bull. Am. Acad. Psychiatry & L. **131** (1991).

Questions for Discussion

1. Should mentally ill offenders remain in the criminal justice system? Should they stay in the general population, for example, at state correctional facilities?
2. Can you add any more myths to this list?
3. What is the source of the public's fascination with the insanity defense?

Kipland Kinkel and his family before he embarked on a shooting rampage in Springfield, Oregon, that killed his father, mother, and two students and wounded 25 others. Kinkel, who pleaded guilty to murder and attempted murder, was sentenced to 111 years imprisonment with no possibility of parole.

admitted that his act was wrong, used the proper words to express his intention to cause no further trouble, and, when asked, said that he would like very much to get out of jail.

He stated that he loved his mother devotedly. "I just kiss her and kiss her ten or twelve times when she comes to see me!" he exclaimed with shallow zeal. These manifestations of affection were so artificial, and, one would even say, unconsciously artificial, that few laymen would be convinced that any feeling, in the ordinary sense, lay in them. Nor was his mother convinced.

A few weeks before this boy was sent to jail he displayed to his mother some rifle cartridges. When asked what he wanted with them he explained that they would fit the rifle in a nearby closet. "I've tried them," he announced. And in a lively tone added, "Why, I could put them in the gun and shoot you. You would fall right over!" He laughed and his eyes shone with a small but real impulse.[43]

Psychologists also have found that psychopaths, like Hans Eysenck's extroverts, have a low internal arousal level; thus psychopaths constantly seek external stimulation, are less susceptible to learning by direct experience (they do not modify their behavior after they are punished), are more impulsive, and experience far less anxiety than nonpsychopaths about any adverse consequences of their acts.[44] Some psychiatrists consider "psychopathy" to be an artificial label for an antisocial personality.[45] To Eysenck and others, it is a major behavioral category that presents significant challenges. Eysenck sums up this view by writing that the psychopath poses the riddle of delinquency. If we could solve the riddle, then we would have a powerful weapon to fight the problem of delinquency.[46]

Crime Surfing

www.psych.org/public_info/INSANI~1.HTML

Interested in the insanity defense? Go to the American Psychiatric Association's website.

TABLE 4.3 Defenses Sometimes Attempted by Defense Lawyers

Defense	Description of Defense
The Twinkie defense (hypoglycemia—too much sugar)	Because he lost his job as a San Francisco supervisor, Dan White gorged on junk food—Twinkies, Coca-Cola, candy. Depressed, he sneaked a gun into City Hall. After killing Mayor Moscone, he killed a leader of the gay community, Supervisor Milk, in 1978.
Defendants or victims with multiple personalities	Many psychiatric experts agree that the disorder exists but disagree on how common it is. If a woman with multiple personalities complains of rape, the defendant might argue that consent to sex was given by one of the personalities. A defendant with multiple personalities might argue that he or she could not control the bad personality.
Sleepwalking and other forms of automatism (unconsciousness)	Automatism is a state in which a person is capable of action but is not conscious of what he or she is doing. This defense is statutorized in some states, including California, and held to be an affirmative defense separate from the insanity defense. *Fulcher v. State*, 633 P.2d 142, 29 CrL 2556 (Wyo. 1981)
Cultural disorientation	Some immigrants to the United States bring with them cultural practices that are in conflict with our criminal codes. For example, some continue the ancient traditions of the medicinal use of opium, the practice of capturing young brides, and the ritual slaughtering of animals. In 1985 when a young Japanese mother of two children learned that her husband was having an affair with another woman, she walked into the Pacific Ocean with her children to commit suicide (*oy ako shinju*). She was saved but the children drowned.
Premenstrual syndrome (PMS) and tension	PMS, a form of emotional and physical stress, afflicts some women before their monthly periods. In certain cases, such stress is so severe that it seriously disrupts the women's lives. In 1982, a British Appeal Court held that PMS could not be used as a defense to a criminal charge but could be used in mitigation to lessen sentences.
Television intoxication	In the 1978 case of *Zamora v. State*, 361 So.2d 776 (Fla. 1978), the defendant was convicted after arguing temporary insanity from "involuntary subliminal television intoxication."
XYY chromosome defense	Everyone has chromosomes. Some have either too few or too many, causing abnormalities. Some scientists believe that the abnormality of the supermale, or XYY in males, can cause such men to exhibit antisocial or criminal conduct. The XYY syndrome is not recognized as a defense unless the requirements of the insanity test of the state are met.

Source: Adapted from Thomas J. Gardner and Terry M. Anderson, *Criminal Law: Principles and Cases* (Belmont, Calif.: Wadsworth, 2000), pp. 100–101.

Psychological Causation

With all this discussion of possible psychological correlates of criminal behavior, it is easy to make what Stephen Morse calls the **fundamental psycholegal error.** This error in thinking or mistaken belief occurs when we identify a cause for criminal behavior and then assume that it naturally follows that any behavior resulting from that "cause" must be excused by law. Think about the kinds of defenses to criminal charges raised by lawyers and ask yourself whether Professor Morse is correct. (See Table 4.3.)

Consider, for example, the likelihood of psycholegal error in cases where lawyers have raised an insanity defense. Park Dietz, a highly regarded forensic psychiatrist, was interviewed recently and revealed just how easy it is to confuse the cause of criminal behavior with an appropriate and legally justifiable defense.

Interviewer: . . . Many defense attorneys argue that sick deeds are born in sick minds, and you have difficulty with that.

PD [Park Dietz]: With rare exceptions, people are responsible for what they do. Killers seldom meet the legal standard for insanity, which is quite different from the way most people use the word every day. Killers may be *disturbed*, but that doesn't necessarily mean that they can't tell right from wrong or are compelled to maim or murder.

Interviewer: But what about someone like Jeffrey Dahmer? People say, "If he wasn't crazy, who is?"

PD: He was certainly *disturbed*, but he knew what he was doing was wrong. He tried to conceal his victims' bodies. He also wore a condom while having sex with the corpses, which indicates that the intensity of his sexual urge was less than many teenagers experience in backseats with their girlfriends.

Interviewer: Still, doesn't that elude the bigger issue, his frame of reference? If I believe that little green men are descending from outer space and the only way to get rid of them is to sprinkle blue cheese on the lawn, and I go out and sprinkle cheese, that would be logical rational behavior given my overarching belief.

PD: And if that were a *crime,* you'd be insane for it.

Interviewer: But Dahmer doesn't fall into that category? It seems to me that while his separate actions may seem rational, he's operating under the idea that he can turn strangers into companions by killing and eating them. Why isn't that insane?

PD: If Dahmer had had the delusion that he'd have companions for life if he killed them and ate them, and that that was somehow a good thing and not *criminal,* that would make him insane. But those weren't the facts at all. Even the defense experts agreed that Dahmer knew it was wrong. In fact, Dahmer was so offended by the idea of killing that he had to get himself drunk to overcome his aversion to doing the killing. It's that point that proves that he did not have an irresistible impulse to kill.[47]

BIOLOGY AND CRIMINALITY

Within the last two decades, biologists have followed in the tradition of Cesare Lombroso, Raffaele Garofalo, and Charles Goring in their search for answers to questions about human behavior. Geneticists, for example, have argued that the predisposition to act violently or aggressively in certain situations may be inherited. In other words, while criminals are not born criminal, the predisposition to be violent or commit crime may be present at birth.

To demonstrate that certain traits are inherited, geneticists have studied

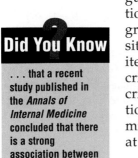

Did You Know

. . . that a recent study published in the *Annals of Internal Medicine* concluded that there is a strong association between low cholesterol levels and violence?

children born of criminals but reared from birth by noncriminal adoptive parents. They wanted to know whether the behavior of the adoptive children was more similar to that of their biological parents than to that of their adoptive parents. Their findings play an important role in the debate on heredity versus environment. Other biologists, sometimes called biocriminologists, take a different approach. Some ask whether brain damage or inadequate nutrition results in criminal behavior. Others are interested in the influence of hormones, chromosomal abnormalities, and allergies. They investigate interactions between brain and behavior, and between diet and behavior.

Modern Biocriminology

Biocriminology is the study of the physical aspects of psychological disorders.[48] It has been known for some time that adults who suffer from depression show abnormalities in brain waves during sleep, experience disturbed nervous system functioning, and display biochemical abnormalities. Research on depressed children reveals the same physical problems; furthermore, their adult relatives show high rates of depression as well. In fact, children whose parents suffer from depression are more than four times more likely than the average child to experience a similar illness.[49] Some researchers believe depression is an inherited condition that manifests itself in psychological and physical disturbances. The important point is that until only recently, physicians may have been missing the mark in their assessment and treatment of depressed children and adults by ignoring the physiological aspects.

Criminologists who study sociology and psychology to the exclusion of the biological sciences may also be missing the mark in their efforts to discover the causes of crime. Recent research has demonstrated that crime does indeed have psychobiological aspects similar to those found in studies of depression—biochemical abnormalities, abnormal brain waves, nervous system dysfunction. There is also evidence that strongly suggests a genetic predisposition to criminality.[50]

The resurgence of interest in integrating modern biological advances, theories, and principles into mainstream criminology began two decades ago. The sociobiological work of Edward Wilson on the interrelationship of biology, genetics, and social behavior was pivotal.[51] So were the contributions of C. Ray Jeffery, who argued that a biosocial interdisciplinary model should become the major theoretical framework for studying criminal behavior.[52]

Criminologists once again began to consider the possibility that there are indeed traits that predispose a person to criminality and that these traits may be passed from parent to child through the genes. Other questions arose as well. Is it possible, for instance, that internal biochemical imbalances or deficiencies cause antisocial behavior? Could too much or too little sugar in the bloodstream increase the potential for aggression? Or could a vitamin deficiency or some hormonal problem be responsible? We will explore the evidence for a genetic predisposition to criminal behavior, the relationship between biochemical factors and criminality, and neurophysiological factors that result in criminal behavior.

Genetics and Criminality

Today the proposition that human beings are products of an interaction between environmental and genetic factors is all but universally accepted.[53] We can stop asking, then, whether nature or nurture is more important in shaping us; we are the products of both. But what does the interaction between the two look like? And what concerns are raised by reliance on genetics to the exclusion of environmental factors? Consider the example of the XYY syndrome.

The XYY Syndrome Chromosomes are the basic structures that contain our genes—the biological material that makes each of us unique. Each human being has 23 pairs of inherited chromosomes. One pair determines gender. A female receives an X chromosome from both mother and father; a male receives an X chromosome from his mother and a Y from his father. Sometimes a defect in the pro-

duction of sperm or egg results in genetic abnormalities. One type of abnormality is the XYY chromosomal male. The XYY male receives two Y chromosomes from his father rather than one. Approximately 1 in 1000 newborn males in the general population has this genetic composition.[54] Initial studies done in the 1960s found the frequency of XYY chromosomes to be about 20 times greater than normal XY chromosomes among inmates in maximum-security state hospitals.[55] The XYY inmates tended to be tall, physically aggressive, and frequently, violent.

Supporters of these data claimed to have uncovered the mystery of violent criminality. Critics voiced concern over the fact that these studies were done on small and unrepresentative samples. The XYY syndrome, as this condition became known, received much public attention because of the case of Richard Speck. Speck, who in 1966 murdered eight nurses in Chicago, initially was diagnosed as an XYY chromosomal male. However, the diagnosis later turned out to be wrong. Nevertheless, public concern was aroused: Were all XYY males potential killers?

Studies undertaken since that time have discounted the relation between the extra Y chromosome and criminality.[56] Although convincing evidence in support of the XYY hypothesis appears to be slight, it is nevertheless possible that aggressive and violent behavior is at least partly determined by genetic factors. The problem is how to investigate this possibility. One difficulty is separating the external or environmental factors, such as family structure, culture, socioeconomic status, and peer influences, from the genetic predispositions with which they begin to interact at birth.

A particular individual may have a genetic predisposition to be violent but be born into a wealthy, well-educated, loving, and calm familial environment. He may never commit a violent act. Another person may have a genetic predisposition to be rule-abiding and nonaggressive yet be born into a poor, uneducated, physically abusive, and unloving family. He may commit violent criminal acts. How, then, can we determine the extent to which behavior is genetically

Separated at birth, the Mallifert twins meet accidentally.

influenced? Researchers have turned to twin studies and adoption studies in the quest for an answer.

Twin Studies To discover whether or not crime is genetically predetermined, researchers have compared identical and fraternal twins. Identical, or **monozygotic (MZ),** twins develop from a single fertilized egg that divides into two embryos. These twins share all their genes. Fraternal, or **dizygotic (DZ),** twins develop from two separate eggs, both fertilized at the same time. They share about half of their genes. Since the prenatal and postnatal family environments are, by and large, the same, greater behavioral similarity between identical twins than between fraternal twins would support an argument for genetic predisposition.

In the 1920s a German physician, Johannes Lange, found 30 pairs of same-sex twins—13 identical and 17 fraternal pairs. One member of each pair was a known criminal. Lange found that in 10 of the 13 pairs of identical twins, both twins were criminal; in 2 of the 17 pairs of fraternal twins, both were criminal.[57] The research techniques of the time were limited, but Lange's results were nevertheless impressive.

Many similar studies have followed. The largest was a study by Karl Christiansen and Sarnoff A. Mednick that included all twins born

between 1881 and 1910 in a region of Denmark, a total of 3586 pairs. Reviewing serious offenses only, Christiansen and Mednick found that the chance of there being a criminal twin when the other twin was a criminal was 50 percent for identical twins and 20 percent for same-sex fraternal twins.[58] Such findings lend support to the hypothesis that some genetic influences increase the risk of criminality.[59] A more recent American study conducted by David C. Rowe and D. Wayne Osgood reached a similar conclusion.[60]

While the evidence from these and other twin studies looks persuasive, we should keep in mind the weakness of such research. It may not be valid to assume a common environment for all twins who grow up in the same house at the same time. If the upbringing of identical twins is much more similar than that of fraternal twins, as it well may be, that circumstance could help explain their different rates of criminality.

Adoption Studies One way to separate the influence of inherited traits from that of environmental conditions would be to study infants separated at birth from their natural parents and placed randomly in foster homes. In such cases we could determine whether the behavior of the adopted child resembled that of the natural parents or that of the adoptive parents, and by how much. Children, however, are adopted at various ages and are not placed randomly in foster homes. Most such children are matched to their foster or adoptive parents by racial and religious criteria. And couples who adopt children may differ in some important ways from other couples. Despite such shortcomings, adoption studies do help us expand our knowledge of genetic influences on human variation.

The largest adoption study conducted so far was based on a sample of 14,427 male and female adoptions in Denmark between 1924 and 1947. The hypothesis was that criminality in the biological parents would be associated with an increased risk of criminal behavior in the child. The parents were considered criminal if either the mother or the father had been convicted of a felony. The researchers had sufficient information on more than 4000 of the male children to assess whether or not both the biological and the adoptive parents had criminal records. Mednick and his associates reported the following findings:

- Of boys whose adoptive and biological parents had no criminal record, 13.5 percent were convicted of crimes.

- Of boys who had criminal adoptive parents and noncriminal biological parents, 14.7 percent were convicted of crimes.

- Of boys who had noncriminal adoptive parents and criminal biological parents, 20 percent were convicted of crimes.

- Of boys who had both criminal adoptive parents and criminal biological parents, 24.5 percent were convicted of crimes.[61]

These findings support the claim that the criminality of the biological parents has more influence on the child than does that of the adoptive parents. Other research on adopted children has reached similar conclusions. A major Swedish study examined 862 adopted males and 913 adopted females. The researchers found a genetic predisposition to criminality in both sexes, but an even stronger one in females. An American study of children who were put up for adoption by a group of convicted mothers supports the Danish and Swedish findings on the significance of genetic factors.[62]

Results of adoption studies have been characterized as "highly suggestive" or "supportive" of a genetic link to criminality. But how solid is this link? There are significant problems with adoption studies. One is that little can be done to ensure the similarity of adopted children's environments. Of even greater concern to criminologists, however, is the distinct possibility of mistaking correlation for causation. In other words, there appears to be a significant correlation between the criminality of biological parents and adopted children in the research we have reviewed, but this correlation does not prove that the genetic legacy passed on by a criminal parent causes an offspring to commit a crime.

So far, research has failed to shed any light on the nature of the biological link that results in the association between the criminality of parents and that of their children. Furthermore, even if we could identify children with a higher-than-average probability of committing offenses as adults on the basis of their parents' behavior, it is unclear what we could do

to prevent these children from following the parental model.

The Controversy over Violence and Genes

At the same time that advances in research on the biological bases of violence shed new light on crime, attacks on such research are calling its usefulness into question. Government-sponsored research plans have been called racist, a conference on genetics and crime was canceled after protests, and a session on violence and heredity at a recent American Association for the Advancement of Science meeting became "a politically correct critique of the research."[63]

Few involved in such research expect to find a "violence gene"; rather, researchers are looking for a biological basis for some of the behaviors associated with violence. As one explanation put it:

> Scientists are . . . trying to find inborn personality traits that might make people more physically aggressive. The tendency to be a thrill seeker may be one such characteristic. So might "a restless impulsiveness, an inability to defer gratification." A high threshold for anxiety or fear may be another key trait. . . . such people tend to have a "special biology," with lower-than-average heart rates and blood pressure.[64]

No one yet has found any direct link between genes and violence. In fact, Sarnoff Mednick, the psychologist who conducted adoption studies of criminal behavior in Denmark, found no evidence for the inheritance of violence. "If there were any genetic effect for violent crimes, we would have picked it up," says Mednick, whose study included 14,427 men.

The controversy over a genetic basis for violent behavior seems to deal less with actual research findings than with the implications of such findings. For example, Harvard psychologist Jerome Kagan predicts that in 25 years biological and genetic tests will make it possible to identify the 15 children in every 1000 who may have violent tendencies. Of those 15, only 1 will actually become violent. The ethical question, then, is what to do with this knowledge. "Do we tell the mothers of all 15 that their kids might be violent?" he asks. "How are the mothers then going to react to their children if we do that?"[65]

A recent National Academy of Science (NAS) report on violence recommended finding better ways to intervene in the development of children who could become violent, and it listed risk factors statistically linked to violence: hyperactivity, poor early grades, low IQ, fearlessness, and an inability to defer gratification, for example.[66]

What frightens those opposed to biological and genetic research into the causes of violence is the thought of how such research could be used by policy makers. If a violent personality can be shown to be genetically determined, crime-prevention strategies might try to identify "potential criminals" and to intervene before their criminal careers begin and before anyone knows if they would ever have become criminals. "Should genetic markers one day be found for tendencies . . . that are loosely linked to crime," explains one researcher, "they would probably have little specificity, sensitivity or explanatory power: most people with the markers will not be criminals and most criminals will not have the markers."[67] On the other hand, when environment—poverty, broken homes, and other problems—is seen as the major cause of violence, crime prevention takes the shape of improving social conditions rather than labeling individuals.

A middle-of-the-road approach is proposed by those who see biological research as a key to helping criminals change their behavior. "Once you find a biological basis for a behavior, you can try to find out how to help people cope," says one such scholar. "Suppose the link is impulsivity, an inability to defer gratification. It might be you could design education programs to teach criminals to readjust their time horizon."[68]

The IQ Debate

A discussion of the association between genes and criminality would be incomplete without paying at least some attention to the debate over IQ and crime. Is an inferior intelligence inherited, and if so, how do we account for the strong relationship between IQ and criminality?

The Research Background   Nearly a century ago scientists began to search for measures to determine people's intelligence, which they believed to be genetically determined. The first test to gain acceptance was developed by a French psychologist, Alfred Binet. Binet's test measured the capacity of individual children to perform tasks or solve problems in relation to the average capacity of their peers.

Between 1888 and 1915, several researchers administered intelligence tests to incarcerated criminals and to boys in reform schools. Initial studies of the relationship between IQ and crime revealed some surprising results. The psychologist Hugo Munsterberg estimated that 68 percent of the criminals that he tested were of low IQ. Using the Binet scale, Henry H. Goddard found that between 25 and 50 percent of criminals had low IQs.[69] What could account for such different results?

Edwin Sutherland observed that the tests were poor and there were too many variations among the many versions administered. He reasoned that social and environmental factors caused delinquency, not low IQ.[70] In the 1950s the psychologist Robert H. Gault added to Sutherland's criticism. He noted particularly that it was "strange that it did not occur immediately to the pioneers that they had examined only a small sample of caught and convicted offenders."[71]

For more than a generation the question about the relationship between IQ and criminal behavior was not studied, and the early inconsistencies remained unresolved. Then in the late 1970s the debate resumed.[72] Supporters of the view that inheritance determines intelligence once again began to present their arguments. The psychologist Arthur Jensen suggested that race was a key factor in IQ differences; Richard J. Herrnstein, a geneticist, pointed to social class as a factor.[73] Both positions spurred a heated debate in which criminologists soon became involved. In 1977 Travis Hirschi and Michael Hindelang evaluated the existing literature on IQ and crime.[74] They cited the following three studies as especially important:

- Travis Hirschi, on the basis of a study of 3600 California students, demonstrated that the effect of a low IQ on delinquent behavior is more significant than that of the father's education.[75]

- Marvin Wolfgang and associates, after studying 8700 Philadelphia boys, found a strong relation between low IQ and delinquency, independent of social class.[76]

- Albert Reiss and Albert L. Rhodes, after an examination of the juvenile court records of 9200 white Tennessee schoolboys, found IQ to be more closely related to delinquency than is social class.[77]

Hirschi and Hindelang concluded that IQ is an even more important factor in predicting crime than is either race or social class. They found significant differences in intelligence between criminal and noncriminal populations within like racial and socioeconomic groups. A lower IQ increases the potential for crime within each group. Furthermore, they found that IQ is related to school performance. A low IQ ultimately results in a youngster's associating with similar nonperformers, dropping out of school, and committing delinquent acts. Hirschi and Hindelang's findings were confirmed by James Q. Wilson and Richard Herrnstein but rejected by criminologist Deborah Denno, who conducted a prospective investigation of 800 children from birth to age 17.[78] Her results failed to confirm a direct relationship between IQ and delinquency.

The Debate: Genetics or Environment?
The debate over the relationship between IQ and crime has its roots in the controversy over whether intelligence is genetically or environmentally determined. IQ tests, many people believe, measure cultural factors rather than the innate biological makeup of an individual.[79] Studies by psychologists Sandra Scarr and Richard Weinberg of black and white adopted children confirmed that environment plays a significant role in IQ development. They found that both black and white children adopted by white parents had comparable IQs and performed similarly.[80] With evidence of cultural bias and environmental influence, why not abandon the use of intelligence tests? The answer is simple: They do predict performance in school and so have significant utility. It appears that this debate will be with us for a long time to come.

Biochemical Factors
Biocriminologists' primary focus has been on the relationship between criminality and bio-

chemical and neurophysical factors. Biochemical factors include food allergies, diet, hypoglycemia, and hormones. Neurophysical factors include brain lesions, brain wave abnormalities, and minimal brain dysfunction.

Food Allergies In 1993, by the time Rachel was 2 years old, she displayed a pattern of behavior that went way beyond the "terrible twos." Without warning, her eyes would glaze over, her speech would develop a lisp, and she'd kick and hit and thrash about wildly until her mother swaddled her tightly and she fell asleep, exhausted. She even developed a "kitty-cat" routine, complete with meowing, stalking, and growling, that often went on for hours.

When Rachel's sister Emma was born later that year, she nursed poorly and never slept through the night. After their mother introduced baby corn into her diet, Emma experienced severe intestinal distress, for which she was hospitalized. After a battery of medical tests proved inconclusive, she was sent home, but the symptoms continued intermittently, without apparent reason.

The following year, in desperation, their mother had Rachel and Emma, then 3 years and 15 months, tested for food allergies. Both showed marked sensitivity to corn, wheat, sugar, preservatives, and dairy products. After those foods were eliminated, Emma's health and well-being improved, and Rachel's perplexing and worrisome behavior all but disappeared.[81]

Over the last decade researchers have investigated the relation between food allergies, aggression, and antisocial behavior. In fact, since 1908 there have been numerous medical reports indicating that various foods cause such reactions as irritability, hyperactivity, seizures, agitation, and behavior that is "out of character."[82] Investigators have identified the following food components as substances that may result in severe allergic reactions:

Phenylethylamine (found in chocolate).
Tyramine (found in aged cheese and wine).
Monosodium glutamate (used as a flavor enhancer in many foods).
Aspartame (found in artificial sweeteners).
Xanthines (found in caffeine).

Each of these food components has been associated with behavioral disorders, including criminality.

Diet

- Susan had been charged with 16 offenses, including criminal damage, solvent abuse, and vehicle theft, by the time she was 13. She had no friends, showed no affection toward her parents, and frequently hit her mother. Her schoolwork deteriorated, and she played truant most days. After 6 months on a changed diet, which excluded burgers, bananas, and chocolate, the number of her offenses dropped to zero. And for the first time since she was a young child, Susan gave her mother a hug.

- Craig, 15, vandalized his home several times and committed numerous petty crimes. He was a bully and was virtually impossible to teach. And his 8-year-old brother was beginning to follow in his footsteps. Both were put on a special diet, cutting out fizzy drinks and sweets, and including more green vegetables and fresh fruit. Within months, says their mother, both were more pleasant and easier to deal with. But Craig has since quit the diet and has reoffended. The bullying and the violence have started again.

- Graham, an 11-year-old, turned from an uncontrollable delinquent into a normal, pleasant boy when pizzas, baked beans, and chocolate in his diet were replaced by fresh vegetables, coconut milk, and carrots. He became less aggressive and argumentative and, reportedly, was "happy" for the first time in his life. Graham's schoolwork improved, and he began to make friends.

Anecdotal reports, in addition to more scientific investigations, link criminality to diets high in sugar and carbohydrates, to vitamin deficiency or dependency, and to excessive food additives.

Criminologist Stephen Schoenthaler conducted a series of studies on the relation between sugar and the behavior of institutionalized offenders. In these investigations inmates were placed on a modified diet that included very little sugar. They received fruit juice in place of soda and vegetables instead of candy. Schoenthaler found fewer disciplinary actions and a significant drop in aggressive behavior in the experimental group.[83] Some individuals charged with crimes have used this finding to build a defense like that of Dan White.

In 1979, San Francisco city supervisor Dan White was on trial for the murder of his fellow supervisor, Harvey Milk, and Mayor George Moscone. White defended himself with testimony on the impact of sugar on his behavior. The testimony showed that when White was depressed, he departed from his normal, healthy diet and resorted to high-sugar junk food, including Twinkies, Coca-Cola, and chocolates. Thereafter, his behavior became less and less controllable. The jury found White guilty of manslaughter, rather than murder, due to diminished capacity. White served 5 years in prison and committed suicide after his release. His defense was promptly dubbed the "junk-food defense," "Dan White's defense," or the "Twinkie defense."

Most subsequent attempts to use the junk-food defense have failed. In a 1989 Ohio case (*Johnson*), it was ruled that the defense may not be used to establish diminished capacity. In 1990, a Cape Cod man was unsuccessful when he defended himself on a charge of stealing (and eating) 300 candy bars (*Callanan*). Nor did this defense (Twinkie and soda pop) succeed in a murder case in Ohio (*McDonald*, 1988). But in a 1987 Florida case, a defendant (*Rosenthal*) was acquitted of drunk-driving charges on evidence that consumption of chocolate mousse after half a glass of sherry caused an unusual blood sugar reaction.

Other researchers have looked for the causes of crime in vitamin deficiencies. One such study found that 70 percent of criminals charged with serious offenses in one Canadian jurisdiction had a greater-than-normal need for vitamin B_6.[84] Other studies have noted deficiencies of vitamins B_3 and B_6 in criminal population samples.

Some investigators have examined the effects of food additives and food dyes on behavior. Benjamin Feingold has argued that between 30 and 60 percent of all hyperactivity in children may be attributable to reactions to food coloring.[85] There is additional support for this hypothesis.[86] Some studies have suggested that a diet deficient in protein may be responsible for violent aggression.

Let us look at the association between the consumption of tryptophan, an amino acid (a protein building block), and crime rates. Tryptophan is a normal component of many foods. Low levels of it have been associated with aggression and, in criminal studies, an increased sensitivity to electric shock. Anthony R. Mawson and K. W. Jacobs reasoned that diets low in tryptophan would be likely to result in higher levels of violent crime, particularly violent offenses such as homicide.

They hypothesized that because corn-based diets are deficient in tryptophan, a cross-national comparison of countries should reveal a positive relationship between corn consumption and homicide rates. Mawson and Jacobs obtained homicide data from the United Nations and the mean per capita corn intake rates of 53 foreign countries from the U.S. Department of Agriculture. They discovered that countries whose per capita rates of corn consumption were above the median had significantly higher homicide rates than countries whose diets were based on wheat or rice.[87]

Hypoglycemia What prompted an otherwise loving father to throw his 20-month-old daughter into a nearby lake? Neighbors knew that something was amiss when they noticed 22-year-old Joe Holt climb on the roof of his duplex in a quiet Orlando suburb. Joe then proceeded to dance, touching power lines in the course of his pantomime. No one sounded the alarm, however, until he disappeared into his lakeside apartment, returning momentarily with his daughter Ashley in his arms. The police arrived on the scene to find Joe in a state of agitation and Ashley facedown in Lake Apopka. Seated in the back of a squad car, handcuffed, the bewildered Joe had no recollection of the preceding events. When his blood was tested, he had a glucose level of 20 milligrams per deciliter of blood. The average is 80 to 120 milligrams. Joe was suffering from severe hypoglycemia. According to a sheriff's

spokesman, "He had virtually no thought process."[88]

Hypoglycemia is a condition that occurs when the level of sugar in the blood falls below an acceptable range. The brain is particularly vulnerable to hypoglycemia, and such a condition can impair its function. Symptoms of hypoglycemia include anxiety, headache, confusion, fatigue, and even aggressive behavior. As early as 1943, researchers linked the condition with violent crime, including murder, rape, and assault. Subsequent studies found that violent and impulsive male offenders had a higher rate of hypoglycemia than noncriminal controls.

Consider the work of Matti Virkkunen, who has conducted a series of studies of habitually violent and psychopathic offenders in Finland. In one such study done in the 1980s he examined the results of a glucose tolerance test (used to determine whether hypoglycemia is present) administered to 37 habitually violent offenders with antisocial personalities, 31 habitually violent offenders with intermittent explosive disorders, and 20 controls. The offenders were found to be significantly more hypoglycemic than the controls.[89]

Hormones Experiments have shown that male animals are typically more aggressive than females. Male aggression is directly linked to male hormones. If an aggressive male mouse is injected with female hormones, he will stop fighting.[90] Likewise, the administration of male hormones to pregnant monkeys results in female offspring who, even 3 years after birth, are more aggressive than the daughters of noninjected mothers.[91]

While it would be misleading to equate male hormones with aggression and female hormones with nonaggression, there is some evidence that abnormal levels of male hormones in humans may prompt criminal behavior. Several investigators have found higher levels of testosterone (the male hormone) in the blood of individuals who have committed violent offenses.[92] Some studies also relate premenstrual syndrome (PMS) to delinquency and conclude that women are at greater risk of aggressive and suicidal behavior before and during the menstrual period. After studying 156 newly admitted adult female prisoners, Katherina Dalton concluded that 49 percent of all their crimes were committed either in the premenstrual period or during menstruation.[93] Recently, however, critics have challenged the association between menstrual distress and female crime.[94]

Neurophysiological Factors

In England in the mid-1950s, a father hit his son with a mallet and then threw him out of a window, killing him instantly. Instead of pleading insanity, as many people expected him to do, he presented evidence of a brain tumor, which, he argued, resulted in uncontrollable rage and violence. A jury acquitted him on the grounds that the brain tumor had deprived him of any control over and knowledge of the act he was committing.[95] Brain lesions or brain tumors have led to violent outbursts in many similar cases. Neurophysiological studies, however, have not focused exclusively on brain tumors; they have included a wide range of investigations: MRI studies of cerebral structure, brain wave studies, clinical reports of minimal brain dysfunction, and theoretical explorations into the relationship between the limbic system and criminality.[96]

EEG Abnormalities   Sam recalled that his wife Janet looked slightly different and that the house smelled funny and he felt out of sorts. During an intimate moment in bed Janet made a funny remark, after which Sam flew into a rage, choked her, and slashed her throat. When he came to his senses, he immediately went to the police and admitted to the crime, although he had little memory of his violent acts. Can EEG tracings explain the behavior of this young U.S. Marine who had returned home on leave? Subsequent tracings were found to be abnormal—indicative of an "intermittent explosive disorder." After reviewing this evidence, the court reduced Sam's charges from first-degree murder to manslaughter.

The EEG (electroencephalogram) is a tracing made by an instrument that measures cerebral functioning by recording brain wave activity with electrodes placed on the scalp. Numerous studies that have examined the brain activity of violent prisoners reveal significant differences between the EEGs of criminals and those of noncriminals. Other findings relate significantly slow brain wave activity to young offenders and adult murderers.[97] When Sarnoff A. Mednick and his colleagues examined the criminal records and EEGs of 265 children in a birth cohort in Denmark, they found that certain types of brain wave activity, as measured by the EEG, enabled investigators to predict whether convicted thieves would steal again.[98]

When Jan Volavka compared the EEGs of juvenile delinquents with those of comparable nondelinquents, he found a slowing of brain waves in the delinquent sample, most prominently in those children convicted of theft. He concluded that thievery "is more likely to develop in persons who have a slowing of alpha frequency than in persons who do not."[99]

Minimal Brain Dysfunction.   Minimal brain dysfunction (MBD) is classified as "attention deficit hyperactivity disorder."[100] MBD produces such asocial behavioral patterns as impulsivity, hyperactivity, aggressiveness, low self-esteem, and temper outbursts. The syndrome is noteworthy for at least two reasons. First, MBD may explain criminality when social theories fail to do so—that is, when neighborhood, peer, and familial associations do not suggest a high risk of delinquency. Second, MBD is an easily overlooked diagnosis. Parents, teachers, and clinicians tend to focus more on the symptoms of a child's psychopathology than on the possibility of brain dysfunction, even though investigators have repeatedly found high rates of brain dysfunction in samples of suicidal adolescents and youthful offenders.[101]

CRIME AND HUMAN NATURE

The criminologist Edward Sagarin has written:

> In criminology, it appears that a number of views . . . have become increasingly delicate and sensitive, as if all those who espouse them were inherently evil, or at least stupidly insensitive to the consequences of their research. . . . In the study of crime, the examples of unpopular orientations are many. Foremost is the link of crime to the factors of genes, biology, race, ethnicity, and religion.[102]

Criticisms of Biocriminology

What is it about linking biology and criminality that makes the subject delicate and sensitive? Why is the concept so offensive to so many people? One reason is that biocriminologists deny the existence of individual free will. The idea of predisposition to commit crimes fosters a sense of hopelessness. But this criticism seems to have little merit. As Diana H. Fishbein has aptly noted, the idea of a "conditioned free will" is widely accepted.[103] This view suggests that individuals make choices in regard to a particular action within a range of possibilities that is "preset" yet flexible. When conditions permit rational thought, one is fully accountable and responsible for one's actions. It is only when conditions are somehow disturbed that free choice is constricted. The child of middle-class parents who has a low IQ might avoid delinquent behavior. But if that child's circumstances changed so that he lived in a lower-class, single-parent environment, he might find the delinquent lifestyle of the children in the new neighborhood too tempting to resist.

Critics have other concerns as well. Some see a racist undertone to biocriminological research. If there is a genetic predisposition to commit crime and if minorities account for a disproportionate share of criminal activity, are minorities then predisposed to commit crime? In Chapter 2 we learned that self-reports reveal that most people have engaged in delinquent or criminal behavior. How, then, do biocriminologists justify their claim that certain groups are more prone than others to criminal behavior? Could it be that the subjects of their investigations are only criminals who have been caught and incarcerated? And is the attention of the police disproportionately drawn to members of minority groups?

How do biocriminologists account for the fact that most criminologists see the structure of our society, the decay of our neighborhoods, and the subcultures of certain areas as determinants of criminality? Are biocriminologists unfairly deemphasizing social and economic factors? (In Chapters 5 through 9 we review theories that attribute criminality to group and environmental forces.)

These issues raise a further question that is at the core of all social and behavioral science: Is human behavior the product of nature (genetics) or nurture (environment)? The consensus among social and behavioral scientists today is that the interaction of nature and nurture is so pervasive that the two cannot be viewed in isolation.

Supporters of biocriminology also maintain that recognizing a predisposition to crime is not inconsistent with considering environmental factors. In fact, some believe that predispositions are triggered by environmental factors. Even if we agree that some people are predisposed to commit crime, we know that the crime rate would be higher in areas that provide more triggers. In sum, while some people may be predisposed to certain kinds of behavior, most scientists agree that both psychological and environmental factors shape the final forms of those behaviors.

An Integrated Theory

In recent years the debate has found a new forum in integrated biocriminological theories, such as the one proposed by James Q. Wilson and Richard Herrnstein. These scholars explain predatory street crime by showing how human nature develops from the interplay of psychological, biological, and social factors. It is the interaction of genes with environment that in some individuals forms the kind of personality likely to commit crimes. The argument takes into account such factors as IQ, body build, genetic makeup, impulsiveness, ability to delay gratification, aggressiveness, and even the drinking and smoking habits of pregnant mothers.

According to Wilson and Herrnstein, the choice between crime and conventional behavior is closely linked to individual biological and psychological traits and to such social factors as family and school experiences. Their conclusion is that "the offender offends not just because of immediate needs and circumstances, but also because of enduring personal characteristics, some of whose traces can be found in his behavior from early childhood on."[104] In essence, they argue that behavior results from a person's perception of the potential rewards and/or punishments that go along with a criminal act. If the potential reward (such as money) is greater than the expected punishment (say, a small fine), the chance that a crime will be committed increases.

REVIEW

When psychologists have attempted to explain criminality, they have taken four general approaches. First, they have focused on failures in psychological development—an overbearing or weak conscience, inner conflict, insufficient moral development, and maternal deprivation, with its concomitant failure of attachment. Second, they have investigated the ways in which aggression and violence are learned through modeling and direct experience. Third, they have investigated the personality characteristics of criminals and found that criminals tend to be more impulsive, intolerant, and irresponsible than noncriminals. Fourth, psychologists have investigated the relation of criminality to such mental disorders as psychosis and psychopathy.

Biocriminologists investigate the biological correlates of criminality, including a genetic predisposition to commit crime. The XYY syndrome, though now generally discounted as a cause of criminality, suggests that aggressive and violent behavior may be at least partly determined by genetic factors. Studies of the behavior of identical and fraternal twins and of the rates of criminality among adopted children with both criminal and noncriminal biological and adoptive parents tend to support this hypothesis. Investigators have also found a strong correlation between low IQ and delinquency. Criminologists are still debating what public policy issues are raised by the possible role of genetics in crime.

Biocriminologists' most recent and perhaps most important discovery is the relation of criminal behavior to biochemical factors (food allergies, dietary deficiencies, hormonal imbalances) and neurophysiological factors (EEG abnormalities and minimal brain dysfunction). Most scientists agree that if some people are biologically predisposed to certain behaviors, both psychological and environmental factors shape the forms of those behaviors.

YOU BE THE CRIMINOLOGIST

For many years psychologists searched for the criminal personality, a common set of personality characteristics associated with criminals. If you were asked to assist in this effort, what methods would you use to capture the criminal personality? Would you use objective personality inventories? If you were successful, what would you do with your findings? How could this common personality profile be used in the criminal justice system?

KEY TERMS

The numbers next to the terms refer to the pages on which the terms are defined.

attachment (89)

behavioral modeling (92)

biocriminology (104)

chromosomes (105)

conditioning (99)

cortical arousal (99)

differential association-reinforcement (97)

dizygotic (DZ) twins (106)

ego (87)

extroversion (99)

fundamental psycholegal error (103)

hypoglycemia (111)

id (87)

minimal brain dysfunction (MBD) (112)

monozygotic (MZ) twins (106)

neuroticism (99)

psychoanalytic theory (87)

psychopathy (100)

psychosis (100)

psychoticism (99)

social learning theory (92)

superego (87)

NOTES

1. See Ronald Blackburn, *The Psychology of Criminal Conduct: Theory, Research, and Practice* (Chichester, England: Wiley, 1993); and Hans Toch, *Violent Men: An Inquiry into the Psychology of Violence*, rev. ed. (Washington, D.C.: American Psychological Association, 1992).
2. See, e.g., Cathy Spatz Widom, "Cycle of Violence," *Science*, **244** (1989): 160–165; and Nathaniel J. Pallone and J. J. Hennessey, *Criminal Behavior: A Process Psychology Analysis* (New Brunswick, N.J.: Transaction, 1992).

3. See, e.g., Sigmund Freud, *A General Intro-duction to Psychoanalysis* (New York: Liv-eright, 1920); and Sigmund Freud, *The Ego and the Id* (London: Hogarth, 1927).

4. August Aichhorn, *Wayward Youth* (New York: Viking, 1935).

5. Kate Friedlander, *The Psycho-Analytic Approach to Juvenile Delinquency* (New York: International Universities Press, 1947).

6. See Hans Eysenck, *The Rise and Fall of the Freudian Empire* (New York: Plenum, 1987).

7. Lawrence Kohlberg, "The Development of Modes of Moral Thinking and Choice in the Years Ten to Sixteen," Ph.D. dissertation, University of Chicago, 1958.

8. Lawrence Kohlberg, "Stage and Sequence: The Cognitive-Developmental Approach to Socialization," in *Handbook of Socialization Theory and Research*, ed. David A. Goslin (Chicago: Rand McNally, 1969).

9. Carol Gilligan has studied moral development in women—extending Kohlberg's role-taking theory of moral development. She found that moral reasoning differed in women. Women, according to Gilligan, see morality as the responsibility to take the view of others and to ensure their well-being. See Carol Gilligan, *In a Different Voice: Psychological Theory and Women's Development* (Cambridge, Mass.: Harvard University Press, 1982).

10. William S. Jennings, Robert Kilkenny, and Lawrence Kohlberg, "Moral Development Theory and Practice for Youthful Offenders," in *Personality Theory, Moral Development, and Criminal Behavior*, ed. William S. Laufer and James M. Day (Lexington, Mass.: Lexington Books, 1983). See also Daniel D. Macphail, "The Moral Education Approach in Treating Adult Inmates," *Criminal Justice and Behavior*, **15** (1989): 81–97; Jack Arbuthnot and Donald A. Gordon, "Crime and Cognition: Community Applications of Sociomoral Reasoning Development," *Criminal Justice and Behavior*, **15** (1988): 379–393; and J. E. LeCapitaine, "The Relationships between Emotional Development and Moral Development and the Differential Impact of Three Psychological Interventions on Children," *Psychology in the Schools*, **15** (1987): 379–393.

11. John Bowlby, *Attachment and Loss*, 2 vols. (New York: Basic Books, 1969, 1973). See also Bowlby's "Forty-Four Juvenile Thieves: Their Characteristics and Home Life," *International Journal of Psychoanalysis*, **25** (1944): 19–52.

12. John Bowlby, *The Making and Breaking of Affectional Bonds* (London: Tavistock, 1979). See also Michael Rutter, *Maternal Deprivation Reassessed* (Harmondsworth, England: Penguin, 1971).

13. Michael Lewis, Candice Feiring, Carolyn McGuffog, and John Jaskir, "Predicting Psychopathology in Six-Year-Olds from Early Social Relations," *Child Development*, **55** (1984): 123–136.

14. L. Sroufe, "Infant Caregiver Attachment and Patterns of Adaptation in Preschool: The Roots of Maladaption and Competence," in *Minnesota Symposium on Child Psychology*, vol. 16, ed. Marion Perlmutter (Hillsdale, N.J.: Erlbaum, 1982).

15. Alicia F. Lieberman, "Preschoolers' Competence with a Peer: Influence of Attachment and Social Experience," *Child Development*, **48** (1977): 1277–1287.

16. Joan McCord, "Some Child-Rearing Antecedents of Criminal Behavior," *Journal of Personality and Social Psychology*, **37** (1979): 1477–1486; Joan McCord, "A Longitudinal View of the Relationship between Paternal Absence and Crime," in *Abnormal Offenders, Delinquency, and the Criminal Justice System*, ed. John Gunn and David P. Farrington (London: Wiley, 1982). See also Scott W. Henggeler, Cindy L. Hanson, Charles M. Borduin, Sylvia M. Watson, and Molly A. Brunk, "Mother-Son Relationships of Juvenile Felons," *Journal of Consulting and Clinical Psychology*, **53** (1985): 942–943; and Francis I. Nye, *Family Relationships and Delinquent Behavior* (New York: Wiley, 1958).

17. Sheldon Glueck and Eleanor T. Glueck, *Unraveling Juvenile Delinquency* (New York: Commonwealth Fund, 1950); Lee N. Robins, "Aetiological Implications in Studies of Childhood Histories Relating to Antisocial Personality," in *Psychopathic Behaviour*, ed. Robert D. Hare and Daisy Schalling (Chichester, England: Wiley, 1970); Lee N.

Review • You Be the Criminologist • Key Terms • Notes

Robins, *Deviant Children Grow Up* (Baltimore: Williams & Wilkins, 1966).

18. Joan McCord, "Instigation and Insulation: How Families Affect Antisocial Aggression," in *Development of Antisocial and Prosocial Behavior: Research Theories and Issues,* ed. Dan Olweus, Jack Block, and M. Radke-Yarrow (London: Academic Press, 1986).

19. Albert Bandura, *Aggression: A Social Learning Analysis* (Englewood Cliffs, N.J.: Prentice-Hall, 1973); Albert Bandura, "The Social Learning Perspective: Mechanism of Aggression," in *Psychology of Crime and Criminal Justice,* ed. Hans Toch (New York: Holt, Rinehart & Winston, 1979).

20. Leonard D. Eron and L. Rowell Huesmann, "Parent-Child Interaction, Television Violence, and Aggression of Children," *American Psychologist,* **37** (1982): 197–211; Russell G. Geen, "Aggression and Television Violence," in *Aggression: Theoretical and Empirical Reviews,* vol. 2, ed. Russell G. Geen and Edward I. Donnerstein (New York: Academic Press, 1983).

21. Leonard D. Eron and L. Rowell Huesmann, "The Control of Aggressive Behavior by Changes in Attitudes, Values, and the Conditions of Learning," in *Advances in the Study of Aggression,* vol. 1, ed. Robert J. Blanchard and D. Caroline Blanchard (Orlando, Fla.: Academic Press, 1984).

22. *National Television Violence Study: Executive Summary* 1994–1995 (Studio City, Calif.: Mediascope, 1996); O. Wiegman, M. Kuttschreuter, and B. Baarda, "A Longitudinal Study of the Effects of Television Viewing on Aggressive and Prosocial Behaviors," *British Journal of Social Psychology,* **31** (1992): 147–164; B. S. Centerwall, "Television and Violence: The Scale of the Problem and Where to Go from Here," *Journal of the American Medical Association,* **267** (1992): 3059–3063; J. E. Ledingham, C. A. Ledingham, and John E. Richardson, *The Effects of Media Violence on Children* (Ottawa, Canada: National Clearinghouse on Family Violence, Health and Welfare, 1993); M. I. Tulloch, M. L. Prendergast, and M. D. Anglin, "Evaluating Aggression: School Students' Responses to Television Portrayals of Institutionalized Violence," *Journal of Youth and Adolescence,* **24** (1995): 95–115.

23. See Gerald R. Patterson, R. A. Littman, and W. Brickler, *Assertive Behavior in Children: A Step toward a Theory of Aggression,* monograph of the Society for Research in Child Development, no. 32 (1976).

24. Bandura, *Aggression.*

25. C. Ray Jeffery, "Criminal Behavior and Learning Theory," *Journal of Criminal Law, Criminology and Police Science,* **56** (1965): 294–300.

26. Ernest L. Burgess and Ronald L. Akers, "A Differential Association-Reinforcement Theory of Criminal Behavior," *Social Problems,* **14** (1966): 128–147. See also Reed Adams, "Differential Association and Learning Principles Revisited," *Social Problems,* **20** (1973): 458–470.

27. See D. W. Andrews and J. Stephen Wormith, "Personality and Crime: Knowledge Destruction and Construction in Criminology," *Justice Quarterly,* **6** (1989): 149–160.

28. William S. Laufer, Dagna K. Skoog, and James M. Day, "Personality and Criminality: A Review of the California Psychological Inventory," *Journal of Clinical Psychology,* **38** (1982): 562–573.

29. Richard E. Tremblay, "The Prediction of Delinquent Behavior from Childhood Behavior: Personality Theory Revisited," in *Facts, Frameworks, and Forecasts: Advances in Criminological Theory,* vol. 3, ed. J. McCord (New Brunswick, N.J.: Transaction, 1992).

30. Michael L. Gearing, "The MMPI as a Primary Differentiator and Predictor of Behavior in Prison: A Methodological Critique and Review of the Recent Literature," *Psychological Bulletin,* **36** (1979): 929–963.

31. Edwin I. Megargee and Martin J. Bohn, *Classifying Criminal Offenders* (Beverly Hills, Calif.: Sage, 1979); William S. Laufer, John A. Johnson, and Robert Hogan, "Ego Control and Criminal Behavior," *Journal of Personality and Social Psychology,* **41** (1981): 179–184; Edwin I. Megargee, "Psychological Determinants and Correlates of Criminal Violence," in *Criminal Violence,* ed. Marvin E. Wolfgang and Neil A. Weiner (Beverly Hills, Calif.: Sage, 1982); Edwin I. Megargee, "The Role of

Inhibition in the Assessment and Understanding of Violence," in *Current Topics in Clinical and Community Psychology*, ed. Charles Donald Spielberger (New York: Academic Press, 1971); Edwin I. Megargee, "Undercontrol and Overcontrol in Assaultive and Homicidal Adolescents," Ph.D. dissertation, University of California, Berkeley, 1964; Edwin I. Megargee, "Undercontrolled and Overcontrolled Personality Types in Extreme Antisocial Aggression," *Psychological Monographs*, **80** (1966); Edwin I. Megargee and Gerald A. Mendelsohn, "A Cross-Validation of Twelve MMPI Indices of Hostility and Control," *Journal of Abnormal and Social Psychology*, **65** (1962): 431–438.

32. See, e.g., William S. Laufer and James M. Day, eds., *Personality Theory, Moral Development, and Criminal Behavior* (Lexington, Mass.: Lexington Books, 1983).

33. Milton Metfessel and Constance Lovell, "Recent Literature on Individual Correlates of Crime," *Psychological Bulletin*, **39** (1942): 133–164.

34. Karl E. Schuessler and Donald R. Cressey, "Personality Characteristics of Criminals," *American Journal of Sociology*, **55** (1950): 476–484.

35. Daniel J. Tennenbaum, "Personality and Criminality: A Summary and Implications of the Literature," *Journal of Criminal Justice*, **5** (1977): 225–235. See also G. P. Waldo and Simon Dinitz, "Personality Attributes of the Criminal: An Analysis of Research Studies, 1950–1965," *Journal of Research in Crime and Delinquency*, **4** (1967): 185–202; and R. D. Martin and D. G. Fischer, "Personality Factors in Juvenile Delinquency: A Review of the Literature," *Catalog of Selected Documents in Psychology*, vol. 8 (1978), ms. 1759.

36. Samuel Yochelson and Stanton Samenow, *The Criminal Personality* (New York: Jason Aronson, 1976).

37. Laufer et al., "Personality and Criminality"; Harrison G. Gough and Pamela Bradley, "Delinquent and Criminal Behavior as Assessed by the Revised California Psychological Inventory," *Journal of Clinical Psychology*, **48** (1991): 298–308.

38. See Anne Campbell and John J. Gibbs, eds., *Violent Transactions: The Limits of Personality* (Oxford: Basil Blackwell, 1986); Lawrence A. Pervin, "Personality: Current Controversies, Issues, and Direction," *Annual Review of Psychology*, **36** (1985): 83–114; and Lawrence A. Pervin, "Persons, Situations, Interactions: Perspectives on a Recurrent Issue," in Campbell and Gibbs, *Violent Transactions*.

39. See Hans J. Eysenck, *Crime and Personality* (London: Routledge & Kegan Paul, 1977); H. J. Eysenck, "Personality and Crime: Where Do We Stand?" *Psychology, Crime and Law*, **2** (1996): 143–152; Hans J. Eysenck, "Personality, Conditioning, and Antisocial Behavior," in Laufer and Day, *Personality Theory*; Hans J. Eysenck, "Personality and Criminality: A Dispositional Analysis," in *Advances in Criminological Theory*, vol. 1, ed. William S. Laufer and Freda Adler (New Brunswick, N.J.: Transaction, 1989); and Hans J. Eysenck and Gisli H. Gudjonsson, *The Causes and Cures of Crime* (New York: Plenum, 1990).

40. Seymour L. Halleck, *Psychiatry and the Dilemmas of Crime* (New York: Harper & Row, 1967); Nicholas N. Kittrie, *The Right to Be Different: Deviance and Enforced Therapy* (Baltimore, Md.: Johns Hopkins Press, 1971).

41. Karl Menninger, *The Crime of Punishment* (New York: Viking, 1968).

42. See Daniel L. Davis et al., "Prevalence of Emotional Disorders in a Juvenile Justice Institutional Population," *American Journal of Forensic Psychology*, **9** (1991): 5–17.

43. Hervey Cleckley, *The Mask of Sanity*, 5/e (St. Louis: Mosby, 1976), pp. 271–272.

44. Ibid., p. 57; Robert D. Hare, *Psychopathy: Theory and Research* (New York: Wiley, 1970); M. Philip Feldman, *Criminal Behavior: A Psychological Analysis* (New York: Wiley, 1978); William McCord and Joan McCord, *Psychopathy and Delinquency* (New York: Wiley, 1956).

45. *The American Psychiatric Association's Diagnostic and Statistical Manual of Mental Disorders*, 3d rev. ed. (DSM III-R) (Washington, D.C., 1987), classifies psychopathy as "antisocial personality." See Benjamin Karpman, "On the Need of Separating Psychopathy into Two Distinct Clinical Types: The Symp-

tomatic and the Idiopathic," *Journal of Criminal Psychopathology*, **3** (1941): 112–137.

46. Eysenck and Gudjonnson, *The Causes and Cures of Crime*. See also Robert D. Hare, "Research Scale for the Assessment of Psychopathology in Criminal Populations," *Personality and Individual Differences*, **1** (1980): 111–119.

47. Anastasia Toufexis, "Dancing with Devils: Forensic Psychiatrist Park Dietz Tracks America's Serial Killers, Bombers and Mass Murderers," *Psychology Today*, **32**(3) (May 1999) p. 54.

48. See, generally, A. J. Reiss, Jr., K. A. Klaus, and J. A. Roth, eds., *Biobehavioral Influences:* vol. 2, *Understanding and Preventing Violence* (Washington, D.C.: National Academy Press, 1994); M. Hillbrand and N. J. Pallone, "The Psychobiology of Aggression: Engines, Measurement, Control," *Journal of Offender Rehabilitation*, **21** (1994): 1–243; J. T. Tedeschi and R. B. Felson, *Violence, Aggression, and Coercive Actions* (Washington, D.C.: American Psychological Association, 1994).

49. J. Puig-Antich, "Biological Factors in Prepubertal Major Depression," *Pediatric Annals*, **12** (1986): 867–878.

50. See, e.g., Guenther Knoblich and Roy King, "Biological Correlates of Criminal Behavior," in McCord, *Facts, Frameworks, and Forecasts;* Diana H. Fishbein, "Biological Perspectives in Criminology," *Criminology*, **28** (1990): 17–40; David Magnusson, Britt af Klinteberg, and Hakan Stattin, "Autonomic Activity/Reactivity, Behavior, and Crime in a Longitudinal Perspective," in McCord, *Facts, Frameworks, and Forecasts;* Frank A. Elliott, "Violence: The Neurologic Contribution: An Overview," *Archives of Neurology*, **49** (1992): 595–603; L. French, "Neuropsychology of Violence," *Corrective and Social Psychiatry and Journal of Behavior Technology Methods and Therapy*, **37** (1991): 12–17; and Elizabeth Kandel and Sarnoff A. Mednick, "Perinatal Complications Predict Violent Offending," *Criminology*, **29** (1991): 519–530.

51. Edward O. Wilson, *Sociobiology: The New Synthesis* (Cambridge, Mass.: Harvard University Press, 1975).

52. C. Ray Jeffery, *Biology and Crime* (Beverly Hills, Calif.: Sage, 1979).

53. P. A. Brennan and S. A. Mednick, "Genetic Perspectives on Crime," *Acta Psychiatria Scandinavia*, **370** (1993): 19–26.

54. See Sarnoff A. Mednick, Terrie E. Moffitt, and Susan A. Stack, *The Causes of Crime: New Biological Approaches* (New York: Cambridge University Press, 1987).

55. A. A. Sandberg, G. F. Koepf, and T. Ishihara, "An XYY Human Male," *Lancet* (August 1961): 488–489.

56. Herman A. Witkin et al., "Criminality, Aggression, and Intelligence among XYY and XXY Men," in *Biosocial Bases of Criminal Behavior*, ed. Sarnoff A. Mednick and Karl O. Christiansen (New York: Wiley, 1977).

57. Johannes Lange, *Verbrechen als Schicksal* (Leipzig: Georg Thieme, 1929).

58. Cf. Gregory Carey, "Twin Imitation for Antisocial Behavior: Implications for Genetic Environment Research," *Journal of Abnormal Psychology*, **101** (1992): 18–25.

59. See Karl O. Christiansen, "A Preliminary Study of Criminality among Twins," in Mednick and Christiansen, *Biosocial Bases of Criminal Behavior.*

60. David C. Rowe and D. Wayne Osgood, "Heredity and Sociological Theories of Delinquency: A Reconsideration," *American Sociological Review*, **49** (1986): 526–540; David C. Rowe, "Genetic and Environmental Components of Antisocial Behavior: A Study of 256 Twin Pairs," *Criminology*, **24** (1986): 513–532.

61. Sarnoff A. Mednick, William Gabrielli, and Barry Hutchings, "Genetic Influences in Criminal Behavior: Evidence from an Adoption Court," in *Prospective Studies of Crime and Delinquency*, ed. K. Teilmann et al. (Boston: Kluwer-Nijhoff, 1983).

62. These and other studies are reviewed in Mednick et al., *The Causes of Crime.*

63. Hannah Bloch and Dick Thompson, "Seeking the Roots of Violence," *Time*, Apr. 19, 1993, pp. 52–53.

64. Daniel Goleman, "New Storm Brews on Whether Crime Has Roots in Genes," *New York Times*, Sept. 15, 1992, p. C1.

65. Hannah Bloch and Dick Thompson, "*Seeking the Roots of Violence.*"

66. Fox Butterfield, "Study Cites Biology's Role in Violent Behavior," *New York Times*, Nov. 13, 1992, p. A7.
67. Goleman, "New Storm Brews on Whether Crime Has Roots in Genes."
68. Ibid.
69. Hugo Munsterberg, *On the Witness Stand* (New York: Doubleday, 1908); Henry H. Goddard, *Feeble-Mindedness: Its Causes and Consequences* (New York: Macmillan, 1914).
70. Edwin H. Sutherland, "Mental Deficiency and Crime," in *Social Attitudes*, ed. K. Young (New York: Henry Holt, 1931).
71. Robert H. Gault, "Highlights of Forty Years in the Correctional Field—and Looking Ahead," *Federal Probation*, **17** (1953): 3–4.
72. Arthur Jensen, *Bias in Mental Testing* (New York: Free Press, 1979).
73. Ibid.; Richard J. Herrnstein, *IQ in the Meritocracy* (Boston: Atlantic–Little, Brown, 1973).
74. Travis Hirschi and Michael J. Hindelang, "Intelligence and Delinquency: A Revisionist Review," *American Sociological Review*, **42** (1977): 571–586.
75. Travis Hirschi, *Causes of Delinquency* (Berkeley: University of California Press, 1969).
76. Marvin E. Wolfgang, Robert F. Figlio, and Thorsten Sellin, *Delinquency in a Birth Cohort* (Chicago: University of Chicago Press, 1972).
77. Albert J. Reiss and Albert L. Rhodes, "The Distribution of Juvenile Delinquency in the Social Class Structure," *American Sociological Review*, **26** (1961): 720–732.
78. James Q. Wilson and Richard Herrnstein, *Crime and Human Nature* (New York: Simon & Schuster, 1985); Deborah W. Denno, "Sociological and Human Developmental Explanations of Crime: Conflict or Consensus?" *Criminology*, **23** (1985): 711–740. See also Deborah W. Denno, "Victim, Offender, and Situational Characteristics of Violent Crime," *Journal of Criminal Law and Criminology*, **77** (1986): 1142–1158.
79. "Taking the Chitling Test," *Newsweek*, July 15, 1968.
80. Sandra Scarr and Richard Weinberg, "I.Q. Test Performance of Black Children Adopted by White Families," *American Psychologist*, **31** (1976): 726–739.
81. See Doris J. Rapp, *Allergies and the Hyperactive Child* (New York: Simon & Schuster, 1981).
82. Diana H. Fishbein and Susan Pease, "The Effects of Diet on Behavior: Implications for Criminology and Corrections," *Research on Corrections*, **1** (1988): 1–45.
83. Stephen Schoenthaler, "Diet and Crime: An Empirical Examination of the Value of Nutrition in the Control and Treatment of Incarcerated Juvenile Offenders," *International Journal of Biosocial Research*, **4** (1982): 25–39.
84. Heather M. Little, "Food May Be Causing Kids' Problems," *Chicago Tribune*, Oct. 29, 1995, p. 1; Abram Hoffer, "The Relation of Crime to Nutrition," *Humanist in Canada*, **8** (1975): 2–9.
85. Benjamin F. Feingold, *Why Is Your Child Hyperactive?* (New York: Random House, 1975).
86. James W. Swanson and Marcel Kinsbourne, "Food Dyes Impair Performance of Hyperactive Children on a Laboratory Test," *Science*, **207** (1980): 1485–1487.
87. Anthony R. Mawson and K. W. Jacobs, "Corn Consumption, Tryptophan, and Cross-National Homicide Rates," *Journal of Orthomolecular Psychiatry*, **7** (1978): 227–230.
88. "Toddler Dies after Being Thrown in Lake by Dad in Diabetic Seizure," *Chicago Tribune*, July 10, 1995, p. 9.
89. Matti Virkkunen, "Insulin Secretion during the Glucose Tolerance Test among Habitually Violent and Impulsive Offenders," *Aggressive Behavior*, **12** (1986): 303–310.
90. E. A. Beeman, "The Effect of Male Hormones on Aggressive Behavior in Mice," *Physiological Zoology*, **20** (1947): 373–405.
91. D. A. Hamburg and D. T. Lunde, "Sex Hormones in the Development of Sex Differences," in *The Development of Sex Differences*, ed. Eleanor E. Maccoby (Stanford, Calif.: Stanford University Press, 1966).
92. A. Booth and D. W. Osgood, "The Influence of Testosterone on Deviance in Adulthood: Assessing and Explaining the Relationship," *Criminology*, **31** (1993): 93–117; L. E. Kreuz and R. M. Rose, "Assessment of Aggressive Behavior and Plasma Testosterone

Review • You Be the Criminologist • Key Terms • Notes

of a Young Criminal Population," *Psychosomatic Medicine,* **34** (1972): 321–332; R. T. Rada, D. R. Laws, and R. Kellner, "Plasma Testosterone Levels in the Rapist," *Psychosomatic Medicine,* **38** (1976): 257–268.

93. Katharina Dalton, *The Premenstrual Syndrome* (Springfield, Ill.: Charles C Thomas, 1971).

94. Julie Horney, "Menstrual Cycles and Criminal Responsibility," *Law and Human Behavior,* **2** (1978): 25–36.

95. *Regina v. Charlson,* 1 A11. E.R. 859 (1955).

96. L. P. Chesterman et al., "Multiple Measures of Cerebral State in Dangerous Mentally Disordered Inpatients," *Criminal Behavior and Mental Health,* **4** (1994): 228–239; Lee Ellis, "Monoamine Oxidase and Criminality: Identifying an Apparent Biological Marker for Antisocial Behavior," *Journal of Research in Crime and Delinquency,* **28** (1991): 227–251.

97. H. Forssman and T. S. Frey, "Electroencephalograms of Boys with Behavior Disorders," *Acta Psychologica et Neurologia Scandinavica,* **28** (1953): 61–73; H. de Baudouin et al., "Study of a Population of 97 Confined Murderers," *Annales Medico-Psychologique,* **119** (1961): 625–686.

98. Sarnoff A. Mednick, Jan Volavka, William F. Gabrielli, and Turan M. Itil, "EEG as a Predictor of Antisocial Behavior," *Criminology,* **19** (1981): 219–229.

99. Jan Volavka, "Electroencephalogram among Criminals," in Mednick et al., *The Causes of Crime.* See also J. Volavka, *Neurobiology of Violence* (Washington, D.C.: American Psychiatric Press, 1995).

100. DSM III-R, 314.01. See also Michael Rutter, "Syndromes Attributed to 'Minimal Brain Dysfunction' in Children," *American Journal of Psychiatry,* **139** (1980): 21–33.

101. Lorne T. Yeudall, D. Fromm-Auch, and P. Davies, "Neuropsychological Impairment of Persistent Delinquency," *Journal of Nervous and Mental Disorders,* **170** (1982): 257–265; R. D. Robin et al., "Adolescents Who Attempt Suicide," *Journal of Pediatrics,* **90** (1977): 636–638.

102. Edward Sagarin, "Taboo Subjects and Taboo Viewpoints in Criminology," in *Taboos in Criminology,* ed. Sagarin (Beverly Hills, Calif.: Sage, 1980), pp. 8–9.

103. Diana H. Fishbein, "Biological Perspectives in Criminology," *Criminology,* **28** (1990): 27–40.

104. Wilson and Herrnstein, *Crime and Human Nature.* Infants develop attachment to mothers, or mother substitutes, for comfort, security, and warmth.

CHAPTER 5
Strain and Cultural Deviance Theories

The early decades of the twentieth century brought major changes to American society. One of the most significant was the change in the composition of the populations of cities. Between 1840 and 1924, 45 million people—Irish, Swedes, Germans, Italians, Poles, Armenians, Bohemians, Russians—left the Old World; two-thirds of them were bound for the United States.[1] At the same time, increased mechanization in this country deprived many American farmworkers of their jobs and forced them to join the ranks of the foreign-born and the black laborers who had migrated from the South to northern and midwestern industrial centers. During the 1920s large U.S. cities swelled with 5 million new arrivals.[2]

Chicago's expansion was particularly remarkable: Its population doubled in 20 years. Many of the new arrivals brought nothing with them except what they could carry. The city offered them only meager wages, 12-hour working days in conditions that jeopardized their health, and tenement housing in deteriorating areas. Chicago had other problems as well: In the late 1920s and early 1930s it was the home of major organized crime groups, which fought over the profits from the illegal production and sale of liquor during Prohibition (as we shall see in Chapter 13).

Teeming with newcomers looking for work, corrupt politicians trying to buy their votes, and bootleggers growing more influential through sheer firepower and the political strength they controlled, Chicago also had a rapidly rising crime rate. The city soon became an inviting urban laboratory for criminologists, who began to challenge the then-predominant theories of crime causation, which were based on biological and psychological factors. Many of these criminologists were associated with the University of Chicago, which has the oldest sociology program in the United States (begun in 1892). By the 1920s these criminologists began to measure scientifically the amount of criminal behavior and its relation to the social turmoil Chicago was experiencing. Since that time, sociological theories have remained at the forefront of the scientific investigation of crime causation. **123**

THE INTERCONNECTEDNESS OF SOCIOLOGICAL THEORIES

The psychological and biological theories of criminal behavior (Chapter 4) share the assumption that such behavior is caused by some underlying physical or mental condition that separates the criminal from the noncriminal. They seek to identify the kind of person who becomes a criminal and to find the factors that caused the person to engage in criminal behavior. These theories yield insight into individual cases, but they do not explain why crime rates vary from one neighborhood to the next, from group to group, within large urban areas, or within groups of individuals. Sociological theories seek the reasons for differences in crime rates in the social environment. These theories can be grouped into three general categories: strain, cultural deviance, and social control.[3]

The strain and cultural deviance theories formulated between 1925 and 1940, and still popular today, focus on the social forces that cause people to engage in criminal activity. These theories laid the foundation for the subcultural theories we discuss in Chapter 6. Social control theories (Chapter 7) take a different approach: They are based on the assumption that the motivation to commit crime is part of human nature. Consequently, social control theories seek to discover why people do not commit crime. They examine the ability of social groups and institutions to make their rules effective.

Strain and cultural deviance theories both assume that social class and criminal behavior are related, but they differ about the nature of the relationship. **Strain theory** argues that all members of society subscribe to one set of cultural values—that of the middle class. One of the most important middle-class values is economic success. Since lower-class persons do not have legitimate means to reach this goal, they turn to illegitimate means in desperation. **Cultural deviance theories** claim that lower-class people have a different set of values, which tend to conflict with the values of the middle class. Consequently, when lower-class persons conform to their own value system, they may be violating conventional or middle-class norms.

ANOMIE: ÉMILE DURKHEIM

Imagine a clock with all its parts finely synchronized. It functions with precision. It keeps perfect time. But if one tiny weight or small spring breaks down, the whole mechanism will not function properly. One way of studying a society is to look at its component parts in an effort to find out how they relate to each other. In other words, we look at the structure of a society to see how it functions. If the society is stable, its parts operating smoothly, the social arrangements are functional. Such a society is marked by cohesion, cooperation, and consensus. But if the component parts are arranged in such a way as to threaten the social order, the arrangements are said to be dysfunctional. In a class-oriented society, for example, the classes tend to be in conflict.

The Structural-Functionalist Perspective

The structural-functionalist perspective was developed by Émile Durkheim (1858–1917) before the end of the nineteenth century.[4] At the time, positivist biological theories, which relied on the search for individual differences between criminals and noncriminals, were dominant. So at a time when science was searching for the abnormality of the criminal, Durkheim was writing about the normality of crime in society. To him, the explanation of human conduct, and indeed human misconduct, lies not in the individual but in the group and the social organization. It is in this context that he introduced the term "anomie," the breakdown of social order as a result of the loss of standards and values.[5]

Throughout his career, Durkheim was preoccupied with the effects of social change. He believed that when a simple society develops into a modern, urbanized one, the intimacy needed to sustain a common set of norms declines. Groups become fragmented, and in the absence of a common set of rules, the actions and expectations of people in one sector may clash with those of people in another. As behavior becomes unpredictable, the system gradually breaks down, and the society is in a state of anomie.

Anomie and Suicide

Durkheim illustrated his concept of anomie in a discussion, not of crime, but of suicide.[6] He suggested several reasons why suicide was more common in some groups than in others. For our purposes, we are interested in the particular form of suicide he called "anomic suicide." When he analyzed statistical data, he found that suicide rates increased during times of sudden economic change, whether that change was major depression or unexpected prosperity. In periods of rapid change people are abruptly thrown into unfamiliar situations. Rules that once guided behavior no longer hold.

Consider the events of the 1920s. Wealth came easily to many people in those heady, prosperous years. Toward the end, through July, August, and September 1929, the New York stock market soared to new heights. Enormous profits were made from speculation. But on October 24, 1929, a day history records as Black Thursday, the stock market crashed. Thirteen million shares of stock were sold. As more and more shares were offered for sale, their value plummeted. In the wake of the crash, a severe depression overtook the country and then the world. Banks failed. Mortgages were foreclosed. Businesses went bankrupt. People lost their jobs. Lifestyles changed overnight. Many people were driven to sell apples on street corners to survive, and they had to stand in mile-long breadlines to get food to feed their families. Suddenly the norms by which people lived were no longer relevant. People became disoriented and confused. Suicide rates rose.

It is not difficult to understand rising suicide rates in such circumstances, but why would rates also rise at a time of sudden prosperity? According to Durkheim, the same factors are at work in both situations. What causes the problems is not the amount of money available but the sudden change. Durkheim believed that human desires are boundless, an "insatiable and bottomless abyss."[7] Since nature does not set such strict biological limits on the capabilities of humans as it does on those of other animals, he argued, we have developed social rules that put a realistic cap on our aspirations.

These regulations are incorporated into the individual conscience and thus make it possible for people to feel fulfilled.

But with a sudden burst of prosperity, expectations change. When the old rules no longer determine how rewards are distributed among members of society, there is no longer any restraint on what people want. Once again the system breaks down. Thus, whether sudden change causes great prosperity or great depression, the result is the same—anomie.

STRAIN THEORY

A few generations after Durkheim, the American sociologist Robert Merton (1910–) also related the crime problem to anomie. But his conception differs somewhat from Durkheim's. The real problem, Merton argued, is created not by sudden social change but by a social structure that holds out the same goals to all its members without giving them equal means to achieve them. This lack of integration between what the culture calls for and what the structure permits, the former encouraging success and the latter preventing it, can cause norms to break down because they no longer are effective guides to behavior.

Merton borrowed the term "anomie" from Durkheim to describe this breakdown of the normative system. According to Merton:

> It is only when a system of cultural values extols, virtually above all else, certain common symbols of success for the population at large while its social structure rigorously restricts or completely eliminates access to approved modes of acquiring these symbols for a considerable part of the same population, that antisocial behavior ensues on a considerable scale.[8]

From this perspective, the social structure is the root of the crime problem (hence the approach Merton takes is sometimes called a *structural explanation*). "Strain theory," the name given by contemporary criminologists to Merton's explanation of criminal behavior, assumes that people are law-abiding but when under great pressure will resort to crime. Disparity between goals and means provides that pressure.

The American anthropologist Kenneth Good committed—for anthropologists—the unpardonable sin of marrying a young woman of the tribe he studied, the Yanomamö. The young bride returned with her husband to suburban New Jersey in 1988, and there they raised their children.(1) But in 1993 the Yanomamö wife slipped back into the Amazon jungle to live among her own people.

Who are the Yanomamö?

When another anthropologist Robert Carneiro went to the Amazon jungle in 1975 to study the Yanomamö, he found them to be a remote, stone-age, people dedicated to frequent intervillage warfare.(2)

Indeed, the Yanomamö are the last major remaining Stone Age people on earth, living their lives in harmony with nature, but also engaging in tribal warfare, according to their customs.

But all went awry in the 1980s, when gold was discovered in the Yanomamö territory.(3) As many as 40,000 prospectors had invaded by 1987, clearing the jungle for airstrips, bringing diseases—venereal and others—against which the Yanomamö had no immunity, importing modern weapons to replace Stone Age clubs, and raising the homicide rate.(4) What once was a nation of 100,000 was reduced to 22,000 (9400 in Brazil; 12,600 in Venezuela). A severe drought in the late 1990s added to the suffering of the Yanomamös, who use ancient incantations to bring rain as well as to quench forest fires and to drive out invaders.(2)

Help is under way and more is promised. The United Nations sent an emergency team of firefighters to deal with the forest fires. The Brazilian government clamped down on encroachments by rogue miners. The U.S. Congress

A Yanomamö man with the trappings of modern civilization.

made some assistance available to protect the rain forests, but did not designate preservation of the Yanomamö territory and lifestyle a priority.

Too little, too late? The Yanomamö's traditional way of life has broken down. The chances that they can withstand the attack of the Western culture invasion are slim. The large deposits of gold, diamonds, tin, and other minerals in the soil of their land will continue to attract invaders, with their attack on the traditional culture. Yanomamös are dying faster than ever before, hunting and fishing are increasingly difficult, alcohol and prostitution are taking their toll, firearms are escalating the death rate, and infant mortality is 24 times that of the United States.(5)

What are we to do about the Yanomamö? It does not seem possible to transplant Yanomamö into suburban

New Jersey. Forcing modern capitalism on them is even more destructive.

Should we just build a fence around the Yanomamö territory and allow them to live their accustomed lifestyle? The spectre of an entrepreneur flying in tourists in jumbo jets and charging admission to view "unspoiled," stone-aged Yanomamö is just too daunting.

Are we witnessing a genocide in the making?

Are you wondering about the Yanomamö wife? Well, you can see her adorned with tribal decoration in a photo at the American Museum of Natural History, Amazon exhibit.

Sources

1. Kenneth Good with David Chernoff, *Into the Heart* (New York: Simon and Schuster, 1991).
2. Robert L. Carneiro, "War and Peace: Alternating Realities in Human History," in *Studying War—Anthropological Perspectives,* ed. S. P. Reyns and R. E. Downs (City: Gordon and Bresch, 1994), pp. 3–27.
3. Lynne Wallis, "Quiet Genocide: Miners Seeking Precious Metals Are Causing Deaths of the Yanomami," *Ottawa Citizen,* June 28, 1993, p. A6.
4. "Aid for an Ancient Tribe," *Newsweek,* Apr. 9, 1990, p. 34.
5. "Genocide in the Amazon," *Newsweek,* Aug. 30, 1993, p. 61.

Questions for Discussion

1. As the Yanomamö culture is being destroyed, how would you expect the tribe's traditional ways of dealing with crime to be affected? Explain.
2. What measures might be effective in protecting indigenous peoples in all parts of the world from suffering a fate similar to that of the Yanomamö?

Merton's Theory of Anomie

Merton argued that in a class-oriented society, opportunities to get to the top are not equally distributed. Very few members of the lower class ever get there. His anomie theory emphasizes the importance of two elements in any society: (1) cultural aspirations, or goals that people believe are worth striving for, and (2) institutionalized means or accepted ways to attain the desired ends. If a society is to be stable, these two elements must be reasonably well integrated; in other words, there should be means for individuals to reach the goals that are important to them. Disparity between goals and means fosters frustration, which leads to strain.

Merton's theory explains crime in the United States in terms of the wide disparities in income among the various classes. Statistics clearly demonstrate that such disparities exist. American families had a median income of $44,568 in 1997. While 12 percent of all families had incomes of $100,000 or more, 10 percent were below the federal government's official poverty level—$16,400 for a family of four. Eleven percent of whites, 26 percent of blacks, and 27 percent of Hispanics live below the poverty level. Twenty percent of the poor are children.[9]

Did You Know

. . . that there are about 2 million full-time poor workers in the United States? In 1998, earnings from full-time, minimum-wage jobs were $2500 below the poverty line for a family of three.

It is not, however, solely wealth or income that determines people's position on a social ladder that ranges from the homeless to the very, very rich who live on great estates. In 1966 Oscar Lewis described the "culture of poverty" that exists in inner-city slums. It is characterized by helplessness, apathy, cynicism, and distrust of social institutions such as schools and the police.[10] A few years later Gunnar Myrdal argued that there is a worldwide "underclass, whose members lack the education and skills necessary to compete with the rest of society."[11] And in 1987, William Julius Wilson depicted the ranks of the underclass as the "truly disadvantaged." This group of urban inner-city dwellers is at the bottom of the ladder. Basic institutions such as the school and the family have deteriorated. There is little community cohesion. The people remain isolated—steeped in their own ghetto culture and the anger and aggression that accompany their marginal existence.[12]

The United States   In our society opportunities to move up the social ladder exist, but they are not equally distributed. A child born to a single, uneducated, 13-year-old girl living in a slum has practically no chance to move up, whereas the child of a middle-class family has a better-than-average chance of reaching a professional or business position. Yet all people in the society share the same goals. And those goals are shaped by billions of advertising dollars spent each year to spread the message that everyone can drive a sports car, take a well-deserved exotic vacation, and record the adventure with a camcorder.

The mystique is reinforced by instant lottery millionaires, the earnings of superstar athletes, and rags-to-riches stories of such people as Ray Kroc. Kroc, a high school dropout, believed that a 15-cent hamburger with a 10-cent bag of French fries could make dining out affordable for low-income families; his idea spread quickly through the United States—and to 116 other countries with 24,500 McDonald's restaurants and their golden arches all over the world. Superstar athletes are another example of American icons. Consider the NBA's Michael Jordan. At age 21 he had a rookie contract of $6 million over 7 years, which increased to the $25 million salary range per season plus $40 million in commercial endorsements. And now in retirement he has yet another multimillion-dollar venture—the famous Michael Jordan's Restaurants in Chicago and in New York, where guests can dine and buy an array of memorabilia in his bustling boutiques. In like manner, record-setting home-run hitter Sammy Sosa already makes over $9 million in salary and $8 million in endorsements. Sosa, now in his 30s, worked as a shoeshine boy in the Dominican Republic to help support his fatherless family. Though Merton argued that lack of legitimate means for everyone to reach material goals like these does create problems, he also made it clear that the high rate of deviant behavior in the United States cannot be explained solely on the basis of lack of means.

India   The world has produced class systems that are more rigid than our own, and societies that place much stricter limitations on people's ability to achieve their goals, without causing the problems the United States faces. In the traditional society of India, for example, the

On the main floor of Michael Jordan's Restaurant in downtown Chicago, fans can buy a slice of Jordan's success: Michael Jordan Cologne, Mike-like Oakleys, golf bags with the restaurant's logo, or even an autographed team jersey featuring four gold logo patches for the championship years.

untouchables at the bottom of the caste system are forbidden by custom (although no longer by law) even to enter the temples and schools used by those above them, while those at the top enjoy immense privileges.

All Hindu castes fall within a hierarchy, each one imposing upon its members duties and prohibitions covering both public and private life. People of high status may give food to people of lower status, for example, but may not receive food from them. One may eat in the home of a person of lower status, but the food must be cooked and served by a person of equal or higher status. Members of such a rigid system clearly face many more restraints than we do. Why, then, does India not have a very high crime rate?

The answer lies in the fact that Indians learn from birth that all people do not and cannot aspire to the same things. In the United States, the egalitarian principle denies the existence of limits to upward mobility within the social structure.[13] In reality, everyone in society experiences some pressures and strains,

and the amounts are inversely related to position in the hierarchy: the lower the class, the higher the strain.

Modes of Adaptation

To be sure, not everyone who is denied access to a society's goals becomes deviant. Merton outlined five ways in which people adapt to society's goals and means. Individuals' responses (modes of adaptation) depend on their attitudes toward the cultural goals and the institutional means of attaining those goals. The options are conformity, innovation, ritualism, retreatism, and rebellion (see Table 5.1).

Merton does not tell us how any one individual chooses to become a drug pusher, for example, and another chooses to work on an assembly line. Instead, he explains why crime rates are high in some groups and low in others.

Conformity   Conformity is the most common mode of adjustment. Individuals accept both the culturally defined goals and the pre-

TABLE 5.1 A Typology of Modes of Individual Adaptation

Mode of Adaptation	Culture Goals*	Institutionalized Means*
Conformity	+	+
Innovation	+	−
Ritualism	−	+
Retreatism	−	−
Rebellion	±	±

*+ = acceptance; − = rejection; ± = rejection and substitution.

Source: Robert K. Merton, *Social Theory and Social Structure* (New York: Free Press, 1957), p. 140.

scribed means for achieving those goals. They work, save, go to school, and follow the legitimate paths. Look around you in the classroom. You will see many children of decent, hardworking parents. After college they will find legitimate jobs. Some will excel. Some will walk the economic middle path. But all those who are conformists will accept (though not necessarily achieve) the goals of our society and the means it approves for achieving them.

Innovation Individuals who choose the adaptation of innovation accept society's goals, but since they have few legitimate means of achieving them, they design their own means for getting ahead. The means may be burglary, robbery, embezzlement, or a host of other crimes. Youngsters who have no parental attention, no encouragement in school, no way to the top—no future—may scrawl their signatures on subway cars and buildings and park benches in order to achieve recognition of a sort. Such illegitimate forms of innovation are certainly not restricted to the lower classes, as evidenced by such crimes as stock manipulation, sale of defective products, and income tax evasion.

Ritualism People who adapt by ritualism abandon the goals they once believed to be within reach and resign themselves to their present lifestyles. They play by the rules; they work on assembly lines, hold middle-management jobs, or follow some other safe routine. Many workers have been catching a bus at the same street corner at the same hour every day for 20 years or more. They have long forgotten why,

except that their jobs are where their paychecks come from. Their great relief is a 2-week vacation in the summer.

Retreatism Retreatism is the adaptation of people who give up both the goals (can't make it) and the means (why try?) and retreat into the world of drug addiction or alcoholism. They have internalized the value system and therefore are under internal pressure not to innovate. The retreatist mode allows for an escape into a nonproductive, nonstriving lifestyle. Some members of the antiwar movement of the 1960s opted to drop out entirely. The pressure was too great; the opportunities were unacceptable. They became addicts or followers of occult religions.

Rebellion Rebellion occurs when both the cultural goals and the legitimate means are rejected. Many individuals substitute their own goals (get rid of the establishment) and their own means (protest). They have an alternate scheme for a new social structure, however illdefined. Many of the so-called militias operating in America today, ranging in size from two to several hundred persons, have lost faith in the legitimacy of the U.S. government and are trying to establish their own alternative quasigovernmental structures.

Merton's theory of how the social structure produces strain that may lead to deviant behavior is illustrated in Figure 5.1. His theory has challenged researchers for half a century.

Tests of Merton's Theory

Merton and his followers (Chapter 6) predict that the greatest proportion of crime will be found in the lower classes because lower-class people have the least opportunity to reach their goals legitimately. Many research studies designed to test the various propositions of strain theory focus on the association between social class and delinquency (an association that evokes considerable controversy). Some studies report a strong inverse relationship: As class goes up, crime rates go down. Others find no association at all between the two variables (Chapter 2).

FIGURE 5.1   Modes of deviant behavior.

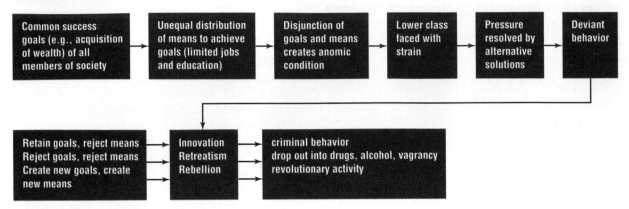

Social Class and Crime   The controversy over the relationship between social class and crime began when researchers, using self-report questionnaires, found more serious and more frequent delinquency among lower-class boys than among those of higher classes.[14] In Chapter 2 we saw that other researchers seriously questioned those findings.[15] When Charles Tittle and his colleagues attempted to clarify the relationship by analyzing 35 empirical studies, they concluded that "class is not now and has not been related to criminality in the recent past."[16] Summarizing the research literature on social class and crime, Gary Jensen and Kevin Thompson wrote: "The safest conclusion concerning class structure and delinquency is the same one that has been proposed for several decades: Class, no matter how defined, contributes little to explaining variation in self-reports of common delinquency."[17]

Once again there was a critical reaction. A summary of more than 100 projects concluded that "lower-class people do commit those direct interpersonal types of crime which are normally handled by the police at a higher rate than middle-class people."[18] But if low social status creates frustration that pushes people to commit crime, why don't all the people in the lowest class commit crimes, or drop out into the drug world, or become revolutionaries? Since they clearly do not, there must be some limitations to the causal relationship between crime and social class.

Nikos Passas answers the question by pointing out that not all those persons exposed to the same problems respond in the same way. In fact, not all people perceive the same situation as a problem. He explains that anomie theorists base their arguments on rates of crime, rather than on individual behavior.[19]

Terence Thornberry and Margaret Farnworth argue that there is no simple connection between class and crime. The relationship, they say, is highly complex; it involves race, seriousness of the offense, education of family and offender, and many other factors.[20] Researchers have also found that low social status promoted delinquency by increasing individuals' strain and by decreasing educational and occupational aspirations, whereas high social status promoted individuals' delinquency by increasing risk taking and decreasing conventional values.[21]

According to a number of studies, we may be able to learn more about the relationship between social class and crime if we look closely at specific types of offenses rather than at aggregate crime (or delinquency) rates. Take homicide, for example: In a study of 190 U.S. cities with populations of 100,000 or more, it was found that both income inequality and poverty are related to homicide rates. The researchers argue that the relationship can be explained "through the legitimate desires of impoverished persons to reduce deprivation and through their decreased ability to compete for legitimate employment."[22] In two large cross-national studies, two teams of Canadian researchers explored the relationship between income inequality and national homicide rates.[23] Both teams reported results that support strain theory. When opportunities or means for success are not provided equally to all members of society (as indicated by crime rates), pressure is exerted on some members of that society to engage in deviant behavior (in this case, homicide). Further analyses by one of the teams showed that the effects of inequality on homicide may be even more pronounced in more democratic societies. The researchers commented: "Income inequality might be more likely to generate violent behavior in more democratic societies because of the coexistence of high material inequality and an egalitarian value system."[24]

David Brownfield also related social class to specific offenses, in this instance to fistfights and brawls among teenagers.[25] His information came from two sources: the Richmond Youth Study, conducted at the University of California at Berkeley, and the Community Tolerance Study, done by a team of researchers at the University of Arizona. Brownfield's analysis of questionnaires completed by 1500 white male students in California and 1300 white male students in Arizona suggests a very strong relation between poverty—as measured by unemployment and welfare assistance—and violent behavior. He concluded that the general public expresses much hostility against the "disreputable poor," a term used by David Matza to describe people who remain unemployed for a long time, even during periods of full employment.[26] In fact, Brownfield suggests, many people hold them in contempt. (He cites a *New York Times*/CBS poll that found that over half of all the respondents believed that most people on welfare could get along without it if they only tried.) This hostility causes the "disreputable poor" to build up frustration, which is made worse by the lack of such fundamental necessities as food and shelter. Such a situation breeds discontent—and violence.

John Hagan argues that youngsters who grow up in a culture where friends are delinquent, parents are criminals, and drug abuse is common, and where early experiences with delinquent activities are widespread, become "embedded" in behaviors that result in later adult unemployment. They are excluded from employment by events that begin early in life. Of course, youngsters can become equally "embedded" in a culture of middle-class values, economic stability, and early work experiences—the foundation for job stability and career success.[27]

Race and Crime   Yet another question that relates to strain theory concerns the relationship between racial inequality and violent crime. Judith and Peter Blau studied data from 125 metropolitan areas in the United States.[28] Their primary finding was that racial inequality—as measured by the difference in socioeconomic status between whites and nonwhites—is associated with the total rate of violent crime. The conclusion fits well with Merton's theory.

The Blaus argued that in a democratic society that stresses equal opportunities for individual achievement but in reality distributes resources on the basis of race, there is bound to be conflict. The most disadvantaged are precisely those who cannot change their situation through political action. In such circumstances, the frustrations created by racial inequalities tend to be expressed in various forms of aggression, such as violent crime. Several researchers have supported these findings. But not all researchers are in agreement.

John Braithwaite examined Uniform Crime Report statistics for a sample of 175 American cities. He compared the rates of violent crime with racial inequality, as measured by the incomes of black families and the incomes of all other families in his sample cities. He concluded that racial inequality does not cause specific crime problems.[29] Perhaps the crucial point is not whether one actually has an equal chance to be successful but rather, how one perceives one's chances. According to this reasoning, people who feel the most strain are those who have not only high goals but also low expectations of reaching them. So far, however, research has not supported this contention.

Evaluation: Merton's Theory
The strain perspective developed by Merton and his followers has influenced both research

and theoretical developments in criminology.[30] Yet, as popular as this theory remains, it has been questioned on a variety of grounds.[31] By concentrating on crime at the lower levels of the socioeconomic hierarchy, for example, it neglects crime committed by middle- and upper-class people. Radical criminologists (see Chapter 8), in fact, claim that strain theory "stands accused of predicting too little bourgeois criminality and too much proletarian criminality."[32]

Other critics question whether a society as heterogeneous as ours really does have goals on which everyone agrees. Some theorists argue that American subcultures have their own value systems (Chapter 6). If that is the case, we cannot account for deviant behavior on the basis of Merton's cultural goals. Other questions are asked about the theory. If we have an agreed-upon set of goals, is material gain the dominant one? If crime is a means to an end, why is there so much useless, destructive behavior, especially among teenagers?

No matter how it is structured, each society defines goals for its members. The United States is far from being the only society in which people strive for wealth and prestige. Yet, while some people in other cultures have limited means for achieving these goals, not all these societies have high crime rates. Two such societies—Japan and Switzerland—are among the most developed and industrialized in the world. Although the United States has quite a bit in common with them, it does not share their very low crime rates.[33]

Despite the many critical assessments, strain theory, as represented primarily by Merton's formulation of anomie, has had a major impact on contemporary criminology. It dominated the delinquency research of the 1950s and 1960s. During the 1970s the theory lost its dominant position as criminologists paid increasing attention to how crime and delinquency were related to individuals' loss of attachment to their social institutions—the family, the school, or the government (see Chapter 7). Then, in the mid-1980s and continuing unabated into the 2000s, there was a resurgence of interest in empirical research and theorizing based on strain concepts.

Institutional Imbalance and Crime

In their book *Crime and the American Dream*, Steven Messner and Richard Rosenfeld agree with Merton that the material success goal is pervasive in American culture. In essence, the American dream is quite clear—succeed by any means necessary, even if those means are illegitimate.[34] The American dream, then, encourages high crime rates. Messner and Rosenfeld expand on Merton's ideas on the relationship between culture, social structure, anomie, and crime rates. High crime, they contend, is more than a matter of striving for monetary gains. It also results from the fact that our major social institutions do not have the capacity to control behavior. These institutions fail to counterbalance the ethos of the American dream. The dominance of economic institutions manifests itself in three ways: devaluation of other institutions, their accommodation to economic institutions, and the penetration of economic norms.

- *The devaluation of noneconomic roles and functions.* Performance in the economic world takes precedence over performance in other institutional settings: Noneconomic functions are devalued. Education is important, for example, only because it promises economic gains. Learning for its own sake is relatively unimportant. In the context of the family, the homeowner is more important than the homemaker. In politics, too, there is a devaluation: If a citizen does not vote, there may be mild disapproval; if an adult citizen does not work, he or she loses status.

- *The accommodation of other institutions to economic needs.* In situations where institutions compete, noneconomic ones **accommodate.** Family life is generally dominated by work schedules. Individuals go to school primarily to get a "good" job. Once out of school, those who return usually do so to get a better job. In political accommodation, government strives to maintain an environment hospitable to business.

- *The penetration of economic norms.* Penetration of economic norms into those of other institutions is widespread. Spouses become partners in "managing" the home, businesspeople/politicians campaign for public office claiming they will "run the country like a corporation," and economic terms such as "accountability" are adopted by educators.

Messner and Rosenfeld contend that as long as there is a disproportionate emphasis on monetary rewards, the crime problem will increase. In fact, if economic opportunities increase, there may be an increase in the preoccupation with material success. Crime will decrease only when noneconomic institutions have the capacity to control behavior.[35]

Freda Adler's study of 10 countries with low crime rates supports this argument. She demonstrates that where economic concerns have not devalued informal social control institutions such as family, community, or religion, crime rates are relatively low and stable. This finding held for nonindustrialized *and* highly industrialized societies.[36]

General Strain Theory

Sociologist Robert Agnew substantially revised Merton's theory in order to make it more broadly explanatory of criminal behavior.[37] The reformulation is called **general strain theory.** Agnew argues that failure to achieve material goals (the focal point of Merton's theory) is not the only reason for committing crime. Criminal behavior may also be related to the anger and frustration that result when an individual is treated in a way he or she does not want to be treated in a social relationship. General strain theory explains the range of strain-producing events.

• *Strain caused by failure to achieve positively valued goals.* This type of strain is based on Merton's view that lower-class individuals are often prevented from achieving monetary success goals through legitimate channels. When people do not have the money to get what they want, some of them turn to illegitimate means to get it.

• *Stress caused by the removal of positively valued stimuli from the individual.* This type of strain results from the actual or anticipated loss of something or someone important in one's life: death of a loved one, breakup with a boyfriend/girlfriend, divorce of parents, move to a new school. Criminal behavior results when individ-

uals seek revenge against those responsible, try to prevent the loss, or escape through illicit drug use.

• *Strain caused by the presentation of negative stimuli.* The third major source of strain involves stressful life situations. Adverse situations and events may include child abuse, criminal victimization, bad experiences with peers, school problems, or verbal threats. Criminal behavior in these situations may result when an individual tries to run away from the situation, end the problem, or seek revenge.[38]

According to Agnew, each type of strain increases an individual's feelings of anger, fear, or depression. The most critical reaction for general strain theory is anger, an emotion that increases the desire for revenge, helps justify aggressive behavior, and stimulates individuals into action.

General strain theory acknowledges that not all persons who experience strain become criminals. Many are equipped to cope with their frustration and anger. Some come up with rationalizations ("don't really need it anyway"); others use techniques for physical relief (a good workout at the gym); and still others walk away from the condition causing stress (get out of the house). The capacity to deal with strain depends on personal experience throughout life. It involves the influence of peers, temperament, attitudes, and, in the case of pressing financial problems, economic resources. Recent empirical tests show preliminary support for general strain theory.[39] By broadening Merton's concepts, general strain theory has the potential to explain a wide range of criminal and delinquent behavior, including aggressive acts, drug abuse, and property offenses, among individuals from all classes in society.

Theory Informs Policy

Strain theory has helped us develop a crime-prevention strategy. If, as the theory tells us, frustration builds up in people who have few means for reaching their goals, it makes sense to design programs that give lower-class people a bigger stake in society.

Head Start It was in the 1960s that President Lyndon Johnson inaugurated the Head Start program as part of a major antipoverty campaign. The goal of Head Start is to make children of low-income families more socially competent, better able to deal with their present environment and their later responsibilities. The youngsters get a boost (or a head start) in a 1-year preschool developmental program that is intended to prevent them from dropping out of society. Program components include community and parental involvement, an 8-to-1 child/staff ratio, and daily evaluation and involvement of all the children in the planning of and responsibility for their own activities.

Since a 1-year program could not be expected to affect the remainder of a child's life, Project Follow Through was developed in an effort to provide the same opportunities for Head Start youngsters during elementary school. What began as a modest summer experience for half a million preschool children has expanded into a year-round program that provides educational and social services to millions of young people and their families. This, then, is a program clearly intended to lower stress in the group most likely to develop criminal behavior.

Some research findings do indicate that the program has had a certain measure of success. In 1997 the National Head Start Association awarded special recognition to newly elected U.S. Representative Loretta Sanchez as a model of success for the Head Start program. She is the first member of Congress to have been a Head Start child. Sanchez, who could not speak until age 4, recalls how Head Start gave her a jump start to a graduate degree in business and to running a successful financial consulting firm.[40] Yet successes of individual Head Start programs are unevenly distributed over the country, depending largely on program and staff quality. Even supporters warn that Head Start's success rates can improve only if these funds are carefully aimed at program improvement, rather than enlargement.

Perry Preschool Project   Another program that tried to ameliorate the disparity between goals and means in society was the Perry Preschool Project, begun in 1962 on the south side of Ypsilanti, Michigan. Its purpose was to develop skills that would give youngsters the means of getting ahead at school and in the

workplace, thereby reducing the amount and seriousness of delinquent behavior. Overall, 123 black children 3 and 4 years old participated for 2 years, 5 days a week, 2½ hours a day. The program provided a teacher for every 5 children, weekly visits by a teacher to a child's home, and a follow-up of every child annually until age 11 and thereafter at ages 14, 15, and 19.

There is little doubt about the effectiveness of the project. By age 19, the participants did better in several areas than a group that had not participated:

- Employment rates doubled.
- Rates of postsecondary education doubled.
- Teenage pregnancy was cut in half.
- The high school graduation rate was one-third higher.
- Arrest rates were 40 percent lower.[41]

Job Corps   Yet another survivor of President Johnson's War on Poverty is the federal Job Corps program. It aims at "the worst of the worst," as Senator Orrin Hatch of Utah said.[42] The program enables neglected teenagers—otherwise headed for juvenile detention or jail—to master work habits that they did not learn at home. In 1999, 68,000 young people were serving in the Job Corps. Most of them had enlisted on the basis of recruitment posters, like those distributed by the armed forces. The average length of stay in the corps is just short of a year, at an annual cost of $18,831. That sounds expensive, but juvenile detention costs $29,600 a year—and residential drug treatment centers cost $19,000. Since its inception in 1964 the program has served 1.8 million people.[43]

Over two-thirds of former Job Corps members get jobs, and 17 percent go on to higher education. Research has shown that the Job Corps returns $1.46 for every dollar spent, because of increased tax revenue and decreased cost of welfare, crime, and incarceration. Over two-thirds of Job Corps members come from minorities; over 80 percent are high school dropouts (see Figure 5.2).

In a report to the United States Congress on which programs prevent crime, researchers at the University of Maryland classified the Job

FIGURE 5.2   A profile of Job Corps members.

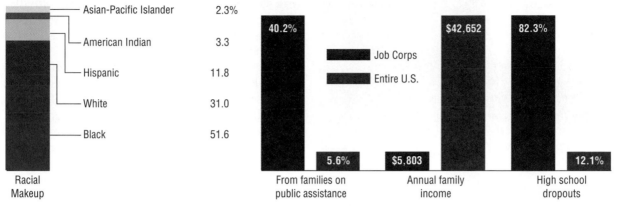

Source: Jane Gross, "Remnant of the War on Poverty, Job Corps Is Still a Quiet Success," *New York Times*, Feb. 17, 1992, p. A14.

Corps program as "promising." Its potential for success includes the resocialization of youth through prosocial role models; a residential requirement that reduces contact with antisocial groups; and the vocational focus and attachment to the job market.[44]

CULTURAL DEVIANCE THEORIES

The programs that emanate from strain theory attempt to give underprivileged children ways to achieve middle-class goals. Programs based on cultural deviance theories concentrate on teaching middle-class values.

Strain theory attributes criminal behavior in the United States to the striving of all citizens to conform with the conventional values of the middle class, primarily financial success. Cultural deviance theories attribute crime to a set of values that exist in disadvantaged neighborhoods. Conformity with the lower-class value system, which determines behavior in slum areas, causes conflict with society's laws. Both strain and cultural deviance theories locate the causes of crime in the marginalized position of those at the lowest stratum in a class-based society.

Scholars who view crime as resulting from cultural values that permit, or even demand, behavior in violation of the law are called cultural deviance theorists. The three major cultural deviance theories are social disorganization, differential association, and culture

conflict. **Social disorganization theory** focuses on the development of high-crime areas in which there is a disintegration of conventional values caused by rapid industrialization, increased immigration, and urbanization. **Differential association theory** maintains that people learn to commit crime as a result of contact with antisocial values, attitudes, and criminal behavior patterns. **Culture conflict theory** states that different groups learn different conduct norms (rules governing behavior) and that the conduct norms of some groups may clash with conventional middle-class rules.

All three theories contend that criminals and delinquents in fact do conform—but to norms that deviate from those of the dominant middle class. Before we examine the specific theories that share the cultural deviance perspective, we need to explore the nature of cultural deviance.

The Nature of Cultural Deviance

When you drive through rural Lancaster County in Pennsylvania, or through Holmes County in Ohio, or through Elkhart and Lagrange Counties in Indiana, in the midst of fertile fields and well-tended orchards, you will find isolated villages with prosperous and well-maintained farmhouses but no electricity. You will see the farmers and their families traveling in horse-drawn buggies, dressed in homespun clothes, and wearing brimmed hats. These people are Amish. Their ancestors came to this

Man with a Hitler tatoo on his back sells white power books at a Ku Klux Klan cross burning rally in Hico, Texas. Deviant hate groups such as these exist throughout the United States and in many foreign countries.

country from the German-speaking Rhineland region as early as 1683 to escape persecution for their fundamentalist Christian beliefs. Shunning motors, electricity, jewelry, and affiliation with political parties, they are a *nonconformist* community within a highly materialistic culture.

Motorcycle gangs made their appearance shortly after World War II. The Hell's Angels was the first of many gangs to be established in slum areas of cities across the country. To become a member of this gang, initiates are subjected to grueling and revolting degradations. They are conditioned to have allegiance only to the gang. Contacts with middle-class society are usually antagonistic and criminal. Motorcycle gangs finance their operations through illegal activities, such as dealing drugs, running mas-

sage parlors and gambling operations, and selling stolen goods. The members' code of loyalty to one another and to their national and local groups makes the gangs extremely effective criminal organizations.

The normative systems of the Amish and the bikers are at odds with the conventional norms of the society in which they live. Both deviate from middle-class standards. Sociologists define **deviance** as any behavior that members of a social group define as violating their norms. As we can see, the concept of deviance can be applied to noncriminal acts that members of a group view as peculiar or unusual (the lifestyle of the Amish) or to criminal acts (behavior that society has made illegal). The Hell's Angels fit the expected stereotype of deviance as negative; the Amish culture demonstrates that deviance is not necessarily bad, just different.

Cultural deviance theorists argue that our society is made up of various groups and subgroups, each with its own standards of right and wrong. Behavior considered normal in one group may be considered deviant by another. As a result, those who conform to the standards of cultures considered deviant are behaving in accordance with their own norms but may be breaking the law—the norms of the dominant culture.

You may wonder whether the Hell's Angels are outcasts in the slum neighborhoods where they live. They are not. They may even be looked up to by younger boys in places where toughness and violence are not only acceptable but appropriate. Indeed, groups such as the Hell's Angels may meet the needs of youngsters who are looking for a way to be important in a disorganized ghetto that offers few opportunities to gain status.

Crime Surfing

www.rcmp-grc.ca/org-crime/motor-gangs.htm

What are the characteristics of outlaw gangs, and how does an individual become a member?

Social Disorganization Theory

Scholars associated with the University of Chicago in the 1920s became interested in so-

FIGURE 5.3 Social disorganization.

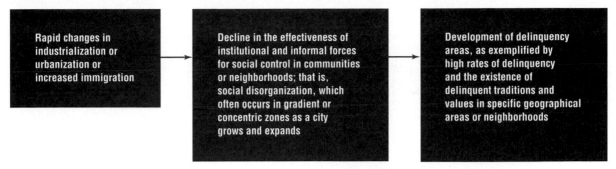

Source: Donald J. Shoemaker, *Theories of Delinquency*, 2d ed. (New York: Oxford University Press, 1990), p. 82.

cially disorganized Chicago neighborhoods where criminal values and traditions replaced conventional ones and were transmitted from one generation to the next. In their classic work *The Polish Peasant in Europe and America,* W. I. Thomas and Florian Znaniecki described the difficulties Polish peasants experienced when they left their rural life in Europe to settle in an industrialized city in America.[45] The scholars compared the conditions the immigrants had left in Poland with those they found in Chicago. They also investigated the immigrants' assimilation.

Older immigrants, they found, were not greatly affected by the move because they managed, even within the urban slums, to continue living as they had lived in Poland. But the second generation did not grow up on Polish farms; these people were city dwellers and they were American. They had few of the old Polish traditions but were not yet assimilated into the new ones. The norms of the stable, homogeneous folk society were not transferable to the anonymous, materially oriented urban settings. Rates of crime and delinquency rose. Thomas and Znaniecki attributed this result to *social disorganization*—the breakdown of effective social bonds, family and neighborhood associations, and social controls in neighborhoods and communities. (See Figure 5.3.)

The Park and Burgess Model Thomas and Znaniecki's study greatly influenced other scholars at the University of Chicago. Among them were Robert Park and Ernest Burgess, who advanced the study of social disorganiza-

tion by introducing ecological analysis into the study of human society.[46] Ecology is the study of plants and animals in relation to each other and to their natural habitat, the place where they live and grow. Ecologists study these interrelationships, how the balance of nature continues and how organisms survive. Much the same approach is used by *social ecologists*, scholars who study the interrelationships of people and their environment.

In their study of social disorganization, Park and Burgess examined area characteristics instead of criminals for explanations of high crime rates. They developed the idea of natural urban areas, consisting of concentric zones extending out from the downtown central business district to the commuter zone at the fringes of the city. Each zone had its own structure and organization, its own cultural characteristics and unique inhabitants (Figure 5.4). Zone I, at the center, called the Loop because the downtown business district of Chicago is demarcated by a loop of the elevated train system, was occupied by commercial headquarters, law offices, retail establishments, and some commercial recreation. Zone II was the zone in transition, where the city's poor, unskilled, and disadvantaged lived in dilapidated tenements next to old factories. Zone III housed the working class, people whose jobs enabled them to enjoy some of the comforts the city had to offer at its fringes. The middle class—professionals, small-business owners, and the managerial class—lived in Zone IV. Zone V was the commuter zone of satellite towns and suburbs.

FIGURE 5.4   Park and Burgess's conception of the "natural urban areas" of Chicago.

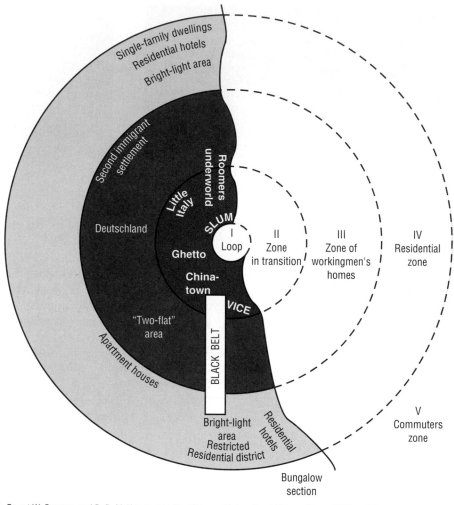

Source: Robert E. Park, Ernest W. Burgess, and R. D. McKenzie, *The City* (Chicago: University of Chicago Press, 1925), p. 55.

Shaw and McKay's Work   Clifford Shaw and Henry McKay, two researchers at Chicago's Institute for Juvenile Research, were particularly interested in the model Park and Burgess had created to demonstrate how people were distributed spatially in the process of urban growth. They decided to use the model to investigate the relationship between crime rates and the various zones of Chicago. Their data, found in 55,998 juvenile court records covering a period of 33 years, from 1900 to 1933, indicated the following:

- Crime rates were differentially distributed throughout the city, and areas of high crime rates had high rates of other

community problems, such as truancy, mental disorders, and infant mortality.

- Most delinquency occurred in the areas nearest the central business district and decreased with distance from the center.

- Some areas consistently suffered high delinquency rates, regardless of the ethnic makeup of the population.

- High-delinquency areas were characterized by a high percentage of immigrants, nonwhites, and low-income families and a low percentage of homeownership.

As the Hale-Bopp comet streaked through the sky over California on March 26, 1997, 39 members of the computer-related cult Gate of Heaven committed suicide at their luxurious Rancho Santa Fe, California, estate. The victims, males between 18 and 24 years old, fully expected to be conveyed to heaven by a waiting spacecraft.(1)

A cult is defined as "a great devotion to a person, idea, or thing, esp.: such devotion regarded as a literary or intellectual fad . . . a usually small circle of persons united by devotion or allegiance to an artistic or intellectual movement or figure" (*Webster's Collegiate Dictionary,* 1981, p. 274). Most cults are marked by

- A dynamic leader.
- The willingness of members to surrender their worldly possessions.
- Strict obedience to the leader.
- A communal social structure, with its own set of norms and values that are in conflict with those of conventional societies.

Experts estimate that there are 1000 to 2000 cults in America with as many as 4 to 6 million members.

Criminologists are interested primarily in destructive cults, such as these:

- An Indian cult has its devotees "marry" their little daughters to a goddess. Upon reaching puberty, the little girls are sold into prostitution for about $200 each.(2)
- Members of the Japanese cult Aun Shinrikyo launched a nerve gas attack in the Tokyo subway system—for unknown reasons—killing 12 and injuring over 5000. (March 20, 1995).
- The Reverend Jim Jones led his cult followers to death at their Jonestown, Guyana, encampment: 914 died;

Shoko Asahara, leader of the Japanese cult Aun Shinrikyo.

those who refused to take the poison were shot (November 18, 1978).

- The Solar Temple cult followers committed 74 murder/suicides in Canada and in Switzerland (1994–1997).
- Of the 107 members of the cult group of David Koresh—called the Branch Davidians—80 died (most committed suicide) in a standoff with federal authorities in Waco, Texas (April 1993).(3)

Some governments (China, Germany, and Russia) have outlawed some cults. The Vatican has issued a strong report exhorting the Church to fulfill the spiritual needs of the people to keep them from seeking salvation in cults.(4) The debate in America centers on First Amendment religious freedom.

However, that constitutional clause does not protect criminally destructive forms of religious expression. What governments, theologians, and criminologists have in common is their determination to bring alienated members of society into the mainstream to keep them out of destructive cults.

Sources

1. Shirley Levung, "Deaths May Be Work of Religious Cult, Expert Says," *Boston Globe,* Mar. 27, 1997, p. A15.
2. "India Sex Cult's 'Handmaidens' Join Tribute to Hindu Goddess, Secret Society Forces Girls Who 'Marry' Yelamma into Prostitution," *Toronto Star,* Jan. 23, 1997, p. A16.
3. Richard Lacayo, "Cult of Death," *Time,* Mar. 15, 1993, p. 36; Sophfionia Scott Gregory, "Children of a Lesser God," *Time,* May 17, 1993, p. 54.
4. E. J. Dionne, "Vatican, Taking Some Blame, Cites Threat of Cults," *New York Times,* May 4, 1986, p. A10.

Questions for Discussion

1. Where and how can we draw the line between those cults that engage in violations of the criminal law (such as murder, arson, incitation to suicide, rape, child abuse, and prostitution) and those that have not (yet) committed any criminal act and therefore enjoy First Amendment privileges?
2. Both theologians and criminologists advocate narrowing the gap between conduct norms of deviant cultures (cults, sects) and the rules of mainstream society. How could either group practically accomplish that goal?

- In high-delinquency areas there was a general acceptance of nonconventional norms, but these norms competed with conventional ones held by some of the inhabitants.[47]

Shaw and McKay demonstrated that the highest rates of delinquency persisted in the same areas of Chicago over the extended period from 1900 to 1933, even though the ethnic composition changed (German, Irish, and English at the turn of the century; Polish and Italian in the 1920s; an increasing number of blacks in the 1930s). This finding led to the conclusion that the crucial factor was not ethnicity but, rather, the position of the group in terms of economic status and cultural values. Finally, through their study of three sets of Cook County juvenile court records—1900 to 1906, 1917 to 1923, and 1927 to 1933—they learned that older boys were associated with younger boys in various offenses and that the same techniques for committing delinquent acts had been passed on through the years. The evidence clearly indicated to them that delinquency was socially learned behavior, transmitted from one generation to the next in disorganized urban areas.[48] This phenomenon is called **cultural transmission.**

Tests of Social Disorganization Theory

Social disorganization, like early strain theory, was overshadowed in the 1970s by social control theorists who turned to explanations of why people do *not* break laws in the face of poor social environments with few means of becoming successful. While these explanations still have widespread impact on the scholarly community, the 1980s and 1990s saw a major resurgence of interest in how neighborhoods affect people's lives. Modern-day social ecologists have once again begun to focus on the interrelationship between individuals and their environment. What are the consequences of rising crime rates in a neighborhood? Ralph Taylor suggests separating these consequences into three categories: psychological and social, behavioral, and economic.[49]

Psychological and Social Effects Life in physically deteriorated neighborhoods with their rat-infested buildings, graffiti-ridden streets, trash-strewn vacant lots, boarded-up windows, and openly conducted drug selling, takes its psychological toll on residents.[50] They feel less emotional investment in their communities, mistrust their neighbors, and harbor increasing desires to "get out." Frustration mounts because they are unable to do so. Many parents are so worried about violence on their streets that they confine their youngsters to the home except for school attendance. Young people refer to this confinement as "lockdown" (a term used to describe the locking of prison cells for security reasons). This desperate move to

protect their children from getting hurt physically has had harmful psychological effects. According to one professor of developmental psychology, in a world where a simple altercation can end as an assault, or even a murder,[51] these "protected" children are at a disadvantage. When they eventually go back on the streets, they don't know how to survive.

Researchers are questioning whether people living in socially disorganized neighborhoods become more fearful. The answer is, they usually do.[52] When word of victimization begins to spread, fear can reach epidemic proportions. Residents begin to stay off the streets, abandoning them to the gangs, drug sellers, and others involved in illicit activities. Fear becomes greatest in communities undergoing rapid age and racial-composition changes.[53]

Fear increases when there is a perception that the police care little about a neighborhood. Douglas Smith looked at police behavior and characteristics of 60 neighborhoods in three large U.S. cities (Rochester, New York; St. Louis, Missouri; Tampa/St. Petersburg, Florida). His major findings suggest that police officers are less likely to file reports of crime incidents in high-crime areas than in low-crime areas and that they are more likely to assist residents and initiate contacts with suspicious-looking people in low-crime neighborhoods.[54]

Todd Clear and Dina Rose link social disorganization to high incarceration rates. They suggest that when large numbers of males are removed through incarceration, local social, political, and economic systems in already disorganized communities become even weaker. In these areas children are more likely to experience lack of supervision, more single-parent families, and few effective guardians. The researchers do not advocate policies that allow those who threaten the personal safety of residents to be on the streets. But, they argue, there are many offenders who can be regulated in the community through various neighborhood-based approaches monitored by collaborative efforts of the police, probation and parole officers, and local groups, leaders, and residents. This crime-control strategy, one that ties the offender to the community, could then strengthen, rather than weaken, already socially disorganized neighborhoods.[55]

Behavioral Effects A 1999 report on an ongoing research project that focuses on 343 urban neighborhoods in Chicago shows that residents overall consider substance abuse and fistfighting "very wrong" to "extremely wrong." Broken down by racial and ethnic groups, minority-group members were more intolerant of deviance than were whites.[56] Regardless of the level of residents' intolerance, however, widespread deviance in a community generally tends to make people limit their participation in efforts to "clean up" the neighborhood. There are, however, communities that fight back with community patrols, anticrime programs, and various activities to protect children. Many would prefer to move away, but few do. Factors besides crime come into play: low income, stage of life cycle, an affordable place to live, or location of employment.[57] Those moving in usually do so because it is the only place they can find an inexpensive place to live.[58]

```
========================================
≡ Crime Surfing                      ≡
========================================
 ⬅   ➡   (STOP)   🏠   ↻
_____
 www.ojp.usdoj.gov/bjs/
_____
 Is the association between        ▲
 victimization levels and          ║
 neighborhoods supported by        ║
 recent survey data?               ▼
```

Economic Effects Crime problems in a community influence assessments of property values by realtors and lenders. Research in Boston suggests that a 5 percent decrease in crime could bring in $7 million to $30 million in increased tax revenue.[59] In another investigation, researchers asked about the impact of Atlantic City casinos and the related increased crime rate on real estate in three southern New Jersey counties.[60] They found a sizable drop in house values. Those communities most accessible to Atlantic City suffered the worst economic consequences.

Middle- and working-class people tend to escape the urban ghetto, leaving behind the most disadvantaged. When you add to those disadvantaged the people moving in from outside who are also severely disadvantaged, over time these areas become places of concentrated poverty, isolated from the mainstream.

Some social ecologists argue that communities, like people, go through life cycles. Neighborhood deterioration precedes rising crime rates. When crime begins to rise, neighborhoods go from owner-occupied to renter-occupied housing, with a significant decline in the socioeconomic status of residents and an increase in population density. Later in the community life cycle, there is a renewed interest on the part of investors in buying up the cheap real estate with the idea of renovating it and making a profit (gentrification).[61]

Evaluation: Social Disorganization Theory

Though their work has made a significant impact, social ecologists have not been immune to challenges. Their work has been criticized for its focus on how crime patterns are transmitted, not on how they start in the first place. The approach has also been faulted for failing to explain why delinquents stop committing crime as they grow older, why most people in socially disorganized areas do not commit criminal acts, and why some bad neighborhoods seem to be insulated from crime. Finally, critics claim that this approach does not come to grips with middle-class delinquency.

Clearly, however, modern criminology owes a debt to social disorganization theorists, particularly to Shaw and McKay, who in the 1920s began to look at the characteristics of people and places and to relate both to crime. There is now a vast body of research for which they laid the groundwork.

Theory Informs Policy

Theorists of the Chicago school were the first social scientists to suggest that most crime is committed by normal people responding in expected ways to their immediate surroundings, rather than by abnormal individuals acting out individual pathologies. If social disorganization is at the root of the problem, crime control must involve social organization. The community, not individuals, needs treatment. Helping the community, then, should lower its crime rate.

The Chicago Area Project Social disorganization theory was translated into practice in 1934 with the establishment of the Chicago Area Project (CAP), an experiment in neighborhood reorganization. The project was initiated by the Institute for Juvenile Research, at which Clifford Shaw and Henry McKay were working. It coordinated the existing community support groups—local schools, churches, labor unions, clubs, and merchants. Special efforts were made to control delinquency through recreational facilities, summer camps, better law enforcement, and the upgrading of neighborhood schools, sanitation, and general appearance.

In 1994 this first community-based delinquency-prevention program could boast 60 years of achievement. South Chicago remains an area of poverty and urban marginalization, dotted with boarded-up buildings and signs of urban decay, though the pollution from the nearby steel mills is under control. But the Chicago Area Project (CAP) initiated by Shaw and McKay is as vibrant as ever, with its three-pronged attack on delinquency: direct service, advocacy, and community involvement. Residents, from clergy to gang members, are working with CAP to keep kids out of trouble, to help those in trouble, and to clean up the neighborhoods. "In fact, in those communities where area projects have been in operation for a number of years, incidents of crime and delinquency have decreased."[62]

Operation Weed and Seed and Others
Operation Weed and Seed is a federal, state, and local effort to improve the quality of life in targeted high-crime urban areas across the country. The strategy is to "weed" out negative influences (drugs, crime) and to "seed" the neighborhoods with prevention and intervention. The key components of the strategy are:

- *Enhanced coordination.* The analysis of neighborhood problems and the development of a law enforcement/community plan to deal with them.

- *Weeding.* The concentrated effort of law enforcement to weed out drug traffickers, violent offenders, and other criminals through arrest, prosecution, adjudication, and supervision.

- *Community policing.* The involvement of police officers in helping the community

solve its problems. By increasing the trust of the community, police and prosecutors join with residents and businesses as partners in enforcing the laws.

- *Seeding.* The focus on eliminating harmful behavior through human services that include youth activities, adult literacy classes, and neighborhood revitalization efforts.

When the program began in 1991 there were three target areas—Kansas City, Missouri; Trenton, New Jersey; and Omaha, Nebraska. By 1999 the number of target areas had increased to 200 sites. An eight-state evaluation showed that the effectiveness of Operation Weed and Seed varied by the original severity of the crime problems, the strength of the established network of community organizations, early seeding with constant weeding, active leadership of key community members, and the formation of partnerships among local organizations.[63]

Another community action project has concentrated on revitalizing a Puerto Rican slum community. Sister Isolina Ferré worked for 10 years in the violent Navy Yard section of Brooklyn, New York. In 1969 she returned to Ponce Plaza, a poverty-stricken area in Ponce, Puerto Rico, infested with disease, crime, and unemployment. The area's 16,000 people had no doctors, nurses, dentists, or social agencies. The project began with a handful of missionaries, university professors, dedicated citizens, and community members who were willing to become advocates for their neighborhood. Among the programs begun were a large community health center, Big Brother/Big Sister programs for juveniles sent from the courts, volunteer tutoring, and recreational activities to take young people off the streets. Young photographers of Ponce Plaza, supplied with a few cameras donated by friends at Kodak, mounted an exhibit at the Metropolitan Museum of Art in New York. Regular fiestas

Did You Know

. . . that preventing one youth from leaving school and turning to a life of crime and drugs saves society approximately $2 million?

Latin Kings gang member teaches gang hand symbols to a child. Social interactions like these are learned and transmitted from one generation to the next.

have given community members a chance to celebrate their own achievements as well.[64]

Programs based on social disorganization theory attempt to bring conventional social values to disorganized communities. They provide an opportunity for young people to learn norms other than those of delinquent peer groups. Let us see how such learning takes place.

Differential Association Theory

What we eat, what we say, what we believe—in fact, the way we respond to any situation—depends on the culture in which we have been reared. In other words, to a very large extent, the social influences that people encounter determine their behavior. Whether a person becomes law-abiding or criminal, then, depends on contacts with criminal values, attitudes, definitions, and behavior patterns. This proposition underlies one of the most important theories of crime causation in American criminology—differential association.

Sutherland's Theory   In 1939 Edwin Sutherland introduced differential association theory in his textbook *Principles of Criminology*. Since then

scholars have read, tested, reexamined, and sometimes ridiculed this theory, which claimed to explain the development of all criminal behavior. The theory states that crime is learned through social interaction. People come into constant contact with "definitions favorable to violations of law" and "definitions unfavorable to violations of law." The ratio of these definitions—criminal to noncriminal—determines whether a person will engage in criminal behavior.[65] In formulating this theory, Sutherland relied heavily on Shaw and McKay's findings that delinquent values are transmitted within a community or group from one generation to the next.

Sutherland's Nine Propositions   Nine propositions explained the process by which this transmission of values takes place:

1. Criminal behavior is learned.

2. Criminal behavior is learned in interaction with other persons in a process of communication. A person does not become a criminal simply by living in a criminal environment. Crime is learned by participation with others in verbal and nonverbal communications.

3. The principal part of the learning of criminal behavior occurs within intimate personal groups. Families and friends have the most influence on the learning of deviant behavior. Their communications far outweigh those of the mass media.

4. When criminal behavior is learned, the learning includes (a) techniques of committing the crime, which are sometimes very complicated, sometimes very simple, and (b) the specific direction of motives, drives, rationalizations, and attitudes. Young delinquents learn not only how to shoplift, crack a safe, pick a lock, or roll a joint but also how to rationalize and defend their actions. One safecracker accompanied another safecracker for 1 year before he cracked his first safe.[66] In other words, criminals, too, learn skills and gain experience.

5. The specific direction of motives and drives is learned from definitions of the legal codes as favorable or unfavorable. In some societies an individual is surrounded by persons who invariably define the legal codes as rules to be observed, while in others he or she is surrounded by persons whose definitions are favorable to the violation of the legal codes. Not everyone in our society agrees that the laws should be obeyed; some people define them as unimportant. In American society, where definitions are mixed, we have a culture conflict in relation to legal codes.

6. A person becomes delinquent because of an excess of definitions favorable to violation of law over definitions unfavorable to violation of law. This is the key principle of differential association. In other words, learning criminal behavior is not simply a matter of associating with bad companions. Rather, learning criminal behavior depends on how many definitions we learn that are favorable to law violation as opposed to those that are unfavorable to law violation.

7. Differential associations may vary in frequency, duration, priority, and intensity. The extent to which associations and definitions will result in criminality is related to the frequency of contacts, their duration, and their meaning to the individual.

8. The process of learning criminal behavior by association with criminal and anticriminal patterns involves all the mechanisms that are involved in any other learning. Learning criminal behavior patterns is very much like learning conventional behavior patterns and is not simply a matter of observation and imitation.

9. While criminal behavior is an expression of general needs and values, it is not explained by those general needs and values, since noncriminal behavior is an expression of the same needs and values. Shoplifters steal to get what they want. Others work to get money to buy what they want. The motives—frustration, desire to accumulate goods or social status, low self-concept, and the like—cannot logically be the same because they explain both lawful and criminal behavior.

Tests of Differential Association Theory

Since Sutherland presented his theory more than 50 years ago, researchers have tried to determine whether his principles lend themselves to empirical measurement. James Short tested a sample of 126 boys and 50 girls at a training school and reported a consistent relationship between delinquent behavior and frequency, duration, priority, and intensity of interactions with delinquent peers.[67] Similarly, Travis Hirschi demonstrated that boys with delinquent friends are more likely to become delinquent.[68] Research on seventh- and eighth-grade students attending Rochester, New York, public schools in the late 1980s and early 1990s shows that gang membership is strongly associated with peer delinquency and the amount of delinquency and drug use.[69] Mark Warr demonstrated that while the duration of delinquent friendships over a long period of time has a greater effect than exposure over a short period, it is recent friendships rather than early friendships that have the greatest effect on delinquency.[70]

Adults have also been the subjects of differential association studies. Two thousand residents of New Jersey, Oregon, and Iowa were asked such questions as how many people they knew personally had engaged in deviant acts and how many were frequently in trouble. They were also asked how often they attended church (assumed to be related to definitions unfavorable to the violation of law). This differential association scale correlated significantly with such crimes as illegal gambling, income tax cheating, and theft.[71]

Evaluation: Differential Association Theory

Many researchers have attempted to validate Sutherland's differential association theory. Others have criticized it. Much of the criticism stems from errors in interpretation. Perhaps this type of error is best demonstrated by the critics who ask why it is that not everyone in heavy, prolonged contact with criminal behavior patterns becomes a criminal. Take, for argument's sake, corrections officers, who come into constant contact with more criminal associations than noncriminal ones. How do they escape from learning to be law violators themselves?

The answer, of course, is that Sutherland does not tell us that individuals become criminal by associating with criminals or even by association with criminal behavior patterns. He tells us, rather, that a person becomes delinquent because of an "excess of definitions favorable to violation of law over definitions unfavorable to violation of law." The key word is "definitions." Furthermore, unfavorable definitions may be communicated by persons who are not robbers or murderers or tax evaders. They may, for example, be law-abiding parents who, over time, define certain situations in such a way that their children get verbal or nonverbal messages to the effect that antisocial behavior is acceptable.

Several scholars have asked whether the principles of differential association really explain all types of crime. They might explain theft, but what about homicide resulting from a jealous

rage?[72] Why do some people who learn criminal behavior patterns not engage in criminal acts? Why is no account taken of nonsocial variables, such as a desperate need for money? Furthermore, while the principles may explain how criminal behavior is transmitted, they do not account for the origin of criminal techniques and definitions. In other words, the theory does not tell us how the first criminal became a criminal.

Differential association theory suggests there is an inevitability about the process of becoming a criminal. Once you reach the point where your definitions favorable to law violation exceed your definitions unfavorable to law violation, have you crossed an imaginary line into the criminal world? Even if we could add up the definitions encountered in a lifetime, could scientists measure the frequency, priority, duration, and intensity of differential associations?

Despite these criticisms, the theory has had a profound influence on criminology.[73] Generations of scholars have tested it empirically, modified it to incorporate psychologically based learning theory (see Chapter 4), and used it as a foundation for their own theorizing (Chapter 6). The theory has also had many policy implications.

Theory Informs Policy

If, according to differential association theory, a person can become criminal by learning definitions favorable to violating laws, it follows that programs that expose young people to definitions favorable to conventional behavior should reduce criminality. Such educational efforts as Head Start and the Perry Preschool Project have attempted to do just that. The same theory underlies many of the treatment programs for young school dropouts and pregnant teenagers.

An innovative Ohio program is trying to break the vicious cycle between poverty–welfare–school dropout–drugs–delinquency and teenage pregnancy. This program, LEAP (for learning, earning, and parenting), provides financial rewards for teenage single parents to stay in, or return to, school and deductions from the welfare checks of those who do not participate in education. A 1993 evaluation found that the program, which costs the state very little, has been moderately successful. Success appears to

American society, like most societies, is stratified in many ways: the haves and the have-nots, the educated and the undereducated, and the law-abiding and the law-violating populations. Unfortunately, millions of American youngsters fall on the negative side of the equation and, in their search for the good life, often end up headed for a career of crime. But what most Americans have in common is their love of sports and, in particular, their love of sports heroes.

These professional sports heroes have recognized the need to reach out to America's youth and offer ways to put these youngsters on a mainstream path to becoming productive members of society. Here are some examples:

"We have been fortunate to be able to reach such a large number of youth through our clinics," said Brian James, assistant coach of the Toronto Raptors, who have held free clinics for young players at various youth centers. "Basketball in Canada is growing and we are proud to help fuel the desire to learn the game."(1)

Many teams conduct weekly community service with their staff members. The Minnesota Timberwolves' community service initiative includes activities at hospitals, schools and non-profit organizations. The team plans to do three service projects a week until the season starts. Recent events include a Habitat for Humanity project and a visit to a women's shelter.(1)

The Indiana Pacers recently hosted fundraising walks to benefit osteoporosis and spinal cord research. In Dallas, the

San Francisco 49ers' Terrell Owens, left, and Lee Harris, reach for a loose ball during the "Hoops That Help" celebrity basketball game on June 19, 1999, at Selland Arena in Fresno, California. The charity event raises money for the Community Intervention and Assistance Foundation, which provides scholarships, job training, and housing.

Mavericks have issued challenges to area schoolchildren to excel in academics. Students with good attendance and who have shown grade improvement are invited to youth training camps hosted by coach and general manager Don

increase with increased counseling and aid services. Several states have instituted similar "learnfare" programs (for example, Virginia, Florida, Maryland, and Oklahoma), while others are considering this option.[74]

Recently, schools in Chicago, New York, Boston, Los Angeles, Tucson, and Washington have introduced conflict resolution into the curriculum. These programs zero in on teaching youngsters to deal with problems nonviolently. For example, by role-playing situations, children practice how to respond when someone insults or challenges them. In the Chicago area alone, 5000 students are going through this antiviolence program, which is supported by the National Institute of Mental Health.[75]

Culture Conflict Theory

Differential association theory is based on the learning of criminal (or deviant) norms or attitudes. Culture conflict theory focuses on the source of these criminal norms and attitudes. According to Thorsten Sellin, **conduct norms**—norms that regulate our daily lives—are rules that reflect the attitudes of the groups to which each of

Nelson and assistant coach Donn Nelson.(1)

The Atlanta Hawks are hosting a series of "Fast Break for Reading" assemblies for kids, while the Cleveland Cavaliers are busy promoting good nutrition and healthy eating habits. The Sacramento Kings are sponsoring a "Stay in School Essay Contest" for middle school students, and the Portland Trail Blazers front office staff helped renovate the exterior of the Blazers Boys and Girls Club. On October 17, 1998, the Miami Heat sponsored the "HEAT Walk Against Domestic Violence."(1)

The Sixers Neighborhood Basketball League (SNBL) presented by First Union and AND 1 is a youth recreation league conducted by the Philadelphia Department of Recreation. The SNBL offers boys and girls from the ages of 9 to 18 the opportunity to participate in an organized, supervised league at one of the 37 Department of Recreation facilities.

Each season more than 5,000 youths compete in more than 60 leagues from December to April. Each player receives an official SNBL T-shirt and is invited to a 76ers game. In addition, 8 SNBL teams have the opportunity to play on the 76ers home court prior to a game and the 76ers coaches lead a special clinic for SNBL coaches.(2)

The 76ers team up with Champion to present 76ers basketball 10, a fast-paced, clinic-style approach to the game of basketball that is available for schools, clubs and special events. One of the 76ers professors of basketball, such as former 76ers star World B. Free, takes the students through a class in basketball fundamentals as well as life lessons. Upon completion of the program, "graduates" are awarded diplomas.(2)

Rockets "Home Team" spokesman Scottie Pippen, along with teammates Othella Harrington, Antoine Carr, Cuttino Mobley and Bryce Drew, participated in the workday by laying sod, planting bushes and installing a basketball hoop for the new homeowners, the Taylor family. Later this month, Tracy and Shelia Taylor and their three children will move into their new home in Fifth Ward.

"It's great to be able to come out here and help a family, to give the people in this community a chance," Pippen said.(3)

Revitalization efforts are made possible each year through a grant to the Fifth Ward Community Redevelopment Corporation from the Fannie Mae Foundation with additional funding from the Rockets Clutch City Foundation. Since the start of the partnership, the Foundation and the Rockets have funded the construction of 23 homes in the Fifth Ward neighborhood. This season the Fannie Mae Foundation donated $75,000 and the Clutch City Foundation contributed $20,600 toward the construction of 12 homes.

"The Rockets and the Fannie Mae Foundation are honored to work side-by-side with families to improve Fifth Ward neighborhoods," Rockets owner Leslie Alexander said.(3)

These efforts to reach out to alienated youngsters and others in socially disorganized communities and neighborhoods are an impressive example of the American credo of helping one another without government participation. But such efforts are just a beginning. Would it not be great if all our American heroes, including all our professional athletes and sports teams, would reach out into all alienated neighborhoods where most youngsters in need of help can be found?

Sources

1. NBA News and Features: NBA Offers Helping Hand. http://www.nba.com/news_feat/community_1098.html
2. Philadelphia 76ers: Philadelphia 76ers Community Programs. http://www.nba.com/sixers/00563776.html
3. Houston Rockets: Rockets Help Community Grow. http://www.nba.com/rockets/hometeam_project.html

Questions for Discussion

Suppose you, as an individual or a member of a college group, wanted to help a socially disorganized community with leadership by a nationally or locally recognized hero (in sports, entertainment, or any other field).

1. How would you go about it? Make a plan.
2. List priorities.
3. Identify, step-by-step, the objectives you have to reach.

us belongs.[76] Their purpose is to define what is considered appropriate or normal behavior and what is inappropriate or abnormal behavior.

Sellin argues that different groups have different conduct norms and that the conduct norms of one group may conflict with those of another. Individuals may commit crimes by conforming to the norms of their own group if that group's norms conflict with those of the dominant society. According to this rationale, the main difference between a criminal and a noncriminal is that each is responding to different sets of conduct norms.

Examples of groups with values significantly deviating from those of the surrounding majority include MOVE, an African-American group concerned with issues like police brutality, animal rights, and African heritage. MOVE, located in a house on Osage Street in Philadelphia, alienated its neighbors by loud and profanity-laced loudspeaker messages. Mutual animosity escalated. Some MOVE members armed themselves. A police officer was killed. Ultimately, the police, armed with arrest warrants for some members, entered the area. The group did not surrender. The police

MOVE members and neighbors watch their houses burn after aerial and ground attacks by the Philadelphia police, May 1985. Over the next 11 years the city has paid more than $30 million to rebuild homes and settle lawsuits of cult members and their families.

attacked: 10,000 rounds of ammunition were fired, and a bomb was dropped from a police helicopter. All but two of the MOVE members died, and all the houses on the street went up in flames.

The last chapter in the MOVE drama was not written until February 1997, when the City of Philadelphia agreed to pay more than $500,000 each to the estates of MOVE founders John Africa and Frank James—after having spent over $30 million to rebuild the houses destroyed by the police bombing, and to settle lawsuits by the estates of nine other MOVE members who had perished.

Another example—far more criminal—was the Solar Temple, founded by a former Gestapo officer, which flourished in Switzerland and Canada. This mystic cult attracted wealthy members who "donated" all their property to the cult, perhaps $93 million in all; much of it was spent for the personal benefit of two cult

leaders. Cult members were heavily armed (and engaged in arms trading) in anticipation of the end of the world. Their end of the world came in the fall of 1994, when the two cult leaders murdered nearly all their followers and then committed suicide.

Sellin distinguishes between primary and secondary conflicts. *Primary conflict* occurs when norms of two cultures clash. A clash may occur at the border between neighboring cultural areas; a clash may occur when the law of one cultural group is extended to cover the territory of another; or it may occur when members of one group migrate to another culture. In a widening gap between cultural norms and generations, Southeast Asian immigrant children are running away from home in increasing numbers. They often run into an informal nationwide network of "safe houses." No one knows how many runaways there are, but it is estimated that at least one-third of all refugee families have had at least one child vanish for days, months, or even longer.

Secondary conflict arises when a single culture evolves into a variety of cultures, each with its own set of conduct norms. This type of conflict occurs when the homogeneous societies of simpler cultures become complex societies in which the number of social groupings multiplies constantly and norms are often at odds. Your college may make dormitory living mandatory for all freshmen, for example, but to follow the informal code of your peer group, you may seek the freedom of off-campus housing. Or you may have to choose whether to violate work rules by leaving your job half an hour early to make a mandatory class or to violate school rules by walking into class half an hour late. Life situations are frequently controlled by conflicting norms, so no matter how people act, they may be violating some rule, often without being aware that they are doing so.

In the next chapter, which deals with the formation and operation of subcultures, we will expand the discussion of the conflict of norms. We will also examine the empirical research that seeks to discover whether there is indeed a multitude of value systems in our society and, if so, whether and how they conflict.

REVIEW

Contemporary criminologists tend to divide the sociological explanation of crime into three categories: strain, cultural deviance, and social control. The strain and cultural deviance perspectives focus on the social forces that cause people to engage in deviant behavior. They assume that there is a relationship between social class and criminal behavior. Strain theorists argue that all people in society share one set of cultural values and that since lower-class persons often do not have legitimate means to attain society's goals, they may turn to illegitimate means instead. General strain theory, a revision of Merton's theory, relates criminal behavior to the anger that results when an individual is treated in a way he or she does not want to be treated in a social relationship. Cultural deviance theorists maintain that the lower class has a distinctive set of values and that these values often conflict with those of the middle class.

Cultural deviance theories—social disorganization, differential association, and culture conflict—relate criminal behavior to the learning of criminal values and norms. Social disorganization theory focuses on the breakdown of social institutions as a precondition for the establishment of criminal norms. Differential association theory concentrates on the processes by which criminal behavior is taught and learned. Culture conflict theory focuses on the specifics of how the conduct norms of some groups may clash with those of the dominant culture.

YOU BE THE CRIMINOLOGIST

A major funding agency has given a large grant for changing the quality of life in a high-crime inner-city neighborhood where residents are afraid to let their children play outside. You are the project director. Whom would you hire as consultants? Would you work with law enforcement? And, finally, what would be your goals, and how would you reach them?

KEY TERMS

The numbers next to the terms refer to the pages on which the terms are defined.

accommodate (132)
conduct norms (146)
cultural deviance theories (124)
cultural transmission (140)
culture conflict theory (135)
deviance (136)
differential association theory (135)
general strain theory (133)
social disorganization theory (135)
strain theory (124)

NOTES

1. Ysabel Rennie, *The Search for Criminal Man* (Lexington, Mass.: Lexington Books, 1978), p. 125.
2. James T. Carey, *Sociology and Public Affairs: The Chicago School* (Beverly Hills, Calif.: Sage, 1975), pp. 19–20.
3. See the discussion of sociological theory in Frank P. Williams III and Marilyn D. McShane, *Criminological Theory* (Englewood Cliffs, N.J.: Prentice-Hall, 1988).
4. Émile Durkheim, *The Division of Labor in Society* (New York: Free Press, 1964).
5. Émile Durkheim, *Rules of Sociological Method* (New York: Free Press, 1966).
6. Émile Durkheim, *Suicide* (Glencoe, Ill.: Free Press, 1951), pp. 241–276.
7. Ibid., p. 247.
8. Robert K. Merton, "Social Structure and Anomie," *American Sociological Review,* **3** (1938): 672–682. For a complete history of the social structure and anomie paradigm, see recent reflections of Merton in Robert K. Merton, "Opportunity Structure: The Emergence, Diffusion, and Differentiation of a Sociological Concept, 1930s–1950s," in *Advances in Criminological Theory: The Legacy of Anomie,* vol. 6, ed. Freda Adler and William S. Laufer (New Brunswick, N.J.: Transaction, 1994), pp. 3–78. Several measures of anomie have been developed. Probably the best-known indicator of anomie at the social level was formulated by Bernard Lander in a study of 8464 cases of juvenile delinquency in Baltimore between 1939 and 1942. Lander devised a measure that included the rate of delinquency, the percentage of nonwhite population in a given area,

and the percentage of owner-occupied homes. According to Lander, those factors were indicative of the amount of normlessness (anomie) in a community. See Bernard Lander, *Towards an Understanding of Juvenile Delinquency* (New York: Columbia University Press, 1954), p. 65.

9. *The World Almanac and Book of Facts, 1999* (Mahwah, N.J.: Primedia Reference, 1999).

10. Oscar Lewis, "The Culture of Poverty," *Scientific American*, **215** (1966): 19–25.

11. Gunnar Myrdal, *The Challenge of World Poverty* (New York: Vintage, 1990).

12. William Julius Wilson, *The Truly Disadvantaged* (Chicago: University of Chicago Press, 1987).

13. Robert K. Merton, *Social Theory and the Social Structure* (New York: Free Press, 1957), p. 187.

14. Albert J. Reiss, Jr., and Albert L. Rhodes, "The Distribution of Juvenile Delinquency in the Social Class Structure," *American Sociological Review*, **26** (1961): 720–732. For the relationship between economic changes and crime, see Pamela Irving Jackson, "Crime, Youth Gangs, and Urban Transition: The Social Dislocations of Postindustrial Economic Development," *Justice Quarterly*, **8** (1991): 380–397.

15. F. Ivan Nye, James F. Short, and Virgil J. Olson, "Socioeconomic Status and Delinquent Behavior," *American Journal of Sociology*, **63** (1958): 381–389.

16. Charles R. Tittle, Wayne J. Villemez, and Douglas A. Smith, "The Myth of Social Class and Criminality: An Empirical Assessment of the Empirical Evidence," *American Sociological Review*, **43** (1978): 652; Charles R. Tittle and Robert F. Meier, "Specifying the SES/Delinquency Relationship by Social Characteristics of Contexts," *Journal of Research in Crime and Delinquency*, **28** (1991): 430–455.

17. Gary F. Jensen and Kevin Thompson, "What's Class Got to Do with It? A Further Examination of Power-Control Theory," *American Journal of Sociology*, **95** (1990): 1009–1023.

18. John Braithwaite, "The Myth of Social Class and Criminality Reconsidered," *American Sociological Review*, **46** (1981): 41. See also Delbert S. Elliott and Suzanne S. Ageton, "Reconciling Race and Class Differences in Self-Reported and Official Estimates of Delinquency," *American Sociological Review*, **45** (1980): 95–110; and Michael W. Neustrom and William M. Norton, "Economic Dislocation and Property Crime," *Journal of Criminal Justice*, **23** (1995): 29–39; and James De Frongo, "Welfare and Homicide," *Journal of Research in Crime and Delinquency*, **34** (1997): 395–406.

19. Nikos Passas, "Anomie, Reference Groups, and Relative Deprivation," in *The Future of Anomie Theory*, ed. Nikos Passas and Robert Ignew (Boston: Northeastern Press, 1997), pp. 64–65.

20. Terence P. Thornberry and Margaret Farnsworth, "Social Correlates of Criminal Involvement: Further Evidence on the Relationship between Social Status and Criminal Behavior," *American Sociological Review*, **47** (1982): 505–518; Thomas J. Bernard, "Control Criticisms of Strain Theories: An Assessment of Theoretical and Empirical Adequacy," *Journal of Research in Crime and Delinquency*, **21** (1984): 353–372; Delbert S. Elliott and David Huizinga, "Social Class and Delinquent Behavior in a National Youth Panel," *Criminology*, **21** (1983): 149–177.

21. Bradley R. Entner Wright, Avshalom Caski, Terrie E. Moffitt, Richard A. Miech, and Phil A. Silva, "Reconsidering the Relationship between SES and Delinquency Causation but Not Correlation," *Criminology* **37** (1999): 175–194.

22. Tomislav V. Kovandzic, Lynne M. Vieraitis, and Mark R. Yeisley, "The Structural Covariates of Urban Homicide: Reassessing the Impact of Income Inequality and Poverty in the Post-Reagan Era," *Criminology*, **36** (1998): 569–600.

23. William R. Avison and Pamela L. Loring, "Population Diversity and Cross-National Homicide: The Effects of Inequality and Heterogeneity," *Criminology*, **24** (1986): 733–749; Harvey Krahn, Timothy F. Hartnagel, and John W. Gartrell, "Income Inequality and Homicide Rates: Cross-National

Data and Criminological Theories," *Criminology*, **24** (1986): 269–295; Richard Fowles and Mary Merva, "Wage Inequity and Criminal Activity: An Extreme Bounds Analysis for the United States, 1975–1990," *Criminology*, **34** (1996): 163–182.

24. Krahn et al., "Income Inequality," p. 288.
25. David Brownfield, "Social Class and Violent Behavior," *Criminology*, **24** (1986): 421–438.
26. David Matza, "The Disreputable Poor," in *Class, Status, and Power*, ed. Reinhard Bendix and Seymour M. Lipset (New York: Free Press, 1966). See also William S. Laufer, "Vocational Interests of Homeless, Unemployed Men," *Journal of Vocational Behavior*, **18** (1981): 196–201; and Chris Hale, "Unemployment and Crime: Differencing Is No Substitute for Modeling," *Journal of Research in Crime and Delinquency*, **28** (1991): 426–429.
27. John Hagan, "The Social Embeddedness of Crime and Unemployment," *Criminology*, **31** (1993): 465–492.
28. Judith R. Blau and Peter M. Blau, "The Cost of Inequality: Metropolitan Structure and Violent Crime," *American Sociological Review*, **47** (1982): 114–129. For a discussion of the relationship of job accessibility and racial inequality to crime rates within racial groups, see Karen F. Parker and Patricia L. McCall, "Structural Conditions and Racial Homicide Patterns: A Look at the Multiple Disadvantages in Urban Areas," *Criminology*, **37** (1999): 447–478. See also Steven F. Messner and Reid M. Golden, "Racial Inequality and Racially Disaggregated Homicide Rates: An Assessment of Alternative Theoretical Explanations," *Criminology*, **30** (1992): 421–446; and James A. Chambers, *Blacks and Crime: A Function of Class* (Westport, Conn.: Praeger, 1995).
29. John Braithwaite, *Inequality, Crime, and Public Policy* (London: Routledge & Kegan Paul, 1979), p. 219.
30. Thomas J. Bernard, "Merton versus Hirshi: Who Is Faithful to Durkheim's Heritage?" in Adler and Laufer, *Advances in Criminological Theory*, vol. 4, pp. 81–91; Nikos Passas, "Continuities in the Anomie Tradition," in Adler and Laufer, *Advances in Criminological*

Theory, vol. 4, pp. 91–112; Scott Menard, "A Developmental Test of Mertonian Anomie Theory," *Journal of Research in Crime and Delinquency*, **32** (1995): 136–174.
31. Gary F. Jensen, "Salvaging Structure through Strain: A Theoretical and Empirical Critique," in Adler and Laufer, *Advances in Criminological Theory*, vol. 4, pp. 139–158; Velmer S. Burton, Jr., Francis T. Cullen, T. David Evans, and R. Gregory Dunaway, "Reconsidering Strain Theory: Operationalization, Rival Theories, and Adult Criminality," *Journal of Quantitative Criminology*, **10** (1994): 213–239.
32. Ian Taylor, Paul Walton, and Jock Young, *The New Criminology* (New York: Harper & Row, 1973), p. 107.
33. Freda Adler, *Nations Not Obsessed with Crime* (Littleton, Colo.: Fred B. Rothman, 1983).
34. Steven F. Messner and Richard Rosenfeld, *Crime and the American Dream* (Belmont, Calif.: Wadsworth, 1994).
35. Mitchell B. Chamlin and John K. Cochran, "Assessing Messner and Rosenfeld's Institutional Anomie Theory: A Partial Test," *Criminology*, **33** (1995): 411–429.
36. Freda Adler, "Synnomie to Anomie: A Macrosociological Formulation," in Adler and Laufer, *Advances in Criminological Theory*, vol. 4, pp. 271–283.
37. Robert Agnew, "Foundations for a General Strain Theory of Crime and Delinquency," *Criminology*, **30** (1992): 47–87.
38. Robert Agnew, "The Contribution of Social-Psychological Strain Theory to the Explanation of Crime and Delinquency," in Adler and Laufer, *Advances in Criminological Theory*, pp. 113–137. See also John P. Hoffman and Alan S. Miller, "A Latent Variable Analysis of General Strain Theory," *Journal of Quantitative Criminology*, **14** (1998): 83–110.
39. Raymond Paternoster and Paul Mazerolle, "General Strain Theory and Delinquency: A Replication and Extension," *Journal of Research in Crime and Delinquency*, **31** (1994): 235–263; Timothy Brezina, "Adapting to Strain: An Examination of Delinquent Coping Responses," *Criminology*, **34** (1996): 39–60; Robert Agnew and Helene Raskin

White, "An Empirical Test of General Strain Theory," *Criminology,* **30** (1992): 475–499. For an examination of gender and delinquent behavior from a general strain theory perspective, see Paul Mazerolle, "Gender, General Strain and Delinquency: An Emperical Examination," *Justice Quarterly,* **15** (1998): 65–91.

40. David Phinney, "Community News Focus: To Head Start Sanchez Serves as 'Model of Success,' " *Los Angeles Times,* Jan. 11, 1997, p. 83.

41. John R. Berrueta-Clement, Lawrence J. Schweinhart, W. Steven Barnett, Ann S. Epstein, and David P. Weekart, *Changed Lives: The Effects of the Perry Preschool Program on Youths through Age 19* (Ypsilanti, Mich.: High/Scope, 1984).

42. Jane Gross, "Remnants of the War on Poverty, Job Corps Is Still a Quiet Success," *New York Times,* Feb. 17, 1992, pp. 1, 14.

43. Tammy Joyner, "Atlanta Job Corps Exec Wins Award," *Atlanta Journal and Constitution,* June 8, 1999, p. 2F.

44. Lawrence W. Sherman, Denise Gottfredson, Doris McKenzie, John Eck, Peter Reuter, and Sharon Bushway, *Preventing Crime: What Works, What Doesn't, What's Promising,* U.S. Department of Justice, Office of Justice Programs, February 1997, chap. 6, p. 40.

45. W. I. Thomas and Florian Znaniecki, *The Polish Peasant in Europe and America* (Boston: Gorham, 1920).

46. Robert E. Park, "Human Ecology," *American Journal of Sociology,* **42** (1936): 1–15.

47. Clifford R. Shaw, Frederick M. Forbaugh, Henry D. McKay, and Leonard S. Cottrell, *Delinquency Areas* (Chicago: University of Chicago Press, 1929).

48. Clifford R. Shaw and Henry D. McKay, *Juvenile Delinquency and Urban Areas* (Chicago: University of Chicago Press, 1942); see also the revised and updated edition: Clifford R. Shaw and Henry D. McKay, *Juvenile Delinquency and Urban Areas: A Study of Delinquency in Relation to Differential Characteristics of Local Communities in American Cities* (Chicago: University of Chicago Press, 1969); and Frederick M. Thrasher, *The Gang* (Chicago: University of Chicago Press, 1927).

49. Ralph B. Taylor, "The Impact of Crime on Communities," *The Annals of the American Academy,* **539** (1995): 28–45.

50. Ralph B. Taylor, Steve D. Gottfredson, and Sidney Brower, "Attachments to Place: Discriminant Validity and Impacts of Disorder and Diversity," *American Journal of Community Psychology,* **13** (1985): 525–542.

51. Michael Marriott, "Living in 'Lockdown,' " *Newsweek,* Jan. 23, 1995, p. 57.

52. Lynn Newhart Smith and Gary D. Hill, "Victimization and Fear of Crime," *Criminal Justice and Behavior,* **18** (1991): 217–239; and Randy L. LaGrange, Kenneth F. Ferraro, and Michael Supancic, "Perceived Risk of Fear of Crime: Role of Social and Physical Incivilities," *Journal of Research in Crime and Delinquency,* **29** (1992): 311–334. For research that measures safety and perceived safety resources in the context of other environmental concerns (as an alternative to measuring fear of crime), see John J. Gibbs and Kathleen J. Hanrahan, "Safety Demand and Supply: An Alternative to Fear of Crime," *Justice Quarterly,* **10** (1993): 369–394.

53. Ralph Taylor and Jeanette Covington, "Community Structural Change and Fear of Crime," *Social Problems,* **40** (1993): 374–392.

54. Douglas A. Smith, "The Neighborhood Context of Police Behavior," in *Communities and Crime,* ed. Albert J. Reiss and Michael Tonry (Chicago: University of Chicago Press, 1986), pp. 313–341; Terance D. Miethe, Michael Hughes, and David McDowall, "Social Change in Crime Rates: An Evaluation of Alternative Theoretical Approaches," *Social Forces,* **70** (1991): 165–185; E. Britt Paterson, "Poverty, Income Inequality, and Community Crime Rates," *Criminology,* **29** (1991): 755–776; Josefina Figueira-McDonough, "Community Structure and Delinquency: A Typology," *Social Service Review,* **65** (1991): 65–91; and Denise C. Gottfredson, Richard J. McNeil, and Gary D. Gottfredson, "Social Area Influence on Delinquency: A Multilevel Analysis," *Journal of Research in Crime and Delinquency,* **28** (1991): 197–226.

55. Dina R. Rose and Todd R. Clear, "Incarceration, Social Capital, and Crime: Implica-

tions for Social Disorganization Theory," *Criminology*, **36** (1998): 441–479.

56. Robert J. Sampson and Dawn Jeglum Bartusch, *Attitudes toward Crime, Police, and the Law: Individual and Neighborhood Differences*, National Institute of Justice Research Preview, June 1999.

57. Steve J. South and Gary D. Deane, "Race and Residential Mobility: Individual Determinants and Structural Constraints," *Social Forces*, **72** (1993): 147–167.

58. See Faith Peeples and Rolf Loeber, "Do Individual Factors and Neighborhood Context Explain Ethnic Differences in Juvenile Delinquency?" *Journal of Quantitative Criminology*, **10** (1994): 141–157; and Thomas A. Petee, Gregory S. Kowlaski, and Don W. Duffield, "Crime, Social Disorganization, and Social Structure: A Research Note on the Use of Interurban Ecological Models," *American Journal of Criminal Justice*, **19** (1994): 117–132.

59. Taylor, "The Impact of Crime on Communities," p. 36.

60. Andrew J. Buck, Simon Hakim, and Ulrich Spiegel, "Casinos, Crime, and Real Estate Values: Do They Relate?" *Journal of Research in Crime and Delinquency*, **28** (1991): 288–303.

61. Robert J. Bursik and Harold G. Grosmick, *Neighborhoods and Crime* (New York: Lexington Books, 1993).

62. Anthony Sorrentino and David Whittaker, "The Chicago Area Project—Addressing the Gang Problem," *FBI Law Enforcement Bulletin*, **63** (1994): 8–12; "Philadelphia Settles with Estates of MOVE Members," *Jet*, Feb. 17, 1997, p. 40; Steven Schlossman, Goul Zellman, and Richard Shavelson, "Delinquency Prevention in South Chicago: A Fifty-Year Assessment of the Chicago Area Project," report prepared for the National Institute of Education by the Rand Corporation, May 1984, p. 1; Solomon Kobrin, "The Chicago Area Project: 25 Years of Assessment," *Annals of the American Academy of Political and Social Science*, **332** (1959): 20–29.

63. Terence Dunworth and Gregory Mills, *National Evaluation of Weed and Seed*, NIJ Research in Brief, June 1999.

64. M. Isolina Ferre, "Prevention and Control of Violence through Community Revitalization, Individual Dignity, and Personal Self-Confidence," *Annals of the American Academy of Political and Social Science*, **494** (1987): 27–36.

65. Edwin H. Sutherland, *Principles of Criminology*, 3d ed. (Philadelphia: Lippincott, 1939).

66. William Chambliss, *Boxmen* (New York: Harper & Row, 1972).

67. James S. Short, "Differential Association as a Hypothesis: Problems of Empirical Testing," *Social Problems*, **8** (1960): 14–15.

68. Travis Hirschi, *Causes of Delinquency* (Berkeley: University of California Press, 1969), p. 95.

69. Beth Bjerregaard and Carolyn Smith, "Patterns of Male and Female Gang Membership," working paper no. 13, Rochester Youth Development Study (Albany, N.Y.: Hindelang Criminal Justice Research Center, 1992), p. 20. For contradictory findings, see Mark D. Reed and Pamela Wilcox Roundtree, "Peer Pressure and Adolescent Substance Abuse," *Journal of Quantitative Criminology*, **13** (1997), 143–180. For the relationship of delinquents to their delinquent siblings, see Janet L. Lauritsen, "Sibling Resemblance in Juvenile Delinquency: Findings from the National Youth Survey," *Criminology*, **31** (1993): 387–409.

70. Mark Warr, "Age, Peers, and Delinquency," *Criminology*, **31** (1993): 17–40.

71. Charles Tittle, *Sanctions and Social Deviance* (New York: Praeger, 1980).

72. Clayton A. Hartjen, *Crime and Criminalization* (New York: Praeger, 1974), p. 51.

73. Ross L. Matsueda, "The Current State of Differential Association," *Crime and Delinquency*, **34** (1988): 277–306; and Craig Reinarman and Jeffrey Fagan, "Social Organization and Differential Association: A Research Note from a Longitudinal Study of Violent Juvenile Offenders," *Crime and Delinquency*, **34** (1988): 307–327.

74. Susan Chira, "A Program That Works for Teen-Age Mothers," *New York Times*, Apr. 28, 1993, p. A12.

75. Fox Butterfield, "Programs Seek to Stop Trouble Before It Starts," *New York Times*, Dec. 30, 1994, A25.

Review • You Be the Criminologist • Key Terms • Notes

76. Thorsten Sellin, *Culture Conflict and Crime,* Bulletin 41 (New York: Social Science Research Council, 1938); Avison and Loring, "Population Diversity and Cross-National Homicide"; Mark R. Pogrebin and Eric D. Poole, "Culture Conflict and Crime in the Korean-American Community," *Criminal Justice Policy Review,* **4** (1990): 69–78; and Ira Sommers, Jeffrey Fagan, and Deborah Baskin, "The Influences of Acculturation and Familism on Puerto Rican Delinquency," *Justice Quarterly,* **11** (1994): 207–228.

CHAPTER 6
The Formation of Subcultures

KEY TERMS
differential opportunity theory
reaction formation
subculture
subcultures of violence

In Fresno, California, the Mongolian Boys Society, a Hmong gang, terrorized, assaulted, and forced girls as young as 12 into prostitution. Hmong gangs are also springing up in Denver, Colorado, where gang members lure Asian girls into motel rooms by offering them a ride and a chance to "party." The gang members do not release the girls until they have had sex with a number of customers. Hmong gang members also kidnapped and gang-raped a 20-year-old University of Colorado student.

Vietnamese gangs in Atlanta smuggle young women and girls into the United States. The cost of the trip, including the promise of legal employment in America, is $40,000. If they are unable to pay the fee, they are forced to be sex slaves in illegal brothels until the amount of passage is paid off, an equivalent of about 600 sex acts.[1]

While Asian gangs represent only a minority of gangs in the United States, their rapid spread to cities such as Denver, as well as to smaller communities, including suburbs and rural areas, demonstrates the increasing prevalence of gangs outside major cities such as New York, Los Angeles, and Chicago. Nationwide 23 cities had known street gangs in 1961. In 1997, the National Youth Gang Center surveyed over 2700 cities, towns, and counties and found 30,500 gangs and 816,000 gang members.[2]

Gang violence, too, is on the rise. Reports about juvenile gang activities fill the files of police departments, juvenile courts, and adult courts as well. How did these groups get started in American society? What keeps them going?

THE FUNCTION OF SUBCULTURES

Strain theorists explain criminal behavior as a result of the frustrations suffered by lower-class individuals deprived of legitimate means to reach their goals. Cultural deviance theorists assume that individuals become criminal by learning the criminal values of the groups to which they belong. In conforming to their own group standards, these people break the laws of the dominant culture. These two perspectives are the foundation for subcultural theory, which emerged in the mid-1950s.

A **subculture** is a subdivision within the dominant culture that has its own norms, beliefs, and values. Subcultures typically emerge when people in similar circumstances find themselves isolated from the mainstream and band together for mutual support. Subcultures may form among members of racial and ethnic minorities, among prisoners, among occupational groups, among ghetto dwellers. Subcultures exist within a larger society, not apart from it. They therefore share some of its values. Nevertheless, the lifestyles of their members are significantly different from those of individuals in the dominant culture.

SUBCULTURAL THEORIES OF DELINQUENCY AND CRIME

Subcultural theories in criminology had been developed to account for delinquency among lower-class males, especially for one of its most important expressions—the teenage gang. According to subcultural theorists, delinquent subcultures, like all subcultures, emerge in response to special problems that members of the dominant culture do not face. Theories developed by Albert Cohen and by Richard Cloward and Lloyd Ohlin are extensions of the strain, social disorganization, and differential association theories. They explain why delinquent subcultures emerge in the first place (strain), why they take a particular form (social disorganization), and how they are passed on from one generation to the next (differential association).

The explanations of delinquency developed by Marvin Wolfgang and Franco Ferracuti and by Walter Miller are somewhat different from those mentioned above. These theorists do not suggest that delinquency begins with failure to reach middle-class goals. Their explanations are rooted in culture conflict theory. The subculture of violence thesis argues that the value systems of some subcultures demand the use of violence in certain social situations. This norm, which affects daily behavior, conflicts with conventional middle-class norms. Along the same lines, Miller suggests that the characteristics of lower-class delinquency reflect the value system of the lower-class culture and that the lower-class values and norms conflict with those of the dominant culture.

Although Miller contends that the lower-class culture as a whole—not a subculture within it—is responsible for criminal behavior in urban slums, his theory is appropriate to our discussion because it demonstrates how the needs of young urban males are met by membership in a street gang. Miller's street gangs, like those of Cohen and of Cloward and Ohlin, condone violent criminal activity as one of the few means of attaining status in a slum.

The Middle-Class Measuring Rod

Albert Cohen was a student of Robert Merton and of Edwin Sutherland, both of whom had made convincing arguments about the causes of delinquency. Sutherland persuaded Cohen that differential association and the cultural transmission of criminal norms led to criminal behavior. From Merton he learned about structurally induced strain. Cohen combined and expanded these perspectives to explain how the delinquent subculture arises, where it is found within the social structure, and why it has the particular characteristics that it does.[3]

According to Cohen, delinquent subcultures emerge in the slum areas of large American cities. They are rooted in class differentials in parental aspirations, child-rearing practices, and classroom standards. The relative position of a youngster's family in the social structure determines the problems the child will have to face throughout life.

Lower-class families who have never known a middle-class lifestyle, for example,

FIGURE 6.1   The process of reaction formation among delinquent boys.

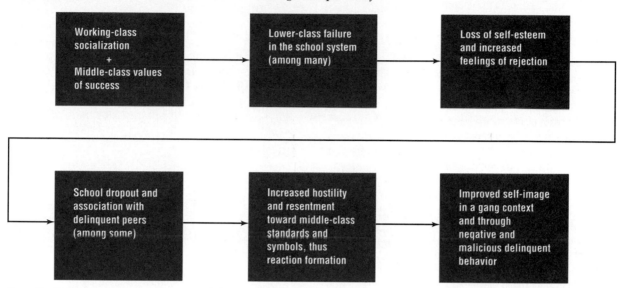

Source: Donald J. Shoemaker, *Theories of Delinquency: An Examination of Explanations of Delinquent Behavior,* 3d ed. (New York: Oxford University Press, 1996), p. 107.

cannot socialize their children in a way that prepares them to enter the middle class. The children grow up with poor communication skills, lack of commitment to education, and an inability to delay gratification. Schools present a particular problem. There, lower-class children are evaluated by middle-class teachers on the basis of a middle-class measuring rod. The measures are based on such middle-class values as self-reliance, good manners, respect for property, and long-range planning. By such measures, lower-class children fall far short of the standards they must meet if they are to compete successfully with middle-class children. Cohen argues that they experience status frustration and strain, to which they respond by adopting one of three roles: corner boy, college boy, or delinquent boy.

Corner Boy, College Boy, Delinquent Boy

Corner boys try to make the best of bad situations. The corner boy hangs out in the neighborhood with his peer group, spending the day in some group activity, such as gambling or athletic competition. He receives support from his peers and is very loyal to them. Most lower-class boys become corner boys. Eventually, they get menial jobs and live a conventional lifestyle.

There are very few *college boys.* These boys continually strive to live up to middle-class standards, but their chances for success are limited because of academic and social handicaps.

Delinquent boys band together to form a subculture in which they can define status in ways that to them seem attainable. Cohen claims that even though these lower-class youths set up their own norms, they have internalized the norms of the dominant class and they feel anxious when they go against those norms. To deal with this conflict, they resort to **reaction formation,** a mechanism that relieves anxiety through the process of rejecting with abnormal intensity what one wants but cannot obtain. These boys turn the middle-class norms upside down, thereby making conduct right in their subculture precisely because it is wrong by the norms of the larger culture (Figure 6.1).

Consequently, their delinquent acts serve no useful purpose. They do not steal things to eat them, wear them, or sell them. In fact, they often discard or destroy what they have stolen. They appear to delight in the discomfort of others and in breaking taboos. Their acts are directed against people and property at random, unlike the goal-oriented activities of many adult criminal groups. The subculture is typi-

A decade ago the Bushwick neighborhood of Brooklyn was one of the most notorious drug bazaars in the country. Today dealers no longer sell on street corners, but use beepers and sell behind closed doors. Businesses are returning to the neighborhood, land once used by drug dealers for pit bull fights is now a garden, children and adults fill the parks by day, and the nightly gunfire in the park has been replaced by the voices of boys arguing over who the greatest baseball player is.

How did this change come about? The generation that started using crack in the 1980s has not stopped using it, but their children are not following in their footsteps. A Harlem resident whose mother was a crack addict noted that children of crack addicts "wanted to get as far away from that drug as [they] could." (1) Using crack is no longer a socially desirable option. In fact, "[p]eople look down on them so much that even crackheads don't want

The neighborhood fights back.

to be crackheads anymore."(1) These comments are reflected in a drug use survey of male arrestees in New York, which found that 35.7 percent of males over the age of 36 had recently used crack, compared with 4 percent of

cally characterized by short-run hedonism, pure pleasure seeking, with no planning or deliberation about what to do, nor where or when to do it. The delinquents hang out on the street corner until someone gets an idea; then they act impulsively, without considering the consequences. The group's autonomy is all-important. Its members are loyal to each other and resist any attempts on the part of family, school, or community to restrain their behavior.

Tests of Cohen's Theory

Criminological researchers generally agree that Cohen's theory is responsible for major advances in research on delinquency.[4] Among them are researchers who have found a relationship between delinquency and social status in our society (Chapter 5). Much evidence also supports Cohen's assumption that lower-class children perform more poorly in school than middle-class children.[5] Teachers often expect them to perform less ably than their middle-class students, and this expectation is one of the components of poor performance.

Researchers have demonstrated that poor performance in school is related to delinquency. When Travis Hirschi studied more than 4000 California schoolchildren, he found that youths who were academically incompetent and performed poorly in school came to dislike school. Disliking it, they rejected its authority; rejecting its authority, they committed delinquent acts (Chapter 7).[6] Delbert Elliott and Harwin Voss also investigated the relationship between school and delinquency. They analyzed annual school performance and delinquency records of 2000 students in California from ninth grade to 1 year after the expected graduation date. Their findings indicated that those who dropped out of school had higher rates of delinquency than those who graduated. They also found that academic achievement and alienation from school were closely related to dropping out of school.[7]

From analysis of the dropout-delinquency relationship among over 5000 persons nationwide, G. Roger Jarjoura concluded that while dropouts were more likely to engage in delinquent acts than graduates, the reason was not always simply the fact that they had dropped

those between the ages of 15 and 20. National surveys reflect the same patterns of use.

The low rate of crack use explains some of the changes in neighborhoods that were once plagued with violence and crack dealers. But can it account for all the changes? Police in New York point to the high number of drug arrests and other law enforcement efforts to explain the decline in violence and street-level dealing. However, violence and street-level dealing have decreased throughout the country, even in major cities that did not increase their police activity.(1) Research suggests an alternative explanation—the stabilization of crack markets. Violence is used as a regulatory mechanism in illicit drug markets. When crack emerged in the 1980s, gangs and other dealers did not have established markets. The unstable nature of the markets opened the door for violence as a tool to establish those markets. This is exemplified by the experience in Milwaukee, where violence increased sharply as rival gangs and individual dealers engaged in a drug war.(2,3)

The decrease in violence in areas that used to be filled with crack markets obviously represents a turn for the better. The question arises as to how to maintain and improve the current situation. Although the answer is likely to vary for each neighborhood, an understanding of what has happened since the mid-1980s may provide some insight into what can and should be done in the future.

Sources

1. Timothy Egan, "A Drug Ran Its Course, Then Hid with Its Users," *New York Times,* Sept. 19, 1999, p. 1.
2. Jeffrey Fagan, "Gangs, Drugs, and Neighborhood Change," in *Gangs in America,* ed. C. Ronald Huff (Thousand Oaks, Calif.: Sage, 1996), pp. 39–74.
3. John M. Hagedorn, "Gang Violence in the Postindustrial Era," in *Youth Violence, Crime and Justice: A Review of Research,* vol. 24 (Chicago: University of Chicago Press, 1998), pp. 365–419.

Questions for Discussion

1. Which explanations for the drop in violence in cities around the country do you think are most valid? What can we do to continue the trend?
2. The residents of Bushwick suggest that using crack is looked down upon, especially by the children of addicts. Why might individuals who grew up with crack addicts as parents feel this way? Do children whose parents used other drugs have a different response?

---

out. Dropping out because of a dislike for school, poor grades, or financial reasons was related to future involvement in delinquency; dropping out because of problems at home was not. Dropping out for personal reasons such as marriage or pregnancy was significantly related to subsequent violent offending.[8] All these findings support Cohen's theory. Other findings, however, do not.

In a study of 12,524 students in Davidson County, Tennessee, Albert Reiss and Albert Rhodes found only a slight relationship between delinquency and status deprivation.[9] This conclusion was supported by the research of Marvin Krohn and his associates.[10] Furthermore, several criminologists have challenged Cohen's claim that delinquent behavior is purposeless.[11] They contend that much delinquent behavior is serious and calculated, and often engaged in for profit.[12] Others have also questioned the consistency of the theory: Cohen argues that the behavior of delinquent boys is a deliberate response to middle-class opinion; yet he also argues that the boys do not care about the opinions of middle-class people.[13]

Evaluation: Cohen's Theory

Researchers have praised and criticized Cohen's work. Cohen's theory answers a number of questions left unresolved by the strain and cultural deviance theories. It explains the origin of delinquent behavior and why some youths raised in the same neighborhoods and attending the same schools do not become involved in delinquent subcultures. His concepts of status deprivation and the middle-class measuring rod have been useful to researchers. Yet his theory does not explain why most delinquents eventually become law-abiding even though their position in the class structure remains relatively fixed. Some criminologists also question whether youths are driven by some serious motivating force or whether they are simply out on the streets looking for fun.[14] Moreover, if delinquent subcultures result from the practice of measuring lower-class boys by a middle-class measuring rod, how do we account for the growing number of middle-class gangs?

Other questions concern the difficulty of trying to test the concepts of reaction formation, internalization of middle-class values, and status deprivation, among others. To answer some of his critics, Cohen, with his colleague James Short, expanded the idea of delinquent subcultures to include not only lower-class delinquent behavior but also such variants as middle-class delinquent subcultures and female delinquents.[15] Cohen took Merton's strain theory a step further by elaborating on the development of delinquent behavior. He described how strain actually creates frustration and status deprivation, which in turn foster the development of an alternative set of values that give lower-class boys a chance to achieve recognition. Since the mid-1950s Cohen's theory has stimulated not only research but the formulation of new theories.

DELINQUENCY AND OPPORTUNITY

Like Cohen's theory, the theory of differential opportunity developed by Richard Cloward and Lloyd Ohlin combines strain, differential association, and social disorganization concepts.[16] Both theories begin with the assumption that conventional means to conventional success are not equally distributed among the socioeconomic classes, that lack of means causes frustration for lower-class youths, and that criminal behavior is learned and culturally transmitted. Both theories also agree that the common solution to shared problems leads to the formation of delinquent subcultures. They disagree, however, on the content of these subcultures. As we have noted, norms in Cohen's delinquent subcultures are right precisely because they are wrong in the dominant culture. Delinquent acts are negative and nonutilitarian. Cloward and Ohlin disagree; they suggest that lower-class delinquents remain goal-oriented. The kind of delinquent behavior they engage in depends on the illegitimate opportunities available to them.

According to Cloward and Ohlin's **differential opportunity theory,** delinquent subcultures flourish in lower-class areas and take the particular forms they do because opportunities for illegitimate success are no more equitably distributed than those for conventional success. Just as means—opportunities—are unequally

distributed in the conventional world, opportunities to reach one's goals are unequally distributed in the criminal world. A person cannot simply decide to join a theft-oriented gang or, for that matter, a violence-oriented one. Cloward and Ohlin maintain that the types of subcultures and of the juvenile gangs that flourish within them depend on the types of neighborhoods in which they develop (Figure 6.2).

In areas where conventional and illegitimate values and behavior are integrated by a close connection of illegitimate and legitimate businesses, *criminal gangs* emerge. Older criminals serve as role models. They teach youngsters the kinds of people to exploit, the necessary criminal skills, the importance of loyal relationships with criminal associates, and the way to make the right connections with shady lawyers, bail bondsmen, crooked politicians, and corrupt police officers. Adolescent members of criminal gangs, like adult criminals in the neighborhood, are involved in extortion, fraud, theft, and other activities that yield illegal income.

This type of neighborhood was described by one of its members in a classic work published in 1930:

> Stealing in the neighborhood was a common practice among the children and approved by the parents. Whenever the boys got together they talked about robbing and made more plans for stealing. I hardly knew any boys who did not go robbing. The little fellows went in for petty stealing, breaking into freight cars, and stealing junk. The older guys did big jobs like stickups, burglary, and stealing autos. The little fellows admired the "big shots" and longed for the day when they could get into the big racket. Fellows who had "done time" were the big shots and looked up to and gave the little fellows tips on how to get by and pull off big jobs.[17]

Neighborhoods characterized by transience and instability, Cloward and Ohlin argue, offer few opportunities to get ahead in organized criminal activities. This world gives rise to *conflict gangs,* whose goal is to gain a reputation for toughness and destructive violence. Thus "one particular biker would catch a bird and then bite off its head, allowing the blood to trickle from his mouth as he yelled 'all right!' "[18] It is

FIGURE 6.2   Factors leading to development of three types of delinquent gangs.

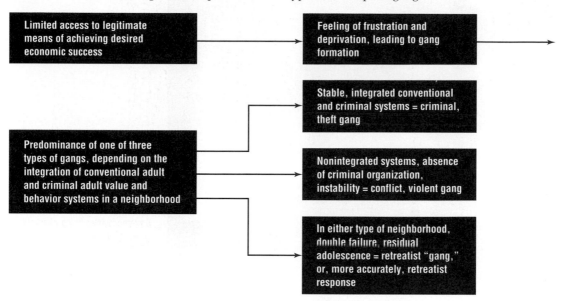

Source: Donald J. Shoemaker, *Theories of Delinquency: An Examination of Explanations of Delinquent Behavior*, 3rd ed. (New York: Oxford University Press, 1996), p. 115.

the world of the warrior: Fight, show courage against all odds, defend and maintain the honor of the group. Above all, never show fear.

Violence is the means used to gain status in conflict gangs. Conventional society's recognition of the "worst" gangs becomes a mark of prestige, perpetuating the high standards of their members. Conflict gangs emerge in lower-class areas where neither criminal nor conventional adult role models exercise much control over youngsters.

A third subcultural response to differential opportunities is the formation of *retreatist gangs*. Cloward and Ohlin describe members of retreatist gangs as double failures because they have not been successful in the legitimate world and have been equally unsuccessful in the illegitimate worlds of organized criminal activity and violence-oriented gangs. This sub-culture is characterized by a continuous search for getting high through alcohol, atypical sexual experiences, marijuana, hard drugs, or a combination of these.

The retreatist hides in a world of sensual adventure, borrowing, begging, or stealing to support his habit, whatever it may be. He may peddle drugs or work as a pimp or look for some other deviant income-producing activity. But the income is not a primary concern; he is interested only in the next high. Belonging to a retreatist gang offers a sense of superiority and well-being that is otherwise beyond the reach of these least successful dropouts.

Not all lower-class youngsters who are unable to reach society's goals become members of criminal, conflict, or retreatist gangs. Many choose to accept their situation and to live within its constraints. These law-abiding youngsters are Cohen's corner boys.

Tests of Opportunity Theory

Cloward and Ohlin's differential opportunity theory presented many new ideas, and a variety of studies emerged to test it empirically.

The first of Cloward and Ohlin's assumptions—that blocked opportunities are related to delinquency—has mixed support. Travis Hirschi, for example, demonstrated that "the greater one's acceptance of conventional (or even quasi-conventional) success goals, the less likely one is to be delinquent, regardless of the likelihood these goals will someday be attained."[19] In

Three suspected members of the Crips, a gang reputed for its toughness and violence, hit the pavement after being chased by SAPD officers and deputies of the Baxar County Gang Unit. The suspects' names were being checked through computers for any outstanding warrants. All three were arrested.

other words, the youngsters who stick to hard work and education to get ahead in society are the least likely to become delinquent, no matter what their real chances of reaching their goals. John Hagedorn disagrees. In late 1992 and early 1993, he conducted interviews with 101 founding members of 18 gangs in Milwaukee. His conclusion: "Most of those we were trying to track appeared to be on an economic merry-go-round, with continual movement in and out of the secondary labor market. Although their average income from drug sales far surpassed their income from legal employment, most Milwaukee male gang members apparently kept trying to find licit work."[20] There is also evidence that both gang and nongang boys believe the middle-class values of hard work and scholastic achievement to be important. Gang boys, however, are more ready to approve of a wide range of behaviors, including aggressive acts and drug use.[21]

The second assumption of differential opportunity theory—that the type of lower-class gang depends on the type of neighborhood in which it emerges—has also drawn the attention of criminologists. Empirical evidence suggests that gang behavior is more versatile and in-

volves a wider range of criminal and noncriminal acts than the patterns outlined by Cloward and Ohlin. Ko-lin Chin's research on New York gangs in 1993 demonstrates that Chinese gangs are engaged in extortion, alien smuggling, heroin trafficking, and the running of gambling establishments and houses of prostitution.[22] A recent report from the Denver Youth Survey showed that while the most frequent form of illegal activity is fighting with other gangs, gang members are also involved in robberies, joyriding, assaults, stealing, and drug sales.[23]

Research does, however, support Cloward and Ohlin's argument that criminal gangs emerge in areas where conventional and illegitimate behavior have a close connection with illegitimate and legitimate businesses. Chinatowns in America, for example, are social, economic, political, and cultural units.[24] All types of organizations, including those that dominate illegal activities, play an important role in the maintenance of order in the community. The illegitimate social order has control of territorial rights, gambling places, heroin trafficking, alien smuggling, and loan-sharking. The illegal order defines

who is in control of particular restaurants, retail shops, garment factories, and the like. Business owners pay a "membership fee" for protection. Adult criminals maintain control of youth gang members by threatening to exclude them from work that pays well. They also resolve conflicts, provide recreational facilities, lend money, and give the young gang members a chance to climb the illegitimate career ladder within the criminal organization. Gang activities are closely supervised by their leaders, who work with the adult crime groups. Elaborate initiation rites are conducted by an adult the youngsters call "uncle"—the link between the gang and the adult sponsoring organization.

Gang members (1015) from California, Illinois, Iowa, Michigan, and Ohio also reported having a variety of legal and illegal income sources, collective gang "treasuries," and mostly adult leaders.[25] Their businesses include dance clubs, billiard halls, and stereo, liquor, jewelry, grocery, cellular phone/beeper, and auto repair shops. They also sell illegal goods: $268 for a 9-mm Glock semiautomatic pistol, $42 for a box of cartridges, $882 for 1 ounce of cocaine, and $155 for a stolen 12-gauge shotgun.[26] These gangs operate somewhat like a union for the underground economy. Members attend meetings, pay dues, follow rules, have their own language, and make collective expenditures (for guns, funerals, attorneys).

Evaluation: Differential Opportunity Theory

For three decades criminologists have reviewed, examined, and revised the work of Cloward and Ohlin.[27] One of the main criticisms is that their theory is class-oriented. If, as Cloward and Ohlin claim, delinquency is a response to blocked opportunities, how can we explain middle-class delinquency? Another question arises from contradictory statements. How can delinquent groups be nonutilitarian, negativistic, and malicious (Cohen)—and also goal-oriented and utilitarian? Despite its shortcomings, however, differential opportunity theory has identified some of the reasons lower-class youngsters may become alienated. Cloward and Ohlin's work has also challenged researchers to study the nature of the subcultures in our society. Marvin Wolfgang and Franco Ferracuti have concentrated on one of them—the subculture of violence.

THE SUBCULTURE OF VIOLENCE

Like Cohen, and like Cloward and Ohlin, Marvin Wolfgang and Franco Ferracuti turned to subcultural theory to explain criminal behavior among lower-class young urban males. All three theories developed by these five researchers assume the existence of subcultures made up of people who share a value system that differs from that of the dominant culture. And they assume that each subculture has its own rules or conduct norms that dictate how individuals should act under varying circumstances. The three theories also agree that these values and norms persist over time because they are learned by successive generations. The theories differ, however, in their focus.

Cohen and Cloward and Ohlin focus on the origin of the subculture, specifically, culturally induced strain. The thrust of Wolfgang and Ferracuti's work is culture conflict. Furthermore, the earlier theories encompass all types of delinquency and crime; Wolfgang and Ferracuti concentrate on violent crime. They argue that in some subcultures behavior norms are dictated by a value system that demands the use of force or violence.[28] Subcultures that adhere to conduct norms conducive to violence are referred to as **subcultures of violence.**

Violence is not used in all situations, but it is frequently an expected response. The appearance of a weapon, a slight shove or push, a derogatory remark, or the opportunity to wield power undetected may very well evoke an aggressive reaction that seems uncalled for to middle-class people. Fists rather than words settle disputes. Knives or guns are readily available, so confrontations can quickly escalate. Violence is a pervasive part of everyday life. Child-rearing practices (hitting), gang activities (street wars), domestic quarrels (battering), and social events (drunken brawls) are all permeated by violence.

Violence is not considered antisocial. Members of this subculture feel no guilt about their aggression. In fact, individuals who do not resort to violence may be reprimanded. The value system is transmitted from generation to generation, long after the original reason for the violence has disappeared. The pattern is very hard to eradicate.

When Wolfgang and Ferracuti described population groups that are likely to respond violently to stress, they posed a powerful question to the criminal justice system. How does one go about changing a subcultural norm? This question becomes increasingly significant with the merging of the drug subculture and the subculture of violence.

Did You Know

. . . that 12 percent of all murders in 1997 had at least one offender who was under the age of 18?

Tests of the Subculture of Violence

Howard Erlanger, using nationwide data collected for the President's Commission on the Causes and Prevention of Violence, found no major differences in attitudes toward violence by class or race. Erlanger concluded that though members of the lower class show no greater approval of violence than middle-class persons do, they lack the sophistication necessary to settle grievances by other means.[29] The subculture of violence thesis has also generated a line of empirical research that looks at regional differences in levels of violent crime.

The South (as you will see in Chapter 11) has the highest homicide rate in the country. Some researchers have attributed this high rate to subcultural values.[30] They argue that the Southern subculture of violence has its historical roots in an exaggerated defense of honor by Southern gentlemen, mob violence (especially lynching), a military tradition, the acceptance of personal vengeance, and the widespread availability and use of handguns.[31]

The problem with many of these studies is that it is difficult to separate the effects of economic and social factors from those of cultural values. Several researchers have sought to solve this problem. Colin Loftin and Robert Hill, for example, using a sophisticated measure of poverty, found that economic factors, not cultural ones, explained regional variation in homicide rates.[32] Similarly, others suggest that high homicide rates and gun ownership may have a great deal to do with socioeconomic conditions, especially racial inequality in the South.[33]

Researchers who support the subculture of violence thesis point to statistics on characteristics of homicide offenders and victims: Lower-class, inner-city black males are disproportionately represented in the FBI's Uniform Crime Reports. In addition:

- The majority of the offenders are young, most in their 20s but many in their late teens.

- Typically, the offender and the victim know each other.

- The offender and the victim are usually in the same age group and of the same race.[34]

Furthermore, in a study of 556 males interviewed at age 26, 19 percent of the respondents, all inner-city males, reported having been shot or stabbed. These victimizations were found to be highly correlated with both self-reported offenses and official arrest statistics. In fact, the best single predictor of committing a violent act was found to be whether or not the individual had been a victim of a violent crime. Though most people in the dominant society who are shot or stabbed do not commit a criminal act in response, it appears that many inner-city males alternate the roles of victim and offender in a way that maintains the values and attitudes of a violent subculture.[35]

Multicultural macho advertisements appeal to young males concerned with showing toughness through masculinity. This billboard suggests that Converse sneakers are not for kids' playgrounds.

Evaluation: The Subculture of Violence Theory

Though empirical evidence remains inconclusive, the subculture of violence theory is supported by the distribution of violent crime in American society.[36] The number of gangs and the violence associated with their activities are growing.[37] Jeffrey Fagan noted that "drug use is widespread and normative" among gangs.[38] Gang warfare, which takes the lives of innocent bystanders in ghetto areas, is a part of life in most of the impoverished, densely populated neighborhoods in such major cities as Los Angeles, New York, Chicago, Miami, Washington, D.C., and Atlanta, and in smaller disintegrating urban centers as well. For example, over the 3 years between 1985 and 1988, Jamaican

"posses"—gangs transplanted from Kingston, Jamaica, to the United States—have been involved in 1400 homicides.[39]

Though not all persons in these subcultures follow the norm of violence, it appears that a dismaying number of them attach less and less importance to the value of human life and turn increasingly to violence to resolve immediate problems and frustrations. (We return to this issue later in the chapter.)

FOCAL CONCERNS: MILLER'S THEORY

All the theorists we have examined thus far explain criminal and delinquent behavior in terms of subcultural values that emerge and are perpetuated from one generation to the next in lower-class urban slums. Walter Miller reasons differently. According to Miller:

> In the case of "gang" delinquency, the cultural system which exerts the most direct influence on behavior is that of the lower-class community itself—a long-established, distinctively patterned tradition with an integrity of its own—rather than a so-called "delinquent subculture" which has arisen through conflict with middle-class culture and is oriented to the deliberate violation of middle-class norms.[40]

To Miller, juvenile delinquency is not rooted in the rejection of middle-class values; it stems from lower-class culture, which has its own value system. This value system has evolved as a response to living in disadvantaged neighborhoods characterized by single-parent households (Figure 6.3). Gang norms are simply the adolescent expression of the lower-class culture in which the boys have grown up. This lower-class culture exists apart from the middle-class culture, and it has done so for generations. The value system, not the gang norms, generates delinquent acts.

Miller has identified six focal concerns, or areas, to which lower-class males give persistent attention: trouble, toughness, smartness, excitement, luck, and autonomy. Concern over *trouble* is a major feature of lower-class life. Staying out of trouble and getting into trouble are daily preoccupations. Trouble can get a person into the hands of the authorities, or it can result in prestige among peers. Lower-class individuals are often evaluated by the extent of their involvement in activities such as fighting, drinking, and sexual misbehaving. In this case, the greater the involvement or the more extreme the performance, the greater the prestige or "respect" the person commands.

These young men are almost obsessively concerned with *toughness;* the code requires a show of masculinity, a denial of sentimentality, and a display of physical strength. Miller argues that this concern with toughness is related to the fact that a large proportion of lower-class males grow up in female-dominated households and have no male figure

FIGURE 6.3 Many children live in poverty, often residing in single-parent households where the head of the household does not have a job.

Percentage of Children Living in Poverty or with No Working Parent

Living Arrangement	No Working Parent	Living in Poverty
Both parents	14%	10%
Single parent	34	43
Mother	37	47
Father	19	22

Source: Juvenile Offenders and Victims: 1999 National Report (Washington, D.C.: Office of Juvenile Justice and Delinquency Prevention, 1999), pp. 6, 8.

from whom to learn the male role. They join street gangs in order to find males with whom they can identify.

Claude Brown's classic 1965 autobiography, *Manchild in the Promised Land,* illustrates the concerns about trouble and toughness among adolescents growing up in an urban slum:

> My friends were all daring like me, tough like me, dirty like me, ragged like me, cursed like me, and had a great love for trouble like me. We took pride in being able to hitch rides on trolleys, buses, taxicabs and in knowing how to steal and fight. We knew that we were the only kids in the neighborhood who usually had more than ten dollars in their pockets. . . . Somebody was always trying to shake us down or rob us. This was usually done by the older hustlers in the neighborhood or by storekeepers or cops. . . . We accepted this as a way of life.[41]

Another focal concern is *smartness*—the ability to gain something by outsmarting, outwitting, or conning another person. In lower-class neighborhoods youngsters practice outsmarting each other in card games, exchanges of insults, and other trials. Prestige is awarded to those who demonstrate smartness.

Many aspects of lower-class life are related to another focal concern, the search for *excitement.* Youngsters alternate between hanging out with peers and looking for excitement, which can be found in fighting, getting drunk, and us-

FIGURE 6.4 The relationship between delinquency and lower-class focal concerns.

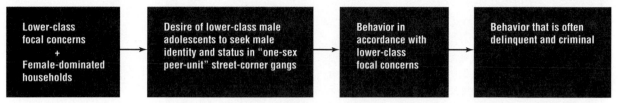

Source: Donald J. Shoemaker, *Theories of Delinquency: An Examination of Explanations of Delinquent Behavior*, 3d ed. (New York: Oxford University Press, 1996), p. 122.

ing drugs. Risks, danger, and thrills break up the monotony of their existence.

Fate, particularly *luck*, plays an important role in lower-class life. Many individuals believe that their lives are subject to forces over which they have little control. If they get lucky, a rather drab life could change quickly. Common discussions center on whether lucky numbers come up, cards are right, or dice are good. Brown recalls:

> After a while [Mama] settled down, and we stopped talking about her feelings, then somebody came upstairs and told her she had hit the numbers. We just forgot all about her feelings. I forgot about her feelings. Mama forgot about her feelings. Everybody did. She started concentrating on the number. This was the first time she'd had a hit in a long time. They bought some liquor. Mama and Dad started drinking: everyone started making a lot of noise and playing records.[42]

Miller's last focal concern, *autonomy*, stems from the lower-class person's resentment of external controls, whether parents, teachers, or police. This desire for personal freedom is expressed often in such terms as "No one can push me around" and "I don't need nobody."[43]

According to Miller, status in every class is associated with the possession of qualities that are valued. In the lower class the six focal concerns define status. It is apparent that by engaging in behavior that affords status by these criteria, many people will be breaking the laws of the dominant society (Figure 6.4).

Tests of Miller's Theory

An obvious question is whether in our urban, heterogeneous, secular, technologically based society any isolated pockets of culture are still to be found. The pervasiveness of mass advertising, mass transit, and mass communication makes it seem unlikely that an entire class of people could be unaware of the dominant value system. Empirical research on opportunity theory has found that lower-class boys share the conventional success goals of the dominant culture. This finding suggests that the idea of isolation from the dominant system does not fit with reality. Empirical research has also found, however, that while gang boys may support middle-class values, they are willing to deviate from them. If an opportunity arises to gain prestige in a fight, gang boys are willing to take the chance that their act will not result in punishment.

Most empirical tests of values question young people on their attachment to middle-class values. Stephen Cernovich expanded this type of research by investigating attachment to lower-class focal concerns.[44] He found that toughness, excitement, trouble, and pleasure seeking were related to self-reported delinquency in all classes. His findings also showed that boys of all classes were committed to delayed gratification, hard work, and education. Cernovich concluded that it is values, rather than class, that are associated with delinquency.

Evaluation: Miller's Theory

Criminologists have been disturbed by Miller's assumption that the lower-class lifestyle is

Violence and police raids are part of everyday life in many inner-city housing projects.

generally focused on illegal activity. In making such an assumption, they say, Miller disregards the fact that most people in the lower class do conform to conventional norms. Moreover, some criminologists ask, if lower-class boys are conforming to their own value system, why would they suffer guilt or shame when they commit delinquent acts?[45]

Perhaps the best support for Miller's ideas is found in qualitative, rather than quantitative, accounts of life in a lower-class slum. In our discussion of cultural deviance and subcultural theories we noted that the values and norms that define behavior in these areas do not change much over time or from place to place. Successive generations have to deal with the same problems. They typically demonstrate similar responses. Angela D'Arpa-Calandra, a former probation officer who now directs a Juvenile Intensive Supervision program, says she recently walked into a New York courtroom and "saw a mother and grandmother sitting with the 14-year-old offender. 'I had the grandmother in criminal court in 1963,' D'Arpa-Calandra says. 'We didn't stop it there. The grandmother was 14

when she was arrested. The mother had this child when she was 14. It's like a cycle we must relive.'"[46]

By and large, descriptions of life in poverty-stricken areas, whether written by people who have lived in them or by people who have studied them, reveal dreary routine, boredom, constant trouble, and incessant problems with drugs, alcohol, and crime. As the father tells his son in Eugene O'Neill's autobiographical play *Long Day's Journey into Night*, "There was no damned romance in our poverty."[47] There still isn't. In 1993, the *New York Times* ran a series of profiles of youth in poverty:

> Derrick White rides through the crumbling asphalt roads of the Hurt Village housing project where he played tag among the steel clotheslines and shot baskets through bent and wobbly hoops. He passes the trash bins where men with black plastic bags mine for cans to sell to a recycling center. He passes the "dope track," where he saw a friend shot in the neck and killed.
>
> Beyond the project he passes the supermarket that refused him a job interview because, he believes, his address marks him as a project kid.[48]

GANGS AT THE TURN OF THE CENTURY

In Los Angeles:

A 7-year-old boy was slain and his 10-month-old brother seriously injured by stray bullets as members of the Crips gang opened fire in a parking lot to avenge shootings that had occurred two hours earlier.[49]

In New York:

An 11-year-old boy was killed as two gang members bicycled up to a crowded playground and opened fire. The goal was to kill a member of a rival gang.[50]

In Washington, D.C.:

An 18-year-old pleaded guilty to first-degree murder of a 12-year-old boy. He beat and shot the victim whom he had warned to stay out of the gang war. When the warning was not heeded, he concluded that the victim "wanted to be dead."[51]

In Santa Monica, California:

Within a 2-week period, gang wars left five people dead and three seriously injured. In the previous year Santa Monica had one homicide.[52]

The new subculture that emerged in the 1980s and continues into the new century combines violence, which has become more vicious than in earlier years, with big business in drug trafficking (Table 6.1).[53] It is estimated that one gang alone, the Eight Trey Gangster Crips, distributed hundreds of kilos of crack and cocaine worth over $10 million on the streets of Los Angeles and five other cities, as far east as Birmingham, Alabama, and Atlanta. The FBI reports that this network is only one of perhaps a hundred more operating across the country.[54] Rival gangs kill for more than simply turf. In cities around the world teenagers are driving BMWs with Uzi submachine guns concealed under the driver's seat and thousands of dollars in their pockets so that they can make bail at any moment. Movies like *Colors, American Me,* and *Boyz in the Hood* provide models for their activities.

Crime Surfing

www.iir.com/nygc/

Would you like to find out more about the prevalence of gangs in various areas?

TABLE 6.1   Gang Control of Drug Distribution in Cities across the United States

Level of Control	Percentage
All	1
More than half	29
Less than half	23
Less than one-fourth	41
None	6

Source: 1996 National Youth Gang Survey (Washington, D.C.: Office of Juvenile Justice and Delinquency Prevention, July 1999), p. 43.

Crime Surfing

www.dc.state.fl.us/pub/gangs/faq.html

Find out more about types of gangs and their affiliations.

Guns and Gangs

It is estimated that between 50 and 70 percent of gang members own or have access to weapons. In fact, gangs often judge each other by their firepower. Their arsenal of weapons includes sawed-off rifles and shotguns, semiautomatic weapons like the Uzi and the AK-47, all types of handguns, body armor, and explosives.[55] Gangs have "treasuries" to buy the sophisticated weapons that are now used on the street for resolving conflicts, for demonstrating bravery, for self-defense, and for protecting turf.

The National Center for Juvenile Justice and the FBI report that:

- From 1989 through 1997 nearly 20,000 juveniles were murdered in the United States.

- More than half of juvenile homicide victims are killed by a firearm.

- The percentage of juveniles killed with a firearm increased from 41 percent in 1980 to 56 percent in 1997.

- The juvenile arrest rate for weapons violations increased 44 percent from 1988 to 1997.[56]

Use of guns rather than knives and clubs turns violent events into life-and-death situations; gangs battle gangs in a kind of street guerrilla warfare. Drive-by shootings, in particular, have become a favored method of operation. A "drive-by" involves members of one gang driving into a rival gang's turf to shoot at someone, followed by a high-speed escape. Gang members take great pride in this hit-and-run technique. Often these encounters occur spontaneously, but they easily spiral into planned events. The sequence may be the following:

> A gang member shoots a rival gang member during an argument. The surviving rival or his friends get a gun and conduct a drive-by on the initial instigator or members of his gang at their home(s). During this retaliatory strike, a friend, family member or gang member is killed or seriously wounded. The original instigatory gang now views itself as the "passive victim" and sets out to get back at the new aggressor. This spiral which, in real time, can result in several drive-by shootings or other murders within a few hours, can and often does lead to protracted gang wars.[57]

Some drive-bys are for "fun," some for defending gang honor, and others for getting rid of competition in the drug business.

FEMALE DELINQUENT SUBCULTURES

Traditionally, gang membership has been limited primarily to young, inner-city males. Theoretical and empirical studies in this area therefore focused on that population. More recently, however, gang membership has been changing. There are increasing numbers of white participants, members younger than 14, members older than 18, and females (see Table 6.2). And more attention has been focused on female gang members. Little was known about female subcultures.

TABLE 6.2 Demographic Profile of Gang Members, 1995

Total number	846,000
Sex	
Male	90%
Female	10
Race-ethnicity	
Hispanic	44%
Black	35
White	14
Asian	5
Other	2
Age	
14 or younger	16%
15–17	34
18–24	37
25 or older	13

Source: Juvenile Offenders and Victims: 1999 National Report (Washington, D.C.: Office of Juvenile Justice and Delinquency Prevention, 1999).

Early Research

In one of the few early studies, done in 1958, Albert Cohen and James Short suggested that female delinquent subcultures, like their male counterparts, were composed of members who had been frustrated in their efforts to achieve conventional goals (respectability, marriage, status). The girls had drifted into a subculture that offered them substitute status, albeit outside legitimate society. Drug use and prostitution became all but inevitable. Since the research that led to this finding was conducted among mostly lower-class black females, Cohen and Short admitted that their findings probably could not be generalized to all female delinquent subcultures.[58]

Recent Studies

Twenty-six years after these tentative findings, Anne Campbell published the first major work on the lifestyle of female gang members in New York. She spent 2 years with three gangs: one Hispanic (the Sex Girls), one black (the Five Percent Nation), and one racially mixed (the Sandman Ladies). Campbell's findings demonstrate that girls, like boys, join gangs for mutual support, protection, and a sense of belonging. They, too, gain status by living up to the value system of their gang. Campbell also noted that these

Psychologist Anne Campbell studied female gangs in New York City and published her findings in her 1984 book, *The Girls in the Gang.* She summarizes some of her observations here:

> All the girls in the gang come from families that are poor. Many have never known their fathers. Most are immigrants from Puerto Rico. As children the girls moved from apartment to apartment as they were evicted or burned out by arsonists. Unable to keep any friends they managed to make and alienated from their mothers, whose lack of English restricted their ability to control or understand their daughters' lives, the girls dropped out of school early and grew up on the streets. In the company of older kids and street-corner men, they graduated early into the adult world. They began to use drugs and by puberty had been initiated into sexual activity. By fifteen many were pregnant. Shocked, their mothers tried to pull them off the streets. Some sent their daughters back to relatives in Puerto Rico while they had their babies. Abortion was out of the question in this Catholic world.
>
> Those who stayed had "spoiled their identity" as good girls. Their reputations were marred before they ever reached adulthood. On the streets, among the gang members, the girls found a convenient identity in the female gang. Often they had friends or distant relatives who introduced them as "prospects." After a trial period, they could undertake the initiation rite: they had to fight an established member nominated by the godmother. What was at issue was not winning or losing but demonstrating "heart," or courage. Gangs do not welcome members who join only to gain protection. The loyalty of other gang members has to be won by a clear demonstration of willingness to "get down," or fight.
>
> Paradoxically, the female gang goes to considerable lengths to control the sexual behavior of its members. Although the neighborhood may believe they are fast women, the girls themselves do not tolerate members who sleep around. A promiscuous girl is a threat to the other members' relationships with their boyfriends. Members can take a boyfriend from among the male gang members (indeed, they are forbidden to take one from any other gang) but they are required to be monogamous. A shout of "Whore!" is the most frequent cause of fistfights among the female members.
>
> On the positive side, the gang provides a strong sense of belonging and sister-hood. After the terrible isolation of their lives, the girls acquire a ready-made circle of friends who have shared many of their experiences and who are always willing to support them against hostile words or deeds by outsiders. Fighting together generates a strong sense of camaraderie and as a bonus earns them the reputation of being "crazy." This reputation is extremely useful in the tough neighborhoods where they live. Their reputation for carrying knives and for solidarity effectively deters outsiders from challenging them. They work hard at fostering their tough "rep" not only in their deeds but in their social talk. They spend hours recounting and embroidering stories of fights they have been in. Behind all this bravado it is easy to sense the fear they work so hard to deny. Terrified of being victims (as many of them have already been in their families and as newcomers in their schools), they make much of their own "craziness"—the violent unpredictability that frightens away anyone who might try to harm them.(1)

Campbell demonstrates the commonality of violence in the lives of female gang members in the early 1980s. Today there is a growing concern over the increasing prevalence and severity of violence in some areas of the country. The number of female gang members and the extent of changes in the use of violence are, however, still debated among researchers.

Los Angeles teenage girl, member of 8-Tray Hoover Crips.

Sources

1. Written by Anne Campbell. Adapted from Anne Campbell, *The Girls in the Gang* (New York: Basil Blackwell, 1984).
2. John M. Hagedorn, "Gang Violence in the Postindustrial Era," in *Youth Violence, Crime and Justice: A Review of Research,* ed. Michael Tonry and Mark H. Moore, vol. 24 (Chicago: University of Chicago Press, 1998), pp. 365–419.
3. Margaret O'Brien, "At Least 16,000 Girls in Chicago's Gangs More Violent Than Some Believe, Report Says," *Chicago Tribune,* Sept. 17, 1999, p. 5.

Questions for Discussion

1. How similar are Campbell's female gangs to the male gangs described in this chapter? Are there any significant differences?
2. Would you expect female gangs to become as involved in criminal activity as male gangs? Why or why not?

youngsters will probably end up, as their mothers have, living on welfare assistance in a ghetto apartment. Men will come and go in their lives, but after their gang days the women feel they have lost their support group and are constantly threatened by feelings of isolation.[59]

Between 10 and 25 percent of gang members nationwide are female. In major cities the number is higher. Among 214 wards of the state of California in 1990, 32 percent were gang members, ages 14 to 21.[60] Among them they had 289 arrests. All but 3 of the women had been arrested for a violent crime—22 murders, 31 armed robberies, and 31 assaults with a deadly weapon.

Many of the female gangs are affiliates of male gangs, often offering support for the young men they refer to as their "homeboys." Initiation rites for females involve either a "jump-in, jump-out" in which they are beaten by four or five gang members or a "sex-in, sex-out" in which they have sexual relations with all male members.[61] Some female affiliate gangs, however, have their own initiation rites (which mimic male ceremonies but are usually much less violent) and their own gang colors. A strong allegiance exists among gang members. For many of these youngsters the gang takes the place of a family. Shorty, a member of Los Angeles's Tiny Diablas, had no family except a grandmother, who had given up on trying to control her. Shorty's mother, who had been a gang member, abandoned her at an early age. Her father overdosed on heroin and was identified by a tattoo of Shorty's name. Her aunt had a teardrop tattoo next to her eye, to signify 1 year in jail; her uncle had two teardrops. Such family ties are not unusual among gang members.[62]

Not all female gangs have male affiliates. In a study of crack sales and violence among gangs in San Francisco, researchers interviewed members of an all-female group, the Potrero Hill Posse (PHP).[63] This independent group was formed in the mid-1980s when the females realized that their gang-affiliated boyfriends were not distributing the profits and labor of their crack sales fairly. The PHP young women run "rock houses" (outlets for crack sales, lent by tenants who receive a small quantity of crack in return), procure other women to provide sex

to male customers, and engage in a major shoplifting business that fills orders placed by people who do not want to pay retail prices.

Gang members rely on the gang for assistance ("Nobody will mess with me . . . because they know that I got back-up. I got back-up. I got my homegirls behind me. And whatever goes down with me, they are going to have to take up with them") and for status ("It [membership] means being bad, being tough, and being able to walk without . . . you know, everybody just respects me because they know I am one of the Potrero Hill Posse girls").[64]

Overall, according to 1992 gang research done as part of the Rochester Youth Development Study, the extent and nature of female participation has changed considerably over the last few decades. The findings show increased participation in gangs (in this study, about equal to that of males) and in gang-related activities, including serious delinquent acts and drug abuse.[65]

Did You Know

. . . that 5 percent of all babies born in 1996 were born to juvenile mothers aged 10 to 17?

MIDDLE-CLASS DELINQUENCY

In Tucson, Arizona, a white middle-class teenager wearing gang colors died, a victim of a drive-by shooting as he stood with black and Hispanic members of the Bloods gang.

At Antelope Valley High School in Lancaster, California, about 50 miles north of Los Angeles, 200 students threw stones at a policeman who had been called to help enforce a ban on the gang outfits that have become a fad on some campuses. . . .

A member of the South Bay Family gang in Hermosa Beach, a 21-year-old surfer called Road Dog, who said his family owned a chain of pharmacies, put it this way: "This is the 90's, man. We're the type of people who don't take no for an answer. If your mom says no to a kid in the 90's, the kid's just going to laugh." He and his friends shouted in appreciation as another gang member lifted his long hair to reveal a tattoo on a bare shoulder: "Mama tried."[66]

FIGURE 6.5 Jurisdictions reporting active gangs. Although the majority of gangs are in major cities, they are becoming more common in less populated areas.

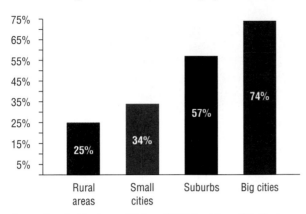

Source: Juvenile Offenders and Victims: 1999 National Report (Washington, D.C.: Office of Juvenile Justice and Delinquency Prevention, 1999), p. 78.

Most people think of gangs as synonymous with inner-city slums, low-income housing projects, turf wars, and a membership that often comes into conflict with law enforcement. But now gang lifestyle is moving to suburbia.[67] (See Figure 6.5.) Affluent youngsters are joining established gangs such as the Crips and the Bloods or forming their own gangs, sometimes referred to as yuppie gangs.[68] Their activities can be as harmless as adherence to a particular dress code or as violent as a drive-by shooting. Experts have identified several types of suburban gangs.[69]

Delinquent Gangs Delinquent gangs are similar to most inner-city gangs. Criminal activities include physical assaults, theft, burglary, and distribution of illegal drugs. The members seek money, peer recognition, the thrill of high-risk behavior, or even protection: "If you want to be able to walk the mall, you have to know you've got your boys behind you."[70] They typically adopt hand signals used by inner-city gangs.

Hate Gangs These gangs, such as skinheads, attach themselves to an ideology that targets racial and ethnic groups. Physical assaults and even murder are justified by their belief system. Their numbers are growing rapidly. In 1988 there were 1000 to 1500 skinheads operating in 12 states. By June 1993, the number was close to 3500, spread across 40 states.[71] According to the FBI, 9861 hate crimes were committed by neo-Nazis, skinheads, and other right-wing extremist groups in 1997. Because of the difficulties in gathering hate-crime statistics, this number is considered only a small percentage of the actual figure.[72]

Satanic Gangs These groups are affiliated with the controversial satanic cults. Their practices include the worship of specific gods, desecration of graveyards, use of a Ouija board to predict the future, ritualistic drug consumption, animal sacrifice, various witchcraft and pagan rituals, and submission to sexual abuse or pain. The common element for these gangs is heavy-metal music. (The name of one heavy-metal group, KISS, stands for Kids [or Knights] in Satan's Service.)[73] Satanic gang members can be identified by their dress: metal-spiked wrist cuffs, belts, anti-Christian items, and T-shirts labeled with heavy-metal band names such as Iron Maidens, Venom, Judas Priest, and Dio.[74]

Crime Surfing

www.ojjdp.ncjrs.org/ccd/

Learn more about current research on delinquency and gangs.

Explanations

Most explanations of middle-class delinquency are extensions of subcultural explanations of lower-class delinquency. Albert Cohen, for example, suggested that changes in the social structure have weakened the value traditionally associated with delay of gratification.[75] Some criminologists say that a growing number of middle-class youngsters no longer believe that the way to reach their goals is through hard work and delayed pleasure. They prefer reaping profits from quick drug sales or shoplifting goods that attract them. Behavior has become more hedonistic and more peer-oriented. While most of this youth subculture exhibits non-delinquent behavior, sometimes the pleasure-seeking activities have led to delinquent acts. Bored and restless, these youngsters seek to break the monotony with artificial excitement

Irish, Italian, and Puerto Rican inner-city gangs have been replaced or augmented by gangs reflecting the new waves of immigrants to America, who seek the protection and group loyalty that gang membership traditionally was thought to have provided.

Most Mexican gang members, for example, are migrants from rural areas where gangs do not exist. At home they had family support. That support all but vanishes when they find themselves in the ghetto neighborhoods of American cities. Other Latin American and Caribbean cultures are also represented in the American gang structure. Jamaican gangs, specializing in the drug and weapons trade, are known for their violence. Colombian gangs have engaged in multiple armed robberies in several states, focusing on jewelers and other businesses. The Colombians have established an arsenal of technologically advanced equipment to commit their robberies and to escape detection. They even use cosmetic surgery to alter their appearances and change their fingerprints. Asian gangs, among them Vietnamese, Korean, Cambodian, Laotian, and Chinese, have sprung up on both coasts and in the middle of the country. Other groups hail from the Pacific Islands. The Tongan Crips gangsters and Sons of Samoa, demonstrating their macho values, have spread fear in once quiet, pastoral Utah. The Vietnamese have established a reputation as "housebreakers"; they burglarize the homes of other, wealthier Vietnamese immigrants.

Chinese gangs have been the greatest surprise for American law enforcement. Traditionally, Chinese-Americans were considered particularly law-abiding. This picture changed drastically with the easing of immigration restrictions that allowed larger numbers of younger Chinese from the mainland, as well as Taiwan and Hong Kong, into the country. These new arrivals have formed gangs.

Chinese gangs, although small in number (an estimated 2000 members nationwide), engage in the smuggling of illegal Chinese immigrants by the tens of thousands annually. Often these immigrants are enslaved until the transportation fee has been paid off. These gangs also engage in major heroin trafficking and protection of the gambling clubs popular in Chinese communities. Their main business is extortion. Their strength, and tradition of ferocious violence, derives from their affiliation with Chinese secret societies known as Triads.

The end of the cold war and the collapse of the Soviet Union have opened new windows of opportunity for Russian entrepreneurs—legal and illegal. A thriving Russian colony in Brighton Beach, New York, is the seat of Russian gangs as ruthless as those of any other ethnic origin. They smuggle gold and Russian army surplus—often passing the goods off as high-grade Japanese products. They deal in bootlegged gasoline. They use extortion and murder to strengthen their operations. Some of the gang leaders are experienced criminals with long histories of economic offenses in Russia. Russians call them "thieves-in-law."

Gangs made up of immigrant Albanians and former Yugoslavians have been committing burglaries along the East Coast since the early 1990s. Their targets are retail shops, banks, and automated teller machines. They specialize in supermarket safes because these stores generally have a great deal of cash on hand. Their techniques are highly sophisticated, not the run-of-the-mill break and enter. The burglars rarely carry guns; every detail is carefully planned (oxygen tanks may be brought for their safe-cracking torches); and they are equipped with an arsenal of tools, gloves, and walkie-talkies. Often they cut phone lines to set off alarms, wait until the police come and go, and then strike.

Some gangs have ties to their homelands; others are independent. Some are national; others are strictly local. Some have memberships of young adults; others, of teenagers. Some are involved in the sale and use of drugs and arms; others are geared primarily toward survival in tough neighborhoods. Indeed, if ethnic gangs have any common characteristic beyond a membership of a single ethnic group, it is probably the diversity of patterns of formation and operation. That diversity is likely to continue as the country's ever-changing immigrant populations result in the emergence of new gangs.

Source:

Jayson Blair, "Killing of Ex-Officer Is Linked to Gang on Nationwide Robbery Spree," *New York Times,* Sept. 12, 1999, p. 37.

Questions for Discussion

1. Dealing with gangs may require infiltrating them. What if there are no young police officers from the gangs' ethnic groups? What else can be done?
2. Are there ways of dealing with ethnic gangs outside the criminal justice system? What of the role of elders, who are highly respected in many ethnic cultures?

and conspicuous indulgence: fast cars, trendy clothes, alcohol, drugs, and sexual activity. Experts note that many affluent gang members come from broken, unstable, or extremely dysfunctional homes. Their problems stem from divorce, separation, physical or sexual abuse, or a drug- or alcohol-addicted parent.[76]

THEORY INFORMS POLICY

Subcultural theory assumes that individuals engage in delinquent or criminal behavior because (1) legitimate opportunities for success are blocked and (2) criminal values and norms are learned in lower-class slums. The theory

Rodney Dailey, left, and Spike Moss appear with other gang members at a press conference held during the National Urban Peace and Justice Summit, Kansas City, 1993.

was translated into action programs during the 1960s. Two presidents, John F. Kennedy and Lyndon Johnson, directed that huge sums of money be spent on programs to help move lower-class youths into the social mainstream.

MOBY

The best-known program, Mobilization for Youth (MOBY), was based on opportunity theory. It provided employment, social services, teacher training, legal aid, and other crime-prevention services to an area on New York's Lower East Side. The cost was over $12 million. MOBY ultimately became highly controversial. Many people accused it of being too radical, especially when neighborhood participants became involved in rent strikes, lawsuits charging discrimination, and public demonstrations. News of the conflict between supporters and opponents, and between the staff and the neighborhood it served, reached Congress, which made it clear that the point of the project was to reduce delinquency, not to reform society.

Little was done to evaluate the program's success. The project was eventually abandoned, and the commission that had established it ceased to exist. The political climate had changed, and federal money was no

longer available for sweeping social programs. However, MOBY's failure does not disprove the opportunity theory on which it was based. In 1995 the Office of Juvenile Justice and Delinquency Prevention (OJJDP) launched the Comprehensive Gang Model, a pilot project based on the same principles as MOBY. It is too early to say whether or not the Comprehensive Gang Model will succeed where MOBY failed, but the OJJDP project reflects the use of pilot projects and research in developing programs.[77]

Other Programs

Many other programs based on subcultural theory have attempted to change the attitudes and behavior of ghetto youngsters who have spent most of their lives learning unconventional street norms. Change is accomplished by setting up an extended-family environment for high-risk youths, one that provides positive role models, academic and vocational training, strict rules for behavior, drug treatment, health care, and other services. For many youths these programs provide the first warm, caring living arrangement they have ever had. One such program is the House of Umoja (a Swahili word for "unity") in Philadelphia.

At any given time about 25 black male teenage offenders live together as "sons" of the founder, Sister Fattah. Each resident signs a contract with Umoja obligating himself to help in the household, become an active part of the family group, study, and work in one of the program's businesses (a restaurant, a moving company, a painting shop) or elsewhere. By many measures this program is successful.

Programs similar to Umoja spread throughout the country; they include Argus in New York's South Bronx; Violent Juvenile Offender Research and Development programs in Chicago, Dallas, New Orleans, Los Angeles, and San Diego; and Neighborhood Anticrime Self-Help programs in Baltimore, Newark, Cleveland, Boston, Miami, and Washington, D.C. All have the same mission: to provide a bridge from a delinquent subcultural value system to a conventional one.[78]

Other means have been used to break up delinquent subcultures. Street workers, many of them former gang members (called OGs, for "original gangsters"), serve as a "street-smart diplomatic corps" in many of the poorest ghettos in the country.[79] In Los Angeles, where gang members control many streets, the OGs work for the Community Youth Gang Service (a government-funded agency). Five nights a week more than 50 of these street workers cover the city, trying to settle disputes between rival gangs and to discourage nonmembers from joining them. They look for alternatives to violence, in baseball games, fairs, and written peace treaties. During a typical evening the street workers may try to head off a gang fight:

> *Parton [street worker]:* Hey, you guys, Lennox is going to be rollin' by here. . . .
>
> *Ms. Diaz [street worker]:* You with your back to the street, homeboy. They goin' to be lookin' for this car, some burgundy car.
>
> *Boy:* If they want to find me, they know where I'm at.

> *Ms. Diaz:* I'm tellin' you to be afraid of them. There are some girls here. You better tell them to move down the street. . . . We are goin' back over there to try to keep them there. Don't get lazy or drunk and not know what you're doin'. I know you don't think it's serious, but if one of your friends gets killed tonight, you will.
>
> *Boy:* It's serious, I know.
>
> *Ms. Diaz:* We're goin' to keep them in their 'hood, you just stay in yours for a while.
>
> *Boy:* All right.[80]

After 2 hours of negotiation, the fight was called off. There was plenty of work left for the team. They would continue the next day to help the gang members find jobs.

Getting Out: Gang Banging or the Morgue

The most difficult problem that counselors and street workers face is the power of gangs over their members. Gangs, through loyalty and terror, make it almost impossible for members to quit. Many gang members would gladly get out, but any move to leave leads to gang banging or the morgue. A Wichita, Kansas, group, the church-sponsored Project Freedom, has created an "underground railroad," a network of local contacts that leads families with gang members to anonymity and freedom out of state.[81]

Gangs, once a local problem, have become a national concern. The federal antigang budget goes primarily to police and prosecution. In 1992 the Department of Justice spent $500 million on law enforcement, while the Department of Health and Human Services spent $40 million on prevention programs over a 3-year period.[82] Experts agree that unless we put more money into educational and socioeconomic programs, there is little likelihood that America's gang problems will lessen as we enter the twenty-first century.

REVIEW

In the decade between the mid-1950s and mid-1960s, criminologists began to theorize about the development and content of youth subcultures and the gangs that flourish within them. Some suggested that lower-class males, frustrated by their inability to meet middle-class standards, set up their own norms by which they could gain status. Often these norms clashed with those of the dominant culture. Other investigators have refuted the idea that delinquent behavior stems from a rejection of middle-class values. They claim that lower-class values are separate and distinct from middle-class values and that it is the lower-class value system that generates delinquent behavior.

Gangs of the 1990s show increasing violence and reliance on guns. They are involved in large profit-making activities such as drug distribution. The number of homicides is rising.

Explanations of female delinquent subcultures and middle-class delinquency are an extension of subcultural explanations of lower-class delinquency. While the theories of reaction formation, the subculture of violence, and differential opportunity differ in some respects, they all share one basic assumption—that delinquent and criminal behaviors are linked to the values and norms of the areas where youngsters grow up.

YOU BE THE CRIMINOLOGIST

You are a consultant called in to address the rise in female gang activity and violence. On what theory or theories would you base your intervention? Are the theories based on male delinquency sufficient? Are gender-based theories necessary?

KEY TERMS

The numbers next to the terms refer to the pages on which the terms are defined.

differential opportunity theory (162)

reaction formation (159)

subculture (158)

subcultures of violence (166)

NOTES

1. Carla Crowder, "Hmong Pipeline Leads to Colorado Authorities Uncovering Trail of Southeast Asian Gangs Who Are Fleeing California," (*Denver*) *Rocky Mountain News*, Sept. 12, 1999, p. A4; R. Robin McDonald, "Human Contraband: Asian Women Expected Jobs, Not Prostitution," *Atlanta Constitution*, Aug. 31, 1999, p. C1.
2. John P. Moore and Craig P. Terrett, "Highlights of the 1997 National Youth Gang Survey," *OJJDP Fact Sheet*, **98** (March 1999). For how gangs spread, see John A. Laskey, "Gang Migration: The Familial Gang Transplant Phenomenon," *Journal of Gang Research*, **3** (1996): 1–15; and Cheryl L. Maxon, "Investigating Gang Migration: Contextual Issues for Intervention," *Gang Journal*, **1** (1993): 1–8.
3. Albert K. Cohen, *Delinquent Boys: The Culture of the Gang* (Glencoe, Ill.: Free Press, 1955).
4. E.g., James F. Short, Jr., and Fred L. Strodtbeck, *Group Process and Gang Delinquency* (Chicago: University of Chicago Press, 1965).
5. Kenneth Polk and Walter B. Schafer, eds., *School and Delinquency* (Englewood Cliffs, N.J.: Prentice-Hall, 1972); Alexander Liazos, "School, Alienation, and Delinquency," *Crime and Delinquency*, **24** (1978): 355–370.
6. Travis Hirschi, *Causes of Delinquency* (Berkeley: University of California Press, 1969).
7. Delbert S. Elliott and Harwin L. Voss, *Delinquency and Dropout* (Lexington, Mass.: Lexington Books, 1974).
8. G. Roger Jarjoura, "Dropping Out of School Enhances Delinquent Involvement? Results from a Large-Scale National Probability Sample," *Criminology*, **31** (1993): 149–172.
9. Albert J. Reiss and Albert L. Rhodes, "Deprivation and Delinquent Behavior," *Sociological Quarterly*, **4** (1963): 135–149.
10. Marvin Krohn, R. L. Akers, M. J. Radosevich, and L. Lanza-Kaduce, "Social Status and Deviance," *Criminology*, **18** (1980): 303–318.
11. Mark Warr, "Organization and Instigation in Delinquent Groups," *Criminology*, **34** (1996): 11–37.

12. David F. Greenberg, "Delinquency and the Age Structure of Society," *Contemporary Crisis*, **1** (1977): 189–223.

13. John I. Kitsuse and David C. Dietrick, "Delinquent Boys: A Critique," *American Sociological Review*, **24** (1959): 208–215.

14. David J. Bordua, "Delinquent Subcultures: Sociological Interpretations of Gang Delinquency," *Annals of the American Academy of Political and Social Science*, **338** (1961): 119–136.

15. Albert K. Cohen and James F. Short, Jr., "Research in Delinquent Subcultures," *Journal of Social Issues*, **14** (1958): 20–37.

16. Richard A. Cloward and Lloyd E. Ohlin, *Delinquency and Opportunity* (Glencoe, Ill.: Free Press, 1960).

17. Clifford R. Shaw, *The Jack-Roller* (Chicago: University of Chicago Press, 1930), p. 54.

18. James R. David, *Street Gangs* (Dubuque, Iowa: Kendall/Hunt, 1982).

19. Hirschi, *Causes of Delinquency*, p. 227.

20. John M. Hagedorn, "Homeboys, Dope Fiends, Legits, and New Jacks," *Criminology*, **32** (1994): 197–219.

21. James Short, Ramon Rivera, and Ray Tennyson, "Perceived Opportunities, Gang Membership, and Delinquency," *American Sociological Review*, **30** (1965): 56–57.

22. Lecture by Ko-lin Chin, Rutgers University, Nov. 22, 1993. See also K. Chin, *Chinese Subculture and Criminality: Nontraditional Crime Groups in America*, Criminology and Penology Series, vol. 29 (Westport, Conn.: Greenwood, 1990); Mark Warr, "Organization and Instigation in Delinquent Groups," *Criminology*, **34** (1996): 11–37; Kevin M. Thompson, David Brownfield, and Ann Marie Sorenson, "Specialization Patterns of Gang and Non-gang Offending: A Latent Structure Analysis," *Journal of Gang Research*, **3** (1996): 25–35.

23. Finn-Aage Esbensen and David Huizinga, "Gangs, Drugs, and Delinquency in a Survey of Urban Youth," *Criminology*, **31** (1993): 565–587; Terence P. Thornberry, Marvin D. Krohn, Alan J. Lizotte, and Deborah Chard-Wierschem, "The Role of Juvenile Gangs in Facilitating Delinquent Behavior," *Journal of Research in Crime and Delinquency*, **30** (1993): 55–87; Malcolm Klein, Cheryl L. Maxson,

and Lea C. Cunningham, " 'Crack,' Street Gangs, and Violence," *Criminology*, **29** (1991): 623–650.

24. K. Chin and J. Fagan, "Social Order and Gang Formation in Chinatown," in *Advances in Criminological Theory*, vol. 6, ed. Freda Adler and William S. Laufer (New Brunswick, N.J.: Transaction, 1994).

25. George W. Knop, Edward D. Tromanhauser, James G. Houston, et al., *The Economics of Gang Life: A Task Force Report of the National Gang Crime Research Center* (Chicago: National Crime Research Center, 1995).

26. Ibid., p. ii.

27. John P. Hoffman and Timothy Ireland, "Cloward and Ohlin's Strain Theory Reexamined: An Elaborated Theoretical Model," in Adler and Laufer, *Advances in Criminological Theory*, vol. 6.

28. Marvin E. Wolfgang and Franco Ferracuti, *The Subculture of Violence* (London: Tavistock, 1967).

29. Howard S. Erlanger, "The Empirical Status of the Subcultures of Violence Thesis," *Social Problems*, **22** (1974): 280–292. For the relationship of the thesis to routine activities, see Leslie W. Kennedy and Stephen W. Baron, "Routine Activities and a Subculture of Violence: A Study on the Street," *Journal of Research in Crime and Delinquency*, **30** (1993): 88–112. For an examination of differences between blacks and whites, see Liqun Cao, Anthony Adams, and Vickie J. Jensen, "A Test of the Black Subculture of Violence Thesis: A Research Note," *Criminology*, **35** (1997): 367–379. For a look at regional differences in punitiveness, see Marian J. Borg, "The Southern Subculture of Punitiveness? Regional Variation in Support for Capital Punishment," *Journal of Research in Crime and Delinquency*, **34** (1997): 25–45.

30. William G. Doerner, "A Regional Analysis of Homicide Rates in the United States," *Criminology*, **13** (1975): 90–101.

31. Jo Dixon and Alan J. Lizotte, "Gun Ownership and the Southern Subculture of Violence," *American Journal of Sociology*, **93** (1987): 383–405.

32. Colin Loftin and Robert Hill, "Regional Subculture of Violence: An Examination of

the Gastril-Hackney Thesis," *American Sociological Review,* **39** (1974): 714–724.

33. Judith Blau and Peter Blau, "Metropolitan Structure and Violent Crime," *American Sociological Review,* **47** (1982): 114–129. For a study that examines the subculture of violence thesis as it relates to three groups—blacks, Hispanics, and American Indians—see Donald J. Shoemaker and J. Sherwood Williams, "The Subculture of Violence and Ethnicity," *Journal of Criminal Justice,* **15** (1987): 461–472.

34. Wolfgang and Ferracuti, *The Subculture of Violence,* pp. 258–265. See also Marvin E. Wolfgang, *Patterns in Criminal Homicide* (Philadelphia: University of Pennsylvania Press, 1958).

35. Marvin E. Wolfgang, Robert M. Figlio, and Thorsten Sellin, *Delinquency in a Birth Cohort* (Chicago: University of Chicago Press, 1972); Simon I. Singer, "Victims of Serious Violence and Their Criminal Behavior: Subcultural Theory and Beyond," *Violence and Victims,* **1** (1986): 61–70. See also Neil Alan Weiner and Marvin E. Wolfgang, "The Extent and Character of Violent Crime in America, 1969 1982," in *American Violence and Public Policy,* ed. Lynn Curtis (New Haven, Conn.: Yale University Press, 1985), pp. 17–39.

36. Steven Messner, "Regional and Racial Effects on the Urban Homicide Rate: The Subculture of Violence Revisited," *American Journal of Sociology,* **88** (1983): 997–1007.

37. Scott H. Decker, "Collective and Normative Features of Gang Violence," *Justice Quarterly,* **13** (1996): 243–264.

38. Jeffrey Fagan, "The Social Organization of Drug Use and Drug Dealing among Urban Gangs," *Criminology,* **27** (1989): 633–666.

39. Joseph B. Treaster, "Jamaica's Gangs Take Root in U.S.," *New York Times,* Nov. 13, 1988, p. 15.

40. Walter B. Miller, "Lower-Class Culture as a Generating Milieu of Gang Delinquency," *Journal of Social Issues,* **14** (1958): 5–19.

41. Claude Brown, *Manchild in the Promised Land: A Modern Classic of the Black Experience* (New York: New American Library, 1965), p. 22.

42. Ibid., p. 129.

43. Miller, "Lower-Class Culture."

44. Stephen A. Cernovich, "Value Orientations and Delinquency Involvement," *Criminology,* **15** (1978): 443–458.

45. Gresham Sykes and David Matza, "Techniques of Neutralization: A Theory of Delinquency," *American Sociological Review,* **22** (1957): 664–673.

46. Barbara Kantrowitz, "Wild in the Streets," *Newsweek,* Aug. 2, 1993, p. 46.

47. Eugene O'Neill, *Long Day's Journey into Night,* in *Great Scenes from the World Theater,* ed. James L. Steffenson, Jr. (New York: Avon, 1965), p. 199.

48. Peter T. Kilborn, "Finding a Way: The Quest of Derrick, 19," *New York Times,* Apr. 22, 1993, p. 1.

49. Jean Merl, "Sentencing and Elegy for Slain Boy Court: Emotional Statements by Victim's Family Have Many in Tears. Three Gang Members Receive Lengthy Terms," *Los Angeles Times,* Sept. 16, 1999, p. B1.

50. Michael Cooper, "17-Year-Old Is Arrested in Boy's Death: Slaying of Bystander Is Linked to Gangs," *New York Times,* Aug. 22, 1999, p. 37.

51. Bill Miller, "Guilty Plea in Slaying of D.C. Boy, 12; Teen Was Triggerman in Gang-Related Case," *Washington Post,* Feb. 21, 1998, p. D01.

52. Rene Sanchez, "Placid Santa Monica Roiled by 5 Gang War Deaths in 2 Weeks," *Washington Post,* Oct. 31, 1998, p. A02.

53. Jeffrey Fagan, "The Political Economy of Drug Dealing among Urban Gangs," in *Drugs and the Community,* ed. Robert Davis, Arthur Lurigio, and Dennis Rosenbaum (Springfield, Ill.: Charles C. Thomas, 1993), pp. 19–54.

54. John Bonfante, "Entrepreneurs of Crack," *Time,* Feb. 27, 1995, p. 22.

55. Beth Bjerregaard and Alan J. Lizotte, "Gun Ownership and Gang Membership," *The Journal of Criminal Law and Criminology,* **86** (1995): 37–58; Alan J. Lizotte, James M. Tesoriero, Terence P. Thornberry, and Marvin D. Krohn, "Patterns of Adolescent Firearms Ownership and Use," *Justice Quarterly,* **11** (1994): 51–74. On the extent of gang organizations, see Scott H. Decker, Tim

Review • You Be the Criminologist • Key Terms • Notes

Bynum, and Deborah Weisel, "A Tale of Two Cities: Gangs as Organized Crime Groups," *Justice Quarterly,* **15** (1998): 395–425.

56. Office of Juvenile Justice and Delinquency Prevention, *Juvenile Offenders and Victims: 1999 National Report* (Washington, D.C.: Office of Juvenile Justice and Delinquency Prevention, 1999), pp. 19, 20, 117; U.S. Department of Justice, Federal Bureau of Investigation, *Uniform Crime Report 1985–1995* (Washington, D.C.: Federal Bureau of Investigation, 1999). See also Alfred Blumstein, "Youth, Violence, Guns and the Illicit Gun Industry," *Journal of Criminal Law and Criminology,* **86** (1995): 10–36.

57. John P. Sullivan and Martin E. Silverstein, "The Disaster within Us: Urban Conflict and Street Gang Violence in Los Angeles," *Journal of Gang Research,* **2** (1995): 11–30 (p. 28).

58. Cohen and Short, "Research in Delinquent Subcultures."

59. Anne Campbell, *The Girls in the Gang* (New York: Basil Blackwell, 1984), p. 267.

60. Jill Leslie Rosenbaum, "A Violent Few: Gang Girls in the California Youth Authority," *Journal of Gang Research,* **3** (1996): 17–23. For reasons girls join gangs, see Finn-Aage Eshensen and Elizabeth Piper Deschenes, "A Multisite Examination of Youth Gang Membership: Does Gender Matter?" *Criminology,* **36** (1998): 799–828.

61. *New Mexico Street Gangs, 1994: Update* (Albuquerque: New Mexico Department of Public Safety, 1994).

62. Seth Mydans, "Life in Girls' Gang: Colors and Bloody Noses," *New York Times,* Jan. 29, 1990, pp. 1, 20.

63. David Lauderback, Joy Hansen, and Dan Waldorf, "'Sisters Are Doin' It for Themselves': A Black Female Gang in San Francisco," *Gang Journal,* **1** (1992): 57–72.

64. Ibid., p. 67.

65. Beth Bjerregaard and Carolyn Smith, *Rochester Youth Development Study: Patterns of Male and Female Gang Membership,* working paper no. 13 (Albany, N.Y.: Hindelang Criminal Justice Research Center, 1992).

66. Seth Mydans, "Not Just the Inner City: Well-to-Do Join Gangs," *New York Times,* Apr. 10, 1990, p. A10.

67. C. Ronald Huff, ed., *Gangs in America* (Newbury Park, Calif.: Sage, 1990).

68. Mydans, "Not Just the Inner City."

69. Dan Korem, *Suburban Gangs: Affluent Rebels* (Richardson, Tex.: International Focus, 1994).

70. As quoted in Mydans, "Not Just the Inner City."

71. Korem, *Suburban Gangs.*

72. Uniform Crime Reports, 1997, p. 60.

73. Wayne S. Wooden, *Renegade Kids, Suburban Outlaws: From Youth Culture to Delinquency* (Belmont, Calif.: Wadsworth, 1995), p. 190.

74. "L.A. Style: A Street Gang Manual of the Los Angeles County Sheriff's Department," in *The Modern Gang Reader,* ed. Malcolm W. Klein, Cheryl L. Maxson, and Jody Miller (Los Angeles: Roxbury, 1995).

75. Albert K. Cohen, "Middle-Class Delinquency and the Social Structure," in *Middle-Class Delinquency,* ed. E. W. Vaz (New York: Harper & Row, 1967), pp. 207–221.

76. Korem, *Suburban Gangs,* p. 50.

77. Jim Burch and Candice Kane, "Implementing the OJJDP Comprehensive Gang Model," *OJJDP Fact Sheet,* **112** (July 1999).

78. Lynn A. Curtis, Preface to "Policies to Prevent Crime: Neighborhood, Family, and Employment Strategies," *Annals of the American Academy of Political and Social Science,* **494** (1987).

79. Robert Reinhold, "In the Middle of L.A.'s Gang Warfare," *New York Times Magazine,* May 22, 1988, p. 31.

80. Ibid., p. 70.

81. Jon D. Hull, "No Way Out," *Time,* Aug. 17, 1992, p. 40.

82. *Time,* June 15, 1992, p. 37.

CHAPTER 7
Social Control Theory

o

Obedience, respect for authority, shared goals and values, commitment to and investment in custom and convention—this is the glue that makes a successful sports team, no less a powerful social order.

In William Golding's novel Lord of the Flies, a group of boys are stranded on an island far from civilization. Deprived of any superior authority—all the grown-ups, their parents, their teachers, the government, that have until now determined their lives—they begin to decide on a structure of government for themselves. Ralph declares:

> "We can't have everybody talking at once. We'll have to have 'Hands up' like at school. . . . Then I'll give him the conch."
>
> "Conch?"
>
> "That's what this shell is called. I'll give the conch to the next person to speak. He can hold it when he's speaking!" . . .
>
> Jack was on his feet.
>
> "We'll have rules!" he cried excitedly. "Lots of rules!"[1]

But do rules alone guarantee the peaceful existence of the group? Who and what ensure compliance with the rules? Social control theorists study these questions.

Strain theories, as we noted, study the question of why some people violate norms, for example, by committing crimes.

Social control theorists are interested in learning why people conform to norms. Control theorists take it for granted that drugs can tempt even the youngest schoolchildren; that truancy can lure otherwise good children onto a path of academic failure and lifetime unemployment; that petty fighting, petty theft, and recreational drinking are attractive features of adolescence and young adulthood. They ask why people conform in the face of so much temptation and peer pressure. The answer is that juveniles and adults conform to the law in response to certain controlling forces in their lives. They become criminals when the controlling forces are weak or absent.

A scene from a film version of Lord of the Flies: *Young boys cast away on an uninhabited island soon invent their own social rules and social controls.*

WHAT IS SOCIAL CONTROL?

What are those controlling forces? Think about the time and energy you have invested in your school, your job, your extracurricular activities. Think about how your academic or vocational ambition would be jeopardized by persistent delinquency. Think about how the responsibility of homework has weighed you down, setting limits on your free time. Reflect on the quality of your relationships with your family, friends, and acquaintances and on how your attachment to them has encouraged you to do right and discouraged you from doing wrong.

Social control theory focuses on techniques and strategies that regulate human behavior and lead to conformity, or obedience to society's rules—the influences of family and school, religious beliefs, moral values, friends, and even beliefs about government. The more involved and committed a person is to conventional activities and values and the greater the attachment to parents, loved ones, and friends, the less likely that person is to violate society's rules and to jeopardize relationships and aspirations.

The concept of social control emerged in the early 1900s in a volume by E. A. Ross, one of the founders of American sociology. According to Ross, belief systems, rather than specific laws, guide what people do and universally serve to control behavior. Since that time, the concept has taken on a wide variety of meanings. Social control has been conceptualized as representing practically any phenomenon that leads to conformity. The term is found in studies of laws, customs, mores, ideologies, and folkways describing a host of controlling forces.[2]

Is there danger in defining social control so broadly? It depends on your perspective. To some sociologists, the vagueness of the term—its tendency to encompass almost the entire field of sociology—has significantly decreased its value as a concept.[3] To others, the value of social control lies in its representation of a mechanism by which society regulates its members. According to this view, social control defines what is considered deviant behavior, what is right or wrong, and what is a violation of the law.

Theorists who have adopted this orientation consider laws, norms, customs, mores, ethics, and etiquette to be forms of social control. Donald Black, a sociologist of law, noted: "Social control is found whenever people hold each other to standards, explicitly or implicitly, consciously or not: on the street, in prison, at home, at a party."[4]

If an example would help, consider that as recently as 20 years ago there were no legal restrictions, norms, or customs regulating the smoking of cigarettes in public places. The surgeon general's declaration in 1972 that secondhand smoke poses a health hazard ushered in two decades of controls over behavior that not too long ago was considered sociable—if not sophisticated and suave.

At present most states have laws restricting or banning smoking in public places. Los Angeles became the thirty-second city in California to outlaw smoking in all its restaurants.[5] The U.S. Supreme Court followed, holding that it is "cruel and unusual punishment" to expose prison inmates to levels of tobacco smoke that place their health at risk. Laws, norms, customs, and etiquette relating to smoking exert strong controls over this behavior.

THEORIES OF SOCIAL CONTROL

Why is social control conceptualized in such different ways? Perhaps because social control has been examined from both a macrosociological and a microsociological perspective. **Macrosociological studies** explore formal systems for the control of groups:

- The legal system, laws, and particularly, law enforcement.
- Powerful groups in society.
- Social and economic directives of governmental or private groups.

These types of control can be either positive—that is, they inhibit rule-breaking behavior by a type of social guidance—or negative—that is, they foster oppressive, restrictive, or corrupt practices by those in power.[6]

The microsociological perspective is similar to the macrosociological approach in that it, too, explains why people conform. **Microsociological studies,** however, focus on informal systems. Researchers collect data from individuals (usually by self-report methods), are often guided by hypotheses that apply to individuals as well as groups, and frequently make reference to or examine a person's internal control system.

The Microsociological Perspective: Hirschi

Travis Hirschi has been the spokesperson of the microsociological perspective since the publication of his *Causes of Delinquency* in 1969. He is not, however, the first scholar to examine the extent of individual social control and its relationship to delinquency. In 1957 Jackson Toby introduced the notion of individual "commitment" as a powerful determining force in the social control of behavior.[7] Scott Briar and Irving Piliavin extended Toby's thesis by advancing the view that the extent of individual commitment and conformity plays a role in decreasing the likelihood of deviance. They noted that the degree of an adolescent's commitment is reflected in relationships with adult authority figures and with friends and is determined in part by "belief in God, affection for conventionally behaving peers, occupational aspirations, ties to parents, desire to perform well at school, and fear of material deprivations and punishments associated with arrest."[8]

Briar and Piliavin were not entirely satisfied with control dimensions alone, however, and added another factor: individual motivation to be delinquent. This motivation may stem from a person's wish to "obtain valued goods, to portray courage in the presence of, or to belong to, peers, to strike out at someone who is disliked, or simply to get his kicks."[9]

Hirschi was less interested in the source of an individual's motivation to commit delinquent acts than in the reasons people do not commit such acts. He claimed that social control theory explains conformity and adherence to rules, not deviance. It is thus not a crime-causation theory in a strict sense but a theory of prosocial behavior used by criminologists to explain deviance.

Social Bonds

Hirschi posited four social bonds that promote socialization and conformity: attachment, commitment, involvement, and belief. The stronger these bonds, he claimed, the less likelihood of delinquency.[10] To test this hypothesis, he administered a self-report questionnaire to 4077 junior and senior high school students in California (see Table 7.1) that measured both

TABLE 7.1   Items from Travis Hirschi's Measure of Social
                Control

1. In general, do you like or dislike school?
   A. Like it
   B. Like it and dislike it about equally
   C. Dislike it

2. How important is getting good grades to you personally?
   A. Very important
   B. Somewhat important
   C. Fairly important
   D. Completely unimportant

3. Do you care what teachers think of you?
   A. I care a lot
   B. I care some
   C. I don't care much

4. Would you like to be the kind of person your father is?
   A. In every way
   B. In most ways
   C. In some ways
   D. In just a few ways
   E. Not at all

5. Did your mother read to you when you were little?
   A. No
   B. Once or twice
   C. Several times
   D. Many times, but not regularly
   E. Many times, and regularly
   F. I don't remember

6. Do you ever feel that "there's nothing to do"?
   A. Often
   B. Sometimes
   C. Rarely
   D. Never

Source: Travis Hirschi, *Causes of Delinquency* (Berkeley: University of
California Press, 1969).

involvement in delinquency and the strength of
the four social bonds. Hirschi found that weakness in any of the bonds was associated with
delinquent behavior.

Attachment   The first bond, **attachment**,
takes three forms: attachment to parents, to
school (teachers), and to peers. According to
Hirschi, youths who have formed a significant
attachment to a parent refrain from delinquency
because the consequences of such an act might
jeopardize that relationship. The bond of affection between a parent and a child thus becomes
a primary deterrent to criminal activities.[11] Its
strength depends on the depth and quality of
parent-child interaction. The parent-child bond
forms a path through which conventional ideals

and expectations can pass. This bond is bol-
stered by:

- The amount of time the child spends with parents, particularly the presence of a parent at times
  when the child is tempted to engage in criminal
  activity.
- The intimacy of communication between parent
  and child.
- The affectional identification between parent and
  child.[12]

Next Hirschi considered the importance of
the school. As we saw in Chapter 6, Hirschi
linked inability to function well in school to
delinquency through the following chain of
events: Academic incompetence leads to poor
school performance; poor school performance
results in a dislike of school; dislike of school
leads to rejection of teachers and administrators
as authorities. The result is delinquency. Thus
attachment to school depends on a youngster's
appreciation for the institution, perception of
how he or she is received by teachers and peers,
and level of achievement in class.

Hirschi found that attachment to parents and
school overshadows the bond formed with peers:

> As was true for parents and teachers, those most
> closely attached to or respectful of their friends are
> least likely to have committed delinquent acts. The
> relation does not appear to be as strong as was the
> case for parents and teachers, but the ideas that
> delinquents are unusually dependent upon their
> peers, that loyalty and solidarity are characteristic
> of delinquent groups, that attachment to adoles-
> cent peers fosters nonconventional behavior, and
> that the delinquent is unusually likely to sacrifice
> his personal advantage to the "requirements of the
> group" are simply not supported by the data.[13]

Commitment   Hirschi's second group of
bonds consists of **commitment** to or investment
in conventional lines of action—that is, support of
and participation in social activities that tie the individual to the society's moral or ethical code.
Hirschi identified a number of stakes in conformity or commitments: vocational aspirations, educational expectations, educational aspirations.

Many programs and institutions currently
strive to nurture and encourage such aspirations. One such institution is the Pioneer

Academy of Electronics, established soon after the 1992 riots in South-Central Los Angeles. Founded on "academic rigor, real work opportunities, decision-making responsibilities, a teacher who serves as a mentor, and a peer group that reinforces positive behavior," the Pioneer Academy gives inner-city high school students an opportunity to immerse themselves in something other than everyday gang activity. The academy's commitment to providing one-on-one interaction and training has changed the aspirations and work ethic of its students. Gilbert Ybarra, a prospective graduate, attests to its positive impact. Before enrollment in the academy, Gilbert opted for play over work, an attitude that was reflected in his high school grades and attendance. Soon thereafter, he was a proud and confident leader among his peers, excelling in his vocational pursuits, and aspiring to be the first in his family to attend college.[14]

Though Hirschi's theory is at odds with the competing theories of Albert Cohen and Richard Cloward and Lloyd Ohlin (Chapter 6), Hirschi provided empirical support for the notion that the greater the aspiration and expectation, the more unlikely delinquency becomes. Also, "students who smoke, those who drink, and those who date are more likely to commit delinquent acts; . . . the more the boy is involved in adult activities, the greater his involvement in delinquency."[15]

Involvement Hirschi's third bond is **involvement,** or preoccupation with activities that promote the interests of society. This bond is derived from involvement in school-related activities (such as homework) rather than in working-class adult activities (such as smoking and drinking). A person who is busy doing conventional things has little time for deviant activities.

Crime Surfing

www.washingtonpost.com/wp-srv/national/longterm/cult/overview90s.htm

There is a dark side to extreme beliefs that defy convention. Can you recall a series of disturbing suicides of cult members that made headlines in the 1990s?

With this premise in mind, several regional schools will soon be following the example set by Parrot Middle School in Southwest Florida. Parrot Middle School currently offers its students an invaluable service. As part of an after-school program that provides counseling and tutoring services, students have been given the opportunity to participate in a diverse range of recreational courses, including martial arts, gymnastics, home economics, computer basics, and art. The program is designed to provide constructive pastimes for youths formerly left unsupervised during the interim between the end of the school day and that of the typical workday.[16]

Belief "This type of prejudice insults me as an individual, but I am helpless because I can't vote. Then again, it's not as if any of the new legislation is affecting me, right? Why should I have any say in my own life? After all, I'm just a teen."

Jeff Lofvers's sentiments reflect much of Florida's teenage population. As of July 1, 1996, the state of Florida enacted a curfew restricting late-night driving for all licensed drivers under the age of 18. Between the hours of 11 P.M. and 6 A.M., 16-year-olds cannot legally drive, unless accompanied by a licensed driver at least 21 years old. The same applies to 17-year-olds between 1 A.M. and 6 A.M. "It amazes me that my friends and I can walk around town as late as we want, yet we're not allowed to be safely locked in our cars past 11 P.M.," protested one angry teen. And another's defiant response when asked to comment on the anticipated effectiveness of this law? "[I]f they (legislators) are trying to trap us in our homes, it won't work."[17]

The last of the bonds, **belief,** consists of assent to the society's value system. The value system of any society entails respect for its laws and for the people and institutions that enforce them. The results of Hirschi's survey lead to the conclusion that if young people no

Crime Surfing

www.street-soldiers.org/

Hirschi identified four social bonds that promote socialization: attachment, commitment, involvement, and belief. How do the programs and resources of the Omega Boys Club promote a commitment to conventional lines of action?

In his attempts to explain the links between respect for authority and criminal behavior, Travis Hirschi quoted developmental psychologist Jean Piaget: "Respect is the source of the law."(1) Hirschi went on to explain:

> "Insofar as the child respects (loves and fears) his parents, and adults in general, he will accept their rules. Conversely, insofar as this respect is undermined, the rules will tend to lose their obligatory character. . . . Lack of respect for the police presumably leads to lack of respect for the law."(1)

Certainly many criminals seem to lack respect for the police, for law, and for their victims. Carjackers provide a good example. The armed theft of cars from drivers, "carjacking" was defined as a violent crime in 1992, when the director of the FBI announced that carjacking was becoming such a serious problem nationwide that it warranted full attention from his bureau.(2) The nation was appalled by a 1992 case in which a Maryland woman was killed when carjackers threw her from her car and then dragged her, tangled in a seat belt, for nearly 2 miles. The carjackers tossed her 22-month-old daughter—in her car seat—into the road, and she was rescued unharmed. But in an example of the extreme lack of respect for authority shown by carjackers, that shocking incident—far from slowing other carjackers—was followed by seven more carjackings in a single day in the Washington area.

Highlights

Annual Average, 1992-96	Total	Carjackings Completed	Attempted
Number of incidents	48,787	24,520	24,267
Number of victimizations	53,452	27,710	25,742
Rate per 10,000 persons	2.5	1.3	1.2
All carjackings	100%	100%	100%
No weapon	17	8*	25
Total with weapon	83	92	75
Firearm	47	72	22*
Knife, other, or unknown	36	20	52
Percent of carjackings			
With injury	16%	23%	10%
Reported to the police	79	100	57

*Based on fewer than 10 sample cases.

- Carjacking is defined as completed or attempted robbery of a motor vehicle by a stranger to the victim. It differs from other motor vehicle theft because the victim is present and the offender uses or threatens to use force.
- Carjackings resulting in murder of the victim(s) are not covered by the National Crime Victimization Survey. According to FBI data, however, each year about 27 homicides by strangers involved automobile theft. These incidents may have been carjackings.
- Between 1992 and 1996 an average of about 49,000 attempted or completed carjackings occurred in the United States each year.
- About half of all carjackings were completed.
- About 7 of 10 completed carjackings involved firearms, compared with 2 of 10 attempted carjackings.
- Most carjackings, completed or attempted, did not result in injury to the victims.
- All the completed carjackings identified by the survey were reported to the police, while more than half of the attempts were reported.

Source: U.S. Department of Justice, Office of Justice Programs, March 1999.

Nearly a year after this 1992 incident in Maryland, carjacking was once again the most talked-about crime in the nation. This time, the father of basketball star Michael Jordan was killed in a carjacking in South Carolina. The murder of Jordan was followed by the carjacking death of two Japanese college students in a parking lot in San Pedro, California, in 1994.(3)

How has carjacking become such a problem? Two scholars, Tod W. Burke

longer believe laws are fair, their bond to society weakens, and the probability that they will commit delinquent acts increases.

Empirical Tests of Hirschi's Theory

Hirschi's work has inspired a vast number of studies. We can examine only a small selection of some of the more significant research.

Michael Hindelang studied rural boys and girls in grades 6 through 12 on the East Coast. His self-report delinquency measure and questionnaire items were very similar to those devised by Hirschi. Hindelang found few differences between his results and those of Hirschi. Two of those differences, however, were significant. First, he found no relationship between attachment to mother and attachment to peers. Hirschi had observed a positive relationship (the stronger the attachment to the mother, the stronger the attachment to peers). Second, involvement in delinquency was positively related to attachment to peers.[18] Hirschi had found an inverse relationship (the stronger the attachment to peers, the less the involvement in delinquency).

Challenging authority and defying it do not always go hand in hand.

period, more than 4188 were stolen "by fear or force," and assailants used handguns, knives, blunt instruments, machetes, simulated guns, and even a broken bottle.(4) Thumbing their noses at authority, carjackers continue to plague the nation with an average of 49,000 attempted or successful carjackings each year between 1992 and 1996.(5)

Sources

1. Travis Hirschi, *Causes of Delinquency* (Berkeley: University of California Press, 1969), pp. 30, 202.
2. "FBI Forms Unit to Battle 'Carjacking,'" *New York Times,* Sept. 16, 1992, p. A21.
3. John L. Mitchell, "Suspect Arraigned in Carjacking Death," *Los Angeles Times,* Apr. 16, 1906, p. B1
4. Tod W. Burke and Charles E. O'Rear, "Armed Carjacking: A Violent Problem in Need of a Solution," *Police Chief,* January 1993, pp. 18–24.
5. Patsy Klaus, *Carjackings in the United States, 1992–96* (Washington, D.C.: Bureau of Justice Statistics, 1999).

Questions for Discussion

1. Could the brazen theory be used to account for crimes other than carjacking? Explain.
2. What approaches to preventing carjacking might serve to increase the amount of respect potential carjackers feel for the police and the law?

and Charles E. O'Rear, offered their theories in a 1993 article.(4) The crime is an outgrowth of simple car theft, which has become less simple as car manufacturers increasingly attempt to prevent theft by providing steering-column locks, sophisticated alarm systems, and tracking devices for stolen vehicles. When the vehicle is occupied, however, such devices are likely to be disengaged, so carjackers specialize in accosting drivers at stop signs, in gas stations, on highway entrance ramps, and in "bump and rob" simulated accidents.

The theory suggested by Burke and O'Rear, and supported by Hirschi's ideas about respect for authority, is the "brazen theory":

The "brazen theory" is based upon the arrogance and self-confidence of the suspects, who tend to believe they are invincible and that their weapons will speak for themselves. Furthermore, with minimal chances of police apprehension and a firm belief that they will beat the system if caught, they consider the risk is worthwhile and cost-effective.

Of 70,000 vehicles stolen in Los Angeles during one recent reporting

In another study, criminologists administered a self-report questionnaire to 3056 male and female students in three Midwestern states. The researchers were critical of Hirschi's conceptualization of both commitment and involvement, finding it difficult to understand how he separated the two. Serious involvement, they argued, is quite unlikely without commitment. They combined commitment and involvement items and ended up with only three bonds: attachment, commitment, and belief.[19]

The study related these bonds to alcohol and marijuana use, use of strong drugs, minor delinquent behavior, and serious delinquent behavior. The results suggested that strong social bonds were more highly correlated with less serious deviance than with such delinquent acts as motor vehicle theft and assault. Also, the social bonds were more predictive of deviance in girls than in boys. Moreover, criminologists who conducted this study noticed that the commitment bond (now joined with involvement) was more significantly correlated with delinquent behavior than were attachment and belief.

Other researchers administered questionnaires to 2213 tenth-grade boys at 86 schools, seeking to answer three questions: First, are Hirschi's four bonds distinct entities? Second, why did Hirschi name only four bonds? Third, why were some factors that are related to educational and occupational aspiration (such as ability and family socioeconomic status) omitted from his questionnaire? The researchers constructed new scales for measuring attachment, commitment, involvement, and belief. They used a self-report measure to assess delinquency. These researchers found little that is independent or distinctive about any of the bonds.[20]

Robert Agnew provided the first longitudinal test of Hirschi's theory by using data on 1886 boys in the tenth and eleventh grades. Eight social control scales (parental attachment, grades, dating index, school attachment, involvement, commitment, peer attachment, and belief) were examined at two periods in relation to two self-report scales (one measuring total delinquency and the other measuring seriousness of delinquency). Agnew found the eight control scales to be strongly correlated with the self-reported delinquency, but the social control measures did little to predict the extent of future delinquency reported at the second testing. Agnew concluded that the importance of Hirschi's control theory has probably been exaggerated.[21]

Most of the recent empirical work on Hirschi's theory explores the relationship between social bonds and other competing theories.[22] Researchers have discovered that the explanatory power of social control theory is enhanced dramatically when joined with other structural and process theories.

Evaluation: Hirschi's Social Control Theory

While social control theory has held a prominent position in criminology for several decades, it is not without weaknesses. For example, social control theory seeks to explain delinquency, not adult crime. It concerns attitudes, beliefs, desires, and behaviors that, though deviant, are often characteristic of adolescents. This is unfortunate because there has long been evidence that social bonds are also significant explanatory factors in postadolescent behavior.[23]

Questions also have been raised about the bonds. Hirschi claims that antisocial acts result from a lack of affective values, beliefs, norms, and attitudes that inhibit delinquency. But these terms are never clearly defined.[24] Critics have also faulted Hirschi's work for other reasons:

- Having too few questionnaire items that measure social bonds.

- Failing to describe the chain of events that results in defective or inadequate bonds.

- Creating an artificial division of socialized versus unsocialized youths.

- Suggesting that social control theory explains why delinquency occurs, when in fact it typically explains no more than 50 percent of delinquent behavior and only 1 to 2 percent of the variance in future delinquency.[25]

Despite the criticisms, Hirschi's work has made a major contribution to criminology. The mere fact that a quarter-century of scholars have tried to validate and replicate it testifies to its importance.

Furthermore, research using and extending Hirschi's constructs has become increasingly sophisticated. Recent research coming from the Rochester Youth Development Study, for example, has considered not only the role of weakened bonds to family and school in promoting delinquency but also the role of delinquent behavior in attenuating the strength of those very bonds. Criminologists have refined Hirschi's constructs so that the effects of social control on delinquency, as well as the effects of delinquency on social control, are considered.[26]

Finally, Hirschi's conception of social bonds has complemented competing explanations of group-level criminality such as gang behavior (see discussion of subcultural theories in Chapter 6). Social control is now discussed in relation to community, family, school, peer group, and individual-level factors (see Table 7.2).

SOCIAL CONTROL AND DRIFT

In the 1960s David Matza developed a different perspective on social control that explains why some adolescents drift in and out of

TABLE 7.2 Risk Factors for Youth Gang Membership

How powerful is social control theory? Consider the premise of this theory in relation to the risk factors for gang membership.

Domain	Risk Factors
Community	Social disorganization, including poverty and residential mobility Organized lower-class communities Underclass communities Presence of gangs in the neighborhood Availability of drugs in the neighborhood Availability of firearms Barriers to and lack of social and economic opportunities Lack of social capital Cultural norms supporting gang behavior Feeling unsafe in neighborhood; high crime Conflict with social control institutions
Family	Family disorganization, including broken homes and parental drug/alcohol abuse Troubled families, including incest, family violence, and drug addiction Family members in a gang Lack of adult male role models Lack of parental role models Low socioeconomic status Extreme economic deprivation, family management problems, parents with violent attitudes, sibling antisocial behavior
School	Academic failure Low educational aspirations, especially among females Negative labeling by teachers Trouble at school Few teacher role models Educational frustration Low commitment to school, low school attachment, high levels of antisocial behavior in school, low achievement test scores, and identification as being learning disabled
Peer group	High commitment to delinquent peers Low commitment to positive peers Street socialization Gang members in class Friends who use drugs or who are gang members Friends who are drug distributors Interaction with delinquent peers
Individual	Prior delinquency Deviant attitudes Street smartness; toughness Defiant and individualistic character Fatalistic view of the world Aggression Proclivity for excitement and trouble *Locura* (acting in a daring, courageous, and especially crazy fashion in the face of adversity) Higher levels of normlessness in the context of family, peer group, and school Social disabilities Illegal gun ownership Early or precocious sexual activity, especially among females Alcohol and drug use Drug trafficking Desire for group rewards, such as status, identity, self-esteem, companionship, and protection Problem behaviors, hyperactivity, externalizing behaviors, drinking, lack of refusal skills, and early sexual activity Victimization

Source: James C. Howell, *Youth Gangs: An Overview* (Washington, D.C.: U.S. Department of Justice, 1998).

The Lambeau Leap, the Ickey Shuffle, the Fun Bunch, and the Sack Dance. Perhaps you were fortunate enough to watch "Monday Night Football" and see a Green Bay Packer leap into a row of Cheesehead fans. Or maybe you have joined others in amazement as Ickey Woods shuffled across the artificial turf, moving side to side, as he passed the football back and forth—to himself. Who could forget the celebratory moves of the Washington Redskins' wide receivers after a touchdown—a collective and well-choreographed high five. What could be worse (or better!) than the New York Jets' Mark Gastineau strutting, stomping, swaggering, gyrating, and wildly pounding his chest in delight over his unparalleled accomplishments?(1) The answer is the cut throat.

The cut throat, also known as the slash, is a simple and less elegant move—just run your hand across your throat in a symbolic gesture that, to Brett Favre, Ricky Watters, Akili Smith, and Keyshawn Johnson, means nothing more than "you cannot stop me" and "in your face." To the National Football League (NFL), however, it means more. The gesture is nothing less than a taunt that crosses the line. This is the line drawn between aggression, confidence, pride, celebration, and sportsmanship on one side—all necessary and important characteristics of the game—and a clear breach of contract between the offending players and fans on the other side. Football players, like their brothers in baseball and hockey, are expected to fight hard to win, to be brutal when necessary, to break bones and teeth when given no other choice, but all within a game that has a set of conventional rules—rules that reflect agreed-upon values; a strong and intractable commitment to the fans, who pay to watch, admire,

and fantasize about playing in a game that is uniquely American. This is a familiar pact.

This pact reflects the very social bonds that promote and sustain our conventional life. That is why all of these violations of convention are so very easy to spot, even when referees fail to throw down their penalty flags. One commentator noted with wonderful sarcasm that there is a reason we do not do the same as Brett, Ricky, Akili, and Keyshawn in "real life." Just imagine:

There is nothing too mundane to lord over a co-worker today. Start with hanging your coat. Turn this nonevent into an in-your-face "gotcha." Scream "This is my house." Let everybody know that you cannot and will not be stopped from putting your coat on that hanger.

If you work in retail—let's say the jewelry counter at a department store—slam the register shut after a transaction, stare at the lady in housewares and menacingly trace a dollar sign in the air. . . .

If you work in an airport control tower, punctuate every safe landing by throwing off your headset so everybody can see your face more clearly. Point up in the sky. Thump your chest.

If you're a surgeon, heckle the patient for needing anesthesia. Don't just remove the tonsils. Say, "I got your tonsils right here." Then spike them.(2)

None of this is done, of course, because places of work reflect our relational attachments, our commitment to convention, a valued involvement in being productive, and our contribution to a shared belief system. With all the effort it takes to succeed—along with the good fortune—few want to lose out on their investment. Few knowingly violate a shared and agreed-to set of values—especially one that has a national time-honored tradition.

Now that the NFL (known in some circles as the "No Fun League") has sent

Brett Favre challenging custom and convention by completing the cutthroat gesture.

letters to all 31 teams warning owners that large fines and significant game penalties will follow the cut throat, will Brett, Ricky, Akili, and Keyshawn conform? Social control theorists would say yes. Not only for fear of fines, but for fear of breaching custom and violating convention, and for fear of losing the admiration of the fans.

Sources

1. Harriet Barovick et al., "Banned Zone," *Time,* Dec. 6, 1999, p. 37.
2. Bud Shaw, "For Many Pro Athletes, Showtime Is All about Me," (New Orleans) *Times-Picayune,* Dec. 12, 1999, p. 7c.

Questions for Discussion

1. As NFL Commissioner, would you impose strict rules on this kind of behavior?
2. Can you think of a sport where custom and convention allow for even more significant demonstrations of individual pride?

---

delinquency. According to Matza, juveniles sense a moral obligation to be bound by the law. A "bind" between a person and the law, something that creates responsibility and control, remains in place most of the time. When it is not in place, the youth may enter into a state of **drift,** or a period when he or she exists in limbo between convention and crime, responding in turn to the demands of each, flirting now with one, now with the other, but postponing commitment, evading decision. Thus, the person drifts between criminal and conventional actions.[27]

If adolescents are indeed bound by the social order, how do they justify their delinquent acts? The answer is that they develop techniques to rationalize their actions. These techniques are defense mechanisms that release the youth from the constraints of the moral order:

- Denial of responsibility. ("It wasn't my fault; I was a victim of circumstances.")

- Denial of injury. ("No one was hurt, and they have insurance, so what's the problem?")

- Denial of the victim. ("Anybody would have done the same thing in my position—I did what I had to do given the situation.")

- Condemnation of the condemner. ("I bet the judge and everyone on the jury has done much worse than what I was arrested for.")

- Appeal to higher loyalties. ("My friends were depending on me and I see them every day—what was I supposed to do?")[28]

Empirical support for drift theory has not been clear. Some studies show that delinquents consider these rationalizations valid,[29] while other research suggests that they do not. Later investigations also demonstrate that delinquents do not share the moral code or values of nondelinquents.[30]

PERSONAL AND SOCIAL CONTROL

Over the last 40 years support has increased for the idea that both social (external) and personal (internal) control systems are important forces in keeping individuals from committing crimes. In other words, Hirschi's social bonds and Matza's drift paradigm may not be enough by themselves to explain why people do not commit crimes.

Failure of Control Mechanisms

Albert J. Reiss, a sociologist, was one of the first researchers to isolate a group of personal and social control factors. According to Reiss, delinquency is the result of (1) a failure to internalize socially accepted and prescribed norms of behavior; (2) a breakdown of internal controls; and (3) a lack of social rules that prescribe behavior in the family, the school, and other important social groups.

To test these notions, Reiss collected control-related data on 1110 juvenile delinquents placed on probation in Cook County (Chicago), Illinois. He examined three sources of information: (1) a diverse set of data on such variables as family economic status and moral ideals and/or techniques of control by parents during childhood; (2) community and institutional information bearing on control, such as residence in a delinquency area and homeownership; and (3) personal control information, such as ego or superego controls, from clinical judgments of social workers and written psychiatric reports. Reiss concluded that measures of both personal and social control seem "to yield more efficient prediction of delinquent recidivism than items which are measures of the strength of social control."[31]

Stake in Conformity

Imagine that your earliest childhood memory conjures up the sound of splintering wood as the police break down your front door, and the image of your grandmother being led away in handcuffs. You are 4 years old. What impact would such an image have on you? What if your formative years were spent in an impoverished urban environment where your mother and grandmother sold heroin out of your living room, your closest friends were high school dropouts with criminal records, and your adolescent confrontations did not involve the school bully demanding your lunch money, but rather the neighborhood drug dealer stopping by to settle overdue debts? Where would you be today?

Six years after the publication of Reiss's study, Jackson Toby proposed a different personal and social control model. Toby discussed the complementary role of neighborhood social disorganization and an individual's own stake in conformity. He agreed that the social disorganization of the slums explains why some communities have high crime rates while others do not: In slums both the community and the family are powerless to control members' behavior. Thieves and hoodlums usually come from such neighborhoods. But a great many law-abiding youngsters come from slums as well. Toby questioned how a theory that explained group behavior could account for individual differences in response to a poor environment. In other words, how can the theory of social disorganization explain why only a few among so many slum youths actually commit crimes?[32]

According to Toby, the social disorganization approach can explain why one neighborhood has a much higher crime rate than another, but not why one particular individual becomes a hoodlum while another does not. What accounts for the difference is a differing stake in **conformity,** or correspondence of behavior to society's patterns, norms, or standards. One person may respond to conditions in a "bad" neighborhood by becoming hostile to conventional values, perhaps because he or she knows that the chances for legitimate success are poor. Another person in the same neighborhood may maintain his or her stake in conformity and remain committed to abiding by the law. Toby reminds us that when we try to account for crime in general, we should look at both group-level explanations (social disorganization) and individual-level explanations (stake in conformity).

Crime Surfing

www.ncjrs.org/pdffiles/163603.pdf

For a discussion of social disorganization and informal social control that confirms many of Toby's early findings, see "Project on Human Development in Chicago Neighborhoods: A Research Update."

CONTAINMENT THEORY

A broad analysis of the relationship between personal and social controls is found in Walter Reckless's presentation of containment theory.[33] **Containment theory** assumes that for every individual there exists a containing external structure and a protective internal structure, both of which provide defense, protection, or insulation against delinquency.

According to Reckless, *outer containment,* or the structural buffer that holds the person in bounds, can be found in the following components:

- A role that provides a guide for a person's activities.
- A set of reasonable limits and responsibilities.
- An opportunity for the individual to achieve status.
- Cohesion among members of a group, including joint activity and togetherness.
- A sense of belongingness (identification with the group).
- Identification with one or more persons within the group.
- Provisions for supplying alternative ways and means of satisfaction (when one or more ways are closed).[34]

Inner containment, or personal control, is ensured by:

- A good self-concept.
- Self-control.
- A strong ego.
- A well-developed conscience.
- A high frustration tolerance.
- A high sense of responsibility.

Reckless suggests that the probability of deviance is directly related to the extent to which internal pushes (such as a need for immediate gratification, restlessness, and hostility), external pressures (such as poverty, unemployment, and blocked opportunities), and external pulls are controlled by one's inner and outer containment. The primary containment factor is found in self-concept, or the way one views oneself in relation to others, and to the world as well. A strong self-concept, coupled with some additional inner controls (such as a strong conscience and sense of responsibility), plus outer controls, makes delinquency highly unlikely.

Table 7.3 shows how the probability of deviance changes as an individual's inner and

TABLE 7.3   The Probability of Deviance as Indicated by
Inner and Outer Containment*

Outer Containment (Social Control)	Inner Containment (Personal Control)	
	Strong	Weak
Strong	+ +	+ −
Weak	+ −	− −

*+ + = very low; + − = average; − − = very high.

Source: Adapted from Walter C. Reckless, "A Non-Causal Explanation:
Containment Theory," *Excerpta Criminologia,* **2** (1962): 131–132.

outer containment weakens. But why is it important to examine inner and outer controls simultaneously? Consider John, a college freshman, who had extensive community ties and strong family attachments and was valedictorian of his high school class. He also was a dealer in cocaine. All efforts to explain John's drug selling would prove disappointing if measures of social control were used alone. In other words, according to Hirschi's social control theory, John should be a conformist—he should focus his efforts on becoming a pharmacist or teacher. Containment theory, on the other hand, would be sensitive to the fact that John, while socially controlled and bonded by external forces, had a poorly developed self-concept, had an immature or undeveloped conscience, and was extremely impulsive. In short, he was driven to selling drugs as a result of a poor set of inner controls.

The idea that both internal and external factors are involved in controlling behavior has interested a number of scholars. Francis Ivan Nye, for example, developed the notion that multiple control factors determine human behavior. He argued that **internalized control,** or self-regulation, was a product of guilt aroused in the conscience when norms have been internalized. **Indirect control** comes from an individual's identification with noncriminals and a desire not to embarrass parents and friends by acting against their expectations.

Nye believes that social control involves "needs satisfaction," by which he means that control depends on how well a family can prepare the child for success at school, with peers, and in the workplace. Finally, **direct control,** a

purely external control, depends on rules, restrictions, and punishments.[35]

Other researchers have looked at direct controls in different ways. Parental control, for example, may depend on such factors as a broken home, the mother's employment, and the number of children in the family; such factors indicate some loss of direct control. Once again we find mixed results. Some studies indicate very little relationship between a broken home and delinquency, except for minor offenses such as truancy and running away.[36] The same can be said about the consequences of a mother's employment and family size.[37] A national study of 1886 males concluded, however, that direct parental control as measured by strictness and punitiveness is indeed correlated with delinquent behavior, and the study warned us not to dismiss this fact lightly. But the question remains open.[38]

Empirical Tests of Containment Theory

"Not when you're 15 and live in a crowded apartment with seven siblings, all younger than 6. Not when your mom has no job, is coming off drugs and belongs to the same gang as you, your drug-addicted dad, and all your relatives belong to. Not when you have to dress so carefully for the trip to class each day, because one mistake could kill. Does Calvin Klein know his logo means "Crips Killer" in Southeast L.A.? Green means you deal drugs. The wrong belt buckle or shoelace knot is big trouble if you meet rival gangs on your way."[39]

How can a child living in this neighborhood grow up to be a good, law-abiding citizen? How is he or she protected from the crime-producing influences lurking around each corner? To answer these questions, Reckless and his associates had high school teachers in a high-crime neighborhood nominate boys they believed would neither commit delinquent acts nor come into contact with police and juvenile court.

The 125 "good boys" scored high on a social responsibility test and low on a delinquency-proneness test. These boys avoided trouble, had good relations with parents and teachers, and had a good self-concept. They thought of themselves as obedient. Reckless concluded that nondelinquent boys follow conventional values even in bad neighborhoods if they maintain a positive self-image. It is this positive self-image that protects them. In a follow-up study the research team compared good boys with those nominated by teachers as "bad boys" (those they believed were headed for trouble). The good boys scored better on parental relation, self-image, and social responsibility tests. Far more of the bad boys had acquired police and juvenile court records.[40]

Did You Know

. . . that most criminologists favor social control theory as an explanation of criminal behavior?

Evaluation: Containment Theory

Containment theory, like Hirschi's social control theory, has received significant criticism.[41] The most damaging has come from Clarence Schrag, who contends that the terminology used is vague and poorly defined, that the theory is difficult to test empirically, and that the theory fails to consider why some poorly contained youths commit violent crimes while others commit property crimes.[42] These criticisms are not easy to answer. And because little empirical research has been done to test the findings of Reckless and his colleagues over the intervening 30 years, there is little evidence of the validity of containment theory.

INTEGRATED THEORIES

Over the past several years a number of attempts have been made to reconceptualize social control theory through the technique of "theoretical integration"—a technical term for the joining, merging, and testing of different theoretical hypotheses and propositions.[43] As Table 7.4 reveals, theoretical criminologists have relied on social control theory to propose developmental, multifactor, and general theories of crime.

Developmental Theories

All developmental theories share one thing in common: explanations for why offending starts (onset), why it continues (continuance), why it

TABLE 7.4　Examples of Integrated Social Control Theories

Life-Course Theories	
Farrington	A combination of multiple personal (e.g., impulsivity), social (e.g., poor parental supervision), and environmental (e.g., low income) factors are associated with crime over the course of a lifetime.
Thornberry	Crime is a function of a dynamic social process that is determined by learning variables (e.g., association with delinquent peers), boundary variables (e.g., attachment and commitment to conventional activities), as well as social class, race, and gender.
Moffitt	Life-course-persistent offending is explained by faulty interactions between children and their parents, resulting in poor self-control and impulsivity. Adolescent-limited offending is traced to social mimicry, antisocial reinforcements and models.
Le Blanc	An integrative, multilayered control theory that borrows heavily from competing perspectives explains criminality, the criminal, and the criminal event in static and developmental terms.
Laub and Sampson	Crime causation must be viewed developmentally—in the context of the turning points in a criminal career.
Multifactor Theories	
Weis	Crime results from an interaction between diminished social controls and influences from delinquent peers.
Elliott	Delinquency is traced to strain, weak social bonds, and deviant subcultures.
General Theories	
Gottfredson and Hirschi	Individual differences in crime commission may be attributed to levels of self-control.

becomes more frequent or serious (escalation), why it de-escalates (de-escalation), and why, inevitably, it stops (desistance). Rather than focusing exclusively on childhood, adolescence, young adulthood, or adulthood, these theories consider each developmental period in relation to the life span of an offender. In an extension of Hirschi's theory to the "life course," for example, Robert J. Sampson and John H. Laub found that family, school, and peer attachments were most strongly associated with delinquency from childhood to adolescence (through age 17).[44] From the transition to young adulthood through the transition to middle adulthood, attachment to work (job stability) and family (marriage) appears most strongly related to crime causation. Sampson and Laub found evidence that these positive personal and profes-

The best predictor of crime in adulthood, according to theorists, is weak social controls as a child. What are the prospects for Nathaniel Abraham, an 11-year-old boy from Michigan, who was convicted as an adult of murder. He was sentenced to a juvenile detention center until age 21, after which he will be freed.

sional relationships build a "social capital" in otherwise vulnerable individuals that significantly inhibits deviance over time.

Another life-course integrated theory combines control with learning theory (Chapter 4). Terence Thornberry argues that the potential for delinquency begins with the weakening of a person's bonds to the conventional world (parents, school, and accepted values). For this potential to be realized, there must be a social setting in which to learn delinquent values. In this setting, delinquents seek each other out and form common belief systems. There is nothing static about this kind of learning. Criminality, according to Thornberry, is a function of a dynamic social process that changes over time.[45]

David Farrington's work with the data from the Cambridge Study of Delinquent Development reveals different explanations for the general tendency to engage in crime (long-term variables) over time, as well as the influences that prompt an individual, at any given time, to engage in crime (short-term variables) (Table 7.4). The former include impulsivity,

low empathy, and belief systems favorable to law violation. The latter consider momentary opportunities and situationally induced motivating factors, such as alcohol consumption and boredom.[46]

In one of the most elegant developmental theories to date, Marc LeBlanc employs social control theory to provide both static (pertaining to a particular time and place) and dynamic (occurring over time) explanations of criminality (the total number of infractions), the criminal (personal characteristics of an offender), and the crime (the criminal event). To construct his models, LeBlanc borrows from a host of disciplines (see Figure 7.1).

Multiple Control Factors

Multiple control factor theories integrate a criminological theory, such as differential association, with a number of social controls. Delbert Elliott and his colleagues have integrated the social bonds of Hirschi's theory of social control with strain theories. These researchers suggest that limited or blocked opportunities

FIGURE 7.1   Control theory at the level of the criminality.

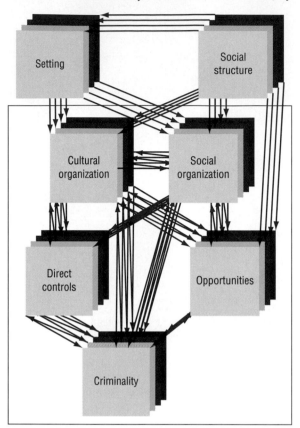

Source: Marc LeBlanc, "A Generic Control Theory of the Criminal Phenomenon:
The Structural and Dynamic Statements of an Integrative Multilayered Control
Theory," in T. P. Thornberry, ed., *Developmental Theories of Crime and
Delinquency: Advances in Criminological Theory,* **7** (1997), p. 238.

FIGURE 7.2   The Gottfredson-Hirschi self-control
model. Gottfredson and Hirschi's model
assumes that poor self-control is an intervening variable that explains all crime, as
well as differences in crime rates, by age,
gender, and race.

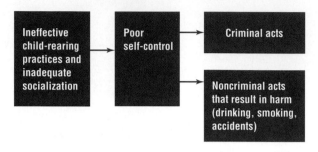

and a subsequent failure to achieve cultural
goals would weaken or even destroy bonds to
the conventional or social order. In other words,
even if someone establishes strong bonds in
childhood, a series of negative experiences in
school, in the community, and at home, along
with blocked access to opportunity, would be
likely to lead to a weakening of those social
bonds. As strain weakens social bonds, the
chance of delinquency increases.[47]

Joseph Weis has proposed a social development model of crime which is an elegant integration of social control and social learning theory. He proposes that delinquency is minimized
when youth who are at risk to commit crime
have the opportunity to engage in conforming
activities, and are rewarded for doing so. Con-

sistent reinforcement maximizes the social
bonds which, in turn, diminish associations
with delinquent peers and reduce crime.[48]

General Theories

In *A General Theory of Crime,* Michael Gottfredson and Travis Hirschi propose a new model of
personal and social control—one designed to
explain an individual's propensity to commit
crime.[49] Gottfredson and Hirschi claim that
their model, unlike earlier conceptualizations,
explains the tendency to commit all crimes,
from crimes of violence such as robbery and
sexual assault to white-collar offenses such as
mail fraud and federal securities violations.[50]

This "general theory" of propensity to commit crimes, shown in Figure 7.2, assumes that
offenders have little control over their own behavior and desires. When the need for momentary pleasure and immediate gratification outweighs long-term interests, crime occurs. In
short, crime is a function of poor self-control.

What leads to poor self-control? Inadequate
socialization and poor child-rearing practices,
coupled with poor attachment, increase the
probability of impulsive and uncontrolled acts.
According to Gottfredson and Hirschi, individuals with low self-control also tend to be involved in noncriminal events that result in
harm, such as drinking, smoking, and most
types of accidents, including auto crashes,
household fires, and unwanted pregnancies.

Most criminologists devote their efforts to learning why people commit crime and why there is so much crime. A few have looked at the question from the opposite perspective: In places with little crime, what accounts for the low crime rate? Using the United Nations' first World Crime Survey (1970–1975), Freda Adler studied the two countries with the lowest crime rates in each of five general cultural regions of the world(1):

Western Europe: Switzerland and the Republic of Ireland

Eastern Europe: The former German Democratic Republic (East Germany) and Bulgaria

Arab countries: Saudi Arabia and Algeria

Asia: Japan and Nepal

Latin America: Costa Rica and Peru(2)

This is an odd assortment of countries. They seem to have little in common. Some are democratic, others authoritarian. Some are republics, others monarchies. Some were ruled by dictators, others by communal councils. Some are rural, others highly urbanized. Some are remote and isolated; others are in the political mainstream. Some are highly religious, some largely atheistic. Some have a very high standard of living,

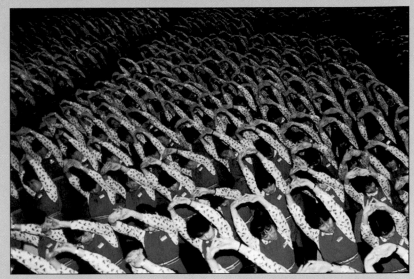

Norm and value convergence at work. Japanese employees showing solidarity in an early morning exercise ritual.

others a very low one. What explains their common characteristic of low crime rates?

Investigations slowly revealed a common factor in all 10 countries: Each appeared to have an intact social control system, quite apart from whatever formal control system (law enforcement) it had. Here are brief descriptions of the types of social control systems identified:

Western Europe: Switzerland fostered a strong sense of belonging to and participating in the local community.(3) The family was still strong in the Republic of Ireland, and it was strengthened by shared religious values.

Eastern Europe: The former German Democratic Republic involved all youths in communal activities, organized by groups and aimed at

---

Evidence in support of this theory is mixed. In the analysis of interviews and breathalizer tests, one study found a definite association between self-control and DUI.[51] Equivocal results, however, were obtained by other researchers who examined interview data from a sample of college students, high school students, adults from Oklahoma City, residents of a Canadian province, and residents of a large southwestern U.S. city.[52] Additional research is establishing the usefulness of this general theory of crime.[53]

It is important to remember that all the integrated theories share one common variable—the social bonds that are at the foundation of social control theory. The ingredients of social control theory have been used quite effectively over the last decade as building blocks in the development and refinement of integrated criminological theories.

THEORY INFORMS POLICY

Social control theory tells us that people commit crimes when they have not developed adequate attachments, have not become involved in and committed to conventional activities, and have not internalized the rules of society (or do not care about them). Efforts to prevent crime must therefore include the teaching of conventional values. It is also necessary to find ways to strengthen individual bonds to society, commitment to the conventional order, and involvement in conventional activities. One way is to strengthen the institutions that socialize people

having young people excel for the glory of self and country. In Bulgaria, industrialization focused on regional industry centers so that the workers would not be dislodged from their hometowns, which served as continuing social centers.

Arab countries: Islam continued to be strong as a way of life and exercised a powerful influence on daily activities, especially in Saudi Arabia. Algeria had, in addition, a powerful commitment to socialism in its postindependence era, involving the citizens in all kinds of commonly shared development activities.

Asia: Nepal retained its strong family and clan ties, augmented by councils of elders that oversaw the community and resolved problems. Highly industrialized Japan had lost some of the social controls of family and kinship, but it found a substitute family in the industrial community, to which most Japanese belonged: Mitsubishi might now be the family that guides one's every step.

Latin America: Costa Rica spent all the funds that other governments devoted to the military on social services and social development, caring for and strengthening its families. Peru went through a process of urbanization in stages: Village and family cohesion marked the lives of people in the countryside, and this cohesion remained with the people as they migrated from Andean villages to smaller towns and then to the big city, where they were received by and lived surrounded by others from their own hometowns.

The study concluded that **synnomie,** a term derived from the Greek *syn* meaning "with" and *nomos* meaning "norms," marked societies with low crime rates.

Sources

1. United Nations, *Report of the Secretary General on Crime Prevention and Control,* A/32/199 (popularly known as the First U.N. World Crime Survey) (New York: United Nations, 1977).
2. Freda Adler, *Nations Not Obsessed with Crime* (Littleton, Colo.: Fred B. Rothman, 1983).
3. Marshall B. Clinard, *Cities with Little Crime: The Case of Switzerland* (Cambridge, Mass.:

Did You Know

. . . that in the most recent World Crime Survey, developing countries reported the highest victimization rates for the following crime categories: burglary with entry, personal theft, robbery, and sexual incidents?

Cambridge University Press, 1978).

Questions for Discussion

1. People in the United States work in factories, live in family groups, go to church, and join youth groups. Why do these institutions not function effectively as forms of social control to keep the crime rate low?
2. How could government or community decision makers use the information presented by this study to help solve crime problems in the United States?

---

and continue to regulate their behavior throughout life—the family, the school, and the workplace.[54]

Family

Experimental school-based parent training programs are offered in many states. The major premise of these programs is that a child's bond to a family is crucial. To develop this bond, parents learned to provide opportunities that would help the child participate and succeed in a social unit such as the school (by demonstrating good study habits, for example) and to reinforce conformity or punish violations of the group's norms. Results suggest that these initiatives decrease children's aggressiveness and increase parental skills.[55]

School

A program called PATHE (Positive Action Through Holistic Education) operates in middle schools and high schools around the United States. Its object is to reduce delinquency by strengthening students' commitment to school and attachment to conforming members—in other words, by bonding young people to the conventional system.

PATHE brings together students, school staff, and community members to plan and implement a program designed to foster a better school climate (encourage more open discussion), improve academic skills, and prepare students for careers. Evaluations of the program reveal higher grades, better attendance, fewer dropouts, and increased commitment to education.[56]

Neighborhood

Historically, church and family have helped protect and maintain the social order in neighborhoods, and instill a sense of pride and comfort in residents. This is no longer the case in many areas. The neighborhood as an institution of informal social control has been very much weakened. Various agencies have tried to reverse this trend with programs to prevent juvenile crime that are implemented through neighborhood-based organizations, for example, in Chicago, Dallas, Los Angeles, New York, New Orleans, and San Diego. Federally funded programs seek to reduce crime by strengthening neighborhood cohesion. Programs assess the needs of residents and then set up crisis intervention centers, mediation (between youngsters and school, family, or police, and between warring gangs), youth training, supervision programs, and family support systems.

Program evaluations reveal that serious juvenile crime decreases.[57] Hundreds of such community crime-prevention projects around the country have been organized by government agencies, private persons, and religious groups.[58] They have made a local impact, but they have not been able to change the national crime rate. The most successful models, however, may offer a plan for crime prevention on a broader, perhaps even a national, scale.

As our understanding of control theory evolves, so will our appreciation of the effects of control interventions. If nothing else, it is fair to say that social control programs and interventions are proliferating and may be found in every state. Here are just a few examples:

Homebuilders (Tacoma, Washington). A family preservation program that seeks to keep at-risk children at home.[59]
Families First (Michigan). A program that strengthens vulnerable families.[60]
S.W.E.A.T. Team (Bridgeport, Connecticut). A project that employs teenagers to create new activities for children who may be tempted into joining gangs or selling drugs.[61]
Learnfare (Ohio, Virginia, Florida, Maryland, and Oklahoma). Programs that provide financial and social support for teenage welfare mothers who attend school.[62]

TABLE 7.5 Violence-Prevention Programs in Boston (Listed by Start Date)

1982
Boston City Hospital Violence Prevention Program

1985
Friends for Life—PSA Campaign Ad Council of Boston
WEATOC Teen Theatre Group Adds Violence Prevention to Its Repertoire

1986
South Boston Boys and Girls Club—Friends for Life Clubs and Violence Prevention Programs

1987
Violence Prevention Curriculum for Adolescents Published for Distribution

1989
Gang Peace

1990
Mayor's Safe Neighborhood Initiative
Teens Against Gang Violence
Citizens for Safety

1992
WBZ-TV Stop the Violence Campaign
Ten-Point Coalition

1994
Louis D. Brown Peace Curriculum
Community Policing in Boston
Adolescent Wellness Program

1995
Ceasefire

1996
Strike Force

Source: Boston Police Department, as cited in *What Can the Federal Government Do to Decrease Crime and Revitalize Communities?* (Washington, D.C.: National Institute of Justice, 1998), p. 60.

Table 7.5 lists programs that Boston, Massachusetts, has initiated since 1982.

Crime-prevention programs like those initiated in Boston, Massachusetts, over the past decade have met with significant success. Most of these efforts are grounded in principles of social control.

CHAPTER 7

REVIEW

The term "social control" has taken on a wide variety of meanings. In general, it describes any mechanism that leads to conformity to social norms. Mainstream studies of social control take one of two approaches. Macrosociological studies focus on formal systems of social control. Most contemporary criminological research takes the microsociological approach, which focuses on informal systems. Travis Hirschi's social control theory has had a long-lasting impact on the scholarly community. Hirschi identified four social bonds that promote adherence to society's values: attachment, commitment, involvement, and belief. The stronger these bonds, Hirschi claimed, the less the likelihood of delinquency.

According to the containment theory of Walter Reckless, every person has a containing external structure (a role in a social group with reasonable limits and responsibilities and alternative means of attaining satisfaction). In addition, each individual has a protective internal structure that depends on a good self-concept, self-control, a well-developed conscience, a tolerance for frustration, and a strong sense of responsibility.

Most investigators today believe that personal (inner) controls are as important as social (external) controls in keeping people from committing crimes. Albert Reiss found that personal controls reinforce social controls. Jackson Toby stressed the importance of a stake in conformity in keeping a person from responding to social disorganization with delinquent behavior. Recent efforts to integrate social control theories with other theories have resulted in developmental, multifactor, and general theories of crime. All share one common variable—the social bonds that constitute social control theory.

As part of an effort to reduce delinquency, a variety of programs at the local and regional levels help parents, schools, and neighborhood groups develop social controls.

YOU BE THE CRIMINOLOGIST

The desire for stability, involvement, belief, and conformity can have a dark side. Consider how mechanisms of social control, narrowly conceived, can support new religious, political, and psychosocial cults or sects. How does social control theory help explain the attraction to Heaven's Gate, the Aum Supreme Truth, the Order of the Solar Temple, or the Branch Davidians?

KEY TERMS

The numbers next to the terms refer to the pages on which the terms are defined.

attachment (188)

belief (189)

commitment (188)

conformity (196)

containment theory (196)

direct control (197)

drift (194)

indirect control (197)

internalized control (197)

involvement (189)

macrosociological studies (187)

microsociological studies (187)

social control theory (186)

synnomie (202)

NOTES

1. William Golding, *Lord of the Flies* (New York: Coward-McCann, 1954), p. 31.
2. Jack P. Gibbs, "Social Control, Deterrence, and Perspectives on Social Order," *Social Forces,* 56 (1977): 408–423. See also Freda Adler, *Nations Not Obsessed with Crime* (Littleton, Colo.: Fred B. Rothman, 1983).
3. Travis Hirschi, *Causes of Delinquency* (Berkeley: University of California Press, 1969).
4. Donald J. Black, *The Behavior of Law* (New York: Academic Press, 1976), p. 105. See Allan V. Horwitz, *The Logic of Social Control* (New York: Plenum, 1990), for an exceptional evaluation of Black's work.
5. Joseph Perkins, "Smoke Signals Taxes, Harsh Rules Go Too Far in Crusade to Snuff Out Habit," *San Diego Union-Tribune,* Mar. 12, 1993, p. B7; editorial, "Smoke Clouds the Political Air in California's City of Angels," *Washington Times,* July 17, 1993, p. C2.
6. Nanette J. Davis and Bo Anderson, *Social Control: The Production of Deviance in the*

Modern State (New York: Irvington, 1983); S. Cohen and A. Scull, eds., *Social Control and the State* (New York: St. Martin's Press, 1983).

7. Jackson Toby, "Social Disorganization and Stake in Conformity: Complementary Factors in the Predatory Behavior of Hoodlums," *Journal of Criminal Law, Criminology, and Police Science,* **48** (1957): 12–17.

8. Scott Briar and Irving Piliavin, "Delinquency, Situational Inducements, and Commitment to Conformity," *Social Problems,* **13** (1965): 41.

9. Ibid, p. 36.

10. Hirschi, *Causes of Delinquency.*

11. See John Bowlby, *Attachment and Loss,* 2 vols. (New York: Basic Books, 1969, 1973); John Bowlby, "Forty-Four Juvenile Thieves: Their Characteristics and Home Life," *International Journal of Psychoanalysis,* **25** (1944): 19–25; and John Bowlby, *The Making and Breaking of Affectional Bonds* (London: Tavistock, 1979).

12. Hirschi, *Causes of Delinquency.*

13. Ibid., p. 145.

14. June Gross, "Successful Program Shows Difficulty of Job Training," *Los Angeles Times,* Apr. 22, 1996, p. 1.

15. Hirschi, *Causes of Delinquency.*

16. Teresa D. Brown, "School Adds After-School Fun," *St. Petersburg Times,* Jan. 12, 1995, p. 3.

17. Jeff Lofvers, "I Don't Understand Why Teens Get Such a Bad Rap," *Orlando Sentinel,* June 5, 1996, p. A13.

18. Michael J. Hindelang, "Causes of Delinquency: A Partial Replication and Extension," *Social Problems,* **20** (1973): 471–487.

19. Marvin D. Krohn and James L. Massey, "Social Control and Delinquent Behavior: An Examination of the Elements of the Social Bond," *Sociological Quarterly,* **21** (1980): 529–544.

20. Michael D. Wiatrowski, David Griswold, and Mary K. Roberts, "Social Control Theory and Delinquency," *American Sociological Review,* **46** (1985): 525–541.

21. Robert Agnew, "Social Control Theory and Delinquency: A Longitudinal Test," *Criminology,* **23** (1985): 47–61. See also Scott Menard, "Demographic and Theoretical Variables in the Age-Period-Cohort Analysis of Illegal Behavior," *Journal of Research in Crime and Delinquency,* **29** (1992): 178–199; Stephen A. Cernovich and Peggy C. Giordano, "School Bonding, Age, Race, and Delinquency," *Criminology,* **30** (1992): 261–291; Kimberly L. Kempf, "The Empirical Status of Social Control Theory," in *New Directions in Criminological Theory,* ed. Freda Adler and William S. Laufer (New Brunswick, N.J.: Transaction, 1993), pp. 143–185; Marc LeBlanc and Aaron Caplan, "Theoretical Formalization, a Necessity: The Example of Hirschi's Bonding Theory," in Adler and Laufer, *New Directions in Criminological Theory,* pp. 237–336; and Orlando Rodriguez and David Weisburd, "The Integrated Social Control Model and Ethnicity: The Case of Puerto Rican American Delinquency," *Criminal Justice and Behavior,* **18** (1991): 464–479.

22. David F. Greenberg, "The Weak Strength of Social Control Theory," *Crime and Delinquency,* **45** (1999): 66–81.

23. Kimberly K. Leonard and S. H. Decker, "The Theory of Social Control: Does It Apply to the Very Young?" *Journal of Criminal Justice,* **22** (1994): 89–105; Karen S. Rook, "Promoting Social Bonding: Strategies for Helping the Lonely and Socially Isolated," *American Psychologist,* **39** (1984): 1389–1407.

24. Milton Rokeach, *The Nature of Human Values* (New York: Free Press, 1973).

25. See Donald J. Shoemaker, *Theories of Delinquency: An Examination of Explanations of Delinquent Behavior,* 2d ed. (New York: Oxford University Press, 1990), pp. 172–207, for an evaluation of social control theory.

26. Terence P. Thornberry, "Toward an Interactional Theory of Delinquency," *Criminology,* **25** (1987): 863–891.

27. David Matza, *Delinquency and Drift* (New York: Wiley, 1964), p. 21.

28. Gresham Sykes and David Matza, "Techniques of Neutralization: A Theory of Delinquency," *American Sociological Review,* **22** (1957): 664–670. For a more recent look at techniques of neutralization, see John Hamlin, "The Misplaced Role of Rational Choice

Review • You Be the Criminologist • Key Terms • Notes

in Neutralization Theory," *Criminology,* **26** (1988): 425–438.

29. Richard A. Ball, "An Empirical Exploration of Neutralization Theory," *Criminologica,* **4** (1966): 103–120. See also N. William Minor, "The Neutralization of Criminal Offense," *Criminology,* **18** (1980): 103–120.

30. Robert Gordon, James F. Short, Jr., D. Cartwright, and Fred L. Strodtbeck, "Values and Gang Delinquency: A Study of Street Corner Groups," *American Journal of Sociology,* **69** (1963): 109–128.

31. Albert J. Reiss, "Delinquency as the Failure of Personal and Social Controls," *American Sociological Review,* **16** (1951): 206.

32. Toby, "Social Disorganization," p. 137.

33. Walter C. Reckless, "A New Theory of Delinquency and Crime," *Federal Probation,* **25** (1961): 42–46; Walter C. Reckless, Simon Dinitz, and E. Murray, "Self-Concept as an Insulator against Delinquency," *American Sociological Review,* **21** (1956): 744–746; Frank R. Scarpitti, Ellen Murray, Simon Dinitz, and Walter C. Reckless, "The Good Boy in a High Delinquency Area: Four Years Later," *American Sociological Review,* **25** (1960): 555–558. See also K. Heimer and R. L. Matsueda, "Role-Taking, Role Commitment, and Delinquency: A Theory of Differential Social Control," *American Sociological Review,* **59** (1994): 365–390.

34. Walter C. Reckless, "A Non-causal Explanation: Containment Theory," *Excerpta Criminologia,* **2** (1962): 131–132.

35. Francis Ivan Nye, *Family Relationships and Delinquent Behavior* (New York: Wiley, 1958).

36. L. Edward Wells and Joseph H. Rankin, "Broken Homes and Juvenile Delinquency: An Empirical Review," *Criminal Justice Abstracts,* **17** (1985): 249–272.

37. Mary Reige, "Parental Affection and Juvenile Delinquency in Girls," *British Journal of Criminology,* **12** (1972): 55–73; Lawrence Rosen, "Family and Delinquency: Structure or Function?" *Criminology,* **23** (1985): 553–573.

38. L. Edward Wells and Joseph H. Rankin, "Direct Parental Controls and Delinquency," *Criminology,* **26** (1988): 263–285. See also Douglas Smith and Raymond Paternoster, "The Gender Gap in Theories of Deviance: Issues and Evidence," *Journal of Research in Crime and Delinquency,* **24** (1987): 140–172; and John Hagan, A. R. Gillis, and John Simpson, "The Class Structure of Gender and Delinquency: Toward a Power-Control Theory of Common Delinquent Behavior," *American Journal of Sociology,* **90** (1985): 1151–1178. See Joan McCord, "Some Child-Rearing Antecedents of Criminal Behavior in Adult Men," *Journal of Personality and Social Psychology,* **36** (1979): 1477–1486. For an examination of the family backgrounds of female offenders, see Jill Leslie Rosenbaum, "Family Dysfunction and Female Delinquency," *Crime and Delinquency,* **35** (1989): 31–44.

39. Betti Jane Levine, "Tender Mercies: They Traded Their Humanity for a Life in Crime," *Los Angeles Times,* June 21, 1996, p. 1.

40. Reckless et al., "Self-Concept as an Insulator"; Scarpitti et al., "The Good Boy in a High Delinquency Area."

41. Gary F. Jensen, "Delinquency and Adolescent Self-Conceptions: A Study of the Personal Relevance of Infraction," *Social Problems,* **20** (1972): 84–103.

42. Clarence Schrag, *Crime and Justice American Style* (Washington, D.C.: U.S. Government Printing Office, 1971), pp. 82–89.

43. Alan Liska, Marvin D. Krohn, and Steven F. Messner, "Strategies and Requisites for Theoretical Integration in the Study of Crime and Deviance," in *Theoretical Integration in the Study of Deviance and Crime: Problems and Prospects,* ed. S. F. Lessner, M. D. Krohn, and A. Liska (New York: SUNYA, 1989), p. 4. See also R. J. Hepburn, "Testing Alternative Models of Delinquency Causation," *Journal of Criminal Law and Criminology,* **67** (1977): 450–460; T. Ross Matsueda, "Testing Control Theory and Differential Association: A Causal Modeling Approach," *American Sociological Review,* **47** (1982): 489–497; Frank S. Pearson and Neil A. Weiner, "Toward an Integration of Criminological Theories," *Journal of Criminal Law and Criminology,* **76** (1985): 116–150; Terrie E. Moffitt, "Adolescence-Limited and Life-Course-Persistent Antisocial Behavior: A Developmental Taxonomy," *Psychological Review,* **100** (1993): 674–701; Terrie E. Moffitt et al., "Childhood-Onset versus

Adolescent-Onset Antisocial Conduct Problems in Males: Natural History from Ages 3 to 18 Years," *Development and Psychopathology*, **8** (1996): 399–424; and Terrie E. Moffitt, "Adolescence-Limited and Life-Course-Persistent Offending: A Complementary Pair of Developmental Theories," in T. P. Thornberry, ed., *Developmental Theories of Crime and Delinquency: Advances in Criminological Theory*, **7** (1997).

44. Robert J. Sampson and John H. Laub, *Crime in the Making: Pathways and Turning Points through Life* (Cambridge, Mass.: Harvard University Press, 1993); R. J. Sampson and J. H. Laub, "Understanding Variability in Lives through Time: Contributions of Life-Course Criminology," *Studies on Crime and Crime Prevention*, **4** (1995): 143–158.

45. Terence P. Thornberry, A. J. Lizotte, and M. D. Krohn, "Delinquent Peers, Beliefs, and Delinquent Behavior: A Longitudinal Test of Interactional Theory," *Criminology*, **32** (1994): 47–83; Terence P. Thornberry, Alan J. Lizotte, Marvin D. Krohn, Margaret Farnsworth, and Sung Juon Jung, "Testing Interactional Theory: An Examination of Reciprocal Causal Relationships among Family, School, and Delinquency," *Journal of Criminal Law and Criminology*, **82** (1991): 3–35; see also Madeline G. Aultman and Charles F. Wellford, "Toward an Integrated Model of Delinquency Causation: An Empirical Analysis," *Sociology and Social Research*, **63** (1979): 316–317; and Thornberry, *Developmental Theories of Crime and Delinquency*.

46. D. S. Nagin and D. P. Farrington, "The Onset and Persistence of Offending," *Criminology*, **30** (1992): 501–524; D. S. Nagin and D. P. Farrington, "The Stability of Criminal Potential from Childhood to Adulthood," *Criminology*, **30** (1992): 235–260; D. P. Farrington, "Explaining the Beginning, Progress, and Ending of Antisocial Behavior from Birth to Adulthood," *Advances in Criminological Theory*, **3** (1992): 253–286.

47. Delbert S. Elliott, Suzanne S. Ageton, and R. J. Canter, "An Integrated Theoretical Perspective on Delinquent Behavior," *Journal of Research in Crime and Delinquency*, **16** (1979):

3–27; S. Menard and Delbert S. Elliott, "Delinquent Bonding, Moral Beliefs, and Illegal Behavior: A Three Wave Panel Model," *Justice Quarterly*, **11** (1994): 173–188.

48. David J. Hawkins and Joseph G. Weis, "The Social Development Model: An Integrated Approach to Delinquency Prevention," *Journal of Primary Prevention*, **6** (1985): 73–97.

49. Michael R. Gottfredson and Travis Hirschi, *A General Theory of Crime* (Stanford, Calif.: Stanford University Press, 1990); Michael Gottfredson and Travis Hirschi, "A Propensity-Event Theory of Crime," in *Advances in Criminological Theory*, vol. 1, ed. W. Laufer and F. Adler (New Brunswick, N.J.: Transaction, 1989); B. J. Arneklev, H. G. Grasmick, and C. R. Tittle, "Low Self-Control and Imprudent Behavior," *Journal of Quantitative Criminology*, **9** (1993): 225–247; D. Brownfield and A. M. Sorenson, "Self Control and Juvenile Delinquency: Theoretical Issues and an Empirical Assessment of Selected Elements of a General Theory of Crime," *Deviant Behavior*, **14** (1993): 243–264; T. Hirschi and M. Gottfredson, "Commentary: Testing the General Theory of Crime," *Journal of Research in Crime and Delinquency*, **30** (1993): 47–54.

50. Travis Hirschi and Michael Gottfredson, "The Significance of White-Collar Crime for a General Theory of Crime," *Criminology*, **27** (1989): 359–371; Darrell Steffensmeier, "On the Causes of 'White Collar' Crime: An Assessment of Hirschi and Gottfredson's Claim," *Criminology*, **27** (1989): 345–358.

51. Carl Keane, Paul S. Maxim, and James J. Teevan, "Drinking and Driving, Self-Control, and Gender: Testing a General Theory of Crime," *Journal of Research in Crime and Delinquency*, **30** (1993): 30–46.

52. See, e.g., A. Sorenson and D. Brownfield, "Adolescent Drug Use and a General Theory of Crime: An Analysis of a Theoretical Integration," *Canadian Journal of Criminology*, **37** (1995): 19–37; J. J. Gibbs and D. Giever, "Self-Control and Its Manifestations among University Students: An Empirical Test of Gottfredson and Hirschi's General Theory," *Justice Quarterly*, **12** (1995): 231–255; Harold G. Grasmick, Charles R.

Review • You Be the Criminologist • Key Terms • Notes

Tittle, and Robert J. Bursik, Jr., "Testing the Core Empirical Implications of Gottfredson and Hirschi's General Theory of Crime," *Journal of Research in Crime and Delinquency,* **30** (1993): 5–29; Hirschi and Gottfredson, "Commentary: Testing the General Theory of Crime"; S. L. Miller and C. Burack, "A Critique of Gottfredson and Hirschi's General Theory of Crime: Selective (In) Attention to Gender and Power Positions," *Women and Criminal Justice,* **4** (1993); M. L. Benson and E. Moore, "Are White-Collar and Common Offenders the Same? An Empirical and Theoretical Critique of a Recently Proposed General Theory of Crime," *Journal of Research in Crime and Delinquency,* **29** (1992): 251–272; and Robert Agnew, "Testing the Leading Crime Theories: An Alternative Strategy Focusing on Motivational Processes," *Journal of Research in Crime and Delinquency,* **32** (1995): 363–398.

53. Don Weatherburn, "On the Quest for a General Theory of Crime," *Australian and New Zealand Journal of Criminology,* **26** (1993): 35–46.

54. See W. Timothy Austin, "Crime and Custom in an Orderly Society: The Singapore Prototype," *Criminology,* **25** (1987): 279–294; J. M. Day and William S. Laufer, eds., *Crime, Values, and Religion* (Norwood, N.J.: Ablex, 1987); and Freda Adler and William S. Laufer, "Social Control and the Workplace," in *US-USSR Approaches to Urban Crime Prevention,* ed. James Finckenauer and Alexander Yakovlev (Moscow: Soviet Academy of State and Law, 1987).

55. David J. Hawkins, Richard F. Catalano, Gwen Jones, and David Fine, "Delinquency Prevention through Parent-Training: Results and Issues from Work in Progress," in *From Children to Citizens:* vol. 3, *Families, Schools, and Delinquency Prevention,* ed. James Q. Wilson and Glenn C. Loury (New York: Springer Verlag, 1987), pp. 186–204.

56. Denise C. Gottfredson, "An Empirical Test of School-Based Environmental and Individual Interventions to Reduce the Risk of Delinquent Behavior," *Criminology,* **24** (1986): 705–731.

57. Jeffrey Fagan, "Neighborhood Education, Mobilization, and Organization for Juvenile Crime Prevention," *Annals of the American Academy for the Advancement of Political and Social Sciences,* **494** (1987): 54–70.

58. For an examination of community social control, see David Weisburd, "Vigilantism as Community Social Control: Developing a Quantitative Criminological Model," *Journal of Quantitative Criminology,* **4** (1988): 137–153.

59. "Fostering the Family: An Intensive Effort to Keep Kids with Parents," *Newsweek,* June 22, 1992, p. 64.

60. Ibid.

61. George Judson, "Fighting Temptations of Summer: Bridgeport Puts Teenagers to Work Helping Other Youths," *New York Times,* Aug. 22, 1992, p. B1.

62. Susan Chirn, "A 'Learnfare' Program Offers No Easy Lessons," *New York Times,* Apr. 28, 1993, p. A12.

CHAPTER 8
Labeling, Conflict, and Radical Theories

KEY TERMS
conflict theory
consensus model
due process
equal protection
labeling theory
penologists
radical criminology
social interactionists

E ach era of social and political turmoil has produced profound changes in people's lives. Perhaps no such era was as significant for criminology as the 1960s. A society with conservative values was shaken out of its complacency when young people, blacks, women, and other disadvantaged groups demanded a part in the shaping of national policy. They saw the gaps between philosophical political demands and reality: Blacks had little opportunity to advance; women were kept in an inferior status; old politicians made wars in which the young had to die. Rebellion broke out, and some criminologists joined it.

These criminologists turned away from theories that explained crime by characteristics of the offender or of the social structure. They set out to demonstrate that individuals become criminals because of what people with power, especially those in the criminal justice system, do. Their explanations largely reject the consensus model of crime, on which all earlier theories rested. Their theories not only question the traditional explanations of the creation and enforcement of criminal law but blame that law for the making of criminals. (See Table 8.1.)

It may not sound so radical to assert that unless an act is made criminal by law, no person who performs that act can be adjudicated a criminal. The exponents of contemporary alternative explanations of crime grant that much. But, justifiably, they also ask: Who makes these laws in the first place? And why? Is breaking such laws the most important criterion for being a criminal? Are all people who break these laws criminals? Do all members of society agree that those singled out by the criminal law to be called "criminals" are criminals and that others are not?

TABLE 8.1 Comparison of Four Criminological Perspectives

Perspective	Origin of Criminal Law	Causes of Criminal Behavior	Focus of Study
Traditional/consensus	Laws reflect shared values.	Psychological, biological, or sociological factors.	Psychological and biological factors (Chap. 4); unequal opportunity (Chap. 5); learning criminal behavior in disorganized neighborhoods (Chap. 5); subculture values (Chap. 6); social control (Chap. 7).
Labeling	Those in power create the laws, decide who will be the rule breakers.	The process that defines (or labels) certain persons as criminals.	Effects of stigmatizing by the label "criminal"; sociopolitical factors behind reform legislation; origin of laws; deviant behavior (Chap. 8).
Conflict	Powerful groups use laws to support their interests.	Interests of one group do not coincide with needs of another.	Bias and discrimination in criminal justice system; differential crime rates of powerful and powerless; development of criminal laws by those in power; relationship between rulers and ruled (Chap. 8).
Radical (Marxist)	Laws serve interests of the ruling class.	Class struggle over distribution of resources in a capitalist system.	Relationship between crime and economics; ways in which state serves capitalist interests; solution to crime problem based on collapse of capitalism (Chap. 8).

LABELING THEORY

The 1950s was a period of general prosperity and pride for Americans. Yet some social scientists, uneasy about the complacency they saw, turned their attention to the social order. They noted that some of the ideals the United States had fought for in World War II had not been achieved at home. Human rights existed on paper but were often lacking in practice. It was clear that blacks continued to live as second-class citizens. Even though the Fourteenth Amendment to the Constitution guaranteed blacks equal rights, neither the law of the country nor the socioeconomic system provided them with equal opportunities.

Nowhere was this fact more apparent than in the criminal justice system. Social scientists and liberal lawyers pressed for change, and the Supreme Court, under Chief Justice Earl Warren, responded. In case after case the Court found a pervasive influence of rules and customs that violated the concepts of **due process,** under which a person cannot be deprived of life, liberty, or property without lawful procedures, and **equal protection,** under which no one can be denied the safeguards of the law. The result of hundreds of Supreme Court decisions was that both black and white citizens now were guaranteed the right to counsel in all criminal cases, freedom from self-incrimination, and other rights enumerated in the first 10 amendments to the Constitution. Nevertheless, a great deal of social injustice remained.

In this social climate, a small group of social scientists, known as *labeling theorists,* began to explore how and why certain acts were defined as criminal or, more broadly, as deviant behavior and others were not, and how and why certain people were defined as criminal or deviant. These theorists viewed criminals not as inherently evil persons engaged in inherently wrong acts but, rather, as individuals who had had criminal status conferred upon them by both the criminal justice system and the community at large.

Viewed from this perspective, criminal acts themselves are not particularly significant; the social reaction to them, however, is. Deviance and its control involve a process of social definition in which the response of others to an individual's behavior is the key influence on subsequent behavior and on individuals' views of themselves. The sociologist Howard S. Becker has written:

> Deviance is not a quality of the act the person commits, but rather a consequence of the application by others of rules and sanctions to an "offender." The deviant is one to whom that label has successfully been applied; deviant behavior is behavior that people so label.[1]

In focusing on the ways in which social inter-actions create deviance, **labeling theory** declares that the reactions of other people and the subse-quent effects of those reactions create deviance. Once it becomes known that a person has engaged in deviant acts, he or she is segregated from con-ventional society, and a label ("thief," "whore," "junkie") is attached to the transgressor. This process of segregation creates "outsiders" (as Becker called them), or outcasts from society, who begin to associate with others like themselves.[2]

As more people begin to think of these peo-ple as deviants and to respond to them accord-ingly, the deviants react to the response by con-tinuing to engage in the behavior society now expects of them. Through this process their self-images gradually change as well. So the key fac-tor is the label that is attached to an individual: "If men define situations as real, they are real in their consequences."[3]

The Origins of Labeling Theory

The intellectual roots of labeling theory can be traced to the post-World War I work of Charles Horton Cooley, William I. Thomas, and George Herbert Mead. These scholars, who viewed the human self as formed through a process of so-cial interaction, were called **social interaction-ists.** In 1918 Mead compared the impact of so-cial labeling to "the angel with the fiery sword at the gate who can cut one off from the world to which he belongs."[4]

Labeling separates the good from the bad, the conventional from the deviant. Mead's inter-est in deviance focused on the social interactions by which an individual becomes a deviant. The person is not just a fixed structure whose action is the result of certain factors acting upon it. Rather, social behavior develops in a continuous process of action and reaction.[5] The way we per-ceive ourselves, our self-concept, is built not only on what we think of ourselves but also on what others think of us.

Somewhat later, the historian Frank Tannen-baum (1893–1969) used the same argument in his study of the causes of criminal behavior. He described the creation of a criminal as a process: Breaking windows, climbing onto roofs, and playing truant are all normal parts of the adoles-cent search for excitement and adventure. Local merchants and others who experience these ac-tivities may consider them a nuisance or per-haps even evil. This conflict is the beginning of the process by which the evil act transforms the transgressor into an evil individual. From that point on, the evil individuals are separated from those in conventional society. Given a criminal label, they gradually begin to think of them-selves as they have been officially defined.

Tannenbaum maintained that it is the process of labeling, or the "dramatization of evil," that locks a mischievous boy into a delin-quent role ("the person becomes the thing he is described as being"). Accordingly, "the entire process of dealing with young delinquents is mischievous insofar as it identifies him to him-self and to the environment as a delinquent per-son."[6] The system starts out with a child in trouble and ends up with a juvenile delinquent.

Basic Assumptions of Labeling Theory

In the 1940s the sociologist Edwin Lemert elabo-rated on Tannenbaum's discussion by formulat-ing the basic assumptions of labeling theory.[7] He reminded us that people are constantly involved in behavior that runs the risk of being labeled delinquent or criminal. But although many run that risk, only a few are so labeled. The reason, Lemert contended, is that there are two kinds of deviant acts: primary and secondary.[8]

Primary deviations are the initial deviant acts that bring on the first social response. These acts do not affect the individual's self-concept. It is the *secondary deviations,* the acts that follow the societal response to the primary deviation, that are of major concern. These are the acts that re-sult from the change in self-concept brought about by the labeling process.[9] The scenario goes somewhat like this:

1. An individual commits a simple deviant act (primary deviation)—throwing a stone at a neighbor's car, for instance.

2. There is an informal social reaction: The neighbor gets angry.

3. The individual continues to break rules (primary deviations)—he lets the neighbor's dog out of the yard.

4. There is increased, but still primary, social reaction: The neighbor tells the youth's parents.

5. The individual commits a more serious deviant act—he is caught shoplifting (still primary deviation).

6. There is a formal reaction: The youth is adjudicated a "juvenile delinquent" in juvenile court.

7. The youth is now labeled "delinquent" by the court and "bad" by the neighborhood, by his conventional peers, and by others.

8. The youth begins to think of himself as "delinquent"; he joins other unconventional youths.

9. The individual commits another, yet more serious, deviant act (secondary deviation)—he robs a local grocery store with members of a gang.

10. The individual is returned to juvenile court, has more offenses added to his record, is cast out further from conventional society, and takes on a completely deviant lifestyle.

According to Lemert, secondary deviance sets in after the community has become aware of a primary deviance. Individuals experience "a continuing sense of injustice, which [is] reinforced by job rejections, police cognizance, and strained interaction with normals."[10] In short, deviant individuals have to bear the stigma of the "delinquent" label, just as English and American convicts, as late as the eighteenth century, bore stigmas, in the form of an M for murder or a T for thief, burned or cut into their bodies to designate them as persons to be shunned.[11] Once such a label is attached to a person, a deviant or criminal career has been set in motion. The full significance of labeling theory was not recognized, either in Europe or in the United States, until political events provided the opportunity.[12]

Labeling in the 1960s

The 1960s witnessed a movement among students and professors to join advocacy groups and become activists in the social causes that were rapidly gaining popularity on college campuses across the nation, such as equal rights for minorities, liberation for women, and peace for humankind. The protests took many forms—demonstrations and rallies, sit-ins and teach-ins, beards and long hair, rock music and marijuana, dropping out of school, burning draft cards.

Arrests of middle-class youths increased rapidly; crime was no longer confined to the ghettos. People asked whether arrests were being made for behavior that was not really criminal. Were the real criminals the legislators and policy makers who pursued a criminal war in Vietnam while creating the artificial crime of draft card burning at home? Were the real criminals the National Guardsmen who shot and killed campus demonstrators at Kent State University? Labeling theorists made their appearance and provided answers. The sociologist Kai Erickson has put it well:

> Deviance is not a property inherent in certain forms of behavior; it is a property conferred upon these forms by audiences which directly or indirectly witness them. The critical variable in the study of deviance, then, is the social audience rather than the individual actor, since it is the audience which eventually determines whether or not any episode or behavior or any class of episodes is labeled deviant.[13]

Edwin Schur, a leading labeling theorist of the 1960s, elaborated on Erickson's explanation:

> Human behavior is deviant to the extent that it comes to be viewed as involving a personally discreditable departure from a group's normative expectation, and it elicits interpersonal and collective reactions that serve to "isolate," "treat," "correct," or "punish" individuals engaged in such behavior.[14]

Schur also expanded on Lemert's secondary deviance with his own concept of "secondary elaboration," by which he meant that the effects of the labeling process become so significant that individuals who want to escape from their deviant groups and return to the conventional world find it difficult to do so. Schur points to members of the gay and drug cultures.[15] The strength of the label, once acquired, tends to exclude such people permanently from the main-

Kent State University protestor grieving over body of fellow student shot and killed by National Guardsmen, Ohio, 1970.

stream culture.[16] Schur found that involvement in activities that are disapproved of may very well lead to more participation in deviance than one had originally planned, and so increase the social distance between the person labeled deviant and the conventional world.[17]

The labeling theorists then asked: Who makes the rules that define deviant behavior, including crime? According to Howard Becker, it is the "moral entrepreneurs"—the people whose high social position gives them the power to make and enforce the social rules by which members of society have to live. By making the rules that define the criminal, Becker argues, certain members of society create outsiders.

The whole process thus becomes a political one, pitting the rule makers against the rule breakers. Becker goes even further, suggesting that people can be labeled simply by being falsely accused. As long as others believe that someone has participated in a given deviant behavior, that individual will experience negative social reaction. People can also suffer the effects of labeling when they have committed a

deviant act that has not been discovered. Since most people know how they would be labeled if they were caught, these secret deviants may experience the same labeling effects as those who have been caught.[18]

Empirical Evidence for Labeling Theory

Empirical investigations of labeling theory have been carried out by researchers in many disciplines using a variety of methodologies. One group of investigators arranged to have eight sane volunteers apply for admission to various mental hospitals. In order to get themselves admitted, the subjects claimed to be hearing voices, a symptom of schizophrenia. Once admitted to the hospital, however, they behaved normally. The experiences of these pseudopatients clearly reveal the effects of labeling.

Doctors, nurses, and assistants treated them as schizophrenic patients. They interpreted the normal everyday behavior of the pseudopatients as manifestations of illness. An early arrival at the lunchroom, for example, was described as exhibiting "oral aggressive" behavior; a patient seen writing something was referred to as a "compulsive note-taker." Interestingly enough, none of the other patients believed the pseudopatients were insane; they assumed they were researchers or journalists. When the subjects were discharged from the hospital, it was as schizophrenics "in remission."

The findings support criminological labeling theory. Once the sane individuals were labeled schizophrenic, they were unable to eliminate the label by acting normally. Even when they supposedly had recovered, the label stayed with them in the form of "schizophrenia in remission," which implied that future episodes of the illness could be expected.[19]

Researchers have also looked at how labels affect people and groups with unconventional lifestyles, whether prohibited by law or not—"gays," "public drunks," "junkies," "strippers," "streetwalkers."[20] The results of research, no matter what the group, were largely in conformity: "Once a _____ , always a _____ ." Labeling by adjudication may have lifelong consequences. Richard Schwartz and Jerome Skolnick, for example, found that employers were reluctant to hire anyone with a court record even though the person had been found not guilty.[21]

The criminologist Anthony Platt has investigated how certain individuals are singled out to receive labels. Focusing on the label "juvenile delinquent," he shows how the social reformers of the late nineteenth century helped create delinquency by establishing a special institution, the juvenile court, for the processing of troubled youths. The Chicago society women who lobbied for the establishment of juvenile courts may have had the best motives in trying to help immigrants' children who, by their standards, were out of control. But by getting the ju-

venile court established, they simply widened the net of state agencies empowered to label some children as deviant.

The state thus aggravated the official problem of juvenile delinquency, which until then had been a neighborhood nuisance handled by parents, neighbors, priests, the local grocer, or the police officer on the street. Juvenile delinquency, according to Platt, was invented. Through its labeling effect, it contributed to its own growth.[22]

The criminologist William Chambliss also studied the question of the way labels are distributed. Consider the following description:

> Eight promising young men [the Saints]—children of good, stable, white upper-middle-class families, active in school affairs, good pre-college students—were some of the most delinquent boys at Hanibal High School. . . . The Saints were constantly occupied with truancy, drinking, wild driving, petty theft and vandalism. Yet not one was officially arrested for any misdeed during the two years I observed them.
>
> This record was particularly surprising in light of my observations during the same two years of another gang of Hanibal High School students, six lower-class white boys known as the Roughnecks. The Roughnecks were constantly in trouble with police and community even though their rate of delinquency was about equal with that of the Saints.[23]

What accounts for the different responses to these two groups of boys? According to Chambliss, the crucial factor is the social class of the boys, which determined the community's reaction to their activities. The Roughnecks were poor, outspoken, openly hostile to authority, and highly visible because they could not afford cars to get out of town. The Saints, on the other hand, had reputations for being bright, they acted apologetic when authorities confronted them, they held school offices, they played on athletic teams, and they had cars to get them out of town. Their behavior went undiscovered, unprocessed, and unpunished.

Chambliss's research reveals what many believe is the inherent discrimination in the juvenile justice system that causes the police and courts to identify the behavior of some as delin-

Psychologist D. L. Rosenhan reported the results of an experiment in which sane volunteers were admitted to psychiatric hospitals after complaining that they had been hearing voices. Length of hospitalization for the volunteers, who stopped "hearing voices" and said they felt fine as soon as they were admitted, ranged from 7 to 52 days, with an average length of 19 days. In this passage, Rosenhan describes how one patient was viewed:

> As far as I can determine, diagnoses were in no way affected by the relative health of the circumstances of a pseudopatient's life. Rather, the reverse occurred: the perception of his circumstances was shaped entirely by the diagnosis. A clear example of such translation is found in the case of a pseudopatient who had had a close relationship with his mother but was rather remote from his father during his early childhood. During adolescence and beyond, however, his father became a close friend, while his relationship with his mother cooled. His present relationship with his wife was characteristically close and warm. Apart from occasional angry exchanges, friction was minimal. The children had rarely been spanked. Surely there is nothing especially pathological about such a history. Indeed, many readers may see a similar pattern in their own experiences, with no markedly deleterious consequences. Observe, however, how such a history was translated in the psychopathological context, this from the case summary prepared after the patient was discharged.

> "This white 39-year-old male . . . manifests a long history of considerable ambivalence in close relationships, which begins in early childhood. A warm relationship with his mother cools during his adolescence. A distant relationship to his father is described as becoming very intense. Affective stability is absent. His attempts to control emotionality with his wife and children are punctuated by angry outbursts and, in the case of the children, spankings. And while he says that he has several good friends, one senses considerable ambivalence embedded in those relationships also."(1)

The facts of the case were unintentionally distorted by the staff to achieve consistency with a popular theory of the dynamics of a schizophrenic reaction. Nothing of an ambivalent nature had been described in relations with parents, spouse, or friends. To the extent that ambivalence could be inferred, it was probably not greater than is found in all human relationships. It is true the pseudopatient's relationships with his parents changed over time, but in the ordinary context that would hardly be remarkable—indeed, it might very well be expected. Clearly, the meaning ascribed to his verbalizations (that is, ambivalence, affective instability) was determined by the diagnosis: schizophrenia. An entirely different meaning would have been ascribed if it were known that the man was "normal."

A psychiatric label has a life and an influence of its own. Once the impression has been formed that the patient is schizophrenic, the expectation is that he will continue to be schizophrenic. When a sufficient amount of time has passed, during which the patient has done nothing bizarre, he is considered in remission and available for discharge. But the label endures beyond discharge, with the unconfirmed expectation that he will behave as a schizophrenic again. Such labels, conferred by mental health professionals, are as influential on the patient as they are on his relatives and friends, and it should not surprise anyone that the diagnosis acts on all of them as a self-fulfilling prophecy. Eventually, the patient himself accepts the diagnosis, with all of its surplus meanings and expectations, and behaves accordingly.

Crime Surfing

www.commonsensepg.com/DiscusPsychiat.html

Examine for a more recent application of "Being Sane in Insane Places."

Source

1. D. L. Rosenhan, "On Being Sane in Insane Places," *Science*, 179 (1973): 253–254.

Questions for Discussion

1. The hospital staff assumed the sane volunteers were schizophrenic, while only 35 of 118 hospital patients in one experiment voiced their suspicions about the pseudopatients' insanity. What accounts for that difference in perception?

2. Have you ever been in a situation in which you felt you had been labeled unfairly or incorrectly and were suffering the consequences? Describe what happened.

quent more so than others. These criminologists state that young minority males are more likely to be arrested and officially processed. This is also true of members of the lower economic classes. Those with wealth or political power, on the other hand, are more likely to be given simply a warning. In this way a Roughneck who spends all his time around other Roughnecks, but does not engage in criminal behavior, would be more likely to be arrested and processed than a Saint who was engaged in illegal activity. Research also seems to indicate that the level of seriousness of the crime committed and the prior record of the individual committing the crime have much influence on delinquency processing.

Up to this point, the contentions of labeling theorists and the evidence they present provide a persuasive argument for the validity of labeling theory. But despite supportive scientific evidence, labeling theory has been heavily criticized.

Evaluation: Labeling Theory

Critics ask: Why is it that individuals, knowing they might be labeled, get involved in socially disapproved behavior to begin with? Most labeled persons have indeed engaged in some act that is considered morally or legally wrong.[24] According to the sociologist Ronald Akers, the impression is sometimes given that people are passive actors in a process by which the bad system bestows a derogatory label, thereby declaring them unacceptable, or different, or untouchable.[25] Critics suggest that the labels may identify real behavior rather than create it. After all, many delinquents have in fact had a long history of deviant behavior, even though they have never been caught and stigmatized. These critics question the overly active role labeling theory has assigned to the community and its criminal justice system and the overly passive role it has assigned to offenders.

Some criminologists also question how labeling theory accounts for individuals who have gone through formal processing but do not continue deviant lifestyles. They suggest that punishment really does work as a deterrent.[26] The argument is that labeling theorists are so intent on the reaction to behavior that they completely neglect the fact that someone has defied the conventions of society.[27] The criminologist Charles Wellford reminds us that, by and large, offenders get into the hands of authorities because they have broken the law. Furthermore, the decisions made about them are heavily influenced by the seriousness of their offenses. He concludes:

> The assumption that labels are differentially distributed, and that differential labelling affects behavior, is not supported by the existing criminological research. In sum, one should conclude that to the degree that these assumptions can be taken to be basic to the labelling perspective, the perspective must be seriously questioned; and criminologists should be encouraged to explore other

ways to conceptualize the causal process of the creation, perpetuation, and intensification of criminal and delinquent behavior.[28]

While most critics believe that labeling theorists put too much emphasis on the system, others of a more radical or Marxist persuasion believe that labeling theorists have not gone far enough. They claim that the labeling approach concentrates too heavily on "nuts, sluts, and perverts," the exotic varieties of deviants who capture public imagination, rather than on "the unethical, illegal and destructive actions of powerful individuals, groups, and institutions of our society."[29] We will look at this argument more closely in a moment.

Empirical evidence that substantiates the claims of labeling theory has been modest. All the same, the theory has been instrumental in calling attention to some important questions, particularly about the way defendants are processed through the criminal justice system. Labeling theorists have carried out important scientific investigations of that system which complement the search of more traditional criminologists for the causes of crime and delinquency.

Some of the criticism of labeling theory can best be countered by one of its own proponents. Howard Becker explains that labeling is intended not as a theory of causation but, rather, as a perspective, "a way of looking at a general area of human activity, which expands the traditional research to include the process of social control."[30] Labeling theory has provided this perspective; it has also spawned further inquiry into the causes of crime.

In a recent extension of labeling theory to a developmental control theory, Sampson and Laub conclude that some delinquency persists because of the reactions that offenders receive to their criminal behavior. Add significant socioeconomic disadvantage, and the result is often a breakdown in social control.[31]

CONFLICT THEORY

Labeling theorists are as well aware as other criminologists that some people make rules and some break them. Their primary concern is the consequences of making and enforcing rules.

One group of scholars has carried this idea further by questioning the rule-making process itself. They claim that a struggle for power is a basic feature of human existence. It is by means of such power struggles that various interest groups manage to control lawmaking and law enforcement.[32] To understand the theoretical approach of these conflict theorists, we must go back to the traditional approach, which views crime and criminal justice as arising from communal consensus.

The Consensus Model

Sometimes members of a society consider certain acts so threatening to community survival that they designate these acts as crimes. If the vast majority of a group's members share this view, the group has acted by consensus. This is the **consensus model** of criminal lawmaking. The model assumes that members of society by and large agree on what is right and wrong and that law is the codification of these agreed-upon social values. The law is a mechanism to settle disputes that arise when individuals stray too far from what the community considers acceptable.

In Durkheim's words, "We can say that an act is criminal when it offends strong and defined states of the collective conscience."[33] Consensus theorists view society as a stable entity in which laws are created for the general good. The laws' function is to reconcile and to harmonize most of the interests that most members of a community cherish, with the least amount of sacrifice.

Deviant acts not only are part of the normal functioning of society but in fact are necessary, because when the members of society unite against a deviant, they reaffirm their commitment to shared values. Durkheim captured this view:

> We have only to notice what happens, particularly in a small town, when some moral scandal has been committed. They stop each other on the street, they visit each other, they seek to come together to talk of the event and to wax indignant in common. From all the similar impressions which are exchanged, for all the temper that gets itself expressed, there emerges a unique temper, more or less determinate according to the circumstances,

which is everybody's without being anybody's in particular. That is the public temper.[34]

Societies in which citizens agree on right and wrong and the occasional deviant serves a useful purpose are scarce today. Such societies could be found among primitive peoples at the very beginning of social evolution. By and large, consensus theory recognizes that not everyone can agree on what is best for society. Yet consensus theory holds that conflicting interests can be reconciled by means of law.[35]

The Conflict Model

With this view of the consensus model, we can understand and evaluate the arguments of the conflict theorists. In the 1960s, while labeling theorists were questioning why some people were designated as criminals, another group of scholars began to ask who in society has the power to make and enforce the laws. Conflict theory, already well established in the field of sociology, thus became popular as an explanation of crime and justice as well.

Like labeling theory, **conflict theory** has its roots in rebellion and the questioning of values. But while labeling theorists and traditional criminologists focused on the crime and the criminal, including the labeling of the criminal by the system, conflict theorists questioned the system itself. The clash between traditional and labeling theorists, on the one hand, and conflict theorists, on the other, became ideological.

Conflict theorists asked: If people agree on the value system, as consensus theorists suggest, why are so many people in rebellion, why are there so many crimes, so many punitive threats, so many people in prison? Clearly conflict is found everywhere in the world, between one country and another, between gay rights and antigay groups, between people who view abortion as a right and others who view it as murder, between suspects and police, between family members, between neighbors. If the criminal law supports the collective communal interest, why do so many people deviate from it?

Conflict theorists answered that, contrary to consensus theory, laws do not exist for the collective good; they represent the interests of specific groups that have the power to get them

The poorest and least powerful have had little influence on the making of laws and on society's reaction to the breaking of laws. Somehow, the poorest have to survive in a society on which they have no apparent impact. In recent years court cases in New York have served as the battleground over what for some is a basic question of survival: Do the poor have a constitutional right to beg?

YES-NO-YES: COURT RULINGS

Yes, said New York federal district court judge Leonard Sand in January 1990, they have a right to panhandle in subway cars.(1) His ruling was overturned by the federal court of appeals in May of the same year, thus denying citizens the right to beg in the New York City subway system.(2) In 1993, when the question concerned the rights of the poor to beg in city streets and public parks, a federal court of appeals decided in favor of the poor.(3)

What did the justices consider in their efforts to decide whether beggars are criminals? Sand's novel ruling stated that panhandling is a form of free speech protected by the First Amendment. "A true test of one's commitment to constitutional principles," he wrote, "is the extent to which recognition is given to the rights of those in our midst who are the least affluent, least powerful and least welcome."(1) The case he decided grew out of attempts by the Metropolitan Transit Authority (MTA) to crack down on panhandling in New York City subway cars and stations. The Legal Action Center for the Homeless had filed a class action against the MTA on behalf of homeless panhandlers.

The court of appeals, in reversing the decision of the district court, criticized the lower court for overlooking the concerns of the MTA's millions of riders. It said that "whether intended as so, or not, begging in the subway often amounts to nothing less than assault, creating in the passengers the apprehension of imminent danger."(2)

CRITICAL COMMENTARY

Judge Sand's ruling created a spate of mostly virulent comments focusing on the judiciary's right to rule on the conduct of those dispossessed of power. One critic, Jill Adler, responded to these attacks:

Judges as the ultimate guardians and interpreters of the Constitution have been charged with the duty of insuring that its fundamental guarantees such as freedom of speech and assembly are not abridged by the government. In this capacity they may sometimes be required to make unpopular decisions.

It is at least arguable that panhandling or begging is a form of symbolic speech—if only because it may be the only avenue of expression open to those society has shunned. Time, place, and manner restrictions, while undoubtedly an important protection for the community, can also be a convenient means of ignoring constitutional guarantees. They will not, however, make the homeless disappear.(4)

Model legislation suggests an increasing interest in curtailing aggressive panhandling by establishing reasonable time, place, and manner restrictions that will not run afoul of the First Amendment. Consider the selected provisions listed below from the Center for Community Interests' (CCI) model legislation on aggressive begging. You should know that CCI calls itself the "common-sense counter to the ACLU—without going to the other extreme."

Section 2. Prohibited acts.
A. No person shall solicit in an aggressive manner in any public place.
B. No person shall solicit on private or residential property without permission from the owner or other person lawfully in possession of such property.

---

enacted.[36] The key concept in conflict theory is power. The people who have political control in any given society are the ones who are able to make things happen. They have power. Conflict theory holds that the people who possess the power work to keep the powerless at a disadvantage. The laws thus have their origin in the interests of the few; these few shape the values, and the values, in turn, shape the laws.[37]

It follows that the person who is defined as criminal and the behavior that is defined as crime at any given time and place mirror the society's power relationships. The definitions are subject to change as other interests gain power. The changing of definitions can be seen in those acts we now designate as "victimless" crimes. Possession of marijuana, prostitution, gambling, refusing to join the armed forces—all have been legal at some times, illegal at others. We may ask, then, whether any of these acts is inherently evil. The conflict theorist would answer that all are *made* evil when they are so designated by those in power and thus defined as crimes in legal codes.

The legal status of victimless crimes is subject to change. But what about murder, a crime considered evil in all contemporary societies? Many conflict theorists would respond that the definition of murder as a criminal offense is also rooted in the effort of some groups to guard their power. A political terrorist may very well become a national hero.

Conflict theorists emphasize the relativity of norms to time and place: Capital punishment is legal in some states, outlawed in others; alcohol consumption is illegal in Saudi Arabia but

Do aggressive panhandlers have a constitutional right to beg? Is asking for money "symbolic" speech protected by the First Amendment? Answers to these questions are increasingly difficult.

connection with such vehicle or otherwise soliciting the sale of goods or services. Provided, however, that this paragraph shall not apply to services rendered in connection with emergency repairs requested by the operator or passenger of such vehicle.(5)

Sources

1. 729 F. Supp. 341 (S.D.N.Y. 1990).
2. 903 F. 2d 146 (2d Cir. 1990).
3. Docket No. 92-9127, United States Court of Appeals for the Second Circuit, July 29, 1993.
4. Andrea Sachs, *Time,* Feb. 12, 1990, p. 55; Jill Adler, *International Herald Tribune,* Feb. 15, 1990, p. 9.
5. http://www.communityinterest. org/backgrounders/indbackg.htm

Questions for Discussion

1. Begging has been regulated throughout history in the United States, and many states currently have statutes that limit or ban begging. What do you suppose the U.S. Supreme Court will do to these statutes?
2. Do you agree that subway begging should be viewed as different from begging on the street?

C. No person shall solicit within twenty feet of public toilets.
D. No person shall solicit within twenty feet of any entrance or exit of any financial institution or check cashing business or within twenty feet of any automated teller machine without the consent of the owner of the property or another person legally in possession of such facilities. Provided,

however, that when an automated teller machine is located within an automated teller machine facility, such distance shall be measured from the entrance or exit of the facility.
E. No person shall solicit an operator or other occupant of a motor vehicle while such vehicle is located on any street, for the purpose of performing or offering to perform a service in

not in the United States. Powerful groups maintain their interests by making illegal any behavior that might be a threat to them. Laws thus become a mechanism of control, or "a weapon in social conflict."[38]

Conflict Theory and Criminology

The sociologist George Vold (1896–1967) was the first theorist to relate conflict theory to criminology. He argued that individuals band together in groups because they are social animals with needs that are best served through collective action. If the group serves its members, it survives; if not, new groups form to take its place. Individuals constantly clash as they try to advance the interests of their particular group over those of all the others. The result is that so-

ciety is in a constant state of conflict, "one of the principal and essential social processes upon which the continuing ongoing of society depends." For Vold, the entire process of lawmaking and crime control is a direct reflection of conflict between interest groups, all trying to get laws passed in their favor and to gain control of the police power.[39]

The sociologist Ralf Dahrendorf and the criminologist Austin Turk are major contemporary contributors to the application of conflict theory to criminology. To Dahrendorf, the consensus model of society is utopian. He believes that enforced constraint, rather than cooperation, binds people together. Whether society is capitalist, socialist, or feudal, some people have the authority and others are subject to it. Society is made up of a large number of interest groups.

221

Conflict: Pro-choice advocates confront right to life supporters over the explosive issue of abortion.

The interests of one group do not always coincide with the needs of another—unions and management, for instance.

Dahrendorf argues that social change is constant, social conflicts are ever-present, disintegration and change are ongoing, and all societies are characterized by coercion of some people by others. The most important characteristics of class, he contends, are power and authority. The inequities remain for him the lasting determinant of social conflict. Conflict can be either destructive or constructive, depending on whether it leads to a breakdown of the social structure or to positive change in the social order.[40]

Austin Turk has continued and expanded this theoretical approach. "Criminality is not a biological, psychological, or even behavioral phenomenon," he says, "but a social status defined by the way in which an individual is perceived, evaluated, and treated by legal authorities." Criminal status is defined by those he calls the "authorities," the decision makers. Criminal status is imposed on the "subjects," the subordinate class. Turk explains that this process works so that both authorities and subjects learn to interact as performers in their dominant

and submissive roles. There are "social norms of dominance" and "social norms of deference." Conflict arises when some people refuse to go along and they challenge the authorities. "Law breaking, then, becomes a measure of the stability of the ruler/ruled relationship."[41] The people who make the laws struggle to hold on to their power, while those who do not make laws struggle to do so.

People with authority use several forms of power to control society's goods and services: police or war power, economic power, political power, and ideological power (beliefs, values).[42] The laws made by the "ins" to condemn or condone various behaviors help shape all social institutions—indeed, the entire culture. Where education is mandatory, for example, the people in power are able to maintain the status quo by passing on their own value system from one generation to the next.[43]

History seems to demonstrate that primitive societies, in their earliest phases of development, tend to be homogeneous and to make laws by consensus. The more a society develops economically and politically, the more difficult it becomes to resolve conflict situations by consensus. For an early instance of criminal law-making by the conflict model, we can go back to 1530, when King Henry VIII of England broke away from the Roman Catholic church because the pope refused to annul Henry's marriage to Catherine of Aragon so that he could marry Anne Boleyn. Henry confiscated church property and closed all the monasteries. Virtually overnight, tens of thousands of people who had been dependent on the monasteries for support were cast out, to roam the countryside in search of a living. Most ended up as beggars. This huge army of vagrants posed a burden on and danger to the establishment. To cope with the problem, Parliament revived the vagrancy laws of 1349, which prohibited the giving of aid to vagrants and beggars. Thus the powerful, by controlling the laws, gained control over the powerless.[44]

Empirical Evidence for the Conflict Model
Researchers have tested several conflict theory hypotheses, such as those pertaining to bias and discrimination in the criminal justice system, differential crime rates of powerful and powerless groups, and the intent behind the development of the criminal law. The findings offer mixed support for the theory.

Alan Lizotte studied 816 criminal cases in the Chicago courts over a 1-year period to test the assumption that the powerless get harsher sentences. His analysis relating legal factors (such as the offense committed) and extralegal factors (such as the race and job of the defendant) to length of prison sentence pointed to significant sentencing inequalities related to race and occupation.[45] When Freda Adler studied the importance of nonlegal factors in the decision making of juries, she found that the socioeconomic level of the defendants significantly influenced their judgment.[46]

While these and similar studies tend to support conflict theory by demonstrating class or racial bias in the administration of criminal justice, others, unexpectedly, show an opposite bias.[47] When we evaluate the contribution of conflict theory to criminological thought, we must keep in mind Austin Turk's warning that conflict theory is often misunderstood. The theory does not, he points out, suggest that most

criminals are innocent or that powerful persons engage in the same amount of deviant behavior as do powerless persons or that law enforcers typically discriminate against people without power. It does acknowledge, however, that behaviors common among society's more disadvantaged members have a greater likelihood of being called "crime" than the activities in which the more powerful typically participate.[48]

Conflict theory does not attempt to explain crime; it simply identifies social conflict as a basic fact of life and as a source of discriminatory treatment by the criminal justice system of groups and classes that lack the power and status of those who make and enforce the laws. Once we recognize this, we may find it possible to change the process of criminalizing people, to provide greater justice. Conflict theorists anticipate a guided evolution, not a revolution, to improve the existing criminal justice system.

RADICAL THEORY
While labeling and conflict theorists were developing their perspectives, social and political conditions in the United States and Europe were changing rapidly and drastically. The youth of America were deeply disillusioned about a political and social structure that had brought about the assassinations of John F. Kennedy, Robert Kennedy, and Martin Luther King, Jr.; the war in Vietnam; and the Watergate debacle. Many looked for radical solutions to social problems, and a number of young criminologists searched for answers to the nation's questions about crime and criminal justice. They found their answers in Marxism, a philosophy born in similar social turmoil a century earlier.

The Intellectual Heritage of Marxist Criminology
The major industrial centers of Europe suffered great hardships during the nineteenth century. The mechanization of industry and of agriculture, heavy population increases, and high rates of urbanization had created a massive labor surplus, high unemployment, and a burgeoning class of young urban migrants forced into the streets by poverty. London is said to have had at

least 20,000 individuals who "rose every morning without knowing how they were to be supported through the day or where they were to lodge on the succeeding night, and cases of death from starvation appeared in the coroner's lists daily."[49] In other cities conditions were even worse.

Engels and Marx

It was against this background that Friedrich Engels (1820–1895) addressed the effects of the Industrial Revolution. A partner in his father's industrial empire, Engels was himself a member of the class he attacked as "brutally selfish." After a 2-year stay in England, he documented the awful social conditions, the suffering, and the great increase in crime and arrests. All these problems he blamed on one factor—competition. In *The Condition of the Working Class in England,* published in 1845, he spelled out the association between crime and poverty as a political problem:

> The earliest, crudest, and least fruitful form of this rebellion was that of crime. The working man lived in poverty and want, and saw that others were better off than he. . . . Want conquered his inherited respect for the sacredness of property, and he stole.[50]

Though Karl Marx (1818–1883) paid little attention to crime specifically, he argued that all aspects of social life, including laws, are determined by economic organization. His philosophy reflects the economic despair that followed the Industrial Revolution. In his *Communist Manifesto* (1848) Marx viewed the history of all societies as a documentation of class struggles: "Freeman and slave, patrician and plebeian, lord and serf, guildmaster and journeyman, in a word, oppressor and oppressed, stood in constant opposition to one another."[51]

Marx went on to describe the most important relationship in industrial society as that between the capitalist bourgeoisie, who own the means of production, and the proletariat, or workers, who labor for them. Society, according to Marx, has always been organized in such a hierarchical fashion, with the state representing not the common interest but the interests of those who own the

means of production. Capitalism breeds egocentricity, greed, and predatory behavior; but the worst crime of all is the exploitation of workers. Revolution, Marx concluded, is the only means to bring about change, and for that reason it is morally justifiable.

Many philosophers before Marx had noted the link between economic conditions and social problems, including crime. Among them were Plato, Aristotle, Virgil, Horace, Sir Thomas More, Cesare Beccaria, Jeremy Bentham, André Guerry, Adolphe Quételet, and Gabriel Tarde (several of whom we met in Chapter 3). But none of them had advocated revolutionary change. And none had constructed a coherent criminological theory that conformed with economic determinism, the cornerstone of the Marxist explanation that people who are kept in a state of poverty will rebel by committing crimes. Not until 1905 can we speak of Marxist criminology.

Crime Surfing

www.soci.niu.edu/~critcrim/dp/dp.html

Do critical criminologists support the death penalty, or are they opposed?

Willem Adriaan Bonger

As a student at the University of Amsterdam, Willem Adriaan Bonger (1876–1940) entered a paper in a competition on the influence of economic factors on crime. His entry did not win; but its expanded version, *Criminality and Economic Conditions,* which appeared in French in 1905, was selected for translation by the American Institute of Criminal Law and Criminology. Bonger wrote in his preface, "[I am] convinced that my ideas about the etiology of crime will not be shared by a great many readers of the American edition."[52] He was right. Nevertheless, the book is considered a classic and is invaluable to students doing research on crime and economics.

Bonger explained that the social environment of primitive people was interwoven with the means of production. People helped each other. They used what they produced. When food was plentiful, everyone ate. When food was scarce, everyone was hungry. Whatever people had, they shared. People were subordinate to nature. In a modern capitalist society, people are much less altruistic. They concentrate on production for profit rather than for the needs of the community. Capitalism encourages criminal behavior by creating a climate that is less conducive to social responsibility. "We have a right," argued Bonger, "to say that the part played by economic conditions in criminality is predominant, even decisive."[53]

Willem Bonger died as he had lived, a fervent antagonist of the evils of the social order. An arch-enemy of Nazism and a prominent name on Hitler's list of people to be eliminated, he refused to emigrate even when the German army was at the border. On May 10, 1940, as the German invasion of Holland began, he wrote to his son: "I don't see any future for myself and I cannot bow to this scum which will now overmaster us."[54] He then took his own life. He left a powerful political and criminological legacy. Foremost among his followers were German socialist philosophers of the progressive school of Frankfurt.

Georg Rusche and Otto Kirchheimer

Georg Rusche and Otto Kirchheimer began to write their classic work at the University of Frankfurt. Driven out of Germany by Nazi persecution, they continued their research in exile in Paris and completed it at Columbia University in New York in 1939. In *Punishment and the Social Structure,* they wrote that punishments had always been related to the modes of production and the availability of labor, rather than to the nature of the crimes themselves.

Consider galley slavery. Before the development of modern sailing techniques, oarsmen were needed to power merchant ships; as a result, galley slavery was a punishment in antiquity and in the Middle Ages. As sailing techniques were perfected, galley slavery was no longer necessary, and it lost favor as a sanction. By documenting the real purposes of punishments through the ages, Rusche and Kirchheimer made **penologists,** who study the penal system, aware that severe and cruel treatment of offenders had more to do with the value of human life and the needs of the economy than with preventing crime.

The names Marx, Engels, Bonger, and Rusche and Kirchheimer were all but forgotten by mainstream criminologists of the 1940s and 1950s, perhaps because of America's relative prosperity and conservatism during those years. But when tranquillity turned to turmoil in the mid-1960s, the forgotten names provided the intellectual basis for American and European radical criminologists, who explicitly stated their commitment to Marxism.

Crime Surfing

www.tile.net/news/altcrimepeacemakingc.html

Do you want to join other critical criminologists? You may do so at their newsgroup.

Radical Criminology since the 1970s

Radical criminology (also called critical, new, and Marxist criminology) made its first public appearance in 1968, when a group of British sociologists organized the National Deviancy Conference (NDC), a group of more than 300 intellectuals, social critics, deviants, and activists of various persuasions. What the group members had in common was a basic disillusion with the criminological studies being done by the British Home Office, which they believed was system-serving and "practical." They were concerned with the way the system controlled people rather than with traditional sociological and psychological explanations of crime. They shared a respect for the interactionist and labeling theorists but believed these theorists had become too traditional. Their answer was to form a new criminology based on Marxist principles.

The conference was followed by the publication in 1973 of *The New Criminology,* the first textual formulation of the new radical criminology. According to its authors, Ian Taylor, Paul Walton, and Jock Young, it is the underclass, the "labor forces of the industrial society," that is controlled through the criminal law and its enforcement, while "the owners of labor will be bound only by a civil law which regulates their competition between each other." The economic institution, then, is the source of all conflicts. Struggles between classes always relate to the distribution of resources and power, and only when capitalism is abolished will crime disappear.[55]

About the time that Marxist criminology was being formulated in England, it was also developing in the United States, particularly at the School of Criminology of the University of California at Berkeley, where Richard Quinney, Anthony Platt, Herman and Julia Schwendinger, William Chambliss, and Paul Takagi were at the forefront of the movement. These researchers were also influenced by interactionist and labeling theorists, as well as by the conflict theories of Vold, Dahrendorf, and Turk.

Though the radical criminologists share the central tenet of conflict theory, that laws are created by the powerful to protect their own interests, they disagree on the number of forces competing in the power struggle. For Marxist criminologists, there is only one dominating segment, the capitalist ruling class, which uses the criminal law to impose its will on the rest of the people in order to protect its property and to define as criminal any behavior that threatens the status quo.[56] The leading American spokesperson for radical criminology is Richard Quinney. His earliest Marxist publications appeared in 1973: "Crime Control in Capitalist Society" and "There's a Lot of Us Folks Grateful to the Lone Ranger."[57]

The second of these essays describes how Quinney drifted away from capitalism, with its folklore myths embodied in individual heroes like the Lone Ranger. He asserts that:

> The state is organized to serve the interests of the dominant economic class, the capitalist ruling class; that criminal law is an instrument the state and the ruling class use to maintain and perpetuate the social and economic order; that the contradictions of advanced capitalism . . . require that the subordinate classes remain oppressed by whatever means necessary, especially by the legal system's coercion and violence; and that only with the collapse of capitalist society, based on socialist principles, will there be a solution to the crime problem.[58]

In *Class, State, and Crime*, Quinney proclaims that "the criminal justice movement is . . . a state-initiated and state-supported effort to rationalize mechanisms of social control. The larger purpose is to secure a capitalist order that is in grave crisis, likely in its final stage of development."[59] Quinney challenges criminologists to abandon traditional ways of thinking about causation, to study what could be rather than what is, to question the assumptions of the social order, and to "ultimately develop a Marxist perspective."[60]

Marxist theory also can be found in the writings of other scholars who have adopted the radical approach to criminology. William Chambliss and Robert Seidman present their version in *Law, Order, and Power:*

> Society is composed of groups that are in conflict with one another and . . . the law represents an institutionalized tool of those in power (ruling class) which functions to provide them with superior moral as well as coercive power in conflict.[61]

They comment that if, in the operation of the criminal justice system by the powerful, "justice or fairness happen to be served, it is sheer coincidence."[62]

To Barry Krisberg, crime is a function of privilege. The rich create crimes to distract attention from the injustices they inflict on the masses. Power determines which group holds the privilege, defined by Krisberg as that which is valued by a given social group in a given historical time.[63] Herman and Julia Schwendinger supported this idea in their summary of the causes of delinquency. They stated that legal relations secure a capitalistic mode of production, while laws are created to secure the labor force. The bourgeoisie are always in a state of being threatened by the proletariats; therefore, while some laws may secure lower-class interests, capitalist interests underlie the basic constitutional laws. Laws in general, according to the Schwendingers, contradict their stated purpose. The Schwendingers went even further in proposing that the state fails to control delinquency because lower-class deviants supply factories with a ready pool of low-wage laborers.[64]

Anthony Platt, in a forceful attack on traditional criminology, has even suggested it would not be "too farfetched to characterize many criminologists as domestic war criminals" because they have "serviced domestic repression in the same way that economics, political sci-

ence, and anthropology have greased the wheels and even manufactured some of the important parts of modern imperialism."[65]

He suggests that traditional criminology serves the state through research studies that purport to "investigate" the conditions of the lower class but in reality only prove, with their probes of family life, education, jobs, and so on, that the members of the lower class are in fact less intelligent and more criminal than the rest of us. Platt claims that these inquiries, based as they are on biased and inaccurate data, are merely tools of the middle-class oppressors.

A number of other areas have come under the scrutiny of Marxist criminologists.[66] They have studied how informal means of settling disputes outside courts actually extend the control of the criminal justice system by adjudicating cases that are not serious enough for the courts; how juvenile court dispositions are unfairly based on social class; how sentencing reform has failed to benefit the lower class; how police practices during the latter half of the nineteenth century were geared to control labor rather than crime; how rape victims are made to feel guilty; how penitentiary reform has benefited the ruling class by giving it more control over the lower class; and how capitalist interests are strengthened by private policing.[67]

Crime Surfing

www.sun.soci.niu.edu/~critcrim

Some scholars question the rule-making process in our society. They claim that a struggle for power is a basic feature of human existence. Many of these scholars belong to the Critical Criminology Division of the American Society of Criminology. What are its purposes?

Evaluation: Marxist Criminological Theory

Critiques of Marxist criminology range from support for the attention the approach calls to the crimes of the powerful to accusations that it is nothing more than a revival of the Robin Hood myth, in which the poor steal from the rich in order to survive.[68] By far the most incisive criticism is that of the sociologist Carl Klockars, who points out that the division of society into social classes may have a beneficial ef-

fect, contrary to Marxist thought. Standards, he argues, are created by some people to inspire the remainder of society. In present-day America, Klockars claims, poverty has lost some of its meaning because luxuries and benefits are spread out over classes. To him, ownership and control of industry are two different things. Anyone who buys a share of stock, for example, can be an owner, while control is handled by bureaucrats who may or may not be owners.[69]

Class Interests versus Interest Groups Klockars attacks Marxists for focusing exclusively on class interests and ignoring the fact that society is made up of many interest groups. This Marxist bias has yielded results that are untrustworthy and predictable, ignore reality, explain issues that are self-evident (some businesspeople are greedy and corrupt), and do not explain issues that are relevant (why socialist states have crime).[70]

Not without a note of sympathy, Richard Sparks summed up the criticism when he said:

> Marxist criminologists tend to be committed to praxis and the desire for radical social reform; but this commitment is not entailed by the scientific claims which Marxists make, and it has sometimes led to those claims being improperly suspect.[71]

Opposition to the new criminology follows many paths, but the most popular, in one way or another, is concerned with its oversimplification of causation by the exclusive focus on capitalism.[72] Critics also attack Marxist criminologists for their assertion that even by studying crime empirically, criminologists are supporting the status quo. That puts Marxist criminologists on the defensive, because if they are not ideologically in a position to expose their theories to empirical research or are unwilling to do so, their assertions will remain just that—assertions with no proof.[73]

Collapse of the Economic Order Even sharper criticism of Marxist theory can be anticipated in the wake of the collapse of the Marxist economic order in the Soviet Union, Poland, Czechoslovakia, Hungary, the German Democratic Republic, Bulgaria, Albania, and Romania, as well as in countries in Africa and

Why has criminology forgotten the systematic decimation of 1 1/2 million Armenians by the Young Turks during World War I, as well as the planned killing of 6 million Jews and the extermination of another 5 million Gypsies, political opponents, mentally ill, retarded, and other "inferior" peoples between 1941 and 1945? How could criminology have neglected an examination of the crimes against humanity that resulted in an estimated 7 million to 16 million deaths over the past 50 years since World War II? You would think that criminology, an academic field concerned with violence, aggression, power, and victimization, would focus on the crime of genocide.

If not in the violence literature, one would expect to find this scholarship in the efforts of conflict, critical, and Marxist theorists in their explanations of organized, state-sanctioned violence and oppression. Criminologists whose life's work is crime prevention also must regularly discuss the causal factors that lead to acts of genocide. If you search through every issue of the journals *Criminology* and *Journal of Criminal Law and Criminology* since their inception, however, you will find only one article on genocide, the most serious of all crimes, and that article was written over 40 years ago. So, why is there no criminology of genocide? Our answers to this question, regrettably, are inadequate.

1. *Genocide is a political act reflecting the will of sovereignty.* Genocide, it has been said, is a political rather than criminal act, most often employed to enhance a country's solidarity and unification. Decisions to liquidate, exterminate, and cleanse a minority population are matters of political policy reflecting the will of sovereignty. The immorality of genocide is tempered by a moral generosity to a sovereign's motivation. The effect of shrouding genocide in a political cloth is to see the annihilation of certain populations as something less than or different from a crime.(1)

2. *Genocide is a breach of international norms and international law.* Several years ago two groups of victims and representatives of victims from Bosnia-Herzegovina brought an action in federal court under the Alien Tort Claims Act against the president and leader of the Bosnian Serb forces for aggravated sexual assault, forced prostitution and impregnation, various acts of extreme torture, and mass execution.(2) The case carried significant symbolic value. Are acts of genocide torts or crimes, violations of international norms or international law? The answers to these questions are far from simple.

3. *Genocide is committed by the state.* Of the many revelations over the past 50 years, criminologists seem to have the most difficulty with the notion that an organization or entity, whether a corporation or nation-state, may commit a crime. When crimes are imputed from an individual to an inanimate entity, the intellectual challenge becomes: Should an individual be blamed as well? The equivocation with bringing those responsible for ethnic cleansing and planned mass murder to justice may be explained, at least in part, by a resistance to the notion that individuals within a "guilty" collective are to blame.

Latin America.[74] Many East European criminologists are no longer quoting Marx in their publications, which tend increasingly to focus on the classical rule-of-law concept. But Quinney has never seen the conditions in those countries as representative of Marxism. According to him, a true Marxist state has not yet been attained, but the ideal is worth pursuing.[75]

To the credit of radical criminologists, it must be said that they have encouraged their more traditional colleagues to look with a critical eye at all aspects of the criminal justice system, including the response of the system to both poor and rich offenders. Their concern is the exercise of power. They ask: Whose power? On whose behalf? For whose benefit? What is the legitimacy of that power? And who is excluded from the exercise of power, by whom, and why? Criminologists have had to address all these questions. Many may not have changed their answers, but the fact that the questions have been raised has ensured clearer answers than had been offered before.

Emerging Explanations

Over the last decade a number of important critical perspectives have emerged that are worthy of attention. These perspectives include radical feminist theory, left realism, abolitionist and anarchist criminology, and peacemaking criminology.

Radical Feminist Theory One significant limitation to critical and Marxist work is an almost exclusive focus on crime committed by males. This limitation has been addressed only recently by both radical and so-

How is it that so many people in countries around the world live in shadows of past genocides and seemingly choose to ignore it?

4. *The magnitude of victimization in genocide defies belief.* The extent of victimization and harm in genocide strains any assessment of seriousness. Who appreciates differences in seriousness when the offense is, for example, 100,000; 250,000; or 500,000 butchered Hutus or Tutsis? Is there a difference in judgments of offense seriousness between the planned killing of 6 million versus 7 million people?

5. *Problems arise regarding both denying and admitting atrocity.* Two prominent themes that emerge from the literature on genocide capture an ambivalence hard-felt by some survivors and refugees of genocide. This ambivalence is captured in the titles of two recently published books on the Holocaust—Deborah Lipstadt's *Denying the Holocaust* and Lawrence L. Langer's *Admitting the Holocaust.*(3) The problem of admission is with the casting of genocide as a historical problem requiring serious study; the effects of intellectualizing mass torture and death; the packaging of the Holocaust neatly into a social science; and the elevation of genocide to a respectable academic discipline of its own, with courses that fit a core curriculum and endow Holocaust professorships. The problem with denial comes from historical revisionists.

Many have commented that the field of criminology has matured. Unfortunately, it has done so without considering the most serious of all crimes.(4)

Sources

1. Irving Louis Horowitz, *Taking Lives: Genocide and State Power* (New Brunswick, NJ: Transaction, 1997).
2. *Kaic v. Karadzic,* 70 F. 3d 232 (2d Cir. 1995).
3. Deborah Lipstadt, *Denying the Holocaust: The Growing Assault on Truth and Memory* (New York: Free Press, 1993); Lawrence L. Langer, Admitting the Holocaust: Collected Essays, (New York: Oxford, 1996).
4. William S. Laufer, "The Forgotten Criminology of Genocide," *Advances in Criminological Theory,* 8 (1999): 45–58.

Questions for Discussion

1. How satisfactory are these answers to you?
2. What could conflict and radical theorists contribute to this dialogue?

---

cialist (Marxist) feminists. The former find the cause of crime in women to be male aggression, as well as men's attempts to control and subordinate women. The latter view female crime in terms of class, gender, and race oppression.[76]

Research by both radical and socialist feminists has revealed important insights into our conceptualization of law, social control, power relationships, and crime-causation theory. They include:

- Reframing the way in which rape is conceptualized (see Chapter 14).

- Acknowledging the fact that the way in which criminologists conceive of and define violence is male-centered.

- Uncovering the relationship between male power, female economic dependency, and battery (for example, spouse abuse).

- Revealing the powerful effect of gender on justice processing.[77]

Left Realism Another critical perspective is left realism.[78] This school of thought emerged over the last decade as a response to the perception that radical criminologists (called "radical idealists" by left realists) place far too much weight on the evils of elite deviance, largely ignoring the fact that the disenfranchised lower classes are persistently victimized by street crime. Radical idealists, it is argued, have developed only weak crime-control strategies. Left realists, on the other hand, recognize street crime as an inevitable outcome of social and political deprivation. They seek a crime-control agenda, capable of being implemented in a capitalist system, that will protect the more vulnerable members of the lower classes from crime, and the fear of crime. The latter, according to

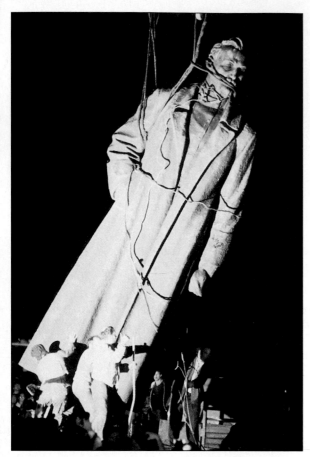

As the Marxist socioeconomic order was toppled, so was the statue of the founder of the KGB, Felix Dzerzhinsky, at the Moscow head-quarters.

left realists, has given conservative right-wing politicians a green light to promote a repressive law-and-order agenda.

Abolitionist and Anarchist Criminology Both abolitionist and anarchist critical theories dispute the existing systems of supremacy. Abolitionism is very much like left realism in its rejection of state controls, as it focuses on the punitive response of segregative punishment. According to abolitionist theory, crime and punishment have a reciprocal effect on each other, with one causing the other. Abolitionist theory advocates the redistribution of power, by returning it to communities and individuals, in order to fix the existing power differential. Similar to this is the anarchist theory of criminology, which also believes that the destruction of communities by the state is at the root of crime. Anarchists, however, reject the sensible and organized opposition to this condition led by abolitionists, opting instead to wage the struggle with chaos and disorder.

Peacemaking Criminology The most recently articulated critical perspective, peacemaking, promotes the idea of peace, justice, and equality in society. The current obsession with punishment and the war on crime suggests an orientation to criminology that only encourages violence. Peacemakers suggest that mutual aid, mediation, and conflict resolution, rather than coercive state control, are the best means to achieve a harmonious, peaceful society.[79] In short, peacemaking criminology advocates humanistic, nonviolent, and peaceful solutions to crime.

The peacemaking perspective is part of an intellectual and social movement toward restorative justice. What is restorative justice? According to Braithwaite restorative justice "means restoring victims, a more victim-centered criminal justice system, as well as restoring offenders and restoring community." This includes restoring:

- Property loss.
- Sense of security.
- Dignity.
- Sense of empowerment.
- Deliberative democracy.
- Harmony based on a feeling that justice has been done.
- Social support.

REVIEW

Labeling theory, conflict theory, and radical theory offer alternative explanations of crime, in the sense that they do not restrict their inquiry to individual characteristics or to social or communal processes. These three theories examine the impact of lawmaking and law enforcement processes on the creation of offenders. The labeling and conflict theories, as critical as they are of the existing system of criminal justice, envisage a system made more just and equitable by reform and democratic processes; radical theory demands revolutionary change. With long historical antecedents, all three theories gained prominence in the 1960s and early 1970s, during an era of rebellion against social, political, and economic inequities.

Labeling theory does not presume to explain all crime, but it does demonstrate that the criminal justice system is selective in determining who is to be labeled a criminal. It explains how labeling occurs, and it blames the criminal justice system for contributing to the labeling process and, therefore, to the crime problem.

Conflict theory goes a step beyond labeling theory in identifying the forces that selectively decide in the first place what conduct should be singled out for condemnation—usually, so it is claimed, to the detriment of the powerless and the benefit of the powerful.

Radical theory singles out the relationship between the owners of the means of production and the workers under capitalism as the root cause of crime and of all social inequities. Radical theory demands the overthrow of the existing order, which is said to perpetuate criminality by keeping the oppressed classes under the domination of the capitalist ruling class.

All three theories have adherents and opponents. Research to demonstrate the validity of the theories has produced mixed results. More important, all these theories have challenged conventional criminologists to rethink their approaches and to provide answers to questions that had not been asked before.

YOU BE THE CRIMINOLOGIST

What kind of crime-prevention program is suggested by critical, Marxist, and labeling theories? How would you go about designing such a program? How would you evaluate its effectiveness?

KEY TERMS

The numbers next to the terms refer to the pages on which the terms are defined.

conflict theory (219)
consensus model (219)
due process (212)
equal protection (212)
labeling theory (213)
penologists (225)
radical criminology (225)
social interactionists (213)

NOTES

1. Howard S. Becker, *Outsiders: Studies in the Sociology of Deviance* (New York: Macmillan, 1963), p. 9.
2. For an excellent discussion of how society controls deviance, see Nicholas N. Kittrie, *The Right to Be Different* (Baltimore: Johns Hopkins University Press, 1972).
3. William I. Thomas, *The Unadjusted Girl* (1923; New York: Harper & Row, 1967).
4. George Herbert Mead, "The Psychology of Punitive Justice," *American Journal of Sociology*, **23** (1918): 577–602. See also Charles Horton Cooley, "The Roots of Social Knowledge," *American Journal of Sociology*, **32** (1926): 59–79.
5. Herbert Blumer, "Sociological Implications of the Thought of George Herbert Mead," in *Symbolic Interactionism*, ed. Blumer (Englewood Cliffs, N.J.: Prentice-Hall, 1969), pp. 62, 65, 66.
6. Frank Tannenbaum, *Crime and the Community* (Boston: Ginn, 1938), p. 27.
7. Edwin M. Lemert, *Social Pathology* (New York: McGraw-Hill, 1951).
8. Edwin M. Lemert, *Human Deviance, Social Problems, and Social Control* (Englewood Cliffs, N.J.: Prentice-Hall, 1967), chap. 3.
9. Lemert, *Social Pathology*, pp. 75–76.
10. Lemert, *Human Deviance*, p. 46. See also Albert K. Cohen, *Deviance and Control* (Englewood Cliffs, N.J.: Prentice-Hall, 1966), pp. 24–25.
11. Erving Goffman, *Stigma: Notes on the Management of Spoiled Identity* (Englewood Cliffs, N.J.: Prentice-Hall, 1963).
12. Gerhard O. W. Mueller, "Resocialization of the Young Adult Offender in Switzerland," *Journal of Criminal Law and Criminology*, **43** (1953): 578–591, at p. 584.
13. Kai T. Erickson, "Notes on the Sociology of Deviance," in *The Other Side: Perspectives on*

Deviance, ed. Howard S. Becker (New York: Free Press, 1964), p. 11.

14. Edwin Schur, *Labeling Deviant Behavior* (New York: Harper & Row, 1971), p. 21.

15. Edwin M. Schur, *Crimes without Victims* (Englewood Cliffs, N.J.: Prentice-Hall, 1965).

16. M. Ray, "The Cycle of Abstinence and Relapse among Heroin Addicts," *Social Problems,* **9** (1961): 132–140.

17. David Matza, *Becoming Deviant* (Englewood Cliffs, N.J.: Prentice-Hall, 1969), pp. 44–53.

18. Becker, *Outsiders,* pp. 18, 20.

19. D. L. Rosenhan, "On Being Sane in Insane Places," *Science,* **179** (1973): 250–258. See also Bruce G. Link, "Understanding Labeling Effects in the Area of Mental Disorders: An Assessment of the Effects of Expectations of Rejection," *American Sociological Review,* **52** (1987): 96–112; and Anthony Walsh, "Twice Labeled: The Effect of Psychiatric Labeling on the Sentencing of Sex Offenders," *Social Problems,* **37** (1990): 375–389.

20. Carol Warren and John Johnson, "A Critique of Labeling Theory from the Phenomenological Perspective," in *Theoretical Perspectives on Deviance,* ed. J. D. Douglas and R. Scott (New York: Basic Books, 1973), p. 77; James P. Spradley, *You Owe Yourself a Drunk: An Ethnography of Urban Nomads* (Boston: Little, Brown, 1979), p. 254.

21. Richard D. Schwartz and Jerome H. Skolnick, "Two Studies of Legal Stigma," *Social Problems,* **10** (1962): 133–138.

22. Anthony Platt, *The Child Savers* (Chicago: University of Chicago Press, 1969). For a further discussion of the effects of stigmatization by the criminal justice system, see Charles W. Thomas and Donna M. Bishop, "The Effect of Formal and Informal Sanctions on Delinquency: A Longitudinal Comparison of Labeling and Deterrence Theories," *Journal of Criminal Law and Criminology,* **75** (1984): 1222–1245.

23. William J. Chambliss, "The Saints and the Roughnecks," *Society,* **11** (1973): 24–31.

24. Walter R. Gove, "Deviant Behavior, Social Intervention, and Labeling Theory," in *The Uses of Controversy in Sociology,* ed. Lewis A. Coser and Otto N. Larsen (New York: Free Press, 1976), pp. 219–227; Ross L. Matsueda,

"Reflected Appraisals, Parental Labeling, and Delinquency: Specifying a Symbolic Interactionist Theory," *American Journal of Sociology,* **97** (1992): 1577–1611.

25. Ronald L. Akers, "Problems in the Sociology of Deviance," *Social Forces,* **46** (1968): 455–465.

26. Ronald L. Akers, *Deviant Behavior: A Social Learning Approach,* 2d ed. (Belmont, Calif.: Wadsworth, 1977); David Ward and Charles R. Tittle, "Deterrence or Labeling: The Effects of Informal Sanctions," *Deviant Behavior,* **14** (1993): 43–64.

27. Jack P. Gibbs, "Conceptions of Deviant Behavior: The Old and the New," *Pacific Sociological Review,* **9** (Spring 1966): 9–14.

28. Charles Wellford, "Labelling Theory and Criminology: An Assessment," *Social Problems,* **22** (1975): 343; Charles F. Wellford and Ruth A. Triplett, "The Future of Labeling Theory: Foundations and Promises," in *Advances in Criminological Theory,* vol. 4, ed. Freda Adler and William S. Laufer (New Brunswick, N.J.: Transaction, 1993).

29. Alexander Liazos, "The Poverty of the Sociology of Deviance: Nuts, Sluts, and Perverts," *Social Problems,* **20** (1972): 103–120.

30. Howard S. Becker, "Labelling Theory Reconsidered," in *Outsiders: Studies in the Sociology of Deviance,* rev. ed., ed. Becker (New York: Free Press, 1973), pp. 177–208. See also Schur, *Labeling Deviant Behavior,* for an excellent review of labeling theory.

31. Robert J. Sampson and John H. Laub, "A Life-Course Theory of Cumulative Disadvantage and Stability of Delinquency," in T. Thornberry, ed., *Developmental Theories of Crime and Delinquency: Advances in Criminology Theory,* **7** (1997).

32. Compare this perspective with the emerging notion of criminology as peacemaking; see Harold E. Pepinsky and Richard Quinney, eds., *Criminology as Peace-Making* (Bloomington: University of Indiana Press, 1991).

33. Émile Durkheim, *The Division of Labor in Society* (New York: Free Press, 1947), p. 80.

34. Ibid., p. 102.

35. Roscoe Pound, *An Introduction to the Philosophy of Law* (Boston: Little, Brown, 1922), p. 98.

36. Richard Quinney, *Crime and Justice in Society* (Boston: Little, Brown, 1969), pp. 26–30.

37. William Chambliss, "The State, the Law, and the Definition of Behavior as Criminal or Delinquent," in *Handbook of Criminology*, ed. Daniel Glaser (Chicago: Rand McNally, 1974), pp. 7–44.

38. Austin Turk, "Law as a Weapon in Social Conflict," *Social Problems*, **23** (1976): 276–291.

39. George Vold, *Theoretical Criminology* (New York: Oxford University Press, 1958), pp. 204, 209.

40. Ralf Dahrendorf, *Class and Class Conflict in Industrial Society* (Stanford, Calif.: Stanford University Press, 1959). See also Ralf Dahrendorf, "Out of Utopia: Toward a Reorientation of Sociological Analysis," *American Journal of Sociology*, **64** (1958): 127.

41. Austin Turk, *Criminality and Legal Order* (Chicago: Rand McNally, 1969), pp. 25, 33, 41–42, 48. See also Thomas O'Reilly-Fleming et al., "Issues in Social Order and Social Control," *Journal of Human Justice*, **2** (1990): 55–74.

42. Austin Turk, *Political Criminality: The Defiance and Defense of Authority* (Beverly Hills, Calif.: Sage, 1982), p. 15.

43. Turk, "Law as a Weapon."

44. William J. Chambliss, "A Sociological Analysis of the Law of Vagrancy," *Social Problems*, **12** (1966): 67–77. For an opposing view on the historical development of criminal law, see Jeffrey S. Adler, "A Historical Analysis of the Law of Vagrancy," *Criminology*, **27** (1989): 209–229; and a rejoinder to Adler: William J. Chambliss, "On Trashing Criminology," ibid., pp. 231–238.

45. Alan Lizotte, "Extra-Legal Factors in Chicago's Criminal Courts: Testing the Conflict Model of Criminal Justice," *Social Problems*, **25** (1978): 564–580. See also Kathleen Daly, "Neither Conflict nor Labeling nor Paternalism Will Suffice: Intersections of Race, Ethnicity, Gender, and Family in Criminal Court Decisions," *Crime and Delinquency*, **35** (1989): 136–168; and Elizabeth Comack, ed., "Race, Class, Gender and Justice," *Journal of Human Justice*, **2** (1990): 1–124.

46. Freda Adler, "Socioeconomic Variables Influencing Jury Verdicts," *New York University Review of Law on Social Change*, **3** (1973): 16–36. See also Martha A. Myers, "Social Background and the Sentencing Behavior of Judges," *Criminology*, **26** (1988): 649–675.

47. Celesta A. Albonetti, Robert M. Hauser, John Hagan, and Ilene H. Nagel, "Criminal Justice Decision-Making as a Stratification Process: The Role of Race and Stratification Resources in Pretrial Release," *Journal of Quantitative Criminology*, **5** (1989): 57–82.

48. Austin Turk, "Law, Conflict, and Order: From Theorizing toward Theories," *Canadian Review of Sociology and Anthropology*, **13** (1976): 282–294.

49. Georg Rusche and Otto Kirchheimer, *Punishment and Social Structure* (New York: Columbia University Press, 1939), p. 93.

50. Friedrich Engels, *"To the Working Class of Great Britain,"* Introduction to The Condition *of the Working Class in England (1845)*, in Karl Marx and Friedrich Engels, *Collected Works*, vol. 4 (New York: International Publishers, 1974), pp. 213–214, 298.

51. Karl Marx and Friedrich Engels, *The Communist Manifesto* (1848; New York: International Publishers, 1979), p. 9.

52. Willem Adriaan Bonger, *Criminality and Economic Conditions*, trans. Henry P. Horton (Boston: Little, Brown, 1916).

53. Ibid., p. 669.

54. J. M. Van Bemmelen, "Willem Adriaan Bonger," in *Pioneers in Criminology*, ed. Hermann Mannheim (London: Stevens, 1960), p. 361.

55. Ian Taylor, Paul Walton, and Jock Young, *The New Criminology: For a Social Theory of Deviance* (London: Routledge & Kegan Paul, 1973), pp. 264, 281. See also Jock Young, "Radical Criminology in Britain: The Emergence of a Competing Paradigm," *British Journal of Criminology*, **28** (1988): 159–183.

56. Gresham Sykes, "The Rise of Critical Criminology," *Journal of Criminal Law and Criminology*, **65** (1974): 206–213.

57. Richard Quinney, "Crime Control in Capitalist Society: A Critical Philosophy of Legal Order," *Issues in Criminology*, **8** (1973): 75–95; Richard Quinney, "There's a Lot of

Review • You Be the Criminologist • Key Terms • Notes

Us Folks Grateful to the Lone Ranger: Some Notes on the Rise and Fall of American Criminology," *Insurgent Sociologist,* 4 (1973): 56–64.

58. Richard Quinney, "Crime Control in Capitalist Society," in *Critical Criminology,* ed. Ian Taylor, Paul Walton, and Jock Young (London: Routledge & Kegan Paul, 1975), p. 199.

59. Richard Quinney, *Class, State, and Crime: On the Theory and Practice of Criminal Justice,* 2d ed. (New York: David McKay, 1977), p. 10.

60. Richard Quinney, *Critique of Legal Order: Crime Control in a Capitalist Society* (Boston: Little, Brown, 1974), pp. 11–13.

61. William Chambliss and Robert Seidman, *Law, Order, and Power* (Reading, Mass.: Addison-Wesley, 1971), p. 503.

62. Ibid., p. 504.

63. Barry Krisberg, *Crime and Privilege: Toward a New Criminology* (Englewood Cliffs, N.J.: Prentice-Hall, 1975).

64. Herman Schwendinger and Julia Schwendinger, "Delinquency and Social Reform: A Radical Perspective," in *Juvenile Justice,* ed. Lamar Empey (Charlottesville: University of Virginia Press, 1979), pp. 246–290.

65. Elliot Currie, "A Dialogue with Anthony M. Platt," *Issues in Criminology,* 8 (1973): 28.

66. Steven F. Messner and Marvin D. Krohn, "Class, Compliance Structures, and Delinquency: Assessing Integrated Structural-Marxist Theory," *American Journal of Sociology,* 96 (1990): 300–328.

67. Lance H. Selva and Robert M. Bohm, "A Critical Examination of the Informalism Experiment in the Administration of Justice," *Crime and Social Justice,* 29 (1987): 43–57; Timothy Carter and Donald Clelland, "A Neo-Marxian Critique, Formulation, and Test of Juvenile Dispositions as a Function of Social Class," *Social Problems,* 27 (1979): 96–108; David Greenberg and Drew Humphries, "The Co-optation of Fixed Sentencing Reform," *Crime and Delinquency,* 26 (1980): 216–225.

68. Jackson Toby, "The New Criminology Is the Old Sentimentality," *Criminology,* 16 (1979): 516–526; Jim Thomas and Aogan O'Maolchatha, "Reassessing the Critical

Metaphor: An Optimistic Revisionist View," *Justice Quarterly,* 6 (1989): 143–171; David Brown and Russell Hogg, "Essentialism, Radical Criminology and Left Realism," *Australian and New Zealand Journal of Criminology,* 25 (1992): 195–230.

69. Carl B. Klockars, "The Contemporary Crises of Marxist Criminology," *Criminology,* 16 (1979): 477–515.

70. Ibid.

71. Richard F. Sparks, "A Critique of Marxist Criminology," in *Crime and Justice: An Annual Review of Research,* ed. Norval Morris and Michael Tonry (Chicago: University of Chicago Press, 1980), p. 159.

72. Milton Mankoff, "On the Responsibility of Marxist Criminology: A Reply to Quinney," *Contemporary Crisis,* 2 (1978): 293–301.

73. Austin T. Turk, "Analyzing Official Deviance: For Nonpartisan Conflict Analysis in Criminology," in *Radical Criminology: The Coming Crisis,* ed. James A. Inciardi (Beverly Hills, Calif.: Sage, 1980), pp. 78–91. See also Sykes, "The Rise of Critical Criminology," p. 212.

74. Philip L. Reichel and Andrzej Rzeplinski, "Student Views of Crime and Criminal Justice in Poland and the United States," *International Journal of Comparative and Applied Criminal Justice,* 13 (1989): 65–81.

75. Quinney, *Class, State, and Crime,* p. 40.

76. Meda Chesney-Lind, "Feminism and Criminology," *Justice Quarterly,* 5 (1988): 497–538; Pat Carlen, "Women, Crime, Feminism, and Realism," *Social Justice,* 17 (1990): 106–123.

77. Sally Simpson, "Feminist Theory, Crime and Justice," *Criminology,* 27 (1989): 605–632; Meda Chesney-Lind, "Judicial Enforcement of the Female Sex Role: The Family Court and the Female Delinquent," *Issues in Criminology,* 8 (1973): 51–69.

78. Martin D. Schwartz and Walter S. DeKeseredy, "Left Realist Criminology: Strengths, Weaknesses and the Feminist Critique," *Crime, Law and Social Change,* 15 (1991): 51–72; John Lowman and Brian D. MacLean, eds., *Realist Criminology: Crime Control and Policing in the 1990s* (Ontario: University of Toronto Press, 1990); Walter S. DeKeseredy and Martin D. Schwartz,

"British and U.S. Left Realism: A Critical Comparison," *International Journal of Offender Therapy and Comparative Criminology,* **35** (1991): 248–262.

79. Pepinsky and Quinney, eds., *Criminology as Peace-Making;* Richard Quinney, "Socialist Humanism and the Problem of Crime," *Crime, Law and Social Change,* **23** (1995): 147–156; Robert Elias et al., Special Issue, "Declaring Peace on Crime," *Peace Review: A Transnational Quarterly,* **6** (1994): 131–254.

Review • You Be the Criminologist • Key Terms • Notes

CHAPTER 9
Targets and Victims of Crime

Riverside, California:

After an hour-long sexual assault during which she thought she was about to die, the 24-year-old Moreno Valley woman testified she turned to her attacker and asked: "Do you think God loves me?"

She then testified that she asked him to tell her mother she loved her if she died.

But she survived to testify in Riverside Superior Court to what police and a prosecutor called one of the most brutal rape cases they ever investigated.

Thursday, Edward Frank Ross, 35, of Moreno Valley, was convicted under the state's tough sexual predator law of six rape and sexual assault counts, including a torture allegation, that could bring an 82-year prison term plus two consecutive life terms.

Deputy District Attorney Tim Schaaf called the Aug. 1, 1995 attack one of the worst he had prosecuted.

"She spent over an hour with this monster," Schaaf said after the eight men and four women returned a verdict following 90 minutes of deliberations. . . .

Although the attack was so violent she was near death from loss of blood, the woman wrapped herself in a sheet and ran from her Moreno Valley apartment in the pre-dawn hours searching for help from a neighbor, Schaaf said. She testified the suspect warned that he would return with his friends.[1]

Arvada, Colorado:

For the second time in two weeks, the Sizzler Steak House . . . has been held up by the same man. In each case, the robber claimed to be armed with a .357 Magnum revolver, demanded money and got an undisclosed amount of cash.

No weapon was seen during the March 25 holdup or in the latest incident Monday night, police said.

The robber was described as a "scruffy" white male in his mid-30s to early-40s, about 6 feet tall and 160 pounds, with blondish-brown hair and glasses. He may be a suspect in several other robberies . . . spokeswoman Susan Rossi said.[2]

Paramus, New Jersey:

A group of car thieves using a limousine as a workshop to make keys for stealing cars . . . would remove a lock cylinder from a car they wanted, go into the limo and file a master key to fit the lock. . . . [T]hey keep working the key and tune it until it fits. They insert the key into the ignition and take off. . . . The most common vehicles stolen have been trucks—not cars—sport-utility vehicles with six-cylinder engines and four-wheel drive, including the Mitsubishi Montero and two Toyota models, the Land Cruiser and 4Runner. . . . Just about any Honda and the Toyota Camry top the thieves' list of desirable passenger cars. . . . The location of Garden State Plaza is enticing. . . . The plaza provides three escape routes, Route 4, Route 17, and the Garden State Parkway.[3]

Here we have three different types of crime, committed in three different jurisdictions—California, Colorado, and New Jersey—involving three different types of harm: nonconsensual intercourse, the taking of property by force and violence, and the loss of automobiles. The prosecutors in these jurisdictions will know what to do. They will identify these crimes under their respective penal codes as sexual assault, robbery, and larceny, respectively, and they will file charges accordingly. But the criminologist, looking more deeply into these crime scenarios, will consider something in addition, something seemingly not of interest to the law, namely, that each of the three crimes occurs at a specific time, at a specific place. The presence of an offender is only one of the necessary components: crimes require many conditions that are independent of the offender, such as the availability of a person to be assaulted or of goods to be stolen.

The three scenarios enable us to see how, up to the actual moment of the crime, the events were a part of everyday life: People sleep in their homes; cars break down, sometimes at odd hours; stores are open for business; and people own Hondas, which must be parked when not being driven. For a full understanding of crime, it is necessary to find out how offenders view the scenes and situations around them as they exercise an option to commit a crime.

In other chapters we have focused on factors explaining why individuals and groups engage in criminal behavior. Now we look at how, in recent years, some criminologists have focused on why offenders choose to commit one offense rather than another at a given time and place. They identify conditions under which those who are prone to commit crime will in fact do so. Current criminological research shows that both a small number of victims and a small number of places experience a large amount of all crime committed. Crimes are events. Criminals choose their targets. Certain places actually attract criminals. Think about the community you live in. Are there some places you hesitate to go to alone? If so, you recognize that some spaces are more dangerous than others. Are there areas that are safe during the day, but not at night? Crime has temporal patterns—some crimes happen more often at night than during the day; others happen more on the weekend than during the rest of the week. There are even what criminologists call seasonal patterns. Certain lifestyles increase people's chances of being victimized. For example, is a drunk person walking alone more likely to be attacked than a sober one? Although victims of crime rarely are to blame for their victimization, they frequently play a role in the crimes that happen to them.

In this chapter we discuss theories of crime and theories of victimization. We will demonstrate how various environmental, opportunity, and victimization theories are interrelated. We will also explore the prevention of crimes against people, places, and valuable goods, presenting current criminological research. In this discussion we include situational crime prevention, diffusion of benefits, routine precautions, and the theoretical and practical implications of focusing on the victims and targets of crime.

TABLE 9.1   Ten Principles of Opportunity and Crime

1. Opportunities play a role in causing all crime.

2. Crime opportunities are highly specific.

3. Crime opportunities are concentrated in time and space.

4. Crime opportunities depend on everyday movements.

5. One crime produces opportunities for another.

6. Some products offer more tempting crime opportunities.

7. Social and technological changes produce new crime opportunities.

8. Opportunities for crime can be reduced.

9. Reducing opportunities does not usually displace crime.

10. Focused opportunity reduction can produce wider declines in crime.

Source: Marcus Felson and Ronald V. Clarke, *Opportunity Makes the Thief: Practical Theory for Crime Prevention,* Police Research Series Paper 98 (London: Home Office, 1998), p. 9.

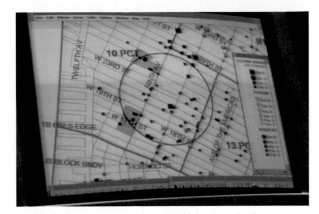

New York Police Department Compstat: Crime mapping is now a powerful tool in the fight against crime. Police departments around the country are developing sophisticated mapping programs to track crime trends, "hot spots," and the pattern of offending.

SITUATIONAL THEORIES OF CRIME

Among the theories of crime that focus on the situation in which a crime occurs, three distinct approaches have been identified: environmental criminology, the rational-choice perspective, and the routine-activity approach. These theories of crime are sometimes called opportunity theories because they analyze the various situations that provide opportunities for specific crimes to occur. (see Table 9.1)

Environmental Criminology

Environmental criminology examines the location of a specific crime and the context in which it occurred in order to understand and explain crime patterns. They ask: Where and when did the crime occur? What are the physical and social characteristics of the crime site? What movements bring offender and target together at the crime site? Environmental criminologists want to know how physical "location in time and space" interacts with the offender, the target/victim, and the law that makes the crime an illegal act.[4]

Contrary to the established criminological theories that explain criminal motivation, environmental criminology begins with the assumption that some people are criminally motivated. Through mapping crimes on global, country, state, county, city, or site-specific levels, such as a particular building or plot of land, environmental criminologists can see crime patterns. They then relate these crime patterns to the number of targets; to the offender population; to the location of routine activities, such as work, school, shopping, or recreation; to security; and to traffic flow.

Mapping crimes and analyzing the spatial crime patterns is not new (Chapter 3). In the nineteenth century, Guerry examined the spatial patterning of crime through his comparison of conviction rates in various regions in France.[5] Quételet tried to establish links between seasonal differences and the probability of committing crime. He found, for instance, that property crimes increase in the winter months in France, whereas "the violence of the passions predominating in summer, excites to more frequent personal collisions" and a rise in crimes against persons (Chapter 3).[6] Contemporary research takes a more focused, crime-specific approach.

Rational-Choice Perspective

The **rational-choice** perspective, developed by Ronald Clarke and Derek Cornish, is based on two main theoretical approaches.[7] The first of these—utilitarianism—was addressed in

Chapter 3. It assumes that people make decisions with the goal of maximizing pleasure and minimizing pain. The second basis for the rational-choice perspective is traditional economic choice theory, which argues that people evaluate the options and choose what they believe will satisfy their needs. According to this perspective, a person decides to commit a particular crime after concluding that the benefits (the pleasure) outweigh the risks and the effort (the pain).[8]

The rational-choice perspective assumes that people make these decisions with a goal in mind, and that they are made more or less intelligently and with free will. This contrasts with the theories of criminality that have an underlying assumption that when people commit a crime, forces beyond their control drive them. Rational choice implies a limited sense of rationality. An offender does not know all the details of a situation; rather, he or she relies on cues in the environment or characteristics of targets. This means the offender may not be able to calculate the costs and benefits accurately, and in hindsight, the decision may seem foolish. Further, an offender may have an impaired ability to make wise choices, perhaps because of intoxication from drugs or alcohol.

According to the rational-choice perspective, most crime is neither extraordinary nor the product of a deranged mind. Most crime is quite ordinary and committed by reasoning individuals who decide that the chances of getting caught are low and the possibilities for a relatively good payoff are high. Since the rational-choice perspective treats each crime as a specific event and focuses on analyzing all its components, it looks at crime in terms of an offender's decision to commit a *specific* offense at *a particular* time and place.

A variety of factors (or characteristics) come into play when an offender decides to commit a crime. These factors are called *choice structuring properties.* With the emphasis of rational-choice theory on analyzing each crime on a crime-specific basis, each particular type of crime has its own set of choice structuring properties (Figure 9.1). Those for sexual assault differ from those for computer crime, and those for burglary differ from those for theft. Nevertheless,

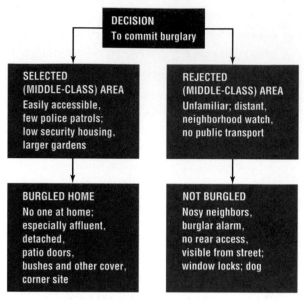

FIGURE 9.1　Event model (*example:* burglary in a middle-class suburb).

Source: Adapted from Ronald V. Clarke and Derek B. Cornish, "Modeling Offenders' Decisions: A Framework for Research and Policy," *Crime and Justice,* vol. 6, ed. Michael Tonry and Norval Morris (Chicago: University of Chicago, 1985), p. 169.

these properties tend to fall into the same seven categories. Thus, a potential thief, before committing a theft, is likely to consider the following aspects (categories):

- The number of targets and their accessibility.
- Familiarity with the chosen method (for example, fraud by credit card).
- The monetary yield per crime.
- The expertise needed.
- The time required to commit the act.
- The physical danger involved.
- The risk of apprehension.

Characteristics fall into two distinct sets: those of the offender and those of the offense. The offender's characteristics include specific needs, values, learning experiences, and so on. The characteristics of the offense include the location of the target and the potential yield. According to rational-choice theory, involvement in crime depends on a personal decision made after one has weighed available information.

FIGURE 9.2 Components of a criminal event: The model of the routine-activity approach.

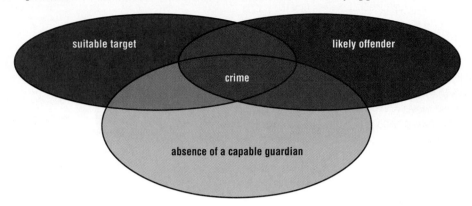

Rational-choice theory, unlike traditional theories, is not concerned with strategies of overall crime prevention. (It leaves those problems to others.) Rather, it is concerned with reducing the likelihood that any given offense will be committed by somebody "involved" in criminal activity. This theory, therefore, has its greatest potential in developing strategies to frustrate perpetrators and to prevent them from committing a crime then and there. It has its greatest challenge in demonstrating that such prevention will not lead to the commission of the intended crime later on, or to the commission of other crimes (displacement). We turn to both of these issues shortly.

Routine-Activity Approach

According to Lawrence Cohen and Marcus Felson, a crime can occur only if there is someone who intends to commit a crime (likely offender), something or someone to be victimized (a suitable target), and no other person present to prevent or observe the crime (the absence of a capable guardian) (Figure 9.2). Later revisions

added a fourth element—no person to control the activities of the likely offender (personal handler). When a suitable target that is unguarded comes together in time and space with a likely offender who is not "handled," the potential for a crime is there.[9] This explanation is called the **routine-activity** approach. It does not explore the factors that influence the offender's decision to commit a crime. Instead, Cohen and Felson focus on the routine or everyday activities of people, such as going to work, pursuing recreation, running errands, and the like. It is through routine activities that offenders come into contact with suitable victims and targets.

The routine-activity approach began with an analysis of crime rate increases in the post-World War II era (1947 to 1974), when socioeconomic conditions had improved in America. The increase was puzzling, since the general public (and some criminologists) expected crime rates to decrease with an increase in prosperity. But the authors of the routine-activity approach demonstrated that certain technological changes and alterations in the workforce created new crime opportunities. They referred to increases in female participation in the labor force, out-of-town travel, automobile usage, and technological advances as factors that account for higher risks of predatory victimization. Further advances in technology create further opportunities for the commission of crime. For example, as television sets, VCRs, personal and laptop computers, and CD players have become more common and lighter to carry, they

It happened long before rational choice and routine activities had been created. Environmental design and situational crime prevention had yet to be invented. Yet there were Volkswagen Beetles the world over.

By 1961 Volkswagen (VW) had produced more than 4 million of these cars, fondly known as lovebugs, according to a popular movie of that time. Close to 1 million were being driven in America, and the rest all over the world. On their hoods, these cars had the distinctive crest of the town of their manufacture: Wolfsburg.

It so happens that soon after the Beetles reached the American market, they lost their crests. Research conducted in 1961 established that 80 percent of the Beetles in the United States had been decrested. The question naturally arose: Who did it (and why)? Police statistics were useless, since VW owners did not feel inclined to report a loss amounting to a little over $3, even though some cars had body damage (the result of removal) many times that amount. Nor did VW owners report the loss to their insurance companies—the value being below the deductible.

The researchers got the help of industry. VW of America made available its sales figures for replacement crests. These figures, statistically analyzed, showed an amazing pattern: The crest thefts started in the east and traveled west within a little over 2 years. The thefts also traveled from the outer perimeters of cities to the suburbs (in less time).

Research established that decrestings were highest in the neighborhood of junior high schools. In collaboration with junior high school administrators and police officials, it was learned that many students had amassed quantities of VW crests (but not those of other motor vehicles). Some were wearing them as necklaces; others had presented them to girlfriends.

Further statistical analysis showed that the fad—for that is what it seemed to be—had spread all over the world—except Brazil. It turned out that VW Beetles manufactured in Brazil were not adorned with the Wolfsburg crest, but the totally different crest of São Paolo, which apparently was not attractive to pubescent males.

A copy of the research report was sent to the VW company. Now everybody knows how reluctant VW was to change its lovebug. But it did: Within a few months the Beetles rolled off VW's assembly line without the crest, but with a slightly longer chrome strip. Problem solved, no more decrestings, no more body damage to the hood.

Source

Gerhard O. W. Mueller, *Delinquency and Puberty: Examination of a Juvenile Delinquency Fad* (New York: Criminal

Law Education and Research Center, 1971; Fred B. Rothman, Distr.).

Questions for Discussion

1. Which of the theories discussed in this chapter best explains the decresting of VW Beetles?
2. What can and should manufacturers of any product do at the design stage to prevent their products from becoming the targets (or instruments) of crime?

---

have become attractive targets for thieves and burglars. The chance that a piece of property will become the target of a theft is based on the value of the target and its weight.[10] One need only compare the theft of washing machines and of electronic goods. Although both washing machines and electronic goods (such as television sets, laptop computers, and compact disc players) are expensive, washing machines are so heavy that their value is estimated at $4 per pound, compared with roughly $400 per pound for a laptop computer. And, of course, cellular phones have increasingly been subject to theft, for resale, for unauthorized telephone use, and for the facilitation of other crimes. Thus, cellular phones, as useful as they are in helping poten-

How can you defeat a motivated offender? Protect and guard the target. Gated communities keep likely offenders out.

Thomas Crown (portrayed by Pierce Brosnan) crafted an extremely clever and well-planned theft of a painting from a well-guarded museum. Of course, not all burglars are so affluent and calculative.

tial crime victims feel more secure, are also used increasingly by drug dealers to reduce the risk of their calls' being traced.[11] It may be concluded that while technological developments help society run more smoothly, they also create new targets for theft, make old targets more suitable, or create new tools for criminals to use in committing their crimes. As people's daily work and leisure activities change with time, the location of property and personal targets also changes.

The logic of the routine-activity argument is straightforward: Routine patterns of work, play, and leisure time affect the convergence in time and place of motivated offenders who are not "handled," suitable targets, and the absence of guardians. If one component is missing, crime is not likely to be committed. And if all components are in place and one of them is strengthened, crime is likely to increase. Even if the proportions of motivated offenders and targets stay the same, changes in routine activities alone—for example, changes of the sort we have experienced since World War II—will raise the crime rate by multiplying the opportunities for crime. This approach has helped explain, among other things, rates of victimization for

specific crimes, rates of urban homicide, and "hot spots"—areas that produce a disproportionate number of calls to police.[12]

Practical Applications of Situational Theories of Crime

The trio of theories discussed here—environmental criminology, rational choice, and routine activities—often work together to explain why a person may commit a crime in a particular situation. We look now at how these theories of crime are used to explain specific varieties of crime, and how the ideas that arise from these theories have practical applications.

Burglars and Burglary Criminologists are increasingly interested in the factors that go into a decision to burglarize: the location or setting of the building, the presence of guards or dogs, the type of burglar alarms and external lighting, and so forth. Does a car in the driveway or a radio playing music in the house have a significant impact on the choice of home to burglarize? George Rengert and John Wasilchick conducted extensive interviews with suburban burglars in an effort to understand their techniques. They found significant differences with respect to several factors[13]:

- *The amount of planning* that precedes a burglary. Professional burglars plan more than do amateurs.

- The extent to which a burglar engages in *systematic selection of a home.* Some burglars examine the obvious clues, such as presence of a burglar alarm, a watchdog, mail piled up in the mailbox, newspapers on a doorstep. More experienced burglars look for subtle clues, for example, closed windows coupled with air conditioners that are turned off.

- The extent to which a burglar pays *attention to situational cues.* Some burglars routinely choose a corner property because it offers more avenues of escape, has fewer adjoining properties, and offers visibility.

Rengert and Wasilchick have also examined the use of time and place in burglary (Figure 9.3). Time is a critical factor to burglars, for three reasons:

- They must minimize the time spent in targeted places so as not to reveal their intention to burglarize.

- Opportunities for burglary occur only when a dwelling is unguarded or unoccupied, that is, during daytime. (Many burglars would call in sick so often that they would be fired from their legitimate jobs; others simply quit their jobs because they interfered with their burglaries.)

- Burglars have "working hours"; that is, they have time available only during a limited number of hours (if they have a legitimate job).

Before committing their offenses, burglars take into account familiarity with the area, fear of recognition, concern over standing out as somebody who does not belong, and the possibility (following some successful burglaries) that a particular area is no longer cost-beneficial. Season, too, plays an important role. One experienced burglar stated that because neighborhoods are populated with children in the sum-

FIGURE 9.3   Crime day of burglar #26.

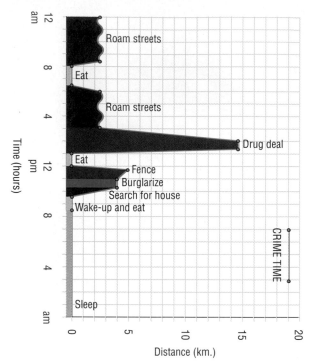

Source: George Rengert and John Wasilchick, *Suburban Burglary: A Time and a Place for Everything* (Springfield, Ill.: Charles C Thomas, 1985), p. 35.

mer, he opted for winter months: "The best time to do crime out here is between 8:00 and 9:00 [A.M.]. All the mothers are taking the kids to school. I wait until I see the car leave. By the time she gets back, I've come and gone."[14]

Recent research demonstrates how important it is for burglars to have prior knowledge of their targets. They obtain such knowledge by knowing the occupants, by being tipped off about the occupants, or by observing the potential target.[15] Some burglars even acquire jobs that afford them the opportunity to observe their potential victims' daily activities; others gain access to the interior of a house, search for valuable goods, and steal them at a later date.

Robbers and Robberies   Richard Wright and Scott Decker conducted in-depth interviews with street robbers and found that they frequently victimize other street-involved individuals—drug dealers, drug users, and gang members—people who, because they are criminals themselves, are unlikely to go to the police.

In response to fear of rising rates of crime on college campuses, security has become a significant issue for administrators, students, and parents. Some colleges and universities have transformed their security services into small and well-trained police forces.

These people are also targeted because they are believed to have a lot of money, jewelry, and other desirable items. Street robbers report that they sometimes specifically target people whom they do not like, or people who have hurt or offended them in the past. When women are targeted, it is because robbers believe they will not resist and are not armed. On the other hand, women are not the desirable targets men are because robbers think women do not carry as much money.[16]

Criminologists also study whether commercial robbers operate the same way as street robbers in their selection of targets. Robbers who target business establishments are interested in some of the same factors that concern burglars. Perpetrators carefully examine the location of the potential robbery, the potential gain, the capability of security personnel, the possibility of intervention by bystanders, and the presence of guards, cameras, and alarms.[17]

Criminologists have found that potential victims and establishments can do quite a bit to decrease the likelihood of being robbed. Following a series of convenience-store robberies in Gainesville, Florida, in 1985, a city ordinance required store owners to clear their windows of signs that obstructed the view of the interior, to position cash registers where they would be visible from the street, and to install approved electronic cameras. Within a little over a year, convenience-store robberies had decreased 64 percent.[18] We will return to this discussion later in this chapter.

Hot Products Why do thieves decide to steal some things and not others? What makes targets attractive? We have examined how burglars select which homes to burglarize, but once they have broken into a residence, how do they decide what to steal? When robbers target victims, they do so believing their chances of making off with something valuable are greater than their chances of not being successful in the robbery attempt. But what is it about things that makes them valuable to robbers? Cohen and Felson argued that items are attractive if they are visible, easy to take away, valuable, and accessible.[19] Twenty years later, Ronald Clarke expanded this idea with his discussion of hot products—those consumer goods that are attractive to thieves. Using an acronym (CRAVED) to organize this idea, Clarke claims that goods are attractive if they are concealable, removable, available, valuable, enjoyable, and disposable (i.e., can be easily fenced). This approach takes into account what thieves do with goods after they are stolen, because that factor figures into their decisions about the attractiveness of items.[20]

College Campus Crime   Crime on college campuses follows patterns that routine-activity theorists would expect, i.e., if you engage in a risky and deviant lifestyle, your risk is significantly increased. Students who party frequently and regularly use recreational drugs are at risk. You are more likely to be a victim of property crime if you are a male aged 17 to 20. If you live in an all-female dorm, you are less likely to experience a theft. Not surprisingly, students who spend several nights per week on campus and full-time students are more vulnerable to property crime than part-time students or those who do not spend as many nights on campus. With respect to target attractiveness, people who spend large amounts of money on nonessential items have a higher risk of on-campus theft than those who spend less.[21]

THEORIES OF VICTIMIZATION

Although the victim is mentioned in many theories of crime, direct consideration of the role that victims play in the criminal event has been of secondary significance. As a result of the "missing victim" in basic criminology, **theories of victimization** have recently been developed for the purpose of understanding crime from the victim's perspective, or with the victim in mind.

The history of victims in criminology can be traced to Hans von Hentig's first article on the subject of victims, in 1941, in which he postulated that crime was an "interaction of perpetrator and victim."[22] Von Hentig, a highly respected scientist, had been a victim of Nazi persecution. It was that experience that made him focus on the significance of the victim. By carefully gathering and analyzing information, he demonstrated that tourist resorts were attractive to criminals who wanted to prey on unsuspecting vacationers. Von Hentig, through his book *The Criminal and His Victim,* published in 1948, founded the criminological subdiscipline of victimology, which examines the role played by the victim in a criminal incident.[23] Nevertheless, it must be acknowledged that the term "victimology" is a year older than von Hentig's book. The term was coined in 1947 by the Romanian lawyer Beniamin Mendelsohn, in

a lecture before the Romanian Psychiatric Association in Bucharest, entitled "New Bio-Psycho-Social Horizons: Victimology."[24] In 1948, Frederic Wertham, an American psychiatrist, first used the term "victimology" in America.[25]

According to Canadian criminologist Ezzat Fattah, "von Hentig insisted that many crime victims contribute to their own victimization be it by inciting or provoking the criminal or by creating or fostering a situation likely to lead to the commission of the crime."[26] Thus, the entire event is regarded as crucial, because criminal behavior involves both the action of the offender and interaction between offender and victim. Nor is it tenable to regard "criminals and victims . . . as different as night and day," because there is an undeniable link between offending and victimization.[27] Many offenders are victimized repeatedly, and victims are frequently offenders.

Such findings may be deemed highly controversial in a time when victims' rights groups have been active, and successful, in securing rights for victims of crimes. It must be understood, however, that *guilt* is not shared by offender and victim. Criminal guilt belongs to the perpetrator of a crime—and it must be proved at trial beyond a reasonable doubt. The victim is free of guilt. Victimology, however, can demonstrate how potential victims, by acting differently, can decrease the risk of being victimized.[28]

We turn now to a discussion of the dominant victimological theories.

Lifestyle Theories

A *lifestyle theory of victimization* was developed by Michael Hindelang, Michael Gottfredson, and James Garofalo in 1978. It argues that because of changing roles (working mother versus homemaker) and schedules (a child's school calendar), people lead different lifestyles (work and leisure activities). Variations in lifestyle affect the number of situations with high victimization risks that a person experiences.[29] The kinds of people someone associates with, such as co-workers, friends, and sexual partners, also affect victimization rates. For instance, someone who has a drug dealer or an insider trader as a friend has a greater chance of being victimized than a person who associates only with law-abiding people. (The similarity of the lifestyle theory of victimization and the routine-activities approach is quite apparent.)

The lifestyle theory of victimization centers on a number of specific propositions that outline the essence of the theory and signal directions for future research[30]:

Proposition 1: The probability of suffering a personal victimization is directly related to the amount of time that a person spends in public places (e.g., on the street, in parks, etc.), and particularly in public places at night.

Proposition 2: The probability of being in public places, particularly at night, varies as a function of lifestyle.

Proposition 3: Social contacts and interactions occur disproportionately among individuals who share similar lifestyles.

Proposition 4: An individual's chances of personal victimization are dependent upon the extent to which the individual shares demographic characteristics with offenders [such as young urban males].

Proposition 5: The proportion of time that an individual spends among nonfamily members varies as a function of lifestyle.

Proposition 6: The probability of personal victimization, particularly personal theft, increases as a function of the proportion of the time that an individual spends among nonfamily members [such as a young man who works a double shift at a factory versus a middle-aged woman who stays home to take care of an elderly parent].

Proposition 7: Variations in lifestyle are associated with variations in the ability of individuals to isolate themselves from persons with offender characteristics [being able to leave high-crime urban areas for sheltered suburbs].

Proposition 8: Variations in lifestyle are associated with variations in the convenience, the desirability, and vincibility of the person as a target for a personal victimization [people who pass within the view of offenders, seem to have what the offender wants, appear unable to resist, or would probably not report the crime to the police].

Both the lifestyle theory of victimization and the routine-activity approach present some basic guidelines for reducing one's chances of victimization. And just as these theories themselves tend to embody common sense, so do the preventive measures derived from them. For instance, people in American society are told not to drive while intoxicated, not to smoke or abuse alcohol or drugs, and not to eat too much greasy food. All these messages are intended to reduce the risks of dying in a motor vehicle accident, or from lung or liver cancer, or from an overdose, or from a heart attack. Although public-service messages designed to protect health may not always be heeded, people do not see them as "blaming the victim." Similarly, messages to prevent criminal victimization, like not walking alone and not frequenting deserted or unfamiliar places late at night, should not be viewed as overly restrictive and intrusive, or as blaming victims who did not heed the advice. The messages directed at preventing victimization are based on theory and research and merely promote living and acting responsibly to ensure a more crime-free existence.

Victim-Offender Interaction

Marvin Wolfgang, one of the preeminent criminologists of his time, studied homicides in Philadelphia during the 1950s. He found that many of the victims had actually brought upon themselves the attack that led to their murder (see Chapter 11 for further discussion of Wolfgang's work). He coined the term "victim precipitation" to refer to situations where victims initiate the confrontations that lead to their death. Wolfgang estimated that as many as one-quarter to one-half of intentional homicides are victim-precipitated.[31] James Tedeschi and Richard Felson put forward a theory of *coercive actions*, which stresses that the way victims and offenders interact plays a large role in violent crime.[32] They argue that people commit violence purposefully. In other words, people don't just lose control. When they are violent, it is with a particular goal in mind. They make a decision to be violent (note the similarity between this theory and the rational-choice perspective) and tend to choose targets who are less powerful than themselves. In unarmed attacks, males are more likely to injure their opponents, while females are more likely to be injured. Gender is not the determinant as much as body size.[33] There are also victims who instigate attacks by irritating others. Schoolyard bullies are a good example.[34]

Repeat Victimization

Not unlike the lifestyle theory of victimization, theories of repeat victimization also focus on the specific characteristics of situations in order to determine which factors account for the initial, as well as for repeat, victimization.[35] Theories of repeat victimization, also called multiple victimization, dispel the myth that crime is uniformly distributed. Research shows that a small number of people and places account for a large amount of the crimes committed. For example, an analysis of the British Crime Survey (a victimization survey) from 1982 to 1992 found that between 24 and 38 percent of all victims of property and personal crime experienced five or more such offenses in a little over a year.[36]

The research literature on repeat victimization is increasing rapidly. A study of police calls for service from 34 fast-food restaurants in San Antonio, Texas, from 1990 to 1992 found that fast-food restaurants had the greatest chance of repeat police calls for service within 1 week of the last call. Thereafter, the number of calls decreases as the time between calls increases.[37] Similar findings have been made in research on the repeat risks of burglary.[38] Risks of a repeat burglary are highest immediately after a previous burglary. In their analysis of repeat victimization for crimes ranging from the repeated physical and sexual abuse of children to repeated credit card fraud, researchers concluded that the rational-choice theory of offender decision making is useful in understanding repeat victimization. Offenders choose targets based on the knowledge they gained in the previous victimization about the risks and rewards of a particular offense.[39]

Formulating strategies to deal with repeat victimizations would certainly be cost-beneficial. Resources could be concentrated on relatively few targets. Unfortunately, police recording systems are not designed to keep track of repeat victimizations. To overcome this problem, several innovative researchers have created their own databases, starting a whole new line of research, called *hot-spots* research.

Hot Spots of Crime

In 1989, Lawrence Sherman, Patrick Gartin, and Michael Buerger published the results of a study that immediately excited the profession. They had analyzed 911 calls for police assistance in Minneapolis, Minnesota, for the period December 15, 1985, to December 15, 1986. After plotting the more than 320,000 calls on a map, they discovered that 3 percent of the addresses and intersections in the city were the subject of 50 percent of the calls received.[40]

They also found that certain types of crime were committed in specific places—for example, all auto thefts at 2 percent of all places. The researchers conclude that attempts to prevent victimization should be focused not on victims, but on the places themselves by making them less vulnerable to crime. Change places, not people! We should identify neighborhood hot spots, reduce social disorder and physical "incivilities," and promote housing-based neighborhood stabilization.[41]

Geography of Crime

Recently, new research based on the idea of hot spots has come into existence. It is labeled "geography of crime." Researchers found that more crime occurs around high schools[42] and blocks with bars,[43] liquor stores,[44] the city center,[45] and abandoned buildings.[46] Higher crime in areas that border high schools and bars is readily explainable: High schools contain a highly crime-prone age group. Bars attract, among others, offenders.[47] Abandoned buildings that are open and unsecured attract illegal users. In city centers there are more opportunities to commit crime and generally fewer social controls in place.

A study on the vulnerability of ports and marinas to vessel and equipment theft found that the proximity of a port or marina to a high-crime area is significant in predicting boat theft.[48] Research on drug markets in Jersey City, New Jersey, shows that areas with illicit drug markets account for a disproportionate amount of arrests and calls for police service.[49] In sum, the discovery that a large amount of crime occurs at a small number of places, and that such places have distinct characteristics, has led criminologists to explain crime in terms of not only who commits it, but also where it is committed.[50]

Interrelatedness of Theories

Environmental criminology, the rational-choice perspective, and the routine-activity approach focus on the interaction between the victim (or target), the offender, and the place. Recently, there has been an integration of these theories of crime with theories of victimization.[51] For example, one study using the lifestyle theory of victimization and the routine-activity approach explores how drinking routines are linked with victimization.[52] It found that alcohol contributed to victimization by making potential victims less able to protect themselves (more suitable targets). Motivated offenders also knew where to find their targets (in bars). Although the evidence on the relationship between alcohol, lifestyle, and increased risks of victimization is not conclusive, this research represents an important attempt at testing the interaction of lifestyle and routine-activity theories.

A further study on the relationship of alcohol and risks of victimization focuses specifically on the "suitable target" portion of routine-activity theory as it relates to sexual assault against women on college campuses.[53] It found that women who were sexually victimized went out more often and drank more when they were out than other women. Moreover, many of the women surveyed had experienced "uncomfortable advances in a bar or restaurant" or "on the street" or had "received obscene or threatening phone calls." In sum, by successfully combining theories of crime, like routine-activity theory, with lifestyle theory, situational factors (e.g., alcohol), and place considerations (e.g., bars and college settings) to examine victimization rates, criminological research has added a new dimension to explaining crime.[54]

PREVENTING CRIMES AGAINST PLACES, PEOPLE, AND VALUABLE GOODS

Situational crime prevention seeks to protect places, people, and valuable goods from victimization. It is rooted in the 1971 work of C. Ray Jeffery's "crime prevention through environmental design" (CPTED)[55] and in Oscar Newman's concept of "defensible space."[56] CPTED posits that environments can be altered, often at little expense, to decrease victimizations. *Defensible space* refers to improved architectural designs, particularly of public housing, in order to provide increased security. Design can enhance surveillance, reduce offenders' escape possibilities, and give residents a feeling of ownership that encourages them to protect their own space.[57] CPTED and defensible space have converged with rational choice and routine activity to form a new approach called *situational crime prevention.*

Crime Surfing

www.preventingcrime.org/report/chapter7.htm

John Eck, contributing to *Crime Prevention: What Works, What Doesn't, What's Promising*, compiled an extremely comprehensive literature review of research into the effectiveness of situational-crime-prevention strategies.

Situational Crime Prevention

Rational-choice theory provides the foundation for designing situational-crime-prevention techniques and their classification (Table 9.2). Situational crime prevention consists of the knowledge of how, where, and when to implement a specific measure that will alter a particular situation in order to prevent a crime from occurring. The routine-activity approach also aims at situational crime prevention by reducing the opportunities for likely offenders to commit crimes. Techniques include protecting suitable targets (making them less suitable) and increasing the presence of capable guardians. Measures such as steering-column locks, vandal-resistant construction, enhanced street lighting, and improved library checkout systems demonstrably

A rash of school shootings during the 1998–1999 academic year (see "School Shootings" in Chapter 11) caused great concern across the nation. Criminologists, police, educators, lawmakers, and parents struggled to figure out why these young men and boys decided to pick up firearms and destroy the lives of their teachers and classmates. Many blamed the easy access to guns; others pointed to the social isolation these students experienced; still others looked to broader sociological explanations.

Although you would not know it, given all the media coverage surrounding these school shooting incidents, as well as experts' premonitions of doom and gloom, we are actually in the midst of a decline in violent crime in American schools. Thirty percent fewer students are carrying weapons to school than in 1991, and the number of student fights has also dropped. The number of school-related violent deaths is one-half what it was 6 years ago. During the 1997–1998 school year, only 34 students died in violent incidents in all the nation's schools. In fact, school is one of the safest places for young people, safer than the streets or even their homes. Young people are far more likely to die in alcohol-related automobile accidents (eight die per day, which represents 40 percent of all deaths of 16- to 20-year-olds), or from unintentional injury or suicide (10 and 13 percent, respectively, of deaths of those aged 10 to 24).(1) Even so, deaths related to school violence get much more press coverage—much of it sensa-

In some inner city schools, security measures rival those used in prison: metal detectors, drug sniffing dogs, frequent searches for weapons, and surveillance cameras that monitor the movement of students in and out of classrooms.

tionalized. As a result, parents, and the community at large, tend to panic.

Target hardening and situational crime prevention in schools are nothing new. Schools in certain parts of some

cities have had metal detectors, doors with alarms, and locker searches for years. Then there are the other schools in towns few have heard of: places like Paducah, Conyers, and Littleton. The

decrease opportunities for crime. These are **target-hardening** techniques.

Rational-choice theorists have recently reviewed their situational-crime-prevention techniques. They have added aspects of the offender's *perception* of a crime opportunity to the catalog of relevant factors, as well as the element of guilt or shame (Table 9.3).[58] The addition of the category of "perception" of opportunity was self-evident. After all, offenders act

only in accordance with what they perceive. The addition of a category called "inducing guilt or shame," on the other hand, is a significant expansion of rational choice.[59] Techniques that induce guilt or shame include the installation of signs saying "shoplifting is stealing" or other measures calculated to prevent common crimes by increasing the personal and social cost in terms of shaming—especially after being caught in the act. For instance, if a high school

image of these suburban schools as safe havens has been shattered. Although the likelihood of a shooting in any particular school is small, officials are not taking any chances. Interestingly, the prevention measures listed below fall squarely into Clarke and Homel's situational-crime-prevention model (see Table 9.2).

Access control
- Intercom systems are being used at locked doors to buzz in visitors.(2)
- Students have to flash or swipe computerized identification cards to get into school buildings.
- Perimeter fences delineate school property and secure cars after hours.

Controlling facilitators
- Students in Deltona, Florida, get an extra set of books to leave at home. The schools have banned backpacks and dismantled lockers to eliminate places to stash weapons. Other school districts are encouraging see-through lockers and backpacks.
- After the Littleton, Colorado, incident, school boards across the country banned trench coats and other oversized garments, apparently to prevent students from hiding weapons on their bodies or in their clothing.

Entry/exit screening
- Handheld and walk-through metal detectors keep anyone with a weapon from entering schools.

Formal surveillance
- Uniformed police officers and private security guards, some of them armed, patrol school halls.
- Schools are installing surveillance cameras in hallways and on school buses.

Surveillance by employees (or, in this case, students)
- Students are carrying small notebooks so that they can log and then report overheard threats.

Identifying property
- Tiny microfilm is hidden inside expensive school property so that it can be identified if stolen.

On the fact of it, these measures seem to make good sense. They can prevent people from bringing weapons into schools and keep unauthorized people out. They increase the ability of school officials to detect crime, identify evildoers, and prevent criminal incidents from happening. But have school officials and others gone too far? Diana Philip is the director of the American Civil Liberties Union of Texas for the northern region, which has filed several lawsuits against schools. She observes that "over the summer, we have had school boards putting together the most restrictive policies we have ever seen. A lot of them are in clear violation of the Fourth Amendment, which guarantees freedom from unreasonable searches."(3)

Chicago Tribune columnist Steve Chapman argues that schools treat students as "dangerous, incorrigible, undeserving of respect" or privacy. He asks, "What's the difference between school and prison? At school, you don't get cable TV."(4)

Sources

1. *Violence in School: The Facts*, Office of the Attorney General, State of Illinois, found at http://www.ag.state.il.us/program/school/facts.htm, Oct. 30, 1999.
2. Jacques Steinberg, "Barricading the School Door," *New York Times*, Aug. 22, 1999, New York section, p. 5.
3. S. C. Gwynne, "Is Anyplace Safe?" *Time*, Aug. 23, 1999. [http://www.pathfinder.com/magazine/time accessed February 10, 2000]
4. Walter Olson, "Dial 'O' for Outrage: The Sequel—Tales from an Over-lawyered America," *Reason*, November 1999, pp. 54 56.

Questions for Discussion

1. Do you think there would be as much concern over school violence if these shooting incidents had happened in urban schools? Why are people more upset when crime happens in places they perceive to be safe (such as in the suburbs)?
2. Does your high school or college campus have any security measures in place? If so, how do they fit into Clarke and Homel's 16 techniques of situational prevention?
3. Is there a point where security measures in schools become so extreme that they can no longer be justified? Have we reached that point yet?

student is leaving the school library with friends and the library checkout system detects a copy of *Rolling Stone* in his bookbag (a magazine that is not allowed to leave the library), two things are expected to happen. First, the librarian will make the student surrender the magazine. Second, the student may be so embarrassed by having the librarian search his bookbag while his friends stand by that he will not try to steal anything from the library again.

There are a number of successful examples of situational crime prevention. For example, situational-crime-prevention techniques have been successfully implemented to prevent crime at Disney World, to stop auto theft, to deter robberies at convenience stores, and to lessen crime in parking facilities.

The Phantom Crime Prevention at Disney World Disney World, home of Donald Duck,

TABLE 9.2 Sixteen Techniques of Situational Prevention

Increasing Perceived Effort	Increasing Perceived Risks	Reducing Anticipated Rewards	Inducing Guilt or Shame
1. *Target hardening:* Slug-rejector device Steering locks Bandit screens	5. *Entry/exit screening:* Automatic ticket gates Baggage screening Merchandise tags	9. *Target removal:* Removable car radio Women's refuges Phonecard	13. *Rule setting:* Harassment codes Customs declaration Hotel registrations
2. *Access control:* Parking lot barriers Fenced yards Entry phones	6. *Formal surveillance:* Burglar alarms Speed cameras Security guards	10. *Identifying property:* Property marking Vehicle licensing Cattle branding	14. *Strengthening moral condemnation:* "Shoplifting is stealing" Roadside speedometers "Bloody-idiots drink and drive"
3. *Deflecting offenders:* Bus stop placement Tavern location Street closures	7. *Surveillance by employees:* Pay phone location Park attendants CCTV systems	11. *Reducing temptation:* Gender-neutral phone lists Off-street parking 12. *Denying benefits:* Ink merchandise tags PIN for car radios Graffiti cleaning	15. *Controlling disinhibitors:* Drinking-age laws Ignition interlock Server intervention
4. *Controlling facilitators:* Credit card photo Caller ID Gun controls	8. *Natural surveillance:* Defensible space Street lighting Cab driver ID		16. *Facilitating compliance:* Improved library checkout Public lavatories Trash bins

Source: Ronald V. Clarke and Ross Homel, "A Revised Classification of Situational Crime Prevention Techniques," in *Crime Prevention at a Crossroads,* ed. Steven P. Lab (Cincinnati, Ohio: Anderson, 1997).

TABLE 9.3 Ten Factors Considered by Commercial Burglars in Suburban Philadelphia

1. *Revenues generated by burglary:*
   Is there a high "payoff"?

2. *Chances of being caught:*
   Can I get away with it?

3. *Location of target:*
   Is the target near a major road or thoroughfare? Commercial burglars like remote targets.

4. *Corner lot:*
   Is the target at the corner?
   Corner properties are easier to get into and out of.

5. *Shopping mall:*
   Is the target in a mall?
   Malls and large retail stores are ideal targets.

6. *Concentration of businesses:*
   Are there other businesses around? The more commercial establishments around, the greater the likelihood of burglary.

7. *Burglar alarm:*
   Is there a visible alarm or alarm sign?

8. *Exterior lighting:*
   How dark is the area around the target?

9. *Length of time the establishment has been in business:*
   Is this a new store?
   New commercial establishments are prime targets.

10. *Retail store:*
    Is the target retail?
    Retail is preferred over wholesale.

Source: Simon Hakim and Yochanan Shachmurove, "Spatial and Temporal Patterns of Commercial Burglaries: The Evidence Examined," *American Journal of Economics and Sociology,* **55** (1996): 443–456.

Even Goofy is part of the Disney crime prevention and control strategy, making Disneyland and Disney World some of the safest locations in the United States.

Mickey and Minnie Mouse, Goofy, and their friends, provides us with an example of environmental/situational crime prevention. Illegal behavior is successfully controlled, yet in an environment that does not have the sterile, fortress-like appearance so often associated with security. How has this been accomplished?[60]

The intricate web of security and crowd control (not visible to the untrained eye) starts at the parking lot with advice to lock your car and remember that you have parked at a particular lot, for example, "Donald Duck 1." With friendly greetings of "have a good time," watchful eyes surround visitors on the rubber-wheeled train into never-never land. Crowd control is omnipresent, yet unobtrusive. Signs guide you through the maze of monorails, rides, and attractions. Physical barriers prevent injury

and regulate the movement of adults and children alike. Mickey Mouse and Goofy monitor movements. Flower gardens, pools, and fountains are pretty to look at; they also direct people toward particular locations. Yet with all these built-in control strategies, few visitors realize the extent to which their choices of movement and action are limited.

Situational Prevention: Auto Theft Let us return to the car theft scenario at the beginning of this chapter to illustrate how action research works in the case of car theft.[61] First, the Paramus Police Department collected information on the specific models and makes of the cars stolen, as well as the particular locations of the thefts. The Toyota Land Cruiser, Toyota 4Runner, and Mitsubishi Montero were the sport utility vehicles preferred by the thieves, while any Honda and the Toyota Camry were the favored cars. Second, information provided by the National Insurance Crime Bureau (see Table 9.4) indicated that some of these makes and models are the most targeted vehicles for theft not only in malls in Bergen County, New Jersey, but throughout the nation.

With this information, situational-crime-prevention practitioners analyze the vehicles

TABLE 9.4   Top 25 Stolen Cars in 1998

1. 1989 Toyota Camry	14. 1997 Ford F150 4×2 Pickup
2. 1988 Toyota Camry	15. 1995 Ford Mustang
3. 1990 Toyota Camry	16. 1989 Chevrolet Caprice
4. 1994 Honda Accord EX	17. 1989 Honda Accord LX
5. 1990 Honda Accord EX	18. 1981 Honda Accord LX
6. 1997 Toyota Corolla	19. 1987 Toyota Camry
7. 1992 Honda Accord LX	20. 1991 Acura Legend
8. 1995 Honda Accord EX	21. 1996 Toyota Corolla
9. 1991 Toyota Camry	22. 1989 Chevrolet C/K 4×2 Pickup
10. 1996 Honda Accord EX	23. 1992 Honda Accord EX
11. 1991 Honda Accord EX	24. 1990 Honda Accord LX
12. 1988 Honda Accord LX	25. 1994 Honda Accord LX
13. 1996 Honda Accord LX	

Source: National Insurance Crime Bureau (NICB) 1997–1998. (Found on the Internet at http://www.crimedoctor.com/autotheft2.htm, Oct. 30, 1999.)

and the specific situational factors that lead to their being targeted for theft. They then devise measures to block the opportunities that give rise to the theft of these particular vehicles, e.g., side window panels that are particularly vulnerable, or key codes in the gas tank compartment (the thief simply writes down the key code and gets a replacement of the "lost" car key).[62]

Devising situational prevention measures, however, is usually not as easy as suggesting to a car manufacturer that the key code be placed in a more secure place. It is important that a researcher also analyze the type of offenders who steal cars (Table 9.5).

Convenience Stores
One of the most successful crime-prevention studies was the Tallahassee Convenience Store Study. In fact, it launched the concept of crime prevention through environmental design. It had long been known that convenience stores, like the 7-Eleven shops, had been prime robbery targets. Researchers studied the vulnerability of these stores in great detail, assessing risks as well as losses, in terms of lives and property. The researchers recommended that stores have two or more clerks on duty, post "limited cash" signs, increase exterior lighting, and restrict es-

Did You Know

. . . that sometimes stealing might result from oversocialization and embarrassment rather than of under-socialization? Research into shoplifting from drug stores shows that the items most commonly stolen include condoms and other birth-control products, as well as medications, such as Preparation H, for "intimate conditions." Similarly, librarians surveyed said that books about sex are among the most stolen items from libraries, apparently because "readers were too embarrassed to borrow such stock legitimately."

TABLE 9.5   Typologies of Frequent Auto Theft Offenders

Acting-out joyrider:
- Most emotionally disturbed of the offenders—derives status from having his peers think he is crazy and unpredictable.
- Engages in outrageous driving stunts—dangerous to pursue—possesses a kamikaze attitude.
- Vents anger via car—responsible for large proportion of the totaled and burned cars.
- Least likely to be deterred—doesn't care what happens.

Thrill-seeker:
- Heavily into drugs—doing crime is a way to finance the habit—entices others to feel the "rush" of doing crime.
- Engages in car stunts and willful damage to cars, but also steals them for transportation and to use in other crimes.
- Steals parts for sale in a loosely structured friendship network.
- Thrill-seeking behavior likely to be transferred to other activities and might be directed to legitimate outlets.

Instrumental offender:
- Doing auto theft for the money—most active of the offenders (5 or more cars a week) but the smallest proportion of the sample—connected to organized theft operations.
- Rational, intelligent—does crimes with least risk—may get into auto theft from burglary—thinks about outcomes.
- Doing crime while young offender status affords them lenient treatment—indicate that they will quit crime at age eighteen.

Source: Zachary Fleming, Patricia Brantingham, and Paul Brantingham, "Exploring Auto Theft in British Columbia," in *Crime Prevention Studies,* vol. 3, ed. Ronald V. Clarke (Monsey, N.Y.: Criminal Justice Press, 1994), p. 62.

THE FAR SIDE   By GARY LARSON

© 1990 FarWorks, Inc./Dist. by Universal Press Syndicate

4-18

Inconvenience stores

Crime Surfing

www.crime-prevention.org.uk/home_office/guide/

This crime-prevention guide by the Home Office in Britain includes details about how one can avoid becoming a crime victim. The Home Office and its staff conduct extensive research on the effectiveness of situational-crime-prevention strategies.

cape routes and potential hiding places for robbers. The study led to the passage of the Florida Convenience Store Security Act (1990), which made certain security measures mandatory.[63] Convenience-store robberies in Florida have dropped by two-thirds.

Parking Facilities[64]   Parking garages are said to be dangerous places: Individuals are alone in a large space, there are many hiding places, the amount of valuable property (cars and their contents) is high, they are open to the public, an offender's car can go unnoticed, and lighting is usually poor. Yet statistics indicate that because of the small amount of time and the relatively limited number of trips that each person takes to and from parking facilities, an individual's chances of being raped, robbed, or assaulted in a parking facility are very low. Nevertheless, the fear of victimization in these facilities is high. Efforts to improve conditions include better lighting, stairways and elevators that are open to the air or glass-enclosed, ticket-booth personnel

monitoring drivers exiting and entering, color-coded signs designating parking areas, elimination or redesign of public restrooms, panic buttons and emergency phones, closed-circuit television, and uniformed security personnel.

Displacement

One important question concerning crime-prevention measures remains. What will happen, for example, if these measures do prevent a particular crime from being committed? Will the would-be offender simply look for another target? Crime-prevention strategists have demonstrated that **displacement**—the commission of a quantitatively similar crime at a different time or place—does not always follow. German motorcycle helmet legislation demonstrates the point. As a result of a large number of accidents, legislation that required motorcyclists to wear helmets was passed and strictly enforced. It worked: Head injuries decreased. But there were additional, unforeseen consequences. Motorcycle theft rates decreased dramatically.[65] The risks of stealing a motorcycle became too high because a would-be offender could not drive it away without wearing a helmet. At this point researchers expected to see a rise in the numbers of cars or bikes stolen. They did not. In other words, there was very little displacement. Of course, some offenders will look for other crime opportunities, but many others will quit for some time, perhaps forever.

THEORY INFORMS POLICY

The study of targets and victims is crucial to preventing crime. Understanding how offenders make decisions helps policy makers allocate resources efficiently. For example, if it is possible to significantly reduce convenience-store robbery by relatively simple measures, isn't it better to spend time and money doing those

The store, part of a small chain, was located in a quasi-residential area next to a park near a two-lane highway. The cashier station was located in the rear of the store, adjacent to a doorway that led to a rear storage room where there was a desk and a safe. Posters and advertisements covered the front windows, and the only outside lighting came from a streetlight across the road.

One night, two men recently released from a state prison held up the store. After forcing the cashier into the rear storage room and making her open the safe, they shot her. As the men were preparing to leave, two people entered the store: a female employee coming to work at the shift change and a young man coming in to make a purchase while his date and another couple waited in the car outside. Seeing the two people enter, the gunman concealed his weapon behind his back and announced that the store was closed. "It can't be," the employee replied. "I work here!" With that, the man revealed his gun, forced the woman and the young man to the rear of the store, and shot them. Both died.

Although the families of the two murdered employees could not sue the employer under workers' compensation laws, the father of the slain young man sued the store, charging that the store failed to provide adequate security:

- The cashier should not have been alone in such an isolated store.
- The counter was located in the rear of the store, which made it difficult for anyone outside to see what was happening within.
- The posters on the windows further isolated the cashier.
- There was no drop safe, which would have removed the incentive for the robbery.
- The second cashier's failure to recognize the threat when she was told by the gunman that the store was closed indicated a failure on the part of store owners to provide proper security training.

Several of these factors involved environmental design: the lighting, the posters, and the location of the cash register. In an interview, which was used as a basis for expert testimony, one of the perpetrators reported that he canvassed the area looking for the "right store" and that he had rejected several because they were brightly lit, the cashier's station was toward the front of the store, and there were no posters to interfere with the view from the parking lot.

This case did not go to trial; it was settled for a substantial sum after expert testimony was submitted. Its usefulness as an example lies in the fact that the criminals acknowledged the importance of environmental design in deciding to strike at this particular store.(1)

Under English common law "landowners had no legal duty to prevent criminal assaults on visitors to their property, and no legal liability could befall them."(2) Tort law, in most jurisdictions in the United States, employs a "totality of the circumstances" test. In deciding whether a civil liability case has merit, judges now examine such factors "as the nature of the business, its surrounding locale, the lack of customary security precautions as an invitation to crime, and the experience of the particular landowner at other locations."(3) The risks of civil liability are high. When life is lost, millions of dollars may be at stake. This is where crime prevention through environmental design (CPTED) comes in. Increasingly, criminologists are analyzing the links between crime-prevention measures according to CPTED factors, which can be instituted at low cost before a criminal event and civil liability suit.

Research indicates that the chance of a lawsuit is positively related to two factors: (1) the classification of a place as high- or low-risk and (2) its financial resources. Investment in crime prevention is driven by the expected costs of a lawsuit. High-risk places that have little

or no financial resources do not expect to be sued and therefore implement fewer crime-prevention measures. But many low-risk places that have more financial resources with which to compensate victims and/or to install crime-prevention or security measures are sued more often.(4)

When companies decide to pursue crime-prevention measures, consideration of lawsuits might seem like a far-fetched idea with few real implications. But large damage awards have become a real threat to many American businesses. Businesses are well advised to consider the low-cost CPTED principles.

Sources

1. Corey L. Gordon and William Brill, "The Expanding Role of Crime Prevention through Environmental Design in Premises Liability," for National Institute of Justice (Washington, D.C.: U.S. Government Printing Office, 1996), p. 4.
2. Ibid., p. 1.
3. Ibid., p. 3.
4. John Eck, "Do Premise Liability Suits Promote Business Crime Prevention?" paper presented at the Business and Crime Prevention Conference, an International Seminar Sponsored by the National Institute of Justice and Rutgers, State University of New Jersey, New Brunswick, N.J., 1996.

Questions for Discussion

1. Of the three types of places that are frequently the subjects of premise liability lawsuits (convenience store, shopping center, and apartment building), is there one that stands out as more responsible for the crimes that occur?

2. If an apartment-building landlord has hired security guards to protect the premises and one of the guards is sleeping while a rape occurs in the building's laundry room, who is responsible?

things rather than trying to prevent crime by focusing exclusively on troubled people (who may or may not rob convenience stores anyway)? If we know that repeat victimization can be prevented by intervening with high-risk people and properties, isn't that the most cost-beneficial way to proceed?

We usually think of crime policy as being made by governments, for only they can control the police, courts, and corrections. Decisions about crime prevention, on the other hand, can be made by small communities, neighborhoods, schools, businesses, and individuals. We discussed how simple precautions lower the risk of convenience-store robbery. This knowledge not only encouraged governments to pass certain laws mandating that stores take those precautions, but led many in private industry to adopt the measures as well. Knowledge about crime prevention is especially valuable to all people because everyone can use these tools to reduce the chances of being a victim.

REVIEW

This chapter focuses on situational theories of crime. These theories, which assume that there are always people motivated to commit crime, try to explain why crimes are being committed by a particular offender against a particular target. They analyze opportunities and environmental factors that prompt a potential perpetrator to act.

We discussed the three most prominent situational theories of crime: environmental criminology, the rational-choice perspective, and the routine-activity approach. We noted that they have merged somewhat, particularly insofar as all these theories aim at preventing victimization by altering external conditions that are conducive to crime.

Theories of victimization view crime as the dynamic interaction of perpetrators and victims (at a given time and place). Here too the aim is to find ways for potential victims to protect themselves. Research into lifestyles, victim-offender interaction, repeat victimization, hot spots, and geography of crime has vast implications for crime control in entire cities or regions. Situational theories of crime and theories of victimization are interrelated.

YOU BE THE CRIMINOLOGIST

Imagine you are a security consultant working for a major department store chain. Recently, one of the stores, located in the downtown area of a large city, has experienced very high levels of shoplifting and employee theft. You must design a comprehensive program to protect merchandise from theft by customers and by people who work at the store. First, identify some of the store's most vulnerable areas (it may help to visit a local department store to observe how it operates). Then, using the 16 techniques of situational crime prevention as a model, prepare a list of prevention strategies.

KEY TERMS

The numbers next to the terms refer to the pages on which the terms are defined.

displacement (255)
environmental criminology (239)
rational choice (239)
routine activity (241)
target hardening (250)
theories of victimization (238)

NOTES

1. Marlowe Churchill, "Jury Finds Man Guilty of One-Hour Sex Attack," Riverside, CA. *The Press-Enterprise,* July 26, 1996, p. B3.
2. "Suburban Digest," *Denver Post,* Apr. 10, 1996, p. B-2.
3. Daniel Sforza, "Thieves Favor Giant Malls When Shopping for Cars," *The Record,* Bergen County, New Jersey, June 26, 1996, pp. A1, A20.
4. Paul J. Brantingham and Patricia L. Brantingham, "Introduction: The Dimensions of Crime," in *Environmental Criminology,* ed. Brantingham and Brantingham (Prospect Heights, Ill.: Waveland, 1991), p. 8. For a discussion on the application of environmental criminology to urban planning, see Paul J. Brantingham and Patricia L. Brantingham, "Environmental Criminology: From Theory to Urban Planning Practice," *Studies on Crime and Crime Prevention,* 7 (1998): 31–60.

5. André M. Guerry, *Essai sur la Statistique Morale de la France* (Paris: Crochard, 1833).

6. Adolphe Quételet, *A Treatise on Man* (Edinburgh: Chambers, 1842), reprinted excerpt Adolphe Quételet, "Of the development of the propensity to crime," in *Criminological Perspectives: A Reader,* ed. John Muncie, Eugene McLaughlin, and Mary Langan (Thousand Oaks, Calif.: Sage, 1996), p. 19.

7. Ronald Clarke and Derek Cornish, "Modeling Offenders' Decisions: A Framework for Research and Policy," in *Crime and Justice,* vol. 6, ed. Michael Tonry and Norval Morris (Chicago: University of Chicago Press, 1985), pp. 147–185; Derek B. Cornish and Ronald V. Clarke, eds., *The Reasoning Criminal* (New York: Springer Verlag, 1986).

8. Jeremy Bentham, *On the Principles and Morals of Legislation* (New York: Kegan Paul, 1789) [reprinted 1948]; Gary S. Becker, "Crime and Punishment: An Economic Approach," *Journal of Political Economy,* **76** (1968): 169–217.

9. Lawrence E. Cohen and Marcus Felson, "Social Change and Crime Rate Trends: A Routine Activity Approach," *American Sociological Review,* **44** (1979): 588–608; Marcus Felson, "Linking Criminal Choices, Routine Activities, Informal Control, and Criminal Outcomes," in *The Reasoning Criminal: Rational Choice Perspectives on Offending,* ed. Derek B. Cornish and Ronald V. Clarke (New York: Springer-Verlag, 1986), pp. 119–128.

10. Marcus Felson, *Crime and Everyday Life: Insights and Implications for Society* (Thousand Oaks, Calif.: Pine Forge Press, 1994), pp. 20–21, 35.

11. Mangai Natarajan, "Telephones as Facilitators of Drug Dealing," paper presented at the Fourth International Seminar on Environmental Criminology and Crime Analysis, July 1995, Cambridge, England; Mangai Natarajan, Ronald V. Clarke and Mathieu Belanger, "Drug Dealing and Pay Phones: The Scope for Intervention," *Security Journal,* **7** (1996) 245–251.

12. Lawrence W. Sherman, Patrick R. Gartin, and Michael E. Buerger, "Hot Spots of Predatory Crime: Routine Activities and the Criminology of Place," *Criminology,* **27** (1989): 27–55; Ronald V. Clarke and Patricia M. Harris, "A Rational Choice Perspective on the Targets of Automobile Theft," *Criminal Behaviour and Mental Health,* **2** (1992): 25–42. See also the following articles in Ronald V. Clarke and Marcus Felson, eds., *Routine Activity and Rational Choice, Advances in Criminological Theory,* vol. 5 (New Brunswick, N.J.: Transaction, 1993): Raymond Paternoster and Sally Simpson, "A Rational Choice Theory of Corporate Crime," pp. 37–58; Richard W. Harding, "Gun Use in Crime, Rational Choice, and Social Learning Theory," pp. 85–102; Richard B. Felson, "Predatory and Dispute-Related Violence: A Social Interactionist Approach," pp. 103–125; Nathaniel J. Pallone and James J. Hennessy, "Tinderbox Criminal Violence: Neurogenic Impulsivity, Risk-Taking, and the Phenomenology of Rational Choice," pp. 127–157; Max Taylor, "Rational Choice, Behavior Analysis, and Political Violence," pp. 159–178; Pietro Marongiu and Ronald V. Clarke, "Ransom Kidnapping in Sardinia, Subcultural Theory and Rational Choice," pp. 179–199; Bruce D. Johnson, Mangai Natarajan, and Harry Sanabria, "'Successful' Criminal Careers: Toward an Ethnography within the Rational Choice Perspective," pp. 201–221.

13. George Rengert and John Wasilchick, *Suburban Burglary: A Time and a Place for Everything* (Springfield, Ill.: Charles C Thomas, 1985).

14. Paul F. Cromwell, James N. Olson, and D'Aunn Webster Avary, *Breaking and Entering: An Ethnographic Analysis of Burglary* (Newbury Park, Calif.: Sage, 1991), pp. 45–46.

15. Richard T. Wright and Scott H. Decker, *Burglars on the Job: Streetlife and Residential Break-Ins* (Boston: Northeastern University Press, 1994), pp. 63–68. See also Alex Piquero and George F. Rengert, "Studying Deterrence with Active Residential Burglars: A Research Note," *Justice Quarterly,* **16** (1999): 451–472.

16. Richard T. Wright and Scott Decker, *Armed Robbers in Action: Stickups and Street Culture* (Boston: Northeastern University Press, 1994). For a feminist analysis of Wright and Decker's ethnographic work on street robbers, see Jody Miller, "Up It Up: Gender and

the Accomplishment of Street Robbery," *Criminology*, **36** (1998): 37–66.

17. Philip J. Cook, *Robbery in the United States: An Analysis of Recent Trends and Patterns*, U.S. Department of Justice (Washington, D.C.: U.S. Government Printing Office, 1983).

18. Wayland Clifton, Jr., *Convenience Store Robbery in Gainesville, Florida* (Gainesville, Fla.: Gainesville Police Department, 1987), p. 15.

19. Lawrence E. Cohen and Marcus Felson, "Social Change and Crime Rate Trends: A Routine Activity Approach," *American Sociological Review*, **44** (1979): 588–608.

20. Ronald V. Clarke, *Hot Products: Understanding, Anticipating and Reducing Demand for Stolen Goods*, Policing and Reducing Crime Unit, Police Research Series Paper 112 (London: Home Office, 1999). For discussions of what drives shoplifters, see Read Hayes, "Shop Theft: An Analysis of Shoplifter Perceptions and Situational Factors," *Security Journal*, **12** (1999): 7–18; and David P. Farrington, "Measuring, Explaining, and Preventing Shoplifting: A Review of British Research," *Security Journal*, **12** (1999): 9–28. For details on measuring and preventing crime against retail business, see a special issue of *Security Journal*, **7** (1996): 1–75.

21. Bonnie S. Fisher, John J. Sloan, Francis T. Cullen, and Chunmeng Lu, "Crime in the Ivory Tower: The Level and Sources of Student Victimization," *Criminology*, **36** (1998): 671–710. For additional research supporting the routine-activity approach, see also Verna A. Henson and William E. Stone, "Campus Crime: A Victimization Study," *Journal of Criminal Justice*, **27** (1999): 295–308.

22. Hans von Hentig, "Remarks on the Interaction of Perpetrator and Victim," *Journal of Criminal Law and Criminology*, **31** (1941): 303–309.

23. Hans von Hentig, *The Criminal and His Victim* (New Haven, Conn.: Yale University, 1948).

24. See Benjamin Mendelsohn, "The Origin of the Doctrine of Victimology," in *Victimology*, ed. Israel Drapkin and Emilio Viano (Lexington, Mass.: Lexington Books, 1974), pp. 3–4.

25. Frederic Wertham, *The Show of Violence* (Garden City, N.Y.: Country Life Press, 1948), p. 259.

26. Ezzat A. Fattah, "Victims and Victimology: The Facts and the Rhetoric," *International Review of Victimology*, **1** (1989): 44–66, at p. 44.

27. Ezzat A. Fattah, "The Rational Choice/Opportunity Perspective as a Vehicle for Integrating Criminological and Victimological Theories," in Clarke and Felson, *Routine Activity and Rational Choice*, pp. 230–231. For an examination of the relationship between lifestyle factors and the victimization of prostitutes, see Charisse Coston and Lee Ross, "Criminal Victimization of Prostitutes: Empirical Support for the Lifestyle/Exposure Model," *Journal of Crime and Justice*, **21** (1998): 53–70.

28. Fattah, "Victims and Victimology," p. 54.

29. Michael J. Hindelang, Michael R. Gottfredson, and James Garofalo, *Victims of Personal Crime: An Empirical Foundation for a Theory of Personal Victimization* (Cambridge, Mass.: Ballinger, 1978), p. 245.

30. Ibid., pp. 251–265.

31. Marvin E. Wolfgang, *Patterns in Criminal Homicide* (Philadelphia: University of Pennsylvania Press, 1958), p. 253.

32. James T. Tedeschi and Richard B. Felson, *Violence, Aggression, and Coercive Actions* (Washington, D.C.: American Psychological Association, 1994).

33. Richard B. Felson, "Big People Hit Little People: Sex Differences in Physical Power and Interpersonal Violence," *Criminology*, **34** (1996): 433–452.

34. Dan Olweus, "Aggressors and Their Victims: Bullying at School," in *Disruptive Behaviors in Schools*, ed. N. Frude and H. Gault (New York: Wiley, 1984), pp. 57–76.

35. Alan Trickett, Dan Ellingworth, Tim Hope, and Ken Pease, "Crime Victimization in the Eighties: Changes in Area and Regional Inequality," *British Journal of Criminology*, **35** (1995): 343–359; Graham Farrell, "Preventing Repeat Victimization," in *Building a Safer Society: Strategic Approaches to Crime Prevention, Crime and Justice*, vol. 19, ed. Michael Tonry and David P. Farrington (Chicago: University of Chicago Press, 1995), pp. 469–534.

36. Dan Ellingworth, Graham Farrell, and Ken Pease, "A Victim Is a Victim Is a Victim? Chronic Victimization in Four Sweeps of the

British Crime Survey," *British Journal of Criminology*, **35** (1995): 360–365.

37. William Spelman, "Once Bitten, Then What? Cross-Sectional and Time-Course Explanations of Repeat Victimization," *British Journal of Criminology*, **35** (1995): 366–383.

38. Natalie Polvi, Terah Looman, Charlie Humphries, and Ken Pease, "The Time-Course of Repeat Burglary Victimization," *British Journal of Criminology*, **31** (1991): 411–414.

39. Graham Farrell, Coretta Phillips, and Ken Pease, "Like Taking Candy: Why Does Repeat Victimization Occur?" *British Journal of Criminology*, **35** (1995): 384–399.

40. Lawrence W. Sherman, Patrick R. Gartin, and Michael E. Buerger, "Hot Spots of Predatory Crime: Routine Activities and the Criminology of Place," *Criminology*, **27** (1989): 27–55.

41. Robert J. Sampson, "The Community," in *Crime*, ed. James Q. Wilson and Joan Petersilia (San Francisco: ICS Press, 1995), pp. 193–216.

42. Dennis W. Roncek and Donald Faggiani, "High Schools and Crime: A Replication," *Sociological Quarterly*, **26** (1985): 491–505.

43. Dennis W. Roncek and Pamela A. Maier, "Bars, Blocks, and Crimes Revisited: Linking the Theory of Routine Activities to the Empiricism of 'Hot Spots,'" *Criminology*, **29** (1991): 725–753.

44. Richard L. Block and Carolyn R. Block, "Space, Place and Crime: Hot Spot Areas and Hot Places of Liquor-Related Crime," in *Crime and Place: Crime Prevention Studies*, vol. 4, ed. John E. Eck and David Weisburd (Monsey, N.Y.: Criminal Justice Press; Washington, D.C.: The Police Executive Research Forum, 1995), pp. 145–183.

45. Per-Olof Wikström, "Preventing City-Center Street Crimes," in Tonry and Farrington, *Building a Safer Society*, vol. 19, pp. 429–468.

46. William Spelman, "Abandoned Buildings: Magnets for Crime?" *Journal of Criminal Justice*, **21** (1993): 481–495.

47. Dennis W. Roncek and Ralph Bell, "Bars, Blocks, and Crimes," *Journal of Environmental Systems*, **11** (1981): 35–47; Roncek and Faggiani, "High Schools and Crime."

48. Jeffrey Peck, G. O. W. Mueller, and Freda Adler, "The Vulnerability of Ports and Marinas to Vessel and Equipment Theft," *Security Journal*, **5** (1994): 146–153.

49. David Weisburd and Lorraine Green with Frank Gajewski and Charles Bellucci, Jersey City Police Department, "Defining the Street Level Drug Market," in *Drugs and Crime: Evaluating Public Policy Initiatives*, ed. Doris Layton MacKenzie and Craig Uchida (Newbury Park, Calif.: Sage, 1994), pp. 61–76. For a discussion of the role of place managers in controlling drug and disorder problems, see Lorraine Green Mazerolle, Colleen Kadleck, and Jan Roehl, "Controlling Drug and Disorder Problems: The Role of Place Managers," *Criminology*, **36** (1998): 371–404. For an analysis of problem-oriented policing in troubled areas, see Anthony A. Braga, David L. Weisburd, Elin J. Waring, Lorraine Green Mazerolle, William Spelman, and Francis Gajewski, "Problem-Oriented Policing in Violent Crime Places: A Randomized Controlled Experiment," *Criminology*, **37** (1999): 541–580.

50. Lawrence W. Sherman, "Hot Spots of Crime and Criminal Careers of Places," in Eck and Weisburd, *Crime and Place*, vol. 4, pp. 35–52.

51. See Fattah, "The Rational Choice/Opportunity Perspective," in Clark and Felson, *Routine Activity and Rational Choice*, pp. 225–258.

52. James R. Lasley, "Drinking Routines/Lifestyles and Predatory Victimization: A Causal Analysis," *Justice Quarterly*, **6** (1989): 529–542.

53. Martin D. Schwartz and Victoria L. Pitts, "Exploring a Feminist Routine Activities Approach to Explaining Sexual Assault," *Justice Quarterly*, **12** (1995): 9–31.

54. Robert F. Meier and Terance D. Miethe, "Understanding Theories of Criminal Victimization," in *Crime and Justice: A Review of Research*, vol. 17, ed. Michael Tonry (Chicago: University of Chicago Press, 1993), pp. 459–499; Richard Titus, "Bringing Crime Victims Back into Routine Activities Theory/Research," paper presented at Fourth International Seminar on Environmental

Criminology and Crime Analysis, July 1995, Cambridge, England.

55. C. Ray Jeffery, *Crime Prevention through Environmental Design* (Beverly Hills, Calif.: Sage, 1971).

56. Oscar Newman, *Defensible Space: Crime Prevention through Urban Design* (New York: Macmillan, 1972).

57. Ronald V. Clarke, "Introduction," in *Situational Crime Prevention: Successful Case Studies,* ed. Ronald V. Clarke (New York: Harrow and Heston, 1992), pp. 3–36.

58. Ronald V. Clarke and Ross Homel, "A Revised Classification of Situational Crime Prevention Techniques," in *Crime Prevention at a Crossroads,* ed. Steven P. Lab (Cincinnati: Anderson, 1997). For a discussion of precipitating factors and opportunity, see Richard Wortley, "A Two-Stage Model of Situational Crime Prevention," *Studies on Crime and Crime Prevention,* **7** (1998): 173–188.

59. See Gresham M. Sykes and David Matza, "Techniques of Neutralization: A Theory of Delinquency," *American Sociological Review,* **22** (1957): 664–670; Harold G. Grasmick and Robert J. Bursik, "Conscience, Significant Others, and Rational Choice," *Law and Society Review,* **34** (1990): 837–861; John Braithwaite, *Crime, Shame and Reintegration* (Cambridge: Cambridge University, 1989).

60. Clifford D. Shearing and Phillip C. Stenning, "From the Panopticon to Disney World: The Development of Discipline," in *Perspectives in Criminal Law: Essays in Honour of John L. J. Edwards,* ed. Anthony N. Doob and Edward L. Greenspan (Aurora: Canada Law Book, 1984), pp. 335–349.

61. See Clarke, "Introduction," in Clarke, *Situational Crime Prevention,* p. 5.

62. Kim Hazelbaker, "Insurance Industry Analyses and the Prevention of Motor Vehicle Theft" paper presented at the Business and Crime Prevention Conference, an International Seminar Sponsored by the National Institute of Justice and Rutgers, State University of New Jersey, New Brunswick, N.J., 1996.

63. Ronald D. Hunter and C. Ray Jeffery, "Preventing Convenience Store Robbery through Environmental Design," in Clarke, *Situational Crime Prevention,* pp. 194–204. See also Lisa C. Bellamy, "Situational Crime Prevention and Convenience Store Robbery," *Security Journal,* **7** (1996): 41–52.

64. All information for this section abstracted from Mary S. Smith, *Crime Prevention through Environmental Design in Parking Facilities,* Research in Brief, for National Institute of Justice (Washington, D.C.: U.S. Government Printing Office, 1996).

65. Patricia Mayhew, Ronald V. Clarke, and David Elliott, "Motorcycle Theft, Helmet Legislation and Displacement," *Howard Journal of Criminal Justice,* **28** (1989): 1–8. For an examination of how preventing repeat victimization can reduce displacement, see Adam C. Bouloukos and Graham Farrell, "On the Displacement of Repeat Victimization," in *Rational Choice and Situational Crime Prevention,* ed. Graeme Newman, Ronald V. Clarke, and S. Giora Shoham (Aldershot, U.K.: Dartmouth, 1997), pp. 219–232.

Review • You Be the Criminologist • Key Terms • Notes

PART III

Types of Crimes

The word "crime" conjures up many images: mugging and murder, cheating on taxes, and selling crack. Penal codes define thousands of different crimes. But all crimes have certain elements in common. All are human acts in violation of law, committed by an actor who acted with a criminal intent to cause a specified harm. The various legal defenses to crime are based on the defendant's alleging that one of the required elements was missing (Chapter 10).

After analyzing the common ingredients of all crimes, we examine specific types of crime: violent crime (Chapter 11); crime against property (Chapter 12); white-collar, corporate, and organized crime (Chapter 13); and crime related to drug and alcohol trafficking and consumption, and to sexual mores (Chapter 14). All these types of crime are explained in terms of legal and criminological perspectives. Their occurrence, frequency, and pervasiveness are also discussed in comparison with the occurrence of crime in other parts of the world. Chapter 15, which is concerned with comparative criminology, includes a discussion of international and transnational crimes.

CHAPTER 10
The Concept of Crime

KEY TERMS

accomplices
criminal attempt
felonies
mens rea
misdemeanors
principals
strict liability
torts
violations

Police in Richmond, California, have an ironclad case against three burglars who had entered the Bermudez family's home and absconded with a tricycle. The ringleader also attacked the only witness to the burglary, beating and kicking him, cracking his skull, and leaving him for dead. In early May 1996, the three were arraigned on charges of having committed burglary. The ringleader was also charged with attempted murder.

What is unusual about the case is that the ringleader is 6 years old, and his companions are 2-year-old twins. The "witness" was a 1-month-old baby! The ringleader obviously is a bad kid, so neighbors concluded. He had unlawfully entered the Bermudez home before; he held a grudge against the Bermudez family; he had harassed other kids in the neighborhood.

Now the three are charged with burglary; and the ringleader, whom his public defender has dubbed a "munchkin," has been charged with attempted murder as well. Journalists, neighbors, and at least some officials are all aflutter: charges of attempted murder and burglary against children that young? "The judicial system has few guidelines for dealing with such youthful *offenders*," wrote *Time*.[1] Are there too "few" guidelines?

This is where the concept of crime becomes relevant. Were crimes committed? What is it that makes a crime? Which crimes were committed?

In trying to answer these questions, we must begin by looking at the law, here the criminal code of the state of California, which defines what is considered a crime in California. This will not get us too far.[2] Codes, for the most part, do not contain theoretical propositions. It is scholars who, over time, have worked out the basics of the concept of crime as these inhere in all the types of crime defined in criminal codes.

THE INGREDIENTS OF CRIME

We begin by examining that part of criminal law that deals with the common legal ingredients, or elements, found in all crimes. With few exceptions, if any one of these elements is not present, no crime has been committed. All the defenses available to a person charged with a crime allege that at least one of these elements is not present.

The Seven Basic Requirements

The American criminal law scholar Jerome Hall has developed the theory that a human event, in order to qualify as a crime, must meet seven basic requirements[3]:

1. The act requirement
2. The legality requirement
3. The harm requirement
4. The causation requirement
5. The mens rea requirement
6. The concurrence requirement
7. The punishment requirement[4]

The Act Requirement

Law scholars have long agreed that one fundamental ingredient of every crime is a human act. In this context, what is an "act"? Suppose a sleepwalker, in a trance, grabs a stone and hurls it at a passerby, with lethal consequences. The law does not consider this event to be an act; before any human behavior can qualify as an act, there must be a conscious interaction between mind and body, a physical movement that results from the determination or effort of the actor. Thus the Model Penal Code (MPC), which the American Law Institute proposed to legislatures in 1962, says that the following behaviors are not voluntary acts:

*   A reflex or convulsion.

*   A bodily movement that occurs during unconsciousness or sleep.

*   Conduct that occurs during hypnosis or results from hypnotic suggestion.

*   A bodily movement that is not determined by the actor, as when somebody is pushed by another person.[5]

Free Will?   This formula gives the impression that the law is based on "free will," the idea that people are accountable only if they freely choose to do something and then consciously do it. But scientists and lawyers have yet to discover an individual who is completely free to make choices. All of us have been molded by factors beyond our control, and our choices are to some extent conditioned by internal and external factors and forces. It is only when choices are overpoweringly influenced by forces beyond our control, such as the case of the sleepwalking stone thrower, that the law will consider behavior irrational and beyond its reach.

Act versus Status   The criminal law, in principle, does not penalize anyone for a status or condition. Suppose the law made it a crime to be more than 6 feet tall or to have red hair. Or suppose the law made it a crime to be a member of the family of an army deserter or to be of a given religion or ethnic background. That was exactly the situation in the Soviet Union under Stalin's penal code, which made it a crime to be related to a deserter from the Red Army. It was also the situation in Hitler's Germany, where in effect it was a crime to be Jewish, and it was punishable by death.

There is thus more to the act requirement than the issue of a behavior's being voluntary and rational: There is the problem of distinguishing between act and status. A California law made it a criminal offense, subject to a jail term, to be a drug addict. In *Robinson v. California* the U.S. Supreme Court held that statute to be unconstitutional. By making a status or condition a crime, the statute violated the Eighth Amendment to the U.S. Constitution, which prohibits "cruel and unusual punishments." Addiction, the Court noted, is a condition, an illness, much like leprosy or venereal disease. Even babies born of addict mothers are addicts. Said the Court: "Even one day in prison would be cruel and unusual punishment for the 'crime' of having a common cold."[6]

In a subsequent case, *Powell v. Texas,* the Supreme Court backed away from its recognition of the act requirement.[7] A Texas statute had made it a crime to be drunk in public. Powell was a chronic alcoholic, prosecuted for being in a public place while drunk. The defense argued that chronic alcoholics cannot refrain from drinking. If they are homeless, they cannot help being in public places. The Supreme Court, however, upheld Powell's conviction, in essence saying that he had not been punished for being a chronic alcoholic but for doing something—for going to a public place in an intoxicated state. This ruling is considered by many to be inconsistent with the *Robinson* decision.

Failure to Act The act requirement has yet another aspect. An act requires the interaction of mind and body. If only the mind is active and the body does not move, we do not have an act: Just thinking about punching someone in the nose is not a crime (Figure 10.1). We are free to think. But if we carry a thought into physical action, we commit an act, which may be a crime.

Then there is the problem of omission, or failure to act. If the law requires that convicted sex offenders register with the police, and such a person decides not to fill out the registration form, that person is guilty of a crime by omission. But he has acted! He told his hand not to pick up that pen, not to fill out the form. Inaction may be action when the law clearly spells out what one has to do and one decides not to do it.

The law in most U.S. states imposes no duty to be a Good Samaritan, to offer help to another person in distress. The Kitty Genovese case is a well-known example. Not one of her 38 neighbors was a Good Samaritan. (See Where Do We Go from Here? on the following page.) The law requires action only if one has a legal duty to act. Lifeguards, for example, are contractually obligated to save bathers from drowning; parents are obligated by law to protect their children; law enforcement officers and firefighters are required to rescue people in distress; baby-sitters must protect babies in their care from harm. In addition, the law imposes a duty to continue rescue operations on anybody who, though not required to do so, has voluntarily come to the aid of a person in need.

The Legality Requirement

Marion Palendrano was charged with, among other things, being a "common scold" because

FIGURE 10.1 Has a crime been committed? Is walking on the grass prohibited by law, subject to punishment? Did the actor commit the act by actually walking on the grass, or did he merely have a criminal intent to do so? Perhaps the actor is incapable of forming a legally relevant intent because he is too young to do so!

© 1962 The Saturday Evening Post

she disturbed "the peace of the neighborhood and of all good and quiet people of this State." Mrs. Palendrano moved that the charge be dismissed, and the Superior Court of New Jersey agreed with her, reasoning:

1. Such a crime cannot be found anywhere in the New Jersey statute books. Hence there is no such crime, although, long ago, the common law of England may have recognized such a crime.

2. "Being a common scold" is so vague a concept that to punish somebody for it would violate constitutional due process: "We insist that laws give the person of ordinary intelligence a reasonable opportunity to know what is prohibited, so that he may act accordingly," ruled the court.[8]

On March 27, 1964, the *New York Times* printed the following story:

For more than half an hour thirty-eight respectable, law-abiding citizens in Queens watched a killer stalk and stab a woman in three separate attacks in Kew Gardens.

Twice the sound of their voices and the sudden glow of their bedroom lights interrupted him and frightened him off. Each time he returned, sought her out and stabbed her again. Not one person telephoned the police during the assault; one witness called after the woman was dead.

That was two weeks ago today. But Assistant Chief Inspector Frederick M. Lussen, in charge of the borough's detectives and a veteran of twenty-five years of homicide investigations, is still shocked.

He can give a matter-of-fact recitation of many murders. But the Kew Gardens slaying baffles him—not because it is a murder, but because the "good people" failed to call the police.

"As we have reconstructed the crime," he said, "the assailant had three chances to kill this woman during a thirty-five-minute period. He returned twice to complete the job. If we had been called when he first attacked, the woman might not be dead now."

This is what the police say happened beginning at 3:30 a.m. in the staid, middle-class, tree-lined Austin Street area:

Twenty-eight-year-old Catherine Genovese, who was called Kitty by almost everyone in the neighborhood, was returning home from her job as manager of a bar in Hollis. She parked her red Fiat . . . turned off the lights of her car, locked the door and started to walk the 100 feet to the entrance of her apartment. . . . Miss Genovese noticed a man at the far end of the lot. . . . She halted. Then, nervously, she headed up Austin Street . . . where there is a call box to the 102d Police Precinct in nearby Richmond Hill.

She got as far as a street light in front of a bookstore before the man grabbed her. She screamed. Lights went on in the ten-story apartment house . . . which faces the bookstore. Windows slid open and voices punctured the early-morning stillness.

Miss Genovese screamed: "Oh, my God, he stabbed me! Please help me! Please help me!"

From one of the upper windows in the apartment house, a man called down: "Let that girl alone!"

The assailant looked up at him, shrugged and walked down Austin Street. . . . Miss Genovese struggled to her feet.

Lights went out. The killer returned to Miss Genovese [and] stabbed her again.

"I'm dying!" she shrieked. "I'm dying!"

Windows were opened again, and lights went on in many apartments. The assailant got into his car and drove away. Miss Genovese staggered to her feet. It was 3:35 a.m.

The assailant returned. By then, Miss Genovese had crawled to the back of the building. . . . The killer . . . saw her slumped on the floor at the foot of the stairs. He stabbed her a third time—fatally.

It was 3:50 by the time the police received their first call from a man who was a neighbor of Miss Genovese. In two minutes they were at the scene.

It was 4:25 a.m. when the ambulance arrived for the body of Miss Genovese. It drove off. "Then," a solemn police detective said, "the people came out."(1)

(1) Where she parked her car.
(2) Place of initial attack.
(3) Place of second attack.
(4) Place of third attack.

Source

1. Excerpted from A. M. Rosenthal, *Thirty-Eight Witnesses* (New York: McGraw-Hill, 1964).

Questions for Discussion

1. Could the Kitty Genovese case happen today? Why or why not?
2. Excuses offered by the witnesses for not calling the police when they first heard screams included "I was tired," "We were afraid," "I didn't want my husband to get involved," and "I don't know." Would you have called the police?

If we want a person to adhere to a standard, the person has to know what that standard is. Thus we have the ancient proposition that only conduct that has been made criminal by law before an act is committed can be a crime; in Latin, this is known as the maxim *nullum crimen sine lege* ("no crime without law"). Police, prosecutors, and courts are not interested in the billions of acts human beings engage in unless such acts have previously been defined by law as criminal. The law is interested only in an act (*actus*) that is guilty, evil, and prohibited (*reus*). Additionally, as Marion Palendrano's case demonstrates, when the law has made some behavior a crime, the language defining it must be clear enough to be understood.

The Harm Requirement

Every crime has been created to prevent something bad (a given harm) from happening. Mur-

The posting of "pooper-scooper" regulations has had its effect. Most inner city residents consider the failure to "pick up" to be a sign of disrespect and a violation of custom.

der is prohibited because we don't want people to be killed. Arson and theft are prohibited because we want people to be secure in their possessions. This detrimental consequence that we are trying to avoid is called *harm.* If the specified harm has not been created by the defendant's act, the crime is not complete. Just think of would-be assassin John W. Hinckley, Jr., who tried to kill President Reagan. He shot Reagan, but the president did not die. The harm envisioned by the law against murder had not been accomplished. (Hinckley could have been found guilty of attempted murder, but he was acquitted by reason of insanity.)

Sometimes the harm is less drastic than a dead person or a burned house. Pooper-scooper laws (you must clean up after your dog) are designed to prevent the harm of dirty streets and sidewalks. In the case of drunk-driving statutes, the harm is not of a physical nature. It consists of the grave danger to the public which driving while intoxicated constitutes. (If the drunk driver kills someone, a more serious charge is brought.)

From a criminological perspective, most crimes are grouped by the harm that each entails. Offenses against the person involve harm to an individual, and offenses against property involve damage to property or loss of its possession.

The Causation Requirement

What is the act of hitting a home run? Of course it is a hit that allows a batter to run to first, second, and third base, and then back to home plate. Actually, it is much more complicated than that. It starts with the decision to swing a bat, at a certain angle, with a particular intensity, in a specific direction, in order to cause a home run. Suppose that at a San Diego Padres home game, the batter hits a ball unusually high into the air. A passing pelican picks it up, flies off with it, and then drops it into the bleachers. Has the batter hit a home run? We doubt it.

It's the same in crime. Causation requires that the actor achieve the result (the harm) through his or her own effort. Suppose that A, in an effort to kill B, wounds him and that B actually dies when the ambulance carrying him to the hospital collides with another vehicle. Despite B's death, A did not succeed in her personal attempt to kill B. Thus the act of murder is incomplete, although A may be guilty of an attempt to kill. The causation requirement, then, holds that a crime is not complete unless the actor's conduct necessarily caused the harm without interference by somebody else, and that it is the proximate cause of the act.[9]

Did You Know

. . . that the concept of guilt (guilty mind, mens rea) is so central to our sense of justice that we symbolized it in the pre-Christian era with the goddess of justice (*justice*) and her scales—to measure guilt and punishment? In the Christian era *Justitia* became a symbol of justice, sometimes referred to as a saint, but certainly no longer a goddess. She is now the lady justice.

Mens Rea: The "Guilty Mind" Requirement

Every crime, according to tradition, requires **mens rea,** a "guilty mind." Let us examine the case of Ms. Lambert. She was convicted in Los Angeles of an offense created by city ordinance: having lived in the city without registering with the police as a person previously convicted of a crime. Ms. Lambert had no idea that Los Angeles had such a registration requirement. Nor could she possibly have known that she was required to register. She appealed all the way to the U.S. Supreme Court, and she won. Said the Court: "Where a person did not know [of the prohibition] (s)he may not be convicted consistent with due process."[10]

Of course, to blame Ms. Lambert for violating the Los Angeles city ordinance would make no sense. Ms. Lambert had no notion that she was doing something wrong by living in Los Angeles and not registering herself as a convicted person. The potential of blame that follows a choice to commit a crime is meant to be a powerful incentive to do the right thing and avoid doing the wrong thing. That is the function of mens rea. (We will return to Ms. Lambert later on.)

With Ms. Lambert's case we have reached a fundamental point: No one can be guilty of a crime unless he or she acted with the knowledge of doing something wrong. This principle always has existed. It is implicit in the concept of crime that the perpetrator know the wrongfulness of the act. It is not required that the perpetrator know the penal code or have personal feelings of guilt. It is enough that the perpetrator knows that he or she had no right to do what he or she did and decided to do it anyway.[11]

In a 1994 landmark decision, a sharply divided U.S. Supreme Court once again expressed its adherence to the mens rea–guilty mind requirement. A married couple, the Ratzlefs, had made cash transactions (to pay a gambling debt) which they should have reported to the Internal Revenue Service. They honestly did not know of their obligation to report—the law had only recently been amended. Prior law required only banks to report.[12] But the majority reached this conclusion only because Congress had used the word "wilful" in defining the crime. That was good enough for Justice Ruth Bader Gins-

burg to conclude that Congress wanted to subject to punishment only those who failed to report, knowing that not to report was wrong. The dissent, in an opinion by Justice Harry A. Blackmun, argued that "wilful" means no more than willing to act (or to omit, as in this case). Yet if that were so, can one conceive of any act that is not wilful by definition? And if that is so, then Congress would have used a self-evident term to describe the act. The controversy over whether "wilfulness" is part of the act requirement, or signals a significant component of the mens rea–knowledge-of-wrongfulness requirement, has led some scholars to argue that the centuries-old distinction between actus reus and mens rea is meaningless and should be abandoned.[13] It does not seem so. The mind has two functions to perform when it comes to the commission of a crime: First, the mind must be on the job when it comes to committing an act; second, the mind must entertain the notion of wrongfulness—and that is mens rea—otherwise, it is not alerted to the threat of punishment.

Anyone who violently attacks another person, takes another's property, invades another's home, forces intercourse, or forges a signature on someone else's check knows rather well that he or she is doing something wrong. All these examples of mens rea entail an intention to achieve harm or a knowledge that the prohibited harm will result. For some crimes, however, less than a definite intention suffices: reckless actions by which the actors consciously risk causing a prohibited harm (for example, the driver who races down a rain-slicked highway or the employer who sends his employees to work without safety equipment, knowing full well that lives are thereby being endangered).

Strict liability is an exception to the mens rea requirement. There is a class of offenses for which legislatures or courts require no showing of criminal intent or mens rea. For these offenses, the fact that the actor makes an innocent mistake and proceeds in good faith does not affect criminal liability. Such offenses are called strict-liability offenses, and they crept into our law with the Industrial Revolution. Most of them involve conduct subject to regulation, conduct that threatens the public welfare as a whole. Strict-liability offenses range all the way from distributing adulterated food to passing a red light. Typically, these offenses are subject to small penalties only, but in a few cases substantial punishments can be and have been imposed.[14]

The efficacy of strict criminal liability is very much in doubt. Vast numbers of persons being found guilty who had no idea of doing something wrong—and in precisely the kind of minor cases which affect the largest portion of the population—can only lead to disrespect for the law.[15]

The Concurrence Requirement

The concurrence requirement states that the criminal act must be accompanied by an equally criminal mind. Suppose a striker throws a stone at an office window in order to shatter it, and a broken piece of glass pierces the throat of a secretary, who bleeds to death. Wanting to damage property deserves condemnation, but of a far lesser degree than wanting to kill. Act and intent did not concur in this case, and the striker should not be found guilty of murder. The law has created many exceptions to the concurrence requirement, one of which, the felony murder rule, we discuss in Chapter 11.

The Punishment Requirement

The last ingredient needed to constitute a crime is that of punishment. An illegal act coupled with an evil mind (criminal intent or mens rea) still does not constitute a crime unless the law subjects it to a punishment. If a sign posted in the park states "Do not step on the grass" and you do it anyway, have you committed a criminal offense? Not unless there is a law that subjects that act to punishment. Otherwise it is simply an improper or inconsiderate act.

The punishment requirement, more than any of the others, helps us differentiate between crimes (which are subject to punishments) and **torts,** civil wrongs for which the law does not prescribe punishment but merely grants the injured party the right to recover damages.

The nature and severity of punishments also help us differentiate between grades of crime. Most penal codes recognize three degrees of severity: **Felonies** are severe crimes, subject to punishments of a year or more in prison or to capital punishment. **Misdemeanors** are less severe crimes, subject to a maximum of 1 year in jail. (For crimes of both grades, fines can also be imposed as punishments.) **Violations** are minor offenses, normally subject only to fines.

THE DEFENSES: EXCUSES

When we turn to the various defenses recognized by law, we discover that each defense simply claims that one or more of the seven basic constituent elements of the crime does not exist. In other words, what at first glance may indicate that a crime was committed—a dead body or a burned building—may turn out not to be a crime after all because, for example, the perpetrator lacked criminal intent or the law granted the actor the right to do what he or she did so that the "illegality" is absent.

A recent analysis by legal scholar and defense counsel Alan Dershowitz demonstrated that in recent years clever defense attorneys have worked 53 new defenses into the legal vocabulary, such as the "black rage defense" or the "everyone-does-it" defense.[16] In October 1999, a defense lawyer in Laramie, Wyoming, posed yet another defense, the "gay panic" defense, for the defendant charged with the killing of Matthew Shepherd. This defense widely publicized the murder trial of a man who alleged that Shepherd had made a gay approach to him. The judge rejected the defense, and the defendant was convicted. (Yet his life was spared after the victim's parents asked the court for mercy.) None of the defenses just noted is a proper legal defense, though all may conjure up pity and compassion. A defense, technically, simply

The killing scene of Matthew Shepherd.

argues the absence of one or more of the seven constituent elements of crime.

The Insanity Defense

On March 30, 1981, a young man stood in front of the Hilton Hotel in Washington, D.C., and mixed with the crowd that had assembled to greet President Reagan. As the president and his entourage left the hotel, the young man drew a revolver and fired several shots, wounding the president, White House Press Secretary James Brady, a secret service agent, and a District of Columbia police officer.[17] All survived, but Brady was permanently disabled.

The young man turned out to be John W. Hinckley, Jr., who had become fascinated with the actress Jodie Foster. She had appeared in a movie that featured a deranged taxi driver who armed himself and killed a political candidate. Hinckley seemed to follow this script: He believed his only hope of winning Miss Foster's admiration lay in killing the president. Hinckley pleaded not guilty by reason of insanity. That plea amounts to saying: "Whatever happened, I am not guilty because I suffered from a mental illness that made me incapable of committing the crime you have charged me with."

In its modern form, the insanity defense was formulated by the House of Lords, following a case that was not very different from Hinckley's. Daniel M'Naghten was obsessed by the idea that the prime minister, Sir Robert Peel, wanted to destroy the liberties of English subjects. In 1829, when Peel was home secretary, with responsibility for security and internal affairs, he created a police force, and in the 1830s and 1840s he used the police to suppress public

John W. Hinckley, Jr., who attempted to assassinate President Reagan in March 1981, holds a pistol to his head in this self-portrait. His defense of insanity at his trial was successful, and he was medically confined to St. Elizabeth Hospital, Washington, D.C. As of 1999, Hinckley was permitted community visits, under guard.

The trial of Daniel McNaughten, whose name is perpetuated in the famous rules on murders by lunatics

M'Naghten, obsessed with the idea that Sir Robert Peel was destroying the liberty of Englishmen by creating a police force, stalked Sir Robert but killed his secretary by mistake. He was acquitted of murder by reason of insanity.

dissent. M'Naghten joined a campaign against Sir Robert. As a consequence of these activities, he became convinced that Sir Robert was spying on and persecuting him. When M'Naghten could no longer stand the pressure of his obsession, he traveled to London and loitered around 10 Downing Street, the prime minister's official residence.

M'Naghten's opportunity came on Friday, January 20, 1843. He shot into the back of the person he thought was Sir Robert. The victim was actually the prime minister's private secretary, Edward Drummond. A few days later Drummond died of the gunshot wounds. The trial of Daniel M'Naghten became a cause célèbre (a notorious case), and aristocratic ladies and gentlemen were frequently in attendance at court.[18] M'Naghten was acquitted by reason of insanity.[19]

The M'Naghten Test After M'Naghten's acquittal the question of insanity was debated in the House of Lords, which is also England's highest court. It formulated the now famous M'Naghten rules:

> The jurors ought to be told in all cases that every man is to be presumed to be sane, and to possess a sufficient degree of reason to be responsible for his crimes, until the contrary is proved to their satisfaction; and that, to establish a defense on the ground of insanity, it must be clearly proved that, at the time

of the committing of the act, the party accused was labouring under such a defect of reason, from disease of the mind, as not to know the nature and quality of the act he was doing; or if he did know it, that he did not know he was doing what was wrong.[20]

This test of insanity can be reduced to the following formula. As a result of mental illness, the accused either:

1. Did not know the nature and quality of his act; that is, the voluntary act requirement was not fulfilled.

Or:

2. Did not know that the act was wrong; that is, the mens rea requirement was not fulfilled.

In either case there can be no crime.[21]

The debate about the M'Naghten test has raged for a century and a half. Some courts have misunderstood the test, believing that the only criterion for insanity was whether the defendant knew the difference between right and wrong. They called it the "right-wrong test." Others thought a test that focuses only on what a person knows fails to capture the complexity of the human mind and its processes.

The Irresistible Impulse Test Imagine a case in which the defendant "knows" perfectly well what he is doing and understands that what he is doing is wrong. But the defendant contends that somehow he lost control over his actions; that is, he lost the power to choose between right and wrong. Some process in his mind compelled him to do what he did. To deal with that kind of situation, some American courts in the second half of the nineteenth century added another component to the M'Naghten rules: If as a result of mental illness the accused was unable to control his or her actions, then he or she must be acquitted. Such loss of self-control has been called an "irresistible impulse."[22]

The Durham or Product Test Judge David Bazelon's opinion in *Durham v. United States* in 1954 developed a new insanity test, partly based on an old New Hampshire case.[23] Under the Durham rule, the defendant was to be acquitted if the crime was the product of mental disease or defect. As soon as the defendant introduced some evidence of disease or defect, the prosecution had to prove the contrary beyond a reasonable doubt. Of all the tests, Durham has met with the most criticism and resistance from the legal community. In order to be acquitted by reason of insanity under the Durham formulation, a defendant simply had to introduce "some" evidence that the crime charged was a "product of" mental illness; that is, a mental disease or defect had the effect of producing the crime. It then became virtually impossible for the prosecution to disprove "some evidence" and the resulting "product."

The Durham or "product" test allowed the medical profession to determine what was included among mental diseases or defects. The list of diseases and defects grew longer and longer. Ultimately, the U.S. Court of Appeals for the District of Columbia, in *United States v. Brawner*, abolished the Durham test in favor of the American Law Institute (A.L.I.) test.[24] Today the Durham test is used in only one jurisdiction: Maine.

The A.L.I. Test The Model Penal Code of the American Law Institute (1962) includes an insanity test that incorporates features of the M'Naghten rules and irresistible impulse. Under this test:

> [A] person is not responsible for criminal conduct if at the time of such conduct as a result of mental

disease or defect he lacks substantial capacity either to appreciate the criminality [wrongfulness] of his conduct or to conform his conduct to the requirements of law.[25]

The special feature of this compromise is that the test leads to an acquittal when the defendant lacks "substantial capacity," whereas M'Naghten is frequently understood as requiring a total lack of capacity. The A.L.I. test is now used in about half of the American states.

Crime Surfing

www.abanet.org

Although criminal law is basically conservative, it does, nevertheless, change. To know more about current developments in criminal law, see the website of the American Bar Association— Criminal Justice section.

The New Federal Test Let us return to the Hinckley case. The acquittal of Hinckley by reason of insanity caused the same kind of public outcry that M'Naghten's acquittal had caused nearly a century and a half earlier. At the time of the Hinckley case, the District of Columbia was using the A.L.I. test. In reaction to Hinckley's acquittal, Congress for the first time debated what the insanity defense should be for the federal courts, just as the House of Lords in 1843 had discussed the same question following M'Naghten's acquittal.

Congress came to the conclusion that the defendant should be acquitted by reason of insanity if "at the time of the commission of the act the defendant, as a result of a severe mental disease or defect, was unable to appreciate the nature and quality or wrongfulness of his act."[26] The new federal test returned to the idea that mental illness, if severe enough, cancels a defendant's criminal act (appreciating the nature and quality) or criminal intent (appreciating the wrongfulness of the act).

The debate about the insanity defense— better called the defense of incapacity for reasons of mental illness—is mostly of academic concern. In practice, this defense is rarely made and even more rarely reaches the jury. A study of 953,000 felony indictment dockets in seven states, for a 4-1/2 year period each, demonstrated that 7299 of those indictees raised the insanity defense, and only 2220 of those who did were acquitted by reason of insanity.[27] Despite the statistical infrequency of the insanity defense, some legislatures have abolished it and others are planning to do so, out of fear that no matter how few such defendants may be, a "guilty" one might go free. When a Montana prisoner claimed that the abolition of the insanity defense is unconstitutional, the Supreme Court refused to hear the case, thereby allowing the states to abolish the insanity defense.[28] Of course, if there is no insanity defense as such, the logical consequence is that the prosecution would have to introduce evidence beyond a reasonable doubt in any case where the defendant has raised doubt about his or her capacity to have formed the requisite actus reus or mens rea.

Guilty but Mentally Ill

A growing number of states have found yet another way to deal with troublesome insanity cases. They have added to the three available verdicts—guilty, not guilty, not guilty by reason of insanity—a fourth one: guilty but mentally ill (in some states, guilty but insane). This somewhat illogical verdict is considered appropriate when a defendant suffers from a mental disease that is not severe enough to warrant acquittal by reason of insanity. It acknowledges the defendant's guilt, and at the same time recognizes as a mitigating factor the presence of a significant but not disabling mental disorder. In practice it permits a guilty verdict for a defendant who, by reason of insanity, has acted without the requisite criminal intent.

Both the abolition of the insanity defense and the verdict "guilty but insane" have two negative consequences: (1) Those who by virtue of mental illness could not formulate the requisite criminal intent are nevertheless condemned as "guilty"; (2) mentally ill persons wind up in prison, rather than psychiatric care facilities which would be far better able to treat them successfully.[29] As might have been expected, the combination of a finding of criminal guilt, but also of insanity, has led to considerable confusion for jurors; nor have acquittals been reduced.[30]

The Intoxication Defense

Can anything other than mental illness affect the mind to such an extent that the accused does not have the required guilty mind or could not fulfill the act requirement? The most prominent example is intoxication, whether by alcohol or by drugs.

In colonial times, the Puritans were extremely averse to excusing the actions of those who drank to excess. In fact, drunkenness itself was an offense. But over time, and as the composition of the population changed, American law changed. The clearest example is "involuntary" intoxication. Suppose that, after taking a prescription drug, a person becomes so disoriented and confused that she loses the capacity to act rationally or to form a criminal intent. Suppose that she then commits a crime. All courts would acquit an involuntarily intoxicated defendant who lacked the capacity to form the required guilty mind. But such cases are extremely rare.

Let us now look at situations in which a perpetrator is voluntarily intoxicated. This is a common problem (as we shall see in Chapter 14). According to a 1991 study of state prison inmates, 49 percent of all inmates were under the influence of drugs, alcohol, or both drugs and alcohol at the time they committed their offense.[31] These figures tell us that alcohol and drugs play an important role in crime. They do not tell us much about the role an intoxicant may have played in any given case. Among those who have acted while under the influence of drugs, we find addicts who have committed offenses to pay for their habits. We also know that most persons who have committed crimes after drinking alcohol are likely to have experienced a lowering of inhibitions induced by the alcohol they drank. These perpetrators might not have acted violently had they not been under the influence of alcohol.

Voluntary intoxication is recognized in most states as a defense of sorts. Occasionally, it may exonerate a defendant if it negates mens rea, but most often it merely reduces the degree of crime charged—from murder in the first degree to murder in the second degree, for example. It is as if the law has retained its original Puritan imprint: Drunkenness is bad, and people who

drink and violate the law do not deserve much leniency.

Infancy

The common law recognized early on that children of tender age cannot "act" in any meaningful way. (Commonly, children below 1 year of age cannot even walk.) Nor can they form "criminal intent" (or mens rea) in any meaningful way. Tantrums may show anger, but they are not a sensible indication of intent to inflict harm. When it comes to causing death or near death, it is questionable whether an infant understands the meaning of death. It would be futile to take young children before a court in order to determine, in each case, whether they had "acted" with the requisite criminal intent. Infants should be recognized as beyond the reach of the criminal law, and left to the custody and care of parents or guardians.

The common law drew the line at age 7, by inventing the defense of "infancy." This age coincides, generally, with beginning school and thus socialization. Under common law the upper limit of infancy was drawn at age 14: Those 14 and older were subject to full adult criminal liability. Again, this age generally coincided with the end of public schooling and entrance into the adult world of work. The period between 7 and 14 was divided into two phases: From 7 to 10-1/2, children were presumed to be incapable of forming a (meaningful, adult-like) criminal intent—but in specific cases the prosecution was allowed to prove the contrary. From 10-1/2 to 14, children were presumed to be capable of forming a criminal intent, but it might be established, on the child's behalf, that this particular child was too immature to form a criminal intent.

In the "munchkin" case with which we started this chapter, the common law simply would not have allowed an inquiry into whether the child could "act" or form a criminal intent. The munchkin, no matter how nasty a little character he may be, was deemed beyond the reach of the criminal law.

Mistake of Fact

A restaurant patron goes to the coatrack to retrieve his raincoat. He verifies the manufacturer's label, takes the coat, and heads toward the exit. Another patron, obviously agitated, jumps up and grabs the coat taker. "You stole my coat!" he shouts. The first man is greatly embarrassed. It turns out that the coat is not his. But is he a thief?

To be a thief, as we shall see in Chapter 12, one has to intend to deprive someone else of his or her property. That is the mens rea requirement. In this instance, did the first patron intend to deprive the owner of his property? No. He is not a thief, because he had no awareness of wrongdoing. That is the essence of the defense of mistake of fact. If there is no mens rea, there is no crime.[32]

Mistake or Ignorance of Law

At this point let us return to Ms. Lambert. Recall that Ms. Lambert had no idea she was doing something wrong when she failed to register as an ex-convict in Los Angeles. Yet a jury convicted her, and the court fined her $250. But does it make any sense to punish Ms. Lambert for what she did, or rather, for what she didn't do? What conceivable purpose could punishment possibly serve under these circumstances?

It is clear that she had no mens rea—no guilty mind—and thus did not commit a crime. But her mistake was not one of fact. Rather, she acted under ignorance of law, and ignorance of the law is no defense, according to an ancient common law maxim. It will be recalled that in the extreme circumstances of Ms. Lambert's case, the Supreme Court ultimately granted her a defense of ignorance of law, and it recognized ignorance of law even in the far less extreme Ratzlaf case.

Obviously, the idea that ignorance or mistake of law is no defense made good sense when the criminal law was restricted to crimes such as clubbing somebody over the head or slaughtering somebody else's cow. People could not claim they did not know that what they had done was forbidden. But times have changed, and who now can know all the laws? Even attorneys often have to do extensive research to find out if and how something is covered by criminal law. And if we all were to refrain from doing anything until we had legal advice, life would come to a standstill. Yet most courts perpetuate the fiction that "everybody is presumed to know the law."

THE DEFENSES: JUSTIFICATIONS

All the defenses discussed so far have one common ingredient: They simply negate the existence of the crime charged because the defendant, in effect, alleges that as a result of some internal or external condition, his or her mind did not participate in the behavior, so he or she did not commit the required act or form the guilty mind. In the next group of defenses the defendant fulfills all the act and intent requirements, and still the law does not impose criminal liability: The act is no longer prohibited by law, since the law itself gives the actor permission to act in exceptional situations, or even demands such action.[33]

Duress

A robber approaches a bank teller with the following demand: "Your money or your life!" A simple choice. The teller probably reaches into the drawer and hands over the cash. Is the teller guilty of larceny or embezzlement? It is not her money. Her job as a teller does not give her the right to steal, to give away, or to embezzle funds entrusted to her.

To deal with such situations, the law has established the defense of duress:

> It is . . . [a] defense that the actor engaged in the conduct charged to constitute an offense because he was coerced to do so by the use of, or a threat to use, unlawful force against his person or the person of another, which a person of reasonable firmness in his situation would have been unable to resist.[34]

This defense applies when the actor has done something the law prohibits. The bank teller took money entrusted to her and gave it to someone else. She was not authorized to do so. All the elements of a crime are there. But the teller had no choice. And that is precisely the point. The law recognizes that we cannot be expected to yield our lives, our limbs, the safety of our relatives, our houses, or our property when we are confronted by a criminal threat that forces us to violate a law. But there is a general requirement that the evil that threatens the actor ("Your money or your life!") and the evil created by the actor (handing over the bank's cash) be commensurate, that is, not out of proportion.

Necessity

As a general rule, necessity is a defense to a criminal charge when one has violated a law in the reasonable belief that the act was necessary to avoid an imminent and greater harm. Suppose two hikers are surprised by a snowstorm. They stumble upon a vacation cottage. Under the rule of necessity, they may break into and enter the cottage and use its provisions to stay alive.

If the necessity defense is to apply, the paramount threat must emanate from a force other than a human aggressor. The cause is, as it has been called, an "act of God"—a storm, a fire, a shipwreck. (If the source of the threat is a human aggressor, the defense is duress.)[35]

The question that has caused the most trouble is whether the defense of necessity ever permits the taking of an innocent life. Courts in England and the United States have reached contrasting solutions. English law does not permit the taking of an innocent life, even under dire necessity. American law permits the taking of innocent lives under certain conditions. A person who has fulfilled all legal obligations may sacrifice innocent human life, by random-lot selection, in order to save more lives.

Public Duty

Jus is the Latin word for law. Thus *justifications* are instances in which the law itself has created a counterlaw. The law prohibits an act; the counterlaw commands or authorizes it (see Table 10.1).

Two cases of lives sacrificed to save others after a shipwreck show the difference between the American and English approaches to necessity as a defense. The descriptions below are from *Outlaws of the Ocean*.(1)

THE AMERICAN CASE

The American packet [passenger vessel] *William Brown* was en route from Liverpool to Philadelphia with a shipload of 65 Scottish and Irish immigrants when she struck an iceberg on April 19, 1841, 250 miles southeast of Race, Newfoundland. She sank rapidly in a howling nor'easter. . . . The first mate and eight sailors manned the longboat, filling it with thirty-two passengers. Even while the longboat was shoving off, they saw the *William Brown* go down, with the remaining passengers screaming, praying, and disappearing in the waves. . . . The first mate managed to keep the longboat afloat, but the seas and wind grew worse. The sea cock plug was lost, and the boat took on more and more water. The crew bailed as much as they could. The first mate shouted to his fellow sailors, "This work won't do. Help me, God. Men, go to work." Finally, the sailors obeyed, throwing a number of passengers overboard, being careful not to separate husband from wife, or mother from child. By such action the longboat was saved, and all still aboard were rescued by a passing vessel.

Holmes, one of the sailors, was tried on a murder charge and found guilty of manslaughter, but only because, as the court said, he had failed to exercise his duties toward passengers by throwing some of them overboard indiscriminately rather than by casting lots. . . . Unlike English law, American law recognizes the defense of necessity in taking

The crew of the vessel Mignonette *in an open lifeboat after the loss of the ship, from sketches by Mr. Stephens, mate, who survived by killing and eating the cabin boy.*

of innocent lives on the high seas under extreme conditions.*

THE ENGLISH CASE

[T]hree shipwrecked sailors had been adrift in an open boat in the doldrums of the equatorial Atlantic. Their predicament had lasted for weeks. They had neither food nor water. They were delirious and the end appeared near, especially for the cabin boy, who was about to expire. In phantasmagoric exasperation, Dudley and Stephens killed the cabin boy and ate his flesh. This enabled them to survive for another few days until they were rescued by a passing vessel. The Court of Kings Bench convicted them of murder. Innocent human life must never be taken even to save one's own life, and even under the most dire necessity. . . . As Chief Justice Lord Coleridge stated: "We are often compelled to set up standards we cannot reach ourselves, and to lay down rules which we could not ourselves satisfy."†

Dudley and Stephens' [capital] sentences were commuted to the misdemeanor range, six months imprisonment.

Source

1. G. O. W. Mueller and Freda Adler, *Outlaws of the Ocean: The Complete Book of Contemporary Crime on the High Seas* [New York: Hearst Marine Books (William Morrow), 1985], pp. 217–218.

Questions for Discussion

1. What other defenses might have applied in these cases? Self-defense? Public duty? Duress? Insanity?
2. Which view of necessity as a defense do you support, the American or the British? Explain your position.

United States v. Holmes, I Wall Jr. I, 26 Fed. Cas. 360 (U.S. Cir. Ct., E.D. Pa., 1842).
†*Regina v. Dudley and Stephens,* 14 Q.B.D. 273 (1884).

TABLE 10.1 Law Prohibition and Counterlaw Justifications

Law Prohibition	Counterlaw Justification
The law prohibits the taking of life (criminal homicide).	The counterlaw requires execution of a convict sentenced to capital punishment.
	The counterlaw permits the shooting of a fleeing felon who is armed and constitutes a threat to life.
The law prohibits the taking of property (as in larceny).	The counterlaw allows impoundment of an illegally parked car.
The law prohibits the seizure of a person (as in false imprisonment or kidnapping).	The counterlaw requires the arrest of a suspect on probable cause.

By far the most frequent justification defense is use of force in law enforcement. Law enforcement officers may use as much force as necessary, for example, to effect an arrest, but no more. The use of deadly force is subject to severe restrictions. Law enforcement officers who use more force than necessary are likely to be committing a criminal offense, such as assault and battery, or a civil rights violation under federal law, as was demonstrated by the federal conviction of the officers who beat Rodney King in Los Angeles.

Self-Defense, Defense of Others, Defense of Property

On the Saturday before Christmas in 1984, Bernhard H. Goetz entered a subway car at the IRT station at Seventh Avenue and Fourteenth Street in Manhattan. He sat down close to four young men in their late teens. One of them offered a "How are ya"; then he approached Goetz and asked for $5. At that point Goetz pulled out a .38-caliber revolver and shot all four youths (one in the back).[36]

Few cases have ignited as much controversy as the Goetz case. Some people saw Goetz as an avenging angel, the city dweller who constantly suffers from crime and the fear of crime. Others labeled him a vigilante. Or was he simply the meek underdog, as his appearance suggested, trying to defend himself against yet another attack on the subway? He could have been any one of those. Goetz was charged with attempted murder, assault, and illegal possession of a weapon. In legal terms, the case simply raised the question of the right to use force, even deadly force, in self-defense, as well as the extent to which the defense still exists if the actor is mistaken about the actual threat that confronts him.

It is safe to say that in most states a person can use as much force as is reasonably necessary to defend himself or herself against what appears to be an immediate threat of violence by another, as long as the following four elements are present:

- The person must have an "honest and reasonable belief" that the force is necessary.

Did Bernard Goetz use reasonable force? Clearly not, if we adopt an objective test. The average person of reasonable intelligence in a like situation would not have used deadly force. But did Goetz believe that the use of deadly force was necessary? Perhaps so.

- The person must believe that the harm threatened will be immediately forthcoming.
- The harm threatened must be unlawful.
- The force used must be reasonable—only as much as appears necessary under the circumstances.[37]

Let us return to the Goetz case. Did Goetz find himself in a life-threatening situation? We will never know. As it turned out, some of his victims had criminal records. They carried no firearms, only screwdrivers, which they said they used to pilfer vending machines. Objectively, it appears that Goetz was in no immediate physical danger. What, then, went on in his mind? He had earlier been the victim of a brutal mugging in similar circumstances. Like many other subway riders, he feared the predators who seemed to be ever present beneath the streets.

The law is very strict when it comes to the application of force in self-defense. The Model Penal Code decrees: "The use of force upon or toward another person is justifiable when the actor believes that such force is immediately necessary for the purpose of protecting himself against the use of unlawful force by such other person on the present occasion."(1)

In recent years an increasing number of women abused by their mates have resorted to deadly force. The law has treated such women leniently in some respects, harshly in others. To begin with, the standard of law is phrased in terms of "protecting himself." How will courts translate the "protecting himself" standard, based on centuries of experience with male self-defense, into a "protecting herself" standard? Lenore E. Walker's study of the battered woman syndrome permitted her to conclude:

> Occasionally (less than 15 percent of all homicides) a woman will kill her abuser while trying to defend herself or her children. Sometimes, she strikes back during a calm period, knowing that the tension is building towards another acute battering incident, where this time she may die. When examining the statistics, we find that more women than men are charged with first or second degree murder. There seems to be a sexist bias operating in which the courts find it more difficult to see justifiable or mitigating circumstances for women who kill. The now classic Broverman et al. (1970) studies demonstrated that the kinds of behaviors and emotions expressed when committing an aggressive act will be viewed as normal for men but not for women. On the other hand, a woman's violence is more likely to be found excusable, if her insanity under the law can be demonstrated. Any changes in the insanity laws will probably have the greatest impact on women and other assault victims who reach a breaking point and no longer appreciate the wrongfulness of their action and/or can no longer refrain from an overpowering impulse to survive.

In most states' criminal codes, self-defense is defined as the justifiable

Minouche Kandel, attorney for the California Coalition of Battered Women in Prison, holds up the clemency petition for imprisoned women who have killed their batterers. News conference May 7, 1996, San Francisco.

commission of a criminal act by using the least amount of force necessary to prevent imminent bodily harm which needs only to be reasonably perceived as about to happen. The perception of how much force is necessary must also be reasonable. Such a definition works against women because they are not socialized to use physical force, are rarely equal to a man in size, strength, or physical training, and may have learned to expect more injury with inadequate attempts to repel a man's attack. Thus, some courts have ruled it would be reasonable for a woman to defend herself with a deadly weapon against a man armed only with the parts of his body he learned to use as a deadly weapon. Courts also have been allowing evidence to account for the cumulative effects of repeated violence in self-defense and diminished-capacity assertions. Expert witness testimony has been admitted in many states to help explain the reasonableness of such perceptions.(2)

It would be rash to conclude that the penal codes need immediate reform to protect women who kill in perceived self-defense. But it is reasonable to expect that penal code reformers review the entirety of penal codes to see that men and women are covered and protected equally, with particular consideration of contemporary life situations.

Sources

1. American Law Institute, Model Penal Code, sec. 3.04.
2. Lenore E. Walker, *The Battered Woman Syndrome* (New York: Springer, 1984), pp. 142–143.

Questions for Discussion

1. Should the difference between men and women in the way threats of violence are perceived be taken into account in self-defense cases?
2. How should the constant threat of violence a battered woman experiences be interpreted in terms of the law's "present occasion" requirement for self-defense?

The defense made a strong case that Goetz was in fear of his life. The legal question was whether he should be judged by a subjective standard (whether he felt in fear of his life) or by an objective standard (whether *a reasonable person* in the same situation would have been in fear of his or her life). The jury resolved this issue by acquitting him of all charges except one: illegal possession of a handgun. But in a subsequent civil suit against Goetz by the paralyzed victim, with a far lesser proof requirement, a jury awarded a multimillion-dollar civil damage award. It was never paid because, in 1996, Goetz was adjudicated a bankrupt.

The right to use reasonable force, and if necessary deadly force, extends to the defense of others. In most jurisdictions, a defender can use as much force on behalf of another as he or she could have used in self-defense. Of course, such defenders must reasonably believe that if they were in the other person's position, they would have the right to defend themselves, and the amount of force used must be necessary. Some states require, in addition, that the person being assisted must also have the right to use force, regardless of the defender's perception.

The law views the protection of property and human life differently (Table 10.2). With few exceptions, the right of self-defense is far more extensive than the right of defense of property. The general rule in this area is that nondeadly force may be used, typically after some request has been made to desist, when it is necessary to stop an intrusion. When there is some indication that the intruder intends to commit a felony on the premises, and a warning to desist has been issued and ignored, deadly force may be used.

ATTEMPT AND ACCESSORYSHIP

The doctrines pertaining to defenses are not the only doctrines of criminal law used to determine criminal charges. Foremost among the remaining doctrines is the one pertaining to attempted crimes. What should the law do to someone who tries to commit a crime but does not succeed? Under early common law, at-

tempts to commit crimes were not considered crimes, because the actus reus was not completed. But a person who tries to complete a crime surely has the same mens rea and thus the same culpability as one who succeeds. Should the would-be perpetrator be treated differently just because he or she did not succeed? In 1784, it was decided in England that an attempt to commit a felony was indeed a crime.[38] That case laid the foundation for our present conceptualization of **criminal attempt:** "an act or omission constituting a substantial step in a course of conduct planned to culminate in the commission of a crime."[39]

The common law also created a sophisticated system for determining the liability of all persons involved in the commission of a crime. When, where, and how the various parties could be prosecuted, and the use of evidence at trial, depended on the type of participation.

Today most states recognize only **principals** (all persons who commit an offense by their own conduct) and **accomplices** (all those who aid the perpetrator). That system has not solved all the problems, because the line between committing a crime and aiding in its commission is a fine one. Though principals and accomplices are usually considered equally culpable, in practice, judges often impose lighter sentences on accomplices.

TYPOLOGIES OF CRIME

The general term "crimes" covers a wide variety of types of crimes, with their own distinct features. Murder and arson, for example, both are crimes. They have the same seven general elements, including a criminal intent (mens rea) and a harm element. But these elements take different forms in different crimes. In murder the criminal intent takes the form of intending to kill another human being wrongfully, while in arson the intent is that of wrongfully burning the property of another. Lawyers and criminologists have searched for a system of grouping the many types of crimes into coherent, rational categories, for ease of understanding, of learning, and of finding them in the law books, and for purposes of studying them from both a legal and a criminological perspective. Such categorizations are called *typologies*.

TABLE 10.2   Justifiable Use of Deadly Force Even if Life Is Not Threatened*

State	To Protect Dwelling	To Protect Property	Against Specific Crime
		Deadly Force May Be Justified	
Alabama	Yes	No	Arson, burglary, rape, kidnapping, robbery
Alaska	Yes	No	Actual commission of felony
Arizona	Yes	No	Arson, burglary, kidnapping, aggravated assaults
Arkansas	Yes	No	Felonies (defined by statute)
California	Yes	No	Unlawful or forcible entry
Colorado	Yes	No	Felonies
Connecticut	Yes	No	Any violent crime
Delaware	Yes	No	Felonious activity
District of Columbia	Yes	No	Felony
Florida	Yes	No	Forcible felony
Georgia	Yes	Yes	Actual commission of a forcible felony
Hawaii	Yes	Yes	Felonious property damage, burglary, robbery, etc.
Idaho	Yes	Yes	Felonious breaking and entering
Illinois	Yes	Yes	Forcible felony
Indiana	Yes	No	Unlawful entry
Iowa	Yes	Yes	Breaking and entering
Kansas	Yes	No	Breaking and entering, including attempts
Kentucky	No	No	—
Louisiana	Yes	No	Unlawful entry, including attempts
Maine	Yes	No	Criminal trespass, kidnapping, rape, arson
Maryland	No	No	—
Massachusetts	No	No	—
Michigan	Yes	No	Case-by-case basis
Minnesota	Yes	No	Felony
Mississippi	Yes	—	Felony, including attempts
Missouri	No	No	—
Montana	Yes	Yes	Any forcible felony
Nebraska	Yes	No	Unlawful entry, kidnapping, rape
Nevada	Yes	—	Actual commission of felony
New Hampshire	Yes	—	Felony
New Jersey	Yes	No	Burglary, arson, robbery
New Mexico	Yes	Yes	Any felony
New York	Yes	No	Burglary, arson, kidnapping, robbery, including attempts
North Carolina	Yes	No	Intending to commit a felony
North Dakota	Yes	No	Any violent felony
Ohio	—	—	—
Oklahoma	Yes	No	Felony within a dwelling
Oregon	Yes	—	Burglary in a dwelling, including attempts
Pennsylvania	Yes	—	Burglary or criminal trespass
Rhode Island	Yes	—	Breaking or entering
South Carolina	No	No	—
South Dakota	Yes	—	Burglary, including attempts
Tennessee	Yes	No	Felony
Texas	Yes	No	Burglary, robbery, or theft at night
Utah	Yes	—	Felony
Vermont	Yes	—	Forcible felony
Virginia	No	No	—
Washington	No	No	—
West Virginia	Yes	No	Any felony
Wisconsin	No	No	—
Wyoming	No	No	—

*All states allow ultimate recourse to deadly force when life is in immediate danger.

Source: U.S. Department of Justice, Report to the Nation on Crime and Justice, 2d ed. (Washington, D.C.: U.S. Government Printing Office, 1988).

Here are some examples: The ancient Romans classified their crimes as those against the gods and those against other human beings. As late as the eighteenth century, some English lawyers simply listed crimes alphabetically. The French of the early nineteenth century created a typology with three categories: serious crimes (which we would call felonies), medium serious crimes (which we would call misdemeanors), and crimes of a petty character (which we would call violations). The more serious crimes were grouped into categories based on the harm those crimes entailed, such as harm against life, against physical integrity, against honor, against property, and so on.

Nowadays the French categorization is generally accepted worldwide, although lawyers and criminologists may differ on the desirability of lumping various crime types together into categories. Lawyers, after all, may be much more interested in the procedural consequences that flow from the categorizations, while criminologists may be much more concerned with criminological implications for studying different types of perpetrators and devising schemes of crime prevention.

There are also political considerations in devising a typology. For example, the criminal codes of the former communist countries had large categories of political crimes, which were given the most prominent place in those codes. They included many crimes that in Western democracies are grouped in other categories, such as property crimes or crimes against the person, or that may have no counterpart at all.

The typology we have chosen for this book seeks to accommodate both the established legal typology—for example, that used in the Model Penal Code—and the criminological objectives that are so important for the study of crime from a sociological and behavioral perspective. These categories are:

- Violent crimes.
- Crimes against property.
- Organizational criminality.
- Drug-, alcohol-, and sex-related crimes.

We discuss these categories in the following chapters.

REVIEW

All crimes can be easily understood if we learn what it is that all crimes have in common. Based on the analysis of Anglo-American common law, scholars have discovered that all crimes are characterized by seven general principles (sometimes called ingredients or elements). Thus, a crime needs (1) an act (actus) that (2) is in violation of law (reus), that (3) causes (4) the harm identified by the law, and that is committed with (5) criminal intent (mens rea, or a guilty mind). In addition, (6) the criminal act must concur with the guilty mind, and (7) the act must be subject to punishment.

Defenses to crime simply negate the existence of one of the seven basic elements, usually the mens rea (as in mistake of fact and insanity), sometimes even the act itself (as in some insanity defenses), and sometimes the unlawfulness of the act (as in justification defenses). These defenses have been grouped into excuses and justifications.

Additional propositions of law explain why and when offenders may incur criminal liability when they try to commit a crime but do not succeed (attempts), and how liability is imposed when several persons act jointly or help each other (accessoryship).

Crimes are usually grouped into categories by severity or type of harm (typologies).

YOU BE THE CRIMINOLOGIST

Having been employed by a victims advocacy group, in order to cut down on victimizations, devise a scheme to make fellow citizens more responsive to the plight of those being criminally attacked. Would you make it a duty to help a person in need or in trouble? Why or why not?

KEY TERMS

The numbers next to the terms refer to the pages on which the terms are defined.

accomplices (281)

criminal attempt (281)

felonies (271)

mens rea (270)

misdemeanors (271)

principals (281)

strict liability (270)

torts (271)

violations (271)

NOTES

1. Anastasia Toufexis and J. Howard Green, "From the Fists of Babes—Can a Six-Year-Old Be Prosecuted for Attempted Murder? A Tragic Beating Tests the Limits of Law," *Time*, May 6, 1996, p. 38; Nadine Joseph, "Just 'A Little Munchkin'—Did a Boy, 6, Try to Kill a Baby?" *Newsweek*, May 6, 1996, p. 38.
2. Paul H. Robinson, "Are Criminal Codes Irrelevant?" *Southern California Law Review,* **68** (1994): 159–202.
3. The Anglo-American concept of crime was developed by a long line of distinguished legal scholars, as discussed in G. O. W. Mueller, *Crime, Law, and the Scholars* (London: Heinemann; Seattle: University of Washington Press, 1969).
4. Jerome Hall, *General Principles of Criminal Law,* 2d ed. (Indianapolis: Bobbs-Merrill, 1960).
5. American Law Institute, Model Penal Code, sec. 2.01(1). The American Law Institute, dedicated to law reform, is an association of some of the most prestigious American lawyers. Between 1954 and 1962 this group sought to codify the best features of the penal codes of the various states. The resultant Model Penal Code (MPC) has had considerable influence on law reform in many states, and has been adopted nearly in full by New Jersey and Pennsylvania. We shall have frequent occasion to refer to the MPC as "typical" American criminal law. See also Gerhard O. W. Mueller, "The Public Law of Wrongs—Its Concepts in the World of Reality," *Journal of Public Law,* **10** (1961): 203–260; Michael Moore, *Act and Crime—The Philosophy of Action and Its Implications for Criminal Law* (Oxford: Clarendon Press, 1993).
6. *Robinson v. California,* 370 U.S. 660 (1962).
7. *Powell v. Texas,* 392 U.S. 514 (1968).
8. *State v. Palendrano,* 120 N.J. Super. 336, 293 A. 2d 747 (1972).
9. G. O. W. Mueller, "Causing Criminal Harm," in *Essays in Criminal Science,* ed. Mueller (South Hackensack, N.J.: Fred B. Rothman, 1961), pp. 167–214.
10. *Lambert v. California,* 355 U.S. 225 (1957). This decision must be approached with care. It does not stand for the proposition that ignorance of the law is an excuse. The Supreme Court was very careful to limit the scope of its decision to offenses by omission of adherence to regulations not commonly known, when the defendant in fact did not know—and had no means of knowing—of the prohibition.
11. G. O. W. Mueller, "On Common Law Mens Rea," *Minnesota Law Review,* **42** (1958): 1043–1104, at p. 1060.
12. *Ratzlaf v. U.S.,* 510 U.S. 135, 114 S. Ct. 655 (1994).
13. See Paul H. Robinson, "Should the Criminal Law Abandon the Actus Reus–Mens Rea Distinction?" in *Action and Value in Criminal Law,* ed. Stephen Shute, John Gardner, and Jeremy Harder (Oxford: Clarendon Press, 1993), pp. 187–211.
14. Wayne R. LaFave and Austin W. Scott, Jr., *Criminal Law* (St. Paul, Minn.: West, 1983), p. 222.
15. H. Lowell Brown, "Vicarious Criminal Liability of Corporations for the Acts of Their Employees and Agents," *Loyola Law Review,* **41** (1995): 279, 328–329.
16. Alan M. Dershowitz, *The Abuse Excuse and Other Cop-Outs, Sob Stories, and Evasions of Responsibility* (Boston: Little, Brown, 1994).
17. Peter W. Low, John Calvin Jeffries, Jr., and Richard J. Bonnie, *The Trial of John W. Hinckley, Jr.* (Mineola, N.Y.: Foundation Press, 1986).
18. Richard Moran, *Knowing Right from Wrong: The Insanity Defense of Daniel McNaughten* (New York: Free Press, 1981), is a fascinating discussion of the M'Naghten case. See also Bernard L. Diamond, "Isaac Ray and the Trial of Daniel M'Naghten," *American Journal of Psychiatry,* **112** (1956): 651–656.
19. In general, see Ralph Slovenko, *Psychiatry and Criminal Culpability* (New York: John Wiley, 1995); Michael L. Perlin, *The Jurisprudence of the Insanity Defense* (Durham, N.C.: Carolina Academic Press, 1994); Finbarr McAuley, *Insanity, Psychiatry and Criminal Responsibility* (Dublin: Round Hall Press, 1993; comparative in coverage).
20. *Daniel M'Naughten's Case,* 10 C.F. 200, 210–211, 8 Eng. Rep. 718, 722–723 (1843).

21. G. O. W. Mueller, "M'Naghten Remains Irreplaceable: Recent Events in the Law of Incapacity," *Georgetown Law Journal*, **50** (1961): 105–119. The literature on the law of insanity is extensive. Noteworthy recent works include Donald H. J. Herfmann, *The Insanity Defense: Philosophical, Historical, and Legal Perspectives* (Springfield, Ill.: Charles C Thomas, 1983); and Michael S. Moore, *Law and Psychiatry: Rethinking the Relationship* (New York: Cambridge University Press, 1984).

22. See *Parsons v. State*, 81 Ala. 577, 2 So. 854 (1887).

23. *Durham v. United States*, 214 F. 2d 862 (D.C. Cir. 1954); *States v. Pike*, 49 N.H. 399 (1869).

24. *United States v. Brawner*, 471 F. 2d 696 (D.C. Cir. 1972).

25. Model Penal Code, sec. 4.01.

26. 18 U.S. Code, sec. 17.

27. Carmen Cincione, "Revisiting the Insanity Defense: Contested or Consensus?" *Bulletin American Academy Psychiatry Law*, **24**(2) (1996):165–176.

28. *Cowan v. Montana*, 114 S. Ct. 1371 (Mem) (1994).

29. Henrik Belfrage, "Variability in Forensic-Psychiatric Decisions—Evidence for a Positive Crime Prevention Effect with Mentally Disordered Violent Offenders?" *Studies on Crime and Crime Prevention*, **4** (1995): 119–124.

30. Kurt M. Bumby, "Reviewing the Guilty but Mentally Ill Alternative: A Case of the Blind 'Pleading' the Blind," *Journal of Psychiatry and Law*, **2** (1993): 191–220.

31. Bureau of Justice Statistics, *Survey of State Prison Inmates, 1991* (Washington D.C.: U.S. Department of Justice, Office of Justice Programs, 1993), p. 26.

32. Paul H. Robinson, *Fundamentals of Criminal Law* (Boston: Little, Brown, 1988), pp. 287 ff.

33. On the disputed distinction between excuses and justifications, see Michael Louis Corrado, ed., *Justification and Excuse in the Criminal Law* (New York: Garland, 1994).

34. Basically, the defense is not available if the actor was at fault by placing himself in the situation: Model Penal Code, sec. 2.09(1).

35. Model Penal Code, Tentative Draft no. 8 (Philadelphia: American Law Institute, 1958), pp. 5–10.

36. For a fascinating legal and factual analysis of the case, see George P. Fletcher, *A Crime of Self-Defense: Bernhard Goetz and the Law on Trial* (New York: Free Press, 1988).

37. Suzanne Unisacke, *Permissible Killing: The Self-Defence Justification of Homicide* (Cambridge: Cambridge University Press, 1994).

38. *Rex v. Scofield* (1784 Cald. 402).

39. Model Penal Code, sec. 5.01(1) (c).

Review • You Be the Criminologist • Key Terms • Notes

CHAPTER 11
Violent Crimes

KEY TERMS

aggravated assault
assault
battery
felony murder
homicide
involuntary manslaughter
justifiable homicide
kidnapping
malice aforethought
manslaughter
mass murder
murder
negligent homicide
rape
robbery
serial murder
simple assault
sociopaths
stranger homicide
terrorism
victim precipitation
voluntary manslaughter

I'D ASK YOU TO HELP
GET GUNS OFF THE STREETS,
BUT I'M DEAD.

I'D ASK YOU TO HELP
GET GUNS OFF THE STREETS,
BUT I'M DEAD.

Vanessa Valerio, age 9, was killed by a burglar armed with a .22 caliber gun. It only took one gun to destroy this life. It only takes one call to destroy a gun. Call 1-800-5 HELP 55

Donald White, age 17, was killed by another 17 year old with a 9mm semi-automatic handgun. It only took one gun to destroy this life. It only takes one call to destroy a gun. Call 1-800-5 HELP 55

To millions of Americans few things are more pervasive, more frightening, more real today than violent crime and the fear of being assaulted, mugged, robbed, or raped. The fear of being victimized by criminal attack has touched us all in some way. People are fleeing their residences in cities to the expected safety of suburban living. Residents of many areas will not go out on the street at night. Others have added bars and extra locks to windows and doors in their homes. Bus drivers in major cities do not carry cash because incidents of robbery have been so frequent. In some areas local citizens patrol the streets at night to attain the safety they feel has not been provided. . . .

There are numerous conflicting definitions of criminal violence as a class of behavior. Police, prosecutors, jurists, federal agents, local detention officials, and behavioral scientists all hold somewhat different viewpoints as to what constitute

acts of violence. All would probably agree, however, as the police reports make abundantly clear, that criminal violence involves the use of or the threat of force on a victim by an offender.[1]

The penal law defines types of violent crime, and each is distinguished by a particular set of elements. We concentrate on criminological characteristics: the frequency with which each type of violent crime is committed, the methods used in its commission, and its distribution through time and place. We also examine the people who commit the offense and those who are its victims. If we can determine when, where, and how a specific type of crime is likely to be committed, we will be in a better position to reduce the incidence of that crime by

devising appropriate strategies to prevent it.

We begin with homicide, since the taking of life is the most serious harm one human being can inflict on another. Serious attacks that fall short of homicide are assaults of various kinds, including serious sexual assault (rape) and the forceful taking of property from another person (robbery). Other patterns of violence are not defined as such in the penal codes but are so important in practice as to require separate discussion. Family-related violence and terrorism, both of which encompass a variety of crimes, fall into this category.

HOMICIDE

Homicide is the killing of one human being by another. Some homicides are sanctioned by law. In this category of **justifiable homicide,** we find homicides committed by law enforcement officers in the course of carrying out their duties (see Chapter 10), homicides committed by soldiers in combat, and homicides committed by a homeowner who has no recourse other than to kill an intruder who threatens the lives of family members. Criminologists are most interested in *criminal homicides*—unlawful killings, without justification or excuse. Criminal homicides are subdivided into three separate categories: murder, manslaughter, and negligent homicide.

Murder

At common law, **murder** was defined as the intentional killing of another person with **malice aforethought.** Courts have struggled with an exact definition of "malice." To describe it, they have used such terms as "evil mind" and "abandoned and malignant heart." Actually, malice is a very simple concept. It is the defendant's awareness that he or she had no right to kill but intended to kill anyway.[2]

Originally the malice had to be "aforethought": The person had to have killed after some contemplation, rather than on the spur of the moment. The concept eventually became meaningless because some courts considered even a few seconds sufficient to establish forethought. The dividing line between planned and spur-of-the-moment killings disappeared. But many legislators believed contemplation was an appropriate concept, because it allowed us to distinguish the various types of murder. They reintroduced it, calling it "premeditation and deliberation." A premeditated, deliberate, intentional killing became murder in the first degree; an intentional killing without premeditation and deliberation became murder in the second degree.

States that had the death penalty reserved it for murder in the first degree. Some state statutes listed particular means of committing murder as indicative of premeditation and deliberation, such as killing by poison or by lying in wait. More recently the charge of murder in the first degree has been reserved for the killing of a law enforcement officer or of a corrections officer and for the killing of any person by a prisoner serving a life sentence. Among the most serious forms of murder is *assassination*, the killing of a head of state or government or of an otherwise highly visible figure.

A special form of murder, **felony murder,** requires no intention to kill. It requires, instead, the intention to commit some other felony, such as robbery or rape, and the death of a person during the commission of, or flight from, that felony. Even accomplices are guilty of felony murder when one of their associates has caused a death. For example, while A and B are holding up a gas station attendant, A fires a warning shot, and the bullet ricochets and kills a passerby. Both A and B are guilty of felony murder. The rule originated in England centuries ago, when death sentences were imposed for all felonies, so it made no difference whether a perpetrator actually intended to kill or merely to rob. Most states today apply the felony murder rule only when the underlying felony is a life-endangering one, such as arson, rape, or robbery.

Manslaughter

Manslaughter is the unlawful killing of another person without malice. Manslaughter may be either voluntary or involuntary.

Voluntary Manslaughter Voluntary **manslaughter** is a killing committed intentionally but without malice—for example, in the heat of passion or in response to strong provocation. Persons who kill under extreme provocation cannot make rational decisions about whether they have a right to kill or not. They therefore act without the necessary malice.[3]

Just as passion, fright, fear, or consternation may affect a person's capacity to act rationally, so may drugs or alcohol. In some states a charge of murder may be reduced to voluntary manslaughter when the defendant was so grossly intoxicated as not to be fully aware of the implications of his or her actions. All voluntary-manslaughter cases have one thing in common: The defendant's awareness of the unlawfulness of the act was dulled or grossly reduced by shock, fright, consternation, or intoxication.

Yolanda Manuel, mother of seven-year-old sexual assault and murder victim Sherrice Iverson, speaks at a rally on U.C. Berkeley campus, 1998. The rally was staged to protest the presence, on the Berkeley campus, of sophomore David Cash, who watched and did nothing as a friend Jeremy Strohmeyer dragged Sherrice into a Las Vegas casino bathroom stall where he killed her.

Involuntary Manslaughter A crime is designated as **involuntary manslaughter** when a person has caused the death of another unintentionally but recklessly by consciously disregarding a substantial and unjustifiable risk that endangered another person's life. Many states have created an additional category, **negligent homicide,** to establish criminal liability for grossly negligent killing in situations where the offender assumed a lesser risk.

Manslaughter plays an increasingly prominent role in our society, with its high concentrations of population, high-tech risks, and chemical and even nuclear dangers. The reach of the crime of involuntary manslaughter was clearly demonstrated in the 1942 Coconut Grove disaster in Boston, in which 491 people perished because of a nightclub owner's negligence in cre-

ating fire hazards. The nightclub was overcrowded, it was furnished and decorated with highly flammable materials, and exits were blocked. The court ruled that a reasonable person would have recognized the risk. If the defendant is so "stupid" as not to have recognized the risk, he is nevertheless guilty of manslaughter.[4]

The Extent of Homicide

Social scientists who look at homicide have a different perspective from that of the legislators who define such crimes. Social scientists are concerned with rates and patterns of criminal activities. (See Table 11.1.)

Homicide Rates in the United States Today The American murder rate always has been high. It reached a peak in 1980 and has been declining erratically since then. In 1997, our population of just over 267 million experienced 18,209 murders and nonnegligent homicides (as reported to the police), or 6.8 per 100,000 of the population.[5] This is the lowest the murder rate has been since 1967, when the murder rate was 7 murders per 100,000 of the population. This rate is not equally distributed over the whole country: Murder rates are higher in the Southern and Western states (8 and 7 per 100,000, respectively) than in the Northeastern and Midwestern states (5 and 6 per 100,000, respectively).[6]

Your chance of becoming a murder victim is much higher if you are male than if you are female: Of all murder victims, 77 percent are male, 23 percent female. Age plays a role—nearly half of all murder victims are between the ages of 20 and 34; so does race—48 percent of all murder victims are white, 49 percent are black, and the remaining 3 percent are of other ethnic origins.[7]

Ninety-four percent of the black murder victims were slain by black offenders, and 85 percent of the white murder victims were killed by white offenders. Intentional criminal homicide apparently is an intraracial crime. But it is not an intragender crime. The data show that males were most often killed by males (88 percent), and 9 out of 10 female victims were murdered by males.[8]

The world continues to watch local law enforcement investigate JonBenet Ramsey's tragic death. Everyone, from her father, mother, and brother, is a suspect.

TABLE 11.1 Where Does Your State Rank According to Rates of Violent Crime (per 100,000 population)?

1996 Violent crime* Rank	State	Rate
United States, total		634.1
1	District of Columbia	2,469.8
2	Florida	1,051.0
3	South Carolina	996.9
4	Maryland	931.2
5	Louisiana	929.1
6	Illinois	886.2
7	California	862.7
8	New Mexico	840.6
9	Nevada	811.3
10	Tennessee	774.0
11	Alaska	727.7
12	New York	727.0
13	Delaware	668.3
14	Texas	644.4
15	Massachusetts	642.2
16	Georgia	638.7
17	Michigan	635.3
18	Arizona	631.5
19	Oklahoma	597.1
20	Missouri	590.9
21	North Carolina	588.1
22	Alabama	565.4
23	Indiana	537.0
24	New Jersey	531.5
25	Arkansas	524.3
26	Mississippi	488.3
27	Oregon	463.1
28	Nebraska	434.7
29	Pennsylvania	432.5
30	Washington	431.2
31	Ohio	428.7
32	Kansas	413.8
33	Connecticut	412.0
34	Colorado	404.5
35	Rhode Island	347.2
36	Virginia	341.3
37	Minnesota	338.8
38	Utah	331.9
39	Kentucky	320.5
40	Hawaii	280.6
41	Iowa	272.5
42	Idaho	267.2
43	Wisconsin	252.7
44	Wyoming	249.7
45	West Virginia	210.1
46	South Dakota	177.2
47	Montana	161.0
48	Maine	124.9
49	Vermont	121.2
50	New Hampshire	118.2
51	North Dakota	84.0

*Murder and nonnegligent manslaughter, robbery, aggravated assault, and forcible rape.

Source: Adapted from *Sourcebook of Criminal Justice Statistics, 1997* (Albany, New York: State University of New York at Albany, 1997), p. 273.

Homicide Rates over Time Researchers have asked what happens to homicide rates over time when the composition of the population changes. What is the effect, for example, of a change in the racial composition of a city? Roland Chilton, using data on offenses committed in Chicago between 1960 and 1980 and census data for those years, found that about 20 percent of the total increase in homicide rates could be explained by increases in the nonwhite male population.[9] The same correlation is found in most major cities in the United States. Chilton argues that the problem will remain because of the poverty and demoralization of the groups involved. We can even expect that it will get worse if municipal governments are unable to improve the schools, reduce unemployment, and extend social services.

In a 1996 article, "Work," sociologist William Julius Wilson explains why America's ghettos

have descended into "ever-deeper poverty and misery." According to him:

> For the first time in the 20th century, a significant majority of adults in many inner-city neighborhoods are not working in a typical week. Inner cities have always featured high levels of poverty, but the current levels of joblessness in some neighborhoods are unprecedented. For example, in the famous black-belt neighborhood of Washington Park on Chicago's South Side, a majority of adults had jobs in 1950; by 1990, only 1 in 3 worked in a typical week. High neighborhood joblessness has a far more devastating effect than high neighborhood poverty. A neighborhood in which people are poor but employed is different from a neighborhood in which people are poor and jobless. Many of today's problems in the inner-city neighborhoods—crime, family dissolution, welfare—are fundamentally a consequence of the disappearance of work.[10]

Until conditions change, what has been poignantly referred to as "the subculture of exasperation" will continue to produce a high homicide rate among nonwhite inner-city males.[11] Coramae Mann has found that although black women make up about 11 percent of the female population in the United States, they are arrested for three-fourths of all homicides committed by females. She argues that given such a disproportionate involvement in violent crime, one has to question whether the subculture of exasperation alone is entirely responsible.[12] But so few studies have been done on the subject that we cannot reach any definitive conclusion. Other investigators agree that homicide rates cannot be explained solely by such factors as poverty; the rates are also significantly associated with cultural approval of a resort to violence.

The Nature of Homicide

Let us take a closer look at killers and their victims and see how they are related to each other. In the 1950s Marvin Wolfgang studied homicide situations, perpetrators, and victims in the Philadelphia area. Victims and offenders were predominantly young black adults of low socioeconomic status. The offenses were committed in the inner city; they occurred primarily in the home of the victim or offender, on weekends, in the evening hours, and among friends or acquaintances.

Building on the pioneering work of Hans von Hentig,[13] Wolfgang found that many of the victims had actually initiated the social interaction that led to the homicidal response, in a direct or subliminal way. He coined the term **victim precipitation** for such instances, which may account for as many as a quarter to a half of all intentional homicides. In such cases it is the victim who, by insinuation, bodily movement, verbal incitement, or the actual use of physical force, initiates a series of events that results in his or her own death. For example:

> During an argument in which a male called a female many vile names, she tried to telephone the police. He grabbed the phone from her hands, knocked her down, kicked her, and hit her with a tire gauge. She ran to the kitchen, grabbed a butcher knife, and stabbed him in the stomach.[14]

A study by Richard Felson and Steven Messner found that victim precipitation is more often seen in cases where women kill their husbands as opposed to incidents in which men kill their wives. However, males tend to be more violent than females in their killing methods.[15]

Other studies have provided additional insight into the patterns of homicide. Robert Silverman and Leslie Kennedy demonstrated that gender relationships, age, means of commission of the act, and location vary with relational distance, from closest relatives (lovers, spouses) to total strangers.[16]

Margaret Zahn and Philip Sagi have developed a model that distinguishes among homicides on the basis of characteristics of victims, offenders, location, method of attack, and presence of witnesses. They conclude that all these characteristics and variables serve to differentiate four categories of homicides: (1) those within the family, (2) those among friends and acquaintances, (3) stranger homicides associated with

A mural made in honor of the memory of more than 140 children killed between 1995 and 2000 by a mass murderer in Pereira, Colombia

felonies, and (4) stranger homicides not associated with felonies.[17]

Stranger Homicides The rate of **stranger homicide**—a killing in which killer and victim have had no known previous contact—has increased by only 1 percent between 1992 (13 percent) and 1997 (14 percent).[18] Marc Riedel, however, found these stranger homicide rates to be considerably understated. The true figures, according to Riedel, ranged from 14 to 29 percent.[19] Furthermore, the impact of stranger homicides on the quality of urban life—especially the fear of crime they engender—is far greater than their relatively small numbers would suggest.[20]

Relatives and Acquaintances Most homicides occur among relatives and acquaintances.[21] One study found that 44 percent of the victims were in intimate relationships with their killers, 26 percent were friends and acquaintances, 11 percent were the offender's own children, and only 7.5 percent were strangers.[26] Of these homicides, those in which women killed their mates have received particular attention. Criminologists take special interest in the factors behind such crimes.[22] Researchers have found a high incidence of long-term abuse suffered by women

who subsequently kill their mates.[23] They also suggest that mate homicides are the result of a husband's efforts to control his wife and the wife's efforts to retain her independence.[24]

Other recent trends are also noteworthy: One study found an increase in women who kill in domestic encounters, more planned killings, and less acceptance of self-defense as a motive in such cases.[25] Children are also at risk of death at the hands of family members. Research suggests that as the age of the child victim increases, so does the level of violence used to fatally injure the child.[26] Also, the closer the family relation to the victim (e.g., mother and child), the more passive the form of homicide (e.g., asphyxiation or abandonment), whereas the more distant a relative is to the victim, the more violent the method used (e.g., stabbing).[27] In most murders of a child under age 15, a family member killed the child, while murder victims aged 15 to 17 are more likely to be killed by an acquaintance of the victim or by someone unknown to the law enforcement authorities.[28] Whether killed by a family member or an acquaintance, boys are more often the victims of violent deaths than are girls.[29]

Young and Old Perpetrators Not surprisingly, the very young and the elderly have low

homicide rates. In 1997, 183 homicide charges were placed against youngsters under 15, but this figure does not include the number of homicides in which the young killers were dealt with by juvenile courts or welfare agencies. Of the 18,290 persons of all ages arrested for homicide in 1997, 1731 were under 18. The elderly, too, are underrepresented among killers. People age 55 and older accounted for only 2.3 percent of all murders in 1997.[30]

Homicide without Apparent Motive In most homicides, the killer has a motive or a reason for killing the victim. Popular fiction tells us that detectives tend to consider a case solved if they can establish the motive. But research shows that in a substantial number of murders, the motive remains unclear. The "unmotivated" murderers are a puzzle—and they constitute 25 percent of all homicide offenders.

Though in most respects the killers without motive are similar to those who kill for a reason, they are more likely to have "(1) no history of alcohol abuse; (2) a recent release from prison; (3) claims of amnesia for the crime; (4) denial of the crime; and (5) a tendency to exhibit psychotic behavior following the crime and to be assessed not guilty of the crime due to mental illness."[31]

Mass and Serial Murders Criminological researchers have paid special attention to two types of murder that are particularly disturbing to the community: **serial murder,** the killing of several victims over a period of time, and **mass murder,** the killing of multiple victims in one event or in very quick succession. Between 1970 and 1993 U.S. police knew of approximately 125 cases of multiple homicides. The literature on the subject is enormous.[32] Some recent serial murderers have become infamous.

Theodore "Ted" Bundy, law student and former crime commission staff member, killed between 19 and 36 young women in the Northwestern states and Florida. David Berkowitz, the "Son of Sam," killed 6 young women in New York. Douglas Clark, the "Sunset Strip killer," killed between 7 and 50 prostitutes in Hollywood. The "Green River killer" of Seattle may have killed more than 45 victims. In the Midwest, Jeffrey Dahmer preserved, and took Polaroid photographs of, the mutilated body parts of his 11 to 17 victims; and on Long Island, Joel Rifkin collected souvenirs—a shoe, an earring, a driver's license—from the more than 13 streetwalkers he claimed as his victims.

In just 1 week in June 1996, two men, both suspected of being serial killers, were captured in New York City. Heriberto Seda, 28, lived a largely solitary life, except for those moments when he would emerge from the apartment he shared with his mother and sister. In two separate crime waves (in 1990, then again during 1992 and 1993), the self-proclaimed Zodiac Killer allegedly shot eight people, killing three (Chapter 4). Larry Stevens, 31, who also lived with his mother, would allegedly trick old people into letting him into their homes. He would beat them or throw them down stairs, and then rob them. He is suspected of killing at least two elderly persons.[33]

Pedro Alonso Lopez, however, is considered the deadliest serial killer of all time, having killed over 300 people in Colombia, Peru, and Ecuador. Lopez has been dubbed the "Monster of the Andes."[34] In 1999, suspected serial killer Angel Leonicio Reyes Maturino Resendez was finally captured. Resendez was referred to as the "railroad killer" since all his slayings occurred near railroad tracks.[35]

Although the most notorious serial killers are men, female serial killers do exist. They are considered to be more difficult to apprehend and to have more complex motivations than their male counterparts.[36]

Throughout the 1990s an unusual number of mass murders occurred. In 1991, an unemployed young man drove his pickup through the glass window of a Texas café and opened fire with a semiautomatic pistol, leaving 22 dead. James Huberty walked into a McDonald's in California and killed 20 people. Colin Ferguson boarded a train where he killed 6 and wounded 17 in the Long Island massacre of 1993. In 1996, Thomas Hamilton entered a school in Dunblane, Scotland, shot and killed 16 kindergarten students and their teacher, and wounded 12 others.[37] In 1998, 5 of the 16 persons shot at a Jonesboro, Arkansas, middle school died. In 1999, there were 15 victims of a

Comedian Bill Cosby discusses the murder of his son, Ennis, in an interview with CBS news anchor Dan Rather. Ennis was shot and killed in Los Angeles on January 16, 1997.

massacre at Columbine High School in Littleton, Colorado, and 7 victims of a mass shooting at a Baptist church in Fort Worth, Texas. Other 1999 incidents include 3 dead in Pelham, Alabama; 12 dead in Atlanta, Georgia; and 2 dead in Salt Lake City, Utah.

Recently, there has been an increase in mass murders in the workplace. From 1992 to 1996, more than 1000 workplace homicides occurred annually.[38] San Franciscan failed businessman Gian Luigi Ferri, who blamed lawyers for his problems, burst into the thirty-fourth-floor law office where he had been a client and, with two pistols, killed eight persons working in the firm. Disgruntled employee Paul Calder returned 8 months after being fired to kill three and wound two at a Tampa insurance company. In 1999, day trader Mark O. Barton, after losing over $100,000 in the stock market in almost 2 months, bludgeoned his wife and two children to death.

He then drove to an office complex in the Buckhead district of Atlanta. There he opened fire inside two brokerage firms where he had been employed. Barton killed a total of 13 people before committing suicide as police were closing in on him.[39] The U.S. Postal Service, where 38 employees died violently between 1986 and 1993, continues to look into ways to reduce employer-employee tension, especially when layoffs are imminent.[40]

It is popularly believed that multiple murderers are mentally ill; their offenses, after all, are often quite bizarre. In many such cases psychiatrists have found severe pathology.[41] Yet juries are reluctant to find these offenders not guilty by reason of insanity. Albert Fish, who cooked and ate the children he murdered, died in the electric chair.[42] Edmund Kemper, who killed hitchhikers as well as his own mother (he used her head as a dartboard), received a life term.[43]

The criminologists Jack Levin and James Fox do not agree with the hypothesis that all mass and serial murderers are mentally diseased (for example, psychotic) and therefore legally insane or incompetent. On the contrary, they say, serial killers are **sociopaths,** persons who lack internal controls, disregard common values, and have an intense desire to dominate others. But psychological characteristics alone cannot explain the actions of these people. They are also influenced by the social environment in which they function: the openness of our society, the ease of travel, the availability of firearms, the lack of external controls and supervision, and the general friendliness and trust of Americans in dealing with each other and with strangers.[44]

The American public is fascinated with the phenomena of mass and serial murder.[45] Levin and Fox suggest that the recent increase in mass and serial murders, despite a general decline in the murder rate, is to some extent attributable to the publicity given to mass murders and the resulting copycat phenomenon, the repetition of a crime as a result of the publicity it receives.[46] When one person killed at random by poisoning Tylenol capsules with cyanide, others copied the idea. This phenomenon has prompted experts to recommend that the media cooperate with the criminal justice system when the circumstances demand discretion.[47] Yet cooperation may be hard to achieve when media help is needed to alert the public to a health hazard (as in the Tylenol cases). In any event, the First Amendment's guarantee of freedom of the press does not permit controls.

Gang Murder Up to this point we have dealt largely with homicides committed by single offenders. But what about homicides by gangs of offenders? Are there any differences between the two types? On the basis of an analysis of data contained in 700 homicide investigation files, researchers found that "gang homicides differ both qualitatively and quantitatively from nongang homicides. Most distinctly, they differ with respect to ethnicity [more likely to be intraethnic], age [gang killers are 5 years younger], number of participants [2 ½ times as many participants], and relationship between the participants [gang killers are twice as likely not to know their victims]."[48] But similarities can also be seen. The causes of gang homicides, like those of single offenders, are often attributable to social disorganization, economic inequality, and deprivation.[49]

Since the 1950s the nature of gang murder has changed dramatically. As we discuss in Chapter 6, besides the major increase in killings, gang homicides have also gotten more brutal. Drive-by and crossfire shootings of intended victims and innocent bystanders are no longer uncommon. From 1989 to 1993, there were 6327 drive-by shootings, 9053 people shot at, and 590 homicides; 47 percent of the people shot at and 23 percent of the homicide victims were innocent bystanders.[50] In Brooklyn, New York, all three brothers in one family fell victim to street violence. Motives also have changed through the years. Once, gang wars, with a few related homicides, took place over "turf," territory that members protected, with knives, rocks, or metal chains as weapons. Now the wars are over drugs, and the weapons are assault rifles and semiautomatic guns.[51]

A Cross-National Comparison of Homicide Rates

The criminal homicides we have been discussing are those committed in the United

FIGURE 11.1 Firearm-related homicide rates for children. The U.S. rate is more than twice that of Finland, the country with the next highest rate.

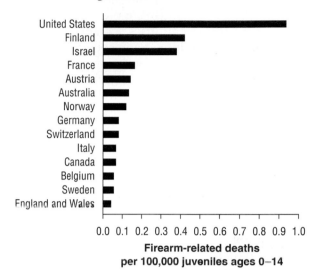

Firearm-related deaths per 100,000 juveniles ages 0–14

Note: Countries with no firearm-related homicide for children: Denmark, Hong Kong, Ireland, Japan, Kuwait, the Netherlands, Northern Ireland, Scotland, Singapore, Taiwan, and Spain.

Source: Adapted from Centers for Disease Control and Prevention's rates of homicide, suicide, and firearm-related death among children—26 industrialized countries, as cited in *Juvenile Offenders and Victims: 1999 National Report.*

States. By comparing homicide rates in this country with those of other countries, we can gain a broader understanding of that crime. In the World Crime Survey ending with the year 1995, the United Nations revealed that the average rate of intentional homicide was 7.2 per 100,000 for developed (industrialized Western) countries and 3.5 per 100,000 for developing countries.[52] The survey figures demonstrate that with the recent decline in U.S. homicide rates to 6.8 per 100,000 from 9 per 100,000 in 1994, the United States no longer has the highest rate among industrialized countries.[53] Recent data, however, show that the number of homicides per 100,000 children under age 15 in the United States was five times the number in the other countries combined. The rate of child homicides involving firearms was 16 times greater in the United States than in the other countries combined (Figure 11.1).[54]

One cross-national study found a moderate association between inequality of income and rate of homicide. It likewise revealed a relationship between a youthful population and the homicide rate. The analysis, the study concluded, "suggests that homicide rates are higher in poorer countries, more culturally diverse countries, in countries which spend less on defense, in less democratic societies, and in countries where fewer young people are enrolled in school."[55] Another researcher who compared the homicide rates in 76 countries with the rate in the United States found that when he took into consideration the differences in the age and sex distributions of the various populations, the United States had a higher rate than all but 15 countries,[56] most of which were experiencing civil war or internal strife.

Did You Know?

. . . that in 1997, on average about six juveniles were murdered daily in the United States?

A comparison of homicide rates with historical and socioeconomic data from 110 nations over a 5-year period led researchers to the following conclusions:

- Combatant nations experience an increase in homicides following cessation of hostilities (violence has come to be seen as a legitimate means of settling disputes).

- The largest cities have the highest homicide rates; the smallest have the lowest homicide rates; but, paradoxically, as a city grows, its homicide rate per capita does not.

- The availability of capital punishment does not result in fewer homicides and in fact often results in more; abolition of capital punishment decreases the homicide rate.[57]

We have seen that murder rates are not distributed equally among countries or within a single country, or even within neighborhoods. As noted earlier, in the United States, homicide rates tend to be higher in the West and the South.[58] A greater proportion of males, young people, and blacks are perpetrators and victims of homicide, which tends to be committed against someone the killer knows, at or near the home of at least one of the persons involved, in the evening or on a weekend. Gang murders are increasing dramatically. A number of experts have found that homicides are related to the everyday patterns of interactions in socially disorganized slum areas.[59]

ASSAULT

The crimes of homicide and serious assault share many characteristics. Both are typically committed by young males, and a disproportionate number of arrestees are members of minority groups. Assault victims, too, often know their attackers. Spatial and temporal distributions are also quite comparable. Assault rates, like those of homicide, are highest in urban areas, during the summer months, in the evening hours, and in the South.

Though the patterns are the same, the legal definitions are not. A murder is an act that causes the death of another person and that is intended to cause death. An **assault** is an attack on another person that is made with apparent ability to inflict injury and that is intended to frighten or to cause physical harm. (An attack that results in touching or striking the victim is called a **battery**.) Modern statutes usually recognize two types of assault: A **simple assault** is one that inflicts little or no physical hurt; a felonious assault, or **aggravated assault,** is one in which the perpetrator inflicts serious harm on the victim or uses a deadly weapon.

Criminologists have looked closely at situations in which assaults are committed. One researcher identified six stages of a confrontational situation that leads to an assault:

1. One person insults another.

2. The insulted person perceives the significance of the insult, often by noting the reactions of others present, and becomes angry.

3. The insulted person contemplates a response: fight, flight, or conciliation. If the response chosen is a fight, the insultee assaults the insulter then and there. If another response is chosen, the situation advances to stage 4.

4. The original insulter, now reprimanded, shamed, or embarrassed, makes a countermove: fight or flight.

Since earliest times the fate of nations and world history have been affected by assassinations. Assassinations were so common in ancient Rome that it became forbidden to carry daggers into the Senate. That did not keep Gaius Julius Caesar's assassins from stabbing him to death in 44 B.C.; their weapons were stilichos, pencil-like tools used to write on wax tablets.

Assassinations are just as likely to occur in politically stable countries as in countries with turmoil, in both developed and developing countries. Is there an effective deterrent? Our penal codes treat the assassination of a head of state or government as a category of homicide distinct from, or higher than, ordinary murder. The Federal Criminal Code, Title 18 U.S. Code 1751, imposes the death penalty for the assassination of the president of the United States, the president-elect, other potential successors, and specially appointed executive staff members. The United States has had more than its share of assassinations. Abraham Lincoln was killed in 1865, and American presidents and political leaders have remained favorite targets: James A. Garfield, 1881; William McKinley, 1901; John F. Kennedy, 1963; Senator Robert F. Kennedy, 1968; Dr. Martin Luther King, Jr., 1968. Presidents Theodore Roosevelt, Franklin Delano Roosevelt, Harry S. Truman, Richard Nixon, Gerald Ford, and Ronald Reagan and Governor George C. Wallace of Alabama have all been the targets of attempted assassinations.

In the past 25 years the number of assassinations around the world appears to have increased. In 1975 President Richard Ratsimandraua of Madagascar, King Faisal of Saudi Arabia, and President Sheik Mujibur Rahman of Bangladesh were assassinated; in 1976 Nigerian head of state General Murtala Ramat Mohammed and Chilean foreign minister Orlando Letelier; in 1977 President Marien Ngouabi of the Congo; in 1978 former Iraqi premier Abdul Razak Al-Naif and former Italian premier Aldo Moro; in 1979 Lord Mountbatten and South Korean president Park Chung Hee; in 1980 Liberian president William R. Tolbert and former Nicaraguan president Anastasio Somoza Debayle; in 1981 Egyptian president Anwar El-Sadat; in 1982 Lebanese president-elect Bishir Gemayel; in 1983 Philippine opposition leader Benigno Acquino; in 1984 Indian prime minister Indira Gandhi; in 1986 Swedish prime minister Olof Palme; in 1988 Lebanese premier Rashid Karami; and in 1992 Indian prime minister Rajiv Gandhi. In the first 4 months of 1993, Sri Lanka's former minister Lalith Athulathmudali, African National Congress leader Chris Hani, Palestinian official Hussein Salem, and Bosnia Herzegovina's deputy prime minister Hakija Turajlik were assassinated. In 1999, assassination attempts were made on the lives of Sauveur Pierre Étienne, the secretary of the Struggling People's Organization in Haiti and on Egyptian president Hosni Mubarak. In the same year, 40-year-old Vazgen Sarkisian, prime minister of Armenia, was killed by an assassin's bullet. Many more assassinations of political leaders have occurred around the world, and hundreds more have been attempted but were not successful.

What prompts people to kill national leaders? Obviously, some assassins are psychologically disturbed. Several recent American assassins fall into that category: Lee Harvey Oswald, who has been identified as the killer of President Kennedy; President Ford's two would-be assassins; and John Hinckley, who tried to kill President Reagan. But some assassins act for political, idealistic reasons, such as the Puerto Rican nationalists Oscar Collazo and Griselio Torresola, who tried to kill President Truman.

Are all political assassins bad? The citizens of the former Federal Republic of Germany commemorate July 20, the day on which Colonel Count Klaus von Stauffenberg in 1944 detonated a bomb in Adolf Hitler's bunker. That was to be the last of 43 attempted assassinations of Hitler, who committed suicide less than a year later—but not before Colonel von Stauffenberg and more than 200 co-conspirators had been summarily tried by Nazi courts and hanged.

Source

James F. Kirkham, Sheldon G. Levy, and William J. Crotty, *Assassinations and Political Violence* (Washington, D.C.: U.S. Government Printing Office, 1969).

Questions for Discussion

1. Do you think assassination should be considered such a serious crime that insanity not be allowed as a defense?
2. Can you think of anything that might serve (or currently serves) as an effective deterrent to would-be assassins?

---

5. If the choice is a fight, the insulter assaults (and possibly kills) the insultee.

6. The "triumphant" party either flees or awaits the consequences (for example, police response).[60]

We can see that crucial decisions are made at all stages, and that the nature of the decisions depends on the context in which they are made. At stage 1, nobody is likely to offer an insult in a peaceful group or situation. At stage 2, the witnesses to the scene could respond in a conciliatory manner. (Let us call this a conflict-resolution situation.) At stage 3, the insulted person could leave the scene with dignity. (A confrontational person would call it flight; a conflict-resolution-minded person would call it a dignified end to a confrontational situation.) Stage 4 is a critical stage, since it calls for a counterresponse. The original aggressor could see this as the last chance to avoid violence and withdraw with apologies. That would be the end of the matter. In a confrontational situation, however, the blows will be delivered now, if none have been dealt already.

A similar pattern was proposed by James Tedeschi and Richard Felson, who developed a theory of aggression as instrumental behavior—that is, goal-oriented behavior carried out intentionally with the purpose of obtaining something. This is a different way of thinking about aggression. For years, criminologists and psychologists have generally accepted that aggression (and the violence that often goes with it) happens when a person reaches a "breaking point." There is little premeditation or thought given to some aggressive or violent behavior. But for Tedeschi and Felson, all aggression occurs after the person has thought about it first, even though these thoughts may be disorganized or illogical and may last for just a fraction of a second.[61]

The National Crime Victimization Survey estimates that 5,224,000 simple assaults were committed in 1998. Assault is the most common of all violent crimes reported to the police. The number of aggravated assaults has risen in recent years, reaching 1,674,000 in 1998.[62] These figures, however, grossly underestimate the real incidence. Many people involved in an assault consider the event a private matter, particularly if the assault took place within the family or household. Consequently, until quite recently little was known about family-related violence. But the focus of recent research is changing that situation rapidly.

FAMILY-RELATED CRIMES

In 1962 five physicians exposed the gravity of the "battered child syndrome" in the *Journal of the American Medical Association*.[63] When they reviewed X-ray photographs of patients in the emergency rooms of 71 hospitals across the country over the course of a year, they found 300 cases of child abuse, of which 11 percent re-

sulted in death and over 28 percent in permanent brain damage. Shortly thereafter, the women's movement rallied to the plight of the battered wife and, somewhat later, to the personal and legal problems of wives who were raped by their husbands.[64]

In the 1960s and 1970s various organizations, fighting for the rights of women and children, exposed the harm that results from physical and psychological abuse in the home. They demanded public action. They created public awareness of the extent of the problem. Psychologists, physicians, anthropologists, and social scientists, among others, increasingly focused attention on the various factors that enter into episodes of domestic violence. Such factors include the sources of conflict, arguments, physical attacks, injuries, and temporal and spatial elements.

Within three decades family violence, the "well-kept secret," has come to be recognized as a major social problem.[65] Family violence shares some of the characteristics of other forms of violence, yet the intimacy of marital, cohabitational, or parent-child relationships sets family violence apart. The physical and emotional harm inflicted in violent episodes tends to be spread over longer periods of time and to have a more lasting impact on all members of the living unit. Moreover, such events tend to be self-perpetuating.

Spouse Abuse

In May 1998, Motley Crüe drummer Tommy Lee was sentenced to 6 months in jail and 3 years probation for battering his wife, former "Baywatch" beauty Pamela Anderson. Lee was also ordered to perform 200 hours of community service and donate $5000 to a battered women's shelter. He had been arrested in February 1998 after Anderson called 911 to report a domestic dispute in which Lee had kicked her in the back while she was holding 7-week-old Dylan Jagger. Lee was charged with spousal abuse, child abuse, and unlawful possession of a firearm. As the result of a plea agreement, all charges except for the spousal abuse charge were dropped.

Media celebrity and former star athlete O. J. Simpson was convicted in 1989 of assaulting his

Rock drummer and Motley Crue band leader Tommy Lee arraigned in Malibu, California, for spousal and child abuse.

Pamela Anderson Lee called 911 with a plea for help.

wife, Nicole Brown Simpson. He served no time in prison, nor was he required to undergo counseling. On June 13, 1994, Nicole Brown Simpson and her friend Ronald Goldman were found lying dead in pools of their own blood, victims of a vicious knife attack. O. J. Simpson was accused of their murder. Following a lengthy, highly publicized, and much-discussed trial, O. J. Simpson was found not guilty by a jury of his peers. The verdict had a wide-reaching impact on various aspects of the criminal justice system. It also made abused women fear for their lives. Concerned that a man who was a convicted batterer could be found not guilty of killing his ex-wife, despite what was perceived by many as convincing evidence, they wondered if they could eventually share the same fate as Nicole Brown Simpson.[66]

The Extent of Spouse Abuse In a national sample of 6002 households, Murray A. Straus and Richard J. Gelles found that about one of

every six couples experiences at least one physical assault during the year.[67] While both husbands and wives perpetrate acts of violence, the consequences of their acts differ.[68] Men, who more often use guns, knives, or fists, inflict more pain and injury. About 60 percent of spousal assaults consist of minor shoving, slapping, pushing; the other 40 percent are considered severe: punching, kicking, stabbing, choking.[69] According to the National Institute of Justice, partner violence is strongly linked to a variety of mental illnesses, a background of family adversity, dropping out of school, juvenile aggression, drug abuse, long-term unemployment, and cohabitation and/or parenthood at a young age. Research also suggests that women who have children by the age of 21 are two times more likely to be victims of domestic violence than are women who are not mothers, and that men who father children by age 21 are three times more likely to be perpetrators of abuse as men who are not fathers.[70]

Researchers agree that assaultive behavior within the family is a highly underreported crime. Data from the National Crime Victimization Survey indicate:

- One-half of the incidents of domestic assault are not reported.

- The most common reason given for failure to report a domestic assault to the police was that the victim considered the incident a private matter.

- Victims who reported such incidents to the police did so to prevent future assaults.

- Though the police classified two-thirds of the reported incidents of domestic violence as simple assaults, half of them inflicted bodily injury as serious as or more serious than the injuries inflicted during rapes, robberies, and aggravated assaults.[71]

The Nature of Spouse Abuse   Before we can understand spouse abuse, we need information about abusers. Some experts have found that interpersonal violence is learned and transmitted from one generation to the next.[72] Studies demonstrate that children who are raised by aggressive parents tend to grow up to be aggressive adults.[73] Other researchers have demonstrated how stress, frustration, and severe psychopathology take their toll on family relationships.[74] A few researchers have also explored the role of body chemistry; one investigation ties abuse to the tendency of males to secrete adrenaline when they feel sexually threatened.[75]

The relationship between domestic violence and the use of alcohol and drugs has also been explored. Abusive men with severe drug and alcohol problems are more likely to abuse their wives or girlfriends when they are drunk or high and to inflict more injury.[76]

Several studies of other societies demonstrate cultural support for the abuse of women. Moroccan researcher Mohammed Ayat reported that of 160 battered women, about 25 percent believed that a man who does *not* beat his wife must be under some magic spell; 8 percent believed that such a man has a weak personality and is afraid of his wife; 2 percent be-

lieved that he must be abnormal; and another 2 percent believed that he doesn't love her or has little interest in her.[77] Wife beating, then, appears to be accepted as a norm by over one-third of the women studied—women who are themselves beaten. It even appears to be an expected behavior. In fact, in a study of 90 cultures, spouse beating was rare or nonexistent in only 15.[78]

Spouse abuse has often been attributed to the imbalance of power between male and female partners. According to some researchers, the historical view of wives as possessions of their husbands persists even today.[79] Until recently, spousal abuse was perceived as a problem more of social service than of criminal justice.[80] Police responding to domestic disturbance calls typically do not make an arrest unless the assailant is drunk, has caused serious injury, or has assaulted the officers. Take, for example, the case of *Thurman v. Torrington.* Tracey Thurman had repeatedly requested police assistance because she feared her estranged husband. Even after he threatened to shoot her and her son, the police merely told her to get a restraining order. Eventually, the husband attacked Thurman, inflicting multiple stab wounds that caused paralysis from the neck down and permanent disfigurement. The police had delayed in responding to her call on that occasion, and the city of Torrington, Connecticut, was held liable for having failed to provide her with equal protection of the laws. In the suit that followed, Ms. Thurman was awarded $2.3 million in damages.[81]

The Thurman case is rare. The majority of assault incidents within the family either are unreported to the police or, if reported, are classified as simple assaults. By and large, the victims of family violence—those who are willing to look for help—have turned to crisis telephone lines and to shelters for battered women (safe havens that first appeared in the early 1970s to provide legal, social, and psychological services).

Whether informal interventions are as effective as the criminal justice system, however, is a matter of controversy.[82] In a study conducted some years ago, the Minneapolis Domestic Violence Experiment, three types of action were taken: (1) The batterer was arrested, (2) the partners were required to separate for a designated period of time, and (3) a mediator intervened between the partners. Over a 6-month period the offenders who were arrested had the lowest recidivism rate (10 percent), those who were required to separate had the highest (24 percent), and those who submitted to mediation fell in between (19 percent).[83] More recently, a 1991 study revealed that neither short-custody arrests for domestic violence in inner-city areas nor longer-term arrests are effective in curbing domestic violence, especially in the long run.[84] Questions on the subject of spouse abuse still far outnumber answers. Personal, ethical, and moral concerns make the issue highly sensitive. Researchers, however, are seeking answers.

Child Abuse

Spouse abuse is closely related to child abuse. One-half to three-quarters of men who batter women also beat their children, and many sexually abuse them as well. Children are also injured as a result of reckless behavior on the part of their fathers while the latter are abusing their mothers. In fact, the majority of abused sons over 14 suffer injuries trying to protect their mothers.[85]

The Extent of Child Abuse Most of the available data on child abuse come from the National Center on Child Abuse and Neglect.[86] Its third *National Incidence Study of Child Abuse and Neglect* (NIS-3) reported that there were nearly 3 million children maltreated or endangered in 1993. Child maltreatment occurs when a parent or parent substitute (e.g., a day care provider) abuses or permits the abuse of a child. Maltreatment includes physical abuse, sexual abuse, emotional abuse (e.g., verbal assaults), physical neglect, emotional neglect (inadequate nurturing), and educational neglect. (See Table 11.2.)

More than half of all victims experienced serious or moderate harm as a result of the maltreatment. Sexual abuse of females was three times greater than among males.[87] The NIS-3 report also shows that the number of children abused, neglected, or endangered almost doubled between 1986 and 1993. Part of the increase

TABLE 11.2 Major Findings of NIS-3 on Maltreated Children

Type of Maltreatment	Percentage of Maltreated Children
Physical neglect	47
Physical abuse	22
Emotional neglect	21
Emotional abuse	19
Sexual abuse	11
Educational neglect	14

Note: One child may experience more than one type of maltreatment.
Source: U.S. Department of Justice, OJJDP, Juvenile Offenders and Victims, 1999 National Report, p. 41.

is due to better reporting, greater public awareness, and improved data collection. It is still very difficult, however, to measure the extent of child abuse. Maltreatment usually takes place in the home, and the child victims rarely notify the police.[88]

The Nature of Child Abuse When child abuse first began to be investigated in the early 1960s, the investigators were predominantly physicians, who looked at the psychopathology of the abusers. They discovered that a high proportion of abusers suffered from alcoholism, drug abuse, mental retardation, poor attachment, low self-esteem, or sadistic psychosis. Later the search for causes moved in other directions. Some researchers pointed out that abusive parents did not know how to discipline children or, for that matter, even how to provide for basic needs, such as nutrition and medical attention. Claims have been made that abusers have themselves been abused; to date, however, the evidence in regard to this hypothesis is mixed.[89]

The list of factors related to child abuse is long. We know, for example, that the rate of child abuse in lower-income families is high.[90] This finding is probably related to the fact that low-income parents have few resources for dealing with the stress to which they are subjected, such as poor housing and financial problems. When they cannot cope with their responsibilities, they may become overwhelmed. Moreover, the risk of abuse is twice as great for children living with single parents as for children living with both parents.[91] The rate of child abuse may also be related to the acceptance of physical responses to conflict situations in what has been termed the "subculture of violence" (Chapter 6). Moreover, since child abuse among poor families is likely to be handled by a public agency, these cases tend to appear in official statistics.

When child abuse is reported to the authorities, the case goes through the criminal justice system just like any other case. However, certain factors are associated with how, and to what extent, these types of cases are prosecuted. One study suggests that, particularly in the case of child sexual abuse, those offenders who are charged with abusing multiple victims are much more likely to be prosecuted than are offenders charged with abusing only one victim. Also, offenders who are strangers to the victim are more likely to be prosecuted than are offenders related to the victim. Cases in which serious abuse was involved and medical evidence of abuse existed were also more likely to be prosecuted.[92]

Some researchers have found that formal action—arrest and prosecution—is the most effective means for limiting repeat offenses in the case of battered wives. The situation seems to be different when children are involved. Several advocates for children oppose any involvement of the criminal justice system. They believe that the parent-child attachment remains crucial to the child's development, and they fear that punishment of parents can only be detrimental to the child's need for a stable family environment. Only in the most extreme cases would they separate children from parents and place them in shelters or in foster homes. The preference is to prevent child abuse by other means, such as self-help groups (Parents Anonymous), baby-sitting assistance, and crisis phone lines.

The results of various types of intervention are characterized by the title of a report on child maltreatment: "Half Full and Half Empty."[93] Rates of repeated abuse are high; yet some families have had positive results, and advances have been made in identifying the best treatment for various types of problems. Although our understanding of the problem has indeed increased, we need to know a great deal more about the offense before we can reduce its occurrence.[94]

Abuse of the Elderly

When the amendments to the Older Americans Act appeared in 1987, they brought with them a federal definition of elder abuse, neglect, and exploitation. The definition is used only as a guideline and not for enforcement purposes. State laws provide their own definitions of elder abuse, and these definitions vary across state jurisdictions. Nevertheless, three basic categories of elder abuse emerged: domestic elder abuse, institutional elder abuse, and self-neglect or self-abuse. Domestic elder abuse results when an older person is maltreated by a person who has a special relationship with the elder, such as a spouse, sibling, child, or friend. Institutional elder abuse occurs in the context of a residential facility, such as a nursing home, in which paid caregivers or other staff are the perpetrators. Self-neglect or self-abuse occurs when elderly persons threaten their own health or safety by, for example, failing to provide themselves with proper amounts of food, clothing, shelter, and medication.[95]

Abuse of the elderly has become an area of special concern to social scientists. The population group that is considered to be elderly is variously defined. The majority of researchers consider 65 the age at which an individual falls into the category "elderly." As health care in the United States has improved, longevity has increased. The population of elderly people has grown larger over the decades: from 4 percent of the total population in 1900 to 12.6 percent in the 1990s.[96] Every day 1000 more people join the ranks. It is estimated that by the year 2020, 20 percent of the population will be elderly.[97]

Elderly persons who are being cared for by their adult children are at a certain risk of abuse. The extent of the problem, however, is still largely unknown. The abused elderly frequently do not talk about their abuse for fear of the embarrassment of public exposure and possible retaliation by the abuser. Congressional hearings on domestic abuse estimate that between 500,000 and 2.5 million elderly people are abused annually.[98] Among the causes of such abuse are caregivers who themselves grew up in homes where violence was a way of life, the stress of caregiving in a private home rather than an institution, generational conflicts, and frustration with

Toys and flowers surround the coffin of 6-year-old Alisa Izquierdo, whose 29-year-old mother was charged with murder and endangering the welfare of a child, Brooklyn, New York, November 1995.

gerontological (old-age) problems of the care receiver, such as illness and senility.[99]

We can see that criminologists share a growing concern about family-related violence. Child abuse has received the attention of scholars for three decades. Spousal abuse has been studied for two decades. The abuse of the elderly has begun to receive attention much more recently. Family abuse is not new; our awareness of the size and seriousness of the problem is. The same could be said about yet another offense. It was not until the 1960s that women's advocates launched a national campaign on behalf of victims of rape. Since then, rape has become a major topic in criminological literature and research.

RAPE AND SEXUAL ASSAULT

The common law defined **rape** as an act of enforced intercourse by a man of a woman (other than the attacker's wife) without her consent. Intercourse includes any sexual penetration, however slight. The exclusion of wives from the crime of rape rested on several outdated legal fictions, among them the propositions that the marriage vows grant implicit permanent rights of sexual access and that spouses cannot testify against each other. The Hale Doctrine, written

in the seventeenth century and recognized judicially in 1857 by the United States, stated specifically that "the husband cannot be guilty of a rape committed by himself upon his lawful wife, for by their mutual matrimonial consent and a contract the wife hath given up herself in this kind unto her husband which she cannot retract."[100]Older laws universally classify rape as a sex crime. But rape has always been much more than that. It is inherently a crime of violence, an exercise of power.

Oddly, as Susan Brownmiller forcefully argues, it really started as a property crime. Men as archetypal aggressors (the penis as a weapon) subjugated women by the persistent threat of rape. That threat forced each woman to submit to a man for protection and thus to become a wife, the property of a man. Rape then was made a crime to protect one man's property—his wife—from the sexual aggressions of other men.[101] But even that view regards rape as a violent crime against the person, one that destroys the freedom of a woman (and nowadays of a man as well) to decide whether, when, and with whom to enter a sexual relationship.

Well over a thousand books, scholarly articles, and papers have been produced on the topic of rape and sexual assault since the 1960s. Much that was obscure and poorly understood has now been clarified by research generated largely by the initiatives of the feminist movement, the National Center for the Prevention and Control of Rape (NCPCR), and other governmental and private funding agencies. While most of the crimes in our penal codes have more or less retained their original form, the law on rape has changed rapidly and drastically. The name of the crime, its definition, the rules of evidence and procedure, society's reaction to it—all have changed.[102] Nevertheless, Americans still regard rape as one of the most serious crimes.

Characteristics of the Rape Event

According to the Uniform Crime Reports, there were 96,122 forcible rapes in 1997. This figure represents 6 percent of the total number of violent crimes.[103] The incidence of rape dropped 9 percent between 1993 and 1997. Of all those arrested for forcible rape, 17 percent were under age 18; 45 percent were under age 25; and 58 percent were white.[104] Most rapes are committed in the summer, particularly in July. Several decades ago, Menachem Amir demonstrated that close to half of all rapes in Philadelphia from 1958 to 1965 were committed by a person known to or even friendly with the victim.[105] Recent victimization data show that the situation has not changed: 48 percent of rapes are committed by men who know their victims.[106] The offender may even be the husband, who in some states can now qualify as a rapist. Nevertheless, marital rape is still minimized by the law. We know little about it except that it often occurs in marriages that are characterized by other forms of violence and in marriages involving alcoholic husbands.[107]

Recently researchers have developed a three-category typology of rape. Stranger rape occurs when the victim has had little or no prior contact with the offender. Predatory rape involves a man who, using deception or force, intends and plans to rape his victim, by pretending to engage in legitimate dating behavior. Date rape involves a legitimate dating situation turned bad, when force is eventually used to gain sex from a woman who is an unwilling participant.[108] In these situations the offenders sometimes use the date rape "drug of choice,"

Rohypnol, commonly referred to as "Roofies." Rohypnol falls into the same class of drugs as marijuana. It is a sedative which is said to be 10 times the strength of Valium. Twenty to thirty minutes after it is consumed, often after being dropped into a drink at a social gathering, this tasteless, odorless drug produces in its victim muscle relaxation, a slowing of psychomotor responses, and amnesia.[109] Some research indicates that as many as 25 percent of all female college students may have experienced rape.[110] Criminologists have difficulty estimating the frequency of date rape, but in all likelihood such rape has increased significantly. It is estimated that only one-tenth of the date rapes committed are reported to the police.

There is an arrest made for all types of forcible rape in about 50 percent of the cases.[111] Many stranger rapists remain at large because they commit their acts in ways that produce little tangible evidence as to their identities. They maintain a distance from the victim by not interacting with her before the attack. The serial rapist also attacks strangers, but because he finds his victims repeatedly in the same places, his behavior is more predictable and so leads to a better arrest rate.[112]

Who Are the Rapists?

Explanations of rape fall into two categories, psychological and sociocultural. While research in these areas has expanded over the last two decades, the causes of rape remain speculative.

Psychological Factors   Several experts view rapists as suffering from mental illness or personality disorders. They argue that some rapists are psychotic, sociopathic, or sadistic, or that they feel deficient in masculinity. Most rapists show hostile feelings toward women, have histories of violence, and tend to attack strangers. They commit the offense because of anger, a drive for power (expressed as sexual conquest), or the enjoyment of maltreating a victim (sadism). Some rapists view women as sex objects whose role is to satisfy them.

Sociocultural Factors   Psychological explanations assume that men who rape are maladjusted in some way. But several studies done in the 1980s demonstrate that rapists are indistinguishable from other groups of offenders.[113] These studies generally conclude that rape is culturally related to societal norms that approve of aggression as a demonstration of masculinity (as we saw in Chapter 6) or that rape is the mechanism by which men maintain their power over women.

The social significance of rape has long been a part of anthropological literature. A cross-cultural study of 95 tribal societies found that 47 percent were rape-free, 35 percent intermediate, and 18 percent rape-prone. In the rape-prone societies women had low status and little decision-making power, and they lived apart from men. The author of this study concluded: "Violence is socially, not biologically, programmed."[114]

Despite anthropologists' traditional interest in gender relationships, it was not until the feminist movement and radical criminology focused on the subject that the relationship of rape, gender inequality, and socioeconomic status was fully articulated. Writing from the Marxist perspective, which we explore in Chapter 9, Julia and Herman Schwendinger posited that "the impoverishment of the working class and the widening gap between rich and poor" create conditions for the prevalence of sexual violence.[115] A test of this hypothesis showed that while the incidence of sexual violence was not related to ethnic inequality, it was significantly related to general income inequality.[116]

A more recent study analyzed these findings and concluded that economic inequality was not the sole determinant of violent crime in our society. Forcible rape was found to be an added "cost" of many factors, including social disorganization.[117] In sum, many factors have been associated with the crime of rape: psychological problems, social factors, and even sociopolitical factors. Some experts suggest that boys are socialized to be aggressive and dominating, that the innate male sex drive leads to rape, and that pornography encourages men to rape by making sex objects of women, degrading women, and glamorizing violence against them. Rape has been explained in such a wide variety of ways that it is extremely difficult to plan preventive strategies and to formulate

crime-control policy. Moreover, it has created major difficulties in the criminal justice system.

Rape and the Legal System

The difficulties of rape prosecutions have their roots in the English common law. Sir Matthew Hale, a seventeenth-century jurist, explained in *Pleas of the Crown* (1685, 1736) how a jury was to be cautious in viewing evidence of rape: "[It] must be remembered . . . that it is an accusation easily to be made and hard to be proved, and harder to be defended, by the party accused, tho never so innocent."[118] This instruction, which so definitively protects the defendant, has until recently been a mandatory instruction to juries in the United States. Along with many other legal and policy changes, many jurisdictions have now cast it aside. The requirement of particularly stringent proof in rape cases had always been justified by the seriousness of the offense and the heavy penalties associated with it, plus the stigma attached to such a conviction.

Difficulties of Prosecution Victims of rape have often been regarded with suspicion by the criminal justice system. The victim's testimony has not sufficed to convict the defendant, no matter how unimpeachable that testimony may have been. There had to be "corroborating evidence," such as semen, torn clothes, bruises, or eyewitness testimony.

Another major issue has been that of consent. Did the victim encourage, entice, or maybe even agree to the act? Was the attack forced? Did the victim resist? Martin Schwartz and Todd Clear sum up the reasons for such questions: "There is a widespread belief in our culture that women 'ask for it,' either individually or as a group." They compared rape victims to victims of other offenses: "Curiously, society does not censure the robbery victim for walking around with $10, or the burglary victim for keeping all of those nice things in his house, or the car theft victim for showing off his flashy new machine, just asking for someone to covet it."[119]

Because defendants in rape cases so often claim that the victim was in some way responsible for the attack, rape victims in the courtroom tend to become the "accused," required to defend their good reputations, their propriety, and their mental soundness. The severity of the assault, the injuries the victim sustains, whether or not the assailant was a stranger, and the victim's social support network all play a role in terms of the rape reporting process.[120] Experts claim that as many as 60 percent of rapes are not reported.[121] In sum, so many burdens are placed on the victim that no one seriously wonders why so few rapes are reported and why so few men accused of rape are convicted.

Legislative Changes   The feminist movement has had a considerable impact on laws and attitudes concerning rape in our country. The state of Michigan was a leader in the movement to reform such laws by creating, in 1975, the new crime of "criminal sexual conduct" to replace the traditional rape laws. It distinguishes four degrees of assaultive sexual acts, differentiated by the amount of force used, the infliction of injury, and the age and mental condition of the victim.

The new law is gender-neutral, in that it makes illegal any type of forcible sex, including homosexual rape. Other states have followed Michigan's lead. Schwartz and Clear have suggested that reform should go one step further. They argue that if rape were covered by the general assault laws rather than by a separate statute on sex crimes, the emphasis would be on the assault (the action of the offender) and not on the resistance (the action of the victim).

Recent legislation has also removed many of the barriers women encountered as witnesses in the courtroom. Thus in states with rape shield laws women are no longer required to disclose their prior sexual activity, and corroboration requirements have been reduced or eliminated; as noted earlier, some states have reversed two centuries of legal tradition by striking down the "marital rape exemption" so that a wife may now charge her husband with rape.[122] But law reform has limits. Unfortunately, prejudices die hard.

Community Response

Women's advocates have taken an interest not only in legislative reform but also in the community's response to the victims of rape. In 1970 the first rape-specific support project, the Bay Area Women Against Rape—a volunteer-staffed emergency phone information service—was established in Berkeley, California.[123] By 1973, similar projects had spread throughout the country. Run by small, unaffiliated groups, they handled crises, monitored agencies (hospitals, police, courts) that came in contact with victims, educated the public about the problems of victims, and even provided lessons in self-defense.

By the late 1970s the number of these centers and their activities had increased dramatically. The mass media reported on their successes. Federal and, later, state and local support for such services rose. As the centers became more professional, they formed boards of directors, prepared detailed budgets to comply with the requirements of funding agencies, hired social workers and mental health personnel, and developed their political action component. But even with increased support, the demand for the services of rape crisis centers far outweighs the available resources.

KIDNAPPING

Kidnapping, as such, was not recognized as a felony under English common law; it was a misdemeanor. Some forms of kidnapping were later criminalized by statute. In the eighteenth century, the most frequent form of kidnapping, according to the great legal scholar Sir William Blackstone, was stealing children and sending them to servitude in the American colonies. Other forms of kidnapping were the "crimping," or shanghaiing, of persons for involuntary service aboard ships and the abduction of women for purposes of prostitution abroad.

All these offenses have elements in common, and together they define the crime of **kidnapping:** abduction and detention by force or fraud and transport beyond the authority of the place where the crime was committed. It was not until the kidnapping of Charles Lindbergh's infant son in 1932 that comprehensive kidnapping legislation was enacted in the United States. In passing the federal kidnapping statute—the so-called Lindbergh act (now 18 U.S. Code [sec.] 1201)—Congress made it a felony to kidnap and transport a victim across a

Stephen Fagan with his daughters after pleading guilty to their kidnapping.

state or national border. The crime was subject to the death penalty, unless the victim was released unharmed.

In the United States kidnapping often involves the abduction of a child from one parent by the other. An interesting case recently appeared in the news. In October 1979, Stephen Fagan kidnapped his two daughters, Lisa (age 2) and Rachael (age 5), from Massachusetts and then moved to Florida. He told his daughters that their mother had died. It was not until 1998 that an anonymous tip led to his arrest in Florida, where he was living the high life as a socialite under the name Dr. William Martin. Fagan claimed that he took his daughters away from his ex-wife, Barbara Kurth, who he believed was an unfit and alcoholic mother. Kurth vehemently denied the allegation. Fagan was charged with kidnapping his daughters even though the crime had occurred 20 years earlier. In a plea agreement, Fagan was spared jail time; instead, he was fined $100,000 and received a suspended 3- to 5-year prison sentence. He must also serve probation for 5 years. The two daughters have stood by their father and have decided not to reunite with their mother.[124]

ROBBERY

Portland (April 26, 1999)—Ethan is shrieking. It would be funny, but he is bleeding from the scro-

tum, and that's just not funny. In the adrenaline rush, he has shoved his dad's gun into his waistband and accidentally shot himself. His best friend Tom has stopped the car, a Chevy Suburban they paid someone $80 to steal for what was supposed to be their big finale. The Oregon teens had planned a major heist, Ethan would later say, maybe half a million that they would tote in athletic bags from the money room at a Nordstrom department store. But that plan didn't work out; in fact, the whole night had gone right to hell. (Why didn't they stick to knocking over Burger Kings?) Tom had worked as a clerk at Nordstrom and— duh—someone recognized him when he and Ethan ambled in. So they walked out without taking a thing. They should have gone home, but after weeks of planning, they were primed. They settled on Rustica, a neighborhood Italian place with a nice sourdough. The petrified manager handed over $500, and it was in the heady aftermath that not far away Ethan shot himself.[125]

Typical robbers? No. Thomas Curtis and Ethan Thrower were two high school superstars who had their fun completing a string of armed robberies.

Robbery is the taking of property from a victim by force and violence or by the threat of violence. The Model Penal Code (Section 222.1) grades robbery as a felony of the second degree, commanding a prison term of up to 10 years. If the robber has intentionally inflicted serious physical injury or attempted to kill, the sentence may be as long as life. In reality, however, the average sentence upon conviction for one charge of robbery is 6 years.[126] In 1997, the number of robbery offenses was 497,950, or 186 robberies per 100,000 of the population, the lowest rate since 1985.[127]

Offenders display weapons, mostly guns and knives, in almost half of all robberies. Since 44 percent of all robberies net the perpetrator less than $50, the overall reporting rate for robbery is only slightly higher than 50 percent. Robberies of individuals occur most frequently on the street (61.3 percent). The remaining robberies take place in parking lots and garages (14 percent), in residences (9.3 percent), in commercial buildings (5.2 percent), in transit stations or on public transportation (3.8 percent), in nightclubs, bars, or restaurants (2.7 percent), and in miscellaneous establishments (3.7 percent).[128]

Characteristics of Robbers

Criminologists have classified the characteristics of robbers as well as the characteristics of robberies. John Conklin detected four types of robbers:

- The *professional robber* carefully plans and executes a robbery, often with many accomplices; steals large sums of money; and has a long-term, deep commitment to robbery as a means of supporting a hedonistic lifestyle.

- The *opportunistic robber* (the most common) has no long-term commitment to robbery; targets victims for small amounts of money ($20 or less); victimizes elderly women, drunks, cab drivers, and other people who seem to be in no position to resist; and is young and generally inexperienced.

- The *addict robber* is addicted to drugs, has a low level of commitment to robbery but a high level of commitment to theft, plans less than professional robbers but more than opportunistic robbers, wants just enough money for a fix, and may or may not carry a weapon.

- The *alcoholic robber* has no commitment to robbery as a way of life, has no commitment to theft, does not plan his or her robberies, usually robs people after first assaulting them, takes few precautions, and is apprehended more often than other robbers.[129]

According to the Uniform Crime Reports, 90 percent of those arrested for robbery in 1997 were males. Approximately 65 percent of the arrestees were under 25 years of age. In terms of race, blacks accounted for 57 percent of all robbery arrests, whites accounted for 41 percent, and all other races constituted the remaining 2 percent of all robbery arrests.[130]

The Consequences of Robbery

Robbery is a property crime as well as a violent crime. It is the combination of the motive for economic gain and the violent nature of robbery that makes it so serious.[131] An estimated $496 million was lost as a result of robbery in 1994 alone. The value of stolen property per incident averaged $801, and the average amount of money stolen ranged from $387 (from convenience stores) to $3551 (from banks).[132] Loss of money, however, is certainly not the only consequence of robbery. The million-odd robberies that take place each year leave psychological and physical trauma in their wake, not to mention the pervasive fear and anxiety that have contributed to the decay of inner cities.

Not all criminologists agree, however, that the high level of fear is warranted. After examining trends in robbery-homicide data from 52 of the largest cities in the United States, one researcher found "little support for the fears that there is a new breed of street criminals who cause more serious injuries and deaths in robberies. Very recent trends point in the other direction. Killing a robbery victim appears to be going out of fashion."[133]

EMERGING PROBLEMS

Some of the more pressing issues we face today include global terrorism, an increase in hate crimes nationwide, the spread of racist and antigovernment militias, and deadly shootings in American schools. In recent years, largely as a result of media attention, these crimes have had a dramatic impact on the public's perception that violence has reached epidemic proportions. In reality, these crimes account for an extremely low proportion of all violent crimes, and rates for two of them (terrorism and violence in schools) have even gone down.

Terrorism

Terrorism is a resort to violence or a threat of violence on the part of a group seeking to accomplish a purpose against the opposition of constituted authority. Crucial to the terrorists' scheme is the exploitation of the media to attract attention to the cause. Many clandestine organizations around the world have sought to draw attention to their causes—the Irish Republican Army (IRA), committed to the cause of uniting the British counties of Northern Ireland with the Republic of Ireland; Islamic fundamentalists committed to the protection of Islam in its purist form against any Western influence; various Palestinian factions opposed to Israeli occupation or to any Mideast peace settlement; radical groups all over the world seeking an end to capitalism or colonialism or the imposition of one or another form of totalitarian rule.

From the outset the member states of the United Nations have been concerned about international terrorism because it endangers or takes innocent lives and jeopardizes fundamental freedoms, such as the freedom to travel and to congregate for public events. The U.N. effort to control international terrorism concentrates on removal of the underlying grievances that provoke people to sacrifice human lives, including their own, in an attempt to effect radical changes.[134] This approach to the control of terrorism is not concerned with the individual motivations of terrorists. Some of them may be highly motivated idealists; others are recruited for substantial rewards. The control effort is directed, rather, at the conditions that give rise to terrorism and at the removal of such conditions.

To the extent that some grievances have been reduced by political action, such as the granting of independence to colonies and the political accord reached in Northern Ireland in

November 1999, terrorism has declined. But other problems remain, especially in the Balkans, India, Central America, Africa, and the West Bank and Gaza Strip occupied by Israel. Crimes of a terrorist nature occur virtually every day and are likely to continue wherever the underlying problems are not resolved. Terrorist activities include but are not restricted to assassinations, hostage taking, and interference with or destruction of ships, aircraft, or means of land transport (see Table 11.3). When funding by clandestine supporters is not forthcoming, terrorists have carried out robberies to finance their operations.

The 1998 bombings of the U.S. embassies in Kenya and Tanzania have increased American awareness of terrorist activities. The impact of the networking of international terrorist groups has become apparent.[135] Osama bin Laden, the reputed mastermind of the embassy bombings, is referred to as the "new model terrorist" and the "chief executive officer" of a network of terrorist groups. He is considered one of the most significant sponsors of Islamic extremist activities in the world today. In fact, bin Laden's so-called terrorist network is considered the most prominent threat to our national security. As of 2000, bin Laden remained a fugitive in Afghanistan. His name is on the FBI's "Ten Most Wanted Fugitives" list, and the United States government has offered a $5 million reward for his capture.[136]

In August 1999, a series of bombings began in Moscow.[137] (See "Window to the World," Chapter 1.) Some researchers suggest that the 15 newly independent states of the former Soviet Union are replacing the Middle East as the primary generator of international terrorism. Of additional concern to the Russians is blood feud terrorism, or acts of retaliation perpetrated solely on the basis of satisfying a vengeance code of a blood feud or clan vendetta, in ethnic communities and regions.[138]

The Extent of Terrorism   The incidence of terrorism may seem slight in the light of overall national crime statistics, especially those of the United States. But the worldwide destructive impact of such acts is considerable. So too are the costs of increased security to combat terrorism.

TABLE 11.3   Terrorist Events against Americans, 1983–1998

- On October 23, 1983, a suicide terrorist in a TNT-laden truck blew up U.S. Marine Corps headquarters in Beirut, Lebanon, killing 241 marines and sailors. A second truck blew up a French paratrooper barracks 2 miles away, killing 58.
- On October 7, 1985, five hijackers seized the Italian cruiseliner *Achille Lauro.* They held some 400 persons for ransom and killed a wheelchair-bound American passenger.
- On April 2, 1986, a bomb exploded aboard TWA flight 840 at Athens airport, killing 4 Americans.
- On April 5, 1986, terrorists exploded a bomb in a West Berlin disco frequented by American service personnel, killing 2 and injuring 200. The incident prompted an American air strike against Libya in retaliation.
- On September 5, 1986, four Pakistani gunmen, followers of Abu Nidal, attempted to hijack a Pan Am 747 in Karachi, Pakistan. After keeping the plane on the runway overnight, the gunmen were overpowered by security; 21 passengers died.
- On December 21, 1988, terrorists exploded Pan Am flight 103, en route from Frankfurt, Germany, to New York, killing 270 passengers, crew, and people on the ground at Lockerbie, Scotland.
- On February 26, 1993, a terrorist bomb in the basement garage of the World Trade Center in New York City killed 6 people, injured over 1000 people, and caused extensive damage to the building.
- On April 19, 1995, a bomb made of fertilizer and diesel fuel exploded in front of the Murrah Federal Building in Oklahoma City, killing 168 and injuring over 600.
- On November 13, 1995, 5 Americans and 2 Indians were killed and 60 injured when a car bomb exploded near a U.S.-run military training facility in Riyahd, Saudi Arabia. Four Saudi Muslim militants were later executed for the attack.
- On June 25, 1996, in Dhahran, Saudi Arabia, a truck bomb exploded in front of a U.S. military barracks; 19 Americans were killed, and 400 people were injured.
- On July 17, 1996, TWA flight 800, en route to Paris from New York City's JFK Airport, went down in a ball of fire into the ocean off Long Island. All 230 passengers and crew aboard were killed. (It appears to be a terrorist attack.)
- On July 27, 1996, during the time that Atlanta was hosting the Olympics, a homemade pipe bomb exploded at a late-night concert held in Atlanta's Centennial Park; 2 people died, and scores more injured by flying shrapnel. The blast cast a pall over the Centennial Olympic Games.
- In late December 1996, 12 letter bombs were mailed to the United States in holiday greeting cards bearing Alexandria, Egypt, postmarks. On January 2, 1997, several of these letter bombs were discovered in the mailrooms of the federal prison in Leavenworth, Kansas, and the Washington, D.C., offices of the Saudi Arabian newspaper *Al-Hayat.*
- On August 7, 1998, the American embassies in Kenya and Tanzania were bombed, killing a total of 224 people, including 12 Americans. Hundreds of others were wounded. Exiled Saudi businessman Osama bin Laden is suspected as the mastermind behind these attacks.

Source: National Center for Health Statistics, World Health Organization, country reports, and media reports; *FBI Report on Terrorism in the United States,* U.S. Government Printing Office, 1997.

The airline industry alone spends $500 million a year for security.[139] After the bombing of the U.S. embassy complex in Beirut, Lebanon, with the loss of the lives of 241 marines and sailors, the strengthening of U.S. embassy security all over the world cost well over $3 billion.

In one year alone (1985) terrorists were responsible for:

4 letter bombs
5 barricade-hostage incidents
9 hijackings
17 specific threats
54 kidnappings
70 attempted attacks
84 armed assaults
165 bombings and arsons

Of these crimes, 12 were committed in Belgium, 14 in Chile, 29 in Colombia, 12 in Cyprus, 35 in West Germany, 12 in France, 29 in Greece, 17 in Italy, 47 in Lebanon, 10 in Peru, 18 in Portugal, 15 in Spain, 10 in the United Kingdom, and 148 in other countries that experienced fewer than 10 incidents each. Regionally, Western Europe was hardest hit (182), followed by the Middle East (70) and South America (62). The remaining incidents were spread all over the other regions, with Asia and the Far East suffering the fewest incidents. Of the targets, 151 were political, 80 were diplomatic, 79 were economic, and the remainder were seemingly random public places, specific persons, and various facilities.[140] It is noteworthy that 31 of the 408 terrorist acts were committed on behalf of governments.

Among the most active terrorist groups were the Islamic Jihad (35 acts), the Fatah Revolutionary Council (24), the West German Red

Army Faction (19), the Portuguese Popular Forces of 25 April (15), and the Chilean Manuel Rodriguez Popular Front (14). In the course of these acts of terrorism, 265 persons were killed, among them 46 Americans, 16 French, 15 British, 11 Germans, 11 Italians, 10 Israelis, and 9 staff members of international organizations. The terrorists suffered fewer deaths.

International Efforts to Control Terrorism
Many years ago the world community agreed on three international conventions to combat terrorism:

- Convention on Offenses and Certain Other Acts Committed on Board Aircraft, signed at Tokyo on September 14, 1963.

- Convention for the Suppression of Unlawful Seizure of Aircraft, signed at The Hague on December 16, 1970.

- Convention for the Suppression of Unlawful Acts against the Safety of Civil Aviation, signed at Montreal on September 23, 1971.

These conventions, which provide for widespread international cooperation in the prevention of airplane hijacking and the pursuit and extradition (surrender to a requesting country) of offenders, produced a dramatic drop in the number of such incidents. Subsequently, the international community agreed on two further conventions to protect diplomats, their families, and their installations:

- Convention on the Prevention and Punishment of Crimes against Internationally Protected Persons, Including Diplomatic Agents, adopted by the General Assembly of the United Nations on December 14, 1973.

- International Convention against the Taking of Hostages, adopted by the General Assembly of the United Nations on December 17, 1979.[141]

It appears that by 1989 several governments that had been supporting "freedom fighters" (elsewhere called terrorist groups) had grown disenchanted with the groups' exercise of arbitrary violence against uninvolved civilian targets, such as airplane passengers, and had ceased to support such groups. In addition, the end of the cold war and breakup of the Soviet bloc have deprived many of these groups of funding; consequently, they are on the decline. Rising in their stead is a new type of terrorist group, more difficult to monitor, and perhaps even more dangerous. The old-style politically motivated mayhem has been replaced with ethnically and religiously inspired violence.

Recently, cults have sprung up whose members believe that a catastrophic war or natural disaster will land the "chosen few" in paradise. These doomsday cults can turn inward, leading to mass suicide or the murder of the membership. Eighty-six of David Koresh's followers at the Branch Davidian compound in Waco, Texas, died a fiery death after a lengthy siege by the FBI. It is still unclear whether the Branch Davidians set the compound on fire themselves, or if the FBI was responsible. Other groups direct their actions at outsiders. In Japan, the Aum Shinrikyo ("Supreme Truth") sect was implicated in the deadly sarin nerve gas attack on the Tokyo subway, which killed 10 and injured over 5000. The leader of the sect, Shoko Asahara, preached about the end of the world, and claimed that sarin would be a primary weapon in the "final world war."[142]

Hate Crimes

In June 1998, James Byrd, an African American, was dragged to his death in Jasper, Texas. Byrd was hitchhiking on a Saturday night when John William King and two friends chained him to their truck and pulled him, alive, for over 2 miles. His head was finally severed from his body. King, who was sentenced to death in March 1999, and his two friends were Ku Klux Klan (KKK) members.

An equally barbaric hate crime occurred in October 1998. Russell Henderson and Aaron McKinney posed as homosexuals and lured gay college student Matthew Shepard out of a bar in Wyoming. They robbed, pistol-whipped, and burned him with cigarettes before leaving him tied to a fence in near freezing temperatures. Shepard died 5 days later in a hospital. The murder trial of Henderson and McKinney

"Michigan Militia" Paramilitary Group training, suspected in Oklamoma City car bombing.

incited further displays of hate, with antigay demonstrators shouting and waving signs that read "God Hates Fags."[143] Only a few months later, in Alabama, Steven Mullins and Charles Butler lured Billy Jack Gaither, another gay male, out of a bar into a secluded area where they beat him and then dumped him into the trunk of their car. They drove about 15 miles, took him out of the trunk, and killed him with an ax handle. Mullins and Butler then placed Gaither's body on top of two old tires that they had set on fire.[144]

In August 1999, Buford O. Furrow, a former member of the Aryan Nation, walked into the lobby of the North Valley Jewish Community Center in the Granada Hills area of Los Angeles, shooting and wounding a receptionist, a camp counselor, and three children. After leaving the scene, Furrow carjacked a person's vehicle, drove to the residential area of Chutsworth, and shot Joseph Ileto, a Filipino-American postman who was in the middle of making his rounds. Furrow later turned himself in.[145]

During the late 1990s, the United States experienced some of the most gruesome displays of hate-crime violence. According to the Uniform Crime Reports, there were 8049 incidents of hate crimes, which involved 9861 separate offenses reported from over 11,000 law enforcement agencies to the FBI. Of the 8049 incidents, 4710 were racially motivated, followed by 1385 religiously motivated offenses, 1102 offenses targeting victims because of their sexual preferences, 836 ethnically motivated offenses, and 12 disability-motivated offenses.[146] According to the Southern Poverty Law Center, the number of hate groups increased from 474 in 1997 to 537 in 1998.[147] It also appears that groups are recruiting more violent members to carry out their messages of hate nationwide. One of the most recent tools used to attract these members is the Internet. Since 1995, over 160 online hate sites have been identified.[148]

Although hate crimes make up only a small percentage of overall criminality, the viciousness of the acts and their impact on broad population groups give them prominence in the media and pose extraordinary challenges to the criminal justice system. Presently, some police departments are forming bias-crime units to further the investigation of these crimes.

Militias

Militias have come to the attention of the American public only within the last decade.

Mary Nell Verrett remembers her brother, James Byrd, Jr., who was brutally murdered in a hate crime in Jasper, Texas.

Most of them are groups whose memberships consist of white, Christian, working- and middle-class Americans whose fundamental belief is that their constitutional right to bear arms (protected under the Second Amendment) is threatened. Members tend to have apocalyptic, paranoid views of U.S. politics and the federal government. Their antigovernment beliefs are intertwined with some forms of white supremacy. They believe leading Democratic politicians are "liberal elitists who betray traditional American values."[149] Members of these groups believe that the federal government is preparing for a war against its own citizens.[150] The movement is a collection of grassroots groups who call themselves Patriots, Militiamen, Freemen, Common-Law Advocates, and Strict Constitutionalists. Although they are often labeled "right-wing," members'

Crime Surfing

www.splcenter.org

The Southern Poverty Law Center is a nonprofit organization that combats hate, intolerance, and discrimination through education and litigation. For more information, visit the center's website.

backgrounds touch all points on the political spectrum. The movement is so fragmented that membership estimates are unreliable. The Southern Poverty Law Center says that members can be found in all 50 states.[151] Some estimates are that as many as 100,000 Americans are involved (Figure 11.2).[152]

Most militia groups are nonviolent. Members have a fondness for wearing battle fatigues, participating in paramilitary maneuvers, and stockpiling firearms. Yet there are growing indications of involvement in illegal activities. The Michigan Militia Corps, for example, one of the nation's largest, with an estimated membership of 10,000 to 12,000, has alleged ties to Timothy McVeigh and Terry Nichols, both charged in the Oklahoma City bombing.[153]

Yet long before this bombing focused attention on the radical right, the FBI had insiders and informants tracking the Freemen of Montana. The Freemen, 13 of whom were indicted for counterfeiting and tax fraud, are reported to have posted $1 million rewards on the heads of local officials, threatened to hang local judges, and intimidated potential jurors in a case against a Freeman. Using bits of the Constitution, the Bible, and the Magna Carta, they put together a doctrine that says the federal government has illegally usurped the common law and power of localities. They also reject the American flag. In their own courts, the Freemen have filed multimillion-dollar "liens" against government officials, and "subpoenaed" public officials to appear before their own grand juries.

For the Freemen, their 960-acre Cranfield County, Montana, farm is sovereign territory that has its own laws, courts, and officials. They also have an armory and a bank. According to federal indictments, the bank turned over $1.8 million in phony money orders and other financial instruments. These were used in fraudulent transactions with credit card companies, mail-order houses, and banks. In 1996, 26 of the antigovernment fanatics holed up in the Freemen's enclaves. Eighty-one days, and millions of dollars later, they all left the compound. The standoff was one of the longest armed sieges in U.S. history.

The media, academics, advocacy groups, and politicians have created what has been described as a hate-crime epidemic. But is the problem really as great as we have been led to believe? Consider that the media can shape public opinion and reinforce the idea that there is an epidemic through the use of these types of headlines:

- "A Cancer of Hatred Afflicts America"(1)
- "Rise in Hate Crimes Signals Alarming Resurgence of Bigotry"(2)

Books and articles are often inflammatory, argue James Jacobs and Jessica Henry.(3) The authors suggest that some scholars simply assume a grave problem exists, in spite of an overwhelming lack of evidence. This can be a dangerous assumption, for the idea of hate crime divides the community and becomes a self-fulfilling prophecy. "Crime sells—so does racism, sexism, and homophobia. Garden-variety crime has become mundane."(3)

Advocacy groups representing blacks, Jews, gays and lesbians, women, and the disabled have embraced the idea of a hate-crime epidemic, much of which is based on dubious statistics. For example, the 1997 Uniform Crime Reports show only 8049 reported hate crimes, less than .001 percent of all reported crimes. Is this an epidemic?

Jacobs and Henry point out that American history shows attacks on racial and ethnic groups started from the moment European settlers arrived and made Native Americans a target. Historically, blacks, Jews, Catholics, and recent immigrants have also been targeted. The 1990s brought a greater intolerance for this behavior, but, Jacobs and Henry say, there still is no epidemic.

Yet it matters little whether the spate of hate crimes is real or merely perceived; significant developments have taken place in consequence: Throughout the 1980s, media reports of increasing numbers of hate-motivated crimes (also known as bias crimes) pressured states to adopt statutes dealing with such crimes. These statutes prohibit acts of ethnically or religiously based intimidation, enhance penalties for these crimes, or raise the level of the crime from a misdemeanor to a felony. In addition, many criminal justice agencies have developed programs for dealing with bias crime, and at the federal level the Hate Crimes Statistics Act of 1990 mandates that local law enforcement agencies compile data on such crimes.

As defined by the federal Hate Crimes Statistics Act of 1990, hate crimes are crimes that show evidence of prejudice against certain group characteristics. The act mandates the collection of data that show evidence of prejudice based on race, sexual orientation, ethnicity, or religion. The Hate Crime Statistics Act was later amended by the Violent Crime and Law Enforcement Act of 1994 to include crimes motivated by bias against persons with disabilities.

Many bias crimes fall into the categories of simple assaults, vandalism, and harassment. Because these are relatively less serious crimes, they ordinarily get little attention. They can, however, have a major impact on the community by increasing the level of fear and hostility between groups. So extra attention to them is warranted.

In the twenty-first century, two trends are likely to continue, with increased challenges for legislators, judges, and criminal justice specialists. First, legislatures are adding sentence enhancements for crimes committed with the motive of hate. Such statutes allow or require judges to add additional prison time for those convicted of crimes committed with a hate motive.

Second, the reach of hate-crime legislation is likely to be expanded. For example, under existing federal law, hate crimes can be prosecuted only if the hate (bias) is directed at religion, sexual orientation, national origin, color, and disability. But under the Hate Crimes Prevention Act (of 1998) the reach has been expanded to any "violent act causing death or bodily injury 'because of the actual or *perceived* race, color, religion, national origin, sexual orientation, *gender,* or disability' of the victim [emphasis supplied]." This act likely will become law and be followed by similar state legislation.

Sources

1. Spencer Rumsey, "A Cancer of Hatred Afflicts America," *Newsday,* May 27, 1993, p. 129.
2. Benjamin J. Hubbard, "Commentary on Tolerance," *Los Angeles Times,* Apr. 4, 1993, p. B9.
3. James B. Jacobs and Jessica S. Henry, "The Social Construction of a Hate Crime Epidemic," *Journal of Criminal Law and Criminology,* 86 (1996): 366–391.

Questions for Discussion

1. Wisconsin's sentence-enhancement law was challenged by a defendant who claimed that his First Amendment (freedom of speech) rights were violated because the statute punishes offenders' bigoted beliefs and not just their acts. Do you agree with the U.S. Supreme Court decision to uphold the Wisconsin statute?
2. An FBI study found that intimidation was the most common type of hate crime, followed by vandalism and assault. Do you think these crimes are serious enough to warrant the extra attention they receive?

Strange things were happening in the woods. Last November agent Jose Wall of the Bureau of Alcohol, Tobacco and Firearms in Phoenix got disturbing information from people who had been through nearby Tonto National Forest. A deer hunter said he had been stopped by a group of men dressed in camouflage and armed with guns. They warned him to turn back, saying they were "security" and hinting they were with the government. The hunter didn't believe them. But something about their eyes, not to mention their weapons, made him think arguing would be imprudent. He ran into other people forced to retreat by the armed men—a Boy Scout troop. After the hunter's call, agent Wall drove out to Tonto. Near an abandoned mine, he found a crater almost big enough to swallow a car. It was recent. Someone had been using powerful explosives.(1)

In July 1996, Alcohol, Tobacco and Firearms agents uncovered a plot by members of "Team Viper" to blow up seven buildings in Phoenix, Arizona, using the same mixture of chemicals used in the Oklahoma City bombing.(1) The agents found an arsenal of two machine guns, six rifles, two pistols, grenades, fuses, blasting caps, and 56 boxes stuffed with 11,463 rounds of ammunition, as well as hundreds of pounds of the chemicals ammonium nitrate and nitromethane, which can be mixed to make a bomb.(1) Group members were charged in federal court for offenses including illegal possession of a machine gun and conspiracy to teach bombing techniques to provoke civil disorder.(2)

The Vipers are white, largely blue-collar, with no significant criminal records, and stuck in dead-end low-paying jobs. They include two janitors, a used-furniture salesman, a telephone company billing representative, an air conditioner repairman, a doughnut baker, an engineer, and a bouncer at a local topless bar. The Vipers reflect the demographics of the antigovernment paramilitary movement.(2) Indeed, in some respects the Vipers are seemingly like many other Americans; in other respects, however, they are extremely different. One member of the group, Dean Pleasant, used to paint grenades with camouflage designs and leave them on the lawn to dry. His roommate, Randy Nelson, slept each night below a Browning machine gun he had mounted over his bed, to which he had given the name "Shirley."(2)

FBI agent Bruce Gebhardt, agent in charge of the Phoenix office, cautioned about the potential danger of a group such as the Vipers: "A lot of these individuals are copycats and wannabes.

They hear the rhetoric of one and repeat it to the other. Are they really expressing their First Amendment rights? There's a line here we have to watch very closely."(1)

What may be most alarming about the Vipers is their obsession with guns that drew them together. This obsession is also driving some of them to devise schemes aimed at the disruption, if not the destruction, of a government based on the rule of law and the right to bear arms.

Sources

1. Christopher John Farley, "A Nest of Vipers," *Time,* July 15, 1996, pp. 24–25.
2. James Brooke, "Volatile Mix in Viper Militia: Hatred Plus a Love for Guns," *New York Times,* July 5, 1996, p. 1.

Questions for Discussion

1. What is it that makes members of groups like the Vipers feel they have a legitimate organization and a legitimate cause?
2. Where should government draw the limit on the legal possession of armament: Super rifles? Machine guns? Mortars? Heavy artillery? Tanks? Submarines?

Violence in Schools

In the nineteenth century, school violence was seen in the form of teachers' inflicting abuse on students, primarily by slapping a student's hand with a ruler. Parents and members of the community looked upon this "violence" as a way to remind students that they must respect authority.

The mid-twentieth century brought a new look to school violence. By the 1950s students were viewed not as the victims but rather as the agents of violence. In response, schools with high levels of violence developed security plans.[154] While overall, violence in schools has decreased, media accounts of school shootings have caused a nationwide panic, and many Americans have lost faith in the ability of the educational system to keep children safe.

Consider the following incidents: it was 12:35 P.M. on March 24, 1998, when the fire alarm bell sounded at Westside Middle School in Jonesboro, Arkansas. The children filed out of their classrooms—as in so many previous drills—and exited into an open area. Then the rifle shots rang out. By 12:39 P.M., 15 students and teachers lay in pools of blood; 4 students and 1 teacher did not survive. The shots were fired from the perimeter of the school grounds by two assailants dressed in army fatigues who had been hiding in the shrubbery. The assailants, 11-year-old Andrew Golden and his 13-year-old accomplice, had planned the attack well. They had arrived in a stolen van, armed with 10 rifles and handguns, plenty of ammunition, and survival gear.[155] That was America's

FIGURE 11.2 Beyond the fringe.

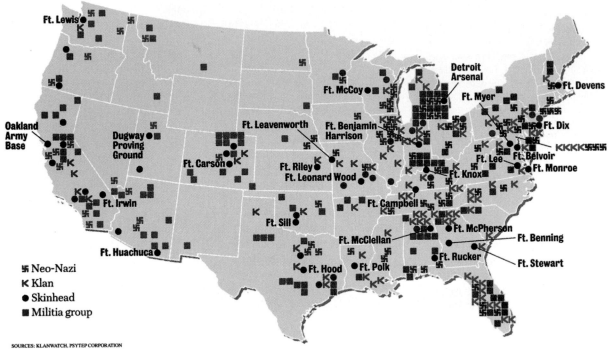

Neo-Nazi
Klan
Skinhead
Militia group

SOURCES: KLANWATCH, PSYTEP CORPORATION

Source: Gregory L. Vistica, "Extremism in the Ranks," *Newsweek*, Mar. 25, 1996, p. 36.

seventh school massacre in little over a year. School massacre eight was not far behind.

> Littleton, Colorado. (April 23, 1999)—"The school's in a panic, and I'm in the library," the teacher is desperately trying to explain to the police dispatcher as she begs for help. "I've got students down."
>
> "Under the table, kids!" she says now, directing her attention back to the students who, moments before, had been quietly studying in the library at Columbine High School. "Kids, under the table. Kids, stay on the floor. . . . Oh, God. Oh, God—kids, just stay down." The teacher's frantic voice, heard as gunfire reverberated in the background, was part of a tape recording released by the police today of some of the emergency calls placed on Tuesday as two students began their lethal rampage.[156]

This 911 call depicts the horror of April 20, 1999. Eric Harris, 18 years old, and Dylan Klebold, 17 years old, executed a massacre they had planned for a year, to occur on Hitler's birthday, at the Littleton, Colorado, Columbine High School. Harris and Klebold were members of a group who referred to themselves as the "Trenchcoat Mafia," a group reportedly known to dislike athletes and minorities. With four firearms and over 30 explosives, they killed 14 students, one teacher, and lastly, themselves.

The media made much of the fact that schools had been turned into killing fields. Fear gripped students and parents all over the country. In fact, shortly after the Columbine shootings, copycat crimes and attempts occurred. In Alberta, Canada, a 14-year-old boy wearing a three-quarter-length parka walked into W. R. Myers High School, whipped out a .22 caliber rifle, killed a 17-year-old boy, and critically wounded another. In Brooklyn, New York, five students were arrested for bragging about plans to blow up the school on graduation day. It was also no surprise when schools in Hillsborough, New Jersey, closed for 1 day after students began receiving e-mail messages stating, "If you think what happened in Col-

Security camera image of Eric Harris and Dylan Klebold during the shoot-out at Columbine High School in Littleton, Colorado.

orado was bad, wait until you see what happens in Hillsborough Middle School on Friday."[157] Yet another incident occurred on December 9, 1999, when a seventh-grade honor student opened fire on his classmates, wounding five, at the Fort Gibson Middle School in Fort Gibson, Oklahoma. Educators called for stricter security, and legislators responded to the media frenzy with proposals ranging from keeping students away from school during all but regular school hours to seeking the death penalty for 11-year-olds.

What is the reality? What do experts tell us? A National School Safety Center research report shows that the probability of being killed by lightning is twice as high as that of being killed at school.[158] And the *1998 Annual Report on School Safety*, the first report of its kind, proclaims that 90 percent of schools are free of serious, violent crime. The most common types of attacks are fights without weapons. This report also claims that there exists less than a 1-in-a-million chance of suffering a school-associated violent death.[159] Yet that is little consolation to the victims of school massacres and their families.

The public looks for scapegoats. Who did what wrong? And what happened to the days when throwing a spitball or an eraser got a student in big trouble? The answer must come from specialists in criminology. All too often, policy and legislation in matters of crime and criminal justice are the result of publicity given to emotion-charged media reports rather than of research data from scientific studies. Experts need to look into the causes of school violence. What do the events have in common? Some say that students are growing up with violence. One survey of inner-city children showed that 43 percent of 7- to 19-year-olds have witnessed a homicide.[160]

What can be done specifically, not only in the aftermath of such events, but also in terms of preventive measures? According to the 1994 Gun Free Schools Act, all schools that receive federal education funding must maintain policies mandating expulsion for any student caught bringing a firearm to school (Figure 11.3).[161] In addition, individual schools are making major changes. Following the shootings at Columbine, new security measures were instituted, including the installation of 16 color

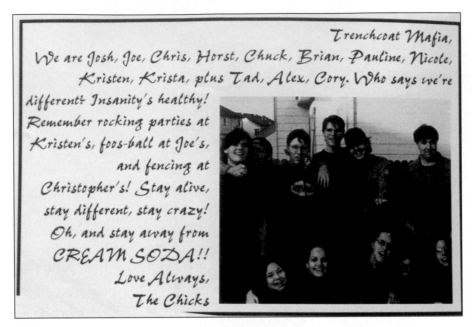

Trenchcoat Mafia,

We are Josh, Joe, Chris, Horst, Chuck, Brian, Pauline, Nicole, Kristen, Krista, plus Tad, Alex, Cory. Who says we're different? Insanity's healthy! Remember rocking parties at Kristen's, foos-ball at Joe's, and fencing at Christopher's! Stay alive, stay different, stay crazy! Oh, and stay away from CREAM SODA!! Love Always, The Chicks

The "Trench Coat Mafia" as they appear in the 1998 Columbine High School Yearbook, Littleton, Colorado.

Kayla Rolland, six years old, was fatally shot in her classroom by a first grade classmate in Mt. Morris, Michigan, on February 29, 2000.

TV cameras to monitor both indoor and outdoor activities, the issuance of identification badges, the restriction of access to locked entryways, and the addition of another uniformed guard to patrol the hallways.[162] Other schools are suggesting the use of computer-coded identification badges.[163] Any way the situation is viewed, there is a noticeable shift from general security in schools to crisis management. Schools are also becoming more militaristic. In some California schools, there are random checks with metal-detector wands. Policies requiring uniforms, or at a minimum, the requirement of tucked-in shirts, are aimed at preventing the carrying of concealed weapons.[164] Still other responses to school violence include the implementation of lockdowns, detector dogs, and rent-a-cops. The entire situation begs the question: Is it truly necessary to turn schools into prisonlike structures? (See also "Of Immediate Concern" in Chapter 9.)

With the implementation of security measure comes an increase in safety, but at what cost? The level of trust between administrators and students dwindles. Innocent and normally well-behaved students feel they are being targeted and their privacy is being invaded. The result could be increased levels of alienation, which in

FIGURE 11.3 Students and guns: a better report card.

Student gun-related expulsions, 1997–98
Number of students expelled per 100,000

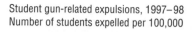

Number of cases ■ 0–9 ■ 10–49 ▨ 50–99 ■ 100+

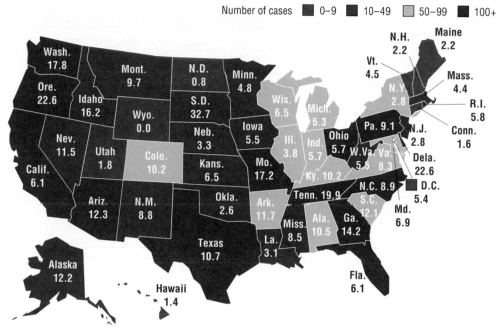

Wash. 17.8
Ore. 22.6
Idaho 16.2
Mont. 9.7
N.D. 0.8
Minn. 4.8
N.H. 2.2
Maine 2.2
Vt. 4.5
Mass. 4.4
N.Y. 2.8
R.I. 5.8
Conn. 1.6
Nev. 11.5
Utah 1.8
Wyo. 0.0
S.D. 32.7
Wis. 6.5
Mich. 5.3
Pa. 9.1
N.J. 2.8
Calif. 6.1
Colo. 10.2
Neb. 3.3
Iowa 5.5
Ill. 3.8
Ind. 5.7
Ohio 5.7
W.Va. 5.5
Va. 8.3
Dela. 22.6
Ariz. 12.3
N.M. 8.8
Kans. 6.5
Mo. 17.2
Ky. 10.2
N.C. 8.9
D.C. 5.4
Okla. 2.6
Ark. 11.7
Tenn. 19.9
S.C. 12.1
Md. 6.9
Texas 10.7
Miss. 8.5
Ala. 10.5
Ga. 14.2
La. 3.1
Alaska 12.2
Hawaii 1.4
Fla. 6.1

Students and Violence, 1997

8.5% said they have carried a weapon at school
7.4% said they were threatened or injured with a weapon at school
4.0% said they felt too unsafe to attend school

Students who said they have...

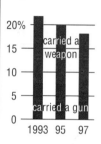

Source: Claudia Kalb, "Schools on the Alert," *Newsweek*, Aug. 23, 1999, p. 42.

some cases lies at the root of most violence. Zero-tolerance policies for weapons, including guns, switchblades, pocketknives, box cutters, razors, ice picks, blackjacks, and chains, are a necessity.[165] High-tech solutions are clearly not the only alternative. Also needed are efforts aimed at increasing communication and interpersonal skills, availability of counseling, and guidance in relationship building. If there is one thing to learn from the recent school shootings, it is that no school is immune to violence. School violence is no longer a problem restricted to inner cities. It is a nationwide concern.

VIOLENCE AND GUN CONTROL

The tragedies of the recent school shootings have fueled the gun-control debate. Estimates indicate that in the wake of the school massacres, more than 80 percent of Americans support stricter gun laws.[166] In fact, following the Columbine High School shooting in Colorado, the National Rifle Association was politely asked by various officials and concerned citizens to cancel its national meeting that was to be held in Denver, Colorado, only weeks after the shootings.[167]

Violence in the United States is frequently attributed to historical conditioning (the need of frontier people to survive in a hostile environment), social factors (poverty, inequities,

Crime Surfing

www.ed.gov/pubs/AnnSchoolRept98/
www.ojp.usdoj.gov/bjs/abstract/iscs99.htm

The Bureau of Justice Statistics and the National Center for Education Statistics collaborate to produce the *Annual Report on School Safety* and *Indicators of School Crime and Safety.* These documents include statistics on the extent of the problem and give examples of programs across the country that address issues such as gangs, bullying, and weapons. See Annual Report on School Safety and Indicators of School Crime and Safety.

and other inner-city problems), and the laxity of the criminal justice system (failure to apprehend and convict enough criminals and to imprison long enough those who are convicted). Some researchers have focused on one common element in a large proportion of violent crime: the availability of firearms in the United States.

One of the hottest and longest political and scholarly debates in our history centers on this point: Should and can Americans drastically restrict the availability of firearms, and would such controls substantially reduce the rate and severity of violent crime?

The Extent of Firearm-Related Offenses

It is difficult to be certain how many guns there are in the United States. Before 1850 less than 10 percent of U.S. citizens were believed to own guns, and between 1800 and 1845, only about 15 percent of all violent deaths were caused by guns.[168] The Bureau of Alcohol, Tobacco and Firearms estimates that from 1899 to 1993, about 223 million guns became available in this country. It is unknown how many of these guns have been seized, destroyed, or lost, or do not work properly.[169] Current estimates indicate there are over 200 million firearms in circulation in the United States, including about 70 million handguns.[170] Half of the handguns are so-called Saturday-night specials (defined by the Bureau of Alcohol, Tobacco and Firearms as small weapons of .32 caliber or less with a barrel length of less than 3 inches and costing $50 or less). The supply of handguns increases by about 1.5 million each year.[171]

The Federal Bureau of Investigation has reported that a handgun is used in about half of all murders and one-third of rapes and robberies (Table 11.4). Two-thirds of police deaths in the line of duty are attributed to the use of handguns. Rates of crime involving guns are far lower in most other developed Western nations than in the United States.[172] According to the Task Force on Firearms of the National Commission on the Causes and Prevention of Violence, the rate of homicide by gun is 40 times higher in the United States than in England and Wales, and our rate of robbery by gun is 60 times higher.

The financial cost of gunshot injury and death, in terms of medical costs, lost produc-

TABLE 11.4 Murdered Juveniles by Age, Gender, and Type of Weapon Used, 1980–1997

		Age of victim			Victim ages 0–17	
Weapon	0–17	0–5	6–11	12–17	Males	Females
Total	100%	100%	100%	100%	100%	100%
Firearm	51	10	42	75	60	31
Knife/blunt object	14	11	19	15	13	17
Personal*	19	48	11	3	15	27
Other	16	30	28	7	12	25

• Three out of four murdered juveniles age 12 or older were killed with a firearm.

• Nearly half (48%) of all murdered children below age 6 were killed by offenders using only their hands, fists, or feet.

• Male murder victims were nearly twice as likely as female victims to be killed with a firearm.

*Personal includes hands, fists, or feet.

Note: Detail may not total 100% because of rounding.

Source: Adapted from the FBI's Supplementary Homicide Reports for the years 1980–1997 [machine-readable data files], as cited in Juvenile Offenders and Victims: 1999 National Report.

tivity, and pain, suffering, and reduced quality of life, was estimated at $63 billion in 1992 alone. The Centers for Disease Control and Prevention estimates that between June 1, 1992, and May 31, 1993, approximately 99,000 nonfatal firearms injuries were treated in U.S. hospital emergency rooms.[173]

Youth and Guns

Three young thugs boarded a city bus in Queens yesterday, brandished guns like Wild West bandits and staged a frontier-style holdup. They strode up and down the aisle, fired shots into the roof, terrorized and robbed 22 passengers, struck a girl in the face with a gun butt and escaped with $300 in cash and fistfulls of jewelry.

The outlaws—one armed with a silver revolver and another with a pair of guns, while a third carried a book bag—made no effort to conceal their faces as they boarded the Q-85 bus at 8:30 a.m. at 140th Avenue and Edgewood Avenue in Springfield Gardens, a residential neighborhood just northeast of Kennedy International Airport.[174]

The "bandits" were three youths age 15 to 19. In a growing number of incidents across the United States, young people are using guns for

Protests outside the Denver NRA Convention in 1999.

robberies, gang warfare, initiation rites (drive-by shootings by wanna-be gang members), random shootings (in fact, James Jordan, father of former basketball star Michael Jordan, fell victim), and protection from their peers.[175]

Concern is mounting over adolescent illegal gun ownership and use. In 1995 the National Institute of Justice interviewed a sample of arrested individuals in Denver, the District of Columbia, Indianapolis, Los Angeles, Phoenix, St. Louis, and San Diego. The study found that juveniles are more likely than arrestees overall to commit crime with a gun. Of the juveniles interviewed, 20 percent said they carried a gun most or all of the time, 25 percent had stolen a gun, and 33 percent who owned a gun had used one in a crime (the percentages were considerably higher for gang members). Eighteen percent of the juveniles agreed that it was appropriate to use a gun "to shoot someone who disrespected you."[176]

Another study, of inner-city high schools in California, Illinois, Louisiana, and New Jersey, found a connection between involvement in drugs and gun carrying.[177] The same study sampled female students as well; 1 in 10 female students owned a gun at some time, and roughly the same percentage carried a gun.[178]

Why have youths turned to guns? When asked, many of them respond the way three teenagers did: "You fire a gun and you can just *hear* the power. It's like *yeah!*" or "It became cool to say you could get a gun," or "Nobody messes with you if they think you may have a gun."[179] While there are many studies on adolescent violent behavior, there are

Crime Surfing

www.atf.treas.gov

The Bureau of Alcohol, Tobacco and Firearms provides information on firearms use, guns in circulation, and programs aimed at reducing the possession of illegal firearms.

few on adolescent illegal gun use. One of the few, a recent study of ninth- and tenth-grade boys, 14- and 15-year-olds, in Rochester, New York, found that most boys who owned illegal guns had friends who owned guns; over half of the illegal gun owners were gang members; and selling drugs was a prime motivation for carrying a gun. Moreover, illegal gun ownership, friends' gun ownership, gang membership, and drug use were closely related to gun crime, street crime, and minor delinquency.[180] Illegal firearms have traditionally been used by youths in low-income urban neighborhoods. The problem, like that of school shootings, is now spreading to the suburbs.

Controlling Handgun Use

While most people agree that gun-related crime is a particularly serious part of our crime problem, there is little agreement on what to do about it. Some want prohibition. Others want comprehensive licensing and registrations.[181] Civic organizations and police associations call for more laws prescribing mandatory sentences for the illegal purchase, possession, or use of firearms. Close to 20,000 laws that regulate firearms already exist in the United States.

A variety of methods of controlling handgun use have been tried:

- In 1996 the Bureau of Alcohol, Tobacco and Firearms established the Youth Crime Gun Interdiction Initiative *to trace crime guns* (those illegally possessed or used in a crime) recovered by law enforcement. Between 1997 and 1998, 76,000 crime guns were traced. Almost half were recovered from persons under the age of 25.[182]

- A *prohibition against carrying guns* in public seemed to be related to a drop in gun crimes in Boston[183] and a leveling off of handgun violence in Detroit.[184]

- In Kansas City, Missouri, a *police gun-confiscation program* was implemented in gun-crime hot spots in the target area, which had a murder rate 20 times the national average. Gun seizures in the target area increased by over 65 percent, while gun crimes decreased by 49 percent. Homicides were also significantly reduced in the target area.[185]

- Some states have passed what are referred to as *sentence-enhancement statutes:* The punishment for an offense is more severe if a person commits it under certain conditions, such as by using a gun. The Massachusetts law (1975) mandates a minimum sentence of 1 year's incarceration upon conviction for the illegal carrying of a firearm.[186] Michigan created a new offense—commission of a felony while possessing a firearm—and added a mandatory 2-year prison sentence to the sentence received for the commission of the felony itself. The state mounted a widespread publicity campaign: "One with a gun gets you two," read the billboards and bumper stickers.[187]

Sentence enhancement has been studied in six U.S. cities. Homicides committed with firearms decreased in all six after sentence-enhancement laws took effect, although the decline in homicides was large in some cities and small in others. Researchers studying sentence enhancement point out that its effectiveness is related to how closely judges follow the law. An additional 3 years in prison may deter criminals from using guns, while an additional month may not.

- Project Exile began in Richmond, Virginia, in 1997. This program specifies that any time a gun is found on a person, whether a drug dealer, drug user, convicted felon, or suspect in a crime, the case will be tried under federal statutes in federal court. By moving gun offenses into the federal system, offenders face mandatory sentences of 5 years without parole. Prison time is increased for repeated or aggravated offenses. This project is advertised all over the city on billboards that in bold letters say, "An Illegal Gun Gets You 5 Years in Federal Prison." Since the implementation of this program, murders in Richmond have dropped significantly, from 140 in 1997 to 94 in 1998 and 32 in the first 6 months of 1999. Project Exile also led to the recovery of almost 500 illegal handguns, indictments against about 400 people on gun charges, and a conviction rate of 86 percent through trials and plea bargains.[188] This Virginia program is being mirrored in other cities as well, with anticipation of a similar effect.[189] The National Rifle Association supports this program, claiming that it is the best alternative to restrictive gun laws.[190]

- A *total ban on handguns* was tried in Washington, D.C., beginning in 1976. Both gun homicides and gun suicides dropped visibly after the ban took effect, while no change occurred in homicides and suicides not committed with guns.[191]

- Some communities have tried *buy-back programs.* St. Louis, San Francisco,

Like father, like son. Dad teaching son how to shoot at the Annual Machine Gun Weekend Tournament at the Knobb Hill Gun Range.

Philadelphia, New York, and several other cities have embarked on such programs to reduce the number of handguns in circulation in the community. Police departments buy guns, no questions asked, for $50 each. In October 1991, the St. Louis Police Department bought 5371 guns from citizens in 10 days. The Philadelphia police received 1044 guns within a 2-week period.

- *Federal legislation* has been passed in an attempt to prevent criminals from buying guns. The Brady bill, named after James Brady, White House press secretary who was injured in the 1981 assassination attempt on President Ronald Reagan, went into effect on February 28, 1994. It calls for a 5-day waiting period and a background check before a handgun can be purchased. Further, the bill prevents certain groups of people, such as convicted felons, fugitives from justice, illegal aliens, juveniles, and the mentally ill, from buying guns. Between February 1994, when the Brady bill was first implemented, and the end of the interim period, November 1998, at which time the permanent provisions of the law became effective,[192] approximately 12.7 million background checks resulted in about 312,000 rejections, a rejection rate of 2.4 percent. The reasons for rejection varied: 63 percent of applicants were rejected as a result of prior felony convictions or current felony indictments; 10 percent of

the applicants were rejected as a result of domestic violence misdemeanor convictions; and 3 percent of applicants were rejected as a result of the presence of domestic violence protection orders. During the interim period, the U.S. Department of Justice established the National Instant Criminal Background Check System, which indexes and accesses criminal justice agency databases that are used in the background check process. When the permanent provisions for the Brady act became effective, presale background checks were expanded to include not only handguns, but all other types of firearms as well.[193] Supporters of the Brady bill claim this shows that fewer felons are managing to obtain handguns. Others argue that felons can still obtain handguns through illegal channels. James Q. Wilson, for example, says the real test of the Brady bill is whether "felons have been stopped from buying guns and then killing people with them."

None of these methods resulted in drastic reductions in the number of handgun-related deaths, although some led to a small decrease. As two gun-control researchers point out, the important question to be answered with regard to gun control is this: How many deaths must be prevented by a gun-control method to justify its use? Very few of the millions of people who own guns commit crimes with them, and control policies will affect legitimate owners as well as criminals. David McDowall and Alan Lizotte ask:

> Is the legitimate happiness of 10 million gun owners worth the lives of 10,000 murder victims? One murder victim? In another context, is a highly restrictive measure that would save 200 lives better than a less restrictive measure that would save 100? There is no obvious answer to these questions, and different people will draw the line in different places.[195]

Perhaps we can learn from the countries with low gun-related homicide rates. Many citizens of Switzerland and Israel, for example, have army-issue firearms at their constant disposal by virtue of citizen-army requirements, yet these weapons

Crime Surfing

www.nra.org

The National Rifle Association maintains its own website, which examines gun-control issues, offers legislative updates, and provides information on state firearm laws.

are rarely used for homicides. What factors control the use of handguns in these countries? Many European countries and Canada maintain strict national gun laws. These countries often require that guns be registered, that owners be licensed, and that guns be stored with the greatest security. In some countries it is mandatory that a gun license applicant pass an examination on gun safety.[196] Even if comparative studies come up with useful findings, some researchers believe the political problems surrounding gun control in the United States will probably continue to hinder the development of nationwide, or even statewide, gun-control policies for some time to come.

The Gun-Control Debate

The battle line on gun control appears to be clearly drawn between the opponents of regulation (including the 3 million members of the National Rifle Association, or NRA, and their supporters) on the one hand and the advocates of control (including the 12 major law enforcement groups, the private organization Handgun Control, and three-quarters of the American public) on the other. The gun lobby likes to say that it is people who kill, not guns, so it is the people who use guns illegally who should be punished. To deter these people, gun enthusiasts say, we need to have stiffer penalties, including mandatory sentences that take these offenders off the streets.

Gun-control opponents often have bumper stickers that read, "When guns are outlawed, only outlaws will have guns." Moreover, most gun owners claim that it is their right to own firearms to protect their homes, especially when they lose confidence in the police and courts.[197] And by controlling guns, they say, the government intrudes in

their private affairs. They interpret the Second Amendment to the Constitution as giving them an individual right "to keep and bear arms." Furthermore, the gun lobby maintains, people may wish to enjoy their guns as collectors or for sport and hunting.

Another argument concerns what is called the *displacement effect:* People who are deterred by gun-control legislation from using guns to commit offenses will use some other weapon to achieve their goals. Or perhaps even more violent offenses will be committed if offenders can rely on the fact that the consequences of a nonfirearm offense are less serious.

Finally, in the face of increasing random violence and a perceived inability of the police to safeguard citizens, more people are routinely carrying guns for self-protection. In many states, it is now becoming easier to do so, as more and more jurisdictions adopt "carrying-concealed-weapons" laws.[198]

Gun-control advocates compare our extremely high homicide rate to the much lower rates of other countries with tighter gun-control laws, including our neighbor Canada. They also argue that the availability of a gun makes homicide and suicide much more probable, because it is easier to produce death with a gun than with any other weapon. Moreover, they claim, better regulation or prohibition of gun ownership is a much faster way to lessen gun-related criminality than such long-term approaches as finding remedies for social problems. Researchers are testing the claims, but thus far no definitive conclusions have been reached.

In a related aspect of the gun-control debate, the gun industry finds itself under pressure. Many lawsuits have been filed against the gun industry on the basis that gun manufacturers have neglected to incorporate safety devices into their products. Gun makers are also cited with allowing their products to be marketed in such ways that both criminals and juveniles can easily obtain them for illicit use.[199] As a response to these lawsuits, many gun makers are attempting to install various safety devices on their products, including trigger locks and cable locks. (Figure 11.4.)

FIGURE 11.4   Companies are trying to make safer guns.

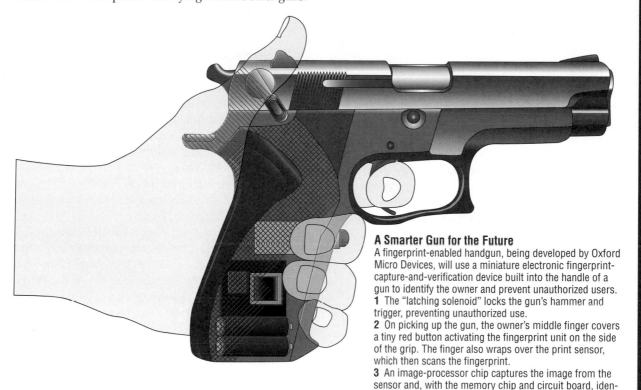

A Smarter Gun for the Future
A fingerprint-enabled handgun, being developed by Oxford
Micro Devices, will use a miniature electronic fingerprint-
capture-and-verification device built into the handle of a
gun to identify the owner and prevent unauthorized users.
1 The "latching solenoid" locks the gun's hammer and
trigger, preventing unauthorized use.
2 On picking up the gun, the owner's middle finger covers
a tiny red button activating the fingerprint unit on the side
of the grip. The finger also wraps over the print sensor,
which then scans the fingerprint.
3 An image-processor chip captures the image from the
sensor and, with the memory chip and circuit board, identifies the fingerprint and unlocks the gun.

Source: "A Nationwide Backlash: State and Local Governments Are Taking Aim at the Gun Industry, Either by Enacting Legislation or by Filing Lawsuits," *Time,*
Aug. 9, 1999, p. 28.

REVIEW

Murder, assaults of various kinds, rape, robbery, kidnapping—all share the common element of violence,
though they differ in many ways: in the harm they cause,
the intention of the perpetrator, the punishment they
warrant, and other legal criteria. Social scientists have
been exploring the frequency with which these crimes
are committed in our society and elsewhere, their distribution through time and place, and the role played by
circumstances, including the environment and behavior
patterns, in facilitating or preventing them.

Such categories as mass murder, serial murder,
gang murder, and date rape are shorthand designations for frequently occurring crime patterns that have
not been specifically identified in penal codes. Another pattern of crime that also is not defined as such
in the penal codes has become so important that it
may be considered in conjunction with the other

crimes of violence: family-related crime. This pattern
encompasses a variety of violent crimes that include
the abuse of spouses, children, and the elderly.

Some of the more pressing problems we face today are global terrorism, an increase in hate crimes
nationwide, the spread of racist and antigovernment
militias, and deadly shootings in American schools.
The media attention given to these crimes has had a
dramatic effect on the public's perception that violence has reached epidemic proportions.

The gun-control controversy demonstrates that
both the definitions of crimes and the social and environmental characteristics associated with them
must be studied in order to develop control and prevention strategies. Our violence-prone society will
have to make serious choices if it is to reach that
level of peaceful living achieved by many other modern societies.

Review • You Be the Criminologist • Key Terms • Notes

YOU BE THE CRIMINOLOGIST

You are the superintendent of schools for your district. Your schools have not experienced any violent incidents, but because of the media hype surrounding the school shootings throughout the country, you are under pressure to take preventive measures. What actions would you take and what programs would you develop to make your schools safe and gun-proof? How would you implement these preventive measures? What are their advantages and disadvantages? How would you target your audience? What are the likely positive and negative reactions to the preventive measures?

KEY TERMS

The numbers next to the terms refer to the pages on which the terms are defined.

aggravated assault (296)

assault (296)

battery (296)

felony murder (288)

homicide (288)

involuntary manslaughter (289)

justifiable homicide (288)

kidnapping (306)

malice aforethought (288)

manslaughter (288)

mass murder (293)

murder (288)

negligent homicide (289)

rape (303)

robbery (307)

serial murder (293)

simple assault (296)

sociopaths (294)

stranger homicide (292)

terrorism (309)

victim precipitation (291)

voluntary manslaughter (288)

NOTES

1. *Crimes of Violence: A Staff Report Submitted to the National Commission on the Causes and Prevention of Violence* (Washington, D.C.: U.S. Government Printing Office, December 1969), vol. 12, p. xxvii; vol. 11, p. 4.
2. G. O. W. Mueller, "Where Murder Begins," *New Hampshire Bar Journal,* **2** (1960): 214–224; G. O. W. Mueller, "On Common Law Mens Rea," *Minnesota Law Review,* **42** (1958): 1043–1104.
3. Wayne R. LaFave and Austin W. Scott, *Handbook on Criminal Law* (St. Paul, Minn.: West, 1972), pp. 572–577.
4. *Commonwealth v. Welansky,* 316 Mass. 383, N.E. 2d 902 (1944), at pp. 906–907. See G. O. W. Mueller, "The Devil May Care—Or Should We? A Reexamination of Criminal Negligence," *Kentucky Law Journal,* **55** (1966–1967): 29–49.
5. Uniform Crime Reports, 1998, p. 15.
6. Ibid., p. 16.
7. Ibid.
8. Ibid.
9. Roland Chilton, "Twenty Years of Homicide and Robbery in Chicago: The Impact of the City's Changing Racial and Age Composition," *Journal of Quantitative Criminology,* **3** (1987): 195–213. See also Carolyn Rebecca Block, *Homicide in Chicago* (Chicago: Loyola University of Chicago, 1986), p. 7; and William Wilbanks, *Murder in Miami* (Lanham, Md.: University Press of America, 1984).
10. William Julius Wilson, "Work," *New York Times Magazine,* Aug. 18, 1996, pp. 27, 28.
11. William B. Harvey, "Homicide among Young Black Adults: Life in the Subculture of Exasperation," in *Homicide among Black Americans,* ed. Darnell F. Hawkins (Lanham, Md.: University Press of America, 1986), pp. 153–171. See also Robert L. Hampton, "Family Violence and Homicide in the Black Community: Are They Linked?" in *Violence in the Black Family,* ed. Hampton (Lexington, Mass.: Lexington Books, 1987), pp. 135–156.
12. Coramae Richey Mann, "Black Women Who Kill," in Hawkins, *Homicide among Black Americans,* pp. 157–186.

13. Hans von Hentig, *The Criminal and His Victim* (New Haven, Conn.: Yale University Press, 1948).
14. Marvin E. Wolfgang, *Patterns in Criminal Homicide* (Philadelphia: University of Pennsylvania Press, 1958), p. 253. See also Marvin E. Wolfgang, "A Sociological Analysis of Criminal Homicide," in *Studies in Homicide,* ed. Wolfgang (New York: Harper & Row, 1967), pp. 15–28.
15. Richard B. Felson and Steven F. Messner, "Disentangling the Effects of Gender and Intimacy on Victim Precipitation in Homicide," *Criminology,* **36** (1998): 405–423.
16. Robert A. Silverman and Leslie W. Kennedy, "Relational Distance and Homicide: The Role of the Stranger," *Journal of Criminal Law and Criminology,* **78** (1987): 272–308. See also Nanci Koser Wilson, "Gendered Interaction in Criminal Homicide," in *Homicide: The Victim/Offender Connection,* ed. Anna Victoria Wilson (Cincinnati: Anderson, 1993), pp. 43–62.
17. Margaret A. Zahn and Philip C. Sagi, "Stranger Homicides in Nine American Cities," *Journal of Criminal Law and Criminology,* **78** (1987): 377–397.
18. Uniform Crime Reports, 1998, p. 19.
19. Marc Riedel, "Stranger Violence: Perspectives, Issues, and Problems," *Journal of Criminal Law and Criminology,* **78** (1987): 223–258.
20. Kenneth Polk, "Observations on Stranger Homicide," *Journal of Criminal Justice,* **21** (1993): 573–582.
21. Coramae Richey Mann, *When Women Kill* (Albany: State University of New York Press, 1996).
22. See, e.g., Colin Loftin, Karen Kindley, Sandra L. Norris, and Brian Wiersema, "An Attribute Approach to Relationships between Offenders and Victims in Homicide," *Journal of Criminal Law and Criminology,* **78** (1987): 259–271.
23. Angela Browne, "Assault and Homicide at Home: When Battered Women Kill," *Advances in Applied Social Psychology,* **3** (1986): 57–79.
24. Martin Daly and Margo Wilson, *Homicide* (New York: Aldine–De Gruyter, 1988), pp. 294–295.
25. Coramae Richey Mann, "Getting Even?: Women Who Kill in Domestic Encounters," *Justice Quarterly,* **5** (1988): 33–51.
26. Martha Smithey, "Infant Homicide: Victim/Offender Relationship and Causes of Death," *Journal of Family Violence,* **13** (1998): 285–297.
27. Ibid.
28. Lawrence A. Greenfeld, *Child Victimizers: Violent Offenders and Their Victims* (Washington, D.C.: Bureau of Justice Statistics, 1996), p. 3.
29. Etienne G. Krug, James A. Mercy, Linda Dahlberg, and Kenneth Powell, "Firearm- and Non-Firearm-Related Homicide among Children: An International Comparison," *Homicide Studies,* **2** (1998): 83–95.
30. Uniform Crime Reports, 1998, pp. 232–233.
31. William R. Holcomb and Anasseril E. Daniel, "Homicide without an Apparent Motive," *Behavioral Sciences and the Law,* **6** (1988): 429–439.
32. See Michael Newton, *Mass Murder: An Annotated Bibliography* (New York: Garland, 1988).
33. N. R. Kleinfield, "Cruelty of Strangers: 3 Men Evoke a Fearsome Trend," *New York Times,* June 23, 1996, p. 27.
34. See <http://www.mayhem.net/crime/serial.html>
35. Daniel Klaidman, "The End of the Line," *Newsweek,* July 26, 1999, p. 71.
36. Michael D. Kelleher and C. L. Kelleher, *Murder Most Rare: The Female Serial Killer* (Westport, Conn.: Praeger, 1998).
37. Daniel Pedersen, "Death in Dunblane," *Newsweek,* Mar. 25, 1996, pp. 24–29.
38. U.S. Department of Justice, Bureau of Justice Statistics, *Workplace Violence, 1992–1996* (Washington, D.C.: U.S. Government Printing Office, 1998).
39. Susan Faludi, "Rage of the American Male," *Newsweek,* Aug. 16, 1999, p. 31. See also <http://www.cnn.com/US/9908/31/atlanta.shooting.03/>
40. See Dawn N. Castillo and E. Lynn Jenkins, "Industries and Occupations at High Risk for Work-Related Homicide," *Journal of Occupational Medicine,* **36** (1994): 125–132.

Review • You Be the Criminologist • Key Terms • Notes

41. David Abrahamsen, *The Murdering Mind* (New York: Harper & Row, 1973).
42. Mel Heimer, *The Cannibal: The Case of Albert Fish* (New York: Lyle Stuart, 1971).
43. Margaret Cheney, *The Co-ed Killer* (New York: Walker, 1976).
44. Jack Levin and James Alan Fox, *Mass Murder: America's Growing Menace* (New York: Plenum, 1985). See also Ronald M. Holmes and Stephen T. Holmes, "Understanding Mass Murder: A Starting Point," *Federal Probation*, **56** (1992): 53–61.
45. James Fox and Jack Levin, "Multiple Homicide: Patterns of Serial and Mass Murder," in *Crime and Justice: A Review of Research*, ed. Michael Tonry (Chicago: University of Chicago Press, 1998), pp. 407–455.
46. James Alan Fox and Jack Levin, *Overkill: Mass Murder and Serial Killing Exposed* (New York: Plenum, 1994); and Philip Jenkins, "African-Americans and Serial Homicide," *American Journal of Criminal Justice*, **17** (1993): 47–60.
47. Ronald M. Holmes and James de Burger, *Serial Murder* (Newbury Park, Calif.: Sage, 1988), p. 155.
48. Cheryl L. Maxson, Margaret A. Gordon, and Malcolm W. Klein, "Differences between Gang and Nongang Homicides," *Criminology*, **23** (1985): 209–222.
49. G. David Curry and Irving A. Spergel, "Gang Homicide, Delinquency, and Community," *Criminology*, **26** (1988): 381–405.
50. Range Hutson, Deirdre Anglin, and Marc Eckstein, "Drive-by-Shootings by Violent Street Gangs in Los Angeles: A Five-Year Review from 1989 to 1993," *Academic Emergency Medicine*, **3** (1996): 300–303.
51. Sam Howe Verhovek, "Houston Knows Murder, but This . . . ," *New York Times*, July 9, 1993, p. A8.
52. Groeme Newman, ed., *Global Report on Crime and Justice* (New York: United Nations; Oxford University Press, 1999), p. 50.
53. Uniform Crime Reports, 1998.
54. U.S. Department of Justice, Office of Juvenile Justice and Delinquency Prevention, *Juvenile Offenders and Victims, 1999 National Report* (Washington, D.C.: U.S. Department of Justice, OJJDP, 1999), p. 17. See also Krug et al., "Firearm-and Non-Firearm-Related Homicide among Children."
55. Harvey Krahn, Timothy F. Hartnagel, and John W. Gartrell, "Income Inequality and Homicide Rates: Cross-National Data and Criminological Theories," *Criminology*, **24** (1986): 269–295.
56. Glenn D. Deane, "Cross-National Comparison of Homicide: Age/Sex-Adjusted Rates Using the 1980 U.S. Homicide Experience as a Standard," *Journal of Quantitative Criminology*, **3** (1987): 215–227.
57. Dane Archer and Rosemary Gartner, *Violence and Crime in Cross-National Perspective* (New Haven, Conn.: Yale University Press, 1984).
58. Candice Nelsen, Jay Corzine, and Lin Corzine-Huff, "The Violent West Reexamined; A Research Note on Regional Homicide Rates," *Criminology*, **32** (1994): 149–161.
59. See Scott H. Decker, "Exploring Victim-Offender Relationships in Homicide: The Role of Individual and Event Characteristics," *Justice Quarterly*, **10** (1993): 585–612. See also Scott H. Decker, "Reconstructing Homicide Events: The Role of Witnesses in Fatal Encounters," *Journal of Criminal Justice*, **23** (1995): 439–450.
60. David F. Luckenbill, "Criminal Homicide as a Situated Transaction," *Social Problems*, **25** (1977): 176–186. Although Luckenbill focused on homicides, the stages he identified are identical in assaults.
61. For a comprehensive, multidisciplinary review of the literature on violence, see James T. Tedeschi and Richard B. Felson, *Violence, Aggression, and Coercive Actions* (Washington, D.C.: American Psychological Association, 1994). See also Barry R. Ruback and Neil Alan Weiner, eds., *Interpersonal Violent Behaviors: Social and Cultural Aspects* (New York: Springer, 1994).
62. U.S. Department of Justice, Bureau of Justice Statistics, *Criminal Victimization, 1998* (Washington, D.C.: U.S. Government Printing Office, 1999), p. 3.
63. C. H. Kempe, F. N. Silverman, B. F. Steele, W. Droegemueller, and H. K. Silver, "The Battered-Child Syndrome," *Journal of the American Medical Association*, **181** (1962): 17–24.

64. Elizabeth Pleck, "Criminal Approaches to Family Violence, 1640–1980," in *Family Violence,* ed. Lloyd Ohlin and Michael Tonry, vol. 2 (Chicago: University of Chicago Press, 1989), pp. 19–57.

65. For a special journal issue on the subject of family violence, see Richard J. Gelles, ed., "Family Violence," *Journal of Comparative Family Studies,* **25** (1994): 1–142.

66. Lyn Nell Hancock, "Why Batterers So Often Go Free," *Newsweek,* Oct. 16, 1995, pp. 61–62.

67. Murray A. Straus and Richard J. Gelles, "How Violent Are American Families?: Estimates from the National Family Violence Resurvey and Other Studies," in *Family Abuse and Its Consequences,* ed. Gerald T. Hotaling, David Finkelhor, John T. Kirkpatrick, and Murray A. Straus (Newbury Park, Calif.: Sage, 1988). See also Ann Goetting, *Homicide in Families and Other Special Populations* (New York: Springer, 1995); and Ronet Bachman, *Violence against Women: A National Crime Victimization Survey Report* (Washington, D.C.: U.S. Bureau of Justice Statistics, 1994).

68. Richard B. Felson, "Big People Hit Little People: Sex Differences in Physical Power and Interpersonal Violence," *Criminology,* **34** (1996): 433–452.

69. Straus and Gelles, "How Violent Are American Families?" p. 17.

70. Terrie E. Moffitt and Avshalom Caspi, *National Institute of Justice, Research in Brief, Findings about Partner Violence from the Dunedin Multidisciplinary Health and Development Study* (Washington, D.C.: U.S. Department of Justice, Office of Justice Programs, National Institute of Justice, July 1999).

71. Patrick A. Langan and Christopher A. Innes, *Preventing Domestic Violence against Women,* for U.S. Department of Justice, Bureau of Justice Statistics (Washington, D.C.: U.S. Government Printing Office, 1986).

72. Marvin E. Wolfgang and Franco Ferracuti, *The Subculture of Violence: Toward an Integrated Theory in Criminology* (London: Tavistock, 1967).

73. Joan McCord, "Parental Aggressiveness and Physical Punishment in Long-Term Perspective," in *Family Abuse and Its Consequences,* pp. 91–98.

74. Margery A. Cassidy, "Power-Control Theory: Its Potential Application to Woman Battering," *Journal of Crime and Justice,* **18** (1995): 1–15.

75. Donald G. Dutton, *The Domestic Assault of Women* (Boston: Allyn and Bacon, 1988), p. 15.

76. Lenore E. Walker, *The Battered Woman Syndrome* (New York: Springer Verlag, 1984); Brenda A. Miller, Thomas H. Nochajski, Kenneth E. Leonard, Howard T. Blane, Dawn M. Gondoli, and Patricia M. Bowers, "Spousal Violence and Alcohol/Drug Problems among Parolees and Their Spouses," *Women and Criminal Justice,* **1** (1990): 55–72.

77. Study conducted by Mohammed Ayat, Atiqui Abdelaziz, Najat Kfita, and El Khazouni Zineb, at the request of UNESCO and the Union of Arab Lawyers, Fez, Morocco, 1989.

78. David Levinson, *Family Violence in Cross-Cultural Perspective* (Newbury Park, Calif.: Sage, 1989).

79. Carolyn F. Swift, "Surviving: Women's Strength through Connections," in *Abuse and Victimization across the Life Span,* ed. Martha Straus (Baltimore: Johns Hopkins University Press, 1988), pp. 153–169.

80. See Christine Rasche, "Early Models for Contemporary Thought on Domestic Violence and Women Who Kill Their Mates: A Review of the Literature from 1895 to 1970," *Women and Criminal Justice,* **1** (1990): 31–53.

81. *Thurman v. Torrington,* 596 F. Supp. 1521 (1985).

82. Jeffrey Fagan, *The Criminalization of Domestic Violence: Promises and Limits* (Washington, D.C.: U.S. National Institute of Justice, 1996).

83. Lawrence W. Sherman and Richard A. Berk, "The Minneapolis Domestic Violence Experiment," *Police Foundation Reports,* **1** (1984): 1–8. See also J. David Hirschel, Ira W. Hutchinson, Charles W. Dean, and Anne-Marie Mills, "Review Essay on the Law Enforcement Response to Spouse Abuse: Past, Present and Future," *Justice Quarterly,* **9** (1992): 247–283; Cynthia Grant Bowman, "The Arrest Experiments: A Feminist Critique," *Journal of Criminal Law and Criminol-*

Review • You Be the Criminologist • Key Terms • Notes

ogy, **83** (1992): 201–208; Albert R. Roberts, "Psychosocial Characteristics of Batterers: A Study of 234 Men Charged with Domestic Violence Offenses," *Journal of Family Violence,* **2** (1987): 81–93; Donald G. Dutton and Susan K. Golant, *The Batterer: A Psychological Profile* (New York: Basic Books, 1995); Lisa A. Frisch, "Research That Succeeds, Policies That Fail," *Journal of Criminal Law and Criminology,* **83** (1992): 209–216; David B. Mitchell, "Contemporary Police Practices in Domestic Violence Cases: Arresting the Abuser: Is It Enough?" *Journal of Criminal Law and Criminology,* **83** (1992): 241–249; and Lawrence W. Sherman, Janell D. Schmidt, Dennis P. Rogan, Patrick R. Gartlin, Ellen G. Cohn, Dean J. Collins, and Anthony R. Bacich, "From Initial Deterrence to Long-Term Escalation: Short Custody Arrest for Poverty Ghetto Domestic Violence," *Criminology,* **29** (1991): 821–850.

84. Lawrence W. Sherman, Janell D. Schmidt, Dennis P. Rogan, Douglas A. Smith, Patrick R. Gartlin, Ellen G. Cohn, Dean J. Collins, and Anthony R. Bacich, "The Variable Effects of Arrest on Criminal Careers: The Milwaukee Domestic Violence Experiment," *Journal of Criminal Law and Criminology,* **83** (1992): 137–169. See also J. David Hirschel and Ira W. Hutchinson III, "Female Spouse Abuse and the Police Response: The Charlotte, North Carolina, Experiment," *Journal of Criminal Law and Criminology,* **83** (1992): 73–119.

85. Joan Zorza, "The Criminal Law of Misdemeanor Domestic Violence, 1970–1990," *Journal of Criminal Law and Criminology,* **83** (1992): 46–72. See also Candace Kruttschnitt and Maude Dornfeld, "Will They Tell? Assessing Preadolescents' Reports of Family Violence," *Journal of Research in Crime and Delinquency,* **29** (1992): 136–147.

86. U.S. Department of Justice, OJJDP, *Juvenile Offenders and Victims, 1999 National Report,* p. 41.

87. Ibid.

88. Edna Erez and Pamela Tontodonato, "Patterns of Reported Parent-Child Abuse and Police Response," *Journal of Family Violence,* **4** (1989): 143–159.

89. Cathy Spatz Widom and M. Ashley Ames, "Criminal Consequences of Childhood Sexual Victimization," *Child Abuse and Neglect,* **18** (1994): 303–318; Carolyn Smith and Terence P. Thornberry, "The Relationship between Childhood Maltreatment and Adolescent Involvement in Delinquency," *Criminology,* **33** (1995): 451–481.

90. U.S. Department of Justice, OJJDP, *Juvenile Offenders and Victims, 1999 National Report,* p. 41.

91. Ibid.

92. Kathleen Brewer, Daryl Rowe, and Devon Brewer, "Factors Related to Prosecution of Child Sexual Abuse Cases," *Journal of Child Sexual Abuse,* **6** (1997): 91–111.

93. Deborah Daro, "Half Full and Half Empty: The Evaluation of Results of Nineteen Clinical Research and Demonstration Projects," *Summary of Nineteen Clinical Demonstration Projects Funded by the National Center on Child Abuse and Neglect, 1978–81* (Berkeley: University of California, School of Social Welfare, 1986).

94. See Candace Kruttschnitt and Maude Dornfeld, "Childhood Victimization, Race, and Violent Crime," *Criminal Justice and Behavior,* **18** (1991): 448–463.

95. See "The Basics: What Is Elder Abuse?" at <www.gwjapan.com/NCEA/basic/index.html> (accessed online Sept. 19, 1999).

96. *U.S. Bureau of the Census, Statistical Abstract of the United States: 1994* (Washington, D.C.: U.S. Government Printing Office, 1994).

97. Craig J. Forsyth and Robert Gramling, "Elderly Crime: Fact and Artifact," in *Older Offenders,* ed. Belinda McCarthy and Robert Langworthy (New York: Praeger, 1988), pp. 3–13.

98. Mildred Daley Pagelow, "The Incidence and Prevalence of Criminal Abuse of Other Family Members," in Ohlin and Tonry, *Family Violence,* p. 267.

99. Jordan I. Kosberg and Juanita L. Garcia, eds., "Elder Abuse: International and Cross-Cultural Perspectives," *Journal of Elder Abuse and Neglect,* **6** (1995): 1–197.

100. See Mark Whatley, "For Better or Worse: The Case of Marital Rape," *Violence and Victims,* **8** (1993): 29–39.

101. Susan Brownmiller, *Against Our Will: Men, Women, and Rape* (New York: Simon & Schuster, 1975), pp. 1–9.
102. Duncan Chappell, "Sexual Criminal Violence," in *Pathways to Criminal Violence*, ed. Neil Alan Weiner and Marvin E. Wolfgang (Newbury Park, Calif.: Sage, 1989), pp. 68–108.
103. Uniform Crime Reports, 1998, pp. 12, 25. For a special issue devoted to an overview of adult sexual assault, see *Journal of Social Issues*, 48 (1992): 1–195, with an Introduction by Susan B. Sorenson and Jacqueline W. White.
104. Ibid., p. 26.
105. Menachem Amir, *Patterns in Forcible Rape* (Chicago: University of Chicago Press, 1977), pp. 233–234.
106. U.S. Department of Justice, Bureau of Justice Statistics, *Highlights from 20 Years of Surveying Crime Victims* (Washington, D.C.: U.S. Government Printing Office, 1993), p. 24.
107. Whatley, "For Better or Worse."
108. Ida Johnson and Robert Sigler, *Forced Sexual Intercourse in Intimate Relationships* (Brookfield, Vt.: Ashgate, 1997).
109. Clark Staten, "Roofies, The New Date Rape Drug of Choice," Jan. 6, 1996 (see <http://www.emergency.com/roofies.htm>).
110. M. P. Koss, C. A. Gidycz, and N. Wisniewski, "The Scope of Rape: Incidence and Prevalence of Sexual Aggression and Victimization in a National Sample of Higher Education Students," *Journal of Consulting and Clinical Psychology*, 55 (1987): 162–170.
111. Uniform Crime Reports 1998, p. 199.
112. James L. LeBeau, "Patterns of Stranger and Serial Rape Offending: Factors Distinguishing Apprehended and At Large Offenders," *Journal of Criminal Law and Criminology*, 78 (1987): 309–326.
113. J. Marolla and D. Scully, *Attitudes toward Women, Violence, and Rape: A Comparison of Convicted Rapists and Other Felons* (Rockville, Md.: National Institute of Mental Health, 1982).
114. Christine Alder, "An Exploration of Self-Reported Sexually Aggressive Behavior,"

Crime and Delinquency, 31 (1985): 306–331; P. R. Sanday, "The Socio-Cultural Context of Rape: A Cross-Cultural Study," *Journal of Social Issues*, 37 (1981): 5–27.
115. Julia R. Schwendinger and Herman Schwendinger, *Rape and Inequality* (Beverly Hills, Calif.: Sage, 1983), p. 220.
116. M. Dwayne Smith and Nathan Bennett, "Poverty, Inequality, and Theories of Forcible Rape," *Crime and Delinquency*, 31 (1985): 295–305.
117. Ruth D. Peterson and William C. Bailey, "Forcible Rape, Poverty, and Economic Inequality in U.S. Metropolitan Communities," *Journal of Quantitative Criminology*, 4 (1988): 99–119.
118. Matthew Hale, *History of the Pleas of the Crown*, vol. 1 (London, 1736), p. 635.
119. Martin D. Schwartz and Todd R. Clear, "Toward a New Law on Rape," *Crime and Delinquency*, 26 (1980): 129–151.
120. Patricia Frazier and Beth Haney, "Sexual Assault Cases in the Legal System: Police, Prosecutor, and Victim Perspectives," *Law and Human Behavior*, 20 (1996): 607–628.
121. Christian Berthelsen, "Women Are Speaking Out to Heal Trauma of Rape," *New York Times*, Apr. 4, 1999, p. 19, Section 1.
122. Cassia C. Spohn and Julie Horney, "The Impact of Rape Law Reform on the Processing of Simple and Aggravated Cases," *Journal of Criminal Law and Criminology*, 86 (1996): 861–884; Gilbert Geis, "Rape-in-Marriage: Law and Law Reform in England, the United States, and Sweden," *Adelaide Law Review*, 6 (1978): 284–303; Joel Epstein and Stacia Langenbahn, *The Criminal Justice and Community Response to Rape* (Washington, D.C.: U.S. National Institute of Justice, 1994).
123. Janet Gornick, Martha R. Burt, and Karen J. Pittman, "Structures and Activities of Rape Crisis Centers in the Early 1980's," *Crime and Delinquency*, 31 (1985): 247–268.
124. Alexis Chiu, "Dad Pleads Guilty to Kidnapping," May 28, 1999 (see <http://more.abcnews.go.com/sections/us/DailyNews/father990527.html>).
125. John Cloud, "Most Likely to Succeed," *Time*, Apr. 26, 1999, p. 72.

Review • You Be the Criminologist • Key Terms • Notes

126. U.S. Department of Justice, *Report to the Nation on Crime and Justice,* 2d ed. (Washington, D.C.: U.S. Government Printing Office, 1988), p. 97.
127. Uniform Crime Reports, 1998.
128. U.S. Department of Justice, Bureau of Justice Statistics, *Criminal Victimization in the United States, 1991* (Washington, D.C.: U.S. Government Printing Office, 1992), p. 76.
129. John Conklin, *Robbery and the Criminal Justice System* (Philadelphia: Lippincott, 1972), pp. 59–78.
130. Uniform Crime Reports, 1998, p. 31.
131. Terry L. Baumer and Michael D. Carrington, *The Robbery of Financial Institutions,* for U.S. Department of Justice (Washington, D.C.: U.S. Government Printing Office, 1986).
132. Uniform Crime Reports, 1994, p. 27.
133. Philip J. Cook, "Is Robbery Becoming More Violent?: An Analysis of Robbery Murder Trends since 1968," *Journal of Criminal Law and Criminology,* **76** (1985): 480–489.
134. Robert J. Kelly and Rufus Schatzberg, "Galvanizing Indiscriminate Political Violence: Mind-Sets and Some Ideological Constructs in Terrorism," *International Journal of Comparative and Applied Criminal Justice,* **16** (1992): 15–41; Jeffrey D. Simon, *The Terrorist Trap: America's Experience with Terrorism* (Bloomington: Indiana University Press, 1993); Brent L. Smith and Gregory P. Orvis, "America's Response to Terrorism: An Empirical Analysis of Federal Intervention Strategies during the 1980s," *Justice Quarterly,* **10** (1993): 661–681.
135. Cindy Combs, *Terrorism in the Twenty-First Century* (Upper Saddle River, N.J.: Prentice-Hall, 1997).
136. See "Bin-Laden Still Sought a Year after Embassy Bombings in Africa," Aug. 6, 1999 (<http://cnn.com/US/9908/06/embassy.bombings>).
137. See "Blast in Moscow Mall Wounds 33," Aug. 31, 1999 (<http://www.cnn.com/wysiwgy://partner/55/http://cnn...europe/9908/31/moscow.blast.08/>).
138. Dennis Pluchinsky, "Terrorism in the Former Soviet Union: A Primer, a Puzzle, a Prognosis," *Studies in Conflict and Terrorism,* **21** (1998): 119–147.
139. Harvey J. Iglarsh, "Terrorism and Corporate Costs," *Terrorism,* **10** (1987): 227–230.
140. Ariel Merari, Tamar Prat, Sophia Kotzer, Anat Kurz, and Yoram Schweitzer, *Inter 85: A Review of International Terrorism in 1985* (Boulder, Colo.: Westview, 1986), p. 106.
141. Noemi Gal-Or, *International Cooperation to Suppress Terrorism* (New York: St. Martin's Press, 1985), pp. 90–96.
142. "A Cloud of Terror and Suspicion," *Newsweek,* Apr. 3, 1995, pp. 36–41. See also Stewart A. Wright, ed., *Armageddon in Waco: Critical Perspectives on the Branch Davidian Conflict* (Chicago: University of Illinois Press, 1995).
143. James Brooke, "Wyoming City Braces for Gay Murder Trial," *New York Times,* Apr. 4, 1999, p. 14.
144. Sylvester Monroe, "A Burning in Alabama," *Time,* Mar. 15, 1999, p. 47.
145. Frank Gibney, Jr., "The Kids Got in the Way," *Time,* Aug. 23, 1999, p. 22.
146. Federal Bureau of Investigation, *Hate Crime Statistics 1998* www.fbi.gov/vcr/98hate.pdf.
147. Matt Bai and Vern E. Smith, "Evil to the End," *Newsweek,* Mar. 8, 1999, p. 22.
148. Rebecca Leung, "Hate Crimes in America: Texas Killing Spotlights Nation's Racial Divide," June 17, 1999 (see <http://abcnews.go.com/sections/us/DailyNews/hatecrimes980611.html>).
149. For discussions of recent events that have shaped the philosophy of militias, see Alan W. Bock, *Ambush at Ruby Ridge: How Government Agents Set Randy Weaver Up and Took His Family Down* (Irvine, Calif.: Dickens Press, 1995).
150. Morris Dees and James Corcoran, *Gathering Storm: America's Militia Threat* (New York: Harper Collins, 1996).
151. Michael Winerip, "Ohio Case Typifies the Tensions between Militia Groups and the Law," *New York Times,* June 23, 1996, p. 1.
152. "The View from the Far Right," *Newsweek,* May 1, 1995, pp. 36–39.
153. Ibid.
154. Gordon Crew and Reid Countes, *The Evolution of School Disturbance in America: Colonial Times to Modern Day* (Westport, Conn.: Praeger, 1997).

155. T. Trent Gepax, Jerry Adler, and Daniel Pedarion, "The Boys behind the Ambush," *Newsweek,* Apr. 6, 1998, pp. 20–24; Geoffrey Cowley, "Why Children Turn Violent," *Newsweek,* Apr. 6, 1998, pp. 24–26; Nadya Lobi, "The Hunter and the Choirboy," *Time,* Apr. 6, 1998, pp. 28–37; Richard Lacayo, "Toward the Root of the Evil," *Time,* Apr. 6, 1998, pp. 38–39.

156. Sam Howe Verhovek, "Sounds from a Massacre: 'Oh God, Kids, Stay Down,' " *New York Times,* Apr. 24, 1999, p. 1.

157. Tammerlin Drummond, "Battling the Columbine Copycats," *Time,* May 10, 1999, p. 29.

158. Vincent Schiraldi, "Hype Aside, School Violence Is Declining." This report appeared in *Newsday, The Washington Post,* and other media, Sept. 30, 1998.

159. U.S. Departments of Education and Justice, *1998 Annual Report on School Safety* (Washington, D.C.: U.S. Department of Education and Justice, 1999), p. 9.

160. Mary Jo Nolin, Elizabeth Davies, and Kathryn Chandler, "Student Victimization at School," *Journal of School Health,* **66** (1996): 216.

161. Samuel Walker, *Sense and Nonsense about Crime and Drugs: A Policy Guide,* 4th ed., (Belmont, Calif.: West/Wadsworth, 1998).

162. Richard Woodbury, "Taking Back the School," *Time,* Aug. 16, 1999, pp. 32–33.

163. Claudia Kalb, "Schools on the Alert," *Newsweek,* Aug. 23, 1999, pp. 42–44.

164. John Cloud, "What Can the Schools Do?" *Time,* May 3, 1999, pp. 38–40.

165. U.S. Department of Justice, Office of Justice Programs, *Promising Strategies to Reduce Gun Violence* (Washington, D.C.: Office of Juvenile Justice and Delinquency Prevention, February 1999).

166. Matt Bai, "Caught in the Cross-Fire," *Newsweek,* June 28, 1999, pp. 31–32.

167. Sam Howe Verhovek, "2 Youths Wanted to 'Destroy the School,' Sheriff Says," *New York Times,* Apr. 23, 1999, p. 1.

168. Roger Rosenblatt, "Get Rid of the Damned Things," *Time,* Aug. 9, 1999, pp. 38–39.

169. Marianne W. Zawitz, *Guns Used in Crime* (Washington, D.C.: Bureau of Justice Statistics, 1995), p. 2.

170. Walker, *Sense and Nonsense about Crime and Drugs.*

171. Ibid.

172. See Martin Killias, "International Correlations between Gun Ownership and Rates of Homicide and Suicide," *Canadian Medical Association Journal,* **148** (1993): 1721–1776; Peter J. Carrington and Sharon Moyer, "Gun Availability and Suicide in Canada: Testing the Displacement Hypothesis," *Studies on Crime and Crime Prevention,* **3** (1994): 168–178.

173. Marianne W. Zawitz, *Firearm Injury from Crime* (Washington, D.C.: Bureau of Justice Statistics, 1996), p. 4.

174. Robert D. McFadden, "On a Bus in Queens, Three Bandits Stage a Frontier Robbery," *New York Times,* July 31, 1993, p. 1.

175. Alan J. Lizotte, James M. Tesoriero, Terence P. Thornberry, et al., "Patterns of Adolescent Firearms Ownership and Use," *Justice Quarterly,* **11** (1994): 51–74.

176. *Juvenile Offenders and Victims, 1999 National Report,* p. 69.

177. Joseph F. Sheley, "Drugs and Guns among Inner-City High School Students," *Journal of Drug Education,* **24** (1994): 303–321.

178. M. Dwayne Smith and Joseph F. Sheley, "The Possession and Carrying of Firearms among a Sample of Inner-City High School Females," *Journal of Crime and Justice,* **18** (1995): 109–128.

179. Jon D. Hull, "A Boy and His Gun," *Time,* Aug. 2, 1993.

180. Alan J. Lizotte, James M. Tesoriero, Terence P. Thornberry, et al., "Patterns of Adolescent Firearms Ownership and Use." See also Joseph F. Sheley and James D. Wright, *In the Line of Fire: Youth, Guns, and Violence in Urban America* (Hawthorne, N.Y.: Aldine de Gruyter, 1995); Joseph F. Sheley and Victoria E. Brewer, "Possession and Carrying of Firearms among Suburban Youth," *Public Health Reports,* **110** (1995): 18–26.

181. James B. Jacobs and Kimberly A. Potter, "Comprehensive Handgun Licensing and Registration: An Analysis and Critique of Brady II, Gun Control's Next (and Last?) Step," *Journal of Criminal Law and Criminology,* **89** (1998): 81–110.

Review • You Be the Criminologist • Key Terms • Notes

182. U.S. Department of Justice, OJJDP, *Juvenile Offenders and Victims, 1999 National Report*, p. 69.

183. Glenn L. Pierce and William J. Bowers, "The Bartley-Fox Gun Law's Short-Term Impact on Crime in Boston," *Annals of the American Academy of Political and Social Science*, **455** (1981): 120–137.

184. Patrick W. O'Carroll, Colin Loftin, John B. Waller, Jr., David McDowall, Allen Bukoff, Richard O. Scott, James A. Mercy, and Brian Wiersema, "Preventing Homicide: An Evaluation of the Efficacy of a Detroit Gun Ordinance," *American Journal of Public Health*, **81** (1991): 576–581.

185. Lawrence W. Sherman, James W. Shaw, and Dennis P. Rogan, *The Kansas City Gun Experiment* (Washington, D.C.: U.S. National Institute of Justice, 1995).

186. James A. Beha II, "And Nobody Can Get You Out: The Impact of a Mandatory Prison Sentence for the Illegal Carrying of a Firearm on the Administration of Criminal Justice in Boston," *Boston University Law Review*, **57** (1977): 96–146, 289–333.

187. Colin Loftin, Milton Heumann, and David McDowall, "Mandatory Sentencing and Firearms Violence: Evaluating an Alternative to Gun Control," *Law and Society Review*, **17** (1983): 288–318.

188. Michael Janofsky, "Fighting Crime by Making Federal Case about Guns," *New York Times*, Feb. 10, 1999, p. A12.

189. Elaine Shannon, "Have Gun? Will Travel," *Time*, Aug. 16, 1999, p. 30.

190. Janofsky, "Fighting Crime by Making Federal Case about Guns."

191. Colin Loftin, David McDowall, Brian Wiersema, and Talbert J. Cottey, "Effects of Restrictive Licensing of Handguns on Homicide and Suicide in the District of Columbia," *New England Journal of Medicine*, **325** (1991): 1615–1620.

192. U.S. Department of the Treasury, Bureau of Alcohol, Tobacco and Firearms, *Implemen-*

tation of the Brady Law. September 1999, (Washington, D.C.: U.S. Government Printing Office).

193. U.S. Department of Justice, Bureau of Justice Statistics, *Presale Handgun Checks, the Brady Interim Period, 1994–1998* (Washington, D.C.: U.S. Government Printing Office, June 1999).

194. Fox Butterfield, "Handgun Law Deters Felons, Studies Show," *New York Times*, Mar. 12, 1995, p. 23. See also *One-Year Progress Report: Brady Handgun Violence Prevention Act* (Washington, D.C.: U.S. Bureau of Alcohol, Tobacco and Firearms, 1995).

195. David McDowall and Alan Lizotte, "Gun Control," in *Introduction to Social Problems*, ed. Craig Calhoun and George Ritzer (New York: Primis Database, McGraw-Hill, 1993).

196. Marjolijn Bijlefeld, ed., *The Gun Control Debate: A Documentary History* (Westport, Conn.: Greenwood Press, 1997).

197. John A. Arthur, "Criminal Victimization, Fear of Crime, and Handgun Ownership among Blacks: Evidence from National Survey Data," *American Journal of Criminal Justice*, **16** (1992): 121–141; Gary S. Green, "Citizen Gun Ownership and Criminal Deterrence: Theory, Research, and Policy," *Criminology*, **25** (1987): 63–81; John A. Arthur, "Gun Ownership among Women Living in One-Adult Households," *International Journal of Comparative and Applied Criminal Justice*, **18** (1994): 249–263; and Wilbur Edel, *Gun Control: Threat to Liberty or Defense against Anarchy?* (Westport, Conn.: Praeger, 1995).

198. *Concealed Carry: The Criminal's Companion. Florida's Concealed Weapons Law—A Model for the Nation?* (Washington, D.C.: Violence Policy Center, 1995).

199. Fox Butterfield, "America under the Gun," *New York Times*, Sept. 16, 1999 (see <http://www.nytimes.com/library/national/091699guns-overview.html>).

CHAPTER 12
Crimes against Property

The motion picture *The Gods Must Be Crazy* introduces us to a society of happy aborigines, remote from the hustle and bustle of modern life. Such tools as they have are shared and can easily be replaced from an abundance of sticks and stones.

High up, a "noisy bird" passes over the camp of these happy people. The pilot of the noisy bird casually throws an empty Coke bottle out of the cockpit. It lands in the middle of the camp. The aborigines stare at this foreign object. They handle it delicately and then discover what a useful object it is: It holds water; it can be used for rolling dough, for hammering, for many things. Everybody needs it and wants it. Fights ensue over who can have it. The peace and tranquillity of this little society are shattered. These people have discovered the concept of property, and they are experiencing all the troubles that go with the possession of property, including property crime.

The film has a happy ending. The aborigines finally get rid of the bottle, and life returns to normal.

We have explored some of the patterns of social interaction and the routine activities of daily life that set the stage for offenders to commit violent crimes and for other people—family members, acquaintances, strangers, airplane passengers—to become victims. We know that if we are to develop effective policies to prevent and control violent crime, we must have a thorough understanding of the characteristics of specific offenses; we need to know where, when, and how they are committed, and which individuals are most likely to commit them. The same is true for property offenses. To develop crime-prevention strategies, we need to study the characteristics that differentiate the various types of offenses which deprive people of their property.

Do such offenses as pocket-picking (pickpocketing), shoplifting, check forgery, theft by use of stolen credit cards, car theft, computer crimes, and burglary have different payoffs and risks? What kinds of resources are needed (weapons, places to sell stolen property)? Are any specific skills needed to carry out these offenses? The opportunities to commit property crime are all but unlimited. Studies demonstrate that if these opportunities are reduced, the incidence of crime is reduced as well.

The traditional property crimes are larceny (theft, or stealing); obtaining property by fraud of various sorts, including false pretenses, confidence games, forgery, and unauthorized use of credit cards; burglary, which does not necessarily involve theft; and arson, which not only deprives the owner of property but also endangers lives. New crime types, such as software piracy, online frauds, and computer viruses, are associated with high-technology equipment. We shall defer until Chapter 13 discussion of the crimes by which criminals deprive people of their property through organizational manipulations—individual white-collar crimes, corporate crimes, and activities related to organized crime.

LARCENY

Larceny (theft, stealing) is the prototype of all property offenses. It is also the most prevalent crime in our society; it includes such contemporary forms as purse-snatching, pickpocketing, shoplifting, art theft, and vehicle theft. In the thirteenth century, when Henry de Bracton set out to collect from all parts of England what was common in law—and thus common law—he learned to his surprise that there was no agreement on a concept of larceny. He found a confusing variety of ancient Germanic laws. So he did what he always did in such circumstances: He remembered what he had learned about Roman law from Professor Azo in Bologna, and simply inserted it into his new text of English law. Thus our common law definition of larceny is virtually identical with the concept in Roman law.[1]

The Elements of Larceny

Here are the elements of **larceny** (or theft, or stealing):

A trespassory
Taking and
Carrying away of
Personal property
Belonging to another
With the intent to deprive the owner of the property permanently

Each of these elements has a long history that gives it its meaning. The first element is perhaps the easiest. There must be a trespass. "Trespass," a Norman-French term, has a variety of meanings. In the law of larceny, however, it simply means any absence of authority or permission for the taking. Second, the property must be taken: The perpetrator must exert authority over the property, as by putting a hand on a piece of merchandise or getting into the driver's seat of the targeted car.

Third, the property must be carried away. The slightest removal suffices to fulfill this element: moving merchandise from a counter, however slightly; loosening the brakes of a car so that it starts rolling, even an inch. Fourth, the property in question, at common law, has to be personal property. (Real estate is not subject to larceny.) Fifth, the property has to belong to another, in the sense that the person has the right to possess that property. Sixth, the taker must intend to deprive the rightful owner permanently of the property. This element is present when the taker (thief) intends to deprive the rightful owner of the property forever. In many states, however, the law no longer requires proof that the thief intended to deprive the owner "permanently" of the property.

The Extent of Larceny

Larceny, except for the most petty varieties, was a capital offense in medieval England.[2] Courts interpreted all its elements quite strictly—that is, in favor of defendants—so as to limit the use of capital punishment. Only once did the courts expand the reach of larceny, when they ruled that a transporter who opens a box entrusted to him and takes out some items has committed larceny by "breaking bulk." For the other forms of deceptive acquisition of property, such as embezzling funds and obtaining property by false pretenses, Parliament had to enact separate legislation.

In the United States the rate of larceny is extraordinarily high. The UCR reported 7.7 million thefts in 1997, or a rate of 2886 for each 100,000 of the population.[3] The NCVS figure, 17.7 million, is more than two times the UCR number, and neither figure includes automobile thefts.[4] The vast majority of thefts are, and always have been, committed furtively and without personal

FIGURE 12.1   Distribution of larcenies known to police, 1997. (Because of rounding, percents may not total 100%.)

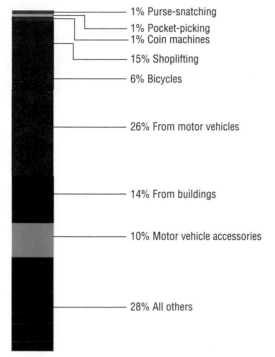

- 1% Purse-snatching
- 1% Pocket-picking
- 1% Coin machines
- 15% Shoplifting
- 6% Bicycles
- 26% From motor vehicles
- 14% From buildings
- 10% Motor vehicle accessories
- 28% All others

Source: Uniform Crime Reports, 1998.

contact with the victims. Thefts involving personal contact—pickpocketing, purse-snatching, and other varieties of larceny—lag behind. Figure 12.1 shows the distribution of all larcenies known to the police in 1997. The estimated dollar value of stolen goods to victims nationally was over $4.5 billion.[5]

Who Are the Thieves?

Nobody knows exactly how many of the total number of thefts are committed by amateurs who lead rather conventional lives and how many are the work of professionals. According to some criminologists, the two types differ considerably.[6]

The Amateur Thief   Amateur thieves are occasional offenders who tend to be opportunists. They take advantage of a chance to steal when little risk is involved. Typically, their acts are carried out with little skill, are unplanned,

and result from some pressing situation, such as the need to pay the rent or a gambling debt.[7] In other words, amateurs resolve some immediate crisis by stealing. Most occasional offenders commit few crimes; some commit only one crime. Many are juveniles who do not go on to commit crimes in adulthood.

Amateur thieves do not think of themselves as professional criminals, nor are they recognized as such by those who do think of themselves as professionals. The lives of amateur thieves are quite conventional: Amateurs work, go to school, have conventional friends, and find little support or approval for their criminal behavior.

The Professional Thief   Professional thieves make a career of stealing. They take pride in their profession. They are imaginative and creative in their work and accept its risks. The most common crimes committed by professional thieves are pickpocketing, shoplifting, forgery, confidence swindling, and burglary. Professional thieves also are involved in art theft, auto vehicle theft, and fraud or theft by use of stolen or forged credit cards, among other crimes.

Thomas Bartholomew Moran, a professional thief who died in a Miami rescue mission in 1971, has been considered the best of American pickpockets. His career began in 1906, when, as a teenager, he started to pick women's purses. Under the careful guidance of Mary Kelly, a well-known pickpocket, he soon sharpened his skills until he could take wallets from pants, jeweled pins from clothing, and watches from vests without alerting the victims. He devoted his life to shoplifting, forgery, and other forms of theft. In 1912 he boarded the Titanic, with the intention of profiting handsomely from proximity to

the more than 300 first-class passengers whose collective wealth exceeded $250 million. His immediate ambitions were dimmed, however, when the Titanic brushed an iceberg in the North Atlantic [and sank] only two hours and forty minutes later. But Moran was among the 705 passengers who managed to find space in one of the ship's twenty lifeboats, and his career in crime continued to flourish for the better part of the 59 remaining years of his life.[8]

The most influential study of professional thieves was conducted by Edwin Sutherland in 1937. Sutherland found that professional thieves share five characteristics:

1. They have well-developed technical skills for their particular mode of operation.

2. They enjoy status, accorded to them by their own subculture and by law enforcement.

3. They are bound by consensus, a sharing of values with their own peers.

4. Not only do they learn from each other, but they also protect each other.

5. They are organized, however loosely.[9]

Subsequent studies have tended to confirm Sutherland's findings.

Shoplifting

Shoplifting, the stealing of goods from retail merchants, is a very common crime; it constitutes about 15 percent of all larcenies. A recent survey in Spokane, Washington, revealed that every twelfth shopper is a shoplifter, and that men and women are equally likely to be offenders.[10] Perhaps shoplifting is so frequent because it is a low-risk offense, with a detection rate of perhaps less than 1 percent.[11] Shoppers are extremely reluctant to report shoplifters to the store management.[12] According to one study, of those apprehended for shoplifting, approximately 45.5 percent are actually prosecuted. It is also estimated that men are slightly more likely than women to be shoplifters, and that 41 percent of offenders are white, 29 percent are black, and 16 percent are Hispanic. More than half of shoplifting events occur between the hours of 12:00 P.M. and 6:00 P.M.[13] Interviews with 740 shoplifters in 50 Minneapolis stores revealed that almost half of those who expressed motivation for stealing said that they stole the merchandise because they liked it and did not have enough money to pay for it.[14] A study conducted in New South Wales with juvenile offenders in detention revealed that their reasons for shoplifting ranged from excitement, peer

pressure, thrills, or fun; to obtaining clothes, food, or money for drugs or alcohol; to relieving boredom or stress.[15]

Mary Owen Cameron found that professional shoplifters largely conform to Sutherland's five characteristics but that amateurs do not. She estimates that of all shoplifters, only 10 percent are professionals—people who derive most of their income from the sale of stolen goods.[16] A broad range of motivations may lead to shoplifting. Among amateurs, need and greed as well as opportunity may precipitate the event.[17] Some researchers point to depression and other emotional disturbances and to the use of various prescription drugs.[18]

To most people, shoplifting is a rather insignificant offense. After all, how much can be stolen? On an individual basis, usually not very much: The average theft amount for each incident was roughly $56.[19] Taken together, however, all shoplifting incidents cost U.S. retail businesses over $10 billion every year.[20] In 1995, approximately $11 million worth of stolen merchandise was recovered. (See Table 12.1.)

As shoplifters decrease store profits, the price of goods goes up; stepped-up security adds even more to costs. Stores typically hire more and more security personnel, although it has been demonstrated that physical or electronic methods of securing merchandise are more cost-effective than the deployment of guards.[21] It is only the amateur shoplifter who is deterred by the presence of guards or store personnel, not the professional.[22]

Given the significantly high costs of shoplifting to retailers, what can be done to reclaim what was stolen? One option, practiced quite often in the United Kingdom, is the use of civil recovery. Civil recovery is an administrative process that enables store owners to utilize the civil law in an attempt to collect restitution from shoplifters directly, whether the shoplifters are customers or store employees. This civil action operates parallel to the criminal process, meaning that stores can both report instances of shoplifting to the police and also file separate civil complaints against the shoplifters to obtain restitution. Those apprehended for shoplifting can then either pay the civil penalty imposed upon them or appear before a civil

TABLE 12.1 Most Frequenlty Shoplifted Items by Store Type

Type of Retailer	Merchandise
Auto-parts stores	Auto accessories
Bookstores	Cassette tapes
Consumer electronics/ computers stores	Compact discs
Department stores	Clothing: Shirts
Discount stores	Clothing, undergarments, compact discs
Drugstores/pharmacies	Cigarettes, batteries, over- the-counter remedies
Fashion merchandise stores	Sneakers
General merchandise stores	Earrings

Grocery stores/supermarkets	Over-the-counter remedies,
	  health and beauty aids,
	  cigarettes

Home centers/hardware stores	Assorted hand tools
Music stores	Compact discs
Shoe stores	Sneakers
Specialty stores	Bed sheets
Specialty apparel stores	Assorted clothes, shoes
Sporting goods stores	Nike shoes
Theme parks	Key chains, jewelry
Toy stores	Action figures
Video stores	Video games
Warehouse stores	Pens, movie videos

Source: Read Hayes, *1996 Retail Theft Trends Report: An Analysis of Customer Theft in Stores* (Winter Park, Fla.: Loss Prevention Specialists, 1996).

court. Research has shown that for amateur shoplifters (as opposed to professionals), the use of civil recovery does not have a significant impact on their initial offense, but does have an impact on preventing them from reoffending.[23]

Art Theft

At the high end of the larceny scale we find art theft. The public knows and seems to care little about art theft, yet it is as old as art itself. Looters have stolen priceless treasures from Egyptian tombs ever since they were built. As prices for antiques and for modern art soar, the demand for stolen art soars. Mexico and other countries with a precious cultural heritage are in danger of losing their treasures to gangs of thieves who destroy what they cannot take with them from historic and archaeological sites.

One of the most grandiose art thefts occurred on May 21, 1986, when a gang of Irish thieves invaded an estate in Ireland with commando precision and made off with 11 paintings, among them a Goya, two Rubenses, a Gainsborough, and a Vermeer.

Art theft, particularly the illicit trade in objects of cultural heritage, has increased significantly worldwide over recent years. Art thieves use a variety of means, including forms of shoplifting, burglary, and robbery, to either steal individual works of art, illegally export pieces of art, or pillage archaeological sites.[24] Despite the widespread incidence of art theft, nobody knows the overall cost. Some paintings are worth $50, others $5000, and others $50 million. Tens of thousands of paintings and other art objects are missing.[25]

In response to the increasing problem of art theft, the Federal Bureau of Investigation (FBI) has created the National Stolen Art File, which consists of a computerized index of stolen art and other forms of cultural property. Once items are reported to either local law enforcement agencies within the United States or law enforcement agencies abroad, the FBI is notified and then incorporates images and physical descriptions of the objects, as well as information specific to the investigation of the particular art theft, into the National Stolen Art File index. The database that is created is used as an analytical tool to investigate and recover these items. According to the FBI, for an object to be entered into the National Stolen Art File, three specific criteria must be met. First, the object must be of artistic or historic significance. This includes fine arts, ethnographic objects, archaeological material, coins, stamps, musical instruments, and the like. Second, the stolen object in question must have a value of $2000 or more. However, if the object is worth less than $2000 but is associated with a major crime, the stolen object will meet the necessary criteria. Finally, the request for inclusion in the National Stolen Art File must be made by a law enforcement agency. Included in the request must be a description of the object, a photograph of the object, and if available, a police report and any other investigative information.[26]

Inasmuch as Hollywood movies are considered art, a new form of art theft has emerged—video piracy. Various video piracy rings exist throughout the country. They produce and sell bootleg tapes of films currently in movie theaters. Enforcement efforts have increased over the past few years. Recently, a New York–based piracy ring operating one of the largest video piracy operations along the East Coast was dismantled, resulting in 11 arrests and the confiscation of approximately 30,000 videotapes. This particular ring earned roughly $50,000 a week after producing and selling bootleg tapes of first-run films. The bootleg tapes sell for between $5 and $10 on the street. Those arrested were charged with trademark counterfeiting and failure to disclose the origin of a recording.[27]

People who commit larceny aim for places and objects that seem to offer the highest and most secure rewards. Our open, mercantile society affords an abundance of opportunities. While shoplifters need little expertise and a low level of professional connection, art thieves must have sophisticated knowledge of art and its value as well as good connections in the art world if they are to dispose of the items they steal. Art thieves methodically select the gallery from which they plan to steal objects of art, paying particular attention to the area in which the gallery is located, the floor of the gallery in which the art is housed, the showrooms with and without closed-circuit television (CCTV), and the number of visitors at the gallery at a particular time.[28] Other types of larceny, such as theft of automobiles and boats, require a moderate degree of skill—but more and more members of the general public are acquiring such skills.

Motor Vehicle Theft

Motor vehicle theft is the largest property crime in the United States. According to the UCR, approximately 1.3 million motor vehicles were stolen in the United States in 1997.[29] These totals are the lowest for this offense since 1987. The value of motor vehicles stolen in 1997 was roughly $5.6 million, with the value of motor vehicles recovered approximately $3.8 million.[30]

In 1997, 77 percent of the vehicles stolen were passenger cars, 18 percent were trucks and buses, and 5 percent were other types of vehicles. The clearance rate (by arrest), as distin-

FIGURE 12.2   Motor vehicle theft. Juvenile arrest rates for motor vehicle theft soared between 1984 and 1989, then decreased through the 1990s.

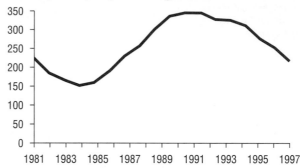

Arrests per 100,000 juveniles ages 10-17

The juvenile arrest rate for motor vehicle theft increased 130 percent between 1983 and 1989. The decline in the 1990s resulted in a 1997 arrest rate that was 50 percent above the 1983 low point and equal to the 1980 rate.

Source: Juvenile Offenders and Victims: 1999 National Report.

guished from the recovery rate of vehicles, is low—about 14 percent. Many cars are stolen during July and August, when schools are not in session. Thirty-nine percent of car thieves are youngsters under 18.[31] Most of their acts amount to *joyriding*, a type of larceny that lacks the element of "intent to deprive the owner of the property permanently." The thieves simply take the vehicle for momentary pleasure or transportation.

More recently, young car thieves have used stolen vehicles for racing, a show of status among peers, or for the "kick" of destroying them (Figure 12.2). At the other end of the spectrum are older, professional auto thieves who steal designated cars on consignment for resale in an altered condition (with identifying numbers changed) or for disposition in "chop shops," which strip the cars for the resale value of their parts.[32] Some estimate that a vehicle is worth three times its value when sold illegally for parts by professional car thieves.[33] In 1997 alone, more than 200,000 vehicles were illegally shipped abroad.[34] Table 12.2 describes the 10 areas in the United States with the highest vehicle theft rates in 1998. The types of vehicles stolen have changed over the years. It is interesting to

TABLE 12.2   The Metropolitan Statistical Areas with the Ten Highest Vehicle Theft Rates

1. Miami, Florida
2. Jersey City, New Jersey
3. Fresno, California
4. Memphis, Tennessee
5. New York, New York
6. Tucson, Arizona
7. Phoenix–Mesa, Arizona
8. Albuquerque, New Mexico
9. Sacramento, California
10. New Orleans, Louisiana

Source: NICB Vehicle Theft Study, 1996 (www.nicb.com/release.htm).

Philadelphia Police officer John Logan carrying "chopped" parts of stolen cars from the city's East Frankford section.

note that sport utility vehicles and pickup trucks are becoming just as popular with thieves as they are with consumers. In fact, 1998 was the second year in a row in which these types of vehicles have made the top 10 stolen vehicles category.

A variety of strategies are used to steal vehicles for financial gain. The "strip and run" occurs when a thief steals a car, strips it for its parts, and then abandons the vehicle. The frame of the car is all that is left. The "scissors job" occurs when scissors are jammed into certain ignition locks in mostly American-made cars, allowing the thief to easily start the car. A "valet theft" takes place when a thief dresses and poses as a valet attendant, opens the car door for the driver, takes the keys, and quickly drives away. Another strategy for vehicle theft is simply the "insurance fraud" scheme, in which a car owner reports his or her car stolen and hides the car for approximately 30 days. Once 30 days have passed without the car's being recovered, insurance claims are often paid without question. After the claim is paid, the cars are often miraculously "found," but are in very poor condition. The owner will then use the money from the insurance claim to purchase a newer car.[35]

Carjacking is considered a combination of motor vehicle theft and robbery. Not only is a car stolen, but it is stolen by use of force or threat of force. Carjacking has become quite a widespread occurrence over the past few years. During each year between 1992 and 1996, there

was an average of about 49,000 completed or attempted nonfatal carjackings. In about half of the incidents, the offender was successful in taking the victim's automobile. Approximately 7 out of 10 completed carjackings involved the use of firearms, whereas about 2 out of 10 attempted carjackings involved the use of firearms. Surprisingly, most carjackings, whether they were completed or attempted, did not result in injury to the victim.[36]

The invention of the ignition key made it harder to steal cars. In recent years, manufacturers of automobiles have tried to make cars more theftproof. Steering-shaft locks, cutoff switches, better door locks, and alarm systems have increased the security of protected cars.

One of the most successful of the high-tech options for car protection may be electronic tracking systems, including the widely known and utilized Lo-Jack. A small electronic transmitter, installed in the car, is activated by police transmitters once a car is reported stolen. A homing signal allows tracking computers in police cruisers to determine the location of the stolen car. A direction finder and a signal-strength meter let the police know how close they are to the stolen car, thereby facilitating the search.[37] A newer type of antitheft device is called the "Unbrakeable Autolock." This particular device, when in place, locks one of the strongest parts of the car, the steel brake pedal. Once the Autolock is in place, the brake pedal cannot be depressed. Most cars built after 1990 feature a component called the "brake pedal shift interlock," which requires that the brake pedal be depressed before the vehicle can be put into gear. Since the Autolock locks the brake, it cannot be depressed, and therefore the car cannot be driven, making theft impossible.[38] One other recently developed antitheft device is the "Silent Scorpion." Unlike many car alarm systems, this device does not emit any sounds upon activation. Instead, it actually prevents the car thief from driving the car more than a quarter mile. The system is activated automatically whenever the driver's door is opened and then closed, while the engine is running. Once the Silent Scorpion is activated, the engine will run normally for about 4 seconds, at which time it will then begin to simulate engine failure. The engine will shudder and, after about 25 seconds, will shut off; the thief will be unable to restart the car.[39]

A recent development by the U.S. Attorney General's office in response to the Motor Vehicle Theft Prevention Act of 1994 is the national "Watch Your Car" program. A car owner can voluntarily display a decal or a special customized license plate on his or her vehicle signifying one of two things: that the car is normally not driven between the hours of 1:00 A.M. and 5:00 A.M. or that the vehicle is normally not driven in the proximity of international land borders or ports. As a member of this program, the car owner con-

U.S. Coast Guard law enforcement team boarding a vessel in American territorial waters.

sents to vehicle stops if the car is being driven under the conditions described above.[40]

Such efforts (as we saw in Chapter 9) are examples of target hardening—that is, designing the target (the car) in such a way that it is harder to steal. Other means of providing for greater car protection include safer parking facilities. Ronald Clarke has demonstrated that parking lots with attendants experience far fewer motor vehicle thefts than unattended lots.[41]

Boat Theft

It is not our purpose to classify all larceny by the type of property stolen. We have singled out automobile theft and art theft to demonstrate the socioeconomic significance of these types of larceny, their dependence on the economic situation, and the challenge of changing the situational conditions that encourage people to commit them. Another type of larceny, the theft

Crime Surfing

www.ojp.usdoj.gov/BJA/html/wycfaq.htm

Check this website for more information on the Watch Your Car program.

While no accurate estimates of worldwide losses from modern-day piracy are possible, knowledgeable experts think the total is probably near $250 million a year. The thieves make off with tons of cement, coffee, sugar, tomato paste, ladies' undergarments, steel, and whatever other cargo they think they can fence on shore. Even more common is the direct attack on the safe in the captain's cabin—pirates may be able to collect $50,000 in cash during a 15-minute job. In 1991 more than 120 pirate attacks were reported worldwide, and it is likely that only 40 percent of the total are reported to authorities.(1)

A downturn of maritime commerce in Nigeria resulted in a decrease of piracies off Lagos. A sharp decrease also occurred in the Malacca Straits, a result of improved security measures. But piracies began to increase again in the mid-1990s, near ports in Cameroon and Angola, and particularly in the Brazilian ports of Santos and Rio de Janeiro. Most affected are vessels at anchor in the roadsteads.

THE LACK OF POLICING

Unfortunately, the world does not yet have an international marine enforce-ment agency to police the oceans. There is no one to spot a vessel dumping nuclear waste into the high seas or into an exclusive economic zone. Who can intercept arms or narcotics smugglers? Even powerful nations, like the United States, have trouble policing their own zones. The problems are much worse for small nations that cannot afford to maintain marine police forces of any size.(2) A look at the Law of the Sea Treaty map indicates that most regions affected by piracy and terrorism are in areas of notoriously underpoliced territorial waters.

THE SCOPE OF CRIME ON THE OCEANS

All these problems are magnified when we realize that piracy is only one of many crimes committed on the oceans. Following are examples of other crimes:

- Frauds in the marine shipping industry have caused severe damage to international trade and threatened the collapse of entire national economies in Africa and Latin America.
- The international drug trade uses the oceans for about half its shipments

from the points of origin or manufacture to the points of distribution.

- Currently about 30,000 American boats are listed in the FBI's Stolen Boat File as having been stolen and not recovered.

Sources

1. G. O. W. Mueller and Freda Adler, *Outlaws of the Ocean* (New York: Hearst Marine Books, 1985, p. 150); Alan Farnham, "Pirates," Fortune, July 15, 1991, pp. 113–118.
2. Roger Villar, *Piracy Today* (London: Conway Maritime Press, 1985), p. 59.

Questions for Discussion

1. What crimes against property are committed by those who engage in maritime fraud?
2. Propose a mechanism to control property crime on the high seas. Defend your proposal.

---

of working and pleasure boats, of little fishing skiffs and rowboats, is similarly tied to socioeconomic conditions.

No statistics were kept on boat theft in the United States before 1970. Obviously, boat thefts have occurred ever since there have been boats, but such thefts attained high proportions only in the 1970s and 1980s. The FBI's National Crime Information Center started a stolen-boat file in 1969. During the first few years this service was little known, and the number of boats listed as stolen was initially small. But by the mid-1970s, law enforcement agencies all over the country had become familiar with this service and had begun reporting the number of stolen boats in their jurisdictions. Between 1975 and 1990 the number of boats stolen and not recovered tripled, from 11,000 to over 30,000, and that number did not include boats eliminated from the file after a given expiration period (of from 1 to 5 years). After 1990, the number of boats stolen declined.

Most boat thefts, both in the water and on land, are linked to the vast increase in the number of boats in the United States. Increased boat ownership among all population groups goes hand in hand with a proliferation of skills in handling boats and outboard motors. The number of automobile thefts rose during the days when automobile ownership and driving skills increased rapidly. Now we are witnessing the same phenomenon with boats. Some of the same crime-specific approaches developed to render cars more theftproof are currently being tried to protect boats and boating equipment—registration, secret and indelible identification numbers, locking devices, alarm systems, marina guards, protection campaigns for boat owners. Already we have some indication that the choices for boat thieves are becoming more

Darlene Gillespie, former Mouseketeer, was convicted of fraud in Los Angeles, California, Federal Court in 1999.

limited and that the thieves are choosing their targets with increasing care.[42]

With the exception of some brazen pickpockets, people who commit larcenies tend to avoid personal contact with their victims. Other criminals seek such contact in order to deprive victims of their property by deception.

FRAUD

Fraud is the acquisition of the property of another person through cheating or deception. In England such crimes owed their existence to the interaction of five circumstances: the advancement of trade and commerce, the inventiveness of swindlers in exploiting these economic advances, the demand of merchants for better protection, the unwillingness of the royal courts to expand the old concept of larceny, and the willingness of Parliament to designate new crimes in order to protect mercantile interests. In brief, medieval England developed a market economy that required the transport of goods by wagon trains across the country, from producer or importer to consumer. Later on, when the Crown sought to encourage settlement of colonies overseas, stock companies were created to raise money for such ventures. People with money to invest acquired part ownership in these companies in the expectation of profit.

Just as some dishonest transporters withheld some of the property entrusted to them for transport, some dishonest investment clerks used funds entrusted to them for their own purposes. Merchants suffered greatly from such losses, yet the royal courts refused to extend the definition of larceny to cover this new means of depriving owners of their property. But merchants demanded protection, and from time to time, as need arose, Parliament designated new, noncapital offenses so that the swindlers could be punished.

Obtaining Property by False Pretenses

The essence of the crime of **obtaining property by false pretenses** is that the victim is made to part with property voluntarily, as a result of the perpetrator's untrue statements regarding a supposed fact. Assume the doorbell rings. A gentleman greets you politely and identifies himself as a representative of a charitable organization, collecting money for disaster victims. On a typed list are the names of all the households in your building, with a dollar amount next to each name. Each household has supposedly contributed an average of $20. Not wanting to be considered cheap, you hand the gentleman a $20 bill. He promptly writes "$20" next to your name and thanks you.

Of course, the gentleman does not represent the charitable organization, there may not even be such a charity, there may not have been a disaster, and you may have been the first victim on his list. The man has obtained property from you by false pretenses. He has not committed a common law larceny because he did not engage in any "trespassory taking" of property.

Cheating was made a crime relatively late in history (in 1757 in England). Until that time the attitude was that people should look out for their own interests. Today obtaining property by false pretenses is a crime in all 50 states, and some states have included it in their general larceny statutes.

Confidence Games and Frauds

In an attempt to protect people from their own greed, a few fraud statutes have included a statutory offense called **confidence game.** In an effort to cover the enormous variety of confidence swindles, legislators have worded the statutory definitions somewhat vaguely. The essence of the offense is that the offender gains the confidence of the victim, induces in the victim the expectation of a future gain, and—by abusing the trust thus created—makes the victim part with some property. In a sense, confidence games are an aggravated form of obtaining property by false pretenses.

To illustrate: A woman (A) sees a shiny object lying on the sidewalk. As she stoops to pick it up, a man (B) grabs it. A dispute ensues over who should have the "lost diamond ring." A third person (C) comes by and offers to mediate. He happens to be a jeweler, he says. C takes a jeweler's loupe out of his pocket, examines the diamond ring, and pronounces it worth $500. At this point, B generously offers his share in the ring to A for a mere $100. A pays—and gets what turns out to be a worthless object. By the time she discovers this fact, B and C are long gone.

Frauds of this sort have been with us for centuries. But frauds change with commercial developments. Some of the more prevalent fraud schemes of today would have been unimaginable a few decades ago, simply because the commercial opportunities for their occurrence had not yet been invented.

Check Forgery

Those motivated to deprive others of their property have always exploited new opportunities to do so. The invention of "instant cash," or credit, by means of a check issued by a creditable, trustworthy person provided just such new opportunities. Ever since checks were invented, they have been abused. All jurisdictions make it a criminal offense to use a counterfeit or stolen check or to pass a check on a nonexisting account, or even on one with insufficient funds,

with intent to defraud. The intent may be demonstrated by the defendant's inability or unwillingness to reimburse the payee within a specified time period.

Another fraud, called **check forging,** consists of altering a check with intent to defraud. The criminologist Edwin Lemert found that most check forgers—or "hot-check artists," as they are frequently called—are amateurs who act in times of financial need or stress, do not consider themselves criminals, and often believe that nobody really gets hurt.[43] With the increase in check forgeries over the past few decades, the primary means of dealing with the problem has been the introduction of identification requirements needed when either cashing a check at a financial institution or presenting a check for payment. The downside of this approach is the annoyance to check users of having to put up with increased restrictions.[44] Some retailers have begun using Telecheck, where a check presented for payment is run through a machine that verifies whether or not the funds presented as payment on the check are in fact available at the time of sale.

Credit Card Crimes

Just as the introduction of checks for payment for goods and services opened up opportunities for thieves to gain illegitimate financial advantage, so did the introduction of "plastic money." Many believe that the widespread use of credit cards, debit cards, and charge cards is quickly making ours a cashless society.[45] There were 7 billion credit card transactions worldwide in 1991; of these, 3 billion took place in the United States. Now, the number of annual credit card transactions is over 21 billion.[46] Visa and MasterCard reported losses from credit card fraud of half a billion dollars in the United States in 1991. This amount has been increasing as the volume of cards in circulation goes up. Losses from credit card crime are expected to surpass all other retailer-reported losses, such as those from bad checks, counterfeit currency, and shoplifting.

Credit card fraud during the 1980s was associated primarily with counterfeiting and lost or stolen cards. Now many cards are stolen while in transit from the issuer to the cardholder. In other instances an offender may simply use false information about a real person to obtain a genuine card. Or a person may make a purchase by mail order or telephone using a genuine card number, but have the goods delivered to an address other than the address of the card owner.[47] Traffickers in stolen cards sell them for cash, with the amount based on the credit limit of the account—a $2000 credit line might bring $250.[48] The availability of new and relatively inexpensive technological equipment, however, keeps transforming the nature of the fraud. Stolen, lost, or expired credit cards are now modified with computers and encoding devices so that they appear to be valid. Totally counterfeit credit cards are also fabricated with the help of laser copiers or other duplicating techniques. And, more recently, credit card account numbers are being stolen from the Internet.

The economic rewards of credit card fraud are quick and relatively easy. The risks are low. Usually merchants do not ask for personal identification; cards are issued in banks that are often in other states or countries; and authorization procedures are weak. Originally, the users of stolen credit cards had the inconvenience of selling the merchandise they obtained with the cards. But when banks introduced the practice of cashing the checks of strangers as long as the transactions were guaranteed by a credit card, perpetrators gained direct access to cash and no longer had to resort to dealers in stolen goods.[49]

The banking industry has studied credit card schemes and has improved the electronic system with target-hardening responses. In 1971 Congress enacted legislation that limited the financial liability of owners of stolen credit cards to $50. Many states have enacted legislation making it a distinct offense to obtain property or services by means of a stolen or forged credit card, while others include this type of fraud under their larceny statutes.

Several fraud-prevention initiatives have been developed in response to the prevalence of credit card fraud. The use of laser-engraved photography and signatures on credit cards makes impersonation more difficult. Other initiatives are the use of increased authorization levels on credit card transactions, as well

Brian Anthony Cox, a 34-year-old engineer pictured with his mother, was charged with creating false identities to open bogus credit-card accounts, racking up more than $25,000 in purchases. Investigators allege that Cox used his technical skills to craft five fake drivers' licenses, based on information found in stolen mail.

as reduced floor limits above which transactions must be authorized to be guaranteed. Better technology has been developed to quickly transmit data on cards that have been reported lost and stolen to retailers worldwide. Further with the ever-increasing "card not present" situations, such as when a person is purchasing items over the Internet, additional methods are being developed to verify the identity of the cardholder.[50]

Insurance Fraud

Insurance fraud is a major problem in the United States. Auto insurance, in particular, has been the target of many dishonest schemes.

About $60 billion is paid in auto insurance claims annually. It is estimated that 10 percent of those claims are fraudulent.[51] The National Automobile Theft Bureau holds manufacturers' records on 188 million vehicles (about 95 percent of U.S. cars); its theft and loss data indicate that 15 percent of all reported thefts are fraudulent.[52] Auto insurance schemes include:

- *Staged claims.* Parts of a car are removed, reported stolen, and later replaced by the owner.
- *Owner dumping.* The car is reported stolen; it is stripped by the owner, and the parts are sold.
- *Abandoned vehicles.* The car is left in a vulnerable spot for theft; then it is reported stolen.[53]
- *Staged accidents.* No collision occurs, but an "accident scene" is prepared with glass, blood, and so forth.
- *Intended accidents.* All parties to the "accident" are part of the scheme.
- *Caused accidents.* The perpetrator deliberately causes an innocent victim in a targeted car to crash into his or her car (often in the presence of "friendly" witnesses).[54]

There are many types of insurance fraud besides that involving automobiles. One rapidly growing type involves filing fraudulent health insurance claims. Various terms have been created to describe the schemes that are used in medical fraud. "Overutilization" involves billing for superfluous and unnecessary tests and other services.[55] "Ping-Ponging" occurs when physicians refer patients to several practitioners when symptoms do not warrant such referrals. "Family ganging" takes place when a doctor extends several unnecessary services to all members of a patient's family. "Steering" is a practice in which doctors direct patients to the clinic's pharmacy to fill un-needed prescriptions. Finally, "upgrading" occurs when a patient is billed for services more extensive than those that were actually performed.[56]

Credit card crimes and insurance schemes are comparatively recent types of fraud, but they are not the last opportunities for swindlers to deprive others of their property. Computer crime, for example, is a growing concern, and technological advances continue to offer new possibilities for theft. Opportunities will always challenge the imagination of entrepreneurs—illegitimate as well as legitimate. In regard to the illegitimate entrepreneurs, the problem invariably is whether they are in violation of existing criminal laws or whether new legislation will have to be drawn up to cover their schemes.

HIGH-TECH CRIMES: CONCERNS FOR TODAY AND TOMORROW

Orange County, California (September 15, 1999). Six Southern California telemarketers have been charged in connection with an Internet gaming scam. Federal prosecutors say the scam took in almost $5 million from more than 500 investors. The six worked for Gecko Holdings. They offered investors stock in Gecko, telling them it was an online gambling business about to go public. Investors were promised that their shares, priced at two dollars, would double or triple the value in a few months. But the stock never went public. Instead, prosecutors say, the owners took off with the money. The six are charged with 26 counts each of mail and wire fraud.[57]

Crimes evolve with the environments we live in. The rise of computers and other high-technology equipment has paved the way for the genesis of new crime types. These present yet another set of challenges for potential victims, law enforcement personnel, criminologists, and other criminal justice professionals.

What exactly is high-technology crime? While there may be debates over the definition of this phenomenon, it is generally agreed that **high-tech crime** involves an attempt to pursue

Crime Surfing

www.ncb.com

Go to this website for more information on the National Crime Bureau and its fight against insurance fraud and vehicle theft.

Consider the case of Ernest Woodson, who fell and broke his eyeglasses on his way out of a supermarket in Cumberland County, New Jersey, and received $250 as compensation for the damage. Was this settlement fair to both parties? One might think so, unless you know that Mr. Woodson executed nearly two dozen similar falls on the premises of various New Jersey merchants in less than a year, filling insurance claims that added up to more than $30,000. When state authorities caught up with him in September of 1999, Woodson entered a guilty plea and was eligible to be sentenced to up to twelve months behind bars.

Ernest Woodson is just one example of insurance fraud in action. Now offenders face not only civil monetary penalties but jail time as well, depending on the extent and type of fraud. With insurance fraud on the rise, particularly health care claims fraud, New Jersey has taken steps to expand its resources and has become one of the few states in this country that has waged such a concentrated effort to combat insurance fraud at all levels. Other states maintain antifraud bureaus, but New Jersey is the first and only state to have a fraud-prevention program headed by a special prosecutor.(1) The handling of suspicious insurance claims and fraud cases was handled formerly by the Insurance Fraud Division (IFD) of the Department of Banking and Insurance. However, with New Jersey's Automobile Insurance Cost Reduction Act of 1998, the Office of the Insurance Fraud Prosecutor (OIFP) was created in the Division of Criminal Justice to "investigate all types of insurance fraud and serve as the focal point for all criminal, civil, and administrative prosecutions of insurance fraud."(2)

After being in business for only 14 months, the Office of the Insurance Fraud Prosecutor is making an impressive name

for itself. During 1998, 66 convictions were won, $2.5 million in fines were imposed, and $1.6 million in restitution was obtained. In the first 8 months of 1999, the OIFP filed charges against 104 people, obtained convictions against 49 people, imposed more than $3.7 million in civil fines, and won nearly $5 million in restitution. As of September 1999, OIFP investigators had sent 11 defendants to jail for a total of 39 years.(1) In addition, as part of its antifraud efforts, a toll-free fraud hot line was instituted so that anyone, including ordinary citizens, who suspects incidents of insurance fraud can report to the OIFP and remain anonymous if he or she chooses. Advertisements about the OIFP and this hot line were heard and seen on radio and television during the fall of 1999.

The following are results of some of the groundbreaking OIFP investigations:

- Karen Lawder, a licensed clinical social worker, received a 3-year prison sentence for committing health care claims fraud. She was the first person prosecuted under the state's new Health Care Claims Fraud Act in December 1998. Lawder had submitted at least five fictitious bills for health care services for which she received over $4000 from health insurers.
- Dr. Jayen Shah was sentenced to 5 years in prison for second-degree attempted theft and third-degree theft. Shah pretended to be wheelchair-bound in order to collect insurance money. After he was caught on tape walking into a restaurant, a sting operation led to his arrest. His medical license was revoked, he paid a $45,000 civil penalty, and he repaid over $70,000 in undeserved disability payments to the Social Security Administration.
- Former psychologist Carl Lichtman received a 5 1/2-year prison sentence for his role in a scheme that involved

more than 200 "patients" and cost 35 insurance carriers and the state of New Jersey more than $3.5 million. North Jersey private-sector employees and school district employees (including a vice-principal, 27 teachers, and 6 custodians) were among 65 people indicted for allegedly receiving kickbacks for being "no-show" patients or for receiving "referral fees" for participating in Lichtman's insurance fraud scheme.(2)

These are just a few examples of how insurance fraud offenders are punished. Other offenders who sell phony insurance cards and file false claims face similar fates. Insurance fraud is no laughing matter. It is estimated that this particular type of fraud may increase insurance bills and premiums as much as 15 percent.(1) Insurance fraud in New Jersey costs over $1 billion a year. Although in its early stages, New Jersey's experiment in fraud-busting is well on its way to success. Other states will likely follow in its footsteps.

Sources

1. Joe Donahue, "Slip and Fall? Better Be Prepared to Prove It," *Star Ledger,* (Newark, N.J.), Sept. 12, 1999, pp. 33–34.
2. Department of Law and Public Safety, Office of the Insurance Fraud Prosecutor, "Initial Report of the Office of the Insurance Fraud Prosecutor: Pursuant to N.J.S.A. 17:33A-24d," Mar. 1, 1999 (http://www.njinsurancefraud.org).

Questions for Discussion

1. What type of punishment is appropriate for an insurance fraud offender?
2. What other types of laws and policies can be created in an attempt to prevent insurance fraud?

illegal activities through the use of advanced electronic media. We shall define "high technology" as "a form of sophisticated electronic device—computer, cellular telephone, and other digital communication—that is in common use today."[58] The new waves of computer crime are perhaps the most illustrative examples of high-technology crime, although sophisticated credit card fraud schemes and cellular telephone scams are also modern problems. In this section, we will refer to crimes relying on modern electronic technology as "high-tech crimes."

Crime Surfing

www.nipc.gov

The National Infrastructure Protection Center, located at FBI headquarters, tracks computer crimes like the famous **Love Bug** virus.

Characteristics of High-Tech Crimes

High-tech crimes have affected the nature of property crimes by taking on a few distinct characteristics:

Role of Victims, Type of Property Criminals engaging in high-tech crimes no longer need actual direct contact with their victims; computers equipped with modems have unlimited range, enabling offenders to victimize people thousands of miles away. The reach of motivated offenders has been considerably extended. Physical movement has been replaced by electronic travel, especially with the recognition that computers are global networks.

The type of property that is stolen or affected is also very different in nature. While other property crimes (arson, vandalism, theft, larceny, burglary) victimize concrete targets, high-tech crimes involve less visible and tangible kinds of property such as information, data, and computer networks. In addition, many victims of high-tech crime realize they have been victimized only long after the crime has taken place. In most other property crimes there is often little time between the actual crime and the realization that a crime has taken place (as in cases of burglary or arson, for example).

Profits of Crime The profits from high-tech crimes are vast. The rise in the incidence of computer crime, for example, is a testament to its efficacy and the profit to be made. The British Banking Association in London estimates the cost of computer fraud worldwide at about $8 billion a year.[59] With the increasing sophistication of equipment, computer hackers are able to steal greater amounts with greater ease, and sometimes a single act can victimize multiple people or places at once.

Detection High-tech crime is also attractive to some individuals because they find evading detection and prosecution relatively easy. Few law enforcement agencies are equipped to detect the high-tech crimes occurring within their jurisdictions. Furthermore, since the nature of high-tech crime allows perpetrators to carry out their illegal activities without any geographic limitations, tracing high-tech criminal activity to the responsible individual is very difficult. Identifying the crime location becomes harder to do since street corners and physical space have been replaced by airwaves, cyberspace, and other electronic media. Often, by the time illegal activity has been detected, the criminals have already moved on to a new target.

Degree of Criminal Complexity Another important aspect of high-technology crimes involves the complicated nature of the crimes being committed. Every day, new crimes are being developed and refined by highly skilled computer users. Traditional law enforcement techniques are not designed to deal with such novel and complex crimes. High-tech criminals are, in a sense, sophisticated criminals. Stealing credit card numbers from the Internet for illicit purposes requires a certain degree of proficiency in Internet navigation, knowledge of how to break into the system to commit the thefts, and, finally, experience in using the stolen credit card numbers for criminal gain—all the while avoiding detection.

International Component Phone companies and computer network systems often advertise that using their services will allow individuals to communicate with people located at the other end of the globe. Such ease of electronic travel is appealing to high-tech criminals, who now participate in a modern phenomenon: global criminality. High-tech crimes can easily go beyond national boundaries, making them transnational crimes, a criminal activity of serious concern for targeted countries. Using a computer, a high-tech criminal can make illegal international money transfers, steal information from a computer located in another country, or diffuse illicit information (such as child pornography or terrorist propaganda) worldwide. The ability to detect and successfully deal with such criminal activities is a major challenge for law enforcement agencies around the world.

Computers and the Internet: Types of Crime[60]

High-tech criminals have also created their own crime types. While some seek the same ends as more traditional property offenders (financial gain), modern technology allows for novel and totally new crimes.

There are three main categories of computer crimes. First, the computer can be used as a storage or communication device whereby information can be created, stored, manipulated, and communicated electronically. In this instance, the computer is incidental, since it is not required for the crime itself, but is used in some way that is connected to the criminal activity. An example is financial records kept on a drug dealer's computer. Second, the computer can be used as an instrumentality or a tool of crime. In this case, the computer is used to commit traditional offenses, such as the creation of counterfeit money or official documents, or newer computer crime offenses, such as the distribution of child pornography, confidence schemes, and illegal gambling networks on the Internet. Finally, a computer can be used as a weapon to commit attacks on the confidentiality, integrity, and availability of information, including theft of information, theft of services, and damage to computer systems.[61] This type of computer crime involves the widespread problem of viruses and other forms of siege attacks, such as those referred to as "denial of service" attacks. The purpose of a denial of service attack is to prevent the normal operation of a digital system. It is often committed by "cyber vandals." Over 50 electronic siege attacks employing some form of denial of service have been initiated against organizations worldwide since January 1993.[62]

Computer Network Break-Ins   There are two types of computer network break-ins. The first is commonly known as "hacking." It is not practiced for criminal gain, and can therefore be considered more mischievous than malicious. Nevertheless, network intrusions have been made illegal by the U.S. federal government. A hacker's reward is being able to tell peers that he or she has managed to break into a network, demonstrating superior computing ability, especially the ability to bypass security measures. Hackers, for the most part, seek entry into a computer system and "snoop around," often leaving no sign of entry. It can be likened to an individual's stealthily gaining entry into another person's house, going through a few personal belongings, and carefully leaving without taking anything.

The second type of break-in is the one done for illegal purposes. A criminal might break into a large credit card company to steal card numbers, or into a network to steal data or sensitive information. Other criminal acts include computer vandalism, whereby individuals break into a system, alter its operating structure, delete important files, change passwords, or plant viruses that can destroy operating systems, software programs, and data.

Did You Know

. . . that online auctions were named the number one Internet fraud problem for 1998?

Industrial Espionage   In an age where information can create power, it should not be surprising that competing industries are very curious to know what the others are doing. "Cyber spies" can be hired to break into a competitor's computer system and gather secret information, often leaving no trace of the intrusion. Once again, these spies have such powerful technology at their disposal that they are able to target computers and information that may be thousands of miles away, making detection even more difficult.

Software Piracy It is estimated by the U.S. Software Publisher's Association that approximately $7.5 billion worth of American software is illegally copied and distributed annually worldwide. Software piracy ranges from friends sharing and occasionally copying software, to international fraudulent schemes whereby software is replicated and passed on as the original product, sometimes at a lower price. Recent research indicates that employees contribute significantly to the presence of illegal software in the workplace, either by bringing software from home (40 percent), downloading unauthorized copies from the Internet (24 percent), or sharing programs with other employees (24 percent).[63] The duplication process is relatively simple, and once mastered, any software can be pirated and copies sold worldwide. Software developers are constantly trying to stay ahead of the pirates by attempting to render their software resistant to such duplication. The advent of the compact disk and digital video disk unfortunately makes casual software piracy relatively easy.

Pornography Online The Internet provides a forum for the display of information. Some individuals, however, see this venue as a means to distribute or seek illegal information such as child pornography. Finding and downloading such material from the Internet is a simple task, even for amateur computer users. While law enforcement agencies occasionally intercept child pornography and those who engage in its dissemination over the airwaves, most offenders are never caught. Also, such material can be strategically hidden or altered to appear to be something else. "Morphing" is a practice that involves using computers to digitally alter pictures. Using such a method, an individual can superimpose two images, or cut and paste parts of one image onto another. This technique has become a tool for child pornographers to evade prosecution. They simply attach the head of an adult to a child's body, and claim the image indeed portrays an adult.

Many cases of online pedophilia have been reported as well. A former employee of Info-

seek, Patrick Naughton was a successful computer guru, who in 1990 helped develop the popular Java programming language at Sun Microsystems. However, his career ended in October 1999 when Naughton faced charges of online pedophilia after he arranged to meet a 13-year-old girl with whom he initiated contact in an online chat room. On arrival at a Santa Monica pier for a rendezvous with his online buddy, Naughton was met by FBI agents. The "13-year-old girl" turned out to be a male FBI agent.[64]

Pornography is finding itself online in other ways as well. In fact, Web pages are being "page-jacked." A recent scheme involved two hackers who cloned legitimate Web pages, including sites such as Audi and Paine Webber. When computer users attempted to reach the legitimate sites, they were "page-jacked" to pornographic websites. When attempting to escape the pornographic sites by clicking on the "Back" or "Home" buttons on their browsers, users were then "mouse-trapped" and sent to additional pornographic websites.[65]

Going after such offenders becomes difficult if different countries are involved in the illegal act. Let us suppose an individual in country A posts pornographic material on the Internet, and in country A, such material is legal. If the same material is retrieved in country B (although the source is country A), where the material is considered illegal, who is to blame, and where has the crime occurred? Jurisdictional questions about information found on the Internet remain largely unresolved. They will surely become more complex with the increasing traffic of illicit information and images.

Mail Bombings Computers can be used to steal money and information. They can also be used for more aggressive purposes. Like the bully told to rough up the new kid in the school yard, computers can be instructed to attack other machines. A common method is that of mail bombings. Mail bombs are the products of computer programs that instruct a computer to literally bombard another computer with information, often irrelevant electronic mail (e-mail). Mail bombs are capable of shutting down computers, and even entire networks, if the amount

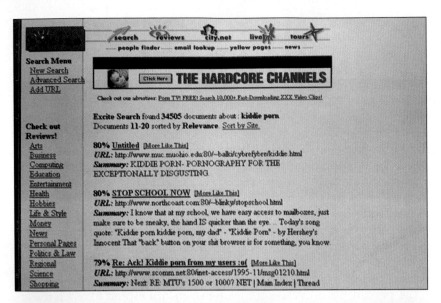

Child pornography is easy to find on the Internet if you know where to go, for example, newsgroups, chatrooms, and bulletin boards. Popular search engines are highly suggestive, but rarely bring you to illegal images. Most "legal" sites are self-regulated, requiring an adult content alert and some form of registration.

of information is too large for the receiving computer to digest.

Password Sniffers   Entry into a computer system often requires a password or some other form of user identification to protect the information it contains. Password sniffers are programs that carefully record the names and passwords of network users as they log in.

With such confidential information, unauthorized users are able to gain unlawful access to the computer and the information it contains. Passwords can also be sold to other users for illegal purposes.

Credit Card Fraud   Computers and the Internet are used more and more to conduct business. It has become commonplace to order merchandise, make payments, and conduct personal banking online. This use of credit cards is very appealing to people involved in credit card fraud. Computers can facilitate credit card fraud in two ways. First, a conventionally stolen credit card can be used to order merchandise online and, because no time is wasted going from store to store, a perpetrator can maximize his or her gain before the card is inactivated. Detection is also reduced since there is no physical contact with sales staff who might alert authorities should they suspect fraud. Second, credit card numbers can be stolen from the Internet as customers are making legitimate purchases. Programs similar to those that are designed to steal passwords from unsuspecting users are often used for this purpose. Another way of stealing credit card numbers is for offenders to access computers located in credit bureaus or financial institutions.

Currently, no one really knows the actual cost of computer crime. Estimates, however, suggest that the costs range from $500 million to $5 billion per year. Computer crime is underdetected and underreported. Furthermore, computer crime is not considered a major priority for many police departments. Greater attention and resources are focused on violent-crime-reduction efforts and, more recently, on community policing. Combating computer crime is not a priority for several reasons: It is difficult to police the Internet, and the necessary resources are not available to adequately handle this type of crime. There is no public outcry against computer crime, since the public is more interested in violent crime. Finally, many police officers feel that they did not choose their profession to police computer crime, but rather to help people and arrest the criminals.[66] Despite these problems, training programs on combating computer crime are being designed and implemented in some police departments.

Crime Surfing

www.sec.gov/consumer/seefraud.htm

Go to this website to report a potential online fraud.

Characteristics of the High-Tech Criminal

While all the crimes and deviant acts discussed so far rely heavily on technology, there are still human offenders behind them. Do these people, however, resemble other property criminals, or do they have distinct characteristics? It is true that modern technology is so widespread that virtually anyone is capable of high-tech crime, but it also remains a fact that most high-tech offenders, especially computer hackers, fit a rather unique profile. These individuals are usually young (14 to 19 years old) white males from middle-class backgrounds. They often possess superior levels of intelligence (IQ over 120), but on a social level they tend to be withdrawn and associate mainly with peers who share their fascination for electronic gadgets and computer-related activities. Some youths also believe that they are part of a counterculture, fighting censorship, liberating information, and challenging big business and major corporations.[67] In a way, they perceive themselves as modern-day Robin Hoods.

The Criminal Justice Problem

High-tech crimes pose a special problem to law enforcement agencies for two reasons. First, these crimes are not easily detected since the offenders can quietly commit them from any computer terminal, usually in the comfort of their own homes. Second, while a few organizations have mobilized to attack high-tech crime, most law enforcement agencies are not equipped to deal with the phenomenon: "Technology changes at an astounding rate while law enforcement techniques, which traditionally are reactionary, do not."[68] It is clear that the police forces of the future need to address this problem by concentrating on detection, and by arming themselves with the technological tools necessary to deal with it. By necessity, computer and/or Internet classes should soon find their way into police academies.

BURGLARY

A "burg," in Anglo-Saxon terminology, was a secure place for the protection of oneself, one's family, and one's property. If the burg protects a person from larceny and assault, what protects the burg? The burghers, perhaps. But there had to be a law behind the burghers. And that was

As we begin the twenty-first century, it has become quite clear just how large a role computers play in our everyday lives, especially for the fastest and cheapest way to communicate worldwide, e-mail. Not unexpectedly, computers have also become weapons for new types of crimes. Computer virus attacks are the latest phenomenon facing computer users worldwide. With computers networked on a global level, the same virus can affect and damage a computer system in Asia and one in North America simultaneously. Computer viruses have many purposes, including the destruction of files and the theft of personal information. And, most recently, these viruses are spread through e-mail.(1)

One of the more infamous virus attacks was that of the Melissa virus, which was created by David L. Smith, a 30-year-old computer programmer, who named the virus after a topless dancer he knew while living in Florida.(2) Smith created the virus from his Aberdeen, New Jersey, apartment. He was arrested and charged with interruption of public communications, theft of computer services, and damage or wrongful access to computer services.

David L. Smith, the 30-year-old computer programmer from New Jersey, who created the "Melissa" virus.

The virus Smith created was executed via e-mail in March of 1999. A computer user affected by the virus received an e-mail message in the in-box that appeared to come from someone he or she knew. The subject line of the e-mail stated: "Here is the document you asked for . . . don't show anyone else ;-)." Attached to the e-mail was a Microsoft Word document entitled "list.doc," which contained a list of pornographic Websites. Once the attachment was opened, the virus was then sent to the first 50 names in the e-mail user's address book.(1)

---

the law of burglary, which made it a crime to break and enter the dwelling of another person at night with the intention of committing a crime therein. (Of course it had to be at night, for during the day the inhabitants could defend themselves, or so it was thought.) The common law defined **burglary** as:

The breaking
And entering
Of the dwelling house
Of another person
At night
With the intention to commit a felony or larceny
    inside

By "breaking," the law meant any trespass (unauthorized entry), but usually one accompanied by a forceful act, such as cracking the lock, breaking a windowpane, or scaling the roof and entering through the chimney. The "entering" was complete as soon as the perpetrator extended any part of his or her body into the house in pursuit of the objective of committing a crime in the house. The house had to be a "dwelling," but that definition was extended to cover the "curtilage," the attached servants' quarters, carriage houses, and barns. The dwelling also had to be that of "another." And as we mentioned, the event had to occur at "night," between sundown and sunup.

The most troublesome element has always been the "intention to commit a felony or larceny" (even a petty or misdemeanor larceny) inside the premises. How can we know what a burglar intends to do? The best evidence of intent is what the burglar actually does inside the premises: Steal jewelry? Commit a rape? Set the house afire? Any crime the burglar commits in-

Once unleashed, Melissa invaded approximately 100,000 corporate and personal computers, including approximately 300 organizations, such as Microsoft, Lucent, Lockheed Martin, and the U.S. Marine Corps.(1) Computer experts had never seen a virus spread so fast. Melissa also caused shutdowns in over 300 computer networks.

After Melissa came the Worm.Explore.Zip virus, which was detected on June 6, 1999, in Israel. This virus was spread by e-mail as well, primarily through the Microsoft e-mail programs Outlook, Outlook Express, and Exchange, and came with a message that stated: "I received your e-mail and I shall send you a reply ASAP. Till then, take a look at the attached zipped docs." Once the recipient launched the zipped files, the system became infected. This particular virus, in a fashion similar to Melissa, sent the infected e-mail to all the addresses in the user's mailbox. In addition, the Worm.Explore.Zip virus wiped out documents, spreadsheets, and other files created by Microsoft programs.(3)

As a result of the damage Melissa caused, which is estimated in the tens of millions of dollars, many companies and computer users began to take precautions. Although Worm.Explore.Zip did infect some companies' computer systems, the damage that occurred was not nearly as bad as it would have been if precautions had not been taken.(1)

With regard to the impact of computer viruses, who gets hurt the most? Experts suggest that individuals, small businesses, and non-Western countries have the most to lose, since they often lack the vast virus-fighting capabilities many large companies maintain.(3) Given the susceptibility of attack, how can ordinary computer users become aware of these viruses and prevent their paths of destruction? Oftentimes, computer users are warned of certain viruses, but only after the viruses have already damaged other systems. In general, however, computer users are constantly warned not to open e-mails and attachments from unrecognized senders. Users are also encouraged to scan all attachments before opening them, as well as to update antivirus software on a regular basis since computer viruses grow at such an alarming rate. The problem of computer viruses has only just begun.

It will be necessary to monitor this type of property crime and to devise measures of counteracting.

Sources

1. Steven Levy, "Biting Back at the Wily Melissa," *Newsweek,* Apr. 12, 1999, pp. 62–64.
2. Janet Kornblum, "Melissa Remedy Shields Many from Worm," *USA Today,* June 14, 1999 (http://www.usatoday.com/life/cyber/tech/ctf379.htm).
3. "Virus Suspect Meant No Harm, Lawyer Says," *New York Times,* Apr. 4, 1999, p. 25.

Question for Discussion

1. Given what is known about computer crimes, particularly the spread of computer viruses in operating systems, how do you think the motivations for this type of property crime differ from those for other property crimes, such as motor vehicle theft and burglary.

---

side is considered evidence of criminal intention at the moment the burglar broke and entered the dwelling.[69]

Today burglary is no longer limited to night attacks, although by statute the crime may be considered more serious if it is committed at night. Statutes have also added buildings other than dwellings to the definition. The UCR defines burglary simply as the unlawful entry into a structure (criminal trespass) to commit a felony or theft. The use of force to gain entry is not a required element of burglary under the UCR.

Burglary rates have consistently declined over the past decade. Even so, in 1997, almost 2.5 million burglaries were reported to the police, with an overall loss of $3.3 billion. These crimes account for nearly a fifth of all Index offenses. Most burglaries (86 percent) are not cleared by arrests.[70]

Criminologists ask questions about the characteristics of offenders who commit burglaries and of the places that are burglarized. Neal Shover described the "good burglar" as one having competence, personal integrity, a specialty in burglary, financial success, and an ability to avoid prison.[71] Another study demonstrated that burglars are versatile, committing a wide range of offenses, but that they do specialize in burglary for short periods of time. Compared with male burglars, female burglars begin offending at a later age, more often commit burglaries with others, and have fewer contacts with the criminal justice system.[72]

Recent research on burglary asks questions not only about who is likely to commit a burglary or what distinguishes one burglar from another. In addition, as we notice in Chapter 9, criminologists are looking, for instance, at the process that leads to the burglary of a particular house in a specific neighborhood—that is, how a burglar discriminates between individual areas and targets when there are so many alternatives—and ways to make the process of burglary more difficult for any burglar.

FENCING: RECEIVING STOLEN PROPERTY

We are treating burglary as a property crime. An occasional burglar enters with the intention of committing rape, arson, or some other felony inside the building. But most burglars are thieves; they are looking for cash and for other property that can be turned into cash. Burglars and thieves depend on a network of fences to turn stolen property into cash.

Jonathan Wild controlled the London underworld from about 1714 until his hanging in 1725. For over 2 1/2 centuries he has captured the imagination of historians, social scientists, and writers. Henry Fielding wrote *The Life of Mr. Jonathan Wild, the Great,* and Mack the Knife in John Gay's *Beggar's Opera* was modeled on Wild. Wild was known as a "thief-taker." Thief-takers made an occupation of capturing thieves and claiming the rewards offered for their arrest. By law, thief-takers were allowed to keep the possessions of the thieves they caught, except objects that had been stolen, which were returned to their owners.

Wild added a devious twist to his trade: He bought stolen goods from thieves and sold them back to their rightful owners. The owners paid much more than the thief could get from the usual fences, so both Wild and the thief made a considerable profit. To thieves, he was a fellow thief; to honest people, he was a legitimate citizen helping them get back their property. Playing both roles well, he ran competing fencing operations out of business, employed about 7000 thieves, and became the most famous fence of all time.[73]

A **fence** is a person who buys stolen property, on a regular basis, for resale. Fences, or dealers in stolen property, operate much like legitimate businesses: They buy and sell for profit. Their activity thrives on an understanding of the law governing the receiving of stolen property, on cooperation with the law when necessary, and on networking. The difference between a legitimate business and a fencing operation is that the channeling of stolen goods takes place in a clandestine environment (created by law enforcement and deviant associates) with high risks and with a need to justify one's activities in the eyes of conventional society.

Carl Klockars's *Professional Fence* and Darrell Steffensmeier's *Fence,* each focusing on the life of a particular fence, present us with fascinating accounts of this criminal business. The proprietors of such businesses deal in almost any commodity. "Oh, I done lots of business with him," said Klockars's fence, Vincent Swazzi. "One time I got teeth, maybe five thousand teeth in one action. You know, the kind they use for making false teeth—you see, you never know what a thief's gonna come up with." And many fences are quite proud of their positions in the community. Said Swazzi, "The way I look at it, this is actually my street. I mean I am the mayor. I walk down the street an' people come out the doors to say hello."[74]

Until recently it was believed that professional thieves and fences were totally interdependent and that their respective illegal activities were mutually reinforcing. Recent research, however, demonstrates a change in the market for stolen goods. D'Aunn Webster Avery, Paul F. Cromwell, and James N. Olson conducted extensive interviews with 38 active burglars, shoplifters, and their fences and concluded that it is no longer the professional fence who takes care of stolen goods but, rather, occasional receivers—otherwise honest citizens—who buy from thieves directly or at flea markets.[75] This willingness to buy merchandise that the buyers must at least suspect has been stolen may indicate that the general public is more tolerant of stealing than previous generations were.

ARSON

The crimes against property that we have discussed so far involve the illegitimate transfer of possession. The property in question is "personal property" rather than real property, or real estate. Only two types of property crime are concerned with real property. Burglary is one; the other is arson.

The common law defined **arson** as the malicious burning of or setting fire to the dwelling of another person. Modern statutes have distinguished degrees of severity of the offense and have increased its scope to include other structures and even personal property, such as automobiles. The most severe punishments are reserved for arson of dwellings, because of the likelihood that persons in the building may be injured or die.

Arson always has been viewed as a more violent crime than burglary. In comparison with burglary, however, arson is a fairly infrequent offense. A total of 81,753 arson offenses were reported in 1997.[76] A national survey of fire departments, however, indicates that the actual number of arson incidents is likely to be far higher than the reported figure.[77]

Buildings were the most frequent targets (49 percent); 29 percent of the targets were mobile property (motor vehicles, trailers, and the like); and crops and timber constituted 23 percent.[78] The annual estimated property loss is over $2 billion. In 1993, 560 civilian lives were lost as a result of suspicious fires.[79]

The seriousness of this crime is demonstrated by a series of spectacular fires set in resort hotels in such cities as San Juan, Puerto Rico (in conjunction with a labor dispute), and Las Vegas, Nevada. Although these fires were not set with the intent to kill any of the people in the buildings, many lives were lost. The inferno created by arsonists in the Du Pont Plaza Hotel in San Juan in 1987 killed 97 people. The arson at the Las Vegas Hilton caused no deaths but did result in $14 million in damages, not including the loss of business.

While insurance fraudsters and organized-crime figures may be responsible for some of the more spectacular arsons, it is juveniles who account for the single most significant share. Consider the following statistics:

- In 1997 juveniles under age 18 accounted for about 50 percent of the arson arrests nationwide.[80]
- Of every 16 persons arrested for arson, 1 is under age 10, and 1 of every 4 persons is under age 15.

- Of children in grades 1 to 8 in Rochester, New York, 38 percent admitted playing with fire.[81]
- Of the 20,000 arrests (adult and juvenile) for arson in 1997, 85 percent were males, 73 percent were white, and 25 percent were black.[82]
- There was a decrease in arson offenses between 1996 and 1997.[83]

Why do children set fires?[84] Recent research suggests that the motive may be psychological pain, anger, revenge, need for attention, malicious mischief, or excitement.[85] Juvenile fire setters have been classified in three groups: the playing with matches fire setter, the crying for help fire setter, and the severely disturbed fire setter.[86] Many juvenile fire setters are in urgent need of help. In response to their needs, juvenile arson intervention programs have been established in recent years.[87]

An interesting English study found that while arsonists were in many respects comparable to offenders classified as violent, they had a lower incidence of interpersonal aggression and rated themselves as less assertive than did violent offenders—perhaps because, as the study showed, arsonists were taken into care at an earlier age.[88] The motives of adult arsonists are somewhat different from those of juveniles. Though here, too, we find disturbed offenders (pyromaniacs) and people who set fires out of spite. We are also much more likely to encounter insurance fraudsters, as well as organized-crime figures who force compliance or impose revenge by burning establishments (the "torches").[89] One classification of fire setters by motive includes:

- Revenge, jealousy, and hatred.
- Financial gain (mostly insurance fraud).
- Intimidation and/or extortion (often involving organized crime).
- Need for attention.
- Social protest.
- Arson to conceal other crimes.
- Arson to facilitate other crimes.
- Vandalism and accidental fire setting.[90]

As arson continues to be a serious national problem, policy makers have been developing two distinct approaches for dealing with it. The offender-specific approach focuses on educational outreach in schools and the early identification of troubled children, for purposes of counseling and other assistance.[91] The offense-specific (geographic) approach focuses on places. It seeks to identify areas with a high potential for arson. The aim is to deploy arson specialists to correct problems and to stabilize endangered buildings and neighborhoods.[92]

COMPARATIVE CRIME RATES

The rates of property crime are much higher than those of the violent crime we discuss in Chapter 11. It is interesting to compare these rates for various regions of the world. If we compare the property-owning, consumer-oriented countries of the industrialized Western world with the still largely agricultural but rapidly urbanizing countries of the Third World, we note a significant discrepancy: The rate of theft per 100,000 in the developed countries was 4200, while the rate in developing countries was 600.[93]

Recall the Coca-Cola bottle that disrupted the lives of the aborigines in *The Gods Must Be Crazy*. We just may have discovered the secret of that bottle: If there is no Coke bottle, no one is going to steal it. The more property people have, especially portable property, the more opportunity other people have to make off with it. Europeans have an old saying: "Opportunity makes thieves." The foremost opportunity for theft may simply be an abundance of property.

REVIEW

Not all crimes against property are aimed at acquiring such property. A burglar invades a dwelling or other structure usually—but not necessarily—to commit a larceny inside. An arsonist endangers the existence of the structure and its occupants. Both amateurs and professionals commit property crimes of all sorts. Each new form of legitimate trade, such as the development of credit cards and computers, offers criminals new opportunities to exploit the situation for gain. It is evident that most high-tech offenders are quite sophisticated and, given the vastness of such technological wonders as the Internet, a new challenge lies ahead for social scientists and criminal justice professionals alike.

Some property-oriented crimes, as we will see in Chapter 13, depend not only on the cunning and daring of the perpetrator who targets a lone victim, but on the normal business operations of legitimate enterprises—and of illegitimate ones as well.

YOU BE THE CRIMINOLOGIST

1. You are the owner of a small, family-run variety store. The only employee working in this store, other than yourself, is your spouse. While conducting monthly inventory checks, you notice a significant amount of missing goods that are inconsistent with the sales records. You and your spouse begin to realize that your store has been the target of shoplifters. What are some of the ways you can attempt to make your small establishment less attractive to shoplifters and prevent future instances of this particular property crime? Consider how routine-activity theory applies to your situation.

2. Computers are now part of our everyday lives at work, or in school, or at home as vehicles to pay bills, shop online, or simply surf the Internet. With the growing use of computers in all facets of our lives, the potential for misuse increases as well. This chapter has discussed some of the most pressing issues at the heart of computer crimes, including online credit card fraud, the use of the Internet in promoting child pornography, viruses and worms that invade the hard drives of computers, and software piracy. Select at least two forms of computer crime. What, in your opinion, are the causes of and the motivations for committing such crimes? What specifically does the offender stand to gain? Describe ways to counteract the problem. What can be done to prevent this emerging type of property crime?

KEY TERMS

The numbers next to the terms refer to the pages on which the terms are defined.

arson (359)

burglary (356)

NOTES

1. J. W. Cecil Turner, *Kenny's Outlines of Criminal Law*, 2d ed. (Cambridge, Mass.: Cambridge University Press, 1958), p. 238.

2. Jerome Hall, *Theft, Law, and Society* (Indianapolis: Bobbs-Merrill, 1935).

3. Uniform Crime Reports, 1998, p. 45.

4. U.S. Department of Justice, Bureau of Justice Statistics, *Criminal Victimization 1998* (Washington, D.C.: U.S. Government Printing Office, 1999), p. 3.

5. Uniform Crime Reports, 1994, p. 46.

6. See Abraham S. Blumberg, "Typologies of Criminal Behavior," in *Current Perspectives on Criminal Behavior*, 2d ed., ed. Blumberg (New York: Knopf, 1981).

7. See John Hepburn, "Occasional Criminals," in *Major Forms of Crime*, ed. Robert Meier (Beverly Hills, Calif.: Sage, 1984), pp. 73–94; and John Gibbs and Peggy Shelly, "Life in the Fast Lane: A Retrospective View by Commercial Thieves," *Journal of Research in Crime and Delinquency*, 19 (1982): 299–330, at p. 327.

8. James Inciardi, "Professional Thief," in Meier, *Major Forms of Crime*, p. 224. See also Harry King and William Chambliss, *Box Man—A Professional Thief's Journal* (New York: Harper & Row, 1972).

9. *The Professional Thief*, annotated and interpreted by Edwin H. Sutherland (Chicago: University of Chicago Press, 1937).

10. Jo-Ann Ray, "Every Twelfth Shopper: Who Shoplifts and Why?" *Social Casework*, 68 (1987): 234–239. For a discussion of who gets caught and what kinds of treatment programs exist, see Gail A. Caputo, "A Program of Treatment for Adult Shoplifters," *Journal of Offender Rehabilitation* 27 (1998): 123–137.

11. Abigail Buckle and David P. Farrington, "An Observational Study of Shoplifting," *British Journal of Criminology*, 24 (1984): 63–73.

12. Donald Hartmann, Donna Gelfand, Brent Page, and Patrice Walder, "Rates of Bystander Observation and Reporting of Contrived Shoplifting Incidents," *Criminology*, 10 (1972): 247–267.

13. Read Hayes, *1996 Retail Theft Trends Report: An Analysis of Customer Theft in Stores* (Winter Park, Fla.: Loss Prevention Specialists, 1996).

14. P. James Carolin, Jr., "Survey of Shoplifters," *Security Management*, 36 (1992): 11–12.

15. Pia Salmelainen, *The Correlates of Offending Frequency: A Study of Juvenile Theft Offenders in Detention* (Sydney, Australia: New South Wales Bureau of Crime Statistics and Research, 1995).

16. Mary Owen Cameron, *The Booster and the Snitch* (New York: Free Press, 1964). See also John Rosecrance, "The Stooper: A Professional Thief in the Sutherland Manner," *Criminology*, 24 (1986): 29–40.

17. Richard Moore, "Shoplifting in Middle America: Patterns and Motivational Correlates," *International Journal of Offender Therapy and Comparative Criminology*, 28 (1984): 53–64. See also Charles A. Sennewald and John H. Christman, *Shoplifting* (Boston: Butterworth-Heinemann, 1992).

18. Trevor N. Gibbens, C. Palmer, and Joyce Prince, "Mental Health Aspects of Shoplifting," *British Medical Journal*, 3 (1971): 612–615.

19. Hayes, *1996 Retail Theft Trends Report*.

20. Roger Griffin, *Shoplifting in Supermarkets* (San Diego, Calif.: Commercial Service Systems, 1988).

21. Barry Poyner and Ruth Woodall, *Preventing Shoplifting: A Study in Oxford Street* (London: Police Foundation, 1987).

22. John Carroll and Frances Weaver, "Shoplifters' Perceptions of Crime Opportunities: A Process-Tracing Study," in *The Reasoning Criminal*, ed. Derek Cornish and Ronald V. Clarke (New York: Springer Verlag, 1986), pp. 19–38.

23. Joshua Bamfield, "Retail Civil Recovery: Filling a Deficit in the Criminal Justice System?"

Review • You Be the Criminologist • Key Terms • Notes

International Journal of Risk Security and Crime Prevention, **3** (1998): 257–267.

24. Truc-Nho Ho, "Prevention of Art Theft at Commercial Art Galleries," *Studies on Crime and Crime Prevention,* **7** (1998): 213–219. See also "FBI—Major Investigations—National Stolen Art File" (http://www.fbi.gov/majcases/arttheft/art.htm).

25. See Truc-Nhu Ho, *Art Theft in New York City: An Exploratory Study in Crime Specificity,* Ph.D. dissertation, Rutgers University, 1992; Christopher Dickey, "Missing Masterpieces," *Newsweek,* May 29, 1989, pp. 65–68.

26. Truc-Nhu Ho, "Prevention of Art Theft at Commercial Galleries."

27. Winnie Hu, "11 Arrested in Video Piracy Crackdown," *New York Times,* Aug. 21, 1999, p. B3.

28. Truc-Nho Ho, "Prevention of Art Theft at Commercial Art Galleries."

29. Uniform Crime Reports, 1998.

30. Ibid.

31. Ibid., p. 238.

32. See Charles McCaghy, Peggy Giordano, and Trudy Knicely Henson, "Auto Theft," *Criminology,* **15** (1977): 367–385.

33. See http://www.lojack.com/theft.htm

34. National Insurance Crime Bureau, *Thieves Target Vehicles in U.S. Coastal and Border Communities,* press release, Mar. 22, 1999 (http://www.nicb.com/release.htm).

35. Kevin Blake, "What You Should Know about Car Theft," *Consumer's Research* (October 1995): 26–28.

36. U.S. Department of Justice, Bureau of Justice Statistics, *Carjackings in the United States, 1992–1996* (Washington, D.C.: U.S. Government Printing Office, 1999), p. 1.

37. Eric Peters, "Anti–Car Theft System Starts in Virginia: D.C., Maryland Next," *Washington Times,* Aug. 13, 1993, p. G2.

38. Lawman Armor Corporation, *New BRAKEthrough Anti-Theft Device from Lawman Armor Corporation Puts the Brakes on Auto Theft,* press release, Sept. 16, 1999 (http://www.biz.yahoo.com/prnews/990917/pa_lawman_1.html).

39. See "The Silent Scorpion" (http://www.carjacking.com).

40. See "The Watch Your Car Program" (http://www.ojp.usdoj.gov/BJA/html/wycfaq.htm).

41. Ronald V. Clarke, "Situational Crime Prevention: Theoretical Basis and Practical Scope," in *Crime and Justice: An Annual Review of Research,* vol. 4, ed. Michael Tonry and Norval Morris (Chicago: University of Chicago Press, 1983).

42. Jeffrey Peck, G. O. W. Mueller, and Freda Adler, "The Vulnerability of Ports and Marinas to Vessel and Equipment Theft," *Security Journal,* **5** (1994): 146–153.

43. Edwin Lemert, "An Isolation and Closure Theory of Naive Check Forgery," *Journal of Criminal Law, Criminology, and Police Science,* **44** (1953–1954): 296–307.

44. Johannes Knutsson and Eckart Kuhlhorn, "Macro Measures against Crime: The Example of Check Forgeries," in *Situational Crime Prevention: Successful Case Studies,* 2d ed., ed. Ronald V. Clarke (Albany, N.Y.: Harrow and Heston, 1997).

45. W. A. Watts, "Credit Card Fraud: Policing Plastic," *Journal of Financial Crime,* **7** (1999): 67–69.

46. Richard Greer, "The Georgia 100," *Atlanta Constitution,* May 19, 1996, p. 13G.

47. Michael Levi and Jim Handley, *A Research and Statistics Directorate Report: The Prevention of Plastic and Cheque Fraud Revisited* (London: Home Office, 1998).

48. Barry Masuda, "Card Fraud: Discover the Possibilities," *Security Management,* **36** (1992): 71–74.

49. Pierre Tremblay, "Designing Crime," *British Journal of Criminology,* **26** (1986): 234–253.

50. Levi and Handley, *A Research and Statistics Directorate Report.*

51. Leonard Sloane, "Rising Fraud Worrying Car Insurers," *New York Times,* Nov. 16, 1991, p. 48.

52. Michael Clarke, "The Control of Insurance Fraud," *British Journal of Criminology,* **30** (1990): 1–23.

53. Sloane, "Rising Fraud Worrying Car Insurers."

54. Edmund J. Pankan and Frank E. Krzeszowski, "Putting a Claim on Insurance

Fraud," *Security Management*, **37** (1993): 91–94.

55. P. Jesilow, H. N. Pontell, and G. Geis, "Physician Immunity from Prosecution and Punishment for Medical Program Fraud," in *Punishment and Privilege*, ed. W. B. Groves and G. R. Newman (New York: N.Y. Harrow and Heston, 1987), p. 8.

56. H. N. Pontell, P. Jesilow, and G. Geis, "Policing Physicians: Practitioner Fraud and Abuse in a Government Medical Program," *Social Problems*, **30** (1982): 117–125.

57. See Yahoo! News, Sept. 15, 1999 (http://www.dailynews.yahoo.com).

58. Larry E. Coutorie, "The Future of High-Technology Crime: A Parallel Delphi Study," *Journal of Criminal Justice*, **23** (1995): 13–27.

59. "Survey Finds Computer Crime Widespread in Corporate America." *The News and Observer*, Raleigh, N.C., Oct. 25, 1995.

60. Natalie D. Voss, "Crime on the Internet," *Jones Telecommunications and Multimedia Encyclopedia*, Drive D: \ Studios, Jones Digital Century (1996). (Found on the Internet at http://www.digitalcentury.com/encyclo/update/crime.html)

61. Marc Goodman, "Why the Police Don't Care about Computer Crime," *Harvard Journal of Law and Technology*, **10** (1997): 465–494.

62. Richard Overill, "Denial of Service Attacks: Threats and Methodologies," *Journal of Financial Crime*, **6** (1999): 351–353.

63. See Yahoo! News, "Employer Beware . . . National Survey Cites Employees as Significant Contributors to Software Piracy in the Workplace," Sept. 16, 1999 (http://www.biz.yahoo.com/bw/990916/dc_bsa_1.html).

64. Brad Stone, "A High Technology Crash," *Newsweek*, Oct. 4, 1999, p. 54.

65. Stephen Labaton, "Net Sites Co-Opted by Pornographers," *New York Times*, Sept. 23, 1999, p. 1.

66. Goodman, "Why the Police Don't Care about Computer Crime."

67. Robert W. Taylor, "Computer Crime," in *Criminal Investigation*, ed. C. R. Swanson, N. C. Chamelin, and L. Tersito (New York: Random House, 1991).

68. Coutorie, "The Future of High-Technology Crime."

69. Kenneth C. Sears and Henry Weihofen, *May's Law of Crimes*, 4th ed. (Boston: Little, Brown, 1948), pp. 307–317.

70. Uniform Crime Reports, 1998.

71. Neal Shover, "Structures and Careers in Burglary," *Journal of Criminal Law and Criminology*, **63** (1972): 540–549.

72. Scott Decker, Richard Wright, Allison Redfern, and Dietrich Smith, "A Woman's Place Is in the Home: Females and Residential Burglary," *Justice Quarterly*, **10** (1993): 143–162.

73. Darrell Steffensmeier, *The Fence: In the Shadow of Two Worlds* (Totowa, N.J.: Rowman & Littlefield, 1986), p. 7.

74. Carl Klockars, *The Professional Fence* (New York: Free Press, 1976), pp. 110, 113.

75. D'Aunn Webster Avery, Paul F. Cromwell, and James N. Olson, "Marketing Stolen Property: Burglars and Their Fences," paper presented at the 1988 Annual Meeting of the American Society of Criminology, Reno, Nev.

76. Uniform Crime Reports, 1998, p. 56.

77. Patrick G. Jackson, "Assessing the Validity of Official Data on Arson," *Criminology*, **26** (1988): 181–195.

78. Uniform Crime Reports, 1994, p. 50.

79. Michael J. Karter, Jr., "Fire Loss in the United States in 1993," *NFPA Journal*, **88** (1994): 59, 62, 64.

80. Uniform Crime Reports, 1998.

81. See Rebecca K. Hersch, *A Look at Juvenile Firesetter Programs*, for U.S. Department of Justice, Office of Justice Programs, Office of Juvenile Justice and Delinquency Prevention (Washington, D.C.: U.S. Government Printing Office, May 1989), p. 1.

82. Uniform Crime Reports, 1998.

83. Ibid.

84. Irving Kaufman and Lora W. Heims, "A Reevaluation of the Dynamics of Firesetting," *American Journal of Orthopsychiatry*, **31** (1961): 123–136.

85. Hersch, *A Look at Juvenile Fire-setter Programs*.

86. Wayne S. Wooden and Martha Lou Berkey, *Children and Arson* (New York: Plenum, 1984), p. 3.

Review • You Be the Criminologist • Key Terms • Notes

87. See Jessica Gaynor and Chris Hatcher, *The Psychology of Child Firesetting* (New York: Brunner/Mazel, 1987).

88. Howard F. Jackson, Susan Hope, and Clive Glass, "Why Are Arsonists Not Violent Offenders?" *International Journal of Offender Therapy and Comparative Criminology*, **31** (1987): 143–151.

89. See Wayne W. Bennett and Karen Matison Hess, *Investigating Arson* (Springfield, Ill.: Charles C Thomas, 1984), pp. 34–38.

90. John M. Macdonald, *Bombers and Firesetters* (Springfield, Ill.: Charles C Thomas, 1977), pp. 198–204.

91. See Federal Emergency Management Agency, U.S. Fire Administration, *Interviewing and Counseling Juvenile Firesetters* (Washington, D.C.: U.S. Government Printing Office, 1979).

92. Clifford L. Karchmer, *Preventing Arson Epidemics: The Role of Early Warning Strategies*, Aetna Arson Prevention Series (Hartford, Conn.: Aetna Life & Casualty, 1981).

93. "Third United Nations Survey of Crime Trends, Operations of Criminal Justice Systems and Crime Prevention Strategies," A/CONF. 144/6, July 27, 1990.

CHAPTER 13
Organizational Criminality

"This is not our proudest day," said Donald J. Carty, Chairman of AMR Corporation, the parent company of American Airlines. Prosecutors in Miami, Florida, felt otherwise. On December 16, 1999, one of the nation's largest airlines pleaded guilty to transporting hazardous and poisonous materials on its passenger jets for more than five years. The passengers and employees of American Airlines were placed at risk by the dangerous handling of hazardous materials, according to Assistant Attorney General Lois Schiffer. The airline was fined $8 million and placed on probation for three years. It agreed to place a full-page advertisement in the Miami Herald apologizing for its actions.

The potential for harm from illegally transporting hazardous materials is a matter of great public concern. This case comes on the heels of the conviction of Sabre Tech, Inc. in federal court on eight counts of recklessly mishandling hazardous materials, leading to the crash of ValuJet Flight 592, in May 1996. The DC-9, on route to Atlanta, plunged into the Everglades after catching on fire. Experts trace the cause of the fire to improperly packaged oxygen canisters in the cargo hold. All 110 people aboard were killed. Sabre Tech, Inc. still faces felony murder charges in state court.[1]

* * *

General Electric has been charged with price fixing and other monopolistic practices not only for its light bulbs, but for turbines, generators, transformers, motors, relays, radio tubes, heavy metals, and lightning arresters. At least 67 suits have been brought against General Electric by the Antitrust Division of the Justice Department since 1911, and 180 antitrust suits were brought against General Electric by private companies in the early 1960's alone. General Electric's many trips to court hardly seem to have "reformed" the company: In 1962, after 50 years' experience with General Electric, even the Justice Department was moved to comment on General Electric's proclivity for frequent and persistent involvement in antitrust violations.[2]

* * *

A Mafia boss found dead last week was involved in the 1992 murder of Cosa Nostra's enemy number one, Judge Giovanni Falcone, Italian state television channels said Sunday.

The reports said Antonino Gioe, who hanged himself with his shoelaces from the bars of his cell Thursday, was at Palermo airport when Falcone arrived there and he had apparently tipped off the Mafia commando which killed the judge minutes later.

Falcone, his wife and three bodyguards died May 23, 1992, when their armor-plated cars were blown up by a huge bomb buried under the highway between Palermo and the airport.

Falcone's murder, followed by that of his colleague Paolo Borsellino two months later, proved a major turning point in Italian politics and provoked a strong state reaction. Leading members of the Mafia were arrested after years on the run.

The reports said Gioe had killed himself because he knew the Mafia had condemned him to death for making too many mistakes. He was apparently hoping his suicide would spare his family any bloody reprisals by his former associates.

According to the reports, investigators traced a call made by Gioe on his mobile phone at Palermo airport two minutes after Falcone and his wife had landed.

The call, to a member of the Madonia clan on whose "territory" the judge was killed, ended only seconds before the killers detonated the bomb. The man Gioe was calling is also under arrest but his name has not been disclosed.

Investigators still do not know who told the Mafia Falcone was making the unannounced trip from Rome to Palermo aboard a secret service plane. The inquiry has centered around a former senior member of the intelligence service and a Sicilian MP.

Gioe, a 37-year-old Mafioso from Corleone, was being kept in solitary confinement in the same wing of Rome's maximum security jail as Salvatore "Toto" Riina, the Mafia godfather arrested last January after 23 years on the run.[3]

What do the crimes of American Airlines, General Electric, and the Cosa Nostra, or Mafia, have in common? According to the criminologist Dwight Smith, white-collar, corporate, and organized crimes all involve business enterprises.[4] An offender—whether a corporation employee, the corporation itself, or a lieutenant in a Mafia family—uses a business enterprise (perhaps an insurance company, a garbage collection company, or a prostitution ring) to profit illegally. It is the use of a legitimate or illegitimate business enterprise for illegal profit that distinguishes organizational crimes from other types of offenses. Organizational offenses are also different in another important respect. Unlike violent crimes and property offenses, which the Model Penal Code classifies quite neatly, organizational offenses are a heterogeneous mix of crimes, from homicide, fraud, and conspiracy to racketeering, gambling, and the violation of a host of federal environmental statutes.

How much white-collar crime is committed each year? What are the attributes of organized crimes? How much crime is committed by major U.S. corporations? Answers to such questions, no matter how preliminary, may provide valuable information to guide efforts to control and prevent white-collar, corporate, and organized crime.

DEFINING WHITE-COLLAR CRIME

Initial reports of a crisis in the U.S. savings and loan (S&L) industry appeared on front pages of newspapers across the country in 1989. They alleged that some savings and loan officers had ruined their institutions financially for personal profit, thereby causing the greatest amount of white-collar crime ever uncovered. Bailing out the insolvent banks may cost an estimated $300 billion to $500 billion by 2021.[5]

But white-collar crime is not a new phenomenon. In ancient Greece public officials reportedly violated the law by purchasing land slated for government acquisition.[6] Much of what we today

By most estimates corporate crime costs more in human lives and in dollars than the more highly publicized, more severely punished, and far more familiar street crime. For example, it is estimated that in the United States 100,000 to 200,000 people die each year from job-related illnesses and injuries. That is a rate five times higher than the number of people murdered by street criminals each year.(1) If you add to this the number of people who die each year from causes related to corporate "oversight," marketing, or profiteering, the rate is far higher. "All things considered," concludes sociologist Sandra Walklate, "this evidence strongly suggests that we are at far more physical risk of being victimized as a result of the activities and inactivities of business and industry than by street crime or burglary."(2)

Victims of corporate crime rarely, it seems, make their victimization known to authorities—sometimes because they don't even realize they *are* victims.(3) In general, corporate crime not only goes unpunished, but also unreported and even undetected. "The majority of those suffering from corporate crime remain unaware of their victimization—either not knowing it has happened to them or viewing their 'misfortune' as an accident or 'no one's fault,' " one researcher explained.(4) "Clearly a major problem in controlling corporate crime is raising victim and public consciousness to a level where the community desires and supports a policy of more active and effective state control and regulation."(4)

"Raising victim and public consciousness" is a problem. When victims are the public at large or another corporation, they do not fit our traditional picture of victims—they are not individuals. Even when the victim is an individual, as in a case of death caused by occupational safety violations, we may not think of him or her as a victim of *crime*. Since we do not know whom in particular to blame (the offender is "depersonalized"), we tend not to blame anyone and to say it was an accident.

According to criminologist David Shichor, several scholars have suggested that social control of corporations will not occur until public opinion toward "big business" has been changed. A better understanding of corporate victimization could improve efforts to educate the public about corporate crime through publicity, "personalization of the harm," "individualization of the victim," and "personalization of the offender." The goal, says Shichor, is "to demonstrate to the public and to corporate executives that many corporate actions and business practices are often more harmful than street crimes, victimize a large number of people, undermine public trust in social institutions and deviate from social and legal norms."(3).

Sources

1. David R. Simon and D. Stanley Eitzen, *Elite Deviance* (Boston: Allyn and Bacon, 1993), p. 40.
2. Sandra Walklate, *Victimology: The Victim and the Criminal Justice Process* (London: Unwin Hyman, 1989), p. 91.
3. David Shichor, "Corporate Deviance and Corporate Victimization: A Review and Some Elaborations," *International Review of Victimology,* **1** (1989): 67–88.
4. S. Box, *Power, Crime and Mystification* (London: Tavistock, 1983), pp. 17, 66.

Questions for Discussion

1. Those injured by corporations may sue the corporation for damages. When an individual is pitted against a giant corporate entity, is the likelihood of a lawsuit an incentive for the corporation to change its practices?
2. Few victims report being victimized. What strategies might induce a larger number of victims of corporate crime to report their victimization to the authorities?

define as white-collar crime, however, is the result of laws passed within the last century. For example, the Sherman Antitrust Act, passed by Congress in 1890, authorized the criminal prosecution of corporations engaged in monopolistic practices.[7] Federal laws regulating the issuance and sale of stocks and other securities were passed in 1933 and 1934. In 1940 Edwin H. Sutherland provided criminologists with the first scholarly account of white-collar crime. He defined it as crime "committed by a person of respectability and high social status in the course of his occupation."[8]

The American Airlines and General Electric cases demonstrate that Sutherland's definition is not entirely satisfactory: White-collar crime can be committed by a corporation as well as by an individual. As Gilbert Geis has noted, Sutherland's work is limited by his own definition. He has a "striking inability to differentiate between the corporations themselves and their executive management personnel."[9] Other criminologists have suggested that the term "white-collar crime" not be used at all; we should speak instead of "corporate crime" and "occupational crime."[10] Generally, however, **white-collar crime** is defined as a violation of the law committed by a person or group of persons in the course of an otherwise respected and legitimate occupation or business enterprise.[11]

Just as white-collar and corporate offenses include a heterogeneous mix of corporate and individual crimes, from fraud, deception, and corruption (as in the S&L case) to pollution of the environment, victims of white-collar crime range from the savvy investor to the unsuspecting consumer. No one person or group is immune.[12] The Vatican lost millions of dollars in a fraudulent stock scheme; fraudulent charities have swindled fortunes from unsuspecting investors; and many banks have been forced into bankruptcy by losses due to deception and fraud.[13]

Crimes Committed by Individuals

As we have noted, white-collar crime occurs during the course of a legitimate occupation or business enterprise. Over time socioeconomic developments have increasingly changed the dimensions of such crimes.[14] Once, people needed only a few business relationships to make their way through life. They dealt with an employer or with employees. They dealt on a basis of trust and confidence with the local shoemaker and grocer. They had virtually no dealings with government.

This way of life has changed significantly and very rapidly during the past few decades. People have become dependent on large bureaucratic structures; they are manipulated by agents and officials with whom they have no personal relationship. This situation creates a basis for potential abuses in four sets of relations:

- Employees of large entities may abuse their authority for private gain by making their services to members of the public contingent on a bribe, a kickback, or some other favor. A corrupt employee of an insurance company, for example, may write a favorable claim assessment in exchange for half of the insurance payment.

- Taking advantage of the complexity and anonymity of a large organization, such as a corporation, employees may abuse the systems available to them or the power they hold within the structure for purposes of unlawful gain, as by embezzlement.

- Members of the public who have to deal with a large organization do not have the faith and trust they had when they dealt with individual merchants. If they see an opportunity to defraud a large organization, they may seize it in the belief that the organization can easily absorb the loss and nobody will be hurt.

- Since the relation of buyer to seller (or of service provider to client) has become increasingly less personal in an age of medical group practice, HMOs, large law firms, and drugstore chains, opportunities for **occupational crimes**—crimes committed by individuals for themselves in the course of rendering a service—have correspondingly increased. Medicare fraud, misuse of clients' funds by lawyers and brokers, substitution of inferior goods—all such offenses are occupational crimes.[15]

Types of White-Collar Crimes

White-collar crimes are as difficult to detect as they are easy to commit.[16] The detection mechanisms on which police and government traditionally rely seem singularly inadequate for this vast new body of crimes. Moreover, though people have learned through the ages to be wary of strangers on the street, they have not yet learned to protect themselves against vast enterprises. Much more scientific study has to be undertaken on the causes, extent, and characteristics of white-collar crimes before we can develop workable prevention strategies.[17]

Eight categories of white-collar offenses committed by individuals can be identified:

- Securities-related crimes.
- Bankruptcy fraud.
- Fraud against the government.
- Consumer fraud.
- Insurance fraud.
- Tax fraud.
- Bribery, corruption, and political fraud.
- Insider-related fraud.[18]

Let us briefly examine each type of crime.

FIGURE 13.1 Common telemarketing scams.

ADVANCE-FEE LOAN OR CREDIT SCHEMES
Telemarketers seek out people with bad credit and offer them loans or credit cards in exchange for fees. Victims offered loans never receive them. Victims offered credit cards usually only get a standard application form or generic information on how to apply.

FOREIGN LOTTERY SCHEMES
Telemarketers offer victims the opportunity to "invest" in tickets in well-known foreign lotteries (e.g., Canada or Australia), or give them a "one in six" chance of winning a substantial prize. This is a common cross-border offense since it plays upon the ignorance of victims of the rules (or even the existence) of foreign lotteries. If offenders purport to sell real lottery chances but deceive victims about their chances of winning, it may be both a gambling offense and fraud. If real chances are sold without deception, it may still be a gambling offense.

INVESTMENT SCHEMES
Victims are sold "investments" in a wide range of merchandise or securities that appear to offer high profit margins. The fraud lies in misrepresenting the true value (or actual existence) of what is being sold, and/or the true extent of the risk in buying it. Common "opportunities" have involved stocks or securities, investment-grade gemstones, precious or strategic metals or minerals, and business opportunities such as oil and gas ventures, pizza ovens, and ostrich farms. These schemes commonly defraud victims more than once (see "reloading" schemes). Once funds have been committed, the victim can be induced to make additional payments to increase the value of the "investment" or avoid its loss (e.g., "margin calls"). Since legitimate investments normally tie up assets for extended periods, victims often do not realize for some time that they have been defrauded.

PRIZE PROMOTION
Telemarketers "guarantee" that the victims have won valuable prizes or gifts, such as vacations or automobiles, but require victims to submit one or more payments for non-existent shipping, taxes, customs or bonding fees, or anything else the offender thinks plausible. Some schemes never provide their victims with any prize or gift, while others provide inexpensive items, often called "gimme gifts" by U.S. telemarketers and "cheap gifts" by Canadian telemarketers.

TELEFUNDING SCHEMES
These prey on the charity of victims by soliciting donations for worthy causes such as antidrug programs or victims of natural disasters. The pitch may simply ask for donations or it may include other inducements, such as donor eligibility for valuable prizes, which never materialize (see "prize promotion" schemes). Charitable donors do not usually expect something in return for their contribution, and may thus never become aware that they have been defrauded.

TRAVEL-RELATED SCHEMES
Fraudulent telemarketers purporting to be travel agencies offer substantial travel packages at comparatively low cost. The use of travel as a commodity makes the long-distance nature of the transaction plausible. The fraud usually involves lies, misrepresentations, or non-disclosure of information about the true value of travel and accommodations, limitations or restrictions on when or where purchasers may go, or what awaits them at the destination. In some cases, the travel proves to be a complete fabrication or has so many terms and conditions as to be completely unusable.

RELOADING AND RECOVERY ROOM SCHEMES
These target the same victims again and again. Persons victimized once are most likely to be deceived repeatedly. Unfortunately, victims' understandable desires to recover their original losses make them more vulnerable to further schemes. This is known as "reloading" or "loading." Those who "invest" money are "reloaded" for more to protect or increase their investment, those asked for customs or shipping fees are "reloaded" for additional charges, and those who give to a spurious "worthy cause" are often "reloaded" for further donations.
    Recovery room schemes exploit the victim's desire to recover losses from previous frauds. Offenders, often from the same organization which defrauded the victim in the first place, call with inside knowledge of the fraud and a promise to recover the losses if "taxes" or "fees" are paid. A common tactic of callers is to represent themselves as law enforcement or other government or professional employees (e.g., bank or stock-exchange officials), using inside knowledge of the victim and the fraud to establish credibility. Recovery room operations frequently deprive victims of their last remaining funds.

Source: http://www.fbi.gov/majcases/db/comscams.htm

Securities-Related Crimes State and federal securities laws seek to regulate both the registration and issuance of a security and the employment practices of personnel in the securities industries. After the stock market crash on October 26, 1929, the federal government enacted a series of regulatory laws, including the Securities Act of 1933 and the Securities Exchange Act of 1934, aimed at prohibiting manipulation and deceptive practices. The 1934 act provided for the establishment of the Securities and Exchange Commission (SEC), an organization with broad regulatory and enforcement powers. The SEC is empowered to initiate civil suits and administrative actions and to refer criminal cases to the U.S. Department of Justice.

Even so, crime in the securities field remains common. Four kinds of offenses are prevalent: churning, trading on insider information, stock manipulation, and boiler-room operations.

Churning is the practice of trading a client's shares of stock frequently in order to generate large commissions. A broker earns a commission on every trade, so whether or not the stock traded increases or decreases in value, the broker makes money. Churning is difficult to prove, because brokers typically are allowed some discretion. Therefore, unless the client has given the broker specific instructions in writing, a claim of churning often amounts to no more than the client's word against the broker's.

Insider trading is the use of material, non-public, financial information to obtain an unfair advantage in trading securities.[19] A person who has access to confidential corporate information may make significant profits by buying or selling stock on the strength of that information. Dennis Levine, a 34-year-old managing director of the securities firm formerly known as Drexel Burnham Lambert, used insider information to purchase stock for himself and others in such corporations as International Telephone and Telegraph, Sperry Corporation, Coastal Corporation, American National Resources, and McGraw Edison. After the SEC found out, Levine implicated other Wall Street executives—including Ivan Boesky, who had made millions of dollars in illegal profits.

Stock manipulation is common in the "pink sheets" over-the-counter market, in which some stocks are traded at very low prices, but it is by no means limited to such stocks. Brokers who have a stake in a particular security may make misleading or even false statements to clients to give the impression that the price of the stock is about to rise and thus to create an artificial demand for it.

Boiler rooms are operations run by stock manipulators who, through deception and misleading sales techniques, seduce unsuspecting and uninformed individuals into buying stocks in obscure and often poorly financed corporations. Significant federal legislation has been passed (Penny Stock Reform Act of 1990) to curtail these operations, but the manipulation continues.

Bankruptcy Fraud   The filing of a bankruptcy petition results in proceedings in which the property and financial obligations of an insolvent person or corporation are disposed of. Bankruptcy proceedings are governed by laws enacted to protect insolvent debtors. Unscrupulous persons have devised numerous means to commit **bankruptcy fraud**—any scam designed to take advantage of loopholes in the bankruptcy laws. The most common are the "similar-name" scam, the "old-company" scam, the "new-company" technique, and the "successful-business" scam.

The *similar-name scam* involves the creation of a corporation that has a name similar to that of an established firm. The objective is to create the impression that this new company is actually the older one. If the trick is successful, the swindlers place large orders with established suppliers and quickly resell any merchandise they receive, often to fences. At the same time the swindlers remove all money and assets of the corporation and either file for bankruptcy or wait until creditors sue. Then they leave the jurisdiction or adeptly erase their tracks.

The *old-company scam* involves employees of an already established firm who, motivated by a desire for quick profits, bilk the company of its money and assets and file for bankruptcy. Such a scam is typically used when the company is losing money or has lost its hold on a market.

The *new-company scam* is much like the similar-name scam: A new corporation is formed, credit is obtained, and orders are placed. Once merchandise is received, it is converted into cash with the assistance of a fence. By the time the company is forced into bankruptcy, the architects of this scheme have liquidated the corporation's assets.

The *successful-business scam* involves a profitable corporation that is well positioned in a market but experiences a change in ownership. After the new owners have bilked the corporation of all its money and assets, the firm is forced into bankruptcy.

Crime Surfing

www.ojp.usdoj.gov/ovc/ncvrw/1999/cost.htm

How much does crime cost society? Consider the estimates of street crimes from a host of different sources. Then determine how you would go about assessing the costs associated with white-collar and corporate crime.

Fraud against the Government   Governments at all levels are victims of a vast amount of fraud, which includes collusion in bidding, payoffs and kickbacks to government officials, expenditures by a government official that exceed the budget, the filing of false claims, the hiring of friends or associates formerly employed by the government, and offers of inducements to government officials.

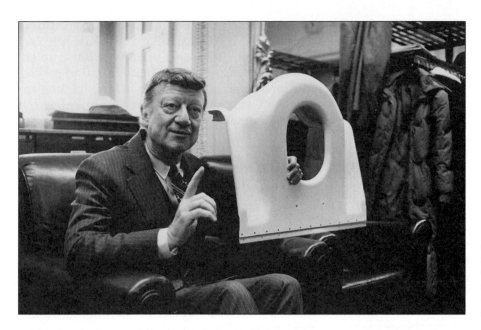

All too frequently, defense contractors and their suppliers have charged outrageous prices for parts used by the military. Senator William Roth (R-Del.) holds up a $640 toilet seat cover.

Consider, for example, the fall of Wedtech—a military contractor with annual sales in excess of $100 million. At one time the Wedtech Corporation was hailed as the first major employer of blacks and Hispanics in New York City's blighted South Bronx. Before its fall from grace, Wedtech was a high flier on the New York Stock Exchange. What fueled the company? As a minority-controlled business, it won defense contracts without the need to bid. But in early 1986 Wedtech lost its status as a minority business, and by the end of that year the company was in ruins.

Wedtech officials had used fraudulent accounting methods, issued false financial reports, and counted profits before they were received. Caught in the cross fire of charges was Congressman Mario Biaggi, who was later convicted of soliciting bribes in order to obtain special government support for Wedtech. Other company and government officials either pleaded guilty or were convicted.[20]

Is the Wedtech scandal an isolated case? Clearly not. From 1986 through 1994, the Department of Defense reported that 138 defense contractors made 325 voluntary disclosures of potential procurement fraud. Recoveries from these disclosures amounted to $290 million.[21]

An important step to curb government contract fraud was taken with the passage of the Major Fraud Act (1988), creating a separate offense of government contract fraud in excess of $1 million. What kinds of activities does this act cover? Federal prosecutors seek indictments against contractors who engage in deceptive pricing or overcharging by submitting inaccurate cost and pricing data; mischarging by billing the government for improper or nonallowable charges; collusion in bidding (a conspiracy between presumed competitors to inflate bids); product substitution or the delivery of inferior, nonconforming, or untested goods; or the use of bribes, gratuities, conflicts of interest, and a whole range of other techniques designed to influence procurement officials.

Clearly there is more to government-related fraud than the manipulation of contractors and consultants.[22] The Inspector General's Office in the Department of Health and Human Services reported that an estimated $20 billion may be lost annually to fraud in the Medicare program alone.[23]

Consumer Fraud **Consumer fraud** is the act of causing a consumer to surrender money through deceit or a misrepresentation of a material fact. Consumer frauds often appear as

confidence games and may take some of the following forms:

- *Home-improvement fraud.* Consumers have
  been defrauded through the promise of low-
  cost home renovation. The homeowners
  give sizable down payments to the
  contractors, who have no plans to complete
  the job. In fact, contractors often leave the
  jurisdiction or declare bankruptcy.

- *Deceptive advertising.* Consumers are often
  lured into a store by an announcement that
  a product is priced low for a limited period
  of time. Once in the store, the customer is
  told that the product is sold out, and he or
  she is offered a substitute, typically of
  inferior quality or at a much higher price.
  Such schemes are known as "bait-and-
  switch advertising."

- *Land fraud.* Consumers are easy prey for
  land fraud swindlers. Here the pitch is that a
  certain piece of vacation or retirement
  property is a worthy investment, many
  improvements to the property will be made,
  and many facilities will be made available in
  the area. Consumers often make purchases
  of worthless or overvalued land.

- *Business opportunity fraud.* The objective of
  business opportunity fraud is to persuade
  a consumer to invest money in a business
  concern through misrepresentation of its
  actual worth. Work-at-home frauds are
  common: Victims are told they can make
  big money by addressing envelopes at
  home or performing some other simple
  task. Consumers lose large sums of money
  investing in such ventures.

Insurance Fraud   There are many varieties
of insurance fraud: Policyholders defraud insurers, insurers defraud the public, management defrauds the public, and third parties defraud insurers. Policyholder fraud is most often
accomplished by the filing of false claims for
life, fire, marine, or casualty insurance. Sometimes an employee of the insurance company is
part of the fraud and assists in the preparation
of the claim. The fraud may be simple—a false
death claim—or it may become complex when
multiple policies are involved.

A different type of insurance fraud is
committed when a small group of people create a "shell" insurance firm without true assets. Policies are sold with no intent to pay legitimate claims. In fact, when large claims are
presented to shell insurance companies, the
firms disband, leaving a trail of policyholder
victims. In yet another form of insurance
fraud, middle- and upper-level managers of
an insurance company loot the firm's assets
by removing funds and debiting them as payments of claims to legitimate or bogus policyholders.[24]

Criminologists Paul Tracy and James Fox
conducted a field experiment to find out how
many auto-body repair shops in Massachusetts
inflate repair estimates to insurance companies, and by how much. These researchers
rented two Buick Skylarks with moderate damage, a Volvo 740 GLE with superficial damage,
and a Ford Tempo with substantial damage.
They then obtained 191 repair estimates, some
with a clear understanding that the car was insured, others with the understanding that there
was no insurance coverage. The results were
unequivocal: Repair estimates for insured vehicles were significantly higher than those for
noncovered cars. This finding is highly suggestive of fraud.[25]

Tax Fraud   The Internal Revenue Code
makes willful failure to file a tax return a misdemeanor. An attempt to evade or defeat a tax,
nonpayment of a tax, or willful filing of a fraudulent tax return is a felony. What must the government prove? In order to sustain a conviction,
the government must present evidence of income tax due and owing, willful avoidance of
payment, and an affirmative act toward tax evasion.[26] How are tax frauds accomplished? Consider the following techniques:

- *Keeping two sets of books.* A person may
  keep one set of books reflecting actual
  profits and losses and another set for the
  purpose of misleading the Internal
  Revenue Service.

- *Shifting funds.* In order to avoid detection,
  tax evaders often shift funds continually
  from account to account, from bank to bank.

• *Faking forms.* Tax evaders often use faked invoices, create fictitious expenses, conceal assets, and destroy books and records.

The IRS lacks the resources to investigate all suspicious tax forms. When the difficulty of distinguishing between careless mistakes and willful evasion is taken into account, the taxes that go uncollected each year are estimated to exceed $100 billion.[27]

Bribery, Corruption, and Political Fraud
Judges who fix traffic tickets in exchange for political favors, municipal employees who speculate with city funds, businesspeople who bribe local politicians to obtain favorable treatment—all are part of the corruption in our municipal, state, and federal governments. The objectives of such offenses vary—favors, special privileges, services, business. The actors include officers of corporations as well as of government; indeed, they may belong to the police or the courts.

Bribery and other forms of corruption are ingrained in the political machinery of local and state governments. Examples abound: Mayors of large cities attempt to obtain favors through bribes; manufacturers pay off political figures for favors; municipal officials demand kickbacks from contractors.[28] In response to the seriousness of political corruption and bribery, Congress established two crimes: It is now a felony to accept a bribe or to provide a bribe.[29] Of course, political bribery and other forms of corruption do not stop at the nation's borders. Kickbacks to foreign officials are common practice (see Table 13.1).[30]

Corruption can be found in private industry as well. One firm pays another to induce it to use a product or service; a firm pays its own board of directors or officers to dispense special favors; two or more firms, presumably competitors, secretly agree to charge the same prices for their products or services.

Insider-Related Fraud Insider-related fraud involves the use and misuse of one's position for pecuniary gain or privilege. This category of offenses includes embezzlement, employee-related thefts, and sale of confidential information.

Embezzlement is the conversion (misappropriation) of property or money with which one is entrusted or for which one has a fiduciary

TABLE 13.1 Which countries are least and best known for having businesspeople who give bribes? The answer: Sweden is perceived to be nearly bribe-free, while China is ranked at the bottom of the list.

Rank	Country	Score
1	Sweden	8.3
2	Australia	8.1
	Canada	8.1
4	Austria	7.8
5	Switzerland	7.7
6	Netherlands	7.4
7	United Kingdom	7.2
8	Belgium	6.8
9	Germany	6.2
	United States	6.2
11	Singapore	5.7
12	Spain	5.3
13	France	5.2
14	Japan	5.1
15	Malaysia	3.9
16	Italy	3.7
17	Taiwan	3.5
18	South Korea	3.4
19	China (including Hong Kong)	3.1

1999 Transparency International Bribe Payers Index (BPI) Ranking 19 Leading Exporters

Source: http://www.transparency.de/documents/cpi/index.html

responsibility. Yearly losses attributable to embezzlement are estimated at over $1 billion.[31]

Employee-related thefts of company property are responsible for a significant share of industry losses. Estimates place such losses between $4 billion and $13 billion each year. Criminologists John Clark and Richard Hollinger have estimated that the 35 percent rate of employee pilferage in some corporations results primarily from vocational dissatisfaction and a perception of exploitation.[32] And not only goods and services are taken; time and money are at risk as well. Phony payrolls, fictitious overtime charges, false claims for business-related travel, and the like, are common.

Finally, in a free marketplace where a premium is placed on competition, corporations must guard against the *sale of confidential information* and trade secrets. The best insurance

TABLE 13.2   Fine and Restitution Imposed on Sentenced Organizations (1998)

Primary Offense	Total		Fine Imposed			Restitution Imposed		
	Number	Percent	Number	Percent	Average	Number	Percent	Average
Antitrust	13	6.1	13	100.0	$16,778,462	0	0.0	—
Archeological damage	1	0.5	1	100.0	500	1	100.0	$ 5,007
Bribery	4	1.9	2	50.0	2,005,000	2	50.0	$6,169,106
Civil rights	3	1.4	3	100.0	10,334	0	0.0	—
Contraband	1	0.5	1	100.0	68,000	1	100.0	104,971
Copyright/trademark infringement	2	0.9	2	100.0	17,500	1	50.0	14,750
Drugs	1	0.5	1	100.0	12,000	0	0.0	—
Environmental (waste discharge)	45	21.1	42	93.3	166,440	13	28.9	101,650
Environmental (wildlife)	9	4.2	7	77.8	12,071	2	22.2	16,236
Export violations	4	1.9	4	100.0	631,875	0	0.0	—
Firearms	2	0.9	1	50.0	50,000	0	0.0	—
Food and drug	4	1.9	3	75.0	106,971	1	25.0	16,941
Fraud	69	32.4	40	58.0	631,694	33	47.8	631,131
Immigration	1	0.5	1	100.0	1,750,000	0	0.0	—
Larceny	8	3.8	4	50.0	184,350	6	75.0	162,085
Motor vehicles/parts	4	1.9	1	25.0	600,000	3	75.0	49,375
Money laundering	16	7.5	6	37.5	957,500	4	25.0	476,266
Obstruction of justice	2	0.9	1	50.0	64,000	0	0.0	—
Tax	24	11.3	21	87.5	236,786	5	20.8	2,958,606
Total	**213**	**100.0**	**154**	**72.3**	**$1,762,250**	**72**	**33.8**	**$ 728,887**

Source: U.S. Sentencing Commission, *Sourcebook of Federal Sentencing Statistics* (Washington, D.C.: U.S. Sentencing Commission, 1999).

policy is employee loyalty. Where there is no loyalty, or where loyalty is compromised, abuse of confidential information is possible. The purchase of confidential information from employees willing to commit industrial espionage is estimated to be a multimillion-dollar business.[33]

CORPORATE CRIME

Corporate crime is a criminal act committed by one or more employees of a corporation that is attributed to the organization itself. On average, between 200 and 350 corporations are convicted each year in federal courts for offenses ranging from tax law violations to environmental crimes (see Table 13.2). The vast majority of these companies are small- to medium-size privately held corporations. In fact, between November 1, 1987, and June 30, 1995, nearly 80 percent of all corporations convicted had fewer than 100 employees. Only 4.7 percent of all convicted corporations had more than 500 employees.

One problem with corporate crime is defining it. In 1989 the supertanker *Exxon Valdez* ran aground in Prince William Sound, Alaska, spilling 250,000 barrels of oil. The spill became North America's largest ecological disaster. Prosecutors were interested in determining the liability of the captain, his officers, and his crew. But there were additional and far-reaching questions. Was the Exxon Corporation liable? If so, was this a corporate crime?

During the Great Depression thousands of unemployed people heard that there was work to be had in the little West Virginia town of Hawk's Nest, where a huge tunnel was to be dug. Thousands of people came to work for a pittance. The company set the men up in crude camps and put them to work drilling rock for the tunnel project—without masks or other safety equipment. The workers breathed in the silicon dust that filled the air. Many contracted silicosis, a chronic lung disease that leads to certain death. They died by the dozens. Security guards dragged the bodies away and buried

Bankrupted Daiwa Bank in Hong Kong.

Toshihide Iguchi, a former bond trader at Daiwa Bank, was sentenced to four years in prison for concealing $1.1 billion in losses from U.S. regulators over a period of more than ten years. Iguchi was ordered to pay $2.57 million in fines and restitution. Iguchi's former supervisor, Masahiro Tsuda, center, was sentenced to two months in prison and was fined $100,000 for assisting in the cover-up.

them secretly. No one was to know. The work went on. The deaths multiplied. Who was to blame? The corporation?[34]

Theories of Corporate Liability

A *corporation* is an artificial person created by state charter. The charter provides such an entity with the right to engage in certain activities—to buy and sell certain goods or to run a railroad, for instance. The charter limits the liability of the persons who own the corporation (the shareholders) to the extent of the value of their investment (their shares). The corporation thus is an entity separate from the people who own or manage it. This convenient form of pooling resources for commercial purposes, with a view toward profiting from one's investment, has had a significant impact on the development of the United States as a commercial and industrial power. Moreover, millions of wage earners whose savings or union funds are invested in corporate stocks and bonds reap dividends from such investments in the form of income or retirement benefits.

But what if a senior official of a corporation engages in unlawful activity? Can we say that the corporation committed the crime? If so, what can be done about it?[35] Initially corporations were considered incapable of committing crimes. After all, crimes require mens rea, an awareness of wrongdoing. Since corporations are bodies without souls, they were deemed to be incapable of forming the requisite sense of wrongdoing. Nor could a corporation be imprisoned for its crimes. Further, corporations were not authorized to commit crimes; they were authorized only to engage in the business for which they had been chartered.

A different theory of corporate criminal liability eventually emerged when courts and legislators began to ask why corporations should not be considered "legal persons" subject to all the laws of "human persons." And so it was decided in 1909.[36] Thereafter, the theory that a corporation can be held accountable for criminal acts was widened, until the Model Penal Code broadly subjected corporations to liability for most criminal offenses, especially those that were "authorized, requested, commanded, performed or recklessly tolerated by the board of directors or by a high managerial agent acting in behalf of the corporation within the scope of his office or employment."[37]

Crime Surfing

www.herring.com/mag/issue22/crime.html

Corporate crime poses serious law enforcement investigatory problems. How much more difficult is the investigation of corporate crime in high-tech industries?

Governmental Control of Corporations

Corporate misconduct is covered by a broad range of federal and state statutes, including the federal conspiracy laws; the Racketeer Influenced and Corrupt Organizations (RICO) Act; federal securities laws; mail-fraud statutes; the Federal Corrupt Practices Act; the Federal Election Campaign Act; legislation on lobbying, bribery, and corruption; the Internal Revenue Code (especially as regards major tax crimes, slush funds, and improper payments); the Bank Secrecy Act; and federal provisions on obstruction of justice, perjury, and false statements.

The underlying theory is that if the brain of the artificial person (usually the board of directors of the corporation) authorizes or condones

the act in question, the body (the corporation) must suffer criminal penalty. That seems fair enough, except for the fact that if the corporation gets punished—usually by a substantial fine—the penalty falls on the shareholders, most of whom had no say in the corporate decision. And the financial loss resulting from the fine may be passed on to the consumer. The counterargument, of course, is that shareholders often benefit from the illegal actions of the corporation. Thus, in fairness, they should suffer some detriment or loss when and if the corporation is apprehended and convicted.

Reliance on Civil Penalties Beginning in the nineteenth century, corporations were suspected of wielding monopolistic power to the detriment of consumers. The theory behind monopoly is simple: If you buy out all your competitors or drive them out of business, then you are the only one from whom people can buy the product you sell. So you can set the price, and you set it very high, for your profit and to the detriment of the consumers. The Sugar Trust was one such monopoly. A few powerful businessmen eliminated all competitors and then drove the price of sugar up, to the detriment of the public. Theodore Roosevelt fought and broke up the Sugar Trust.

In 1890 Congress passed the **Sherman Antitrust Act,** which effectively limited the exercise of monopolies.[38] The act prohibited any contract, conspiracy, or combination of business interests in restraint of foreign or interstate trade. This legislation was followed by the Clayton Antitrust Act (1914), which further curbed the ability of corporations to enrich their shareholders at the expense of the public, by prohibiting such acts as price-fixing.[39] But the remedies this act provided consisted largely of splitting up monopolistic enterprises or imposing damages, sometimes triple damages, for the harm caused. In a strict sense, this was not a use of the criminal law to govern corporate misconduct.

Criminal Liability A movement away from exclusive reliance on civil remedies was apparent in the 1960s, when it was discovered that corporate mismanagement or negligence on the part of officers or employees could inflict vast harm on identifiable groups of victims. Negligent management at a nuclear power plant can result in the release of radiation and injury to thousands or millions of people. The marketing of an unsafe drug can cause crippling deformities in tens of thousands of bodies.[40] Violation of environmental standards can cause injury and suffering to generations of people who will be exposed to unsafe drinking water, harmful air, or eroded soil. The manufacture of hazardous products can result in multiple deaths.[41]

The problem of corporate criminal liability since the 1960s, then, goes far beyond an individual death or injury. Ultimately, it concerns the health and even the survival of humankind. Nor is the problem confined to the United States. It is a global problem. It thus becomes necessary to look at the variety of activities attributable to corporations which in recent years have been recognized as particularly harmful to society.

When it comes to proving corporate criminal liability, prosecutors face formidable problems: Day-to-day corporate activity has a low level of visibility. Regulatory agencies that monitor corporate conduct have different and uncoordinated recording systems. Offending corporations operate in a multitude of jurisdictions, some of which regard a given activity as criminal, while others do not. Frequently, the facts of a case are not adjudicated at a trial; the parties may simply agree on a settlement approved by the court. Those corporations that are convicted tend to be first offenders without an effective compliance program.

Did You Know?

. . . that more than 95 percent of all corporations convicted of crimes each year in federal courts are small, privately held entities? Why do you suppose that this is a consistent finding over time?

Investigating Corporate Crime

We know very little about the extent of economic criminality in the United States. There is no national database for the assessment of corporate criminality, and corporations are not likely to release information about their own wrongdoing. The situation is worse in other countries, especially in the developing countries of Africa south of the Sahara, where few national crime statistics are kept and where corporations are least subject to governmental control. Yet the evidence in regard to corporate crime is gradually coming in.[42]

As we noted earlier, the first American criminologist who was alert to the potential for harm in corporate conduct was Edwin Sutherland, who described the criminal behavior of 70 of the 200 largest production corporations in his 1946 book *White Collar Crime.*[43] An even more ambitious study was completed by Marshall B. Clinard and Peter C. Yeager, who investigated corporations within the jurisdiction of 25 federal agencies during 1975 and 1976. Of 477 major American corporations whose conduct was regulated by these agencies, 60 percent had violated the law. Of the 300 violating corporations, 38 (or 13 percent) accounted for 52 percent of all violations charged in 1975 and 1976, an average of 23.5 violations per firm.[44] Large corporations were found to be the chief violators, and a few particular industries (pharmaceutical, automotive) were the most likely to violate the law.

According to Clinard and Yeager, what makes it so difficult to curb corporate crime is the enormous political power corporations wield in the shaping and administration of the laws that govern their conduct. This is particularly the case in regard to multinational corporations that wish to operate in developing countries. The promise of jobs and development by a giant corporation is a temptation too great for the governments of many such countries to resist. They would rather have employment opportunities that pollute air and water than unemployment in a clean environment. Government officials in some Third World countries can be bribed to create or maintain a legal climate favorable to the business interests of the corporation, even though it may be detrimental to the people of the host country.

The work of Sutherland, Clinard and Yeager, and other traditional scholars, as well as that of a group of radical criminologists;[45] hearings on white-collar and corporate crime held by the Subcommittee on Crime of the House Judiciary Committee, under the leadership of Congressman John Conyers, Jr., in 1978; the

TABLE 13.3   Characteristics of Organizations Sentenced in Federal Courts (1998)

Characteristic	Number	Percent
Involvement in or tolerance of criminal activity by substantial authority personnel		
Involvement/tolerance in an organization/unit of 5000+ employees	1	0.8
Involvement/tolerance in an organization/unit of 1000+ employees	2	1.7
Involvement/tolerance in an organization/unit of 200+ employees	8	6.8
Involvement in an organization of 50+ employees	21	17.8
Involvement in an organization of 10 or more employees	37	31.4
No involvement/tolerance or fewer than 10 employees	49	41.5
TOTAL	118	100.0
Prior history		
One similar criminal/two similar administrative violations within 5 years	1	0.8
Organization had no prior record	117	99.2
TOTAL	118	100.0
Violation of an order		
Organization did violate an order	0	0.0
Organization did not violate an order	118	100.0
TOTAL	118	100.0
Obstruction of justice		
Organization obstructed justice	8	6.8
Organization did not obstruct justice	110	93.2
TOTAL	118	100.0
Effective program to prevent and detect violations of law		
Organization did have an effective program	0	0.0
Organization did not have an effective program	118	100.0
TOTAL	118	100.0
Self-reporting, cooperation, and acceptance of responsibility		
Self-reported offense	0	0.0
Cooperated with investigation	64	54.2
Accepted responsibility	36	30.5
Organization did not self-report, cooperate, or accept responsibility	18	15.3
TOTAL	118	100.0

Source: U.S. Sentencing Commission, *Sourcebook of Federal Sentencing Statistics* (Washington, D.C.: U.S. Sentencing Commission, 1999).

consumer protection movement, spearheaded by Ralph Nader; and investigative reporting by the press have all contributed to public awareness of large corporations' power to inflict harm on large population groups.

In 1975 James Q. Wilson still considered such crime to be insignificant,[46] but more recent studies show that the public considers corporate criminality at least as serious as, if not more serious than, street crime. Marvin Wolfgang and his associates found in a national survey that Americans regard illegal retail price-fixing (the artificial setting of prices at a high level, without regard for the demand for the product) as a more serious crime than robbery committed with a lead pipe.[47] Within the sphere of corporate criminality perhaps no other group of offenses has had so great an impact on public consciousness as crimes against the environment. As we shall see, however, enforcement of major environmental statutes has been weak in the past. There is some evidence that this is changing.

Environmental Crimes

Warren D. Mooney makes life sweet—sodas, candies. His company, Liquid Sugars Inc., is the confection in Jelly Belly, the gourmet bean that everyone chewed after presidential candidate Ronald Reagan said they were his favorite.

On Friday, Mooney was indicted by the federal grand jury in Sacramento on nine felony counts, including conspiracy to pollute. Prosecutors say they are strictly enforcing the law; the defense calls it "justice run amok."

If found guilty of violating the Clean Water Act, Mooney could be sentenced to 29 years in jail and be fined $2.25 million. The company faces a fine of $4.5 million.

The indictments concluded a two-year investigation into Liquid Sugars, a company headquartered in Emeryville, managed by Mooney and accused of violating water-pollution laws at its Port of Stockton facility. The company blends sweeteners for manufacturers—its most notable client being Jelly Belly maker Herman Goelitz Candy Co. of Fairfield.

Mooney and Liquid Sugars are charged with dumping into the Stockton sewer waste water trucked from Goelitz's Fairfield facility. The waste was water contaminated with sweetener from washing down the equipment that produces exotically flavored beans—buttered popcorn, toasted marshmallow, piña colada.

Similarly, the indictment said the company trucked in waste water from a second customer, pickle-maker G. L. Mezzetta of Sonoma.

In addition to conspiracy, Liquid Sugars is charged with violating regulations imposed on industries that dump waste into sewers: four counts of dumping into the sewer waste hauled in from elsewhere, and four counts of dumping into the system waste with a pH below 5.[48]

The world's legal systems include few effective laws and mechanisms to curb destruction of the environment. The emission of noxious fumes into the air and the discharge of pollutants into the water have until recently been regarded as common law nuisances at the level of misdemeanors, commanding usually no more than a small fine. Industrial polluters could easily absorb such a fine and regard it as a kind of business tax. Only in 1969 did Congress pass the National Environmental Policy Act (NEPA). Among other things, the act created the Environmental Protection Agency (EPA). It requires environmental impact studies so that any new development that would significantly affect the environment can be prevented or controlled.

The EPA is charged with enforcing federal statutes and assisting in the enforcement of state laws enacted to protect the environment. The agency monitors plant discharges all over the country and may take action against private industry or municipal governments. Yet during the first 5 years of its existence, the EPA referred only 130 cases to the U.S. Department of Justice for criminal prosecution, and only 6 of those involved major corporate offenders.[49] The government actually charged only one of the corporations, Allied Chemical, which admitted responsibility for 940 misdemeanor counts of discharging toxic chemicals into the Charles River in Virginia, thereby causing 80 people to become ill.[50]

A 1979 report of the General Accounting Office stated that the EPA inadequately monitored, inaccurately reported, and ineffectively enforced the nation's basic law on air pollution, although the agency's chief at that time contended that corrective action had been taken during the previous year.[51] The situation improved during the 1990s, but the environment is far from safe. Catastrophic releases of toxic and even nuclear substances, usually attributable to inadequate safeguards and human negligence, pose a particularly grave hazard, as the disasters at Bhopal in India and at Chernobyl in the former Soviet Union have demonstrated.

Enforcing Legislation The difficulties of enforcing legislation designed to protect the environment are enormous. Consider the 250,000 barrels of oil spilled by the *Exxon Valdez* in 1989. What legislation could have prevented the disaster?

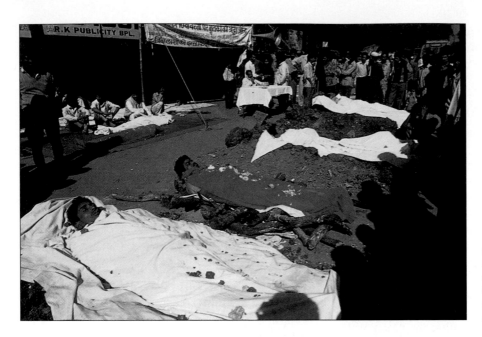

A catastrophic explosion at the Union Carbide plant in Bhopal, India, on December 2, 1984, spewed clouds of deadly gas, causing nearly 6500 fatalities and more than 20,000 injuries.

Developing effective laws to protect the environment is a complex problem. It is far easier to define the crimes of murder and theft than to define acts of pollution, which are infinitely varied. A particular challenge is the separation of harmful activities from socially useful ones. Moreover, pollution is hard to quantify. How much of a chemical must be discharged into water before the discharge is considered noxious and subjects the polluter to punishment? Discharge of a gallon by one polluter may not warrant punishment, and a small quantity may not even be detectable. But what do we do with a hundred polluters, each of whom discharges a gallon?

Many other issues must be addressed as well. For instance, should accidental pollution warrant the same punishment as intentional or negligent pollution? Since many polluters are corporations, what are the implications of penalties that force a company to install costly antipollution devices? To cover the costs, the corporation may have to increase the price of its product, and so the consumer pays. Should the company be allowed to lower plant workers' wages instead? Should the plant be forced or permitted to shut down, thereby increasing unemployment in the community? The company may choose to move its plant to another state or country that is more hospitable.

Addressing Sensitive Issues Fines imposed on intentional polluters have been increased so that they can no longer be shrugged off as an ordinary cost of doing business. The General Electric Company was fined $7 million and the Allied Chemical Corporation $13.2 million for pollution offenses. Fines of such magnitude are powerful incentives to corporations to limit pollution. But since many of the enterprises that are likely to pollute are in the public sector, or produce for the public sector, the public ultimately will have to pay the fine in the form of increased gas or electricity bills.[52]

In the Third World, problems of punishing and preventing pollution are enormous. Industries preparing to locate there have the power to influence governments and officials, surreptitiously and officially, into passing legislation favorable to the industry. The desire to industrialize outweighs the desire to preserve the environment. Some countries find ways to address the problem, only to relinquish controls when they prove irksome. While Japan was trying to establish its industrial dominance, for example, it observed a constitutional provision stating: "The conservation of life environment shall be balanced against the needs of economic development."[53] This provision was deleted in 1970, when Japan had achieved economic strength.

Developing Effective Legislation U.S. legislators have several options in developing legislation to protect the environment:

- *The independent use of the criminal sanction: direct prohibition of polluting activities.* This is the way American legislators have typically tried to cope with the problem in the past. They simply made it a criminal offense to maintain a "nuisance," that is, an ongoing activity that pollutes the water, the soil, or the air.

- *The dependent-direct use of the criminal sanction: prohibition of certain polluting activities that exceed specified limits.* This is a more sophisticated legislative method. If pollution is to be kept at a low level, no one person or company can be allowed to emit more than an insignificant amount of noxious waste into the environment. This amount is fixed by administrative regulation. Anyone who exceeds the limit commits a criminal offense.

- *The dependent-indirect approach: criminal sanction reserved for firms that fail to comply with specific rulings rendered by administrative organs against violators of standards.* Under this option, polluters have already been identified by regulatory agencies, and they are now under order to comply with the agencies' requirements. If they violate these orders, a criminal punishment can be imposed.

- *The preventive use of the criminal sanction: penalties imposed for failure to install or maintain prescribed antipollution equipment.* This is the newest and most sophisticated means of regulating polluting industries. The law determines what preventive and protective measures must be taken (to filter industrial waste water, to put chemical screens on smokestacks, and so on). Any firm that fails to take the prescribed measures is guilty of a violation.[54]

In the past, legal systems relied primarily on the independent use of the criminal sanction. More recent legislation has concentrated on administrative orders and technological prevention.

Curbing Corporate Crime

Laws and regulations prescribing criminal sanctions have been passed and continue to be passed to guard the public against the dangers rooted in the power of corporate enterprise. Recently, for example, Congress passed new sentencing guidelines for corporations in federal courts. These guidelines significantly increased corporate sanctions, but at the same time allowed companies large reductions in fines where there was evidence of organizational due diligence—that is, implementation of effective ethics compliance programs.[55] While such laws, regulations, and guidelines may provide some disincentives for illegal acts, many governments recognize that criminal justice systems are not well prepared to deal with economic crimes, in terms of both strategy and resources.[56] They also recognize the importance of attacking this problem at the international level, perhaps by designing strategies, standards, and guidelines that may be helpful to all governments.[57]

A disturbing thought remains: Is the imposition of criminal liability for the conduct of corporations on the corporations themselves really the best way to curb corporate misconduct? If corporations act on the decisions of their principal officers or agents, might it not be appropriate to restrict the reach of the law to these corporate actors rather than to subject the innocent and uninformed shareholders to financial loss? Why not rely more on administrative and civil proceedings? Both can and often do contain penalties that exceed those of the criminal law.

ORGANIZED CRIME

Earlier we noted that all forms of organizational criminality have in common the use of business enterprises for illegal profit. We have recognized some significant problems not only with existing definitions and conceptualizations of white-collar and corporate crime but with the criminal justice response to such offenses. Similar problems arise in efforts to deal with organized crime. It, too, depends on business enterprises. And like corporate crime, organized crime comes in so many varieties that attempts to define it precisely lead to frustration.

What kind of person would illegally dump hazardous waste into the waterways and landscapes of America? Many would guess it might be a sinister organized crime operator. Some past published works on hazardous waste crime have, in fact, described this area of crime as being synonymous with syndicate crime.

This is the introduction to criminologist Donald J. Rebovich's controversial book *Dangerous Ground: The World of Hazardous Waste Crime,* in which he reports the results of an empirical study of hazardous waste offenders in four states.(1) He continues:

> Surprisingly enough, the study has found that, most commonly, the criminal dumper is an ordinary, profit-motivated businessman who operates in a business where syndicate crime activity may be present but by no means pervasive. The research uncovers a criminal world of the hazardous waste offender unlike any theorized in the past. It is a world where the intensity, duration, and methods of the criminal act will be more likely determined by the criminal opportunities available in the legitimate marketplace than by the orders of a controlling criminal syndicate.

Rebovich's portrait of hazardous waste crime replaces our ideas about midnight dumping and masked dumpers with straightforward descriptions of hazardous waste treatment/storage/disposal (TSD) facilities failing to comply with state and federal regulations:

> The mark of a successful hazardous waste criminal—one who can maintain his criminal lifestyle for a lengthy duration—is his skill in effectively analyzing the potential threats to his livelihood and his versatility in adapting to those threats. For many TSD-facility operators, the serious game of working the system was played out by eluding the regulatory inspectors by capitalizing on either the inspectors' unfamiliarity with treatment apparatus or their lack of diligence in inspecting thoroughly.
>
> TSD-facility offenders did have to contend with monitoring devices, installed by regulators, that were used to gauge volume and properties of effluents released into local sewer systems to determine compliance with existing discharge standards. The mechanisms were intended to sample effluents randomly but, in reality, offenders found the system seriously flawed and did not hesitate to seize their opportunities to work the system in a new way. . . . The tests were simply rigged to elicit a false impression of the toxicity of the substances discharged into the sewer.

Rebovich makes this prediction:

> The characteristics of future hazardous waste offenders, and the crimes that they commit, will more than likely be determined by developments in several areas external to the criminal act: (1) pressure from the general public and public interest groups for stricter enforcement, (2) legislative expansion of the scope of legal coverage, (3) redesigned enforcement, and (4) future availability of affordable disposal outlets. These areas can be seen as the components of an equation that could lead to a reduction in hazardous waste crime.

Source

1. Donald J. Rebovich, *Dangerous Ground: The World of Hazardous Waste Crime* (New Brunswick, N.J.: Transaction, 1992).

Questions for Discussion

1. Illegal hazardous waste practices may be punished by fining the company or industry. Should individuals be punished as well?
2. Some TSD-facility operators have claimed that they were forced to use illegal practices because it is economically impossible to take care of hazardous wastes under current regulations. What is your reaction to such a defense?

The difficulty of gaining access to information on organized crime has also hindered attempts to conceptualize the problems posed by this kind of law violation. Finally, law enforcement efforts have been inadequate to control the influence of organized crime. As will be evident, a greater effort must be made to uncover the nature, pattern, and extent of organized crime.

The History of Organized Crime

Organized crime had its origin in the great wave of immigrants from southern Italy (especially from Sicily) to the United States between 1875 and 1920. These immigrants came from an environment that historically had been hostile to them. Suppressed by successive bands of invaders and alien rulers dating back some 800 years before Christ, Sicily was first coveted as a strategic location between major Mediterranean trade routes by the Greeks and Phoenicians. In later centuries Roman, Byzantine, Arab, Norman, German, Spanish, Austrian, and French soldiers all laid siege and claim to Sicily. Exploited by mostly absentee landlords with their armies, Sicilians had learned to survive by relying on the strength of their own families. Indeed, these families had undergone little change since Greco-Roman times, two millennia earlier.

A traditional Sicilian family has been described as an extended family, or clan; it includes lineal relations (grandparents, parents, children, grandchildren) and lateral relations through the paternal line—uncles, aunts, and cousins as far as the bloodline can be traced. This *famiglia* is hierarchically organized and administered by the head of the family, the *capo di famiglia* (the Romans called him *pater familias*), to whom all members owe obedience and loyalty. Strangers, especially those in positions of power in state or church, are not to be trusted. The importance of the family is evident in the famous Sicilian proverb: *"La legge e' per l ricchi, La forca e' per l poveri, E la giustizie e' per l buffoni."* (The law is for the rich, the gallows are for the poor, and justice is for the fools.) For Sicilians all problems are resolved within the family, which must be kept strong. Its prestige, honor, wealth, and power have to be defended and strengthened, sometimes through alliances with more distant kin.[58]

Throughout history these strong families have served each other and Sicily. Upon migration to the United States, members of Sicilian families soon found that the social environment in their new country was as hostile as that of the old. Aspirations were encouraged, yet legitimate means to realize them were often not available. And the new country seemed already to have an established pattern for achieving wealth and power by unethical means. Many of America's great fortunes—those of the Astors, the Vanderbilts, the Goulds, the Sages, the Stanfords, the Rockefellers, the Carnegies, the Lords, the Harrimans—had been made by cunning, greed, and exploitation.

As time passed, new laws were enacted to address conspiracies in restraint of trade and other economic offenses. Yet by the time the last wave of Sicilian immigrants reached the United States, the names of the great robber barons were connected with major universities, foundations, and charitable institutions.[59] At the local level, the Sicilian immigrants found themselves involved in a system of politics in which patronage and protection were dispensed by corrupt politicians and petty hoodlums from earlier immigrant groups—German, Irish, and Jewish. The Sicilian family structure helped its members survive in this hostile environment. It also created the organizational basis that permitted them to respond to the opportunity created when, on January 16, 1920, the Eighteenth Amendment to the Constitution outlawed the manufacture, sale, and transportation of alcoholic beverages.

Howard Abadinsky explains what happened:

> Prohibition acted as a catalyst for the mobilization of criminal elements in an unprecedented manner. Pre-prohibition crime, insofar as it was organized, centered around corrupt political machines, vice entrepreneurs, and, at the bottom, gangs. Prohibition unleashed an unparalleled level of competitive criminal violence and changed the order—the gang leaders emerged on top.[60]

During the early years of Prohibition, the names of the most notorious bootleggers, mobsters, and gangsters sounded German, Irish, and Jewish: Arthur Flegenheimer (better known as "Dutch Schultz"), Otto Gass, Bo and George Weinberg, Arnold Rothstein, John T. Nolen (better known as "Legs Diamond"), Vincent "Mad Dog" Coll, Waxey Gordon, Owney Madden, and Joe Rock. By the time Prohibition was repealed, Al Capone, Salvatore Luciana (better known as "Lucky Luciano"), Frank Costello, Johnny Torrio, Vito Genovese, Guiseppe Doto (better known as "Joe Adonis"), and many other Sicilians were pre-eminent in the underworld. They had become folk heroes and role models for young boys in the Italian ghettos, many of whom were to seek their own places in this new society.

Sicilian families were every bit as ruthless in establishing their crime empires as the earlier immigrant groups had been. They were so successful in their domination of organized crime that, especially after World War II, organized crime became virtually synonymous with the Sicilian Mafia.

The term "Mafia" appears to derive from an Arabic word denoting "place of refuge." The concept, which was adopted in Sicily during the era of Arab rule, gradually came to describe a mode of life and survival. Sicilians trace the word to a tale of revenge that took place on Easter Monday, 1282. On this day, a French soldier who was part of a band of marauding foreigners raped a Sicilian woman on her wedding day. Following the assault, bands of Sicilians went to the streets of Palermo to slaughter hundreds of Frenchmen, spurred on by the screams of the young girl's mother: "Ma fia, ma fia" ("My daughter, my daughter").[61]

Have you ever asked yourself (or anyone else) what the world's largest business is? Oil? Autos? Computers? Steel? It's none of these: Drug and arms trafficking by major crime syndicates take first and second place.(1) The United Nations estimates that the combined annual sales from organized crime range from $700 billion to $1000 billion annually. Trafficking in narcotics alone exceeds $300 billion each year.(1, p. 22)

Much of the expansion of organized crime in recent years has been made possible by the fragile political and economic situation of developing and transitional countries. A prime example is post–cold war Russia. Enticed by the weakened judicial system, reduced law enforcement, and a susceptible bureaucracy, organized-crime groups such as the Russian and Sicilian Mafias have established a firm hold on the ex-Soviet states. Organized crime has moved in, shielded by the need for foreign capital investment. The Russian Mafia alone, with over 3 million members in 5700 gangs, controls approximately one-quarter of the commercial and retail banks, as well as tens of thousands of other legitimate businesses. Gangs traffic in everything from raw material to nuclear weapons.

The infiltration of organized crime into legitimate businesses poses a particularly significant threat to the emerging economic order of transitional economies. Politically and economically, the Mafia is becoming part of the business culture in certain markets. "Instead of being a threat to the legal order, the Mafia is becoming its rival and even its replacement. Wherever and whenever the state fails to fulfill the basic needs of its people, this creates a vacuum which the criminals can exploit."(2)

The effects of the infiltration of organized crime are unmistakable. On November 21, 1994, member states of the United Nations gathered in Naples, Italy, at the World Ministerial Conference on Organized Crime. One conclusion was very clear: "Traditionally insular and clannish, the world powers of crime—the Hong Kong–based Triads, the Cali Cartel of Colombia, the Italian Mafia, the Japanese Yakuza, the Russian Vory v. Zakonye and affiliated newcomers, and rapidly expanding West African crime groups—are now making deals with each other and taking tentative steps to maximize their operations."(1) The cooperative nature of organized crime has changed the realities of law enforcement efforts. The policing of organized crime is no longer a regional or local endeavor. To control the effects of the single largest business in the world, law enforcement efforts must also be transnational and cooperative.

Among the steps called for at the conference:

- Global assessment and regular monitoring of organized transnational crime.
- New legislation, both substantive (against the crimes) and procedural (against the criminals).
- Special cooperative programs and preventive strategies.
- A concerted attack on money laundering to chip away at the economic advantage of organized transnational crime and criminals.

Here is why the steps are needed: Each national criminal group, as the table that follows shows, is allied with most of the others across the globe.

Ultimately, the **Mafia** became the entirety of those Sicilian families that were loosely associated with one another in operating organized crime, both in America and in Sicily.[62] The first realistic depiction of the organization of the Mafia came with the testimony of Joseph Valachi before the Senate's McClellan Committee in 1963. Valachi, a disenchanted soldier in New York's Genovese crime family, was the first member of Italian organized crime to describe a quasi-military secret criminal syndicate. From that point on, the Mafia has also been referred to as *La Cosa Nostra*, literally translated as "this thing of ours."[63]

Despite Valachi's testimony and later revelations, some scholars still doubt the existence of a Sicilian-based American crime syndicate. To the criminologist Jay Albanese, for instance:

> [I]t is clear . . . that despite popular opinion which has for many years insisted on the existence of a se-

cret criminal society called "the Mafia," which somehow evolved from Italy, many separate historical investigations have found no evidence to support such a belief.[64]

The Structure and Impact of Organized Crime

Americans have felt the impact of organized crime, and they have followed the media coverage of the mob wars and their victims with fascination. But little was known about the Mafia's actual structure in the United States until a succession of government investigations began to unravel its mysteries. The major investigations were conducted by the Committee on Mercenary Crimes, in 1932; the Special Senate Committee to Investigate Organized Crime in Interstate Commerce (the Kefauver crime committee), from 1950 to 1951; the Senate Permanent Subcommittee on Investigations (the

Organization	Size	Major Activities	International Ties
Colombian cartels	Hundreds of men	Drug trafficking—manage entire cycle from production to distribution	U.S. and Sicilian Cosa Nostra, Chinese Triads, Japanese Yakuza
Chinese Triads (Hong Kong and Taiwan)	150,000 in 5 groups	Drugs, usury, illegal immigration, gambling, racketeering, prostitution, money laundering	Colombian cartels, Japanese Yakuza, U.S. groups
Russian Mafia	3 million in 5700 gangs	Trafficking in everything—army weapons, nuclear materials, drugs, money laundering, prostitution, counterfeiting	Settlements in the U.S., Colombian cartels, Sicilian Cosa Nostra
Sicilian Cosa Nostra	5000 members	International drug trafficking clearinghouse, money laundering on a grand scale, arms trafficking, extortion	U.S. Cosa Nostra, Colombian cartels, Mafia families in Western Europe, Russian Mafia, Chinese Triads
U.S. Cosa Nostra	3000 soldiers in 25 families	Drug and arms trafficking, illegal gambling, prostitution, extortion, business activities	Colombian cartels, Russian Mafia, Sicilian Cosa Nostra
Japanese Yakuza	60,000 full-time, 25,000 associates, in 1246 clans	Amphetamine traffic in Asia and U.S., extortion, prostitution	Chinese Triads, Colombian cartels, German groups, Russian Mafia, U.S. Cosa Nostra

Sources

1. ANSA News Agency Dossier on Organized Crime, *U.N. World Ministerial Conference on Organized Transnational Crime,* Naples, Italy, Nov. 21–23, 1994.

2. "Russian Organized Crime," *Jane's Intelligence Review,* 8 (May 1, 1996): 195.

Questions for Discussion

1. Why is organized crime the world's largest business?

2. What efforts to control the rise of organized crime seem most promising?

John Gotti Jr., 35, acting head of New York City's Gambino crime family, assumed the reigns of the family firm in 1994. In 1999, "John Junior" worked a deal with federal prosecutors by pleading guilty to racketeering, extortion, and tax evasion. He was sentenced to six and one-half years, with parole eligibility in 2004.

"I TAKE IT YOU'RE ALSO IN THE FEDERAL WITNESS-PROTECTION PROGRAM."

McClellan committee), from 1956 to 1963; President Lyndon Johnson's Commission on Law Enforcement and Administration of Justice (the Task Force on Organized Crime), from 1964 to 1967; and the President's Commission on Organized Crime, which reported to President Reagan in 1986 and 1987.[65]

The findings of these investigations established the magnitude of organized crime in the United States. It had become an empire almost beyond the reach of government, with vast resources derived from a virtual monopoly on gambling and loan-sharking, drug trafficking, pornography and prostitution, labor racketeering, murder for hire, the control of local crime activities, and the theft and fencing of securities, cars, jewels, and consumer goods of all sorts.[66] Above all, it was found that organized crime had infiltrated a vast variety of legitimate businesses, such as stevedoring (the loading and unloading of ships), the fish and meat industries, the wholesale and retail liquor industry (including bars and taverns), the vending machine business, the securities and investment business, the waste disposal business, and the construction industry.[67]

Specific legislation and law enforcement programs have allowed governmental agencies to assert some measure of control over organized crime. Cases have been successfully prosecuted under the **Racketeer Influenced and Corrupt Organizations (RICO) Act** of 1970.[68] This statute attacks racketeering activities by prohibiting the investment of any funds derived from racketeering in any enterprise that is engaged in interstate commerce. In addition, the **Federal Witness Protection Program,** established under the Organized Crime Control Act of 1970, has made it easier for witnesses to testify in court by guaranteeing them a new identity, thus protecting them against revenge. Currently 14,000 witnesses are in the program.[69]

The information provided by the governmental commissions, in combination with scholarly research, has established that the structure of an organized crime group is similar to that of a Sicilian family. Family members are joined by "adopted" members; the family is then aided at the functional level by nonmember auxiliaries.[70] The use of military designations such as *caporegima* ("lieutenant") and "soldier" does not alter the fact that a criminal organization is rather more like a closely knit family business enterprise than like an army.[71] On the basis of testimony presented by Joseph Valachi in 1963, the commission's Task Force on Organized Crime was able to construct an organization chart of the typical Mafia, or Cosa Nostra, family (Figure 13.2).

Relations among the various families, which were formerly determined in ruthlessly fought gang wars, have more recently been facilitated by a loosely formed coordinating body called "the Commission." By agreement, the country has been divided into territorial areas of jurisdiction, influence, and operation. These arrangements are subject to revision from time to time, by mutual agreement. Likewise, rules of conduct have become subject to control or regulation by the heads of the various crime families. They consider, for example, to what extent each family should enter the hard-drug market, how much violence should be used, and how each will deal with public officials and the police.[72]

Informants at the "convention" of the so-called Apalachin conspirators provided a rare opportunity to learn about the way crime fami-

FIGURE 13.2   Organization chart of the typical Mafia family.

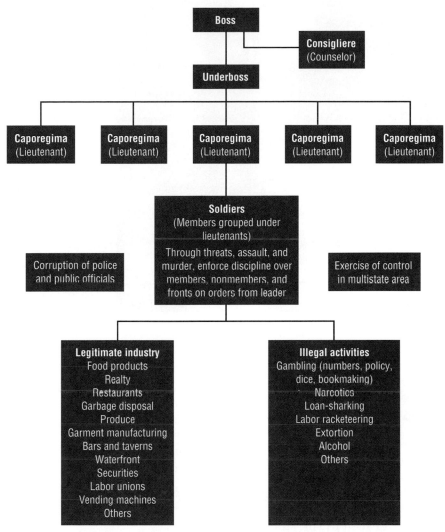

Source: President's Commission on Law Enforcement and Administration of Justice, *Task Force Report: Organized Crime* (Washington, D.C.: U.S. Government Printing Office, 1967), p. 9.

lies reach agreement on their operations. On November 14, 1957, 63 of the country's most notorious underworld figures were arrested in Apalachin, New York, at or near the home of Joseph M. Barbara, a well-known organized-crime figure. Participants included New York's Vito Genovese, Carlo Gambino, Paul Castellano, and Joe Bonano. Also arrested were Florida's don, Santo Trafficante, Jr.; Sam ("Momo") Giancana of Chicago; Detroit boss Joe Zerilli; and the boss of the Buffalo rackets, Stefano Magaddino. Apparently, they had congregated at Barbara's home to settle a dispute among the families, which had three weeks earlier resulted in the assassination of Mangano family boss Albert Anastasia (the Mangano family was predecessor to the largest contemporary crime family in the United States, the Gambino crime family) and the attempted murder in May 1957 of Francesco Castiglia, better known as Frank Costello, by the current godfather of the Genovese crime family, Vincent "The Chin" Gigante.

The presence of so many out-of-state license plates on brand new Cadillacs and Lincolns in

The funeral procession of Chinatown crime boss Benny Ong, August 19, 1994. Ong was the undisputed leader of New York City's Chinese gangs.

this small upstate New York town caught the attention of New York State Police Sergeant Edgar Croswell, an amateur organized-crime buff. Croswell, already somewhat suspicious of the true nature of Barbara's business dealings, put in a call to federal authorities and arranged to have a roadblock set up to guard against any of the participants leaving without being questioned. The police presence didn't go unnoticed by the gangsters, who rushed to make a quick escape back to their fiefdoms.

The comical scene of men in silk suits and fedora hats running through the forest was enough for Croswell. He caught as many as he could and placed them under arrest. None of the conspirators, however, publicly revealed the true nature of their meeting. Some suggested that, quite by coincidence, all had simply come to visit their sick friend Joe Barbara, who would die of a heart attack 2 years later. All were indicted and convicted for refusing to answer the grand jury's questions about the true purpose of the meeting. The convictions were subsequently reversed.[73]

Certain core business matters were decided at that meeting:

- Carlo Gambino was given the leadership of the New York crime family that still

bears his name, a family made famous by the more recent exploits of John Gotti.

- As a vote of confidence for Vito Genovese, Frank Costello was asked to go into semiretirement to pave the way for Genovese to take over the family that Lucky Luciano had started.

- A ban was placed on any "made man" trafficking in drugs. "If you deal, you die" was the slogan that resonated throughout organized crime as of the late 1950s. Although widely ignored, the ban still exists today.

The activities of the Mafia appear to have shifted from the once extremely violent bootlegging and street crime operations to a far more sophisticated level of criminal activity.[74] Modern organized crime has assumed international dimensions.[75] It extends not only to international drug traffic, but also to such legitimate enterprises as real estate and trade in securities, as well as to many other lucrative business enterprises. This transition has been accomplished both by extortion and by entry with laundered money derived from illegitimate activity. It is tempting to wonder whether we may be witnessing the same kind of metamorphosis that

FIGURE 13.3   Time line of New York City's Chinese gangs: 1960–1990.

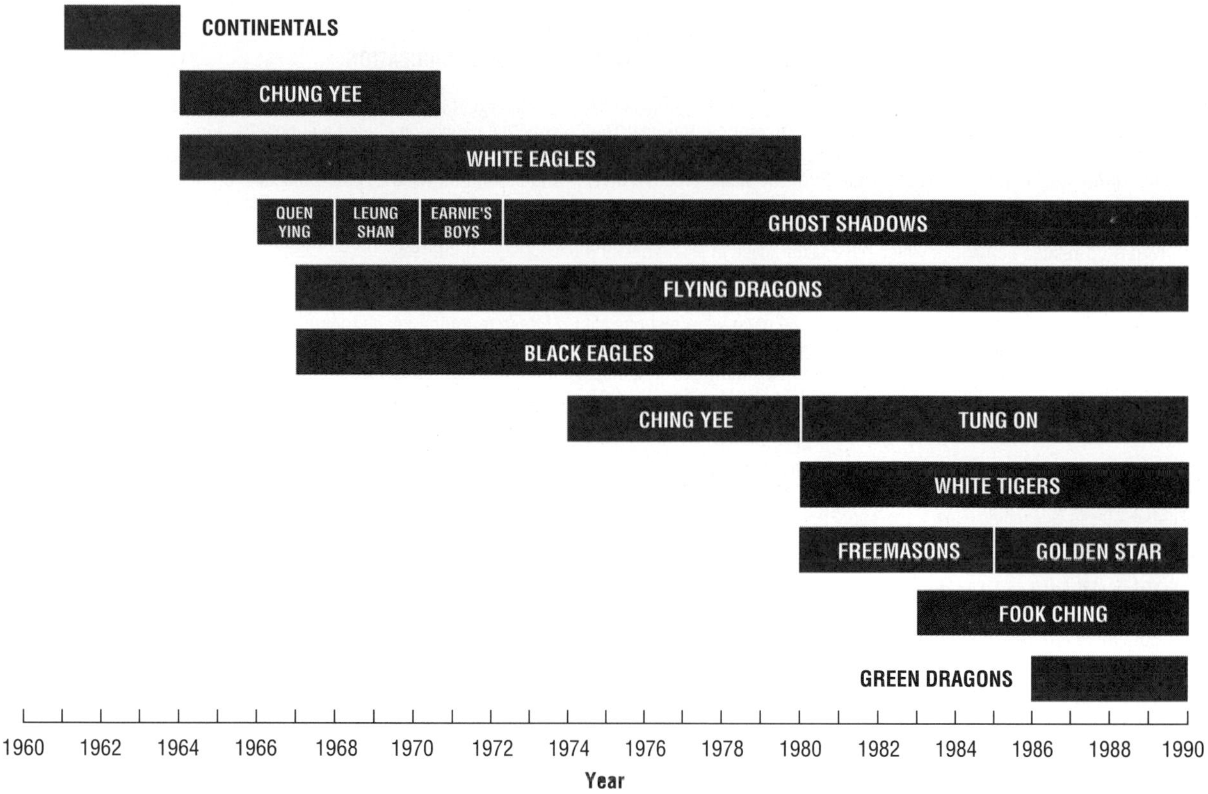

CONTINENTALS

CHUNG YEE

WHITE EAGLES

QUEN YING | LEUNG SHAN | EARNIE'S BOYS | GHOST SHADOWS

FLYING DRAGONS

BLACK EAGLES

CHING YEE | TUNG ON

WHITE TIGERS

FREEMASONS | GOLDEN STAR

FOOK CHING

GREEN DRAGONS

1960 1962 1964 1966 1968 1970 1972 1974 1976 1978 1980 1982 1984 1986 1988 1990

Year

Source: Ko-lin Chin, *Chinese Subculture and Criminality* (New York: Greenwood Press, 1990), p. 76.

occurred a century ago, when the robber barons became legitimate business tycoons and, ultimately, philanthropists.

The New Ethnic Diversity in Organized Crime

Organized crime is not necessarily synonymous with the Mafia. Other groups also operate in the United States. Foremost among them are the Colombian crime families, whose brutality is unrivaled by any other organized-crime group, and Bolivian, Peruvian, and Jamaican crime families, which since the 1970s have organized the production, transportation, and distribution within the United States of cocaine and marijuana.

Another form of organized crime, initiated by disillusioned veterans of the Korean War and reinforced by veterans of Vietnam, appears in the outlaw motorcycle gangs. Among them are the Hell's Angels, the Pagans, the Outlaws, the Sons of Silence, and the Bandidos. All are organized along military lines; all are devoted to violence; all are involved in the production and distribution of narcotics and other drugs. Many members are also involved in other criminal activities, including extortion and prostitution, trafficking in stolen motorcycles and parts, and dealing in automatic weapons and explosives.

Among other organized groups engaged in various criminal activities are Chinese gangs (see Figure 13.3), the so-called Israeli Mafia, the recently emerging Russian-Jewish Mafia, Jamaican posses, and the "Tattooed Men" of Japan's Yakuza, whose Yamaguchi-Gumi family alone has over 56,000 members, or nearly 20 times the number of fully initiated Italian organized-crime members in all the crews of all the families in the United States. All these groups have demonstrated potential for great social disruption.[76]

FBI ALERT
POISON CLAN
RICHMOND TASK FORCE "CRACKS" COCAINE ORGANIZATION

•

The "Poison Clan," a Brooklyn-based Jamaican gang that established itself in Richmond in 1988, was considered one of the largest and most violent drug distribution organizations in Richmond, Virginia. The Poison Clan network included a supply base in Brooklyn/Queens, New York, and had known distribution points including Richmond, Norfolk, Boston, Baltimore, and Raleigh. This gang, however, was no match for the Richmond Violent Criminal Homicide Task Force (RVCHTF), who brought down the "crack" cocaine organization. The RVCHTF is a joint cooperative effort among the Richmond FBI, Richmond Police Department and the Virginia State Police, which began in 1995. The purpose of the Richmond Violent Criminal Homicide Task Force is to combine resources in the investigation of selected unsolved drug-related homicides which have taken place in Richmond and have a federal interest.

It is estimated that the Poison Clan distributed well over 100 kilos of crack cocaine in the Richmond area in one year alone. The task force was able to determine that members of the gang were responsible for fifteen murders, which took place over an eight-year period, and responsible for a kidnapping and five aggravated assaults. This gang was responsible for bringing in more than just drugs to the Richmond area. Members also trafficked Uzi submachine guns, .9 millimeter pistols, rifles, and revolvers, including a .357 magnum and a .44 caliber magnum revolver. As a result of this investigation, the task force identified over 100 people who were either directly involved with or associated with the Poison Clan.

Fifteen months after RVCHTF initiation of the investigation, simultaneous arrests took place in [locations under the jurisdictions of] the Richmond, New York, New Haven and Miami Field Offices. The two Poison Clan leaders, brothers Devon and Dean Beckford, were arrested later in Oceanside, New York, and Rochester, New York.

During 1997, the leaders of this organization were convicted and sentenced to numerous life sentences. In addition, twenty-six other defendants were convicted on drug conspiracy and harboring charges. Those defendants received sentences ranging from two years to life.

To date there are three remaining fugitives:

Mervin Benjamim
aka: "Benji"
date of birth: 8/10/1965
race: black
sex: male

Charles O. Brackett
aka: "Charlie," "Chase"
date of birth: 8/28/1964
race: black
sex: male

Fabian O'Neal Littlejohn
aka: "Jack," "Fatta," "Jack Fatta"
date of birth: 2/1/1969
race: black
sex: male

All three are believed to be traveling back and forth from the Caribbean Islands to the New York City and Miami areas.

Source: http://www.fbi.gov/majcases/poison/poison.htm

REVIEW

Organizational crimes are characterized by the use of a legitimate or illegitimate business enterprise for illegal profit. As American corporations grew in the nineteenth and twentieth centuries, they amassed much of the nation's wealth. Many corporations abused their economic power. Government stepped in to curb such abuses by legislation.

Edwin Sutherland, who provided the first scholarly insight into the wrongdoing of corporations, originated the concept of white-collar crime. Subsequent scholars have distinguished white-collar crime, committed by individuals, from corporate crime, committed by business organizations. Corporate or individual white-collar offenses include securities-related crimes, such as misrepresentation and churning; bankruptcy fraud of various kinds; fraud against the government, in particular contract and procurement fraud; consumer fraud; insurance fraud; tax fraud; bribery and political fraud; and insider-related fraud. In the twentieth century, corporations have been subjected to criminal liability for an increasing number of offenses, including common law crimes and environmental as well as other statutory offenses.

Organized crime got its start in this country when Sicilian immigrants replicated their traditional family structure in organizing criminal activities in their new home. These families and their associates were so successful in controlling bootlegging, gambling, prostitution, loan-sharking, labor racketeering, drug trafficking, and other illegal enterprises that they were able to assume control of many legitimate businesses. In recent years members of other ethnic groups—Latin Americans, Jamaicans, Russian Jews, Japanese, Chinese—have challenged the Sicilian Mafia for supremacy.

 ## YOU BE THE CRIMINOLOGIST

For obvious reasons the extent of corporate crime is difficult to assess and measure. But criminologists do not shy away from significant challenges. How would you approach the problem of assessing and measuring crimes committed by corporations?

KEY TERMS

The numbers next to the terms refer to the pages on which the terms are defined.

bankruptcy fraud (372)

boiler rooms (372)

churning (371)

consumer fraud (373)

corporate crime (376)

embezzlement (375)

Federal Witness Protection Program (388)

insider trading (372)

Mafia (386)

occupational crimes (370)

Racketeer Influenced and Corrupt Organizations (RICO) Act (388)

Sherman Antitrust Act (378)

stock manipulation (372)

white-collar crime (369)

NOTES

1. Matthew L. Wald, "Airline Pleads Guilty to Illegal Storage of Hazardous Waste," *New York Times*, Dec. 17, 1999, p. 27; "ValuJet Jury Got It Right," *Chicago Tribune*, Dec. 17, 1999, p. 16.
2. Marshall B. Clinard and Peter C. Yeager, *Corporate Crime* (New York: Free Press, 1980), pp. 59–60.
3. "Mafia Chief Tied to Crime-Busting Judge's Murder," Reuters, Aug. 1, 1993.
4. Dwight Smith, "White-Collar Crime, Organized Crime, and the Business Establishment: Resolving a Crisis in Criminological Theory," in *White Collar and Economic Crime*, ed. Peter Whickman and Timothy Dailey (Lexington, Mass.: Lexington Books, 1982).
5. Michael Binstein and Charles Bowden, *Trust Me: Charles Keating and the Missing Billions* (New York: Random House, 1993); Kitty Calavita and Henry N. Pontell, " 'Other People's Money' Revisited: Collective Embezzlement in the Savings and Loan and Insurance Industries," *Social Problems*, **38** (1991): 94–112; Kitty Calavita and Henry N. Pontell, " 'Heads I Win, Tails You Lost': Deregulation, Crime, and Crisis in the Savings and Loan Industry," *Crime and Delinquency*, **36** (1990): 309–341.

6. P. Renfrew, "Introduction to Symposium on White Collar Crime," *Memphis State University Law Review,* **10** (1980): 416.

7. Sally S. Simpson, "Strategy, Structure, and Corporate Crime: The Historical Context of Anticompetitive Behavior," in *Advances in Criminological Theory,* vol. 4, ed. Freda Adler and William S. Laufer (New Brunswick, N.J.: Transaction, 1993), pp. 71–93. See also Melissa Baucus and Terry Moorehead-Dworkin, "What Is Corporate Crime? It Is Not Illegal Corporate Behavior," *Law and Policy,* **13** (1991): 231–244; Ron Boostrom, *Enduring Issues in Criminology* (San Diego, Calif.: Greenhaven Press, 1995).

8. Edwin H. Sutherland, "White Collar Criminality," *American Sociological Review,* **5** (1940): 1–20.

9. Gilbert Geis, *On White Collar Crime* (Lexington, Mass.: Lexington Books, 1982), p. 9.

10. Marshall B. Clinard and Richard Quinney, *Criminal Behavior Systems,* 2d ed. (New York: Holt, Rinehart & Winston, 1982); Marshall B. Clinard, *Corporate Corruption: The Abuse of Power* (Westport, Conn.: Praeger, 1990); Gilbert Geis and Paul Jesilow, eds., "White-Collar Crime," *Annals of the American Academy of Political and Social Science,* **525** (1993): 8–169; David Weisburd, Stanton Wheeler, and Elin Waring, *Crimes of the Middle Classes: White-Collar Offenders in the Federal Courts* (New Haven, Conn.: Yale University Press, 1991); John Braithwaite, "Poverty, Power, White-Collar Crime and the Paradoxes of Criminological Theory," *Australian and New Zealand Journal of Criminology,* **24** (1991): 40–48; Frank Pearce and Laureen Snider, eds., "Crimes of the Powerful," *Journal of Human Justice,* **3** (1992): 1–124; Hazel Croall, *White Collar Crime: Criminal Justice and Criminology* (Buckingham, England: Open University Press, 1991); Stephen J. Rackmill, "Understanding and Sanctioning the White Collar Offender," *Federal Probation,* **56** (1992): 26–33; Brent Fisse, Michael Bersten, and Peter Grabosky, "White Collar and Corporate Crime," *University of New South Wales Law Journal,* **13** (1990): 1–171; Susan P. Shapiro, "Collaring the Crime Not the Criminal: Reconsidering the Concept of White-Collar Crime," *American Sociological Review,* **55** (1990): 346–365; Kip Schlegel and David Weisburd, eds., *White-Collar Crime Reconsidered* (Boston: Northeastern University Press, 1992); David Weisburd, Stanton Wheeler, Elin Waring, et al., *Crimes of the Middle Classes: White-Collar Offenders in the Federal Courts* (New Haven, Conn.: Yale University Press, 1991); David Weisburd, Ellen F. Chayet, and Elin J. Waring, "White-Collar Crime and Criminal Careers: Some Preliminary Findings," *Crime and Delinquency,* **36** (1990): 342–355; David Weisburd, Elin Waring, and Stanton Wheeler, "Class, Status, and the Punishment of White-Collar Criminals," *Law and Social Inquiry,* **15** (1990): 223–243; Lisa Maher and Elin J. Waring, "Beyond Simple Differences: White Collar Crime, Gender and Workforce Position," *Phoebe,* **2** (1990): 44–54; John Hagan and Fiona Kay, "Gender and Delinquency in White-Collar Families: A Power-Control Perspective," *Crime and Delinquency,* **36** (1990): 391–407.

11. See James W. Coleman, *The Criminal Elite: The Sociological White-Collar Crime,* 2d ed. (New York: St. Martin's Press, 1989); and Michael L. Benson and Elizabeth Moore, "Are White-Collar and Common Offenders the Same? An Empirical and Theoretical Critique of a Recently Proposed General Theory of Crime," *Journal of Research in Crime and Delinquency,* **29** (1992): 251–272. See also Lori A. Elis and Sally S. Simpson, "Informal Sanction Threats and Corporate Crime: Additive versus Multiplicative Models," *Journal of Research in Crime and Delinquency,* **32** (1995): 399–424. For a view of white-collar offending in which the risks and rewards are considered by potential offenders, see David Weisburd, Elin Waring, and Ellen Chayet, "Specific Deterrence in a Sample of Offenders Convicted of White-Collar Crimes," *Criminology,* **33** (1995): 587–605.

12. Not only are governments at all levels victimized by corporate crimes, governments of all nations are also victimized; see Karlhans Liebl, "Developing Trends in Economic Crime in the Federal Republic of Germany," *Police Studies,* **8** (1985): 149–162.

CHAPTER 13

See also Jurg Gerber and Susan L. Weeks, "Women as Victims of Corporate Crime: A Call for Research on a Neglected Topic," *Deviant Behavior,* **13** (1992): 325–347; Elizabeth Moore and Michael Mills, "The Neglected Victims and Unexamined Costs of White-Collar Crime," *Crime and Delinquency,* **36** (1990): 408–418.

13. August Bequai, *White Collar Crime: A 20th-Century Crisis* (Lexington, Mass.: Lexington Books, 1978), p. 3; Linda Ganzini, Bentson McFarland, and Joseph Bloom, "Victims of Fraud: Comparing Victims of White Collar and Violent Crime," *Bulletin of the American Academy of Psychiatry and the Law,* **18** (1990): 55–63.

14. For the relationship between patterns of crimes in the savings and loan industry and those in organized crime, see Kitty Calavita and Henry N. Pontell, "Savings and Loan Fraud as Organized Crime: Toward a Conceptual Typology of Corporate Illegality," *Criminology,* **31** (1993): 519–548.

15. For an international perspective on consumer fraud, see U.S. Senate Committee on Governmental Affairs, *International Consumer Fraud: Can Consumers Be Protected?* (Washington, D.C.: U.S. Government Printing Office, 1994); Gilbert Geis, Henry N. Pontell, and Paul Jesilow, "Medicaid Fraud," in *Controversial Issues in Criminology and Criminal Justice,* ed. Joseph E. Scott and Travis Hirschi (Beverly Hills, Calif.: Sage, 1987); Maria S. Boss and Barbara Crutchfield George, "Challenging Conventional Views of White Collar Crime: Should the Criminal Justice System Be Refocused?" *Criminal Law Bulletin,* **28** (1992): 32–58. See also Richard M. Titus, Fred Heinzelmann, and John M. Boyle, "Victimization of Persons by Fraud," *Crime and Delinquency,* **41** (1995): 54–72. For a description of fraud in an organizational setting presented from the perspective of the perpetrator, fellow employees, and the organization itself, see Steve W. Albrecht, Gerald W. Wernz, and Timothy L. Williams, *Fraud: Bringing Light to the Dark Side of Business* (Burr Ridge, Ill.: Irwin Professional Publishing, 1995).

16. For an outline of a general theory of crime causation applicable to both street crime and white-collar crime, see Travis Hirschi and Michael Gottfredson, "Causes of White-Collar Crime," *Criminology,* **25** (1987): 949–974; James W. Coleman, "Toward an Integrated Theory of White Collar Crime," *American Journal of Sociology,* **93** (1987): 406–439; and James R. Lasley, "Toward a Control Theory of White Collar Offending," *Journal of Quantitative Criminology,* **4** (1988): 347–362.

17. Donald R. Cressey, "The Poverty of Theory in Corporate Crime Research," in *Advances in Criminological Theory,* vol. 1, ed. William Laufer and Freda Adler (New Brunswick, N.J.: Transaction, 1989), for a response, see John Braithwaite and Brent Fisse, "On the Plausibility of Corporate Crime Theory," in *Advances in Criminological Theory,* vol. 2, ed. William Laufer and Freda Adler (New Brunswick, N.J.: Transaction, 1990). See also Travis Hirschi and Michael Gottfredson, "The Significance of White-Collar Crime for a General Theory of Crime," *Criminology,* **27** (1989): 359–371; and Darrell Steffensmeier, "On the Causes of 'White Collar' Crime: An Assessment of Hirschi and Gottfredson's Claims," *Criminology,* **27** (1989): 345–358.

18. Bequai, *White Collar Crime.* Bequai also includes antitrust and environmental offenses, which are corporate crimes, discussed in the next section.

19. Kenneth Polk and William Weston, "Insider Trading as an Aspect of White Collar Crime," *Australian and New Zealand Journal of Criminology,* **23** (1990): 24–38. In a report before Congress, insider trading scandals were said to have cost the securities industry nearly half a billion dollars in the early 1970s; see U.S. Congress House Select Committee on Crime, *Conversion of Worthless Securities into Cash* (Washington, D.C.: U.S. Government Printing Office, 1973). For a review of the insider trading that persists on Wall Street, see Gene G. Marcial, *Secrets of the Street: The Dark Side of Making Money* (New York: McGraw-Hill, 1995); Martin Mayer, *Nightmare on Wall Street: Salomon Brothers and the Corruption of the Marketplace* (New

York: Simon & Schuster, 1993); Nancy Reichman, "Insider Trading," in Michael Tonry and Albert J. Reiss, Jr., eds., *Beyond the Law: Crime in Complex Organizations* (Chicago: University of Chicago Press, 1993).

20. For a more extensive review of the Wedtech debacle, see Mark S. Hamm, "From Wedtech and Iran-Contra to the Riots at Oakdale and Atlanta: On the Ethics and Public Performance of Edwin Meese III," *Journal of Crime and Justice,* **14** (1991): 123–147; Marilyn W. Thompson, *Feeding the Beast: How WedTech Became the Most Corrupt Little Company in America* (New York: Charles Scribner's Sons, 1990); William Power, "New York Rep. Biaggi and Six Others Indicted as Wedtech Scandal Greatly Expands," *Wall Street Journal,* June 4, 1987, p. 9.

21. See http://www.fas.org/man/gao/gao9621.htm.

22. For a discussion of the many ways in which a person may be defrauded, see Phil Berger and Craig Jacob, *Twisted Genius: Confessions of a $10 Million Scam Man* (New York: Four Walls Eight Windows, 1995). For an Australian perspective of fraud, see M. Kapardis and A. Kapardis, "Co-regulation of Fraud Detection and Reporting by Auditors in Australia: Criminology's Lessons for Non-compliance," *Australian and New Zealand Journal of Criminology,* **28** (1995): 193–212.

23. Bequai, *White Collar Crime,* pp. 70–71.

24. For a European perspective on insurance fraud, with a particular focus on the enforcement activities in France and Belgium, see Andre Lemaitre, Rolf Lemaitre, Rolf Arnold, and Roger Litton, "Insurance and Crime," *European Journal on Criminal Policy,* **3** (1995): 7–92. For a description of insurance fraud prevalent in the American insurance industry, see Kenneth D. Myers, *False Security: Greed & Deception in America's Multibillion-Dollar Insurance Industry* (Amherst, N.Y.: Prometheus Books, 1995); Andrew Tobias, *The Invisible Banker* (New York: Washington Square Press, 1982).

25. Paul E. Tracy and James A. Fox, "A Field Experiment on Insurance Fraud in Auto Body Repair," *Criminology,* **27** (1989): 589–603.

26. Kathleen F. Brickey, *Corporate Criminal Liability,* 2 vols. (Wilmette, Ill.: Callaghan, 1984). See also Thomas Gabor, *Everybody Does It! Crime by the Public* (Toronto: University of Toronto Press, 1994). For a uniquely British perspective, see Doreen McBarnet, "Whiter Than White Collar Crime: Tax, Fraud, Insurance and the Management of Stigma," *British Journal of Sociology,* **42** (1991): 323–344.

27. Alan Murray, "IRS Is Losing Battle against Tax Evaders Despite Its New Gain," *Wall Street Journal,* Apr. 10, 1984, p. 1.

28. Ralph Salerno and John S. Tompkins, "Protecting Organized Crime," in *Theft of the City,* ed. John A. Gardiner and David Olson (Bloomington: Indiana University Press, 1984); Edwin Sutherland, *The Professional Thief* (Chicago: University of Chicago Press, 1937).

29. 18 U.S.C. [sec] 166(b) and (c).

30. Bequai, *White Collar Crime,* p. 45.

31. Ibid., p. 87. See Virginia Department of Social Services, *Report of the Financial Exploitation of Older Adults and Disabled Younger Adults in the Commonwealth* (Richmond, Va.: Senate Document no. 37, 1994). For steps to take to avoid being a victim of embezzlement, see Russell B. Bintliff, *Complete Manual of White Collar Crime Detection and Prevention* (Englewood Cliffs, N.J.: Prentice Hall, 1993). For a historic account of embezzlement in the United Kingdom from 1845 to 1929, see George Robb, *White Collar Crime in Modern England: Financial Fraud and Business Morality, 1845–1929* (Cambridge: Cambridge University Press, 1992).

32. John Clark and Richard Hollinger, *Theft by Employees in Work Organization* (Washington, D.C.: U.S. Government Printing Office, 1983).

33. Bequai, *White Collar Crime,* p. 89.

34. M. David Ermann and Richard J. Lundman, "Corporate and Governmental Deviance: Origins, Patterns, and Reactions," in *Corporate and Governmental Deviance: Problems of Organizational Behavior in Contemporary Society,* 3d ed., ed. M. David Ermann and Richard J. Lundman (New York: Oxford University Press, 1996). A school of thought holds that, unlike people, corporations have

no personality, no conscience, and no shame. See, for example, Thomas Donaldson, *Corporations and Morality* (Englewood Cliffs, N.J.: Prentice-Hall, 1982); Donald R. Cressey, "The Poverty of Theory in Corporate Crime Research," in Laufer and Adler, *Advances in Criminological Theory*, vol 1. Over 100 years ago a New York court in *Darlington v. The Mayor*, 31 N.Y. 164 (1865), observed: "A corporation, as such, has no human wants to be supplied. It cannot eat, drink, or wear clothing, or live in houses." Steven Walt and William S. Laufer, "Corporate Criminal Liability and the Comparative Mix of Sanctions," in *White-Collar Crime Reconsidered*, ed. Kip Schlegel and David Weisburd (Boston: Northeastern University Press, 1992), describe corporations as being given a life and a moral personhood that clouds the distinction between crimes attributable to individuals (hourly employees, line managers, corporate officers, etc.) and those attributable to the corporate entity. John Braithwaite and Brent Fisse, "On the Plausibility of Corporate Crime Theory," in Laufer and Adler, *Advances in Criminological Theory*, vol. 2.

35. Nearly a century ago D. R. Richberg asked the question, "Should it not be the effort of all legislation dealing with corporations, to place them as nearly as possible on a plane of equal responsibility with individuals?" D. R. Richberg, "The Imprisonment of the Corporation," *Case and Comment*, **18** (1912): 512–529. Saul M. Pilchen discovered that although notions of corporate criminal culpability have been broadened over the years, initial prosecutions under the federal sentencing guidelines for organizations generally have been limited in scope. Saul M. Pilchen, "When Corporations Commit Crimes: Sentencing under the Federal Organizational Guidelines," *Judicature*, **78** (1995): 202–206. Daniel R. Fischel and Alan O. Sykes, "Corporate Crime," *The Journal of Legal Studies*, **xxv** (1996): 319–349. Ronald L. Dixon believes, "No corporation should be unaware of these statutes or of the theories upon which criminal liability can be established. Corporations must realize that no

one is immune from criminal liability, and corporate practices must reflect this fact." Ronald L. Dixon, "Corporate Criminal Liability," in *Corporate Misconduct: The Legal, Societal, and Management Issues*, ed. Margaret P. Spencer and Ronald R. Sims (Westport, Conn.: Quorum Books, 1995). For a British perspective on corporate liability, see "Great Britain, The Law Commission," in *Criminal Law: Involuntary Manslaughter: A Consultation Paper*, no. 135 (London: Her Majesty's Stationery Office, 1994). For a general overview of the corporate crime problem, see Francis T. Cullen, William J. Maakestad, and Gray Cavender, *Corporate Crime under Attack: The Ford Pinto Case and Beyond* (Cincinnati: Anderson, 1987), pp. 37–99.

36. *New York Central and Hudson River Railroad v. United States*, 212 U.S. 481 (1909); *State v. Lehigh Valley R. Co.*, 90 N.J. Law 372, 103 A. 685 (1917).

37. Model Penal Code, sec. 2.07(1) (c).

38. Sherman Antitrust Act, Act of July 2, 1890, c. 647, 26 Stat. 209, 15 U.S.C. [sec] 1-7 (1976).

39. Clayton Antitrust Act, Act of Oct. 15, 1914, c. 322, 38 Stat. 730, 15 U.S.C. [sec] 12-27 (1976); Robinson-Patman Act, Act of June 19, 1936, c. 592, [sec] 1, 49 Stat. 1526, 15 U.S.C. [sec] 13(a) (1973). See also Brickey, *Corporate Criminal Liability*.

40. Phillip Knightly, Harold Evans, Elaine Potter, and Marjorie Wallace, *Suffer the Children: The Story of Thalidomide* (New York: Viking, 1979).

41. The Ford Pinto case is fully described in Cullen et al., *Corporate Crime under Attack*. For more information on crimes against consumer safety, see Raymond J. Michalowski, *Order, Law, and Crime* (New York: Random House, 1985), pp. 334–340. For a description of corporate greed in its most vile form, see James S. Kunen, *Reckless Disregard: Corporate Greed, Government Indifference, and the Kentucky School Bus Crash* (New York: Simon & Schuster, 1994).

42. For an examination of corporate criminality in the United States and the response of the criminal justice system of America, see Spencer and Sims, *Corporate Misconduct*. See also Russell Mokhiber, *Corporate Crime and*

Violence: Big Business Power and the Abuse of the Public Trust (San Francisco: Sierra Club, 1988); Susan P. Shapiro, *Wayward Capitalists: Target of the Securities and Exchange Commission* (New Haven, Conn.: Yale University Press, 1984); M. David Ermann and Richard J. Lundman, *Corporate and Governmental Deviance: Problems of Organizational Behavior in Contemporary Society,* 2d ed. (New York: Oxford University Press, 1982); Cullen et al., *Corporate Crime under Attack;* Knightly et al., *Suffer the Children;* and W. Byron Groves and Graeme Newman, *Punishment and Privilege* (New York: Harrow & Heston, 1986).

43. See Edwin Sutherland, *White Collar Crime* (1946). Sutherland had earlier published articles on the topic, including "White Collar Criminality," *American Sociological Review,* **5** (1940): 1–12, and "Is White Collar Crime 'Crime'?" *American Sociological Review,* **10** (1945): 132–139.

44. See Gary E. Reed and Peter Cleary Yeager, "Organizational Offending and Neoclassical Criminology: Challenging the Reach of a General Theory of Crime," *Criminology,* **34** (1996): 357–382; Clinard and Yeager, *Corporate Crime,* p. 116. See also Peter C. Yeager, "Analysing Corporate Offences: Progress and Prospects," *Research in Corporate Social Performance and Policy,* **8** (1986): 93–120. For similar findings in Canada, see Colin H. Goff and Charles E. Reasons, *Corporate Crime in Canada* (Scarborough, Ontario: Prentice-Hall, 1978).

45. Richard Quinney, *Critique of Legal Order: Crime Control in Capitalist Society* (Boston: Little, Brown, 1974); Richard Quinney, *Class, State, and Crime: On the Theory and Practice of Criminal Justice* (New York: David McKay, 1977); Ian Taylor, Paul Walton, and Jock Young, *The New Criminology: For a Social Theory of Deviance* (London: Routledge & Kegan Paul, 1973); William Chambliss and Robert Seidman, *Law, Order, and Power,* 2d ed. (Reading, Mass.: Addison-Wesley, 1982).

46. James Q. Wilson, *Thinking about Crime* (New York: Basic Books, 1975). For a competing school of thought, see Gilbert Geis, "Criminal Penalties for Corporate Criminals," *Criminal Law Bulletin,* **8** (1972): 377–392;

Chamber of Commerce of the United States, *White Collar Crime* (Washington, D.C.: U.S. Government Printing Office, 1974); John Collins Coffee, Jr., "Beyond the Shut-Eyed Sentry: Toward a Theoretical View of Corporate Misconduct and an Effective Legal Response," *Virginia Law Review,* **63** (1977): 1099–1278; Gilbert Geis and Robert F. Meier, *White-Collar Crime: Offenses in Business, Politics, and the Professions* (New York: Free Press, 1977); Marshall B. Clinard, *Illegal Corporate Behavior* (Washington, D.C.: U.S. Government Printing Office, 1979); Miraim S. Saxon, *White-Collar Crime: The Problem and the Federal Response* (Report no. 80-84 EPW, Library of Congress, Congressional Research Service, Washington, D.C., Apr. 14, 1980); Laura S. Schrager and James F. Short, Jr., "How Serious a Crime? Perceptions of Organizational and Common Crimes," in *White-Collar Crime: Theory and Research,* ed. Gilbert Geis and Ezra Stotland (Beverly Hills, Calif.: Sage, 1980). Contemporary works include James W. Coleman, *The Criminal Elite: The Sociology of White-Collar Crime* (New York: St. Martin's Press, 1989); Laureen Snider, "The Regulatory Dance: Understanding Reform Processes in Corporate Crime," *International Journal of the Sociology of Law,* **19** (1991): 209–236; Kip Schlegel and David Weisburd, *White-Collar Crime: The Parallax View* (Boston: Northeastern University Press, 1993); Michael Tonry and Albert J. Reiss, *Beyond the Law: Crime in Complex Organizations* (Chicago: University of Chicago Press, 1993); Robert Tillman and Henry Pontell, "Organizations and Fraud in the Savings and Loan Industry," *Social Forces,* **73** (1995): 1439–1463.

47. Patsy Klaus and Carol Kalish, *The Severity of Crime,* Bureau of Justice Statistics Bulletin NCJ-92326 (Washington, D.C.: U.S. Government Printing Office, 1984). See also Schrager and Short, "How Serious a Crime?" Francis Cullen, B. Link, and C. Polanzi, "The Seriousness of Crime Revisited," *Criminology,* **20** (1982): 83–102; Francis Cullen, R. Mathers, G. Clark, and J. Cullen, "Public Support for Punishing White Collar Crime: Blaming the Victim Revisited," *Journal of Criminal Justice,*

11 (1983): 481–493; Richard Sparks, Hazel G. Genn, and David Dodd, *Surveying Victims* (New York: Wiley, 1977).

48. Jim Mayer, "Confection Maker Indicted in Dumping," *Sacramento Bee,* July 10, 1993.

49. Mark A. Cohen, "Environmental Crime and Punishment: Legal/Economic Theory and Empirical Evidence on Enforcement of Federal Environmental Statutes," *Journal of Criminal Law and Criminology,* **82** (1992): 1054–1108. See, for an early treatment, Timothy R. Young, "Criminal Liability under the Refuse Act of 1899 and the Refuse Act Permit Program," *Journal of Criminal Law, Criminology and Police Science,* **63** (1972): 366–376. For a global perspective on the prevention of environmental crime, see Boon Khoo Hui, Prathan Watanavanich, Edgar Aglipay, et al., *Effective Countermeasures against Crimes Related to Urbanization and Industrialization: Urban Crime, Juvenile Delinquency and Environmental Crime* (Tokyo: Report for 1993 and Resource Material Series no. 45, UNAFEI, 1994).

50. Clinard and Yeager, *Corporate Crime,* p. 92, citing *New York Times* survey of July 15, 1979.

51. Gerhard O. W. Mueller, "Offenses against the Environment and Their Prevention: An International Appraisal," *Annals of the American Academy of Political and Social Science,* **444** (1979): 56–66.

52. Ibid., p. 60.

53. Ryuichi Hirano, "The Criminal Law Protection of Environment: General Report," Tenth International Congress of Comparative Law, Budapest, 1978. For a discussion of the problems of multinational corporations operating in developing countries, see Richard Schaffer, Beverly Earle, and Filiberto Agusti, *International Business Law and Its Environment,* 2d ed. (St. Paul, Minn.: West, 1993). For a discussion of corporate crime in Japan, see Harold R. Kerbo and Mariko Inoue, "Japanese Social Structure and White Collar Crime: Recruit Cosmos and Beyond," *Deviant Behavior,* **11** (1990): 139–154.

54. Kerbo and Inoue, "Japanese Social Structure and White Collar Crime."

55. John Braithwaite, "Challenging Just Deserts: Punishing White-Collar Criminals," *Journal of Criminal Law and Criminology,* **73** (1982): 723–763; Stanton Wheeler, David Weisburd, and Nancy Boden, "Sentencing the White-Collar Offender," *American Sociological Review,* **47** (1982): 641–659. For a thoughtful analysis of corporate illegality, see Nancy Frank and Michael Lombness, *Corporate Illegality and Regulatory Justice* (Cincinnati: Anderson, 1988); Kip Schlegel, *Just Deserts for Corporate Criminals* (Boston: Northeastern University Press, 1990); and John C. Coffee, Jr., Mark A. Cohen, Jonathan R. Macey, et al., "A National Conference on Sentencing of the Corporation," *Boston University Law Review,* **71** (1991): 189–453.

56. Sally S. Simpson and Christopher S. Koper, "Deterring Corporate Crime," *Criminology,* **30** (1992): 347–375; Genevra Richardson, *Policing Pollution: A Study of Regulation and Enforcement* (Oxford: Clarendon, 1982); Albert J. Reiss and Albert D. Biderman, *Data Sources on White-Collar Law-Breaking* (Washington, D.C.: National Institute of Justice, 1980); Susan Shapiro, "Detecting Illegalities: A Perspective on the Control of Securities Violations," Ph.D. dissertation, Yale University (University Microfilms), 1980. See also Brian Widlake, *Serious Fraud Office* (London: Little, Brown, 1995).

57. Dan Magnuson, ed., *Economic Crime: Programs for Future Research* (Stockholm: National Council for Crime Prevention, 1985); Michael L. Benson, Francis T. Cullen, and William A. Maakestad, *Local Prosecutors and Corporate Crime: Final Report* (Washington, D.C.: National Institute of Justice, 1991); Michael L. Benson, Francis T. Cullen, and William J. Maakestad, "Local Prosecutors and Corporate Crime," *Crime and Delinquency,* **36** (1990): 356–372.

58. William Balsamo and George Carpozi, Jr., *Under the Clock: The Inside Story of the Mafia's First 100 Years* (Far Hills, N.J.: New Horizon Press, 1988). Some legal historians trace the appearance of organized crime in the United States to the early 1860s; see Humbert S. Nelli, "A Brief History of American

Review • You Be the Criminologist • Key Terms • Notes

Syndicate Crime," in *Organized Crime in America: Concepts and Controversies*, ed. Timothy S. Bynum (Monsey, N.Y.: Criminal Justice Press, 1987). See also Richard Gambino, *Blood of My Blood: The Dilemma of the Italian American* (Garden City, N.Y.: Doubleday, 1974), p. 3; Luigi Barzini, "Italians in New York: The Way We Were in 1929," *New York Magazine*, Apr. 4, 1977, p. 36; Howard Abadinsky, *Organized Crime*, 2d ed. (Chicago: Nelson Hall, 1985).

59. Abadinsky, *Organized Crime*, pp. 43–53.

60. Ibid., p. 91. For a description of some of the more colorful characters of the Prohibition era, see David E. Ruth, *Inventing the Public Enemy* (Chicago: University of Chicago Press, 1996); Joseph McNamara, "Dapper Bootlegger," *New York Daily News*, Oct. 15, 1995, p. 42; Charles Rappleye and Ed Becker, *All American Mafioso: The Johnny Roselli Story* (New York: Barricade Books, 1995); Mary M. Stolberg, *Fighting Organized Crime: Politics, Justice, and the Legacy of Thomas E. Dewey* (Boston: Northeastern University Press, 1995); Colin Wilson, Ian Schott, Ed Shedd, et al., *World Famous Crimes* (New York: Carroll & Graf, 1995); Jay Robert Nash, *World Encyclopedia of Organized Crime* (New York: Paragon House, 1992); Robert J. Schoenberg, *Mr. Capone: The Real and Complete Story of Al Capone* (New York: William Morrow, 1992); Robert Lacey, *Little Man: Meyer Lansky and the Gangster Life* (Boston: Little, Brown, 1991).

61. James Inciardi, *Careers in Crime* (Chicago: Rand McNally, 1975), p. 113; Norman Lewis, *The Honored Society: A Searching Look at the Mafia* (New York: Putnam, 1964), p. 25.

62. For a European perspective on the harms generated by the Sicilian Mafia, see John Follain, *A Dishonoured Society: Sicilian Mafia's Threat to Europe* (London: Little, Brown, 1995); Brian Freemantle, *The Octopus: Europe in the Grip of Organized Crime* (London: Orion Books, 1995). For a description of the Sicilian Mafia's reach into the former Soviet Union, see Werner Raith, *Das Neue Mafia-Kartell: Wie de Syndikate den Osten Erober* (The New Mafia Cartel: How the Syndicates Conquer the East) (Berlin:

Rowohlt, 1994). For a global perspective, see Phil Williams and Ernesto U. Savona, "Problems and Dangers Posed by Organized Transnational Crime in the Various Regions of the World," *Transnational Organized Crime*, **1** (1995): 1–42; Louise I. Shelley, "Transnational Organized Crime: An Imminent Threat to the Nation-State?" *Journal of International Affairs*, **48** (1995): 463–489; Raimondo Catanzaro, *Men of Respect: A Social History of the Sicilian Mafia* (New York: Free Press, 1992); Pino Arlacchi, *Men of Dishonor: Inside the Sicilian Mafia* (New York: William Morrow, 1992). For a description of how the Sicilian Mafia attempted to join forces with the Colombian cocaine cartels, see William Gately and Yvette Fernandez, *Dead Ringer: An Insider's Account of the Mob's Colombian Connection* (New York: Donald I. Fine, 1994); Abadinsky, *Organized Crime*, pp. 56–62.

63. Ronald Goldfarb, *Perfect Villains, Imperfect Heros: Robert F. Kennedy's War against Organized Crime* (New York: Random House, 1995); Annelise Graebner Anderson, *The Business of Organized Crime: A Cosa Nostra Family* (Stanford, Calif.: Hoover Institution Press, 1979); Peter Maas, *The Valachi Papers* (New York: Putnam, 1968); U.S. Senate Committee on Governmental Affairs, Subcommittee on Investigations, *Organized Crime: 25 Years after Valachi* (Washington, D.C.: U.S. Government Printing Office, 1990).

64. Jay Albanese, *Organized Crime in America* (Cincinnati: Anderson, 1985), p. 25. See also Francis A. J. Ianni, *A Family Business: Kinship and Social Control in Organized Crime* (New York: Russell Sage, 1972); Joseph Albini, *The American Mafia: Genesis of a Legend* (New York: Irvington, 1971); Merry Morash, "Organized Crime," in *Major Forms of Crime*, ed. Robert F. Meier (Beverly Hills, Calif.: Sage, 1984), pp. 191–220. For a response, see Claire Sterling, *Octopus: The Long Reach of the International Sicilian Mafia* (New York: W. W. Norton, 1990); Ralph Blumenthal, *Last Days of the Sicilians: At War with the Mafia* (New York: Pocket Books, 1994). See also Shana Alexander, *The Pizza Connection* (New York: Weidenfeld & Nicolson, 1988).

65. For a perceptive analysis of the changing focus of the two most recent commission reports, see Jay S. Albanese, "Government Perceptions of Organized Crime: The Presidential Commissions, 1967 and 1987," *Federal Probation,* **52** (1988): 58–63.

66. For a popular account of how a Sicilian Mafia associate infiltrated and almost destroyed one of the largest movie studios in Hollywood, see "The Predator: How an Italian Thug Looted MGM, Brought Credit Lyonnais to Its Knees, and Made the Pope Cry," *Fortune Magazine,* July 8, 1996, p. 128. Despite the denial of generations of Italian and Sicilian organized-crime figures concerning the trafficking of illegal narcotics, criminologists have discussed the involvement of all major American syndicates; see Peter A. Lupsha, "La Cosa Nostra in Drug Trafficking," in Bynum, *Organized Crime in America.* See also Dwight Smith, *The Mafia Mystique* (New York: Basic Books, 1975).

67. P. Beseler, Wayne Brewer, and Julienne Salzano, "Focus on Environmental Crimes," *FBI Law Enforcement Bulletin,* **64** (1995): 1–26; Joel Epstein, Theodore M. Hammett, and Laura Collins, *Law Enforcement Response to Environmental Crime,* (Washington, D.C.: U.S. National Institute of Justice, 1995). For a global perspective on environmental stability, see Norman Myers, *Ultimate Security: The Environmental Basis of Political Stability* (New York: W. W. Norton & Company, 1993). For a uniquely Italian organized-crime perspective on the illegal disposal of toxic wastes throughout the United States, see Frank R. Scarpitti and Alan A. Block, "America's Toxic Waste Racket: Dimensions of the Environmental Crisis," in Bynum, *Organized Crime in America.* For a discussion of predicting which legitimate businesses will be infiltrated by organized crime, see Jay S. Albanese, "Predicting the Incidence of Organized Crime: A Preliminary Model," in Bynum, *Organized Crime in America,* pp. 103–114.

68. Past efforts to develop civil and criminal causes of action against corporations are found in RICO legislation. See Racketeer Influenced and Corrupt Organizations (RICO) Provisions of the Organized Crime Control Act of 1970 [Act of Oct. 15, 1970, Public Law 91-452, Section 901 (a), 84 Stat. 941, 18 U.S. Code Sections 1961 through 1968, effective Oct. 15, 1970, as amended Nov. 2, 1978, Public Law 95-575, Sec. 3 (c), 92 Stat. 2465 and Nov. 6, 1978, Public Law 95-598, Sec. 314 (g), 92 Stat. 2677]. For a discussion of the pros and cons of RICO, see Donald J. Rebovich, "Use and Avoidance of RICO at the Local Level: The Implementation of Organized Crime Laws," in *Contemporary Issues in Organized Crime,* ed. Jay Albanese (Monsey, N.Y.: Criminal Justice Press, 1995).

69. Fred Montanino, "Protecting Organized Crime Witnesses in the United States," *International Journal of Comparative and Applied Criminal Justice,* **14** (1990): 123–131.

70. For a description of the contemporary leadership of New York's five Italian-American organized-crime families, see Jeffrey Goldberg, "The Mafia's Morality Crisis," *New York Magazine,* Jan. 9, 1995, p. 22. See also Donald Cressey, *Theft of the Nation* (New York: Harper & Row, 1969).

71. Abadinsky, *Organized Crime,* pp. 8–23; Donald Cressey, in President's Commission, *Task Force Report,* pp. 7–8; Gay Talese, *Honor Thy Father* (New York: World, 1971).

72. For a discussion of "Commission" membership, mores, and dispute resolution, see William F. Roemer, Jr., *Accardo: The Genuine Godfather* (New York: Donald I. Fine, 1995); Sidney Zion, *Loyalty and Betrayal: The Story of the American Mob* (San Francisco: Collins, 1994); John H. Davis, *Mafia Dynasty: The Rise and Fall of the Gambino Crime Family* (New York: HarperCollins, 1993); Sam Giancana and Chuck Giancana, *Double Cross: The Explosive, Inside Story of the Mobster Who Controlled America* (New York: Warner Books, 1992); John Cummings and Ernest Volkman, *Goombata: The Improbable Rise and Fall of John Gotti and His Gang* (Boston: Little, Brown, 1990).

73. *United States v. Bonanno,* 180 F. Supp. 71 (S.D.N.Y. 1960), upholding the Apalachin roundup as constitutional; *United States v. Bonanno,* 177 F. Supp. 106 (S.D.N.Y. 1959),

sustaining the validity of the conspiracy indictment; *United States v. Bufalino*, 285 F. 2d 408 (2d Cir. 1960), reversing the conspiracy conviction.

74. James Walston, "Mafia in the Eighties," *Violence, Aggression, and Terrorism*, **1** (1987): 13–39. For a look into organized crime's once mighty and still lingering hand on gambling in the United States, see Jay Albanese, "Casino Gambling and Organized Crime: More Than Reshuffling the Deck," in Albanese, *Contemporary Issues in Organized Crime*; Ronald A. Farrelland and Carole Case, *The Black Book and the Mob: The Untold Story of the Control of Nevada's Casinos* (Madison: University of Wisconsin Press, 1995); Nicholas Pileggi, *Casino: Love and Honor in Las Vegas* (New York: Simon & Schuster, 1995); David Johnston, *Temples of Chance: How America Inc. Bought Out Murder Inc. to Win Control of the Casino Business* (New York: Doubleday, 1992).

75. Organized-crime activities are certainly not limited to local communities. Rather, an ever-evolving organized-crime syndicate feeds off ever-increasing global opportunities; see Petrus van Duyne and Alan A. Block, "Organized Cross-Atlantic Crime: Racketeering in Fuels," *Crime, Law and Social Change*, **22** (1995): 127–147; Umberto Santino, "The Financial Mafia: The Illegal Accumulation of Wealth and the Financial-Industrial Complex," *Contemporary Crises*, **12** (1988): 203–243.

76. For a description of the damage inflicted on society by contemporary Russian organized-crime figures, see New York State Organized Crime Task Force, New York State Commission of Investigation, New Jersey State Commission of Investigation, *An Analysis of Russian-Émigré Crime in the Tri-State Region* (White Plains, N.Y.: New York State Organized Crime Task Force, June 1996); Dennis J. Kenny and James O. Finckenauer, *Organized Crime in America* (Belmont, Calif.: Wadsworth, 1995).

CHAPTER 14
Public Order Crimes

In cities across the country and around the world, people buying and selling illicit goods and services congregate in certain areas that are easily identifiable by theater marquees advertising live sex shows. Shops feature everything from child pornography to sadomasochistic slide shows; prostitutes openly solicit clients; drunks propped up in doorways clutch brown bags; drug addicts deal small amounts of whatever they can get to sell to support their habits. The friendly locals will deliver virtually any service to visitors, for a price.

The activities involved—prostitution, drunkenness, sex acts between consenting adults for money, drug use—were commonly called "victimless" crimes. Perhaps that is because it was assumed that people who engage in them rationally choose to do so and do not view themselves as victims. Often no one complains to the police about being victimized by such consensual activity. But contemporary forms of such activities and their ramifications may entail massive victimizations: How many murders are committed during drug gang wars? How many thefts are committed by addicts seeking to support their habits? How much damage is done to persons and property by drunken drivers? Does pornography encourage physical abuse? And what of the future of children sold for prostitution?

FIGURE 14.1 National spending for drug control.

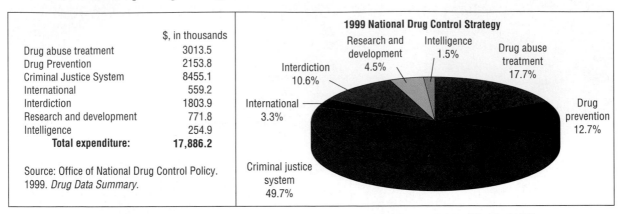

	$, in thousands
Drug abuse treatment	3013.5
Drug Prevention	2153.8
Criminal Justice System	8455.1
International	559.2
Interdiction	1803.9
Research and development	771.8
Intelligence	254.9
Total expenditure:	**17,886.2**

Source: Office of National Drug Control Policy. 1999. *Drug Data Summary.*

1999 National Drug Control Strategy

Research and development 4.5%
Intelligence 1.5%
Drug abuse treatment 17.7%
Interdiction 10.6%
International 3.3%
Drug prevention 12.7%
Criminal justice system 49.7%

Source: Office of National Drug Control Policy, *Fact Sheet: Drug Data Summary* (Washington, D.C.: U.S. Government Printing Office, April 1999).

DRUG ABUSE AND CRIME

A woman arrives at the airport in Los Angeles with very few belongings, no hotel reservations, no family or friends in the United States, and a passport showing eight recent trips from Bogotá, Colombia. A pat-down and strip search reveal a firm, distended abdomen, which is discovered to hold 88 balloons filled with cocaine.[1] In New York City, a heroin addict admits that "the only livin' thing that counts is the fix . . . : Like I would steal off anybody—anybody, at all, my own mother gladly included."[2] In Chicago, crack cocaine has transformed some of the country's toughest gangs into ghetto-based drug-trafficking organizations that guard their turf with automatic weapons and assault rifles.[3]

On a college campus in the Northeast a crowd sits in the basement of a fraternity house drinking beer and smoking pot through the night. At a beachfront house in Miami three young professional couples gather for a barbecue. After dinner they sit down at a card table in the playroom. On a mirror, someone lines up a white powdery substance into rows about ⅛ inch wide and 1 inch long. Through rolled-up paper they breathe the powder into their nostrils and await the "rush" of the coke. In a quiet suburban home two middle school students inhale paint thinner after school.

These incidents demonstrate that when we speak of the "drug problem," we are talking about a wide variety of conditions that stretch be-

yond our borders, that involve all social classes, that in one way or another touch most people's lives, and that cost society significant sums of money (Figure 14.1). The drug scene includes manufacturers, importers, primary distributors (for large geographical areas), smugglers (who transport large quantities of drugs from their place of origin), dealers (who sell drugs on the street and in crack houses), corrupt criminal justice officials, users who endanger other people's lives through negligence (train engineers, pilots, physicians), and even unborn children (Table 14.1).

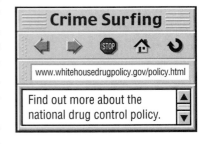

Crime Surfing

www.whitehousedrugpolicy.gov/policy.html

Find out more about the national drug control policy.

The drug problem is further complicated by the wide diversity of substances abused, their varying effects on the mind and body, and the kinds of dependencies users develop. There is also the much-debated issue of the connection between drug use and crime—an issue infinitely more complex than the stereotype of maddened addicts committing heinous acts because they either were under the influence of drugs or needed to get the money to support a habit. Many of the crimes we have discussed in earlier chapters are part of what has been called the nation's (or the world's) drug problem. Let us examine this problem in detail.

TABLE 14.1 Roles and Functions in the Drug Distribution Business Compared with Those in Legitimate Industry

Approximate Role Equivalents in Legal Markets	Roles by Common Names at Various Stages of the Drug Distribution Business	Major Functions Accomplished at This Level
Grower producer	Coca farmer, opium farmer, marijuana grower	Grow coca, opium, marijuana: the raw materials
Manufacturer	Collector, transporter, elaborator, chemist, drug lord	All stages for preparation of heroin, cocaine, marijuana as commonly sold
Traffickers		
Importer	Multikilo importer, mule, airplane pilot, smuggler, trafficker, money launderer	Smuggling of large quantities of substances into the U.S.
Wholesale distributor	Major distributor, investor, "kilo connection"	Transportation and redistribution of multi-kilograms and single kilograms
Dealers		
Regional distributor	Pound and ounce men, weight dealers	Adulteration and sale of moderately expensive products
Retail store owner	House connections, suppliers, crack-house supplier	Adulteration and production of retail-level dosage units (bags, vials, grams) in very large numbers
Assistant manager, security chief, or accountant	"Lieutenant," "muscle men," transporter, crew boss, crack-house manager/proprietor	Supervises three or more sellers, enforces informal contracts, collects money, distributes multiple dosage units to actual sellers
Sellers		
Store clerk, salesmen (door-to-door and phone)	Street drug seller, runner, juggler	Makes actual direct sales to consumer; private seller responsible for both money and drugs
Low-Level Distributors		
Advertiser, security guards, leaflet distributor	Steerer, tout, cop man, lookout, holder runner, help friend, guard, go-between	Assists in making sales, advertises, protects seller from police and criminals, solicits customers; handles drugs or money but not both
Servant, temporary employee	Run shooting gallery, injector (of drugs), freebaser, taster, apartment cleaner, drug bagger, fence, money launderer	Provides short-term services to drug users or sellers for money or drugs; not responsible for money or drugs

Source: Bruce D. Johnson, Terry Williams, Kojo A. Dir, and Harry Sanabria, "Drug Abuse in the Inner City: Impact on Hard-Drug Users and the Community," in *Drugs and Crime,* vol. 13: *Crime and Justice,* ed. Michael Tonry and James Q. Wilson (Chicago: University of Chicago Press, 1990), p. 19. © 1990 by the University of Chicago Press. All rights reserved. From U.S. Department of Justice, *Drugs, Crime and the Justice System* (Washington, D.C.: U.S. Government Printing Office, 1992).

The History of Drug Abuse

The use of chemical substances that alter physiological and psychological functioning dates back to the Old Stone Age.[4] Egyptian relics from 3500 B.C. depict the use of opium in religious rituals. By 1600 B.C. an Egyptian reference work listed opium as an analgesic, or painkiller. The Incas of South America are known to have used cocaine at least 5000 years ago. Cannabis, the hemp plant from which marijuana and hashish are derived, also has a 5000-year history.[5]

Since antiquity, people have cultivated a variety of drugs for religious, medicinal, and social purposes. The modern era of drug abuse in the United States began with the use of drugs for medicinal purposes. By the nineteenth century the two components of opium, which is derived from the sap of the opium poppy, were identified and given the names "morphine" and "codeine." Ignorant of the addictive properties of these drugs, physicians used them to treat a wide variety of human illnesses. So great was their popularity that they found their way into almost all patent medicines used for pain relief and were even incorporated in soothing syrups for babies (Mother

Barley's Quieting Syrup and Mumm's Elixir were very popular).

During the Civil War the use of injectable morphine to ease the pain of battle casualties was so extensive that morphine addiction among veterans came to be known as the "soldier's disease."[6] By the time the medical profession and the public recognized just how addictive morphine was, its use had reached epidemic proportions. Then in 1898 the Bayer Company in Germany introduced a new opiate, supposedly a nonaddictive substitute for morphine and codeine. It came out under the trade name Heroin; yet it proved to be even more addictive than morphine.[7]

When cocaine, which was isolated from the coca leaf in 1860, appeared on the national drug scene, it too was used for medicinal purposes. (Its use to unblock the sinuses initiated the "snorting" of cocaine into the nostrils.) Its popularity spread, and soon it was used in other products: Peruvian Wine of Coca ($1 a bottle in the Sears, Roebuck catalog), a variety of tonics, and, the most famous of all, Coca-Cola, which was made with coca until 1903.[8]

As the consumption of opium products (narcotics) and cocaine spread, states passed a variety of laws to restrict the sale of these substances. Federal authorities estimated that there were 200,000 addicts in the early 1900s. Growing concern over the increase in addiction led in 1914 to the passage of the Harrison Act, designed to regulate the domestic use, sale, and transfer of opium and coca products. Though this legislation decreased the number of addicts, it was a double-edged sword: By restricting the importation and distribution of drugs, it paved the way for the drug smuggling and black-market operations that are so deeply entrenched today.

It was not until the 1930s that the abuse of marijuana began to arouse public concern. Because marijuana use was associated with groups outside the social mainstream—petty criminals, jazz musicians, bohemians, and, in the Southwest, Mexicans—a public outcry for its regulation arose.[9] Congress responded with the Marijuana Tax Act of 1937, which placed a prohibitive tax of $100 an ounce on the drug. With the passage of the Boggs Act in 1951,

penalties for possession of and trafficking in marijuana (and other controlled substances) increased. Despite all the legislation, the popularity of marijuana continued.

As the drugs being used proliferated to include glue, tranquilizers (such as Valium and Librium), LSD, and many others, the public became increasingly aware of the dangers of drug abuse. In 1970 another major drug law, the Comprehensive Drug Abuse Prevention and Control Act (the Controlled Substances Act), updated all federal drug laws since the Harrison Act.[10] This act placed marijuana in the category of the most serious substances. The 1970 federal legislation made it necessary to bring state legislation into conformity with federal law. The Uniform Controlled Substances Act was drafted and now is the law in 48 states, the District of Columbia, Puerto Rico, the Virgin Islands, and Guam.

Most of the basic federal antidrug legislation has been drawn together in Title 21 of the United States Code, the collection of all federal laws. It includes many amendments passed since 1970, especially the Anti-Drug Abuse Act of 1988, which states: "It is the declared policy of the United States Government to create a drug-free America by 1995."[11]

Title 21, as amended, has elaborate provisions for the funding of national and international drug programs; establishes the Office of National Drug Control Policy, headed by a so-called drug czar; and provides stiff penalties for drug offenses. The manufacture, distribution, and dispensing of listed substances in stated (large) quantities are each subject to a prison sentence of 10 years to life and a fine (for individuals) of $4 million to $10 million. Even simple possession now carries a punishment of up to 1 year in prison and a $100,000 fine. Title 21, along with other recent crime-control legislation, defines many other drug crimes as well and provides for the forfeiture of any property constituting or derived from the proceeds of drug trading.

The Extent of Drug Abuse

Historically, the substance (other than alcohol) most frequently abused in the United States has been marijuana. In annual surveys, high school seniors were asked whether they ever used marijuana. Between 1975 and 1991, the percentage answering yes ranged from a high of 51 percent in 1979 to a low of 37 percent in 1991. The survey also found that in 1991, 24 percent had used marijuana in the past year, and 14 percent in the past month.[12]

The most recent national household survey shows a slight decrease in drug use among youths between the ages of 12 and 17 after almost a decade of rising rates. Almost 10 percent of America's youths report the recent use of illegal drugs, and an estimated 13.6 million Americans, or 6.2 percent of the population over age 12, reported recent drug use. After dramatic increases in the use of marijuana, cocaine, LSD, and other hallucinogens between 1992 and 1995, the rate of use for all these drugs has stabilized.[13]

In the 1980s cocaine constituted the country's major drug problem. An estimated 22 million people had tried the substance, and another 4 million were using it regularly. In 1998 the number of regular users had dropped to 1.5 million.[14] The use of heroin is much less pervasive; the number of users is estimated to be about 600,000.[15] Other drugs on the market are crack (a derivative of cocaine) and the so-called *designer drugs*—substances that have been chemically altered in such a way that they no longer fall within the legal definition of controlled substances.[16]

It is difficult to measure how many people abuse drugs in any given period. The national household survey has shown a decline in the use of illicit drugs between 1979 and 1991, followed by an increase. The most recent data demonstrate a leveling off of drug use by high school students (Table 14.2 and Figure 14.2).[17]

Patterns of Drug Abuse

New and more potent varieties of illicit substances, as well as increasing levels of violent crime associated with drug abuse, have led researchers to ask many questions about the phenomenon. Is drug abuse a symptom of an underlying mental or psychological disorder that makes some people more vulnerable than others? Some investigators argue that the addict is characterized by strong dependency needs,

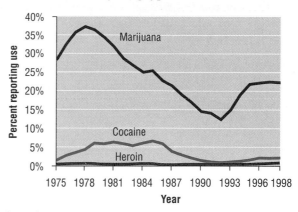

FIGURE 14.2 Past year drug use by high school seniors, by drug type, 1975–1998.

Source: Office of National Drug Control Policy, *Fact Sheet: Drug Use Trends* (Washington, D.C.: U.S. Government Printing Office, June 1999).

feelings of inadequacy, a need for immediate gratification, and lack of internal controls.[18] Or is it possible that addicts lack certain body chemicals and that drugs make them feel better by compensating for that deficit?

Perhaps the causes are environmental. Is drug abuse a norm in deteriorated inner cities, where youngsters are learning how to behave from older addicted role models? Do people escape from the realities of slum life by retreating into drug abuse?[19] If so, how do we explain drug abuse among the upper classes?

Just as there are many causes of drug abuse, there are many addict lifestyles—and the lifestyles may be linked to the use of particular substances. During the 1950s, heroin abuse began to increase markedly in the inner cities, particularly among young black and Hispanic males.[20] In fact, it was their drug of choice throughout the 1960s and early 1970s. Heroin addicts spend their days buying heroin, finding a safe place to shoot the substance into a vein with a needle attached to a hypodermic syringe, waiting for the euphoric feeling, or rush, that follows the injection, and ultimately reaching a feeling of overall well-being known as a high, which lasts about 4 hours.[21] The heroin abuser's lifestyle is typically characterized by poor health, crime, arrest, imprisonment, and temporary stays in drug treatment programs.[22] Today AIDS, which is spread, among other ways, by

TABLE 14.2   Highlights of the 1998 National Household Survey

Illicit Drug Use
• In 1998, an estimated 13.6 million Americans were current illicit drug users, meaning they had used an illicit drug in the month prior to the interview. This number represents a slight decrease from 1997, when the estimate was 13.9 million. The number of illicit drug users was at its highest level in 1979, when there were 25 million. • Between 1997 and 1998, the rate of past-month illicit drug use among youths decreased from 11.4 percent to 9.9 percent. The rate is still twice what it was in 1992. • In 1998, youth marijuana use decreased slightly from its 1997 level, from 9.4 percent to 8.3 percent. • The overall number of current cocaine users did not change significantly between 1997 and 1998 (1.8 million in 1998 and 1.5 million in 1997). However, use is down from a peak of 5.7 million in 1985. • There were an estimated 1.1 million new hallucinogen users in 1997. The rate of initiation among youths ages 12 to 17 increased between 1991 and 1995, from 11.1 to 25.0 per thousand potential new users, and was constant from 1995 to 1997 (23.9 percent). • In 1997, an estimated 81,000 people used heroin for the first time. The rate of initiation for youths between 1994 and 1997 was at the highest level since the early 1970s. • An estimated 2.1 million persons first used marijuana in 1997. This number represents a significant decrease since 1996. • In 1997 and 1998 an estimated 4.1 million people met diagnostic criteria for dependence on illicit drugs, including 1.1 million youths ages 12 to 17.
Alcohol Use
• In 1998, 113 million Americans age 12 and older had used alcohol in the past month. About 33 million engaged in binge drinking (five or more drinks on at least one occasion in the past month), and about 12 million were heavy drinkers (drinking five or more drinks per occasion on 5 or more days in the past 30 days). • There were no changes in rates of alcohol use between 1997 and 1998. • About 10.5 million drinkers were under age 21 in 1998. Of these, 5.1 million were binge drinkers, including 2.3 million heavy drinkers.
Cigarette Use
• An estimated 60 million Americans were current smokers in 1998. This number represents a smoking rate of 27.7 percent, which is a significant decrease from 1997 (29.6 percent). • Among youths ages 12 to 17, rates of smoking did not change between 1997 and 1998. An estimated 18.2 percent (4.1 million) of youths ages 12 to 17 were smokers in 1998. • Current smokers are more likely to be heavy drinkers and illicit drug users than are nonsmokers. Youths ages 12 to 17 who currently smoked cigarettes were 11.4 times more likely to use illicit drugs and 16 times more likely to drink heavily than nonsmoking youths. • In 1997, an estimated 2.1 million people became daily smokers. More than half of these new smokers were under age 18 (3000 new youth smokers per day).

the shared use of needles, has become the most serious health problem among heroin addicts.

During the 1960s marijuana became one of the major drugs of choice in the United States, particularly among white, middle-class young people who identified themselves as antiestablishment. Their lifestyles were distinct from those of the inner-city heroin addicts. What began as a hippie drug culture in the Haight-Ashbury area of San Francisco spread quickly through the country's college campuses.[23] In fact, a Harvard psychologist, Timothy Leary, traveled across the country in the 1960s telling students to "turn on, tune in, and drop out." Young marijuana users tended to live for the moment. Disillusioned by what they perceived

as a rigid and hypocritical society, they challenged its norms through deviant behavior. Drugs—first marijuana, then hallucinogens (principally LSD), amphetamines, and barbiturates—came to symbolize the counterculture.[24]

In the 1960s and 1970s, attitudes toward recreational drug use became quite lax, perhaps as a result of the wide acceptance of marijuana.[25] By the 1980s, cocaine, once associated only with deviants, had become the drug of choice among the privileged, who watched (and copied) the well-publicized drug-oriented lifestyles of some celebrities and athletes. Typical cocaine users were well-educated, prosperous, upwardly mobile professionals in their twenties and thirties. They were lawyers and architects, editors and

Actor Robert Downey, Jr., in a Malibu, California, courtroom just prior to being sentenced to six months in jail for violating parole on a prior drug conviction.

stockbrokers. They earned enough money to spend at least $100 an evening on their illegal recreational activities. By and large they were otherwise law-abiding, even though they knew their behavior was against the law.

The popularity of cocaine waned toward the end of the 1980s. The same is not true for crack, however, which spread to the inner-city population that had abused heroin in the latter part of the 1980s.[26] Crack is cheaper than powdered cocaine, fast-acting, and powerful. Though individual doses are inexpensive, once a person is hooked on crack, a daily supply can run between $100 and $250.

Drug addicts continually search for new ways to extend their highs. In 1989 a mixture of crack and heroin, called "crank," began to be used. Crank is smoked in a pipe.[27] It is potentially very dangerous, first, because it prolongs the brief high of crack alone and, second, because it appeals to younger drug addicts who are concerned about the link between AIDS and the sharing of hypodermic needles. The history of drug abuse is evolutionary. "Crank" is now the name of methamphetamine—also known as "ice," "crystal," "chalk," and "speed."

Crime-Related Activities

Many researchers have examined the criminal implications of addiction to heroin and, more recently, cocaine. James Inciardi found that 356 addicts in Miami, according to self-reports, committed 118,134 offenses (27,464 Index crimes) over a 1-year period.[28] A national program, Drug Use Forecasting, found that in 1996, 49 to 82 percent of arrestees in 24 major U.S. cities had used drugs. Cocaine remains the most prevalent drug used.[29] Official statistics on drug-related offenses make it quite clear that street crime is significantly related to drug abuse.

The nature of the drug-crime relationship, however, is less clear. Is the addict typically an adolescent who never committed a crime before he or she became hooked, but who thereafter was forced to commit crimes to get money to support the drug habit? In other words, does drug abuse lead to crime?[30] Or does criminal behavior precede drug abuse? Another possibility is that both drug abuse and criminal behavior stem from the same factors (biological, psychological, or sociological).[31] The debate continues, and many questions are still unanswered. But on one point most researchers agree: Whatever the temporal or causal sequence of drug abuse and crime, the frequency and seriousness of criminality increase as addiction increases. Drug abuse may not "cause" criminal behavior, but it does enhance it.[32]

Until the late 1970s most investigators of the drug-crime relationship reported that drug abusers were arrested primarily for property offenses. Recent scholarly literature, however, presents a different perspective. There appears to be an increasing amount of violence associated with drugs, and it may be attributable largely to the appearance of crack. Drug wars became more frequent during the 1980s. Cities across the country have been divided into distinct turfs. Rival drug dealers settle disputes with guns, power struggles within a single drug enterprise lead to assaults and homicides, one dealer robs another, informers are killed, their associates retaliate, and bystanders, some of them children, get caught in the cross fire.[33]

The use of performance-enhancing drugs, "doping," is not new in athletic competitions. Nor is it limited to the use of anabolic steroids by weight lifters and others seeking to increase strength and muscle mass. Doping is used in such sports as cycling, running, tennis, swimming, and Nordic skiing. The increased publicity surrounding sports and the huge sums of money offered to medal winners for endorsing products creates pressures on athletes that go beyond winning their events. Several athletes admit that doping is common among world-class competitors; however, testing athletes and sanctioning them has proved problematic.

The experience of cyclist Erwan Menthéour demonstrates the role of doping and the means athletes and their trainers use to attempt to circumvent detection. In 1997 Menthéour was selected for random drug testing during the Tour de France. Just before the competition he had taken erythropoietin (EPO), an endurance-enhancing drug that works by increasing the number of red blood cells. When Menthéour was notified that he would be tested, his trainer and doctor tried to thin out his blood by using an IV drip of chilled glucose and by bleeding him. Despite their efforts, Menthéour tested positive and was thrown off the racing circuit for 2 weeks. He claimed that his red blood cell count was high because he had had diarrhea and was dehydrated. Menthéour stated, "For two years I took EPO, growth hormone, anabolic steroids, testosterone, amphetamine. Just about everything. That was part of the job."(1)

The harmful effects of doping include physical changes and health problems such as heart disease, muscle and bone disfigurement, liver cancer, and impotence. Mixing drugs into "drug cocktails" to achieve better performance is especially risky because of interaction effects. EPO use alone has killed 18 Belgian and Dutch cyclists since 1987.

While athletes who test positive for enhancement drugs are not allowed to continue in a competition, relatively few are severely sanctioned.(2) Some, however, have been banned from competition for life. There appears to be some reluctance on the part of the International Olympic Committee (IOC) and other governing organizations to take action against doping. Detection is part of the problem. The IOC currently uses urine testing rather than blood testing, which is more invasive, requires refrigeration, and has some religious objections. With urine testing, it is more difficult to detect the presence of drugs in the system, which allows athletes to use techniques that hide doping. Athletes and coaches are also in a race against officials to create new performance-enhancing agents that are not yet banned. Some officials have suggested freezing urine samples and retesting them as new tests become available. This approach would allow officials to regulate doping retroactively and, theoretically, to deter the use of new substances.

It is still unclear what the IOC intends to do to prevent doping among Olympic athletes. Possible options include random drug testing while athletes are not in competition, along with a "doping passport," which would require athletes to prove that they have undergone several out-of-competition drug tests to be eligible to compete at the Olympics.(3) Even if doping passports do become a requirement for Olympic competition and do cut down on doping among Olympic athletes, they would address only part of the problem. Measures must still be devised to deal with doping among professional athletes as well as amateur athletes, including those at middle school, high school, and college levels.

Sources

1. Sharon Begley and Martha Brant, "The Real Scandal," *Newsweek*, Feb. 15, 1999, pp. 48–54.

After running 100 meters in 9.84 seconds and breaking the world record at the 1988 Seoul Olympics, Canadian track star Ben Johnson was required to give back his gold medal when tests revealed that he was using banned anabolic steroids.

2. Department of Life Sciences, "Doping and Sports Collective Expert Assessment," December 1998 (http://www.uiuc.edu/cnrs/ English/Compresse/dopage/ dopage2.html).
3. Stephen Wilson, " 'Doping Passport' Issue Pushed," Oct. 2, 1999 (http://www.dailynews.yahoo.com/ h/ap/19991002/sp/oly_ioc_ meetings_7.html).

Questions for Discussion

1. How important is it to prevent the use of performance-enhancing drugs? Does the level of competition make a difference (e.g., high school vs. Olympic level)?
2. What kinds of measures should be taken to prevent doping? What can be done to decrease the pressures on athletes to use performance-enhancing drugs?

The International Drug Economy

The drug problem is a worldwide phenomenon, beyond the power of any one government to deal with.[34] Nor are drugs a concern simply of law enforcement agencies. Drugs influence politics, international relations, peace and war, and the economies of individual countries and of the world. Let us take a look at the political

A Lahu hill tribe girl in Myanmar holds opium poppies as she assists her tribe in eradicating illegal poppies.

and economic impact of the international drug trade, specifically as it concerns cocaine, heroin, and marijuana. Figure 14.3 shows the sources of these drugs and some shipping routes.

Cocaine Today the largest cocaine producer is Peru, although harvests have been decreasing since 1995. Annual harvests of 95,600 to 130,200 metric tons of coca leaves yield from 178 to 242 tons of pure cocaine. Cocaine production in Colombia has increased in recent years, with annual yields of 118 to 151 tons.[35] Colombia also exports more than any other country—over half the world's supply—because much of the raw coca of Peru and other coca producers, such as Bolivia, is refined into cocaine in Colombia. The "cocaine cartel," which controls production and distribution, is said to be composed of no more than 12 families, located principally in Colombia and Bolivia. However, organized-crime interests in other South American countries are establishing themselves in the market.

Each year nearly half of all cocaine seized was shipped to the United States on private planes. Small planes evade controls and land on little-used airstrips or drop their cargos offshore to waiting speedboats.[36] Boats carrying drugs then mingle with local pleasure craft and bring the cargo to shore. Wholesalers who work for the Colombian cartels take care of the nationwide distribution. Some of the estimated 100,000 Colombians living illegally in the United States are thought to belong to the distribution apparatus.

Heroin "Just five years ago, almost all of the heroin seized came from Asia. Today, 32 percent of heroin seized can be traced to South America, with an estimated 20,000 hectares of opium poppies being cultivated in Colombia alone." This statement, made by the former head of the Justice Department's Drug Enforcement Administration, Thomas Constantine, sheds light on the recent expansion in scope of Colombia's cash crop. This diversification is a direct result of simple economics— while 1 kilogram of cocaine sells for $10,000 to $40,000 on the streets, an equal amount of South American heroin fetches anywhere from $85,000 to $180,000.

Production of heroin in all countries is organized by local warlords, illegitimate traders,

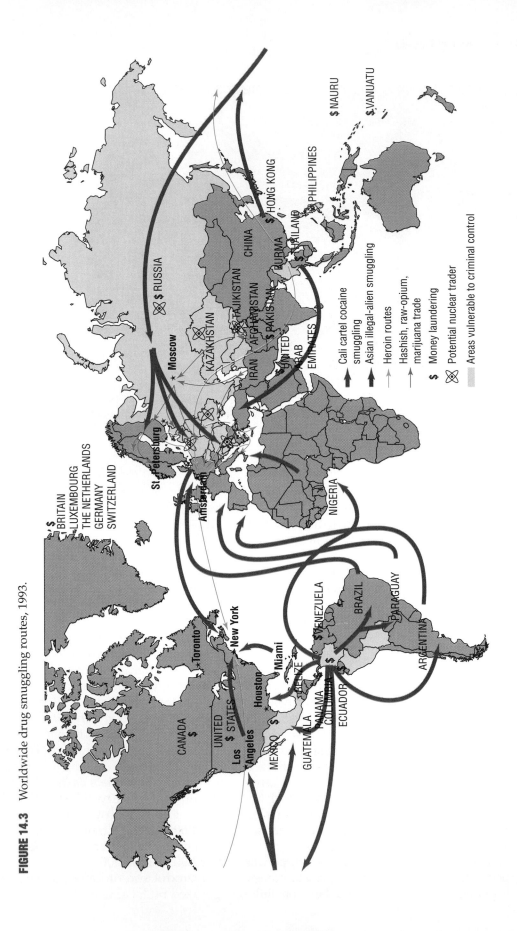

FIGURE 14.3 Worldwide drug smuggling routes, 1993.

Legend:
- Cali cartel cocaine smuggling
- Asian illegal-alien smuggling
- Heroin routes
- Hashish, raw-opium, marijuana trade
- $ Money laundering
- ⊗ Potential nuclear trader
- Areas vulnerable to criminal control

Labels on map: BRITAIN, LUXEMBOURG, THE NETHERLANDS, GERMANY, SWITZERLAND, RUSSIA, Moscow, KAZAKHSTAN, TAJIKISTAN, AFGHANISTAN, IRAN, PAKISTAN, UNITED ARAB EMIRATES, CHINA, BURMA, THAILAND, HONG KONG, PHILIPPINES, NAURU, VANUATU, St. Petersburg, Amsterdam, NIGERIA, CANADA, UNITED STATES, Toronto, New York, Los Angeles, Houston, Miami, MEXICO, BELIZE, GUATEMALA, PANAMA, COLOMBIA, ECUADOR, VENEZUELA, BRAZIL, PARAGUAY, ARGENTINA

414

and corrupt administrators; it is tending to come increasingly under the control of *triads*—organized-crime families of Chinese origin based in Hong Kong and Taiwan. More and more, heroin in the United States comes from Mexico. Most of the heroin from the Golden Crescent and Golden Triangle enters the United States on commercial aircraft, whereas Mexican heroin comes overland. In Europe and in the United States the traditional Sicilian Mafia families have assumed significant roles in the refining and distribution of heroin.

Did You Know

. . . that white intravenous drug users outnumber black users 5 to 1? However, for every 100 white addicts there are 5 arrests, compared with 20 arrests for every 100 black addicts.

Marijuana Because marijuana is bulky, smugglers initially transported it on oceangoing vessels. From January through October 1986, 87 percent of the total volume of marijuana seized was taken from privately owned pleasure craft or charter vessels not engaged in commercial trade. Today, most of the Colombian marijuana—about one-third of all marijuana imported into the United States—is shipped by sea. Mexican marijuana, trucked overland, makes up another third, and the remainder comes in by private plane from such countries as Belize and Jamaica. Hashish, a concentrated form of marijuana that comes predominantly from Pakistan (60 to 65 percent) and Lebanon (25 to 30 percent), is brought in by noncommercial ships.

Money Laundering The illegal drug economy is vast. Annual sales are estimated to be between $300 billion and $500 billion. The American drug economy alone generates $40 billion to $50 billion in sales. Profits are enormous, and no taxes are paid on them. Because the profits are "dirty money," they must undergo **money laundering.** Typically, the cash obtained from drug sales in the United States is physically smuggled out of the country because it cannot be legally exported without disclosure (Table 14.3).

Smuggling cash is not easy—$1 million in $20 bills weighs 100 pounds—yet billions of

TABLE 14.3 A Typical Money-Laundering Scheme

La Mina, The Mine, reportedly laundered $1.2 billion for the Colombian cartels over a 2-year period.

Currency from selling cocaine was packed in boxes labeled "jewelry" and sent by armored car to Ropex, a jewelry maker in Los Angeles.

↓

The cash was counted and deposited in banks but few suspicions were raised because the gold business is based on cash.

↓

Ropex then wire-transferred the money to New York banks in payment for fictitious gold purchased from Ronel, allegedly a gold bullion business.

↓

Ronel shipped Ropex bars of lead painted gold to complete the fake transaction. Ropex used the alleged sale of this gold to other jewelry businesses to cover further currency conversions.

↓

Ronel then transferred the funds from American banks to South American banks where the Colombian cartel could gain access to them.

Source: Adapted from "Getting Banks to Just Say 'No,'" *Business Week*, Apr. 17, 1989, p. 17; and Maggie Mahar, "Dirty Money: It Triggers a Bold New Attack in the War on Drugs," *Barron's*, **69** (June 1989): 6–38, at p. 7. From the U.S. Department of Justice, *Drugs, Crime and the Justice System* (Washington, D.C.: U.S. Government Printing Office, 1992).

dollars are exported, in false-bottomed suitcases and smugglers' vests, to countries that allow numbered bank accounts without identification of names (the Cayman Islands, Panama, Switzerland, Austria, and Liechtenstein, among others).

New methods of laundering drug profits, not involving physical transfer of cash, have recently been devised, such as bogus real estate transactions; purchase of gold, antiques, and art; and cybercurrency (microchip-based electronic money), which utilizes the Internet. Such transactions permit electronic transfer of drug funds worldwide with minimum chance of detection. Once deposited in foreign accounts, the funds are "clean" and can be returned to legitimate businesses and investments. They may also be used for illegal purposes, such as the purchase of arms for export to terrorist groups.

The Political Impact The political impact of the drug trade on producer countries is devastating. In the late 1970s and early 1980s, the government of Bolivia became completely corrupt.

The minister of justice was referred to as the "minister of cocaine." In Colombia, drug lords and terrorists combined their resources to wrest power from the democratically elected government. Thirteen supreme court judges and 167 police officers were killed; the minister of justice and the ambassador to Hungary were assassinated.

The message was that death was the price for refusal to succumb to drug corruption. In 1989 a highly respected Colombian presidential candidate who had come out against the cocaine cartel was assassinated. The government remained fragile and the situation precarious. Over the years, the scandal aroused by liaisons between notorious drug lords and high-ranking government officials has endured. A recent scandal, perhaps most injurious to diplomatic relations with the United States, was that involving Colombia's former president Ernesto Samper. Samper received $6 million toward his 1994 campaign fund from the renowned Cali cartel—the leader in cocaine trafficking. Despite his exoneration by Colombia's House of Representatives, the United States government sent an unequivocal message to President Samper by revoking his U.S. visa and decertifying Colombia (the United States "certifies" countries considered an ally in the drug war).

Nor is Colombia alone in its efforts to cope with the drug problem. Before General Manuel Noriega was arrested in a U.S. invasion of Panama to face charges of drug smuggling, he had made himself military dictator of Panama. By 1996 (7 years later), however, little had really changed:

President Ernesto Perez Balladares has admitted that his 1994 campaign received $51,000 from a Colombian businessman later jailed on drug charges. Other donations to the President are also under scrutiny. . . . Seven years after the military intervention, Panama's banking system once again is a conduit for drug traffickers laundering their profits. Secret numbered accounts, legal in Panama, prevent prosecutors from putting a name to a number. Lawyers create shell corporations with little more than a stroke of a pen and about $1,000. Those behind the companies remain a mystery. The collapse earlier this year of a Panamanian bank, under investigation in the US for money laundering, with links to two senior aides of the

president underscored, for many, the pervasiveness of the problem.[37]

Corruption and crime rule in all drug-producing countries. Government instability is the necessary consequence. Coups replace elections. The populations of these countries are not immune to addiction themselves. Several South American countries, including Colombia, Bolivia, and Peru, are now experiencing major addiction problems; Peru alone has some 60,000 addicts. The Asian narcotics-producing countries, which thought themselves immune to the addiction problem, also became victims of their own production. Pakistan now counts about 200,000 addicts.[38]

One of the more remarkable aspects of the expansion of the drug trade has been the spread of addiction and the drug economy to the Third World and to the newly democratic, formerly socialist countries. Of all political problems, however, the most vicious is the alliance that drug dealers have forged with terrorist groups in the Near East, in Latin America, and in Europe.[39]

Drug Control

In September 1989 President George Bush unveiled his antidrug strategy. On the international level, the president sought modest funding for the United Nations effort to combat the international narcotics drug traffic. He also called for far greater expenditures for bilateral cooperation with other countries to deal with producers and traffickers. This effort extends to crop eradication programs.[40] He singled out Colombia, Bolivia, and Peru for such efforts and immediately sent U.S. Army assistance, including helicopters and crews, to Colombia for use in that country's very difficult battle with the Medellín cartel.

On the national level, the strategy focused on federal aid to state and local police for street-level attacks on drug users and small dealers, for whom alternative punishments such as house arrest (confinement in one's home rather than in a jail cell) and boot camps (short but harsh incarceration with military drill) were started. It also called for rigorous enforcement of forfeiture laws, under which money is confiscated from offenders if it can be established that it came from the drug trade; property purchased with such money is also forfeited.[41] The Bush war on drugs followed a host of federal drug-control initiatives. All of them, like the Bush administration initiatives, have been at best only slightly effective.[42]

The Bush plan continued the American emphasis on law enforcement options for drug control. Treatment and prevention received only a fraction of the money allocated to traditional law enforcement efforts throughout the 1980s and early 1990s. The Clinton administration's approach, unveiled on February 9, 1994, earmarked $13 billion for a national strategy that emphasized antidrug education as well as treatment programs. His 1995 strategy, which targeted four major initiatives, was advanced by the current drug czar, Barry McCaffrey. McCaffrey placed a decided emphasis on treatment, prevention, domestic law enforcement, interdiction, and international control. The White House established a budget of almost $18 billion for the 1999 drug-control strategy, which continued to focus on law enforcement, education, and treatment, as well as on reducing the supply of drugs coming into the country.

Treatment The treatment approach to drug control is not new. During the late 1960s and into the 1970s, hope for the country's drug problem centered on treatment programs. These programs took a variety of forms, depending on the setting and modality, for example, self-help groups (Narcotics Anonymous, Cocaine Anonymous), psychotherapy, detoxification ("drying out" in a hospital), "rap" houses (neighborhood centers where addicts can come for group therapy sessions), various community social-action efforts (addicts clean up neighborhoods, plant trees, and so on), and—the two most popular—residential therapeutic communities and methadone maintenance programs.[43]

The *therapeutic community* is a 24-hour, total-care facility where former addicts and professionals work together to help addicts become drug-free. In *methadone maintenance* programs, addicts are given a synthetic narcotic, methadone, which prevents withdrawal symptoms (physical and psychological pain associ-

ated with giving up drugs), while addicts reduce their drug intake slowly over a period of time. Throughout the program addicts receive counseling designed to help them return to a normal life.

It is difficult to assess the success of most treatment programs. Even if individuals appear to be drug-free within a program, it is hard to find out what happens to them once they leave it (or even during a week when they do not show up). In addition, it may well be that the addicts who succeed in drug treatment programs are those who have already resolved to stop abusing drugs before they voluntarily come in for treatment; the real hard-core users may not even make an effort to become drug-free.

A program to divert drug offenders (users and purchasers) from criminal careers is the drug court, in which the judge has the option to divert nonviolent drug offenders to a counseling program in lieu of incarceration. Since the first drug court was established in Dade County, Florida, in 1989, 400 similar courts have been established in counties throughout the country. The S.T.O.P. program in Portland, Oregon, diverted 944 cases within an 18-month period and has a rearrest rate of 6 percent for the first year following completion of the program. Other drug courts enjoy similar success rates. The most recent diversion program is in Arizona, where all nonviolent drug offenders were diverted to treatment and probation in 1998. The program has not only had a high success rate in keeping people drug-free, but also saved the state an estimated $2.5 million during the first year of operation.[44]

Crime Surfing

http://www.bostoncoalition.org/

Interested in what major cities can do to combat drugs and violence? Find out what Boston is doing.

Education While drug treatment deals with the problem of addiction after the fact, education tries to prevent people from taking illegal drugs in the first place. The idea behind educational programs is straightforward: People who have information about the harmful effects of illegal drugs are likely to stay away from them. Sometimes the presentation of the facts has been coupled with scare techniques. Some well-known athletes and entertainers have joined the crusade with public-service messages ("a questionable approach," says Howard Abadinsky, "given the level of substance abuse reported in these groups").[45]

The educational approach has several drawbacks. Critics maintain that most addicts are quite knowledgeable about the potential consequences of taking drugs but think of them as just a part of the "game."[46] Most people who begin to use drugs believe they will never become addicted, even when they have information about addiction.[47] Inner-city youngsters do not lack information about the harmful effects of drugs. They learn about the dangers from daily exposure to addicts desperately searching for drugs, sleeping on the streets, going through withdrawal, and stealing family belongings to get money.[48]

Did You Know

. . . that under federal law a cocaine user with 100 grams of cocaine receives the same sentence as someone caught with 1 gram of crack, a cocaine derivative?

Legalization Despite increases in government funding for an expanded war on drugs, the goal of a drug-free society in the 1990s was not achieved and is hardly likely to be achieved within the next decade. There is much evidence that all the approaches, even the "new" ones, have been tried before with little or no effect. Some experts are beginning to advocate a very different approach—legalization. Their reasoning is that since the drug problem seems to elude all control efforts, why not deal with heroin and cocaine the same way we deal with alcohol and tobacco? In other words, why not subject these drugs to some government control and restrictions, but make them freely available to all adults?[49]

They argue that current drug-control policies impose tremendous costs on taxpayers without demonstrating effective results. In addition to spending less money on crime control, the government would make money on tax revenue from the sale of legalized drugs. This is, of course, a hotly debated issue. Given the dangers of drug abuse and the moral issues at stake, legalization surely offers no easy solution and has had little public support. However, the surgeon general of the United States, in 1994, mentioned the option of legalization—only to be rebuffed by the president.

ALCOHOL AND CRIME

Alcohol is another substance that contributes to social problems. One of the major differences between alcohol and the other drugs we have been discussing is that the sale and purchase of alcohol are legal in most jurisdictions of the United States. The average annual consumption of alcoholic beverages by each individual 14 years of age and over is equivalent to 591 cans of beer, or 115 bottles of wine, or 35 fifths of liquor; this is more than the average individual consumption of coffee and milk.[50] Alcohol is consumed at recreational events, business meetings, lunches and dinners at home, and celebrations; in short, drinking alcohol has become the expected behavior in many social situations.

Drinking is widespread among young people, but the rate of use has been fairly steady since 1994. Recent research demonstrates that 10.5 million current drinkers (9.2 percent of current drinkers) were 12 to 20 years old. Of this group, nearly 50 percent (5.1 million) engaged in binge drinking and over 20 percent (2.3 million) were classified as heavy drinkers. Individuals between the ages of 18 and 20 are the heaviest users; 53 percent reported using alcohol in the past 30 days. This amount is equivalent to the rate of use reported by those age 35 and older.[51] (See Table 14.2.)

The History of Legalization

Alcohol consumption is not new to our culture; in colonial days alcohol was considered safer and healthier than water. Still, the history of alcohol consumption is filled with controversy. Many people through the centuries have viewed it as wicked and degenerate. By the turn of the twentieth century, social reformers linked liquor to prostitution, poverty, the immigrant culture, and corrupt politics.

Various lobbying groups, such as the Women's Christian Temperance Union and the American Anti-Saloon League, bombarded politicians with demands for the prohibition of alcohol.[52] On January 16, 1920, the Eighteenth Amendment to the Constitution went into force, prohibiting the manufacture, sale, and transportation of alcoholic beverages. The Volstead Act of 1919 had already defined as "intoxicating liquor" any beverage that contained more than ½ of 1 percent alcohol.

Historians generally agree that no law in America has ever been more widely violated or more unpopular. Vast numbers of people continued to consume alcohol. It was easy to manufacture and to import. The illegal business brought tremendous profits to suppliers, and it could not be controlled by enforcement officers, who were too inefficient, too few, or too corrupt. The unlawful sale of alcohol was called "bootlegging." The term originated in the early practice of concealing liquor in one's boot to avoid payment of liquor taxes.

Bootlegging created empires for such gangsters as Al Capone and Dutch Schultz, as we saw in Chapter 13. Private saloons, or "speakeasies," prospered. Unpopular and unenforceable, the Eighteenth Amendment was repealed 13 years after its birth—on December 5, 1933. Except for a few places, the manufacture and sale of alcohol have been legal in the United States since that time.

Crime-Related Activities

The alcohol-related activities that have become serious social problems are violent crime, drunk driving, and public intoxication.

Violence National surveys of inmates in jails and prisons show the following:

- About 40 percent of the convicted offenders incarcerated for violent crimes used alcohol immediately before the crimes.
- About 40 percent of prison inmates engaged in binge drinking in the past.
- Over one-third of prison inmates have gotten into a physical fight while drinking or directly afterwards.

- About one-third of state inmates convicted of violent crimes described themselves as daily drinkers.[53]

For many decades criminologists have probed the relationship between alcohol and violence. Marvin Wolfgang, in a study of 588 homicides in Philadelphia, found that alcohol was present in two-thirds of all homicide cases (both victim and offender, 44 percent; victim only, 9 percent; offender only, 11 percent).[54] Similar findings were reported from northern Sweden: Two-thirds of the offenders who committed homicide between 1970 and 1981 and almost half of their victims were intoxicated when the crime was committed.[55]

Many other offenses show a significant relationship between alcohol and violence. In the United States, 58 percent of those convicted for assault and 64 percent of offenders who assaulted police officers had been drinking.[56] In about one-third of rapes, the offender, the victim, or both had been drinking immediately before the attack.[57] The role of alcohol in violent family disputes has been increasingly recognized. Among 2413 American couples, the rate of severe violence by the husband was 2.10 per 100 couples in homes where the husbands were never drunk and 30.89 per 100 couples in homes where the husbands were drunk "very often."[58]

Many explanations have been offered for the relationship between alcohol and violence.[59] Some studies focus on the individual. When people are provoked, for example, alcohol can reduce restraints on aggression.[60] Alcohol also escalates aggression by reducing awareness of consequences.[61] Other studies analyze the social situation in which drinking takes place. Experts argue that in some situations aggressive behavior is considered appropriate or is even expected when people drink together.[62]

Drunk Driving The effect of alcohol on driving is causing continuing concern. The incidence of drunk driving, referred to in statutes as "driving under the influence" and "driving while intoxicated" (depending on the level of alcohol found in the blood), has been steadily rising. Statistics indicate the extent of the problem:

- Between 1990 and 1997 the number of arrests for driving under the influence decreased 19 percent, while the number of licensed drivers increased nearly 15 percent.

- Before arrest for driving while intoxicated (DWI), the majority of convicted offenders drink at least 4 ounces of pure alcohol within 4 hours.

- About 45 percent of prison inmates have driven while intoxicated.

- In 1996 there were an estimated 17,126 alcohol-related traffic fatalities (40.9 percent of all traffic fatalities for that year).

- The annual cost of drunk driving (property damage, medical bills, and so on) is estimated at $24 billion.

- There were 1,477,300 arrests for driving under the influence in 1997.[63]

Cari Lightner, age 13, was killed in May 1980 by a drunk driver while she was walking on a sidewalk.[64] The driver had been arrested only a few days before on a DUI charge. The victim's mother, Candy, took action almost immediately to push for new legislation that would mandate much stiffer penalties for drunk driving. It was difficult at first to get government to respond, but she did get the attention of journalists. By the end of the year in which Cari died, Mrs. Lightner had organized the Governor's Task Force on Drinking and Driving in California.

And her own advocacy group, Mothers Against Drunk Driving (MADD), was in the national spotlight. MADD's members were people who themselves had been injured or whose family members had been injured or killed in an accident involving an intoxicated driver. The organization has grown to more than 300 chapters.[65] Remove Intoxicated Drivers (RID) and Students Against Drunk Drivers (SADD) have joined the campaign.

The citizens' groups called public attention to a major health and social problem, demanded action, and got it. Congress proclaimed one week each December to be Drunk and Drugged Awareness Week, and the Presidential Commission on Drunk Driving was formed. Candy Lightner was appointed a commissioner. The federal government attached the distribution of state highway funds to various anti-drunk-driving measures, thereby pressuring the states into putting recommendations into action. Old laws have been changed, and new laws have been passed.

After the ratification in 1971 of the Twenty-Sixth Amendment to the U.S. Constitution, which lowered the voting age to 18 years, many states lowered their minimum-age requirement for the purchase and sale of alcoholic beverages. By 1983, 33 states had done so; but by 1987, all but one state had raised the minimum drinking age back to 21. Under New York's Civil Forfeiture Law, the government can take any car involved in a felony drunk-driving case, sell it, and give the money to the victims. Texas has a similar law.[66] Tuscarawas County in Ohio places brightly colored orange plates on cars of drivers whose licenses have been suspended for drunk driving.[67]

Other objectives of legislation have been to limit the "happy hours" during which bars serve drinks at reduced prices, to shorten hours when alcoholic beverages can be sold, to make hosts and bartenders liable for damages if their guests or patrons drink too much and become involved in an accident, to limit advertisements, and to put health warnings on bottles. Most states have increased their penalties for drunk driving to include automatic license suspension, higher minimum fines, and even mandatory jail sentences.

Thus far the results of such legislation are mixed. A study carried out in Seattle, Minneapolis, and Cincinnati found that such measures did indeed lower the number of traffic deaths, while other investigations did not show positive results.[68] Nevertheless, drunk driving has achieved national attention, and even modern technology is being used in the effort to find solutions: Japanese and American technicians have come up with a device that locks the ignition system and can be unlocked only when the attached Breathalyzer (which registers alcohol in the blood) indicates that the

Alcohol intoxication plays a part in some of the most significant tragedies of our time. In 1997, Princess Diana died in an accident in which the driver's blood-alcohol level was more than three times the legal limit. His blood level was compounded with prescription drugs including the antidepressant Prozac.

driver is sober.[69] California, Washington, Texas, Michigan, and Oregon have passed legislation authorizing its use.

SEXUAL MORALITY OFFENSES

All societies endeavor to regulate sexual behavior, although what specifically is considered not permissible has varied from society to society and from time to time. The legal regulation of sexual conduct in Anglo-American law has been greatly influenced by both the Old and the New Testaments. In the Middle Ages the enforcement of laws pertaining to sexual morality was the province of church courts. Today, to the extent that immorality is still illegal, it is the regular criminal courts that enforce such laws.

Morality laws have always been controversial, whether they seek to prevent alcohol abuse or to prohibit certain forms of sexual behavior or its public display or depiction. Sexual activity other than intercourse between spouses for the purpose of procreation has been severely penalized in many societies and until only recently in the United States. Sexual intercourse between unmarried persons ("lewd cohabitation"), seduction of a female by promise of marriage, and all forms of "unnatural" sexual rela-

tions were serious crimes, some carrying capital sentences, as late as the nineteenth century. In 1962 the Model Penal Code proposed some important changes. Fornication and lewd cohabitation were dropped from the list of offenses, as was homosexual intercourse between consenting adults.

The idea behind these changes is that the sexual relations of consenting adults should be beyond the control of the law, not only because throughout history such legal efforts have proved ineffective but also because the harm to society, if any, is too slight to warrant the condemnation of law. "The state's power to regulate sexual conduct ought to stop at the bedroom door or at the barn door," said sex researcher Alfred Kinsey four decades ago.[70]

Although the Model Penal Code (MPC) has removed or limited sanctions for conduct among consenting adults, the code retains strong prohibitions against sexual activities involving children. Penalties are severe for **statutory rape** (intercourse by an adult male with an underage female regardless of consent), deviate sexual intercourse with a child, corruption of a minor, sexual assault, and endangering the welfare of a child. Of course, the recommendations of the American Law Institute are not always accepted by state legislatures.

Let us take a close look at three existing offenses involving sexual morality: "deviate sexual intercourse by force or imposition," prostitution, and pornography.

"Deviate Sexual Intercourse by Force or Imposition"

The Model Penal Code defines "deviate sexual intercourse" as "sexual intercourse per os or per anum [by mouth or by anus] between human beings who are not husband and wife, and any form of sexual intercourse with an animal" [sec. 213.2(1)]. The common law called such sexual acts **sodomy,** after the biblical city of Sodom, which the Lord destroyed for its wickedness, presumably because its citizens had engaged in such acts. The common law dealt harshly with sodomy, making it a capital offense and referring to it as *crimen innominatum*—a crime not to be mentioned by name.

Yet other cultures, including ancient Greece, did not frown on homosexual activities. And Alfred Kinsey reminded us that homosexual (from the Greek word *homos,* meaning "same") relations are common among all mammals, of which humans are but one species.[71] The MPC subjects "deviate sexual intercourse" between two human beings to punishment only if it is accomplished by severe compulsion or if the other person is incapable of granting consent or is a child less than 10 years old. To conservative lawmakers, this model legislation is far too liberal; to liberals, it does not go far enough. Generally, liberal thinkers prefer the law not to interfere with the sexual practices of consenting adults at all.

The gay and lesbian rights movements have done much to destigmatize consensual, private adult sexual relationships. Yet legislatures have been slow to respond, and the U.S. Supreme Court has taken a conservative stance as well. In 1986 the Court sustained a Georgia statute that criminalizes consensual sexual acts between adults of the same gender, even if they are performed in the privacy of one's home.[72]

Prostitution

Not so long ago it was a crime to be a prostitute.[73] The law punished women for a status acquired on the basis of sexual intercourse with more than one man. Under some statutes it was not even necessary to prove that money was paid for the sexual act. The Supreme Court ruled in 1962—in a case involving the status of being a drug addict—that criminal liability can be based only on conduct, that is, on doing something in violation of law.[74] This decision would seem to apply to prostitution as well. Therefore, one can no longer be penalized for being a prostitute. But soliciting for sex is an act, not a status, and nearly all states make solicitation of sex for money the misdemeanor of **prostitution.**

The Uniform Crime Reports recorded 101,900 arrests for prostitution and commercialized vice during 1997.[75] This represents a steady increase in arrests since 1994 (Figure 14.4).

The number would be extremely high if we were to include all acts of sexual favor granted in return for some gratuity. Even if the number were limited to straightforward cash transactions (including, nowadays, credit card transactions), there is no way of arriving at a figure. Many persons may act as prostitutes for a while and then return to legitimate lifestyles. There are part-time and full-time prostitutes, male and female prostitutes, itinerant and resident prostitutes, street hookers and high-priced escorts who do not consider themselves prostitutes.[76]

Many law enforcement agencies do not relish the task of suppressing prostitution. In some jurisdictions the police have little time to spend on vice control, given the extent of violent and property crimes. Thus, when prostitutes are arrested, it is likely to be in response to demands by community groups, business establishments, or church leaders to "clean up the neighborhood." Occasionally, the police find it expedient to arrest prostitutes because they may divulge information about unsolved crimes, such as narcotics distribution, theft, receiving stolen property, or organized crime.

Prostitution encompasses a variety of both acts and actors. The prostitute, female or male, is not alone in the business of prostitution. A **pimp** provides access to prostitutes and protects and exploits them, living off their proceeds. There are still madams who maintain houses of prostitution. And finally, there are the patrons of prostitutes, popularly called "johns."

FIGURE 14.4 Estimated number of prostitution arrests in the United States, 1970–1997.

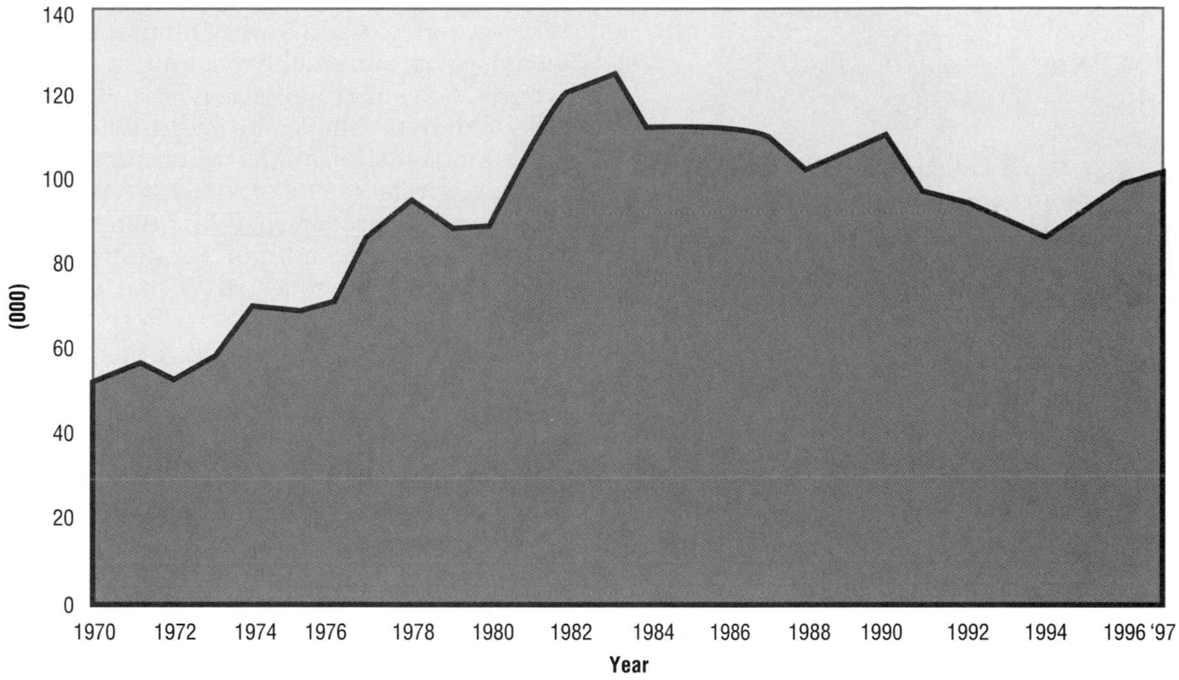

Source: Uniform Crime Reports, 1994–1998.

Ordinarily, it is not a criminal offense to patronize a prostitute; yet the framers of the MPC proposed to criminalize this act. The section was hotly debated before the American Law Institute. A final vote of the members rejected criminalization.

Researchers have found that many prostitutes come from broken homes and poor neighborhoods and are school dropouts. Yet all social classes contribute to the prostitution hierarchy. High-priced call girls, many of them well-educated women, may operate singly or out of agencies. The television "blue channels" that broadcast after midnight in most metropolitan areas carry commercials advertising the availability of call girls, their phone numbers, and sometimes their specialties. At the next lower level of the prostitution hierarchy are the massage parlor prostitutes. When Shirley, a masseuse, was asked, "Do you consider yourself a prostitute?" she answered: "Yes, as well as a masseuse, and a healer, and a couple of other things."[77] One rung lower on the prostitution ladder are the "inmates" (a term used by the MPC) of the houses of prostitution, locally called bordellos, whorehouses, cathouses, or red-light houses.

According to people "in the life" (prostitution), the streetwalkers are the least-respected class in the hierarchy. They are the "working girls" or "hookers." They are found clustered on their accustomed street corners, on thoroughfares, or in truck and bus depots, dressed in bright attire, ready to negotiate a price with any passerby. Sexual services are performed in vehicles or in nearby "hot-sheet" hotel rooms. Life for these prostitutes—some of whom are transvestite males—is dangerous and grim. Self-reports suggest that many are drug addicts and have been exposed to HIV.[78] Other varieties of prostitution range from the legal houses that a few counties permit to operate in Nevada to troupes of prostitutes who travel from one place of opportunity to another (work projects, farm labor camps, construction sites) and bar ("B") girls who entertain customers in cocktail lounges and make themselves available for sexual activities for a price.

Popular, political, and scientific opinions on prostitution have changed, no doubt largely

For years, the Mustang Ranch was one of many legal brothels in Las Vegas. Bureau of Land Management officials in Nevada, however, are interested in taking over the Mustang Ranch, reopening it as a visitor center. The Ranch property was forfeited to the federal government several years ago after guilty verdicts were obtained against the ranch's owner in a fraud and racketeering trial.

because prostitution has changed. Around the turn of the century it probably was true that a large number of prostitutes had been forced into the occupation by unscrupulous men. Indeed, it was this pattern that led to the enactment of the White Slave Traffic Act (called the Mann Act, after the senator who proposed the bill), prohibiting the interstate transportation of females for purposes of prostitution. There is some evidence that today the need for money, together with few legitimate opportunities to obtain it, prompts many young women and men to become prostitutes.

Sex researcher Paul Gebhard found in 1969 that only 4 percent of U.S. prostitutes were forced into prostitution. More recently

Jennifer James found that the majority entered the life because of its financial rewards.[79] Whatever view we take of adult prostitutes as victims of a supposedly victimless criminal activity, one subgroup clearly is a victimized class: children, female and male, who are enticed and sometimes forced into prostitution, especially in large cities. Some are runaways, picked up by procurers at bus depots; some are simply "street children"; and others have been abused and molested by the adults in their lives.[80]

Pornography

Physical sexual contact is a basic component of both sodomy and prostitution. **Pornography** requires no contact at all; it simply portrays sexually explicit material. Statutes in all states make it a criminal offense to produce, offer for sale, sell, distribute, or exhibit pornographic (sometimes called obscene, lewd, or lascivious) material. Federal law prohibits the transportation of such material in interstate commerce and outlaws the use of the mails, the telephone, radio, and television for the dissemination of pornographic material.[81]

The Problem of Definition The term "pornographic" is derived from the Greek *pornographos* ("writing of harlots," or descriptions of the acts of harlots). The term "obscene" comes from the Latin *ob* ("against," "before") plus *caenum* ("filth"), or possibly from *obscena* ("offstage"). In Roman theatrical performances, disgusting and offensive parts of plays took place offstage, out of sight but not out of hearing of the audience.[82] Courts and legislators have used the two terms interchangeably, but nearly all statutes and decisions deal with pornography (with the implication of sexual arousal) rather than with obscenity (with its implication of filth).[83]

Scholars generally agree that the statutes in existence appear to be addressed primarily to pornographic materials.[84] What, then, is the contemporary meaning of "pornography"? The Model Penal Code (1962) says that a publication is pornographic (obscene or indecent) "if, considered as a whole, its predominant appeal is to prurient inter-

- The dean of the Harvard Divinity School recently resigned his post after a computer tech discovered an extensive collection of hard-core pornography on his Harvard-owned computer. This Lutheran minister, divinity school dean, scholar, and father of two committed no crime, but his actions violated the school's ban on having materials that are "inappropriate, obscene, bigoted or abusive" on school computers.(1) The case received widespread media coverage.

- A deputy sheriff from Palmdale, California, was indicted on federal charges for child pornography. The evidence was found on his hard drive. Also, he allegedly tried to solicit sex via the Internet from a person he thought was a 13-year-old girl. The deputy sheriff faces up to 15 years in prison if convicted.(2)

- A Cub Scout leader from Long Island was arrested for having child pornography on his computer, which he downloaded from the Internet and reportedly swapped with other porn peddlers.(3)

- A 23-year-old woman started her own porn website 2 years ago as a hobby. She expects to make about $50,000 a week on the site in the next year. This money will allow her to cut back on making movies and dancing at clubs. She is one of many women in the porn industry who have set up their own websites as alternative businesses.(4)

- Some men find themselves "addicted" to cyberporn, spending as much as 80 hours per week online. Their real sex lives and relationships are damaged as online sex becomes more important and fulfilling than the real thing, leading some marriages to end in divorce.(5)

The Internet provides an ever-increasing number of avenues for the distribution of pornography. For entrepreneurs setting up porn sites, the Internet is proving quite lucrative. However, some of those who use it find themselves in legal trouble when they go beyond legal pornography to child pornography or use sex chat rooms to solicit sex with children. Even those who stick to legal porn may face problems related to their jobs or their personal relationships. It is unlikely that pornography—both legal and illegal—on the Internet will decrease in the years to come.

Of all the issues regarding pornography on the Internet, one of the most hotly debated is censorship. While some programs exist that limit access to porn sites, they do not prevent the exploitation of children or keep those who wish to access the sites from doing so. Child pornographers are creative and adaptable, shying away from explicit child pornography. Many frequent preteen and teen nudism news groups and sites, where thousands of photographs of nude children await them in an apparently "constitutionally protected" cyberspace. The question remains as to what can be done to limit children's access to pornographic sites as well as to prevent their exploitation on the Internet.

Sources

1. Trent Gegax. "An Odd Fall from Grace: Computer Porn Undoes a Divinity-School Dean," *Newsweek*, May 31, 1999, p. 70.
2. "Deputy in Custody Allegedly Tried to Solicit Sex in Internet Chat Room," *City News Service*. Oct. 22, 1999.
3. "Scout Leader Accused of Child Pornography," *New York Times*, Oct. 22, 1999. p. B14.
4. John Leland, "More Bang for the Buck: How Sex on the Internet Has Transformed the Business of Pornography," *Newsweek*, Oct. 11, 1999, p. 73.
5. Greg Gutfield, "The Sex Drive: Web Pornography Has Turned Computers into Sex Objects, and Men, by the Millions, Are Hooking Up, Should You?" *Men's Health*, Oct. 1, 1999, p. 116.

Questions for Discussion

1. Why do you think seemingly normal individuals procure child pornography on the Internet or become "addicted" to cyberporn?
2. What can society do to limit the damage to children by child pornographers who use the Internet as a means of distribution? What should be done with those who are caught?

---

ests," and if, "in addition, it goes substantially beyond customary limits in describing or representing such matters" (sec. 251.4). This definition, which is full of ambiguities, was to play a major role in several Supreme Court decisions.

Two presidential commissions were no more successful in defining the term. The Commission on Obscenity and Pornography (1970) avoided a definition and used instead the term "explicit sexual material."[85] The Attorney General's Commission on Pornography (1986) gave no definition.[86] The definition created by a British parliamentary committee in 1979 seems to describe pornography best:

> A pornographic representation combines two features: It has a certain function or intention, to arouse its audience sexually, and also a certain content, explicit representation of sexual materials (organs, postures, activity, etc.).[87]

This definition indicates nothing about any danger inherent in pornography. The law will step in

"I thought I was going to work as a waitress," a young Dominican, transported to Greece, told BBC television, her eyes welling with tears. "Then they said if I didn't have sex, I'd be sent back to Santo Domingo without a penny. I was beaten, burned with cigarettes. I knew nobody. I was a virgin. I held out for five days, crying, with no food. [Eventually] I lost my honor and my virginity for $25."(1)

This woman's story is a common one. While some women become pros-

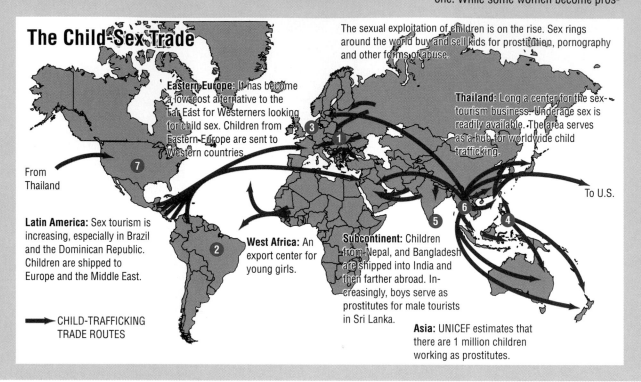

The Child-Sex Trade

The sexual exploitation of children is on the rise. Sex rings around the world buy and sell kids for prostitution, pornography and other forms of abuse.

Eastern Europe: It has become a low-cost alternative to the Far East for Westerners looking for child sex. Children from Eastern Europe are sent to Western countries.

Thailand: Long a center for the sex-tourism business. Underage sex is readily available. The area serves as a hub for worldwide child trafficking.

From Thailand

To U.S.

Latin America: Sex tourism is increasing, especially in Brazil and the Dominican Republic. Children are shipped to Europe and the Middle East.

West Africa: An export center for young girls.

Subcontinent: Children from Nepal, and Bangladesh are shipped into India and then farther abroad. Increasingly, boys serve as prostitutes for male tourists in Sri Lanka.

Asia: UNICEF estimates that there are 1 million children working as prostitutes.

→ CHILD-TRAFFICKING TRADE ROUTES

---

only when pornography is exhibited or distributed in a manner calculated to produce harm.

Historically, that harm has been seen as a negative effect on public morals, especially those of children. That was the stance taken by many national and local societies devoted to the preservation of public morality in the nineteenth century. More recently, the emphasis has shifted to the question of whether the availability and use of pornography produce actual, especially violent, victimization of women, children, or, for that matter, men.

Pornography and Violence The National Commission on Obscenity and Pornography in 1970 and the Attorney General's Commission on Pornography in 1986 reviewed the evidence of an association between pornography, on the one hand, and violence and crime, on the other. The National Commission provided funding for more than 80 studies to examine public attitudes toward pornography, experiences with pornography, the association between the availability of pornography and crime rates, the experience of sex offenders with pornography, and the relation between pornography and behavior. The commission concluded:

> [E]mpirical research designed to clarify the question has found no evidence to date that exposure to explicit sexual materials plays a significant role in the causations of delinquent or criminal behavior among youth or adults. The Commission cannot conclude that exposure to erotic materials is a factor in the causation of sex crimes or sex delinquency.[88]

Between 1970 (when the National Commission reported its findings) and 1986 (when the Attorney General's Commission issued its report), hundreds of studies have been conducted on this question. For example:

- Researchers reported in 1977 that when male students were exposed to erotic stimuli, those stimuli neither inhibited nor

titutes by choice, many are forced into it. The growing sex trade around the world needs a constant supply of bodies, and it is getting them however it can. The statistics are horrifying: For the brothels of Bombay, some 7000 adolescents from Nepal's Himalayan hill villages are sold to slave traders each year. In Brazil the number of girls forced into prostitution in mining camps is estimated at 25,000. Japan's bars feature approximately 70,000 Thai "hostesses" working as sex slaves. Some 200,000 Bangladeshi women have been kidnapped into prostitution in Pakistan.(1)

The numbers of underage prostitutes are equally shocking, whether the children were sold into slavery or are trying to survive in a harsh world by selling their bodies: 800,000 in Thailand; 400,000 in India; 250,000 in Brazil; and 60,000 in the Philippines. Child prostitution recently has increased in Russian and East European cities, with an estimated 1000 youngsters working in Moscow alone.(2) In Vietnam, fathers may act as pimps for their daughters to get money for the family to survive:

> Dr. Hoa, [a] pediatrician from Vietnam, said she asked the fathers of her young patients why they sold their daughters' services. "One father came with his 12-year-old daughter," Dr. Hoa recalled. "She was bleeding from her wounds and as torn as if she had given birth. He told me, 'We've earned $300, so it's enough. She can stop now.' "(3)

The physical wounds suffered by underage prostitutes are part of the terrible irony of the growing market for sex with children. Customers request children under the mistaken belief that they are less likely to be infected with the virus that causes AIDS. In fact, because children are so likely to incur injuries in intercourse, they are more vulnerable to infection.(2)

Experts at a 1993 conference on the sex trade and human rights cited the global AIDS epidemic, pornography, peep shows, and "sex tours" as factors responsible for the increasing demand for child prostitutes.(3) Organized sex tours form a large part of the market for bodies of any age; Taiwan, South Korea, the Philippines, and Thailand have been favorite destinations for sex tourists, and many other places are gaining in popularity.

Sources

1. Margot Hornblower, "The Skin Trade," *Time*, June 21, 1993, pp. 45–51.
2. Michael S. Serrill, "Defiling the Children," *Time*, June 21, 1993, pp. 53–55.
3. Marlise Simons, "The Sex Market: Scourge on the World's Children," *New York Times*, Apr. 9, 1993, p. A3.

Questions for Discussion

1. How would you begin to fight the exploitation of women and children in the sex market?
2. What are some of the forces at work that would make such a fight difficult?

had any effect on levels of aggression. When the same research team worked with female students, they found that mild erotic stimuli inhibited aggression and that stronger erotic stimuli increased it.[89]

• Researchers who exposed students to sexually explicit films during six consecutive weekly sessions in 1984 concluded that exposure to increasingly explicit erotic stimuli led to a decrease in both arousal responses and aggressive behavior. In short, these subjects became habituated to the pornography.[90]

After analyzing such studies, the Attorney General's Commission concluded that nonviolent and nondegrading pornography is not significantly associated with crime and aggression. It did conclude, however, that exposure to pornographic materials:

> (1) leads to a greater acceptance of rape myths and violence against women; (2) results in pronounced effects when the victim is shown enjoying the use of force or violence; (3) is arousing for rapists and for some males in the general population; and (4) has resulted in sexual aggression against women in the laboratory.[91]

The Feminist View: Victimization To feminists, these conclusions supported the call for greater restrictions on the manufacture and dissemination of pornographic material. The historian Joan Hoff has coined the term "pornerotic," meaning:

> any representation of persons that sexually objectifies them and is accompanied by actual or implied violence in ways designed to encourage readers or viewers that such sexual subordination of women (or children or men) is acceptable behavior or an innocuous form of sex education.[92]

Hoff's definition also suggests that pornography, obscenity, and erotica may do far more than offend sensitivities. Such material may victimize not only the people who are depicted but all women (or men or children, if they are the people shown). Pornographers have been accused of promoting the exploitation, objectification, and degradation of women. Many people who call for the abolition of violent pornography argue that it also promotes violence toward women. Future state and federal legislation is likely to focus on violent and violence-producing pornography, not on pornography in general.

The Legal View: Supreme Court Rulings

Ultimately, defining pornographic acts subject to legal prohibition is a task for the U.S. Supreme Court. The First Amendment to the Constitution guarantees freedom of the press. In a series of decisions culminating in *Miller v. California* (1973), however, the Supreme Court articulated the view that obscenity, really meaning pornography, is outside the protection of the Constitution. Following the lead of the Model Penal Code and reinterpreting its own earlier decisions, the Court announced the following standard for judging a representation as obscene or pornographic:

- The average person, applying contemporary community standards, would find that the work, taken as a whole, appeals to prurient interests.

- The work depicts or describes, in a patently offensive way, sexual conduct specifically defined by the applicable state law.

- The work, taken as a whole, lacks serious literary, artistic, political, or scientific value.[93]

While this proposed standard is flexible enough to be expanded or contracted as standards change over time and from place to place, its terms are so vague that they give little guidance to local law enforcement officers or to federal and state courts. In 1987 the Supreme Court addressed this problem and modified the Miller decision. In *Pope v. Illinois* the Court ruled that the third aspect of Miller (that the work has "no value") may be judged by an objective test rather than by local community standards. Justice Byron White wrote for the majority:

> The proper inquiry is not whether an ordinary person of any given community will find serious lit-

erary, artistic, political, or scientific value in the allegedly obscene material, but whether a reasonable person would find such value in the material, taken as a whole.[94]

Whether this test will make juries' tasks easier when they must decide whether a film or magazine is pornographic or obscene is still not clear.

Pornography and the Internet

Warning! This site contains sexually oriented material intended for consenting adults at least 21 years old.

Any child with basic knowledge of a computer and a minimal amount of curiosity can, with a few clicks of a mouse, open a doorway to the world of cyberporn: pictures of adults having sexual intercourse, adults having intercourse with animals, video clips of adults having sex with children, and guides to bordellos, massage parlors, and various pleasure districts—both local and international.[95]

Censorship of the Internet has been a heavily debated issue in recent times. Almost everyone agrees that access of minors to pornographic material over the Internet should be restricted, but the primary point of contention remains: Who should be responsible for policing access to such material? Parents? Educators? The government? Responding to a nationwide outcry, Congress passed the Communications Decency Act (CDA) on February 8, 1996. This portion of the Telecommunications Decency Act of 1996 made it a felony to "knowingly use a telecommunications device or interactive computer to send an indecent communication to a child or to use a computer to display indecent material in a manner accessible to a child." Violations of this act are punishable by up to 2 years' imprisonment and a fine of $250,000.

Four months after the passage of this law, however, a federal court in Philadelphia ruled that it is in conflict with the constitutional right to free speech. According to the court, blocking enforcement of the CDA was justified because

Anyone with a computer and a modem can access cyber pornography. Pornography of all sorts—from child pornography to bondage and S & M—is available on binary files in newsgroups, chat rooms, bulletin boards, and individual websites. The FBI, U.S. Customs Service, Department of Justice, and U.S. Postal Service have committed significant resources to investigate and prosecute distributors and consumers of child pornography.

(1) the term "indecent" was found to be impermissibly vague; and (2) while the CDA could restrict Americans from disseminating "indecent" material, it had no jurisdiction over communications originating outside the United States and would thus be ineffective. Existing federal and state laws, however, still ban the sale and possession of child pornography.

One of the biggest issues surrounding government regulation of pornography on the Internet is the lack of global cooperation. The recent conviction of the head of the German division of the American online service CompuServe for the spread of child pornography on the Internet highlights this fact. Legislation on pornography varies around the world, and thus means that pornography can be easily sent across borders. Strategies are currently being developed by several international agencies to increase communication, provide hot lines for users to report illegal material, make laws more unified, and prevent the exploitation of children on a global scale.

Another significant issue is the fine line between what some call eroticism and others call child pornography. Perhaps the most famous photographer of young girls—David Hamilton—prides himself on belonging to an elite group of art photographers. His books—which no doubt appeal to child pornographers—are carried by most large chain bookstores and are "on" the Internet. But is this art or child pornography? Is it constitutionally protected or should it be criminally prosecuted? These two questions will be at the forefront of a debate about pornography on and off the Web.

In the wake of the continued controversy over "cybersmut," several computer programs have been developed to assist parents and educators in regulating children's access to the Internet. Programs such as Net Nanny, Cyber Patrol, and Surf Watch are designed to block access to sites deemed inappropriate for children.

These programs, however, are far from effective. The software must be continually updated to keep up with the new sites added on a daily basis. If activated by certain keywords, access may also be limited to potentially educational sites (such as those related to sexual harassment). Also, the cost of implementing such programs in a particular school district could run into tens of thousands of dollars.

The Gap between Behavior and Law
When we examine sexual morality offenses, we note an enormous gap between the goals of law and actual behavior. As long ago as the late 1940s and early 1950s the pioneering Kinsey reports brought us evidence about this gap. Ac-

cording to these studies, of the total white male population in the United States:

- 69 percent had had some experience with prostitutes.
- Between 23 and 37 percent had had extramarital intercourse.
- 37 percent had had at least one homosexual experience.[96]

Among women:

- 26 percent could be expected to have extramarital intercourse by age 40.

- 19 percent had had some physical contact with other females which was deliberately and consciously, at least on the part of one of the partners, intended to be sexual.[97]

Morton Hunt noted that the frequency with which Americans were breaking legally imposed moral standards had increased significantly by the 1970s, yet far fewer American men were buying sex from prostitutes than had done so in the 1940s.[98] This finding raised the question of whether the sexual revolution of the 1960s and 1970s made access to sexual partners more freely available.

REVIEW

Intoxicating substances have been used for religious, medicinal, and recreational purposes throughout history. Lifestyles of people who use them are as varied as the drugs they favor.

Governments have repeatedly tried to prevent the abuse of these substances. The drug problem today is massive, and it grows more serious every year. Heroin and cocaine in particular are associated with many crimes. A vast international criminal empire has been organized to promote the production and distribution of drugs. Efforts of law enforcement and health agencies to control the drug problem take the forms of international cooperation in stemming drug trafficking, treatment of addicts, education of the public, and arrest and incarceration of offenders. Some observers, comparing the drug problem with the wide evasion of the Prohibition amendment and the consequent rise in crime, believe that drugs should be legalized.

Legalization of alcoholic beverages, however, has not solved all problems related to alcohol. The abuse of alcohol has been reliably linked to violence, and the incidence of drunk driving has increased so alarmingly that citizen groups have formed to combat the problem.

The legal regulation of sexual conduct has undergone striking changes in recent decades. Many sexual "offenses" once categorized as capital crimes no longer concern society or government. In this sphere, research has done much to influence public opinion and, consequently, legislation. Pornography, however, remains a hotly debated issue.

YOU BE THE CRIMINOLOGIST

Significant debate continues over how to reduce drug use and what to do with users and dealers. If you were to make a recommendation to the president on how to design the next drug-control strategy, what would you recommend? On what evidence would you base your recommendations?

KEY TERMS

The numbers next to the terms refer to the pages on which the terms are defined.

money laundering (415)

pimp (422)

pornography (424)

prostitution (422)

sodomy (422)

statutory rape (421)

NOTES

1. Christopher S. Wren, "A Pipeline of the Poor Feeds the Flow of Heroin," *New York Times,* Feb. 21, 1999, p. 37.
2. Arthur Santana, "For Liz, a Heroin User, Time Is Running Out—Health Officials Estimate 15,000 Addicts in King County," *Seattle Times,* July 12, 1999, p. B1.
3. David Heinzmann, "Violence No Stranger Where Boy Shot; 4-Year-Old Victim of Gun

Battle in Good Condition," *Chicago Tribune,* Oct. 9, 1999, p. 5. See also Robert C. Davis and Arthur J. Lurigio, *Fighting Back: Neighborhood Antidrug Strategies* (Thousand Oaks, Calif.: Sage, 1996); Bureau of Justice Statistics, *Guns Used in Crime* (Washington, D.C.: U.S. Department of Justice, 1995); Susan J. Popkin, Lynn M. Olson, Arthur J. Lurigio, et al., "Sweeping Out Drugs and Crime: Residents' Views of the Chicago Housing Authority's Public Housing Drug Elimination Program," *Journal of Research in Crime and Delinquency,* **41** (1995): 73–99.

4. Mark D. Merlin, *On the Trail of the Ancient Opium Poppy* (Rutherford, N.J.: Fairleigh Dickinson University Press, 1984). For a historic account of alcohol consumption, see Harvey A. Siegal and James A. Inciardi, "A Brief History of Alcohol," in *The American Drug Scene: An Anthology,* ed. James A. Inciardi and Karen McElrath (Los Angeles: Roxbury, 1995).

5. Howard Abadinsky, *Drug Abuse: An Introduction* (Chicago: Nelson Hall, 1989), pp. 30–31, 54. For the medicinal benefits of marijuana, see Lester Grinspoon and James Bakalar, "Marijuana: The Forbidden Medicine," in Inciardi and McElrath, *The American Drug Scene.*

6. Michael D. Lyman, *Narcotics and Crime Control* (Springfield, Ill.: Charles C Thomas, 1987), p. 8. See also F. E. Oliver, "The Use and Abuse of Opium," in *Yesterday's Addicts: American Society and Drug Abuse, 1865–1920,* ed. H. Wayne Morgan (Norman: University of Oklahoma Press, 1974).

7. W. Z. Guggenheim, "Heroin: History and Pharmacology," *International Journal of the Addictions,* **2** (1967): 328. For a history of heroin use in New York City, from just after the turn of the twentieth century into the late 1960s, see Edward Preble and John J. Casey, "Taking Care of Business: The Heroin Addict's Life on the Street," *International Journal of the Addictions,* **4** (1969): 1–24.

8. Abadinsky, *Drug Abuse,* p. 52.

9. Ibid., p. 56.

10. Lyman, *Narcotics and Crime Control,* p. 10.

11. Public Law 100-690, of Nov. 18, 1988; 102 Stat. 4187.

12. Lloyd D. Johnston, Patrick M. O'Malley, and Jerald G. Bachman, *Drug Use among American High School Seniors, College Students, and Young Adults, 1975–1990,* vols. 1–2, for U.S. Department of Health and Human Services, National Institute on Drug Abuse (Washington, D.C.: U.S. Government Printing Office, 1991). For an early treatment, see James D. Preston and Patricia A. Fry, "Marijuana Use among Houston High School Students," *Social Science Quarterly,* **52** (1971): 170–178. For a look into how teen drug use can influence presidential elections, see Stewart Ugelow, "Drug Use Is Surging among Teenagers, and Dole Makes It a Campaign Issue," *Wall Street Journal,* Aug. 21, 1996, p. A4.

13. Office of National Drug Control Policy, *Fact Sheet: Drug Use Trends* (Washington, D.C.: U.S. Government Printing Office, June 1999); Department of Health and Human Services, *Annual Drug Survey Results Released: Youth Drug Use Decreases; Overall Rates Remain Level,* Aug. 18, 1999 (http://www.health.org/pubs/nhsda/98hhs/nhs98rel.htm). For an early treatment of the extent of illegal drug use in Britain, see Pierce I. James, "Drug Abuse in Britain," *Medicine, Science and the Law,* **13** (1973): 246–251.

14. Lyman, *Narcotics and Crime Control,* p. 21. For a German perspective on cocaine use, see Reiner Kaulitzki, "Cocaine Crisis? Myths, Moral Panics and Symbolic Politics," *Kriminologisches Journal,* **27** (1995): 134–158. See also Substance Abuse and Mental Health Services Administration, *1998 National Household Survey on Drug Abuse,* August 1999 (http://www.health.org/pubs/nhsda/98hhs/facts/factsheet.htm).

15. National Institute on Drug Abuse, *National Household Survey* (Washington, D.C.: U.S. Government Printing Office, 1996), p. 9; see Robert J. Michaels, "The Market for Heroin before and after Legalization," in *Dealing with Drugs,* ed. Ronald Hamowy (Lexington, Mass.: Lexington Books, 1987), pp. 311–318.

16. Mark A. de Bernardo and Marci M. DeLancey, *Guide to Dangerous Drugs: Everything You Should Know about Marijuana, Cocaine, Alcohol, Depressants, Amphetamines, Heroin and Other Opiates, Inhalants and Hallucinogens* (Washington, D.C.: Institute for a Drug-Free Workplace, 1994); Abadinsky,

Review • You Be the Criminologist • Key Terms • Notes

Drug Abuse, p. 107; Lyman, *Narcotics and Crime Control*, pp. 33–34. For a description of emerging new drugs and availability, see Dana Hunt, *Pulse Check: National Trends in Drug Abuse* (Washington, D.C.: Office of National Drug Control Policy, 1996).

17. Lloyd D. Johnston, Patrick M. O'Malley, and Jerald G. Bachman, *The National Survey Results on Drug Use from the Monitoring the Future Study, 1975–1993*, vol. 1, National Institutes of Health (Washington, D.C.: U.S. Government Printing Office, 1994). Office of National Drug Control Policy, *Fact Sheet*; Department of Health and Human Services, *Annual Drug Survey Results Released*. See also Allan L. McCutcheon and George Thomas, "Patterns of Drug Use among White Institutionalized Delinquents in Georgia: Evidence from a Latent Class Analysis," *Journal of Drug Education*, **25** (1995): 61–71; Bruce A. Jacobs, "Anticipatory Undercover Targeting in High Schools," *Journal of Criminal Justice*, **22** (1994): 445–457; Joseph F. Sheley, "Drugs and Guns among Inner-City High School Students," *Journal of Drug Education*, **24** (1994): 303–321; Ken C. Winters, Christine L. Weller, and James A. Meland, "Extent of Drug Abuse among Juvenile Offenders," *Journal of Drug Issues*, **23** (1993): 515–524. For a perspective on drug use among 12- and 19-year-olds living in England and Wales, see Joy Mott and Catriona Black Mirrlees, *Self-Reported Drug Misuse in England and Wales: Findings from the 1992 British Crime Survey* (London: Home Office, Research and Planning Unit, 1995). See, as an early treatment, Lloyd Johnson and Jerald G. Bachman, *Drug Use among American High School Students, 1975–1977* (Washington, D.C.: U.S. Government Printing Office, 1978); Henry Wechsler, "Alcohol Intoxication and Drug Use among Teen-Agers," *Journal of Studies on Alcohol*, **37** (1976): 1672–1677; U.S. House of Representatives, Select Committee on Crime, *Drugs in Our Schools. Hearings, September 21–23, 1972, Chicago, Illinois* (Washington, D.C.: U.S. Government Printing Office, 1972).

18. Lisa Maher, Eloise Dunlap, Bruce D. Johnson, and Ansley Hamid, "Gender, Power, and Alternative Living Arrangements in the Inner-City Crack Culture," *Journal of Research in Crime and Delinquency*, **33** (1996): 181–205; H. Virginia McCoy, Christine Miles, and James A. Inciardi, "Survival Sex: Inner-City Women and Crack-Cocaine," in Inciardi and McElrath, *The American Drug Scene*; Jody Miller, "Gender and Power on the Streets: Street Prostitution in the Era of Crack Cocaine," *Journal of Contemporary Ethnography*, **23** (1995): 427–452; Ann Sorenson and David Brownfield, "Adolescent Drug Use and a General Theory of Crime: An Analysis of a Theoretical Integration," *Canadian Journal of Criminology*, **37** (1995): 19–37. For a summary of psychiatric approaches, see Marie Nyswander, *The Drug Addict as a Patient* (New York: Grune & Stratton, 1956), chap. 4.

19. Richard Cloward and Lloyd Ohlin, *Delinquency and Opportunity* (New York: Free Press, 1960), pp. 178–186. See also Jeffrey A. Fagan, "The Social Organization of Drug Use and Drug Dealing among Urban Gangs," *Criminology*, **27** (1989): 633–669. See also Marcia R. Chaiken, *Identifying and Responding to New Forms of Drug Abuse: Lessons Learned from "Crack" and "Ice"* (Washington, D.C.: National Institute of Justice, 1993).

20. D. F. Musto, "The History of Legislative Control over Opium, Cocaine, and Their Derivatives," in Hamowy, *Dealing with Drugs*.

21. Marsha Rosenbaum, *Women on Heroin* (New Brunswick, N.J.: Rutgers University Press, 1981), pp. 14–15; Jeannette Covington, "Theoretical Explanations of Race Differences in Heroin Use," in *Advances in Criminological Theory*, vol. 2, ed. William S. Laufer and Freda Adler (New Brunswick, N.J.: Transaction). See also U.S. Senate Judiciary Committee, Subcommittee to Investigate Juvenile Delinquency, *The Global Connection: Heroin Entrepreneurs. Hearings, July 28 and August 5, 1976* (Washington, D.C.: U.S. Government Printing Office, 1976).

22. Freda Adler, Arthur D. Moffett, Frederick G. Glaser, John C. Ball, and Diana Horwitz, *A Systems Approach to Drug Treatment* (Philadelphia: Dorrance, 1974).

23. Erich Goode, *Drugs in American Society* (New York: Basic Books, 1972). See also Ned

Polsky, *Hustlers, Beats, and Others* (Chicago: Aldine, 1967).

24. Norman E. Zinberg, "The Use and Misuse of Intoxicants: Factors in the Development of Controlled Abuse," in Hamowy, *Dealing with Drugs*, p. 262.

25. Abadinsky, *Drug Abuse*, p. 53. See also, as an early treatment, Hope R. Victor, Jan Carl Grossman, and Russell Eisenman, "Openness to Experience and Marijuana Use in High School Students," *Journal of Consulting and Clinical Psychology*, **41** (1973): 78–85; U.S. Narcotics and Dangerous Drugs Bureau, *Marijuana: An Analysis of Use, Distribution and Control* (Washington, D.C.: U.S. Government Printing Office, 1971); California Department of Public Health and Welfare, Research and Statistics Section, *Five Mind-Altering Drugs: The Use of Alcoholic Beverages, Amphetamines, LSD, Marijuana, and Tobacco, Reported by High School and Junior High School Students, San Mateo County, California, Two Comparable Surveys, 1968 and 1969* (San Mateo: California Department of Public Health, 1969); Erich Goode, "Multiple Drug Use among Marijuana Smokers," *Social Problems*, **17** (1969): 48–64.

26. Bruce A. Jacobs, "Crack Dealers' Apprehension Avoidance Techniques: A Case of Restrictive Deterrence," *Justice Quarterly*, **13** (1996): 359–381; Bruce A. Jacobs, "Crack Dealers and Restrictive Deterrences: Identifying Narcs," *Criminology*, **34** (1996): 409–431; Bruce D. Johnson, Andrew Golub, and Jeffrey Fagan, "Careers in Crack, Drug Use, Drug Distribution, and Nondrug Criminality," *Journal of Crime and Delinquency*, **41** (1995): 275–295; Abadinsky, *Drug Abuse*, p. 83. See also Jeffrey A. Fagan, "Initiation into Crack and Powdered Cocaine: A Tale of Two Epidemics," *Contemporary Drug Problems*, **16** (1989): 579–618; Jeffrey A. Fagan, Joseph G. Weis, and Y. T. Cheng, "Drug Use and Delinquency among Inner City Youth," *Journal of Drug Issues*, **20** (1990): 349–400; and James A. Inciardi et al., "The Crack Epidemic Revisited," *Journal of Psychoactive Drugs*, **24** (1992): 305–416. See also B. D. Johnson, M. Natarajan, E. Dunlap, and E. Elmoghazy, "Crack Abusers and Noncrack Abusers: A Comparison of Drug Use, Drug Sales, and Nondrug Criminality," *Journal of Drug Issues*, **24** (1994): 117–141. Smoking crack is certainly not limited to the inner cities of America. For a description of crack use in the tropical paradise of Hawaii, see Gordon James Knowles, "Dealing Crack Cocaine: A View from the Streets of Honolulu," *The FBI Law Enforcement Bulletin*, July 1996: 1–7.

27. Michael Marriott, "Potent Crack Blend on the Streets Lures a New Generation to Heroin," *New York Times*, July 13, 1989, pp. A1, B3.

28. James Inciardi, "Heroin Use and Street Crime," *Crime and Delinquency*, **25** (1979): 335–346; Bruce D. Johnson, Paul J. Goldstein, Edward Preble, James Schmeidler, Douglas S. Lyston, Barry Spunt, and Thomas Miller, *Taking Care of Business: The Economics of Crime by Heroin Abusers* (Lexington, Mass.: Heath, 1985); James Inciardi, *The War on Drugs: Heroin, Cocaine, Crime, and Public Policy* (Palo Alto, Calif.: Mayfield, 1986); Eric Wish and Bruce Johnson, "The Impact of Substance Abuse on Criminal Careers," in *Criminal Careers and Career Criminals*, ed. Alfred Blumstein, Jacqueline Cohen, Jeffrey A. Roth, and Christy A. Visher (Washington, D.C.: National Academy Press, 1986), pp. 52–58.

29. National Institute of Justice, *Drug Use Forecasting 1996: Annual Report on Adult and Juvenile Arrestees* (Washington, D.C.: U.S. Government Printing Office, June 1997). See also U.S. Sentencing Commission, *Cocaine and Federal Sentencing Policy* (Washington, D.C.: U.S. Sentencing Commission, 1995).

30. For a determination of the causal link between drug use and crime, see Bruce L. Benson and David W. Rasmussen, *Illicit Drugs and Crimes* (Oakland, Calif.: The Independent Institute, 1996); James A. Inciardi, Duane C. McBride, and James E. Rivers, *Drug Control and the Courts* (Thousand Oaks, Calif.: Sage, 1996); Inciardi and McElrath, *The American Drug Scene*; Sybille M. Guy, Gene M. Smith, and P. M. Bentler, "The Influence of Adolescent Substance Use and Socialization on Deviant Behavior in Young Adulthood," *Criminal Justice and Behavior*, **21** (1994): 236–255.

31. George Speckart and M. Douglas Anglin found that criminal records preceded drug use; see their "Narcotics Use and Crime: An Overview of Recent Research Advances," *Contemporary Drug Problems*, **13** (1986): 741–769, and "Narcotics and Crime: A Causal Modeling Approach," *Journal of Quantitative Criminology*, **2** (1986): 3–28. See also Cheryl Carpenter, Barry Glassner, Bruce D. Johnson, and Julia Loughlin, *Kids, Drugs, and Crime* (Lexington, Mass.: Heath, 1988). See also Louise L. Biron, Serge Brochu, and Lyne Desjardins, "The Issue of Drugs and Crime among a Sample of Incarcerated Women," *Deviant Behavior*, **16** (1995): 25–43.

32. James A. Inciardi and Anne E. Pottieger, "Kids, Crack, and Crime," *Journal of Drug Issues*, **21** (1991): 257–270; David N. Nurco, Thomas E. Hanlon, Timothy W. Kinlock, and Karen R. Duszynski, "Differential Criminal Patterns of Narcotics Addicts over an Addiction Career," *Criminology*, **26** (1988): 407–423; M. Douglas Anglin and George Speckart, "Narcotics Use and Crime: A Multisample, Multimethod Analysis," *Criminology*, **26** (1988): 197–233; M. Douglas Anglin and Yining Hser, "Addicted Women and Crime," *Criminology*, **25** (1987): 359–397.

33. Paul Goldstein, "Drugs and Violent Crime," in *Pathways to Criminal Violence*, ed. Neil Alan Weiner and Marvin E. Wolfgang (Newbury Park, Calif.: Sage, 1989), pp. 16–48.

34. This section is based on Inciardi, *The War on Drugs*. See also Fernando Cepeda Ulloa, "International Cooperation and the War on Drugs," in *Drug Trafficking in the Americas*, ed. Bruce M. Bagley and William O. Walker III (Coral Gables, Fla.: North-South Center Press, University of Miami, 1996); Ronald Kessler, *The FBI* (New York: Pocket Books, 1993); *United States v. Celio*, 945 F.2d 180 (7th Cir. 1991), where the U.S. Court of Appeals for the Seventh Circuit acknowledged the need for a concerted effort on behalf of various law enforcement agencies to combat international drug-trafficking cartels.

35. Office of National Drug Control Policy, *Fact Sheet: Drug Use Trends* (Washington, D.C.: U.S. Government Printing Office, April 1999).

36. *The Illicit Drug Situation in the United States and Canada* (Ottawa: Royal Canadian Mounted Police, 1984–1986), p. 19. See also William Gately and Yvette Fernandez, *Dead Ringer: An Insider's Account of the Mob's Colombian Connection* (New York: Donald I. Fine, 1994).

37. Colin McMahon, "Panama's Future Uncertain as Ever; Corruption Persists in Post-Noriega Era," *Chicago Tribune*, Aug. 25, 1996, p. 17.

38. United Nations, "Commission on Narcotic Drugs, Comprehensive Review of the Activities of the United Nations Fund for Drug Abuse Control in 1985," E/CN.7/1986/CRP.4, Feb. 4, 1986. See also Elaine Sciolino, "U.N. Report Links Drugs, Arms, and Terror," *New York Times*, Jan. 12, 1987.

39. John Warner, "Terrorism and Drug Trafficking: A Lethal Partnership," *Security Management*, **28** (1984): 44–46. See, as an early treatment, U.S. Congress, House Public Health and Environment Subcommittee, *Production and Abuse of Opiates in the Far East* (Washington, D.C.: U.S. Government Printing Office, 1971).

40. For a review of drug enforcement policies aimed directly at the users of illicit narcotics, see Richard Lawrence Miller, *Drug Warriors and Their Prey: From Police Power to Police State* (Westport, Conn.: Praeger, 1996). For a comprehensive guide to state agencies that address drug abuse concerns, see Bureau of Justice Statistics, *State Drug Resources: 1994 National Directory* (Washington, D.C.: U.S. Department of Justice, 1994).

41. James A. Inciardi, *The War on Drugs II: The Continuing Epidemic of Heroin, Cocaine, Crack, Crime, AIDS, and Public Policy* (Mountain View, Calif.: Mayfield, 1992).

42. Even before President Bush's drug initiatives, government agencies recognized the ineffectiveness of narcotic countermeasures during the 1970s; see U.S. Comptroller General, *Gains Made in Controlling Illegal Drugs, Yet the Drug Trade Flourishes* (Washington, D.C.: U.S. Government Printing Office, 1979).

43. See Rae Sibbitt, *The Ilps Methadone Prescribing Project* (London: Home Office, 1996); Paul J. Turnbull, Russell Webster, and Gary

Stillwell, *Get It While You Can: An Evaluation of an Early Intervention Project for Arrestees with Alcohol and Drug Problems* (London: Home Office, 1996); Ira Sommers, Deborah R. Baskin, and Jeffrey Fagan, "Getting out of the Life: Crime Desistance by Female Street Offenders," *Deviant Behavior*, **15** (1994): 125–149; Sandra L. Tunis, *The State of the Art in Jail Drug Treatment Programs* (San Francisco: National Council on Crime and Delinquency, 1994).

44. Peter Finn and Andrea K. Newlyn, *Miami's "Drug Court,"* National Institute of Justice (Washington, D.C.: U.S. Government Printing Office, 1993); Christopher S. Wren, "Arizona Finds Cost Savings in Treating Drug Offenders," *New York Times*, Apr. 21, 1999; Bureau of Justice Assistance, *Two Special Drug Court Models: Dedicated Drug Treatment vs. Speedy Trial and Differentiated Case Management (DCM)—The Program Concept* (Washington, D.C.: U.S. Government Printing Office, 1998); Jonathan Alter, "The Buzz on Drugs," *Newsweek*, September 6, 1999, 25–28.

45. Abadinsky, *Drug Abuse*, p. 171.

46. David N. Nurco, Norma Wegner, Philip Stephenson, Abraham Makofsky, and John W. Shaffer, *Ex-Addicts' Self-Help Groups: Potentials and Pitfalls* (New York: Praeger, 1983); Harold I. Hendler and Richard C. Stephens, "The Addict Odyssey: From Experimentation to Addiction," *International Journal of the Addictions*, **12** (1977): 25–42.

47. For a perspective on how corporate America educates employees on the risks of drug abuse, see Mark A. de Bernardo, *What Every Employee Should Know about Drug Abuse* (Washington, D.C.: Institute for a Drug-Free Workplace, 1993); Troy Duster, *The Legislation of Morality: Law, Drugs, and Moral Judgment* (New York: Free Press, 1970), p. 192.

48. Dan Waldorf, "Natural Recovery from Opiate Addiction," *Journal of Drug Issues*, **13** (1983): 237–280.

49. See James A. Inciardi, Duane C. McBride, Clyde B. McCoy, et al., "Violence, Street Crime and the Drug Legalization Debate: A Perspective and Commentary on the U.S. Experience," *Studies on Crime and Crime Pre-*

vention, **4** (1995): 105–118; Steven Foy Luper, Curtis Brown, et al., *Drugs, Morality, and the Law* (New York: Garland, 1994); Robert J. MacCoun, James P. Kahan, and James Gillespie, "A Content Analysis of the Drug Legalization Debate," *Journal of Drug Issues*, **23** (1993): 615–629; Arnold S. Trebach and James A. Inciardi, *Legalize It? Debating American Drug Policy* (Washington, D.C.: American University Press, 1993).

50. James B. Jacobs, *Drunk Driving: An American Dilemma* (Chicago: University of Chicago Press, 1989), p. xiii.

51. Substance Abuse and Mental Health Services Administration, *1998 National Household Survey on Drug Abuse*.

52. James Inciardi, *Reflections on Crime* (New York: Holt, Rinehart & Winston, 1978), pp. 8–10. For an even earlier perspective, see Herbert Berger and Andrew A. Eggston, "Should We Legalize Narcotics?" *Coronet*, **38** (June 1995): 30–34.

53. Lawrence A. Greenfield, *Alcohol and Crime: An Analysis of National Data on the Prevalence of Alcohol Involvement in Crime* (Washington, D.C.: U.S. Government Printing Office, 1998); Christopher J. Mumola, *Substance Abuse and Treatment, State and Federal Prisoners, 1997* (Washington, D.C.: U.S. Government Printing Office, January 1999).

54. Marvin E. Wolfgang, *Patterns in Criminal Homicide* (New York: Wiley, 1966).

55. P. Linquist, "Criminal Homicides in Northern Sweden, 1970–81: Alcohol Intoxication, Alcohol Abuse, and Mental Disease," *International Journal of Law and Psychiatry*, **8** (1986): 19–37. See also Roland Gustafson, "Is It Possible to Link Alcohol Intoxication Causally to Aggression and Violence? A Summary of the Swedish Experimental Approach," *Studies on Crime and Crime Prevention*, **4** (1995): 22–42.

56. D. Mayfield, "Alcoholism, Alcohol Intoxication, and Assaultive Behavior," *Diseases of the Nervous System*, **37** (1976): 288–291; C. K. Meyer, T. Magendanz, B. C. Kieselhorst, and S. G. Chapman, *A Social-Psychological Analysis of Police Assaults* (Norman: Bureau of Government Research, University of Oklahoma, April 1978).

Review • You Be the Criminologist • Key Terms • Notes

57. For the role of alcohol consumption in violent episodes against intimates and women, see Christine A. Scronce and Kevin J. Corcoran, "The Influence of the Victim's Consumption of Alcohol on Perceptions of Stranger and Acquaintance Rape," *Violence against Women*, **1** (1995): 241–253; Bureau of Justice Statistics, *Violence between Intimates* (Washington, D.C.: U.S. Department of Justice, 1994); Bureau of Justice Statistics, *Violence against Women: A National Crime Victimization Survey Report* (Washington, D.C.: U.S. Department of Justice, 1994); S. D. Johnson, L. Gibson, and R. Linden, "Alcohol and Rape in Winnipeg, 1966–1975," *Journal of Studies on Alcohol*, **39** (1987): 1877–1894; Menachem Amir, *Patterns of Forcible Rape* (Chicago: University of Chicago Press, 1971), p. 99.

58. D. H. Coleman and M. A. Straus, "Alcohol Abuse and Family Violence," in *Alcohol, Drug Abuse, and Aggression*, ed. E. Gottheil, K. A. Druley, T. E. Skoloda, and H. M. Waxman (Springfield, Ill.: Charles C Thomas, 1983).

59. See Maggie Sumner and Howard Parker, *Law in Alcohol: A Review of International Research into Alcohol's Role in Crime Causation* (Manchester, U.K.: Department of Social Policy and Social Work, University of Manchester, 1995); Klaus A. Miczek et al., "Alcohol, Drugs of Abuse, Aggression, and Violence," in *Understanding and Preventing Violence*, ed. Albert J. Reiss, Jr., and Jeffrey A. Roth (Washington, D.C.: National Academy Press, 1993).

60. K. E. Leonard, "Alcohol and Human Physical Aggression," *Aggression*, **2** (1983): 77–101. See also Matthew W. Lewis, Jon F. Merz, Ron D. Hays, et al., "Perceptions of Intoxication and Impairment at Arrest among Adults Convicted of Driving under the Influence of Alcohol," *Journal of Drug Issues*, **25** (1995): 141–160.

61. C. M. Steele and L. Southwick, "Alcohol and Social Behavior: I. The Psychology of Drunken Excess," *Journal of Personality and Social Psychology*, **48** (1985): 18–34. See also Peter B. Wood, John K. Cochran, Betty Pfefferbaum, et al., "Sensation-Seeking and Delinquent Substance Use: An Extension of Learning Theory," *Journal of Drug Issues*, **25** (1995): 173–193.

62. S. Ahlstrom-Laakso, "European Drinking Habits: A Review of Research and Time Suggestions for Conceptual Integration of Findings," in *Cross-Cultural Approaches to the Study of Alcohol*, ed. M. W. Everett, J. O. Waddell, and D. Heath (The Hague: Mouton, 1976).

63. Uniform Crime Reports, 1992, p. 168; 1989, p. 224; Lawrence A. Greenfeld, *Drunk Driving*, for Bureau of Justice Statistics (Washington, D.C.: U.S. Government Printing Office, February 1988), p. 1; William K. Stevens, "Deaths from Drunken Driving Increase," *New York Times*, Oct. 29, 1987, p. 12. See also Gwen W. Bramlet, "DUI Offenders, Drug Users, and Criminals: A Comparison," *Journal of Crime and Justice*, **18** (1995): 59–78; Greenfield, *Alcohol and Crime*; and Mumola, *Substance Abuse and Treatment*.

64. Joseph R. Gusfield, "The Control of Drinking-Driving in the United States: A Period of Transition," in *Social Control of the Drinking Driver*, ed. Michael D. Lawrence, John R. Snortum, and Franklin E. Zimring (Chicago: University of Chicago Press, 1988).

65. Jacobs, *Drunk Driving*, p. xvi.

66. Faye Silas, "Gimme the Keys," *American Bar Association Journal*, **71** (1985): 36.

67. Atic Press, "The Menace on the Roads," *Newsweek*, Dec. 21, 1987, p. 42.

68. Brandon K. Applegate, Francis T. Cullen, Bruce G. Link, Pamela J. Richards, and Lonn Lanza-Kaduce, "Determinants of Public Punitiveness toward Drunk Driving: A Factorial Survey Approach," *Justice Quarterly*, **13** (1996): 57–79; Stephen D. Mastrofski and R. Richard Ritti, "Police Training and the Effects of Organization on Drunk Driving Enforcement," *Justice Quarterly*, **13** (1996): 291–320.

69. *The Effectiveness of the Ignition Interlock Device in Reducing Recidivism among Driving under the Influence Cases* (Honolulu: Criminal Justice Commission, 1987).

70. Personal communication, 1951. See, as additional early treatments, Dr. Eustace Chesser, *Strange Loves: The Human Aspects of Sexual Deviation* (New York: William Mor-

row, 1971); David Reuben, *Everything You Always Wanted to Know about Sex: But Were Afraid to Ask* (New York: David McKay, 1969). Contemporary works include Samuel S. Janus and Cynthia L. Janus, *The Janus Report on Sexual Behavior: The First Broad-Scale Scientific National Survey since Kinsey* (New York: Wiley, 1993).

71. Alfred C. Kinsey, Wardel B. Pomeroy, and Clyde E. Martin, *Sexual Behavior in the Human Male* (Philadelphia: Saunders, 1948), p. 613. See also Judith A. Reisman and Edward W. Eichel, *Kinsey, Sex and Fraud: The Indoctrination of a People* (Lafayette, La.: Huntington House, 1990).

72. *Bowers v. Hardwick*, 478 U.S. 186; reh. denied, 478 U.S. 1039 (1986).

73. Nickie Roberts, *Whores in History: Prostitution in Western Society* (London: HarperCollins, 1992).

74. *Robinson v. California*, 370 U.S. 660 (1962).

75. Uniform Crime Reports, 1997, p. 222.

76. See Cudore L. Snell, *Young Men in the Street: Help-Seeking Behavior of Young Male Prostitutes* (Westport, Conn.: Praeger, 1995); Sari van der Poel, "Solidarity as Boomerang: The Fiasco of the Prostitutes' Rights Movement in the Netherlands," *Crime, Law and Social Change*, **23** (1995): 41–65; Barbara Sherman Heyl, "The Madam as Teacher: The Training of House Prostitutes," in *Deviant Behavior*, ed. Delos H. Kelly, (New York: St. Martin's Press, 1993); Sari van der Poel, "Professional Male Prostitution: A Neglected Phenomenon," *Crime, Law, and Social Change*, **18** (1992): 259–275; David F. Luckenbill, "Deviant Career Mobility: The Case of Male Prostitutes," *Social Problems*, **33** (1986): 283–296.

77. Jeremiah Lowney, Robert W. Winslow, and Virginia Winslow, *Deviant Reality—Alternative World Views*, 2d ed. (Boston: Allyn and Bacon, 1981), p. 156. For a law enforcement perspective on countering prostitution in New York City, where female undercover police officers are used to seek out the patrons of prostitutes, see Dean Chang, "Dear John, It's a Bust: Cops Target Sex Clients," *New York Daily News*, June 26, 1994, p. 10.

78. Bureau of Justice Statistics, *HIV in Prisons 1994* (Washington, D.C.: U.S. Department of Justice, 1996); Bureau of Justice Statistics, *HIV in Prisons and Jails, 1993* (Washington, D.C.: U.S. Department of Justice, 1995); James A. Inciardi, Anne E. Pottieger, Mary Ann Forney, et al., "Prostitution, IV Drug Use, and Sex-for-Crack Exchanges among Serious Delinquents: Risks for HIV Infection," *Criminology*, **29** (1991): 221–236; Joseph B. Kuhns III and Kathleen M. Heide, "AIDS-Related Issues among Female Prostitutes and Female Arrestees," *International Journal of Offender Therapy and Comparative Criminology*, **36** (1992): 231–245; David J. Bellis, "Reduction of AIDS Risk among 41 Heroin Addicted Female Street Prostitutes: Effects of Free Methadone Maintenance," *Journal of Addictive Diseases*, **12** (1993): 7–23; L. Maher and R. Curtis, "Women on the Edge of Crime: Crack Cocaine and the Changing Contexts of Street-Level Sex Work in New York City," *Crime, Law, and Social Change*, **18** (1992): 221–258; Edward V. Morse, Patricia M. Simon, Stephanie A. Baus, et al., "Cofactors of Substance Use among Male Street Prostitutes," *Journal of Drug Issues*, **22** (1992): 977–994.

79. Paul Gebhard, "Misconceptions about Female Prostitution," *Medical Aspects of Human Sexuality*, **3** (1969): 28–30; Jennifer James, "Prostitutes and Prostitution," in *Deviants: Voluntary Action in a Hostile World*, ed. Edward Sagarin and F. Montamino (Glenview, Ill.: Scott, Foresman, 1977), p. 384.

80. R. Karl Hanson, Heather Scott, and Richard A. Steffy, "A Comparison of Child Molesters and Nonsexual Criminals: Risk Predictors and Long-Term Recidivism," *Journal of Research in Crime and Delinquency*, **32** (1995): 325–337; Dennis Howitt, *Paedophiles and Sexual Offences against Children* (Chichester, U.K.: Wiley, 1995); Human Rights Watch: Asia, *Rape for Profit: Trafficking of Nepali Girls and Women to India's Brothels* (New York: Human Rights Watch, 1995).

81. See Gerhard O. W. Mueller, *Legal Regulation of Sexual Conduct* (New York: Oceana, 1961), pp. 139–147, tables 9A, 9B. Note, however, that some states have amended their statutes since these data were collected.

Review • You Be the Criminologist • Key Terms • Notes

82. Edward Donnerstein et al., *The Question of Pornography: Final Report of the Attorney General's Commission on Pornography* (Nashville, Tenn.: Rutledge Hill Press, 1986), p. 147.
83. For the now famous Justice Potter Stewart comment on pornography, where he couldn't truly define obscenity, but stated he knew it when he saw it, see *Jacobellis v. Ohio*, 378 U.S. 184 (1964). Joel Feinberg, "Pornography and Criminal Law," in *Pornography and Censorship*, ed. D. Copp and S. Wendell (New York: Prometheus, 1979).
84. See Susan M. Easton, *The Problem of Pornography: Regulation and the Right to Free Speech* (London: Routledge, 1994); Donald A. Downs, *The New Politics of Pornography* (Chicago: University of Chicago Press, 1989). See also Donnerstein et al., *The Question of Pornography*, chap. 7; and Gordon Hawkins and Franklin E. Zimring, *Pornography in a Free Society* (New York: Cambridge University Press, 1988), p. 26.
85. *The Report of the Commission on Obscenity and Pornography* (Washington, D.C.: U.S. Government Printing Office, 1970).
86. U.S. Department of Justice, *Attorney General's Commission on Pornography, Final Report*, vols. 1 and 2 (Washington, D.C.: U.S. Government Printing Office, 1986). For comments on the scientific underpinnings of this report, see Edward Donnerstein, "The Pornography Commission Report: Do Findings Fit Conclusions?" *Sexual Coercion and Assault Issues and Perspectives*, **1** (1986): 185–188.
87. Home Office, *Report of the Committee on Obscenity and Film Censorship* (London: Her Majesty's Stationery Office, 1979), p. 103. See also Dennis Howitt and Guy Cumberbatch, *Pornography: Impacts and Influences: A Review of Available Research Evidence on the Effects of Pornography* (London: Research and Planning Unit, U.K. Home Office, 1990).
88. *The Report of the Commission on Obscenity and Pornography.*
89. R. A. Barron and P. A. Bell, "Sexual Arousal and Aggression by Males: Effects of Type of Erotic Stimuli and Prior Provocation," *Journal of Personality and Social Psychology*, **35** (1977): 79–87. For a more current study, see Scot B. Boeringer, "Pornography and Sexual Aggression: Associations of Violent and Nonviolent Depictions with Rape and Rape Proclivity," *Deviant Behavior*, **15** (1994): 289–304.
90. Dolf Zillman and Jennings Bryant, "Pornography, Sexual Callousness, and the Trivialization of Rape," *Journal of Communication*, **32** (1984): 10–21. See also Berl Kutchinsky, "Evidence Proves That Pornography Does Not Promote Rape," in the Current Controversies series, *Violence against Women*, ed. Karin L. Swisher, Carol Wekesser, and William Barbour (San Diego: Greenhaven Press, 1994); Cynthia S. Gentry, "Pornography and Rape: An Empirical Analysis," *Deviant Behavior*, **12** (1991): 277–288.
91. Donnerstein et al., *The Question of Pornography*, esp. pp. 38–47. See also Swisher, Wekesser, and Barbour, Myriam Miedzian, "How Rape Is Encouraged in American Boys and What We Can Do to Stop It," in *Transforming a Rape Culture*, ed. Emilie Buchwald, Pamela R. Fletcher, and Martha Roth (Minneapolis: Milkweed Editions, 1993); Judith A. Reisman, *Images of Children, Crime and Violence in Playboy, Penthouse and Hustler* (Washington, D.C.: Office of Juvenile Justice and Delinquency Prevention, Office of Justice Assistance, Research and Statistics, U.S. Department of Justice, 1990).
92. Joan Hoff, "Why Is There No History of Pornography?" in *For Adult Users Only: The Dilemma of Violent Pornography*, ed. Susan Gubar and Joan Hoff (Bloomington: Indiana University Press, 1989), p. 18. See also Franklin Mark Osanka and Sara Lee Johann, "Pornography Contributes to Violence against Women," in Swisher, Wekesser, and Barbour, *Violence against Women*.
93. *Miller v. California*, 413 U.S. 15 (1973). See also Laura Lederer, Richard Delgado, et al., *The Price We Pay: The Case against Racist Speech, Hate Propaganda, and Pornography* (New York: Hill and Wang, 1995).
94. *Pope v. Illinois*, 481 U.S. 497 (1987). See also Adele M. Stan et al., *Debating Sexual Correctness: Pornography, Sexual Harassment, Date Rape, and the Politics of Sexual Equality* (New

York: Dell, 1995); Bill Thompson, *Soft Core: Moral Crusades against Pornography in Britain and America* (London: Cassell, 1994); Catherine Itzen et al., *Pornography: Women, Violence and Civil Liberties* (Oxford: Oxford University Press, 1993).

95. Laura Davis, Marilyn D. McShane, and Frank P. Williams III, "Controlling Computer Access to Pornography: Special Conditions for Sex Offenders," *Federal Probation*, **59** (1995): 43–48; Marty Rimm, "Marketing Pornography on the Information Superhighway: A Survey of 917,410 Images, Descriptions, Short Stories and Animations Downloaded 8.5 Million Times by Consumers in Over 2,000 Cities in Forty Countries, Provinces, and Territories," *Georgetown Law Journal*, **83** (1995): 1849–2008;

Great Britain House of Commons, *Computer Pornography* (London: Her Majesty's Stationery Office, 1994). For a perspective on the government's plan to police the Internet's superhighway, see James Aley, "How Not to Help High Tech," *Fortune Magazine*, May 16, 1994, p. 100.

96. Kinsey et al., *Sexual Behavior in the Human Male.*

97. Alfred C. Kinsey, Wardel B. Pomeroy, Clyde E. Martin, and Paul H. Gebhard, *Sexual Behavior in the Human Female* (Philadelphia: Saunders, 1953), p. 453.

98. See Jules Older, "Mother Nature's Dirty Trick: Our Bodies Design Bespeaks Promiscuous Urges," *Los Angeles Times*, March 12, 1988, p. 8.

Review • You Be the Criminologist • Key Terms • Notes

CHAPTER 15
Comparative Criminology

KEY TERMS
comparative criminology
international crimes
international criminal court
transnational crime

In June 1993 the FBI arrested eight "skinheads" who had been plotting to bomb the First African Methodist Episcopal Church in Los Angeles and shoot worshipers. American skinheads have become notorious for their random assaults on blacks, Jews, gays, immigrants, minority groups—anybody they perceive as different and whom they therefore dislike. They revere Hitler and his terror, delight in overt racist music, display swastikas and Nazi flags, and serve as shock troops for more established racist organizations. Between 3300 and 3500 skinheads are scattered in 160 or so groups in 40 states. They have become so dangerous that the FBI had to withdraw some undercover agents who had infiltrated their ranks.[1]

Few people had heard of skinheads prior to May 1985, when groups from Britain, Belgium, Denmark, and France staged a riot at a soccer game in Belgium, which left 38 people of color dead and another 200 wounded. Since then, skinheads have become a daily news item in many countries. During the Persian Gulf War, 1990 to 1991, skinheads burned 20 mosques to the ground in the London area.

By 1995, an estimated 70,000 youths, in 33 countries, on six continents, adhered to the neo-Nazi skinhead movement, with the largest concentrations in Germany, Hungary, the Czech Republic, the United States, Poland, the United Kingdom, Brazil, Italy, and Sweden (listed in descending order).[2]

Hardest hit has been Germany, the birthplace of Nazism, where the homes of Jewish families have been firebombed and hundreds of foreign workers and asylum seekers have been attacked or killed. The skinheads attack with screams of "Heil Hitler," waving their favorite symbol, the old German imperial flag.

Their ideology, if that is the word, is primitive . . . they know nothing about Hitler, or the war, beyond the fact that Hitler exterminated people who were "different" which is what they like to do themselves. They do not even know about the "ethnic cleansing" going on . . . in Bosnia now. They do not read newspapers. They read killer comic books and listen to Oi music, which is a kind of heavy-metal rock about the pleasures of "genocide."[3]

Neo-Nazi groups march in Germany on the anniversary of the death of Rudolf Hess, one of Hitler's best-known associates and one of the few Nazis to serve a long prison term.

In 1990–1991 it had been the mosques of the London region. By 1994–1995 the torch was turned on some 70 African-American churches in the American South, nearly all with the hallmark of hate crime. In France hate has now reversed. The new "enemy," born of the suburban ghettos, is of mostly African origin, a ragtag subcultural group. Their common language is "hip-hop." Their roots are "in the Bronx and Kingston, Jamaica; in South-Central Los Angeles and Brixton, London; in Dakar and Algiers, in Islam and the N.B.A."[4] Its hallmarks are rage, graffiti, drug dealing, and firearms. For the time being, this movement has been dubbed the "guerrilla renaissance." What has caused the rise of neo-Nazism and the formation of skinhead groups, of torchers of houses of worship, and of "guerrilla renaissance," almost simultaneously, in so many different parts of the world? Who defines the often bizarre ideology of such groups? Do adherents communicate with each other across borders?

To answer these questions, criminologists must engage in comparative research. But so far, there are few answers. For the skinheads, criminologist Mark Hamm has begun this process with his work *American Skinheads—The*

Criminology and Control of Hate Crime, which presents the phenomenon in an international perspective. He traces American developments to earlier occurrences in England and to the ideological background of Nazism in Germany.[5] Yet much more comparative research remains to be done to explain the almost simultaneous occurrence of identical crime problems in many parts of the world.

We begin this chapter on comparative criminology with an attempt to define it. We look next at the history of comparative criminology in order to identify its purpose and goals. Later in the chapter we focus on the prerequisites for comparative criminological research, the process itself, and the challenges globalization is posing to comparative criminology.

WHAT IS COMPARATIVE CRIMINOLOGY?

Comparison is something all human beings do every day. In choosing a home, for example, you compare such elements as number of rooms and price; location; access to transportation, shopping, and recreation; age of the structure;

beauty of the surroundings; and so on. This comparison can become a science if it is done in a systematic manner. And so it is with comparative criminology.[6]

The Definition of Comparative Criminology

What is **comparative criminology?** Simply put, it is the cross-cultural or cross-national study of crime and crime control applying the comparative method in the science of criminology.[7]

Many criminologists use comparisons. Just think of a study comparing one group with another group, a control group. But this is not what we mean by comparative criminology; it requires comparison across cultures or nations. A comparative study of victimization rates between Montana and Mississippi is not comparative criminology, because the two states are part of one nation and of one basic culture. But if we were to compare the role of alcohol in the escalation of violence among the Cheyenne nation, in Montana or Wyoming, with that among the people of the rest of the state, we might well have a cross-cultural comparison, because the Cheyenne have a distinct legal system, and a culture of their own.

The History of Comparative Criminology

Comparative criminology is not new. When the Romans had a crime problem in the fifth century B.C., they sent a delegation to the more advanced nation of Greece to learn better techniques for dealing with crime, such as the publication of laws. In the late Middle Ages and during the Renaissance (fourteenth to sixteenth centuries), all of continental Europe became a vast comparative laboratory as laws that had developed in the various principalities and cities were compared against the rediscovered laws of the old Roman Empire.

It was also during this era that crime-control methods became ever more brutal. The situation did not change until the eighteenth century, when—again through comparison, cooperation, and transfer—the work of the classical school (see Chapter 3) began to introduce rationality and humanitarian principles into crime control in Europe and America. In the nineteenth century, as communications im-

proved, policy makers and scholars of criminology compared approaches and introduced into one another's systems what seemed to work. Such ideas as the juvenile court, the penitentiary, the reformatory, probation, and parole gained worldwide acceptance as a result of comparison. Yet the comparisons of the nineteenth and early twentieth centuries lacked scientific rigor; they were impressionistic and often emotional. For example, the juvenile court, first established in Chicago in 1899, seemed such a good idea that it gained acceptance in many parts of the world. But as later experience showed, it did not necessarily work everywhere.

The founders of criminology, including those of American criminology, were, for the most part, comparatists. They would gather at international meetings and trade ideas; they would visit each other and stimulate criminological thought. But truly comparative studies, measuring up to scholarly standards, could not be done until criminology itself became a science. Throughout the first half of the twentieth century internationalism met resistance from isolationism. Comparatists were regarded as dreamers, and the comparative approach was seen as not very practical.

The Global Village: Advantages Now circumstances have changed drastically. Comparative criminologists have become a necessity, simply because the world has become a "global village." Consider these figures from the U.S. Department of Commerce: In 1960 U.S. exports amounted to $19,659 million. By 1998 that figure had increased 35 times to $683,000 million. Similarly, in 1960 imports amounted to $15,073 million. By 1998 that figure had increased 62 times to $944,600 million. And that is only part of the global trade picture.

World economies have become totally integrated and interdependent. The Japanese car you own was probably manufactured in the United States, and your American car may have parts made in more than 30 countries. Your shirt may come from Hong Kong, your shoes from Italy, and your Swiss watch from the American Virgin Islands. The situation is no different abroad, where Coke and Pepsi and American fast-food chains are only the most visible aspects of economic globalization.

Communications likewise have become global. Sitting in your living room before a TV, you participate in world events as they happen. Phone and fax and computer networking have made instant personal and business communications possible. Transportation advances, especially since the introduction of jumbo jets, together with the opening of frontiers, have made it possible for millions of people to move across oceans within hours. Air-traffic volume increased from 26 billion passenger miles in 1960 to close to 2 trillion by the end of 2000.

Europe is feeling the effects of globalization even more intensely than the rest of the world. The collapse of Communist dictatorships in Central and Eastern Europe[8] and the virtual abolition of frontiers within Europe[9] have brought crime problems until now unheard of in Europe. Consequently, national criminology had to become international criminology. Criminology has in fact been globalized.[10]

The Global Village: Disadvantages While many aspects of the global village are beneficial, others have brought great problems. Instant communication promotes not only the spread of benefits, in goods, lifestyles, and useful knowledge, but also the dissemination of dysfunctional ideas and values—like the skinhead phenomenon. Economic globalization, as much as it promotes useful commerce, also aids organized crime and fosters the global spread of frauds that were once confined to smaller localities or single countries.

Jet planes transport not just legitimate travelers but also illegal aliens, criminal entrepreneurs, drug dealers, money launderers, and terrorists. Airlines themselves have become the targets of international criminals. Moreover, the industrialization of the world brings not just economic benefits but threats to the world ecology so severe that, unless checked, they could compromise the food, water, and clean air supply for all people. It is little wonder, then, that criminologists too must look across borders to study crime and crime-control efforts, and to search for internationally acceptable solutions to common problems.

The Goals of Comparative Research

Before the 1970s there was very little literature on comparative research in criminology. Since then, however, it has been growing rapidly. That is attributable to (1) a realization that we will learn more about crime if we test our theories under diverse cultural conditions and (2) renewed interest in trying to discover what we can learn from the experience of other nations.[11]

Comparative criminology, then, has both theoretical and practical goals. It helps us better understand crime causation and find successful means of crime control, so that no nation need repeat costly mistakes made elsewhere. Presently, a large number of U.N. and affiliated organizations are engaged in the task of establishing international measures to deal with dangers that threaten people of all cultures. (See Table 15.1.)

Before we discuss the implementation of comparative research, we must look at the methods used by comparative criminologists.

ENGAGING IN COMPARATIVE CRIMINOLOGICAL RESEARCH

Comparative research requires special preparatory work to ensure that research data and information are in fact comparable. Empirical research presents additional obstacles.

Preparatory Work

Studying Foreign Law Before beginning a comparative study, the researcher must become familiar with the laws of the country or culture to which the comparison extends. Every country belongs to one or more of the world's great families of law, or legal systems (Table 15.2):

- *The civil law system.* This system grew out of the Roman legal tradition, was refined by scholars, and was codified under Napoleon in the early nineteenth century. Today it is found in systematic codes of law. The countries of continental Europe belong to this family of law, as do their former colonies in Africa, Latin America, and Asia, including Japan and China (now socialist), which chose the civil law system when they modernized.

TABLE 15.1 United Nations Organizations and Affiliates: Solving Worldwide Crime Problems

Center for Informational Crime Prevention, in the Office for Drug Control and Crime Prevention (of the U.N. Secretariat at Vienna, Austria): Reports to the U.N. Commission on Crime Prevention and Criminal Justice and conducts the quinquennial U.N. Congress on the Prevention of Crime and the Treatment of Offenders; provides extensive reports, research, documentation, and technical assistance; is responsible for U.N. standards and guidelines in criminal justice; conducts worldwide statistical surveys.

UNICRI—United Nations Interregional Crime and Justice Research Institute (heretofore located in Rome, Italy): Research arm of the U.N. Secretariat in crime prevention and criminal justice; is responsible for extensive research and publications.

UNAFEI—United Nations Asia and Far East Institute for the Prevention of Crime and the Treatment of Offenders (Tokyo, Japan): Services the region with training, technical assistance, research, and publications.

ILANUD—United Nations Latin American Institute for the Prevention of Crime and the Treatment of Offenders (San José, Costa Rica): Services the region with training, technical assistance, research, and publications.

UNAFRI—United Nations African Regional Institute for the Prevention of Crime and the Treatment of Offenders (Kampala, Uganda): Services the region with training and technical assistance.

HEUNI—Helsinki European Institute for Crime Prevention and Control; affiliated with the United Nations (Helsinki, Finland): Provides extensive research, training, research publications, and technical assistance services on behalf of European countries for both developed and developing countries.

AIC—Australian Institute of Criminology (Canberra, Australia): Under agreement with the U.N., provides research, publication, training, and technical assistance services for Oceania, including Australia and New Zealand.

Arab Security Studies and Training Centre (Riyadh, Saudi Arabia): In close cooperation with the U.N., provides extensive educational and training services, research, publications, and development and technical assistance to Arab countries.

International Centre for Criminal Law Reform and Criminal Justice Policy (Vancouver, B.C., Canada): Newly established, by agreement with the U.N., to provide services within its sphere of expertise.

ISPAC—International Scientific and Professional Advisory Council of the United Nations Crime Prevention and Criminal Justice Programme (Milan, Italy): By agreement with the U.N., provides advisory services to the U.N. with respect to data and information, both in general and on specific subjects falling within the mandate of the U.N.

UNCJIN—United Nations Crime and Justice Information Network (Albany, N.Y.): In close cooperation with *WCJLN*—World Criminal Justice Library Network (Newark, N.J.)—assembles, integrates,

and disseminates criminal justice information and data worldwide, with a view to complete electronic accessibility.

NIJ—The National Institute of Justice, of the U.S. Department of Justice: By an agreement with the United Nations signed in 1995, joined the Network of U.N.-affiliated institutes to make the services of the National Criminal Justice Reference Service—especially its UNOJUST computer services—available to the U.N. community, through its international center.

NGOs—Nongovernmental organizations in consultative status with the United Nations Economic and Social Council: International organizations whose expertise is made available to the U.N. They include many major scientific, professional, and advocacy groups, such as:
- International Association of Penal Law
- International Penal and Penitentiary Foundation (special status)
- International Society of Criminology
- International Society of Social Defense
- Institute of Higher Studies in Criminal Sciences
- Centro Nazionale di Prevenzione e Difesa Sociale
- International Association of Chiefs of Police
- International Prisoners Aid Association
- Amnesty International

NGO Alliances in Crime Prevention and Criminal Justice (New York, N.Y., and Vienna, Austria): Made up of the headquarters' representatives of NGOs; provide coordination and research services to the U.N.

U.N. agencies: Concerned with various aspects of crime and justice. The agencies include:
- Centre for Human Rights (Geneva, Switzerland)
- UNICEF, United Nations Children's Fund (New York, N.Y.)

The United Nations Centre for International Drug Control: Concerned with various aspects of international drug control and drug abuse prevention. The programs include:
- Division on Narcotic Drugs
- International Narcotics Drug Control Board
- U.N. Fund for Drug Abuse Control

Regional intergovernmental organizations: Have organizational units and/or conduct programs concerned with crime prevention and criminal justice. Examples include:
- Council of Europe
- European Union (EU)
- Organization of American States
- Organization of African Unity
- North Atlantic Treaty Organization

- *The common law system.* Common law originated in England and then spread to the various English colonies. Today it is the legal system not only of the United Kingdom but also of the United States, Canada (except Quebec), Australia, New Zealand, India, many of the Caribbean islands, and African and Asian countries that were once English colonies. Although common law is now found in written form, it originated from case law, and case precedents still play a determining role.

- *Other legal systems.* (See Table 15.2.)

TABLE 15.2   Dominant Criminal Justice Systems

Roman (Civil) Law	Common Law	Other Legal Systems
Law and procedure governed by separate, comprehensive, systematized codes, which are forward-looking, wishing to anticipate new problems.	Law and procedure governed by laws and precedents, which, if codified at all, simply organize past experiences.	*Islamic Law.* Called the Sharia; based in part on the Koran; of divine origin; covers all aspects of a Muslim's life; interpreted by judges and legal scholars; reasoning by analogy.
Codes based on scholarly analysis and conceptualizations.	Laws reflect experience of practitioners, on a case-by-case basis.	*Customary Law.* Also called tribal law; administered by elders; often exists side by side with civil or common law.
Supreme courts interpret nuances of law.	Supreme courts develop law.	
Legal proceedings must establish entire truth.	Truth finding strictly limited by pleadings and rules of evidence.	*Socialist Law.* Basically civil law; legal propositions subject to social/political policy.
Judges free to find and interpret facts.	Rules of evidence limit fact-finding process. Parties produce evidence.	*Mixed Systems.* A mix of civil and common law; may exist within a province or in a nation as a whole.
Very little lay participation.	Grand and petit juries play strong role.	
Originally, no presumption of guilt or innocence. Now presumption of innocence recognized.	Presumption of innocence.	

Having identified the legal system to which the country under study belongs, the comparatist studies the applicable law and its precise interpretation. Foreign legal systems, just like that of the United States, contain penal codes, codes of criminal procedure, constitutions, and case reports. But they also include special legislation on such topics as environmental protection and money laundering. In federal countries both federal and state legislation may have to be studied.

Then there is the problem of finding the country's laws. For the English-speaking researcher this need not be an insurmountable task. The laws, court decisions, and textbooks of English-speaking countries, for the most part, are accessible in libraries. The constitutions,[12] criminal codes,[13] and codes of criminal procedure[14] of many other countries are available in English. For a number of non-English-speaking countries there are English-language texts about their criminal law or procedure.[15] But since there is always a gap between the law on the books and the law in action, the comparatist must also consult the criminal justice research literature.

Understanding Foreign Criminal Justice Systems   Laws function within a country's criminal justice system. It is the practitioners of the system who make the laws function. There are reports from around the world based on their experience.[16] There is also a considerable amount of periodical literature and statistical information in English describing the functioning of criminal justice systems in a variety of countries (Table 15.3).[17]

Contemporary cross-cultural texts and treatises contain descriptions of the developments in criminology and criminal justice for over 50 countries.[18] In addition to the descriptions of entire criminal justice systems, there are accounts of the functioning of subsystems. For example, a five-volume series examines the area of delinquency and juvenile justice in more than two dozen countries and regions throughout the world.[19] Other aspects of criminal justice have been investigated by specialists in such areas as policing,[20] corrections,[21] and the incidence of female criminality.[22]

Learning about a Foreign Culture   Comparatists may have an understanding of their own culture. To do comparative work, they must study a foreign culture: They must become familiar with its history, politics, economy, and social structure. Scholars of comparative criminology—such as Marshall B.

TABLE 15.3 English-Language Periodical Literature for Comparative Criminology

Abstracting Services
Criminal Justice Abstracts
Criminology, Penology, and Police Science Abstracts

Periodicals
Crime Prevention and Criminal Justice Newsletter (U.N.)
Criminal Justice International
Criminal Justice—The International Journal of Policy and Practice (2001)
Criminal Law Forum: An International Journal
Dutch Penal Law and Policy
EuroCriminology
European Journal of Crime, Criminal Law and Criminal Justice
European Journal on Criminal Policy and Research
Forensic Science International
Home Office Research and Planning Unit Research Bulletin
International Annals of Criminology
International Criminal Justice Review
International Criminal Police Review
International Journal of Comparative and Applied Criminal Justice
International Journal of Law and Psychiatry
International Journal of Offender Therapy and Comparative Criminology
International Journal of the Addictions
International Journal on Drug Policy
International Review of Criminal Policy (U.N.)
International Review of Victimology
Japanese Journal of Sociological Criminology
Police Practice and Research: An International Journal
Revue de Science Criminelle et de Droit Penal Comparée
Revue Internationale de Criminologie et de Police Technique
Revue Internationale de Droit Penal
Studies in Conflict and Terrorism
Studies on Crime and Crime Prevention (Norway)
Terrorism
UNAFEI Resource Material Series
Violence, Aggression and Terrorism
Violence and Victims

Clinard, working in Switzerland as well as India and other developing countries,[23] Louise I. Shelley, working in Eastern European socialist countries and elsewhere,[24] and William Clifford, having worked in several African countries as well as Japan[25]—have successfully demonstrated that the immersion in the cultures under study that comparative research requires can be accomplished without losing the objectivity of the detached scientific researcher.

Collecting Data Research, as we emphasized in Chapter 2, requires factual information. Although some countries do not yet have the resources for systematically collecting information on their crime problems,[26] the great majority send statistics to the International Criminal Police Organization (Interpol), which publishes the data biannually,[27] or participate in the United Nations Surveys of Crime Trends, Operation of Criminal Justice Systems and Crime Prevention Strategies. The U.N. surveys, published in 5-year cycles, began with data for the year 1970 and by now include statistics from well over 100 countries on prevalence of crime and the operation of criminal systems.[28]

Several other international databases are available to the researcher, including the homicide statistics of the World Health Organization;[29] the private-initiative Comparative Crime Data File, which covers 110 sovereignties (published 1984);[30] and the Correlates of Crime (published 1989).[31]

International (or nation-by-nation) crime statistics suffer from the same problems as American UCR statistics, only magnified several times.[32]

Consequently, to obtain a more accurate picture of the crime situation in various countries, researchers have devised two additional statistical instruments:

1. The International Crime Victim Survey (ICVS). Beginning in 1989 and working through 1997, a group of researchers from various countries and research centers has conducted three victimization surveys in numerous developed (industrialized) and developing countries; 130,000 people were interviewed around the world, in 40 languages.[33]

2. A self-report study has measured delinquency among 14- to 21-year-old

FIGURE 15.1 Police and victim survey data. Comparison between police data of U.N. Crime and Justice Survey (UNCJS) and victim survey data (ICVS), percent change in reported crime 1988–1995.

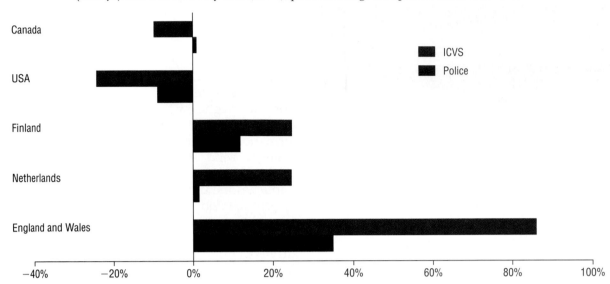

Source: *Global Report on Crime and Justice* (New York: United Nations, 1999), p. 69.

subjects in 12 countries, extending to property, violence, and drug criminality. This 1992 survey did not include developing countries.[34]

A comparison between the "official" crime rates of the U.N. surveys and the victimization rates shows that the two are reasonably related, although victimization studies usually show higher crime rates and tend to fluctuate over the years more than the U.N. survey rates. (See Figure 15.1.) One may cautiously conclude that the U.N. survey rates provide a fairly reasonable account of crime rates for most countries.

Comparative Research

Up to this point we have reviewed the general approach to doing comparative criminological research: studying foreign law, criminal justice systems, cultures, and available data. Comparative criminological research begins only after these requirements have been met. It is at this point that the comparatist sets sail for uncharted seas. The comparatist meets two problems right at the outset: the interdependence of

all crime and criminal justice phenomena, and culture specificity.

Interdependent Phenomena Think of an elaborately assembled mobile hanging from the ceiling. All the parts are in perfect balance. If you remove a single part, the whole mobile will shift out of balance. It is the same with problems of crime and justice in any society: The existence of each is related to all the others and is explainable by reference to the others. Bicycle thefts may exist in countries like China, Denmark, and the Netherlands—all of which rely heavily on bicycle transportation—as well as in the United States or Mexico. But such theft plays a different role in the various countries, generates different responses, and leads to different consequences.

Is the bicycle theft problem comparable around the world? What could be learned from a comparison, and what factors must be considered? Would it be more useful to compare the Chinese bicycle theft problem with the Italian automobile theft problem? How do these problems fit in their countries' respective crime and justice mobiles?

The preferred means of transportation during rush hour in the streets of Beijing, China.

Culture-Specific Phenomena   The task of a comparative criminologist is like that of a surgeon about to transplant a heart or a liver. The surgeon studies a great variety of factors to be sure the donor's organ is compatible with the recipient's body. If we want to compare Japan's low crime rates with the high crime rates in the United States, we must consider many factors, such as the role of shame in Japanese society. Misconduct brings shame not only on individual Japanese wrongdoers, but also on their families, schools, and companies: Could shaming, as a sanction, play a role in American criminal justice, or is it too culture-specific? It is easier to ask such questions than it is to answer them, since research experience in comparative criminology is still limited.

Comparative Research Tools and Resources

The first book entitled *"Comparative" Criminology* appeared as recently as 1965. Its author, the late German-English scholar Hermann Mannheim, relied on his vast cross-cultural experience in criminology but offered no guide to the comparative method.[35] Re-

searchers and teachers of the field now have at their disposal a variety of reference works,[36] textbooks,[37] scholarly books,[38] and book-length informative coverage of United Nations activities in the field, of which the *Global Report on Crime and Justice* is the most significant.[39]

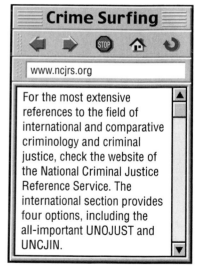

Crime Surfing

www.ncjrs.org

For the most extensive references to the field of international and comparative criminology and criminal justice, check the website of the National Criminal Justice Reference Service. The international section provides four options, including the all-important UNOJUST and UNCJIN.

The Special Problems of Empirical Research

Criminologists who cannot find or rely upon comparative data must generate their own, usually by parallel field investigations proceeding more or less simultaneously. They confront three problems: first, the identification of comparable problems; second, the identification of sources of information; and third, the selection

It was in the summer of 1935 that Karl N. Llewellyn, renowned legal philosopher, and his friend E. Adamson Hoebel, noted anthropologist, visited the northern Cheyennes on the Tongue River Reservation at Lame Deer, Montana. High Forehead of the Cheyennes served as their interpreter. Sitting in a circle with several Cheyennes, a chief filled the pipe and held it to the five directions. After the pipe had been passed around, he asked why the two white men had come.(1)

"To learn of your laws," answered the visitors. There was silence and more pipe puffing. Obviously the term "laws" meant nothing. Llewellyn went on, "For example, your rules on homicide . . . ?" More silence, more puffing. "Well," said Llewellyn, making another attempt, "what happens when there is trouble because one of your warriors has killed another man of the tribe?"

At this there was a smile of recognition, and Calf Woman spoke:

Cries Yia Eya had been gone from the camp for three years because he had killed Chief Eagle in a whiskey brawl. The chiefs had ordered him away for his murder, so we did not see anything of him for that time. Then one day he came back, leading a horse packed with bundles of old-time tobacco. He stopped outside the camp and sent a messenger in with the horse and tobacco who was to say to the chiefs for him, "I am begging to come home."

The chiefs all got together for a meeting, and the soldier societies were told to convene. The tobacco was divided up and chiefs' messengers were sent out to invite the soldier chiefs to come to the lodge of the tribal council. "Here is the tobacco that that man sent in," [the big chiefs] told the soldier chiefs. "Now we want you soldiers to decide if you think we should accept his request. If you decide that we should let him return, then it is up to you to convince his family that it is all right." (The relatives of Chief Eagle had told everybody that they would kill Cries Yia Eya on sight if they ever found him.) The soldier chiefs took the tobacco and went out to gather their troops. Each society met in its own separate lodge to talk among themselves.

At last one man said, "I think it is all right. I believe the stink has blown from him. Let him return!" This view was passed around, and this is the view that won out among the soldiers. Then the father of Chief Eagle was sent for and asked whether he would accept the decision. "Soldiers," he replied, "I shall listen to you. Let him return! But if that man comes back, I want never to hear his voice raised against another person. If he does, we come together."

Cries Yia Eya had always been a mean man, disliked by everyone, but he had been a fierce fighter against the enemies. After he came back to the camp, however, he was always good to the people.(2)

Llewellyn and Hoebel went on to collect hundreds of anecdotes of Cheyenne "conflict and case law." While they knew that the Cheyennes had structured institutions, they were surprised at the "juristic beauty" that the research revealed. In the introduction to their work on the subject, *The Cheyenne Way*, the authors comment:

Three years of puzzlement went into the analysis of the material before order emerged; and this happened (as it does in modern case law) when the data of sixty or eighty years were arranged not on a flat time-plane, but against the moving time-perspective of the culture and the individual life.(2)

Source

1. As told in class, ca. 1950, by Karl N. Llewellyn, University of Chicago.
2. Calf Woman's story is excerpted from K. N. Llewellyn and E. Adamson Hoebel, *The Cheyenne Way* (Norman: University of Oklahoma Press, 1941), pp. 12–13.

Questions for Discussion

1. What are some of the problems of doing criminological research in other cultures?
2. What are the best ways of ensuring that those problems are overcome?

---

of a research method compatible in the countries under comparison.

Identification of Comparable Problems
Researchers of New York University's Comparative Criminal Law Project, in the 1960s, compared the prevalence of delinquency in several cultures. To their surprise, they learned that Egypt had a high rate of delinquency for railroad offenses. Only local assistance could provide a plausible answer: The long railroad line running parallel to the Nile River is a favored haunt for local youths. Their delinquent acts were recorded as railroad offenses, rather than as delinquency.[40] These "railroad offenses" had to be made comparable to nonrailroad delinquencies in both Egypt and the other countries under comparison.

Identification of Sources of Information
The social groups of one society may not be comparable to those of another. American junior high school students may represent American youngsters of that age range as a whole, but Haitian junior high school students would not. What groups are comparable to such favorite research subjects as American college students, blue-collar workers, and self-

employed small-business people? What is a fair cross section of any country's population?

Police records may be highly reliable in Belgium, but are they in Mali and Malawi or in Armenia? And if they are not, what comparable substitutes can the comparatist find? Such problems challenge the researcher's ingenuity.

Selection of Compatible Research Methods Criminologist James Finckenauer, studying attitudes toward legal and other values among American and Russian youngsters, was at first confronted with the reluctance of Russian administrators to ask youngsters to report (even anonymously) their own delinquencies. The Soviet culture had blocked any such initiative. The problem was overcome only by indirect questions to the youngsters, such as: "How wrong would it be (to do this, that, or the other)?" This was followed by further semidirect questions, such as: "Do your peers (parents, and so on) view you as a good kid, bad kid, or something in between?" It was only after the end of communism in 1992 that Finckenauer could administer a self-report delinquency questionnaire.

Certain research methods simply are unknown in many other countries or, if known, are frowned upon. In a study of perceptions of police power in four cultures, for example, the commanding officer of a foreign police department was asked to have some questionnaires distributed to his officers. At first the officer responded: "You don't seem to understand our police! It is we who ask the questions!" Finally, he agreed and distributed the questionnaires. After the results were analyzed, the researchers were astonished to find that all the answers were identical. Apparently, all the questionnaires had been reviewed and "corrected" by an attorney to make sure they were "accurate."[41]

THEORY TESTING

As we noted earlier, the cross-cultural testing of criminological theories has become one of the major goals of comparative criminology. Recent studies have extended to several of the crime-causation theories discussed in this book. Yet cross-cultural theory testing requires utmost caution.[42]

Validation of Major Theories

After Sheldon and Eleanor Glueck had completed *Unraveling Juvenile Delinquency* (1950),[43] their work was criticized as too culture-specific because it was based on a sample of American children. In response, scholars replicated the Glueck research in different cultural settings—Puerto Rico, Germany, and Japan. As the Gluecks themselves put it, "All these [studies] . . . have provided the most definite of all proofs, that of applicability to other samples by other researchers."[44] These cross-cultural validations of the Gluecks' delinquency-prediction system are some of the earliest empirical, comparative criminological studies.

More recently, criminologist Obi Ebbe has reviewed the Gluecks' studies and found their theories applicable to juvenile delinquents in Nigeria.[45] He has also examined the cross-cultural validity of other American theories, such as differential association, social control, and culture conflict. During the last few years other scholars have tested opportunity theory,[46] situational characteristics of crime,[47] routine-activity theory,[48] differential opportunity theory,[49] social control and strain theory,[50] the synnomie explanation of low crime rates,[51] and Durkheim's anomie theory.[52] Most of these studies have shown the theories to have moderate to significant validity.[53]

The Socioeconomic Development Perspective

Cross-cultural researchers have devoted particular attention to the recently developed hypothesis that modernization and urbanization lead to increases in crime[54] as well as to the general question of whether socioeconomic development necessarily brings an increase in crime.[55] Several have noted a connection between rapid development and an increase in certain types of crime, especially property crime.[56] Other research has demonstrated that sudden urbanization and industrialization have not led to increased crime in some countries,[57] but that unguided socioeconomic and political changes, such as the current transformation from a socialist to a market economy in Central and Eastern Europe, do produce an increase in crime.[58] The complexity of the relation between development and crime has prompted some comparative criminologists to warn that, as yet, there is no universal theoretical framework linking crime and development.[59]

PRACTICAL GOALS

Learning from Others' Experiences

With increasing globalization, the similarity of crime problems increases as well. It is natural that criminologists would look at the experiences of other countries in their search for solutions, especially the experiences of countries that seem to have found workable solutions.[60] For the worldwide drunk-driving problem, for example, comparative research has been done in Australia, Norway, and the United States.[61] One gun-control study investigated the situation in 7 nations[62]; another, in 26.[63] Insurance fraud researchers have looked at the situation in 8 countries[64]; insider-trading researchers, in 3.[65]

A recent symposium compared differential methods of dealing with ecological crime in the United States, Germany, Austria, Japan, and Taiwan.[66] Comparative criminological research has also been done on violent crime, such as homicides of children,[67] spousal homicides,[68] homicides among young males,[69] and urban violence.[70] For the past 25 years, much attention has been devoted to the comparative study of the problem of juvenile delinquency.[71]

By now there is also a considerable body of cross-cultural research on various aspects of crime-control policy. One of the earliest studies in this area examined the perception of police power among divergent population groups in four countries.[72] The perception of law was studied in six cultures,[73] and teenagers' perception of crime and criminal justice was the subject of a more recent two-country study.[74]

Issues in policing[75] as well as sanctions[76] occupy the attention of comparatists in their search for "what works." Victimologists have been particularly active in cross-cultural study.[77]

Developing International Strategies

Comparative criminology reveals that most crime problems are not unique to a single country. So we are challenged to develop strategies jointly with other countries in order to establish crime-prevention and crime-control programs to benefit all. This is particularly necessary for those crime problems that have international implications. For the sake of convenience, we can group crime problems reaching beyond national borders into three categories:

- Internationally induced local crime problems.
- Transnational crime.
- International crime.

Internationally Induced Local Crime Problems   The skinhead phenomenon is a prime example of the simultaneous appearance of a similar type of crime in various parts of the world.[78] As yet, little is known about what causes such simultaneous appearances, although instantaneous reporting in the mass media may aid the process,[79] and some international organizational connections also may play a role. Recently, the Internet has come to play a role in connecting people pursuing common criminal goals. (Yet none of these factors was present in another simultaneous occurrence of a crime problem, namely, piracy in several widely separated waterways of the world in the mid-1970s, perpetrated in large part by rootless young offenders.[80]) The skinheads are part of the broader problem of crimes of discrimination against minorities, which itself is fueled by vastly increased intracontinental and intercontinental migrations. The appearance of new ethnic minorities within heretofore mono-ethnic communities often results in the victimization of minorities. These population migrations have also resulted in the migration of crime perpetrated by migrants—often against their fellow migrants, but also against the indigenous population. Consequently, criminologists have had to look for new ways to deal with these new forms and dimensions of crime.[81]

Internationally induced local crime problems can be far greater than hate crimes or other forms of crime associated with culture conflict and migration. Consider that drugs produced abroad and distributed locally create a vast problem of crime: Not only is drug dealing illegal, but a considerable portion of street crime is associated with narcotics. Ultimately, it could be said that there are very few crime problems that are not associated with persons and events abroad over which we have no direct control. Although the problem is a vast, yet largely uncharted territory, a number of criminal activities with foreign connections have recently been identified and given the title "transnational crime."

Transnational Crime   Criminologists use the term **transnational crime** to refer to criminal activities, transactions, or schemes that violate the laws of more than one country or have a direct impact on a foreign country. Neither individually, nor by type, nor collectively by category do transnational crimes conform to the definitions and categorizations found in penal codes.

In a recent questionnaire sent to all the world's national governments, and in a subsequent report on the results, the United Nations, for the first time in history, demonstrated the existence and prevalence of transnational crime.[82] Eighteen categories of transnational criminality emerged. While it is conceivable that all these activities could be committed within a single jurisdiction, and/or by individual perpetrators, it is the hallmark of all that they are typically perpetrated by means of transnational activities and by organized groups of perpetrators.[83]

1. *Money laundering.* This category ranks number 1 on the list because of its massive impact on the economy of the entire world. Money laundering is an activity aimed at making illegally obtained funds seem legitimate, so that such funds can be spent or invested in the legitimate economy without arousing suspicion. Consider that a substantial part of the financial gain of the world's citizens is ill-gotten, for example, by bribery, by corruption, by black-market activities and transactions outside the tax laws, and especially by dealing in contraband.

The drug barons and others who have illegitimate income have devised many schemes to

Terrorism or pilot suicide? Egyptian Air Flight 990 disaster off Nantucket, Massachusetts, in November 1999.

launder dirty money, including bogus real estate transactions, purchases of gold (many times consisting of lead bars with a coating of gold), and sales (real or fictitious) of art and antiques. But the standard method remains the physical transfer of cash out of the country (by planes or ships or by trucks and trailers with false bottoms), deposit of such cash abroad, followed by a series of international (electronic) transfers, at the end of which the source is untraceable, and the money seems clean and legitimately invested in the economy (Figure 15.2).

The true dimensions of money laundering are largely unknown. Estimates are as high as $500 billion annually.[84] Nevertheless, policy research (especially the Financial Transactions Task Force of the Group of Seven [highly industrialized countries]) has resulted in some remedies.

2. *Terrorist activities.* Americans had been largely unaware of the international scope of terrorist activities, primarily because their

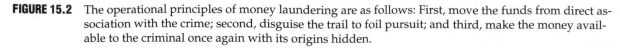

FIGURE 15.2   The operational principles of money laundering are as follows: First, move the funds from direct association with the crime; second, disguise the trail to foil pursuit; and third, make the money available to the criminal once again with its origins hidden.

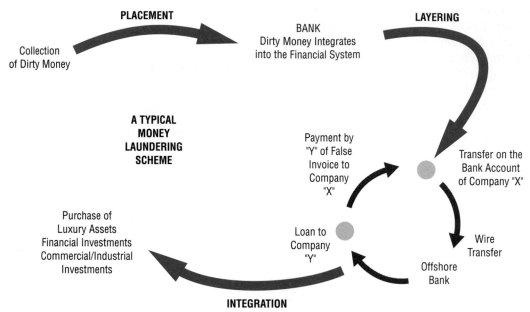

Source: United Nations Office for Drug Control and Crime Prevention, *United Nations Global Programme against Money Laundering* (New York: United Nations, 1998), pp. 18, 19.

homeland had remained unaffected. This naiveté changed with the growing awareness that Americans, and American interests and installations abroad, have become targets of international terrorists. But only the bombing of the World Trade Center in New York City in February 1993 by an organized group of Middle Eastern terrorists alerted Americans to the vulnerability of their own country. Of course, the victimization of air transport to and from America is a continuing reminder of terrorists' capability to harm American interests. The terrorist bombing of Pan Am Flight 103 over Lockerbie, Scotland, in December 1988, and more recently the destruction of Egypt Air Flight 990, which crashed 60 miles south of Nantucket en route from New York to Cairo on October 31, 1999, killing all 217 people aboard, demonstrate the point. In the latter case preliminary evidence points to an act of sabotage or terrorism. In the wake of this latest disaster, the Federal Aviation Administration released an overdue report on airport safety, which shows that considerable

shortcomings still exist. It may well take years to provide near-perfect safety from terrorism in air transportation.[85]

Much scholarly inquiry has been directed at understanding and explaining international terrorism.[86] And there have been legislative responses. As a matter of fact, a network of international conventions is in place to deal with international terrorism. International judicial and police cooperation have been vastly improved. Yet there is no international machinery in operation to ensure the arrest or adjudication of international terrorists, and criminologists have yet to arrive at theoretically sound explanations that would help deal with a problem that knows no boundaries.

3. *Theft of art and cultural objects.* This category obtained a number 3 ranking because of its potential for robbing entire cultures and nations of their cultural heritage. Tombs and monuments have been plundered since the time of the pharaohs. But with the development of modern tools and the high demand for cultural objects,

Two hundred and seventeen people lost their lives plunging into the Atlantic Ocean.

as well as the ease of transport, international thieves have developed systems that can strip an entire region or country of its heritage—as well as the work of contemporary artists. There is no country that has not been victimized. An estimated $4.5 billion worth of fine art is stolen every year for sale on the international market. A database lists 45,000 stolen art objects, with an increase of 2000 items a month.[87] With few exceptions,[88] criminologists have paid scant attention to this phenomenon, though the art industry has endeavored to come up with some practical solutions.[89]

4. *Theft of intellectual property.* Theft of intellectual property includes the unauthorized use of the rights of authors and performers, and of copyrights and trademarks. There is obviously a high temptation to reproduce works of protected originators at a fraction of franchise (or similar) costs, especially in countries with relatively unregulated economies. Yet the destructive impact on the economies of producing or originating countries is immediately apparent—though hard to assess in monetary terms. One type of theft of intellectual property, namely the illegal copying of software, has been quantified by the U.S. Software Publishers Association: It amounts to an astounding loss of $7.5 billion annually.[90] Despite international agreements, this transnational crime category is a problem without a solution.

5. *Illicit traffic in arms.* Local, regional, or national armed conflicts, which plague us today in every part of the globe, would not be imaginable without an international network of weapons producers and suppliers. This is a shadowy world beyond the reach of statistical assessment. Criminological information on the illegal arms trade is also lacking. Yet the largest portion of the world's homicides is potentially traceable to the illegal trade in arms.

The most lethal part of the world's illegal arms trade centers on the transfer of nuclear materials. It is clear now that during the past few years several relatively small quantities of nuclear material, including pure plutonium, have been diverted from nuclear facilities in former Soviet republics and offered for sale in Germany and other countries west of Russia.

First indications are that the diversions of nuclear material that have occurred so far were carried out by small groups of individuals, rather than organized crime, for motives of individual gain (or possibly to assist in financing totally underfunded former Soviet laboratories and scientists). Most of the efforts were amateurish, and none of the material apparently reached a viable buyer. Indeed, most ended up in sting operations. However, quantities of nuclear material seized by authorities are not insubstantial. In September 1999, Georgian authorities seized 2.2 pounds of uranium 235 at the Georgian-Turkish border.[91] In several cases the thieves, transporters, and the public have been exposed to radiation hazards—in itself a not insubstantial danger.[92] Criminologists have been caught by surprise. As yet, there have been few criminological responses.[93] At this point, governments have cooperated to control nuclear materials at the source.

6. *Aircraft hijacking.* The system for curbing and responding to the illegal interception of aircraft is in place and has proved largely effective. The number of hijackings has declined significantly, yet incidents still occur with regularity.

The airline industry had been plagued by aircraft hijackings in the 1970s and into the 1980s. While a few such incidents were attributable to individuals who demanded ransom, most were political statements with typical terrorist characteristics, seeking to demonstrate the ability of the terrorist organization to strike at vulnerable targets almost anywhere in the world.

Since the entire world community was affected, especially diplomats and politicians, whose mobility depends on air travel, the reaction to the flood of hijackings was swift. The industry itself reacted effectively by increasing security measures.

The criminological literature on this phenomenon is considerable, centering on the profiles of hijackers, causes, regions, carriers involved, and the like, all of which has led to the improvement of controls. Unfortunately, the phenomenon of aircraft hijacking has been upstaged by the terrorist destruction of aircraft in flight.

7. *Sea piracy.* Virtually forgotten until the mid-1970s, sea piracy has resurfaced on two fronts since then:

- The illegal narcotics drug smuggling from South and Central America into the United States initially relied heavily on yachts and fishing vessels captured at sea or in port, after owners and crews were killed.

Several thousand vessels were victimized. As the drug trade became prosperous, smugglers began to rely on purchased or illegally chartered vessels.

- At the roadstead of Lagos, Nigeria, and the narrow shipping channel of the Malacca Straits—as well as in several other comparable sea lanes—the opportunity of deriving some benefit by attacking commercial vessels at anchor or slow speed attracted thousands of marginalized young men in Africa, Southeast Asia, and Latin America. Such piracies (often not piracies in the international law sense, since they occurred in the territorial waters of states) reached a high level of frequency (one a day in the 1980s), but are on the decline now, thanks largely to the research and policy activities of the International Maritime Bureau (London) of the International Chamber of Commerce (Paris), the International Maritime Organization (U.N.), and research by a number of criminologists.[94] (See "Window to the World," Chapter 12.)

While the problem has been ameliorated, it has by no means ended. Prudent shipping lines order "piracy watches" on their vessels in affected waters. National and regional maritime law enforcement agencies maintain closer watch, and the International Maritime Bureau maintains a special branch office in Kuala Lumpur to monitor developments.

8. *Land hijacking.* The inclusion of land hijacking in the list of transnational crimes was a surprise. At the national level, hijacking of trucks had been well documented as a form of robbery or theft. But the world economy has changed. Long-distance trucking from Eastern to Western Europe, or from the Central Asian republics to the Baltic States, now is a reality, and involves a high percentage of goods transported transnationally. The opportunity to divert such cargos has increased proportionately.

It is telling that only four countries responded to this item on the U.N. questionnaire. At this point the evidence is entirely episodic but seems to point to the involvement of organized groups. Predictably, the problem will increase as a result of the openness of borders, the growth of organized crime (especially in Eastern Europe), and the lack of data and criminological analysis.

9. *Insurance fraud.* The insurance industry is internationally linked, especially through reinsurance and other methods of spreading risks and benefits. Thus, local insurance fraud ultimately affects all insurers, and all insured, worldwide. The global dimensions of the problem have not been calculated, but for the United States alone the loss likely amounts to $100 billion annually.[95]

10. *Computer crime.* Just as computers serve legitimate commerce, governments, and researchers, the global Internet is also accessible for criminal schemes, exploitation, and use by organized crime. Current estimates of losses through computer crime range up to $8 billion annually.[96] Unfortunately, on this issue we lack information, though criminologists take an increasing interest in the development of legal and other protections.

11. *Environmental crime.* Well into the middle of the twentieth century, harming the environment was regarded as a matter to be controlled by local authorities. It was not until the United Nations Congress on the Environment (Stockholm, 1972) that the global dimensions of environmental destruction, and thus the need for its control, were recognized. In the three decades since Stockholm, much has been achieved in recognizing environmental dangers, quantifying them, and devising control mechanisms (by treaties, legislation, and ultimately, technology) in order to avert these dangers. Criminological research has contributed a great deal in this regard.[97]

12. *Trafficking in persons.* Original forms of trafficking in persons included the slave trade and the white slave trade (traffic in women). While the slave trade may be a matter of the past, the traffic in persons is on the increase, including:

- The transport of illegal immigrants, often resulting in involuntary servitude.
- The transport of women and young children for purposes of prostitution.

- The transport of migratory laborers to work under slavelike conditions.
- The transport of household workers from developing countries.
- The transfer of children for adoptions not sanctioned by law.

For the most part, laws are in place to prevent the illegal trafficking in persons. Their enforcement is another matter. The problem is bound to increase as the populations of a stagnant Third World press to emigrate to the relatively prosperous countries.

Much of the illegal population flow is controlled by organized crime.[98] The newcomers in the industrialized countries, being largely unemployable, are forming a new marginalized class, likely to be exploited, but also contributing to crime and unrest.

13. *Trade in human body parts.* The first kidney transplant was performed in 1954, the first lung transplant in 1963, and the first heart transplant in 1967. By now close to half a million kidneys have been transplanted. Transplant surgery has become a highly specialized branch of medicine, and the supply of transplantable organs has spawned a very large industry. In the United States, 69 transplant agencies have been established, and federal and state laws seek to control their activities.

Yet, at any given moment, 35,000 people are waiting for a transplant (and the number increases by 14 percent annually); thus, the demand far outstrips the supply. (The number of potential donors in the United States is estimated at about 12,000.) An illegitimate industry has sprung up to provide a service. Recipients are flown to a country where organs can be procured virtually on demand. "Donors" may in fact have been murdered for their organs, or they are children of poor parents sold for their organs, at extremely low prices.

14. *Illicit drug trafficking.* Illicit traffic in narcotic drugs is entirely controlled by organized-crime networks, loosely related with each other geographically, as well as at the various levels of production and marketing and by type of narcotic drugs.[99] The criminological literature exploring this phenomenon from every angle is vast but by no means clear in terms of policy implications.[100]

With the Single Convention on Narcotic Drugs (1961), the Convention on Psychotropic Substances (1971), and the United Nations Convention against Illicit Traffic in Narcotic Drugs and Psychotropic Substances (1988), a theoretically perfect international legal structure to control this traffic is in place. Yet its application and enforcement suffer from the following shortcomings:

- The U.N. structure to oversee this treaty scheme is inadequate, primarily due to underfunding.

- Similarly underfunded are comparable national and regional programs.

- Nations differ vastly in their emphases (interdiction versus repression and control versus tolerance versus treatment approaches).

- Some of the most important countries of origin suffer from corruption at all levels—due to the vast income base of the trade—thus affecting enforcement.

- Corruption similarly affects law enforcement in many countries.

- Most developing and newly democratic countries lack the legal and technical infrastructure necessary to implement the treaties.

No other form of transnational and organized crime is as costly in terms of human and national financial suffering as the illicit trade in narcotic drugs.

15. *Fraudulent bankruptcy.* The internationalization of commerce has turned fraudulent bankruptcy from a local to a transnational crime. The dimensions of the phenomenon are largely unknown. Evidence is anecdotal but includes information that organized crime, after acquiring an enterprise, may subject it to bankruptcy when the gains from bankruptcy exceed the expectations of profit. There is a need to strengthen national enforcement efforts and to coordinate these efforts internationally.

16. *Infiltration of legal business.* This is the logical and temporal sequence of money laundering, the principal objective of which is seemingly legitimate investment. At this point the existing information permits no quantitative or qualitative

assessment of the phenomenon, but it must be considered that the drug trade alone has between $200 billion and $500 billion to invest in the market. At this rate one could theoretically predict a time at which the world's economy would be controlled by organized crime.[101]

Crime Surfing

www.ravel.ifs.univie.ac.at/~uncjin/uncjin.html

How does the United States crime rate compare with that of the world as a whole? You will find this information in the U.N. Survey of Crime Trends and Operations of Criminal Justice Systems.

17. *Corruption and bribery of public officials, party officials, and elected representatives.* While bribery of party officials is not punishable in several countries, all other forms of bribery encompassed by this title are prohibited by penal codes. The problem lies with the enforceability of such laws, in both developed and developing countries, particularly with respect to international investments and trade. Disguised as "commissions," "consultancies," and agency or attorneys' fees, bribes have become a necessary cost of doing business worldwide. Nor is the practice universally condemned. Traders and investors have often proclaimed that it cannot be their business to improve the business or political ethics in countries with which they have commercial relations.[102] A recently established international organization, Transparency International (Berlin), has undertaken the formidable task of investigating international business ethics. Among its accomplishments are:

- Publishing a country-by-country bribery index.

- Pressing for national legislation abolishing the tax deductibility of bribes.

- Seeking international governmental cooperation in criminalizing the bribing of officials.

- Strengthening international cooperation among nongovernmental organizations, such as the International Chamber of Commerce.

- Creating independent watchdog mechanisms.

Where Do We Go from Here?

Transnational Criminality: And Now They Deal in Human Body Parts!

True to his conviction that the measurement of body and brain is the key to distinguishing between criminals and noncriminals, Cesare Lombroso, the founder of positivist criminology, willed his body to science. Today, many people donate their organs to other human beings who need them to live. Yet the demand for donated organs far outstrips the supply. Where do the donated organs come from? Who are the donors?

In 1988 a German physician attended a medical congress in Rio de Janeiro, Brazil. Unknown perpetrators attacked him from behind and knocked him unconscious. Several days later he found himself on a park bench, awakening from obvious anesthesia. He noticed that he had been professionally bandaged. A medical examination revealed that he was missing a kidney.

THE SCOPE OF THE PROBLEM

In Barranquilla, Colombia, the chief of the University Security Force confessed to 50 murders, committed to obtain organs for transplants. In many parts of Latin America, hospital patients, upon discharge, find out that organs have been needlessly removed; the organs are sold for transplants at exorbitant prices! It has been reported that children's homes in Brazil have been established as "organ farms."(1) President Rafeal Callejas of Honduras has appointed a commission to investigate charges that Honduran children had been sold abroad for illegal adoptions and organ transplants.(2) A member of the European Parliament

asked for international police action to stop "barbaric practices" that included "the murder of children whose bodies are butchered for their organs," which are used for transplants in American and European clinics.(3) The Russian parliament (Supreme Soviet) passed legislation in the face of allegations "that organs for transplants are being illegally harvested on a massive scale and that criminal forces are at work in this."(4) The Mexico City weekly *Proceso* revealed the existence of "baby farms" in several Mexican states; the children are used for adoptions abroad and for organ transplants in 17 clinics in Mexican border cities.(5)

The trade in body parts is now worldwide, criminal, organized, and extremely lucrative. An advertisement in a German newspaper offered kidney transplants for $80,000, including cost of the operation and airfare for two persons to an undisclosed clinic in Asia. The "donor" of the kidney will receive little if anything for his or her organ. The risks for recipients are high: Of 130 patients who had traveled to India for a kidney transplant, 8 died on the operating table and another 17 died within a year, mostly of viral and bacterial infections contracted under the unsanitary conditions of the transplant clinics. Less is known about the fate of donors. Yet the poorest inhabitants of the Third World continue to offer skin, an eye, or one or more of their other body parts to transplant clinics catering to foreign recipients. In November 1999, a group of American

medical ethicists and researchers formed an agency called Organs Watch to monitor the international traffic in human organs, aimed at curbing abusive, exploitative, and corrupt practices.(6)

Sources

1. Britta Buse and Katja Donges, "Illegaler Organhandel," *Magazin für die Polizai*, **203** (1993): 4–7.
2. "Honduran Official Charges Children's Organs Sold," *Orlando Sentinel Tribune,* Apr. 17, 1993, p. A12.
3. "Euro MPs Seek Transplant Laws," *Press Association Limited, Press Association News File,* Sept. 14, 1993.
4. Svetlana Tutorskaya, "Henceforth, Donated Organs Cannot Be Bought and Sold," *Current Digest of the Post Soviet Press,* **45** (1993): 25.
5. "Latin Children Sold in the United States, Study Claims," *Inter Press Service,* Feb. 16, 1993.
6. "Researchers to Monitor Trade in Human Organs," *New York Times,* Nov. 4, 1999, p. 22.

Questions for Discussion

1. Based on the examples given above, what laws are violated by those who deal in human body parts or transplant illegally obtained organs?
2. What type of laws or international conventions are needed to stop "barbaric practices" in organ transplants, without hurting those who desperately need a transplant?

18. *Other offenses committed by organized criminal groups.* This catchall category permitted governments to report problems that could not be easily included in the 17 other categories. For example, both North America and Western Europe are experiencing large-scale automobile theft, with the stolen vehicles being transported abroad. These activities are controlled by international organized criminal groups. They affect not just individual owners, but the insurance industry of each country.

This review of the 18 categories of transnational criminality demonstrates the vast impact these criminal activities have on individuals, various branches of the economy, and the world economy itself. Individuals and individual commercial enterprises can do relatively little to protect themselves from these dangers, and

Crime Surfing

www.interpol.com

. . . If you want to find out
how the International
Criminal Police Organization
(ICPO-Interpol) helps in the
fight against transnational
crime (or anything else you
ever wanted to know about
Interpol), access the
organization's website.

increased international cooperation among nations has been recognized as absolutely necessary. But international action must be preceded by research. Thus, comparative criminological research will increasingly focus on transnational crime.[103]

International Crime

International crimes are the major criminal offenses so designated by the community of nations for the protection of interests common to all humankind. They may be found in precedent (much like the Anglo-American common law of crimes) or in written form in international conventions. They can be tried in the courts of countries that recognize them, or they can be tried by international courts. The war crimes tribunals that tried German and Japanese war criminals after World War II were such courts. In 1993, the U.N. Security Council ordered the establishment of an international tribunal, to sit in the Netherlands, for war crimes committed on the territory of the former Yugoslavia; a court for the trial of persons charged with genocide in Rwanda was added. These courts have issued several hundred indictments—the exact number is unknown because they are sealed. Several trials have been held, leading to convictions as well as acquittals. Those in custody pending trial include General Momir Talic, the chief of staff of the Bosnian Serb army, who was arrested in Austria, on August 24, 1999. Some other powerful indicted war criminals are still in hiding, but they cannot leave the small territories under their control, for fear of likewise being taken into custody under outstanding international arrest warrants.

For five decades, the world's governments have tried to reach agreement for the establishment of a permanent **international criminal court,** with jurisdiction over the most heinous international crimes. While such an agreement

Investigators excavate one of many mass grave sites in the former Yugoslavia, October 1995.

was impossible during the era of the cold war, the governments of the world, meeting in Rome in July 1998, agreed by a vast majority vote to establish the Permanent International Criminal Court. This court will become functional when 60 governments have signed the treaty establishing the court. The handful of countries that have not yet approved the court include the United States, China, and a few small—so-called rogue—countries. The jurisdiction of the new international criminal court extends only to the most serious international crimes, such as crimes against humanity, genocide, and war crimes. Concerned countries have the right to bring persons accused of these crimes to trial in their own courts, or to hand them over to the Permanent International Criminal Court. Except for the few major international crimes over

"Massive fraud." "World's biggest banking crash." "Financial deception of 'epic proportions.'" Journalists had a field day characterizing the magnitude of the collapse of the Bank of Credit & Commerce International (BCCI), which failed in July 1991. But let's talk numbers instead of adjectives:

- Founded in Pakistan, the international financial institution owed some $2 billion when it folded.
- A senior official admitted to playing a major role in frauds totaling $1.242 billion.
- Thousands of creditors, both businesses and individuals, lost every penny of the money they had deposited.
- In 1991, BCCI agreed to forfeit $550 million to begin compensating depositors worldwide and to salvage institutions the corporation owned secretly in the United States.
- The U.S. investigation that preceded the prosecution of a single person accused of participating in the scandal cost a whopping $20 million.
- In England alone, BCCI had a staff of 1200 and 45,000 customers—personnel who lost their jobs and customers who lost their life savings when the bank failed.

Big numbers! What are the crimes that led to this scandal of "epic proportions"? In the United States, BCCI pleaded guilty to federal and state charges of racketeering, fraud, and money laundering. Individuals have been charged with withholding information in a scheme to defraud federal and state bank regulators and depositors. In Britain, charges against bank officials include false accounting, the furnishing of false information, and conspiracy to defraud.

HOW IT WORKED

A picture of the corporation's operations has unfolded since the crash:

> BCCI's reported profits had been "falsely inflated" by $614 million between January 1983 and December 1985. The misuse of clients' funds by the bank amounted to another $627 million by the end of 1985. . . . By the early 1980s the bank needed to demonstrate its profitability and a healthy balance sheet to maintain the confidence of banking regulators and current and potential investors. In desperation, the bank's founder and his senior officers turned to the trading of commodities as a likely source of funds and began a series of high-risk speculations trading in futures. Most of these were in options on large-scale purchases of silver, which went badly wrong when the price of the metal turned sharply downwards. As money was lost upon money, the frauds became more widespread. The methods involved to maintain the pretense of solidity included filing accounts in which commissions on silver-trading deals that had never taken place were recorded as profits. . . . Accounts were falsified and large sums of customers' money diverted using a financial labyrinth to fool auditors into thinking the bank was solvent when it was actually hugely in deficit.(1)

A HARD LESSON

While the settlement in the United States provided funds for the compensation of some depositors, many more will never see their money again. Some consider this a "school of hard knocks" lesson about the inability of the criminal justice system to deal effectively with international fraud. Gathering the documents needed to provide evidence ranges from difficult to impossible. After one trial in the United States, a *Chicago Tribune* editorial commented: "International financial transactions can be made so complex as to effectively conceal what is really going on; key officials can always flee the jurisdiction and take vital evidence with them."(2) One lawyer summed up his observation of the outcomes of big international cases very succinctly: "No one gets caught but huge sums of money disappear."(3)

Sources

1. Ben Fenton and Sonia Purnell, "Bank Official Admits $750m Fraud, 'Financial Juggler' Was at the Heart of BCCI Scandal," *Daily Telegraph,* Sept. 28, 1993, p. 1.
2. "BCCI Still a Mystery," *Chicago Tribune,* Aug. 27, 1993, p. 23.
3. Peter Blackman, "The BCCI Problem; System's Flaws Stymie Probes of Foreign Banks," *New York Law Journal,* Aug. 26, 1993, p. 5.

Questions for Discussion

1. How could depositors be protected from losing their money in international scams like BCCI's?
2. Would an international criminal court be better able to deal with massive international fraud?

Crime Surfing

www.igc.epc.org/icc/index.html

For the latest developments on the establishment of the permanent International Criminal Court, check their website.

which the international criminal court has jurisdiction, all others are triable only before national criminal courts.

Which crimes are listed as international crimes? The Draft Code of Crimes lists the following as crimes against the peace and security of humanity:

- Crimes against humanity.
- Aggression (by one state against another).
- Threat of aggression.
- Intervention (in the internal or external affairs of another state).
- Colonial domination and other forms of alien domination.

- Genocide (destroying a national, ethnic, racial, or religious group).
- Apartheid (suppression of a racial or an ethnic group).
- Systematic or mass violations of human rights.
- Exceptionally serious war crimes.
- Recruitment, use, financing, and training of mercenaries (soldiers of fortune).
- International terrorism.
- Illicit traffic in narcotic drugs.
- Willful and severe damage to the environment.[104]

Did You Know

. . . that the United Nations started in 1945 with 51 Member States? By fall 1999, there were 188 Member States, united "to achieve international cooperation in solving economic, social, cultural and humanitarian problems," including the prevention of crime. The 189th Member State, Tuvalu, is the latest to be approved.

These crimes occur in many forms. For example, "systematic or mass violations of human rights" may be organized, large-scale rapes of women in occupied territories, as in Bosnia in 1992 and 1993.[105]

In addition to the listed international crimes, many others are recognized by convention; these include the cutting of undersea cables, the transportation of women for purposes of prostitution ("white slavery"), and fisheries offenses. There is now a considerable body of research and scholarship on international crimes.[106]

Globalization versus Ethnic Fragmentation

We have entered the twenty-first century. Comparative criminologists view the new millennium with some uneasiness. Globalization raises great hopes for a better future for all human beings. Yet it brings with it grave dangers in terms of the internationalization of crime. Comparative criminology has a significant role to play in the investigation of new forms of transnational crime. Researchers can apply the methods used when such crimes were strictly local or national, but using the sophistication of the science of comparative criminology.

The new millennium presents additional hazards arising from the trend toward balkanization. *Balkanization,* the opposite of globalization, is the breakup of nation-states into ethnic entities. Many ethnic groups are striving for the independence and sovereignty denied to them when they were incorporated in larger nation-states, as in the former Soviet Union or Yugoslavia; or when they were joined arbitrarily with other groups in colonial times, as in Africa; or when other accidents of history included them within empires, as in Western Europe. Frequently, such ethnic groups had to abide by laws and customs that were not of their own choosing and had to suppress their own languages and cultures. Now they are searching for identities, territories, and criminal justice systems of their own. Unfortunately, the struggle has brought with it human rights violations, war crimes, and genocide on a massive scale. This is the latest challenge for criminologists and criminal justice specialists working on the international level.

REVIEW

Comparative criminology, despite its historical antecedents, is a young science, a subspecialty of criminology. In view of the globalization of the world—brought about by recent technological advances and the enormous increase in international commerce, both legal and illegal—comparative studies in criminology have become a necessity. Comparatists are called upon to assist governments in devising strategies to deal with a wide variety of international and transnational crimes.

In this chapter we traced the history of comparative criminology, sought to define it, and attempted to identify its goals. These goals may be theoretical, like the cross-cultural testing of prominent theories of crime. They can also be very practical, like the search for transplantable crime-fighting strategies or for techniques to deal with specific transnational and international crimes.

There are a number of requirements for successful comparative research: studying foreign law, understanding foreign criminal justice systems, learning about a foreign culture, collecting reliable data, engaging in comparative research, and, when needed, doing cross-cultural empirical research.

We paid special attention to three dimensions that pose special challenges to comparative criminology: internationally induced local crime, transnational crime, and international crime. There is much research to be conducted before progress can be expected in these three areas.

The accomplishments of criminologists who have engaged in comparative studies form the foundation for further research. The tools of comparative criminology should prove useful in helping both individual nations and the United Nations solve some of their common crime problems. The United Nations and its agencies continue to do very practical work to help nations deal with crime on a worldwide basis.

YOU BE THE CRIMINOLOGIST

What advice would you give to the U.S. Congress regarding how to alleviate the global crime problem as it affects U.S. citizens? Should the United States go it alone? Enter into bilateral arrangements? Attempt to find global solutions? Explain your recommendations.

KEY TERMS

The numbers next to the terms refer to the pages on which the terms are defined.

comparative criminology (443)

international crimes (460)

international criminal court (460)

transnational crime (453)

NOTES

1. Peter Applebome, "Skinhead Violence Grows, Experts Say," *New York Times,* July 18, 1993, p. 25.
2. *The Skinhead International: A World-Wide Survey of Neo-Nazi Skinheads* (New York: Anti-Defamation League of B'nai B'rith, 1995).
3. Jane Kramer, "Neo-Nazis: A Chaos in the Head," *New Yorker,* July 14, 1993, pp. 52–70, at p. 53. See also Marie C. Douglas, "Ausländer Raus! Nazi Raus! An Observation of German Skins and Jugendgangen," *International Journal of Comparative and Applied Criminal Justice,* **16** (1992): 129–134.
4. John Leland and Marcus Mabry, "Toasting the 'Head,'" *Newsweek,* Feb. 26, 1996, pp. 42–43.
5. Mark S. Hamm, *American Skinheads—The Criminology and Control of Hate Crime* (Westport, Conn.: Praeger, 1993).
6. Piers Beirne and David Nelken, eds., *Issues in Comparative Criminology* (Aldershot, U.K.: Dartmouth, 1997, is a useful anthology of scientific issues in comparative criminology.
7. The term "comparative criminology" appears to have been coined by Sheldon Glueck. See Sheldon Glueck, "Wanted: A Comparative Criminology," in *Ventures in Criminology,* ed. Sheldon Glueck and Eleanor Glueck (London: Tavistock, 1964), pp. 304–322.
8. James O. Finckenauer, *Russian Youth: Law, Deviance and the Pursuit of Freedom* (New Brunswick, N.J.: Transaction, 1995); Nanci Adler, "Planned Economy and Unplanned Criminality: The Soviet Experience," *International Journal of Comparative and Applied Criminal Justice,* **17** (1993): 189–201; Wojciech Cebulak, "White-Collar Crime in Socialism: Myth or Reality?" *International Journal of Comparative and Applied Criminal Justice,* **15** (1991): 109–120; Klaus Sessar, "Crime Rate Trends before and after the End of the German Democratic Republic—Impressions and First Analyses," in *Fear of Crime and Criminal Victimization,* ed. Wolfgang Bilsky, Christian Pfeiffer, and Peter Wetzels (Stuttgart, Germany: Ferdinand Enke Verlag, 1993), pp. 231–244; Louise I. Shelley et al., "East Meets West in Crime," *European Journal on Criminal Policy and Research,* **3** (1995): 7–107. As China is undergoing a transformation, mostly economic, changes in that country are noteworthy. See Yue Ma, "Crime in China: Characteristics, Causes and Control Strategies," *Journal of Comparative and Applied Criminal Justice,* **34** (1994): 54–68.
9. Martin Kilias et al., "Cross-Border Crime," *European Journal on Criminal Policy and Research,* **1** (1993): 7–134.
10. William F. McDonald, "The Globalization of Criminology: The New Frontier Is the

Frontier," *Transnational Organized Crime*, **1** (1995): 1–12.

11. Piers Beirne and Joan Hill, *Comparative Criminology—An Annotated Bibliography* (New York: Greenwood, 1991), pp. vii–viii.

12. See especially Albert P. Blaustein and G. H. Flenz, *Constitutions of the Countries of the World*, 21 vols. (updated) (Dobbs Ferry, N.Y.: Oceana, 1971 and continuing).

13. The Comparative Criminal Law Project at Wayne State University Law School (formerly at New York University School of Law) has published 21 criminal codes in *The American Series of Foreign Penal Codes*, ed. G. O. W. Mueller, cont. by Edward M. Wise (Littleton, Colo.: Fred B. Rothman, since 1960); G. O. W. Mueller and Fré Le Poole Griffiths, *Comparative Criminal Procedure* (New York: New York University Press, 1969); Albin Eser and George Fletcher, *Justification and Excuse—Comparative Perspectives*, 2 vols. (Freiburg, Germany: Max Planck Institut, 1987); Edward M. Wise and G. O. W. Mueller, eds., *Studies in Comparative Criminal Law*, Comparative Criminal Law Project Publications Series, vol. 9 (Littleton, Colo.: Fred B. Rothman, 1975); Marc Ancel, *Social Defense: The Future of Penal Reform*, Comparative Criminal Law Project Publications Series, vol. 16 (Littleton, Colo.: Fred B. Rothman, 1987). For a historical survey, see G. O. W. Mueller, *Comparative Criminal Law in the United States*, Comparative Criminal Law Project Monograph Series, vol. 4 (South Hackensack, N.J.: Fred B. Rothman, 1970).

14. Seven codes of criminal procedure have appeared in Mueller and Wise, *The American Series of Foreign Penal Codes*.

15. E.g., Shigemitsu Dando, *Japanese Criminal Procedure*, Comparative Criminal Law Project Publications Series, vol. 4 (Littleton, Colo.: Fred B. Rothman, 1965).

16. UNAFEI, 1–26 Harumicho, Fuchu, Tokyo, Japan. There are now 51 volumes.

17. Kristiina Kangaspunta, ed., *Profiles of Criminal Justice Systems in Europe and North America* (Helsinki: HEUNI, 1995); Matti Joutsen, *Criminal Justice Systems in Europe: Finland* (Helsinki: HEUNI, 1995).

18. Dae H. Chang, *Criminology: A Cross-Cultural Perspective*, 2 vols. (Durham, N.C.: Carolina Academic Press, 1976); George F. Cole, Stanislaw J. Frankowski, and Marc G. Gertz, *Major Criminal Justice Systems—A Comparative Survey*, 2d ed. (Newbury Park, Calif.: Sage, 1987); Richard J. Terrill, *World Criminal Justice Systems*, 2d ed. (Cincinnati: Anderson, 1985); Robert Heiner, ed., *Criminology—A Cross-Cultural Perspective* (Minneapolis/St. Paul: West, 1996); Obi N. I. Ebbe, ed., *Comparative and International Criminal Justice Systems* (Boston: Butterworth-Heinemann, 1996); Charles B. Fields and Richter H. Moore, eds., *Comparative Criminal Justice: Traditional and Non-traditional Systems of Law and Control* (Prospect Heights, Ill.: Waveland Press, 1996).

19 V. Lorne Stewart, *Justice and Troubled Children around the World*, vols. 1–5 (New York: New York University Press, 1980–1983).

20. David H. Bayley, *Patterns of Policing—A Comparative International Analysis* (New Brunswick, N.J.: Rutgers University Press, 1985).

21. Roy Walmsley, *Prison Systems in Central and Eastern Europe* (Helsinki: HEUNI, 1996).

22. Freda Adler, ed., *The Incidence of Female Criminality in the Contemporary World* (New York: New York University Press, 1984).

23. Marshall B. Clinard, *Cities with Little Crime: The Case of Switzerland* (London: Cambridge University Press, 1978).

24. Louise I. Shelley, *Crime and Modernization: The Impact of Industrialization and Urbanization on Crime* (Carbondale: Southern Illinois University Press, 1981).

25. William Clifford, *Crime Control in Japan* (Lexington, Mass.: Lexington Books, 1976).

26. G. O. W. Mueller, *World Survey on the Availability of Criminal Justice Statistics*, Internet-UNCJIN-ftp238.33.18WSAYL. See also G. O. W. Mueller, "International Criminal Justice: Harnessing the Information Explosion—Coasting Down the Electronic Superhighway," *Journal of Criminal Justice Education* (Fall 1996), 7(2):253–261.

27. Interpol, located in Lyons, France, has published the crime statistics supplied to it by member states since 1951.

28. First survey: 1970–1975, A/32/199; second survey: 1975–1980, A/Conf. 121/18; third survey: 1980–1986, A/Conf. 144/6; fourth survey: 1986–1990, A/Conf. 169/15 and Add. 1; fifth survey (see United Nations, *Global Report on Crime and Justice*). See "Window to the World" in Chapter 2.

29. World Health Organization, "Homicide Statistics," in *World Health Statistics* (Geneva: World Health Organization, annually).

30. Dane Archer and Rosemary Gartner, *Violence and Crime in Cross-National Perspective* (New Haven, Conn.: Yale University Press, 1984).

31. Richard R. Bennett, *Correlates of Crime: A Study of Nations, 1960–1984* (Ann Arbor, Mich.: Inter-University Consortium for Political and Social Research, 1989).

32. Richard R. Bennett and James P. Lynch, "Does a Difference Make a Difference?" *Criminology*, **28** (1990): 155–182; Carol B. Kalish, *International Crime Rates* (Washington, D.C.: Bureau of Justice Statistics, 1988).

33. Jan J. M. Van Dijk, Pat Mayhew, and Martin Killias, *Experiences of Crime across the World: Key Findings from the 1989 International Crime Survey* (Deventer, Netherlands: Kluwer, 1990); Richard R. Bennett and R. Bruce Wiegand, "Observations on Crime Reporting in a Developing Nation," *Criminology*, **32** (1994): 135–148; Ugljesa Zvekic and Anna Albazzi del Frate, eds., *Criminal Victimization in the Developing World* (Rome: United Nations Interregional Crime and Justice Research Institute, 1995); Gail Travis et al., "The International Crime Surveys: Some Methodological Concerns," *Current Issues in Criminal Justice*, **6** (1995): 346–361; Van Dijk, Box 0.9 in *Global Report on Crime and Justice*, p. 9.

34. Josine Junger-Tas, Gert-Jan Terlouw, and Malcolm W. Klein, *Delinquent Behavior among People in the Western World* (Amsterdam: RDC Ministry of Justice, Kugler Publ., 1994); Junger-Tas, Box 0.10 in *Global Report on Crime and Justice*, p. 16.

35. Hermann Mannheim, *Comparative Criminology* (Boston: Houghton Mifflin, 1965).

36. See Jerome L. Neapolitan, *Cross-National Crime—A Research Review and Sourcebook* (Westport, Conn.: Greenwald Press, 1997); Dennis Benamati, Phyllis Schultze, Adam Bouloukos, and Graeme Newman, *Criminal Justice Information: How to Find It, How to Use It* (Phoenix, Ariz.: Onyx Press, 1997); Harry R. Dammer and Philip L. Reichel, eds., *Teaching about Comparative/International Criminal Justice—A Resource Manual* (Highland Heights, N.Y.: Academy of Criminal Justice Sciences, 1997).

37. Elmer H. Johnson, ed., *International Handbook of Contemporary Developments in Criminology*, 2 vols. (Westport, Conn.: Greenwood Press, 1983); George F. Cole, Stanislaw J. Frankowski, and Marc G. Gertz, *Major Criminal Justice Systems—A Comparative Survey*, 2d ed. (Newbury Park, Calif.: Sage, 1987); Richard J. Terrill, *World Criminal Justice Systems: A Survey* (Cincinnati: Anderson, 1984); Obi N. Ignatius Ebbe, *Comparative and International Criminal Justice Systems* (Boston: Butterworth, 1996); Philip L. Reichel, *Comparative Criminal Justice Systems: A Topical Approach* (Upper Saddle River, N.J.: Prentice Hall, 1994); Brunon Holyst, *Comparative Criminology* (Lexington, Mass.: Lexington Books, 1979); Louise I. Shelley, ed., *Readings in Comparative Criminology* (Carbondale: Southern Illinois University Press, 1981).

38. United Nations, *The United Nations Crime Prevention and Criminal Justice Program: Formulation of Standards and Efforts at Their Implementation* (Philadelphia: University of Pennsylvania, 1994); Benedict Alper and Jerry F. Boren, *Crime: International Agenda* (Lexington, Mass.: Lexington Books, 1972); Ethan N. Nadelman, *Cops across Borders* (University Park: Penn State Press, 1993); André Bossard, *Transnational Crime and Criminal Law* (Chicago: Office of International Criminal Justice, 1990).

39. Graeme Newman, ed., *Global Report on Crime and Justice*, United Nations Office for Drug Control and Crime Prevention, Centre for International Crime Prevention (New York: Oxford University Press, 1999). See also, *The United Nations and Crime Prevention: Seeking Security and Justice for All* (New York: UNDPI, 1996); and *The United Nations and Criminal Justice, 1946–1996: Resolutions,*

Review • You Be the Criminologist • Key Terms • Notes

Reports, Documents and Publications, International Review of Criminal Policy, Issue 47–48 (Vienna: United Nations, 1996/97).

40. G. O. W. Mueller, Michael Gage, and Lenore R. Kupperstein, *The Legal Norms of Delinquency: A Comparative Study,* Criminal Law Education and Research Center Monograph Series, vol. 1 (South Hackensack, N.J.: Fred B. Rothman, 1969).

41. Anastassios Mylonas, *Perception of Police Power: A Study in Four Cities,* Comparative Criminal Law Project Monograph Series, vol. 8 (South Hackensack, N.J.: Fred B. Rothman, 1973).

42. Setsuo Miyazawa, "The Enigma of Japan as a Testing Ground for Cross-Cultural Criminological Studies," *Annales Internationales de Criminologie,* 32 (1994): 81–103; B. Hebenton and J. Spencer, "The Contribution and Limitations of Anglo-American Criminology to Understanding Crime in Central-Eastern Europe," *European Journal of Crime, Criminal Law and Criminal Justice,* 2 (1994): 50–61.

43. Sheldon Glueck and Eleanor Glueck, *Unraveling Juvenile Delinquency* (New York: The Commonwealth Fund; Cambridge, Mass.: Harvard University Press, 1950).

44. Sheldon Glueck and Eleanor Glueck, *Of Delinquency and Crime—A Panorama of Years of Search and Research,* Publications of the Criminal Law Education and Research Center, vol. 8 (Springfield, Ill.: Charles C Thomas, 1974), p. 332.

45. Obi N. I. Ebbe, "Juvenile Delinquency in Nigeria: The Problem of Application of Western Theories," *International Journal of Comparative and Applied Criminal Justice,* 16 (1992): 353–370.

46. Rosemary Gartner, "The Victims of Homicide: A Temporal and Cross-National Comparison," *American Sociological Review,* 55 (1990): 92–106.

47. Gary LaFree and Christopher Birkbeck, "The Neglected Situation: A Cross-National Study of the Situational Characteristics of Crime," *Criminology,* 29 (1991): 73–98.

48. Richard R. Bennett, "Routine Activities: A Cross-National Assessment of a Criminological Perspective," *Social Forces,* 70 (1991): 147–163.

49. Richard R. Bennett and P. Peter Basiotis, "Structural Correlates of Juvenile Property Crime: A Cross-National, Time-Series Analysis," *Journal of Research in Crime and Delinquency,* 28 (1991): 262–287.

50. Sam S. Souryal, "Juvenile Delinquency in the Cross-Cultural Context: The Egyptian Experience," *International Journal of Comparative and Applied Criminal Justice,* 16 (1992): 329–352.

51. Adel Helal and Charisse T. M. Coston, "Low Crime Rates in Bahrain: Islamic Social Control—Testing the Theory of Synnomie," *International Journal of Comparative and Applied Criminal Justice,* 15 (1991): 125–144.

52. Gregory C. Leavitt, "General Evaluation and Durkheim's Hypothesis of Crime Frequency: A Cross-Cultural Test," *Sociological Quarterly,* 33 (1992): 241–263; Suzanne T. Ortega, Jay Corzine, and Cathleen Burnett, "Modernization, Age Structure, and Regional Context: A Cross-National Study of Crime," *Sociological Spectrum,* 12 (1992): 257–277.

53. Christopher Birkbeck, "Against Ethnocentrism: A Cross-Cultural Perspective on Criminal Justice Theories and Policies," *Journal of Criminal Justice Education,* 4 (1993): 307–323.

54. Shelley, *Crime and Modernization.*

55. David Shichor, "Crime Patterns and Socio-Economic Development: A Cross-National Analysis," *Criminal Justice Review,* 15 (1990): 64–78; John Arthur, "Development and Crime in Africa: A Test of Modernization Theory," *Journal of Criminal Justice,* 19 (1991): 499–513.

56. "New Perspectives in Crime Prevention and Criminal Justice and Development: The Role of International Co-operation," working paper prepared by the Secretariat, United Nations, 1980, A/Conf. 87/10.

57. Freda Adler, *Nations Not Obsessed with Crime,* Comparative Criminal Law Project Publications Series, vol. 15 (Littleton, Colo.: Fred B. Rothman, 1983).

58. See Note 8.

59. See Ugljesa Zvekic, ed., *Essays on Crime and Development* (Rome: U.N. Interregional Crime and Justice Research Institute, 1990).

60. V. Lee Hamilton and Joseph Sanders, *Everyday Justice: Responsibility and the Individual in Japan and the United States* (New Haven, Conn.: Yale University Press, 1992); Hans Joachim Schneider, "Crime and Its Control in Japan and in the Federal Republic of Germany, a Comparative Study," *International Journal of Offender Therapy and Comparative Criminology,* **36** (1992): 47–63.

61. Dale E. Berger et al., "Deterrence and Prevention of Alcohol-Impaired Driving in Australia, the United States, and Norway," *Justice Quarterly,* **7** (1990): 453–465.

62. David B. Kopel, *The Samurai, the Mountie, and the Cowboy: Should America Adopt the Gun Controls of Other Democracies?* (Buffalo, N.Y.: Prometheus, 1992).

63. Robert L. Nay, *Firearms Regulations in Various Foreign Countries* (Washington, D.C.: Law Library of Congress, 1990).

64. Michael Clarke, "The Control of Insurance Fraud: A Comparative View," *British Journal of Criminology,* **30** (1990): 1–23.

65. Kenneth Polk and William Weston, "Insider Trading as an Aspect of White Collar Crime," *Australian and New Zealand Journal of Criminology,* **23** (1990): 24–38.

66. Yü-Hsiu Hsü, ed., *International Conference on Environmental Criminal Law* (Taipei: Taiwan/ROC Chapter of the International Association of Penal Law, 1992).

67. Rosemary Gartner, "Family Structure, Welfare Spending, and Child Homicide in Developed Democracies," *Journal of Marriage and the Family,* **53** (1991): 231–240.

68. Margo I. Wilson and Martin Daly, "Who Kills Whom in Spouse Killings? On the Exceptional Sex Ratio of Spousal Homicides in the United States," *Criminology,* **30** (1992): 189–215.

69. Lois A. Fingerhut and Joel C. Kleinman, "International and Interstate Comparisons of Homicide among Young Males," *Journal of the American Medical Association,* **263** (1990): 3292–3295.

70. F. H. McClintock and Per-Olof H. Wikstrom, "The Comparative Study of Urban Violence—Criminal Violence in Edinburgh and Stockholm," *British Journal of Criminology,* **32** (1992): 505–520.

71. Dae H. Chang and Galan M. Janeksela, eds., "Special Issue on Comparative Juvenile Delinquency," *International Journal of Comparative and Applied Criminal Justice,* **16** (1992): 135–170, with contributions by Gaban M. Janeksela, David P. Farrington, Alison Hatch and Curt T. Griffiths, Günther Kaiser, Josine Junger-Tas, Paul C. Friday, James O. Finckenauer and Linda Kelly, Hualing Fu, Michael S. Vaughn and Frank F. Y. Huang, Byung In Cho and Richard J. Chang, Clayton A. Hartjen and Sesharajani Kethineni, Sam S. Souryhal, and Obi N. I. Ebbe.

72. Mylonas, *Perception of Police Power.*

73. Graeme Newman, *Comparative Deviance: Perception and Law in Six Cultures* (New York: Elsevier Scientific, 1976).

74. Russel P. Dobash, R. Emerson Dobash, Scott Balliofyne, Karl Schuman, Reiner Kaulitzki, and Hans-Werner Guth, "Ignorance and Suspicion: Young People and Criminal Justice in Scotland and Germany," *British Journal of Criminology,* **30** (1990): 306–320.

75. Ronald D. Hunter, "Three Models of Policing," Police Studies, 13 (1990): 118–124; R. I I. Mawby, *Comparable Policing Issues: The British and American Experience in International Perspective* (London: Unwin Hyman, 1990).

76. Leslie T. Wilkins, *Punishment, Crime and Market Forces* (Aldershot, England: Dartmouth, 1991); Dennis Wiechman, Jerry Kendall, and Ronald Bae, "International Use of the Death Penalty," *International Journal of Comparative and Applied Criminal Justice,* **14** (1990): 239–259.

77. See Gunther Kaiser, Helmut Kury, and Hans-Jorg Albrecht, eds., *Victims and Criminal Justice,* 3 vols. (Freiburg, Germany: Max Planck Institut, 1991); Emilio C. Viano, ed., *Critical Issues in Victimology— International Perspectives* (New York: Springer Verlag, 1992).

78. Jack Levin and Jack McDevitt, *Hate Crimes—The Rising Tide of Bigotry and Bloodshed* (New York: Plenum, 1993).

79. See Hans-Dieter Schwind et al., "Causes, Prevention and Control of Violence," *Revue Internationale de Criminologie et de Police Technique,* **43** (1990): 395–520.

Review • You Be the Criminologist • Key Terms • Notes

80. Gerhard O. W. Mueller and Freda Adler, *Outlaws of the Ocean: The Complete Book of Contemporary Crime on the High Seas* (New York: Hearst Marine Books, 1985); Gerhard O. W. Mueller and Freda Adler, "A New Wave of Crime at Sea," *The World and I* (February 1986): 96–103.

81. Mike King, *Towards Federalism: Policing the Borders of a "New" Europe* (Leicester, United Kingdom: University of Leicester, 1993); H. Lensing, "The Federalization of Europe: Towards a Federal System of Criminal Justice," *European Journal of Crime, Criminal Law and Criminal Justice*, 1 (1993): 212–229; Ethan A. Nadelman, *Cops across Borders: The Internationalization of U.S. Criminal Law Enforcement* (University Park: Penn State University Press, 1994).

82. See fourth U.N. Survey, 1986–1990, A/Conf.169/15 and Add. 1.

83. See, for example, Jonathan Reuvid, ed., *The Regulation and Prevention of Economic Crime Internationally* (London: Kogan Page, 1995).

84. United Nations Office for Drug Control and Crime Prevention, *United Nations Global Programme against Money Laundering* (New York: United Nations, 1998), p. 19.

85. Laurence Zuckerman and John Sullivan, "An FAA Study Shows Few Gains in Improving Security at Airports," *New York Times*, Nov. 5, 1999, p. 30.

86. Several journals are devoted entirely to terrorism. See *Terrorism* (New York); *Studies in Conflict and Terrorism* (London); *Violence, Aggression, Terrorism* (Danbury, Conn.).

87. "High-Tech Art Sleuths Snare Thieves," *C.J. International*, 9 (1993): 4:6.

88. Truc-Nhu Ho, *Art Theft in New York City: An Explanatory Study in Crime Specificity*, Ph.D. dissertation, Rutgers University, 1992.

89. Ralph Blumenthal, "Museums Getting Together to Track Stolen Art," *New York Times*, July 16, 1996, pp. C13, C15.

90. Natalie D. Voss, "Crime on the Internet," *Jones Telecommunications and Multimedia Encyclopedia*, Drive D:\Studio, Jones Digital Century, 1996.

91. Michael R. Gordon, "Stolen Uranium Intercepted by Georgia in the Caucasus," *New York Times*, Sept. 24, 1999, p. 6.

92. "For Sale—Nukes: Deadly Plutonium from Russia's Vast Nuclear Network Is Turning Up on the European Market. Who Is Buying—and Can They Be Stopped?" *Newsweek*, Aug. 29, 1994, pp. 30–31; Bruce W. Nolan, "Formula for Terror," *Time*, Aug. 29, 1994.

93. Les Johnston, "Policing Plutonium: Issues in the Provision of Policing Services at Nuclear Facilities and for Related Materials in Transit," *Policing and Society*, 4 (1994): 53–72; Phil Williams and Paul H. Woessnar, *Nuclear Material Trafficking: An Interim Assessment* (Pittsburgh: Ridgway Center for International Security Studies, 1995).

94. Eric Ellen, "The Dimensions of International Maritime Crime," in *Issues in Maritime Crime: Mayhem at Sea*, ed. Martin Gill (Leicester, United Kingdom: Perpetuity Press, 1995), pp. 4–11; Martin Gill, *Crime at Sea: A Forgotten Issue in Police Co-operation* (Leicester, United Kingdom: Centre for the Study of Public Order, 1995); Gerhard O. W. Mueller and Freda Adler, "Piraterie: le 'Jolly Roger' flotte à nouveau les Corsaires des Caribes," *Revue Internationale de Criminologie et de Police Technique*, 4 (1992): 408–424.

95. National Insurance Crime Bureau, fax of July 29, 1996.

96. British Banking Association estimate. See Larry E. Coutoria, "The Future of High-Technology Crime: A Parallel Delphi Study," *Journal of Criminal Justice*, 23 (1995): 13–27.

97. E.g., Sally M. Edwards, Terry D. Edwards, and Charles B. Fields, eds., *Environmental Crime and Criminality* (New York: Garland, 1996).

98. Ko-lin Chin, *Chinese Subculture and Criminality: Non-traditional Crime Groups in America* (Westport, Conn.: Greenwood, 1990); Alex P. Schmid, ed., *Migration and Crime* (Milan, Italy: International Scientific and Professional Advisory Council of the United Nations Crime Prevention and Criminal Justice Programme, 1998).

99. Michael Woodiwiss, "Crime's Global Reach," in *Global Crime Connections*, ed. Frank Pearce and Michael Woodiwiss (Houndmills, United Kingdom: Macmillan, 1993), pp. 1–31.

100. Raphael F. Perl, ed., *Drugs and Foreign Policy: A Critical Review* (Boulder, Colo.: Westview Press, 1994); Günther Kaiser, "International Experiences with Different Strategies of Drug Policy," *EuroCriminology,* **7** (1994): 3–29.

101. See Frederick T. Martens, "Transnational Enterprise Crime and the Elimination of Frontiers," *International Journal of Comparative and Applied Criminal Justice,* **15** (1991): 99–107; Wojciech Cebulak, "The Antitrust Doctrine: How It Was Internationalized," *International Journal of Comparative and Applied Criminal Justice,* **14** (1990): 261–267.

102. See "Crime Prevention and Criminal Justice in the Context of Development: Realities and Perspectives of International Cooperation," *International Review of Criminal Policy,* **41/42** (1993): 1–19.

103. Gerhard O. W. Mueller, "Transnational Crime: An Experience in Uncertainties," in *Organized Crime: Uncertainties and Dilemmas,* ed. S. Einstein and M. Amir (Chicago: Office of International Criminal Justice, 1999), pp. 3–18.

104. Draft Articles of the Draft Code of Crimes against the Peace and Security of Mankind, adopted by the International Law Commission on First Reading, United Nations, New York, 1991. For a complete listing, see M. Cherif Bassiouni, *International Criminal Law—A Draft International Criminal Code* (Alphen an den Rijn, Netherlands: Sijthoff & Noordhoff, 1980).

105. Shana Swiss and Joan E. Giller, "Rape as a Crime of War," *Journal of the American Medical Association,* **270** (1993): 612–615.

106. For an analysis of all international crimes, see M. Cherif Bassiouni, ed., *International Criminal Law:* vol. 1, *Crimes,* 2d ed. (Ardsley, N.Y.: Transnational, 1999); M. Cherif Bassiouni, *A Draft International Criminal Code and Draft Statute for an International Criminal Tribunal* (Dordrecht, Netherlands: Martinus Nijhoff, 1987); Farhad Malekian, *International Criminal Law,* 2 vols. (Motala, Sweden: Borgstroms Trycker, 1991); Gerhard O. W. Mueller and Edward M. Wise, *International Criminal Law,* Comparative Criminal Law Project, Publications Series, vol. 2 (South Hackensack, N.J.: Fred B. Rothman, 1965).

Review • You Be the Criminologist • Key Terms • Notes

PART IV

A Criminological Approach to the Criminal Justice System

When a crime appears to have been committed and authorities have been notified, a legal apparatus is set in motion. This apparatus is called the criminal justice system, and its processes have been studied closely. Extensive research has made it possible to understand the system and its component parts. This research provides the basis for efforts to make the system more rational, more cost-beneficial, and more humane (Chapter 16). The law enforcement component of the criminal justice system is by far the most visible and costly one, because it employs the most personnel. The operations and tactics of the police, the images and perceptions of law enforcement, and its successes and failures are explained in terms of contemporary criminological research (Chapter 17).

The functions and tasks of the judiciary—the second component of the criminal justice system—are examined in the light of criminological studies (Chapter 18). Much blame for America's high crime rate is bestowed, justly as well as unjustly, on the third component of the criminal justice system: corrections (Chapter 19). Corrections include institutional corrections (prisons and jails), juvenile institutions, and community-based facilities, as well as noninstitutional responses, such as fines, community service sentences, probation, and parole. The functioning, success, and failure of all the correctional responses are examined on the basis of research findings.

CHAPTER 16
Processes and Decisions

KEY TERMS
direct file
exclusionary rule
Miranda warning
parens patriae
plea bargaining
preliminary hearing
prima facie case
probable cause
reasonable suspicion

The great novelist Franz Kafka, in one of his most famous works, *The Trial,* portrayed the criminal justice process with a profound understanding of the frustrations and despair experienced by a person caught in its machinery. Escape doors seem blocked; a step ahead is prevented by a step that one should not have taken earlier. No one has a map to chart the way. One can only submit without hope to a fate that seems arbitrary.

Are today's criminal defendants in America as bewildered and frustrated as Kafka's litigant three-quarters of a century ago? As we explore the criminal justice system in the United States, Kafka will be much on our minds because many aspects of the U.S. criminal justice process seem bewildering and pointless to the uninitiated. Criminological research has revealed a logical structure, but one that can accommodate bias, arbitrariness, mistakes, and caprice. Moreover, in many large and congested urban areas, this system of criminal justice suffers from delay, overcrowding, indifference, and lack of funding.[1]

FIGURE 16.1   The paths of the criminal justice system.

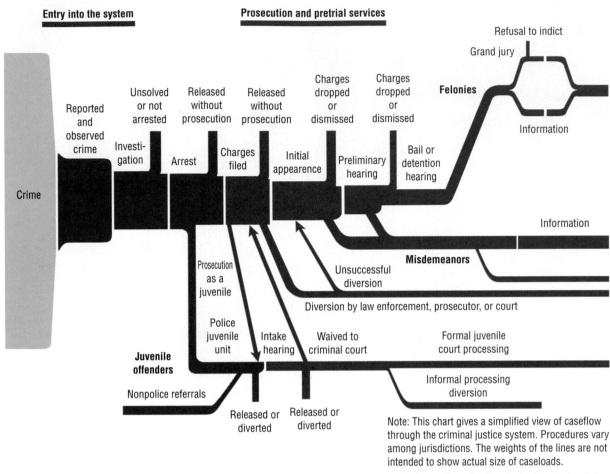

Note: This chart gives a simplified view of caseflow through the criminal justice system. Procedures vary among jurisdictions. The weights of the lines are not intended to show actual size of caseloads.

Source: Adapted from the President's Commission on Law Enforcement and Administration of Justice, *The Challenge of Crime in a Free Society* (Washington, D.C.: U.S. Government Printing Office, 1967), pp. 8–9, Revised, 1997.

THE STAGES OF THE CRIMINAL JUSTICE PROCESS

Until the 1960s, criminal justice procedures from arrest to conviction were generally not seen as an orderly process. The various sectors of the system seemed to exist in isolation. In the 1960s, criminal justice came to be seen as a process similar to the production system in industry. In 1967 the President's Commission on Law Enforcement and the Administration of Justice first depicted the criminal justice system as an apparatus by which a product is produced in an orderly process (Figure 16.1).[2] Some people regard that product as justice, others as the reduction of crime; still others recognize both as the system's outputs.

If criminal justice is a system, or a process, we should be able to assess its costs and benefits. To some extent we can, though assessing the cost is somewhat easier. For Montana, for example, it has been established that the total aggregate cost of processing an average offender in a simple case amounts to $4047 (including police costs, $561; court processing, $1511; jail detention, $1511). In complicated, serious felony cases, the cost jumps to $45,312.[3] The benefits, or performance measures, are harder to calculate. Should we look for indicators such as crime and recidivism prevention, or should we utilize "soft" indicators, such as perceptions of justice, feelings of security, satisfaction of victims, or conflict resolution?[4]

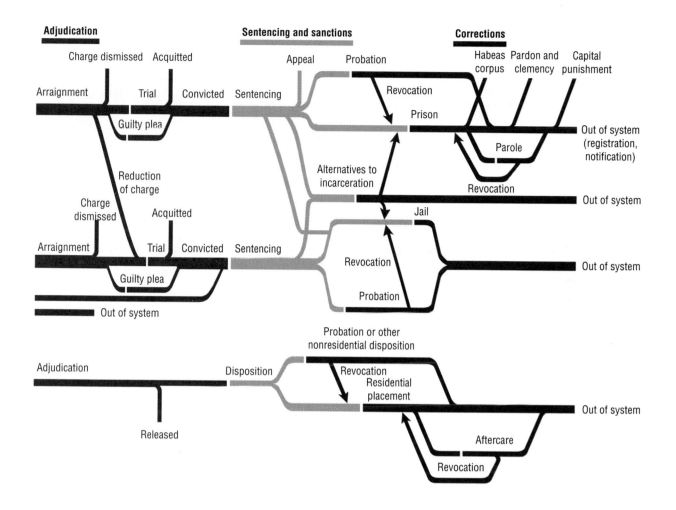

Some scholars characterize criminal justice systems in terms of their predominant features, rather than their goals. For example, Herbert Packer distinguished between the *crime-control model* for criminal justice systems, in which effectiveness and efficiency are emphasized, and the *due process model*, which is oriented more to the rights of defendants.[5] Most criminologists would agree that the ideal criminal justice system should embody both these concepts.

The President's Commission depicts the criminal justice system as composed of five phases. Every criminal case may potentially flow through all five phases, though most do not, as we shall see.

In the first phase, called *entry into the system*, citizens bring criminal events to the attention of

the police. The police, by investigating the case and identifying a suspect, play a crucial role. The judiciary participates by issuing search and arrest warrants.

The second phase, *prosecution and pretrial services*, is dominated by government lawyers called prosecutors, who prepare the charges; grand juries, which indict defendants; and judges, who conduct a series of hearings, including the initial appearance of an arrested person at court and a preliminary hearing.

Crime Surfing

www.aclu.org

For a fascinating view of criminal justice topics—from a civil liberties perspective— go to American Civil Liberties Union website.

The third phase, *adjudication*, begins with the arraignment, at which the officially accused person pleads to (answers) the indictment or information (formal charges) against him or her, and ends with a judgment of guilty or not guilty. This phase is conducted by a judge, with or without a jury. The prosecutor, representing the state and the people, and the defense lawyer play the most active roles in this phase.

The fourth phase consists of *sentencing and sanctions*. In most cases, in most states, jurors do not participate in sentencing. The judge imposes the sentence, usually after hearing a presentence investigation (PSI) report prepared by a probation officer. Prosecutors, defense lawyers, and defendants have their say, and in some states victims have their say as well.

The fifth and final phase, *corrections*, is in the hands of the executive branch of government, whose department of corrections executes the sentence imposed by the court. When called upon to do so, however, courts play a considerable role in ensuring compliance with law in the correctional phase.

The revised system flowchart devised by the President's Commission indicates three different paths through the system. The first path is that for major crimes, or felonies; the second is for minor crimes, or misdemeanors. These differ in some respects: Misdemeanors normally require no grand-jury indictment and no trial by jury, and the sanctions imposed are jail sentences of 1 year or less or fines rather than imprisonment for more than a year. The third path is that for juveniles. It resembles the paths for adults in many respects, except that the proceedings are less formal and rarely include juries. There may well be additional distinct paths, such as those for international criminals or for violators of regulatory, economic, and environmental laws.

As the flowcharts indicate, the various paths through the criminal justice system and the juvenile justice system do not end at a single exit; they lead to many exits at various points. An offender's path through the system is not inexorable or predestined. The direction that path takes depends on individual decisions all along the way, including decisions by the offender. Michael R. Gottfredson and Don M. Gottfredson point out that decision making throughout the system results in a very large attrition rate. Many more crimes are reported than are adjudicated; many more offenders are arrested than are ultimately sent to prison.[6] In this chapter we examine the consequences of decision making at the various stages of the process.

Crime Surfing

www.tqd.advanced.org/2760/homep.htm

Anatomy of a murder: Follow a defendant through the process of a criminal trial. What decisions were made by criminal justice actors? What other outcomes of the case were possible?

Entry into the System

In the entry stage, three kinds of decisions are made: Citizens decide to bring suspected criminal events to the attention of the police. The police decide whether or not to investigate the allegation and seek an arrest warrant. The judiciary participates by granting or refusing to grant search and arrest warrants.

Decisions by Victims Intake into the criminal justice system begins when a crime becomes known to the police (see Figure 16.1). As we noted in Chapter 2, the number of crimes reported does not correspond with the actual number of crimes committed. First, many events reported as crimes are not crimes—some wallets reported as stolen have actually been lost; some automobiles reported as stolen have in fact been abandoned for purposes of collecting insurance benefits. Such reports tend to inflate crime statistics. Second, many crimes are not reported to the police by the victims (see Chapter 2). Victims' decisions to invoke the criminal justice process by a report to the police are related to the seriousness of the crime, the victim's attitude toward the police, the gender of the victim, and other assorted factors.[7]

Decisions by the Police Once information about a possible crime has come to the attention of the police, a decision has to be made about whether or not to investigate the case to determine if a crime has been committed and who committed it. The police cannot possibly investigate every complaint. Under the pressure of heavy caseloads, the police give priority to the investigation of major crimes.

Other factors also affect police decisions to make an arrest or to seek an arrest warrant. Police will consider, for example, public ambivalence about the significance of a given statute, the probability that a witness will or will not cooperate, and whether arrest may be too harsh a response. There are alternatives to arrest, ranging from outright release, to release with a citation, to release of a youngster into the custody of parents or guardians.[8]

Legal Criteria   What legal criteria determine when and whether a suspect can be taken into the criminal justice system? When may the system do something to or about a suspect? There are legal criteria for processing a suspect from one phase to the next in the criminal justice process. The Constitution, as interpreted by the Supreme Court, provides some of these criteria.

The Constitution states that nobody may be "seized" (taken into the criminal justice process) except on a warrant issued on the basis of **probable cause** of having committed a crime. For almost two centuries the probable-cause requirement has been deemed to establish the point at which potential guilt is likely enough to justify taking a person into custody. Ideally, the determination is made by a judge or magistrate on the basis of the testimony of witnesses (including the police), delivered under oath, that a given suspect has committed a given crime. In practice, the decision more frequently is made by a law enforcement officer at the scene of the crime.

Neither magistrates who issue warrants of arrest nor police officers who make an arrest without a warrant are guided by any precise standard of probable cause. The Supreme Court has ruled that the police have probable cause to take a suspect into custody when:

> the facts and circumstances within their knowledge and of which they [have] reasonable trust-

worthy information [are] sufficient to warrant a prudent man in believing that the [suspect] had committed or was committing an offense.[9]

This definition, relying as it does on such vague terms as "reasonable trustworthy information" and "prudent man," lacks precision. Nevertheless, arrests made without probable cause, or not resting on a warrant issued on sworn testimony before a judge and based on a determination of probable cause, are considered unreasonable seizures of the person, and thus in violation of the Fourth Amendment.

Evidence seized in the course of such an illegal arrest can be barred from trial. This is called the **exclusionary rule.** Its intent is to deter the police from engaging in illegal practices and to keep the courts from condoning such conduct. The Supreme Court ruled in 1961, in *Mapp v. Ohio,* that all courts in the country must apply the exclusionary rule.[10]

Civil libertarians view this ruling as a necessary safeguard against police misconduct. Conservatives argue that the rule is an arbitrary measure that handcuffs the police. These two positions exemplify the fundamental issues that are balanced in a Fourth Amendment analysis—that is, the need for effective law enforcement versus individual rights and liberties. Conservatives call for unhampered law enforcement, and liberals ask for the assurance of rights. Research, on the whole, establishes that law enforcement has not been seriously hindered by the exclusionary rule. On the contrary, the result has been improved legal training for law enforcement officers and consequently, some argue, improved police behavior.[11]

Recent Supreme Court decisions have strengthened police powers—unduly so, some critics say. Faced with mounting public concern over street crime in the 1960s, the Supreme Court was under pressure to legitimize prudent police action for the purpose of preventing a specific crime about to be committed, even when an officer had no probable cause to make an arrest. In 1968 the Supreme Court acknowledged the propriety of police intervention when evidence against a suspect fell short of probable cause. If a police officer has **reasonable suspicion** that a person might be engaged in the com-

Obtaining custody over a person charged with a crime is particularly difficult when the accused is an international/transnational perpetrator with the ability to hide almost anywhere on the globe. Take the case of Carlos the Jackal.

Illyich Ramirez Sanchez, better known as "Carlos the Jackal," is now serving a life sentence in France for the murder of three people in 1975. For two decades, until his arrest in August 1994 in the Sudan, this Venezuelan revolutionary was the world's most fabled and most wanted terrorist. Had he been dedicated to a single ideological cause, he might still be regarded as the world's most famous, most dedicated terrorist, but he was a gun for hire, a playboy terrorist enamored of his own exploits.

While actively appealing his life sentence, Sanchez has been tried on other charges during his incarceration, including his recent acquittal for the bombing of a Paris drugstore. His most famous exploit was the capture, in 1975, of 11 OPEC ministers in Vienna, Austria. At the time he proclaimed: "To get anywhere, you have to walk over the corpses." Indeed, in that exploit there were three corpses, and the living were ransomed for millions of dollars, which was used to finance further terrorist activities. Above all, the Jackal wanted to make the point that he could strike any target, anywhere, anytime. Unknown to most of the world, Carlos tried in 1980 to capture the world's crime fighters assembled at Caracas, Venezuela (Carlos' hometown), for the Sixth United Nations Congress on the Prevention of Crime.

No sooner had they arrived in Caracas when two of the leaders of the Congress were threatened by phone: "You will not leave Caracas alive." The threats continued. The U.N. congress site at Caracas, being U.N. territory by agreement between the United Nations and Venezuela, was virtually unprotected. U.N. security staff from New

The many guises of terrorist Carlos the Jackal in a Hungarian newspaper.

York were flown in—but promptly (and without precedent) disarmed at the airport. A last-minute appeal to the government of Venezuela brought in the Venezuelan marines, who surrounded the conference site and protected the delegates. Carlos failed. But that was not his only failure: Security agencies around the world have compiled a long list of failed Jackal operations all over Europe and the Middle East. Carlos's legend is greater than his legacy.

Nevertheless, for two decades he wrought havoc, cashing in on the goodwill of all the governments then supporting terrorism against Western targets. He worked with the Bader-Meinhoff gang (his wife was one of its members), the Brigadi Rossi (Red Brigade) of Italy, the Japanese Red Army, as well as the Haddad terrorist group of the Middle East. He spread terror pointedly and randomly—most of his victims were innocent bystanders, and perhaps most of his operations were badly bungled.

Who was there to keep track of the Jackal's real exploits? Was there any "world cop" to track him down? Police and intelligence agencies of many

countries followed his trail, but solid leads did not surface until the collapse of the Iron Curtain, when East German intelligence files fell into the hands of Western law enforcement. The French—hardest hit by the Jackal's killing spree—had kept the closest surveillance. Ultimately, however, it was the course of world history, with the collapse of terrorism-sponsoring agencies, that proved the Jackal's downfall. Having run out of countries in which to hide, Carlos moved to the Sudan. He had not counted on the Sudanese Minister of Justice, a long-time participant in United Nations efforts, to extradite him for trial in France.

Questions for Discussion

1. Carlos the Jackal has violated the laws of many countries. Which country should have the right to try him? Would the laws of each country treat his crimes similarly?
2. Terrorism is an international problem. What kind of system is needed to make international prosecution possible?

FIGURE 16.2   The Miranda warning.

MIRANDA WARNING

1. You have the right to remain silent.
2. Anything you say can and will be used against you in a court of law.
3. You have the right to talk to a lawyer and have him present with you while you are being questioned.
4. If you cannot afford to hire a lawyer, one will be appointed to represent you before any questioning, if you wish one.
5. You may stop answering questions at any time.
6. Do you understand each of these rights I have explained to you?
7. Having these rights in mind, do you wish to talk to us now?

mission of a crime, the officer is authorized to stop such a person, to ask questions, and to frisk him or her to make sure that the suspect is not armed and dangerous to the officer.[12] This is called the *stop-and-frisk rule.* With an ever more conservative Supreme Court, police powers to make searches and seizures have increased,[13] leading some observers to call for a return to judicial integrity and greater concern for individual rights.[14]

In some circumstances law enforcement officers can intervene even short of reasonable suspicion. The highest court of New York, the New York Court of Appeals, stated in the case of *People v. de Bour* that police officers have the right and duty to approach a person for purposes of making an inquiry on the basis of "articulable facts" that "crime is afoot."[15]

The Miranda Warning   Assume that a police officer or a magistrate has made the decision to arrest a suspect and that a suspect has in fact been arrested. What happens now?

Immediately after the arrest, when the arrestee is in custody, the arresting officer will recite the **Miranda warning** (Figure 16.2). The term derives from one of the Supreme Court's most important rulings, which laid down the standards of procedural fairness mandated by the Fourth, Fifth, and Sixth Amendments to the

Constitution.[16] If the warning is not given, the courts may exclude from evidence at trial any statement the arrestee may have made and any evidence that has resulted from it.[17] In a controversy similar to that surrounding the exclusionary rule, conservatives and liberals disagree over the use of the warning, while studies of its impact have yielded conflicting results.[18]

Once a suspect has been taken into custody, the processing of the event and of the offender begins—booking, fingerprints and mug shots (identifying photographs), filling out of forms—and the suspect waits in a holding pen (police lockup) for the next step.

The Right to Counsel and Counsel's Decisions   In *Gideon v. Wainwright* (1963) the Supreme Court laid down the rule that every person charged with a crime that may lead to incarceration has the right to an attorney and that the state must pay for that service if the defendant cannot afford to do so.[19] The Gideon case, involving an indigent Florida defendant, established the universal right to free defense counsel for the poor. It subsequently was reflected in the Miranda warning. The Supreme Court requirement has been implemented nationwide by the provision of assigned counsel, public defenders, contract counsel, or legal aid. As we shall see, however, these defense lawyers, working on tremendous caseloads and with ever-decreasing budgets, may sometimes be inclined to pressure their clients into unfavorable plea bargains.[20] Thus their decisions, too, have a considerable impact on the flow of the process.

Prosecution and Pretrial Services

During the prosecution and pretrial services phase, prosecutors and judges make the decisions. Far fewer persons are processed through this phase than are entered into the system. Many arrested persons have already been diverted out of the system; others will be diverted at this stage, when charges are dropped or cases dismissed. Charges may be dismissed for many reasons: Perhaps the evidence is not strong enough to support probable cause. Perhaps the arrested person is a juvenile who should be

Serial murderer Jeffrey Dahmer arrives in a Milwaukee courtroom in January 1992 for a pretrial hearing. In 1994, he was beaten to death in prison by a fellow inmate.

dealt with by the juvenile justice system or a mentally disturbed person who requires hospitalization. Perhaps the judge or prosecutor believes that justice is best served by compassion.

The Judicial Decision to Release After an arrest, the arrested person must be taken before a magistrate, a local judge, who makes a determination that probable cause exists. As a judge, the magistrate will use a standard of probable cause that is likely to be a bit tougher than the police officer's. The magistrate must also repeat the Miranda warning and then decide whether:

- To permit the defendant to be released on bail or on percentage bail. (With the latter, the defendant deposits with the court only a stipulated percentage of the bail set.) Normally, bail money is available in the form of commercial surety bail, through bail bond companies.[21]

- To release on recognizance, or ROR. (No bail is required, on condition that the defendant appear for trial and behave lawfully in the meantime.)

- To release the defendant into someone's custody.

- To detain the defendant in jail pending further proceedings.

In making the decision to release, judges or magistrates are strongly influenced by prosecutors' views about whether a given defendant is a safe risk for release. In some states, release criteria have been enacted into law. Historically, however, the only criterion for release on bail has been whether the defendant can be relied on to appear for the next court appearance. In practice, judges tend to rely on such factors as the gravity of the charge and the probability that the defendant may commit a crime or harass victims if he or she is released.

The District of Columbia and a few other jurisdictions permit preventive detention when there is a high probability that the defendant may commit a crime if he or she is released. Despite the difficulty of predicting anyone's behavior, the Supreme Court has ruled it to be constitutionally proper to deny bail to a person who is considered dangerous.[22] A large number of studies have been conducted to assess factors related to release decisions. The seriousness of the charge was found to be the single most important factor in the decision. Both rearrest rates and rates of failure to appear are quite low, especially if trial follows within a short time after pretrial release.[23] This finding might indicate that judges have done well in assessing the risk of releasing defendants. It could also mean that judges might want to liberalize their risk assessments. The issue requires further research.

The Preliminary Hearing   In many states, the next step in the process is the **preliminary hearing,** a preview of the trial in court before a judge, in which the prosecution must produce enough evidence to convince the judge that the case should proceed to trial or to the grand jury. In many jurisdictions the preliminary hearing is officially considered another probable-cause hearing. But what emerges is more than probable cause: In this proceeding, conducted with some of the rights afforded at trials—cross-examination of witnesses and the introduction of evidence under stringent rules—enough evidence must be produced to "bind the defendant over" to the grand jury. In other words, the evidence must constitute a reasonable inference of guilt or reasonable grounds to believe that the defendant is guilty.

In the preliminary hearing, in which the defense need not present any evidence, the defendant gains the advantage of finding out how the prosecution's case is being developed. The defense attorney's decision to enter a plea or to engage in plea negotiations depends very much on what happens during the preliminary hearing.

The Decision to Charge   No matter what the result of the preliminary hearing, the decision to charge the defendant with a crime rests with the prosecutor. Even in states where a grand jury must determine whether a defendant is to be indicted for a felony, it is the prosecutor who decides in the first place whether to place a case before the grand jury. The prosecutor also decides what evidence to present to the grand jury and how to present it.

In a major study based on data from the Prosecutor's Management Information System (PROMIS), researchers found that prosecutors' reasons for not proceeding after an arrest vary by offense. Of all reasons given for not proceeding with robbery cases, 43 percent were "witness problem(s)"; 35 percent, "insufficiency of evidence"; and 22 percent, "other." For nonviolent property offenses, 25 percent of the reasons were "witness problems"; 37 percent, "insufficiency of evidence"; and 36 percent, "other."[24]

As soon as the prosecutor has made a decision to charge the defendant and has informed the defense counsel accordingly, the stage is set for plea bargaining. This process is inherent in the Anglo-American system, under which a trial always proceeds in accordance with the prosecution's charge and the defendant's agreement (guilty plea) or disagreement (not-guilty plea) with that charge.

The Plea-Bargaining Process   Every criminal defendant exercises some power over the way the case is to be conducted. A defendant who pleads guilty admits all the facts alleged in the accusation, whether it is an indictment or an information, and all their legal implications: He or she admits to being guilty as charged. No trial has to be conducted. A defendant who pleads not guilty denies all the facts and their legal implications and puts the government—the prosecutor—to great expense to prove guilt in an elaborate criminal trial.

The idea arose centuries ago that both sides, prosecution and defense, could benefit if they were to agree on a plea that would save the government the expense of a trial and the defendant the risk of a very severe punishment if he or she were found guilty. By the mid-twentieth century it had become common practice in the United States for prosecutors and defense attorneys to engage in **plea bargaining,** that is, to discuss the charges against defendants and to agree on a reduced or modified plea that would spare the state the cost of a trial and guarantee the defendant a sentence more lenient than the original charge warranted.

Did You Know

. . . that the "Alford plea" allows criminal defendants to maintain their innocence while admitting that the state has enough evidence to convict on a charge?

At first, such plea negotiations were secret and officially denied. In fact, when accepting a plea, the judge would always inquire whether the plea was freely made, and the defendant always answered yes, when in fact the plea was the result of a bargain in which defendant and prosecutor manipulated each other into a deal. Contemporary legislation, federal and state, recognizes the plea-bargaining process, and simply requires guarantees that no one is coerced and that all pleas are voluntarily entered, with full awareness of the consequences.

Nevertheless, plea bargaining invites injustices of many sorts. Defendants who are morally or legally not guilty, for example, may feel inclined to accept a plea bargain in the face of strong evidence. Other defendants may plead guilty to a lesser charge even though the evidence was obtained in violation of constitutional guarantees. In some cases, by "overcharging" (charging murder instead of manslaughter, for example), a prosecutor may influence a defendant to plead guilty to the lower charge, in effect forcing him or her to relinquish the right to a jury trial.

The practice of plea bargaining is widespread. A Bureau of Justice Statistics report has estimated that in urban areas, guilty pleas outnumbered trials by about 17 to 1, and nearly all those guilty pleas were negotiated.[25] Research on why defendants accept plea bargains and on the factors that affect the decisions is inconclusive. Nevertheless, there appears to be agreement that plea bargains:

- Are necessary devices to keep the courts from getting hopelessly clogged with criminal cases.

- Are desirable means of compensating for the harshness of the sanctions provided by the penal codes.

- Allow for adjustment of inadequately developed legal rules regarding defenses, such as mistake, insanity, or self-defense.

- Reduce the negative effects of net widening—that is, the tendency to include more and more offenders within the sweep of the criminal justice system.

- Allow for consideration of legally irrelevant but factually important factors, ranging from poverty and despair to intense emotional distress.

Abolishing plea bargaining would require broad changes in criminal law and procedure and thus in the entire criminal justice system. Until such reforms are achieved, the system will continue to rely on the decisions of prosecutors and defense counsels to agree on a plea.

If prosecutor and defense counsel have agreed on a plea bargain—for example, by reducing the charge from murder to manslaughter or by reducing the number of charges from four counts of larceny to one—the judge will have to decide whether that bargain is in the interest of justice. In considering the defendant's bargained plea, the judge must do the following:

1. Inform the defendant of the implications of the plea (that the defendant can now be sentenced).

2. Ascertain that the facts support the plea.

3. Accept the plea.[26]

4. Impose sentence.

The second requirement is particularly important, as it requires the judge to adjudicate the facts of the case in order to determine whether the plea of guilty is warranted. This determination of fact may amount to a minitrial.

If no plea bargain is agreed upon, the case will be set for submission to the grand jury whenever a defendant has the right to trial on indictment by a grand jury. Normally, this right is restricted to felony cases.

The Grand Jury's Decision to Indict   The grand jury is one of the oldest institutions of our criminal justice system. It dates to Magna Carta in A.D. 1215. It has been abolished in England, but in most American states it continues, in serious (felony) cases, to screen the prosecution's evidence in secret hearings and decide whether the defendant should be formally charged with crime.

Increasingly, the grand jury is being viewed as a cumbersome institution which, at great expense, no longer serves its original function of sparing innocent citizens a burdensome trial. Two-thirds of the states have eliminated grand-jury participation in all but the most serious felony cases, and New York is on the verge of following suit.[27]

Federal grand juries are composed of 16 to 23 citizens, and indictment requires the concurrence of at least 12 grand jurors.[28] State rules are similar. The indictment must rest on evidence indicating a *prima facie* case against the defendant.

New York police officer Sean Carroll cries as he testifies in court about the shooting of Amadou Diallo. Carroll and three other New York City police officers were acquitted of all charges in connection with the shooting of Diallo.

A **prima facie case** exists when there seems to be sufficient evidence to convict the defendant. The prima facie case may be defeated by evidence at trial that raises reasonable doubt or constitutes a legal excuse. Since that is a strong evidentiary requirement, most indicted defendants are inclined to make a plea bargain at this point. Indeed, the conviction rate of those who stand trial is high. Of every 16 persons indicted, 10 plead guilty (usually in a plea bargain) and 4 go to trial; 3 of the 4 are convicted; only 1 is acquitted, dismissed by the judge, or dismissed by the prosecutor.[29] If, after the indictment has been presented in open court, the defendant pleads not guilty, the stage is set for trial.

Adjudication Decisions

Defendants may choose to be tried by a judge (a bench trial) or by a jury (consisting usually of 12 citizens but as few as 6 in some states for lesser offenses).[30] In a jury trial the judge rules on matters of law, instructs the jurors about relevant legal questions and definitions, and tells them how to apply the law to the facts of the case.

A defendant may prefer a jury trial or a bench trial for any number of reasons. When the defense is based largely on the application and interpretation of technical legal propositions, a judge is likely to be the choice. If the defense appeals more to sympathy and emotion, a jury is likely to be the better choice.

Considerable research has been done on the functions and functioning of judges and juries, beginning with the University of Chicago Jury Project in the 1950s.[31] Much of the research has focused on whether jurors differ widely in their decisions. Apparently they do not. Most juries come to a unanimous verdict.[32] That was believed to be the general requirement under American law. In a surprise decision in 1972, however, the Supreme Court ruled that a conviction decided upon by fewer than all 12 jurors is constitutionally acceptable.[33]

The widely publicized and televised 1995 jury trial of O. J. Simpson, in Los Angeles, has once again raised the question of the fairness of jury trials in "open court." Whereas televised justice has become an entertainment vehicle,[34] the scholarly research on its impact on the trial process has yielded conflicting results.[35]

Sentencing Decisions

If a defendant has not been diverted out of the system, has pleaded not guilty, and has been tried and convicted, the next step in the process is the imposition of a sentence. In some states, with respect to some crimes, the statute leaves the sentencing judge no choice: A fixed sentence is imposed by law. But in most states judges still have some choice. The judge must decide whether to place the defendant on probation and, if so, what type of probation; whether to impose a sentence of incarceration and, if so, for what length of time; whether to impose a minimum or maximum term (or both) or to leave the sentence open-ended (indeterminate) within statutory limits; whether to impose a fine and, if so, how much; whether to order compensation for the victims; whether to impose court costs; and so on.

In making their sentencing decisions, judges are guided by presentence reports prepared by the court's probation department. After evaluating the probation officer's presentence investigation report, the judge may decide to place the person on probation, usually with specified conditions—that the person not commit another offense, not leave the county without permission, make payments to the victim, attend meetings of Alcoholics Anonymous, or whatever other conditions may be appropriate. In deciding on sentences, judges are supposed to consider what the presentence reports reveal about offenders' personal characteristics, their past and potential future, their problems, and their needs. What do judges actually consider when they decide on sentences? The National Academy of Sciences, having reviewed most of the research on sentencing, has found that two criteria predominate:

> [O]ffense seriousness and offender's prior record emerge consistently as the key determinants of sentences. The more serious the offense and the worse the offender's prior record, the more severe the sentence. The strength of this conclusion persists despite the potentially severe problems of pervasive biases arising from the difficulty of measuring—or even precisely defining—either of these complex variables. This finding is supported by a wide variety of studies using data of varying quality in different jurisdictions and with a diversity of measures of offense seriousness and prior record.[36]

To avoid bias that results in dissimilar sentences for more or less similar offenders, several researchers have developed, and several legislatures have adopted, sentencing guidelines. These guidelines assign specific values to the important sentencing criteria—principally, the seriousness of the offenses and possibly, prior record and other factors (Chapter 18). These guidelines are meant to help judges select the length and type of punishment.

Don Gottfredson and Bridget Stecher conducted research on what factors judges actually take into consideration when they select an "appropriate" sentence. In studying 17 judges who sentenced 982 adult offenders, they found that the main objective was rehabilitation (in 36 percent of the cases), followed by "other purposes including general deterrence" (34 percent), retribution (17 percent), special deterrence (9 percent), and incapacitation (4 percent).[37]

Corrections Decisions

The two traditional corrections choices are incarceration (the institutional choice) and routine probation (the community choice). Today there are a number of community alternatives, as well as different types of incarceration and release/parole decisions.

Decisions in the Community The court's sentence may transfer an offender to the executive part of government, the correctional authorities. This happens when the sentence is one of incarceration. Yet far more offenders are sentenced to serve their time in the community, on probation. In that case the person remains subject to the control of the court, and the sentence is supervised by the court's probation department.

Recently, many states have experimented with a variety of alternatives to the two traditional choices of incarceration and routine probation. Among these alternatives are placement in restitution programs, intensive supervision programs (ISPs), shock incarceration, and regimented discipline programs (RDPs, also called "boot camps"). Such programs are usually operated by the correctional service, rather than the probation department.

A good deal of research has been done on the success or failure of traditional probation with various types of offenders. The newer programs have not been in existence long enough to permit reliable evaluation. Initial research (discussed in Chapter 19) indicates that some types may be cost-beneficial and somewhat successful in lowering recidivism (repeat-offense) rates.[38]

Crime Surfing

www.usdoj.gov/

The criminal justice process stretches across a vast system of organizations. What is the structure of the federal criminal justice system?

Decisions in Institutions   The correctional sector of the criminal justice system is composed of institutions of varying degrees of security, with varying programs, and of quasi-institutional as well as community-based programs. Within the limitations of law, the correctional staff decides where to place sentenced offenders in view of security requirements, the availability of treatment and rehabilitation programs, and organizational needs.

All inmates must be classified in accordance with the placements that are available.[39] Such decisions are not easy. It is difficult to predict the types of security precautions an inmate will require. Nor is it possible to accurately predict the success of education, vocational training, or any other treatment program.

It is perhaps easier to decide where to assign inmates in terms of the institutional jobs that keep the institution running. Inmates do clerical and classification work, provide legal aid, and perform maintenance work; they work in the library, the infirmary, the laundry, the kitchen. But even these decisions require consideration of other factors, especially safety. All such decisions have to be reviewed on the basis of the information gathered, and new decisions have to be made from time to time.

Release and Parole Decisions   To the extent that the system permits any leeway, the most important decision is whether to release an individual from the institution. There are two types of release from the correctional system. In the first, at the expiration of his or her sentence, the inmate must be released. Although correctional administrators have little choice in this type of release, the expiration point depends to some degree on their decisions. In the course of disciplinary proceedings, correctional administrators must decide whether an inmate will lose "good-time" benefits because of violations of the institution's rules. An inmate who violates the rules loses the benefit of the early release that comes with good behavior. Today release decisions are further complicated by policy decisions made at higher governmental levels. They are also made by judges, who frequently order prisoners released to make space for new ones in order to relieve prison overcrowding.

The second way an inmate may be released is through parole. In its original and ideal form, parole was a benefit bestowed on a prisoner for good behavior in prison and a promise of good conduct after discharge. Success was to be achieved with the aid of a parole officer. As parole officers' caseloads increased, however, that ideal faded; today parole is simply an early release from prison based on the decision of a parole board. Parole boards have little information to rely on in making their decisions. Conduct in the institution, however, has been demonstrated to relate to behavior outside it.[40]

Some progress has been made in the development of devices to predict success on parole; these devices are called base expectancy scales.[41] Nevertheless, parole decisions remain difficult. Statistics show that arrest rates of released inmates are very high, as are rates of reconviction and reincarceration (Chapter 19).[42] Variations in these rates depend on the number of previous incarcerations, the types of crimes committed, ethnic background, education, length of the prison term served, time elapsed since release, and other factors. Some states have abolished parole, and others are using it with steadily declining frequency. (Several special forms of parole, such as intensive-supervision parole with and without electronic monitoring, are discussed in Chapter 19.)

FIGURE 16.3   The funnel effect: Reported crimes through prison sentence, 1965 and 1997.

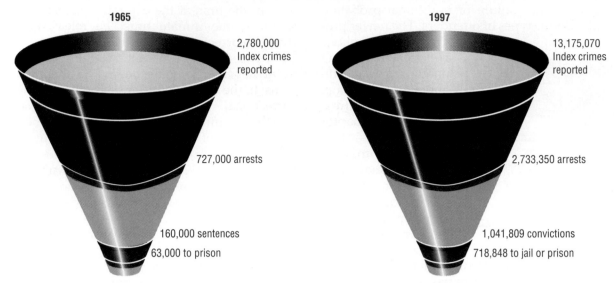

Source: President's Commission on Law Enforcement and Administration of Justice, *Task Force Report on Science and Technology* (Washington D.C.: U.S. Government Printing Office, 1967), p. 61. Total number of reported Index offenses and arrests adapted from *Crime in the United States, 1997* (Washington, D.C.: U.S. Government Printing Office, 1998), p. 222. Total number of convictions and number of persons sent to jail or prison adapted from Jodi M. Brown and Patrick A. Langan, *Felony Sentences in the United States, 1996* (Washington, D.C.: Bureau of Justice Statistics Bulletin, 1999), pp. 2 and 5, tables 2 and 4.

Diversion out of the System

Throughout the criminal justice process, the number of persons within the system steadily decreases. This phenomenon is called the *attrition rate,* or the "mortality rate." The President's Commission on Law Enforcement and the Administration of Justice depicted the criminal justice system as a funnel. In the mid-1960s, 727,000 defendants entered the funnel—roughly 1 for every 4 of the 2.78 million Index crimes reported. Slightly more than 1 in 5 of the arrestees were convicted.[43] More than three decades later, by the late 1990s, the 1965 numbers had almost quintupled, yet the proportion remained essentially the same, roughly 1 for every 5 of the 13.2 million Index crimes reported (Figure 16.3).

As we have seen, there are two reasons for the enormous amount of diversion from the system at various stages. First, decision makers may, for a variety of reasons, consider a case inappropriate for further processing within the normal flow of the criminal justice system. If they did not do so, the system would come to a halt. Moreover, this exercise of discretion keeps an already punitive system from being overly punitive. Thus compassion is added to the mix. Second, if a legal standard of proof is not met, the case must leave the criminal justice process. In such situations decision makers have no choice. At each stage of the process the authorities must meet a legal standard of proof. These standards become progressively tighter as the case proceeds through the various stages of the process (Figure 16.4).

A very broad standard of proof—reasonable suspicion—permits a large intake into the criminal justice system. A very tight standard of proof—guilt beyond a reasonable doubt—results in persons ultimately to be convicted and retained in the system. Various intermediate standards determine whether a person should be processed to the next stage.

There is something very troublesome about our system. On the one hand, it supposedly protects us against interference by government until we are proved guilty of a crime by evidence beyond a reasonable doubt.[44] On the other hand, ever greater intrusions are authorized, on a sliding scale, as the probability of potential guilt increases. What is worse, even the ultimate standard of guilt—conviction on evidence of

FIGURE 16.4   The funnel effect of the standard of proof.

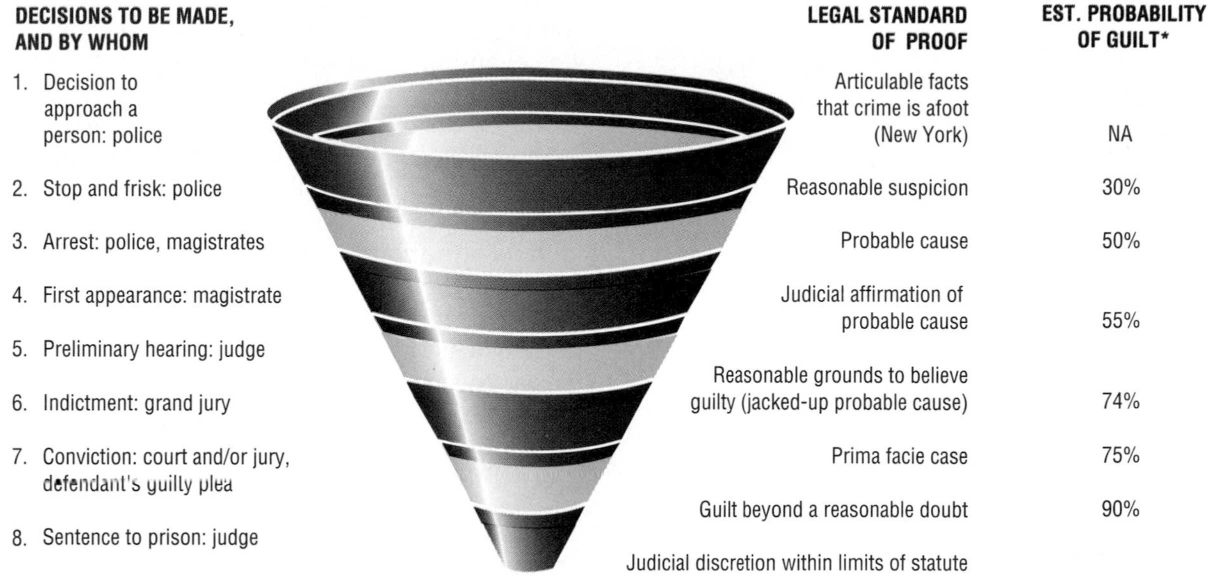

DECISIONS TO BE MADE, AND BY WHOM	LEGAL STANDARD OF PROOF	EST. PROBABILITY OF GUILT*
1. Decision to approach a person: police	Articulable facts that crime is afoot (New York)	NA
2. Stop and frisk: police	Reasonable suspicion	30%
3. Arrest: police, magistrates	Probable cause	50%
4. First appearance: magistrate	Judicial affirmation of probable cause	55%
5. Preliminary hearing: judge		
6. Indictment: grand jury	Reasonable grounds to believe guilty (jacked-up probable cause)	74%
7. Conviction: court and/or jury, defendant's guilty plea	Prima facie case	75%
	Guilt beyond a reasonable doubt	90%
8. Sentence to prison: judge	Judicial discretion within limits of statute	

*Based on a survey of 171 federal judges.

Source: Probabilities adapted from C. M. A. McCauliff, "Burdens of Proof: Degrees of Belief, Quanta of Evidence, or Constitutional Guarantees?" *Vanderbilt Law Review,* **35** (1982): 1293–1335.

guilt beyond a reasonable doubt—is not even a certain measure. A group of federal judges estimated (very reluctantly) the probability of true guilt to be only 90 percent (see Figure 16.4). That would mean 10 percent of convicts are wrongfully convicted. But even if researchers who have established that our system is accurate in convicting at a rate of 99.5 percent are to be believed, there would still be 10,000 wrongful convictions per year.[45] The implications are particularly troublesome in capital cases after executions, when there is no chance of correcting errors.

JUVENILE JUSTICE

The juvenile justice system is very large and must cope with a sizable number of juvenile offenders, starting at intake with the 1.7 million juveniles arrested (1997).[46] Table 16.1 indicates the proportion of arrests for Index crimes committed by juveniles in 1997. Among the eight UCR Index crimes, the percentage ranges from a low of 7.8 percent for murder and nonnegligent manslaughter to a

TABLE 16.1   Index Crimes Cleared by Arrest of Juveniles, 1997

Index Crimes	Percent of Total Arrests
Murder, nonnegligent manslaughter	7.8
Forcible rape	11.5
Robbery	17.4
Aggravated assault	11.5
Burglary	20.2
Larceny-theft	23.9
Motor vehicle theft	20.5
Arson	46.3
All violent crime	12.4
All property crime	23.0
All Index crimes	20.0

Source: U.S. Department of Justice, *Crime in the United States, 1997* (Washington, D.C.: U.S. Government Printing Office, 1998), p. 219.

high of 46.3 percent for arson. The juveniles under 18 arrested for all Index crimes represented 20.2 percent, or one-fifth, of all persons arrested for such crimes. In that same year, juveniles were involved in 17 percent of violent crime Index arrests and 35 percent of property crime Index arrests.[47]

FIGURE 16.5   Delinquency cases judicially waived to criminal court.

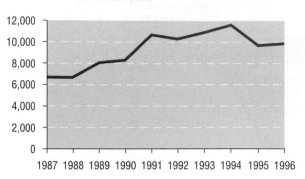

- Between 1987 and 1994, the number of delinquency cases judicially waived to criminal court grew 73 percent (from 6800 to 11,700). By 1996, the number of cases was down to 10,000, a drop of 15 percent.
- One reason for the decline after 1994 was that a larger number of serious cases bypassed the juvenile justice system under newly enacted statutory exclusion and prosecutor discretion provisions.

Source: Juvenile Offenders and Victims: 1999 National Report, Washington, DC: Office of Juvenile Justice and Delinquency Prevention, 1999, p. 170.

The Development of the Juvenile Justice System

The roots of our system of juvenile justice can be traced to classical Roman law. There are two roots, one clearly punitive, the other supportive and caring. The punitive root brought the imposition of adult criminal liability on children. In the Middle Ages, under the law of the church, the Roman law classification of children with respect to criminal liability took definite shape and was taken over by the common law.

This classification scheme potentially subjected children between ages 7 and 14 to the rigors of adult criminal liability, proceedings, and punishments. It still affects our thinking, and its impact can be seen in the laws of many states. Theoretically, today a 10-year-old can be tried as an adult in Vermont, a 12-year-old in Colorado, and a 13-year-old in Georgia, Illinois, and Mississippi (see Table 16.2). Juvenile courts waived 47 percent more delinquency cases to criminal court in 1996 than in 1987 (Figure 16.5).

The second root, also originating in Roman law, is that of concern for troubled children. We find its traces in the concepts used today in juvenile court proceedings. It was very much present in the concept of **parens patriae,** which to the Romans meant that the emperor, and in medieval times the king or queen, could exercise "parental power" *in loco parentis* ("in the

place of a parent" deemed incapable or unworthy) over children in trouble or in danger of becoming wayward. The power of the monarch was eventually transferred to the people of the state, as represented by the juvenile court judge.

These doctrines guided American practice for dealing with troubled children after 1838 and the case *Ex parte Crouse*. On the petition of her mother, a young girl, Mary Ann Crouse, had been committed by the court to the Philadelphia House of Refuge as wayward and incorrigible. When Mary Ann's father, who was estranged from his wife, learned what had happened, he sought a writ of habeas corpus to secure the release of his daughter, who, so he alleged, had been imprisoned without a jury trial. The Pennsylvania Supreme Court rejected this argument, reasoning that under the parens patriae doctrine the state has every right to protect children from improper upbringing.[48]

Houses of refuge designed to care for the impoverished, "dangerous" street people of the time were based on an earlier English model. In reality, these houses were little more than prisons to which individuals could be sent without trial. The houses of refuge proved a dismal failure. They neither educated nor reformed anybody. In them, children were subjected to harsh discipline.

Reformatories   Massachusetts tried a new approach in 1854, with the creation of the Massachusetts Industrial School for Girls. In a cottage-style setting, surrogate families were created, with the goal of reforming girls who were considered "wayward and delinquent." Other states followed Massachusetts's lead. The problem with this approach was the lack of a judicial determination that a given child had indeed violated the law and therefore was in need of some remedial placement.

The all-important change occurred in Chicago, where Timothy D. Hurley, a judge and former probation officer, and Julia Lathrop, of the Illinois Board of Charities, advocated abandonment of the system that placed child offenders and wayward children in adult jails and prisons and removed children who had been arbitrarily declared wayward from the custody of their parents and placed them in prisonlike institutions. Hurley and Lathrop lobbied for the creation of a juvenile court. With the help of the Catholic Visitation and Aid Society and the Chicago Bar Association, they succeeded. The

TABLE 16.2   Minimum Age for Criminal Liability

State	Minimum Age for Judicial Waiver	Judicial Waiver Offense and Minimum Age Criteria, 1997							
		Any Criminal Offense	Certain Felonies	Capital Crimes	Murder	Certain Person Offenses	Certain Property Offenses	Certain Drug Offenses	Certain Weapon Offenses
Alabama	14	14							
Alaska	NS	NS				NS			
Arizona	NS		NS						
Arkansas	14		14	14	14	14			14
California	14	16	16		14	14	14	14	
Colorado	12		12		12	12			
Connecticut	14		14	14	14				
Delaware	NS	NS	15^a		NS	NS	16^b	16^b	
Dist. of Columbia	NS	15	15		15	15	15		NS
Florida	14	14							
Georgia	13	15		13	14^c	14^c	15^b		
Hawaii	NS		14		NS	NS			
Idaho	NS	14	NS		NS	NS	NS	NS	
Illinois	13	13	15						
Indiana	NS	14	NS^b		10			16	
Iowa	14	14	15						
Kansas	10	10	14			14		14	
Kentucky	14		14	14					
Louisiana	14				14	14			
Maine	NS		NS		NS				
Maryland	NS	15		NS					
Michigan	14	14							
Minnesota	14		14						
Mississippi	13	13							
Missouri	12		12						
Montana	NS	NS							
Nevada	14	14	14			14			
New Hampshire	13		15		13	13		15	
New Jersey	14	14^b			14	14	14	14	14
North Carolina	13		13	13					
North Dakota	14	16	14^b		14	14		14	
Ohio	14		14		14	14	16		
Oklahoma	NS		NS						
Oregon	NS		15		NS	NS	15		
Pennsylvania	14		14		15	15			
Rhode Island	NS		16	NS	17	17			
South Carolina	NS	16	14		NS	NS		14	14
South Dakota	NS		NS						
Tennessee	NS	16			NS	NS			
Texas	14		14	14				14	
Utah	14		14			16	16		16
Vermont	10				10	10	10		
Virginia	14		14		14	14			
Washington	NS	NS							
West Virginia	NS		NS		NS	NS	NS	NS	
Wisconsin	14	15	14		14	14	14	14	
Wyoming	13	13							

Examples: Alabama allows waiver for any delinquency (criminal) offense involving a juvenile age 14 or older. Arizona allows waiver for any juvenile charged with a felony. New Jersey allows waiver for juveniles age 14 or older who are charged with murder or certain person, property, drug, or weapon offenses. In New Jersey, juveniles age 14 or older who have prior adjudications or convictions for certain offenses can be waived regardless of the current offense.

Note: Ages in minimum age column may not apply to all offense restrictions, but represent the youngest possible age at which a juvenile may be judicially waived to criminal court. "NS" indicates that in at least one of the offense restrictions indicated, no minimum age is specified.

^{a}Only if committed while escaping from specified juvenile facilities.
^{b}Requires prior adjudication(s) or conviction(s), which may be required to have been for the same or a more serious offense type.
^{c}Only if committed while in custody.

Source: Adaptation of Griffin et al.'s *Trying Juveniles as Adults in Criminal Court: An Analysis of State Transfer Provisions.*
Source: Juvenile Offenders and Victims: 1999 National Report, Washington, D.C.: Office of Juvenile Justice and Delinquency Prevention, 1999, p. 104.

On June 8, 1964, in Gila County, Arizona, Mrs. Cook complained to Deputy Sheriff Flagg about obscene phone calls she had received, which she attributed to a neighborhood kid, Gerald Francis Gault, age 15. The deputy sheriff knew Gerry Gault; he was on probation, having been found in the company of another youngster who had lifted a wallet from a woman's handbag.

Deputy Sheriff Flagg promptly went to Gerry's home, arrested him, and placed him in the juvenile detention facility. When Gerry's mother returned home that night and found Gerry gone, she sent her elder son out to find him. He learned from acquaintances that Gerry was in detention. Gerry's mother promptly went to the detention center. She did not get to see Gerry. The deputy told her of the arrest and informed her that there would be a hearing in juvenile court at 3 P.M. the next day. On that day, the deputy filed an application with the court noting that Gerry, as a minor, is "in need of the protection of the honorable court, as he is delinquent." The application contained no reference to Mrs. Cook's complaint. The hearing took place before Judge McGhee of juvenile court. Present were Deputy Sheriff Flagg in his capacity as a probation officer, Gerry, and his mother and elder brother. Mrs. Cook was absent.

In a formless proceeding, Gerry denied ever having made the phone calls. The judge returned Gerry to the detention facility. A second hearing was held 1 week later. Gerry's mother was informed about the hearing by a hand-written note left on her door by Deputy Sheriff Flagg. The second hearing was as formless as the first. There was no complaining witness, and Judge McGhee ruled that none was necessary. The court declared that it had been proved that Gerry made the calls. If an adult had been convicted of this crime, the penalty would have been a fine of $5 to $50 and a jail term of up to 2 months. Juveniles, however, could not be punished. Judge McGhee declared Gerry to be a habitual juvenile offender,

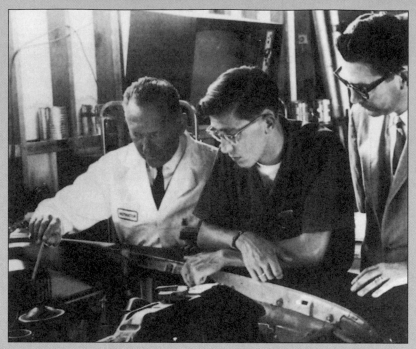

Gerald Gault (center), whose Supreme Court victory guaranteed due process to all future juvenile defendants.

because 3 years earlier, Gerry had been accused of the theft of a baseball glove (although no charges were ever filed), and declared that Gerry had lied when he denied the accusation. In the final ruling, Gerry was found to be a juvenile delinquent, not to be punished, but sent to a juvenile correctional facility for 6 years—until he reached the age of 21.

After Gerry's parents finally engaged an attorney, the case gained widespread publicity. Everything seemed to have gone wrong with the case, yet all the appeals courts had upheld Judge McGhee's ruling. With the help of civil libertarians and members of some of the most prestigious law faculties, the case reached the U.S. Supreme Court 3 years after Gerry's incarceration. In the case of *In re Gault,* Justice Abe Fortas wrote in his opinion that children have as much right to the protection of the Constitution as adults. Never again would a child be sentenced to 6 years of incarceration for an act that would have received 2 months of incarceration for an adult.

Since the ruling of *In re Gault,* a number of Supreme Court decisions have granted juveniles more constitutional rights, but they still do not enjoy the full set of rights guaranteed to adults. Whereas there is considerable debate over how to treat America's juveniles, the demise of parens patriae has left juveniles in a rather awkward position—not quite children and not quite adults, but in either case, not fully extended the protections of due process.

Source

In re Gault, 387 U.S. 1 (1967).

Questions for Discussion

1. What constitutional rights were denied to Gerry Gault that now must be guaranteed in juvenile court?
2. What due process rights are currently still denied to juveniles? What rights have been only partially granted? How might the denial or restriction of these rights affect the legal process and the juvenile?

Illinois legislature created the nation's first juvenile court, in Chicago, in 1899.

The Juvenile Court The concepts that guided the operation of the Chicago juvenile court and subsequent similar courts were straightforward:

- All dependent, neglected, and delinquent children under 16 years of age could be brought under the jurisdiction of the juvenile court.

- Delinquency included any act that, if committed by an adult, would be a crime.

- The juvenile court did not find youngsters guilty of anything, but simply determined their status as dependent, neglected (in a very broad, sweeping sense), or delinquent.

- The juvenile court judge acted as a surrogate parent, conducting informal proceedings (in contrast to the formal adversarial proceedings in criminal court).

- Exercising much discretion, the juvenile court judge gave first consideration to the best interest of the child.

- Dispositions by the court were not punishments; they might include only friendly probation, in the child's own home, or placement in a suitable foster home or training in an industrial school.

There were two problems with this approach. First, the definition of behavior that brought a child under the jurisdiction of the juvenile court was still extremely broad. "Dependency" and "neglect" are vague terms. Nor are these conditions the youngster's fault; they are the parents' fault. Moreover, the concept of delinquency embraced not only acts that would be crimes if an adult committed them but also behavior that would not be considered deviant in adults, such as truancy or running away from home. When dependency and neglect were included in the definition of delinquency, neglect itself became a status offense. A neglected child was by definition delinquent.

Second, while the motivations for the informality of the proceedings in the juvenile justice system were praiseworthy, they led to intolerable abuses. Not all children's rights were violated in all cases, but abuses were frequent. Most juvenile court judges sincerely regarded the informality of their proceedings as in the best interest of the child.[49]

This system dominated until 1967, when the Supreme Court at last ruled that children, too, have rights that are protected by the Constitution. In the case *In re Gault* the Court ruled that virtually all the guarantees of the Fourth, Fifth, and Sixth Amendments, made applicable to the states under the due process clause of the Fourteenth Amendment, must be extended to juveniles.

These guarantees include the right to be informed of the charges, freedom from unreasonable seizure (arrest), the right to have an attorney, and the right to be confronted by and to examine witnesses.[50] Later the Court ruled that proof of juvenile delinquency, like that of a crime charged to an adult, must be established beyond a reasonable doubt. Only the right to a jury trial need not be accorded to juveniles, perhaps to preserve some of the informality of the juvenile court.[51] These decisions subjugated parens patriae to the rule of law and to constitutional due process (Figure 16.6).

A Junior Criminal Justice System Juvenile court judges viewed the Supreme Court's decisions with mixed emotions. Some thought the juvenile court movement had come to an end. But as time passed, it became evident that juvenile courts can function well in administering juvenile justice even while abiding by the due process guarantees of the Constitution. There is some evidence, however, that many children and parents do not claim the procedural rights to which they are constitutionally entitled, frequently out of ignorance.[52]

The transformation of juvenile justice proceedings into a junior model of adult criminal justice had a peculiar consequence. If juveniles are to have the rights of adults charged with crime, should they not also have the responsibilities? In 1977 an influential joint committee of the Institute of Judicial Administration at New York University and the American Bar Association formulated a set of standards for juvenile justice.

FIGURE 16.6 U.S. Supreme Court decisions. A series of U.S. Supreme Court decisions made juvenile courts more like criminal courts but maintained some important differences.

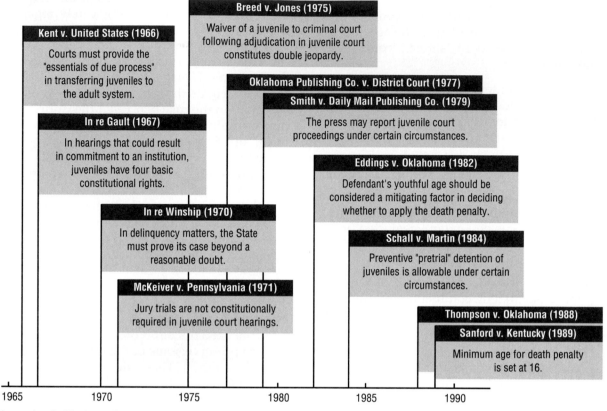

Source: *Juvenile Offenders and Victims: 1999 National Report,* Office of Juvenile Justice and Delinquency Prevention, 1999, p. 91.

The committee proposed that juvenile dispositions be based on the seriousness of the offense, not merely on the court's view of the juvenile's needs.[53] With these standards the punitive movement of the mid-1970s reached juvenile justice. The resulting punitiveness manifested itself in six developments:

1. *Lowering the age at which juveniles are subject to adult criminal liability.* Twenty states chose 14 as the age at which juveniles are liable; two states lowered the age to 10; two allowed no judicial waiver; and fourteen do not specify an age.[54]

2. *Reducing the upper age at which juveniles are subject to original juvenile court jurisdiction:*

   In . . . 37 states and the District of Columbia, juvenile courts are initially responsible for all law violations committed by youth under 18. In other words, the juvenile court's "upper age of original jurisdiction" is 17. In 10 states, the upper age of original juvenile court jurisdiction is set at 16 years. . . . In three states . . . the upper age of jurisdiction is 15, which means that all youth age 16 or older face criminal prosecution for any arrest. . . .

   [In recent years] other states have considered reducing the upper age of juvenile court jurisdiction. . . . If more states follow this trend, large numbers of young offenders will be excluded from juvenile court and automatically handled in adult court.[55]

3. *Excluding certain serious offenses from the jurisdiction of juvenile courts altogether* (see Table 16.3). In many states, prosecutors are empowered to bring charges against juveniles directly in criminal court, bypassing the juvenile justice system altogether. In Florida, where this method

TABLE 16.3   Offenses Excluded from Juvenile Court Jurisdiction*

Offenses	States†
Murder**	Connecticut, Delaware, District of Columbia, Georgia, Idaho, Illinois, Indiana, Louisiana, Minnesota, Nevada, New Mexico, New York, North Carolina, Ohio, Oklahoma, Pennsylvania, Utah, Vermont.
Rape	Delaware, District of Columbia, Georgia, Idaho, Illinois, Indiana, Louisiana, New York.
Kidnapping	Delaware, Louisiana, Vermont.
Burglary	District of Columbia, Georgia, Louisiana, Vermont.
Armed robbery	District of Columbia, Georgia, Idaho, Illinois, Indiana, Louisiana, Maryland, Vermont.
Other‡	Alabama, Connecticut, Florida, Idaho, Illinois, Indiana, Kansas, Kentucky, Nebraska, Rhode Island, Vermont, Washington.
Hawaii:	Class A felonies if one violent prior, or two violent priors in the past two years.
Maryland:	Any crime punishable by the death penalty.
Mississippi:	Any crime punishable by the death penalty.

*Criminal courts can try juveniles for such crimes provided they have reached minimum age.
†Because of the different offense categories, some states are listed more than once.
**This category includes various degrees of criminal homicide, including attempted murder in some states.
‡This category includes offense categories such as "any offense."
Source: Barry C. Feld, "The Juvenile Court Meets the Principle of the Offense: Legislative Changes in Juvenile Waiver Statutes," *Journal of Criminal Law & Criminology 78* (1987): pp. 512–514. Reprinted by special permission of Northwestern University, School of Law.

Tonya Kline, 15, is led by her mother Deborah Harter to family court in South Carolina. A family court judge allowed Kline to remain tethered to her mother until she is sentenced on truancy, shoplifting, and burglary charges. The alternative was time in a state detention facility.

is particularly popular, 7000 juvenile cases were direct filed in criminal court in 1995, nearly equaling the number of juvenile cases waived by judges *nationwide.*[56]

4. *Investing prosecutors with the power to* **direct file** *juveniles for trial in adult criminal courts* (mostly for serious offenses).

5. *Increasing family responsibility.* A number of states have passed parental responsibility laws that subject parents to criminal liability (for failure to control) for the criminal acts of their children.

6. *Placing juveniles in adult jails and prisons.* Under "three strikes" (for juvenile

offenses) and other legislative provisions, juveniles have been placed in adult jails and prisons. There they are subject to sexual exploitation by adult prisoners, receive no treatment, and return far more likely to commit crimes upon release than if placed in juvenile correctional facilities.[57] It has been pointed out—unsuccessfully— that this policy violates the treaty obligation of the United States (Article 10, [United Nations] International Covenant on Civil and Political Rights).[58] The policy also contravenes everything research has established.

The Juvenile Justice Process

Let us now turn to the flowchart for the juvenile justice process (see Figure 16.1). Having entered the juvenile justice system, the individual will be processed according to its procedures.

Did You Know

. . . that under international human rights standards, persons under age 18 at the time of the commission of a capital crime cannot be executed. Nevertheless, the United States puts the limit at age 16.

Entry into the System It has been said that "citizens . . . largely determine delinquency rates," because it is the citizens' tolerance level and perceptions that determine the decision to call the police.[59] Perceptions and tolerance levels vary from area to area and neighborhood to neighborhood, but on the whole, they are more lenient in the case of juvenile misconduct. We noted earlier that crimes actually committed far outnumber those reported to the police. It appears that as far as crimes committed by juveniles are concerned, the difference is even greater than that in adult crimes because of the reluctance of other juveniles, and of adults who remember their own youth, to bring juvenile misconduct to the attention of the authorities.

Invoking the Juvenile Justice Process Once juvenile misconduct has been brought to the attention of the authorities, usually the police, the next step is a decision to investigate, to arrest, and to process. There is no uniform stan-

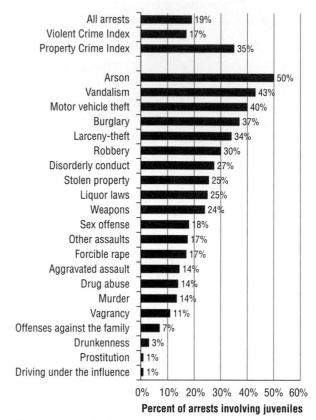

FIGURE 16.7   Juvenile arrests by offense type.

- All arrests — 19%
- Violent Crime Index — 17%
- Property Crime Index — 35%
- Arson — 50%
- Vandalism — 43%
- Motor vehicle theft — 40%
- Burglary — 37%
- Larceny-theft — 34%
- Robbery — 30%
- Disorderly conduct — 27%
- Stolen property — 25%
- Liquor laws — 25%
- Weapons — 24%
- Sex offense — 18%
- Other assaults — 17%
- Forcible rape — 17%
- Aggravated assault — 14%
- Drug abuse — 14%
- Murder — 14%
- Vagrancy — 11%
- Offenses against the family — 7%
- Drunkenness — 3%
- Prostitution — 1%
- Driving under the influence — 1%

0% 10% 20% 30% 40% 50% 60%

Percent of arrests involving juveniles

Note: Running away from home and curfew and loitering violations are not presented in this figure because, by definition, only juveniles can be arrested for these offenses.

Data source: Crime in the United States 1997 (Washington, D.C.: U.S. Government Printing Office, 1998), table 38.

Source: Howard N. Snyder, *Juvenile Arrests 1997* (Washington, D.C.: Office of Juvenile Justice and Delinquency Prevention, 1998).

dard as to whether the taking of a juvenile into custody is in fact an arrest. In some states it is; in others it is not; and in still others the issue is not clear. But in all states the taking of a juvenile into custody requires compliance with the constitutional mandates of *In re Gault*, including the probable-cause requirement and administration of the Miranda warning. (See Figure 16.7.)

Generally, the police have broad power when a juvenile is taken into custody for reasons other than criminal conduct, such as being in danger, in trouble, or in violation of a juvenile court's order. But police officers are both reluctant and poorly prepared to make decisions in such instances.[60] After an arrest or detention, usually by a patrol officer, the juvenile is ordinarily handed over to a juvenile officer, a member of a specially trained police unit. Such units exercise far broader discretion than their colleagues who process adult criminal cases. They may decide to release a juvenile into the custody of parents or otherwise involve parents, who may be called to the station house to discuss the matter.

Once a juvenile has been taken into custody, the police juvenile unit must also decide, guided by law, whether to process the youngster as an adult offender and take him or her before a magistrate for a first appearance, to choose the juvenile path and take the suspect before a juvenile court judge, or to deal with the case in a less formal manner.

If the case is not informally disposed of by the police or the juvenile probation department, it moves before a juvenile court judge for an intake hearing. In large metropolitan areas the juvenile court judge usually is a specialist in juvenile matters. In the more rural parts of the country the criminal court judge doubles as juvenile court judge.

The juvenile court then decides, on the basis of the report of the intake department (juvenile court officers and probation intake officers), whether sufficient grounds exist for filing a petition requesting an adjudicatory hearing (juvenile court trial), whether the case should be waived to criminal court, whether the juvenile should be transferred to a social agency, or whether the case should be dismissed. Juvenile court judges have broad discretion in making these decisions.

Adjudication   If the juvenile court has retained jurisdiction, the case moves into the adjudicatory hearing, which is equivalent to a trial in criminal court. As we noted earlier, under the terms of *In re Gault* the juvenile is entitled to nearly all the procedural guarantees that protect adults charged with crime.

In the adjudicatory hearing, the juvenile court judge must decide whether the facts warrant a decision in accordance with the petition. If the petition alleges that the juvenile has committed an act which, if committed by an adult, would be a crime or that the juvenile is a status

offender by being a truant, a runaway, or ungovernable (or some other such term), and if the facts support the petition, the court will adjudicate the juvenile to be a delinquent.

In order not to stigmatize individuals with the label "delinquent," some states have created such categories as "persons in need of supervision" (PINS), "juveniles in need of supervision" (JINS), "children in need of supervision" (CHINS), or "dependent and neglected children," all of which have simply become new labels. Juveniles so charged will be adjudicated as such if the facts warrant this. The judge will then proceed to the second part of the adjudication process, which corresponds to sentencing in criminal court.

The Dispositional Hearing   In finding an appropriate disposition, the court is guided by any relevant information, especially that provided by the juvenile probation officer. The juvenile court judge must reconcile the child's interest with society's interest in being protected from dangerous and disruptive persons; guide delinquent children into a socially acceptable path; set an example for other children on the path of delinquency; make children responsible for their harmful actions; and set an example of love, care, and forgiveness for children who have broken the law.[61]

In choosing a disposition, juvenile court judges have broader discretion than criminal court judges.[62] The judge may choose probation, with numerous conditions; commitment to a juvenile correctional facility; restitution; or fines. Placement in a foster home or in a special program may also be decreed.

Juvenile Corrections   The juvenile court may decide that the only option is to place the juvenile in an institution. There has been considerable debate over whether placement in an institution is ever an appropriate response to juvenile wrongdoing.

Jerome Miller, as head of the Massachusetts juvenile correction system, tried to prove the point by closing down all the state's juvenile detention facilities.[63] The experiment did not last. Policy makers determined that some juvenile offenders must be segregated for the protection of the community. Although researchers continue to demonstrate that the jailing of juvenile offenders has no appreciable effect on the juvenile crime rate,[64] all states maintain facilities for their confinement and hoped-for rehabilitation.

Most inmates of juvenile facilities (74 percent) have committed crimes. Only 12 percent are adjudicated juvenile status offenders, but a surprising 14 percent are juveniles classified as nonoffenders, including dependent, neglected, and abused children. Even more surprising, the total number of residents in juvenile facilities grows by 6 to 9 percent annually.[65]

A study conducted by the Office of Juvenile Justice and Delinquency Prevention (OJJDP) revealed that for 1997, 125,805 youths were assigned beds in 1121 public and 2310 private facilities in the United States. In that same year, the rate of custody for juveniles was 368 juveniles for every 1000 persons in the population. Over 30 percent of all juveniles in custody are located in three states—California, Texas, and Florida.[66]

The juvenile facilities encompass a wide spectrum: detention centers, training schools, reception or diagnostic centers, shelters, ranches, forestry camps or farms, halfway houses, and group homes. Most of the 3432 facilities in the nation are privately operated. Yet the majority of juvenile offenders are being held in public facilities, which are far more security-minded than the private ones.

Juvenile facilities range from serene, campuslike complexes with understanding counselors to sordid, prisonlike establishments. Criminologists have argued that incarceration of juveniles will do more harm than good unless the conditions of detention are radically reformed and the population is kept at a minimum through reduced admissions. This is one of the tasks of the science of criminology.

Arguments about the future of juveniles placed in detention facilities have reached an impasse in the courts. In the case of *Schall v. Martin* (1984) it was argued before the Supreme Court that a New York law permitting the incarceration of juveniles predicted to constitute a danger was unconstitutional because social science cannot make such predictions. In addressing the question, the Supreme Court affirmed its belief "that there is nothing inher-

ently unattainable about a prediction of future conduct."[67] To some researchers it is still apparent that juvenile correctional treatment is largely unsuccessful,[68] yet a surprising number of juvenile correctional programs have established acceptable success records.[69] This raises the question of whether greater benefits are to be gained by diverting juveniles out of the juvenile justice system.

Diversion out of the Juvenile System
There is significant attrition in the juvenile system. For every 1000 delinquency cases referred to juvenile courts in 1996, 197 were dismissed and 244 were handled through informal disposition. Of those detained and subsequently adjudicated, 175 were placed on probation, 91 were placed in detention, 43 received other sanctions, 14 were released, and 6 were waived to criminal court.[70]

Comparisons of the juvenile and adult attrition rates reveal more significant diversion in the adult criminal justice system. This is remarkable given that the juvenile court was originally designed as a diversion from the adult court. Moreover, literally thousands of diversionary programs were created in the 1970s to filter out juveniles who would "do better" outside the system.

Over the last two decades, some observers have found a wide gap between diversion in theory and diversion in practice. According to some scholars, diversionary programs were originally conceived as alternatives to the formal juvenile justice system—they were to be privately run ("nonlegal"), community-based programs. But most diversionary programs ended up being sponsored or supervised by state or local justice agencies. The result seemed to be only a widening of the net of the juvenile justice system—an increase in the reach of state-sponsored social control. Evidence emerged that diversionary programs were in fact sometimes coercive. Finally, to the extent that diversionary programs became government-sponsored, the benefit of using such programs so that children would avoid stigmatization was all but lost.[71] Nevertheless, there has been progress in deinstitutionalizing juvenile offenders so that, with a greater political commitment, the current trend toward imprisoning young offenders could be reversed.[72]

There is general agreement that our juvenile justice system is far from perfect but that improving it is within our reach.[73] The real problem, however, is not necessarily in the juvenile justice system but rather in the social and economic conditions that produce delinquency in the first place. Reforms, therefore, must aim primarily at the root causes of delinquency.

VICTIMS AND CRIMINAL JUSTICE

Victims of crime play a crucial role in invoking the criminal and juvenile justice processes. An old proverb states: "Where there is no complainant, there is no judge." Victims play an equally significant role at the later stages of the process, as witnesses. Without their testimony, convictions usually cannot be obtained. Until recently, however, the role and plight of victims seemed to have been overlooked by the criminal justice system.

That plight was recognized by the earliest legal systems. The Code of Hammurabi in the eighteenth century B.C. provided that the victims of highway robbers had to be compensated for their losses out of the governor's treasury.[74] Until the Middle Ages many acts that are crimes today were considered torts—that is, civil wrongs—which entitled the victim to compensation from the wrongdoer. Later on, powerful monarchs claimed compensation for themselves for the harm done to the real victim. Fines to the government replaced compensation to actual victims, who were forced to seek compensation in civil court proceedings.

Victims' Rights

Victims played no role in the Anglo-American criminal process, except as witnesses. On the European continent they were only slightly better off; they could join the prosecution in a criminal trial and, if the defendant was convicted, would recover damages as part of the judgment.

The "forgotten" victim began to receive recognition in the 1950s when Margery Fry, an English intellectual, made the case for victim compensation.[75] In America it was the Hungarian-born scholar Stephen Schafer (a victim of Nazi and Stalinist oppression) who placed the crime victim squarely into the criminal process,[76] beginning with the creation of victim compensation schemes. As of now, there are such laws in 45 American states. Many states also enacted a variety of laws intended to ease the lot of victims.[77] Domestic violence and rape crisis centers were created in the late 1960s and early 1970s. These initial efforts were followed by the establishment of victim-witness units, first in the District of Columbia courts and then elsewhere, which ensure respectful treatment for victims and witnesses involved in the criminal justice system. Such units perform a wide variety of services:

Crime Surfing

www.ncvc.org/law/

The website of the National Center for Victims of Crime contains information and research about crime victims. What differences can you find between the federal victims' bill of rights and those of the states?

- Assisting victims who report crimes.
- Responding at the scene of a crime in order to provide crisis counseling.
- Providing 24-hour telephone hot line service to victims and witnesses.
- Making emergency monetary aid available to victims.
- Providing victims with referral services to appropriate agencies.
- Helping victims obtain the return of property.
- Assisting victims and witnesses throughout their court appearances.

Similar programs have been established throughout the country to make it easier for crime victims to participate in the criminal justice process, to secure their participation, and ultimately to provide satisfaction for them. The laws and programs focusing on victims' rights have had a profound impact on the administration of criminal justice in general, and on the

TABLE 16.4   Victim Ratings of Criminal Justice Processing

	Percentage of Victims Who Rate Processing More Than Adequate or Completely Inadequate *			
	Strong-Protection States		*Weak-Protection States*	
Aspect of Processing	**More Than Adequate**	**Completely Inadequate**	**More Than Adequate**	**Completely Inadequate**
Efforts to apprehend the perpetrator	44	6	27	11
Efforts to inform the family about progress on the case	29	9	13	19
Ability to have input in the case	21	15	9	25
Thoroughness of case preparation	28	10	14	20
Fairness of the trial	20	11	10	20
Fairness of the verdict or plea	17	21	6	28
Fairness of the sentence	14	25	5	34
Speed of the process	17	15	6	27
Support services	16	15	8	22

*The ratings continuum was "more than adequate," "adequate," "somewhat less than adequate," and "completely inadequate."
Note: All figures are statistically significant at the 0.05 level or less.
Source: Dean G. Kilpatrick, David Beatty, and Susan Smith Howley, *The Rights of Crime Victims—Does Legal Protection Make a Difference?* (Washington, D.C.: National Institute of Justice, 1998).

role and plight of victims during the course of the process in particular.[78] One study has shown that victims in states with strong victim-protection legislation are generally more satisfied with criminal justice processes than are victims in states with weak legislative protection (see Table 16.4).

The Victim's Role in the Criminal Justice Process

Once again we present a flowchart through the criminal justice process, adapted from the one constructed by the President's Commission, but this time geared to the role of the victim (Figure 16.8). The criminal justice process, as we will see, looks quite different from the victim's perspective.

Entry into the System The victim virtually determines the course of the criminal justice process by his or her willingness to report a victimization and to testify before the authorities, especially at trial.[79] As we noted in Chapter 2, for a wide variety of reasons, many victims are reluctant or unwilling to report their victimization and to participate in the process; yet without a victim's complaint, the process normally cannot start.

Because, at the point of entry into the system, crime victims are inexperienced, vulnerable, and helpless, the creation of "victim advocates" has been proposed. This position would parallel the role of counsel for indigent defendants, with the prime responsibility of securing to victims the rights due them under law.[80]

Prosecution and Pretrial Services The victim must appear at a police precinct at least once. The police may have to interview the victim at home. The victim is likely to have to appear at the district attorney's office to answer the same questions. Accommodations for victims are not comfortable. Interview offices are typically dingy and crowded. Confrontations with the accused, however brief, are disquieting. Actual or anticipated harassment by the perpetrator may instill fear in the victim. Many victims get frustrated and stop showing up for scheduled hearings; many do not appear at the trial.

Adjudication In most criminal proceedings, a plea negotiation takes the place of a criminal trial. In the past, victims played no role in plea bargaining. Recently, however, the American Bar Association has directed prosecuting attorneys to "make every effort to remain advised of the attitudes and sentiments of victims" be-

It happened at a training course on sentencing and corrections for trial judges from all over the country, at the National Judicial College in Reno, Nevada. Present were 40 judges and 10 consultants, "cons" for short, whom we had recruited at the Nevada State Penitentiary to help us give judges an idea of what sentencing and corrections are all about from a prisoner's perspective.

Toward the end of the evening session one of the more senior judges got a little angry with us, saying: "You professors give us all that academic perspective, and the cons complain about life in prison. Why don't we have any victims here?"

That night the two of us went to the sheriff's station, waiting for victims/complainants to come in. We didn't have to wait long. Two victims accepted our invitation to come to the Judicial College the next morning.

One was a rather robust lady who managed a supermarket. She told her story: "This guy comes around and approaches my desk; it's like a glass cage, a bit elevated. He pulls a tire iron out from under his windbreaker and says: 'Give me the cash or I bash your brains in!' So I gave him a little wad of bills, he looks at them and I quickly grab my revolver and start shooting at him. But I missed. He ran out of the store like a jackrabbit."

Question by first judge: "Ma'am, wouldn't you like to see this guy locked up and the key thrown away?"

Answer: "Sure would!"

Question by second judge: "Ma'am, what went through your mind when you shot at him?"

Answer: "I should'a took target practice!"

Question by third judge: "How would you like it if I were to sentence this guy to work for you for nothing, for a year, to stack the shelves every night?"

Answer: "Now let me think about that. That's not a bad idea. It would save me— let me think—about 3000 bucks. Sure, I'd accept that, as long as I can keep my gun."

Guess what? All the judges and nine of the cons nodded their heads! The tenth con blurted out, "I wouldn't want to work for that tough lady." To which the third judge responded: "You may just have to and you may even get to like that tough lady!"

The third judge's suggestion is "restorative justice." Restorative justice has been a feature of justice systems for a long time, though it was little used until a group of criminologists in the United States and the Commonwealth countries brought the idea back to life.

In a restorative paradigm, the crime is viewed as a violation of or harm to people and relationships, as opposed to a violation of the law. The aim of justice is to identify obligations, to meet needs, and to promote healing, as opposed to establishing blame and administering punishment. The process of justice involves the victims, offenders, and the community in an effort to identify solutions among the parties, as opposed to a conflict between adversaries in a win-lose situation.

If a paradigm of restorative justice were adopted, where would that leave us with respect to the traditional goals of criminal justice?

1. As to retribution, we would still be limited to never imposing a sanction that outweighs the harm done.
2. As to incapacitation, even the most staunch advocates of restorative justice recognize that some offenders are far too dangerous to be returned to the community, but the prison population could be vastly reduced.
3. As to rehabilitation, the very idea is built into restorative justice, which aims at restoring the community.

Is restorative justice the emerging paradigm for criminal justice? A number of programs that aim at making restorative justice a reality have been established and tested over the years, with a particular focus on its use as an alternative in juvenile justice. At the end of 1995, 24 states had adopted or were examining new procedures that incorporated the tenets of restorative justice. Some programs, such as the ones pioneered by the Hudson Institute in Indianapolis, have shown promising results. Its overall effectiveness, however, has been called into question by several researchers. Despite the debate over its use, there is a growing interest in programs based on restorative justice, which may signal its lead in the race to transform justice in America.

Sources

1. Incident at National Judicial College conference (as told by Professors G. O. W. Mueller and Freda Adler, 1977).
2. Howard Zehr, "Justice as Restoration, Justice as Respect," *The Justice Professional*, **11**, no. 1–2 (1998): 71–87.
3. Edmund F. McGarrell, *Restorative Justice Conferences* (Indianapolis: Hudson Institute, 1999).
4. Peter Freivalds, "Balanced and Restorative Justice Project (BARJ): Fact sheet #42" (Washington, D.C.: Office of Juvenile Justice and Delinquency Prevention, 1996).

Further Readings

1. Bruce A. Arrigo and Robert C. Schehr, "Restoring Justice for Juveniles: A Critical Analysis of Victim-Offender Mediation," *Justice Quarterly*, **15** (1998): 629–666.
2. Lode Walgrave, ed., *Restorative Justice for Juveniles: Potentialities, Risks and Problems* (Leuven, Belgium: Leuven University Press, 1998).

Questions for Discussion

1. Could the tenets of restorative justice be a realistic goal of the criminal justice system? What problems might arise if a paradigm of restorative justice was adopted in America?
2. If it were adopted, should it be applied to juvenile justice only? How would this paradigm affect the increasing use of waiver to transfer juveniles to adult criminal courts?
3. If restorative justice is truly the future of American criminal justice, how should it be applied and to which types of offenses? What role should victims play in the process, and how much input should they have regarding the types of sentences that offenders receive?

fore reaching a plea agreement.[81] Several researchers have studied victim participation in the plea-bargaining process. One study found that only one-third of victims chose to participate, and their participation was minor.[82] Another researcher, by contrast, found victims to be very active in the plea-bargaining process, as demonstrated by the fact that 46 percent of the victims asked for the maximum punishment.[83]

If a case goes to trial, the victim is likely to be called as a witness. Though the defendant, handcuffed and in a holding pen, may be less comfortable and more anxious than the victim-witness, the anxiety of the victim and the lack of comfort in a courthouse corridor can be painful experiences. During the trial the victim is subject to cross-examination by defense counsel, whose strategy it may be to impugn the credibility of the witness.

The victims' rights movement has spurred the development of legislation and services that are responsive to the plight of victims called to testify in court. Several states have increased witness fees from the previous low of $5 a day to as much as $30 a day. Some states have created procedures to notify victims of court proceedings and guarantee them the right to speedy disposition of their cases. Forty-one states and Congress have enacted laws or provided guidelines requiring that victims and witnesses be informed of the scheduling and cancellation of criminal proceedings. Thirty-three states and the federal government permit victims to participate in criminal proceedings by oral or written testimony.[84] These developments have vastly improved the role of the victim in the adjudication process. Nevertheless, the plight of victims during the crim-

FIGURE 16.8   The path of the victim through the criminal justice process.

ENTRY INTO THE SYSTEM   PROSECUTION AND PRETRIAL SERVICES

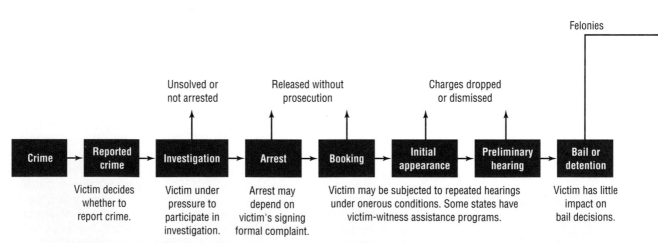

Source: Gerhard O. W. Mueller, "A System-Wide Approach to Criminal Justice Management," in The International Committee for Coordination—ICC, *Criminal Justice and Police Systems: Management and Improvement of Police and Other Law Enforcement Agencies, Prosecution, Courts and Corrections and the Role of Lawyers,* Milan, Italy: Centro Nazionale di Prevenzioue e Difesa Sociale, 1994, pp. 65–67, 76–77.

inal trial process—especially in cases of notoriety—remains unsatisfactory and calls for rigorous reform.[85]

Sentencing   In the common law tradition the victim has no role in the imposition of a sentence. In 30 states, however, victims now have the right to state their views at sentencing hearings.[86] Yet on average only 10 percent of victims make use of this right, which in some jurisdictions is exercised by a written victim impact statement (VIS), in others by presenting evidence at the sentencing hearing. The results have not been overly encouraging, but at least the predicted adverse effects, such as harsher sentences, have not been observed.[87] At this stage it is also possible to join the punishment of the offender with the satisfaction of the victim. Ideally, a sentence can be fashioned to satisfy both the victim's

sense of outrage and his or her need to be compensated for losses caused by the crime.[88]

In several states, for example, a defendant may be sentenced to a community restitution facility instead of a prison. At a sentencing hearing it can be made clear to a victim who demands a stiff prison sentence for the defendant that such a sentence will not result in compensation for any loss the victim has sustained. A sentence to a community restitution facility, however, guarantees that the offender will make payments to the victim for the harm inflicted. Victims are likely to agree to this seemingly less punitive but more rewarding sentence.

A promising new strategy for involving victims in the sentencing process is the opportunity of reconciling victim and offender in some cases, with or without compensation for the victim.[89] One such victim-offender reconciliation program

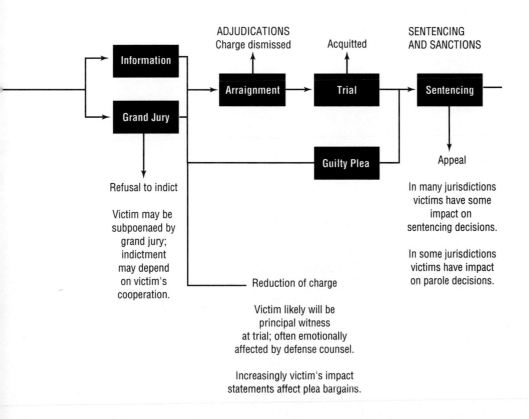

(VORP) began operating in 1992 at the Graterford, Pennsylvania, Correctional Institution and now conducts conferences for the benefit of other practitioners. But the emotional problems involved require further study before such programs can be put into practice on a large scale.[90]

Corrections and Release   The correctional system implements any victim compensation sentence that is imposed. If the sentence makes no provision for compensation, in several states the victim at least has one more opportunity to affect an important decision: the parole hearing.[91] Parole boards tend to give great weight to a victim's opposition to a prisoner's release on parole.

Victims could be given a far greater opportunity to pursue their legitimate interests, especially to obtain compensation for the harm they have suffered. The European criminal justice process has always offered the victim an opportunity to "join" the prosecution. The objective is to have the judge award compensation to the victim in conjunction with the sentence imposed on the offender.[92] American law has not yet adopted this practice, although the American system now offers a variety of civil justice remedies apart from victim compensation schemes.[93] But no matter what the compensation scheme, actual collection of compensation by victims remains a major problem.[94]

Nevertheless, great improvements have been made in our system to accommodate victims of crime. The drive for recognition of the role of the victim in the criminal justice process has had powerful effects in America and all over the world. Undoubtedly, it will create further changes in our criminal justice system as criminology continues to widen its focus to include the victim as well as the offender. The ultimate aim is, as Senator Joseph Biden put it in his speech on the Brady bill, on August 11, 1993, "to create a victim-friendly" system of criminal justice.

REVIEW

The criminal justice system has been perceived as a system for only a generation. Like any other system, it has components that are related and interdependent. The criminal justice process begins with the perception that a crime has been committed. After the crime has been reported, laws and standards guide authorities in following up. This process may lead to an arrest of a suspect and the presentation of charges. When the facts warrant a grand-jury indictment or a prosecutor's information, the case moves to trial. Yet at this stage a plea agreement may be reached under which the defendant avoids trial and receives a reduced sentence in return for a plea of guilty to a lesser charge or to fewer charges. The conviction rate of defendants who go to trial is high.

The movement through the criminal justice system is not automatic and inevitable. At each stage of the process it is dependent on decisions made by criminal justice officials and by the defendant. These decisions may lead to diversion out of the system at any stage. The criminal justice path has many exits. These multiple exits explain the high attrition rate: Only a fraction of the offenders who enter the criminal justice system wind up in corrections.

A juvenile's path through the criminal justice system differs from an adult's. Juveniles are now granted constitutional rights that a generation ago were denied them. But they have also been increasingly subjected to some of the rigors of the adult criminal justice system. Juvenile justice has become punitive.

The emergence of the victims' rights movement has drawn attention to the role and plight of victims. Legislation in most states has facilitated victims' participation in the criminal justice process, eased the burden on victims, and provided compensation for their losses.

YOU BE THE CRIMINOLOGIST

A large amount of discretion is granted to criminal justice actors at every stage of the system. Choose an area of the criminal justice system in which an attempt should be made to limit the amount of discretion used. What methods are in place now and how effective are they? What procedures can be devised to improve these methods or replace them?

KEY TERMS

The numbers next to the terms refer to the pages on which the terms are defined.

direct file (493)

exclusionary rule (477)

Miranda warning (479)

parens patriae (488)

plea bargaining (481)

preliminary hearing (481)

prima facie case (483)

probable cause (477)

reasonable suspicion (477)

NOTES

1. See Golan M. Janeksela, "Analysis of Justice Systems," *Criminal Justice Policy Review,* **5** (1991): 114–120.

2. President's Commission on Law Enforcement and the Administration of Justice, *The Challenge of Crime in a Free Society* (Washington, D.C.: U.S. Government Printing Office, 1967). See also John A. Conley, ed., *The 1967 President's Crime Commission Report: Its Impact 25 Years Later* (Cincinnati: Anderson, 1994).

3. David E. Olson, *Per-Unit and Per-Transaction Expenditures in the Montana Criminal Justice System* (Helena: Montana Board of Crime Control, 1993).

4. John J. DiIulio et al., *Performance Measures for the Criminal Justice System* (Washington, D.C.: U.S. Bureau of Justice Statistics, 1993).

5. Herbert Packer, *The Limits of the Criminal Sanction* (Stanford, Calif.: Stanford University Press, 1968).

6. Michael R. Gottfredson and Don M. Gottfredson, *Decision Making in Criminal Justice: Toward the Rational Exercise of Discretion,* 2d ed. (New York: Plenum, 1988); Lloyd E. Ohlin and Frank J. Remington, eds., *Discretion in Criminal Justice: The Tension between Individualization and Uniformity* (Albany: State University of New York Press, 1993). The exercise of discretion frequently involves an assessment of the perceived dangerousness of a given offender. See Dean J. Champion, *Measuring Offender Risk: A Criminal Justice Sourcebook* (Westport, Conn.: Greenwood Press, 1994).

7. Champion, *Measuring Offender Risk,* chap.2.

8. Ibid., chap. 3.

9. *Beck v. Ohio,* 379 U.S. 89 (1964).

10. *Mapp v. Ohio,* 367 U.S. 643 (1961).

11. Comptroller General of the United States, *Impact of the Exclusionary Rule on Federal Criminal Prosecutions* (Washington, D.C.: U.S. General Accounting Office, Apr. 19, 1979).

12. *Terry v. Ohio,* 392 U.S. 1 (1968).

13. Craig M. Bradley, "The Court's 'Two Model' Approach to the Fourth Amendment: Carpe diem," *Journal of Criminal Law and Criminology,* **84** (1993): 429–461.

14. Robert M. Bloom, "Judicial Integrity: A Call for its Re-emergence in the Adjudication of Criminal Cases," *Journal of Criminal Law and Criminology,* **84** (1993): 462–501.

15. *People v. de Bour,* 40 N.Y. 2d 210 (1976).

16. *Miranda v. Arizona,* 384 U.S. 436 (1966).

17. But there is an exception to this rule: When public safety is at risk, the warning may be postponed. See *New York v. Quarles,* 467 U.S. 649 (1984).

18. See Richard A. Leo, "The Impact of Miranda Revisited," *Journal of Criminal Law and Criminology,* **86** (1996): 621–692; Paul G. Cassell and Richard Fowles, "Handcuffing the Cops? A Thirty-Year Perspective on Miranda's Harmful Effects on Law Enforcement," *Stanford Law Review,* **50** (1998): 1055–1145.

19. *Gideon v. Wainwright,* 372 U.S. 335 (1963), as amplified by, *int. al., Argersinger v. Hamlin,* 407 U.S. 25 (1972), and *Strickland v. Washington,* 446 U.S. 668 (1984) (counsel must be competent). See also Anthony Lewis, *Gideon's Trumpet* (New York: Vintage, 1966).

20. Robert Hermann, Eric Single, and John Boston, *Counsel for the Poor* (Lexington, Mass.: Lexington Books, 1977), esp. p. 153; Alissa Pollitz Worden, "Counsel for the Poor: An Evaluation of Contracting for Indigent Criminal Defense," *Justice Quarterly,* **10** (1993): 613–637; Richard Klein and Robert Spangenberg, *The Indigent Defense Crisis* (Washington, D.C.: Section of

Criminal Justice, American Bar Association, 1993).

21. See *Commercial Surety Bail: Assessing Its Role in the Pretrial Release and Detention Decision* (Washington, D.C.: Pretrial Services Resource Center, 1994).

22. *United States v. Salerno*, 481 U.S. 739 (1987).

23. Gottfredson and Gottfredson, *Decision Making in Criminal Justice*, chap. 4.

24. Brian E. Forst, J. Lucianovic, and S. Cox, *What Happens after Arrest*, Institute for Law and Social Research Publication no. 4 (Washington, D.C.: U.S. Government Printing Office, 1977), p. 67.

25. "Only 3 of every 100 arrests went to trial in 1986, whereas 52 resulted in a guilty plea": U.S. Department of Justice, Bureau of Justice Statistics, *Annual Report*, Fiscal 1988 (Washington, D.C.: U.S. Government Printing Office, 1989), p. 49.

26. Federal Rules of Criminal Procedure, Rule 11.

27. Jan Hoffman, "No Longer Judicially Sacred, Grand Jury Is under Review," *New York Times*, Mar. 30, 1996, pp. 1, 28; Blanche Davis Blank, *The Not So Grand Jury: The Story of the Federal Grand Jury System* (Lanham, Md.: University Press of America, 1993).

28. Federal Rules of Criminal Procedure, Rule 6.

29. Forst et al., *What Happens after Arrest*, p. 17.

30. Held constitutional in *Williams v. Florida*, 399 U.S. 25 (1972).

31. See Harry Kalven, Jr., and Hans Zeisel, *The American Jury* (Chicago: University of Chicago Press, 1966).

32. Marta Sandys and Ronald C. Dillehay, "First-Ballot Votes, Predeliberation Dispositions, and Final Verdicts in Jury Trials," *Law and Human Behavior*, **19** (1995): 175–195.

33. *Apodica v. Oregon*, 406 U.S. 404 (1972).

34. Paul Thaler, *The Watchful Eye: American Justice in the Age of the Television Trial* (Westport, Conn.: Praeger, 1994).

35. For further discussion, see Ruth Ann Strickland and Richter H. Moore, Jr., "Cameras in State Courts: A Historical Perspective," *Judicature*, **78** (1994): 128–135, 160; Norbert L. Kerr, "The Effects of Pretrial Publicity on Jurors," *Judicature*, **78** (1994): 120–277; Marjorie Cohn and David Dow, *Cameras in the Courtroom: Television and the Pursuit of Justice* (Jefferson, N.C.: McFarland, 1998); Ronald Goldfarb, *TV or Not TV: Television, Justice, and the Courts* (New York: New York University Press, 1998); and Samuel H. Pillsbury, "Time, TV and Criminal Justice: Second Thoughts on the Simpson Trial," *Criminal Law Bulletin*, **33** (1997): 3–28.

36. Alfred Blumstein, Jacqueline Cohen, Susan E. Martin, and Michael H. Tonry, eds., *Research on Sentencing: The Search for Reform*, vol. 1 (Washington, D.C.: National Academy Press, 1983), p. 11.

37. Don Gottfredson and Bridget Stecher, "Sentencing Policy Models," unpublished manuscript, School of Criminal Justice, Rutgers University, 1979.

38. Joan Petersilia, *Expanding Options for Criminal Sentencing* (Santa Monica, Calif.: Rand Corporation, 1987). See also National Council on Crime and Delinquency, *Probation: An Effective Tool for the Future* (San Francisco: National Council on Crime and Delinquency, 1998).

39. Hans Toch, *Living in Prison* (New York: Free Press, 1977).

40. Michael R. Gottfredson and K. Adams, "Prison Behavior and Release Performance: Empirical Reality and Public Policy," *Law and Policy Quarterly*, **4** (1982): 373–391.

41. Gottfredson and Gottfredson, *Decision Making in Criminal Justice*, chap. 8.

42. Allen J. Beck and Bernard E. Shipley, *Recidivism of Young Parolees: Special Report*, for U.S. Department of Justice, Bureau of Justice Statistics (Washington, D.C.: U.S. Government Printing Office, 1987).

43. For a discussion of this study, see Charles Silberman, *Criminal Violence, Criminal Justice* (New York: Random House, 1978), pp. 257–261.

44. William S. Laufer, "The Rhetoric of Innocence," *Washington Law Review*, **70** (1995): 329–421.

45. Ronald C. Huff, Arye Rattner, and Edward Saparin, *Convicted but Innocent: Wrongful Conviction and Public Policy* (Thousand Oaks, Calif.: Sage, 1996); Clive Walker and Keir Starmer, eds., *Justice in Error* (London: Blackstone Press, 1993).

46. Uniform Crime Report, 1997.

47. Ibid., p. 116.

48. *Ex parte Crouse,* 4 Wharton, Pa., 9 (1838).

49. Sanford Fox, "Juvenile Justice Reform: An Historical Perspective," *Stanford Law Review,* **22** (1970): 1187–1239; Anthony M. Platt, *The Child Savers: The Invention of Delinquency,* 2d ed. (Chicago: University of Chicago Press, 1977).

50. *In re Gault,* 387 U.S. 1 (1967).

51. *In re Winship,* 397 U.S. 358 (1970); *McKeiver v. Pennsylvania,* 403 U.S. 528 (1971).

52. Norman Lefstein, Vaughan Stapleton, and Lee Teitelbaum, "In Search of Juvenile Justice: Gault and Its Implementation," *Law and Society Review,* **3** (1969): 491; H. Ted Rubin, "The Juvenile Court's Search for Identity and Responsibility," *Crime and Delinquency,* **23** (1977): 1–13.

53. Institute of Judicial Administration–American Bar Association, *Juvenile Justice Standards: A Summary and Analysis,* 2d ed., ed. Barbara Danziger Flicker (Cambridge, Mass.: Ballinger, 1982), p. 47.

54. Eric Fritsch and Craig Hemmens, "Juvenile Waiver in the United States, 1979–1995: A Comparison and Analysis of State Waiver Statutes," *Juvenile and Family Court Journal,* **46,** no. 3 (1995): 7–35.

55. Jeffrey A. Butts and Adele V. Harrell, *Delinquents or Criminals: Policy Options for Young Offenders* (Washington, D.C.: Urban Institute, 1998), pp. 5, 6.

56. Ibid., p. 6.

57. Fox Butterfield, "Republicans Challenge Notion of Separate Jails for Juveniles," *New York Times,* June 24, 1996, pp. 1, 13.

58. Peter J. Spiro, "On Juveniles, U.S. Has Treaty Obligations," *New York Times,* June 26, 1996, p. 18. See also Editorial, "Wrong Approach to Teen Age Crime," *New York Times,* June 30, 1996, p. E14.

59. Richard J. Lundman, Richard E. Sykes, and John P. Clark, "Police Control of Juveniles: A Replication," in *Police Behavior: A Sociological Perspective,* ed. Richard J. Lundman (New York: Oxford University Press, 1980), pp. 130–151.

60. Samuel M. Davis, *Rights of Juveniles: The Juvenile Justice System,* 2d ed. (New York: Clark Boardman, 1980), pp. 3–9.

61. *State ex. Rel. D.D.H. v. Dostert,* 165 W.Va. 448, 269 S.E. 2d 401 (1980). See also Institute of Judicial Administration—American Bar Association, *Juvenile Justice Standards;* and Franklin E. Zimring, "Toward a Jurisprudence of Youth Violence," in *Youth Violence,* ed. Michael Tonry and Mark H. Moore (Chicago: University of Chicago Press, 1998), pp. 477–501.

62. Don M. Gottfredson, Michael R. Gottfredson, Stephen D. Gottfredson, et al., eds., *Improving Information for Rational Decision Making in Juvenile Justice* (Sacramento, Calif.: Justice Policy Research Corp., 1994).

63. See Lloyd E. Ohlin, Robert B. Coates, and Alden D. Miller, "Radical Correctional Reform: A Case Study of the Massachusetts Youth Correctional System," *Harvard Educational Review,* **44** (1974): 74–111.

64. Denise C. Gottfredson and William H. Barton, "Deinstitutionalization of Juvenile Offenders," *Criminology,* **31** (1993): 591–611.

65. U.S. Department of Justice, Bureau of Justice Statistics, *Report to the Nation on Crime and Justice,* 2d ed. (Washington, D.C.: U.S. Government Printing Office, 1988), pp. 95, 103, 105.

66. Snyder and Sickmund, *Juvenile Offenders and Victims: 1999 National Report,* pp. 186, 189.

67. *Schall v. Martin,* 467 U.S. 253 (1984). For further discussion, see Alex M. Holsinger and Edward J. Latessa, "An Empirical Evaluation of a Sanction Continuum: Pathways through the Juvenile Justice System," *Journal of Criminal Justice,* **27** (1999): 155–172; and Donna Rau Sawicki, Beatrix Schaeffer, and Jeanie Thies, "Predicting Successful Outcomes for Serious and Chronic Juveniles in Residential Placement," *Juvenile and Family Court Journal,* **50** (1999): 21–31.

68. Steven P. Lab and John T. Whitehead, "An Analysis of Juvenile Correctional Treatment," *Crime and Delinquency,* **34** (1988): 60–83.

69. Imogene M. Montgomery, Patricia McFall Torbet, Diane A. Malloy, et al., *What Works: Promising Interventions in Juvenile Justice: Program Report* (Washington, D.C.: Office of Juvenile Justice and Delinquency Prevention, 1994).

Review • You Be the Criminologist • Key Terms • Notes

70. Snyder and Sickmund, *Juvenile Offenders and Victims: 1999 National Report*, p. 162.

71. James Austin and Barry Krisberg, "Wider, Stronger and Different Nets: The Dialectics of Criminal Justice Reform," *Journal of Research in Crime and Delinquency*, **18** (1981): 165–196; Edwin M. Lemert, "Diversion in Juvenile Justice: What Hath Been Wrought," *Journal of Research in Crime and Delinquency*, **18** (1981): 35–46.

72. Dan Macallair, "Disposition Case Advocacy in San Francisco's Juvenile Justice System: A New Approach of Deinstitutionalization," *Crime and Delinquency*, **40** (1994): 84–95.

73. Barry Krisberg, *Juvenile Justice—Improving the Quality of Care* (San Francisco: National Council on Crime and Delinquency, 1992); *Guide for Implementing the Comprehensive Strategy for Serious, Violent, and Chronic Juvenile Offenders* (Washington, D.C.: Office of Juvenile Justice and Delinquency Prevention, 1995).

74. See Gerhard O. W. Mueller, "Compensation for Victims of Crime: Thought before Action," *Minnesota Law Review*, **50** (1965): 213–221.

75. Margery Fry, "Justice for Victims," (*London*) *Observer*, May 7, 1957, p. 8. See also Margery Fry, *Arms of the Law* (London: Gollancz, 1951). For an assessment of the current state of crime victim compensation, see Robert J. McCormack, "Compensating Victims of Violent Crime," *Justice Quarterly*, **9** (1991): 329–346.

76. Stephen Schafer, *Restitution to Victims of Crime* (London: Stevens & Sons, 1960). See also Gerhard O. W. Mueller and H. H. A. Cooper, *The Criminal, Society, and the Victim*, Law Enforcement Assistance Administration (Washington, D.C.: U.S. Government Printing Office, 1973).

77. See Peggy M. Tobolowsky, "Victim Participation in the Criminal Justice Process: Fifteen Years after the President's Task Force on Victims of Crime," *New England Journal on Criminal and Civil Confinement*, **25** (1999): 21–105; and National Network to End Domestic Violence, *Survey of State Laws and Constitutional Provisions Regarding Crime Victims' Rights* (Washington, D.C.: National Network to End Domestic Violence, 1997).

78. See Robert J. McCormack, "United States Crime Victim Assistance: History, Organization and Evaluation," *International Journal of Comparative and Applied Criminal Justice*, **8** (1994): 202–220.

79. Mary S. Knudten and Richard P. Knudten, "What Happens to Crime Victims and Witnesses in the Justice System?" in *Perspectives on Crime Victims*, ed. Burt Galaway and Joe Hudson (St. Louis: Mosby, 1981), pp. 52–72.

80. Andrew Carmen, "Towards the Institutionalization of a New Kind of Justice Professional: The Victim Advocate," *Justice Professional*, **9** (1995): 1–15.

81. A. M. Heinz and W. A. Kerstetter, "Victim Participation in Plea Bargaining: A Field Experiment," in *Plea Bargaining*, ed. W. F. McDonald and J. A. Cramer (Lexington, Mass.: Heath, 1979), pp. 167–177.

82. William F. McDonald, "The Victim's Role in the American Administration of Criminal Justice: Some Developments and Findings," in *The Victim in International Perspective*, ed. Hans Joachim Schneider (New York: De Gruyter, 1982), pp. 397–407.

83. U.S. Department of Justice, Bureau of Justice Statistics, *Report to the Nation*, p. 82.

84. Donald J. Hall, "The Role of the Victim in the Prosecution and Disposition of a Criminal Case," in Galaway and Hudson, *Perspectives on Crime Victims*, pp. 318–342.

85. George P. Fletcher, *With Justice for Some: Victims' Rights in Criminal Trials* (New York: Addison-Wesley, 1995).

86. Ibid.; Ellen K. Alexander and Janice Harris Lord, *Impact Statements—A Victim's Right to Speak . . . A Nation's Responsibility to Listen* (Arlington, Va.: National Victim Center, 1994).

87. Edna Erez, Pamela Tontodonato, Matti Joutsen, et al., "Victim Participation in Sentencing," *International Review of Victimology*, **3** (1994): 17–166; Edna Erez and Leigh Roeper, "The Effect of Victim Impact Statements on Sentencing Patterns and Outcomes: The Australian Experience," *Journal of Criminal Justice*, **23** (1995): 363–375; Valerie Finn-DeLuca, "Victim Participation at Sentenc-

ing," *Criminal Law Bulletin*, **30** (1994): 403–428; Robert C. Davis and Barbara E. Smith, "Victim Impact Statements and Victim Satisfaction: An Unfulfilled Promise," *Journal of Criminal Justice*, **22** (1994): 1–12.

88. Stephen Schafer, "The Victim and Correctional Theory: Integrating Victim Reparation with Offender Rehabilitation," in McDonald and Cramer, *Plea Bargaining*, pp. 227–236.

89. See Dorothy (Edmonds) McKnight, "The Victim-Offender Reconciliation Project," in Galaway and Hudson, *Perspectives on Crime Victims*, pp. 292–298.

90. See Janet Rifkin, "Mediation in the Justice System: A Paradox for Women," *Women and Criminal Justice*, **1** (1989): 41–54.

91. Hall, "The Role of the Victim."

92. See Irene Melup, ed., "UN Regulations on Victims of Crime," *International Review of Victimology*, **2** (1991): 28–72.

93. Morris Dees, Lenore E. A. Walker, Frederica L. Lehrman, et al., "Victims and Violence: Civil Justice Remedies," *Trial*, **31** (1995): 20–71.

94. See Robert E. Crew, Jr., and Mary Vancore, "Managing Victim Restitution in Florida: An Analysis of the Implementation of FS 775.089," *Justice System Journal*, **17** (1994): 241–248.

CHAPTER 17
Enforcing the Law: Practice and Research

KEY TERMS
community policing
constable
frankpledge
genetic fingerprinting
justices of the peace
night watchmen
police subculture
problem-oriented policing
sheriff
sting operation
team policing
tithing

Crime is rampant. Pickpockets and purse snatchers lurk on every street. To protect their money from muggers, people now carry their wallets on a leather strap around their necks. Just the other day a noted wit said: "Only a fool would go out to dinner without having made his will." The police are sparse in the neighborhoods. The city even installed dummy police officers, at highway intersections and school crossings, to serve as an alert to the presence of law enforcement. Citizens bought locks to protect their homes. You have never seen so many "Beware of Dog" signs! The more affluent hired private security agencies to protect their premises. Public officials don't even ride around in public anymore without security agents in front, in back, and on the sides. Neighborhoods have formed citizens' watch groups. And every-

body is upset about the lack of police presence.[1]

What city is being described? Chicago? Washington? New York? Or Denver? Seattle? Dallas? Although it could be any of these or other cities in the United States, this was reported about Rome of 2000 years ago.

No country or city is capable of ensuring an orderly, secure life for its citizens unless it polices itself. This idea is so ancient that the Greeks used the same word for "city" and for "police": *polis*. Through their presence the police, whether the lictors of

ancient Rome or the men and women in blue in modern America, are supposed to maintain peace in the community. But their mere presence cannot prevent crime and disorder unless it is backed by enforcement power. This power cannot be merely reactive; it has to include preventive and protective functions, as well as the right and duty to investigate, to assemble facts, and to prepare these facts for judicial disposition. These duties can be categorized as peace-keeping and crime-fighting functions. Yet as we shall see, relatively little police time is devoted to these duties. Far more time is devoted to social services, such as helping people in distress; answering requests for information; responding to emergencies, disasters, and accidents; and maintaining an orderly traffic flow.

There is general agreement that the police are a multifunction service agency equipped to respond to civic problems and to fight crime. But there is disagreement on the political and social role police should play in a democratic society. The debate is marked by fear that civil liberties may be lost if the police power to take away personal freedom—by arrest, search, or use of force—is abused. The controversy, which almost prevented the English from creating their first police force in 1829, has surfaced intermittently in the United States since the early nineteenth century. It reached particular intensity in the 1960s, when aggressive policing against demonstrators and minorities resulted in claims that some police agencies were biased and infringed on the rights of citizens. Assertions regarding police abuses of power against minority citizens have resurfaced in the 1990s. The Rodney King case presented the public with a disturbing example—excessive use of force by members of the Los Angeles Police Department.[2]

Their strategic position at the gateway of the criminal justice process, their numerical strength in comparison with that of all other agents of criminal justice, and their constant contact with the public give the police prominence in the criminal justice process.

THE HISTORY OF POLICING

Some cultures can proudly point to ancient documentation for their police. The Egyptians, for example, recruited Nubians for their Medjay police nearly 4000 years ago and established a maritime police about 1340 B.C. We do not even have a record of the existence of our Anglo-Saxon ancestors at that time.

The English Heritage

The earliest records of policing in Anglo-American history can be found in the laws of the Danish king Canute (d. 1035), who governed England in the first quarter of the eleventh century, be-

fore the Norman Conquest. In a system called **frankpledge,** members of a **tithing,** an association of 10 families, were bound together by a mutual pledge to keep the peace. Every male over age 12 was part of the system. Over time the frankpledge system was strengthened by the establishment of the king's representative, the *reeve,* in each county or shire. The shire reeve, or **sheriff,** presided over the shire's court, executed summonses, and enforced the laws. A force of able-bodied citizens, called a *posse comitatus* (Latin for "power of the county"), assisted the sheriff and could be convened at his command. (The use of sheriff's posses persisted well into the twentieth century in the western and southern United States.)

The Statute of Winchester in 1285 established the office of **constable,** a royal official charged with suppressing riots and violent crimes in each county. By the thirteenth century a night watch system developed in larger towns and cities. The **night watchmen** were untrained citizens who patrolled at night, on the lookout for disturbances. In 1326 the first **justices of the peace** were commissioned. They were untrained men, usually nobles, who investigated and tried minor cases. Law enforcement by sheriffs, constables, hired assistants, justices of the peace, and night watchmen changed very little in England until the eighteenth century.[3]

But then came industrialization and urban growth. The system that had worked in rural and feudal England proved inadequate in the rapidly growing cities. At the beginning of the eighteenth century there was little law and order in London. Henry Fielding (1707–1754), the author of *Tom Jones* and a justice of the peace, led efforts to establish a uniformed, armed standing police force. In response to research conducted by Fielding and reported in his *Enquiry into the Causes of the Late Increase of Robbers* (1751), Parliament granted him funds to recruit England's first professional police force. The experiment failed, and it was not until 1829 that such a system was established.

In that year the Act for Improving the Police in and near the Metropolis was steered through Parliament by England's home secretary (and later prime minister), Sir Robert Peel (1788–1850). This bill established the Metropolitan Constabulary, originally composed of 1000 men. These officers were unarmed but uniformed and well disciplined: They were taught "that there is no qualification more indispensable to a police officer, than a perfect command of temper, never suffering himself to be moved in the slightest degree, by any language or threats that may be used."[4] Sir Robert's officers came to be known as "little Roberts," or "bobbies." The experiment proved such a success in London that by 1856 all counties and boroughs in England were required to have their own professional police.[5]

Despite rising crime rates, urban chaos, and the humanitarian reforms instituted by Peel, some scholars believe that the real reason for the establishment of the English police was not the crime problem but the elite's desire to control the poor. Vagrants and idle persons, after arrest and conviction, could be a source of cheap labor for the Industrial Revolution's large factories.[6]

Policing in the United States

Colonial America used a system of policing much like that of early England. County sheriffs were the principal law enforcement officers. They were supplemented by town marshals, constables, and night watchmen. Sheriffs received no salaries but were paid standard fees for various services (collecting taxes, supervising elections, and so forth).[7] Sheriffs were assisted by deputies, and in case of need they could convene posses composed of ordinary citizens. This system lasted until the early nineteenth century, when the rapid growth of cities brought the need for a better and more formal law enforcement system.[8]

Politics and Policing In a time of migration and immigration, rapid industrialization, social unrest, hostility toward minorities, and mob violence, American cities organized their first uniformed police forces. In 1838 Boston established its force. New York followed in 1844, and Philadelphia 10 years later. The police were expected to keep the peace, to prevent crime,

and to defuse social conflict. Their duties extended to such activities as caring for orphans and derelicts, operating soup kitchens, and maintaining sanitary conditions in overcrowded neighborhoods.

Appointments to the police were made by political bosses. Police commissioners changed with every election, as did many of the men on the force. Often the officers were, in fact, tools of ward politicians. Throughout the nineteenth century, the conduct of the police in the United States was an ongoing scandal. As a group, they were corrupt, powerful, often poorly trained, without standards for admission to the force (not even health or age), unsupervised, and frequently abusive.[9] Police brutality appeared to be tolerated by the middle class because it was used in large measure against social outcasts.

At the turn of the twentieth century, the situation changed. Progressive reformers attacked social and urban problems, including the police. August Vollmer developed the concept of police professionalism. Vollmer's model of police organization and activity, based on crime fighting as the primary role of the police, was not challenged until the 1960s.

The Progressive Era The Progressives were educated upper- and middle-class Americans determined to stamp out corruption wherever they found it. Among the many places they found it were the police forces. The Progressives worked to professionalize law enforcement by taking it out of politics and introducing modern technology. Their slogan was "The police have to get out of politics, and politics has to be out of the police."[10]

One reformer, Theodore Roosevelt, who accepted the presidency of the New York City Board of Police Commissioners in 1895, immediately effected a change in police standards by failing over half of the applicants on the physical examination and 30 percent on the mental examination in a 10-month period.[11] Despite the many reforms the Progressives brought about, some historians of criminology have argued that the Progressives' interest in a more efficient police force was grounded less in a desire to reform than in their fear that newer immigrant groups might be gaining too much power in local government and thus too much control in the cities.

Vollmer and Wilson: Pioneers of Police Professionalization   August Vollmer, who developed the professional model of policing in the early twentieth century, was a first-generation American with a limited education who became one of the most prominent figures in the history of American policing. He began his career in 1904 as police marshal in Berkeley, California. Within 5 years he was made chief of police, a position he held until 1932.

To Vollmer, a professional police force had to be nonpolitical, well recruited, well trained, well disciplined, and equipped with modern technology. Its members had to be part of the civil service, selected and advanced by merit. The police officers' major role was to fight crime. Vollmer's book *The Police and Modern Society* (1936) remained a guide for police professionals for decades. The American Society of Criminology gave his name to its most prestigious award for outstanding achievement in law enforcement and criminal justice.

Another pioneer in modern policing, Orlando W. Wilson, a student and protégé of Vollmer, stands out for his contribution to the modern management and administrative techniques used in policing. Wilson, who obtained a degree in criminology from the University of California in 1924, became chief of police in Fullerton, California (1924–1928), and Wichita, Kansas (1928–1939). He served as professor of police administration (1939–1960) and as founding dean of the University of California, Berkeley, School of Criminology (1953). He retired in 1967 from his position as superintendent of the Chicago Police Department, which he had transformed from one of the least reputable in the country to one of the very best.

The Wickersham Commission   While the pioneers were professionalizing police forces, several crime commissions at the local, state, and national levels began to investigate the extent of crime and the criminal justice system's response to it. Former attorney general George W. Wickersham was appointed to head the United States National Commission on Law Observance and Enforcement from 1929 to 1932.[12] The commission retained practitioners and academicians to observe and analyze the state of law enforcement in the country, particularly in connection with the futile attempts to enforce the Prohibition laws.

The result of the inquiry was devastating: Many police forces were corrupt, training was superficial, and recruitment was inadequate. Communications, statistics, and information sharing were chaotic. Constitutional guarantees were largely ignored. The report of the Wickersham Commission provided solid evidence that America's early reform efforts had not reached far enough or deep enough.

The crime-fighting model of policing lasted until it was challenged in the 1960s, in the wake of civil unrest. Before we discuss how police departments began to improve their image and try to deal more effectively with the public, let us look at their organizational structure.

LAW ENFORCEMENT AGENCIES

Today there are more than 20,000 separate law enforcement agencies in the United States at the federal, state, and local levels. The majority of these are located at the local level—county, city, town, and village. The number of officers in these departments can range from as few as 1 sworn officer to as many as 43,000 sworn officers. As of 1996, 921,978 full-time employees, including 663,535 sworn personnel, and 97,770 part-time personnel served state and local agencies.[13] The number of full-time employees has been increasing since the early 1990s (Figure 17.1).

American policing differs from that found in most other countries in its diversity of forces and lack of central coordination and command. The idea that federal and state police functions are separate is basic to our system of federalism. Even within the states there has always been concern that any central command not only would violate local autonomy but also might put a dangerous concentration of power in the hands of the chief executive. So most policing takes place at the municipal level, where the

In 1914 Prince Albert I of Monaco responded to the increasing international mobility of criminals by organizing the First International Criminal Police Congress, which recommended the establishment of an international police force. Founded in 1923, that force evolved into what we now know as the International Criminal Police Organization, called "Interpol" after its telegraphic code name. Membership today stands at 158 states, with a staff of some 300.

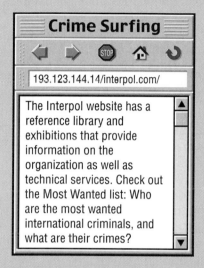

Crime Surfing

193.123.144.14/interpol.com/

The Interpol website has a reference library and exhibitions that provide information on the organization as well as technical services. Check out the Most Wanted list: Who are the most wanted international criminals, and what are their crimes?

As a police organization, Interpol is unique in that it has no police officers. It is, in fact, a complex communications network. It provides information on criminals and handles requests for wanted criminals. Each member state has a police department that serves as the country's national central bureau (NCB) for Interpol. The NCB replies to requests from other NCBs and from the Interpol General Secretariat and coordinates large-scale police actions when necessary. In the United States, the U.S. National Central Bureau (USNCB), located in the Department of Justice in

Washington, D.C., handles all Interpol requests. The bureau may be asked to locate a fugitive, check a license, or supply a criminal record.(1)

The bureau also issues "red notices," which are international notices for fugitives who are wanted by the United States. In fiscal year 1992, the NCB issued 60 red notices for U.S. fugitives. Twenty-six of these fugitives were wanted for drug-related crimes; the remainder were sought for offenses that included mail and wire fraud, kidnapping, and murder.(2)

The goals of Interpol are carefully defined:

- To ensure and promote the widest possible mutual assistance between all criminal police authorities, within the limits of the laws existing in the different countries and in the spirit of the Declaration of Human Rights.
- To establish and develop all institutions likely to contribute effectively to the prevention and suppression of ordinary law crimes.

Interpol is not allowed to undertake "any intervention or activities of a political, military, religious or racial character,"(3) yet it is not always easy to separate "ordinary law crimes" from political crimes. For example, drug crimes are regarded as "ordinary law crimes," and in fact, the control of drug-related criminality is one of Interpol's major activities. But traffic in narcotic drugs also can be a highly political affair: It can support some governments and destabilize others. Interpol's annual general assemblies of member states help draw the boundaries between ordinary and political criminality.

Interpol works to assist member states in preventing the exploitation of children and in devising measures to deal with international organized crime, the firearms and explosives trade,

terrorism, traffic in human beings, missing persons, disaster victim identification, and counterfeiting. Perhaps one of Interpol's most important functions is its continuing activity in the criminal intelligence area—receiving, processing, and disseminating international notices and messages that may lead to crime clearance and arrest of wanted persons in any member state.

Interpol, now headquartered in Lyons, France, has no precinct houses at which a citizen could file a complaint. Unlike any other police organization, Interpol works solely at the intergovernmental level, serving its member states and ultimately benefiting the whole world.

Sources

1. "From the Parc Monceau to the Parc de la Tete d'Or," *International Criminal Police Review* (November–December 1989): 6–8; Fenton Bresler, *Interpol* (London: Sinclair Stevenson, 1992).
2. U.S. General Accounting Office, *Interpol—Information on the Red Notice System* (Washington, D.C.: General Accounting Office, March 1993), p. 3.
3. Richard Bell, "The History of Drug Prohibition and Legislation," *International Criminal Police Review* (September–October 1991): 2–6.

Questions for Discussion

1. Why should ordinary citizens not have the right to file a complaint with Interpol if the crime they wish to report has international dimensions?
2. What stands in the way of Interpol's having its own sworn officers, with power to arrest an international criminal anywhere in the world?

control rests, for the most part, with an elected police commissioner and an appointed chief, superintendent, or director who handles the administrative responsibilities.

Although there are many levels of public law enforcement agencies, each with specialized units, they often must work together to solve cases. A major narcotics operation, for

FIGURE 17.1   Full-time employees in state and local law enforcement agencies, 1992 and 1996.

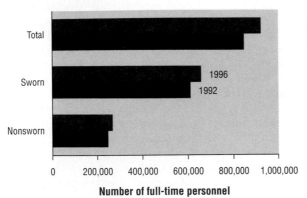

Number of full-time personnel

Source: Brian A. Reaves and Andrew L. Goldberg, *Census of State and Local Law Enforcement Agencies, 1996* (Washington D.C.: Bureau of Justice Statistics, 1998).

example, may involve federal agencies like the DEA, the Coast Guard, and the FBI; the state police; county officials; and local police. The 1996 investigation into the bombing of TWA flight 800 is an example of multilevel interagency cooperation among law enforcement. Local, state, federal, and international police organizations worked collaboratively and individually to investigate this case.

Federal Law Enforcement

The framers of the Constitution did not envisage the need for any federal law enforcement agency. But it soon became clear that the federal government needed an enforcement system to perform its mandated functions. The first federal police force to be established was the United States Coast Guard, which in 1790 was assigned the task of policing the coasts to prevent smuggling and ensure the collection of import duties. Other federal police forces were added, particularly after 1870, when the Department of Justice became aware of its law enforcement obligations. The federal agency with the broadest range of duties is the FBI.

The Federal Bureau of Investigation   In 1908 President Theodore Roosevelt, angered by Congress's failure to adopt legislation to regulate political and business corruption, estab-

lished the Department of Justice's Bureau of Investigations. Initially, the Bureau was staffed by 35 employees. They were empowered to investigate bankruptcy fraud, antitrust violations, and other violations of federal law.

During the late 1920s—the heyday of Prohibition—citizens became frustrated by the inability of local and state law enforcement agencies to stem the growth of organized crime. Incidents such as the Lindbergh kidnapping added to this frustration. But at that point the Bureau had no authority to investigate or apprehend fleeing felons who crossed state lines.

In the face of arguments favoring the establishment of a national, or federal, police force, J. Edgar Hoover, whom President Calvin Coolidge had appointed to head the Bureau in 1924, argued that state and local police should retain their own jurisdictions and sovereignty, but that new federal legislation was needed to give the Bureau jurisdiction over criminals who operate across state lines. In 1934 Congress passed such legislation. One year later, in 1935, the Bureau adopted a new name—the Federal Bureau of Investigation.[14]

Over the years the FBI has played a highly publicized role in the investigation and capture of such criminals as Baby Face Nelson, Doc Barker, John Dillinger, Pretty Boy Floyd, Al Capone, Bonnie Parker, and Clyde Barrow. Under Hoover, the FBI acquired its sterling image as the chief investigative branch of the Department of Justice. This image was tarnished in the 1960s when it was revealed that FBI agents had been wiretapping national leaders, including Martin Luther King, Jr.; opening mail; and discrediting political radicals as "enemies of the government."[15]

In the early 1990s the FBI's handling of a variety of cases was called into question and subjected to review. The Bureau was harshly criticized for its handling of a confrontation with the Branch Davidians in Waco, Texas, in 1993. The standoff between the Bureau and the Davidians came to an end on April 19 after the FBI and other federal law enforcement officers shot tear gas shells into the compound.[16] The tragic result was that 75 Davidians, including 25 children, died in a fire that ensued. The FBI and the other federal agencies involved (such as the Bureau of

Dennis Fritz and his daughter, Elizabeth, hug after District Court Judge Tom Landrith announced his life sentence for murdering Debra Carter would be dismissed. Fritz had spent twelve years in prison. DNA tests established his innocence.

Alcohol, Tobacco and Firearms) have learned from this tragedy and, based on advice from experts on extremist groups, have altered some of their procedures.[17] These revised procedures have helped federal agencies respond more effectively in similar situations. For example, federal agencies peacefully resolved a 1996 standoff with a group of federal tax protestors who had barricaded themselves in an Arizona ranch.

Incidents such as these illustrate how the orientation of the Bureau has changed over the years. In addition to dealing with extremist groups and investigating acts of domestic terrorism (such as the bombing of the Federal Building in Oklahoma City on April 19, 1995), it also focuses on white-collar crime, public corruption, organized crime, and drug offenses.

The Bureau, headquartered in Washington, D.C., has a staff of more than 27,000, including 11,400 special agents in 56 offices nationwide as well as 34 foreign posts.[18] The FBI also develops and maintains advanced forensic research capabilities, training facilities, and extensive databases of information on crime and criminals. The Laboratory Division collects and analyzes evidence for its own investigations as well as for other federal, state, and local law enforcement agencies. In 1996 alone, the lab conducted 696,543 forensic examinations of evidence and 2,184,998 latent fingerprint comparisons. The Forensic Science Research and Training Center provides advanced forensic training to FBI staff and other law enforcement personnel, including a technical training course in the implementation of new DNA technology (sometimes referred to as **genetic fingerprinting**) in criminal investigations.

DNA evidence has been introduced in hundreds of cases to convict the guilty and free the innocent. In fact, there are more than 10 state-run laboratories around the country that contribute DNA samples of convicted sex offenders to a national FBI database that searches for evidentiary matches in an attempt to solve murders, rapes, and other violent crimes. The labs evaluate blood, semen, and tissue samples taken from crime scenes.[19]

Regular fingerprints are still maintained in the Identification Division that was established in 1924. Today, the bureau's files contain more than 214 million fingerprint cards, representing 74 million individuals.[20] More than 96 million of these cards contain criminal history data on some 24 million people. Approximately 31,000 additional fingerprint cards arrive at the Identification Division every day. The FBI also maintains the National Crime Information Center (NCIC), a nationwide network of criminal justice information. Available to law enforcement agencies in all 50 states, the NCIC contains records on stolen property, wanted persons with outstanding arrest warrants, criminal histories on persons arrested for serious offenses, and records of certain missing persons. More than 900,000 transactions are processed per day at the NCIC.[21]

In 1985, the bureau established the National Center for the Analysis of Violent Crime (NCAVC), a research and training center that provides assistance to law enforcement agencies faced with violent crimes that are unusual and/or particularly vicious or repetitive in nature, such as sexually-oriented serial murders or child molestation cases involving multiple victims. The FBI also investigates police corruption. Finally, the FBI National Academy, located at Quantico, Virginia, provides training free of charge to state, local, and foreign law enforcement officials. These courses are given to more than 1000 state and local law enforcement administrators annually. The Bureau also collects and disseminates crime statistics nationwide, known as the Uniform Crime Reports (see Chapter 2).

Other Federal Law Enforcement Agencies
The Department of Justice maintains other agencies that also fulfill law enforcement duties:

- The *Drug Enforcement Administration (DEA)*, which is charged with the enforcement of laws controlling the use, sale, and distribution of narcotics and other controlled substances.

- The *Immigration and Naturalization Service (INS)*, which has the dual authority of policing U.S. borders to prevent aliens from entering illegally and overseeing the admission, naturalization, exclusion, and deportation of aliens. The INS employs the largest number of federal officers (see Figure 17.2).

- The *United States Marshal Service*, which provides protection for relocated witnesses and administrative support and security

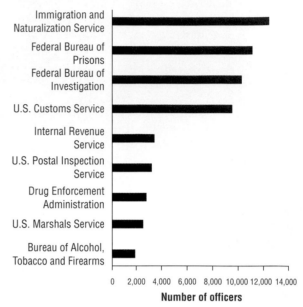

FIGURE 17.2   Major employers of federal officers, 1996.

Source: Brian A. Reaves, *Federal Law Enforcement Officers, 1996* (Washington, D.C.: Bureau of Justice Statistics, 1998).

services for federal district courts and the U.S. courts of appeals.

Most of the other departments of the federal government operate law enforcement agencies as well. The Treasury Department maintains a law enforcement agency within the Internal Revenue Service (IRS). The Treasury also operates the Secret Service, which protects governmental officials and investigates forgery and counterfeiting, and the Bureau of Alcohol, Tobacco and Firearms (ATF), which enforces federal laws regulating the importation, distribution, and use of alcohol, tobacco, and firearms. The Department of Transportation is responsible for the U.S. Coast Guard (in peacetime). The Federal Trade Commission (FTC), the Securities and Exchange Commission (SEC), the Department of Labor, and the United States Postal Service all maintain their own law enforcement agencies.

State Police

In 1835 the first state police agency, the Texas Rangers, was established. Its primary purpose was to control the Mexican border. Thirty years later Massachusetts created a similar force. It was not until the turn of the twentieth century that states across the country followed suit—Connecticut in 1903, Arizona and Pennsylvania in 1905, New Jersey in 1921. The Pennsylvania Constabulary (state police) became a model for the nation. It is a highly centralized, quasi-military force, which had to overcome its initial reputation as being an antilabor, pro-big-business police.

Today all states except Hawaii have their own state police forces, whose primary function is to control traffic on the highways. These forces also fill gaps in rural and suburban policing, respond to the statewide mobility of crime (for example, by pursuing offenders crossing jurisdictional boundaries), aid in crowd control, and provide centralized services for local police forces (tracing stolen cars, statewide record keeping, laboratory assistance). Distrust of centralized police power has generally kept state police forces from assuming any duties of local officials.

County Police

The sheriff's office, at the county level, is responsible for countywide policing outside municipalities. In Westerns, the sheriff is portrayed as a tough, fearless, fair, and incorruptible official, clearly distinguishable by his "tin star" and his agility with pistols. He was indeed a powerful figure on the frontier. During the westward expansion in the nineteenth century, the sheriff was often the only legal authority over vast areas.

Today sheriff's departments range from small offices with an appointed sheriff to large departments staffed by trained, professional personnel (as in Los Angeles County, California). Most sheriff's forces perform functions that extend beyond crime prevention and control to such traditional county services as tax assessment and collection, court duty, jail administration, inspection services, the serving of court orders, and the overseeing of public buildings, highways, bridges, and parks. In some places the sheriff may even serve as the coroner.[22]

Municipal Police

In modern urban America, as in urbanized ancient Greece, the city is the societal unit with which most people identify. Its most visible government representatives are the municipal police. Citizens rely on the police for advice, service, and protection around the clock. No wonder, then, that municipal police forces are among the largest governmental employers and account for so large a proportion of the budget. A recent survey has estimated that 13,578 local police agencies employed approximately 583,438 people, including 410,956 sworn officers.[23]

The distribution of personnel is uneven, however, ranging from departments with 1 or 2 employees to the New York City police department with a force of 43,976 employees, including 36,813 sworn officers,[24] the largest in the country. In fact, as of 1996 only 4 percent of local police departments employed 100 or more full-time sworn personnel.[25]

The expenditures of some of the larger departments are intimidating. In fiscal year 1997, the New York City police department's operating expenditures totaled $2,424,000,000; the expenditures for Chicago totaled $702,194,102; and those for Los Angeles totaled $552,512,202.[26] Yet fiscal management, with its constant crises, revenue shortfalls, and budget-cutting exercises, is only one of the many challenges facing a police department. Controlling crime, controlling officers, and facing constant pressures from all segments of society make the management of large urban departments one of the most difficult governmental tasks.

The limited size of small-town departments means that they differ from their big-city counterparts in several ways. Officers who work in small departments usually work as generalists, and there is a much less formal chain of command than that found in the large municipal departments. The chief of police might be found on patrol, and a detective might be making traffic stops. These departments usually have a smaller proportion of civilian employees than do those in cities.[27] City residents would probably be surprised to realize that the continuous presence and round-the-clock availability of police officers to which they are accustomed is not the norm in many departments. Agencies staffed by as few as one or two officers simply cannot provide service 24 hours a day, 7 days a week.[28]

The small-town police officer has sometimes been depicted in popular culture as a good-natured figure whom nobody takes very seriously as a law enforcement officer. Some recent research, however, suggests that, in fact, investigative effectiveness, as measured by clearance rates, is greater in smaller departments than in larger ones.[29] Additional research is required before we can conclude that small-town police are more effective than those in large cities and, if they are, before we can determine what factors account for the difference.

Special-Purpose Police

Throughout the country, agencies that are not part of the local department possess police powers within specified jurisdictional limits that may cut across political boundaries. Special police forces include transit police, public housing police, airport police, public school police, and park police (see Table 17.1). Special police forces were often regarded as inferior to municipal forces. Indeed, some of them started out as guard services. By now, however, most special forces are as well recruited and trained as their municipal counterparts. Some have better training, given the highly specialized nature of their duties. The New York–New Jersey Port Authority Police, for example, have some of the highest standards of recruitment, training, and performance.

Private Police

Security guards, alarms, closed-circuit surveillance systems, and antitheft devices are everywhere in American life today. At work, at home, or at leisure, Americans are now the object of surveillance or protection furnished by the private security industry more often than at any previous time. Clifford Shearing and Philip Stenning, who have written extensively on the subject, note that the widespread acceptance of private police, or private security, has significantly extended the reach of social control.[30] Given the extent and significance of this phenomenon, any discussion of policing in the

TABLE 17.1   Special Police Agencies and Full-Time Sworn Personnel, by Type of Jurisdiction, June 1996

Type of Special Jurisdiction	Agencies	Full-Time Sworn Personnel
Total	1,316	43,082
College/university campus	699	10,496
Natural resources/conservation laws	79	8.395
Public school district	117	5,247
Transportation system/facilities	28	4,274
Parks/recreation facilities	68	2,595
Criminal Investigations	72	2,515
Airport	84	2,407
Waterways/harbors/ports	38	1,291
Public housing	13	1,245
Alcoholic beverage control	17	1,199
State capitol/government buildings	24	988
Medical school/facility	42	894
Fire investigations	14	448
Agricultural/livestock laws	6	300
Commercial vehicle laws[a]	1	197
Public sanitation district	3	193
Gaming/racing laws	5	190
Court services[b]	1	140
Other	5	68

Note: The table includes both state-level and local-level agencies.

[a]Arkansas Highway Patrol

[b]Hawaii Department of Public Safety.

Source: Brian A. Reaves and Andrew L. Goldberg, *Census of State and Local Law Enforcement Agencies, 1996* (Washington, D.C.: Bureau of Justice Statistics, 1998).

United States would be incomplete without reference to private security forces, even though they are not part of the publicly financed system of law enforcement.[31]

Private security today includes guard and patrol services, private investigators, alarm companies, armored-car and -courier services, and security consulting services for loss-prevention strategies, computer security systems, and executive-protection strategies. Private security forces even provide protection to entire communities, and some compare very favorably with the public police in surrounding neighborhoods in terms of crime prevention and lower levels of fear of crime.[32]

The costs of private security are about $401 billion,[33] while the expenditure figures for police protection at all levels of government amount to only about $41 billion.[34] Today the U.S. private security industry employs over 1.5 million people, more than federal, state, and local governments combined.[35] Many of those employed in private security have a background in public law enforcement. In fact, research conducted for the National Institute of Justice indicated that almost one-quarter (24 percent) of public police personnel also work off-duty in private security.[36]

The widespread use of private security forces has raised a number of issues. One is the fitness of security personnel, especially of guards. Training is usually minimal, and few states had standards until recently.[37] Another concern is the question of equity. Is it fair for those who can afford it to have more protection than those who cannot? One reason for public police is to provide equal protection to all; the idea that the wealthy can buy added services seems to violate this principle and raises troubling questions about the willingness of the wealthy to support tax-financed public police.[38] The employment of off-duty police officers by

private security companies also raises a number of issues, including questions of police department liability for the actions of its officers while engaged in private duty, potential tarnishing of the image of police if officers give the appearance of serving private interests only, and the possibility of conflicts of interest.[39]

COMMAND STRUCTURE

A prototype for a well-organized municipal police department, developed by the President's Commission on Law Enforcement and the Administration of Justice, has become the model for urban agencies (Figure 17.3). A department performs basically two types of functions: line

functions (bureaus of operational services, of investigative services, of technical services) and nonline functions (administration and technical service bureaus).

Line functions include patrol duties, investigation, traffic control, and various specialized services (juvenile, vice, domestic dispute). Most officers are assigned to patrol duties. The *nonline functions* include the staff duties that one finds in most large organizations, public or private, such as planning, research, administration and training, budgeting, purchasing, public relations, inspections. Nonline functions also increasingly include the complex tasks of supporting line functions with high-tech services in communications, identification, laboratory work, and data processing, as well as such routine services as building and grounds maintenance, repair services, supply provisioning, and jail administration.

Police departments are not democratic organizations. They are organized largely along the lines of a military command, with military ranks and insignia. Patrol officers are responsible to their sergeants, sergeants to lieutenants, lieutenants to captains, captains to inspectors, inspectors to their chief or director. The structure of operational units is similar to that of other governmental departments. A bureau is at the highest level (a bureau of police within a department of public safety, for instance); divisions (such as a criminal investigation division) are at the next lower level; and sections and/or units are at the lowest level (the art theft unit, for example). The goal of this type of organization is efficient performance. The day-to-day and night-to-night operations of line officers are carried out in shifts, or watches, usually of 8 consecutive hours but often lasting longer.

Operations Bureau: Patrol

Patrol officers on the beat are usually the first law enforcement persons on the scene of a crime. They conduct the initial search, block off the crime scene for later investigation, interview victims and witnesses, and make a report of the facts. Small police agencies may have only patrol officers. In larger agencies, the

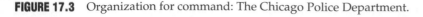

FIGURE 17.3 Organization for command: The Chicago Police Department.

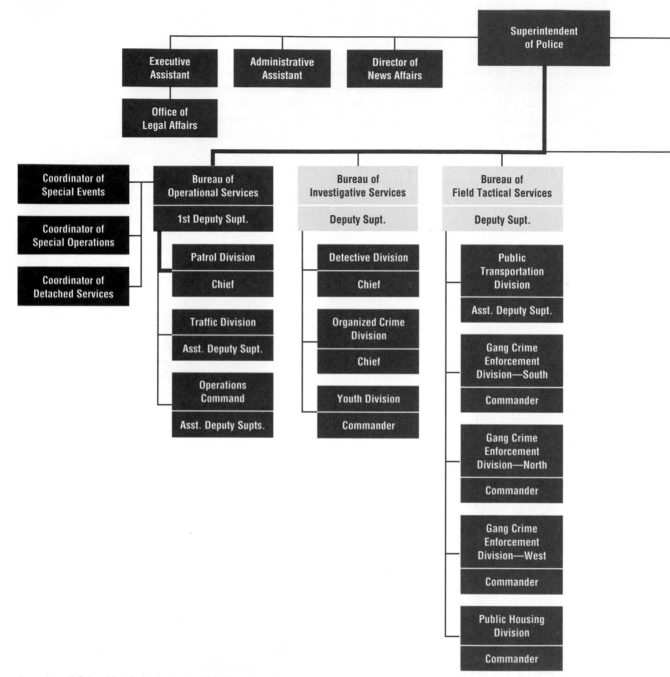

Source: Larry K. Gaines, Mittie D. Southerland, and John E. Angell, *Police Administration* (New York: McGraw-Hill, 1991), p. 82.

patrol unit is made up of about two-thirds of the officers.

The functions of this unit are to deter crime by the presence of officers on the street, to check on suspicious activities, to respond to calls for aid, to enforce laws, and to maintain order. The public is more familiar with patrol officers than with officers of other units because the former are the ones who walk or cruise the neighborhoods, and constantly come into contact with residents. The pa-

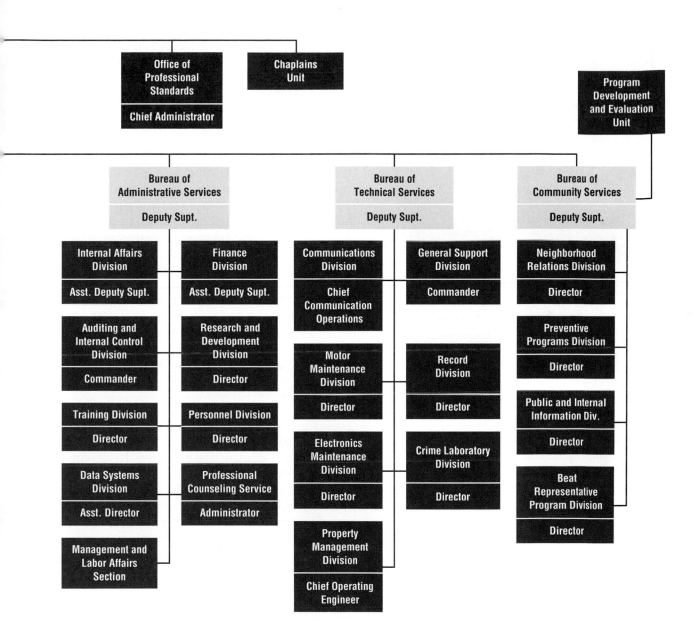

trol officer on the beat is very important to the relations between the police and the community.

Operations Bureau: Investigation

With only a few clues, a magnifying glass, a bumbling friend, and a good bit of intuition, Sherlock Holmes always solved the crime. Television and motion pictures have promoted the romanticized version of the detective as a tough "loner" stalking suspects until they end up in handcuffs or dead after a hair-raising shootout. In reality, however, the role of the detective is quite different. Most detectives are trained in modern investigative techniques and in the laws of evidence and procedure. They interact with many other individuals or police units, such as the traffic, vice, juvenile, and homicide divisions. And they spend most of their time on

"Notice all the computations, theoretical scribblings, and lab equipment, Norm. ... Yes, curiosity killed these cats."

rather routine chores involving quite a bit of paperwork and not much excitement.

Detectives, however, occupy a more prestigious position in a police department than do patrol officers. They receive better salaries, they have more flexible hours, they do not wear uniforms, and they can act more independently. After a crime is reported, detectives investigate the facts in order to determine whether a crime has been committed and whether they have enough information to indicate that the case warrants further investigation. If a full-scale investigation is undertaken, detectives reinterview witnesses, contact informants, check crime files, and so on.

Modern detective work sometimes includes **sting operations,** which are undercover operations in which police pretend to involve themselves in illegal acts to trap a suspect. They may pose as fences in order to capture thieves or as wealthy businesspeople offering money to those suspected of taking bribes. Sting operations have been highly criticized by researchers, who find that this particular method borders on illegal entrapment.[40] However, there is an important legal and psychological difference between a sting operation—or, for that matter, a *decoy operation,* in which a police officer poses as a vulnerable victim—on the one hand, and an entrapment, on the other. *Entrapment* involves police conduct in which an originally unwilling person is actively induced to commit a crime. That is illegal, as the U.S. Supreme Court has ruled.[41]

The Rand Corporation has studied how efficient detectives are at clearing cases. Data from 153 large detective bureaus demonstrated that too much time was spent on paperwork and too little on detecting.[42] Another analysis of 5336 cases reported to suburban police departments reached a different conclusion: The solution of most crimes does not require detective work.[43] Finally, a Police Executive Research Forum (PERF) study had contradictory findings: Data on 3360 burglaries and 320 robberies in De Kalb County, Georgia; St. Petersburg, Florida; and Wichita, Kansas, show that both initial investigation by patrol officers and follow-up work by detectives are necessary to find suspects.[44]

Specialized Units

Metropolitan police departments have specialized units to deal with specific kinds of problems. The traffic unit, for example, is responsible for investigation of accidents, control of traffic, and enforcement of parking and traffic laws. Since police departments have neither the resources to enforce all traffic laws nor the desire to punish all violators, they have a policy of selective enforcement: They target specific problem intersections or highways with high accident or violation rates for stiffer enforcement. Traffic law enforcement has an important influence on community relations because of the amount of contact with the public that this task requires. Most large city departments also have a vice squad. It enforces laws against such activities as gambling, drug dealing, and prostitution. This type of work requires undercover agents, informants, and training in the legal procedures that govern their duties.

FIGURE 17.4   Contact with police. Number of residents age 12 or older with face-to-face contact with police during 1996, by reason for contact.

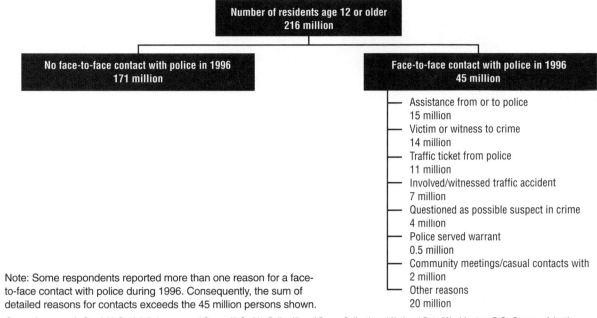

Note: Some respondents reported more than one reason for a face-to-face contact with police during 1996. Consequently, the sum of detailed reasons for contacts exceeds the 45 million persons shown.

Source: Lawrence A. Greefeld, Patrick A. Langan, and Steven K. Smith, *Police Use of Force: Collection of National Data* (Washington, D.C.: Bureau of Justice Statistics, 1997).

Nonline Functions

Every department also needs administrators to recruit officers, to plan, to run the budget, to keep records, and to teach. The training of officers has gained particular significance. Today all police agencies have training programs, and in each state there is a Police Officer Standards and Training (POST) Commission that sets mandatory minimum requirements for training. As yet there is a great deal of difference among the states. Some mandate 16 weeks of training; others require only 3 weeks. Depending on the length of time, training programs range from basic training (handling of weapons) to academic courses.[45] Before 1969, only 10 states required preservice training for their officers.[46]

POLICE FUNCTIONS

The police have three categories of functions: law enforcement, order maintenance, and community service. As the most highly visible members of the criminal justice system, local police play a major role in instilling a sense of security among

citizens and in maintaining good relations between the police and the community. During the civil unrest of the 1960s, police departments began to look for ways to improve their image in order to establish better relations with the public. Police administrators realized that officers had to do more than just enforce the law; they needed to concentrate on maintaining order and providing services as well (see Figure 17.4).

Law Enforcement

The law enforcement function, which involves intervention in situations in which the law has been broken, predominated well into the 1960s, under the strong influence of Vollmer, Wilson, and their like-minded contemporaries. Crime was to be controlled by concentration on serious offenses, and police performance was assessed by the number of felony arrests. There was not much concern about routine, minor violations, like public drunkenness and groups of noisy teenagers.

Crime was to be suppressed in the most efficient way possible, and that way depended on

FIGURE 17.5   Police workload in Wilmington, Delaware: Unit activity file.

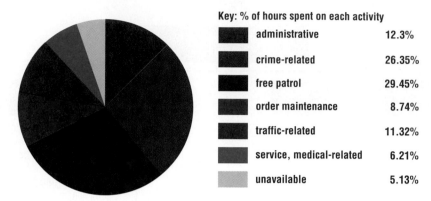

Key: % of hours spent on each activity

	administrative	12.3%
	crime-related	26.35%
	free patrol	29.45%
	order maintenance	8.74%
	traffic-related	11.32%
	service, medical-related	6.21%
	unavailable	5.13%

Source: Jack R. Greene and Carl B. Klockars, "What Police Do," in *Thinking about Police,* 2d ed., ed. Carl B. Klockars and Stephen D. Mastrofski (New York: McGraw-Hill, 1991), pp. 273–274, 279.

maximum coverage of an officer's beat. A beat, the argument ran, was covered better in a car than on foot, and one-officer cars were twice as efficient as two-officer cars. So police departments shifted from foot patrol to car patrol and made large investments in communications equipment.

As depersonalized as the car-patrol beats became, they were made even more so by frequent rotation in an effort to minimize the corruption that might tempt officers if they got to know their constituents too well. The result of all these changes, suggest James Q. Wilson and George Kelling, was that the personal relationship between the people in the neighborhood and the cop of former days was lost.[47] But not all criminologists agree with Wilson and Kelling. Samuel Walker, for example, contends that the "good old days" of policing never existed. When communications were primitive, officers could avoid supervision, neglect their responsibilities, and engage in corrupt practices.

Walker also points out that at the same time that police were put into patrol cars to depersonalize the system, the widespread use of the telephone increased the number of contacts with individuals. When police were on foot patrol, they had more in-person contact with people, but mainly in public places. They seldom went into private homes, for the good reason that a person in trouble at home had no way to call for help.[48] Empirical studies have confirmed the impor-

tance of the telephone. It is estimated that when citizens ask for police help, close to 90 percent of the requests are made by phone.[49]

Order Maintenance

Several researchers have studied police work, usually by observing police on duty or by reviewing and categorizing the nature of the incidents with which police officers deal, based on the calls they receive and the incident reports they file. Specific numbers may vary, but analyses of the types of incidents reveal that the majority usually do not involve law enforcement (Figure 17.5). Egon Bittner, for instance, found that patrol officers average about one arrest per month. Many of the calls relate to what has been called order maintenance, peacekeeping, or conflict management (for example, dispersing a group of rowdy teenagers or warning an aggressive panhandler to move on).[50] In maintaining order, officers usually can exercise discretion in deciding whether a law has been broken.

Wilson and Kelling described this police function in an article titled "Broken Windows: The Police and Neighborhood Safety."[51]

Police issue tickets to the homeless for offenses like carrying open containers of alcohol or trespassing. Most have gone unpaid.

Though literally "broken windows" refers to the run-down, burned-out, deteriorated conditions of buildings in many inner-city neighborhoods, the phrase has a symbolic meaning as well. It refers to the quality of life in a neighborhood and the attitudes of the people who live in it. According to Wilson and Kelling, as policing in America became more professional, increasing emphasis was placed on crime fighting (the law enforcement model) and less on the type of policing that enhances harmonious relationships within the community, reduces fear of crime, and fosters cooperation between citizens and police (the order maintenance function).[52]

Community Service

As the government's frontline response to social problems and emergencies, the police are called on to provide service to those members of the community who, by reason of personal, economic, social, or other circumstances, are in need of immediate aid.[53] The duties of the police bring them in contact with knife and gunshot wounds, drug overdoses, alcoholic delirium, and routine medical problems from heart attacks to diabetic comas. They return runaway children to their parents and remove cats from trees. Research done in a city of 400,000 found, in fact, that social service and administrative tasks accounted for 55 percent of officers' time; crime

fighting accounted for 17 percent.[54] Another study found that of 18,000 calls to a Kentucky police department over a 4-month period, 60 percent were for information, 13 percent concerned traffic, 2.7 percent dealt with violent crime, and 1.8 percent involved property crime.[55] Although there are differences in the services and duties of police officers in urban, suburban, and rural departments, findings from a sample of 38 different police departments revealed these differences to be rather small.[56]

THE POLICE AND THE COMMUNITY

The successful performance of the law enforcement, order maintenance, and community service functions requires that the police have the trust and cooperation of the public. The manner in which the police perform these three functions, especially order maintenance and community service, determines the community's respect for and trust in its police. If such respect exists, citizens are much more likely to assist the police in their law enforcement function. Yet good police community relations had all but vanished during the era of professionalization. This became apparent during the late 1960s and early 1970s when citizens, especially in inner-city ghetto areas, rebelled against government

In August 1999, a man with a high-powered gun burst into the North Valley Jewish Community Center near downtown Los Angeles and sprayed the lobby with twenty to thirty shots, wounding five people, including three boys attending camp. Police arrested Buford O. Furrow, Jr., who was later charged with the killing of a postal worker just hours after he allegedly stormed the community center.

policy in general and law enforcement in particular. The revolts prompted large-scale efforts to restore police-community relations.

Community Policing

The most widely accepted strategy for improving police-community relations is that of community policing. **Community policing** generally consists of programs and policies based on a partnership between the police and the community they serve. Some observers have used the term "community wellness" to describe the philosophy behind this kind of policing.[57] The emphasis is on working in collaboration with residents to determine community needs and the best way to address them and to involve citizens as "co-producers of public safety."[58] Among the goals of community policing are a reduction in fear of crime, the development of closer ties with the community, the engagement of residents in a joint effort to prevent crime and maintain order, and an increase in the level of public satisfaction with police services. Many types of programs have been described as community policing, including increased use of foot patrol, storefront police stations, community surveys, police-sponsored youth activities, and Neighborhood Watch programs.[59]

The idea of community policing is neither new nor unique to the United States. Although there has been a substantial increase in America's interest in community policing, many other countries have much more active programs.[60] In Japan, for example, officers are stationed in a mini-police station (called a *koban*) in each neighborhood. They receive complaints, search for runaways, patrol on bike or foot, and provide security through constant contact. The koban has a reception room, a small kitchen, an interview area, and a lost-and-found service; it serves the important function of soliciting recommendations for what the police might do to help the community.[61] Norway and Singapore also have such mini-police stations.[62]

The idea behind this approach is that communities have different needs and priorities that the police have to be aware of if efforts to prevent crime are to be effective. New York City established the Community Patrol Officers (CPOs) program in July 1984. Individual officers were taken from their routine line duties and appointed CPOs. A CPO was to make rounds, on foot, and "to function as a planner, problem solver, community organizer, and information link between the community and the police."[63]

On April 23, 1998, New Jersey state troopers opened fire on four youths during a traffic stop on the New Jersey Turnpike. Initial reports claimed that the officers had stopped the van for speeding and began firing when the driver attempted to back up over the officers. The department later admitted that the officers did not have radar in their cruiser, raising the question of why the officers really stopped the van. The youths charge that they were initially stopped because of their race. The case is currently being reviewed by a grand jury. The incident itself, however, has sparked national debate and investigation of police officers' use of race as probable cause to stop and search persons and vehicles. Other cases of profiling include:

California. Shawn Lee, who plays for the San Diego Chargers football team, and his girlfriend were pulled over and detained in handcuffs for half an hour on Interstate 15. Officers claimed the vehicle driven by Lee (a Jeep Cherokee) matched the description of a stolen vehicle. The stolen vehicle, however, was a Honda sedan.

Florida. Orange County sheriff's deputies pulled over Aaron Campbell on the Florida Turnpike for an illegal lane change and obscured tags. Mr. Campbell, a fellow police officer, identified himself to the deputies. The incident ended when Mr. Campbell was wrestled to the ground, pepper-sprayed, and arrested.

Maryland. Nelson Walker was pulled over by Maryland state police for not wearing a seatbelt. He and his two passengers were detained for 2 hours as officers searched for illegal drugs, weapons, and other contraband. When the search of the car revealed nothing, officers then dismantled parts of the vehicle, but failed to uncover anything. Upon leaving, officers handed Mr. Walker a screwdriver and reportedly said, "You're going to need this."

What do these and countless similar cases have in common? All the drivers and passengers of these vehicles were members of a minority group. The allegations of profiling, however, do not end with vehicular stops. The New York Police Department and its Street Crime Unit, for example, are currently under federal investigation for charges of violating minority citizens' constitutional rights through stop-and-frisks and other tactics. The larger debate over profiling, however, stems from claims of racism versus aggressive policing tactics.

The most recent report from the New Jersey attorney general admits that "minority motorists have been treated differently than non-minority motorists during the course of traffic stops on the New Jersey Turnpike." The New Jersey ACLU concludes that problems of racial profiling are not limited to the state police, but are found in various other departments throughout the state as well.

Defenders of profiling argue that these stops are consistent with crime data revealing minority groups to be more heavily involved in illegal drug and gun activity. They also contend that officers have successfully used traffic stops and stop-and-frisks as tools in lowering crime rates and removing weapons and drugs in their communities.

Are these cases symptomatic of a national epidemic of profiling? In view of the recent findings in New Jersey, a number of studies are currently being conducted in other states to investigate similar charges. Congress is also in the process of introducing legislation to fund a national analysis of traffic stops by law enforcement officers. Until the results of these studies become available, the question of racial profiling will remain open to debate.

Sources

1. ACLU of New Jersey, "New Jersey 1999: Statewide Crisis in Policing," (NJ: ACLU, 1999).
2. Interim Report of the State Police Review Team Regarding Allegations of Racial Profiling (NJ: State Attorney General, 1999).
3. Mark Hosenball, "It Is Not the Act of a Few Bad Apples," *Newsweek,* May 17, 1999.
4. Benjamin Weiser, "Stop-and-Frisk Policy Faces U.S. Scrutiny," *New York Times,* Mar. 19, 1999.

Questions for Discussion

1. What is the danger of allowing officers to stop and search citizens without probable cause? Should official statistics be used to cite a suspect's race as probable cause that a crime has been committed?
2. If racial profiling is indeed a national problem, what can be done nationally and within state and local jurisdictions to ensure that the practice is stopped?

The CPO evaluation project conducted by the Vera Institute focused on the functioning of CPOs in relation to the command structure of normal policing. It concluded that if the program was to work, changes would need to be made in traditional operational functioning—changes that would take into account the aspirations of the residents, the diversity of their problems, and the resources in the neighborhoods patrolled.[64]

A recent evaluation of community policing programs in eight cities revealed that "forays into community policing produced only minimal, and often transient, effects on drug trafficking, drug-related crime, and fear of crime. And perhaps even more important were the findings that these eight sites experienced common implementation problems that hampered their ability to have the desired impacts."[65]

TABLE 17.2   Citizen Perception of Community Policing, 1998

Percent of Residents Who Said Police Are Doing Community Policing*	
Chicago, IL	67
Kansas City, MO	52
Knoxville, TN	42
Los Angeles, CA	50
Madison, WI	47
New York, NY	51
San Diego, CA	57
Savannah, GA	48
Spokane, WA	54
Springfield, MA	64
Tucson, AZ	46
Washington, DC	53

*Question: "Community policing involves police officers working with the community to address the causes of crime in an effort to reduce problems themselves and the associated fear, through a wide range of activities. Based on this definition, do you think police in your neighborhood practice community policing?"

Source: Steven K. Smith, Greg W. Steadman, Todd D. Minton, and Meg Townsend, Criminal Victimization and Perceptions of Community Safety in 12 Cities, 1998 (Washington, D.C.: Bureau of Justice Statistics and the Office of Community Oriented Policing Services, 1999).

Others have pointed out that aside from implementation difficulties, the success of community policing is largely contingent on the cooperation and coordination of citizens, social agencies, political leaders, and the media.[66] Unfortunately, such cooperation and coordination are often lacking. However, there may be some evidence that these new initiatives are affecting citizen perspectives. Table 17.2 reports the findings of one recent survey of 12 U.S. cities, which shows that citizen perceptions of policing may be changing.

The success of community policing reform efforts remains uncertain. Several of the nation's large police departments have recently implemented community policing strategies. Perhaps the most significant problem is that the term "community policing" is so broadly defined and ambiguous that it loses its meaning. Mark Moore disagrees, noting that the ambiguity is a virtue, as it encourages police departments to experiment with different styles of policing.[67]

Foot Patrol   Another effort to improve police-community relations involved the reintroduction of the pre–World War II practice of "walking the beat." It was felt that patrol cars isolated officers from citizens and that if police were put back on the streets, people would get to know them and feel a greater sense of security.[68] A number of cities, including Houston, Newark, and Flint, Michigan, carried out experiments to test the effectiveness of foot patrol. They found that crime rates generally did not go down significantly, but citizen fear of crime did. Moreover, better citizen cooperation resulted in more job satisfaction among officers and fewer calls for assistance.[69] Foot patrol remains a common element of community policing, permitting officers to have direct contact with the citizens of the neighborhood they police.[70]

Team Policing   In the early 1970s a strategy called **team policing** became a popular way to enhance contacts between citizens and police. Team policing was a response to the riots in the inner cities, the perception of the police as an army of occupation, and the limited familiarity on the part of officers with the needs of the neighborhoods they served. It was hoped that if the image of the police was changed from that of enemy to that of friend, law enforcement activities would be a great deal more effective.

In team policing, a team of officers, rather than individual officers, carries out the policing responsibilities. The team, a group of officers and a supervisor, is in charge of a specific neighborhood on a 24-hour basis. Team members decide how to divide up the work, what methods to use to cover an area, and how to maximize communication with community members. The communication is accomplished by a variety of means, including meetings between community leaders and team representatives, storefront mini-police stations that encourage citizens to drop in, and programs in which community volunteers work as block watchers to report suspicious situations. Team members meet regularly to discuss neighborhood problems, to keep each other informed, and to decide on common policy.

Like most innovations, team policing has its advocates and its critics. Some observers say that it has neither prevented crimes nor increased the number solved.[71] Others question whether it really differs much from routine patrol activities.[72] Nevertheless, other experts argue, team policing has indeed helped to encourage crime control through better police-community relations.[73]

Problem-Oriented Policing Another way in which police can enhance community relations is through **problem-oriented policing.** In this approach police work with citizens to identify and respond to community problems. Herman Goldstein warns that police too often focus on specific incidents. Their object is to get to places fast, to stabilize the situation, and to get back into service quickly. Most administrators want their officers available to respond to emergency calls as rapidly as possible. But, argues Goldstein, police cannot reduce or prevent crime this way. They need to be more problem-oriented and less incident-oriented. They should analyze local social problems, help design solutions, advocate programs to change the situation, and monitor effects.[74]

Goldstein's approach has been tried in many communities. In Madison, Wisconsin, police were called regularly to deal with people behaving strangely at a shopping mall. The press characterized the mall as a haven for vagrants and put their number at 1000. The public began to stay away. Business suffered. The police looked into the problem and discovered that the individuals in question had been under psychiatric supervision and were disruptive when they did not take their medication. The police worked with mental health professionals to set up better supervision. Within a short time the problem was solved, customers returned, and business went back to normal.

In 1982 the Baltimore County Police Department created three teams of officers to solve recurring problems. The teams, called Citizen-Oriented Police Enforcement (COPE) teams, worked with local patrol officers to pinpoint conditions that appeared to be creating problems. For example, each spring burglaries increased, and one item, baseball gloves, was consistently stolen. When a program was instituted to provide baseball equipment to low-income families, the burglary rate fell significantly.[75]

As with many recent community policing initiatives, problem-oriented policing (P.O.P.) has met with some resistance from both police and the community. Implementation has been difficult as well.[76] Problem-oriented strategies have focused on a variety of crime problems, including guns, violent crime, and especially, drugs and drug-related crime. There have been several recent applications of P.O.P. in an effort to disrupt local drug markets and street-level drug dealing.[77] P.O.P. initiatives have also been extended to address youth gun violence. The Boston Police Department, in collaboration with researchers from Harvard University and an interagency working group, conducted research into Boston's youth violence problem and gun markets, and then crafted a citywide interagency problem-solving strategy. An evaluation is forthcoming.[78]

Policing Hot Spots of Crime Lawrence Sherman and David Weisburd decided to replicate the Kansas City study but with a different focus. They argued that allocating more police to entire neighborhoods did not have a deterrent effect because not all areas of a neighborhood are at high risk for crime. The police presence, rather than being distributed over the whole neighborhood, should be intensified in hot spots, particular places within neighborhoods that are the source of the most calls to police. In Minneapolis, for example, 5 percent of the locations were the sources of 64 percent of the calls.[79]

The Minneapolis Hotspots experiment was designed to test whether increased police patrol in these high-crime hot spots would reduce crime. Using an experimental design, the city's 110 hot spots were split into two groups of 55. The experimental group of hot spots received twice as much patrol presence as the control group of hot spots. The results of this experiment indicated that there was a reduction in crime calls for service and a reduction in disorder in the areas with stronger police presence.[80] Although crime was deterred in the hot-spot areas that received increased police enforcement, it is possible that it may have shifted to other areas.[81]

Recently the hot-spots approach has been widely applied to policing guns and drugs.[82] To aid in their identification of crime hot spots, many large police departments have implemented computerized mapping technologies. By mapping out those areas with the most calls for service and police activity, for particular crimes, hot spots can be identified and addressed.[83]

Crime Surfing

www.ojp.usdoj.gov/emree/pfmaplab@policefoundation.org

What is crime mapping? Check out the Crime Mapping Research Center at the National Institute of Justice website or the Police Foundation's Computer Mapping Lab.

Preventive Patrol   It has long been argued that preventive patrol, which entails an increase in police presence and visibility, deters criminals from committing crimes and thereby reduces citizen fear and fosters good police-community relations. Between October 1, 1972, and September 30, 1973, the Kansas City Police Department conducted the Kansas City Preventive Patrol Experiment. Fifteen police beats covering a population of close to 150,000 inhabitants were divided into three sections. Each section was subjected to a different type of patrol: intensified routine patrol (two to three times more officers were on the beat), decreased patrol (officers came into the area only when they were called for service), and routine patrol (the area maintained its usual number of police). The results were unexpected: Increased patrol levels had no effect on crime rates, citizens' fear of crime, citizens' satisfaction with police, or the amount of time it took to respond to calls.[84]

Police-Community Relations Programs

A final strategy for enhancing public perception of the police consists of police-community relations programs. These programs do not change the basic method of policing; but by reaching out into the community, they have had good results:

- Increased likelihood of citizen cooperation in providing information to assist in law enforcement.

- More voluntary compliance with the law.

- Improved relations with minority groups.[85]

- Community support for budget appropriations in an environment of competing demands.[86]

A recent inventory of programs in different jurisdictions showed that department-sponsored activities include "ride-along" programs in which citizens accompany the police on patrols, citizenship awards, citizen citation programs to recognize meritorious acts, liaison programs with the clergy, police headquarters tours, and public-speaking programs.[87]

Citizen Review Boards   In recent years, one type of program designed to enhance community relations—the citizen review board—has grown dramatically, nationwide. Citizen review is a procedure for handling civilian complaints against police in which cases are heard by a panel of other citizens.[88] In the past, citizen complaints about police misconduct, including brutality, were reviewed by police internal investigative units. This practice resulted in very few rulings favoring complainants: One study found that, nationwide, only 10 percent of internal police reviews ended in rulings in favor of the citizen complainants.[89]

Popular dissatisfaction with these outcomes prompted demands for civilian input into the reviewing process. By 1994, 66 police departments had citizen review procedures—a 400 percent increase over 1980.[90] Though their approaches—in terms of organizational structure, role, mission, and staffing—vary greatly, these groups share the overarching goal of improving responsiveness between police departments and the communities they serve. For example, in 1991 the Berkeley, California, Police Review Commission was made up of nine volunteer members. They handled 60 inquiries informally—providing mediation between the complainant and the officer—and investigated 104 cases. In 1990, police officer misconduct was found in 17 percent of the cases. Such findings can result in a variety of sanctions, including suspension.[91] But many questions about the effectiveness of civilian review boards have yet to be answered. Do they promote more thorough investigation of police misconduct? Does their existence in fact improve police-community relationships?

THE RULE OF LAW IN LAW ENFORCEMENT

National investigative commissions in the 1930s and again in the 1960s found American policing to be defective in six distinct areas:

- Constitutional due process.
- Civil rights.
- Use of deadly force and police brutality.
- Abuse of discretion.
- Corruption.
- Police-community relations (as discussed above).

Restoration and maintenance of the rule of law to which the American system of government is devoted required reforms in all these areas.

Constitutional Due Process

Largely as a result of the demonstrated systematic lawlessness of some police officers, the United States Supreme Court, under the leadership of Chief Justice Earl Warren, played the leading role in the reform movement. In case after case the Supreme Court reversed convictions that had been obtained in violation of constitutional restraints. The provisions in the Bill of Rights, which had been applied only to federal law enforcement, were extended to cover state actions as well through the Fourteenth Amendment, which guarantees that no one shall be deprived of life, liberty, or property without due process of law (Chapter 16). These rights include protection against unreasonable searches and seizures (Fourth Amendment), protection against self-incrimination (Fifth Amendment), and the right to counsel (Sixth Amendment). Some people hailed the Court's decisions; others saw them as handcuffing the police in their efforts to enforce the law.

Civil Rights

In the 1960s, American policing also suffered from increasing tensions between black citizens who demanded their civil rights and police who tried to maintain the status quo. Police officers gave the appearance of a force removed from the community, encapsulated in a professional cocoon, insensitive to community moods and needs. This was especially the case in the inner cities.

On July 16, 1964, a white New York City officer shot and killed a black teenager. Demonstrators marched to the Twenty-Eighth Precinct headquarters, and 2 days of rioting followed. The rioting spread to Rochester, Jersey City, and Philadelphia, and in the next year to Los Angeles, Chicago, and San Diego. Then Cleveland, San Francisco, Atlanta, Detroit, and Newark were affected. In the same years, college students were demonstrating against the Vietnam war. In all cases, the police were called in to restore order, a process that culminated in many confrontations and some deaths.

During these years of turmoil, in 1966, Lyndon B. Johnson established the President's Commission on Law Enforcement and the Administration of Justice. The commission reported findings of racism, unequal justice, and police brutality. This report led to the enactment of the Omnibus Crime Control and Safe Streets Act of 1968, which created the Law Enforcement Assistance Administration (LEAA). During its brief existence (1967–1982) the agency spent $7 billion in an effort to upgrade law enforcement and criminal justice in the United States.

Though the LEAA has been criticized for its vast expenditures on hardware and on speculative research and development, among other things, it has also been praised for its enormous positive effects on American criminal justice.[92] LEAA funds established advanced training in law enforcement and criminal justice and, directly and indirectly, resulted in the creation of more than 600 academic programs of criminal justice in the United States.

Use of Deadly Force and Police Brutality

In *Tennessee v. Garner* the United States Supreme Court was confronted with a tragic situation. A father was suing a Memphis police officer, as well as governmental agencies, for the loss of the life of his 17-year-old son. The son, according to the undisputed facts, had burglarized a home. The police responded instantly to the homeowner's call. An officer spotted the suspect fleeing across the backyard and ordered him to stop. The officer saw that the suspect was unarmed. The youngster made an effort to jump over a high fence. The officer shot and killed him. The common law rule of England and the United States, as well as the law of Tennessee, had always been that the police may use deadly force to stop a fleeing felon whether or not he or she is in possession of a weapon. The officer had acted properly when he shot and killed the suspect, and the Supreme Court found that the officer could not be prosecuted or sued for wrongful death.

The Court reached a different conclusion, however, with respect to governmental liability. The Court reasoned that when all felonies in England were capital crimes, perhaps such a rule on the use of deadly force made sense, because an offender found guilty at trial could be sentenced to death. But the taking of the life of a suspect who, if convicted, might receive only a relatively short prison sentence makes no sense and constitutes an unreasonable seizure of the person in violation of the Fourth Amendment.

The Police Foundation was allowed to file an *amicus curiae* ("friend of the court") brief in which it supported abandonment of the harsh common law rule. The brief demonstrated through research that the shoot-to-kill rule for fleeing felons does not prevent crime or enhance the protection of police officers and thus is unreasonable as a law enforcement tool. Consequently, the Supreme Court overturned the common law rule as violating the due process clause of the Fourteenth Amendment.[93]

Did You Know?

. . . that more officers are killed in the line of duty each year, nationwide, than the number of civilians killed by officers each year?

Deadly force may not be used unless it is necessary to prevent the escape of a suspect who the officer has probable cause to believe poses a significant threat of death or serious injury to the officer or others. As we noted, use of deadly force by police officers has been a major issue in police-minority relations. James J. Fyfe writes, "As most police recruits learn in the academy, the cop on the street . . . carries in his holster more power than has been granted the Chief Justice of the Supreme Court."[94] If this power is used improperly, it can lead to riots, deaths, litigation against the police, and the downfall of entire city administrations.

The issue had been confronted by two presidential commissions, the Commission on Civil Disorders (1968) and the President's Commission on Law Enforcement and the Administration of Justice (1967). Both had suggested that use of deadly force was the immediate reason for urban riots. Before the work of these commissions, little had been done in the way of empirical research.[95] Since then, a number of scientists have studied the issue. One, John Goldkamp, explains it this way. There are two conflicting perspectives: One is that the disproportionately high number of minority persons shot and killed by police can be explained by police officers' irresponsible use of deadly force and the differential administration of law enforcement toward minorities. The other is that the disproportionately high number of minority persons shot and killed by police can be explained by disproportionately high arrest rates among minorities for crimes of violence.[96]

There is evidence to support both sides. Catherine Milton and her associates point out that 70 percent of the people shot by police in the seven cities that they studied were black, although blacks made up about 39 percent of the population.[97] Betty Jenkins and Adrienne Faison showed that 52 percent of the persons killed by police over a 3-year period were black and 21 percent Hispanic.[98] Paul Takagi sums up this side of the controversy: "The news gets around the community when someone is killed by police. It is part of a history—a very long history of extralegal justice that included whippings and lynchings."[99]

The other side of the argument—that larger proportions of minority individuals are shot by police because they live in high-crime areas, are more likely to own guns, and more often commit violent crime—also finds support. James Fyfe's study of New York City shootings, for example, showed that in many incidents in which a shooting took place, police officers themselves were killed or wounded. He also found that minorities were more likely than whites to be involved in incidents in which guns were used.[100]

With the nation still reeling over the issue of police brutality in the Rodney King incident in Los Angeles, the focus shifted to the New York Police Department. Two highly publicized cases demonstrate a rising fear of the police, at a time when, with starkly falling crime rates, fear of crime is decreasing. The two cases, known by their victims' names, are those of Abner Louima and Amadou Diallo. It is noteworthy that both victims were black immigrants. All police officers involved were white.

Abner Louima was arrested in August 1997 outside a New York nightclub and taken to a Brooklyn precinct, where he was handcuffed, beaten, and sodomized with a broken broomstick. One officer in the incident has been convicted and sentenced to 30 years in prison. This officer apologized for his brutal act. A second officer has pleaded guilty. (Three of the officers involved are currently on trial for a cover-up conspiracy.)

Amadou Diallo was shot at 41 times and hit 19 times, in February 1999, while confronted by 4 police officers of the street crime unit, standing in the vestibule of his apartment building. Charged with murder as well as lesser included offenses, the 4 officers were tried and acquitted in February 2000.

Both incidents sparked several days of protests, claims of racism, and calls for New York to investigate its police department and the practices of its officers. While seemingly similar, the two cases nevertheless raise different issues. The Louima case is one of outright police brutality, demonstrating that despite improved recruitment procedures, psychological testing, etc., some candidates totally unfit for police work find their way into the ranks. There are criminals in all organizations.

Tensions flare when protestors demonstrate against the brutalization of Abner Louima by New York City Police officers.

The Diallo case, while affected by the issue of racism (racial profiling), raises another issue: the extent to which officers are socialized into operating procedures that emphasize proactive use of deadly force over restraint in officer-citizen confrontations. As one letter to the editor of *The New York Times* put it: "The culture of the police force must be reformed, so that bullies who demand instant obedience are not in positions where they can hurt innocent people."(1)

So, while in the Louima torture case we are confronted with at least two clearly guilty police officers, and in the Diallo case with four acquitted police officers, behind them is a potentially guilty city and its police department, which now must own up to its obligation toward the citizenry.

New York City has begun by focusing on improvements within its street crime unit, including mandatory racial sensitivity classes and recruitment of minority residents to the force. Unhappily, "street crime arrests are down 62 percent since the concentration on the Diallo case. And here's what we have to be concerned about: in the places that street crime arrests are down, shootings and murders are up."(2) And that, in turn, increases citizens' fear of crime. So, does it necessarily follow that when fear of crime decreases, fear of the police increases; or, put the other way, when fear of the police decreases, the fear of crime (and crime itself) increases?

Sources

1. Steven Landev, "To the Editor," *New York Times,* Mar. 1, 2000, p. 22.
2. David M. Herszenhorn, "Arrests Drop and Shootings Rise as the Police, Giuliani Says, Are Distracted," *New York Times,* Mar. 29, 1999.

Questions for Discussion

1. Is the drop in New York City's crime rate related to the increase of citizen complaints against officers?
2. Which side of the argument do you agree with: If you agree with the practice of aggressive law enforcement, what procedures can officers be required to use to ensure that they are, while upholding the constitutional rights of citizens, controlling crime? If you agree that discrimination contributes to acts of police brutality, what procedures can be used to identify and prevent such acts in the future? Can discrimination be controlled or identified?

Official inquiries and empirical studies of police use of deadly force continue. Lawrence Sherman maintains that there have been some positive developments. Data obtained from surveys of killings of civilians by police in 59 cities between 1970 and 1984 show that such killings have decreased by 50 percent.[101] Nonetheless, even with improved training, controversial incidents still occur and often polarize an entire county or city. For example, on April 10, 1990, a black teenager named Phillip Pannell was shot and killed by a white Teaneck, New Jersey, police officer. The shooting resulted in riots throughout Teaneck and polarized Bergen County, New Jersey, for nearly 2 years.[102]

The use of uncalled-for deadly or overwhelming physical force against persons, frequently suspects, who are deemed not to respect the power of the police is what we call police brutality. Who can forget the image of Rodney King being beaten mercilessly, without any apparent reason, by four Los Angeles police officers?[103] But Los Angeles is not an exception. A similar amateur videotape recorded a beating inflicted by a Trenton, New Jersey, police officer on Thomas Downing, who had simply inquired why his stepson was being arrested.[104] In New York City, in August 1997, Haitian immigrant Abner Louima was sodomized by police officers with a broomstick. Repeated surgery was necessary to keep him alive.[105] In the wake of these high-profile cases, efforts to address and prevent the misuse of force have been heightened. Many police departments are attempting to improve their initial screening of officer candidates, enhance police training, and increase the mechanisms to ensure police accountability.

Force must be used in law enforcement, but democracies always put limits on that use. The best-known abuse historically was probably the "third degree"—torture for the purpose of extracting a confession. Torture by police may be rare in the United States today, but it remains a significant problem in many other countries around the world, even with the adoption of the United Nations Code of Conduct for Law Enforcement Officials, which prohibits all police abuses.[106] We have a long way to go before the ideals found in that code guide police practice in every nation.[107]

Abuse of Discretion

Yet another defect in the functioning of American policing has been and still is the potential abuse of discretion in making decisions about whom to arrest. How does police discretion work in the case of young, poor, minority males? While discretionary power may be regulated officially, the reality of the patrol

Javier Ovando, convicted of assaulting police and sentenced to more than 23 years in prison, was ordered released from prison in September 1999, at the request of prosecutors. Startling revelations from a former Los Angeles Police officer revealed that he and a partner shot the unarmed 19-year-old man, planted a gun on him, and then testified that Ovando threatened them with an assault weapon during a stakeout on gang turf.

situation is such that officers have considerable autonomy.[108]

Several studies show that discretionary police decision making discriminates against blacks.[109] But there is no clear-cut pattern: Some researchers conclude that the neighborhood is the best predictor of arrest. Police make more arrests in low-income areas.[110] Others clarify the importance of neighborhood by adding that in black communities police are more punitive toward whites than blacks. The reverse is also true. In predominantly white neighborhoods, police are more punitive to black offenders.[111]

Other determinants of racial disparity in arrests are revealed by an array of studies that have examined such factors as income differences between neighborhood residents and suspects, personal characteristics of the victim, the demeanor (attitude and appearance) of the suspect, real differences in rates of offending, and the choice of the people who make the complaints (blacks more often than whites request that an officer make an arrest).[112]

Christy Visher found that police are more likely to arrest a woman whose attitudes and actions differ from the stereotype of a "lady" and that older white women are less likely to be arrested than young black women.[113] Marvin Krohn and his colleagues disagree. In a study conducted between 1948 and 1976 involving 10,723 police contacts, they found a trend toward more equal treatment of girls (compared with boys) for juvenile misdemeanors and of women (compared with men) for both misdemeanors and felonies.[114]

Many efforts have been made to control abuse of discretion. The courts have placed limits on what police are permitted to do when they investigate and question suspects. Police administrators have tried to establish guidelines for behavior in the field. But the task is difficult: Police officers perform a wide variety of duties under a wide range of conditions, and we have little detailed information on what factors actually influence their decisions.

Corruption

At the turn of the century the Progressives thought that the civil service system would eliminate corruption and incompetence among the police. Yet after a century of reforms, police corruption persists. In the early 1970s a New York City police lieutenant, then sergeant, David Durk, and his partner, Detective Frank Serpico, discovered massive corruption among fellow officers and superiors. They collected the evidence and reported it to higher authorities within the department. Neither there nor at the highest level of the department was any action taken. Durk and Serpico ultimately reported their findings directly to the mayor. Still nothing happened. In frustration they released their information to the press. Durk and Serpico were attacked by fellow officers for "dirtying their own nest," "washing dirty laundry in public," "tarnishing their shields," and worse. The result of their revelations was the creation of the Knapp Commission, which unraveled the existing police cor-

ruption in New York City and recommended measures to avoid it in the future.[115]

The term "corruption" covers a wide range of conduct patterns. The Knapp Commission itself distinguished—in typical police jargon—between "meat eaters," who solicit bribes or actually cooperate with criminals for personal gain, and "grass eaters," who accept payoffs for rendering police services or for looking the other way when action is called for. Subsequent empirical and analytical studies have provided additional classifications and descriptions of police misconduct, including solicitation and acceptance of bribes, dereliction of duty, and street crime offenses such as larceny, embezzlement, and coercion.[116]

Despite the efforts of the Knapp Commission in 1972 and the National Advisory Commission on Criminal Justice Standards and Goals in 1973, corruption continues. According to experts, corruption may be even more serious now than it was in the 1970s. In the late 1990s an elite Los Angeles Police Department (LAPD) antigang unit known as CRASH (Community Resources Against Street Hoodlums) became involved in a scandal that set off one of the largest internal investigations in decades, and even brought the FBI in to look for civil rights violations. The news broke when a rogue cop, caught stealing cocaine from police evidence lockers, bargained for a lighter sentence by blowing the whistle on CRASH—with a story of police officers involved in brutality, perjury, planted evidence, attempted murder, and drug sales. He stated that in one incident an officer shot an unarmed gang member and then planted a rifle on the unconscious suspect to make the shooting look legal. The victim, confined to a wheelchair for life because of the shooting, has now filed a $20 million suit against the city and a number of officers. He has also been freed from prison, where he would have served a 23-year sentence for assault of the officer.[117]

The LAPD is not alone in battling corruption among its own. More than 100 Miami police officers were implicated in corrupt drug-related activities. A federal grand jury indicted 10 of them for their involvement in a $13 million theft of cocaine from a boat anchored in the Miami River. A Philadelphia officer who was heading a corruption investigation was given an 18-year prison sentence on evidence that he received $50,000 a month from operators of illegal electronic poker machines.[118]

The ancient Romans had a phrase, *Quis enim custodiet custodes?*—"Who then watches the watchmen?" Modern policing relies on internal and external controls to maintain its professionalism and its integrity. We have discussed some of the external controls. The court system, especially the Supreme Court, plays a role in policing the police by holding law enforcement activities to strict constitutional standards.

Another external-control mechanism is the civilian police review boards that were established to fulfill a review function. But many police departments rely on internal controls to police themselves. Yet if internal controls are to be effective, experts argue, law enforcement professionals need to change their thinking about self-policing. In the past, departmental whistle-blowers were regarded with derision. Such attitudes need to be replaced by intolerance toward those who abuse the public trust and the power of the shield by engaging in abuses, corruption, and other forms of criminality. Studies indicate, however, that more officers than not are unwilling to report misconduct by other officers.[119]

This raises the question of whether there is anything special or different about the personality of police officers and the culture in which they function that sets them apart from the rest of the population. The question of how to alter the police culture—which some argue breeds corruption—remains a difficult one. Having recently been called upon to investigate and develop strategies to address corruption in New York City, the Mollen Commission recommended:

> that a permanent, independent body outside the department's control be charged with uncovering corruption, and that the department enact reforms to: improve screening, recruitment and integrity training; reinvent the enforcement of command accountability; enhance sanctions and disincentives for corruption and brutality; strengthen intelligence-gathering efforts; solicit police union support for anti-corruption efforts; and minimize the corruption hazards of community policing.[120]

FIGURE 17.6   Higher-education requirements. Percent of law enforcement agencies that required new officers to have a 2-year or 4-year college degree, 1993 and 1997.

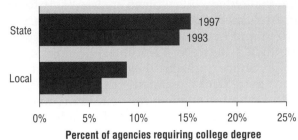

Law enforcement agencies with 100 or more full-time sworn personnel

Percent of agencies requiring college degree

Source: Brian A. Reaves and Andrew L. Goldberg, *Law Enforcement Management and Administrative Statistics, 1997: Data for Individual State and Local Agencies with 100 or More Officers* (Washington, D.C.: Bureau of Justice Statistics, 1999).

POLICE OFFICERS AND THEIR LIFESTYLE

If we want to find out whether police officers are different, we must find out who it is police departments accept into their ranks. We must then understand the police culture in which the officers live and function.

Qualifications

Most departments require that new recruits be in good physical condition, have no criminal record, and have a high school diploma. Other criteria for selection, used to varying degrees by different departments, are a written exam (78 percent), an interview (97 percent), a lie detector test (40 percent), weight and height standards (42 percent), and a background check (99 percent). Some require intelligence and psychological tests also (68 percent).[121] So as not to discriminate against the hiring of women and some ethnic groups, standards of height and weight have virtually disappeared.[122] By the mid-1990s, 8 percent of local law enforcement agencies required new officers to have a 2-year or 4-year college degree (Figure 17.6).

The question of whether police officers should have a college degree, although it has been recommended by national commissions since 1931, is still controversial. In a survey of law enforcement agencies conducted by the Police Executive Research Forum and supported by the Ford Foundation, some consistent themes emerged. Those in favor of higher education argued that college-educated officers:

Communicate better with the public.
Show more initiative.
Write better reports.
Make better decisions.
Have greater sensitivity to minorities.
In general, perform better.[123]

Those who questioned higher-education requirements for police officers argued that college-educated officers:

Might leave police work.
Are more prone to question orders.
Expect preferential treatment.
Cause animosity within the ranks.
Feel dissatisfied with the job.[124]

Changing Composition of the Police Force

The political and social crises of the 1960s challenged Americans to reaffirm their commitment to equality before the law. Title VII of the Civil Rights Act of 1964 prohibited the private sector from discriminating in employment on the basis of race, gender, religion, or national origin. In 1972, the Equal Employment Opportunity Act amended the Civil Rights Act to include the public sector. The 1972 act also required that federal agencies develop affirmative action programs. Besides federal legislation, state and local laws prohibit discrimination on the basis of race, national origin, religion, and gender. Two states and over 60 cities go even further by prohibiting discrimination on the basis of sexual preference.[125]

These social and legal changes have had a major impact on the composition of the police force. First, the laws made it easier for individuals to bring employer discrimination suits against police agencies. Many did. In fact, over the last 20 years, most of the largest police departments in the country have been sued. Second, to comply with federal guidelines, police departments had to make an effort to attract minority and female applicants.[126] And third, the community has continued to put pressure on the

police administration to make policy changes with respect to the recruitment of minorities.

Minority Groups in Policing   The first minority police officer was hired in Washington, D.C., in 1861.[127] By 1940, only 1 percent of all police officers in the United States came from minority groups; in 1950, only 2 percent.[128] Nicholas Alex wrote in *Black in Blue* (1969) that black officers were pressured in two ways: by racism on the part of white colleagues and by the expectation of black citizens that they would get a break from a black officer.[129]

Changes began to occur in the 1960s. Civil unrest at the time showed that if police officers were recruited from a limited segment of the overall population, there was a risk of alienating those groups that were not represented in law enforcement.[130] Recruitment drives to hire minorities began in most major metropolitan police departments. The issue was highly controversial during the initial phase, and progress has been slow.[131] In the face of outright discrimination in examination and appointment procedures, court action had to be resorted to in many instances to open the doors to blacks and Hispanics who wanted to join the ranks.

In 1997, among departments with 100 or more officers, the overall percentage of minorities on the police force was 23 percent for county police departments, 19 percent for municipal police departments, 17 percent for sheriff's agencies, and 12 percent for state police agencies. The actual numbers vary greatly from department to department.[132]

Although changes have occurred—many police departments are headed by blacks, for example—the ethnic problem has not yet been resolved.[133] Well-founded discrimination suits continue to be brought by minority-group officers. In 1989 Hispanic police officers in New York City complained about discrimination in the promotion of patrol officers to sergeants.[134] The Federal Bureau of Investigation, found by a federal court to have engaged in discriminatory practices, is revamping its practices so as to be in compliance with the Equal Employment Opportunity Act of 1972. This act prohibits discriminatory hiring practices by state and local governments. It also prohibits job discrimination against women.

Women in Policing The First American woman to serve as a sworn police officer was Lola Baldwin, who joined the Portland, Oregon, police department in 1905. Like the few police matrons of the nineteenth century, she dealt primarily with women and children. In fact, she was originally granted the police power so that she could manage women and children at the Ohio State Exposition. Five years later, in 1910 in Los Angeles, Alice Stebbin Wells became the first officially classified policewoman, assigned to "supervising and enforcing laws concerning dance halls, skating rinks, and theaters; monitoring billboard displays; locating missing persons; and maintaining a general bureau for women seeking advice on matters within the scope of the police department."[135] In 1915 she founded the International Association of Police Women.

More than 60 police departments had women on their staffs by 1919; 145 had women by 1925. But women's police roles remained restricted. Women did not attain patrol officer status until the 1960s. There were no female sergeants until 1965, after a successful lawsuit against New York City.[136] With the emergence of the drive for the equality of women in the late 1960s and early 1970s and the passage of Title VII of the Civil Rights Act of 1972, many departments began to recruit women. Others resisted. Serious obstacles and stereotypes had to be overcome: that women were physically weak, irrational, and illogical; that they lacked the toughness needed to deal with work on the streets. Some people argued that the association of female with male officers would cause complications in both job and family life.

By 1980, according to the Uniform Crime Reports, the number of policewomen was still low—under 4 percent of all officers. By 1993, that proportion had more than doubled to 9.5 percent, but the rates are increasing slowly. As of 1998, women held only 13.8 percent of all sworn law enforcement positions nationwide, and held top command positions in slightly over 30 percent of all police agencies.[137] Most recent surveys of personnel practices have found that eligibility criteria and mechanisms used to recruit, screen, and select candidates have changed dramatically, enlarging the pool of eligible women. This change appears to be happening worldwide, not just in the United States, according to an international survey sponsored by the United Nations.[138]

Despite the advances that women have made in policing, they are still not fully accepted by their male colleagues or the public. Most of the resistance stems from the belief that the physical strength of women does not allow them to perform well in violent situations.[139] However, some police scholars argue that resistance is based on more than just the issue of strength: "Women are perceived as a threat to the men's physical safety, group solidarity, and occupational identity as macho crime fighters. In addition, women's presence undermines the close association of their work with masculinity and men's control over social order."[140] Responding to these concerns, many police departments continue to assign women to clerical duties or to specific types of problems, such as domestic disputes and runaways. Research has demonstrated, however, that these fears are ungrounded. Female officers make almost as many successful arrests as male officers, their overall work performance has been rated extremely satisfactory by superiors, their level of strength is well within the acceptable range for the profession, and they may be more pleasant and respectful with the public than their male counterparts.[141]

As to the way policewomen perceive themselves, it appears that they enter the force self-confident and a bit idealistic but gradually become disillusioned by others' beliefs that they are flirtatious and ineffective.[142] In sum, policewomen have indeed made their mark on the police force, but it may be some time before their male colleagues accept them as equal partners.

The Police Subculture

While there continue to be many differences—in numbers, seniority, and positions, for example—between black, Hispanic, and female police officers on the one hand, and white male police officers on the other, one thing that they all have in common is job-related stress. Where their police work is concerned, they rely heavily on each other as partners.

A matter of judgment: Police departments around the country are relying more frequently on simulated firearms training to increase the skill level of their officers when facing deadly force situations.

Michael K. Brown describes how police officers stick together when they work the streets because of the constant stress and anxiety that goes along with the job. These working conditions, plus the entry requirements, training, citizen expectations, and behavioral norms (officers are required to be respectful yet to be in control of a situation, for instance), combine to produce a similarity of values—a **police subculture.**[143]

The process of socialization into the culture begins as soon as new recruits enter the academy. They get to know not only the formal rules of policing but also the informal norms that a person has to abide by in order to be accepted into the group. They learn very quickly that loyalty—the obligation to support a fellow officer—is the first priority. Respect for police authority, honor, individualism, and group solidarity also rank high among esteemed values.[144]

One of the primary reasons for the existence of a subculture that is characterized by very strong in-group ties is the nature of police work. Officers often view the external community as hostile and threatening. They are caught in a bind. Their job calls for them to discipline the people they serve, and they are allowed to use force to do it. The police uniform also isolates officers. Easily recognizable, they are constantly approached by people who know what is going on and want to tell them about it or who want to complain.

When they are off duty, police officers also tend to isolate themselves from the community, spending most of their time with other officers and their families. William Westley says that police officers are isolated from the rest of society behind a "blue curtain."[145] Police officers are often viewed as suspicious, authoritative, and cynical.[146] Their working environment may be responsible for the development of these traits.[147] Police work is potentially dangerous, so officers need to be constantly aware of what is happening around them. At the academy they are warned about what happens to officers who are too trusting. They learn about the many officers who have died in the line of duty because they did not exercise proper caution. It would be surprising if they did not become suspicious.

As George Kirkham, police officer and professor, argues: "Chronic suspiciousness is something that a good cop cultivates in the interest of going home to his family each evening."[148] The second trait, authoritativeness, is another response to the police working environment. Uniforms, badges, and guns signify authority. But even more important is the fact that officers need to gain immediate control of potentially dangerous situations in order to do their job.

And what about cynicism? In a study of 220 New York City police officers, Arthur Niederhoffer found that 80 percent of the new recruits believed that the department was a smoothly operating, effective organization. Within a couple of months, fewer than one-third still held that belief. Moreover, cynicism increased with length of service and among those of the more highly educated who did not get promoted.[149]

The working environment that we have described quite often leads to stress, which results in emotional and physical problems. A study of 2300 officers in 20 departments found that 37 percent had serious marital problems, 36 percent suffered physical ailments, 23 percent abused alcohol, 20 percent indicated problems among their children, and 10 percent abused drugs.[150] Since the 1970s there has been increasing concern over these stress-related problems. Many departments, especially the large ones, are trying to provide more medical attention, more psychological counseling, and a greater range of disability and retirement benefits, and to give higher priority to community-oriented policing, which lessens tension between officer and citizenry.[151]

REVIEW

In tenth-century England, policing was done by all males over age 12, who were bound to keep the peace and track down criminals. Through the centuries the system became more formal, with sheriffs, night watchmen, and justices of the peace. Colonial America adopted a similar system. It was not until 1829 that the first professional police force came into existence in England.

Today there are more than 20,000 separate public law enforcement agencies in the United States. About 50 are federal, some 200 are state, and the rest are local. But although there are many levels of law enforcement agencies, each with specialized units, they often work together on major operations. The federal agency with the broadest range of duties is the FBI. At the state level, all states except Hawaii have centralized, quasi-military forces. At the county level, the sheriff's office is responsible for countywide policing outside municipalities. Municipal police forces range in size from small-town 1- or 2-person departments to the New York City department, which with almost 40,000 officers is the largest in the country. There are also specialized police forces, like housing police, and a growing number of private security police.

Police departments are organized largely along the lines of a military command, with units that parallel those of other government departments: bureaus, divisions, and sections or units. Police perform three categories of functions: law enforcement, order maintenance, and community service. Because the focus on crime fighting and law enforcement tended to alienate police from the community, the social unrest of the 1960s resulted in a great deal of tension and distrust of the police. Departments sought ways to change their image by using innovative methods such as community policing, team policing, foot and bicycle patrols, and problem-oriented policing.

Defects in the functioning of American police forces, in addition to community relations, include maintenance of the rule of law (due process protections and civil rights), use of deadly force and brutality, abuse of discretion, and corruption.

Departments also sought to broaden their community base by recruiting members of various ethnic and minority groups, including women. Today the composition of American police forces is changing rapidly. Although there continue to be many differences in numbers, seniority, and position, for example, between black, Hispanic, and female police officers on the one hand, and white male officers on the other, they all have in common the stress of their jobs. They rely heavily on one another at work and tend to spend most of their off-duty time with other officers and their families.

YOU BE THE CRIMINOLOGIST

Keep in mind the issues related to diversity of American police agencies. What areas must be addressed in the creation of an international police force? Which problems might be reduced or exacerbated by the creation of an international police force? Would such a force eliminate or increase the need for other police agencies?

KEY TERMS

The numbers next to the terms refer to the pages on which the terms are defined.

community policing (526)

constable (510)

frankpledge (510)

genetic fingerprinting (515)

justices of the peace (510)

night watchmen (510)

police subculture (539)

problem-oriented policing (529)

sheriff (510)

sting operation (522)

team policing (528)

tithing (510)

NOTES

1. Based on Martin A. Kelly, "Citizen Survival in Ancient Rome," *Police Studies*, **11** (1988): 195–201, a delightful historical police vignette, which we recommend to all our readers. The quote is from Juvenal (A.D. 40–120).

2. Jerome H. Skolnick and James J. Fyfe, *Above the Law: Police and the Excessive Use of Force* (New York: Free Press, 1993), pp. 1–22.

3. See Daniel Devlin, *Police Procedure, Administration, and Organization* (London: Butterworth, 1966).

4. Metropolitan Police Force, *Instruction Book* (London, 1829), as quoted in William H. Hewitt, Robert S. Getz, and Oscar H. Ibele, *British Police Administration* (Springfield, Ill.: Charles C Thomas, 1965), p. 32.

5. Patrick Pringle, *Hue and Cry: The Story of Henry and John Fielding and the Bow Street Runners* (New York: Morrow, 1965). Also see Philip Rawlings, "The Idea of Policing: A History," *Policing and Society*, **5** (1995): 129–149.

6. Drew Humphries and David F. Greenberg, "The Dialectics of Crime Control," in *Crime and Capitalism: Readings in Marxist Criminology*, ed. David Greenberg (Palo Alto, Calif.: Mayfield, 1981), pp. 209–254.

7. Samuel Walker, *Popular Justice: A History of American Criminal Justice* (New York: Oxford University Press, 1980), p. 18.

8. Roger Lane, "Urban Police and Crime in Nineteenth-Century America," in *Crime and Justice: A Review of Research*, vol. 15, ed. Michael Tonry and Norval Morris (Chicago: University of Chicago Press, 1992), pp. 1–50; Roger Lane, *Policing the City: Boston, 1822–1885* (Cambridge, Mass.: Harvard University Press, 1967), p. 26.

9. Walker, *Popular Justice*, pp. 61–62.

10. George F. Cole, *The American System of Criminal Justice* (Pacific Grove, Calif.: Brooks/Cole, 1989), p. 177.

11. Samuel Walker, *A Critical History of Police Reform* (Lexington, Mass.: Lexington Books, 1977), pp. 45–46; Bruce Smith, *Police Systems in the United States*, rev. ed. (New York: Harper, 1949). For a complete discussion of Theodore Roosevelt as police commissioner, see Jay Stuart Berman, *Police Administration and Progressive Reform: Theodore Roosevelt as Police Commissioner of New York* (New York: Greenwood, 1987).

12. National Commission on Law Observance and Enforcement, *Report on Lawlessness in Law Enforcement*, no. 11 (Washington, D.C.: U.S. Government Printing Office, 1931).

13. Brian A. Reaves and Andrew L. Goldberg, *Census of State and Local Law Enforcement*

Agencies, 1996 (Washington, D.C.: Bureau of Justice Statistics, 1998), p. 1.

14. James D. Calder, *The Origins and Development of Federal Crime Control Policy: Herbert Hoover's Initiatives* (Westport, Conn.: Praeger, 1993).

15. Walker, *Popular Justice,* p. 238.

16. U.S. Department of Justice, *Report to the Deputy Attorney General on the Events at Waco, Texas, February 28 to April 19, 1993* (Washington, D.C.: U.S. Government Printing Office, 1993).

17. U.S. Department of Justice, *Recommendations of Experts for Improvements in Federal Law Enforcement after Waco* (Washington, D.C.: U.S. Government Printing Office, 1993).

18. Federal Bureau of Investigation, "FBI Mission, History and Organization: Organizational Structure and Budget," p. 2, Nov. 1, 1999 (see *http://www.fbi.gov/yourfbi/facts/fbimission.htm*).

19. See William S. Laufer, "The Rhetoric of Innocence," *Washington Law Review,* **70** (1995): 329–421; and Laura Lefay, "New Evidence Exonerates Rape Convict, Expert Says," *The Virginian-Pilot,* Oct. 12, 1994, p. B1.

20. *99 Frequently Asked Questions about the FBI,* July 29, 1998 (see http://www.fbi.gov/faq/fbifaq.htm).

21. *FBI: Facts and History* (Washington, D.C.: U.S. Department of Justice, Federal Bureau of Investigation, 1990).

22. David R. Struckhoff, *The American Sheriff* (Joliet, Ill.: Justice Research Institute, 1993).

23. Reaves and Goldberg, *Census of State and Local Law Enforcement Agencies, 1996,* p. 2.

24. Ibid., p. 6.

25. Ibid., p. 5.

26. Brian A. Reaves and Andrew L. Goldberg, *Law Enforcement Management and Administrative Statistics, 1997: Data for Individual State and Local Agencies with 100 or more Officers,* table 6a (Washington, D.C.: U.S. Department of Justice, 1999).

27. See John P. Crank, "Civilianization in Small and Medium Police Departments in Illinois, 1973–1986," *Journal of Criminal Justice,* **17** (1989): 167–177.

28. Victor H. Sims, *Small Town and Rural Police* (Springfield, Ill.: Charles C Thomas, 1988);

Jay Bass, "Rural Policing: Patterns and Problems of 'Micro' Departments," *Justice Professional,* **9** (1995): 59–74. Also see Ralph A. Weisheit, David N. Falcone, and L. Edward Wells, "Rural Crime and Rural Policing," *National Institute of Justice, Research in Action* (Washington, D.C.: National Institute of Justice, October 1994).

29. Gary W. Cordner, "Police Agency Size and Investigative Effectiveness," *Journal of Criminal Justice,* **17** (1989): 145–155.

30. Clifford D. Shearing and Philip C. Stenning, "Private Security: Implications for Social Control," *Social Problems,* **30** (1983): 493–506.

31. For a brief history of the private security industry, see Milton Lipson, *On Guard—The Business of Private Security* (New York: Quadrangle, 1975); and Robert D. McCrie, "The Development of the U.S. Security Industry," *Annals of the American Academy of Political and Social Science,* **498** (1988): 23–33. Also see Harvey N. Morely and Robert S. Fong, "Can We All Get Along? A Study of Why Strained Relations Continue to Exist between Sworn Law Enforcement and Private Security," *Security Journal,* **6** (1995): 85–92.

32. William F. Walsh and Edwin J. Donovan, "Private Security and Community Policing: Evaluation and Comment," *Journal of Criminal Justice,* **17** (1989): 187–197.

33. William C. Cunningham, John J. Strauchs, and Clifford W. Van Meter, *Private Security: Patterns and Trends, Research in Brief* (Washington, D.C.: National Institute of Justice, August 1991).

34. Sue A. Lindgren, *Justice Expenditures and Employment, 1990* (Washington, D.C.: U.S. Government Printing Office, 1992), p. 3.

35. David A. Sklansky, "The Private Police," *UCLA Law Review,* **46** (1999): 1165–1287.

36. William C. Cunningham and Todd H. Taylor, *Crime and Protection in America: A Study of Private Security and Law Enforcement Resources and Relationships—Executive Summary* (Washington, D.C.: National Institute of Justice, 1985); Charles P. Nemeth, *Private Security and the Investigative Process* (Cincinnati: Anderson, 1992).

37. Fifth United Nations Congress on the Prevention of Crime and the Treatment of Of-

fenders, *Report Prepared by the Secretariat*, A/Conf. 56/10 (New York: United Nations, 1976), p. 29.

38. See Hubert Williams, "Trends in American Policing: Implications for Executives," *American Journal of Police*, **9** (1990): 139–149.

39. Clifford D. Shearing, "The Relation between Public and Private Policing," in Tonry and Morris, *Crime and Justice*, pp. 399–434; Albert J. Reiss, Jr., "Private Employment of Public Police," *NIJ Reports* (Washington, D.C.: National Institute of Justice, 1988), pp. 2–6.

40. C. Cotter and J. Burrows, *Proper Crime Program, A Special Report: Overview of the STING Program and Project Summaries*, for U.S. Department of Justice (Washington, D.C.: U.S. Government Printing Office, 1981); Carl B. Klockars, "Jonathan Wild and the Modern Sting," in *History and Crime: Implications for Criminal Justice Policy*, ed. James C. Inciardi and Charles Faupel (Beverly Hills, Calif.: Sage, 1980), pp. 225–260; John Kleinig, *The Ethics of Policing* (New York: Cambridge University Press, 1996); Mark R. Pogrebin and Eric D. Poole, "Vice Isn't Nice: A Look at the Effects of Working Undercover," *Journal of Criminal Justice*, **21** (1993): 383–394.

41. *Sherman v. United States*, 356 U.S. 369 (1958).

42. Peter Greenwood and Joan Petersilia, *The Criminal Investigation Process*: vol. 1, *Summary and Policy Implications* (Santa Monica, Calif.: Rand Corporation, 1975).

43. Mark T. Willman and John Snortum, "Detective Work: The Criminal Investigation Process in a Medium-Sized Police Department," *Criminal Justice Review*, **9** (Spring 1984): 33–39.

44. John E. Eck, *Solving Crimes: The Investigation of Burglary and Robbery* (Washington, D.C.: Police Executive Research Forum, 1983). For a study of factors that influence time spent on investigation of burglaries and robberies, see Steven G. Brandl, "The Impact of Case Characteristics on Detectives' Decision Making," *Justice Quarterly*, **10** (1993): 395–415.

45. Kenneth E. Christian and Steven M. Edwards, "Law Enforcement Standards and Training Councils: A Human Resource Planning Force in the Future," *Journal of Police Science and Administration*, **13** (1985): 1–9. For changes over time in police training, see Thomas M. Frost and Magnus J. Seng, "Police Recruit Training in Urban Departments: A Look at Instructors," *Journal of Police Science and Administration*, **11** (1983): 296–302. For a methodology of police training evaluation, see Richard A. Talley, "A New Methodology for Evaluating the Curricula Relevancy of Police Academy Training," *Journal of Police Science Administration*, **14** (1986): 112–120. For a discussion of police academy instructors currently teaching in America, see Bruce L. Berg, "Who Should Teach Police: A Typology and Assessment of Police Academy Instructors," *American Journal of Police*, **9** (1990): 79–100.

46. Samuel Walker, *The Police in America* (New York: McGraw-Hill, 1983), p. 265.

47. James Q. Wilson and George L. Kelling, "Broken Windows: The Police and Neighborhood Safety," *Atlantic Monthly* (March 1982): 29–38; Mark H. Moore and George L. Kelling, "To Serve and Protect: Learning from Police History," *Public Interest*, **70** (Winter 1983): 49–65.

48. Samuel Walker, "'Broken Windows' and Fractured History: The Use and Misuse of History in Recent Police Patrol Analysis," *Justice Quarterly*, **1** (1984): 76–90.

49. Albert Reiss, Jr., *The Police and the Public* (New Haven, Conn.: Yale University Press, 1971), p. 11. Research evidence is crucial to police work. See Lawrence W. Sherman, "Evidence-Based Policing," *Ideas in American Policing*, The Police Foundation, July 1998.

50. See, e.g., James Q. Wilson, *Varieties of Police Behavior* (Cambridge, Mass.: Harvard University Press, 1968); Eric J. Scott, *Calls for Service: Citizen Demand and Initial Police Response* (Washington, D.C.: U.S. Government Printing Office, 1981); Steven P. Lab, "Police Productivity: The Other Eighty Percent," *Journal of Police Science and Administration*, **12** (1984): 297–302. See also David H. Bayley and James Garofalo, "The Management of Violence by Police Patrol Officers," *Criminology*, **27** (1989): 1–25.

Review • You Be the Criminologist • Key Terms • Notes

CHAPTER 17

51. Wilson and Kelling, "Broken Windows."

52. George L. Kelling, "Order Maintenance, the Quality of Urban Life, and Police: A Line of Argument," in *Police Leadership,* ed. William A. Gelles (Chicago: American Bar Association, 1985), p. 297.

53. Reiss, *The Police and the Public,* pp. 70–72.

54. John Webster, "Police Task and Time Study," *Journal of Criminal Law, Criminology, and Police Science,* **61** (1970): 94–100.

55. J. Robert Lilly, "What Are the Police Now Doing?" *Journal of Police Science and Administration,* **6** (1978): 51–60. See also Wilson, *Varieties of Police Behavior,* chap. 7; Egon Bittner, *The Function of the Police in Modern Society* (Chevy Chase, Md.: National Institute of Mental Health, 1970).

56. David H. Bayley, *Police for the Future* (New York: Oxford University Press, 1994).

57. Robert C. Wadman and Robert K. Olson, *Community Wellness: A New Theory of Policing* (Washington, D.C.: Police Executive Research Forum, 1990). See also Mark H. Moore, "Problem-Solving and Community Policing," in Tonry and Morris, *Crime and Justice,* pp. 99–158; "Introduction," in *Themes and Variations in Community Policing: Case Studies of Community Policing. Police Executive Research Forum* (Washington, D.C.: Police Executive Research Forum, 1996), pp. 1–13; and John E. Eck and Dennis P. Rosenbaum, "The New Police Order: Effectiveness, Equity and Efficiency in Community Policing," in *The Challenge of Community Policing: Testing the Promises,* ed. Dennis P. Rosenbaum (Thousand Oaks, Calif.: Sage, 1994), pp. 3–26.

58. Gary W. Cordner and Robert C. Trojanowicz, "Patrol," in *What Works in Policing? Operations and Administration Examined,* ed. Gary W. Cordner and Donna C. Hale (Highland Heights, Ky.: Academy of Criminal Justice Sciences; Cincinnati: Anderson, 1992), p. 11.

59. Jerome H. Skolnick and David H. Bayley, *Community Policing: Issues and Practices around the World* (Washington, D.C.: National Institute of Justice, May 1988). See also Susan Sadd and Randolph Grinc, "Innovative Neighborhood Oriented Policing: An Evaluation of Community Policing Programs in Eight Cities," in Rosenbaum, *The Challenge of Community Policing,* pp. 27–52; Deborah Lamm Weisel and John E. Eck, "Toward a Practical Approach to Organizational Change: Community Policing Initiatives in Six Cities," in Rosenbaum, *The Challenge of Community Policing,* pp. 53–72; Arthur J. Lurigio and Dennis P. Rosenbaum, "An Inside Look at Community Policing Reform: Definitions, Organizational Changes, and Evaluation Findings," *Crime and Delinquency,* **40** (1994): 299–314. For further discussion, see Lawrence W. Sherman, Denise Gottfredson, Doris MacKenzie, John Eck, Peter Reuter, and Shawn Bushway, *Preventing Crime: What Works, What Doesn't, What's Promising* (Washington, D.C.: National Institute of Justice, 1997).

60. Jihong Zhao, Nicholas Lovrich, and Quint Thurman, "The Status of Community Policing in American Cities," *Policing: An International Journal of Police Strategies and Management,* **22** (1998): 139–156.

61. Freda Adler, *Nations Not Obsessed with Crime* (Littleton, Colo.: Fred B. Rothman, 1983), p. 101; Dieter Dolling and Thomas Feltes, eds., *Community Policing—Comparative Aspects of Community Oriented Police Work* (Holzkirchen/ Obb, Germany: Felix Verlag, 1993). See also David H. Bayley, "International Differences in Community Policing," in Rosenbaum, *The Challenge of Community Policing,* pp. 278–281.

62. Skolnick and Bayley, *Community Policing,* p. 8; David H. Bayley, *A Model of Community Policing: The Singapore Story* (Washington, D.C.: National Institute of Justice, 1989).

63. Jerome E. McElroy, Colleen A. Cosgrove, and Susan Sadd, *CPOP, The Research: An Evaluative Study of the New York City Community Patrol Officer Program* (New York: Vera Institute of Justice, 1990). See also Antony M. Pate and Penny Shtull, "Community Policing Grows in Brooklyn: An Inside View of the New York City Police Department's Model Precinct," *Crime and Delinquency,* **40** (1994): 384–410.

64. David Weisburd and Jerome E. McElroy, "Enacting the CPO Role: Findings from the

New York City Pilot Program in Community Policing," in *Community Policing: Rhetoric or Reality?* ed. Jack R. Greene and Stephen D. Mastrofski (New York: Praeger, 1988), pp. 89–101; McElroy, Cosgrove, and Sadd, *CPOP, The Research.*

65. Sadd and Grinc, "Innovative Neighborhood Oriented Policing."

66. Robert C. Trojanowicz, "The Future of Community Policing," in Rosenbaum, *The Challenge of Community Policing,* pp. 258–262. For further discussion, see Lawrence F. Travis III and Craig N. Winston, "Dissension in the Ranks: Officer Resistance to Community Policing, Cynicism, and Support for the Organization, "*Journal of Crime and Justice,* **21** (1998): 139–156; Michael Resig and Andrew Giacomazzi, "Citizen Perceptions of Community Policing: Are Attitudes toward Police Important?" *Policing: An International Journal of Police Strategies and Management,* **21** (1998): 547–561; Albert P. Cardarelli, Jack McDevitt, and Katrina Baum, "The Rhetoric and Reality of Community Policing in Small and Medium-Sized Cities and Towns," *Policing: An International Journal of Police Strategies and Management,* **21** (1998): 397–415; and Todd J. Dicker, "Tension on the Thin Blue Line: Police Officer Resistance to Community Oriented Policing," *American Journal of Criminal Justice,* **23** (1998): 59–82.

67. Mark H. Moore, "Research Synthesis and Policy Implications," in Rosenbaum, *The Challenge of Community Policing,* pp. 285–299. See also Robert Trojanowicz and Bonnie Bucqueroux, "The Ten Principles of Community Policing," in *Classics in Policing,* ed. Steven G. Brandl and David E. Barlow (Cincinnati: Anderson, 1993), pp. 353–356.

68. Hubert Williams and Antony M. Pate, "Returning to First Principles: Reducing the Fear of Crime in Newark," *Crime and Delinquency,* **33** (1987): 53–70.

69. *The Effects of Police Fear Reduction Studies: A Summary of Findings from Houston and Newark* (Washington, D.C.: Police Foundation, 1986); *The Newark Foot Patrol Experiment* (Washington, D.C.: Police Foundation, 1981); Lee P. Brown and Mary Ann Wycoff,

"Policing Houston: Reducing Fear and Improving Service," *Crime and Delinquency,* **33** (1987): 71–89; Frans Willem Winkel, "The Police and Reducing Fear of Crime: A Comparison of the Crime-Centered and the Quality of Life Approaches," *Police Studies,* **11** (1988): 183–189.

70. Lawrence W. Sherman, "The Police," in *Crime,* ed. James Q. Wilson and Joan Petersilia (San Francisco: ICS Press, 1995), p. 339.

71. William J. Bopp, *Police Personnel Administration* (Boston: Holbrook, 1974), pp. 48–51.

72. Lawrence W. Sherman, Catherine H. Milton, and Thomas V. Kelly, *Team Policing: Seven Case Studies* (Washington, D.C.: Police Foundation, 1973).

73. John P. Kenney, *Police Administration* (Springfield, Ill.: Charles C Thomas, 1972).

74. Herman Goldstein, *Problem-Oriented Policing* (New York: McGraw-Hill, 1990), pp. 14–31.

75. Gard W. Cordner, "The Baltimore County Citizen-Oriented Police Enforcement (COPE) Project: Final Evaluation," paper presented to the American Society of Criminology, San Diego, 1985.

76. Michael E. Buerger, "The Problems of Problem-Solving: Resistance, Interdependencies, and Conflicting Interests," *American Journal of Police,* **13** (1994): 1–36.

77. Timothy J. Hope, "Problem Oriented Policing and Drug Market Locations: Three Case Studies," in *Crime Prevention Studies,* vol. 4, ed. Ronald V. Clarke (Monsey, N.Y.: Willow Tree Press, 1995), pp. 5–32; Sandra S. Stone, "Problem Oriented Policing Approach to Drug Enforcement: Atlanta as a Case Study," Ph.D. dissertation, Emory University (Ann Arbor, Mich.: University Microfilms International, 1993); U.S. Bureau of Justice Assistance, *Problem-Oriented Drug Enforcement: A Community-Based Approach for Effective Policing* (Washington, D.C.: Bureau of Justice Assistance, 1993).

78. David M. Kennedy, Anne M. Piehl, and Anthony A. Braga, "Youth Gun Violence in Boston: Gun Markets, Serious Youth Offenders, and a Use Reduction Strategy," *Working Paper,* John F. Kennedy School of Government, Program in Criminal Justice Policy and Management (Cambridge, Mass.:

Review • You Be the Criminologist • Key Terms • Notes

Harvard University, 1996). For further discussion, see Tara O'Connor Shelley and Anne C. Grant, eds., *Problem Oriented Policing: Crime-Specific Problems, Critical Issues, and Making POP Work* (Washington, D.C.: Police Executive Research Forum, 1998).

79. Lawrence W. Sherman and David Weisburd, "General Deterrent Effects of Police Patrol in Crime 'Hot Spots': A Randomized, Controlled Trial," *Justice Quarterly*, **12** (1995): 625–648.

80. Lawrence W. Sherman, "Hot Spots of Crime and Criminal Careers of Places," in Clarke, *Crime Prevention Studies*, pp. 35–52; Michael E. Buerger, Ellen G. Cohn, and Anthony Petrosino, "Defining the 'Hot Spots of Crime'; Operationalizing Theoretical Concepts for Field Research," in Clarke, *Crime Prevention Studies*, pp. 237–558.

81. Geoffrey C. Barnes, "Defining and Optimizing Displacement," in Clarke, *Crime Prevention Studies*, pp. 95–114.

82. Lawrence W. Sherman and Dennis P. Rogan, "Effects of Gun Seizures on Gun Violence: 'Hot Spots' Patrol in Kansas City," *Justice Quarterly*, **12** (1995): 673–694; James W. Shaw, "Community Policing against Guns: Public Opinion of the Kansas City Gun Experiment," *Justice Quarterly*, **12** (1995): 695–710; David Weisburd and Lorraine Green, "Policing Drug Hot Spots: The Jersey City Drug Market Analysis Experiment," *Justice Quarterly*, **12** (1995): 711–736. Also see Lorraine Green, "Policing Places with Drug Problems: The Multi-Agency Response Team Approach," in Clarke, *Crime Prevention Studies*, pp. 199–216.

83. Nancy G. LaVigne, "Computerized Mapping as a Tool for Problem-Oriented Policing," *Crime Mapping News*, **1** (Winter 1999), The Police Foundation, Washington, D.C.; Nancy LaVigne and Julie Wartell, eds., *Crime Mapping Case Studies: Success in the Field* (Washington, D.C.: Police Executive Research Forum, 1998); David Weisburd and Tom McEwen, eds., *Crime Mapping and Crime Prevention* (Monsey, N.Y.: Criminal Justice Press, 1997).

84. George L. Kelling, *What Works—Research and the Police, Crime File Study Guide,* for U.S. Department of Justice, National Institute of Justice (Washington, D.C.: U.S. Government Printing Office, 1988); George L. Kelling, Antony Pate, Duane Dieckman, and Charles E. Brown, *The Kansas City Preventive Patrol Experiment: A Summary Report* (Washington, D.C.: Police Foundation, 1974). See also David F. Greenberg, Ronald C. Kessler, and Colin Loftin, "The Effect of Police Employment on Crime," *Criminology,* **21** (1983): 375–394; Charles R. Wellford, "Crime and the Police: A Multivariate Analysis," *Criminology,* **12** (1974): 195–213; Craig Uchida and Robert Goldberg, *Police Employment and Expenditure Trends,* for U.S. Department of Justice, Bureau of Justice Statistics (Washington, D.C.: U.S. Government Printing Office, 1986); and Colin Loftin and David McDowall, "The Police, Crime, and Economic Theory: An Assessment," *American Sociological Review,* **47** (1982): 393–401.

85. For recent surveys of attitudes of minority-group members toward the police, see James R. Davis, "A Comparison of Attitudes toward the New York City Police," *Journal of Police Science and Administration,* **17** (1990): 233–243; and Komanduri S. Murty, Julian B. Roebuck, and Joann D. Smith, "The Image of the Police in Black Atlanta Communities," *Journal of Police Science and Administration,* **17** (1990): 250–257.

86. See Earl M. Sweeney, *The Public and the Police: A Partnership in Protection* (Springfield, Ill.: Charles C Thomas, 1982); and Louis A. Radelet, *The Police and the Community* (New York: Macmillan, 1986).

87. Thomas A. Johnson, Gordon E. Misner, and Lee P. Brown, *The Police and Society: An Environment for Collaboration and Confrontation* (Englewood Cliffs, N.J.: Prentice-Hall, 1981). See also Fred I. Klyman and Joanna Kruckenberg, "A National Survey of Police-Community Relations Units," *Journal of Police Science and Administration,* **7** (1979): 72–79. For the importance of municipal police organization to police-community relations, see Thomas A. Johnson, *A Study of Police Resistance to Police Community Relations in a Municipal Police Department* (Ann Arbor, Mich.: University Microfilms, 1971).

88. Samuel Walker, *Citizen Review Resource Manual* (Washington, D.C.: Police Executive Research Forum, 1995).

89. Antony M. Pate and Lorie A. Fridell, *Police Use of Force: Official Reports, Citizen Complaints and Legal Consequences*, vol. II (Washington, D.C.: Police Foundation, 1993). For further discussion, see M. L. Dantzker, ed., "Public Perceptions of Policing," *Journal of Contemporary Criminal Justice*, **15** (1999): 131–204.

90. Samuel Walker and Betsy Wright, "Citizen Review of the Police, 1994: A National Survey," *Fresh Perspectives* (Washington, D.C.: Police Executive Research Forum, 1995).

91. Douglas W. Perez, *Common Sense about Police Review* (Philadelphia: Temple University Press), pp. 127–138.

92. See Richard S. Allinson, "LEAA's Impact on Criminal Justice: A Review of the Literature," *Criminal Justice Abstracts*, **11** (1979): 608–648.

93. *Tennessee v. Garner*, 471 U.S. 887 (1985). For a recent review of the impact of the Garner decision on police shootings, see Abraham N. Tennenbaum, "The Influence of the *Garner* Decision on Police Use of Deadly Force," *Journal of Criminal Law and Criminology*, **81** (1994): 241–260.

94. James J. Fyfe, "Police Use of Deadly Force: Research and Reform," *Justice Quarterly*, **5** (1988): 165–205.

95. With the exception of, e.g., Gerald D. Robin, "Justifiable Homicide by Police Officers," *Journal of Criminal Law, Criminology, and Police Science*, **54** (1963): 225–231; and *Police Power vs. Citizens' Rights* (New York: American Civil Liberties Union, 1966).

96. John S. Goldkamp, "Minorities as Victims of Police Shootings: Interpretations of Racial Disproportionality and Police Use of Deadly Force," *Justice System Journal*, **2** (1976): 169–183. Also see Dennis M. Rome, in Soo Son and Mark S. Davis, "Police Use of Excessive Force: Does the Race of the Suspect Influence Citizens' Perceptions?" *Social Justice Research*, **8** (1995): 41–56. For the association between economic inequality and police-caused homicides, see Johnathan R. Sorensen, James W. Marquart, and Deon E. Brock, "Factors Related to Killings of Felons by Police Officers: A Test of the Community Violence and Conflict Hypothesis," *Justice Quarterly*, **10** (1993): 417–440.

97. Catherine Milton, J. W. Halleck, J. Lardner, and G. L. Abrecht, *Police Use of Deadly Force* (Washington, D.C.: Police Foundation, 1977).

98. Betty Jenkins and Adrienne Faison, *An Analysis of 248 Persons Killed by New York City Policemen* (New York: Metropolitan Applied Research Center, 1974).

99. Paul Takagi, "Death by Police Intervention," in *A Community Concern: Police Use of Deadly Force*, ed. R. N. Brenner and M. Kravitz (Washington, D.C.: U.S. Government Printing Office, 1979), p. 34.

100. James J. Fyfe, "Race and Extreme Police-Citizen Violence," in *Race, Crime, and Criminal Justice*, ed. R. L. McNeely and C. E. Pope (Beverly Hills, Calif.: Sage, 1981), pp. 89–108; and Skolnick and Fyfe, *Above the Law*. See also Kleinig, *The Ethics of Policing*, pp. 96–122; Arnold Binder and Peter Scharf, "Deadly Force in Law Enforcement," *Crime and Delinquency*, **28** (1982): 1–23; and Reiss, *The Police and the Public*.

101. Lawrence W. Sherman, *Citizens Killed by Big City Police, 1970–1984* (Washington, D.C.: Crime Control Institute, Crime Control Research Corporation, 1986).

102. Anthony Desletano et al., "NJ Cop Innocent: Slain Teen's Mom Falters after Verdict," *Newsday*, July 12, 1992, p. 3; John Kifner, "Evidence Shows Youth's Hands Up When Teaneck Officer Killed Him," *New York Times*, Aug. 2, 1990, p. 1.

103. The four officers whom a videotape showed beating the black driver were acquitted. Thereupon the Los Angeles riots occurred, resulting in over 50 deaths and the destruction of nearly $1 billion worth of property. See Carl E. Pope and Lee E. Ross, "Race, Crime and Justice: The Aftermath of Rodney King," *Criminologist*, **17** (1992): 1–10; Helen Taylor Green, "Black Perspectives

Review • You Be the Criminologist • Key Terms • Notes

on Police Brutality," in *African-American Perspectives on Crime Causation, Criminal Justice Administration and Crime Prevention,* ed. Anne T. Sulton (Englewood, Colo.: Sulton Books, 1994), pp. 139–147. And for an excellent overview of issues relating to police abuse of force, see William A. Geller and Hans Toch, eds., *And Justice for All: Understanding and Controlling Police Abuse of Force* (Washington, D.C.: Police Executive Research Forum, 1995).

104. Jerry Gray, "In Police Brutality Case, One Videotape but Two Ways to View It," *New York Times,* Dec. 13, 1991, p. B7. A jury subsequently found the police officers not guilty of official misconduct; see "Videotape Discounted in Beating," *New York Times,* Feb. 20, 1993, p. A25. But two of these officers were subsequently found guilty in federal court of having abused King's constitutional rights. In August 1993, King himself was again arrested on a drunk-driving charge, having smashed his car into a wall while under the influence of alcohol.

105. Alan Feuer, "Charges Are Traded in Summations at 'Officers' Cover-Up Trial in Louima Torture," *New York Times,* March 1, 2000, p. B5; Geller and Toch, *And Justice for All;* and Pate and Fridell, *Police Use of Force,* vol. II. For a discussion of psychological screening issues, see Ellen M. Scrivner, "Controlling Police Use of Force: The Role of the Police Psychologist," *NIJ Research in Brief* (Washington, D.C.: National Institute of Justice, October 1994).

106. U.N. General Assembly Resolution 34/169, Dec. 17, 1979. On the difficulties of research on police violence, see Jeffrey Ian Ross, "The Outcomes of Public Violence: A Neglected Research Agenda," *Police Studies,* **15** (1992): 1–12.

107. See Bayley, *Police for the Future.*

108. Samuel Walker, *Taming the System: The Control of Discretion in Criminal Justice, 1950–1990* (New York: Oxford University Press, 1993), pp. 21–53; Kleinig, *The Ethics of Policing,* pp. 96–122.

109. Cecil L. Willis and Richard H. Wells, "The Police and Child Abuse: An Analysis of Police Decisions to Report Illegal Behavior," *Criminology,* **26** (1988): 695–716; Charles J. Ogletree, Mary Prosser, Abbe Smith, et al., *Beyond the Rodney King Story: An Investigation of Police Conduct in Minority Communities* (Boston: Northeastern University Press, 1995); John R. Hepburn, "Race and the Decision to Arrest: An Analysis of Warrants Issued," *Journal of Research in Crime and Delinquency,* **15** (1978): 54; Douglas A. Smith and Christy A. Visher, "Street-Level Justice: Situational Determinants of Police Arrest Decisions," *Social Problems,* **29** (1981): 167–177; Dale Dannefer and Russell K. Schutt, "Race and Juvenile Justice Processing in Court and Police Agencies," *American Journal of Sociology,* **87** (1982): 1113–1132.

110. Carl Werthman and Irving Piliavin, "Gang Members and the Police," in *The Police: Six Sociological Essays,* ed. David Bordua (New York: Wiley, 1967), pp. 75–83.

111. Dennis D. Powell, "Race, Rank, and Police Discretion," *Journal of Police Science and Administration,* **9** (1981): 383–389. For recent research findings confirming disproportionate police punitiveness against minorities, see Dana M. Nurge, Anthony A. Braga, Lorraine Greene, and David Weisburd, "The Influence of Race on Narcotics Enforcement in Jersey City, New Jersey," paper presented at the American Society of Criminology Annual Meetings, Miami, October 1994; Major Nelson Oramas, *Drug Enforcement in Minority Communities: The Minneapolis Police Department, 1985–1990* (Washington, D.C.: Police Executive Research Forum, 1994); and Sandra Browning, Francis T. Cullen, Liqun Cao, et al., "Race and Getting Hassled by the Police: A Research Note," *Police Studies,* **17** (1994): 1–11.

112. Douglas Smith and Jody Klein, "Police Control of Interpersonal Disputes," *Social Problems,* **21** (1984): 468–481; Richard C. Hollinger, "Race, Occupational Status, and Pro-active Police Arrest for Drinking and Driving," *Journal of Criminal Justice,* **12** (1984): 173–183; Douglas A. Smith,

Christy A. Visher, and Laura A. Davidson, "Equity and Discretionary Justice: The Influence of Race on Police Arrest Decisions," *Journal of Criminal Law and Criminology*, **75** (1984): 234–249; Donald Black, "The Social Organization of Arrest," *Stanford Law Review*, **23** (1971): 1087–1098; Alfred Blumstein, "On the Racial Disproportionality of United States' Prison Populations," *Journal of Criminal Law and Criminology*, **73** (1982): 1259–1281; Richard J. Lundman, Richard E. Sykes, and John P. Clark, "Police Control of Juveniles: A Replication," *Journal of Research in Crime and Delinquency*, **15** (1978): 74–91.

113. Christy A. Visher, "Gender, Police Arrest Decisions, and Notions of Chivalry," *Criminology*, **21** (1983): 5–28.

114. Marvin D. Krohn, James P. Curry, and Shirley Nelson-Kilger, "Is Chivalry Dead? An Analysis of Changes in Police Dispositions of Males and Females," *Criminology*, **21** (1983): 417–437. See also Imogene L. Moyer, "Police/Citizen Encounter: Issues of Chivalry, Gender and Race," in *The Changing Roles of Women in the Criminal Justice System*, ed. Moyer (Prospect Park, Ill.: Waveland, 1992), pp. 69–80.

115. Whitman Knapp, chairman, *Commission Report* (New York: Commission to Investigate Allegations of Police Corruption and the City's Anticorruption Procedures, 1972); *Knapp Commission Report on Police Corruption* (New York: Braziller, 1973).

116. Herman Goldstein, *Police Corruption: A Perspective on Its Nature and Control* (Washington, D.C.: Police Foundation, 1975); Lawrence Sherman, *Police Corruption: A Sociological Perspective* (Garden City, N.Y.: Doubleday, 1974); Ellwyn Stoddard, "Blue Coat Crime," in *Thinking about Police: Contemporary Readings*, ed. Carl Klockars (New York: McGraw-Hill, 1983), pp. 338–349; Michael Johnston, *Political Corruption and Public Policy in America* (Monterey, Calif.: Brooks/Cole, 1982), p. 75.

117. Andrew Murr, "L.A.'s Dirty War on Drugs," *Newsweek*, Oct. 11, 1999. See also Robert J. McCormack, "Confronting Police Corruption: Organizational Initiatives for Internal Control," in *Managing Police Corruption: International Perspectives*, ed. Richard H. Ward and Robert McCormack (Chicago: Office of International Criminal Justice, University of Illinois at Chicago, 1987), pp. 151–165; Dale K. Sechrest and Pamela Burns, "Police Corruption: The Miami Case," *Criminal Justice and Behavior*, **19** (1992): 294–313.

118. Cole, *The American System of Criminal Justice*, p. 277.

119. William Westley, *Violence and the Police: A Sociological Study of Law, Custom, and Morality* (Cambridge, Mass.: M.I.T. Press, 1970); Paul Chevigny, *Police Power: Police Abuses in New York City* (New York: Pantheon, 1969); Sherman, *Police Corruption*.

120. Richard S. Allinson, ed., *Criminal Justice Abstracts* (Monsey, N.Y.: Willow Tree Press, September 1994), p. 420; *Commission Report* (New York: Commission to Investigate Allegations of Police Corruption, 1994). For a journalistic account of the recent corruption scandal in New York City, see Mike McAlary, *Good Cop, Bad Cop: Detective Joe Trimboli's Heroic Pursuit of New York City Police Department Officer Michael Dowd* (New York: Pocket Books, 1994). For an overview of current strategies designed to eliminate corruption in New York City, see William J. Bratton, *Policing Strategy Number Seven: Rooting out Corruption: Building Organizational Integrity in the New York City Police Department* (New York, 1995). For a historical overview of police corruption in England, see James Morton, *Bent Coppers: A Survey of Police Corruption* (London: Little, Brown, 1993).

121. Jack Aylward, "Psychological Testing and Police Selection," *Journal of Police Science and Administration*, **13** (1985): 201–210. Also see Joan E. Pynes, "Police Officer Selection Procedures: Speculation on the Future," *American Journal of Police*, **13** (1994): 103–112; Peter B. Ainsworth, *Psychology and Policing in a Changing World* (New York: Wiley, 1995), pp. 129–145. And for a discussion of polygraph screening of police officers, see Frank Horvath,

Review • You Be the Criminologist • Key Terms • Notes

"Polygraph Screening of Candidates for Police Work in Large Police Agencies in the United States: A Survey of Practices, Policies, and Evaluative Comments," *American Journal of Police,* **12** (1993): 1993.

122. James J. Fyfe, Jack R. Greene, William F. Walsh, O. W. Wilson, and Roy Clinton McLaren, *Police Administration,* 5th ed. (Boston: McGraw-Hill, 1997), p. 281.

123. David L. Carter, Allen D. Sapp, and Darrell W. Stephens, *The State of Police Education: Policy Direction for the 21st Century* (Washington, D.C.: Police Executive Research Forum, 1989), p. 38; Chris Eskridge, "College and the Police: A Review of the Issues," in *Police and Policing: Contemporary Issues,* ed. Dennis Jay Kenney (New York: Praeger, 1989), pp. 18–25. See also Lee H. Bowker, "A Theory of Educational Needs of Law Enforcement Officers," *Journal of Contemporary Criminal Justice,* **1** (1980): 17–24. For a discussion of the best type of college education for law enforcement officers, see Lawrence W. Sherman and Warren Bennis, "Higher Education for Police Officers: The Central Issues," *Police Chief,* **44** (August 1977): 32. See also Lawrence Sherman et al., *The Quality of Police Education* (San Francisco: Jossey-Bass, 1978).

124. Elizabeth Burbeck and Adrian Furnham, "Police Officer Selection: A Critical Review of the Literature," *Journal of Police Science and Administration,* **13** (1985): 58–69.

125. Samuel Walker, *The Police in America,* 2d ed. (New York: McGraw-Hill, 1992), p. 313.

126. Marvin Dulaney, *Black Police in America* (Bloomington: Indiana University Press, 1996); Candice McCoy, "Affirmative Action in Police Organizations: Checklist for Supporting a Compelling State Interest," *Criminal Law Bulletin,* **20** (1984): 245–254; Timothy Stroup, "Affirmative Action and the Police," in *Police Ethics: Hard Choices in Law Enforcement,* ed. W. C. Heffernan and Timothy Stroup (New York: John Jay, 1985). See also Isaac C. Hunt, Jr., and Bernard Cohen, *Minority Recruiting in the New York City Police Department* (New York: Rand Institute, 1971).

127. Jack L. Kuykendall and David E. Burns, "The Black Police Officer: An Historical Perspective," *Journal of Contemporary Criminal Justice,* **1** (1986): 4–12.

128. James J. Fyfe, "Police Personnel Practices," *Baseline Data Reports,* vol. 15 (Washington, D.C.: International City Management Association, 1983).

129. Nicholas Alex, *Black in Blue: A Study of the Negro Policeman* (New York: Appleton-Century-Crofts, 1969).

130. Bruce L. Berg, Edmond J. True, and Marc G. Gertz, "Police, Riots, and Alienation," *Journal of Police Science and Administration,* **12** (1984): 186–190.

131. See U.S. Commission on Civil Rights, *Who Is Guarding the Guardians? A Report on Police Practices* (Washington, D.C.: U.S. Government Printing Office, 1981).

132. Reaves and Goldberg, *Law Enforcement Management and Administrative Statistics, 1997;* see table 3a for detailed listing of departmental data.

133. Dulaney, *Black Police in America;* Ellen Hochstedler, "Impediments to Hiring Minorities in Public Police Agencies," *Journal of Police Science and Administration,* **12** (1984): 227–240.

134. David E. Pitt, "Racial Tensions in Police Ranks Work Three Ways Now," *New York Times,* Feb. 19, 1989, p. E6.

135. Daniel J. Bell, "Policewomen: Myths and Reality," *Journal of Police Science and Administration,* **10** (1982): 112–120. On the history of women in policing, see Kerry Segrave, *Policewomen: A History* (Jefferson, N.C.: McFarland, 1995); Jenis Marie Appier, "Gender and Justice: Women Police in America: 1910–1946," doctoral dissertation, University of California, Riverside (Ann Arbor, Mich.: University Microfilms International, 1993); Jenis Marie Appier, "Preventive Justice: The Campaign for Women Police, 1910–1940," *Women and Criminal Justice,* **4** (1992): 3–36.

136. Samuel S. Janus, Cynthia Janus, Leslie K. Lord, and Thomas Power, "Women in Police Work—Annie Oakley or Little

Orphan Annie?" *Police Studies*, **11** (1988): 124–127; Susan E. Martin, *Women on the Move? A Report on the Status of Women in Policing* (Washington, D.C.: Police Foundation, 1989).

137. National Center for Women and Policing, *Equality Denied: The Status of Women in Policing* (Los Angeles: National Center for Women and Policing, 1998).

138. United Nations report, A/Conf. 121/17, July 1, 1985, with a comprehensive analysis of women in law enforcement by Edith Flynn, who served as U.N. consultant on the topic.

139. Kenneth W. Kerber, Steven M. Andes, and Michele B. Mittler, "Citizen Attitudes Regarding the Competence of Female Police Officers," *Journal of Police Science and Administration*, **5** (1977): 337–347. On the variegated forms of gender discrimination, see Inger J. Sagatun, "Gender Discrimination in Criminal Justice: Relevant Law and Future Trends," *Women and Criminal Justice*, **2** (1990): 63–81.

140. Susan Ehrlich Martin and Nancy C. Jurik, *Doing Justice, Doing Gender: Women in Law and Criminal Justice Occupations* (Thousand Oaks, Calif.: Sage, 1996), pp. 72–73.

141. Merry Morash and Jack Greene, "Evaluating Women on Patrol: A Critique of Contemporary Wisdom," *Evaluation Review*, **10** (1986): 230–255. A study of female police officers' perceptions of their handling of violent and dangerous situations noted their strong survival skills for managing difficult situations: Frances Heidensohn, " 'We Can Handle It Out Here': Women Officers in Britain and the USA and the Policing of Public Order," *Policing and Society*, **4** (1994): 293–303. A study of patrol teams in New York City found policewomen less likely to injure citizens or to be injured; see Sean Grennan, "Findings on the Role of Officer Gender in Violent Encounters with Citizens," *Journal of Police Science and Administration*, **15** (1988): 78–85. A Texas and Oklahoma study found arrest rates of male and female officers almost alike; see James A. Davis, "Perspectives of Policewomen in Texas

and Oklahoma," *Journal of Police Science and Administration*, **12** (1984): 395–403. See also Robert J. Homant and Daniel B. Kennedy, "Police Perceptions of Spouse Abuse: A Comparison of Male and Female Officers," *Journal of Criminal Justice*, **13** (1985): 29–47; Michael T. Charles, "Women in Policing: The Physical Aspects," *Journal of Police Science and Administration*, **10** (1982): 194–205; James A. Davis, "Perspectives of Policewomen in Texas and Oklahoma," *Journal of Criminal Justice*, **13** (1985): 49–64; and Peter Bloch and Deborah Anderson, *Police Women on Patrol: Final Report* (Washington, D.C.: Urban Institute, 1974).

142. Sally Gross, "Women Becoming Cops: Developmental Issues and Solutions," *Police Chief*, **51** (January 1984): 32–35.

143. Michael K. Brown, *Working the Street* (New York: Russell Sage, 1981). For further discussion, see Steve Herbert, "Police Subculture Reconsidered," *Criminology*, **36** (1998): 343–369.

144. Westley, *Violence and the Police*, p. 226.

145. Ibid.

146. Arthur Niederhoffer, *Behind the Shield: The Police in Urban Society* (Garden City, N.Y.: Doubleday, 1967); Richard Lundman, *Police and Policing* (New York: Holt, Rinehart & Winston, 1980); Jerome H. Skolnick, *Justice without Trial* (New York: Wiley, 1966); John P. Crank, Robert M. Regoli, Eric D. Poole, and Robert G. Culbertson, "Cynicism among Police Chiefs," *Justice Quarterly*, **3** (1986): 343–352. For different "types" of officers, see William F. Walsh, "Patrol Officer Arrest Rates: A Study of the Social Organization of Police Work," *Justice Quarterly*, **3** (1986): 271–290.

147. See Michael J. Leiber, Makesh K. Nalla, and Margaret Farnworth, "Explaining Juveniles' Attitudes toward the Police," *Justice Quarterly*, **15** (1998): pp. 151–174.

148. George Kirkham, "A Professor's Street Lessons," in *Order under Law*, ed. R. Culbertson and M. Tezak (Prospect Heights, Ill.: Waveland, 1981), p. 81.

149. Niederhoffer, *Behind the Shield*. For changes over time attributed to occupational

socialization, see Jesse L. Maghan, "The 21st-Century Cop: Police Recruit Perceptions as a Function of Occupational Socialization," Ph.D. dissertation, City University of New York, 1988.

150. John Blackmore, "Are Police Allowed to Have Problems of Their Own?" *Police Magazine*, **1** (1978): 47–55. See also John M. Violanti and Fred Aron, "Police Stressors: Variations in Perception among Police Personnel," *Journal of Criminal Justice*, **23** (1995): 287–294; Clement Mihanovich, "The Blue Pressure Cooker," *Police Chief*, **47** (February 1980): 20–21; Mary Hageman, "Occupational Stress and Marital and Family Relationships," *Journal of Police Science and Administration*, **6** (1978): 402–416; Francis T. Cullen, Terrence Lemming, Bruce G. Link, and John F. Wozniak, "The Impact of Social Supports on Police Stress," *Criminology*, **23** (1985): 503–522; W. Clinton Terry III, "Police Stress: The Empirical Evidence," *Journal of Police Science and Administration*, **9** (1981): 61–75; T. E. Malloy and G. L. Mays, "The Police Stress Hypothesis: A Critical Evaluation," *Criminal Justice and Behavior*, **11** (1984): 197–226; Merry Morash and Robin N. Haarr, "Gender, Workplace Problems, and Stress in Policing," *Justice Quarterly*, **12** (1995): 113–140; B. A. Vulcano, G. E. Barnes, and L. J. Breen, "The Prevalence and Predictors of Psychosomatic Symptoms and Conditions among Police Officers," *Psychosomatic Medicine*, **45** (1983): 277–293; R. C. Trojanowicz, *The Environment of the First-Line Police Supervisor* (Englewood Cliffs, N.J.: Prentice-Hall, 1980); W. Clinton Terry III, "Police Stress as a Professional Self-Image," *Journal of Criminal Justice*, **13** (1985): 501–512; Katherine W. Ellison and John L. Genz, *Stress and the Police Officer* (Springfield, Ill.: Charles C Thomas, 1983); William H. Kroes, *Society's Victims—The Police*, 2d ed. (Springfield, Ill.: Charles C Thomas, 1985); Steven Stack and Thomas Kelley, "Police Suicide: An Analysis," *American Journal of Police*, **13** (1994): 73–90. An entire organization devoted to the study of police stress (the International Law Enforcement Stress Association) has been founded; it publishes its own journal, *Police Stress*.

151. Jack R. Greene, "Police Officer Job Satisfaction and Community Perceptions: Implications for Community-Oriented Policing," *Journal of Research in Crime and Delinquency*, **26** (1989): 168–183.

CHAPTER 18
The Nature and Functioning of Courts

KEY TERMS
arraignment
certiorari, writ of
challenges for cause
defense counsel
deterrence
directed verdict
habeas corpus
indictment
information
just deserts
mandatory sentence
motions
motion to dismiss
peremptory challenges
plead
presumptive sentence
prosecutor
rehabilitation
restorative justice
retribution
selective incapacitation
sentencing commissions
vindication
voir dire

C ourtroom drama is an integral part of our popular culture, drawing the audience in like no moving network miniseries or big-screen motion picture could. Real-life voyeurism with real-life scripts and, unfortunately, real-life victims. The facts of sensation-alized cases often repulse us, yet we read about and watch the courtroom proceedings with unparalleled fascination. These are the trials of the last half-century, the cases that captured our attention, obsessed the media, and, for many, provided milestones for our lives.

- Jeffrey Dahmer, a serial killer who committed at least 17 murders, drugged, strangled, and killed his victims, only to have sex with them before freezing and dining on their remains, was tried and convicted in a surreal courtroom drama. He was later killed in prison by a fellow inmate.
- Danny Rolling, a 39-year-old serial murderer, shocked the Gainesville campus of University of Florida as he savagely slashed, executed, and dismembered four female students and one male student over the course of a lengthy killing spree. Rolling willingly confessed to the crimes. The proceedings were devastating to watch.
- Erik and Lyle Menendez, brothers living in Beverly Hills, shot and killed their parents. Their trial painted two irreconcilable portraits of the brothers: Were they sexually abused and emotionally tortured children who acted out of self-defense, or cold-hearted, money-driven upper-class kids, desperate for a $14 million inheri-tance? Some watched the trial with pity, others with disgust.
- Jenny Jones, a popular TV talk show host, found herself on the other side of the fray, this time accused of causing the death of Scott Amedure, a guest on her highly rated show. Amedure was a guest in an

British nanny Louise Woodward was found guilty of second degree murder in the death of 8-month-old Matthew Eappen after the child was rushed to the hospital with brain injuries consistent with shaken baby syndrome and blunt trauma. Woodward's conviction was subsequently reduced to manslaughter.

episode on "Same-Sex Secret Crushes," where he confessed his affection for his unknowing neighbor, another guest, Jonathan Schmitz. Schmitz was enraged—humiliated beyond his control—and later shot and killed Amedure. In a strange blend of fiction and nonfiction, the trial itself was to many viewers an entertaining daytime show.

- Rodney King, severely beaten by four white police officers (captured on videotape), sought justice in a California courtroom. The case was unremarkable, but the controversial verdict led to rioting and looting in South Central Los Angeles, leaving 54 people dead, hundreds injured, and more than 800 buildings completely destroyed.

- Dr. Jack Kevorkian ("Dr. Death") encouraged the criminal justice system to confront his practice of assisted suicide by having CBS film his "therapeutic" lethal injection of a patient suffering from Lou Gehrig's disease. Kevorkian was later convicted in a trial that raised significant

philosophical (as well as practical) questions about life and death.

- Louise Woodward, a seemingly mild-mannered British nanny, was far more interested in a social life than in caring for 8-month-old Matthew Eappen, according to prosecutors. To make their case, they had to prove beyond a reasonable doubt that Woodward fatally shook and threw the baby onto the floor, fracturing his skull. The defense claimed that the cause of death was a combination of a previous head injury and a congenital brain defect. Woodward's emotionally charged trial, her subsequent conviction, and the light sentence prompted cries for justice both here and abroad.

- O. J. Simpson, former football star, sportscaster, and actor, went on trial for the murder of his ex-wife and a friend of hers in perhaps the most watched and talked about case in our history. You remember the facts. You know the verdict.

It is all too easy to think that criminal cases that reach courtrooms around the United States are like Woodward's, Kevorkian's, or Simpson's—dramatic episodes of well-acted and emotionally charged scripts. It is all too easy to think that the average criminal case pits good against bad, clearly reveals the innocent and the guilty, and results in a just and fair decision. It is all too easy and very wrong. What can be said with assurance is that courts of law are entrusted with the responsibility of resolving controversies arising under civil law and determining the legal or guilt innocence of a party charged with the violation of a criminal law.

To an ordinary citizen charged with a crime, the experience of going to court can be confusing, frightening, and frustrating. Courts follow legal rules and procedures that only lawyers and judges fully understand. The court system is intricate and often complex. Defendants are frightened because they experience a loss of control over their own destiny. The experience is frustrating because the court system does not always function as effectively as it should. In many jurisdictions delay is inevitable. Bargains and deals made by prosecutor and defense counsel are common. Bias, discrimination, and arbitrariness are just part of the system.

In this chapter we will examine the structure, function, rules, and procedures of courts. We will review their origins, the various types of court systems, the trial court process, and issues relating to the sentencing of convicted offenders.

THE ORIGINS OF COURTS

The word "court" is derived from the Latin of classical Rome (a contraction of *co*, meaning "together," and *hortus*, meaning "garden" or "yard"). Later, emperors, kings, dukes, and other nobles had estates or castles that were referred to as "courts"—the court of the king of England, the court of the queen of Spain, and so on. Important business was conducted at the court, including the business of resolving disputes and adjudging the guilt or innocence of persons accused of crime.

The earliest trial methods seem very strange to us today. In trial by combat, for example, the accuser and the accused, or their hired professional fighters, fought on foot or on horseback and in armor; the last person alive was the win-

ner. Trial was a game at court, very much like games played on basketball courts and tennis courts. What all these court games have in common is the fact that they are played in established public places, in accordance with established rules, and are judged by umpires or judges in the presence of the public. A nineteenth-century English cartoonist captured the spirit of an Anglo-American trial court proceeding when he depicted it as if it were a game of tennis. Opposing counsel bounce their arguments back and forth in front of the judge, who makes sure that the game is being played according to the rules. When the game is over, the judge pronounces the winner.

An American jurist and philosopher, Jerome Frank, has questioned the American "game" approach to the resolution of disputes in court.[1] Such an approach encourages advocates for the people or state (prosecutors) and for the defendant (defense counsel) to adopt and argue extreme positions. A judge is thus required to mediate between two inconsistent and often incompatible interpretations of fact and law. Is the truth really discovered when opposing counsel for the prosecution and defense argue it out, sometimes overstepping the bounds of propriety? Defenders of Anglo-American trial theory hold that a contest between combatants in open court will indeed resolve the issues fairly.

Some changes have been made in criminal procedure over the centuries, but the basic idea still holds: Anglo-American criminal trials are a game played by competitors; the players are combatants defending opposing positions, they are adversaries, and it is at court that the contest is fought.

THE U.S. COURT SYSTEM

The basic premises of the Anglo-American criminal process were well established in the fifteenth and sixteenth centuries and were ready to be imported into the North American colonies in the seventeenth century. The American colonies followed the British common law model. The courts of the colonies were common law courts, applying the common law of England with certain limitations that contributed to the drive for independence. When independence was declared, these courts became common law courts of the several states, subject only to the laws of the state legislatures. They still are: We have 50 state court systems in the United States.

The courts of these 50 jurisdictions are common law courts, the heirs of the common law of England as of 1776, applying the law in the common law fashion, as modified and amplified by state legislatures. There is, however, one big difference. In forming the United States, the original colonies granted the federal government the right to make and enforce, through federal courts, those laws that Congress was empowered to make. Consequently, we have two legal systems, one implemented by the state courts and another implemented by the federal courts.

State Courts

Most states have three distinct levels of courts of law: courts of limited or special jurisdiction, courts of general jurisdiction, and appellate courts, often at two levels (see Figure 18.1).

Courts of Limited or Special Jurisdiction
Courts of limited jurisdiction are limited by law as to the kinds of cases they can hear. Every town or city is likely to have a court with a justice of the peace, magistrate, or judge, not necessarily trained in law, who handles minor criminal cases (misdemeanors or violations), less serious civil suits (involving small sums of money), traffic and parking violations, and health law violations. These courts are called municipal courts, justice of the peace courts, and magistrate's courts. Courts of special jurisdiction include family courts, juvenile courts, and probate courts (which deal with estate matters).

Courts of General Jurisdiction At the next state level are the courts of general jurisdiction. These are a state's major trial courts. They have regular jurisdiction over all cases and controversies involving civil law and criminal law. Courts of general jurisdiction are county courts or, in less populous states, courts of a region that includes several counties. These

FIGURE 18.1   State court systems.

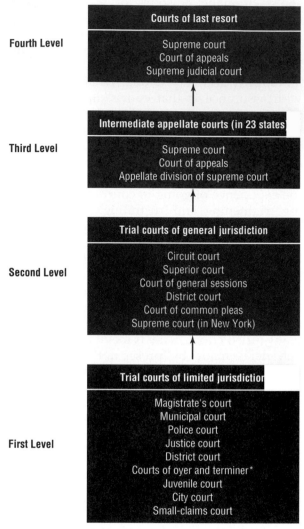

*As limited-jurisdiction courts are called in some states.

Source: Adapted from Abraham S. Blumberg, *Criminal Justice: Issues and Ironies* (New York: New Viewpoints, 1979), p. 150.

are called superior courts or district courts. The judges of such courts are law school graduates, often with extensive experience at the bar. They are elected or appointed. In criminal cases, the law grants a defendant the right to a jury trial. When a defendant chooses a jury trial, the court is composed of a judge, to deal with matters of law, and a jury, to deal with the facts of the case and to apply to them the law as laid down by the judge. All felony cases are heard in courts of

TABLE 18.1   Felony Sentences in State Courts

- State courts convicted 997,970 adults of a felony in 1996. That total represents an average growth of approximately 5 percent every year since 1988 (667,366).

- Drug offenders were 35 percent of felons convicted in state courts in 1996. Property offenders made up 30 percent; violent offenders, 17 percent; those convicted of weapons offenses and other nonviolent crimes made up the rest (18 percent).

- State courts sentenced 38 percent of convicted felons to a state prison, 31 percent to a local jail, and 31 percent to straight probation with no jail or prison time to serve.

- The 38 percent of convicted felons given a prison sentence in 1996 was the lowest percentage in all the years that the survey has been conducted.

- The average sentence to local jail was 6 months. The average probation sentence was almost 3 1/2 years. A fine was imposed on 20 percent of convicted felons, restitution on 14 percent, and community service on 6 percent; treatment was ordered for 6 percent.

- The average sentence length to state prison has decreased since 1988, but felons sentenced in 1996 were likely to serve more of that sentence before release.

- Trial convictions accounted for 9 percent of felony convictions in 1996. Guilty pleas accounted for the remaining 91 percent. Since 1988 guilty pleas have remained at about 90 percent of felony convictions.

- Nationally, of the felons convicted in 1996, 54 percent were white, 44 percent were black, and 2 percent were other races. The average age of felons convicted in state courts in 1996 was 31.

- Females account for an increasing portion of felons convicted in state courts. In 1988, females were 13 percent of convicted felons; in 1996, 16 percent.

- In 1996 the average time from arrest to sentencing was just over 7 months (219 days). Possibly because of increased workload (977,970 cases in 1996 versus 667,366 in 1988), courts took an average of 11 days longer to process cases in 1996 than in 1988.

Source: Jodi Brown, Patrick A. Langan, and David Levin, *Felony Sentences in State Courts, 1996* (Washington, D.C.: Bureau of Justice Statistics, 1998, revised July 30, 1999), p. 1.

general jurisdiction. Table 18.1 presents the highlights of felony sentences in courts across the United States.

Appellate Courts   All states have developed elaborate procedures of appeal for parties who are unsuccessful at trial. In some states the only appellate court is the state's supreme court; others provide an intermediate court of appeals. A person convicted of a crime has the right to appeal to an appellate court and ultimately to the court of last resort, the state supreme court, whenever the trial court is alleged to have erred on a point of law.

Federal Courts

The primary function of the federal courts is to apply and enforce all federal laws created by Congress. These statutes include a large body of federal criminal laws, which range from violations of the Migratory Bird Act to treason and piracy. Most of the federal criminal laws can be found in Title 18 of the U.S. Code. The federal courts have a second and perhaps even more important function: They are continually called upon to test the constitutionality of federal and state legislation and of court decisions.[2] For example, can a state pass and enforce a statute making it a criminal offense for black and white citizens to intermarry? In *Loving v. Virginia* (1967) the Supreme Court of the United States ruled no.[3] The states cannot create such a crime because it violates the equal protection clause of the Fourteenth Amendment to the U.S. Constitution.

In other words, the Supreme Court (a federal court) has the power to hold as a matter of law that a state cannot enact a statute that violates the U.S. Constitution. Consider another example: Can a state court receive in evidence at trial an object seized by state or local law enforcement officers in violation of the Fourth Amendment to the U.S. Constitution, which protects citizens against unreasonable searches and seizures? The Supreme Court ruled that doing so would be a violation of the due process guarantee of the Fourteenth Amendment, which protects all people in the United States.[4] Thus federal courts often ensure that citizens are afforded the rights that the U.S. Constitution guarantees them. And just as in the state systems, there are several levels of federal courts.

Federal Magistrates   At the lowest level of jurisdiction are the federal magistrates, formerly called United States commissioners. The magistrates not only have trial jurisdiction over minor federal offenses but also have the important right to issue warrants, such as arrest warrants.

United States District Courts   The trial courts in the federal system, called United States district courts, have both civil and criminal jurisdiction. There are 94 federal district courts, including those in Guam, the Virgin Islands, the Northern Marianas, and Puerto Rico. Every state

FIGURE 18.2 Number of defendants in criminal cases terminated in U.S. district court, by category of offense, 1982–1998.

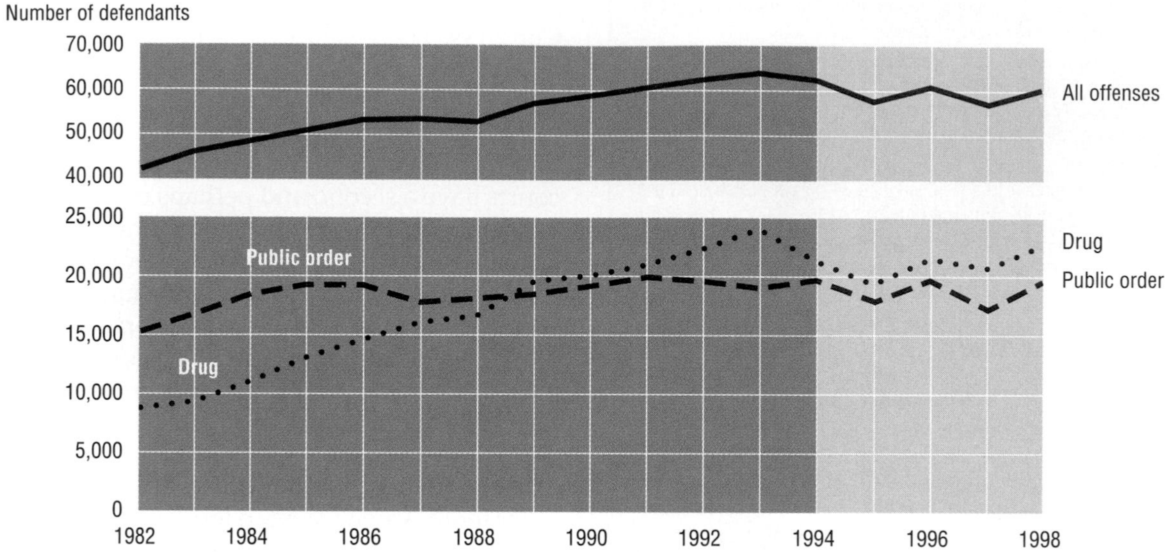

Number of defendants

All offenses

Drug

Public order

Note: Data for 1982 through 1993 are based on a 12-month calendar year reporting period ending December 31. Beginning in 1994, data are reported on the federal fiscal year running from October 1 through September 30.

Source: Federal Criminal Case Processing, 1998 (with trends 1982–98) (Washington, D.C., Bureau of Justice Statistics, 1999), p. 10.

has at least one such court, and the populous states have more than one. A total of 576 presidentially appointed judges sit in these courts. Increasingly, federal district courts are hearing drug and public-order cases (e.g., weapons and immigration cases). (See Figure 18.2.)

United States Circuit Courts of Appeals
An appeal of a conviction in a federal district court is heard by a United States circuit court of appeals. There are 13 appeals courts in the country: one in each of 11 areas (circuits) of the country plus one in the District of Columbia and another, also in Washington, D.C., called the Federal Circuit. It handles appeals that originate anywhere in the country when they pertain to such matters as patents and copyrights, some tax disputes, and suits against the federal government. There are 156 federal appeals court judges.

The original designation of states included within the federal circuits was made when most of the business of the federal courts was in the populous East and in the Midwest (Figure 18.3). With shifts in population to the West Coast, the Ninth Circuit, which covers a vast area, now has more business than any of the other courts.

The Supreme Court of the United States
The Supreme Court of the United States occupies a unique position in our system of government. It is the highest level of the third branch of government, the judiciary, and occupies a place of honor not equaled in any other country. Its chief justice is not just the chief justice of the Supreme Court but the chief justice of the United States. The chief justice and the eight associate justices are appointed by the president of the United States, with the advice and consent of the Senate.

The United States Supreme Court is the ultimate authority in interpreting the Constitution as it applies to both federal and state law; it also is the final authority in interpreting federal law. Thus, both federal and state cases may reach the Supreme Court.

Interaction between State Courts and Federal Courts

It is important not to view state and federal court systems as wholly independent or mutually exclusive. A legal controversy that arises in a state court may raise matters of federal law, especially

FIGURE 18.3   United States circuit courts of appeal.

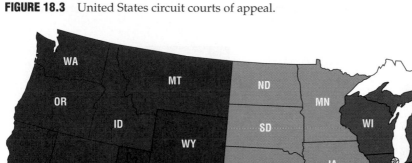

Not shown: D.C. Circuit, Washington, D.C.
            Federal Circuit, Washington, D.C.

constitutional questions. In such a case, a federal court may be asked to hear the case.

Suppose that on the tip of an anonymous informer, with no other corroborating evidence, a local magistrate issues a warrant authorizing the search of a college dormitory room for marijuana. Let us further suppose that a small bag of marijuana is found in the drawer of a desk that is used by two students. Both are arrested, tried in a local court, and convicted of the crime of possession of a controlled substance. Defense counsel claims that the search warrant was ille-

gally issued, because it was not based on the legally required evidence showing probable cause that a crime was committed. Therefore, the evidence, the marijuana, should never have been admitted in court. Let us suppose that the state trial judge does not agree with this defense.

Appeal and the Writ of Certiorari   The students decide to appeal their conviction, claiming that the trial judge committed a legal error by not excluding the evidence. Suppose that the state court of appeals (if there is one) rules against the

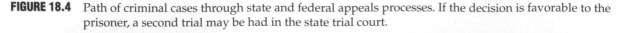

FIGURE 18.4   Path of criminal cases through state and federal appeals processes. If the decision is favorable to the prisoner, a second trial may be had in the state trial court.

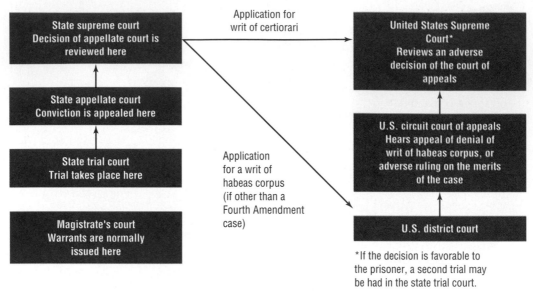

*If the decision is favorable to the prisoner, a second trial may be had in the state trial court.

students. They next appeal to the state supreme court. If the state supreme court rejects the argument as well, the next option is to appeal to the United States Supreme Court. The basis of this appeal is that the federal constitutional right to be free from search and seizure except on a warrant issued on the basis of probable cause (Fourth Amendment) was violated. This option is exercised by an application for a **writ of certiorari,** an order issued by a higher court (in this case the U.S. Supreme Court) directing a lower court (the state supreme court) to send to it the records of a case.

The Supreme Court may accept this case because it has established the rule that a search warrant issued on the basis of an unreliable informant's tip does not meet the reasonableness and probable-cause requirements of the Fourth Amendment.[5] But the U.S. Supreme Court gets thousands of appeals and applications for writs of certiorari every year; it can consider only very few. Normally the Court chooses to review a case only if it involves a substantial unresolved constitutional question, particularly one on which the findings of the various federal courts of appeals have diverged.

Habeas Corpus   Having been denied a writ of certiorari by the United States Supreme Court, the students may then apply for a writ of

habeas corpus at the federal district court. Historically, under the common law of England, a prisoner's detention could be tested by a judicial writ (command) to a jailer for an inquiry. Written in Latin, the writ contained the crucial words "habeas corpus," which means "you have the body [person] of." The text of the writ concluded with a request to produce the prisoner before the reviewing judge and to explain by what lawful authority the prisoner is being detained.[6] Used throughout the history of Anglo-American law, such inquiries still determine whether the Constitution was violated during the trial that resulted in the conviction that led to the imprisonment.

In our hypothetical case, until 1976, the students could have applied to the federal district court for a writ of habeas corpus. But in that year the Supreme Court held that the writ was no longer available in Fourth Amendment search-and-seizure cases because the federal courts were so flooded with applications for the writ that they could not manage the caseload.[7] Whenever the alleged constitutional violation pertains to issues other than search and seizure, the writ is still available, though on a restricted basis since 1996.

If the district court denies the writ of habeas corpus, the prisoner can appeal that decision to a

TABLE 18.2 Prosecutors' Offices with Districts Serving a Population of 1 Million or More, 1996

State	Office	Population	State	Office	Population
California	Los Angeles	9,127,751	California	Riverside	1,417,425
Illinois	Cook	5,096,540	Massachusetts	Middlesex District	1,412,561
Texas	Harris	3,126,966	Ohio	Cuyahoga	1,401,552
California	San Diego	2,655,463	New York	Suffolk	1,356,896
California	Orange	2,636,888	California	Alameda	1,328,139
Arizona	Maricopa	2,611,327	Texas	Bexar	1,318,322
New York	Kings	2,273,966	Texas	Tarrant	1,305,185
Florida	11th Judicial Circuit	2,076,175	New York	Nassau	1,303,389
Michigan	Wayne	2,039,819	Pennsylvania	Allegheny	1,296,037
Texas	Dallas	2,000,192	New York	Bronx	1,193,775
New York	Queens	1,980,643	Florida	6th Judicial Circuit	1,180,443
Washington	King	1,619,411	Michigan	Oakland	1,162,098
California	Santa Clara	1,599,604	California	Sacramento	1,117,275
California	San Bernardino	1,598,358	Minnesota	Hennepin	1,058,746
New York	New York	1,533,774	Nevada	Clark	1,048,717
Pennsylvania	Philadelphia	1,478,002	Ohio	Franklin	1,013,724
Florida	17th Judicial Circuit	1,438,228	Missouri	St. Louis	1,003,807

Note: 34 prosecutor's offices serve 24 percent of the U.S. population.

Source: Carol J. DeFrances and Greg W. Steadman, *Prosecutors in State Courts, 1996* (Washington, D.C.: Bureau of Justice Statistics, 1998), p. 4.

U.S. circuit court of appeals. If that court does not overrule the district court, the prisoner can appeal again to the U.S. Supreme Court. Figure 18.4 depicts the entire process.

Lawyers in the Court System

In every criminal case an attorney represents the government, whether county, city, or state. That attorney is called a **prosecutor.** (See Table 18.2.) On the other side of the case is the lawyer who has been retained by the person charged with an offense or who has been assigned by the court if the defendant is indigent. That attorney is called the **defense counsel.**

Prosecutors and Their Duties Prosecutors are government officials who represent the people of a particular jurisdiction. They may be appointed or elected. Prosecutors are responsible for some of the most important initial responses to crime. They screen suspects arrested by the police, decide whether or not to press charges, argue the case on behalf of the government, and often make recommendations regarding sentencing. More than 8000 state and local agencies are involved in prosecution. They include the offices of district attorney, city corporation counsel, and state attorney general. Federal crimes are prosecuted by United States attorneys, who are appointed by the president.

Prosecutorial Discretion Prosecutors can exercise a variety of options that have far-reaching effects on an individual's freedom, life, property, reputation, and well-being. This power is unmatched by that of any other official in the American criminal justice system. Prosecutors are relatively free to choose their causes, cases, and targets for prosecution.[8] They have complete discretion in three areas of pretrial decision making: (1) whether or not to file a criminal charge, (2) how to set the level of seriousness of the offense to be charged, and (3) when to cease prosecution.[9] In most jurisdictions, prosecutors are empowered by statute to "prosecute for all offenses." As the legal scholar Abraham S. Goldstein has noted, however, this exclusive authority to prosecute does not confer an obligation to do so in every case.[10] Prosecutors have discretion in the way they handle cases.

Prosecutorial Roles   Prosecutors play a variety of functional and occupational roles, which are not necessarily specified by law. Abraham Blumberg has identified several such roles:

- *Collection agent.* In smaller communities, prosecutors collect and dispense money to cover debts, such as family support payments, proceeds from bad checks, and debt arising from fraud.

- *Dispenser of justice/power broker–fixer.* Prosecutors weigh the available penalties associated with certain charges and, by using their discretion, dispense justice. In political situations, they mediate between disputants by the use and threat of sanctions.

- *Political enforcer.* A prosecutor may prosecute a case for reasons and purposes other than a desire to achieve a just conviction—perhaps to seek vengeance or notoriety, to deter certain conduct, or to damage a reputation.

- *Overseer of police.* The prosecutor is also known to act as a magistrate, continually reviewing the work of the police.[11]

Defense Counsel.   All persons accused of a crime for which jail or prison is the possible penalty have a right to counsel under the Sixth Amendment to the U.S. Constitution.[12] A defense attorney ensures that the legal rights of an accused person are fully protected at every stage in the criminal justice process. Defendants who can afford counsel retain an attorney of their choice or, very rarely, choose to represent themselves. An accused person who is unable to afford an attorney may be represented free of charge by counsel coming from any of three sources, depending on the jurisdiction:

Crime Surfing

www.courttv.com/

Catch the latest and greatest trial on the Web.

- A *public defender program.* Statewide and local public defenders belong to public or private nonprofit organizations that provide free legal counsel.

- *An assigned-counsel system.* Judges appoint attorneys who are in private practice as they are needed.

- *A contract system.* Contracts are awarded to bar associations, private law firms, or individual attorneys who agree to provide legal counsel on a regular basis.

THE ROLE OF THE TRIAL JUDGE

In discussing the criminal justice process, we noted the important role judges play during proceedings before trial. They grant release at various stages, preside over first appearances of arrested persons in court and over preliminary hearings, issue orders and rule on motions, accept plea bargains, impanel grand juries, and instruct juries in their tasks.

The role traditionally associated with a judge is that of a person who presides over trials.

Arraignment

A trial begins with the **arraignment,** a formal proceeding in open court at which the grand jury hands down its indictment. Not all states, however, require a grand-jury indictment to initiate prosecutions.

At the arraignment, in the presence of the defendant and the defense counsel, the person named in the **indictment** (accusation by the grand jury) or **information** (accusation by the prosecutor) is asked to **plead** to the charge. The defendant has two or sometimes three options:

- The defendant may plead *guilty* to the charges contained in the various counts of the indictment, thereby admitting all the facts alleged to have occurred, as well as their legal implications. Under those circumstances no trial is necessary. The trial judge need only make certain that the pleas have been advisedly taken and that the facts indeed support the guilt of the defendant. The judge may then accept the plea of guilty and sentence the offender.

- The defendant may plead *not guilty,* thereby denying everything and putting

An artist's drawing shows Unabomber suspect Theodore J. Kaczynski, center on monitor at left, during a video hearing in Newark, New Jersey, on December 10, 1996, where he pleaded not guilty to charges that he sent a mail bomb that killed a New Jersey advertising executive. Kaczynski was in a courtroom in Sacramento, California. He was subsequently convicted and sent to a psychiatric prison.

on the prosecution the burden of proving beyond a reasonable doubt all the facts alleged in the indictment.

- In most jurisdictions, the defendant may also plead *no contest,* or *nolo contendere,* with the approval of the prosecution and the court. By this plea the defendant admits criminal liability for the purposes of the immediate proceeding only. This procedure has the practical advantage of avoiding the implications of guilt in other proceedings (a civil suit for damages, for example).

Did You Know

... that DNA evidence is admissible in criminal trials in 46 states? Maine, North Dakota, Rhode Island, and Utah exclude such evidence.

Pretrial Motions

Counsel for either side, defense or prosecution, may make a multitude of **motions,** or official requests to the judge, at any appropriate moment from arrest until after the trial is over. The majority of such motions are made before trial; each requires a hearing and sometimes a separate minitrial. Among the many types of motions are the following:

- A motion for a severance, by which a defendant claims that it would be prejudicial to his or her case to be tried together with other defendants charged in the indictment.

- A motion for a change of venue, which is made when pretrial publicity makes it impossible to get a fair trial in the county where the crime was committed.

- A motion to quash the indictment on the grounds that the evidence presented is insufficient to establish probable cause.

- A motion for a sanity hearing, which is made when the defendant claims that mental illness deprives him or her of legal responsibility.

- A motion to suppress illegally obtained evidence.

- A motion for discovery of evidence in the hands of the prosecution.

- A motion to dismiss the case for want of adequate evidence or for some other cause.

Release Decisions

Once again the trial judge must decide whether to release the defendant, this time for the period

TABLE 18.3   Types of Pretrial Release

Financial Bond	Alternative Release Options
Fully secured bail. The defendant posts the full amount of bail with the court.	*Release on recognizance (ROR).* The court releases the defendant on his promise that he will appear in court as required.
Privately secured bail. A bondsman signs a promissory note to the court for the bail amount and charges the defendant a fee for the service (usually 10% of the bail amount). If the defendant fails to appear, the bondsman must pay the court the full amount. Frequently the bondsman requires the defendant to post collateral in addition to the fee.	*Conditional release.* The court releases the defendant subject to his following specific conditions set by the court, such as attending drug treatment therapy or staying away from the complaining witness.
Percentage bail. The courts allow the defendant to deposit a percentage (usually 10 percent) of the full bail with the court. The full amount of the bail is required if the defendant fails to appear. The percentage bail is returned after disposition of the case, although the court often retains 1 percent for administrative costs.	*Third-party custody.* The defendant is released into the custody of an individual or agency that promises to ensure his appearance in court. No monetary transactions are involved in this type of release.
Unsecured bail. The defendant pays no money to the court but is liable for the full amount of bail should he fail to appear.	

Source: U.S. Department of Justice, Bureau of Justice Statistics, *Report to the Nation on Crime and Justice: The Data* (Washington, D.C.: U.S. Government Printing Office, 1983), p. 58.

between the arraignment and the main phase of the trial—a period that may last weeks. The decision has far-reaching consequences, summarized by the President's Commission on Law Enforcement and the Administration of Justice:

> The importance of this decision to any defendant is obvious. A released defendant is one who can live with and support his family, maintain his ties to his community, and busy himself with his own defense by searching for witnesses and evidence and by keeping in close touch with his lawyer. An imprisoned defendant is subjected to the squalor, idleness, and possible criminalizing effect of jail. He may be confined for something he did not do; some jailed defendants are ultimately acquitted. He may be confined while presumed innocent only to be freed when found guilty; many jailed defendants, after they have been convicted, are placed on probation rather than imprisoned. The community also relies on the magistrate for protection when he makes his decision about releasing a defendant. If a released defendant fails to appear for trial, the law is flouted. If a released defendant commits crimes, the community is endangered.[13]

The various types of pretrial release are summarized in Table 18.3.

In view of the large number of indigent defendants today, is it reasonable to base release decisions on financial means? A movement to ensure fairness in bail decisions began in the early 1960s in response to the perception of discrimination against defendants who could not afford bail. The Manhattan Bail Project, sponsored by the Vera Institute of Justice, found that it was possible to minimize no-shows and to predict with reasonable accuracy whether an accused would return to court on the basis of the person's offense history, family ties, and employment record. The project's early findings revealed a low default rate.

Through the 1960s and early 1970s, similar programs flourished throughout the country. Perhaps the most promising reform attempt may be credited to the criminologist John Goldkamp, who, with the assistance of Michael Gottfredson, designed uniform guidelines for bail decision makers (see Figure 18.5).[14] By creating a two-dimensional grid on which they could plot the severity of the offense against a series of variables, such as type of crime, number of arrests, age, and community ties, these criminologists enabled judges to reduce significantly the disparities in decisions regarding bail.

Recent studies show that the pretrial release rate has been fairly high for several years—namely, 63 to 66 percent of persons indicted for felonies in state courts, but only 24 percent of murder defendants, 48 percent of rape defendants, 50 percent of robbery defendants, and 51

FIGURE 18.5 Guidelines for bail decision makers.

			LEAST SERIOUS CHARGES				MOST SERIOUS CHARGES									"n" negative / "p" positive		
LOWEST RISK OF FAILURE TO APPEAR AND REARREST	ROR 01*	ROR 06	ROR 11	ROR 16	ROR 21	ROR 26	ROR 31	ROR $1,500 36	ROR- $1,500 41	$800- $3,000 46	$1,000- $3,000 51	$2,000- $7,500 56	I (+ 19 to + 13)	Risk Severity Dimension — Risk Groups	CONSTANT		4
	ROR 02	ROR 07	ROR 12	ROR 17	ROR 22	ROR 27	ROR 32	$500- $1,500 37	ROR $1,500 42	$800- $3,000 47	$1,000- $3,000 52	$2,000- $7,500 57	II (+ 12 to + 10)		crim categ		
															arrests		
	ROR 03	ROR 08	ROR 13	ROR 18	ROR 23	ROR 28	ROR- $500 33	ROR- $1,500 38	$500- $1,500 43	$1,000- $3,000 48	$1,000- $3,000 53	$2,000- $7,500 58	III (+ 9 exactly)		cr + arrs		
GREATEST RISK OF FAILURE TO APPEAR AND REARREST															pend'g chgs		
	ROR 04	ROR 09	ROR 14	ROR- $1,000 19	$500- $1,000 24	$500- $1,500 29	$500- $1,500 34	$500- $2,000 39	$800- $2,500 44	$1,000- $5,000 49	$1,000- $5,000 54	$2,500- $7,500 59	IV (+ 8 to + 4)		FTA's		
															age of def't		
	ROR 05	ROR- $500 10	ROR- $1,000 15	$500- $1,000 20	$500- $1,000 25	$500- $1,500 30	$500- $2,000 35	$500- $2,000 40	$800- $3,000 45	$1,000- $5,000 50	$1,500- $5,000 55	$3,000- $10,000 60	V (+ 3 to − 13)		age + FTA's		
															Comm'ty ties		
															Col Total		
	1	2	3	4	5	6	7	8	9	10	11	12	RISK GROUPS (points)		Subtract "n" (if smaller) TOTAL POSITIVE		

Charge Severity Dimension — Charge Levels

(*Nos & ltrs for coding purposes)

Selected Guidelines Range:

⟹

Actual Decision:

☐ ROR   ☐

_____ (amount)

IF OUTSIDE GUIDELINES, CHECK REASON BELOW:

A* B C D E N/A N/A F
☐ ☐ ☐ ☐ ☐   ☐

IF YOU GO BELOW THE GUIDELINES AMOUNT—SHOW REASON [DEPARTING FROM GUIDELINES BY USING A LOWER FIGURE (ROR, or lower financial bail, than in the guidelines decision) CHECK THE APPLICABLE BOX(ES) ACROSS TO THE LEFT].

(LIKELY) Prosecution Will Be Withdrawn
(GOOD)
(VERY UNLIKELY)
Sponsor at Prel. Arr.
Court Room Demeanor of Defendant
Physical or Mental Health Concerns
Interference with Witness(es)
VERSUS
CURRENT/OUTSTANDING Warrants/Detainers/Wanted Cards
POSSIBILITY of Mandatory Sentence
Cause Guardian to Be Notified of Arrest
OTHER (Indicate DIRECTION OF DEPARTURE)

(Show REASON to Right) ⟹ _____

_____

_____

REASONS ⟹

[DEPARTING FROM GUIDELINES BY USING A HIGHER BAIL AMOUNT(money bail instead of ROR, or a greater money amount than within guidelines) CHECK BOX(es) TO RIGHT]
IF YOU GO ABOVE THE GUIDELINES AMOUNT—SHOW REASON

Will Be Convicted (LIKELY)
VERSUS

☐ ☐ ☐ ☐ ☐ ☐ ☐ ☐
G H I J K L M N

Guidelines Decision By _____ J.

Source: John Goldkamp and Michael Gottfredson, *Judicial Decision Guidelines for Bail: The Philadelphia Experiment* (Washington, D.C.: National Institute of Justice, 1983).

percent of burglary defendants. Of those released, 14 percent were rearrested while on pretrial release, but only 10 percent of those on a felony charge. Another 3 percent failed to appear in court.[15] It appears that nonfinancial release mechanisms can be used without increasing the risk of pretrial misconduct.[16]

Despite efforts to make the bail system equitable, the tide has shifted toward placing restraints on pretrial release and instituting provisions for pretrial detention. Many states now place significant restrictions on pretrial release decisions. Some jurisdictions, such as Washington, D.C., have instituted preventive detention statutes that authorize judges to deny bail to apparently dangerous offenders and keep them in custody. In fact, the Bail Reform Act of 1984 permits preventive detention in the federal system where "no condition or combination of conditions will reasonably assure the appearance of the person as required and the safety of any other person, and the community."[17]

Plea Bargaining

The arraignment gives prosecutor and defense counsel their last significant opportunity to offer the court a negotiated plea. As we noted in Chapter 16, the vast majority of defendants prefer to plead guilty to a lesser charge at any step of the process before trial. The inclination to make such a bargain is particularly great at arraignment, when the defendant may realize he or she stands a good chance of being convicted. Though an acquittal cannot be ruled out, the near certainty of a significant period of incarceration if convicted is an incentive to bargain or negotiate. Statistics support such considerations. While the conviction rate in felony cases that go to trial varies from jurisdiction to jurisdiction, it is generally high. A study of 26 jurisdictions found a median conviction rate of 73 percent.[18] Prosecutors are concerned about the expense of a trial, a shortage of staff, and perhaps a long wait for available courtroom space and a trial judge.

Plea bargains may provide efficiency in the criminal justice system, but their use on such a large scale is fraught with considerable danger. Not the least of which is the use of the plea bar-

gain as a mechanism of control that is exercised to discipline a highly visible section of society, those who are swept off the street and into jails, and then given 15 seconds to accept a plea bargain.[19]

The National Advisory Commission on Criminal Justice Standards and Goals recommended in 1971 that the practice of plea bargaining be abolished: "As soon as possible, but in no event later than 1978, negotiations between prosecutors and defendants—either personally or through their attorneys—concerning concessions to be made in return for guilty pleas should be prohibited."[20] According to the commission, abolishing plea bargaining would remove the incentive for prosecutors to charge an offender with a crime more serious than they expect to be able to prove; it would increase the number of trials only insignificantly; and, most important, it would increase the rationality and fairness of the criminal trial process.[21]

Abolition of plea bargaining might also restore the constitutional right to a trial by jury, which defendants are now manipulated into giving up. It would prevent the prosecution from achieving victory on the basis of insufficient or even illegally obtained evidence, which it can currently hide in a plea bargain.

But would the elimination of plea bargaining really have only an insignificant effect on the caseloads of judges, juries, prosecutors, and defense counsel? Only a 10 percent increase in trials, some experts claim, might cause the court apparatus to stop functioning.[22] But it also has been argued, on the basis of the experience of the few jurisdictions that have abolished plea bargaining—Alaska, New Orleans, El Paso, Blackhawk County in Iowa, Maricopa County in Arizona, Oakland County in Michigan, and Multnomah County in Oregon—that most defendants who consider themselves guilty will plead guilty anyway in the hope of a lighter sentence.[23]

Some evidence on the impact of the abolition of plea bargaining is beginning to come in, most notably for Alaska, for which it was reported that, despite abolition, plea bargaining is alive and well.[24] Rather than abolish plea bargaining, most jurisdictions have made it more open, more regulated, and fairer. The Supreme Court has insisted that the voluntariness of the plea and an understanding of its implications must be demonstrated in open court and that the prosecution must stick to its part of the bargain.[25] In federal courts the plea-bargaining process has actually been turned into a minitrial, consisting of such an "inquiry as shall satisfy [the court] that there is a factual basis for the plea."[26]

THE TRIAL

Trial courts are established to find and express the communal judgment under law as to the guilt or innocence of an accused person. The public, in whose name the judgment is rendered, is supposed to participate actively in the process. Indictments read "The People of the State of . . . versus John Doe" or "Jane Roe."

What specifically is meant by "the people"? One answer is that the judge, who is elected by the people or appointed by somebody who was elected by the people, represents a consensus of the people. When an indictment is handed down and a jury trial held, the people are directly represented by a cross section of the community participating in the grand jury that indicts the defendant and the trial jury that tries the defendant. Any citizen is allowed into the courtroom to witness the proceedings, and seats for spectators are provided. Indeed, in pioneer days, trial day at the county seat was major entertainment. In some states, television coverage of court proceedings has taken the place of direct and total community participation.

Selecting the Jury: Voir Dire

After a plea of not guilty, the first step is the impaneling of the jury, which is called the *petit*, or *petty*, jury, in contrast to the grand jury. Twelve is the traditional number of trial jurors. Some states use fewer jurors for trials involving crimes of lesser seriousness. Ordinarily, several alternate jurors are selected to take the place of any juror who might become disabled during the trial.

Jury selection is usually guided by three objectives. Attorneys have to:

- Determine whether prospective jurors meet the minimum qualifications to sit as jurors (age and residency requirements).

- Determine the impartiality of prospective jurors.

- Obtain sufficient information on prospective jurors to enable the attorneys to exclude "for cause" any who may be prejudiced for or against the defendant.

The process by which lawyers and the judge examine a prospective juror to determine his or her acceptability is known as **voir dire.** Attorneys for each side attempt to pick jurors who might be just a little more understanding or sympathetic to their arguments. They can exclude people they think will be unsympathetic by means of **peremptory challenges,** or objections to potential jurors for which no explanation is required. Each side has a fixed number of such challenges; usually the defense has more than the prosecution. Either side may use an unlimited number of **challenges for cause,** which are intended to keep persons with a conflict of interest off the jury. A person related by birth or by marriage to any of the parties connected with the case, for example, would almost certainly be challenged for cause.

Jury selection has yet another aspect: Skilled attorneys believe they can subliminally inject certain biases into potential jurors to ensure that evidence introduced at trial will be understood in a particular way. In a sense, they attempt to create sympathetic understanding for the position of the prosecution or the defense, as the case may be. The psychologists David Suggs and Bruce Sales, however, have noted:

> [S]uggestions from the legal literature [on ways to ensure sympathetic jurors] for the most part are based on hypotheses and folklore. Very little, if any, empirical work has been performed to substantiate the reliability and validity of the [jury selection] techniques proposed by legal writers.[27]

Nevertheless, consulting firms make their services available to attorneys, to assist them in selecting sympathetic jurors and in influencing them to see the case sympathetically.

The Proceedings

Once a jury has been chosen or the defendant has waived a jury trial and consented to a trial by the judge alone, proceedings begin. The prosecution makes an opening statement, outlining the case and previewing what it proposes to prove and how. The defense may then make or postpone its opening statement. It is the prosecution's burden to introduce the evidence against the defendant. All evidence necessary to prove the case must be introduced in court directly and in compliance with the rules of evidence.

Evidence The rules of evidence have evolved over centuries. One prominent rule says that hearsay cannot be used because, when information is repeated and obtained through third parties, it tends to become distorted. The exclusionary rule prohibits the introduction of any evidence that does not meet the strict standards of the law of evidence.[28] But the exclusionary rule is also used to keep out of court evidence that was obtained in violation of constitutional rights. For example, if a suspect is not given the Miranda warnings, any evidence obtained through police-initiated questioning after arrest may be excluded from trial. On constitutional issues, the exclusionary rule, for example, is a legal standard that binds not only the federal courts but all state courts as well.[29]

Evidence found as a result of illegally received information cannot be introduced as evidence at trial either. It is regarded as "the fruit of the poisonous tree" and thus is tainted.[30] The Supreme Court has made exceptions to the constitutional exclusionary rule, for example, by creating the "inevitable discovery" rule. Under this rule, evidence obtained in violation of a constitutional prohibition is admissible if it would have been discovered anyway.[31]

During the entire evidentiary stage of the trial, the defense watches the prosecution carefully, objecting immediately when it appears that one of the rules of evidence may have been violated. If the breach of the rule is so grave that the defendant's chance of a fair trial has been prejudiced, the defense may even move for a mistrial. If that motion is granted, the prosecution will have to start over again before a new jury. The judge rules on all motions and objections. If the judge rules against the defendant, defense counsel will have the ruling placed on record as a potential cause to appeal a verdict and judgment of guilty. Every witness called by

either party is subject to cross-examination by the other party.

When the prosecution has completed its case, the defense has several options. If the evidence against the defendant is poor, the defense may move for a directed verdict of acquittal or a motion to dismiss. A **directed verdict** is a verdict pronounced by the judge. A **motion to dismiss** is a request that the proceedings be terminated. The defense can also address the jury in a postponed opening statement to influence an acquittal.

But the defense is more likely to present its own evidence—alibi witnesses, expert witnesses, character witnesses, even the defendant. The defendant is under no obligation to testify in his or her own behalf. A defendant who does testify is subject to cross-examination by the prosecution.

The Task of the Jury In the normal course of a trial, after both sides have presented their evidence, closing arguments are presented by the defense and the prosecution. The jurors then must apply the law to the facts that they have heard and determine the guilt or innocence of the defendant. So that they may do so responsibly, the judge gives them instructions—directions concerning the way they should go about deciding the case. Often both the prosecution and the defense will offer the judge instructions on the law that they propose should be given to the jury.

Defense and prosecution usually differ on how the jury should be instructed, especially on how the instructions should be phrased. Once again the judge takes ultimate responsibility for instructing the jury and may even prefer his or her own version of the instructions to those offered by defense and prosecution. If the defense counsel objects to the proposed instructions on grounds of law, the objections are noted for a potential appeal.

After receiving their instructions, the jurors retire to the jury room for their deliberations, which are guided by a foreman—one of their number whom they select to preside over their deliberations. The majority of juries have little difficulty in arriving at a verdict: guilty, not guilty, guilty of the crime charged in a lesser degree, or guilty of some but not all of the crimes charged. Some juries, however, do have difficulty reaching

a verdict. In the celebrated "preppy murder case" (*People v. Chambers*), the jury wavered for 9 days between overwhelming majorities for and against the defendant, until defense and prosecution both realized the dilemma and agreed on a plea bargain, thus taking the jury out of the picture.[32]

Jury Decision Making

For several decades psychologists have studied juror decision making, courtroom testimony, and eyewitness identification and testimony.[33] In examining the power of eyewitness testimony, psychologist Elizabeth Loftus conducted a mock-trial experiment in which subjects played the roles of jurors, listened to testimony, and were asked to reach a verdict. The mock jurors received a detailed description of a grocery store robbery in which the store's owner and granddaughter were killed.

Loftus presented three versions of the evidence. One group of subjects was informed that there was no eyewitness, only circumstantial evidence. The second group was told a store clerk had testified that the defendant shot the two victims. The third group was told of the store clerk's identification but was informed that on cross-examination his testimony was discredited because he had not been wearing his glasses and his eyesight was poor. The result: 18 percent of the first group, 72 percent of the second group, and 68 percent of the third group found the defendant guilty. The results of this research suggest that eyewitness testimony, even if contradicted or impeached, can be very persuasive to jurors.

Psychologists have also studied the influence of personal prejudice and expectations on the validity of eyewitness accounts. To address this question, Albert H. Hastorf and Hadley Cantrill showed a film of a football game between Dartmouth and Princeton to students at each school and asked them to note the number of infractions. Princeton students reported twice as many infractions by Dartmouth as their own team had made, and twice the number that Dartmouth students noted about their own team.[34] This study and the hundreds that followed it demonstrate the weakness of eyewitness accounts. Consider the findings of just a few of these other studies:

- The accuracy of older eyewitnesses is reduced in certain situations.[35]
- Both whites and blacks do better at identifying suspects of their own race.[36]
- Experience in recalling details of events witnessed (such as a police officer might have) does not necessarily improve recall.[37]
- The credibility of a witness is increased significantly by a display of confidence.[38]

There is a large body of research evaluating the process of juror decision making and whether or not extralegal issues influence jurors. Studies have demonstrated that jurors are sometimes influenced by their own personal characteristics (age, race, gender, occupation) and by the characteristics of defendant and victim. In fact, mock jurors who evaluated the culpability of attractive versus unattractive defendants charged with identical crimes ascribed greater guilt to the unattractive ones.[39] Other studies that considered the character of the victim found that such variables as marital status, unorthodox lifestyle, and past sexual experience can play a role in jurors' decision making.

If class and race affiliation appear to influence jurors' verdicts, then the question becomes: What is a jury of one's peers? Must race and social status be reflected in the composition of a jury? Are we headed for a jury quota system? The jury verdicts in cases that led to and arose out of the 1992 Los Angeles race riots, and in the 1995 O. J. Simpson case, underline the significance of this question.

SENTENCING: TODAY AND TOMORROW

Sentencing has been characterized as the most controversial of all the stages in the criminal justice process.[40] This is not surprising. At earlier stages the defendant benefits from the presumption of innocence, and certain safeguards are built into the adversarial system: due process, fundamental fairness, and impartiality. Once the defendant is convicted, however, the focus shifts away from these concerns to the imposition of punishment.

For over 50 years the International Court of Justice, an organ of the United Nations, located at The Hague in the Netherlands, has been adjudicating disputes among nations. The Court's 15 judges have handled the cases before them with great dignity, and with success—except in rare cases where nations refused to comply with a decision. This court has no jurisdiction in criminal matters, although questions of criminal law sometimes play a role in decision making.

Following World War II, two international tribunals, established by the Allied Powers, tried German and Japanese war criminals, in Nuremberg and Tokyo, respectively. These were ad hoc, or temporary, tribunals that ceased to exist when their job was done, although policy makers had recommended that those courts be made permanent, for future emergencies.

These policy makers were right. In 1993 the U.N. Security Council found it necessary to establish another ad hoc tribunal, the International Criminal Tribunal for the Former Yugoslavia, followed shortly by the establishment of another such tribunal for Rwanda. There is now a great deal of evidence before these courts of massive criminal violations of human rights law, war crimes, genocide, torture, mass rapes, and other crimes.

The tribunal for the former Yugoslavia, also located at The Hague, has indicted over 90 persons, mostly Bosnian Serbs, but also some Croats and Muslims. The number of defendants actually in the custody of the court started with zero, and skeptics called the work of the court an exercise in futility. Yet by the beginning of 2000, nearly 50 percent of those indicted were in custody, and their number continues

The United Nations International Tribunal in The Hague produced its first conviction and handed down a 10-year prison sentence for crimes against humanity in late November 1996. Drazen Erdemovic, a 25-year-old foot soldier in the Bosnian Serb Army, was convicted for his participation in a massacre. His unit took Muslim men in groups of 10 and shot them; they killed 1200 men in 5 hours.

to increase. There will always be some defendants whom the court will not reach. Their fate, however, is not a happy one. Shunned and hunted, they will be unable to leave their lairs for fear of being arrested when they step across their territorial borders.

The Rwanda tribunal has the opposite problem: Not too few, but too many defendants are in custody—about 70,000. The inadequately funded U.N. tribunal is struggling to sort the evidence and prepare indictments. At present, 36 suspects have been indicted.

Meanwhile, a treaty that created a permanent international criminal court was approved at a U.N. conference in July 1998. The jurisdiction of the court, which will be based in The Hague,

extends to many already existing international crimes, principally genocide, war crimes, terrorism, and possibly international narcotic drug trafficking. The court has no jurisdiction over domestic crimes as contained in the penal codes of all countries.

Questions for Discussion

1. Suppose that in an effort to reach a peace accord, the cooperation of persons likely to be indicted by an international criminal court is needed. Should the court grant immunity from prosecution or engage in plea bargaining?

2. In whose custody should convicted war criminals be kept? Where? By what standards?

Judges can choose from a variety of sentencing options, ranging from the death penalty to the imposition of a fine:

- *Death penalty.* In 37 jurisdictions, judges may impose a sentence of death for any offense designated a capital crime, most commonly murder.

- *Incarceration.* A defendant may be sentenced to serve a term in a state or federal prison or in a local jail.

FIGURE 18.6   What factors explain a judge's prediction of risk and decision to incarcerate?

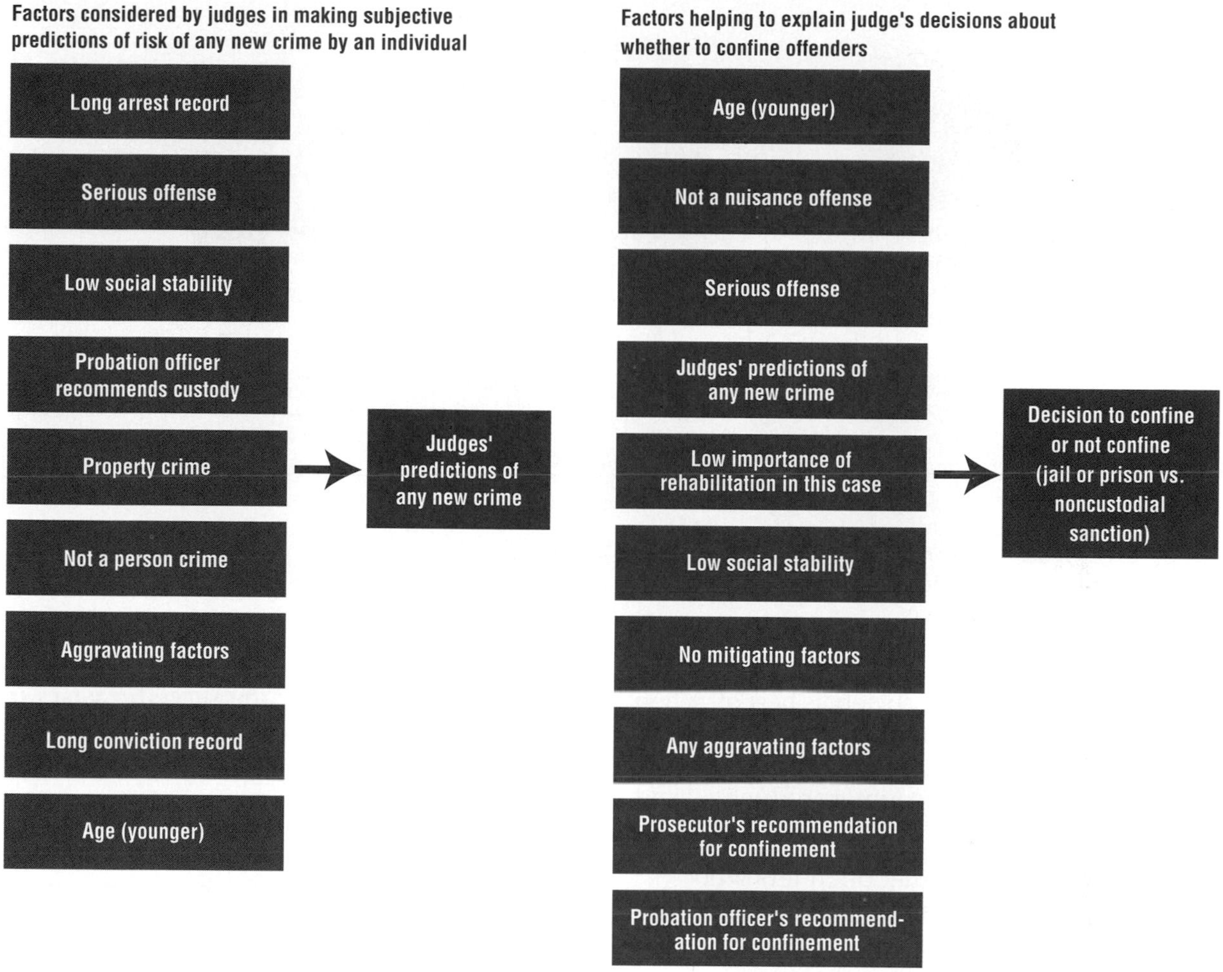

Factors considered by judges in making subjective predictions of risk of any new crime by an individual

- Long arrest record
- Serious offense
- Low social stability
- Probation officer recommends custody
- Property crime
- Not a person crime
- Aggravating factors
- Long conviction record
- Age (younger)

→ Judges' predictions of any new crime

Factors helping to explain judge's decisions about whether to confine offenders

- Age (younger)
- Not a nuisance offense
- Serious offense
- Judges' predictions of any new crime
- Low importance of rehabilitation in this case
- Low social stability
- No mitigating factors
- Any aggravating factors
- Prosecutor's recommendation for confinement
- Probation officer's recommendation for confinement

→ Decision to confine or not confine (jail or prison vs. noncustodial sanction)

Source: Don M. Gottfredson, *Effects of Judges' Sentencing Decisions on Criminal Careers* (Washington, D.C.: National Institute of Justice, 1999), pp. 5, 8.

- *Probation.* A defendant may be sentenced to a period of community supervision with special limitations. Violation of these conditions may result in incarceration.

- *Split sentence.* A judge may split the sentence between a period of incarceration and a period of probation.

- *Restitution.* An offender may be required to provide financial reimbursement to cover the cost of a victim's losses.

- *Community service.* A judge may require an offender to spend a period of time performing public-service work.

- *Fine.* The offender may be required to pay a certain sum of money as a penalty

and/or as an alternative to or in conjunction with incarceration.

What determines which option will be chosen? More often than not, judges are given discretion and thus are guided by their own sentencing philosophy and perception of risk (see Figure 18.6). Their discretion may be limited by a statute that prescribes a prison term of a specified length or a range of prison terms. Before we consider the various limits and guidelines, we need to review the most prominent philosophies of punishment: incapacitation, deterrence, retribution, rehabilitation, and just deserts.

Incapacitation

"Lock 'em up and throw away the key" reflects the belief that, given the frequency with which

"*Your Honor, we the jury blame the victim.*"

offenders commit crime, society is best off when criminals are incarcerated for long periods of time—or incapacitated. Yet long sentences may be unjust, unnecessary, counterproductive, and inappropriate:

- They are unjust if other offenders who have committed the same crime receive shorter sentences.

- They are unnecessary if the offender is not likely to offend again.

- They are counterproductive whenever prison increases the risk of habitual criminal behavior.

- They are inappropriate if the offender has committed an offense entailing insignificant harm to the community.

Research evidence on incapacitation is equivocal. Joan Petersilia and Peter Greenwood, for example, suggest that the crime rate could be reduced by as much as 15 percent if every convicted felon were imprisoned for 1 year.[41] Earlier investigations provided widely different estimates. Revel Shinnar and his colleagues projected that an 80 percent reduction in violent crime rates was possible if everyone

convicted of a violent crime served 5 years in prison. Another study, however, concluded that only a 4 percent reduction would result from that policy.[42]

Most of the empirical research in the area of incapacitation focuses on criminal behavior that persists over many years. Such research examines how criminal careers begin, how they progress, and why they terminate. As we saw in Chapter 2, Marvin Wolfgang and his associates determined that two-thirds of all violent crimes and more than one-half of all crimes were committed by 6 percent of the birth cohort they investigated. This evidence, in conjunction with Peter Greenwood's findings that recidivists often manage to stay out of prison by plea bargaining, suggests that if prosecutors could identify recidivists and prosecute them vigorously, and if judges imposed long prison sentences on them, serious crime might be reduced significantly.

Some believe that a policy of **selective incapacitation**—that is, the targeting of high-risk, recidivist offenders for prosecution and incarceration—may be worth pursuing.[43] Implementation of such a policy, however, is limited by the state of criminological research. In the words of Joan Petersilia and her colleagues:

For an incapacitative crime control strategy to be effective, we need to know, first, whether there is a group of offenders who commit large numbers of offenses over a substantial period, and second, whether we can identify them. The first condition can be met. There is a small group of persistent offenders. . . . The second condition—ability to predict—cannot now be met.[44]

There are other problems as well, such as the false identification of high-risk offenders (false positive) and the release of defendants mistakenly labeled low-risk (false negative). In sum, as a recent study by Gottfredson and Gottfredson established, the preconditions for a successful collective or selective incapacitation strategy are not met, for a variety of reasons.[45]

Deterrence

The theory of **deterrence** holds that fear of punishment will cause potential offenders to refrain from committing crimes. This seemingly simple proposition has many theoretical and practical implications. In the first place, it seems clear that most people do not engage in prohibited conduct for reasons other than fear of punishment. Consider a recent study by Ronald V. Clarke: 16.4 million cars traveling on a rural Illinois highway with a speed limit of 65 mph (lightly enforced) were clocked. The vast majority did indeed travel at the posted speed, with a very small minority traveling faster or slower.[46] It could be concluded that deterrence works even when the chances of being caught are slight. It could also be concluded that most people do not need deterrence to do the right thing. Or was it that the Illinois legislature did the right thing by posting a reasonable and acceptable speed limit? Or should we conclude that deterrence does not work precisely on that small group of people who are prone to nonconformity?

Deterrence has a selective aim: It tries to reach those whose normal controls do not keep them within the bounds of the law. There are clearly two types of persons in that small group, those who could be deterred if the right sanction had been devised and were to be enforced, and the group of nondeterrables. The latter can be a very large por-tion of the population, varying with psychosociological circumstances, economic conditions, and other factors, but especially with the type of crime thought to be deterred. Here are some examples.

Researchers have investigated instances in which policing was terminated and others in which policing was significantly strengthened. A classic example of the former situation occurred in Denmark in 1944, when the German occupation forces arrested the entire Danish police force. An examination of insurance claims showed that fraud crimes and embezzlement did not increase but that larcenies and burglaries rose tenfold.[47] During a strike by the Montreal police force in 1969, crimes of revenge and vandalism increased significantly.[48] Yet research on the effect of police strikes in the 1970s on the crime rates of 11 American cities provided very little support for the hypothesis that removal of the police presence raises crime rates.[49]

The evidence on the effects of intensified policing is no clearer. In 1982, New York City's Transit Police force was strengthened to combat subway crime. Additional officers were posted in subway stations on virtually all trains between 8 P.M. and 4 A.M. The results were inconclusive.[50] In a citywide program in 1990, Mayor Rudolph Giuliani and Police Commissioner William Bratton significantly increased the visibility of the police in troubled areas, increased the number of arrests for quality-of-life crimes, and used other techniques to make deterrence theory publicly believable. It has been claimed that a significant drop in serious crimes—especially homicides—is directly attributable to the strategy, though we should await criminological evaluations.[51]

Researchers have studied the effects of increasing the threatened punishments for some crimes. Massachusetts mandated a minimum prison term of 1 year for carrying a firearm without a permit. This law had a measurable deterrent effect.[52] But the deterrent effect of criminal sanctions is limited.

In a study of deterrence by the Criminal Law Education and Research Center at New York University, three types of warning stickers were attached to parking meters in three comparable areas. One sticker threatened a $50 fine for the use of slugs in parking meters. The second threatened a $250 fine and 3 months' imprisonment. The third threatened a $1000 fine and 1 year in prison. Slug use decreased substantially where the threatened sanction was lowest and thus realistic. The highest sanction appeared so unrealistic that slug use actually increased, although only slightly. In another area, where newly installed parking meters had coin-view windows that revealed what had been inserted into the meter, slug use decreased substantially.[53]

Overall, research on deterrence is still inconclusive, largely because the opportunities for making controlled studies are extremely limited, but also because some crimes and some criminals are more easily deterred than others.[54] It is important to note that deterrence assumes rational choice. Supporters of deterrence-based strategies argue that criminals weigh the relative benefits and risks of engaging in crime and choose not to do so because they are deterred by a greater chance of being caught.

Retribution

In many preliterate societies victims retaliated fiercely against anybody or anything that had caused them harm—another person, an animal, a tree. In early literate societies such uncontrolled revenge gave way to a measured response to wrongdoing. In the Mosaic laws we find a limitation on revenge: The punishment should be comparable to the harm inflicted ("an eye for an eye"). This *lex talionis* ("retaliation law") marks the birth of the idea of **retribution**.[55]

Under the retributive system of the nineteenth and early twentieth centuries, all punishments were determined by legislative act, and the judge had little choice in sentencing. Every type of crime was given a fixed punishment. In fixing these punishments, legislatures took into account the perceived gravity of each type of crime. Thus murder commanded a more severe punishment than robbery, and robbery a more severe punishment than larceny.

In the early part of this century attitudes began to change. This was a period of great expectations, of great advances in medicine and

in psychology. Especially in the United States, anything seemed possible, even changing criminals into law-abiding citizens. In this climate the classical retributive idea of punishment seemed to be inherently flawed. The idea of punishment as retribution was based on the assumption that all offenders who had violated the same provision of the penal law were alike and thus deserved the same punishment. But behavioral scientists point out that no two offenders who have committed the same crime are completely alike in capacity, depravity, intelligence, and potential for rehabilitation.

Rehabilitation

Dissatisfaction with retribution led to a new emphasis on the rehabilitative ideal. As a sentencing strategy or option, **rehabilitation** is based on the premise that through correctional intervention (educational and vocational training and psychotherapeutic programs), an offender may be changed and returned to society as a productive citizen (see Chapter 19). Punishment now became individualized: The court could select a sentence ranging from a minimum to a maximum length of incarceration or impose an indeterminate sentence. The parole board was established to decide when the convicted person should be released and under what conditions.

Although correctional systems did experiment with rehabilitation, more often than not the efforts were perfunctory. Yet judges believed in the promise of rehabilitation and sentenced offenders accordingly. In the 1970s, researchers increasingly attacked the rehabilitative ideal as a failure. In 1974 Robert Martinson wrote: "[W]ith few and isolated exceptions, the rehabilitative efforts that have been reported so far have had no appreciable effect on recidivism."[56] After Martinson's devastating analysis, a number of criminologists and research organizations responded with comparable findings and conclusions.[57] The result was a temporary vacuum in sentencing theory. In practice, however, most states had adopted the sentencing policies of the Model Penal Code and tried to abide by them.

Model Penal Code Sentencing Goals

The Model Penal Code describes the general purposes of the provisions governing the sentencing of offenders as follows:

1. To prevent and condemn the commission of offenses.

2. To promote the correction and rehabilitation of offenders.

3. To ensure the public safety by preventing the commission of the offenses through the deterrent influence of sentences imposed and the confinement of offenders when required in the interest of public protection.

4. To safeguard offenders against excessive, disproportionate, or arbitrary punishment.

5. To give fair warning of the nature of the sentences that may be imposed on conviction of an offense.

6. To differentiate among offenders with a view to a just individualization in their treatment.

7. To advance the use of generally accepted scientific methods and knowledge in sentencing offenders.[58]

Thus the Model Penal Code set as goals the prevention of crime through deterrence and incapacitation; condemnation of the commission of offenses, which may be called **vindication** of the law; correction and rehabilitation of the offender; and retribution if sentences are properly individualized.

These sentencing objectives have been with us for a long time. Each objective has been given more or less emphasis at various times. As we have noted, some have been supported or even partially validated by research. The difficulty comes in trying to combine objectives. Legislatures, in providing appropriate punishments for the various offenses in the code, are supposed to consider the interplay of the multiple goals. Judges, acting within the legislative framework, likewise are supposed to consider all the goals when they mete out individual sentences. But the goals are not necessarily compatible; in fact, they may be contradictory. For example, a long prison term may be necessary to remove an offender from society (incapacitation), but a long prison sentence can be incompatible with the goal of rehabilitation. Or incapacitation may be wholly unnecessary, yet retribution demands a long sentence.

Just Deserts

In the wake of the perceived failure of rehabilitation, the wide differences in sentences for like crimes under indeterminate sentencing laws became apparent. Andrew von Hirsch, Richard Singer, and other scholars began to promote a return to retribution.[59] Their model is called **just deserts.** Underlying the concept of just deserts is the proposition that the punishment must be based on the gravity of the offense and the culpability of the perpetrator.

Utilitarian aims, such as general or individual deterrence, incapacitation, and rehabilitation, can only result in variations among the sentences imposed on offenders who deserve identical punishment. Moreover, it can be established that such extralegal factors as the characteristics of judges, race, socioeconomic status, sex, age, geographic area of the trial, and type of defense counsel cause wide differences in sentences imposed.[60] Just-deserts advocates further hold that courts simply do not have the capacity to discriminate between those who can be deterred, reformed, or incapacitated and those who cannot. Parole boards likewise have been found to be poorly prepared to make sound decisions about which offenders are good risks for release and which are not.

The system of rehabilitation was based on the capacity of prisons—"correctional" institutions—to correct or rehabilitate, but they did not do so in most cases. There is therefore no choice but to return to retribution, which at least guarantees just or like sentences for like crimes. Any rehabilitative efforts in prisons should be made only within the terms of the fixed sentence and with the consent of the convicted person.[61]

The just-deserts approach has been successful in minimizing disparity in sentences and in curbing judicial arbitrariness. But it has its problems as well: It has been blamed for prison overcrowding. It has been attacked for insensitivity to the social problems that lead a large proportion of offenders to crime. It has been criticized for refusal to acknowledge the fact

In 1994 two young Americans were sentenced to the punishment of whipping (caning, flogging) for relatively minor offenses. One of the cases made the headlines of most major newspapers and magazines. The other, when mentioned at all, was buried in the back pages. In the first of these cases, the president of the United States intervened with the government that had imposed the sentence—Singapore. In the second case, there was no intervention—that sentence was executed by a Native-American tribal court, one supposedly subject to the U.S. Constitution.

There are detailed accounts of the caning of the American youngster in Singapore: the process of being stripped and tied, the forceful and well-aimed hits of the cane, the ripping of the flesh of the buttocks, the intense pain, and the repeat strokes—though the government of Singapore reported that, after the execution, the convict smiled, shook hands with his executioner, sat through a post-sentence interview, and was given medical attention.(1)

No account of the other flogging, that of a young American tribal woman, is available, and because, oddly, the case gained no favor with the media, there was no public reaction to the American whipping. What explains the difference in attention? Is it differential bias? Do we expect more of others than we are willing to render to our own?

Surprisingly, while the media condemned the Singapore caning—even calling for a boycott of Singapore-made products—the American public reacted otherwise. Mail and phone calls to talk shows and other media by far favored caning as a punishment for graffiti spraying. Why? Is it disgust with America's high crime rate, revulsion against graffiti, or envy of Singapore, that highly prosperous and practically crime-free (by our standards) little island country? Or is it that not so long ago, caning was a legal punishment in Delaware (abolished in 1972), flogging of sailors ended only in 1874, and

slaves and former slaves had been whipped both before and after the 1863 Emancipation Proclamation? In fact, in the United States paddling apparently is still a legal form of school discipline in 23 states.

WHAT IS THE GOAL OF PUNISHMENT?

The U.S. Constitution (Eighth Amendment) prohibits the infliction of "cruel and unusual punishment," as does the Universal Declaration of Human Rights. Yet we permit the capital execution of youngsters aged 16, which is contrary to international standards (which posit a minimum age of 18). Suppose that caning were proved to be an effective deterrent to vandalism (which is unproved) and that capital punishment were proved an effective deterrent to juvenile murderers (which is unproved): Should we embrace such punishments?

As recently as 1984, a distinguished—indeed, highly respected—American criminologist published a reasoned argument for a return to flogging as the principal punishment for all offenders except incorrigibles and the like who, he posited, should be given one of only two alternative punishments, either 15 years or life in prison.(2) His book produced rather mixed reactions. For one thing, controlled studies about the effectiveness of flogging are not available and are hard to construct. For another, there is a widespread revulsion against corporal punishments (even in a society as physical as our own, as evidenced by our predilection for contact sports, violent entertainment, and everyday physical reactions to conflict situations).

An American legal philosopher once posited the case of a defendant "convicted of treasonable utterances by which he successfully sought to impair the morale and obedience of combat soldiers in time of war. The sentence of the court [was] that he be compelled to submit to a surgical operation on his vocal cords so that thereafter he [could] only bark like a dog."(3)

Singapore uses caning as punishment for a variety of offenses, including immigration violations, sex offenses, and vandalism. Those caned are strapped to a wooden frame and lashed with a long rattan cane. In 1994, American teenager Michael Fay was sentenced to six strokes for spray-painting cars. The sentence was subsequently reduced to four strokes after an appeal from President Clinton.

Where should we draw the line on what is cruel and unusual? And whose conscience should prevail on legislators?

Sources

1. Melinda Liu interview of Michael Fay, "I Tried to Ignore the Pain," *Newsweek,* July 4, 1994, p. 36; "Singapore: After the Caning, 'Mike's in Pain.' " *Newsweek,* May 16, 1994, p. 41.
2. Graeme Newman, *Just and Painful: A Case for the Corporal Punishment of Criminals* (London: Macmillan, New York: 1984).
3. Edmond Cahn, *The Sense of Injustice* (New York: New York University Press, 1949), p. 17.

Questions for Discussion

1. Why do Americans sense injustice in corporal punishment when the methods of capital punishment (e.g., electrocution or the use of a gas chamber) are so cruel?
2. Do you think that corporal punishment deters criminals from committing future offenses?

that education, in the broadest sense, can affect values, attitudes, and behavior. It also has been called unscientific because of its rejection of scientific efforts to identify the types of offenders whose leanings toward crime are said to be demonstrable. Critics also have complained that the just-deserts concept is superficial in its rejection of the rehabilitative ideal: It ignores the fact that rehabilitation has been condemned on the basis of flawed evaluations.

Restorative Justice

Just-deserts theory may have reached its potential, in both its theoretical refinement and the willingness of legislatures to put it into practice. There is a search on for a new paradigm, though as yet it is unclear what its dimensions might be. In the confusing clash between ever more punitive thinking on the one hand and a search for better ways of protecting the victims of crime, including victimized communities, on the other, what emerges is a model called **restorative justice.**[62] A harsh retributive sentence may satisfy the desire for revenge, but it does not buy a loaf of bread for the victim, nor does it really restore a community's sense of wholeness. Restorative justice seeks to serve both goals: restoring all those who suffered from crime to their original sense of well-being, but in a way that makes it clear that justice in itself is being restored (which may call for a sentence popularly regarded as adequate). Restorative justice may be "new wine in old wineskins," yet as a penal theory it is somewhat novel.[63]

Sentencing Limits and Guidelines

Presumptive and Mandatory Sentencing
The federal courts and at least 12 state court systems have judges who are virtually deprived of the power to determine the lengths of sentences.[64] The law determines what the punishment ought to be, often by a **presumptive** (presumed to be most appropriate) **sentence.** The length of such a sentence is regulated by statute—there is a definite sentence for each class of crimes, and it cannot ordinarily be adjusted for mitigating or aggravating circumstances. In some limited cases a judge may modify the sentence slightly on the basis of such circumstances, provided the reasons are detailed in a written explanation. When **sentences** are **mandatory,** judges have no discretion to alter them.

Most state prison inmates are serving presumptive sentences and thus, in 90 percent of all cases, can estimate their release date. There is, however, a wide disparity in sentence lengths among the states.[65] Researchers have found that appellate review of sentencing decisions would enhance uniformity within jurisdictions.[66] Efforts are under way to improve the uniformity of sentences, and estimates of their length, by "truth-in-sentencing" policies. Under such laws those convicted would be required to serve at least 85 percent of their sentence, or periods 2.3 times longer than they serve currently.[67]

Mandatory sentencing has been opposed by both the judiciary[68] and the research community. The cost of incarceration invariably increases, reducing cost-effectiveness; massive unfairness is introduced (no two offenders are alike); and crime control is not achieved.[69] The return to mandatory sentencing has been called a "betrayal of sentencing reform."[70] In fact, just as a quarter-century ago, researchers had nothing positive to report on judicial sentencing discretion and the rehabilitative ideal, so nothing positive is forthcoming from the researchers on any form of structured[71] or determinative sentencing.[72]

All the problems of the past, associated with both determinate and indeterminate sentencing schemes, were meant to be resolved with the invention of sentencing guidelines.

Sentencing Guidelines   Sentencing guidelines provide a relatively fixed punishment that corresponds with prevailing notions of harm and allows for upward or downward adjustment on the basis of specific aggravating or mitigating circumstances. In the United States, the movement toward sentencing guidelines began with a plea by federal district judge Marvin E. Frankel in the early 1970s for an independent sentencing commission to study sentences and assist in the formulation and enactment of detailed guidelines for use by judges.[73] Since then, a number of states have adopted guidelines, and several have created **sentencing commissions,** which are independent agencies authorized by state legislatures to create guidelines. In 1984 the United States Sentencing Commission was established by Congress, and in 1987 it delivered its guidelines for the sentencing of individual defendants.[74] In November 1991, Congress adopted guidelines proposed by the U.S. Sentencing Commission for organizations, especially for corporations.[75]

At the heart of all guidelines is a sentencing grid, most often in the form of a matrix, in which a ranking of the severity of the offense is combined with a defendant's criminal history or other characteristics to arrive at a recommended sentence or sentence range (Figure 18.7). Guidelines usually allow for mitigating or aggravating circumstances associated with the specific offense. They typically indicate which offenses should be sanctioned by a prison term (the "in/out" decision) and the length of the sentence.

A judge simply calculates a defendant's history and the severity of the offense, plus or minus mitigating or aggravating circumstances (where allowed), and, with the exactness of a computer, has a sentence to impose. In practice, some guidelines can be fairly complicated to use because of the number of factors that must be included in calculating the sentence. Every U.S. probation office and U.S. attorney's office has been provided with a computer program to assist in calculating recommended sentences in accordance with the federal sentencing guidelines.[76]

Types of Guidelines There are two types of sentencing guidelines: voluntary and presumptive. *Voluntary* guidelines are created by the judiciary rather than mandated by the legislature. They are sometimes referred to as "descriptive guidelines" because they describe, rather than prescribe, recommended sentences. Denver developed a voluntary system in 1976; subsequently it was tried in other cities, such as Newark, Chicago, and Phoenix. Michigan, Massachusetts, and New Jersey pioneered the use of voluntary systems on a statewide basis. Such voluntary systems have been tried at the state or local level in almost every state. However, evaluations have shown that they have had little effect on judges' sentencing patterns,

and interest in them seems to have diminished.[77]

The other form of sentencing guideline is referred to as *presumptive* because the appropriate sentence for an offender is presumed to fall within the range of sentences specified by the guidelines. Judges are expected to choose from a range of available sentences, and all deviations must be documented in writing. The federal sentencing guidelines and those of Minnesota, Pennsylvania, and Washington are all considered presumptive schemes.

Pennsylvania's system, unlike the others, still allows for indeterminate sentences because the sentencing commission sought to incorporate a rehabilitative philosophy into its guidelines, along with goals related to deterrence, incapacitation, and just deserts. For offenders in Pennsylvania who are to be incarcerated, the judge must specify a minimum and a maximum sentence chosen from a wide range allowed in the guidelines. The parole board then decides the actual release date. Minnesota and Washington, emphasizing a retributive approach, have made the range for a given offense narrower than that in Pennsylvania.[78]

Some Criticisms Sentencing commissions and sentencing guidelines both have met with significant resistance, perhaps because the state commissions are independent of the judicial and the legislative branches. Some of the proposed guidelines or recommendations were simply rejected by the legislatures.[79] The Connecticut commission developed a guidelines system but went on record as strongly opposed to its adoption and instead recommended statutory-determinate sentences.[80] At the federal level, opposition to individual guidelines came chiefly from the judges themselves.

The federal guidelines for individuals took effect on November 1, 1987, but many judges found them unconstitutional. They reasoned that, since the U.S. Sentencing Commission was created by Congress, the guidelines were a violation of the separation of powers. In January 1989, the United States Supreme Court upheld the constitutionality of the U.S. Sentencing Commission and the guidelines.[81] Between the time the guidelines went into effect and this

FIGURE 18.7   The dispositional line on Minnesota's sentencing grid.

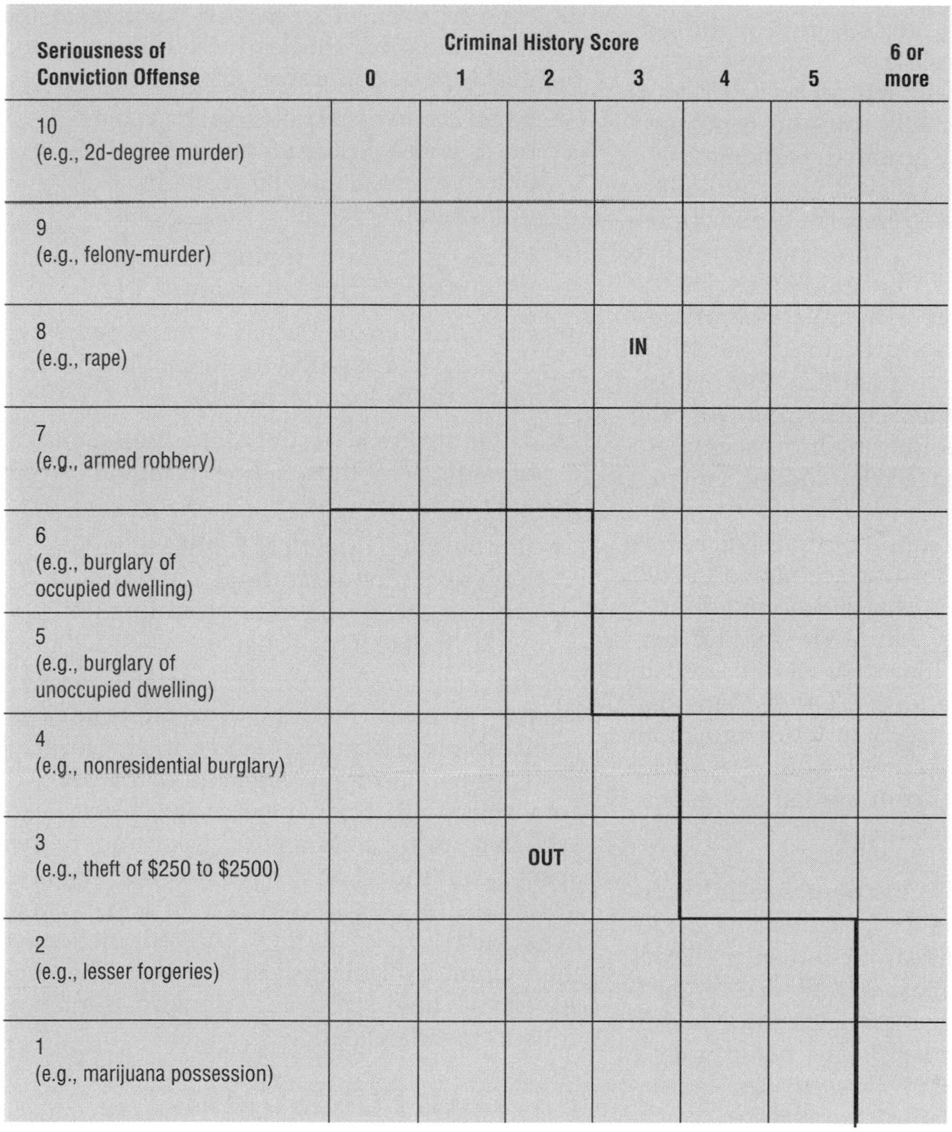

Seriousness of Conviction Offense	Criminal History Score						6 or more
	0	1	2	3	4	5	
10 (e.g., 2d-degree murder)							
9 (e.g., felony-murder)							
8 (e.g., rape)				IN			
7 (e.g., armed robbery)							
6 (e.g., burglary of occupied dwelling)							
5 (e.g., burglary of unoccupied dwelling)							
4 (e.g., nonresidential burglary)							
3 (e.g., theft of $250 to $2500)			OUT				
2 (e.g., lesser forgeries)							
1 (e.g., marijuana possession)							

Source: Andrew von Hirsch, Kay A. Knapp, and Michael Tonry, *The Sentencing Commission and Its Guidelines* (Boston: Northeastern University Press, 1987), p. 91.

Supreme Court decision, more than 150 federal district judges refused to use the guidelines on the grounds that they might be unconstitutional. An evaluation of the initial use of the guidelines at the federal level showed that lawyers also opposed them. Only probation officers, who are responsible for preparing presentence investigation reports, seemed to have mastered the intricacies of the system.[82]

Like statutory-determinate sentencing schemes, guidelines represent an attempt to overcome the inequities and uncertainties associated with indeterminate sentences. Critics of presumptive sentencing guidelines, however, fear that their use will lead to harsher sentences and make the already serious problem of prison overcrowding worse. Others suggest that discretion in sentencing will simply move from the judge to the prosecutor. Defendants will seek bargains that move their charges to the "out" side of the in/out line or to a location on the sentencing grid that carries a more lenient sentence. The pressure to bargain will also lead defendants to avoid trials. Finally, some are concerned that judges will simply ignore the guidelines.

Two decades have passed since guideline sentencing has been used in some jurisdictions. Assessments of its impact show mixed results. Michael Tonry reports that guidelines are the most effective prescription against arbitrariness and discrimination in sentencing.[83] But other researchers discovered unanticipated shortcomings. Law enforcement may circumvent the guidelines during the investigation stage.[84] In Minnesota, which pioneered guideline sentencing, inequality is reported to have returned.[85] While the prison population of that state seems to have been kept stable, displacement occurred by considerable increases in jail populations.[86] On the whole, the best that can be said for sentencing guidelines is that they can be used to control prison populations.[87] Other than that, these guidelines have become more and more rigid. The idea has suffered from the outset from the effort to transform human beings into a two-dimensional grid.[88]

Three Strikes and Other Sentence Enhancements   While the debate over sentencing guidelines continues, a political movement is under way to increase the severity of sentences, regardless of guidelines, and oblivious to the evidence of the research community. This new punitive movement has resulted in "three-strikes" legislation and sentence-enhancement statutes. Washington State was the first to pass legislation generally called "three strikes and you're out." By early 2000, 24 states had passed such legislation, and a federal enactment encouraged such state legislation by funding support.

The more carefully crafted three-strikes statutes provide for an enhanced (possibly life) term of imprisonment for the third violent felony conviction. Under more sloppily drafted statutes, a two-time loser can be given a life term for taking a slice of pizza from a kid at a pizza parlor, as happened in California. Although the three-strikes statutes have been touted by politicians as a significant crime and violence reducer, at great cost savings to the public, evaluation studies have demonstrated these laws to be counterproductive:

- Small crime reductions can be achieved, but at a vast cost (e.g., more than $5.5 billion over the next 25 years, in California).

- Plea bargains are dropping rapidly, increasing the number of trials beyond capacity.

- Civil cases are neglected at the expense of criminal trials, with vast negative implications for civil justice.

- Three-strikes laws aim at the wrong end of offending—at those whose criminal careers are rapidly declining.

- By confining offenders for life (long past the age of their offending), such laws create a vast problem of providing for geriatric care in prisons.[89]

Yet another effort on the part of legislators seeking to curry favor with a presumptively punitive-minded public comes in the form of sentence-enhancement legislation for offenses committed with a gun, near certain places (e.g., schools), during certain periods, or under other special conditions. Such laws had been favored in the twelfth century (crimes on holy days or near sacred places); they proved ineffective then. Crime control was not achieved. The same seems to hold true for modern sentence-enhancement legislation.[90]

CAPITAL PUNISHMENT

A judge's most awesome sentencing alternative for those convicted of a capital crime is the imposition of the death sentence. Capital punishment is a controversial issue, and one that poses particular challenges to the judiciary. After all, it is the only sentence that, once executed, is irreversible and final: It deprives the convicted person of an ultimate appeal.

Daniel Frank's execution in 1622 was the first on record in America. He was executed in the colony of Virginia for the crime of theft.[91] Scholars have estimated that since that year, between 18,000 and 20,000 people in America

- Gay college student Matthew Shepard was tied to a fence and beaten to death by his attackers.
- Self-identified neo-Nazis killed two African-American residents of Fayetteville, North Carolina, for kicks.
- Two African-American men killed a white father of three in Lubbock, Texas, in their search for a white victim.
- Two men in Houston, Texas, killed a gay man by stabbing him 35 times.
- A Brooklyn real estate office was fire-bombed for showing properties to African Americans.
- A North Hollywood school was painted with swastikas and slurs against Jews by young vandals.

The stories are as chilling as the headlines. In Hillsborough County, Florida, two white males kidnapped a black man from a shopping center, forced him at gunpoint to drive 16 miles to an isolated spot, poured gasoline over him, and then lit four matches. When the matches went out, they continued with a cigarette lighter to ignite the fire that burned 40 percent of the victim's body. Charles Rourk, 33, and Mark Kahut, 27, two friends from Illinois who shared an interest in hard-rock music, motorcycles, and action movies and lived in a trailer park with their pet dog, Caesar, a pit bull, were sentenced to life-plus for the horrific attack.

An 18-year-old leader of a skinhead gang, the S.S. Action Group, became disenchanted with racism, dropped out of the New Jersey group, and fed information on its activities to the authorities. He described how the skinheads thrived on hostility against minorities; the sounds of racist music from Britain and Germany, known as oi; and fascist demonstrations where members dressed in military fatigues and, with arms raised straight in the Nazi salute, taunted spectators with a call for white supremacy.(1)

Four whites were charged with breaking into a home and badly beating a deaf black mother and her teenage son with baseball bats. It was not the first racially motivated attack on the family of this 39-year-old substitute teacher at a school for the deaf. Just 18 months earlier, shortly after they had moved into their new home (they were the only black family on the street), a Molotov cocktail had been tossed into a window.

Destruction of property, arson, vandalism, assault, and attempted homicide—all fit the definition of "hate crime," or "bias crime": crimes committed against a person or property because of the race, religion, color, disability, sexual orientation, national origin, or ancestry of the victim. The National Hate Crime Statistics Act of 1990 mandates comprehensive reports on bias crimes, and in early 1993 the first such report was issued by the FBI. Although fewer than a fifth of the nation's law enforcement agencies contributed data for the report, 4558 hate-crime incidents reported in 1991 were included in the study. The FBI found that blacks are the targets of the most hate crimes (36 percent), followed by whites (19 percent) and Jews (17 percent). Religious bias motivated 2 of every 10 incidents reported, with ethnic and sexual-orientation bias accounting for 1 of every 10. Racial bias was responsible for the greatest number of incidents by far—6 of every 10. By 1997 the number of reported hate crimes rose to 9861, with more than 60 percent motivated by racial bias. Most of the prosecutions have been initiated under state criminal laws.(2)

Two trends will continue into the next century, posing a great challenge to legislators, judges, and criminal justice specialists. First, jurisdictions around the United States are adding sentence enhancements to hate-crimes statutes. Such amendments either allow or require judges to add additional prison time for those convicted of hate crimes. Second, jurisdiction for prosecuting hate crimes is expanding rapidly. For example, under current federal law, hate crimes may be prosecuted only if there is a crime motivated by bias based on religion, national origin, or color. With the Hate Crimes Prevention Act of 1998, however, Congress is debating the expansion of the definition of a "hate crime" to include a violent act causing death or bodily injury "because of the actual or perceived race, color, religion, national origin, sexual orientation, gender, or disability" of the victim. This expansion of federal jurisdiction will no doubt increase the number of prosecutions—at a time when we are made increasingly aware of the vulnerability of diversity in our very own neighborhoods.

Sources

1. Clifford J. Levy, "Crusading for Harmony as a Skinhead Spy," *New York Times,* Apr. 4, 1994, pp. B1, B8.
2. David Van Biema, "When White Makes Right," *Time,* Aug. 9, 1993, p. 40.

Questions for Discussion

1. Are the acts that we characterize as hate crimes increasing in frequency?
2. Is there a definite need for a new class of federal hate crimes?

have suffered state-sanctioned execution for crimes including train wrecking, aggravated murder, and rape.[92] (The latest estimate puts the total at 14,570.[93]) Countless others have died at the hands of lynch mobs.[94] During the last century, Western countries have employed six methods of execution: firing squad, lethal gas, hanging, decapitation by ax or guillotine, electrocution, and lethal injection. Decapitation is the only one of these methods that has never been used in the United States.

Between 1976, when the death penalty was reinstated in the United States after a short moratorium, and January 2000, 598 convicted

Rubin "Hurricane" Carter, once a contender for the middleweight boxing crown, spent nineteen years in prison for a crime that most say he never committed. In 1985 U.S. District Judge H. Lee Sarokin in Newark, New Jersey, vacated Carter's convictions, finding that the prosecution committed "grave constitutional violations" and that the convictions were based on "racism rather than reason and concealment rather than disclosure." According to Sarokin, "human decency mandates his immediate release."

criminals have been executed (Figure 18.8). Thirty-eight states and the federal government now have death penalty laws in effect.

The arguments surrounding capital punishment are deceptively simple. What makes them deceptive is that abolitionist or retentionist views of the death penalty often influence assessments of the penalty's utility and effectiveness. Abolitionists find little empirical evidence of a deterrent effect, and retentionists claim that sophisticated studies can be conducted only after executions have been resumed at a steady pace. They argue, in other words, that it is impossible to tell whether deterrence is fact or fiction until we execute all inmates sentenced to death.

The Deterrence Argument

Social scientists have long debated whether and to what extent executions deter murder. The de-

FIGURE 18.8   Death sentences and executions in the United States.

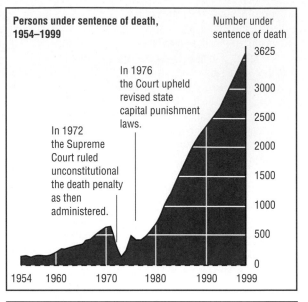

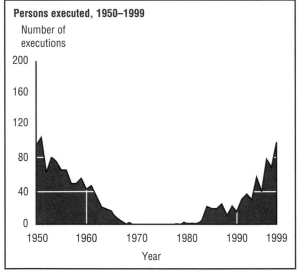

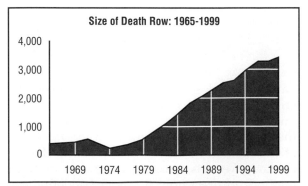

Source: Death Penalty Information Center (http://www.essential.org/dpic/dpicexec.htm).

TABLE 18.4 Arguments Against and For the Death Penalty

Argument	Rationale
	Against
Arbitrary-use argument	With over 2600 inmates on death row, the process by which an inmate is selected to die is entirely arbitrary; it is not determined by the seriousness of the crime committed or any other objective measure.
Mistakes argument	Studies have documented cases in which individuals were wrongly convicted and thus executed in error.[a] It is impossible to be entirely certain that a person is truly guilty. Are we willing to permit mistakes?[b]
Religious argument	Organizations representing most of the major religions have called for an end to the death penalty. Interreligious task forces have voiced concern over issues of ethics and guilt in the putting to death of human beings.[c]
Cost-benefit argument	The cost of trying and appealing a capital case, plus the cost of maintenance on death row, is far higher than the cost of trying and maintaining a lifer.[d]
Risk argument	Convicted murderers behave well in prison and, if paroled, rarely commit violent offenses again.
Morality argument	Examinations of the relation between moral development and attitudes toward capital punishment show that the more developed one's sense of morality, the less likely one is to favor the death penalty.
	For
Economic argument	The cost of maintaining an inmate in prison for life places an unfair burden on taxpayers and the state.
Retribution argument	Any individual who kills another human being must pay for the crime.
Community protection argument	It is always possible that a person on death row may escape and kill again or may kill another inmate or a correctional officer. Thus the community cannot be fully protected unless the person is executed.[e]
Public opinion argument	Standards of decency, the criteria by which courts judge the humaneness of a punishment, are continually evolving. Two decades ago public opinion was not in favor of the death penalty. Today Americans have mixed reactions.[f]

[a]Hugo Adam Bedau and Michael J. Radelet, "Miscarriages of Justice in Potentially Capital Cases," *Stanford Law Review,* **40** (1987): 21–129.

[b]Between 1973 and 1993, 48 inmates have been released from death row after their innocence had been acknowledged. U.S. Congress, Committee on the Judiciary, Subcommittee on Civil and Constitutional Rights, *Innocence and the Death Penalty: Assessing the Danger of Mistaken Executions* (Washington, D.C.: U.S. Government Printing Office, 1993).

[c]Yet the New Christian Right is more favorably disposed toward capital punishment, based on a literal interpretation of the Bible. Harold G. Grasmick, Robert J. Buisick, Jr., and Brenda Sims Blackwell, "Religious Beliefs and Public Support for the Death Penalty for Juveniles and Adults," *Journal of Crime and Justice,* **16** (1993): 59–86.

[d]Actually, the cost of appeals and maintenance of a person on death row is far higher than the cost of maintaining a prisoner sentenced to life imprisonment—approximately $3 million. See Andrew P. Malcolm, "Capital Punishment Is Popular, but So Are Its Alternatives," *New York Times,* Sept. 10, 1989, p. E4; see also Philip J. Cook and Donna B. Slawson, *The Costs of Processing Murder Cases in North Carolina* (Dunham, N.C.: Sanford Institute of Public Policy, 1993).

[e]Thorsten Sellin's research demonstrated that this argument is specious. Convicted murderers behave exceedingly well in prison and, if released, have very good parole records. Repeat homicides are statistically rare. See Sellin, *The Death Penalty* (Philadelphia: American Law Institute), pp. 69–79.

[f]Public opinion polls with a simple favor/oppose response have produced inaccurate results. When a "no opinion" category is added, the results shift dramatically. See Peter R. Jones, "It's Not What You Ask, It's the Way That You Ask It: Question Form and Public Opinion on the Death Penalty," *Prison Journal,* **74** (1994): 32–50.

bate focuses on two questions: Do would-be murderers decide not to kill out of fear of being put to death? If the threat of execution is in fact a deterrent, would the threat of life imprisonment be just as effective?

The results of studies designed to answer these questions are inconclusive. Many researchers have found little evidence that homicide rates are affected by executions.[95] On the other hand, Isaac Ehrlich, an economist, has found what does appear to be a deterrent effect:

specifically, that each execution prevents between 8 and 20 murders. His study, however, has been criticized on a number of methodological grounds.[96]

Recent research on the deterrent effect of the death penalty has focused on the relationship between publicity about executions and homicide rates. If deterrence works, the argument goes, then publicized executions should result in lower numbers of murders because of greater awareness of the risk of being sentenced to death. Here again, the results of research are not clear: Some studies show that publicity does have some deterrent effect (although much weaker than other factors associated with the homicide rate),[97] and others conclude that neither newspaper nor television coverage of executions has had any deterrent effect,[98] or may even be counterproductive by increasing the homicide rate.[99]

The legal scholar Charles L. Black has noted that it is extremely difficult to design methodologically sound deterrence studies. How can we estimate the number of people who refrained from committing murder in a jurisdiction with a death penalty or in one without a death penalty? According to Black:

> After all possible inquiry, we do not know, and for systematic and easily visible reasons cannot know, what the truth about this "deterrent" effect may be. A "scientific"—that is to say, a soundly based—conclusion is simply impossible, and no methodological path out of this tangle suggests itself.[100]

The Discrimination Argument

In the early 1970s Marvin Wolfgang and Mark Riedel identified an anomaly in the use of the death penalty. Since the 1950s it had become clear that death sentences in some Southern states had been given disproportionately to blacks convicted of the rape of white women. Wolfgang and Riedel noted: "Of the 3,859 persons executed for all crimes since 1930, 54.6 percent have been black or members of other racial minority groups. Of the 455 executed for rape alone, 89.5 percent have been non-white."[101]

Though the discrimination question has been at the core of legal challenges to the constitutionality of many death sentences, it remained in the background until the legal scholar David Baldus and his colleagues conducted a comprehensive and methodologically sound analysis of discrimination in capital sentencing in Fulton County, Georgia.[102] This study, which clearly demonstrated that a black defendant is 11 times more likely to be sentenced to death for killing a white person than is a white for killing a black, was presented to the U.S. Supreme Court in *McKlesky v. Kemp* (1985).[103]

Warren McKlesky asked the Supreme Court to invalidate the Georgia capital punishment statute because of this proven discrimination. The Court refused to do so because defense attorneys had not shown that McKlesky himself had been discriminated against. Further, the Court ruled that if there is such racial bias, it is at a tolerable level. But a level that is tolerable is difficult to specify. For over 50 years research on sentencing disparity has found racial discrimination in both capital and noncapital cases. This does not suggest that all judges discriminate; rather, some judges discriminate and some do not.[104] Furthermore, differences based on race are not just the result of judicial decision making. Research has found evidence indicating that prosecutors are more likely to request the death penalty for black killers of white people.[105] That by itself is some indication of discrimination.

The latest research on race and capital punishment is unanimous in finding that the U.S. Supreme Court has not succeeded in removing racial bias in capital cases. African-Americans continue to be discriminated against.[106]

Other Arguments

Other arguments have been advanced for and against the death penalty. They are based on everything from religious concerns to a calculation of the cost of imprisonment. Table 18.4 lists some of these arguments and gives the rationales for them.

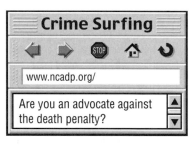

Crime Surfing

www.ncadp.org/

Are you an advocate against the death penalty?

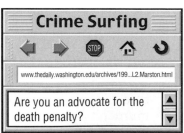

Crime Surfing

www.thedaily.washington.edu/archives/199...L2.Marston.html

Are you an advocate for the death penalty?

Trends in American Capital Punishment

After a persistent decline in capital executions (and a Supreme Court–imposed moratorium, 1972–1976), the number of executions increased, but not yet to the level of the 1930s and 1940s, despite a sharp increase in the

FIGURE 18.9   Public feelings about the death penalty. (a) Increasing support for alternative punishments; (b) doubts about its efficacy.

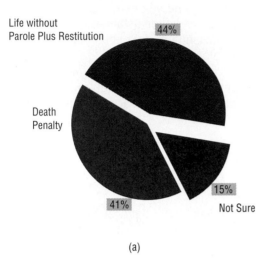

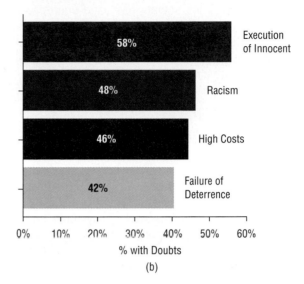

(a)   (b)

Source: Death Penalty Information Center, Washington, D.C., Mar. 29, 1995, p. 5.

number of persons sentenced to death. The number of death-row inmates—disproportionately male and from minority groups—has far exceeded 3000. The number of executions has increased sharply,[107] as a result of the efforts by Congress and the U.S. Supreme Court to reduce the availability of appeals, including the writ of habeas corpus (by the 1996 Antiterrorism and Effective Death Penalty Act, as upheld by the Supreme Court on June 28, 1996, in *Fekar v. Turpin*, no. 95-8836).[108]

There is a fundamental ambivalence about the death penalty in America (Figure 18.9). Only recently, Americans seemed confident that capital punishment might be a solution to the crime problem—a view still held by Congress, state legislators, and many judges. But public confidence is now giving way to doubts and concerns, even in legislative quarters. An opinion poll of Indiana legislators has shown such doubts. A majority of these lawmakers, despite high general support for the death penalty, now state a preference for life without parole coupled with work and restitution to victims' families.[109]

There remains the retribution-vengeance argument: A killer deserves to be killed, a phi-

losophy the Supreme Court, as currently constituted, seems to endorse.[110]

Of the world's major industrialized nations, only the United States, Japan, and South Africa retain the death penalty. Much of the rest of the world shows an opposite trend: 70 countries have abolished the death penalty altogether, and 13 abolished it for "ordinary crimes" (crimes other than those under military codes or those enforced in time of war). The trend in the former communist countries is toward abolition.[111]

The lessons learned from the countries where capital punishment has been abolished might be useful in this country when the future of the death penalty is discussed. The deterrence argument would predict that homicide rates should go up when the death penalty is abolished. An analysis of murder rates in 14 abolitionist nations showed that homicide rates actually declined after abolition.[112]

Did You Know

. . . that California (551) and Texas (458) had the most death-row inmates as of September 1999? New York (3) and Wyoming (2) had the least.

REVIEW

Since earliest times society has used courts to resolve disputes among individuals and between a society and its members. With the emergence of government under strong rulers, the establishment of courts became a sovereign prerogative. In the common law family of legal systems, to which the United States belongs, the adversary system prevails. In criminal cases the prosecution, as one of the adversaries, presents evidence against the defendant in an effort to establish guilt beyond a reasonable doubt. The defendant, as the other adversary, has the right to contest the prosecution's evidence. The judge ensures the fairness of the proceedings.

The United States has two legal systems, one implemented by the state courts and the other implemented by the federal courts. In most of the 50 state systems, there are three distinct levels of courts of law: courts of limited or special jurisdiction, courts of general jurisdiction, and appellate courts. The federal system has several levels as well: federal magistrates, United States district courts, United States circuit courts of appeal, and the United States Supreme Court.

In the United States, criminal cases are tried in state courts when the crime charged is one that violates state law and in federal courts when a violation of federal law is charged. Both state and federal convictions may be appealed within each system, with federal review of state cases when certain federal constitutional issues are raised.

The roles and decision-making processes of all participants in the criminal process—defendants and defense counsel, prosecutors, judges, and jurors—have been subjected to increasing scientific scrutiny. The research reveals that the system does not measure up to expectations. Plea bargaining, in particular, undermines confidence in the court process, yet it may well be the only way to deal with vastly increased caseloads that make it impossible to grant a jury trial in most cases.

Legislative and judicial policies in sentencing convicted offenders are currently in turmoil. Evidence of grossly disproportionate punishments meted out for comparable offenders has led to large-scale abandonment of the rehabilitative goal in sentencing and to a return of the retributive (just-deserts) and incapacitative approaches. But sentencing policies continue to change, with some signs of a rebirth of the rehabilitative goal. At the moment, many states operate with sentencing guidelines that seek to curb abuses of judicial discretion, incorporate just-deserts ideas, and allow some degree of flexibility for aggravating and mitigating circumstances.

Capital punishment as a sentencing option remains a problem for policy makers and the general public. The United States is the only major Western democracy to have returned to capital punishment, without any clear evidence that it promotes public safety

YOU BE THE CRIMINOLOGIST

Amnesty International has created "The Death Penalty Quiz: National Edition" (http://www.patweb.com/dpquiz/index.htm), that will test your knowledge of this ultimate sanction. The objective is to make you more sensitive to the social and systemwide issues surrounding the execution of convicted criminals. Put aside your beliefs about the death penalty for a moment. Then take the quiz and see if you have the substantive knowledge necessary to be a criminologist.

KEY TERMS

The numbers next to the terms refer to the pages on which the terms are defined

arraignment (564)

certiorari, writ of (562)

challenges for cause (569)

defense counsel (563)

deterrence (575)

directed verdict (570)

habeas corpus (562)

indictment (564)

information (564)

just deserts (577)

mandatory sentence (579)

motions (565)

motion to dismiss (570)

peremptory challenges (569)

plead (564)

NOTES

1. See, e.g., Jerome Frank, *Courts on Trial: Myth and Reality in American Justice* (Princeton, N.J.: Princeton University Press, 1949).
2. *Marbury v. Madison*, 1 Cr. 137 (1803).
3. *Loving v. Virginia*, 388 U.S. 1 (1967).
4. *Mapp v. Ohio*, 367 U.S. 643 (1961).
5. *Draper v. United States*, 358 U.S. 307 (1961).
6. Habeas Corpus Act of 1679, 31 Car. II, c. 2.
7. In *Stone v. Powell*, 428 U.S. 465 (1976), the Court ruled that in Fourth Amendment cases (search and seizure), federal habeas corpus is not available to a state prisoner when the alleged due process violation has been fully and fairly litigated in the state court system.
8. Frank Miller, *Prosecution: The Decision to Charge a Suspect with a Crime* (Boston: Little, Brown, 1969); Martha Myers and John Hagan, "Private and Public Trouble: Prosecutors and the Allocation of Court Resources," *Social Problems*, **26** (1979): 439–451.
9. Celesta A. Albonetti, "Prosecutorial Discretion: The Effects of Uncertainty," *Law and Society Review*, **21** (1987): 291–313.
10. Abraham S. Goldstein, *The Passive Judiciary: Prosecutorial Discretion and the Guilty Plea* (Baton Rouge: Louisiana State University Press, 1981).
11. Abraham S. Blumberg, *Criminal Justice: Issues and Ironies* (New York: New Viewpoints, 1979), p. 123.
12. *Gideon v. Wainright*, 375 U.S. 335 (1963); *Argersinger v. Hamlin*, 407 U.S. 25 (1972).
13. President's Commission on Law Enforcement and the Administration of Justice, *Task Force Report: Courts* (Washington, D.C.: U.S. Government Printing Office, 1967), p. 131.
14. John S. Goldkamp, *Two Classes of Accused: A Study of Bail and Detention in American Justice* (Cambridge, Mass.: Ballinger, 1979).
15. Brian A. Reaves and Jacob Perez, *Pretrial Release of Felony Defendants, 1992* (Washington, D.C.: Bureau of Justice Statistics, 1994).
16. Peggy M. Tobolowsky and James F. Quinn, "Pretrial Release in the 1990s: Texas Takes Another Look at Nonfinancial Release Conditions," *New England Journal on Criminal and Civil Confinement*, **19** (1993): 267–327.
17. Bail Reform Act of 1984, 18 U.S.C. §§3141–3150 (1984).
18. U.S. Department of Justice, Bureau of Justice Statistics, *Report to the Nation on Crime and Justice* (Washington, D.C.: U.S. Government Printing Office, 1988), p. 24.
19. Mike Conville and Chester Missky, "Guilty Plea Courts: A Social Discipline Model of Criminal Justice," *Social Problems*, **42** (1995): 216–234.
20. National Advisory Commission on Criminal Justice Standards and Goals, *A National Strategy to Reduce Crime* (Washington, D.C.: U.S. Government Printing Office, 1971), p. 43.
21. See Douglas Smith, "The Plea Bargaining Controversy," *Journal of Criminal Law and Criminology*, **77** (1986): 949–967.
22. Barbara Boland, *Prosecution of Felony Arrests*, for Bureau of Justice Statistics (Washington, D.C.: U.S. Government Printing Office, 1986).
23. Teresa Carns and John Kruse, *Alaska's Plea Bargaining Ban Re-evaluated: Executive Summary* (Anchorage: Alaska Judicial Council, 1991); Malcolm D. Holmes, Howard C. Daudistel, and William A. Taggart, "Plea Bargaining Policy and State District Court Caseloads: An Interrupted Time Series Analysis," *Law and Society Review*, **26** (1992): 139–159; William McAllister, James Atchinson, and Nancy Jacobs, "A Simulation Model of Pretrial Felony Case Processing: A Queuing System Analysis," *Journal of Quantitative Criminology*, **7** (1991): 291–314.
24. Otwin Marenin, "The State of Plea Bargaining in Alaska," *Journal of Crime and Justice*, **18** (1995): 167–197.
25. *Boykin v. Alabama*, 395 U.S. 238 (1964); *Santobello v. New York*, 404 U.S. 257 (1971).

Review • You Be the Criminologist • Key Terms • Notes

26. Rule 11(f), Federal Rules of Criminal Procedure. See also Samuel Walker, *Taming the System: The Control of Discretion in Criminal Justice, 1950–1990* (New York: Oxford University Press, 1993).

27. David Suggs and Bruce Sales, "The Art and Science of Conducting the Voir Dire," *Professional Psychology,* **9** (1978): 362–388.

28. *Mapp v. Ohio,* 367 U.S. 643 (1961).

29. The Mapp decision made the Fourth Amendment's exclusionary rule applicable to the states through the Fourteenth Amendment's due process clause. See note 4 above.

30. See, e.g., *Wong Sun v. United States,* 371 U.S. 471 (1923); and *People v. Defore,* 242 N.Y. 13 at 21 (1926).

31. *Nix v. Williams,* 467 U.S. 431 (1984).

32. Linda Wolfe, *Wasted: The Preppie Murder* (New York: Simon & Schuster, 1989).

33. See Reid Hastie, *Inside the Jury* (Cambridge, Mass.: Harvard University Press, 1983); Elizabeth F. Loftus, *Eyewitness Testimony* (Cambridge, Mass.: Harvard University Press, 1979); Elizabeth F. Loftus and James M. Doyle, *Eyewitness Testimony: Civil and Criminal* (New York: Kluwer, 1987).

34. Albert H. Hastorf and Hadley Cantrill, "They Saw the Game: A Case Study," *Journal of Abnormal and Social Psychology,* **49** (1954): 129–134.

35. J. C. Bartlett and J. E. Leslie, "Aging and Memory for Faces versus Single Views of Faces," *Memory and Cognition,* **14** (1986): 371–381.

36. Kenneth A. Deffenbacher and Elizabeth F. Loftus, "Do Jurors Share a Common Understanding Concerning Eyewitness Behavior?" *Law and Human Behavior,* **6** (1982): 15–30.

37. J. C. Yuille, "Research and Teaching with Police: A Canadian Example," *International Review of Applied Psychology,* **33** (1984): 5–23.

38. R. K. Bothwell, J. Brigham, and M. A. Piggott, "An Exploratory Study of Personality Differences in Eyewitness Memory," *Journal of Social Behavior and Personality,* **2** (1987): 335–343.

39. C. A. Visher, "Juror Decision-Making: The Importance of Evidence," *Law and Human Behavior,* **11** (1987): 1–17.

40. See Gerhard O. W. Mueller, *Sentencing: Process and Purpose* (Springfield, Ill.: Charles C Thomas, 1977).

41. See, e.g., Joan Petersilia, Peter Greenwood, and Marvin Lavin, *Criminal Careers of Habitual Felons,* for LEAA (Washington, D.C.: U.S. Government Printing Office, 1978).

42. Revel Shinnar and S. Shinnar, "The Effects of the Criminal Justice System on the Control of Crime: A Quantitative Approach," *Law and Society Review,* **9** (1975): 581–611.

43. See, e.g., Peter Greenwood, *Selective Incapacitation* (Santa Monica, Calif.: Rand Corporation, 1982).

44. Petersilia et al., *Criminal Careers of Habitual Felons,* p. 5.

45. Stephen D. Gottfredson and Don M. Gottfredson, *Incapacitation Strategies and the Criminal Career* (Sacramento, Calif.: Information Center, California Division of Law Enforcement, 1992).

46. Ronald V. Clarke, "The Distribution of Deviance and Exceeding the Speed Limit," *The British Journal of Criminology,* **36** (1996): 169–181.

47. Johannes Andenaes, *Punishment and Deterrence* (Ann Arbor: University of Michigan Press, 1974), p. 51.

48. William G. Bailey, ed., *The Encyclopedia of Police Science* (New York: Garland, 1989), p. 600.

49. Edwin H. Pfuhl, Jr., "Police Strikes and Conventional Crime," *Criminology,* **21** (1983): 489–503.

50. Ari L. Goldman, "In Spite of Dip, Subway Crime Nears a Record," *New York Times,* Nov. 20, 1982, pp. 1, 26.

51. See Chapter 2.

52. James A. Beha II, "And Nobody Can Get You Out: The Impact of a Mandatory Prison Sentence for the Illegal Carrying of a Firearm on the Administration of Criminal Justice in Boston," *Boston University Law Review,* **57** (March 1977): 96–146.

53. Robert P. Barry, "To Slug a Meter: A Study of Coin Fraud," *Criminology,* **4** (1969): 40–47; John F. Decker, "Curbside Deterrence," *Criminology,* **10** (1972): 127–142.

54. Steven R. Burkett and David A. Ward, "A Note on Perceptual Deterrence, Religiously

Based Moral Condemnation, and Social Control," *Criminology*, **31** (1993): 119–134; David Ward and Charles R. Tittle, "Deterrence or Labeling: The Effects of Informal Sanctions," *Deviant Behavior*, **14** (1993): 43–64; Ronet Bachman, Raymond Paternoster, and Sally Ward, "The Rationality of Sexual Offending: Testing a Deterrence/Rational Choice Conception of Sexual Assault," *Law and Society Review*, **26** (1992): 343–372; Chester L. Britt III, Michael R. Gottfredson, and John S. Goldkamp, "Drug Testing and Pretrial Misconduct: An Experiment on the Specific Deterrent Effects of Drug Monitoring Defendants on Pretrial Release," *Journal of Research in Crime and Delinquency*, **29** (1992): 62–78; Daniel Nagin and Raymond Paternoster, "The Preventive Effects of the Perceived Risk of Arrest: Testing an Expanded Conception of Deterrence," *Criminology*, **29** (1991): 561–587; Lawrence W. Sherman, Janell D. Schmidt, Dennis P. Rogan, et al., "From Initial Deterrence to Long-Term Escalation: Short Custody Arrest for Poverty Ghetto Domestic Violence," *Criminology*, **29** (1991): 821–850; Ruth D. Peterson and William C. Bailey, "Felony Murder and Capital Punishment: An Examination of the Deterrence Question," *Criminology*, **29** (1991): 367–395.

55. Immanuel Kant, *Critique of Pure Reason* (n.p., 1781).

56. Robert Martinson, "What Works? Questions and Answers about Prison Reform," *Public Interest*, **35** (Spring 1974): 25. See also James Q. Wilson, "'What Works?' Revisited: New Findings on Criminal Rehabilitation," *Public Interest*, **61** (Fall 1980): 1.

57. See Francis T. Cullen, Edward J. Latessa, Velmer S. Burton, Jr., and Lucien X. Lombardo, "The Correctional Orientation of Prison Wardens: Is the Rehabilitative Ideal Supported?" *Criminology*, **31** (1993): 69–92.

58. Model Penal Code, sec. 1.02(b).

59. Andrew von Hirsch, *Doing Justice: The Choice of Punishments* (New York: Hill & Wang, 1976). Also see Andrew von Hirsch, *Past or Future Crimes: Deservedness and Dangerousness in the Sentencing of Criminals* (New Brunswick, N.J.: Rutgers University Press, 1985).

60. Willard Gaylin, *Partial Justice* (New York: Knopf, 1974).

61. Norval Morris, *The Future of Imprisonment* (Chicago: University of Chicago Press, 1974).

62. Aleksander Fatic, *Punishment and Restorative Crime-Handling: A Social Theory of Trust* (Aldershot, United Kingdom: Avebury, 1995); Gordon Bazemore and Mark Umbreit, "Rethinking the Sanctioning Function in Juvenile Court: Retributive or Restorative Responses to Youth Crime," *Crime and Delinquency*, **41** (1995): 296–316; Sally Merry and Neal Milner, eds., *The Possibility of Popular Justice: A Case Study of Community Mediation in the United States* (Ann Arbor: University of Michigan Press, 1995); Kayleen M. Hazelhurst, ed., *Popular Justice and Community Regeneration: Pathways of Indigenous Reform* (Westport, Conn.: Praeger, 1995).

63. Daniel W. Van Ness and Andrew Ashworth, "New Wine and Old Wineskins: Four Challenges to Restorative Justice," *Criminal Law Forum*, 4 (1993): 251–306.

64. David W. McDowall, Colin Loftin, and Brian Wiersema, *A Comparative Study of the Preventive Effects of Mandatory Sentencing Laws for Gun Crimes* (Washington, D.C.: U.S. Government Printing Office, 1992); U.S. Sentencing Commission, *Special Report to the Congress: Mandatory Minimum Penalties in the Federal Criminal Justice System* (Washington, D.C.: U.S. Government Printing Office, 1991).

65. Lawrence A. Greenfield, *Prison Sentences and Time Served for Violence* (Washington, D.C.: Bureau of Justice Statistics, 1995).

66. Jimmy J. Williams, "Controlling the Judge's Discretion: Appellate Review of Departures," *Justice System Journal*, **17** (1994): 229–240; *A Plan for Felony Sentencing in Ohio* (Columbus: Ohio Criminal Sentencing Commission, 1993).

67. James Wotton, *Truth in Sentencing: Why States Should Make Violent Criminals Do Their Time* (Washington, D.C.: Heritage Foundation, 1993).

68. E.g., Lois G. Forer, *A Rage to Punish: The Unintended Consequences of Mandatory Sentencing* (New York: W. W. Norton, 1994).

Review   •   You Be the Criminologist   •   Key Terms   •   Notes

69. Mary K. Shilton, Vincent L. Boderick, and Walter Dickey, "Mandatory Minimum Sentencing," *IARCA Journal on Community Corrections*, **6** (1994): 4–35; *Mandatory Minimum Sentences: Are They Being Imposed and Who Is Receiving Them?* (Washington, D.C.: U.S. General Accounting Office, 1993).

70. Henry Scott Wallace, "Mandatory Minimums and the Betrayal of Sentencing Reform: A Legislative Dr. Jekyll and Mr. Hyde," *Federal Probation*, **57** (1993): 9–19.

71. James Austin, Charles Jones, John Kramer, et al., *National Assessment of Structured Sentencing: Final Report* (Washington, D.C.: Bureau of Justice Statistics, 1995).

72. Thomas B. Marvell and Carlisle E. Moody, "Determinative Sentencing and Abolishing Parole: The Long-Term Impacts on Prisons and Crime," *Criminology*, **34** (1996): 107–128; Pamela L. Griset, "Determinative Sentencing and Agenda Building: A Case Study of the Failure of a Reform," *Journal of Criminal Justice*, **23** (1995): 349–362; Pamela L. Griset, "Determinate Sentencing and the High Cost of Overblown Rhetoric: The New York Experience," *Crime and Delinquency*, **40** (1994): 532–548; *Arizona Criminal Code and Corrections Study: Final Report to the Legislative Council* (Phoenix, Ariz.: Institute for Rational Public Policy, 1991).

73. Marvin E. Frankel, *Criminal Sentences* (New York: Hill and Wang, 1973).

74. Andrew von Hirsch, Kay A. Knapp, and Michael Tonry, *The Sentencing Commission and Its Guidelines* (Boston: Northeastern University Press, 1987).

75. Sally S. Simpson and Christopher S. Koper, "Deterring Corporate Crime," *Criminology*, **30** (1992): 347–373; William S. Laufer, "Culpability and the Sentencing of Corporations," *Nebraska Law Review*, **71** (1992): 1049–1094.

76. See Eric Simon, Gerry Gaes, and William Rhodes, "ASSYST—The Design and Implementation of Computer-Assisted Sentencing," *Federal Probation*, **55** (1991): 46–55.

77. See Michael Tonry, "The Politics and Processes of Sentencing Commissions," *Crime and Delinquency*, **37** (1991): 307–329; Alfred Blumstein, Jacqueline Cohen, Susan E. Martin, and Michael H. Tonry, *Research on Sentencing: The Search for Reform* (Washington, D.C.: National Academy Press, 1983); and Joann L. Miller, Peter H. Rossi, and Jon E. Simpson, "Felony Punishments: A Factorial Survey of Perceived Justice in Criminal Sentencing," *Journal of Criminal Law and Criminology*, **82** (1991): 396–422.

78. See John H. Kramer, Robin L. Lubitz, and Cynthia A. Kempinen, "Sentencing Guidelines: A Quantitative Comparison of Sentencing Policies in Minnesota, Pennsylvania, and Washington," *Justice Quarterly*, **61** (1989): 565–587.

79. For a complete account of the fate of New York's sentencing commission, see Pamala L. Griset, *Determinate Sentencing: The Promise and the Reality of Retributive Justice* (Albany: State University of New York Press, 1991).

80. Michael Tonry, "Sentencing Guidelines and Their Effects," in von Hirsch, Knapp, and Tonry, *The Sentencing Commission and Its Guidelines*, pp. 16–43; Laura Lein, Robert Rickards, and Tony Fabelo, "The Attitudes of Criminal Justice Practitioners toward Sentencing Issues," *Crime and Delinquency*, **38** (1992): 189–203.

81. *Mistretta v. U.S.*, 488 U.S. 361 (1989).

82. Stephen J. Schulhofer and Ilene H. Nagel, "Negotiated Pleas under the Federal Sentencing Guidelines: The First Fifteen Months," *American Criminal Law Review*, **27** (1989): 231–288.

83. Michael Tonry, "Sentencing Commissions and Their Guidelines," *Crime and Justice: A Review of Research*, vol. 17 (Chicago: University of Chicago Press, 1993).

84. Eric P. Berlin, "The Federal Sentencing Guidelines' Failure to Eliminate Sentencing Disparity: Governmental Manipulations before Arrest," *Wisconsin Law Review* (1993): 187–230.

85. Lisa Stalzenberg and Stewart J. D'Alessio, "Sentencing and Unwarranted Disparity: An Empirical Assessment of the Long-Term Impact of Sentencing Guidelines in Minnesota," *Criminology*, **32** (1994): 301–310.

86. Lisa Stalzenberg and Stewart J. D'Alessio, "The Unintended Consequence of Linking

Sentencing Guidelines to Prison Populations—A Reply to Moody and Marvell," *Criminology,* **34** (1996): 269–279; and Carlisle E. Moody and Thomas B. Marvell, "The Uncertain Timing of Innovations in Time Series: Minnesota Sentencing Guidelines and Test Sentences—A Comment," *Criminology,* **34** (1996): 257–267.

87. Thomas B. Marvell, "Sentencing Guidelines and Prison Population Growth," *Journal of Criminal Law and Criminology,* **85** (1995): 696–709.

88. Michael Tonry, *Sentencing Matters* (New York: Oxford University Press, 1996).

89. Edith E. Flynn et al., "Task Force Report on 'Three Strikes' Legislation," *Critical Criminal Justice Issues, Task Force Reports from the American Society of Criminology to Attorney General Reno* (Washington, D.C.: Compiled by the National Institute of Justice, 1995).

90. See, e.g., Thomas B. Marvell and Carlisle E. Moody, "The Impact of Enhanced Prison Terms for Felonies Committed with Guns," *Criminology,* **33** (1995): 247–281.

91. Sara T. Dike, "Capital Punishment in the United States, Part I: Observations on the Use and Interpretation of the Law," *Criminal Justice Abstracts,* **13** (1981): 283–311; Hugo A. Bedau, *The Death Penalty in America* (New York: Oxford University Press, 1984).

92. William Bowers, *Executions in America* (Lexington, Mass.: Lexington Books, 1974).

93. Victoria Schneider and John Ortiz Smykla, "A Summary Analysis of *Executions in the United States: 1608–1978: The Espy File,*" in *The Death Penalty in America: Current Research,* ed. Robert M. Bohm (Cincinnati: Anderson; Highland Heights, Ky.: Academy of Criminal Justice Sciences, 1991), pp. 1–20.

94. Sandra Nicolai, Karen Riley, Rhonda Christensen, Patrice Stych, and Leslie Greunke, *The Question of Capital Punishment* (Lincoln, Neb.: Contact, 1980).

95. Thorsten Sellin, *The Death Penalty* (Philadelphia: American Law Institute, 1959); Thorsten Sellin, *Capital Punishment* (New York: Harper & Row, 1967); Thorsten Sellin, *The Penalty of Death* (Beverly Hills, Calif.: Sage, 1980); Hans Zeisel, "The Deterrent Ef-

fect of the Death Penalty: Facts v. Faith," in *The Supreme Court Review,* ed. P. E. Kurland (Chicago: University of Chicago Press, 1976), pp. 317–343; Darrel Cheatwood, "Capital Punishment and the Deterrence of Crime in Comparable Counties," *Criminal Justice Review,* **18** (1993): 165–181; Raymond Paternoster, *Capital Punishment in America* (New York: Lexington Books, 1991); Louis D. Bilionis, "Moral Appropriateness, Capital Punishment, and the 'Lockett' Doctrine," *Journal of Criminal Law and Criminology,* **82** (1991): 283–333; Robert M. Bohm, Louise J. Clark, and Adrian F. Aveni, "Knowledge and Death Penalty Opinion: A Test of the Marshall Hypotheses," *Journal of Research in Crime and Delinquency,* **28** (1991): 360–387.

96. Isaac Ehrlich, "The Deterrent Effect of Capital Punishment: A Question of Life and Death," *American Economic Review,* **65** (1975): 397–417; Gennaro F. Vito, Pat Koester, and Deborah G. Wilson, "Return of the Dead: An Update on the Status of *Furman*-Commuted Death Row Inmates," in Bohm, *The Death Penalty in America,* pp. 89–99; Thomas J. Keil and Gennaro F. Vito, "Fear of Crime and Attitudes toward Capital Punishment: A Structures Equation Model," *Justice Quarterly,* **8** (1991): 447–464; Robert M. Bohm, "Retribution and Capital Punishment: Toward a Better Understanding of Death Penalty Opinion," *Journal of Criminal Justice,* **20** (1992): 227–236.

97. See Steven Stack, "Publicized Executions and Homicide, 1950–1980," *American Sociological Review,* **52** (1987): 532–540; and David J. Phillips, "The Deterrent Effect of Capital Punishment: New Evidence on an Old Controversy," *American Journal of Sociology,* **86** (1980): 139–148.

98. See William C. Bailey and Ruth D. Peterson, "Murder and Capital Punishment: A Monthly Time-Series Analysis of Execution Publicity," *American Sociological Review,* **54** (1989): 722–743; and William C. Bailey, "Murder, Capital Punishment, and Television: Execution Publicity and Homicide Rates," *American Sociological Review,* **55** (1990): 628–633.

99. Steve Stock, "Execution Publicity and Homicide in Georgia," *American Journal of Criminal Justice,* **18** (1994): 25–39.

Review • You Be the Criminologist • Key Terms • Notes

100. Charles L. Black, *Capital Punishment: The Inevitability of Caprice and Mistake* (New Haven, Conn.: Yale University Press, 1984); Herb Haines, "Flawed Executions, The Anti–Death Penalty Movement, and the Politics of Capital Punishment," *Social Problems,* **39** (1992): 125–138.

101. Marvin Wolfgang and Mark Riedel, "Race, Judicial Discretion, and the Death Penalty," *Annals of the American Academy of Political and Social Sciences,* **407** (1973): 119–133. See also Joseph E. Jacoby and Raymond Paternoster, "Sentencing Disparity and Jury Packing: Further Challenges to the Death Penalty," *Journal of Criminal Law and Criminology,* **73** (1982): 379–387; Robert L. Young, "Race, Conceptions of Crime and Justice, and Support for the Death Penalty," *Social Psychology Quarterly,* **54** (1991): 67–75; and Elizabeth Rapaport, "The Death Penalty and Gender Discrimination," *Law and Society Review,* **25** (1991): 367–383.

102. David Baldus, Charles Pulaski, and George Woodworth, "Comparative Review of Death Sentences: An Empirical Study of the Georgia Experience," *Journal of Criminal Law and Criminology,* **74** (1983): 661–678.

103. *McKlesky v. Kemp,* 478 U.S. 109 (1985); Thomas J. Keil and Gennaro F. Vito, "Race and the Death Penalty in Kentucky Murder Trials: An Analysis of Post-Gregg Outcomes," *Justice Quarterly,* **8** (1990): 189–207. On the overall use of social science data by the Supreme Court in capital cases, see James R. Acker, "Social Science in Supreme Court Death Penalty Cases: Citation Practices and Their Implications," *Justice Quarterly,* **8** (1991): 422–446.

104. Blumberg, *Criminal Justice.*

105. Michael L. Radelet and Glenn L. Pierce, "Race and Prosecutorial Discretion in Homicide Cases," *Law and Society Review,* **19** (1985): 587–621; Paige H. Ralph, Jonathan R. Sorensen, and James W. Marquart, "A Comparison of Death-Sentenced and Incarcerated Murderers in Pre-*Furman* Texas," *Justice Quarterly,* **9** (1992): 185–209.

106. Gregory D. Russell, *The Death Penalty and Racial Bias: Overturning Supreme Court Assumptions* (Westport, Conn.: Greenwood Press, 1994); Robert M. Bohm, "Capital Punishment in Two Judicial Circuits in Georgia: A Description of the Key Actors and the Decision-Making Process," *Law and Human Behavior,* **18** (1994): 319–338; Adalberto Aguirre and David V. Baker, "Racial Prejudice and the Death Penalty: A Research Note," *Social Justice,* **20** (1993): 150–155; Steven E. Barkan and Steven F. Cohen, "Racial Prejudice and Support for the Death Penalty by Whites," *Journal of Research in Crime and Delinquency,* **31** (1994): 202–209; Jonathan R. Sorensen and Donald H. Wallace, "Arbitrariness and Discrimination in Missouri Criminal Cases: An Assessment Using the Barnett Scale," *Journal of Crime and Justice,* **18** (1995): 21–57; U.S. Congress, Committee on the Judiciary, Subcommittee on Civil and Constitutional Rights, *Racial Disparities in Federal Death Penalty Prosecutions 1988–1994* (Washington, D.C.: U.S. Government Printing Office, 1994).

107. Robert M. Bohm, Louise J. Clark, and Adrian F. Aveni, "The Influence of Knowledge on Reasons for Death Penalty Opinions: An Experimental Test," *Justice Quarterly,* **7** (1990): 175–188.

108. See Victor E. Flango, *Habeas Corpus in State and Federal Courts* (Williamsburg, Va.: National Center for State Courts, 1994).

109. Marta Sandys and Edmund F. McGarrell, "Attitudes toward Capital Punishment among Indiana Legislators: Diminished Support in Light of Alternative Sentencing Options," *Justice Quarterly,* 11 (1994): 651–675.

110. Kenneth C. Haas, "The Triumph of Vengeance over Retribution: The United States Supreme Court and the Death Penalty," *Crime, Law and Social Change,* **21** (1994): 127–154.

111. Roger Hood, *The Death Penalty: A World-Wide Perspective* (New York: Oxford University Press, 1989); Dennis Wiechman, Jerry Kendall, and Ronald Bae, "International Use of the Death Penalty," *International Journal of Comparative and Applied Criminal Justice,* **14** (1990): 239–260.

112. Hugo Adam Bedau, *Death Is Different* (Boston: Northeastern University Press, 1987).

CHAPTER 19
A Research Focus on Corrections

KEY TERMS
conjugal visits
corrections
employment prisons
fee system
good-time system
inmate code
intensive-supervision probation
(ISP)
parole
penitentiary
prisonization
probation
shock incarceration (SI)

To the uninitiated observer, the sentencing of the convicted person is the end of the judiciary's role in the process of reacting to crime and the beginning of the role of the executive branch of government—the execution of the court-imposed sentence. Such a view was official doctrine as late as 1958, when Justice Felix Frankfurter, in *Gore v. United States,* pronounced that "in effect, we are asked to enter the domain of penology. . . . This Court has no such power."[1]

Much has changed since then. Prisoners have acquired the right to appeal judgment and sentence and the conditions of their confinement. In many states, courts have intervened by ordering changes in the way sentences are being executed. In some jurisdictions the courts have actually assumed control and management of prison systems, through court-appointed masters. The tasks of the courts never end. From the moment a sentence has been imposed until the last minutes of its execution, the courts have the power and duty to intervene in the correctional system. Courts and corrections may be separate organizational entities

and represent different branches of government; yet they are quite interdependent, in that corrections executes and implements the orders of courts—the sentences—in compliance with standards of law.

Justice Frankfurter's choice of words was as outdated as his reasoning. He referred to penology as the domain of those who deal with offenders

after sentence has been imposed. "Penology" was a term used in the nineteenth century and the first half of the twentieth to describe the science of applying punishment for retributive or utilitarian purposes. Today criminologists speak of **corrections** when they refer to the implementation and execution of sentences imposed by courts, and to the

597

system that administers those sentences. The switch was more than a change of name; it was a change of outlook and approach, from a punitive to a rehabilitative philosophy.

The meaning of "corrections" varies with the context. Professors make corrections on term papers. Eyeglasses or contact lenses make corrections in vision. Ignorance may be corrected by education. In each of these contexts, "correction" implies some form of improvement. After centuries of exploiting and punishing criminals, the penologists of the nineteenth century concluded that criminals needed correction more than punishment. "Penologists" became "correctional specialists," and the "penal system" became a "correctional system."

PUNISHMENT AND CORRECTIONS: AN HISTORICAL OVERVIEW

From Antiquity to the Eighteenth Century

It is common to equate corrections with a prison system. That equation is not accurate today, nor was it ever accurate in the past. Nomadic people have no prisons, because buildings cannot be carried on the trek. Yet nomadic people do have means of correcting or punishing offenders. The Romans, once nomads, did not use prisons for punishment even after they settled and built the city and state of Rome. Roman criminals were punished primarily by being sentenced to hard labor for a specified period of time or for life. The Romans also had capital punishment of various forms for very serious crimes that offended not only the Roman state but also the gods. Prisons were simply places of detention for offenders awaiting trial or criminals about to be transported to the place where their sentence was to be carried out.

From the fifth to the eleventh centuries, under Germanic law homicides were dealt with by *blood feuds*, revenge killings by the victimized family against the offender's family. These feuds were not viewed as private revenge. In fact, the law demanded and sanctioned the feud as punishment. But the feud was lawful only if it was completed in a timely manner and if it did not exceed in measure the harm done. Any

revenge committed thereafter or any that exceeded the limit was considered unlawful and would lead to legal proceedings.[2] Some unlawful killings could also be compensated by payment of *wergeld*, money to compensate for the loss of a warrior.[3]

The late Middle Ages in Europe were marked by the emergence of strong rulers who gained increasing control over the punishment of wrongdoers. Punishment, except that inflicted within the family, became a function of the state. By converting compensation money into fines and by claiming the estates of persons sentenced to death, rulers enriched themselves. Consequently, the number of capital offenses and of executions increased sharply. During the reign of Henry VIII in England (1509–1547), the number of executions rose rapidly, though not to the 72,000 that some writers have claimed.[4]

The forms of punishment became ever more cruel. Those sentenced to death were hanged, burned at the stake, drawn and quartered, disemboweled, boiled, broken on the wheel, stoned to death, impaled, drowned, pressed to death in a spiked container, and torn by red-hot tongs. Noncapital punishments also rose to a level of unprecedented cruelty; prisoners were branded, dismembered, flogged, and tortured, even for offenses that today are considered trivial. This state-sanctioned brutality apparently did not reduce the crime rate, but it did condition the population to accept cruelty as part of daily life.

During the reign of Queen Elizabeth I (1558–1603) the English began to experiment with additional forms of punishment. Galley slavery was introduced.[5] Queen Elizabeth characterized it as a "more merciful" form of punishment.[6] Many city-states on the Continent also used this form of punishment, selling their prisoners as galley slaves to the fleets of Italian city-states.[7] Slave galleys were maintained by France, Spain, Denmark, and other European countries well into the eighteenth century. Conditions on the galleys were anything but merciful. Chained to crowded rowing benches, exposed to all kinds of weather conditions, whipped by brutal overseers, and fed on hard rations, the galley slaves often welcomed death.

Imprisonment was not a principal means of punishment in England or on the Continent.

The penal code of the Holy Roman emperor Charles V (1532) mentions punitive incarceration only once. Gradually, however, incarceration evolved from the practice of forced labor, a popular punishment because it supplied rulers with cheap workers. It was necessary to confine forced laborers at night in secure places. Ultimately, imprisonment came to be the primary punishment and forced labor the secondary punishment. By the mid-sixteenth century, the old English castle of Bridewell had been converted into a "house of occupations, or rather a house of correction—for repression of the idle and sturdy vagabond and common strumpet."[8] "Bridewells" were later established in all the counties of England.

Reformers in other countries created similar institutions. The Dutch, for example, established a *tuchthuis,* a house of discipline, in 1589. Germany, Denmark, and Sweden soon followed. The purpose of imprisonment was to make offenders useful members of the community through hard labor and religious worship. But soon after prisons were established, they became overcrowded. The English addressed the problem by establishing the prison hulk. Decommissioned and deteriorated warships were converted into prisons, most of which were docked in the river Thames. In the 1840s the British government had about 12 hulks that housed up to 4000 inmates.[9]

Hulks made no contribution to the correction of offenders. They were overcrowded, unsanitary places of confinement, with high death rates due to communicable diseases. Today the world community is in agreement that at least prisoners of war should not be confined on prison ships.[10]

The Bridewells and the houses of correction never measured up to the ideals of the reformers. In fact, they became slave-labor camps in which the offenders' cheap labor contributed to the wealth of the rulers. In 1832 prison inmates still worked on treadmills, holding on to a wooden bar above their heads and treading steadily as the steps went round to produce power to move millstones.[11] In the eighteenth century England invented yet another way to deal with convicted persons: It sentenced them to be "transported" to the colonies. Virginia and the other southern colonies received many such persons who labored for the development of towns and plantations. After the American colonies won their independence, England transported offenders to Australia, which is proud to acknowledge its debt to their labor.[12]

Punishment in the New World

The first settlers of New England were Puritans opposed to the primacy of the Church of England. Rejecting English law, they nevertheless imported the English means of punishment, including the stocks and the pillory. Their religious beliefs were similar to those of the Calvinists of the Netherlands, the country in which the *Mayflower* group prepared for the crossing to America. The *tuchthuis,* which they saw in the Netherlands, must have stuck in their minds as a means of correcting wrongdoers.

It was not in New England, however, but in Pennsylvania that the American correctional movement began.[13] It started there with William Penn's "Great Law" of December 4, 1682, which provided for the establishment of houses of correction. Penn's law restricted corporal and capital punishment, though it retained whipping for the more severe offenses.[14]

After the colonies declared their independence, Pennsylvania continued the liberal spirit of William Penn. In Philadelphia the physician William Rush (1745–1813) took up the cause of penal reform. He worked to abolish capital punishment and to introduce penitentiaries. Rush helped organize the Pennsylvania Society for the Abolition of Slavery, and he became instrumental in the creation of the Philadelphia Society for Alleviating the Miseries of Public Prisons (1787). As a result, a small **penitentiary** wing was added to the Walnut Street Jail in 1790. Extended solitary confinement in a cell, it was thought, would bring the offender to penitence. Even at work prisoners were not allowed to communicate with one another.

The Quaker idea of penitence and labor in lieu of capital punishment seemed persuasive. For a few years after the creation of the Walnut Street penitentiary wing, the crime rate appeared to drop. New York (1791), Virginia (1800), Kentucky (1800), New Jersey (1798), and later other states adopted the penitentiary concept and reduced the use of capital punishment. These reforms reflected the Quaker philosophy of redemption through penitence. They must also be viewed as an extension of the Enlightenment reforms advocated by Cesare Beccaria in Italy and by John Howard, Jeremy Bentham, and Elizabeth Fry in England (Chapter 3).

The Pennsylvania System: Separate Confinement Although the experiment at first seemed to be successful, barely a decade after the penitentiary wing was constructed at the Walnut Street Jail, the visiting committee of the Philadelphia Society for Alleviating the Miseries of Public Prisons reported "Idleness, Dirt, and Wretchedness" in the facility.[15] These conditions were the result of overcrowding and management's failure to cope with it. Prisoners were not at all penitent, useful labor could not be provided, and the authorities were unable to maintain the institution in a condition conducive to the improvement of prisoners.

New solutions were sought—better prisons, with better conditions and better management. Dr. Rush was in the forefront of the search. After his death in 1813 and after much lobbying by the Philadelphia Society, the Pennsylvania legislature approved the construction of two new penitentiaries, the Western in Pittsburgh and the Eastern in Philadelphia. They received their first inmates in 1826 and 1829, respectively.

The Western Penitentiary was a round building, permitting control of all cells from a central point. It was constructed more sturdily than any fortress then in existence. The prisoners were housed in small, tomblike cells that were furnished with Bibles. The prisoners had to work in their cells and were permitted only 1 hour of exercise daily. Even then they were not allowed to communicate with one another. The system proved disastrous: Anxiety increased; psychoses were rampant. The prison soon had to be rebuilt at great cost to allow some daylight into the cells. The Eastern Penitentiary functioned along similar lines. Solitary confinement, work in cells, religious instruction, and penitence were the principal features. Yet harsh discipline was not tolerated.

The Auburn System: Congregate Labor An alternative approach to imprisonment was developed in New York at the Auburn Penitentiary. Silence and labor, key features of the Pennsylvania system, were adopted. But one innovation was added—congregate labor. Younger offenders were permitted to work and eat in groups, although they were not allowed to talk to or even to glance at one another. Since the Pennsylvania system, which permitted inmates to work only in their cells, also proved extremely expensive, most states adopted the Auburn system. Congregate labor was cost-beneficial. Many penitentiaries even made a profit.

The Reformatory Movement

After the Civil War, Americans became disenchanted with both types of penitentiaries. Penitence rarely resulted from incarceration. Brutality and corruption were common. Operating costs rose. In 1870 a group of prison administrators met in Cincinnati to discuss their problems. These corrections leaders included Gaylord Hubbell, warden of Sing Sing Prison in New York; Enoch C. Wines, secretary of the New York Prison Association; Franklin Sanborn, Massachusetts correctional administrator; and Zebulon Brockway, of the Michigan House of Corrections, Detroit. The group enthusiastically adopted the reform ideas of two English penal reformers, Captain Alexander Maconochie and Sir Walter Crafton.

Maconochie and Crafton had called for an end to the vindictive imposition of suffering and embraced the ideas of treatment, moral regeneration, and reformation. The approach had to be scientific, starting with classification of inmates. Sentences had to be indeterminate, and release was to be the reward for having reformed in the "reformatory." The new reform spirit was to be kept alive by the National

Crime Surfing

www.libertynet.org/e-state/

Find out more about Eastern State Penitentiary.

Prison Association, founded at that conference. Within a few years, nearly all states had constructed reformatories, primarily for younger prisoners. The Elmira Penitentiary in New York (1876) was used as a model. Optimism disappeared, however, as it became apparent that reformatories did not reform.[16]

The Medical Treatment Model

After World War I, a new corrections philosophy appeared. During the war, draftees had been subjected to psychological testing. Psychiatry was widely accepted as a means of dealing with individual and social problems. Psychiatrists (especially psychoanalysts) and psychologists became involved in the treatment of criminals and the reform of the penal system. Individual and group therapy was practiced in American prisons. This medical model flourished until World War II.

Despite the good intention of treating inmates as if they were medical patients, conditions of imprisonment changed very little. Inmates were permitted to leave their cells only for exercise, congregate work, chapel, therapy, and meals. Silence was enforced. Movements from cell to yard, to mess hall, to chapel took place in controlled groups that marched in lockstep. A particularly harsh form of military discipline had taken over. Indeed, many members of the prison staff were recruited from the military. The slightest infraction of the rules was severely punished, often by flogging.

After World War II the medical model lingered on under such titles as the therapeutic approach and the rehabilitative model. California was the leader in this movement, but nearly all states instituted group and individual therapy programs, counseling services, and behavior modification programs of various sorts, including shock therapy and revulsion therapy. Many of these programs raised serious civil liberties issues. Most were underfunded and inadequately staffed. They reached only a small number of inmates, and the results were disappointing.

Community Involvement

At the same time, American corrections experienced yet another change. With the realization that prisons did not rehabilitate offenders and at best rendered them fit to survive in a prison environment, efforts were made to integrate the offender into the community. Representatives of the community came into prisons, and offenders were diverted out of prisons. Increasing use was made of probation, parole, and halfway houses. Later on, work-release and community projects became popular. Yet in all these approaches prisoners were simply the objects of the system and had to take what came to them.

The Prisoners' Rights Movement

The mid- and late 1960s witnessed rapid social change all over the world. In the United States minority groups demanded equality, women wanted equal treatment in public and private life, students rebelled against complacent educational systems, and the young rebelled against their elders. Prisoners, too, demanded their rights. But the correctional system was not prepared to respond. A riot broke out on September 9, 1971, at New York's Attica State Prison, an institution holding 2200 inmates. Prisoners took over most of the facility and held correctional officers as hostages. Governor Nelson Rockefeller ordered an attack by the state police. Helicopters dropped bombs and gas canisters. After 4 days and 43 deaths, "peace" was restored.[17]

Why had prisoners revolted? As a list of their demands revealed, they had been denied many of the fundamental rights guaranteed them under the Constitution. G. O. W. Mueller and Douglas J. Besharov compared the list of demands by the inmates with the United Nations Standard Minimum Rules for the Treatment of Prisoners, to which all countries, including the United States, had agreed. These standards pertain to diet, the handling of complaints, hygiene, religious freedom, contact with the outside world, treatment, education, legal assistance, recreation, medical care, minority-group personnel, inmate funds, resentencing and parole, and discipline. Most of the prisoners' demands were justified by the minimum standards guaranteed to them.[18]

The Attica experience was a shock to administrators. Prisoners' rights litigation had

Attica in the aftermath of the 1971 uprising: Inmates ordered to lie down in a yard, prior to a skin search. As the area became crowded, they were made to crawl away from the door on their bellies, hands locked behind their heads, to make room for more.

been initiated in the early 1960s, but the Attica rebellion opened the floodgates to lawsuits by prisoners testing not only the right of access to the courts but the particular conditions of their confinement.[19] Until the middle of the twentieth century, the penal codes of many states provided that felony imprisonment amounted to civil death: The felon lost virtually all civil rights, including the right to vote; the spouse of the prisoner was even entitled to have the marriage annulled.

The courts did not interfere with the management of prisons. In 1951 a federal circuit court ruled in the case of the "Birdman of Alcatraz," a prisoner who had become a highly respected ornithologist in prison, that "it is not the function of the courts to superintend the treatment and discipline of persons in penitentiaries."[20] This was called the "hands-off" doctrine.

In the 1960s the National Prison Project of the American Civil Liberties Union, the NAACP Legal Defense and Educational Fund, and the Legal Services of the federal government's Office of Economic Opportunity, as well as countless volunteers from the legal profession and hundreds of self-trained jailhouse lawyers, succeeded in overturning the hands-off doctrine.[21] Since then, hundreds of decisions establishing various rights have been handed

down. Prisoners now have the right to humane living conditions, legal assistance and law libraries, and freedom of religious practice. The rights guaranteed by the Constitution were finally granted to prisoners.[22]

Prisoners' rights litigation had a profound impact on the American correctional system. Some correctional administrators welcomed these decisions. Under court order, or the threat of court order, they could finally make improvements they had long considered necessary. Others regarded court-ordered changes in prison management as undue interference with their authority (see Table 19.1).

During the 1980s and 1990s the number of suits reaching the Supreme Court declined, for several reasons: (1) The Supreme Court has taken a more restrictive view of such litigation. (2) Prison administrators, whether directly affected by lawsuits or not, have made an effort (although often unsuccessful) to comply with mandated standards. (3) Many prison systems have set up alternative means to improve relations, such as grievance procedures, mediation, and review boards. (4) While trial courts have

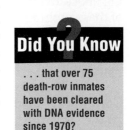

Did You Know

. . . that over 75 death-row inmates have been cleared with DNA evidence since 1970?

TABLE 19.1   Benchmarks in Rights for Prisoners

Year	Case	Ruling
1958	*Gore v. United States*, 357 U.S. 386	*The hands-off doctrine.* The court has no right to enter the domain of penology.
1964	*Cooper v. Pate*, 378 U.S. 546	*End of the hands-off doctrine.* Prisoners may bring civil action for violation of their civil rights under the Civil Rights Act of 1871.
1964	*Rouse v. Cameron*, 373 F. 2d 452 (D.C. Cir.)	*Right to treatment.* A person incarcerated for "treatment" has a right to such treatment; otherwise, he or she must be discharged.
1968	*Lee v. Washington*, 390 U.S. 333	*Equal protection (Fourteenth Amendment).* Racial discrimination in prison is unconstitutional.
1969	*Johnson v. Avery*, 393 U.S. 499	*Right to legal defense.* Prisoners have a right to assistance from jailhouse lawyers.
1970	*Goldberg v. Kelly*, 397 U.S. 254	*Due process rights (Fourteenth Amendment).* Prisoners have a right to due process when threatened with a loss resulting from arbitrary or erroneous official decisions.
1972	*Cruz v. Beto*, 405 U.S. 319	*Freedom of religion (First Amendment).* Religious freedom must be granted equally to inmates of all faiths.
1974	*Wolff v. McDonnell*, 418 U.S. 539	*Due process in disciplinary proceedings.* When faced with serious disciplinary action, prisoners are entitled to procedural due process.
1974	*Procunier v. Martinez*, 416 U.S. 396	*Freedom of speech (First Amendment).* Prisoners' mail may be opened only by "legitimate," "least-restrictive" means. Relative freedom from censorship.
1976	*Estelle v. Gamble*, 429 U.S. 97	*Medical treatment.* Deliberate indifference to prisoners' serious medical needs is cruel and unusual punishment.
1977	*Bounds v. Smith*, 430 U.S. 817	*Legal assistance.* Prison law libraries must be adequately staffed to provide legal assistance to inmates in need.
1978	*Hutto v. Finney*, 437 U.S. 678	*Prohibition of cruel and unusual punishment (Eighth Amendment).* Confinement in a segregation cell for 30 days is cruel and unusual punishment. (Totality of circumstances test.)
1992	*Hudson v. McMillian*, 112 S. Ct. 995, 117 L. Ed. 2d 156	*Use of excessive force.* Beating of a prisoner by guards, or use of excessive force, may constitute cruel and unusual punishment even if not resulting in serious injury.

Source: Based on Geoffrey P. Albert, ed., *Legal Rights of Prisoners* (Beverly Hills, Calif.: Sage, 1980).

been as busy ruling for prisoners' rights as ever, most administrators prefer not to take the costly route of appeal. (5) Most state correctional systems have been under court order to improve conditions of confinement.

CORRECTIONS TODAY

The prisoners' rights movement was one of two factors that changed the nature of American corrections. The other was the rebirth in the mid-1970s of the retribution philosophy in the form of the just-deserts model. This rebirth had an immediate effect on corrections. As sentencing became oriented toward punitive and proportionate prison sentences, corrections became punitive and custodial. Politicians and lawmakers began advocating a "no frills" approach for prisons, calling for the banning of such things as gym equipment, television, basketball, martial arts, air conditioning, conjugal visits, cigarettes, and educational programs.[23] Most rehabilitation programs, already discredited, were abandoned. Prisoners were "doing time" in proportion to the gravity of their crime. They were not incarcerated to be rehabilitated or to be reformed.[24]

This more punitive attitude toward offenders had an unfortunate consequence: Legislators passed more punitive sentencing laws, and parole boards became more reluctant to grant parole or were abolished altogether. Table 19.2 identifies the significant stages in the evolution of corrections and their relation to important criminological phenomena.

Types of Incarceration

There are two categories of prison facilities: detention facilities and correctional facilities. *Detention facilities* normally do not house convicted

TABLE 19.2 Significant Stages in the Evolution of Corrections

Time Frame	Culture: Socioeconomic-Political Development	Theory of Crime Causation	Intervention Modes
Prehistoric, preliterate, Stone Age	Clans, tribes of hunter-gatherers, early agriculture	Fate, spirits	Sacrifices to spirits, appeasement, outlawry
Starting around 3500 B.C.	Near-Eastern cities and kingdoms, commerce and agriculture	Personal motivation, rebellion	Elaborate rituals, capital punishment, compensation
Ca. 1200 B.C.	Ancient Israelites	Personal wrongdoing, offending God	Talionic punishment (an eye for an eye)
Ca. 1110 B.C.–A.D. 375	Graeco-Roman (classical period)	Ranging from fate (deities) to personal guilt (free will, pleasure/pain)	Severe punishments, slave labor (mines, galleys), capital and corporal punishment
A.D. 400–1500	Europe, Middle Ages (Inquisition, beginning twelfth century)	Rebellion against the Lord and the lords, the devil	Blood feuds, capital punishment, cruel and severe punishment, galley slavery
A.D. 1500–1800	Age of discovery and commercial expansion; development of sovereign states	Personal responsibility, laziness, bad habits, rebellion	Galley slavery, capital punishment, disfigurement, houses of correction, transportation to penal colonies
Late eighteenth century	American and French revolutions, Age of Enlightenment	Free will: Beccaria, Bentham, the Classical School	Fixed and proportionate prison punishments, decrease of capital punishment, transportation, fines
Nineteenth century	Industrial Revolution, rise of middle class	Social problems (Marx, Engels); free-will theory continues	Reformation, control; work houses, penitentiaries, probation, parole
Late nineteenth century	Evolutionism (Darwin), the scientific age	Positivist school (Lombroso), the born criminal	Control, imprisonment and community sentences, classification of convicts
First quarter, twentieth century	The rise of psychology and psychiatry	Lombroso's theory disproved (Goring); biological-psychological factors	Individualized punishments, start of indeterminate prison sentences
Mid-twentieth century	From Depression to recovery, era of world wars	Sociological, ecological factors and learning theory	Individualized sentencing, treatment, with harsh imprisonment
Third quarter, twentieth century	Civil rights movement and due process revolution	Strain, culture deviance, subculture theory	The treatment approach, rehabilitation
Fourth quarter, twentieth century	Rapid socioeconomic development, worldwide internationalization (esp. of culture)	Labeling theory, radical theory, conflict and social control theories	Retribution (fixed, mandatory sentences), return to social intervention, tough alternative sentences Reemergence of restorative justice (victim-focused resolution plans)

persons; they are not, technically, correctional facilities. They house persons arrested and undergoing processing, awaiting trial, or awaiting transfer to a correctional facility after conviction. *Correctional facilities* include county jails and state and federal prisons. In county jails, persons convicted of misdemeanors normally serve sentences of not more than 1 year. State and federal prisons house persons sentenced for felonies to terms of longer than 1 year.

But there are numerous exceptions to the rules. Many jails operated by counties and cities serve two purposes: They house persons awaiting trial or transfer, and they also hold those serving misdemeanor sentences. Moreover, since a large number of state prisons are overcrowded, many states have found it necessary to house in county jails those sentenced to state prison for felonies. Local variations cloud the distinctions even further.

Palden Gyatso is an elderly Buddhist monk and a disciple of the Dalai Lama, exiled leader of Tibet. The monk wept as he told of his time in a Chinese-run Tibetan prison. He told of electric batons that were placed in the prisoners' mouths or on their genitals. Prison guards placed the baton in Gyatso's mouth, and the electric shock was so strong that his teeth fell out. Other tortures included fires lit under the feet of hanging prisoners or boiling water poured over them. The Chinese captors also used "finger-cuffs," where shackles were put over the prisoner's thumbs, with one hand over his shoulders and the other behind his back.(1)

Gyatso's captors were torturing him and others because they were in favor of Tibet's independence from China. The monk spent 33 years in such institutions, being tortured and forced into hours of hard labor every day. During torture sessions, prisoners were asked if they still favored Tibetan independence. Affirmative answers or silence led to continuation of suffering. Despite criticism, the Chinese government is continuing to mistreat political prisoners.

MEXICO

A United Nations representative issued a report on Mexico's prison system in early 1998 that stated: "Torture and analogous mistreatment occur with frequency in many parts of Mexico,

although the information received by the Special Rapporteur does not permit the conclusion that it is a systematic practice in all parts of the country."(2) The United Nations reported that torture tends to take place during interrogation.

IRAN

A German citizen who was arrested by Iranian authorities for allegedly spying claimed that "he was tortured without a stop from the moment he was arrested. He says that he was blindfolded and that he was repeatedly slapped in the face by his interrogator. He was subjected to such abuse on a daily basis for four weeks. . . . He was tied to a wooden pole and was beaten repeat-edly on the soles of the feet with a copper cable. 'They pounded me like crazy.' He ended up signing a confes-sion. He says that he heard men and women being tortured screaming for hours on end." The Iranian government responded by saying that the German was a spy and is not credible.(3)

UNITED STATES

Correctional officers from California's Corcoran State Prison shot 50 prisoners, most of whom were unarmed, between 1988 and 1998. Federal authorities indicted eight officers for having inmates fight gladiator-style and then breaking up the altercations by firing rifles at them. In July 1998, the state government began an investigation into 36 of the fatal and serious shootings that occurred at Corcoran. Complaints of officer abuse of

inmates have also been received from prisoners in other states.(4)

Sources

1. Marie O'Halloran, "Tearful Monk Tells of His Torture in Tibetan Prison," *Irish Times,* Apr. 28, 1995.
2. Human Rights Watch, *Human Rights Developments: Mexico* (New York: Human Rights Watch, 1999).
3. United Nations, *Report on the Situation of Human Rights in the Islamic Republic,* U.N. Economic and Social Council, 1995.
4. Human Rights Watch, *Human Rights Developments: United States* (New York: Human Rights Watch, 1999).

Questions for Discussion

1. Most governments have acceded to the Convention against Torture and Other Cruel, Inhuman or Degrading Treatment or Punish-ment, making prison conditions such as those described here crimes. What could prisoners do to hold their governments respon-sible under this convention?
2. In any given country you will find some correctional institutions to be models of decency, while others are as described here. How would you design a research project that could identify the factors accounting for differences, in an effort to correct the worst conditions?

Jails Criminologists generally consider the conditions in jails inferior to those in prisons. Most jails are not sanitary, have few services or programs for inmates, and do not separate dangerous from nondangerous prisoners.[25] They are often overcrowded and underfunded.[26]

There are 3304 jails in the United States. A jail in one state may be as large as the entire prison system of another state. The Men's Central Jail of Los Angeles has a rated capacity of 5800 inmates; it usually holds more. Cook County Jail in Chicago has a rated capacity of

4600. Many jails in rural counties, by contrast, are small and operate under a **fee system,** by which the county government pays a modest amount of money for each prisoner per day. That amount usually constitutes the entire op-erating budget of the jail. As a result, there are movements to create central jails for neighbor-ing counties, which can then share the cost of operation.

The movement to deinstitutionalize mental patients, begun in the 1960s, added an addi-tional burden to the criminal justice system,

Supermax prisons became popular in the early 1990s, when correctional officials examined different ways to prevent and contain inmate violence. In supermax, there is little inmate-to-inmate interaction. The typical cell configuration: walls of solid concrete, cement bed, and a table, a toilet, a sink, and a shower nozzle on the wall. Inmates are fed in their cells.

especially to jails. It was demonstrated in a study of county jails in New Jersey that 10.9 percent of inmates had a history of mental hospitalization. That figure did not include inmates who were confined on special tiers reserved for those exhibiting grossly bizarre, irrational, or violent behavior patterns.[27] The inmates on the segregated tiers were even more likely to have some history of mental institutionalization.

Jail staff, whether law enforcement or corrections employees, cannot be expected to have the expertise required to deal with such a massive problem.[28] Experts argue that if public policy dictates that jails deal with emotionally disturbed and mentally ill offenders, a far better program of identification, diagnosis, crisis intervention, and case management at release is called for.[29]

Crime Surfing

www.stadt.corrections.com/links/

Find out what state departments of corrections do.

Prisons Whatever they are called, whether state or federal prisons, penitentiaries, or correctional institutions, prisons for the most part have had better management than jails and better education, recreation, and employment programs. But this is not surprising. After all, prisons are larger, have many more inmates, and thus have much bigger budgets. A prison normally has three distinct custody levels for inmates, based on an assessment of their perceived dangerousness:

- *Maximum security prisons* are designed to hold the most dangerous and aggressive inmates. They have high concrete walls or double-perimeter fences, gun towers with armed guards, and strategically placed electronic monitors.

- *Medium security prisons* house inmates who are considered less dangerous or escape-prone than those in maximum security facilities. These less imposing structures typically have no outside wall, only a series of fences. Many medium security inmates are housed in dormitories rather than cells.

- *Minimum security prisons* hold inmates who are considered the lowest security risks. Very often these institutions operate without armed guards and without perimeter walls or fences. The typical inmate in such an institution has proved to be trustworthy in the correctional setting, is nonviolent, and/or is serving a short prison term.

There is a new form of maximum security: the supermax prison. Among their populations are convicted spies, organized-crime figures, ultraviolent offenders (sexual and mass murderers), and other highly dangerous convicts. The United States currently has 57 supermax units in 42 states.[30] They are extremely expensive to build and to operate. The one in Florence, Colorado, for example, cost $60 million. It has 1400 electronically controlled steel gates, countless rolls of lethal razor wire, the latest in audio and visual monitoring equipment, antihelicopter devices, and six bullet-proof towers for gun-carrying guards. Inmates live in a "row of cells connected by a narrow walkway like a kennel."[31] During the 1-hour-a-week outdoor exercise time, "alone in a wire cage about 30 ft. square . . . you can see them running around the perimeter of the cage, sometimes they pace up and down like a distressed animal in the zoo."[32]

The Size and Cost of the Correctional Enterprise

The correctional enterprise encompasses a very large number of people and requires a huge budget. By midyear 1998, there were 1,302,019 prisoners residing in over 1500 state and federal prisons, the highest number in our history.[33] There were also 592,462 persons in locally administered jails.[34] (See Figure 19.1.) If we add the number of children in custody, which stood at 108,746, over 2 million persons were incarcerated on any given day in the United States, or about 1 in every 149 residents.[35]

This figure does not include the 41,874 persons arrested daily for Index crimes or the many more arrested for misdemeanors and disorderly charges.[36] Most of these were being detained on any given day (usually for several days) in the country's 13,500 police lockups, holding pens, and other local facilities operated by police and sheriff's departments.[37]

Most of the prisoners are male. State and federal correctional facilities held only 82,700 female prisoners in 1998, as compared with 1,195,100 male prisoners. Since 1981 the number of women incarcerated has risen from 4.2 to 6.4 percent of the total prison population.[38] The number of white persons in state or federal pris-

FIGURE 19.1   Number of inmates in prison. From year-end 1985 to midyear 1998, the number of inmates in the nation's prisons and jails grew by more than 1,058,000, an annual increase of 7.3 percent.

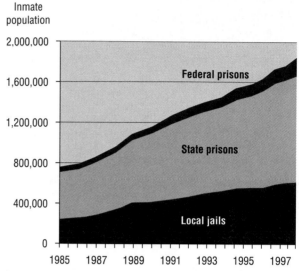

Source: Bureau of Justice Statistics, *Prison and Jail Inmates at Midyear 1998* (Washington, D.C.: U.S. Department of Justice, March 1999), p. 2.

Crime Surfing

http://www.ojp.usdoj.gov

Find out how many state prisoners undergo substance abuse treatment in prison.

ons in 1997 was 578,000, while the number of black persons in prison was 584,400.[39] The rate of incarceration for blacks is eight times the rate for whites. In 1997 blacks were incarcerated at a rate of 3209 per 100,000 black residents; whites were incarcerated at a rate of 401 per 100,000 white residents.[40] (See Figure 19.2.)

In addition to offenders in correctional institutions, there are those who are sentenced to non-institutional, or community, corrections. Principally, these are persons on probation, which provides for the sentence to be served in the community in lieu of imprisonment, and on parole, which permits a convict to serve the tail end of a prison sentence in the community. By year-end 1997, there were 3,261,888 adults on probation and 685,033 on parole. Consequently, over 5 million adult men and women, or 2.9 percent of the U.S. residents age 18 or older, were being serviced

FIGURE 19.2   Percent of U.S. adult population in state or federal prisons or in local jails, by race and sex, 1984–1996.

Percent of U.S. adult
population for each group

Black males (6.6%)

White males (0.94%)
Black females (0.47%)
White females (0.07%)

1984 1986 1988 1990 1992 1994 1996

Source: Bureau of Justice Statistics, *Correctional Populations in the United States, 1996* (Washington, D.C.: U.S. Department of Justice, April 1999), p. 4.

by the correctional system.[41] Fox Butterfield, in a *New York Times* article, questions whether there will soon be more prisoners than college students in America.[42] The number of people under correctional supervision is fast approaching 6 million—the number of full-time college students.

The U.S. rate of incarceration—668 imprisoned in prisons and jails per 100,000 residents[43]—is exceeded only by that of Russia (685 per 100,000). Other countries with high rates are Belarus (505), Kazakhstan (495), and South Africa (320). Those high figures contrast with Western European incarceration rates, for example, Germany (90), the Netherlands (85), Italy (85), and Norway (56). Of the major industrialized countries, Japan (40) has one of the lowest rates.[44] (See Figure 19.3.)

The cost of running the entire federal and state correctional enterprise in 1996 was $24.5

FIGURE 19.3   Incarceration rates for selected nations, 1998.

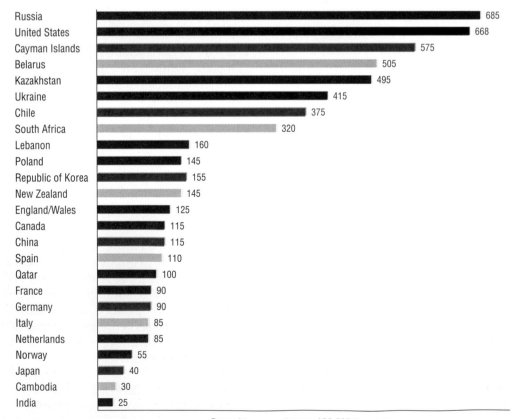

Nation	Rate
Russia	685
United States	668
Cayman Islands	575
Belarus	505
Kazakhstan	495
Ukraine	415
Chile	375
South Africa	320
Lebanon	160
Poland	145
Republic of Korea	155
New Zealand	145
England/Wales	125
Canada	115
China	115
Spain	110
Qatar	100
France	90
Germany	90
Italy	85
Netherlands	85
Norway	55
Japan	40
Cambodia	30
India	25

Rate of Incarceration per 100,000 Population

Source: Adapted from Roy Walmsley, *World Prison Population List, Research Findings,* no. 88, Home Office Research Development, 1998.

billion, an 83 percent and a 160 percent increase for state and federal systems, respectively.[45] This may sound like a lot of money, but it is actually only 1 percent of all government spending. While there is considerable variation among the states, on average, prison officials report that it costs about $20,000 a year to house, feed, clothe, and supervise a prisoner. Because this estimate does not include indirect costs, the true annual expenditure probably exceeds $30,000 per prisoner.[46]

The other significant cost is construction. We divide the total construction cost of any one institution by the number of prisoners it houses to get the cost per "bed." This cost may be as low as $7000 per year for a minimum security prisoner to as high as $155,000 for a maximum security prisoner.

The Problem of Overcrowding

At a recent international conference of criminal justice specialists, a Japanese correctional administrator asked, "With half of our prison cells being empty and our prisoner population declining, do I have a future in my chosen profession, corrections?" American corrections specialists do not have that worry. The U.S. inmate population has been increasing since the early 1970s, and the rise does not appear to be related to crime rates (Figure 19.4).

Some experts argue that incarceration rates rose because punitiveness increased, perhaps fueled by fear of drug crime and crime in general, supported by increasing media attention to crime. Once this fear was generated, it had a snowball effect. Scholars began to argue in favor of punitiveness, against the rehabilitative idea, and in support of just deserts. These arguments prompted legislative programs that severely curtailed judicial discretion in sentencing by mandating specific sentences for specific crimes. Between 1980 and 1996 the number of state prisoners serving drug sentences more than tripled (Figure 19.5), and the number of federal prisoners serving time for drug crimes more than doubled.[47] Moreover, legislation such as "three strikes and you're out" continues to add lifers to the rising inmate population.

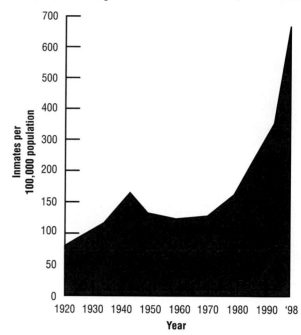

FIGURE 19.4   U.S. prison incarceration rates, 1920–1998.

Source: U.S. Department of Justice, Bureau of Justice Statistics, *Report to the Nation on Crime and Justice,* 2d ed. (Washington, D.C.: U.S. Government Printing Office, 1988), p. 104; *Prisoners in 1992,* Bureau of Justice Statistics Bulletin (Washington, D.C.: U.S. Government Printing Office, May 1993); Bureau of Justice Statistics, *Prisoners in 1998* (Washington, D.C.: U.S. Department of Justice, March 1999), p. 1.

An alternative hypothesis seeks to explain the escalating prison population in demographic terms. The most crime-prone population group is made up of 18- to 25-year-old males, a group whose numbers have grown rapidly since 1960. But this explanation is not entirely satisfactory, since the increase in the prison population was greater than the increase in the prison-prone population group.[48]

The enormous prison overcrowding over the past two decades contributed significantly to the increase in prisoners' rights litigation.[49] At year-end 1997 our state prisons were operating between 13 and 22 percent above capacity, while federal prisons were operating at 27 percent above capacity.[50] All jurisdictions are nearing their breaking points. By the end of 1997, 32 states and the federal prison system reported overcrowding.[51] The situation is growing worse.

FIGURE 19.5 Percent of sentenced prisoners admitted to state prisons, by offense type, 1980–1996.

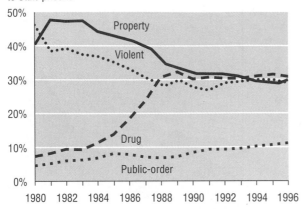

Percent of new court commitments to State prisons

Source: Bureau of Justice Statistics, *Trends in U.S. Correctional Population* (Washington, D.C.: National Institute of Justice, July 1999), p. 13.

Prison Culture and Society

For over half a century social scientists have studied the prison as a social entity with its own traditions, norms, language, and roles. Inmates constitute a unique social group. They live together, but not voluntarily. They live in extremely close quarters, often sharing all space other than a bed. They must stay in the group even if they fear for their safety.

The Deprivation Model Some experts argue that the traditions, norms, languages, and roles that develop in prison result from the deprivations of prison life (the *deprivation model*). Donald Clemmer, who has described the prison subculture and how inmates adapt to it, uses the term **prisonization** to describe the complex process by which new inmates learn the ways of the prison society and what is expected of them. Inmates are first reduced in status from civilians to anonymous figures, numbers in a common uniform, subject to institutional rules and the prison's rigid hierarchy. After a while they begin to accept the inferior role; to take on new habits of eating, sleeping, and working; and to learn that they do not owe anything to anybody for their subsistence.[52]

Building on Clemmer's work, Gresham M. Sykes described the "pains of imprisonment"

new inmates suffer.[53] First, inmates are deprived of liberty and cut off from friends and family. The results are lost emotional relationships, boredom, and loneliness. Second, inmates are deprived of goods and services. While it is true that an inmate will get "three squares and clean sheets," the standard of living inside a prison is very low.

Third, inmates are deprived of heterosexual relations. Criminologists have identified a number of psychological problems that result from this deprivation. The worst of these problems expresses itself in the homosexual enslavement of younger prisoners by older, aggressive inmates. To deal with the problem, many correctional systems have instituted programs of **conjugal visits,** which allow inmates to stay with their spouses for a given number of hours.

Fourth, convicts are deprived of personal autonomy. Their lives are regulated and controlled 24 hours a day. But the control by corrections staff is selective. The fifth pain of imprisonment is the deprivation of security. When a prisoner shares a small space with other inmates, some of whom are likely to be violent, aggression, violence, and sexual exploitation are inevitable.[54]

To cope with these pains of imprisonment, an inmate needs to live by the **inmate code,** a set of rules that reflect the values of the prison society ("Don't interfere with inmate interests," "Don't trust the guards," "Don't weaken," and so on).[55] The prison culture is a distinct culture that develops because of the nature of confinement.

Did You Know

. . . that in all but four states convicted felons lose their right to vote until their sentences are complete? Felons in 12 states lose their right to vote for life.

The Importation Model Clarence Schrag has offered an opposing explanation of prison cultures. In his view, the values found within the prison are precisely those values found on the streets from which the offenders come.[56] This model, called the *importation model*, suggests that the inmate subculture is not formed within the prison but is brought in from the outside.

Research Studies   Many researchers have tested the ideas of Clemmer, Sykes, and Schrag. Charles W. Thomas, for example, found support for the importation model.[57] Stanton Wheeler tested Clemmer's prisonization concept empirically and found that prisonization follows a U-shaped pattern during a period of incarceration: It is mild at the beginning, increases in intensity, and then decreases as release becomes imminent.[58]

The psychologist Hans Toch and his colleagues determined that most inmates serve trouble-free terms and that prison misbehavior is characteristic of youthful offenders sentenced to long terms. Misbehavior dissipates as prisoners age. To Toch, the goal of any prison system is to reduce violence through the creation of a climate that defuses it and to deal with residual violence through a person-centered approach.[59]

Reformers traditionally have been concerned with the physical environment in which prisoners serve their sentences. They have expressed the belief that prisoners cannot be reformed unless they are provided with more decent, more humane, and more refined settings.[60] Others disagree that more attractive facilities make prisoners feel better about their surroundings.[61]

The modern prison, according to James Jacobs, can be understood only in terms of the interaction between the institution and the larger society. He claims that there are still unique conditions in the prison environment which require special adaptation (as described by Clemmer and Sykes), but that the isolation of inmates from the world outside the prison walls is decreasing. Television, radio, newspapers, more visitation, and increased legal representation account for the changes. Jacobs says the idea that "prison subculture" means a group that is "isolated, separate, and opposed to the dominant culture" may no longer be true.[62]

Some researchers argue that changes in the prison population since the 1960s have created a new prison society. Contemporary prisons now house a more heterogeneous group of inmates, and it appears that a single inmate code for the whole population no longer exists. Race plays the dominant role in inmate relationships. In many state prison systems competition among black, Hispanic, Native American, and white power blocs often leads to alliances that resemble international treaties among nations.[63]

Prison Violence   The new prison society may be characterized as a culture of violence. On February 2, 1980, the New Mexico Penitentiary in Santa Fe exploded in the most violent and destructive riot since 43 inmates and hostages were killed at Attica in 1971. In Attica, the disturbance was tightly controlled by a small group of powerful inmates; the New Mexico inmates were leaderless and out of control. Fourteen guards were held hostage while hundreds of prisoners roamed the prison smashing and burning everything in sight. At least seven of the hostages were severely beaten, and several were repeatedly raped.

But the inmates reserved the brunt of their rage for each other. Thirty-three inmates were killed, some after being brutally tortured and mutilated. As many as 200 other inmates were beaten and raped. The terror was so pervasive and uncontrolled that the majority of 1136 inmates fled and sought safety among the state police and National Guard personnel ringing the penitentiary. The level of inmate-to-inmate violence was unprecedented.

When the riot was over, officials acknowledged that the New Mexico corrections system had long been neglected. Maximum-custody inmates, including some labeled psychotic, were mixed with young and vulnerable first offenders, often in dormitories holding as many as 90 men each.[64]

The increasing violence in prisons has been attributed to the younger age of inmates, overcrowding, and warring racial groups. It appears that the subculture of violence has moved from the streets into the prison.[65]

Prison Gangs   Over the past 30 years prison gangs have evolved from small groups of inmates associated for mutual protection into self-perpetuating criminal gangs with the characteristics of organized-crime syndicates.[66] The first prison gang, the Gypsy Jakers, started at Washington State penitentiary, Walla Walla,

During an interview with a reporter, Frank M. Crose, warden of Garner Correctional Institution in Connecticut, remarked: "Staff should have a reasonable expectation that they'll leave at the end of the day looking pretty much like they did when they came in. . . . There was a while when we really couldn't guarantee that, and it was all gang-related."(1) Many wardens and staff members in correctional facilities nationwide can relate to the anxiety that Crose mentioned when it comes to dealing with prison gangs. Gang violence is increasing in almost all large prisons nationwide.(2)

Since they began tracing membership in 1993, jail officials have identified 1200 members of the Ñetas and the Latin Kings in New York City jails. Gang members show their affiliation by wearing their gang colors—black and gold beads for Latin Kings; and white, red, and black for the Ñetas. They use hand signals to communicate—a tactic that allows them to defy corrections officers. There were 60 stabbings with homemade knives in 1 year among inmates in the 450-bed high-security unit at Rikers Island.(3)

It is estimated that the United States now has about 13,000 prison gang members. While they account for a small proportion of all inmates, they create over half the problems. Among the many problems prison gangs present for prison officials are violence, drug trafficking, gang wars, contract murders, rapes, co-opting of guards, confrontation between gang members and nonmembers, and the difficulties in gaining information about secret activities. Gang-related problems may increase as more and more street gang members wind up in prison. For example, the Bloods and Crips, two well-publicized Los Angeles–based street gangs, will

Members of the "Aryan Brotherhood," a white supremacist gang in Furgeson Prison (Texas). Initiation rites into the Brotherhood often require killing an African-American inmate, called the "spilling of blood" or getting a "blood tie."

eventually add many from their ranks to the prison gang population—and to the wars with other dominant prison gangs.

Prison administrators are currently working to combat gang-related problems in prison, particularly those involving violence. Some prevention measures include phone monitoring, mail monitoring, and disciplinary sanctions for possession of gang-related materials. Some states, such as Connecticut, have constructed special gang units. While in these units, members stay in their cells 23 hours a day. The only way out is to enter counseling sessions and classes that teach inmates how to survive outside of gangs. Members who complete the classes must take one more important step before rejoining the general population: They must renounce their gang membership in writing. Failure to do so results in the inmate's spending the remainder of his sentence in lockdown 23 hours a day.(1)

Sources

1. George Judson, "A Prison Blurs Gang Colors to Reduce Violence," *The Keepers' Voice,* 1995 (available at http://www.acsp.uic.edu).
2. Peter Scharf, "Empty Bars: Violence and the Crisis of Meaning in Prison," in *Prison Violence in America,* 2d ed., ed. Michael C. Braswell, Reid Montgomery, Jr., and Lucien Lombardo (Cincinnati: Anderson, 1994), pp. 11–26.
3. Mireya Navarro, "The Inmate Gangs of Rikers Island," *New York Times,* May 8, 1994, pp. 29, 36.

Questions for Discussion

1. What else can prison administrators do to prevent gang-related violence?
2. Why would an inmate who was never before involved in a gang decide to join one in prison?
3. How do gangs serve some sort of useful purpose in prisons?

in 1950. In the 1960s, racial turmoil in American society spilled into the prisons, sometimes resulting in inmate race wars. Gangs provided protection for their members. At San Quentin, for example, there were the Aryan Brotherhood, created supposedly to protect white inmates; the Black Guerrilla Family, a militant gang associated with the Black Panther party; the Mexican Mafia, with members from East Los Angeles; and their bitter rivals, Nuestra Familia, consisting of rural Chicanos.

Gangs developed in Illinois in the late 1960s, and by the 1970s and 1980s prison gangs had spread throughout the country. A recent survey indicates that there are "security threat groups," commonly known as prison gangs, in 40 state systems and the federal corrections system. The American Correctional Association reported that prison gangs tripled in size, from 12,624 members in 1985 to 46,190 in 1992.[67] A total of 763 different groups have been identified. The most common are the Aryan Brotherhood, Crips, Bloods, and Skinheads. Racial tension has led to power struggles that permeate prisons. One officer at the Men's Central Jail in Los Angeles refers to some of the gang members as "scorpions" who will attack anyone, anywhere.[68]

Correctional Officers

Prison life is largely determined by the interactions among the prisoners themselves. The role of correctional officers appears secondary. The popular perception is that the correctional staff must control prisoners by brute force. Yet officers rarely carry weapons inside the prison because inmates might take the weapons away from them if they did.

Controlling Inmates   Correctional officers survive by earning respect and resorting, when necessary, to unarmed coercion.[69] James W. Marquart designed an innovative study to address this issue. In order to understand inmate coercion, Marquart became a correctional officer for 19 months in a prison housing nearly 3000 inmates. He worked throughout the institution, collecting data on social control and order. He was able to observe how the officers meted out official and unofficial punishments, co-opted inmate

elites to act as prisoner correctional officers, cultivated snitches, and engaged in other activities.

Marquart developed relations with more than 20 key informants, who helped him interpret events. His research revealed the following on officers' use of force:

> [G]uard violence was not idiosyncratic nor a form of self-defense and was relatively unprovoked. Instead, force was used against inmates as a means of physical punishment by a small but significant percentage of the guards. These officers were primarily hall officers and sergeants with relatively low-ranking positions in the guard hierarchy. It also demonstrated that force served not only as a control mechanism, but also induced group cohesion, maintained status and deference, and facilitated promotions.[70]

Stun Shield: A correction's officer in Riker's Island (New York) displays the latest technology for disorienting and disabling problem inmates. The shield emits a six-second shock with 50,000 volts of electricity.

Correctional administrators have searched for years for the most effective means of curbing prison violence. Recent experiments have proved successful. For example, on Rikers Island, the New York City prison, disciplinary control by trained and motivated officers, through thorough and frequent searches and frisks, has resulted in the removal of most makeshift weapons. Offenders have been arrested for violations inside the prison. Inmates who have slashed others now have their hands clamped inside foot-long protective tubes, known as "the mitts." Those suspected of hiding razor blades in body cavities are placed on a chair with ultrasensitive sensors that detect all metal. The rate of violent assaults has been drastically reduced—by 90 percent in 5 years.[71]

Types of Correctional Officers   The life of a correctional officer is not easy. In some communities, such as Moundsville, West Virginia, and Elmira, New York, it is a tradition for sons, and now daughters as well, to follow in a father's footsteps and seek employment with the state correctional authority. In many towns the prison is the principal employer.

The stressful quality of the job determines the types of personalities that serve in correctional institutions. One researcher found five types, based on their attitudes toward the inmates and the other officers:

Pollyannas (optimists). Positive toward both groups.
Burnouts. Negative toward both groups.
Functionaries. Ambivalent toward both groups.
Hard asses. Negative toward inmates, positive toward officers.
White hats. Positive toward inmates, negative toward officers.[72]

Programs in Penal Institutions

With this understanding of prison life and institutional culture, we are better able to assess contemporary programs in American corrections: labor, treatment, and rehabilitation.

Labor   The overpowering demand to save taxpayers' money has led to massive programs to employ prisoners for profit. In the nineteenth century, American prisoners were farmed out to private entrepreneurs. The products of their labor were sold at a profit, which was shared by the entrepreneur and the state.

When the lease system was finally abolished in the 1920s, the legislatures of Southern states enacted statutes permitting state highway authorities to use prison labor in chain gangs on the roads. Several Southern states established plantation prisons, where, to save money, armed prisoner "trusties" replaced guards. Conditions were brutal.

The exploitation of prison labor came to a gradual halt in the early 1930s when federal legislation prohibited the interstate sale of prison-made goods (some prisons continue to manufacture license plates). In the 1970s prison administrators once again realized the potential profitability of prison industries. The U.S. Department of Justice now authorizes state prison systems that have met certain standards to ship prison-made goods in interstate commerce. At present, more than 30 private-sector industry projects are in operation. Companies such as Best Western International (hotels), Wahlers Company (office furniture), and Utah Printing and Graphics have set up shops in prisons around the country. Prisoners manufacture disk drives, airplane parts, light-metal products, and condensing units. They also operate computer terminals. California uses prison labor to help out in various emergency situations, such as forest fires, earthquakes, and toxic spills. In several states, private, nonprofit corporations operate all or parts of prison industries. The wages paid to most prisoners, however, are less than those paid to free workers.

In 1995 the chain gang reemerged on our nation's fields and highways. Alabama, Arizona, and Florida were first to revive the practice. In Alabama the men are shackled together at the ankle while working 12-hour shifts. In Phoenix, Arizona, women in ankle chains and bright orange jumpsuits clean the streets. There is a major debate about the real goals of chain gangs. Many argue against them. They say that the practice is used to humiliate inmates and to satisfy the public's desire for retribution. Some passersby even seem to enjoy the spectacle. Still others maintain that the chain gang is degrad-

September 19, 1996: Prisoner Annette Torrez takes a drink of water during a brief break from cleaning the sidewalks in downtown Phoenix, Arizona. Torrez is one of 15 prisoners in a female chain gang that pulls weeds and picks up trash on the city streets.

ing, will result in violence, and is a cruel and unusual punishment.

Among the states that have successfully experimented with productive prison labor are New York and Florida. New York State's Corcraft, a corporation empowered to run its prison industries, has proved economically beneficial for the state.[73] Florida created Prison Rehabilitative and Diversified Enterprises (PRIDE), a nonprofit corporation that since 1982 has operated all prison industries at double the income that was made before it took over. It appears also to have lowered the recommitment rate for prisoners who participate in the program.[74]

The question of prison labor is intricate and bothersome. The return to prison industry seemed to offer a means to deal with the budget crisis in which American corrections found itself. Overall, it has not worked. Moreover, troublesome questions persist about issues like compensation, industrial safety, unionization, and the absence of benefits.

Treatment and Rehabilitation Progressive criminologists regard the principal objective of the correctional system to be reformation, the voluntary, self-initiated transformation of an individual, lacking in social or vocational skills, into a productive, normally functioning citizen. Offenders are, according to this view, in need of rehabilitation. They may be psychologically disturbed, addicted to alcohol or drugs, or simply lacking in the basic skills necessary to survive in a complex society. As evidence, a 1992 survey by the Educational Testing Service found that inmates fall far behind the general population in terms of literacy skills. Fully one-third fall into the lowest literacy skill classification.[75] They therefore need educational, psychological, and vocational programs.

Other criminologists have little faith in rehabilitation programs or are philosophically opposed to the emphasis on treating and correcting behavior. With the recent focus on retribution and just deserts, some criminologists have promoted the incarceration of offenders in humane conditions with few efforts to change them, either through work or through involvement in therapeutic programs. But even those opposed to compulsory rehabilitation would not deny prisoners the right to participate in voluntary programs.

Rehabilitation has been broadly defined as the result of any social or psychological intervention intended to reduce an offender's further criminal activity (see Chapter 18).[76] By this standard, the true test of success is noninvolvement in crime following participation in an intervention program. This is why criminologists traditionally have examined recidivism (repeat offenses) rates of offenders who have and have not been exposed to rehabilitative intervention. Supporters of rehabilitation hope to see lower recidivism rates, while those who seek warehousing of inmates anticipate no such change.

Three types of programs are typically in use in prisons in the United States: psychological (psychotherapy and behavior therapy), educational (general equivalency diploma), and vocational (for example, food preparation) programs. In a novel program called Fresh Start, at Riker's Island in New York City, inmates can learn how to cook from the city's best chefs, how to wait tables, and how to wash dishes. The men who complete the program apply for a food handler's license and are given job-placement assistance upon release.

Evaluation of Rehabilitation

Innovative rehabilitation programs are generally begun with great enthusiasm; then disillusion sets in when they are subjected to critical examination. Most programs promise more than they can deliver.[77] The most devastating evaluation, commonly referred to as "nothing works," was that by Douglas Lipton, Robert Martinson, and Judith Wilks in 1974 (see Chapter 18).[78] As a result, the treatment philosophy was discredited, programs were dismantled, and the vacuum in corrections was filled by the just-deserts approach. Later some criminologists scrutinized Martinson's evaluations and found them methodologically flawed.[79]

The expectation that appropriate efforts may yield some success in changing recidivism rates has been rekindled.[80] After a thorough review of biomedical, diversion, family intervention, education, get-tough, and work programs initiated between 1981 and 1987, the researchers stated:

> [I]t is downright ridiculous to say "nothing works." This review attests that much is going on to indicate that offender rehabilitation has been, can be, and will be achieved.[81]

In a study of the psychology of criminal behavior, Nathaniel Pallone and James Hennessy conclude that the future of rehabilitation will be found in models of education and reeducation developed for behavior therapy. These approaches seek incremental changes in behavior through incentives and disincentives.[82]

Other researchers argue that prison education programs reduce recidivism and help manage prisons in the process. A large-scale 1994 study looked at 14,000 inmates in Texas and concluded that a substantial reduction in recidivism is possible when programs focus on the most educationally disadvantaged inmates.[83] Despite such results, college programs for inmates have lost much support recently because of federal and state governments' reducing or eliminating tuition assistance.[84]

At present criminologists are ambivalent about the future of the rehabilitative approach; they agree only that therapy can never again be forced on convicts. Integration of the treatment approach with the widely accepted just-deserts model seems hard to achieve. Above all, criminologists are wary of viewing treatment as the solution to the crime problem.

Medical Problems: AIDS, TB, and Mental Illness

At year-end 1996, a total of 24,881 prisoners (2.3 percent of the prison population) were HIV positive.[85] Because of the higher concentration among inmates of people with histories of high-risk behaviors for contracting the disease, particularly IV drug use, the rate of confirmed AIDS patients among the prison population is six times higher than that of the general population in the United States.[86] In 1996, 907 state and federal inmates died of AIDS-related illnesses, and since 1991, AIDS has been the second most common cause of death among state prisoners.

With no cure for AIDS and no vaccine to protect against the virus that causes it, long-term health care for infected inmates and long-range plans for minimizing transmission are important. The fear of contagion is great, both among prison guards and among inmates, raising questions about isolation or quarantine of AIDS-infected prisoners. There is little risk of HIV infection through assault and none through casual contact, but correctional officers often are afraid of dealing with HIV-infected inmates.

When the rehabilitative model was created, nobody could anticipate the enormous financial burden that the AIDS crisis would impose on corrections. The cost of caring for a terminal AIDS patient has been estimated to be $500,000. AIDS patients are shunned by other prisoners and by officers. In a recent case (*Dow v. State of New York*), $5.4 million in damages was awarded to a 42-year-old nurse who tested positive for HIV after being jabbed by an intravenous needle that came loose while she tried to restrain an AIDS-infected inmate being treated in a community hospital. Nurses testified that they had screamed 50 times for help from correctional officers who were standing in the doorway and did nothing.[87]

How can the system control prisoners dying of AIDS, who have nothing to lose? Prison hospitals are not equipped to provide adequate care for terminal patients. Placement in community hospitals poses grave risks. Successful treatment programs have not yet been established. Officials are still searching for solutions.[88]

Tuberculosis (TB) has also been a significant problem for the correctional system. The incidence of TB inside correctional facilities has declined in recent years from 1065 in 1994 to 729 in 1997, but is still higher than that of the overall U.S. population.[89] Prisons are challenged to provide isolation wards for those affected and to improve ventilation for all prisoners. There is also the danger of infection for the community at large from released TB-infected offenders.

In addition to inmates with physical illnesses, correctional administrators are faced with a large number of mentally ill offenders. A recent study found that 238,800 inmates have severe mental illnesses.[90] The Los Angeles County Jail has become the nation's largest mental institution, with 1500 to 1700 severely mentally ill inmates housed

Did You Know

... that almost 10 percent of prisoners are sentenced to life behind bars?

there daily.[91] Before being sent to jail or prison, many mentally ill offenders were homeless and unable to get the medication they need.[92]

The Elderly Inmate

A news article describes the life of an elderly inmate in Alabama:

> Grant Cooper knows he lives in prison, but there are days when he cannot remember why. His crimes flit in and out of his memory like flies through a hole in a screen door, so that sometimes his mind and conscience are blank and clean.[93]

There are nearly 75,000 inmates over the age of 50, and the elderly prison population is expected to increase dramatically within the coming decades.[94] The growth of this "new" group of prisoners may be explained by the increase in lengthy sentences, sentences without the possibility of parole, "three-strikes" legislation, and the increased life span of people in general.

This growth poses many challenges to prison administrators. These offenders often experience family conflict, depression, suicidal thoughts, and the fear of dying while incarcerated.[95] Prison staffs are not adequately trained to deal with their problems. Elderly inmates require extensive and costly medical care. They may need protection from other inmates, and activities tailored to their age. In "The Greying of America's Prison Population," Edith Flynn strongly recommends special housing and programming for three reasons: (1) to meet the increasing numbers, (2) to avoid litigation, and (3) to protect the health and safety of a vulnerable group.[96]

Most elderly inmates were incarcerated for a serious crime when they were young; some were incarcerated later in life for white-collar or sexual crimes. Still others may be habitual criminals who continue to offend and have served numerous sentences. Experts argue that incarcerating the elderly is a waste of valuable prison space, since the chances that these inmates will offend again, if released, are slim. Others maintain that these inmates should serve their time, and that they act as stabilizing influences in the volatile prison environment. Releasing these inmates brings other problems: People who have been incarcerated for their entire adult lives often find that they have lost the ability to make decisions for themselves.

Women in Prison

Most prisons are male institutions in which male offenders are guarded and receive services from a male staff. Until the mid-nineteenth century there were no separate prisons for women in the United States. The relatively few women prisoners were housed in male institutions, though usually in segregated sections. The first prison for women was opened in 1835 at Mt. Pleasant, New York, next to and under the supervision of Sing Sing Prison for men. Indiana started the next prison for women in 1873. During most of the twentieth century, women were imprisoned exclusively in women's prisons. These institutions tend to be smaller and less threatening in appearance and operation than male prisons (for example, no high walls or guard towers, and less regimentation). Yet, being smaller, they also lack many of the facilities of male institutions.

Currently, the population in women's prisons resembles that in men's prisons. Prisoners come predominantly from the uneducated, urban, poor sections of the population. Most women are incarcerated for nonviolent offenses, typically property and drug offenses.[97] Women in prison often adapt to prison life by creating surrogate families among themselves. These kinship networks provide mutual support and stable relationships and help alleviate the deprivation caused by separation from their real families. Investigators disagree on the extent and nature of homosexual relationships. Programs available in women's prisons are also different from those in male prisons.[98] They tend to emphasize society's traditional "women's work": cooking, sewing, cosmetology, and office work, to which recently, computer programming has been added.

There is an additional burden on women in institutions. More than 76 percent are mothers. They leave behind an estimated 167,000 children.[99] Many give birth in prison. The mother-child relationship poses problems the correctional system has not resolved.[100] Programs for mother-child contact are woefully inadequate;

mothers may keep their newborns for only a few weeks, and children's visits are typically limited because of the distance from the children's homes and the restricted visiting hours.

Nearly a century and a half after the first U.S. prison for women was opened, an effort to use facilities in a cost-effective manner led to the establishment of the first co-correctional institutions, sometimes referred to as coed prisons, in which men and women, segregated at night, participate in joint daytime programs of work, recreation, and meals. Physical contact is limited to hand holding. Infraction of the rules leads to transfer to separate institutions. The federal system has played a leading role in operating co-correctional prisons; nearly two-thirds of federal women offenders serve their sentences in such facilities. For the country as a whole, however, the majority of the women prisoners are serving their time in institutions for women.

Privatization of Corrections

So far we have viewed punishment as the exclusive right of the state, and the correctional system as a governmental institution for dealing with convicted offenders. This state monopoly of the penal system has existed since the Middle Ages. In the current era of free enterprise, state monopolies in many areas of government are gradually giving way to private enterprise. The delivery of letters is no longer exclusively in the hands of the U.S. Postal Service; much of it has been taken over by private courier companies. A great deal of government's police function has been taken over by private security firms. A similar movement is discernible in corrections.

Frustration over the low success rates of prisons, usually measured by recidivism rates, coupled with incredibly high expense to the taxpayers, has prompted policy makers to search for alternatives to government-

Crime Surfing

www.ojp.usdoj.gov

Find out which state has the highest number of offenders on probation.

operated prisons. One is to turn over the administration of prisons to private entrepreneurs, who expect to run prisons at a profit.[101] The first private enterprise prison was established in 1975, when RCA, under contract with the Commonwealth of Pennsylvania, opened a training school for delinquents in Weaversville. In 1996, approximately 50,000 adults were incarcerated in 126 privately run prisons. Private juvenile facilities were in operation in 12 states.[102]

A report prepared for the National Institute of Justice, based on a survey of private-sector corrections in all states, is fairly optimistic about the future of private prisons:

- Idleness is reduced at low cost.
- Prisons have access to private-sector economic expertise.
- The prison environment is improved.
- Prisoners may earn real wages and obtain vocational training useful after their release.
- Taxpayers benefit because the wages of prisoners help offset the cost of incarceration.
- Victims have a better chance of obtaining compensation out of prisoners' earnings.[103]

Regardless of success, privatization raises some troubling questions:

What standards will be used to operate the institution?
Who will monitor the facility?
Will the public still have access?
What can members of the public do if they do not approve of how the institution is operated?
Who will be responsible for maintaining security if the private personnel go on strike?
Where will the responsibility for prison disciplinary procedures lie?
Will the company be able to refuse to accept certain inmates, such as those who have contracted AIDS or tuberculosis?
What options will be available to the government if the corporation substantially raises its fees?
What will happen if the company declares bankruptcy or simply goes out of business because there is not enough profit?[104]

These questions underline the legal problems inherent in privatization. The most disturbing and basic question that must be addressed is whether the sovereign right of the people, as represented by their government, to punish those found guilty of violating the people's code should ever be transferred to private hands.

COMMUNITY ALTERNATIVES

The public equates punishment and corrections with prisons and jails. Incarceration is, in fact, the most painful, enduring contemporary punishment. In terms of the number of sentenced offenders, however, incarceration is far less significant than noninstitutional control of offenders through probation, parole, and other alternatives to confinement.

Probation

John Augustus, born in Woburn, Massachusetts, in 1784, moved to Lexington at the age of 21, learned the shoemaking trade, and by 1827 had become a successful craftsman in Boston. He often visited the courts, where he was appalled by what he saw. Judges filled the jails with petty criminals simply because the miscreants could not pay the small fines imposed. So Augustus stepped forward to pay the fines himself. Sheldon Glueck, nearly a century later, described how John Augustus worked:

> His method was to bail the offender after conviction, to utilize this favor as an entering wedge to the convict's confidence and friendship, and through such evidence of friendliness as helping the offender to obtain a job and aiding his family in various ways, to drive the wedge home. When the defendant was later brought into court for sentence, Augustus would report on his progress toward reformation, and the judge would usually fine the convict one cent and costs, instead of committing him to an institution.[105]

John Augustus promoted his new approach through his Washington Total Abstinence Society, and the Boston courts endorsed the idea. Thus was born the concept of **probation,** the release of a prison-bound offender into the community under the supervision of a trustworthy person and bound by certain conditions, such as not to violate the law, not to leave the jurisdiction, and to maintain employment. Probation was greeted as a welcome alternative to prisons in the mid-nineteenth century, when the demand for prison space was greater than the supply, the first disenchantment about the capacity of penitentiaries to reform their inmates had set in, and the exorbitant cost of imprisonment was first perceived.

The purpose of probation has always been to integrate offenders, under supervision, into law-abiding society. By 1956 all states had established a probation system. Most operate throughout a county, but some are statewide.[106] Probation is now one of the most widely used correctional dispositions. In fact, approximately four times as many offenders are placed on probation as are sent to prison.

Probation serves the dual purpose of protecting the community through continued court supervision and rehabilitating the offender. Only minor restrictions are imposed on the probationer's life. There are many benefits: (1) Not all types of offenses are serious enough to require costly incarceration; (2) probationers can obtain or maintain employment and pay taxes; and (3) offenders can care for their families and comply with their other financial responsibilities without becoming burdens on the state.

As we noted in Chapter 18, the trial judge, in order to determine a convicted defendant's eligibility for probation, requests a presentence investigation (PSI) report. This report is prepared by a probation officer, who focuses on such factors as the nature of the offense (violent or nonviolent), the defendant's version of the offense, prior criminal record, employment history, family background, financial situation, health, religious involvement, length of current residence, and community ties. On the basis of such factors, the judge then decides whether to impose a prison sentence or probation.

The probation concept as it works in practice has two major flaws. First, judges generally do not have the time, the information, or the capacity to determine whether a given offender is a good prospect for probation. They frequently view probation simply as a means of limiting the prison population by keeping less serious

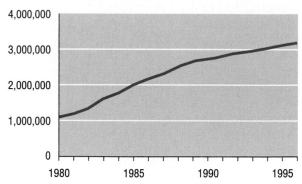

FIGURE 19.6 Correctional population on probation, 1980–1996.

Source: Adapted from Bureau of Justice Statistics Correctional Surveys (The National Probation Data Survey) as presented in *Correctional Populations in the United States, 1996,* reprinted from Bureau of Justice Statistics, *Trends in U.S. Correctional Populations* (Washington, D.C.: National Institute of Justice, July 1999), p. 1.

offenders out of prison or jail. Second, the probationer (the person put on probation) does not have the assistance and guidance John Augustus considered essential for success.

By the end of 1997 there were 3,261,888 people on probation[107] (Figure 19.6). There are 30,606 probation officers in the United States, each with an average caseload of 115 probationers at any given moment. Some officers supervise many more. And the cases are constantly changing. The officer has no chance to provide guidance and assistance. Under the circumstances, we would expect failure rates to be very high, but this is not so. In 1996, nationwide, 708,602 offenders successfully completed their terms of probation, while 196,916 were returned to incarceration.[108]

The unmet challenge is to exclude from routine probation those 20 to 23 percent of offenders who do constitute a danger. Better presentence screening may provide an answer, since probationers (except property offenders) for whom the PSI recommends probation are less likely to offend than those placed on probation against the investigator's recommendation.

Treatment programs in general and probation programs in particular depend greatly on the personality of the person providing the service. The relative success of probation programs may be attributable to the people who

TABLE 19.3   Probation versus Parole

Probation	Parole
An offender is sentenced to a period of probation *in lieu of prison.*	A prisoner is *released from prison* and placed on parole.
Probation is a front-end measure.	Parole is a tail-end measure.
The court imposes the sentence of probation.	A parole board grants release on parole.
The court retains jurisdiction.	A parole board retains jurisdiction.
A probation officer is an officer of the court and is employed by a county or district.	A parole officer is a state officer employed by the state government.
Probation is an alternative sentence for less serious cases.	Originally, serious offenders could earn parole through good conduct in prison.
Eligibility depends on a favorable PSI report.	Eligibility depends on successful service of a specific part of the prison sentence.

have joined the probation service. Probation officers have relatively low levels of job stress. Most like what they are doing, except for the endless preoccupation with administrative procedures.

Parole

The concept of parole was introduced about the same time as that of probation. In the 1840s Captain Alexander Maconochie administered an English penal colony on Norfolk Island, a speck of land in the Pacific Ocean, 900 miles east of Australia. He observed:

> [A] man under a time sentence thinks only how he is to cheat that time and while it away; he evades labor, because he has no interest in it whatsoever, and he has no desire to please the officers under whom he is placed, because they cannot serve him essentially; they cannot in any way promote his liberation.

Maconochie created a "scheme of marks awarded for industry, labor, and good conduct, [which] gave prisoners an opportunity to earn their way out of confinement."[109] Release from confinement proceeded through several stages of ever-greater freedom from control.

On the surface, **parole,** the supervised release of a prisoner before expiration of the prison sentence, may appear to be similar to probation. Both programs provide periods in which an offender lives in the community instead of serving time in a prison. Both programs require that the person be under supervision to ensure his or her good conduct. When the condition is violated, confinement results. But here the similarity ends (see Table 19.3).

The idea of parole was introduced in the United States at the first National Prison Association Congress in Cincinnati in 1870. Warden Zebulon Brockway of the Elmira Reformatory began using parole in 1876. Promising offenders were released into the care of private reform groups before their terms had expired. Later on, correctional officers were assigned to supervise the parolees. By 1900, 20 states and the federal government had parole systems in place. Ultimately, all jurisdictions instituted parole.

Parole success rates have never been great. Perhaps parole is granted too late. Don M. Gottfredson and his colleagues at the National Council on Crime and Delinquency found that success on parole diminishes as the length of time served in prison increases.[110] In 1996, of the 704,709 parolees, 179,875 successfully completed their terms and 155,624 were returned to incarceration.[111]

The high failure rate is not the only reason parole has come under attack in recent years. First, parole is supposed to be a reward for rehabilitation in prison; yet prisons do not promote rehabilitation. Second, the parole system has long been plagued by a lack of valid criteria that parole boards can use when they decide whether to release a prisoner. Though 19 jurisdictions have had guidelines for parole decisions since federal guidelines were instituted in 1973, parole decision making nevertheless remains a mysterious process that increases the anxiety of inmates.

The system is also criticized because it is subject to political manipulation and lobbying. For example, the governor may pressure the parole board to grant more parole releases when prisons are overcrowded. Lobbyists may exert pressure against a parole decision when a notorious convict comes up for parole. Parole, like probation, depends for its success on assistance and supervision. Yet caseloads are so great that such assistance is not available in the ordinary case.

In a broad attack on the parole system, Andrew von Hirsch and Kathleen J. Hanrahan argued for its abolition. The decision to release an offender, they say, should not be based on questions of treatment or likelihood of offending again; rather, prison time should be correlated with responsibility for the current offense. Parole supervision and the potential for revocation of parole disturb von Hirsch and Hanrahan particularly on grounds of fairness and appropriateness. They propose instead a fixed release date, rather than one that can change after a large portion of the sentence has been served.[112]

These criticisms have led some jurisdictions to terminate discretionary releases by parole boards. They have substituted mandatory release, either through determinate sentencing or through parole guidelines. Some jurisdictions use both methods, and some have returned to the "good-time" system.

The **good-time system** entails a procedure by which the length of the sentence is shortened by specific periods if the prisoner performs in accordance with the expectations of prison authorities. Many risks, especially to public safety, may inhere in the good-time system, and much has yet to be learned about it before it can be considered a sensible means of dealing with prison overcrowding. An opinion survey has found strong public approval for the use of good time and community-based corrections; construction of more prisons received only moderate support; and shortening sentences and increasing parole boards' authority were disapproved.

The Search for Cost-Beneficial Alternatives

Probation and parole have always been regarded as cost-beneficial alternatives to imprisonment.

As we noted, however, their success rates are mixed. In an era when crimes of violence are increasing, policy makers and the public view routine probation and parole as unsuitable solutions to the problem of prison overcrowding.

The search has begun for cost-beneficial alternatives consistent with the public's demand for security and the punitive philosophy that marks the current era.[113] The search has focused on penal or correctional measures that:

- Are less costly than confinement in a prison or jail.

- Are not perceived by the population as a cop-out, a lessening of the message conveyed by a jail or prison term.

- Do not pose a threat to the community.

- Do not have the negative effect on offenders that prison terms normally entail, but may actually benefit the offenders, their families, and their communities.

Experimentation has shown some promising possibilities, among them intensive-supervision programs, home confinement programs, shock programs, restitution programs, fines, and community service programs.

Intensive-Supervision Probation   As originally conceived, probation programs were aimed at prison-bound offenders for whom it was thought that safety considerations did not require confinement and for whom association with others in confinement would do more harm than good. Traditional probation required intensive supervision, but such supervision has become impossible because the number of probationers is so enormous. Some states continue to use token or routine probation for low-risk cases, but many have introduced **intensive-supervision probation (ISP)** for those who do not qualify for routine probation.

The experience of the New Jersey ISP program has been particularly encouraging. The New Jersey program, directed by the Administrative Office of the Courts since 1983, is designed to handle 500 offenders, the equivalent of the population of one prison. Only nonviolent offenders are eligible for the program, so it excludes robbers, murderers, and all sex offenders. Those who want to be considered for the program must apply after 30 days and before 60 days from the day of imprisonment. This period is considered desirable for shock incarceration, a method to be discussed below.

Each applicant must develop a personal plan, describing his or her own problems, plans, community resources, and contacts. A community sponsor must be identified with whom the offender will live during the early months after release and who will help the offender fulfill the program's objectives. Applicants must also identify several other people in the community who can be relied on for help. These people are called the *network team.*

The offender's ISP plan and the persons identified in it are closely checked. All information is placed before the ISP screening board, which includes the ISP director, correctional staff, and community representatives. If the screening board's decision is positive, the application goes to a three-judge resentencing panel. A positive decision by this panel results in a 90-day placement in the ISP program; the placement is renewable after 90 days. Each participant must serve a minimum of 1 year in the program, including time on parole after release, during which period he or she is on bench warrant status and thus subject to immediate arrest should a violation occur.

Program conditions center on employment and hard work. They include:

- At least 16 hours of community service per week.
- Multiple weekly contacts with the ISP officer and the community sponsor.
- Maintenance of a daily diary detailing accomplishments.
- Immediate notification of the ISP officer of any police contact or arrest.
- Participation in weekly counseling activities, if ordered.
- Maintenance of employment or participation in a vocational training program.
- Participation in any treatment program (for example, drug, alcohol) designated by the ISP officer.

- Adherence to curfew requirements (normally 10 P.M. to 6 A.M.).
- Subjection to electronic monitoring, if ordered.
- Payment of all obligations, such as the cost of electronic monitoring ($5 to $18 daily), court costs, fines, victim compensation payments, and child support, to the extent ordered by the court.

The failure rate in the New Jersey program has been far lower than anybody expected. Only 5 percent of ISP participants committed a felony during the average 18 months of the program's duration. This rate is considered a success rate, as it tends to prove that intensive supervision is capable of detecting those who may abuse the privilege of participating in the ISP program.

Among the program's greatest benefits are these:

- Rather than costing the state $17,000 per year, ISP costs $7000, thus saving the state $10,000 per offender per year.
- The offender earns a living, pays taxes, and pays the cost of electronic monitoring, fines, fees, and other obligations.
- Though it is too soon to make definite pronouncements, there is an indication that ISP program participants can do better after discharge than comparable prison inmates, thus saving the community some of the costs of crime.[114]

New Jersey's program is particularly punitive and demanding and thus more costly than any other state's ISP program. The Illinois program, for instance, aims at offenders who constitute a lesser risk and costs only $2500 per person. ISP programs in some other jurisdictions have proved similarly cost-beneficial (see Figure 19.7). An evaluation of Minnesota's intensive-supervision program indicates that participants pose no greater risk to public safety than those sentenced to prison and later released.[115] The Colorado ISP program also successfully diverted offenders from prison, at a cost much lower than either community corrections or prison.[116]

FIGURE 19.7 Annual cost of sentencing options, exclusive of construction costs.

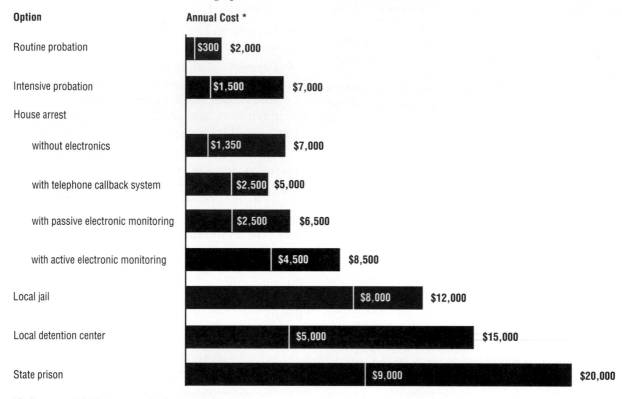

*Dollar amounts indicate range of actual costs.

Source: Joan Petersilia, *Expanding Options for Criminal Sentencing* (Santa Monica, Calif.: Rand Corporation, 1987), p. 32.

Intensive Supervision of Parolees Intensive supervision appears to be effective and cost-beneficial for offenders who are eligible for parole but who might pose undue risks and are therefore denied release on routine parole. In such cases, release into an intensive-supervision parole program, structured along the same lines as front-end programs, frees prison bed space and provides the same financial rewards to the community as front-end programs. As of 1996, there were 24,885 parolees around the United States under intensive supervision.[117] Judgment on the effectiveness of these types of programs awaits further research.

Home Confinement Programs In view of the high cost of incarcerating a criminal in a public prison, many state administrators have thought it cheaper to "imprison" a person at a place where the "rent" is cheaper. The person's home, or an alternative such as a group home or shelter, has been viewed as a viable option. Thus *house arrest*, to which over 50,000 American offenders have already been sentenced, came into existence.

> House arrest is a sentence imposed by the court whereby offenders are legally ordered to remain confined in their own residences for the duration of their sentence. House arrestees may be allowed to leave their homes for medical reasons, employment, and approved religious services. They may also be required to perform community service and to pay victim restitution and probation supervising fees. In selected instances, electronic monitoring equipment may be used to monitor an offender's presence in a residence where he or she is required to remain.[118]

Technical problems in the original electronic monitoring systems caused some initial difficulties, but these have now been largely resolved. As to psychological difficulties, it appears that other household members can accept their family member's house arrest, but many people have an aversion to electronic monitoring of human beings.[119] Michigan, Nevada, and Oklahoma have experimented with residential confinement programs whose participants are drawn from the prison population. Most states with such programs use them for diversion from prison.

The advantages of home confinement programs are that they are seen as sufficiently punitive, that the retribution and deterrence goals of punishment are satisfied, and that the offender is still allowed to maintain employment as well as close family ties, which can be particularly important when the family includes young children. Day reporting centers are another alternative to incarceration. This program allows the offender to live at home. Rather than using electronic surveillance, the offender is required to report regularly to a facility where the focus is often on treatment.[120] It is too early to know how successful home programs will be.[121]

Shock Programs Under both retribution theory of the past and the current just-deserts theory, punishment is measured by the length of time to be spent in confinement, a period determined by the gravity of the offense and the guilt or culpability of the perpetrator. Some corrections specialists believe that punishment should also be measured by the punitiveness and severity of incarceration. The intensity of a short, sharp shock incarceration may be as severe as a longer, "easy-time" confinement in a prison. Moreover, the shorter incarceration may avoid the detrimental prisonization effects of a longer prison sentence.

Shock incarceration (SI) attempts to "shock" offenders out of criminal behavior by subjecting them to short periods (90 to 180 days) of intense drills, hard work, and character-building exercises. Some ISP programs include shock incarceration; other types of programs are based entirely on the shock model. Similar to Marine Corps or Army training programs, shock programs are sometimes referred to as "boot camps."[122]

Boot camp programs are politically attractive because they are cost-effective and demonstrate to the public that offenders are undergoing an intense disciplinary experience. Their popularity has spread across the country. The programs have generally been used only for young (under age 30) male offenders, but this group traditionally constitutes two-thirds of all inmates. The number of correctional boot camps tripled between 1990 and 1995, increasing from 22 to 65 facilities.[123]

Evaluation research on boot camps yields discouraging findings. Although Illinois, Alabama, and Oregon indicate substantial financial savings,[124] a comprehensive 1994 evaluation of eight programs in eight states found that the boot camps had little effect on reducing recidivism. Furthermore, no substantial amount of prison bed space was saved.[125]

Restitution Programs In theory, victims of crime always have some recourse against their victimizers, traditionally in the form of a civil suit. Most offenders, however, are too poor to pay damages. Incarceration aggravates the situation by depriving them of the employment that could provide the money for restitution. Policy makers have begun to recognize this problem. Restitution programs have become increasingly popular since 1973, when a team of American corrections specialists visited Radbruch Haus, a former prison in Frankfurt, Germany, that had been converted into an employment-detention facility.

Half of the district's prison inmates had been selected at random to reside in this no-security facility. They were obligated to go to work every day. Their wages were carefully budgeted by correctional staff (guards retrained as accountants) to pay for court costs, confinement costs, victim restitution, support of their families, transportation to work, and so forth. The walk-away rate was low. Inmates who did walk off were placed in a secure prison.[126]

Among the American visitors was Kenneth C. Schoen, then head of the Minnesota correctional system, who pioneered the first American restitution program at the Minnesota Restitution Center. Offenders lived at a community correctional center after making a contractual agreement with the victim that itemized the amount, schedule, and form of restitution.

By now several jurisdictions have experimented successfully with **employment prisons,** or minimum security restitution centers. Low-risk offenders bound for prison may be placed in such facilities, which are usually located in or near the cities where they live and work. At night, the prisoners must remain in the facility. During working hours, they pursue their employment. Wages are administered by the correctional staff and applied to the cost of incarceration and to all other financial obligations, including compensation to the victim when it has been ordered.

Research confirms that restitution may achieve the utilitarian goal of punishment as well as the goal of ensuring just deserts. Victims and the public at large strongly support restitution programs.

Straight Fines, Day Fines, and Community Service Forced labor to pay the treasury and fines to reimburse the government for its trouble in dealing with or punishing an offender have been part of the system since the Middle Ages. Most offenders today are too poor to pay fines. Even a dollar is a lot for a person who has no income. A *straight fine*—a fixed sum—can be a burden to a factory worker but no burden to a manager. Fixed sums of money mean different things to people in different income brackets.

To compensate for income differentials among offenders, the Nordic countries (Sweden, Denmark, Norway, Finland, and Iceland) have long used the *day-fine system,* according to which the amount of the fine is measured in days of earnings. For a drunk-driving offense, the fine may be 10 days' earnings. For the corporate executive, this fine may amount to 10 times $500, or $5000; for a factory worker it may amount to 10 times $50, or $500. This scheme, which approximates that of the graduated income tax, helps the public treasury. The offender is in the community and is able to meet other obligations, such as supporting children and making car payments. And the offender is not subjected to prisonization.

Fines are predicted to play a far greater role in American corrections than they have done in the past. In view of the large number of unemployed and unemployable minor offenders, however, fines have their limitations.[127] Whether vocational training can bring these people into the group of finable offenders is yet to be seen.

When the payment of money is inappropriate, an order of *community service* may be an alternative.[128] One of the first jurisdictions in the United States to use community service orders was Alameda County, California. In October 1966 the Alameda County court agreed to permit misdemeanants to serve their sentences as volunteers for community organizations. Since then, thousands of minor offenders have served time by performing many hours of service for health and welfare organizations.

The benefits of such programs are clear:

- Offenders have opportunities to engage in constructive activities.

- Offenders may undergo a change of attitude through the experience of volunteer work.

- Community service is a sentence uniquely appropriate to indigent offenders.

- It can also be an appropriate sentence for persons in higher-income brackets whose offenses merit a public humbling.

Evaluation of Community Alternatives

Prison overcrowding in America has become such a problem both socially and financially that the established system can no longer cope with it. Criminologists were challenged to devise cost-beneficial alternatives to incarceration and the standard forms of probation and parole that also met the contemporary demand for punitiveness and public security.

In an amazingly short time, several such alternatives were developed and instituted in various states. Heralded as cost-beneficial, punitive, and secure, these programs were accepted at face value and replicated in other states on very little evidence of success in achieving the stated goals. We have pointed to some of the early evaluations, fully aware that they do not provide an accurate measure of the success of these programs.

To correctional innovators it seemed like a natural idea: if the armed forces can turn relatively undisciplined young persons, in their late teens or early twenties, into disciplined, motivated, and dedicated soldiers, why not use the same method for the same population group—though even less disciplined—to turn delinquents and young criminals into good citizens? And so military style boot camps for young offenders were designed. Prison-bound convicts, most of them undisciplined high school dropouts with histories of alcohol and drug abuse, are selected for these programs, called regimented (or regimental) inmate discipline (RID).

The first such program was established in Oklahoma in 1983. Along with the usual strict discipline and drill of all RID programs, inmates there spend several hours daily in educational, vocational, drug abuse treatment, and counseling programs. Inmates go from the program to probation or to a halfway house.(1) A similar program in Georgia subjects inmates to 8 hours a day of hard labor in addition to the usual boot camp activities. Some boot camps include more extensive therapy programs or community service experiences.(2)

Boot camp programs have been used only for young male offenders, but this group traditionally constitutes two-thirds of all inmates. The Oklahoma RID program has a success rate (individuals crime-free 12 months after discharge) of 85 percent.

Boot camp programs have been attacked as creators of "Rambos," but the use of such programs in the United States is too new a phenomenon to allow us to judge. Perhaps the experience of other countries can give insights into the effects of boot camp programs. Germany's thorough militarization until 1918 extended to the prison system, where inmates wore military-style uniforms, marched in lockstep from place to place, and had orders barked at them by drill sergeants. Their education was confined to military manuals. One prisoner's story—that of "the captain of Koepenik"—has been retold in several books and movies. Upon discharge, the prisoner bought himself an infantry captain's uniform in a secondhand

Prison boot camps employ military and para-military training and techniques to give specially selected inmates discipline and structure. In exchange, conditions in boot camps tend to be better than those in the general prison population.

clothing store, changed into the uniform in the men's room of the railroad station, and emerged as a man of authority. He promptly assumed command of a passing platoon of soldiers, marched them to city hall, arrested the mayor, and retrieved his confiscated passport—all this just so he could get out of the country.

It is surprising that, despite discouraging evaluation findings, federal and state funding is still made available to operate and create more correctional boot camps. Several studies have found that military-style basic training does not reduce repeat offending any more than traditional sanctions, such as probation or parole.(3) Although studies have not reported that the released offenders turn into Rambos or captains of Koepenik upon release, researchers have emphasized that in order to accomplish the goal of reduced recidivism, "softer" forms of correctional treatment (drug counseling, education, aftercare, and the like) should be used, either in conjunction with or as a substitution for boot camps.(4)

Sources

1. Dale Parent, *Shock Incarceration: An Overview of Existing Programs* (Washington, D.C.: National Institute of Justice, 1989).

2. Roberta C. Cronin, *Boot Camps for Adult and Juvenile Offenders: Overview and Update* (Washington, D.C.: National Institute of Justice, 1994).

3. Lawrence W. Sherman, Denise Gottfredson, Doris L. MacKenzie, John Eck, Peter Reuter, and Shawn D. Bushway, *Preventing Crime: What Works, What Doesn't, What's Promising* (Washington, D.C.: National Institute of Justice, July 1998), p. 9.

4. Ernest Cowles, Thomas C. Castellano, and Laura A. Gransky, *"Boot Camp" Drug Treatment and Aftercare Interventions. An Evaluation Review* (Washington, D.C.: National Institute of Justice, 1995).

Questions for Discussion

1. Do you think the addition of educational and counseling sessions to the boot camp–style discipline of RID programs serves to dilute the "shock effect" or to prevent inmates from becoming captains of Koepenik?

2. Would you expect boot camp graduates to continue on their careers crime-free for longer than 1 year after release, or will the effect of the boot camp experience wear off with time?

REVIEW

Throughout history, systems of punishment have often served the economic purposes of the state, first as a source of slave labor, later as a source of fines. During the past two centuries many well-meaning efforts by reformers to rehabilitate offenders turned out to be fruitless, but they shaped the correctional system into the form it has today, a mix of punishment and reform efforts.

Prison overcrowding is a particularly American phenomenon, resulting from punitiveness fueled by the drug problem and its corresponding violence along with the growing number of elderly inmates serving life sentences without parole. The traditional forms of alternative corrections, probation and parole, are still used, but recognition of their limitations has led to the development of innovative forms of intermediate corrections, such as intensive-supervision probation programs, home confinement, shock programs, restitution, fine systems, and community service programs.

Having recently gone through a period in which the need for rehabilitation determined the measure of punishment, and after a brief return to straight time (the just-deserts movement), we seem to be headed for a new era in which the measure of punishment is also likely to include the need to protect society, the need to compensate society for losses due to crime, and the need to compensate victims of crime for their losses.

YOU BE THE CRIMINOLOGIST

You are a jail warden. There have recently been several acts of violence by inmates toward corrections officers and other inmates. What can you do to prevent further acts of violence in your jail?

KEY TERMS

The numbers next to the terms refer to the pages on which the terms are defined.

conjugal visits (610)

corrections (597)

employment prisons (626)

fee system (605)

good-time system (622)

inmate code (610)

intensive-supervision probation (ISP) (622)

parole (621)

penitentiary (599)

prisonization (610)

probation (619)

shock incarceration (SI) (625)

NOTES

1. *Gore v. United States,* 357 U.S. 386 (1958), at 393.
2. Rudolf His, *Deutsches Strafrecht bis zur Karolina* (Munich: R. Oldenbourg, 1928), pp. 58–60.
3. Georg Rusche and Otto Kirchheimer, *Punishment and Social Structure* (New York: Columbia University Press, 1939), p. 9.
4. Thorsten Sellin, "Two Myths in the History of Capital Punishment," *Journal of Criminal Law and Criminology,* **50** (1959): 114–117.
5. Thorsten Sellin, *Slavery and the Penal System* (New York: Elsevier, 1976), p. 54.
6. George Ives, *A History of Penal Methods* (1914; Montclair, N.J.: Patterson Smith, 1970), p. 104.
7. Sellin, *Slavery and the Penal System,* pp. 54–55.
8. Ibid., p. 71.
9. Ibid., pp. 77, 101.
10. Geneva Convention Relative to the Treatment of Prisoners of War, Aug. 12, 1949, art. 22.
11. Sellin, *Slavery and the Penal System,* p. 101.
12. It is estimated that 100,000 offenders were transported from England to the American colonies and Australia over a period of nearly 200 years. See J. J. Tobias, *Nineteenth-Century Crime: Prevention and Punishment* (Newton, Mass.: David and Charles, 1972); and C. R. Henderson, *Penal and Reformatory Institutions* (New York: Charities, 1910).
13. Norval Morris and David J. Rothman, eds., *The Oxford History of the Prison: The Practice of Punishment in Western Society* (Oxford: Oxford University Press, 1995).
14. Graeme R. Newman, *The Punishment Response* (Philadelphia: Lippincott, 1978), p. 121.
15. Harry Elmer Barnes and Negley K. Teeters, *New Horizons in Criminology,* rev. ed. (New York: Prentice-Hall, 1945), p. 505.

16. See Alexander W. Pisciotta, "A House Divided: Penal Reform at the Illinois State Reformatory, 1891–1915," *Crime and Delinquency,* **37** (1991): 165–185.

17. *Attica: The Official Report of the New York Special Commission on Attica* (McKay Commission Report) (New York: Bantam, 1972).

18. Gerhard O. W. Mueller and Douglas J. Besharov, "The Demands of the Inmates of Attica State Prison and the United Nations Standard Minimum Rules for the Treatment of Prisoners: A Comparison," *Buffalo Law Review,* **21** (1972): 839–854.

19. James B. Jacobs, *New Perspectives on Prisons and Imprisonment* (Ithaca, N.Y.: Cornell University Press, 1983).

20. *Stroud v. Swope,* 187 F. 2d 850 (9th Cir. 1951).

21. Rudolph Alexander, Jr., "Hands-Off, Hands-On, Hands Semi-Off: A Discussion of the Current Legal Test Used by the United States Supreme Court to Decide Inmates Rights," *Journal of Crime and Justice,* **17** (1994): 103–128.

22. For a discussion of court treatment of women inmates' rights claims, see Barbara B. Knight, "Women in Prison as Litigants: Prospects for Post-prison Futures," *Women and Criminal Justice,* **4** (1992): 91–116.

23. Amanda Wunder, "The Extinction of Inmate Privileges: Survey Summary," *Corrections,* **20** (1995): 5–24.

24. Francis T. Cullen, "Assessing the Penal Harm Movement," *Journal of Research in Crime and Delinquency,* **32** (1995): 338–358.

25. Hans Mattick, "The Contemporary Jail in the United States," in *Handbook of Criminology,* ed. Daniel Glaser (Chicago: Rand McNally, 1974).

26. Michael T. Charles, Sesha Kethineni, and Jeffrey L. Thompson, "The State of Jails in America," *Federal Probation,* **56** (1992): 56–62. See also Wayne N. Welsh, Henry N. Pontell, Matthew C. Leone, and Patrick Kinkade, "Jail Overcrowding: An Analysis of Policy Makers' Perceptions," *Justice Quarterly,* **7** (1990): 339–370; Robert R. Smith, John H. Clark, Sandra I. Corliss, and Maria Lawrence, "Jail Health Care: Current Issues," *American Jails,* **8** (1994): 11–26. For an historical description, see Lois A. Guyon and

Helen Fay Greer, "Calaboose: Small Town Lockup," *Federal Probation,* **54** (1990): 58–62.

27. Freda Adler, "Jails as a Repository for Former Mental Patients," *International Journal of Offender Therapy and Comparative Criminology,* **30** (1986): 225–236.

28. See John J. Gibbs, "Symptoms of Psychopathology among Jail Prisoners: The Effects of Exposure to the Jail Environment," *Criminal Justice and Behavior,* **14** (1987): 288–310.

29. Paula N. Rubin and Susan W. McCampbell, *The Americans with Disabilities Act and Criminal Justice: Mental Disabilities and Corrections,* National Institute of Justice Research in Action (Washington, D.C.: U.S. Government Printing Office, September 1995).

30. James Brooke, "'Supermax' Isolates the 'Worst of the Worst' from Federal Prisons," *New York Times,* June 13, 1999.

31. Reg Tyre, "Hard Times for the Don," *Newsday,* Nov. 22, 1992, p. 4.

32. Russell Miller, "The Tallest Jail in the World," *Sunday Times,* May 23, 1993.

33. Bureau of Justice Statistics, *Prisoners in 1998* (Washington, D.C.: U.S. Department of Justice, August 1999), p. 1; Bureau of Justice Statistics, *Census of State and Federal Correctional Facilities, 1995* (Washington, D.C.: U.S. Department of Justice, August 1997), p. 1.

34. Bureau of Justice Statistics, *Prison and Jail Inmates at Midyear 1998* (Washington, D.C.: U.S. Department of Justice, March 1999), p. 1; Michael Welch, *Corrections: A Critical Approach* (New York: McGraw-Hill, 1996).

35. Bureau of Justice Statistics, *Prisoners in 1998,* p. 4.

36. Uniform Crime Reports, 1998, p. 1.

37. Todd R. Clear and George F. Cole, *American Corrections* (Belmont, Calif.: Wadsworth, 1994), p. 144.

38. Bureau of Justice Statistics, *Prisoners in 1998,* p. 4.

39. Ibid., p. 9.

40. Bureau of Justice Statistics, *Prison and Jail Inmates at Midyear 1998,* p. 9.

41. Bureau of Justice Statistics, *Nation's Probation and Parole Population Reached New High Last Year* (Washington, D.C.: U.S. Department of Justice, March 1998), p. 1.

Review • You Be the Criminologist • Key Terms • Notes

42. Fox Butterfield, "More in U.S. Are in Prisons, Report Says," *New York Times,* Aug. 10, 1995, p. A14.

43. Bureau of Justice Statistics, *Prison and Jail Inmates at Midyear 1998,* p. 1.

44. Roy Walmsley, *World Prison Population List, Research Findings,* no. 88, Home Office Research Development, 1998.

45. Bureau of Justice Statistics, *State Prison Expenditures, 1996* (Washington, D.C.: U.S. Department of Justice, August 1999), p. 1.

46. Ibid.

47. Bureau of Justice Statistics, *Correctional Populations in the United States, 1996* (Washington, D.C.: U.S. Department of Justice, April 1999), p. 6.

48. See Clear and Cole, *American Corrections,* p. 465.

49. Jack E. Call, "Prison Overcrowding Cases in the Aftermath of *Wilson v. Seiter,*" *Prison Journal,* **75** (1995): 390–405.

50. Bureau of Justice Statistics, *Prisoners in 1998,* p. 2.

51. Bureau of Justice Statistics, *Prisoners in 1997* (Washington, D.C.: U.S. Department of Justice, March 1998), p. 2.

52. Donald Clemmer, *The Prison Community* (New York: Holt, Rinehart and Winston, 1965).

53. Gresham M. Sykes, *The Society of Captives: A Study of a Maximum Security Prison* (Princeton, N.J.: Princeton University Press, 1958).

54. Dennis J. Stevens, "The Depth of Imprisonment and Prisonization: Levels of Security and Prisoners' Anticipation of Future Violence," *Howard Journal of Criminal Justice,* **33** (1994): 137–157; and L. Thomas Winfree, Jr., G. Larry Mays, Joan E. Crowley, and Barbara J. Peat, "Drug History and Prisonization: Toward Understanding Variations in Inmate Institutional Adaptations," *International Journal of Offender Therapy and Comparative Criminology,* **38** (1994): 281–296.

55. Gresham M. Sykes and Sheldon L. Messinger, "The Inmate Social System," in *Theoretical Studies in Social Organization of the Prison,* ed. Richard A. Cloward et al. (New York: Social Science Council, 1960).

56. Clarence Schrag, "Some Foundations for a Theory of Corrections," in *The Prison: Studies in Institutional Organization and Change,* ed. Donald R. Cressey (New York: Holt, Rinehart and Winston, 1961). For a comparative analysis, see William G. Archambeault and Charles Fenwick, "A Comparative Analysis of Culture, Safety, and Organizational Management Factors in Japan and U.S. Prisons," *Prison Journal,* **68** (1988): 3–23.

57. Charles W. Thomas, "Prisonization or Resocialization: A Study of External Factors Associated with the Impact of Imprisonment," *Journal of Research in Crime and Delinquency,* **10** (1973): 13–21.

58. Stanton L. Wheeler, "Socialization in Correctional Institutions," in *Handbook of Socialization Theory and Research,* ed. D. A. Goslin (Chicago: Rand McNally, 1969). For adjustment to prison, see Kevin N. Wright, "A Study of Individual, Environmental, and Interactive Effects in Explaining Adjustment to Prison," *Justice Quarterly,* **8** (1991): 216–242.

59. Hans Toch, Kenneth Adams, and Douglas J. Grant, *Coping: Maladaptation in Prisons* (New Brunswick, N.J.: Transaction, 1989).

60. Gerhard O. W. Mueller, "Economic Failures in the Iron Womb: The Birth of Rational Alternatives to Imprisonment," in *Sentencing: Process and Purpose,* ed. Mueller (Springfield, Ill.: Charles C Thomas, 1977), pp. 110–143; Richard C. McCorkle, Terance D. Miethe, and Kriss A. Drass, "The Roots of Prison Violence: A Test of the Deprivation, Management, and 'Not-So-Total' Institution Models," *Crime and Delinquency,* **41** (1995): 317–331.

61. James F. Houston, Don C. Gibbons, and Joseph F. Jones, "Physical Environment and Jail Social Climate," *Crime and Delinquency,* **34** (1988): 449–466.

62. James B. Jacobs, "Prisons: Prison Subculture," in *Encyclopedia of Crime and Justice,* ed. Sanford H. Kadish (New York: Free Press, 1983), p. 1224.

63. R. G. Leger, "Perception of Crowding, Racial Antagonism, and Aggression in a Custodial Prison," *Journal of Criminal Justice,* **16** (1988): 167–181; John Irwin, *Prisons in Turmoil* (Boston: Little, Brown, 1980).

64. Michael S. Serrill and Peter Katel, "New Mexico: The Anatomy of a Riot," *Corrections Magazine,* **6** (1980): 6–7; R. Arjen Boin

and Menno J. Van Duin, "Prison Riots as Organizational Failures: A Managerial Perspective," *Prison Journal*, **75** (1995): 357–379.

65. Matthew Silberman, *A World of Violence: Corrections in America* (Belmont, Calif.: Wadsworth, 1995); Lenore M. J. Simon, "Prison Behavior and the Victim-Offender Relationship among Violent Offenders," *Justice Quarterly*, **10** (1993): 489–506; Edith E. Flynn, "From Conflict Theory to Conflict Resolution: Controlling Collective Violence in Prison," *American Behavioral Scientist*, **23** (1980): 745–776; Darrell Bryan, "Emergency Response Teams: A Prison's First Line of Defense," *Corrections Compendium*, **20** (1995): 1–13.

66. Alan T. Harland, Salvador Buentello, and George W. Knox, "Prison Gangs," *Prison Journal*, **71** (1993): 1–66; Robert S. Fong, Ronald E. Vogel, and Salvador Buentello, "Blood in, Blood out: The Rationale behind Defecting from Prison Gangs," *Journal of Gang Research*, **2** (1995): 45–51.

67. American Correctional Association, *Gangs in Correctional Facilities: A National Assessment* (Laurel, Md.: American Correctional Association, 1993).

68. Seth Mydans, "Racial Tensions in Los Angeles Jails Ignite Inmate Violence," *New York Times*, Feb. 6, 1995, p. A13.

69. Patricia Van Voorhis, "Measuring Prison Disciplinary Problems: A Multiple Indicators Approach to Understanding Prison Adjustment," *Justice Quarterly*, **11** (1994): 679–709; Christopher Howard, L. Thomas Winfree, Jr., G. Larry Mays, Mary K. Stohr, and Dennis L. Clason, "Processing Inmate Disciplinary Infractions in a Federal Correctional Institution: Legal and Extralegal Correlates of Prison-Based Violence," *Prison Journal*, **74** (1994): 5–31; Dorothy Spektorov McClellan, "Disparity in the Discipline of Male and Female Inmates in Texas Prisons," *Women and Criminal Justice*, **5** (1994): 71–97.

70. James W. Marquart, *Cooptation of the Kept: Maintaining Control in a Southern Penitentiary* (Ann Arbor, Mich.: University Microfilms, 1983). See also Jeffery T. Walker, "Police and Correctional Use of Force: Legal and Policy Standards and Implications," *Crime and Delinquency*, **42** (1996): 144–156.

71. Christopher Drew, "An Iron Hand at Rikers Island Drastically Reduces Violence," *New York Times*, Nov. 9, 1999, pp. A1, B6.

72. Kelsey Kaufman, *Prison Officers and Their World* (Cambridge, Mass.: Harvard University Press, 1988); Mary K. Stohr, Nicholas P. Lovrich, and Gregory L. Wilson, "Staff Stress in Contemporary Jails: Assessing Problem Severity and the Payoff of Progressive Personnel Practices," *Journal of Criminal Justice*, **22** (1994): 313–327. For a discussion of women officers in male prisons, see Linda L. Zupan, "The Progress of Women Correctional Officers in All-Male Prisons," in *The Changing Roles of Women in the Criminal Justice System*, ed. Imogene L. Moyer (Prospect Park, Ill.: Waveland, 1992), pp. 323–343. For a discussion of men guarding women, see Linda L. Zupan, "Men Guarding Women: An Analysis of the Employment of Male Correction Officers in Prisons for Women," *Journal of Criminal Justice*, **20** (1992): 297–309.

73. *The Economic Impact of Corcraft Correctional Industries in New York State* (Alexandria, Va.: Institute for Economic and Policy Studies, 1988).

74. Committee on Corrections, *Probation and Parole, Oversight Report on PRIDE* (Tallahassee: Florida House of Representatives, 1988). See also Dianne Carter, "The Status of Education and Training in Corrections," *Federal Probation*, **55** (1991): 1723.

75. Paul E. Barton and Richard J. Coley, *Captive Students: Education and Training in America's Prisons* (Princeton, N.J.: Educational Testing Service Policy Information Center, 1996).

76. For an examination of the role of religion in prison, see James M. Day and William S. Laufer, eds., *Crime, Values and Religion* (Norwood, N.J.: Ablex, 1987); and Harry Dammer III, *Prisoners, Prisons and Religion*, Ph.D. dissertation, Rutgers University, 1992.

77. Daniel Glaser, *The Effectiveness of a Prison and Parole System* (Indianapolis: Bobbs-Merrill, 1964); Freda Adler, Arthur D. Moffett, Frederick B. Glaser, John C. Ball,

and Diane Horwitz, *A Systems Approach to Drug Treatment* (Philadelphia: Dorrance, 1974).

78. Douglas Lipton, Robert Martinson, and Judith Wilks, *The Effectiveness of Correctional Treatment: A Survey of Treatment Evaluation Studies* (New York: Praeger, 1975).

79. Ted Palmer, "Martinson Revisited," *Journal of Research in Crime and Delinquency*, **12** (1975): 133–152.

80. Daniel H. Antonowicz and Robert R. Ross, "Essential Components of Successful Rehabilitation Programs for Offenders," *International Journal of Offender Therapy and Comparative Criminology*, **38** (1994): 97–104.

81. Paul Gendreau and Robert R. Ross, "Revivification of Rehabilitation: Evidence from the 1980s," *Justice Quarterly*, **4** (1987): 395.

82. Nathaniel J. Pallone and James J. Hennessy, *Criminal Behavior—A Process Psychology Analysis* (New Brunswick, N.J.: Transaction, 1991), pp. 362–363.

83. Kenneth Adams, Katherine J. Bennett, Timothy J. Flanagan, James W. Marquart, Steven J. Cuvelier, Velmer S. Burton, Jr., Eric Fritsch, Jurg Gerber, and Dennis R. Longmire, "A Large-Scale Multidimensional Test of the Effect of Prison Education Programs on Offenders' Behavior," *Prison Journal*, **74** (1994): 433–449; Anne Morrison Piehl, *Learning While Doing Time* (Cambridge, Mass.: John F. Kennedy School of Government, Harvard University, 1995).

84. Jamie Lillis, "Prison Education Programs Reduced," *Corrections Compendium*, **19** (1994): 1–4; Sylvia G. McCollum, "Prison College Programs," *Prison Journal*, **74** (1994): 51–61.

85. Theodore M. Hammett, Patricia Harmon, and Laura M. Marushcak, *1997–1998 Update: HIV/AIDS, STDs, and TB in Correctional Facilities* (Washington D.C.: National Institute of Justice, July 1999), p. 6.

86. Ibid.

87. John O'Brien, "Record Award in HIV Needle Case," *New York Law Journal*, July 14, 1992, p. 1.

88. Eileen Kelly, "Expanding Prisoners' Access to AIDS-Related Clinical Trials: An Ethical and Clinical Imperative," *Prison Journal*, **75**

(1995): 48–68; Katherine J. Mahaffey and David K. Marcus, "Correctional Officers' Attitudes toward AIDS," *Criminal Justice and Behavior*, **22** (1994): 91–105.

89. Hammett, Harmon, and Marushcak. *1997–1998 Update*, p. 85.

90. Fox Butterfield, "Experts Say Study Confirms Prison's New Role as Mental Hospital," *New York Times*, July 12, 1999.

91. Fox Butterfield, "By Default, Jails Become Mental Institutions," *New York Times*, Mar. 5, 1998.

92. Butterfield, "Experts Say Study Confirms Prison's New Role as Mental Hospital."

93. Rick Bragg, "Where Alabama Inmates Fade into Old Age," *New York Times*, Nov. 1, 1995, p. 1.

94. Camille Graham Camp and George M. Camp, *The Corrections Yearbook, 1997* (South Salem, N.Y.: Criminal Justice Institute, 1997), p. 20.

95. Ronald H. Aday, "Aging in Prison: A Case Study of New Elderly Offenders," *International Journal of Offender Therapy and Comparative Criminology*, **38** (1994): 79–91.

96. Edith Flynn, "The Greying of America's Prison Population," *Prison Journal*, **72** (1992): 77–96.

97. Barbara Bloom, Russ Immarigeon, and Barbara Owen, eds., "Special Issue: Women in Prisons and Jails," *Prison Journal*, **75** (1995): 131–272; Louise L. Biron, Serge Brochu, and Lyne Desjardins, "The Issue of Drugs and Crime among a Sample of Incarcerated Women," *Deviant Behavior*, **16** (1995): 25–43.

98. Allison Morris and Chris Wilkinson, "Responding to Female Prisoners' Needs," *Prison Journal*, **75** (1995): 295–305; LaMont W. Flanagan, "Meeting the Special Needs of Females in Custody: Maryland's Unique Approach," *Federal Probation*, **49** (1995): 49–53.

99. Peter Appleborne, "U.S. Prisons Challenged by Women behind Bars," *New York Times*, Nov. 30, 1992, p. A10.

100. Judith Clark, "The Impact of the Prison Environment on Mothers," *Prison Journal*, **75** (1995): 306–329.

101. David Shichor and Dale K. Sechrest, "Quick Fixes in Corrections: Reconsider-

ing Private and Public For-Profit Facilities," *Prison Journal,* **75** (1995): 457–478.

102. Kathleen Maguire and Ann L. Pastore, eds., *Sourcebook of Criminal Justice Statistics—1996* (Washington, D.C.: U.S. Department of Justice, Bureau of Justice Statistics, 1997), p. 92.

103. Barbara J. Auerbach et al., *Work in American Prisons: The Private Sector Gets Involved,* for National Institute of Justice (Washington, D.C.: U.S. Government Printing Office, 1988).

104. Ira P. Robbins, "Privatization of Corrections: Defining the Issues," *Federal Probation,* **50** (1986): 24–30.

105. Sheldon Glueck, Introduction to *John Augustus, First Probation Officer* (New York: National Probation Association, 1939), p. xvi.

106. Harry Allen, Chris Eskridge, Edward Latessa, and Gennaro Vito, *Probation and Parole in America* (New York: Free Press, 1985).

107. Bureau of Justice Statistics, *Nation's Probation and Parole Population Reached New High Last Year,* p. 1.

108. Bureau of Justice Statistics, *Correctional Populations in the United States, 1996,* p. 30.

109. Alexander Maconochie as quoted in Barnes and Teeters, *New Horizons in Criminology,* p. 548.

110. Don M. Gottfredson, M. G. Neithercutt, Joan Nuffield, and Vincent O'Leary, *Four Thousand Lifetimes: A Study of Time Served and Parole Outcomes* (Davis, Calif.: National Council on Crime and Delinquency, Research Center, 1973).

111. Bureau of Justice Statistics, *Correctional Populations in the United States, 1996,* p. 116.

112. Andrew von Hirsch and Kathleen J. Hanrahan, *The Question of Parole: Retention, Reform, or Abolition?* (Cambridge, Mass.: Ballinger, 1979).

113. See William B. Lawless and Gerhard O. W. Mueller, *Report of the Commission to Advise the Nevada Legislature on the Question of Prison Overcrowding* (Reno, Nev.: National Judicial College, 1989).

114. New Jersey Criminal Disposition Commission, "Report to the Governor and Legislature, 1987," on file at NCCD Library, Rutgers University.

115. Elizabeth Piper Deschenes, Susan Turner, and Joan Petersilia, "A Dual Experiment in Intensive Community Supervision: Minnesota's Prison Diversion and Enhanced Supervised Release Programs," *Prison Journal,* **75** (1995): 330–356.

116. Kim English, Susan M. Chadwick, and Suzanne K. Pullen, *Colorado's Intensive Supervision Probation: Report of Findings* (Denver: Colorado Division of Criminal Justice, 1994).

117. Bureau of Justice Statistics, *Correctional Populations in the United States, 1996,* p. 116.

118. Joan Petersilia, *Expanding Options for Criminal Sentencing* (Santa Monica, Calif.: Rand Corporation, 1987), p. 32.

119. Dorothy K. Kagehiro and Ralph Taylor, "A Social Psychological Analysis of Home Electronic Confinement," in *Handbook of Psychology and Law,* ed. D. K. Kagehiro and W. S. Laufer (New York: Springer Verlag, 1992).

120. See David W. Diggs and Stephen L. Pieper, "Using Day Reporting Centers as an Alternative to Jail," *Federal Probation,* **58** (1994): 9–12; and Dale Parent, Jim Byrne, Vered Tsarfaty, Laura Valade, and Julie Esselman, *Day Reporting Centers,* vol. 1 (Washington, D.C.: U.S. National Institute of Justice, 1995).

121. Stephen J. Rackmill, "An Analysis of Home Confinement as a Sanction," *Federal Probation,* **58** (1994): 45–52; Darren Gowen, "Electronic Monitoring in the Southern District of Mississippi," *Federal Probation,* **59** (1995): 10–13; Michael P. Brown and Preston Elrod, "Electronic House Arrest: An Examination of Citizen Attitudes," *Crime and Delinquency,* **41** (1995): 332–346.

122. Doris Layton MacKenzie and James Shaw, "The Impact of Shock Incarceration on Technical Violations and New Criminal Activities," *Justice Quarterly,* **10** (1993): 463–487; James Austin, Michael Jones, and Melissa Bolyard, *The Growing Use of Jail Boot Camps: The Current State of the Art* (Washington, D.C.: National Institute of Justice, 1993); Carol Poole and Peggy Slavick, *Boot Camps: A Washington State Update and Overview of National Findings* (Olympia: Washington State Institute for Public Policy, 1995).

Review • You Be the Criminologist • Key Terms • Notes

123. Bureau of Justice Statistics, *Census of State and Federal Correctional Facilities, 1995,* p. 15.

124. Steven P. Karr and Robert J. Jones, *Impact Incarceration Program* (Springfield: Illinois Department of Corrections, 1994); Jerald C. Burns and Gennaro F. Vito, "An Impact Analysis of the Alabama Boot Camp Program," *Federal Probation,* **49** (1995): 63–67; David K. Blanchard and Gary Perlstein, *A Program Evaluation of the Oregon Summit Boot Camp Program* (Portland, Oreg.: Portland State University, 1995); Ronald Corbett and Gary T. Marx, "Critique: No Soul in the New Machine: Technofallacies in the Electronic Monitoring Movement," *Journal of Offender Monitoring,* **7** (1994): 1–9.

125. Doris Layton MacKenzie and Claire Souryal, *Multisite Evaluation of Shock Incarceration—A Final Summary Report* (Washington, D.C.: National Institute of Justice, 1994).

126. Criminal Law Education and Research Center, *International Conference of Correctional Policy Makers* (New York: New York University School of Law, 1973).

127. James F. Nelson, "A Dollar or a Day: Sentencing Misdemeanants in New York State," *Journal of Research in Crime and Delinquency,* **31** (1994): 183–201.

128. Richard D. Majer, "Community Service: A Good Idea That Works," *Federal Probation,* **58** (1994): 20–23.

A

Accommodate   In regard to achieving the American Dream, to adjust noneconomic needs so that they are secondary to and supportive of economic ones.

Accomplice   A person who helps another commit a crime.

Aggravated assault   An attack on another person in which the perpetrator inflicts serious harm on the victim or uses a deadly weapon.

Aging-out phenomenon   A concept that holds that offenders commit less crime as they get older because they have less strength, initiative, stamina, and mobility.

Anomie   A societal state marked by normlessness, in which disintegration and chaos have replaced social cohesion.

Arraignment   First stage of the trial process, at which the indictment or information is read in open court and the defendant is requested to respond.

Arson   At common law, the malicious burning of the dwelling house of another. This definition has been broadened by state statutes and criminal codes to cover the burning of other structures or even personal property.

Assault   At common law, an unlawful offer or attempt with force or violence to do a corporal hurt to another or to frighten another.

Atavistic stigmata   Physical features of a human being at an earlier stage of development, which—according to Cesare Lombroso—distinguish a born criminal from the general population.

Attachment   The bond between a parent and child or between individuals and their family, friends, and school.

B

Bankruptcy fraud   A scam in which an individual falsely attempts to claim bankruptcy (and thereby erase financial debts) by taking advantage of existing laws.

Battery   A common law crime consisting of the intentional touching of or inflicting of hurt on another.

Behavioral modeling   Learning how to behave by fashioning one's behavior after that of others.

Belief   The extent to which an individual subscribes to society's values.

Biocriminology   The subdiscipline of criminology that investigates biological and genetic factors and their relation to criminal behavior.

Birth cohort   A group consisting of all individuals born in the same year.

Boiler room   An operation run by one or more stock manipulators who, through deception and misleading sales techniques, seduce the unsuspecting and uninformed public into buying stocks in obscure and often poorly financed corporations.

Born criminal   According to Lombroso, a person born with features resembling an earlier, more primitive form of human life, destined to become a criminal.

Burglary   A common law felony, the nighttime breaking and entering of the dwelling house of another, with the intention to commit a crime (felony or larceny) therein.

C

Case study   An analysis of all pertinent aspects of one unit of study.

Certiorari, writ of   A writ issued by a higher court directing a lower court to prepare the record of a case and send it to the higher court for review.

Challenge for cause   A challenge to remove a potential juror because of his or her inability to render a fair and impartial decision in a case. *See also* Peremptory challenges; Voir dire.

Check forging   The criminal offense of making or altering a check with intent to defraud.

Chromosomes   Basic cellular structures containing genes, i.e., biological material that creates individuality.

Churning   Frequent trading, by a broker, of a client's shares of stock for the sole purpose of generating large commissions.

Classical school of criminology   A criminological perspective suggesting that (1) people have free will to choose criminal or conventional behavior; (2) people choose to commit crime for reasons of greed or personal need; and (3) crime can be controlled by criminal sanctions, which should be proportionate to the guilt of the perpetrator.

Commitment   A person's support of and participation in a program, cause, or social activity, which ties the individual to the moral or ethical codes of society.

Community policing   A strategy that relies on public confidence and citizen cooperation to help prevent crime and make the residents of a community feel more secure.

Comparative criminology   The study of crime in two or more cultures in an effort to gain broader information for theory construction and crime-control modeling.

Conditioning   The process of developing a behavior pattern through a series of repeated experiences.

Conduct norms   Norms that regulate the daily lives of people and that reflect the attitudes of the groups to which they belong.

Confidence game   A deceptive means of obtaining money or property from a victim who is led to trust the perpetrator.

Conflict model   A model of crime in which the criminal justice system is seen as being used by the ruling class to control the lower class. Criminological investigation of the conflicts within society is emphasized.

Conformity   Correspondence of an individual's behavior to society's patterns, norms, or standards.

Conjugal visits   A program that permits prisoners to have contact with their spouses or significant others in order to maintain positive relationships.

Consensus model   A model of criminal lawmaking that assumes that members of society agree on what is right and wrong and that law is the codification of agreed-upon social values.

Constable   An officer, established by the Statute of Winchester in 1285, who was responsible for suppressing riots and violent crimes in each county; later, a local law enforcement officer, lowest rank in some police hierarchies.

Consumer fraud   An act that causes a consumer to surrender money through deceit or a misrepresentation of a material fact.

Containment theory   A theory positing that every person possesses a containing external structure and a protective internal structure, both of which provide defense, protection, or insulation against delinquency.

Corporate crime   A crime attributed to a corporation, but perpetrated by or on the authority of an officer or high managerial agent.

Corrections   Implementation and execution of sentences imposed by the courts; also, the system that administers those sentences.

Cortical arousal   Activation of the cerebral cortex, a structure of the brain that is responsible for higher intellectual functioning, information processing, and decision making.

Crime   An act in violation of law that causes harm, is identified by law, is committed with criminal intent, and is subject to punishment.

Crimes against property   Crimes involving the illegal acquisition or destruction of property. *See* Crime.

Crimes against the person   Crimes violative of life or physical integrity. *See* Crime.

Criminal attempt   An act or omission constituting a substantial step in a course of conduct planned to culminate in the commission of a crime.

Criminal careers   A concept that describes the onset of criminal activity, the types and amount of crime committed, and the termination of such activity.

Criminology   The body of knowledge regarding crime as a social phenomenon. It includes within its scope the process of making laws, of breaking laws, and of reacting toward the breaking of laws (Sutherland). Thus, criminology is an empirical, social-behavioral science that investigates crime, criminals, and criminal justice.

Cultural deviance theories   Theories positing that crime results from cultural values which permit, or even demand, behavior in violation of the law.

Cultural transmission A theory that views delinquency as a socially learned behavior transmitted from one generation to the next in disorganized urban areas.

Culture conflict theory A theory positing that two groups may clash when their conduct norms differ, resulting in criminal activity.

D

Data Collected facts, observations, and other pertinent information from which conclusions can be drawn.

Defense counsel A lawyer retained by an individual accused of a crime, or assigned by the court if the individual is unable to pay.

Deterrence The theory of punishment which envisages that potential offenders will refrain from committing crimes out of fear of punishment (sometimes called *general prevention*).

Deviance A broad concept encompassing both illegal behavior and behavior that departs from the social norm.

Differential association-reinforcement A theory of criminality based on the incorporation of psychological learning theory and differential association with social learning theory. Criminal behavior, the theory claims, is learned through associations and is contained or discontinued as a result of positive or negative reinforcements.

Differential association theory A theory of criminality based on the principle that an individual becomes delinquent because of an excess of definitions learned that are favorable to violation of law over definitions learned that are unfavorable to violation of law.

Differential opportunity theory A theory that attempts to join the concept of anomie and differential association by analyzing both legitimate and illegitimate opportunity structures available to individuals. It posits that illegitimate opportunities, like legitimate opportunities, are unequally distributed.

Direct control An external control that depends on rules, restrictions, and punishments.

Direct file Prosecutor's power to try juveniles directly in adult criminal court.

Directed verdict A verdict of acquittal pronounced by the judge when the evidence against the accused is so poor that acquittal is the only possible verdict.

Displacement In the event that a crime has been prevented, the commission of a quantitatively similar crime at a different time or place.

Dizygotic (DZ) twins Fraternal twins, who develop from two separate eggs fertilized at the same time. *See also* Monozygotic twins.

Drift According to David Matza, a state of limbo in which youths move in and out of delinquency and in which their lifestyles can embrace both conventional and deviant values.

Due process According to the Fourteenth Amendment of the U.S. Constitution, a fundamental mandate that a person should not be deprived of life, liberty, or property without reasonable and lawful procedures.

E

Ego The part of the psyche that, according to psychoanalytic theory, governs rational behavior; the moderator between the superego and the id.

Embezzlement The crime of withholding or withdrawing (conversion or misappropriation), without consent, funds entrusted to an agent (e.g., a bank teller or officer).

Employment prison A prison for low-risk offenders. Prisoners work at jobs outside the prison during the day but return to prison after work.

Equal protection A clause of the Fourteenth Amendment to the U.S. Constitution that guarantees equal protection of the law to everyone, without regard to race, origin, economic class, gender, or religion.

Eugenics A science, based on the principle of heredity, that has for its purpose the improvement of the race.

Exclusionary rule A rule prohibiting use of illegally obtained or otherwise inadmissible evidence in a court of law.

Experiment A research technique in which an investigator introduces a change into a process in order to make measurements or observations that evaluate the effects of the change.

Extroversion According to Hans Eysenck, a dimension of the human personality; describes individuals who are sensation-seeking, dominant, and assertive.

F

False pretenses, obtaining property by   Leading a victim to part with property on a voluntary basis through trickery, deceit, or misrepresentation.

Federal Witness Protection Program   A program, established under the Organized Crime Control Act of 1970, designed to protect witnesses who testify in court by relocating them and assigning to them new identities.

Fee system   A system, used in some rural areas, in which the county government pays a modest amount of money for each prisoner per day as an operating budget.

Felony   A severe crime, subject to punishment of 1 year or more in prison or to capital punishment.

Felony murder   The imposition of criminal liability for murder upon one who participates in the commission of a felony that is dangerous to life and that causes the death of another.

Fence   A receiver of stolen property who resells the goods for profit.

Field experiment   An experiment conducted in a real-world setting, as opposed to one conducted in a laboratory.

Frankpledge   An ancient system whereby members of a tithing, an association of 10 families, were bound together by a mutual pledge to keep the peace. Every male over age 12 was part of the system.

Fraud   An act of trickery or deceit, especially involving misrepresentation.

G

General strain theory   A criminological theory positing that criminal behavior can result from strain caused by failure to achieve positively valued goals, stress caused by the removal of positively valued stimuli from the individual, or strain caused by the presentation of negative stimuli.

Good-time system   A system under which time is deducted from a prison sentence for good behavior within the institution.

H

Habeas corpus   A writ requesting that a person or an institution that is detaining a named prisoner bring him or her before a judicial officer and give reasons for the prisoner's capture and detention so that the lawfulness of the imprisonment may be determined.

High-tech crime   The pursuit of illegal activities through the use of advanced electronic media.

Homicide   The killing of one person by another.

Hypoglycemia   A condition that may occur in susceptible individuals when the level of blood sugar falls below an acceptable range, causing anxiety, headaches, confusion, fatigue, and aggressive behavior.

Hypothesis   A proposition set forth as an explanation for some specified phenomenon.

I

Id   The part of the personality that, according to psychoanalytic theory, contains powerful urges and drives for gratification and satisfaction.

Index crimes   The eight major crimes included in Part I of the Uniform Crime Reports: criminal homicide, forcible rape, robbery, aggravated assault, burglary, larceny-theft, auto theft, and arson.

Indictment   Accusation against a criminal defendant rendered by a grand jury on the basis of evidence constituting a prima facie case.

Indirect control   A behavioral influence that arises from an individual's identification with noncriminals and his or her desire to conform to societal norms.

Information   Accusation against a defendant prepared by a prosecuting attorney.

Inmate code   An informal set of rules that reflects the values of the prison society.

Insider trading   The use of material nonpublic financial information to obtain an unfair advantage in trading securities.

Intensive-supervision probation (ISP) An alternative to prison for convicted nonviolent offenders who do not qualify for routine probation.

Internalized control Self-regulation of behavior and conformity to societal norms as a result of guilt feelings arising in the conscience.

International crimes The major criminal offenses so designated by the community of nations for the protection of interests common to all humankind.

International criminal court A court that would have jurisdiction over the most heinous international crimes.

Involuntary manslaughter Homicide in which the perpetrator unintentionally but recklessly causes the death of another person by consciously taking a grave risk that endangers the person's life.

Involvement An individual's participation in conventional activities.

J

Just deserts A philosophy of justice which asserts that the punishment should fit the crime and culpability of the offender. *See also* Retribution.

Justice of the peace Originally (established in 1326), an untrained man, usually of the lower nobility, who was assigned to investigate and try minor cases; presently, a judge of a lower local or municipal court with limited jurisdiction.

Justifiable homicide A homicide, permitted by law, in defense of a legal right or mandate.

K

Kidnapping A felony consisting of the seizure and abduction of a person by force or threat of force and against the victim's will. Under federal law, the victim of a kidnapping is one who has been taken across state lines and held for ransom.

L

Labeling theory A theory that explains deviance in terms of the process by which a person acquires a negative identity, such as "addict" or "ex-con," and is forced to suffer the consequences of outcast status.

Larceny The trespassory (unconsented) taking and carrying away of personal property belonging to another with the intent to deprive the owner of the property permanently.

Laws of imitation An explanation of crime as learned behavior. Individuals are thought to emulate behavior patterns of others with whom they have contact.

Longitudinal study An analysis that focuses on studies of a particular group conducted repeatedly over a period of time.

M

Macrosociological study The study of overall social arrangements, their structures, and their long-term effects.

Mafia The entirety of those Sicilian families which, in both the United States and Sicily, are loosely associated with one another in operating organized crime.

Malice aforethought The mens rea requirement for murder, consisting of the intention to kill with the awareness that there is no right to kill. *See also* Mens rea.

Mandatory sentence A sentence that is specified by law and that a judge has no power to alter.

Manslaughter Criminal homicide without malice, committed intentionally after provocation (voluntary manslaughter) or recklessly (involuntary manslaughter).

Mass murder The killing of several persons, in one act or transaction, by one perpetrator or a group of perpetrators.

Mens rea (Latin, "guilty mind") Awareness of wrongdoing; the intention to commit a criminal act or behave recklessly.

Microsociological study The study of everyday patterns of behavior and personal interactions.

Minimal brain dysfunction (MBD) An attention-deficit disorder that may produce such asocial behavior as impulsivity, hyperactivity, and aggressiveness.

Miranda warning A warning that explains the rights of an arrestee. An arresting officer is required by law to recite the warning at the time of the arrest.

Misdemeanor A crime less serious than a felony and subject to a maximum sentence of 1 year in jail or a fine.

Money laundering The process by which money derived from illegal activities (especially drug sales) is unlawfully taken out of the country, placed in a numbered account abroad, and then transferred as funds no longer "dirty."

Monozygotic (MZ) twins Identical twins, who develop from a single fertilized egg that divides into two embryos. *See also* Dizygotic twins.

Motion An oral or written request to a judge that asks the court to make a specified ruling, finding, decision, or order. It may be presented at any appropriate moment from arrest until the end of the trial.

Motion to dismiss A request by the defense that the trial proceedings be terminated.

Murder The unlawful (usually intentional) killing of a human being with malice aforethought.

N

Neuroticism A personality disorder marked by low self-esteem, excessive anxiety, and wide mood swings (Eysenck).

Night watchman Originally, a thirteenth-century un-trained citizen who patrolled at night on the lookout for disturbances.

Nonparticipant observation A study in which investigators observe closely but do not become participants.

O

Occupational crime A crime committed by an individual for his or her own benefit, in the course of performing a profession.

P

Parens patriae (Latin, "father of the fatherland") Assumption by the state of the role of guardian over children whose parents are deemed incapable or unworthy.

Parole Supervised conditional release of a convicted prisoner before expiration of the sentence of imprisonment.

Participant observation Collection of information through involvement in the social life of the group a researcher is studying.

Penitentiary A prison or place of confinement and correction for persons convicted of felonies; originally, a place where convicts did penance.

Penologist A social scientist who studies and applies the theory and methods of punishment for crime.

Peremptory challenges Challenges (limited in number) by which a potential juror may be dismissed by either the prosecution or the defense without assignment of reason. *See also* Challenge for cause; Voir dire.

Phrenology A nineteenth-century theory based on the hypothesis that human behavior is localized in certain specific brain and skull areas. According to this theory, criminal behavior can be determined by the bumps on the head.

Physiognomy The study of facial features and their relation to human behavior.

Pimp A procurer or manager of prostitutes who provides access to prostitutes and protects and exploits them, living off their proceeds.

Plea bargaining Making an agreement between defense and prosecution for certain leniencies in return for a guilty plea.

Plead To respond to a criminal charge. Forms of pleas are guilty, not guilty, and nolo contendere.

Police subculture The result of socialization and bonding among police officers due to the stress and anxiety produced on the job.

Population A large group of persons in a study.

Pornography The portrayal, by whatever means, of lewd or obscene (sexually explicit) material prohibited by law.

Positivist school of criminology A criminological perspective that uses the scientific methods of the natural sciences and suggests that human behavior is a product of social, biological, psychological, or economic forces.

Preliminary hearing A preview of a trial held in court before a judge, in which the prosecution must produce sufficient evidence of guilt for the case to be bound over for the grand jury or to proceed to trial.

Presumptive sentence A sentence whose length is specified by law but which may be modified by a judge under limited circumstances.

Prima facie case A case in which there is as much evidence as would warrant the conviction of the defendant if properly proved in court, unless contradicted; a case that meets evidentiary requirements for grand-jury indictment.

Primary data Facts and observations that researchers gather by conducting their own measurements for a study.

Principals Perpetrators of a criminal act.

Prisonization A socialization process in which new prisoners learn the ways of prison society, including rules, hierarchy, customs, and culture.

Probable cause A set of facts that would induce a reasonable person to believe that an accused person committed the offense in question; the minimum evidence requirement for an arrest, according to the Fourth Amendment to the U.S. Constitution.

Probation An alternative to imprisonment, allowing a person found guilty of an offense to stay in the community, under conditions and with supervision.

Problem-oriented policing A strategy to enhance community relations and to improve crime prevention whereby police work with citizens to identify and respond to problems in a given community.

Prosecutor An attorney and government official who represents the people in proceedings against persons accused of criminal acts.

Prostitution The practice of engaging in sexual activities for hire.

Psychoanalytic theory In criminology, a theory of criminality that attributes delinquent and criminal behavior to a conscience that is either so overbearing that it arouses excessive feelings of guilt or so weak that it cannot control the individual's impulses.

Psychopathy A condition in which a person appears to be psychologically normal but in reality has no sense of responsibility, shows disregard for truth, is insincere, and feels no sense of shame, guilt, or humiliation (also called sociopathy).

Psychosis A mental illness characterized by a loss of contact with reality.

Psychoticism A dimension of the human personality describing individuals who are aggressive, egocentric, and impulsive (Eysenck).

R

Racketeer Influenced and Corrupt Organizations (RICO) Act A federal statute that provides for forfeiture of assets derived from a criminal enterprise.

Radical criminology A criminological perspective that studies the relationships between economic disparity and crime, avers that crime is the result of a struggle between owners of capital and workers for the distribution of power and resources, and posits that crime will disappear only when capitalism is abolished.

Random sample A sample chosen in such a way as to ensure that each person in the population to be studied has an equal chance of being selected. *See also* Sample.

Rape At common law, a felony consisting of the carnal knowledge (intercourse), by force and violence, by a man of a woman (not his wife) against her will. The stipulation that the woman not be the man's wife is omitted in modern statutes. Many states now call rape "sexual assault."

Rational choice A theory stating that crime is the result of a decision-making process in which the offender weighs the potential penalties and rewards of committing a crime.

Reaction formation An individual response to anxiety in which the person reacts to a stimulus with abnormal intensity or inappropriate conduct.

Reasonable suspicion Warranted suspicion (short of probable cause) that a person may be engaged in the commission of a crime.

Rehabilitation A punishment philosophy that asserts that through proper correctional intervention, a criminal can be reformed into a law-abiding citizen.

Restorative justice An approach to sentencing that seeks both to restore those who suffered from a crime to their original sense of well-being and to make it clear that justice in itself is being restored.

Retribution An "eye for an eye" philosophy of justice. *See also* Just deserts.

Robbery The taking of the property of another, or out of his or her presence, by means of force and violence or the threat thereof.

Routine activity A theory stating that an increase or decrease in crime rates can be explained by changes in the daily habits of potential victims; based on the expectation that crimes will occur where there is a suitable target unprotected by guardians.

S

Sample A selected subset of a population to be studied. *See also* Random sample.

Secondary data Facts and observations that were previously collected for a different study.

Selective incapacitation The targeting of high-risk and recidivistic offenders for rigorous prosecution and incarceration.

Self-report survey A survey in which respondents answer in a confidential interview or, most often, by completing an anonymous questionnaire.

Sentencing commission An independent agency authorized by a legislature to create sentencing guidelines.

Serial murder The killing of several victims over a period of time by the same perpetrator(s).

Sheriff The principal law enforcement officer of a county.

Sherman Antitrust Act An act (1890) of Congress prohibiting any contract, conspiracy, or combination of business interests in restraint of foreign or interstate trade.

Shock incarceration (SI) Short-term, high-intensity confinement intended to shock convicts into disciplined lifestyles.

Shoplifting Stealing goods from stores or markets.

Simple assault An attack that inflicts little or no physical harm on the victim.

Social control theory An explanation of criminal behavior that focuses on control mechanisms, techniques, and strategies for regulating human behavior, leading to conformity or obedience to society's rules, and which posits that deviance results when social controls are weakened or break down, so that individuals are not motivated to conform to them.

Social disorganization theory A theory of criminality in which the breakdown of effective social bonds, primary-group associations, and social controls in neighborhoods and communities is held to result in development of high-crime areas.

Social interactionists Scholars who view the human self as formed through a process of social interaction.

Social learning theory A theory of criminality that maintains that delinquent behavior is learned through the same psychological processes as nondelinquent behavior, e.g., through reinforcement.

Sociopath A person who has no sense of responsibility; shows disregard for truth; is insincere; and feels no sense of shame, guilt, or humiliation.

Sodomy Sexual intercourse by mouth or anus; a felony at common law.

Somatotype school of criminology A criminological perspective that relates body build to behavioral tendencies, temperament, susceptibility to disease, and life expectancy.

Statutory rape Sexual intercourse with a person incapable of giving legally relevant consent, because of immaturity (below age), mental, or physical condition.

Sting operation An undercover operation in which police officers attract likely perpetrators by posing as criminals.

Stock manipulation An illegal practice of brokers in which clients are led to believe that the price of a particular stock will rise, thus creating an artificial demand for it.

Strain theory A criminological theory positing that a gap between culturally approved goals and legitimate means of achieving them causes frustration which leads to criminal behavior.

Stranger homicide Criminal homicide committed by a person unknown and unrelated to the victim.

Strict liability Liability for a crime or violation imposed without regard to the actor's guilt; criminal liability without mens rea. *See also* Mens rea.

Subculture A subdivision within the dominant culture that has its own norms, beliefs, and values.

Subculture of violence A subculture with values that demand the overt use of violence in certain social situations.

Superego In psychoanalytic theory, the conscience, or those aspects of the personality that threaten the person or impose a sense of guilt or psychic suffering and thus restrain the id.

Survey The systematic collection of information by asking questions in questionnaires or interviews.

Synnomie A societal state, opposite of anomie, marked by social cohesion achieved through the sharing of values.

T

Target hardening A crime-prevention technique that seeks to make it more difficult to commit a given offense, by better protecting the threatened object or person.

Team policing A strategy for improving contacts between citizens and police, whereby a team of officers is responsible for a specific neighborhood on a 24-hour basis.

Terrorism The use of violence against a target to create fear, alarm, dread, or coercion for the purpose of obtaining concessions or rewards or commanding public attention for a political cause.

Theories of victimization Theories that explain the role that victims play in the crimes that happen to them.

Theory A coherent group of propositions used as principles in explaining or accounting for known facts or phenomena.

Tithing In Anglo-Saxon law, an association of 10 families bound together by a frankpledge, for purposes of crime control. *See also* Frankpledge.

Tort An injury or wrong committed against a person's property, subject to compensation; an infringement of the rights of an individual that is not founded on either contract or criminal law prohibition.

Transnational crime A criminal act or transaction violating the laws of more than one country, or having an impact on a foreign country.

U

Utilitarianism A criminological perspective positing that crime prevention and criminal justice must serve the end of providing the greatest good for the greatest number; based on the rationality of lawgivers, law enforcers, and the public at large.

V

Variables Changeable factors.

Victim precipitation Opening oneself up, by either direct or subliminal means, to a criminal response.

Victimization survey A survey that measures the extent of crime by interviewing individuals about their experiences as victims.

Vindication Condemnation of the commission of offenses.

Violation Minor criminal offense, usually under a city ordinance, commonly subject only to a fine.

Voir dire A process in which lawyers and a judge question potential jurors in order to select those who are acceptable, i.e., those who are unbiased and objective in relation to the particular trial. *See also* Challenge for cause; Peremptory challenges.

Voluntary manslaughter Homicide in which the perpetrator intentionally, but without malice, causes the death of another person, as in the heat of passion, in response to strong provocation, or possibly under severe intoxication.

W

White-collar crime A sociological concept encompassing any violation of the law committed by a person or group of persons in the course of an otherwise respected and legitimate occupation or business enterprise.

"Did You Know?"
Sources

7: G. O. W. Mueller and Freda Adler, *Outlaws of the Ocean,* (New York: Hearst Marine Books, 1985), Ch. 17; **11:** T. F. T. Plucknett, *A Concise History of The Common Law,* 5th edition (London: Butterworth and Co., 1956), pp. 15, 156, 323, 355; **29:** *Juvenile Offenders and Victims: 1999 National Report,* Office of Juvenile Justice and Delinquency Prevention, September 1999; **39:** *Juvenile Offenders and Victims: 1999 National Report,* Office of Juvenile Justice and Delinquency Prevention, September 1999; **64:** http://www.utm.edu/research/rep/b/beccarea.htm; **70:** http://www.epub.orgbr/cm/m01/frenolog/frenmod.htm; **86:** Former FBI Agent Jack Douglas, quoted in Kevia Johnson, "Several Serial Killers Said to Be At Large," *USA Today,* July 1, 1999, p. 12A; **92:** "Cholesterol and Violence: Is There a Connection?" *Annals of Internal Medicine,* **128** (1998): 478–487; **127:** Daryl Rothman, "Minimum-Wage Workers Remain in Poverty," *St. Louis Post-Dispatch,* Apr. 16, 1998, p. B7; **142:** *Juvenile Offenders and Victims: 1999 National Report,* Office of Juvenile Justice and Delinquency Prevention, September, 1999; **166:** *Juvenile Offenders and Victims: 1999 National Report,* Office of Juvenile Justice and Delinquency Prevention, 1999, p. 53; **174:** *Juvenile Offenders and Victims: 1999 National Report,* Office of Juvenile Justice and Delinquency Prevention, 1999, p. 9; **198:** Anthony Walsh and Lee Ellis, "Political Ideology and American Criminologists' Explanations for Criminal Behavior," *Criminologist,* **24** (1999): 1; **202:** http://www.ifs.univie.ac.at/~pr2gq1/85275.html#funsoc; **241:** Marcus Felson and Ronald V. Clarke, "Routine Precautions, Criminology, and Crime Prevention," in *Crime and Public Policy: Putting Theory to Work,* ed. Hugh D. Barlow, Boulder, Colo.: Westview Press, 1995; **254:** Ronald V. Clarke, *Hot Products: Understanding, Anticipating and Reducing Demand for Stolen Goods,* Policing and Reducing Crime Unit, Police Research Series Paper 112 (London: Home Office, 1999); John Burrow and D. Cooper, *Theft and Loss from UK Libraries,* Police Research Group Crime Prevention Unit Series Paper 37 (London: Home Office, 1992); **291:** *Juvenile Offenders and Victims: 1999 National Report,* Office of Juvenile Justice and Delinquency Prevention, 1999, p. 16; **296:** *Juvenile Offenders and Victims: 1999 National Report,* Office of Juvenile Justice and Delinquency Prevention, 1999, p. 17; **352:** "1998 Internet Fraud Statistics" (http://www.fraud.org/internet/9923stat.htm); **415:** Editorial Observer, "Why Some Get Busted and Some Go Free," *New York Times,* May 10, 1999; **418:** Anti–Drug Abuse Act of 1986, 21 USC 801; **565:** Edward Connors et al., *Convicted by Juries, Exonerated by Science: Case Studies in the Use of DNA Evidence to Establish Innocence after Trial* (Washington, D.C.: U.S. Department of Justice, 1999); **587:** Death Penalty Information Center (http://www.essential.org/dpic/dpic5.html); **602:** Bill Deman, "DNA Tests Are Freeing Scores of Prison Inmates," *New York Times,* Apr. 19, 1999, p. 12; **610:** Sasha Abramsky, "When They Get Out," *Atlantic Monthly,* June 1999 (http://www.theatlantic.com); **617:** Sasha Abramsky, "When They Get Out," *Atlantic Monthly,* June 1999 (http://www.theatlantic.com).

Chapter 1

Figure 1.2 Adapted from Jack D. Douglas and Frances C. Waksler, *The Sociology of Deviance*, p. 11. (Boston: Little, Brown, & Company, 1982). Reprinted by permission of the authors.

Table 1.1 From Carl Fox, "Some Major Marine Oil Spills," *Albuquerque Journal*, February 20, 1996, p. 6. Data from *Golub's Oil Pollution Bulletin*. Reprinted by permission of The Associated Press.

Of Immediate Concern Excerpt from Tupac Shakur, "If I Die 2nite," written by Willie James Clarke, Norman A. Durham, Tupac Amaru Shakur, and Betty Regina Wright. Published by EMI Longitude Music. Recorded by Death Row Records. International copyright secured. All rights reserved. Reprinted by permission.

Of Immediate Concern Excerpt from Tupac Shakur, "Ain't Hard to Find," written by Brandt Keith Jones, Michael Mosley, Tupac Amaru Shakur, Danelle Stevens, Ricardo Thomas, and Shawn Thomas. Published by EMI Blackwood Music. Recorded by Death Row Records. International copyright secured. All rights reserved. Reprinted by permission.

Of Immediate Concern From Frank Williams, "The Living End," *The Source: The Magazine of Hip-Hop Music, Culture, and Politics*, November 1996, p. 103. Copyright by Source Publications, Inc. Reprinted by permission.

Window to the World From Douglas Waller, "Counterterrorism: Victim of Success?" *Newsweek*, July 5, 1993, pp. 22–23. © 1993 Newsweek, Inc. All rights reserved. Reprinted by permission.

Chapter 2

Figure 2.1 From Richard F. Sparks, H. G. Genn, and D. J. Dodd, *Surveying Victims: A Study of the Measurement of Criminal Victimization, Perceptions of Crime, and Attitudes to Criminal Justice*, p. 6. Copyright © 1977. John Wiley & Sons, Ltd. Reprinted by permission.

Window to the World Figure from Fifth United Nations Crime and Justice Survey, 1994. Reprinted by permission.

Chapter 3

Where Do We Go from Here? From Ron Rosenbaum, "The Great Ivy League Nude Posture Photo Scandal," originally published in *New York Times Magazine*, January 15, 1995, p. 26. © 1995 by Ron Rosenbaum. All rights reserved. Reprinted by permission.

Chapter 4

Table 4.1 Adapted from Robert S. Feldman, *Understanding Psychology*, p. 378. Copyright 1987. Reprinted by permission of The McGraw-Hill Companies.

Table 4.3 From J. Federman (ed.), *National Television Violence Study*, Vol. 3. Copyright 1998. Reprinted by permission of Sage Publications.

Table 4.4 Adapted from Thomas J. Gardner and Terry M. Anderson, *Criminal Law: Principles and Cases*. Copyright 2000. Reprinted by permission of Belmont Publishers.

Of Immediate Concern Excerpt from Hannah Bloch and Jeanne McDowell, "When Kids Kill Abusive Parents," *Time*, November 23, 1992. © 1992 Time Inc. Reprinted by permission.

Window to the World Quotation from Thomas Collins, "In China, The Carnage That Never Was," *Newsday*, June 14, 1989, p. 67. Copyright 1989 Newsday, Inc. Reprinted by permission.

Cartoon, p. 94 Cartoon by Jeff Stahler. © Newspaper Enterprise Association (NEA) 1996. Reprinted by permission of United Feature Syndicate.

Quote, p. 100 Excerpt from Hervey Cleckley, *The Mask of Sanity*, 5th edition, pp. 271–272. Copyright 1976, 1988. Published by Emily S. Cleckley, 3024 Fox Spring Road, Augusta, GA 30909.

Quote, p. 107 From Anastasia Toufexis, "Dancing with Devils: Forensic Psychiatrist Park Dietz Tracks America's Serial Killers, Bombers and Mass Murderers," *Psychology Today*, **32** (3), May 1999, p. 54. Copyright © 1999. Sussex Publishers, Inc. Reprinted by permission.

Cartoon, p. 106 Cartoon by Charles Addams. © 1981 The New Yorker Magazine, Inc. Reprinted by permission of www.cartoonbank.com.

Quote, p. 112 Excerpt from Daniel Goleman, "New Storm Brews on Whether Crime Has Roots in Genes," *New York Times*, September 15, 1992, p. C1. Copyright 1992. Reprinted by permission of The New York Times Company.

Chapter 5

Figure 5.2 From Jane Gross, "Remnant of the War on Poverty, Job Corps Is Still a Quiet Success," *New York Times*, February 17, 1992, p. A14. Copyright © 1992 by The New York Times Company. Reprinted by permission.

Figure 5.3 From Donald J. Shoemaker, *Theories of Delinquency*, 3rd edition. Copyright © 1996 Oxford University

Chapter 6

Chapter 7

Chapter 8

Chapter 9

Chapter 10

Chapter 11

Times, April 24, 1999, p. 1. Copyright 1999. Reprinted by permission of The New York Times Company.

Quote, p. 320 Excerpt from Robert D. McFadden, "On a Bus in Queens, Three Bandits Stage a Frontier Robbery," *New York Times,* July 31, 1993, p. 1. Copyright 1993. Reprinted by permission of The New York Times Company.

Quote, p. 323 Excerpt from David McDowell and Alan Lizotte, "Gun Control," in Craig Calhoun and George Ritzer (eds.), *Introduction to Social Problems,* Primis Database. Copyright 1993. Reprinted by permission of The McGraw-Hill Companies.

Chapter 12

Table 12.1 From Read Hayes, *1996 Retail Theft Trends Report: An Analysis of Customer Theft in Stores.* Copyright 2000 Read Hayes. Reprinted by permission of Loss Prevention Specialists, Winter Park, FL.

Table 12.2 From National Insurance Crime Bureau, *NICB Vehicle Theft Study, 1996.* Available at http://nicb.com/release.htm. © National Insurance Crime Bureau. Reprinted by permission.

Quote, p. 340 Excerpt from James Inciardi, "Professional Thief," in Robert F. Meier (ed.), *Major Forms of Crime,* p. 224. Copyright 1984. Reprinted by permission of Sage Publications.

Quote, p. 349 Excerpt from http://dailynews.yahoo.com. Copyright September 15, 1999. Reprinted by permission of yahoo-inc.com.

Quote, p. 354 Adult content alert. Copyright © 1998, 1999 Infoseek Corporation. All rights reserved.

Chapter 13

Figure 13.3 From Ko-lin Chin, *Chinese Subculture and Criminality,* p. 76. Copyright © 1990. Reprinted by permission of Greenwood Publishing Group, Inc., Westport, CT.

Table 13.1 From http://www.transparency.de/documents/cpi/index.html. Copyright 1999. Reprinted by permission of Transparency International.

Of Immediate Concern From Donald J. Rebovich, *Dangerous Ground: The World of Hazardous Waste Crime.* Copyright 1992. Reprinted by permission of Transaction Publishers.

Quote, p. 367 Excerpt from Chicago Tribune, "ValuJet Jury Got It Right," *Chicago Tribune,* December 17, 1999, p. 16. Copyright 1999. Reprinted by permission.

Quote, p. 367 Excerpt from Matthew L. Wald, "Airline Pleads Guilty to Illegal Storage of Hazardous Waste," *New York Times,* December 17, 1999, p. 27. Copyright 1999. Reprinted by permission of The New York Times Company.

Quote, p. 368 Excerpt from "Mafia Chief Tied to Crime-Busting Judge's Murder," *Reuters,* August 1, 1993.

Copyright 1993. Reprinted by permission of Reuters Limited Reuters Information.

Quote, p. 381 Excerpt from Jim Mayer, *Sacramento Bee,* July 10, 1993. Copyright, The Sacramento Bee, 1993. Reprinted by permission.

Cartoon, p. 388 Cartoon by Sidney Harris. © 1997 by Sidney Harris. Reprinted by permission.

Chapter 14

Window to the World Map from World Congress Against Sexual Exploitation of Children, *Newsweek,* September 2, 1996, p. 11. © 1996 Newsweek, Inc. All rights reserved. Reprinted by permission.

Window to the World Excerpt from Marlise Simons, "The Sex Market: Scourge on the World's Children," *New York Times,* April 9, 1993, p. A3. Copyright 1993. Reprinted by permission of The New York Times Company.

Quote, p. 416 Excerpt from Colin McMahon, "Panama's Future Uncertain as Ever; Corruption Persists in Post-Noriega era," *Chicago Tribune,* August 25, 1996, p. 17. Copyright 1996 Chicago Tribune Company. All rights reserved. Reprinted by permission.

Chapter 15

Of Immediate Concern From K. N. Llewellyn and E. A. Hoebel, *The Cheyenne Way,* pp. 12–13. Copyright 1941. University of Oklahoma Press, Norman. Reprinted by permission.

Chapter 16

Figure 16.4 Probabilities adapted from C. M. A. McCauliff, "Burdens of Proof: Degrees of Belief, Quanta of Evidence, or Constitutional Guarantees?" *Vanderbilt Law Review,* **35** (1982), pp. 1293–1335. Copyright © 1982 Vanderbilt Law Review. Used by permission.

Table 16.2 From Barry C. Feld, "The Juvenile Court Meets the Principle of the Offense: Legislative Changes in Juvenile Waiver Statutes," *Journal of Criminal Law and Criminology,* **78** (1987), pp. 512–514. Reprinted by permission of Northwestern University School of Law.

Chapter 17

Figure 17.3 From Larry K. Gaines, Mittie D. Southerland, and John E. Angell, *Police Administration,* p. 82. Copyright 1991. Reprinted by permission of The McGraw-Hill Companies.

Figure 17.5 From Jack R. Greene and Carl B. Klockars, "What Police Do," in Carl B. Klockars and Stephen D. Matrofski, *Thinking about Police,* 2nd edition, pp. 273–274,

279. Copyright 1991. Reprinted by permission of The McGraw-Hill Companies.

Cartoon, p. 522 Cartoon by Gary Larson. © 1985 Far-Works Inc./Distributed by Universal Press Syndicate.

Chapter 18

Figure 18.1 Adapted from Abraham S. Blumberg, *Criminal Justice: Issues and Ironies*, p. 150. Copyright 1979. Reprinted by permission of New Viewpoints.

Figure 18.7 From Andrew von Hirsch, Kay A. Knapp, and Michael Tonry, *The Sentencing Commission and Its Guidelines*, p. 91. Copyright 1987 by Andrew von Hirsch, Kay A. Knapp, and Michael Tonry. Reprinted by permission of Northeastern University Press, Boston.

Figure 18.8 From Death Penalty Information Center, http://www.essential.org/dpic/dpicexec.htm. Reprinted by permission.

Figure 18.9 From Death Penalty Information Center, March 29, 1995, p. 5. Reprinted by permission.

Quote, p. 564 From Abraham S. Blumberg, *Criminal Justice: Issues and Ironies*, p. 123. Copyright 1979. Reprinted by permission of New Viewpoints.

Cartoon, p. 574 Cartoon by Dana Fradon. © 1992 The New Yorker. Reprinted by permission of www.cartoonbank.com.

Chapter 19

Figure 19.3 Adapted from Roy Walmsley, *World Prison Population List, Research Findings*, no. 88. Copyright 1998. Reprinted by permission of Home Office Research Development, U.K.

Figure 19.7 From Joan Petersilia, *Expanding Options for Criminal Sentencing*, p. 32. Copyright 1987. Reprinted by permission of Rand Corporation.

Table 19.1 Based on Geoffrey P. Albert (ed.), *Legal Rights of Prisoners*. Copyright 1980. Reprinted by permission of Sage Publications.

Quote, p. 624 Excerpt from Joan Petersilia, *Expanding Options for Criminal Sentencing*, p. 32. Copyright 1987. Reprinted by permission of Rand Corporation.

Name Index